JEFFREY S. NEVID
St. John's University

BEVERLY GREENE
St. John's University

LINDA J. KNIGHT
John Abbott College

PAUL A. JOHNSON

STEVEN TAYLOR
University of British Columbia

Essentials of Abnormal Psychology

IN A CHANGING WORLD

FOURTH CANADIAN EDITION

DSM 5

Pearson

VICE PRESIDENT, EDITORIAL: Anne Williams
EXECUTIVE ACQUISITIONS EDITOR: Kimberley Veevers
MARKETING MANAGER: Lisa Gillis
CONTENT MANAGER: Madhu Ranadive
PROJECT MANAGER: Susan Johnson
CONTENT DEVELOPER: Katherine Goodes
PRODUCTION SERVICES: iEnergizer Aptara®, Ltd.

PERMISSIONS PROJECT MANAGER: Kathryn O'Handley
PHOTO PERMISSIONS RESEARCH: Integra Publishing Services, Inc.
TEXT PERMISSIONS RESEARCH: Integra Publishing Services, Inc.
INTERIOR DESIGNER: Anthony Leung
COVER DESIGNER: Anthony Leung
COVER IMAGE: Butterfly Hunter/Shutterstock

Pearson Canada Inc., 26 Prince Andrew Place, North York, Ontario M3C 2H4.

ISBN 978-0-13-404870-3

Library and Archives Canada Cataloguing in Publication
Nevid, Jeffrey S., author
 Essentials of abnormal psychology in a changing world / Jeffrey S. Nevid, Beverly Greene, Linda Knight, Paul A. Johnson, Steven Taylor. — Fourth edition.

ISBN 978-0-13-404870-3 (softcover)

 1. Psychology, Pathological—Textbooks. 2. Textbooks. I. Greene, Beverly, author II. Knight, Linda J. (Linda Jocelyne), 1960-, author III. Johnson, Paul A., author IV. Taylor, Steven, 1960-, author V. Title. VI. Title: Abnormal psychology in a changing world.

RC454.E88 2018   616.89   C2017-907063-0

To Sam, Scott, and Derek
—LK

To Anna, Alex, and Amy
—ST

BRIEF CONTENTS

CONTENTS

Abnormal psychology is among the most popular areas of study in psychology for good reason. The problems it addresses are of immense personal and social importance—problems that touch the lives of us all in one way or another. They include problems that are all too pervasive, such as depression, anxiety, sexual dysfunctions, and alcohol and substance use disorders. They include problems that are less common but have a profound impact on all of us, such as schizophrenia.

The problems addressed in this book are thus not those of the few. The majority of us will experience one or more of them at some time or another, or a friend or loved one will. Even those who are not personally affected by these problems will be touched by society's response—or lack of response—to them. We hope that this text will serve both as an educational tool and as a vehicle to raise awareness among students and general readers alike.

Essentials of Abnormal Psychology in a Changing World, Fourth Canadian Edition, uses case examples and self-scoring questionnaires; a clear and engaging writing style that is accessible but does not compromise rigour; research-based and comprehensive coverage; superior pedagogy; and integration of sociocultural material throughout, including coverage of issues relating to Canadian cultural diversity, gender, and lifestyle.

Essentials of Abnormal Psychology provides students with the basic concepts in the field in a convenient 11-chapter format. These chapters cover historical and theoretical perspectives, approaches to psychological assessment and treatment, and the major types of psychological disorders—including eating disorders, anxiety disorders, depressive and bipolar disorders, substance-related disorders, personality disorders, gender dysphoria and sexual dysfunctions, schizophrenia, and disorders of childhood, adolescence, and aging. Throughout the text, we highlight important Canadian research, case examples, and societal and legal perspectives on abnormal psychology. We also present the best international research from a Canadian perspective.

NEW TO THE FOURTH CANADIAN EDITION

Welcome to the fourth Canadian edition of *Essentials of Abnormal Psychology in a Changing World.* We continue to bring readers the latest research developments that inform contemporary understandings of abnormal behaviour in a way that both stimulates student interest and makes complex material understandable. Highlights of this new edition include the following:

- **Enhanced Integration of DSM-5**
  This new edition has been revised to better reflect the organizational structure of DSM-5.

- **A Continued Focus on Mental Health in Canada**
  Since our third edition, Canada has made significant strides in recognizing and planning for the mental health needs of our population, including the homeless and Indigenous communities.

- Here is a sample of the documents that have been recently released and that are integrated into this new edition:

  o Employment and Social Development Canada:

     • Homelessness Partnering Strategy Coordinated Canadian Point-in-Time Count

     • Highlights of the National Shelter Study 2005–2014

- o Mental Health Commission of Canada:
  - Changing Directions, Changing Lives: The Mental Health Strategy for Canada
  - Informing the Future: Mental Health Indicators for Canada, 2015
  - Advancing the Mental Health Strategy for Canada: A Framework for Action (2017–2022)
  - National At Home/Chez Soi Project Final Report
  - o Public Health Agency of Canada:
    - Report from the Canadian Chronic Disease Surveillance System: Mental Illness in Canada, 2015
  - o Canadian Institute for Health Information:
    - Care for Children and Youth with Mental Disorders, 2015
  - o Statistics Canada:
    - Mental and Substance Use Disorders in Canada
    - Prevalence and Correlates of Marijuana Use in Canada, 2012
    - 2011 National Household Survey Aboriginal Demographics, Educational Attainment and Labour Market Outcomes
    - Immigration and Ethnocultural Diversity in Canada, 2016
    - First Nations & Inuit Health, 2016
    - Population Size and Growth in Canada: Key Results from the 2016 Census

- **Integration of Latest Scientific Developments**
  The text integrates the latest research findings and scientific developments in the field that inform our understanding of abnormal psychology. We present these research findings in a way that makes complex material engaging and accessible to the student.

- **Integration of Social and Cultural Diversity**
  We examine abnormal behaviour patterns in relation to factors of diversity, such as ethnicity, culture, and gender. We believe students need to understand how issues of diversity affect the conceptualization of abnormal behaviour as well as the diagnosis and treatment of psychological disorders.
  Here are a few examples:
  - o Cultural factors in defining and assessing mental illness
  - o Eating disorders in non-Western countries
  - o Sociocultural perspective on depression in women
  - o Differences in youth suicide rates across various countries
  - o The psychological effects of female genital mutilation
  - o Sociocultural issues in gender dysphoria
  - o The Indigenous healing perspective
  - o Traditional Indigenous ceremonies and practices
  - o The Canadian Indigenous suicide crisis

- **Emphasis on Mental Illness as a Continuum**
  - o Continuum Chart
    We recognize that mental illnesses are on a continuum and that the delineation between "normal" and "abnormal" is not always clear. In order to emphasize this continuum, we have introduced a continuum chart at the beginning of each chapter to emphasize the dimensional aspect of mental disorders.
  - o Dimensional versus Categorical Approach to Diagnoses
    Our present method of diagnosing (DSM) continues to be categorical despite increasing criticisms and debates. In order to promote critical thinking, we introduce students to these controversial issues and alternative approaches.

- **Increased Emphasis on Student Learning**
  - Interactive Concept Maps
    Students learn best when they are actively engaged in the learning process. To engage students in active learning, we converted the Concept Maps in this edition to an interactive format. The maps are presented in a matching format in which key words and terms are omitted so that students can fill in the missing pieces to complete these knowledge structures.
  - Multiple-choice questions have also been added to the end of each chapter.

GENERAL APPROACH

We approached the writing of this text with the belief that a textbook should do more than offer a portrait of a field of knowledge. It should be a teaching device—a means of presenting information in ways that arouse interest and encourage understanding and critical thinking. To these ends, we speak to the reader in a clear expository style. We attempt to render complex material accessible. We put a human face on the subjects we address by including many case examples drawn from our own clinical files, those of other mental health professionals, and those from DSM casebooks. We stimulate and involve students through carefully chosen pedagogical features, questionnaires, highlights, and applications. We also include built-in study tools designed to help students master difficult material. And yes, we keep abreast of our ever-changing subject by bringing to our readers a wealth of new scientific information drawn from leading scientific journals and organizations. To summarize the material covered in each chapter in an easy-to-remember visual format, we also include Concept Maps at the end of each chapter.

Essentials of Abnormal Psychology exposes students to the multiple perspectives that inform our present understandings of abnormal behaviour—the psychological, sociocultural, and biological domains. We adopt an interactionist approach, which recognizes that abnormal behaviour typically involves a complex interplay of multiple factors representing different domains. Because the concept of integrating diverse perspectives is often difficult for beginning students to grasp, the unique "Tying It Together" features interspersed through the text help students explore how multiple factors interact in the development of psychological disorders.

FEATURES OF THE TEXT

Textbooks walk balance beams, as it were, and they can fall off in three directions, not just two. That is, they must do justice to their subject matter while also meeting the needs of both instructors and students.

In subject matter, *Essentials of Abnormal Psychology* is comprehensive, providing depth and breadth as well as showcasing the most important new research discoveries. It covers the history of societal response to abnormal behaviours, historical and contemporary models of abnormal behaviours, methods of assessment, psychological and biological models of treatment, contemporary issues, the comprehensive range of problem behaviours set forth in the DSM, and a number of other behavioural problems that entail psychological factors—most notably in the interfaces between psychology and health.

Canadian Content

The fourth Canadian edition of *Essentials of Abnormal Psychology in a Changing World* showcases a wealth of Canadian content. We chose to do this for several reasons. First and foremost, there is a great deal of important, internationally acclaimed Canadian work being done on the research and treatment of abnormal behaviour. In other words, we have tried to present the best research on abnormal psychology while at the same time alerting our readers to the fact that much of this work comes from Canada. Why would we do this? The answer is to help our readers understand that there is important, relevant research being conducted right where they live, and quite likely on their own campus. Our Canadian focus helps readers understand that key research does not originate just in other countries—it's happening in students' own backyards, perhaps being done by the professor who is teaching their course.

The second reason for highlighting Canadian content is to refute the myth that mental disorders are things that happen to people who live someplace else, such as in other regions or countries. Mental disorder touches all of us; there are people in our country and communities and on our campuses who are afflicted with psychological problems. By citing Canadian examples of people who have battled psychological problems, we hope to bring home the fact that mental illness can reach any of us. Fortunately, effective treatments are available for many of these disorders.

Our third reason for a Canadian focus is pragmatic. The prevalence of mental disorders differs from country to country, as do the treatments of and laws regarding mental disorders and patient rights. Some disorders, such as dependence on crack cocaine, are much more common in the United States than in Canada. Substance use disorders in Canada more commonly involve other substances. The health-care system in Canada is also different from systems in other countries. Accordingly, it is important to have a Canadian focus so that readers can understand how people with mental health problems are treated in Canada.

Finally, the issues regarding mental disorders and the law are different in Canada than in many other countries. For example, in the United States, a person might be deemed to be "not guilty by reason of insanity." In Canada, such a judgment would be "not criminally responsible on account of a mental disorder." In other words, the Canadian courts often recognize that an accused is guilty of a given crime but not responsible because he or she is under the influence of a mental disorder.

This text illustrates the important fact that abnormal psychology does not occur in a cultural vacuum; the expression and treatment of psychological problems are strongly influenced by cultural factors. Our task of updating and Canadianizing this text was made much easier by the fact that so much of the key research on abnormal behaviour has been conducted in Canada.

"Did You Know That" Chapter Openers

Each chapter begins with a set of "Did You Know That" questions designed to whet students' appetites for specific information contained in the chapter and to encourage them to read further. These chapter-opening questions (e.g., "Did You Know That . . . you can become psychologically dependent on a drug without becoming physically addicted?" or ". . . as many as 17% of people will suffer from an anxiety disorder at some point in their lives?") also encourage students to think critically and evaluate common conceptions in light of scientific evidence.

"Normal/Abnormal" Features

Instructors often hear the question "So what is the difference between normal behaviour and a psychological disorder?" In an effort to bring the material back to real life and to separate normal emotional distress from a psychological disorder, we've introduced case comparisons called "Normal/Abnormal Behaviour"—for example, "Alcohol Use: No Disorder" and "Alcohol Abuse: Disorder," "Normal Perfectionism: No Disorder" and "OCPD: Disorder." These have been written to inspire discussion and engagement with students in class. Students will encounter a variety of symptom severities and can discuss the differences between the cases. These cases are not meant to encourage labelling but are designed to show real-life examples written in nonclinical language. The cases have been written by Dr. Karen Rowa, Assistant Professor,

McMaster University, and Associate Director at St. Joseph's Healthcare Clinical Psychology Residency Program.

"Focus on Diversity" Features

The fourth Canadian edition of *Essentials of Abnormal Psychology* helps broaden students' perspectives so that they understand the importance of issues relating to gender, culture, ethnicity, and lifestyle in the diagnosis and treatment of psychological disorders. Students will see how behaviour deemed normal in one culture could be labelled abnormal in another, how states of psychological distress might be experienced differently in other cultures, how some abnormal behaviour patterns are culture-bound, and how therapists can cultivate a sensitivity to cultural factors in their approach to treating people from diverse backgrounds. Multicultural material is incorporated throughout the text and is highlighted in boxed "Focus on Diversity" features that cover specific topics, including the following:

- Mental Health Issues in Canadian Indigenous Communities (Chapter 1)
- Culture-Bound Syndromes (Chapter 2)
- Traditional Indigenous Ceremonies and Practices (Chapter 2)
- Canadian Multicultural Issues in Psychotherapy (Chapter 2)
- Koro and Dhat Syndromes: Asian Somatic Symptom Disorders? (Chapter 5)
- Ethnicity and Alcohol Abuse (Chapter 7)

"A Closer Look" Features

The Closer Look features highlight cutting-edge developments in the field (e.g., virtual reality therapy) and in practice (e.g., suicide prevention) that enable students to apply information from the text to their own lives. Here is a quick preview of features:

- Canadian Mental Health Promotion (Chapter 1)
- The Homeless in Canada (Chapter 1)
- DSM-5: Points of Controversy (Chapter 2)
- A New Vision of Stigma Reduction and Mental Health Support for Young Adults (Chapter 2)
- Virtual Therapy (Chapter 3)
- Concussions, Depression, and Suicide Among NHLers (Chapter 4)
- Suicide Prevention (Chapter 4)
- Personality Disorders—Categories or Dimensions? (Chapter 6)
- The Controlled Social Drinking Controversy (Chapter 7)
- Correctional Service Canada's National Sex Offender Programs (Chapter 9)
- A New View of Women's Sexual Dysfunctions? (Chapter 9)
- Psychosis Sucks! Early Psychosis Intervention Programs (Chapter 10)
- A Canadian Definition of Learning Disabilities (Chapter 11)

Self-Scoring Questionnaires

Self-scoring questionnaires (for example, "The Body Shape Questionnaire" in Chapter 8 and the "An Inventory of Dissociative Experiences" in Chapter 5) involve students in the discussion at hand and permit them to evaluate their own behaviour. In some cases, students may become more aware of troubling concerns, such as states of depression or problems with drug or alcohol use, which they may wish to bring to the attention of a professional. We have screened the questionnaires to ensure that they will provide students with useful information to reflect on and to serve as a springboard for class discussion.

Review It: In-Chapter Study Breaks

Essentials of Abnormal Psychology contains a built-in study break for students. These in-chapter study breaks conclude each major section in the chapters. This feature provides students with the opportunity to review the material they have just read and gives them a review break before moving on to a new section.

Define It: End-of-Chapter Glossary Terms

Key terms introduced throughout the text are listed here, with page references for easy retrieval and to help students as they study.

Think About It: End-of-Chapter Discussion Material

End-of-chapter questions ask students to think critically about the issues that were raised in the preceding passages of the text and invite students to relate the material to their own experiences.

Recall It

End-of-chapter multiple-choice questions enable students to test their understanding of the material.

Concept Maps

Concept Maps are diagrams at the end of each chapter that summarize key concepts and findings. Refreshed and revised for this edition, the Concept Maps provide readers with a "big picture" and are a useful way of understanding and remembering the material covered in each chapter.

SUPPLEMENTS

No matter how comprehensive a textbook is, today's instructors require a complete educational package to advance teaching and comprehension. These instructor supplements are available for download from a password-protected section of Pearson Canada's online catalogue (https://pearson.com/higher-education). Navigate to your book's catalogue page to view a list of those supplements that are available. Speak to your local Pearson Canada sales representative for details and access.

Essentials of Abnormal Psychology is accompanied by the following supplements:

MYTEST   from Pearson Canada is a powerful assessment generation program that helps instructors easily create and print quizzes, tests, and exams, as well as homework or practice handouts. Questions and tests can all be authored online, allowing instructors ultimate flexibility and the ability to efficiently manage assessments at any time, from anywhere. MyTest for *Essentials of Abnormal Psychology in a Changing World*, Fourth Canadian Edition, includes over 3500 fully referenced multiple-choice, true/false, and essay questions. Each question is accompanied by a difficulty level, type designation, topic, and answer justification. Instructors can access MyTest at "http://www.pearsonmytest.com".

TEST ITEM FILE.   The MyTest questions in multiple-choice, true/false, and essay formats are also provided in a Word document.

INSTRUCTOR'S RESOURCE MANUAL   The Instructor's Resource Manual is a true "course organizer," integrating a variety of resources for teaching abnormal psychology. It includes a summary discussion of the chapter content, a full chapter outline, lecture and discussion questions, a list of learning goals for students, demonstrations, and activities.

POWERPOINT® PRESENTATIONS Students often learn visually, and in a world where multimedia is almost an expectation, a full set of PowerPoint presentations will help you present course material to students.

IMAGE LIBRARY Electronic versions of key figures and tables in the text are available for your use.

LEARNING SOLUTIONS MANAGERS Pearson's Learning Solutions Managers work with faculty and campus course designers to ensure that Pearson technology products, assessment tools, and online course materials are tailored to meet your specific needs. This highly qualified team is dedicated to helping schools take full advantage of a wide range of educational resources by assisting in the integration of a variety of instructional materials and media formats. Your local Pearson Canada sales representative can provide you with more details on this service program.

ACKNOWLEDGMENTS

The field of abnormal psychology is a moving target, because the literature base that informs our understanding is continually expanding. We are deeply indebted to a number of talented individuals who helped us hold our camera steady in taking a portrait of the field, focus in on the salient features of our subject matter, and develop our snapshots through prose.

First, we thank Tracey Carr at the University of Saskatchewan, who reviewed and updated the previous edition to address changes in the DSM-5 criteria.

Second, we thank our professional colleagues, who reviewed chapters from earlier Canadian editions: Mark Benner, Fanshawe College; Beverley Bouffard, York University; Kristen Buscaglia, Niagara College; Kathy Foxall, Wilfrid Laurier University; Stephane Gaskin, Dawson College; Stuart Keenan, Sir Sandford Fleming College; Thomas Keenan, Niagara College; Ronald Laye, University of the Fraser Valley; Jocelyn Lymburner, Kwantlen University College; Rajesh Malik, Dawson College; Jillian Esmonde Moore, Georgian College; Karen Moreau, Niagara College; Ravi Ramkissoonsingh, Niagara College; Joanna Sargent, Georgian College; Sandy Schlieman, Algonquin College; Dana Shapero, University of Windsor; Carolyn Szostak, University of British Columbia-Okanagan; and Abe Worenklein, Dawson College.

Third, we are thankful to those who provided feedback to develop this new fourth Canadian edition: Anastasia Blake, St. Clair College; Leonard George, Capilano University; and Cathy Lountis, Camplain College.

And finally, thank you to the publishing professionals at or collaborating with Pearson Canada who helped guide the development, editing, proofreading, and marketing of this edition, including Kim Veevers (Acquisitions); Madhu Ranadive and Katherine Goodes (Development); Darcey Pepper (Marketing); Susan Johnson (Production); and the various people who contributed by copyediting and proofreading the manuscript and researching permissions and photos.

ABOUT THE AUTHORS

JEFFREY S. NEVID is Professor of Psychology at St. John's University in New York, where he directs the Doctoral Program in Clinical Psychology, teaches at the undergraduate and graduate levels, and supervises doctoral students in clinical practicum work. He received his PhD in Clinical Psychology from the State University of New York at Albany and was a staff psychologist at Samaritan Hospital in Troy, New York. He later completed a National Institute of Mental Health Post-Doctoral Fellowship in Mental Health Evaluation Research at Northwestern University. He holds a Diplomate in Clinical Psychology from the American Board of Professional Psychology, is a Fellow of the American Psychological Association and the Academy of Clinical Psychology, and has served on the editorial boards of several journals and as Associate Editor of the *Journal of Consulting and Clinical Psychology*. His publications have appeared in journals such as *Journal of Consulting and Clinical Psychology, Health Psychology, Journal of Occupational Medicine, Behavior Therapy, American Journal of Community Psychology, Professional Psychology: Research and Practice, Journal of Clinical Psychology, Journal of Nervous and Mental Disease, Teaching of Psychology, American Journal of Health Promotion*, and *Psychology and Psychotherapy*. Dr. Nevid is also author of the book *Choices: Sex in the Age of STDs* and the introductory psychology text *Psychology: Concepts and Applications*, as well as several other college texts in the fields of psychology and health co-authored with Dr. Spencer Rathus. Dr. Nevid is also actively involved in a program of pedagogical research focusing on helping students become more effective learners.

BEVERLY GREENE is Professor of Psychology at St. John's University, a fellow of seven divisions of the American Psychological Association, and a fellow of the American Orthopsychiatric Association and the Academy of Clinical Psychology. She holds a Diplomate in Clinical Psychology and serves on the editorial boards of numerous scholarly journals. She received her PhD in Clinical Psychology from Adelphi University and worked in public mental health for over a decade. She was founding co-editor of the APA Society for the Study of Lesbian, Gay, and Bisexual Issues series, *Psychological Perspectives on Lesbian, Gay and Bisexual Issues*. She is also co-author of the recent book *What Therapists Don't Talk About and Why: Understanding Taboos That Hurt Ourselves and Our Clients* and has more than 80 professional publications that are the subject of nine national awards. Dr. Greene was recipient of the APA 2003 Committee on Women in Psychology Distinguished Leadership Award; 1996 Outstanding Achievement Award from the APA Committee on Lesbian, Gay, and Bisexual Concerns; the 2004 Distinguished Career Contributions to Ethnic Minority Research Award from the APA Society for the Study of Ethnic Minority Issues; the 2000 Heritage Award from the APA Society for the Psychology of Women; the 2004 Award for Distinguished Senior Career Contributions to Ethnic Minority Research (APA Division 45); and the 2005 Stanley Sue Award for Distinguished Professional Contributions to Diversity in Clinical Psychology (APA Division 12). Her co-edited book *Psychotherapy with African American Women: Innovations in Psychodynamic Perspectives and Practice* was also honoured with the Association for Women in Psychology's 2001 Distinguished Publication Award. In 2006, she was the recipient of the Janet Helms Award for Scholarship and Mentoring from the Teacher's College, Columbia University

Cross Cultural Roundtable, and of the 2006 Florence Halpern Award for Distinguished Professional Contributions to Clinical Psychology (APA Division 12). In 2009, she was honoured as recipient of the APA Award for Distinguished Senior Career Contribution to Psychology in the Public Interest. She is an elected representative to the APA Council and member at large of the Women's and Public Interest Caucuses of the Council.

LINDA J. KNIGHT has been teaching psychology at John Abbott College in Sainte-Anne-de-Bellevue, Quebec, since 2001. She teaches in both the Psychology Department and the Youth & Adult Correctional Intervention department and supervises students in clinical practicum work. She served on the Innovative Research and Development Committee and the Teaching and Learning Environmental Committee. She received her PhD in Clinical Psychology from Queen's University in Kingston, Ontario, and was a staff psychologist at the London Psychiatric Hospital, London, Ontario, and the Child and Family Assessment and Treatment Centre of Brant County, Brantford, Ontario. She also practised as a clinical psychologist in Vancouver, British Columbia, and in Montreal, Quebec. In addition to a private practice, she conducted intake and parole assessments at various correctional facilities in Quebec. Dr. Knight served as a reviewer for the first three Canadian editions of *Essentials of Abnormal Psychology in a Changing World*.

PAUL A. JOHNSON has 25 years' experience in post-secondary education as a professor, program co-ordinator, and curriculum and program validation adviser at Confederation College. Paul recently served on the Ontario Ministry of Training, Colleges and Universities (MTCU) committee that developed the new provincial college curriculum standards for general education and essential employability skills. He has received international recognition for academic leadership from the Chair Academy and the National Institute for Staff and Organizational Development (NISOD). Paul has also practised psychology in the Psychotherapy and Psychiatric departments of St. Joseph's Hospital in Thunder Bay. As well, he has been a health-promotion consultant in his community for many years. Along with Helen Bee and Denise Boyd, Paul co-authored *Lifespan Development* (Pearson Education Canada), now in its fourth Canadian edition.

STEVEN TAYLOR, PHD, ABPP, is a professor and clinical psychologist in the Department of Psychiatry at the University of British Columbia and is editor-in-chief of the *Journal of Cognitive Psychotherapy*. He serves on the editorial board of several journals, including the *Journal of Consulting and Clinical Psychology*. He has published over 200 journal articles and book chapters, and over a dozen books on anxiety disorders and related topics. Dr. Taylor has received career awards from the Canadian Psychological Association, the British Columbia Psychological Association, the Association for Advancement of Behaviour Therapy, and the Anxiety Disorders Association of America. He is a fellow of several scholarly organizations, including the Canadian Psychological Association, the American Psychological Association, the Association for Psychological Science, and the Academy of Cognitive Therapy. His clinical and research interests include cognitive-behavioural treatments and mechanisms of anxiety disorders and related conditions, as well as the behavioural genetics of these disorders.

1

What Is Abnormal Psychology?

Did You Know That...

- About one in five adults in Canada will be diagnosed with a psychological disorder at some point in their lives?

- Behaviour we consider abnormal may be perceived as perfectly normal in another culture?

- The modern medical model of abnormal behaviour can be traced to the work of a Greek physician some 2500 years ago?

- A night on the town in London, Ontario, in the 19th century may have included peering at the residents of a local asylum?

- At one time, there were more patients occupying psychiatric hospital beds than there were patients in hospital beds due to all other causes?

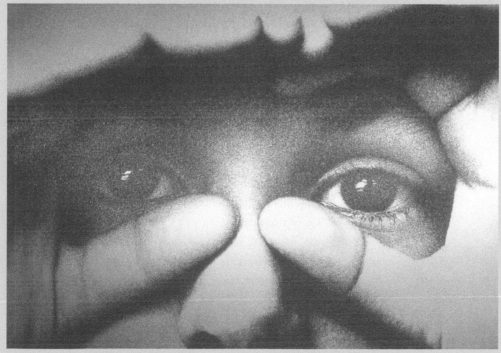

Tomek Sikora/The Image Bank/Getty Images

clinical psychologist Person with graduate training in psychology who specializes in abnormal behaviour. He or she must be registered and licensed with a provincial psychological regulatory body in order to provide psychological services in that province.

psychiatrist Physician who specializes in the diagnosis and treatment of mental disorders.

psychological disorders Disturbances of psychological functioning or behaviour associated with states of personal distress or impaired social, occupational, or interpersonal functioning. Also called *mental disorders*.

abnormal psychology Branch of psychology that deals with the description, causes, and treatment of abnormal behaviour patterns.

medical model Biological perspective in which abnormal behaviour is viewed as symptomatic of underlying illness.

Abnormal behaviour might appear to be the concern of only a few. After all, only a minority of the population will ever be admitted to a psychiatric hospital. Most people never seek the help of a **clinical psychologist** or **psychiatrist**. Only a few people plead not criminally responsible on account of a mental disorder. Many of us have what we call an "eccentric" relative, but few of us have relatives we would consider truly bizarre.

The truth of the matter is abnormal behaviour affects virtually everyone in one way or another. Abnormal behaviour patterns that involve a disturbance of psychological functioning or behaviour are classified as **psychological disorders** (also called *mental disorders*). According to the Canadian Community Health Survey, about 33% of Canadians experience a psychological disorder at some time in their lives. The survey also reported psychological disorders were most common among people in the 45- to 64-year age range, followed by those in the 25- to 44-year range (Statistics Canada, 2012b). In 2015, the Mental Health Commission of Canada (MHCC) released a document titled "Informing the Future: Mental Health Indicators for Canada," which provided a snapshot of mental health and mental illness in Canada. According to this report, close to 12% of Canadian adults in 2011/2012 between the ages of 20 and 64 were diagnosed as having either an anxiety or a depressive disorder. These rates were two and a half times greater among lesbian, gay, and bisexual individuals. In this same year, over 322 000 individuals in Canada were providing care for a family member with a mental illness (MHCC, 2015). So if we include the mental health problems of our family members, friends, and co-workers, then perhaps none of us remains unaffected.

Abnormal psychology is the branch of the science of psychology that addresses the description, causes, and treatment of abnormal behaviour patterns. Let's pause for a moment to consider our use of terms. We prefer to use the term *psychological disorder* when referring to abnormal behaviour patterns associated with disturbances of psychological functioning, rather than *mental disorder*. There are a number of reasons why we have adopted this approach. First, *psychological disorder* puts the study of abnormal behaviour squarely within the purview of the field of psychology. Second, the term *mental disorder* is generally associated with the **medical model** perspective, which considers abnormal behaviour patterns to be symptoms of underlying mental illnesses or disorders. Although the medical model remains a prominent perspective for understanding abnormal behaviour patterns, we shall see that other perspectives, including psychological and sociocultural perspectives, also inform our understanding of abnormal behaviour. Third, *mental disorder* as a phrase reinforces the traditional distinction between mental and physical phenomena. As we'll see, there is increasing awareness of the interrelationships between the body and the mind that calls into question this distinction.

In this chapter, we first address the task of defining abnormal behaviour. We see that throughout history, and even in prehistory, abnormal behaviour has been viewed from different perspectives or according to different models. We chronicle the development of concepts of abnormal behaviour and its treatment. We see that, historically speaking, *treatment* usually referred to what was done *to*, rather than *for*, people with abnormal behaviour. Finally, we'll introduce you to current perspectives on abnormal behaviour.

HOW DO WE DEFINE ABNORMAL BEHAVIOUR?

Most of us become anxious or depressed from time to time, but our behaviour is not deemed abnormal. It is normal to become anxious in anticipation of an important job interview or a final examination. It is appropriate to feel depressed when you have lost someone close to you or when you have failed at a test or on the job. But when do we cross the line between normal and abnormal behaviour?

One answer is emotional states like anxiety and depression may be considered abnormal when they are not appropriate to the situation. It is normal to feel down because of failure on a test, but not when one's grades are good or excellent. It is normal to feel anxious during a job interview, but not whenever entering a department store or boarding a crowded elevator.

Abnormal behaviour may also be suggested by the magnitude of the problem. Although some anxiety is normal enough before a job interview, feeling your heart hammering away so relentlessly that it feels like it might leap from your chest—and consequently cancelling the interview—is not. Nor is it normal to feel so anxious in this situation that your clothing becomes soaked with perspiration.

Criteria for Determining Abnormality

Abnormal behaviour thus has multiple definitions. Depending on the case, some criteria may be weighted more heavily than others. But in most cases, a combination of these criteria is used to define abnormality. Precisely how mental health professionals assess and classify abnormal behaviour is described in Chapter 2, "Assessment, Classification, and Treatment of Abnormal Behaviour."

Psychologists generally apply some combination of the following criteria in making a determination that behaviour is abnormal:

1. *Behaviour is unusual.* Behaviour that is unusual is often considered abnormal. Only a few of us report seeing or hearing things that are not really there; "seeing things" and "hearing things" are almost always considered abnormal in our culture, except, perhaps, in cases of religious experience. Yet **hallucinations** are not deemed unusual in some non-Western cultures. Being overcome with feelings of panic when entering a department store or when standing in a crowded elevator

hallucinations Perceptions that occur in the absence of an external stimulus and that are confused with reality.

Eviled/Shutterstock

Air Images/Shutterstock

When is anxiety abnormal? Negative emotions such as anxiety are considered abnormal when they are judged to be excessive or inappropriate to the situation. Anxiety is generally regarded as normal when it is experienced during a job interview, so long as it is not so severe that it prevents the interviewee from performing adequately. Anxiety is deemed to be abnormal if it is experienced whenever one boards an elevator.

is also uncommon and considered abnormal. But uncommon behaviour is not in itself abnormal. Only one person can hold the record for swimming or running the fastest 100 metres. The record-holding athlete differs from the rest of us but, again, is not considered abnormal.

2. *Behaviour is socially unacceptable or violates social norms.* All societies have norms (standards) that define the kinds of behaviours acceptable in given contexts. Behaviour deemed normal in one culture may be viewed as abnormal in another. In our society, standing on the street corner and repeatedly shouting "Kill 'em!" to passersby would be labelled abnormal; shouting "Kill 'em!" in the arena at a professional wrestling match is usually within normal bounds.

Although the use of norms remains one of the important standards for defining abnormal behaviour, we should be aware of some limitations of this definition.

paranoid Having irrational suspicions.

One implication of basing the definition of abnormal behaviour on social norms is that norms reflect relative cultural standards, not universal truths. What is normal in one culture may be abnormal in another. For example, Canadians who assume strangers are devious and will try to take advantage are usually regarded as distrustful, perhaps even **paranoid**. But such suspicions were justified among the Mundugumor, a tribe of cannibals in Papua New Guinea studied by anthropologist Margaret Mead (1935). Within that culture, male strangers, even the male members of one's own family, *were* typically spiteful toward others.

Clinicians such as psychologists and psychiatrists need to weigh cultural differences in determining what is normal and abnormal. In the case of the Mundugumor, this need is more or less obvious. Sometimes, however, differences are subtler. For example, what is seen as normal, outspoken behaviour by most Canadian women might be interpreted as brazen behaviour when viewed in the context of another, more traditional culture. Moreover, what strikes one generation as abnormal may be considered by others to fall within the normal spectrum. For example, until the mid-1970s, homosexuality was classified as a mental disorder by the psychiatric profession (see Chapter 9, "Gender Dysphoria, Paraphilic Disorders, and Sexual Dysfunctions"). Today, however, the psychiatric profession no longer considers homosexuality a mental disorder. Indeed, roughly two thirds of Canadians now express approval of same-sex relationships (Bibby, 2006). Another implication of basing normality on compliance with social norms is the tendency to brand nonconformists as mentally disturbed.

delusions Firmly held but inaccurate beliefs that persist despite evidence they have no basis in reality.

ideas of persecution A form of delusional thinking characterized by false beliefs that one is being persecuted or victimized by others.

3. *Perception or interpretation of reality is faulty.* Normally speaking, our sensory systems and cognitive processes permit us to form fairly accurate mental representations of the environment. But seeing things or hearing voices that are not present are considered hallucinations, which in our culture are often taken as signs of an underlying disorder. Similarly, holding unfounded ideas or **delusions**, such as **ideas of persecution** that the Mounties or the Mafia are out to get you, may be regarded as signs of mental disturbance—unless, of course, they *are*.

It is normal in Canada to say one "talks" to God through prayer. If, however, a person claims to have literally seen God or heard the voice of God—as opposed to, say, being divinely inspired—we may come to regard her or him as mentally disturbed.

4. *The person is in significant personal distress.* States of personal distress caused by troublesome emotions, such as anxiety, fear, or depression, may be considered abnormal. As noted earlier, however, anxiety and depression are sometimes appropriate responses to a situation. Real threats and losses occur from time to time, and the *lack* of an emotional response to them would be regarded as abnormal. Appropriate feelings of distress are considered normal unless they become prolonged or persist long after the source of anguish has been removed (after most people would have adjusted) or if they are so intense they impair the individual's ability to function.

Christof Stache/AP Photo/CP Images

Is this abnormal? One of the criteria used to determine whether behaviour is abnormal is whether it deviates from acceptable standards of conduct or social norms. The behaviour and attire of these spectators might be considered abnormal in the context of a classroom or workplace, but perhaps not at a sporting event.

5. *Behaviour is maladaptive or self-defeating.* Behaviour that leads to unhappiness rather than self-fulfillment can be regarded as abnormal. Behaviour that limits our ability to function in expected roles or to adapt to our environments may also be considered abnormal. According to these criteria, then, heavy alcohol consumption that impairs health or social and occupational functioning may be viewed as abnormal. **Agoraphobia**, behaviour characterized by an intense fear of venturing into public places, may be considered abnormal in that it is uncommon and also maladaptive because it impairs the individual's ability to fulfill work and family responsibilities.

6. *Behaviour is dangerous.* Behaviour that is dangerous to oneself or other people may be considered abnormal. Here, too, social context is crucial. In wartime, people who sacrifice themselves or charge the enemy with little apparent concern for their own safety may be characterized as courageous, heroic, and patriotic. But people who threaten or attempt suicide because of the pressures of civilian life are usually considered abnormal.

Football and hockey players (and even adolescents) who occasionally get into altercations may be normal enough. Given the cultural demands of these sports, nonaggressive football and hockey players would not last long in varsity or professional ranks. But individuals involved in frequent unsanctioned fights may be regarded as abnormal.

Let's look more in depth at the importance of cultural beliefs and expectations in determining which behaviour patterns are deemed abnormal.

agoraphobia A fear of places and situations from which it might be difficult or embarrassing to escape in the event of panicky symptoms or of situations in which help may be unavailable if such problems occur.

Cultural Bases of Abnormal Behaviour

As noted, behaviour that is normal in one culture may be deemed abnormal in another. Australian Aborigines believe they can communicate with the spirits of their ancestors and that other people, especially close relatives, share their dreams (Glaskin, 2011). These beliefs are considered normal within Aboriginal culture. But were such beliefs to be expressed in a Western culture, they would likely be deemed delusions, which professionals regard as a common feature of schizophrenia. Thus, the standards we use in making judgments of abnormal behaviour must take into account cultural norms.

Abnormal behaviour patterns take different forms in different cultures. According to Hofmann and Hinton (2014), these differences may reflect cultural beliefs of how the body functions. During an anxiety attack, Westerners' catastrophic cognitions usually centre on symptoms associated with a heart attack. Cambodians, in contrast, fear death from the blockage of "tubes" that carry blood and wind throughout the body. As a result, symptoms of anxiety for Cambodians include tightness and soreness in the legs, cold hands and feet, and a sore neck.

The very words we use to describe psychological disorders—words such as *depression* or *anxiety*—have different meanings in other cultures, or no equivalent meaning at all. This doesn't mean that depression or anxiety doesn't exist in other cultures. Rather, it suggests we need to learn how people in different cultures experience emotional distress rather than imposing our perspectives on their experiences. People in China and other countries in the Far East generally place greater emphasis on the physical or somatic symptoms of depression, such as headaches, fatigue, or weakness, than on feelings of guilt or sadness, as compared to people from Western cultures (Ryder et al., 2008; Zhou et al., 2011).

Cultural differences in how abnormal behaviour patterns are expressed lead us to realize we must ensure our concepts of abnormal behaviour are recognizable and valid before we apply them to other cultures. The reverse is equally true. The concept of "soul loss" may characterize psychological distress in some non-Western societies but has little or no relevance to North Americans. Research efforts along these lines have shown that the abnormal behaviour pattern associated with our concept of schizophrenia exists in countries as wide-ranging as Colombia, India, China, Denmark, Nigeria, and the former Soviet Union, as well as many others (Jablensky, Sartorius, Ernberg, & Anker, 1992; Vespia, 2009). Furthermore, rates of schizophrenia appear similar among the countries studied. However, differences have been observed in some of the features of the disorder across cultures (Myers, 2011).

Societal views or perspectives on abnormal behaviour also vary across cultures. In our society, models based on medical disease and psychological factors have achieved prominence in explaining abnormal behaviour. But in traditional cultures, concepts of abnormal behaviour often invoke supernatural causes, such as possession by demons or the devil (Stefanovics et al., 2016). For example, in Filipino folk society, psychological problems are often attributed to the influence of "spirits" or the possession of a "weak soul" (Edman & Johnson, 1999). In Nigeria, over 30% of individuals surveyed in a community sample attributed mental illness to possession by evil spirits (Adewuya & Makanjuola, 2008).

The Continuum between Normal and Abnormal Behaviour

Although our discussion has centred on how to determine whether or not a behaviour pattern is considered abnormal, it is important to recognize that most behaviours are on a continuum from normal to abnormal, and a precise line delineating the threshold between the two is not clear (Cuijpers, 2014). Keep in mind that you may have experienced some of the symptoms of the disorders discussed in the following chapters, but not necessarily in the range that would be considered abnormal. For this reason, we will introduce a continuum chart at the beginning of each chapter to emphasize the dimensional aspect of mental disorders. As you will see in Chapter 2, our present approach to diagnosis is categorical, in that an individual either meets the criteria for a particular mental disorder or does not.

It is one thing to recognize and label behaviour as abnormal; it is another to understand and explain it. Philosophers, physicians, natural scientists, and psychologists have

Continuum between Normal and Abnormal Behaviour

Does not meet criteria		Meets criteria		
NO SYMPTOMS	STRUGGLING	MILD	MODERATE	SEVERE

used various approaches, or *models*, in an effort to explain abnormal behaviour. Some approaches have been based on superstition; others have invoked religious explanations. Some current views are predominantly biological; others are psychological. Let's now consider various historical and contemporary approaches to understanding abnormal behaviour.

FOCUS ON DIVERSITY

Mental Health Issues in Canadian Indigenous Communities

Canadian census data show our Indigenous population continues to be the fastest-growing segment of the population. The highest concentrations of Canada's more than 1.4 million Indigenous peoples are in the North and West, and more than half are now living in urban centres throughout Canada (Statistics Canada, 2013a). Along with rapid population growth, there is evidence of the resurgence of Canadian Indigenous cultures, especially in the arts, the media, education, commerce, and health (Aboriginal Planet, 2002; Arthur & Stewart, 2001; Letendre, 2002).

Despite this optimistic outlook, Indigenous peoples in Canada are still dealing with the effects of generations of physical, mental, emotional, and spiritual distress caused by the decimation of their communities, lands, and cultural identities. Consequently, both on- and off-reserve Indigenous peoples have to contend with extensive mental health, addiction, and medical issues in their communities as compared to the rest of Canadians. In particular, Canadian Indigenous peoples suffer from disproportionately higher rates of major depression, anxiety, posttraumatic stress disorder, alcoholism and substance abuse, sexual abuse, family violence, chronic disease such as heart disease and diabetes, lower life expectancy, and suicide (Kielland & Simeone, 2014).

According to Menzies (2014), the trauma experienced by one generation affects subsequent generations. Centuries of extreme social, cultural, and geographic disruption have contributed to the distress suffered by Indigenous peoples. The arrival of European settlers resulted in an estimated 90% decline in Indigenous populations (Trigger & Swagerty, 1996). The remaining Indigenous people were exposed to widespread, inescapable social and cultural disruption caused by government-sanctioned separation of children from their parents and communities plus systematic efforts to force Indigenous people to take on non-Indigenous cultural values at the cost of becoming disconnected from their own. This process of cultural assimilation was enforced by the relocation and social regrouping of Indigenous peoples onto remote reserves, by placing Indigenous children into residential boarding schools, and by unwittingly creating a forced dependence on government support. Poverty and powerlessness further marginalized Indigenous peoples and their cultural traditions from mainstream society (Poonwassie & Charter, 2001). Indigenous peoples' survival of and recovery from this long-standing personal and social devastation are a testament to their strength and long-suffering determination. Moreover, it gives credence to the significance and legitimacy of their perception of life.

On June 11, 2008, Prime Minister Stephen Harper apologized, on behalf of the Government of Canada, to former students of Indian residential schools (IRS). An Indian Residential Schools Resolution Health Support Program was established to provide mental health services to former IRS students and their families. Health Canada continues to work collaboratively with the Assembly of First Nations and the Inuit Tapiriit Kanatami to develop and implement mental health, addiction, and youth suicide prevention strategies (Health Canada, 2015a).

How Do We Define Abnormal Behaviour?

- **What are the criteria used by mental health professionals to define abnormal behaviour?** Psychologists generally consider behaviour abnormal when it meets some combination of the following criteria: (1) unusual; (2) socially unacceptable or in violation of social norms; (3) fraught with misperceptions or misinterpretations of reality; (4) associated with states of severe personal distress; (5) maladaptive or self-defeating; and (6) dangerous.
- **What are psychological disorders?** Psychological disorders (also called *mental disorders*) involve abnormal behaviour patterns associated with disturbances in mental health or psychological functioning.
- **How are cultural beliefs and norms related to the classification and understandings of abnormal behaviour?** Behaviours deemed normal in one culture may be considered abnormal in another. Concepts of health and illness may have different meanings in different cultures. Abnormal behaviour patterns may also take different forms in different cultures, and societal views or models explaining abnormal behaviour vary across cultures as well.

HISTORICAL PERSPECTIVES ON ABNORMAL BEHAVIOUR

worldview Prevailing view of the times. (English translation of the German *Weltanschauung*.)

possession In demonology, a type of superstitious belief in which abnormal behaviour is taken as a sign that the individual has become possessed by demons or the devil, usually as a form of retribution or the result of making a pact with the devil.

trephining Harsh prehistoric practice of cutting a hole in a person's skull, possibly as an ancient form of surgery for brain trauma, or possibly as a means of releasing the demons prehistoric people may have believed caused abnormal behaviour in the afflicted individuals.

demonological model The model that explains abnormal behaviour in terms of supernatural forces.

Throughout the history of Western culture, concepts of abnormal behaviour have been shaped, to some degree, by the prevailing **worldview** of the time. Throughout much of history, beliefs in supernatural forces, demons, and evil spirits held sway. Abnormal behaviour was often taken as a sign of **possession**. In more modern times, the predominant—but by no means universal—worldview has shifted toward beliefs in science and reason. Abnormal behaviour has come to be viewed in our culture as the product of physical and psychosocial factors, not demonic possession.

The Demonological Model

Let's begin our journey with an example from prehistory. Archaeologists have unearthed human skeletons from the Stone Age with egg-size cavities in the skulls. One interpretation of these holes is our prehistoric ancestors believed abnormal behaviour reflected the invasion of evil spirits. Perhaps they used this harsh method—called **trephining**—to create a pathway through the skull to provide an outlet for those irascible spirits. Fresh bone growth indicates some people managed to survive the ordeal.

Threat of trephining may have persuaded people to comply with group or tribal norms to the best of their abilities. Because no written records or accounts of the purposes of trephination exist, other explanations are possible. Perhaps trephination was used as a primitive form of surgery to remove shattered pieces of bone or blood clots that resulted from head injuries (Maher & Maher, 1985).

Explanation of abnormal behaviour as a result of supernatural or divine causes is termed the **demonological model**. Ancient peoples explained natural forces in terms of divine will and spirits. The ancient Babylonians believed the movements of the stars and planets were fashioned by the adventures and conflicts of the gods. The ancient Greeks believed their gods toyed with humans; when aroused to wrath, the gods could unleash forces of nature to wreak havoc on disrespectful or arrogant humans, even clouding their minds with madness.

Origins of the Medical Model: An "Ill Humour"

Not all ancient Greeks believed in the demonological model. The seeds of naturalistic explanations of abnormal behaviour were sown by Hippocrates and developed by other physicians in the ancient world, especially Galen.

Hippocrates (ca. 460–377 BC), the celebrated physician of the Golden Age of Greece, challenged the prevailing beliefs of his time by arguing that illnesses of the body and mind were the result of natural causes, not of possession by supernatural spirits. He believed the health of the body and mind depended on the balance of **humours** or vital fluids: phlegm, black bile, blood, and yellow bile. An imbalance of humours, he thought, accounted for abnormal behaviour. A lethargic or sluggish person was believed to have an excess of phlegm, from which we derive the word **phlegmatic**. An overabundance of black bile was believed to cause depression, or **melancholia**. An excess of blood created a **sanguine** disposition: cheerful, confident, and optimistic. An excess of yellow bile made people "bilious" and **choleric**—that is, quick tempered.

Hippocrates's theory of bodily humours is of historical importance because of its break from demonology. It also foreshadowed the development of the modern medical model, the view that abnormal behaviour results from underlying biological processes. Medical schools continue to pay homage to Hippocrates by having new physicians swear the Hippocratic oath in his honour.

humours Four fluids in the body: phlegm, black bile, blood, and yellow bile. Hippocrates believed the health of the body and mind depended on their balance.

phlegmatic Slow and stolid.

melancholia State of severe depression.

sanguine Cheerful.

choleric Having or showing bad temper.

Medieval Times

The Middle Ages, or medieval times, cover the millennium of European history from about AD 476 through AD 1450. Belief in supernatural causes, especially the doctrine of possession, increased in influence and eventually dominated medieval thought. The doctrine of possession held that abnormal behaviours were a sign of possession by evil spirits or the devil. This belief was embodied within the teachings of the Roman Catholic Church, which became the unifying force in Western Europe following the decline of the Roman Empire. Although belief in possession dates from before the Church and is found in ancient Egyptian and Greek writings, the Church revitalized it. The treatment of choice for abnormal behaviour was **exorcism**. Exorcists were employed to persuade evil spirits that the bodies of their intended victims were basically uninhabitable. Their methods included prayer, waving a cross at the victim, beating and flogging, and even starving the victim. If the victim still displayed unseemly behaviour, there were yet more powerful remedies, such as the rack, a device of torture. It seems clear that recipients of these "remedies" would be motivated to behave acceptably as much as possible.

exorcism Ritual intended to expel demons or evil spirits from a person believed to be possessed.

Witchcraft

The late 15th through the late 17th centuries were especially dangerous times to be unpopular with your neighbours. These were times of massive persecutions of people, particularly women, who were accused of witchcraft. Officials of the Roman Catholic Church believed witches made pacts with the devil, practised satanic rituals, and committed heinous acts such as eating babies and poisoning crops. In 1484, Pope Innocent VIII decreed witches must be executed. Two Dominican priests compiled a manual for witch hunting, called the *Malleus Maleficarum* ("The Witches' Hammer"), to help inquisitors identify suspected witches. More than 100 000 accused witches were killed in the next two centuries.

Modern scholars once believed the so-called witches of the Middle Ages and the Renaissance were actually people who were mentally disturbed. They were believed to have been persecuted because their abnormal behaviour was taken as evidence they were in league with the

Shutterstock

Exorcism. This medieval woodcut illustrates the practice of exorcism, which was used to expel evil spirits who were believed to have possessed people.

devil. It is true that many suspected witches confessed to impossible behaviours; however, most of these confessions can be discounted because they were extracted under torture by inquisitors who were bent on finding evidence to support accusations of witchcraft (Spanos, 1978). Accusations of witchcraft appeared to be a convenient means of disposing of social nuisances and political rivals, of seizing property, and of suppressing heresy (Spanos, 1978). In English villages, many of the accused were poor, unmarried elderly women who were forced to beg their neighbours for food. If misfortune befell people who declined to help, the beggar might be accused of causing misery by having cast a curse on the uncharitable family (Spanos, 1978). If the woman was generally unpopular, accusations of witchcraft were more likely to be followed up.

Historical trends do not follow straight lines. Although the demonological model held sway during the Middle Ages and much of the Renaissance, it did not universally replace belief in naturalistic causes (Schoeneman, 1984). In medieval England, for example, demonic possession was only rarely invoked as the cause of abnormal behaviour in cases in which a person was held to be insane by legal authorities (Neugebauer, 1979). Most explanations of unusual behaviour involved natural causes, such as illness or trauma to the brain. In England, in fact, some disturbed people were kept in hospitals until they were restored to sanity (Alldderidge, 1979). The Renaissance Belgian physician Johann Weyer (1515–1588) also took up the cause of Hippocrates and Galen by arguing that abnormal behaviour and thought patterns were caused by physical problems.

Asylums in Europe and the New World

By the late 15th and early 16th centuries, asylums, or *madhouses*, began to crop up throughout Europe. Many were former leprosariums that were no longer needed as a result of the decline in leprosy that occurred in the late Middle Ages. Asylums often gave refuge to beggars as well as the disturbed, and conditions were generally appalling. Residents were often chained to their beds and left to lie in their own waste or wander about unassisted. Some asylums became public spectacles. In the 19th century, it was standard operating procedure at many Ontario asylums (found in Toronto, Hamilton, and London) to open to public viewing from noon until 3 p.m. every day (Miron, 2006).

The first asylum in what is now North America was the Hôtel Dieu in Quebec City. It was founded in 1639 by the Duchesse d'Aiguillon to care for people with psychological disorders and intellectual disabilities, as well as the poor, the destitute, and the physically disabled. The Catholic community took responsibility for the treatment of patients and oversaw the development of other asylums throughout Quebec (Hurd et al., 1916). Outside Quebec, however, people with psychological disorders received little treatment and were commonly shut away in jails, poorhouses, charity shelters, or another convenient stronghold. No means of addressing their needs came until well into the 19th century, when mental hospitals began to appear in other parts of Canada (Sussman, 1998).

Jerry Cooke/Science Source/Getty Images

Madhouse, spectacle, or hospital? Standard operating procedure in many Ontario asylums was to allow the public to view the patients, making the hospitals a public spectacle.

The Reform Movement and Moral Therapy in Europe and North America

The modern era of treatment can be traced to the efforts of individuals such as the Frenchmen Jean-Baptiste Pussin and Philippe Pinel in the late 18th and early 19th centuries. They argued that people who behave abnormally suffer from diseases and should be treated humanely. This view

The unchaining of inmates at La Bicêtre by 18th-century French reformer Philippe Pinel. Continuing the work of Jean-Baptiste Pussin, Pinel stopped harsh practices such as bleeding and purging and moved inmates from darkened dungeons to sunny, airy rooms. Pinel also took the time to converse with inmates in the belief that understanding and concern would help restore them to normal functioning.

Bettmann/Getty Images

was not popular at the time. Deranged people were generally regarded by the public as threats to society, not as sick people in need of treatment.

From 1784 to 1802, Pussin (1746–1811), a layman, was placed in charge of a ward for people considered "incurably insane" at La Bicêtre, a large mental hospital in Paris. Although Pinel is often credited with freeing the inmates of La Bicêtre from their chains, Pussin was actually the first official to unchain a group of the "incurably insane." These unfortunates had been considered too dangerous and unpredictable to be left unchained. But Pussin believed if they were treated with kindness, there would be no need for chains. As he predicted, most of the shut-ins became manageable and calm when their chains were removed. They could walk the hospital grounds and take in fresh air. Pussin also forbade the staff from treating the residents harshly, and he discharged employees who ignored his directives.

Pinel (1745–1826) became medical director for the incurables' ward at La Bicêtre in 1793 and continued the humane treatment Pussin had begun. Pinel also spent hours talking to inmates, in the belief that showing understanding and concern would help restore them to normal functioning.

The philosophy of treatment that emerged from these efforts was labelled **moral therapy** (a mistranslation of the words for "well-being" or "morale") (Dix, 1999). It was based on the belief that providing humane treatment in a relaxed, decent, and encouraging environment could restore functioning. Similar reforms were instituted at about this time in England by William Tuke and later in the United States and Canada by Dorothea Dix.

Dix (1802–1887), a Boston schoolteacher, travelled throughout the United States, Europe, and Canada decrying the deplorable conditions in jails and charitable housing, where deranged people were often placed. As a direct result of her social activism, mental hospitals were established in Canada outside of Quebec, initially in the Maritimes during the 1840s and later in the century in the other provinces.

moral therapy A 19th-century treatment philosophy emphasizing that hospitalized mental patients should be treated with care and understanding in a pleasant environment, not shackled in chains.

Drugs and Deinstitutionalization: The Exodus from Provincial Psychiatric Hospitals

An important factor that spurred the exodus from psychiatric hospitals was the advent of a new class of drugs—**phenothiazines**. The phenothiazines, a group of antipsychotic drugs that helped suppress the most flagrant behaviour patterns associated with schizophrenia, were introduced in Canada in the early 1950s. Two psychiatrists, unbeknownst to each other, had begun experimenting with chlorpromazine, a drug that was being

phenothiazines Group of antipsychotic drugs or "major tranquillizers" used in the treatment of schizophrenia.

used in conjunction with anaesthetics for surgery. They were curious about its soothing qualities and potential worth as a treatment for psychotic symptoms, and it wasn't long before their pioneering research produced far-reaching outcomes. In 1954, Dr. Ruth Kajander was the first in North America to publicly report on the drug's therapeutic value (Sussman, 1999). A month later, McGill University psychiatrist Heinz Lehmann published the first research paper for the North American audience describing his success in using chlorpromazine to treat schizophrenia (Griffin, 1993; Sussman, 1999). As a result of Kajander's and Lehmann's research, the widespread use of chlorpromazine as an antipsychotic drug in Canada and the United States quickly followed. Chlorpromazine reduced the need for indefinite hospital stays and permitted many people with schizophrenia to be discharged to less restrictive living arrangements in their community, such as halfway houses, group homes, and independent living arrangements. This was a crucial moment in the mental health-care system in Canada.

In response to the growing call for reform in the mental health system, the Canadian Mental Health Association (CMHA) published a book, *More for the Mind: A Study of Psychiatric Services in Canada* (Tyhurst et al., 1963), that recommended mental illness be treated as a medical condition in a medical facility. This report paved the way for long-term custodial care patients (the so-called back-ward patients in bleak institutions) to be integrated into community general hospitals. This policy of **deinstitutionalization** was based on the belief—the hope, perhaps—that psychiatric patients would benefit from the opportunity to lead more independent and fulfilling lives in the community while relying on general hospitals for short-term care during episodes of illness. Indeed, the psychiatric hospital population across Canada plummeted from more than 50 000 in 1960 to 15 000 by 1975 (Wasylenki, 2001).

In the initial stages, during the 1960s and 1970s, there was a shift from long stays in provincial psychiatric hospitals to shorter but more frequent stays in general hospital psychiatric units. However, although the number of general hospital beds used for this purpose rose, it failed to match the shrinking number of psychiatric hospital beds. At the same time, the availability of more community mental health supports and services lagged far behind the rapid exodus of mental health patients from psychiatric hospitals (Sealy & Whitehead, 2004). The general hospital psychiatric units treated patients with less severe forms of mental disorders, while patients with severe and persistent mental disorders had to rely on the much-scaled-down provincial psychiatric hospital system. In effect, this created a two-tier mental health-care system, whereby middle- and upper-class patients had easier access to psychiatrists and general hospital psychiatric care than less fortunate Canadians, who were relegated to shrinking psychiatric hospital services or, worse, were left to lead a barely sufficient existence in the community (Kirby & Keon, 2004).

Services continued to be narrow in focus and were not well coordinated, thus making it difficult for patients to receive adequate and consistent care. The community programs and services that were supposed to replace institutional care have thus far been inadequate (Kirby & Keon, 2004; Wasylenki, 2001). Deinstitutionalization in Canada has left mental patients to rely on dramatically fewer hospital beds and a fragmented system of community services and supports. In "A Closer Look: The Homeless in "Canada" on page 16, we consider the plight of the homeless Canadians with mental health issues who got lost in the shuffle between the movement toward the closure of psychiatric institutions and the promised, but thus far inadequate, community mental health-care system.

Until recently, Canada lacked a comprehensive mental health-care policy. In 2006, senators Michael Kirby and Wilbert Keon conducted the most comprehensive study of its kind in Canada on mental health, mental illness, and addiction. Their report, *Out of the Shadows at Last: Transforming Mental Health, Mental Illness and Addiction Services in Canada,* focused squarely on mental health promotion, prevention of mental illness, and the creation of a continuum of care for those who suffer from mental illness and addiction. Based on the recommendations from this report, a Canadian Mental Health Commission was established in 2007 to implement a national mental health-care strategy (see "A Closer Look: Canadian Mental Health Promotion").

deinstitutionalization Practice of discharging large numbers of hospitalized mental patients to the community and reducing the need for new admissions through the development of alternative treatment approaches such as halfway houses and crisis intervention services.

Canadian Mental Health Promotion

PROMOTING MENTAL HEALTH

Mental health promotion is a proactive, holistic, multilevelled, synergistic process that fosters resilience as one progresses toward an optimal sense of well-being (see Figure 1.1 in this box) (Johnson, 1989). It is proactive in that it builds up knowledge, resources, and strengths for overall wellness and improves the capacity of individuals to take control of their lives (Health Canada, 2003). Through education, community efforts, and government policy, mental health promotion champions optimal mental health, reduces the stigma of mental illness, and promotes a mental wellness lifestyle (Baylis, 2002). Mental health promotion also moves beyond the commonly held notion that mental health is the mere absence of mental illness (Kahan & Goodstadt, 2002). Moreover, it applies equally to all people, sick or well, disabled or not, problematic or not (Health Canada, 2003). The holistic nature of mental health promotion places high importance on mental, emotional, social, physical, and spiritual functioning (World Health Organization, n.d.). It considers the interactive nature of these personal domains on multiple levels, including the physical environment, family, community, culture, politics, and economics (Health Canada, 2003; Kahan & Goodstadt, 2002). As is true with risk factors, there is a synergistic effect among

health-promoting factors. Exposure to a combination of mental health promotion factors can be greater than the sum total effect of the individual factors (Dryden, Johnson, Howard, & McGuire, 1998).

MENTAL HEALTH PROMOTION INITIATIVES

Canada is sitting on the cusp of change when it comes to mental health promotion and prevention, and psychology's role will likely expand across all health-related areas (Arnett, 2006). Below are just some of the initiatives that cover the full spectrum of mental health promotion services and supports:

- In their report *Out of the Shadows at Last: Transforming Mental Health, Mental Illness and Addiction Services in Canada*, Canadian senators Kirby and Keon (2006) recommended a Canadian mental health commission be established for mental health promotion and prevention of mental illness. The Mental Health Commission of Canada (MHCC) was established in 2007.
- Among its initiatives, the MHCC created the country's first mental health strategy, *Changing Directions, Changing Lives*, released in May 2012. It aims to help improve the mental health and well-being of all people living in Canada and to create a

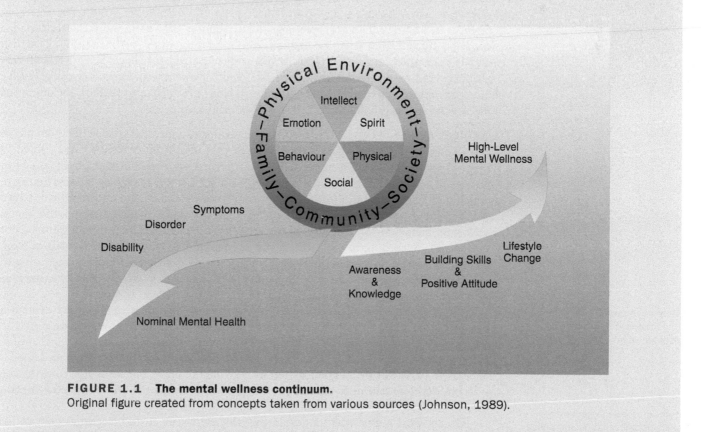

FIGURE 1.1   The mental wellness continuum.
Original figure created from concepts taken from various sources (Johnson, 1989).

mental health system that can truly meet the needs of people living with mental health problems and illnesses and their families (MHCC, 2012).

- A first phase of work was completed in 2009 with the release of *Toward Recovery and Well-Being: A Framework for a Mental Health Strategy for Canada*, which put forward a vision and broad goals for transforming the mental health system (MHCC, 2009). The strategy translates this vision into 26 priorities and 109 recommendations for action, grouped under the following six strategic directions:

1. Promote mental health across the lifespan in homes, schools, and workplaces, and prevent mental illness and suicide wherever possible.
2. Foster recovery and well-being for people of all ages living with mental health problems and illnesses, and uphold their rights.
3. Provide access to the right combination of services, treatments, and supports when and where people need them.

4. Reduce disparities in risk factors and access to mental health services, and strengthen the response to the needs of diverse communities and Northerners.
5. Work with First Nations, Inuit, and Métis to address their mental health needs, acknowledging their distinct circumstances, rights, and cultures.
6. Mobilize leadership, improve knowledge, and foster collaboration at all levels.

- In 2016, the MHCC released *Advancing the Mental Health Strategy for Canada: A Framework for Action*. This document represents the MHCC's strategic plan (2017–2022) to identify key areas for action based on the objectives outlined in *Changing Directions, Changing Lives* (MHCC, 2016).

Source: Mental Health Commission of Canada. (2012) *Changing directions, changing lives: The mental health strategy for Canada*. Calgary, AB: Author.

Pathways to the Present: From Demonology to Science

Beliefs in possession or demonology persisted until the rise of the natural sciences in the late 17th and early 18th centuries. Society at large began to turn toward reason and science as ways of explaining natural phenomena and human behaviour. The emerging sciences of biology, chemistry, physics, and astronomy offered promise that knowledge could be derived from scientific methods of observation and experimentation. The 18th and 19th centuries witnessed rapid developments in medical science. Scientific discoveries uncovered the microbial causes of some kinds of diseases and gave rise to preventive measures. Emerging models of abnormal behaviour also began to surface, including the medical model, psychological models, and sociocultural models.

MEDICAL MODEL   Against the backdrop of advances in medical science, German physician Wilhelm Griesinger (1817–1868) argued that abnormal behaviour was rooted in diseases of the brain. Griesinger's views influenced another German physician, Emil Kraepelin (1856–1926), who in 1883 wrote an influential textbook on psychiatry in which he likened mental disorders to physical diseases. Griesinger and Kraepelin paved the way for the development of the modern medical model, which attempts to explain abnormal behaviour on the basis of underlying biological defects or abnormalities, not evil spirits. According to the medical model, people behaving abnormally suffer from mental illnesses or disorders that can be classified, like physical illnesses, according to their distinctive causes and symptoms and whose features can be conceptualized as symptoms of underlying disorders, whatever their cause.

dementia praecox Term used by Emil Kraepelin to describe the disorder we now call *schizophrenia*.

Kraepelin specified two main groups of mental disorders or diseases: **dementia praecox** (from roots meaning "precocious [premature] insanity"), which we now call *schizophrenia*, and *manic-depressive psychosis*, which is now labelled *bipolar disorder*. Kraepelin believed dementia praecox was caused by a biochemical imbalance and manic-depressive psychosis by an abnormality in body metabolism. But his major contribution was the development of a classification system that forms the cornerstone of current diagnostic systems.

general paresis Degenerative brain disorder that occurs during the final stage of syphilis.

The medical model was supported by evidence that a form of derangement called **general paresis** represented an advanced stage of syphilis in which the syphilis bacterium directly invades brain tissue. Scientists grew optimistic that other biological causes, as well as treatments, would soon be discovered for other so-called mental disorders. This early optimism has remained largely unfulfilled because the causes of most patterns of abnormal behaviour remain obscure.

Much of the terminology in current use reflects the influence of the medical model. Because of the medical model, many professionals and laypeople speak of people whose behaviour is deemed abnormal as being mentally *ill*. It is because of the medical model that so many speak of the *symptoms* of abnormal behaviour rather than its *features* or *characteristics*. Other terms spawned by the medical model include *mental health*, *syndrome*, *diagnosis*, *patient*, *mental patient*, *mental hospital*, *prognosis*, *treatment*, *therapy*, *cure*, *relapse*, and *remission*.

The medical model is a major advance over demonology. It inspired the idea that abnormal behaviour should be treated by learned professionals and not be punished. Compassion replaced hatred, fear, and persecution.

PSYCHOLOGICAL MODELS Although the medical model was gaining influence in the 19th century, there were those who believed that organic factors alone could not explain the many forms of abnormal behaviour. In Paris, a highly respected neurologist, Jean-Martin Charcot (1825–1893), experimented with the use of **hypnosis** in treating **hysteria** (which is now called *conversion disorder*), a condition in which people present with physical symptoms such as paralysis or numbness that cannot be explained by any underlying physical cause. The thinking at the time was they must have an affliction of the nervous system that caused their symptoms. Yet Charcot and his associates demonstrated these symptoms could be removed in hysterical patients or actually induced in normal patients by means of hypnotic suggestion.

Among those who attended Charcot's demonstrations was a young Austrian physician named Sigmund Freud (1856–1939). Freud reasoned that if hysterical symptoms could be made to disappear or appear through hypnosis—the mere "suggestion of ideas"—they must be psychological in origin (Jones, 1953). He concluded that whatever psychological factors give rise to hysteria, they must lie outside the range of conscious awareness. This was the kernel of the idea that underlies his model of abnormal behaviour, the **psychodynamic model**, which holds that the causes of abnormal behaviours lie in the interplay of forces within the unconscious mind. "I received the proudest impression," Freud wrote of his experience with Charcot, "of the possibility that there could be powerful mental processes which nevertheless remained hidden from the consciousness of men" (cited in Sulloway, 1983, p. 32).

Freud's theoretical model was the first major psychological model of abnormal behaviour. As we'll see later in this chapter, other psychological perspectives on abnormal behaviour soon followed, based on behavioural, humanistic, and cognitive approaches. We'll also see that each of these psychological perspectives, as well as the physiological perspective, spawned particular forms of therapy to treat psychological disorders.

SOCIOCULTURAL MODELS Sociocultural theorists believe that to better understand the roots of abnormal behaviour, we must consider the broader social contexts in which behaviour occurs. They believe the causes of abnormal behaviour may be found in the failures of society rather than of the person. Psychological problems may be rooted in the social ills of society, such as poverty, lack of economic opportunity, rapidly changing social values and morals, and racial and gender discrimination. This view of abnormal behaviour will be addressed further later in this chapter.

According to the more radical sociocultural theorists, such as the psychiatrist Thomas Szasz, mental illness is no more than a myth—a label used to stigmatize and subjugate people whose behaviour is socially deviant (Szasz, 1961). Szasz argues that so-called mental illnesses are really "problems in living," not diseases in the sense that influenza, hypertension, and cancer are. Nearly half a century later, Canadian psychiatrist Gordon Warme (2006) has rekindled these sentiments by claiming that biological explanations of abnormal behaviour are still unconvincing and "most, if not all, of the effects of psychiatry are magical" (p. 2).

Sociocultural theorists maintain that once the label of "mental illness" is applied it is difficult to remove. The label also affects other people's responses to the "patient."

hypnosis Trance-like state, induced by suggestion, in which one is generally passive and responsive to the commands of the hypnotist.

hysteria Former term for *conversion disorder*.

psychodynamic model Theoretical model of Freud and his followers in which behaviour is viewed as the product of clashing forces within the personality.

While it is true that many provincial psychiatric hospitals closed their doors and general hospitals reduced the number of psychiatric beds beginning in the 1990s, problems arose when provinces failed to adequately fund or integrate community support services intended to replace the need for long-term hospitalization (Muckle & Turnbull, 2006). Far too often, homeless people with a range of psychological problems fell through the cracks of the mental health and social services systems and were left largely to fend for themselves. In particular, there has been an ongoing lack of available housing, transitional care facilities, and effective case management for homeless Canadians who have psychological disorders and addictions (Kirby & Keon, 2006).

FACING THE CHALLENGE OF MENTAL HEALTH PROMOTION FOR HOMELESS PEOPLE

Projections indicate that up to 200 000 Canadians are homeless annually (Goering et al., 2014). Although difficult to measure, it is estimated that up to 67% of homeless people have had a mental health problem in their lifetime (Goering et al., 2014). A year-long study of Toronto homeless shelter users found that about one third (31%) of homeless people were experiencing both psychological and substance use disorders, while roughly equal numbers were experiencing either a psychological disorder (19%) or a substance use disorder (21%) (Tolomiczenko & Goering, 1998). In 5% of cases, a severe psychological disorder, primarily schizophrenia, was found. From 2010 to 2014, approximately 450 000 people in Canada used an emergency shelter. Although the number of people using shelters did not increase from 2005 to 2014, there was an increase in the average length of stay and the number of families using shelters. Close to 90% of families who used a shelter were single-parent families headed by women. The rate of shelter use for Indigenous peoples is 10 times greater than the general population (ESDC, 2016).

In April 2007, the Homelessness Partnering Strategy (HPS) was launched. Its aim was to prevent and reduce homelessness by providing support and funding to communities throughout Canada. In 2008, the federal government invested in a research demonstration project to test the benefits of a housing-first approach to helping individuals who were both mentally ill and homeless. Typically, individuals who are homeless are expected to resolve their substance and mental health problems prior to being assisted in finding housing. In this reversed approach, individuals are moved into permanent housing and provided with case management and professional services to help them with their mental health issues and reintegration into the community.

Use with the permission of Paul W. Liebhardt

Homeless with mental health issues. A multifaceted effort is needed to meet the needs of the psychiatric homeless population, including access to affordable housing and to medical, drug and alcohol, and mental health treatment, as well as other social services. Far too often, homeless people with a range of psychological problems fall through the cracks of the mental health and social services systems and are left largely to fend for themselves.

This project, named At Home/Chez Soi, was implemented by the MHCC in five cities in Canada (Vancouver, Winnipeg, Toronto, Montreal, and Moncton) between 2009 and 2013. The results revealed that those who participated in the project had increased housing stability and higher levels of community involvement than a control group. Participants also reported greater gains in quality of life (Goering et al., 2014). Based on these findings, the Government of Canada's Economic Action Plan 2013 committed nearly $600 million over five years (2014–2019) toward a renewed HPS that would implement a housing-first approach across Canada (ESDC, 2016).

In 2016, the Government of Canada conducted the first coordinated point-in-time homelessness count across 32 communities in Canada. A point-in-time count is an estimate of the number of people who are either in emergency shelters, transitional housing, or living on the street on the day of the count. The count identified 4579 homeless individuals across these communities. The majority (47%) were staying in a shelter, 29% were in

>

transitional housing, and 24% were living on the street. Close to 57% had been homeless for six or more months. Among adults between the ages of 25 to 49, the most common reason given for their most recent housing loss was addiction or substance use. This was

the second most common reason among youth ages 14 to 24, following conflict with a parent or guardian (ESDC, 2017). A second count is planned for the spring of 2018 to assess the effectiveness of interventions aimed at reducing homelessness.

Mental patients are stigmatized and socially degraded. Job opportunities may be denied, friendships may dissolve, and the "patient" may become increasingly alienated from society. Szasz argues that treating people as mentally ill strips them of their dignity because it denies them responsibility for their own behaviour and choices. He claims troubled people should be encouraged to take more responsibility for managing their lives and solving their problems (Szasz, 1961).

Although not all sociocultural theorists subscribe to Szasz's more radical views, they alert us to consider the importance of taking sociocultural factors relating to gender, race, ethnicity, lifestyle, and social ills such as poverty and discrimination into account in understanding people whose behaviour leads them to be perceived as mentally ill or abnormal. It should come as no surprise that the effects of stigma and discrimination remain a daily experience for many Canadians diagnosed with psychological or addictive disorders—a topic we'll come back to in Chapter 2, "Assessment, Classification, and Treatment of Abnormal Behaviour."

REVIEW IT

Historical Perspectives on Abnormal Behaviour

- **How have views about abnormal behaviour changed over time?** Ancient societies attributed abnormal behaviour to divine or supernatural forces. There were some authorities in ancient times, such as the Greek physicians Hippocrates and Galen, who believed abnormal behaviour reflected natural causes. In medieval times, belief in possession held sway, and exorcists were used to rid people who behaved abnormally of the evil spirits that were believed to possess them. The 19th-century German physician Wilhelm Griesinger argued that abnormal behaviour was caused by diseases of the brain. He and another German physician who followed him, Emil Kraepelin, were influential in the development of the modern medical model, which likens abnormal behaviour patterns to physical illnesses.

- **How has the treatment of people with psychological disorders changed over time?** Asylums, or madhouses, began to crop up throughout Europe in the late 15th and early 16th centuries. Conditions in these asylums were dreadful, and in some, such as Bethlehem Hospital in England and 19th-century hospitals in Ontario, a circus atmosphere prevailed. With the rise of moral therapy in the 19th century, largely spearheaded by the Frenchmen Jean-Baptiste Pussin and Philippe Pinel, conditions in mental hospitals improved. Proponents of moral therapy believed mental patients could be restored to function-

ing if they were treated with dignity and understanding. The decline of moral therapy in the latter part of the 19th century led to a period of apathy and to the belief that the "insane" could not be successfully treated. Conditions in mental hospitals deteriorated, and they offered little more than custodial care.

- Not until the middle of the 20th century did public outrage and concern over the plight of mental patients mobilize a change in government policy. As a consequence, psychiatric services were commonly relocated to general hospital psychiatric units as an alternative to long-term hospitalization. This movement toward deinstitutionalization was spurred by the introduction of psychoactive drugs, called *phenothiazines*, that curbed the more flagrant features of schizophrenia.

- **What are the roles of psychiatric hospitals and general hospital psychiatric units today?** The hospitals provide a structured treatment environment for people in acute crisis and for those who are unable to adapt to community living. Mental health care in a hospital today aims to restore patients to community functioning. Community mental health-care services are meant to provide continuing care outside of the hospital to people with psychological disorders.

- **What is deinstitutionalization and how successful has it been?** Deinstitutionalization is the policy of reducing the need for long term hospitalization of mental patients by shifting care to community-based settings. Although deinstitutionalization has greatly reduced the population in provincial psychiatric hospitals, it has not yet fulfilled its promise of restoring people with psychological disorders to a reasonable quality of life in the community. One example of the challenges yet to be met is the number of homeless people with psychological and substance use problems who are not receiving adequate care in the community.

CURRENT PERSPECTIVES ON ABNORMAL BEHAVIOUR

Biological Perspectives on Abnormal Behaviour

The medical model, inspired by physicians from Hippocrates through Kraepelin, remains a powerful force in contemporary understanding of abnormal behaviour, representing a biological perspective. We prefer to use the term *biological perspective* rather than *medical model* to refer to approaches that emphasize the role of biological factors in explaining abnormal behaviour and the use of biologically based components in treating psychological disorders.

Knowledge of the biological underpinnings of abnormal behaviour has grown rapidly in recent years, and exciting advances are being made in genetics, epigenetics, and stem cell research that are taking us to an entirely new level of understanding of abnormal behaviour. We know that other biological factors, especially the functioning of the nervous system, are also involved in many forms of abnormal behaviour. To better understand the role of biological systems in abnormal behaviour patterns, we first need to learn the basics of how molecular structures alter and regulate cellular function, how the nervous system is organized, and how nerve cells communicate with each other.

genetics Science of heredity.

genes Units found on chromosomes that carry heredity.

polygenic Traits or characteristics that are determined by more than one gene.

chromosomes Structures found in the nuclei of cells that carry the units of heredity, or *genes*.

DNA Deoxyribonucleic acid is a double-strand complex molecule of helical structure that contains the genetic instructions for building and maintaining living organisms.

genotype The set of traits specified by our genetic code.

phenotype Representation of the total array of traits of an organism, as influenced by the interaction of nature (genetic factors) and nurture (environmental factors).

proteins Organic compounds consisting of amino acids that perform most life functions and make up the majority of cellular structures.

GENETICS Heredity plays an important role in human behaviour. From a biological perspective, heredity is described in terms of **genetics**—the study of how traits are passed down from one generation to the next and how these traits affect the way we look, function, and behave. **Genes** are the basic building blocks of heredity. They are the structures that regulate the development of traits. Some traits, such as blood type, are transmitted by a single pair of genes, one of which is derived from each parent. Other traits, referred to as **polygenic**, are determined by complex combinations of genes. **Chromosomes**, the rod-shaped structures that house our genes, are found in the nuclei of the body's cells. Each consists of more than a thousand genes. A normal human cell contains 46 chromosomes, organized into 23 pairs. Chromosomes consist of large complex molecules of deoxyribonucleic acid (**DNA**). Genes occupy various segments along the length of chromosomes. There are about 20 000 to 25 000 genes in every cell in our bodies.

The set of traits specified by our genetic code is referred to as our **genotype**. However, our appearance and behaviour are not determined by our genotype alone. We are also influenced by environmental factors such as nutrition, exercise, accident and illness, learning, and culture. The constellation of our actual or expressed traits is called our **phenotype**. Our phenotype represents the interaction of genetic and environmental influences.

We'll begin this section by looking at the latest groundbreaking research on the role genetics plays in the origin of abnormalities.

The Human Genome   A genome comprises all the genetic material encoded in the DNA located in the nucleus of cells in living organisms (see Figure 1.2). DNA—the long, complex molecular structures that make up the genome—is characterized by essential organic compounds that determine our unique genetic code. In each of our cells, there are an estimated 2.8 billion of the base-pair compounds that form the familiar DNA double-helix structures of the human genome.

Most of our genes contain the cellular instructions for combining 20 standard amino acids to build a wide array of **proteins** (35000 or so). Each protein is a unique

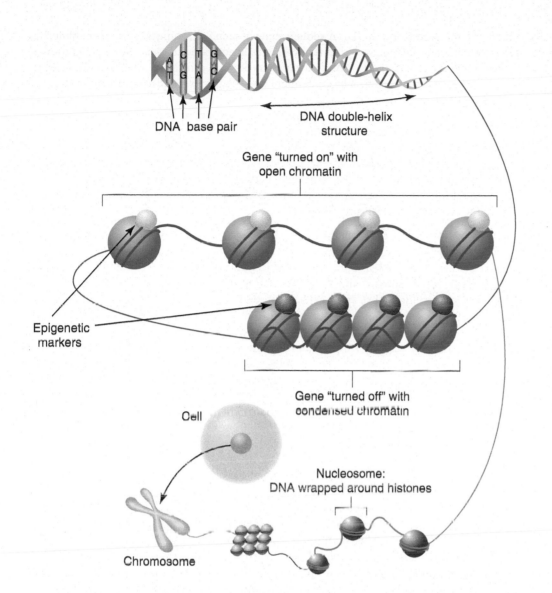

DNA base pair

DNA double-helix structure

Gene "turned on" with open chromatin

Epigenetic markers

Gene "turned off" with condensed chromatin

Cell

Nucleosome:
DNA wrapped around histones

Chromosome

FIGURE 1.2   The genome and the epigenome.
The genome is all the hereditary information or all the information necessary to build and maintain life. Each cell contains the same genetic code. The genome is actually made up of chromosomes, found in each nucleus of each cell, that are further segmented into genes, which are then wrapped around histones. Gene-coiled histones are called *nucleosomes*, and groups of these look like beads on a necklace. Along the nucleosomes are epigenetic markers that regulate the gene—in gene expressions or gene silencing. It is in this process that epigenetic errors happen and interfere with normal gene regulation.

combination of amino acids, and every cell in our body is constructed and maintained by proteins. For example, different proteins are used to build everything from bones, muscles, and organs to brain cells. In addition, all biological processes—metabolism, immune function, muscle contraction, and neurotransmission—rely on proteins.

Genetic errors occur when the number or order of the DNA base pairs is wrong. When the DNA sequence is interrupted, the result can be an alteration or breakdown of a cell's normal protein production, maintenance, and repair processes. If these errors are serious enough, bodily structures and functions can become abnormal or fail.

Epigenetics   Recent genetics research has revealed that DNA errors tell only one part of the story when it comes to explaining the causes of human diseases and disorders. Each of your body's cells contains an identical DNA code. But if each cell carries the same genetic code (your genotype), how is it they come to differentiate into specialized cell types (your phenotype), such as muscle, skin, or brain cells? The answer seems to be found in a molecular structure that overlays the genome called the **epigenome** (Callinan & Feinberg, 2006).

Epigenetics research, particularly in recent years (Labonté et al., 2012; Murphy, Slavich, Rohleder, & Miller, 2013; Weinhold, 2006), has shown the epigenome plays a vital role in gene regulation through two key means: **gene expression** and **gene silencing**. Under normal circumstances, some genes are expressed (turned on) while others are silenced (turned off). So, for example, although a person's muscle cells and brain cells

epigenome The sum total of inherited and acquired molecular variations to the genome that lead to changes in gene regulation without changing the DNA sequence of the genome itself.

epigenetics The study of the heritable and acquired changes in gene regulation (phenotype) that occur without affecting DNA sequence (genotype).

gene expression The process by which a gene sequence becomes activated ("turned on") and is translated into the proteins that determine the structure and functions of body cells.

gene silencing The process of preventing or suppressing ("switching off") a gene sequence from being translated into proteins.

both have the same genome (DNA sequence), it is each cell's unique epigenome that dictates which pattern of genes within that cell will be activated. Simply put, we could say it is the epigenome that causes "brain" genes to be active in brain cells but silenced in muscle cells, and vice versa. The epigenome also regulates hundreds of other critically precise tasks in our cells.

In the area of mental health, Canadian researchers are at the forefront of investigating the role epigenetics plays in the origin and course of psychological disorders such as schizophrenia, bipolar disorder, Alzheimer's disease, and eating disorders (Booij et al., 2015; Schumacher & Petronis, 2006). Epigenetics has suddenly provided scientists with a significant reinterpretation of the interplay between genes and the environment. We are just now beginning to understand what may well be the next revolution in the theory and treatment of human disease and disorders.

Stem Cells   Stem cell research has recently opened up new avenues for studying the development and treatment of various conditions such as schizophrenia, autism, and bipolar disorder. Stem cells, found in all multicellular organisms, are biological cells that can divide (through mitosis) and differentiate into diverse specialized cell types and can self-renew to produce more stem cells. Stem cells can now be artificially grown and transformed through cell culture into specialized cell types with characteristics consistent with cells of various tissues, such as muscles or nerves.

The inability to actually watch living human brain cells in action has hampered scientists in their efforts to understand psychiatric disorders. However, researchers have identified a promising new approach that may revolutionize the study and treatment of conditions. A team led by researchers at the Salk Institute for Biological Studies in La Jolla, California, took skin cells from a patient with schizophrenia, turned them into adult stem cells, and then grew those stem cells into neurons (Brennand et al., 2011). The resulting tangle of brain cells gave neuroscientists their first real-time glimpse of human schizophrenia at the cellular level.

Scientists have used the disease-in-a-dish strategy to gain insight into sickle-cell anemia and heart arrhythmias. But the Salk team, led by neuroscientist Fred H. Gage, was the first to apply the approach to a genetically complex neuropsychiatric disorder. The group found that neurons derived from patients with schizophrenia formed fewer connections with one another than those derived from healthy patients; they also linked the deficit to the altered expression of nearly 600 genes, four times as many as had been previously implicated. The approach may eventually improve therapy, allowing psychiatrists to screen a variety of drugs to find the one that would be most effective for each patient.

THE NERVOUS SYSTEM   Perhaps you would not be nervous if you did not have a nervous system, but even calm people have nervous systems. The nervous system is made up of nerve cells called **neurons**. Neurons communicate with one another, or transmit "messages." These messages somehow account for events as diverse as sensing an itch from a bug bite, coordinating a figure skater's vision and muscles, composing a symphony, solving an architectural equation, and in the case of hallucinations, hearing or seeing things that are not really there.

Every neuron has a cell body, or **soma**, dendrites, and an axon (see Figure 1.3). The cell body contains the nucleus of the cell and metabolizes oxygen to carry out its work. Short fibres called **dendrites** project from the cell body to receive messages from adjoining neurons. Each neuron has a single **axon** that projects trunk-like from the cell body. Axons can extend over a metre if they are conveying messages between the toes and the spinal cord. They may branch and project in various directions. Axons terminate in small branching structures aptly called **terminals**. Swellings called **knobs** occupy the tips of axon terminals. Neurons convey messages in one direction, from the dendrites or cell body along the axon to the axon terminals. The messages are then conveyed from terminal knobs to other neurons, muscles, or glands.

Neurons transmit messages to other neurons by means of chemical substances called **neurotransmitters**. Neurotransmitters induce chemical changes in receiving neurons. These changes cause axons to conduct the messages in electrical form.

neurons Nerve cells.

soma Cell body.

dendrites Root-like structures at the end of a neuron that receive nerve impulses from other neurons.

axon Long, thin part of a neuron along which nervous impulses travel.

terminals In neuropsychology, the small branching structures found at the tips of axons.

knobs Swollen endings of axon terminals.

neurotransmitters Chemical substances that serve as a type of messenger by transmitting neural impulses from one neuron to another.

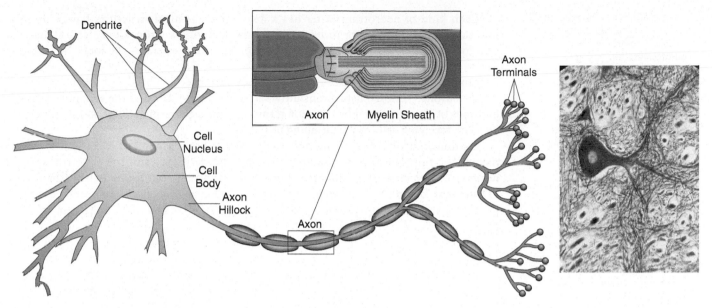

FIGURE 1.3   Anatomy of a neuron.
Neurons typically consist of cell bodies (or somas), dendrites, and one or more axons. The axon of this neuron is wrapped in a myelin sheath, which insulates it from the bodily fluids surrounding the neuron and facilitates transmission of neural impulses (messages that travel within the neuron).

The junction between a transmitting neuron and a receiving neuron is called a **synapse**. A transmitting neuron is termed *presynaptic*. A receiving neuron is said to be *postsynaptic*. A synapse consists of an axon terminal from a transmitting neuron, a dendrite of a receiving neuron, and a small fluid-filled gap between the two called the *synaptic cleft*. The message does not jump the synaptic cleft like a spark. Instead, axon terminals release neurotransmitters into the cleft like myriad ships casting off into the seas (see Figure 1.4).

synapse Junction between the terminal knob of one neuron and the dendrite or soma of another through which nerve impulses pass.

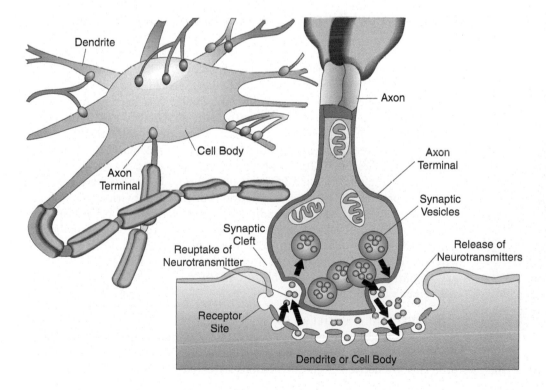

FIGURE 1.4   Transmission of neural impulses across the synapse.
Neurons transmit messages or neural impulses across synapses, which consist of the axon terminal of the transmitting neuron; the gap, or synaptic cleft, between the neurons; and the dendrite of the receiving neuron. The "message" consists of neurotransmitters released by synaptic vesicles (sacs) into the synaptic cleft and taken up by receptor sites on the receiving neuron. Finally, neurotransmitters are broken down and reabsorbed by the axon terminal (reuptake) to be recycled.

receptor site Part of a dendrite on the receiving neuron that is structured to receive a neurotransmitter.

norepinephrine Type of neurotransmitter of the catecholamine class.

Alzheimer's disease Progressive brain disease characterized by gradual loss of memory and intellectual functioning, personality changes, and eventual loss of ability to care for oneself.

acetylcholine Type of neurotransmitter involved in the control of muscle contractions. Abbreviated *ACh*.

dopamine Neurotransmitter of the catecholamine class that is believed to play a role in schizophrenia.

serotonin Type of neurotransmitter, imbalances of which have been linked to depressive and bipolar disorders and anxiety.

Each kind of neurotransmitter has a distinctive chemical structure. It will fit only into one kind of harbour or **receptor site** on the receiving neuron. Consider the analogy of a lock and key. Only the right key (neurotransmitter) operates the lock, causing the postsynaptic neuron to forward the message.

Once released, some molecules of a neurotransmitter reach port at receptor sites of other neurons. "Loose" neurotransmitters may be broken down in the synaptic clefts by enzymes or be reabsorbed by the axon terminal (a process termed *reuptake*) so as to prevent the receiving cell from continuing to fire.

Malfunctions in neurotransmitter systems in the brain are linked to various kinds of mental health problems. For example, excesses and deficiencies of the neurotransmitter **norepinephrine** have been connected to depressive and bipolar disorders (see Chapter 4, "Depressive Disorders, Bipolar and Related Disorders, and Suicide") and eating disorders (see Chapter 8, "Feeding and Eating Disorders and Sleep–Wake Disorders"). **Alzheimer's disease,** which involves the progressive loss of memory and cognitive functioning, is associated with reductions in the levels in the brain of the neurotransmitter **acetylcholine.** Irregularities involving excessive availability of the neurotransmitter **dopamine** appear to be involved in schizophrenia (see Chapter 10, "Schizophrenia Spectrum and Other Psychotic Disorders"). **Serotonin,** another neurotransmitter, is linked to various psychological disorders, including anxiety disorders (see Chapter 3, "Anxiety, Obsessive-Compulsive and Trauma- and Stressor-Related Disorders"), depressive and bipolar disorders (see Chapter 4), sleep disorders (see Chapter 8), and feeding and eating disorders (see Chapter 8). Although neurotransmitters are believed to play a role in various psychological disorders, precise causal relationships have not yet been determined.

REVIEW IT

Biological Perspectives

- **What is the distinguishing feature of the biological perspectives on abnormal behaviour?** Biological perspectives focus on the biological underpinnings of abnormal behaviour, including the roles of genetics, neurotransmitter functioning, and brain abnormalities and defects.

Psychological Perspectives on Abnormal Behaviour

Researchers are investigating whether the combination of psychological and drug treatments for problems such as depression, anxiety disorders, and substance use disorders may increase the therapeutic benefits of either of the two approaches alone. Although Canadian psychiatry has become increasingly medicalized in recent years, some within the psychiatric community have warned their colleagues not to overlook the role of psychological factors in explaining and treating mental health problems (Leszcz, MacKenzie, el-Guebaly, Atkinson, & Wiesenthal, 2002).

At about the time biological models of abnormal behaviour were beginning to achieve prominence with the contributions of Kraepelin, Griesinger, and others, another approach to understanding the bases of abnormal behaviour began to emerge. This approach emphasized the psychological roots of abnormal behaviour and was most closely identified with the work of Freud. Over time, other psychological models would emerge from the behaviourist, humanistic-existential, and cognitivist traditions. Let's begin our study of psychological perspectives with Freud's contribution and the development of psychodynamic models.

PSYCHODYNAMIC MODELS Psychodynamic theory is based on the contributions of Sigmund Freud and his followers. The psychodynamic model espoused by Freud, called **psychoanalytic theory,** is based on the belief that psychological problems are derived from unconscious psychological conflicts, which can be

SPL/Science Source

Sigmund Freud at about the age of 30.

traced to childhood. Freud held that much of our behaviour is driven by unconscious motives and conflicts of which we are unaware. These underlying conflicts revolve around primitive sexual and aggressive instincts or drives and the need to keep these primitive impulses out of direct awareness. Why? Because awareness of these primitive impulses, including murderous urges and incestuous impulses, would flood the conscious self with crippling anxiety.

The Structure of the Mind   Freud's clinical experiences led him to conclude that the mind is like an iceberg (see Figure 1.5). Only the tip of an iceberg is visible above the surface of the water. The great mass of the iceberg lies below the surface, darkening the deep. Freud came to believe that people, similarly, perceive but a few of the ideas, wishes, and impulses that dwell within them and determine their behaviour. Freud held that the larger part of the mind, which includes our deepest wishes, fears, and instinctual urges, remains below the surface of consciousness. Freud labelled the region that corresponds to our present awareness the **conscious** part of the mind. The regions that lie beneath the surface of awareness were labelled the **preconscious** and the **unconscious**.

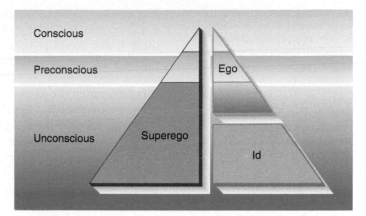

FIGURE 1.5   The parts of the mind, according to Sigmund Freud.
According to psychodynamic theory, the mind is akin to an iceberg in that only a small part of it rises to conscious awareness at any moment in time. Although material in the preconscious mind may be brought into consciousness by focusing our attention on it, the impulses and ideas in the unconscious tend to remain veiled in mystery.

In the preconscious mind, memories of experience can be found that are not in awareness but can be brought into awareness with focus. Your telephone number, for example, remains in the preconscious until you focus on it. The unconscious mind, the largest part of the mind, remains shrouded in mystery. Its contents can be brought to awareness only with great difficulty, if at all. Freud believed the unconscious is the repository of biological drives or instincts such as sex and aggression.

The Structure of Personality   According to Freud's **structural hypothesis**, the personality is divided into three mental entities or **psychic** structures: the id, ego, and superego. Psychic structures cannot be seen or measured directly, but their presence is suggested by observable behaviour and expressed in thoughts and emotions.

The **id** is the only psychic structure present at birth. It is the repository of our baser drives and instinctual impulses, including hunger, thirst, sex, and aggression. The id, which operates completely in the unconscious, was described by Freud as "a chaos, a cauldron of seething excitations" (1933/1964, p. 73). The id follows the **pleasure principle**. It demands instant gratification of instincts without consideration of social rules or customs or the needs of others. It operates by **primary process thinking**, which is a mode of relating to the world through imagination and fantasy. This enables the id to achieve gratification by conjuring up a mental image of the object of desire.

During the first year of life, the child discovers that its every demand is not instantly gratified. It must learn to cope with delay of gratification. The **ego** develops during this first year to organize reasonable ways of coping with frustration. Standing for "reason and good sense" (Freud, 1933/1964, p. 76), the ego seeks to curb the demands of the id and to direct behaviour in keeping with social customs and expectations. Gratification can thus be achieved, but not at the expense of social disapproval. The id floods your consciousness with hunger pangs. Were it to have its way, the id might also prompt you to wolf down any food at hand or even to swipe someone else's plate. But the ego creates the ideas of walking to the refrigerator, making yourself a sandwich, and pouring a glass of milk.

The ego is governed by the **reality principle**. It considers what is practical and possible, as well as the urgings of the id. The ego engages in **secondary process thinking**—the remembering, planning, and weighing of circumstances that permit a compromise between the fantasies of the id and the realities of the world outside. The ego lays the groundwork for the development of the conscious sense of the **self**.

During middle childhood, the **superego** develops. The moral standards and values of parents and other key people become internalized through a process of **identification**.

psychoanalytic theory Theoretical model of personality developed by Freud. Also called *psychoanalysis*.

conscious In psychodynamic theory, the part of the mind that corresponds to our present awareness.

preconscious In psychodynamic theory, descriptive of material that lies outside of present awareness but can be brought into awareness by focusing attention. See also *unconscious*.

unconscious (1) In psychodynamic theory, pertaining to impulses or ideas that are not readily available to awareness, in many instances because they are kept from awareness by means of *repression*. (2) Also in psychodynamic theory, the part of the mind that contains repressed material and primitive urges of the id. (3) More generally, a state of unawareness or loss of consciousness.

structural hypothesis In Freud's theory, the belief that the clashing forces within the personality could be divided into three psychic structures: the id, the ego, and the superego.

psychic (1) Relating to mental phenomena. (2) A person who claims to be sensitive to supernatural forces.

id In psychodynamic theory, the unconscious psychic structure present at birth. The id contains instinctual drives and is governed by the pleasure principle.

pleasure principle In psychodynamic theory, the governing principle of the id, involving the demands for immediate gratification of instinctual needs.

primary process thinking In psychodynamic theory, the mental process in infancy by which the id seeks gratification of primitive impulses by means of imagining it possesses what it desires. Thinking that is illogical and magical and fails to discriminate between reality and fantasy.

ego In psychodynamic theory, the psychic structure corresponding to the concept of the self. The ego is governed by the reality principle and is responsible for finding socially acceptable outlets for the urgings of the id. The ego is characterized by the capacity to tolerate frustration and delay gratification.

reality principle In psychodynamic theory, the governing principle of the ego that involves consideration of what is socially acceptable and practical in gratifying needs.

secondary process thinking In psychodynamic theory, the reality-based thinking processes and problem-solving activities of the ego.

self Centre of consciousness that organizes sensory impressions and governs one's perceptions of the world. The sum total of a person's thoughts, sensory impressions, and feelings.

superego In psychodynamic theory, the psychic structure that represents the incorporation of the moral values of parents and important others and floods the ego with guilt and shame when it falls short of meeting those standards. The superego is governed by the moral principle and consists of two parts: the conscience and the ego ideal.

The superego operates according to the **moral principle**—it demands strict adherence to moral standards. The superego represents the moral values of an ideal self, called the **ego ideal**. It also serves as a conscience or internal moral guardian that monitors the ego and passes judgment on right and wrong. It metes out punishment in the form of guilt and shame when it finds the ego has failed to adhere to the superego's moral standards. Ego stands between the id and the superego. It endeavours to satisfy the cravings of the id without offending the moral standards of the superego.

Freud believed there is a thin line between normal and abnormal. Both normal and abnormal behaviour are motivated or driven by irrational drives of the id. The difference may be largely a matter of degree. Normality is a matter of the balance of energy among the psychic structures of id, ego, and superego. In normal people, the ego has the strength to control the instincts of the id and to withstand the condemnation of the superego. The presence of acceptable outlets for the expression of some primitive impulses, such as the expression of mature sexuality in marriage, decreases the pressures within the id and at the same time lessens the burdens of the ego in repressing the remaining impulses. Being reared by reasonably tolerant parents might prevent the superego from becoming overly harsh and condemnatory.

Defence Mechanisms   Although part of the ego rises to consciousness, some of its activity is carried out unconsciously. In the unconscious, the ego serves as a kind of gatekeeper or censor that screens impulses from the id. It uses **defence mechanisms** (psychological defences) to prevent socially unacceptable impulses from rising into consciousness. If it were not for these defence mechanisms, the darkest sins of our childhoods, the primitive demands of our ids, and the censures of our superegos might disable us psychologically. **Repression,** or motivated forgetting (banishment of unacceptable ideas or motives to the unconscious), is considered the most basic of the defence mechanisms. A number of these defence mechanisms are described in Table 1.1.

TABLE 1.1

Major Defence Mechanisms in Psychodynamic Theory

Type of Defence Mechanism	Description	Example
Repression	Expulsion from awareness of unacceptable ideas or motives.	A person remains unaware of harbouring hateful or destructive impulses toward others.
Regression	The return of behaviour that is typical of earlier stages of development.	Under stress, a university student starts biting his nails or becomes totally dependent on others.
Displacement	The transfer of unacceptable impulses away from threatening individuals toward safer or less threatening objects.	A worker slams a door after his boss chews him out.
Denial	Refusal to recognize a threatening impulse or desire.	A person harshly rebukes his or her spouse but denies feeling angry.
Reaction formation	Behaving in a way that is the opposite of one's true wishes or desires in order to keep these repressed.	A sexually frustrated person goes on a personal crusade to stamp out indecency.
Rationalization	The use of self-justifications to explain unacceptable behaviour.	A woman says, when asked why she continues to smoke, "Cancer doesn't run in my family."
Projection	Imposing one's own impulses or wishes onto another person.	A sexually inhibited person misinterprets other people's friendly approaches as sexual advances.
Sublimation	The channelling of unacceptable impulses into socially constructive pursuits.	A person channels aggressive impulses into competitive sports.

The use of defence mechanisms to cope with feelings like anxiety, guilt, and shame is considered normal. These mechanisms enable us to constrain impulses from the id as we go about our daily business. Freud noted that slips of the tongue and ordinary forgetfulness could represent hidden motives that are kept out of consciousness by repression. If a friend means to say "I hear what you're saying" but it comes out "I hate what you're saying," perhaps the friend is expressing a repressed emotion. If a lover storms out in anger but forgets his umbrella, perhaps he is unconsciously creating an excuse for returning. Defence mechanisms may also give rise to abnormal behaviour, however. The person who regresses to an infantile state under pressures of enormous stress is clearly not acting adaptively to the situation.

Perpetual vigilance and defence take their toll. The ego can weaken and, in extreme cases, lose the ability to keep a lid on the id. **Psychosis** results when the urges of the id spill forth into consciousness, untempered by an ego that either has been weakened or is underdeveloped. The fortress of the ego is overrun, and the person loses the ability to distinguish between fantasy and reality. Behaviour becomes detached from reality. Psychoses are characterized, in general, by more severe disturbances of functioning than neuroses, by the appearance of bizarre behaviour and thoughts, and by faulty perceptions of reality, such as hallucinations ("hearing voices" or seeing things that are not present). Speech may become incoherent and there may be bizarre posturing and gestures.

Freud equated psychological health with the abilities to love and to work. The normal person can care deeply for other people, find sexual gratification in an intimate relationship, and engage in productive work. Other impulses must be channelled (sublimated) into socially productive pursuits, such as work, enjoyment of art or music, or creative expression. When some impulses are expressed directly and others are sublimated, the ego has a relatively easy time repressing those that remain in the boiling cauldron.

Other Psychodynamic Theorists Freud left a rich intellectual legacy that has stimulated the thinking of many theorists. Psychodynamic theory has been shaped over the years by the contributions of other theorists who are sometimes referred to collectively as **neo-Freudians** (Carl Jung, Alfred Adler, Karen Horney, and Harry Stack Sullivan are a few of the more famous). They shared certain central tenets in common with Freud, such as the belief that behaviour reflects unconscious motivation, inner conflict, and the operation of defensive responses to anxiety. They tended to de-emphasize the roles of basic instincts such as sex and aggression, however, and placed greater emphasis on roles for conscious choice, self-direction, and creativity.

Evaluating Psychodynamic Perspectives Psychodynamic theory has had a pervasive influence not only on concepts of abnormal behaviour but more broadly on art, literature, philosophy, and the general culture. It has focused attention on our inner lives—our dreams, fantasies, and hidden motives. People unschooled in Freud habitually look for the symbolic meanings of each other's slips of the tongue and assume that abnormalities can be traced to early childhood. Terms like *ego* and *repression* have become commonplace, although their everyday meanings do not fully overlap with those intended by Freud.

One of the major contributions of the psychodynamic model was the increased awareness that people may be motivated by hidden drives and impulses of a sexual or aggressive nature. Freud's beliefs about childhood sexuality were both illuminating and controversial. Before Freud, children were perceived as pure innocents, free of sexual desire. Freud recognized, however, that young children, even infants, seek pleasure through stimulation of the oral and anal cavities and the phallic region.

Yet for all the criticism and skepticism directed at psychoanalytic theory, new research shows support for some of Freud's specific predictions and claims. For example, modern cognitive psychology has confirmed that through repetition our behaviour can become automatic, and as a consequence we perform many everyday tasks with minimal conscious awareness (Power, 2000). Neuropsychological studies are also helping us better understand conscious and unconscious mental processes and how early life experiences can influence one's susceptibility to abnormal behaviour (Stein, Solms, & van Honk, 2006).

identification (1) In psychodynamic theory, the process of incorporating the personality or behaviour of others. (2) In social learning theory, a process of imitation by which children acquire behaviours similar to those of role models.

moral principle In psychodynamic theory, the principle that governs the superego to set moral standards and enforce adherence to them.

ego ideal In Freud's view, the configuration of higher social values and moral ideals embodied in the superego.

defence mechanisms In psychodynamic theory, the reality-distorting strategies used by the ego to shield itself from conscious awareness of anxiety-evoking or troubling material.

repression In psychodynamic theory, a type of defence mechanism involving the ejection from awareness of anxiety-provoking ideas, images, or impulses without the conscious awareness that one has done so.

psychosis A severe form of disturbed behaviour in which people show impaired ability to interpret reality and difficulties in meeting the demands of daily life. Schizophrenia is a prominent example of a psychotic disorder. Plural: *psychoses*.

neo-Freudians Term used to describe the "second generation" of theorists who followed in the Freudian tradition. On the whole, neo-Freudians (such as Jung, Adler, Horney, and Sullivan) placed greater emphasis on the importance of cultural and social influences on behaviour and lesser importance on sexual impulses and the functioning of the id.

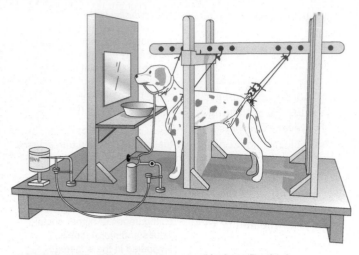

FIGURE 1.6   The apparatus used in Ivan Pavlov's experiments on conditioning.
Pavlov used an apparatus such as this to demonstrate the process of conditioning. To the left is a two-way mirror, behind which a researcher rings a bell. After the bell is rung, meat is placed on the dog's tongue. Following several pairings of the bell and the meat, the dog learns to salivate in response to the bell. The animal's saliva passes through the tube to a vial, where its quantity may be taken as a measure of the strength of the conditioned response.

behaviourism School of psychology that defines psychology as the study of observable or overt behaviour and focuses on investigating the relationships between stimuli and responses.

conditioned response (1) In classical conditioning, a learned or acquired response to a previously neutral stimulus. (2) A response to a conditioned stimulus. Abbreviated *CR*.

unconditioned stimulus Stimulus that elicits an instinctive or unlearned response from an organism. Abbreviated *US* or *UCS*.

unconditioned response Unlearned response or a response to an unconditioned stimulus. Abbreviated *UR* or *UCR*.

conditioned stimulus Previously neutral stimulus that comes to evoke a conditioned response following repeated pairings with a stimulus (unconditioned stimulus) that had already evoked that response. Abbreviated *CS*.

BEHAVIOURAL PERSPECTIVES   The psychodynamic models of Freud and his followers were the first major psychological theories of abnormal behaviour, but other relevant psychologies were also taking shape early in the 20th century. Among the most important was the behavioural perspective, or **behaviourism**, which is identified with contributions by the Russian physiologist Ivan Pavlov (1849–1936), the discoverer of the conditioned reflex, and the American psychologists John B. Watson (1878–1958) and B. F. Skinner (1904–1990). The behavioural perspective focuses on the role of learning in explaining both normal and abnormal behaviour. From a learning perspective, abnormal behaviour represents the acquisition or learning of inappropriate, maladaptive behaviours. Abnormal behaviour can also be described in terms of not learning or underlearning appropriate, adaptive behaviours.

From the medical and psychodynamic perspectives, abnormal behaviour is symptomatic, respectively, of underlying biological or psychological problems. From the behavioural perspective, however, abnormal behaviour need not be symptomatic of anything. The abnormal behaviour itself is the problem. Abnormal behaviour is regarded as learned in much the same way as normal behaviour. Why, then, do some people behave abnormally? One reason is found in situational factors. For example, harsh punishment for early exploratory behaviour, such as childhood sexual exploration in the form of masturbation, might give rise to adult anxieties over autonomy or sexuality. Poor child-rearing practices, such as a lack of praise or rewards for good behaviour and harsh and unpredictable punishment of misconduct, might give rise to antisocial behaviour. Then, too, children with abusive or neglectful parents might learn to pay more attention to inner fantasies than to the world outside, giving rise, at worst, to difficulty in separating reality from fantasy.

Watson, Skinner, and other behaviourists believed human behaviour is basically the product of genetic endowment and environmental or situational influences. Like Freud, Watson and Skinner discarded concepts of personal freedom, choice, and self-direction. But whereas Freud saw us as driven by irrational unconscious forces, behaviourists see us as products of environmental influences that shape and manipulate our behaviour. To Watson and Skinner, even the belief that we have free will is determined by the environment, just as surely as is raising our hand in class before speaking. Behaviourists focus on the roles of two major forms of learning in shaping normal and abnormal behaviour: classical conditioning and operant conditioning.

Role of Classical Conditioning   Pavlov discovered the conditioned reflex (now called a *conditioned response*) quite by accident. In his laboratory, he harnessed dogs to an apparatus like that in Figure 1.6 to study their salivary response to food. Yet he observed the animals would start salivating and secreting gastric juices even before they started eating. These responses appeared to be elicited by the sounds made by his laboratory assistants when they wheeled in the food cart. So Pavlov undertook a clever experimental program to show that animals could learn to salivate to other stimuli, such as the sound of a bell, if these stimuli were associated with feeding.

Because dogs don't normally salivate to the sound of bells, Pavlov reasoned they had acquired this response, called a **conditioned response** (CR) or conditioned reflex, because it had been paired with a stimulus, called an **unconditioned stimulus** (US)—in this case, food—which naturally elicits salivation (see Figure 1.7). The salivation to food, an unlearned response, is called the **unconditioned response** (UR), and the bell, a previously neutral stimulus, is called the **conditioned stimulus** (CS). Can you recognize classical

FIGURE 1.7 **Schematic diagram of the process of classical conditioning.**

Before conditioning, food (an unconditioned stimulus, or US) placed on a dog's tongue will naturally elicit salivation (an unconditioned response, or UR). The bell, however, is a neutral stimulus that may elicit an orienting response but not salivation. During conditioning, the bell (the conditioned stimulus, CS) is rung while food (the US) is placed on the dog's tongue. After several conditioning trials have occurred, the bell (the CS) will elicit salivation (the conditioned response, or CR) when it is rung, even though it is not accompanied by food (the US). The dog is said to have been conditioned or to have learned to display the conditioned response (CR) in response to the conditioned stimulus (CS). Learning theorists have suggested that irrational excessive fears of harmless stimuli may be acquired through principles of classical conditioning.

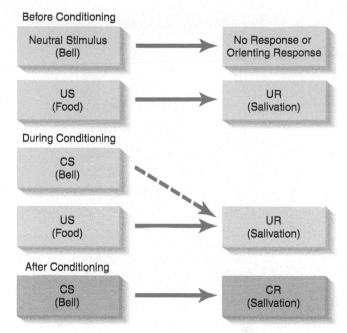

Before Conditioning

Neutral Stimulus (Bell) → No Response or Orienting Response

US (Food) → UR (Salivation)

During Conditioning

CS (Bell)

US (Food) → UR (Salivation)

After Conditioning

CS (Bell) → CR (Salivation)

conditioning in your everyday life? Do you flinch in the waiting room at the sound of the dentist's drill? The drill sounds may be conditioned stimuli for conditioned responses of fear and muscle tension.

A now-famous study was conducted in a laboratory by John B. Watson and his assistant, Rosalie Rayner (Watson & Rayner, 1920). The participant in this study, known as "Little Albert," was a healthy and emotionally stable infant. When tested initially, he showed no fear except of the loud noise Watson made by striking a hammer against a steel bar. Rayner then presented Little Albert with a white rat, in the hope of conditioning him to associate the rat with a loud noise. This pairing was repeated until Albert jumped violently, fell forward, and began to whimper. A week later, the rat was paired with the loud noise five more times. At the sight of the white rat alone, Albert began to cry. This is a great example (albeit highly unethical by today's standards) of how phobias or excessive fears may be acquired by classical conditioning.

For instance, a person may develop a phobia for riding on elevators following a traumatic experience while riding on an elevator. In this example, a previously neutral stimulus (elevator) becomes paired or associated with an aversive stimulus (trauma), which leads to the conditioned response (phobia). From the learning perspective, normal behaviour involves responding adaptively to stimuli—including conditioned stimuli.

Role of Operant Conditioning   Operant conditioning involves the acquisition of behaviours, called *operant behaviours*, that are emitted by an organism and operate upon or manipulate the environment to produce certain effects. Skinner (1938) showed that food-deprived pigeons would learn to peck buttons when food pellets drop into their cages as a result. It takes a while for the birds to happen on the first peck, but after a few repetitions of the association between button pecking and food, pecking behaviour, an operant response, becomes fast and furious until the pigeons have had their fill.

In operant conditioning, organisms acquire responses or skills that lead to **reinforcement**. Reinforcers are changes in the environment (stimuli) that increase the frequency of the preceding behaviour.

Positive reinforcers boost the frequency of behaviour when they are presented. Food, money, social approval, and the opportunity to mate are examples of positive reinforcers. **Negative reinforcers** increase the frequency of behaviour when they are removed. Fear, pain, discomfort, and social disapproval are examples of negative reinforcers. We learn responses that lead to their removal (like learning to turn on the air conditioner to remove unpleasant heat and humidity from a room).

reinforcement Stimulus that increases the frequency of the response it follows. See *positive reinforcers, negative reinforcers, primary reinforcers,* and *secondary reinforcers*.

positive reinforcers Types of reinforcers that increase the frequency of a behaviour when they are presented. Food and social approval are generally, but not always, positive reinforcers. Contrast with *negative reinforcers*.

negative reinforcers Reinforcers whose removal increases the frequency of an operant behaviour. Anxiety, pain, and social disapproval often function as negative reinforcers; that is, their removal tends to increase the rate of the immediately preceding behaviour. Contrast with *positive reinforcers*.

Everett Collection Historical/Alamy Stock Photo

B. F. Skinner. American psychologist, author, and pioneer of operant conditioning.

primary reinforcers Natural reinforcers or stimuli that have reinforcement value without learning. Water, food, warmth, and relief from pain are examples of primary reinforcers. Contrast with *secondary reinforcers*.

secondary reinforcers Stimuli that gain reinforcement value through their association with established reinforcers. Money and social approval are typically secondary reinforcers. Contrast with *primary reinforcers*.

punishments Unpleasant stimuli that suppress the frequency of the behaviours they follow.

behaviour therapy A learning-based model of therapy.

Adaptive, normal behaviour involves learning responses or skills that permit us to obtain positive reinforcers and escape or avoid negative reinforcers. But if our early learning environments do not provide opportunities for learning new skills, we might be hampered in our efforts to develop the skills needed to obtain reinforcers. A lack of social skills, for example, may reduce opportunities for social reinforcement (approval or praise from others), especially when a person withdraws from social situations. This may lead to depression and social isolation. In Chapter 4, "Depressive Disorders, Bipolar and Related Disorders, and Suicide," we examine links between changes in reinforcement levels and the development of depression.

We can also differentiate primary and secondary, or conditioned, reinforcers. **Primary reinforcers** influence behaviour because they satisfy basic physical needs. We do not learn to respond to these basic reinforcers; we are born with that capacity. Food, water, sexual stimulation, and escape from pain are examples of primary reinforcers. **Secondary reinforcers** influence behaviour through their association with established reinforcers. Thus, we learn to respond to secondary reinforcers. People learn to seek money—a secondary reinforcer—because it can be exchanged for primary reinforcers like food and heat (or air conditioning).

Punishments are aversive stimuli that decrease or suppress the frequency of the preceding behaviour when they are applied. Negative reinforcers, by contrast, increase the frequency of the preceding behaviour when they are removed. A loud noise, for example, can be either a punishment (if by its introduction the probability of the preceding behaviour decreases) or a negative reinforcer (if by its removal the probability of the preceding behaviour increases).

Reinforcing desirable behaviour is generally preferable to punishing misbehaviour. But reinforcing appropriate behaviour requires paying attention to it, and not just to misbehaviour. Some children who develop conduct problems can gain the attention of other people only by misbehaving. They learn that by acting out, others will pay attention to them. For them, getting scolded may actually serve as a positive reinforcer, increasing the rate of response of the behaviour it follows. Learning theorists point out that it is not sufficient to expect good conduct from children. Instead, adults need to teach children proper behaviour and regularly reinforce them for performing it.

Evaluating Behavioural Perspectives   One of the principal values of behavioural models, in contrast to psychodynamic approaches, is their emphasis on observable behaviour and environmental factors, such as reinforcers and punishments, that can be systematically manipulated to observe their effects on behaviour. Learning perspectives have spawned a major model of therapy called **behaviour therapy** (also called *behaviour modification*), which involves the systematic application of learning principles to help people make adaptive behavioural changes. Behaviour therapy techniques have been applied to helping people overcome a wide range of psychological problems, including phobias and other anxiety disorders, sexual dysfunctions, and depression. Moreover, reinforcement-based programs are now widely used in helping parents learn better parenting skills and helping children learn in the classroom.

Critics contend that behaviourism cannot explain the richness of human behaviour and human experience cannot be reduced to observable responses. Many learning theorists, especially social-cognitive theorists, have been dissatisfied with the strict behaviouristic view that environmental influences—reinforcements and punishments—mechanically control our behaviour. Humans experience thoughts and dreams and formulate goals and aspirations; behaviourism seems not to address much of what it means to be human.

A NEO-HUMANISTIC PERSPECTIVE Psychologist Leslie Greenberg of York University has been at the forefront of advancing the humanistic approach, which has been influenced by contemporary developments in the areas of neuroscience and cognitive theory. A key feature of his neo-humanistic approach is that it attempts to reconcile the theoretical differences between the major psychological theories we have discussed so far in this chapter. For example, Greenberg (2002a, 2002b) views humans as comprising multiple facets—emotions, motivations, cognitions, and actions—each of which is valuable for survival. In comparison, the different psychological theories have traditionally emphasized that one domain of human functioning is superior to the others (Greenberg, 2002a, 2002b). This theoretical competition has created major theoretical dilemmas by pitting emotions against reason, conscious against unconscious processes, conformity against self-determination, and mind against both behaviour and biology, to name a few. Accordingly, each theory has given rise to divergent therapeutic approaches. However, despite their serious differences, they all have a common therapeutic goal: to regulate and minimize undesirable emotions (Greenberg, 2002a, 2002b). Greenberg's theory, instead of emphasizing the mere reduction of unpleasant emotions, embraces the notion that emotions—both pleasant and unpleasant—serve essential adaptive purposes and should therefore be heeded. For example, emotions have survival value when they warn us of potentially dangerous situations, aid us in interpersonal communication (especially nonverbal), and enhance learning by arousing attention and motivation. To suppress or radically modify our emotions is to deny ourselves this important survival function.

The cornerstone of this approach is our **emotional intelligence**. Emotional intelligence dictates how well we experience and express our emotions in a purposeful way to cope with life. Strengthening our emotional intelligence leads to well-being, and this is the premise for a neo-humanistic therapy referred to as *emotion-focused therapy*.

The strengths of humanistic-existential perspectives in understanding abnormal behaviour lie largely in their focus on conscious experience and their innovation of therapy methods that assist people along pathways of self-discovery, self-acceptance, and self-determination. The humanistic-existential movement put concepts of purpose, free choice, inherent goodness, responsibility, and authenticity back on centre stage and brought them into modern psychology. Ironically, the primary strength of the humanistic-existential approach—its focus on conscious experience—may also be its primary weakness. Conscious experience is private and subjective. Therefore, the validity of formulating theories in terms of consciousness has been questioned. How can psychologists be certain they accurately perceive the world through the eyes of their clients?

There is now a Canadian initiative to study these types of issues. Founded in Langley, British Columbia, in 1998, the International Network on Personal Meaning (INPM; see www.meaning.ca) is an organization of 300 members in 30 countries dedicated to the scientific research and advancement of the role of meaning in our daily lives (Wong, 2002). This multidisciplinary society addresses, through scholarly and educational activities, our needs for health, spirituality, and community. The INPM has also spawned a professional branch of its organization to advance the role of existential psychology and therapy within psychology, the International Society for Existential Psychology and Psychotherapy, and it launched a peer-reviewed journal in 2004, the *International Journal of Existential Psychology and Psychotherapy*.

Critics suggest that neo-humanistic intervention is best suited for personal growth and development, and, indeed, Greenberg (2002a) agrees it is inappropriate for acute conditions such as panic disorder or disorders of impulse control. Nonetheless, it has been shown to be effective in the treatment of moderate depression, of disorders related to

Used with the permission of Leslie Greenberg.

Dr. Leslie Greenberg. Psychology professor at York University and the director of the Emotion-Focused Therapy Clinic, which is affiliated with the York University Psychology Clinic. Dr. Greenberg is one of the originators of emotion-focused therapy for individuals and couples.

emotional intelligence "involves the ability to monitor one's own and others' feelings and emotions, to discriminate among them, and to use this information to guide one's thinking and actions" (Salovey, 2008, p. vii).

Used with the permission of The Albert Ellis Institute.

Albert Ellis. Psychologist who developed rational-emotive behaviour therapy (REBT), in which therapists help people adjust their thinking and behaviour to treat emotional and behavioural problems. Ellis is considered one of the originators of cognitive-behavioural therapy.

childhood maltreatment and trauma, of interpersonal problems, and in couples therapy.

COGNITIVE-BEHAVIOURAL PERSPECTIVES In their attempt to turn psychology into a scientific discipline, the early behaviourists focused on outward measurable behaviour and denied the legitimacy of internal mental processes in human behaviour. But the pioneering Canadian psychologist Donald Hebb (1904–1985) thought differently. He believed "psychology without thought was unthinkable," notes fellow McGill University psychologist Peter Milner (2006, p. 36). In *The Organization of Behavior*, Hebb (1949/2002) outlined his pivotal theory describing how mental processes could be explained by neural functioning, and this opened the way for cognition to become a worthy scientific field of study (Milner, 2006).

The word *cognitive* derives from the Latin *cognitio*, meaning "knowledge." Cognitive-behaviour theorists study the cognitions—the thoughts, beliefs, expectations, and attitudes—that accompany and may underlie abnormal behaviour. They focus on how reality is coloured by our expectations, attitudes, and so forth, and how inaccurate or biased processing of information about the world—and our place within it—can give rise to emotional difficulties and dysfunctional behaviours. Cognitive-behaviour theorists believe our interpretations of the events in our lives, and not the events themselves, determine our emotional states and actions.

Albert Ellis Psychologist Albert Ellis (1913–2007) (1977, 1993, 2003) was a prominent cognitive-behaviour theorist who believed troubling events in themselves do not lead to anxiety, depression, or disturbed behaviour. Rather, it is the irrational beliefs about unfortunate experiences that foster negative emotions and maladaptive behaviour. Consider someone who gets fired from a job, becomes anxious and despondent about it, and spends the day just moping around the house. It may seem that being fired is the direct cause of the person's misery, but the misery actually stems from the person's beliefs about the loss and not directly from the loss itself.

Ellis used an "ABC approach" to explain the causes of the misery. Being fired is an activating event (A). The ultimate outcome or consequence (C) is a dysfunctional emotional, physiological, and behavioural response (Ellis, 2003; Harris, Davies, & Dryden, 2006). But the activating event (A) and the consequences (C) are mediated by various beliefs (B). Some of these beliefs might include "That job was the major thing in my life," "What a useless washout I am," "My family will go hungry," "I'll never be able to find another job as good as that one," or "I can't do a thing about it." These exaggerated and irrational beliefs compound depression, nurture helplessness, and distract us from evaluating what to do. For instance, the beliefs "I can't do a thing about it" and "What a useless washout I am" promote helplessness.

The situation can be diagrammed like this:

Activating events ⟶ Beliefs ⟶ Consequences

Ellis emphasized that apprehension about the future and feelings of disappointment are perfectly normal when people face losses. However, the adoption of irrational beliefs leads people to **catastrophize** the magnitude of losses, leading in turn to profound distress and states of depression. By intensifying emotional responses and nurturing feelings of helplessness, such beliefs impair coping ability.

Ellis asserted that there are three core irrational beliefs held by many people worldwide:

catastrophize To exaggerate or magnify the negative consequences of events; to "blow things out of proportion."

1. "I must be thoroughly competent, adequate, achieving, and lovable at all times, or else I am an incompetent worthless person. . . ."

2. "Other significant people in my life must treat me kindly and fairly at all times, or else I can't stand it, and they are bad, rotten, and evil persons who should be severely blamed, damned, and vindictively punished for their horrible treatment of me. . . ."

3. "Things and conditions absolutely must be the way I want them to be and must never be too difficult or frustrating. Otherwise life is awful, terrible, horrible, catastrophic, and unbearable. . . ." (Ellis, 2003, pp. 236–237)

Ellis noted that the desire for others' approval is understandable, but it is irrational to assume you cannot survive without it. It would be marvellous to excel in everything we do, but it's absurd to demand it of ourselves. Sure, in tennis it would be great to serve and volley like a pro, but most people haven't the leisure time nor the aptitude to perfect the game. Insisting on perfection deters people from playing simply for fun.

Ellis developed a model of therapy called *rational-emotive behaviour therapy* (REBT) to help people dispute these conditioned habitual irrational beliefs and substitute more rational ones. Ellis admitted that childhood experiences are involved in the origins of irrational beliefs but stated that cognitive appraisal—the here and now—causes people misery. For most people who are anxious and depressed, the ticket to greater happiness lies not in discovering and liberating deep-seated conflicts but in recognizing and modifying irrational self-demands.

Aaron Beck Another prominent cognitive theorist, psychiatrist Aaron Beck (1921–), proposed that depression may result from "cognitive errors" such as judging oneself entirely on the basis of one's flaws or failures and interpreting events in a negative light (as though wearing bluecoloured glasses) (Beck, Rush, Shaw, & Emery, 1979). Beck stresses the pervasive roles of four basic types of cognitive errors that contribute to emotional distress, which are explained in Table 1.2.

Like Ellis, Beck has developed a major model of therapy, called *cognitive therapy* (now commonly referred to as *cognitive-behavioural therapy*), that focuses on helping individuals with psychological disorders identify and correct faulty ways of thinking.

Social-cognitive theorists, who share much in common with the cognitive-behaviour theorists, focus on the ways in which social information is encoded. Let's now consider social-cognitive theory, which broadens the focus of both traditional behaviourist and cognitive theories by considering the role of social factors in learning and behaviour.

Used with the permission of Aaron T. Beck, M.D.

Aaron Beck. One of the leading cognitive theorists. His theories are used in the treatment of clinical depression. Beck developed the widely used self-report inventories called the Beck Depression Inventory and the Beck Anxiety Inventory.

TABLE 1.2

Beck's Four Cognitive Errors

Cognitive Error	Description
Selective abstraction	People may selectively abstract (focus exclusively on) the parts of their experiences that reflect on their flaws and ignore evidence of their competencies.
Overgeneralization	People may overgeneralize from a few isolated experiences. For example, they may see their futures as hopeless because they were laid off or believe they will never marry because they were rejected by a dating partner.
Magnification	People may blow out of proportion or magnify the importance of unfortunate events. Students may catastrophize a bad test grade by jumping to the conclusion that they will flunk out of university and their lives will be ruined.
Absolutist thinking	People see the world in black-and-white terms rather than in shades of grey. Absolutist thinkers may assume any grade less than a perfect "A" or a work evaluation less than a rave is a total failure.

Cheriss May/NurPhoto/Sipa USA/Newscom

Albert Bandura. A Canadian/American psychologist whose greatest contribution to the field is his social learning theory, which later became social-cognitive theory. He played a crucial role in the transition between behaviourism and cognitive psychology.

social-cognitive theory A broader view of learning theory that emphasizes both situational determinants of behaviour (reinforcements and punishments) and cognitive factors (expectancies, values, attitudes, beliefs, etc.).

reciprocal determinism The ongoing process of two-way interactions among personal factors (cognitive abilities— expectancies, values, attitudes, and beliefs—as well as affective and biological characteristics), behaviours (skills, talents, habits, and interpersonal relations), and environmental factors (physical surroundings and other people).

expectancies In social-cognitive theory, a personal variable describing people's predictions of future outcomes.

Albert Bandura   **Social-cognitive theory** represents the contributions of theorists such as Alberta-born Albert Bandura (1925–) (Zimmerman & Schunk, 2002). Social-cognitive theorists emphasize the roles of thinking or cognition and of learning by observation or modelling in human behaviour. For example, social-cognitive theorists suggest that phobias may be learned vicariously, by observing the fearful reactions of others in real life or as shown on television or in movies.

Social-cognitive theorists also view people as affecting their environment, just as the environment affects them. They see people as self-aware and purposeful learners who seek information about their environment, who do not just respond automatically to the stimuli that impinge on them. Bandura (1986, 1989, 2001) uses the term **reciprocal determinism** to describe how a person's behaviour both acts upon and is influenced by one's personal and environmental factors. For example, if you were lost and approached someone for help, you might elicit a different reaction from a stranger depending on whether you came across as friendly or as fearful or threatening. In turn, the stranger's reaction to your request for help might, in part, be influenced by his or her interpretation of your intentions based on your behaviour. As well, the circumstances play a role—the intentions of a smiling stranger may be viewed quite differently on a dimly lit street corner than in a shopping mall.

Social-cognitive theorists concur with traditional behaviourists that theories of human nature should be tied to observable behaviour. They assert, however, that factors within a person should also be considered in explaining human behaviour. For example, behaviour cannot be predicted from situational factors alone (Rotter, 1972). Whether or not people behave in certain ways also depends on certain cognitive factors, such as the person's **expectancies** about the outcomes of behaviour. For example, we see in Chapter 7 that people who hold more positive expectancies about the outcomes of using drugs are more likely to use them and to use them in larger quantities.

Donald Meichenbaum   University of Waterloo professor emeritus Donald Meichenbaum (1940–) is a co-founder of cognitive-behavioural modification. Like the other cognitive behaviourists, Meichenbaum's perspective (1976, 1977) considers the interdependence of thoughts, emotions, and actions (interpersonal in particular). Aggressive boys and adolescents, for example, are likely to incorrectly encode other people's behaviour as threatening (see Chapter 11, "Abnormal Behaviour across the Lifespan"). They assume other people intend them ill when they do not. Aggressive children and adults may behave in ways that elicit coercive or hostile behaviour from others, which serves to confirm their aggressive expectations (Meichenbaum, 1993). Information may also be distorted by what cognitive-behaviour therapists call *cognitive distortions,* or errors in thinking. For example, people who are depressed tend to develop an unduly negative view of their personal situation by exaggerating the importance of unfortunate events they experience (Meichenbaum, 1993). From Meichenbaum's perspective, behavioural interventions can be used to initiate change anywhere along the chain of cognitive, affective, and behavioural events.

Evaluating Cognitive-Behavioural Perspectives   As we'll see in later chapters, cognitive-behavioural theorists have had an enormous impact on our understanding of abnormal behaviour patterns and the development of therapeutic approaches. The overlap between the behavioural-based and cognitive approaches is best represented by the emergence of cognitive-behavioural therapy (CBT), a form of therapy that focuses on modifying self-defeating beliefs in addition to overt behaviours. A major issue concerning cognitive-behavioural perspectives is their range of applicability. Cognitive-behavioural therapists have largely focused on emotional disorders relating to anxiety and depression but have had less impact on the development of treatment approaches or conceptual models for more severe forms of disturbed behaviour, such as schizophrenia. Moreover, in the case of depression, it remains unclear, as we see in Chapter 4, to what extent distorted thinking patterns are causes of depression or effects of depression.

REVIEW IT

Psychological Perspectives

- **What are the major psychological perspectives on abnormal behaviour?** Psychodynamic perspectives reflect the views of Freud and his followers, who believed that abnormal behaviour stems from psychological causes involving underlying psychic forces within the personality. Learning theorists posit the principles of learning can be used to explain both abnormal and normal behaviour. Humanistic-existential theorists believe it is important to understand the obstacles people encounter as they strive toward self-actualization and authenticity. Cognitive-behavioural theorists focus on the role of distorted and self-defeating thinking in explaining abnormal behaviour.

Sociocultural Perspectives on Abnormal Behaviour

To what extent does abnormal behaviour arise from forces within a person, as the psychodynamic theorists propose, or from the learning of maladaptive behaviours, as the learning theorists suggest? The sociocultural perspective informs us that a fuller accounting of abnormal behaviour requires that we also consider the impact of social and cultural factors, including factors relating to ethnicity, gender and social roles, and poverty. Sociocultural theorists seek causes of abnormal behaviour that may reside in the failures of society rather than in the person.

Acadia University community psychologist Patrick O'Neill (2004) contends that when dealing with social problems, it is important to keep the focus on dysfunctional social systems rather than on an individual's dysfunction. O'Neill cautions that it is easy for social researchers to inadvertently divert their attention toward an individual's "problem" rather than focus on the social causes of that problem, and doing so contributes to a "blame the victim" mentality. For example, if we were to consider the problem of drug abuse from a sociocultural perspective, we should focus on the social structures that underlie substance use problems instead of on the personal characteristics or "failings" of the drug addict. The former requires sweeping social changes that, for example, would reduce poverty and improve living conditions. The latter perpetuates interventions that deal with the problem of drug dependence one drug user or one drug dealer at a time.

EVALUATING SOCIOCULTURAL PERSPECTIVES As you recall from the discussion of homelessness, low-income Canadians experience higher rates of mental health problems than the rest of society. The reasons why are not easy to determine. One line of thinking suggests poverty gives rise to mental illness. Psychosocial stress resulting from chronic unemployment, financial difficulties, or inadequate housing can create a sense of futility or emotional upset that may lead to the development of mental illness (Hudson, 2005; Wadsworth & Achenbach, 2005). Additionally, low-income Canadians have less access to mental health counselling opportunities than higher-income individuals, and this creates a further barrier to getting well (Rudnick et al., 2014).

An alternative view is the **downward drift hypothesis**, which suggests mental illness leads to poverty. According to this perspective, having a mental illness makes it difficult to hold down a well-paying job. The lack of gainful employment may lead people to drift downward in social status, thereby explaining the linkage between low socioeconomic status and severe behaviour problems (Poole, Higgo, & Robinson, 2014).

downward drift hypothesis The belief that people with psychological problems may drift downward in socioeconomic status.

Yet another view posits that the connections are not so simple. There may be one or more other variables that influence both poverty and mental illness, such as discrimination, dysfunctional family relationships, interpersonal conflict, or a lack of social support networks.

All in all, the sociocultural theorists have focused much-needed attention on the social stressors that may lead to abnormal behaviour. Throughout this text, we consider how sociocultural factors relating to gender, race, ethnicity, and lifestyle better inform our understanding of abnormal behaviour and our response to people deemed mentally ill.

REVIEW IT

Sociocultural Perspectives

- **What is the basic idea that underlies sociocultural perspectives?** Sociocultural theorists believe we need to broaden our outlook on abnormal behaviour by taking into account the role of social ills in society, including poverty, racism, and lack of opportunity, in the development of abnormal behaviour patterns.

Interactionist Perspectives

We have seen several models or perspectives for understanding and treating psychological disorders. The fact that there are different ways of looking at the same phenomenon does not mean one model must be right and the others wrong.

No one theoretical perspective can account for the complex forms of abnormal behaviour we encounter in this text. Each of the perspectives we have discussed—the biological, psychological, and sociocultural frameworks—contributes something to our understanding, but none offers a complete view. We are only beginning to uncover the subtle and often complex interactions involving the multitude of factors that give rise to abnormal behaviour patterns.

Many theorists today adopt an interactionist perspective. They believe we need to take into account the interaction of multiple factors representing biological, psychological, sociocultural, and environmental domains to explain abnormal behaviour. We'll describe two prominent interactionist models next—the diathesis-stress and the biopsychosocial models.

THE DIATHESIS-STRESS MODEL   The leading interactionist model is the **diathesis-stress model**, which holds that psychological disorders result from the combination or interaction of a diathesis (vulnerability or predisposition) with stress (see Figure 1.8). The model proposes that some people possess a vulnerability, or **diathesis**, possibly genetic in nature, that increases their risk of developing a particular disorder. Yet whether they develop the disorder depends on the kinds and level of stress they

diathesis-stress model Model of abnormal behaviour positing that abnormal behaviour patterns, such as schizophrenia, involve the interaction of genetic and environmental influences. In this model, a genetic or acquired predisposition, or *diathesis*, increases an individual's vulnerability to developing the disorder in response to stressful life circumstances. If, however, the level of stress is kept under the person's particular threshold, the disorder may never develop, even among people with the predisposition.

diathesis A predisposition or vulnerability.

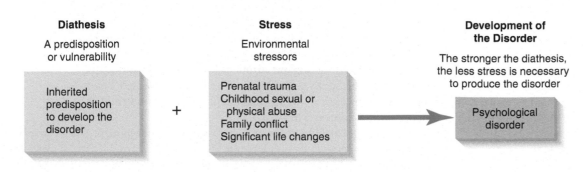

FIGURE 1.8   The diathesis-stress model.

experience. Stress may take the form of biological events, such as prenatal trauma, birth complications, or physical illness; psychosocial factors, such as childhood sexual or physical abuse or family conflict; and negative life events, such as prolonged unemployment or loss of loved ones. This model is crucial to an understanding of the development of mental health issues.

In some cases, people with a diathesis for a particular disorder may remain free of the disorder or develop a milder form of the disorder if the level of stress in their lives remains low or they develop effective coping responses for handling the stress they encounter. However, the stronger the diathesis, the less stress is generally needed to produce the disorder. In some cases the diathesis may be so strong that the disorder develops even under the most benign life circumstances.

The diathesis-stress hypothesis was originally developed as an explanatory framework for understanding the development of schizophrenia (see Chapter 10). It has since been applied to other psychological disorders, such as depression. Although the term *diathesis* generally refers to an inherited predisposition, a diathesis may involve psychological factors such as dysfunctional thinking patterns or personality traits. For example, a dysfunctional pattern of thinking may put individuals at greater risk of developing depression in the face of upsetting or stressful life events, such as prolonged unemployment or divorce (see Chapter 4).

THE BIOPSYCHOSOCIAL (SYSTEMS) MODEL   The diathesis-stress model is not the only interactionist account of how abnormal behaviour patterns develop. Another prominent interdisciplinary approach is the **biopsychosocial model**, which, compared to the diathesis-stress model, expands and more clearly delineates the number of factors and dynamic interactions between a person and his or her environment. The biopsychosocial model encompasses the dynamic interplay of three major systems or domains. Two systems can be thought of as being internal: the biological, which includes genetic, epigenetic, and neurophysiologic factors; and the psychological, which includes psychoanalytic, behavioural, humanistic-existential, and cognitive-behavioural factors. The third system consists of what is considered to be external or outside of us: the sociocultural and environmental factors. Together, these biopsychosocial systems determine the range of known variables involved in the development of abnormal behaviour (Schumacher & Petronis, 2006; Szyf, 2006; Weir, 2012).

biopsychosocial model A conceptual model emphasizing that human behaviour is linked to complex interactions among biological, psychological, and sociocultural factors.

EVALUATING INTERACTIONIST PERSPECTIVES   Research shows how biopsychosocial factors play a major role in the aging process, diseases, and abnormal behaviour. Indeed, the discovery of epigenetic factors and the pivotal role they play in our overall well-being may prove to be the proverbial "missing link" that helps us explain how psychological, sociocultural, and environmental factors interact with our genetic code. Throughout the rest of this text, you will also find many forms of abnormal behaviour involve a complex interplay of multiple influences that include psychological, biological, and/or sociocultural factors.

REVIEW IT

Interactionist Perspectives

- **What is the distinguishing feature of the interactionist perspectives?** The diathesis-stress model posits that some people have predispositions (diatheses) for particular disorders, but whether these disorders actually develop depends on the type and severity of the stressors these people experience. The biopsychosocial approach examines the interplay of biological, psychological, and sociocultural factors in abnormal behaviour. External and internal factors can alter epigenetic patterns, which can affect gene expression. This can lead to an increased risk of both physical and psychological disorders.

Define It

abnormal psychology, 2	expectancies, 32	preconscious, 23
acetylcholine, 22	gene expression, 19	primary process thinking, 24
agoraphobia, 5	general paresis, 14	primary reinforcers, 28
Alzheimer's disease, 22	genes, 18	proteins, 18
axon, 20	gene silencing, 19	psychiatrist, 2
behaviour therapy, 28	genetics, 18	psychic, 23
behaviourism, 26	genotype, 18	psychoanalytic theory, 23
biopsychosocial model, 35	hallucinations, 3	psychodynamic model, 15
catastrophize, 30	humours, 9	psychological disorders, 2
choleric, 9	hypnosis, 15	psychosis, 25
chromosomes, 18	hysteria, 15	punishments, 28
clinical psychologist, 2	id, 24	reality principle, 24
conditioned response, 26	ideas of persecution, 4	receptor site, 22
conditioned stimulus, 26	identification, 25	reciprocal determinism, 32
conscious, 23	knobs, 20	reinforcement, 27
defence mechanisms, 25	medical model, 2	repression, 25
deinstitutionalization, 12	melancholia, 9	sanguine, 9
delusions, 4	moral principle, 25	secondary process thinking, 24
dementia praecox, 14	moral therapy, 11	secondary reinforcers, 28
demonological model, 8	negative reinforcers, 27	self, 24
dendrites, 20	neo-Freudians, 25	serotonin, 22
diathesis, 34	neurons, 20	social-cognitive theory, 32
diathesis-stress model, 34	neurotransmitters, 20	soma, 20
DNA, 18	norepinephrine, 22	structural hypothesis, 23
dopamine, 22	paranoid, 4	superego, 24
downward drift hypothesis, 33	phenothiazines, 11	synapse, 21
ego, 24	phenotype, 18	terminals, 20
ego ideal, 25	phlegmatic, 9	trephining, 8
emotional intelligence, 29	pleasure principle, 24	unconditioned response, 26
epigenetics, 19	polygenic, 18	unconditioned stimulus, 26
epigenome, 19	positive reinforcers, 27	unconscious, 23
exorcism, 9	possession, 8	worldview, 8

Recall It

1. Which of the following statements is NOT true?
   a. Abnormal behaviour patterns are identical in almost all respects in every culture researchers have studied.
   b. Behaviour considered normal in one culture may be deemed abnormal in another.
   c. Beliefs about the nature of health and illness often vary across cultures.
   d. The words we use to describe abnormal behaviour patterns may have different meanings in other cultures.

2. Which is NOT true of the policy of deinstitutionalization?
   a. It has led to a major reduction in the patient population of psychiatric hospitals.
   b. It was instituted to help correct past abuses of patients confined to mental hospitals.
   c. It has mostly eliminated the problem of homeless people with mental health issues.
   d. It has caused people with serious psychological disorders to rely increasingly on community support services.

3. According to Freud, the part of the mind that plans ways of satisfying basic impulses in socially acceptable ways is called the _____.
   a. id
   b. ego
   c. superego
   d. conscious self

4. The chemical substances that enable neurons to transmit messages to each other are called _____.
   a. epigenomic promoters
   b. hormones

c. neurotransmitters
d. neuropeptides

5. The psychological model that holds that abnormal behaviour patterns involve a combination of a biological predisposition and exposure to stress is the _____ model.

a. perceived self-efficacy
b. diathesis-stress
c. neural sensitivity
d. genetic-stress

Think About It

- What criteria would you use to distinguish abnormal behaviour from normal behaviour?
- What behaviours in your own cultural group might be considered abnormal by members of other groups?
- Do you believe abnormal behaviour is a function more of nature (biology) or of nurture (environment)? Explain.

- Do you believe biology is destiny? Why or why not?
- What role did hypnotism play in the development of psychological models of abnormal behaviour?
- What do you believe should be done about the problem of homelessness for people with psychological disorders?

Weblinks

Canadian Psychological Association (CPA)
www.cpa.ca
The homepage for Canada's national psychological association. It is the central source for information about the profession of psychology in Canada.

Canadian Psychiatric Association (CPA)
www.cpa-apc.org
The homepage for Canada's national professional association for psychiatrists. It contains psychiatric e-journals and information on a variety of professional matters.

Canadian Mental Health Association (CMHA)
www.cmha.ca
The CMHA is a voluntary organization dedicated to the promotion of mental health for all Canadians. Its website contains a diverse selection of mental health resources.

Mental Health Commission of Canada (MHCC)
www.mentalhealthcommission.ca
The MHCC promotes mental health in Canada and works with stakeholders to change the attitudes of

Canadians toward mental health problems and to improve services and support. Its website contains reports and videos.

Mental Health Page at Health Canada
https://www.canada.ca/en/public-health/topics/mental-health-wellness.html
This website provides convenient access to a range of online materials related to the promotion of mental health, mental health programs and services in Canada, and the mental health issues, problems, and disorders encountered by Canadians.

Centre for Addiction and Mental Health (CAMH)
www.camh.net
CAMH is Canada's largest teaching and research centre for mental health and addiction problems. The site contains resources on a wide range of mental health and addiction concerns.

Answers to Recall It

1. a   2. c   3. b   4. c   5. b

What Is Abnormal Psychology?

Test your understanding of the key concepts by filling in the blanks with the correct statements chosen from the list that follows. The answers are found at the end of the chapter.

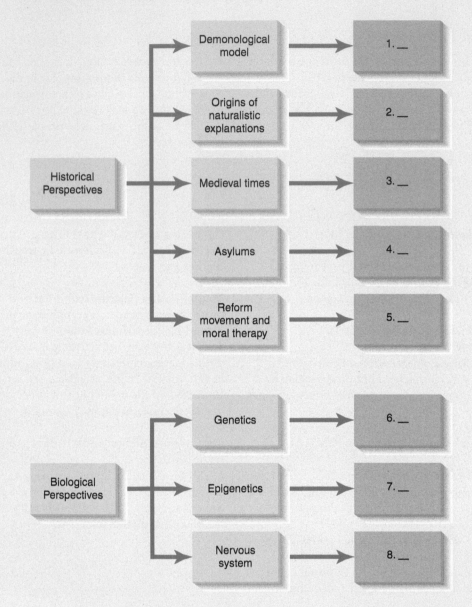

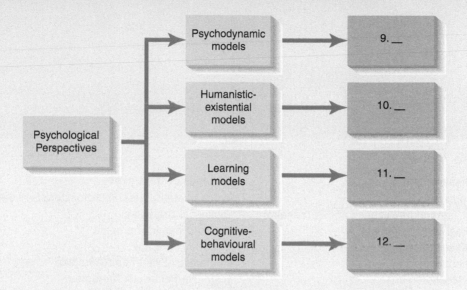

a. Models that focus on the role of learning in explaining both normal and abnormal behaviour

b. The model that explains abnormal behaviour in terms of supernatural forces

c. The science of heredity

d. Theories based on the belief that psychological problems are derived from unconscious psychological conflicts that can be traced to childhood

e. Comprised of nerve cells called neurons, which transmit messages to other neurons by means of chemical substances called neurotransmitters

f. Attributed to Hippocrates, who believed abnormal behaviour was caused by an imbalance of vital bodily fluids

g. The study of the heritable and acquired changes in gene regulation that occur without affecting DNA sequence

h. Belief in demonic possession predominated during this period, and exorcists were used to rid people who behaved abnormally of the evil spirits believed to possess them

i. Models that focus on thoughts, beliefs, expectations, and attitudes that accompany and may underlie abnormal behaviour

j. Theories that focus on self-actualization and living authentically

k. A refuge for both beggars and the disturbed

l. Proponents believed mental patients could be restored to functioning if they were treated with dignity and understanding

Answers: 1. b, 2. f, 3. h, 4. k, 5. l, 6. c, 7. g, 8. e, 9. d, 10. j, 11. a, 12. i

2

Assessment, Classification, and Treatment of Abnormal Behaviour

Did You Know That...

- The most widely used personality inventory includes a number of questions that bear no obvious relationship to the traits the instrument purports to measure?

- Some clinicians form diagnostic impressions on the basis of how people interpret inkblots?

- Researchers today can probe the workings of the brain without surgery?

- One form of treatment for depression involves electrical impulses transmitted through electrodes deep within the brain?

- People can't be committed to a psychiatric hospital just because they're eccentric?

- Despite beliefs to the contrary, the insanity defence (which is called "not criminally responsible on account of a mental disorder" in Canada) is used in very few trials and is successful in fewer still?

- Psychologists and other mental health professionals are not very accurate when it comes to predicting dangerousness?

Hemera Technologies/AbleStock.com/Thinkstock/Getty Images.

The diagnosis of psychological or mental disorders represents a way of classifying patterns of abnormal behaviour on the basis of their common features or symptoms. Abnormal behaviour has been classified since ancient times. Hippocrates classified abnormal behaviours according to his theory of humours (vital bodily fluids). Although his theory proved to be flawed, Hippocrates's classification of some types of mental health problems generally corresponds to diagnostic categories clinicians use today (see Chapter 1). His description of melancholia, for example, is similar to current conceptions of depression. The 19th-century German physician Emil Kraepelin was the first modern theorist to develop a comprehensive model of classification on the basis of distinctive features, or symptoms, associated with abnormal behaviour patterns (see Chapter 1). The most commonly used classification system in North America is largely an outgrowth and extension of Kraepelin's work: the *Diagnostic and Statistical Manual of Mental Disorders*, published by the American Psychiatric Association.

Why is it important to classify abnormal behaviour? For one thing, classification is the core of science. Without labelling and organizing patterns of abnormal behaviour, researchers could not communicate with one another, and progress toward understanding these disorders would come to a halt. Moreover, important decisions are made on the basis of classification. Certain psychological disorders respond better to one therapy or drug than others. Classification also helps clinicians predict behaviour. Some patterns of abnormal behaviour, such as schizophrenia, follow more or less predictable courses of development. Classification also helps researchers identify populations with similar patterns of abnormal behaviour. By classifying groups of people as depressed, for example, researchers might be able to identify common factors that help explain the origins of depression.

One concern about classifying abnormal behaviour is the potential for stigmatization of people labelled with psychiatric diagnoses. Our society is strongly biased against people who are labelled as mentally ill (Everett, 2006). They are often shunned by others and treated unfairly when it comes to many aspects of daily living, such as finding safe and adequate housing, landing employment, or obtaining insurance benefits. This, in turn, impedes their prospects for social integration and can contribute to a cycle of social disadvantages, including unemployment, family discord, divorce, and substance abuse (Kirby & Keon, 2006; Stuart, 2005). Stigma also affects individuals directly when they internalize negative stereotypes, which can contribute to feelings of guilt, shame, and inferiority and to the wish to conceal their condition (Everett, 2006; Stuart, 2005). Indeed, the burden of stigmatization has been portrayed as causing greater and longer-lasting suffering than the mental disorder itself (Schulze & Angermeyer, 2003). Even family members, by association, may adopt attitudes of self-loathing and self-blame when they share in the negative stereotyping of people identified as mentally ill.

This chapter reviews the classification and assessment of abnormal behaviour, beginning with the psychological assessment, whereby the clinician develops a summary of the symptoms and problems using psychological tests, observations, and interviews. We then introduce you to the major systems clinicians use in Canada to classify and report abnormal behaviour patterns: the *Diagnostic and Statistical Manual of Mental Disorders* (DSM) and the *International Classification of Diseases* (ICD), followed by the treatment methods that you will see later in the text alongside the specific disorders. Finally, we consider psychiatric commitment and other issues that arise from society's response to abnormal behaviour, such as the rights of patients in institutions, the use of the insanity defence in criminal cases, and the responsibility of professionals to warn individuals who may be placed at risk by the dangerous behaviour of their clients.

METHODS OF ASSESSMENT

Here we explore methods of assessment that clinicians use to arrive at diagnostic impressions, including interviews, psychological testing, self-report questionnaires, behavioural measures, and physiological measures. The role of assessment, however, goes further than classification. A careful assessment provides a wealth of information about clients' personalities and cognitive functioning. This information helps clinicians acquire a broader understanding of their clients' problems and recommend appropriate forms of treatment.

The Clinical Interview

The clinical interview is the most widely used means of assessment. The interview is usually a client's first face-to-face contact with a clinician. Clinicians often begin by asking clients to describe the presenting complaint in their own words. They may say something like, "Can you describe to me the problems you've been having lately?" The clinician will then usually probe aspects of the presenting complaint, such as behavioural abnormalities and feelings of discomfort, the circumstances regarding the onset of the problem, the history of past episodes, and how the problem affects the client's daily functioning. The clinician may explore possible precipitating events, such as changes in life circumstances, social relationships, employment, or schooling. The interviewer encourages the client to describe the problem in her or his own words in order to understand it from the client's point of view.

Although the format of an intake process may vary from clinician to clinician, most interviews cover topics such as the following:

1. *Identifying data.* Sociodemographic characteristics: marital status, age, gender, racial/ethnic characteristics, religion, employment, family composition, and so on.
2. *Description of the presenting problem(s).* How does the client perceive the problem? What troubling behaviours, thoughts, or feelings are reported? How do they affect the client's functioning? When did they begin?
3. *Psychosocial history.* Information describing the client's developmental history: educational, social, and occupational history; early family relationships.
4. *Medical/psychiatric history.* History of medical and psychiatric treatment and hospitalizations. Is the present problem a recurrent episode of a previous problem? How was the problem handled in the past? Was treatment successful? Why or why not?
5. *Medical problems/medication.* Description of present medical problems and present treatment, including medication.

INTERVIEW FORMATS Of course, every interviewer brings his or her own theoretical orientation to the assessment; however, interviewing skills and techniques have a few features in common. Psychologists and other professionals are trained to establish rapport with and feelings of trust on the part of a client. These feelings help put the client at ease and encourage candid communication. Effective interviewers do not pressure clients to disclose sensitive information. Clients are generally more willing to disclose their personal feelings and experiences to someone who shows concern and understanding, someone they feel they can trust.

There are three general types of clinical interviews: unstructured interviews, semi-structured interviews, and structured interviews. In an **unstructured interview**, the clinician adopts his or her own style of questioning rather than following any standard format. In a **semi-structured interview**, the clinician follows a general outline of

unstructured interview Type of clinical interview in which interviewers determine which questions to ask rather than following a standard interview format.

semi-structured interview Type of clinical interview in which interviewers are guided by a general outline but are free to modify the order in which questions are asked and to branch off in other directions.

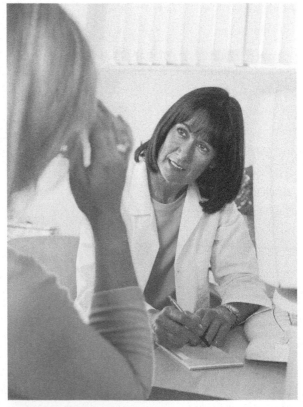

Digital Vision/Photodisc/Getty Images

The clinical interview. During the clinical interview, the format might vary, but it typically includes gathering information about present complaints, possible precipitating events, and how the problem affects the person's daily functioning.

questions designed to gather essential information but is free to ask the questions in any order and to branch off in other directions to follow up on clinically important information. In a **structured interview,** the interview follows a preset series of questions in a particular order.

The major advantage of the unstructured interview is its spontaneity and conversational style. There is an active give-and-take between the interviewer and the client because the interviewer is not bound to follow any specific set of questions. The major disadvantage is the lack of standardization. Different interviewers may ask questions in different ways. For example, one interviewer might ask, "How have your moods been lately?" and another might pose the question "Have you had any periods of crying or tearfulness during the past week or two?" Client response may depend to a certain extent on how the questions are asked. Another drawback is that the conversational flow of the interview may fail to touch on important clinical information needed to form a diagnostic impression.

Structured interviews (also called *standardized interviews*) provide the highest level of reliability and consistency in reaching diagnostic judgments, which is why they are used frequently in research settings. Yet many clinicians prefer using a semi-structured approach because of its greater flexibility. A leading example of structured interview protocol is the Structured Clinical Interview for the DSM (SCID). The SCID includes closed-ended questions to determine the presence of behaviour patterns that suggest specific diagnostic categories and open-ended questions that allow clients to elaborate on their problems and feelings. Evidence supports the reliability of the SCID across various clinical settings (Lobbestael, Leurgans, & Arntz, 2011; Roelofs, Muris, Braet, Arntz, & Beelen, 2015; Zanarini et al., 2000).

In the course of an interview, a clinician may also conduct a more formal assessment of the client's cognitive functioning by administering a **mental status examination.** This involves a formal assessment of the client's appearance (appropriateness of attire and grooming), mood, attention, perceptual and thinking processes, memory, orientation (knowing who they are, where they are, and the present date), level of awareness or insight into their problems, and judgment in making life decisions. The interviewer compiles all the information available from the interview and review of the client's background and presenting problems to arrive at a diagnostic impression.

Psychological Tests of Intelligence and Personality

Psychological tests are structured methods of assessment used to evaluate reasonably stable traits such as intelligence and personality. Tests are usually standardized on large numbers of subjects and provide norms that compare clients' scores with an average. By comparing test results from samples of people who are free of psychological disorders with those of people who have diagnosable psychological disorders, we may gain some insight into the types of response patterns that are indicative of abnormal behaviour.

INTELLIGENCE TESTS   The assessment of abnormal behaviour often includes an evaluation of intelligence. Formal tests of intelligence are used to help diagnose intellectual disability. They evaluate the intellectual impairment that may be the result of other disorders, such as organic mental disorders caused by damage to the brain. They also provide a profile of a client's intellectual strengths and weaknesses, which helps in the development of a treatment plan suited to the client's competencies.

Intelligence is a controversial concept in psychology, however. Even attempts at definition stir debate. David Wechsler, the originator of a widely used series of intelligence tests, defined intelligence as "capacity . . . to understand the world . . . and . . . resourcefulness to cope with its challenges" (1975). From his perspective, intelligence has to do with the ways in which we (1) mentally represent the world and (2) adapt to its demands.

The Stanford-Binet Intelligence Scale was originated by Frenchmen Alfred Binet (1857–1911) and Théodore Simon (1872–1961) in 1905 in response to the French public

structured interview Means by which an interviewer obtains clinical information from a client by asking a fairly standard series of questions concerning such issues as the client's presenting complaints or problems, mental state, life circumstances, and psychosocial or developmental history.

mental status examination Structured clinical evaluation to determine various aspects of a client's mental functioning.

intelligence (1) Global capacity to understand the world and cope with its challenges. (2) Trait or traits associated with successful performance on intelligence tests.

mental age Age equivalent that corresponds to the person's level of intelligence, as measured by performance on the Stanford-Binet Intelligence Scale. Abbreviated *MA*.

intelligence quotient Measure of intelligence derived on the basis of scores on an intelligence test. Called a *quotient* because it was originally derived by dividing a respondent's mental age by her or his actual age. Abbreviated *IQ*.

deviation IQ Intelligence quotient derived by determining the deviation between the individual's score and the norm (mean).

school system's quest for a test that could identify children who might profit from special education. The initial Binet-Simon scale yielded a score called a **mental age** (MA) that represented a child's overall level of intellectual functioning. A child who received an MA of eight was said to be functioning as a typical eight-year-old. Children received "months" of credit for correct answers, and their MAs were determined by adding them up.

Lewis Terman of Stanford University adapted the Binet-Simon test for American children in 1916, and it became known by its full current name: the Stanford-Binet Intelligence Scale (SBIS). The SBIS also yielded an **intelligence quotient** (IQ), which reflected the relationship between a child's MA and chronological age (CA) according to this formula:

$$IQ = MA/CA \times 100$$

Examination of this formula shows that children who received identical mental age scores might differ markedly in IQ, with a younger child attaining a higher IQ.

Today, the SBIS is used for children and adults, and test-takers' IQ scores are based on their deviation from the norms of their age group. A score of 100 is defined as the mean. People who answer more items correctly than the average obtain IQ scores above 100; those who answer fewer items correctly obtain scores of less than 100.

This method of deriving an IQ score, called the **deviation IQ**, was used by psychologist David Wechsler (1896–1981) in developing various intelligence tests for children and adults, known as the *Wechsler scales*. The Wechsler scales group questions into subtests like those shown in Table 2.1, each of which measures a different intellectual task. The Wechsler scales are thus designed to offer insight into a person's relative strengths and weaknesses, and not simply to yield an overall score.

TABLE 2.1

Examples of Subtests from the Wechsler Adult Intelligence Scale

Verbal Subtests	Performance Subtests
Information Who wrote the *Iliad*?	**Digit Symbol** Fill in as many boxes as you can with symbols corresponding to particular numbers within the time allowed.
Comprehension Why do people need to obey traffic laws? What does the saying "The early bird catches the worm" mean?	**Picture Completion** Determine the missing parts of a picture.
Arithmetic John wanted to buy a shirt that cost $31.50, but he only had $17.00. How much more money would he need to buy the shirt?	**Block Design** Use blocks like those in Figure 2.1 to match particular designs.
Similarities How are a stapler and a paper clip alike?	**Picture Arrangement** Arrange storybook pictures in the correct order to tell a coherent story.
Digit Span (Forward order) Listen to this series of numbers and repeat them back to me in the same order: 4 7 5 6 (Backward order) Listen to this series of numbers and then repeat them backward: 3 9 7 1	**Symbol Search** Determine whether either of two target shapes matches those presented in a row of shapes. **Object Assembly** Arrange the pieces of a puzzle so that they form a meaningful object.
Vocabulary What does *capricious* mean?	
Letter–Number Sequencing Listen to this series of numbers and letters and repeat them back, first saying the numbers from least to most, and then saying the letters in alphabetical order.	

Subtest examples from the *Wechsler Adult Intelligence Scale*, Third Edition (WAIS-III). Copyright © 1997 NCS Pearson, Inc. Reproduced with permission. All rights reserved.

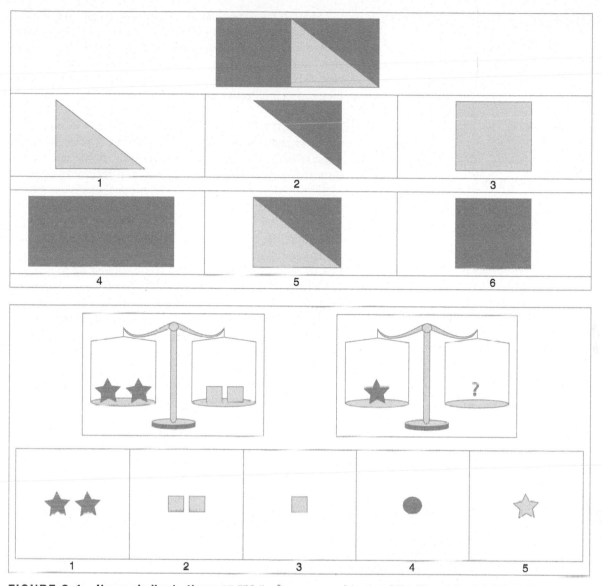

FIGURE 2.1 Items similar to those on the performance subtests of the Weschler Adult Intelligence Scale IV.

Source: Wechsler Adult Intelligence Scale—Fourth Edition (WAIS-IV). Copyright © 2008, NCS Pearson, Inc. Reproduced with permission. All rights reserved. "Wechsler Adult Intelligence Scale" and "WAIS" are trademarks, in the US and/or other countries, of Pearson Education, Inc., or its affiliates.

Wechsler's scales include both verbal and performance subtests. Verbal subtests generally require knowledge of verbal concepts; performance subtests rely more on spatial-relations skills. (Figure 2.1 shows items similar to those on performance subtests of the Wechsler scales.) Wechsler's scales allow for computation of verbal and performance IQs.

Students from various backgrounds yield different profiles. Postsecondary students, generally speaking, perform better on verbal subtests than on performance subtests. Australian Aboriginal children outperform white Australian children on performance-type tasks that involve visual-spatial skills (Kearins, 1981). Such skills are likely to foster survival in the harsh Australian outback. Intellectual attainments, like psychological adjustment, are connected with the demands of particular sociocultural and physical environmental settings.

Wechsler IQ scores are based on how respondents' answers deviate from those attained by age-mates. The mean whole test score at any age is defined as 100. Wechsler distributed IQ scores so that 50% of the scores of a population would lie within a "broad average" range of 90 to 110.

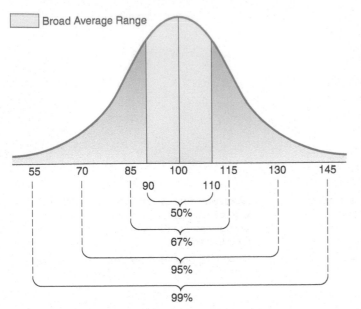

Broad Average Range

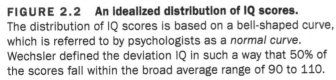

FIGURE 2.2   An idealized distribution of IQ scores.
The distribution of IQ scores is based on a bell-shaped curve, which is referred to by psychologists as a *normal curve*. Wechsler defined the deviation IQ in such a way that 50% of the scores fall within the broad average range of 90 to 110.

objective tests Tests that allow a limited, specified range of response options or answers so that they can be scored objectively.

forced-choice formats Method of structuring test questions that requires respondents to select among a set number of possible answers.

validity scales Groups of test items that serve to detect whether the results of a particular test are valid or whether a person responded in a random manner or in a way intended to create a favourable or unfavourable impression.

Most IQ scores cluster around the mean (see Figure 2.2). Just 5% are above 130 or below 70. Wechsler labelled people who attained scores of 130 or above as "very superior," and those with scores below 70 as "intellectually deficient." IQ scores below 70 are one of the criteria used in diagnosing intellectual disability.

PERSONALITY TESTS   Clinicians use various formal tests to assess personality. We consider two types of personality tests: self-report tests and projective tests. Some self-report tests are intended to measure a particular trait or construct, such as anxiety or depression. Here, our focus is on multi-dimensional self-report personality tests or inventories, as represented by the most widely used of these instruments, the Minnesota Multiphasic Personality Inventory (MMPI).

Do you like automobile magazines? Are you easily startled by noises in the night? Are you bothered by periods of anxiety or shakiness? Self-report inventories use structured items similar to these to measure personality traits such as anxiety, depression, emotionality, hypomania, masculinity–femininity, and introversion. Comparison of clients' responses on scales measuring these traits to those of a normative sample reveals their relative standing.

Self-report personality inventories are also called **objective tests**. They are objective in that the range of possible responses to items is limited. Empirical objective standards—rather than psychological theory—are also used to derive test items. Tests might ask respondents to check adjectives that apply to them, to mark statements as true or false, to select preferred activities from lists, or to indicate whether items apply to them "always," "sometimes," or "never." Tests with **forced-choice formats** require respondents to mark which of a group of statements is truest for them or to select their most preferred activity from a list. They cannot answer "none of the above." Forced-choice formats are commonly used in interest inventories, as in this item:

> I would rather
> a. be a forester.
> b. work in an office setting.
> c. play in a band.

With objective personality tests, items are selected according to some empirical standard. The MMPI-2 contains more than 500 true–false statements that assess interest patterns, habits, family relationships, somatic complaints, attitudes, beliefs, and behaviours characteristic of psychological disorders. It is widely used as a test of personality as well as assisting in the diagnosis of abnormal behaviour patterns. The MMPI-2 consists of a number of individual scales comprising items that tend to be answered differently by members of carefully selected diagnostic groups, such as patients diagnosed with schizophrenia or depression, than by members of normal comparison groups.

Many items that distinguish normal people from clinical groups are transparent in meaning, such as "I feel down much of the time." Some items are subtler in meaning or bear no obvious relationship to the measured trait.

The clinical scales are described in Table 2.2. The MMPI-2 also has **validity scales** that assess tendencies to distort test responses in a favourable ("faking good") or unfavourable ("faking bad") direction.

MMPI profiles may suggest possible diagnoses that can be considered in light of other evidence. Moreover, instead of making a full diagnosis, many clinicians use the MMPI to gain general information about respondents' personality traits and attributes that may underlie their psychological problems.

The validity of the original and revised MMPI is supported by a large body of research demonstrating its ability to discriminate between control and psychiatric

TABLE 2.2
Sample Clinical Scales of the MMPI-2

Scale Number	Scale Label	Items Similar to Those Found on MMPI Scale	Sample Traits of High Scorers
1.	Depression	Nothing seems to interest me anymore. My sleep is often disturbed by worrisome thoughts.	Depressed mood; pessimistic, worrisome, despondent, lethargic
2.	Hysteria	I sometimes become flushed for no apparent reason. I tend to take people at their word when they're trying to be nice to me.	Naive, egocentric, little insight into problems, immature; develops physical complaints in response to stress
3.	Psychopathic Deviate	My parents often disliked my friends. My behaviour sometimes got me into trouble at school.	Difficulties incorporating values of society, rebellious, impulsive, antisocial tendencies; strained family relationships; poor work and school history
4.	Paranoia	I would have been more successful in life but people didn't give me a fair break. It's not safe to trust anyone these days.	Suspicious, guarded, blames others, resentful, aloof, may have paranoid delusions
5.	Social Introversion	I don't like loud parties. I was not very active in school activities.	Shy, inhibited, withdrawn, introverted, lacks self-confidence, reserved, anxious in social situations

samples and between groups composed of people with different types of psychological disorders, such as anxiety versus depressive disorders (Butcher, 2011; Graham, 2011).

The Personality Assessment Inventory (PAI) is a commonly used objective personality test. The PAI has several subscales, including ones that have treatment implications (e.g., they measure potential for harm to self or others, level of stress, and motivation for treatment). The validity of the PAI is about equal to that of the MMPI (Braxton, Calhoun, Williams, & Boggs, 2007; Kurtz & Blais, 2007), but the PAI can be completed in almost half the time—an important feature for clients who may have difficulty staying on a task for extended periods of time, such as those who are cognitively impaired, impulsive, or depressed.

Self-report tests have the benefits of relative ease and economy of administration. Once the examiner has read the instructions to clients and ascertained that they can read and comprehend the items, clients can complete the tests on their own. Such tests often uncover information that might not be revealed during a clinical interview or by observing a person's behaviour.

A disadvantage of self-rating tests is that they rely on clients themselves as the source of data. Test responses may therefore reflect underlying response biases, such as tendencies to answer items in a socially desirable direction, rather than accurate self-perceptions. For this reason, self-report inventories like the MMPI contain validity scales to help uncover response biases. Yet even validity scales may not detect all sources of bias (Nelson, Sweet, & Heilbronner, 2007). Examiners may also look for additional supporting information, such as by interviewing others who are familiar with a client's behaviour.

Psychodynamically oriented critics suggest that self-report instruments tell us little about possible unconscious processes. The use of such tests may also be limited to relatively high-functioning individuals who can read well, respond to verbal material, and focus on a potentially tedious task. Clients who are disorganized, unstable, or confused may not be able to complete these tests.

PROJECTIVE PERSONALITY TESTS Projective tests, unlike objective tests, offer no clear, specified answers. Clients are presented with ambiguous stimuli, such as vague drawings or inkblots, and are usually asked to describe what the stimuli look like or to relate stories about them. The tests are called *projective* because they were derived from

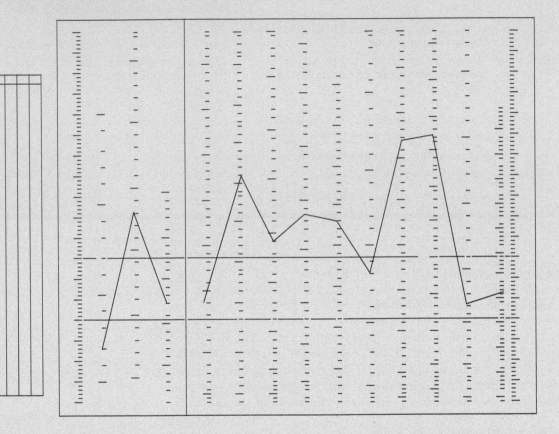

FIGURE 2.3 MMPI form.

Source: MMPI® -2(Minnesota Multiphasic Personality Inventory® -2) Manual for Administration, Scoring, and Interpretation, Revised Edition. Copyright © 2001 by the Regents of the University of Minnesota. Used by permission of the University of Minnesota Press. All rights reserved. "MMPI" and "Minnesota Multiphasic Personality Inventory" are trademarks owned by the Regents of the University of Minnesota.

Figure 2.3 reflects the profile of a patient referred to [a] clinic by a physician. The physician was concerned about possible schizophrenic ideations, level of depression, and possible suicidal tendencies. It was interpreted by a senior psychologist who specializes in the MMPI, and who knew only the patient's sex, age, level of education, and marital status. This is called a *blind interpretation*.

REPORT

This is the blind analysis of an MMPI profile completed by Mr. Smith. This profile is valid. The MMPI profile completed by Mr. Smith suggests that he is currently experiencing a considerable amount of psychological distress in the form of tension, worry, and anxiety. He is a passive, dependent man who is having considerable

difficulty coming to grips with his underlying dependency needs. It would not be unusual for such an individual to form very strong passive relationships. He is an angry man, whose anger is modified somewhat by his own self-image as a soft, esthetically inclined individual who has rejected the traditionally masculine role. However, he pays for this role rejection with a high level of anxiety and tension, and also experiences a moderate level of depression.

Although the level of anxiety may produce some interference in his thinking, it is unclear from the profile whether a thought disorder exists. It would be necessary to definitively ascertain this from other data sources.

However, he is a ruminative and obsessive man, who tends to externalize sources of anger. He is subtly suspicious of the motives of others but feels uncomfortable in stating

>

this directly. Again, this is reflective of his own difficulty in dealing with anger in a direct, but still very controlled, way.

Individuals with profiles such as this often do engage in self-destructive behaviour. However, I would suspect Mr. Smith would give some warning about any such acts. It should be noted that he is highly vulnerable to loss and does have the potential to become seriously disorganized

around such issues. Should he sustain the loss of a significant other person, or significant function, he may become actually suicidal.

Source: A Closer Look The MMPI: A Sample Profile: Abnormal Psychology, David A. Dozois, Philip Firestone, ©2010, page 69-73, Pearson Canada. Used with the permission of Pearson Canada.

the psychodynamic projective hypothesis, the belief that people impose or "project" their psychological needs, drives, and motives, much of which may lie in the unconscious, onto their interpretations of unstructured or ambiguous stimuli.

The psychodynamic model holds that potentially disturbing impulses and wishes, often of a sexual or aggressive nature, are frequently hidden from consciousness by defence mechanisms. Defence mechanisms may thwart direct probing of threatening material. Indirect methods of assessment, however, such as projective tests, may offer clues to unconscious processes. More behaviourally oriented critics contend that the results of projective tests are based more on clinicians' subjective interpretations of test responses than on empirical evidence.

The two most prominent projective techniques are the Rorschach inkblot test and the Thematic Apperception Test. The Rorschach test, in which a person's responses to ink-blots are used to reveal aspects of his or her personality, was developed by Swiss psychiatrist Hermann Rorschach (1884–1922). As a child, Rorschach was intrigued by the game of dripping ink on paper and folding the paper to make symmetrical figures. He noted that people saw different things in the same blot, and he believed that their percepts reflected their personalities as well as the stimulus cues provided by the blot. Five of the inkblots are black and white and the other five have colour (see Figure 2.4). Each inkblot is printed on a separate card, which is handed to subjects in sequence. Subjects are asked to tell the examiner what the blot might be or what it reminds them of. A follow-up inquiry explores what features of the blot (its colour, form, or texture) the person used in forming an impression of what it resembled.

Clinicians who use the Rorschach tend to interpret responses in the following ways. Clients who use the entire blot in their responses show ability to perceive part–whole relationships and integrate events in meaningful ways. People whose responses are based solely on minor details of the blots may have obsessive-compulsive tendencies that, in psychodynamic theory, protect them from having to cope with the larger issues in their lives. Clients who respond to the negative (white) spaces tend to see things in their own way, suggestive of negativism or stubbornness.

The validity of the Rorschach has been the subject of extensive debate. While the Rorschach is widely used, its use is controversial and the empirical basis of its use is regularly questioned. For example, research refutes the idea that the Rorschach test is sensitive in discriminating psychopaths from nonpsychopaths (Wood et al., 2010).

One concern with the Roscharch is the lack of a standard scoring procedure. Interpretation of a person's responses is not objective; it depends to some degree on the subjective judgment of the examiner. Two examiners may interpret the

PH College/Pearson Education

FIGURE 2.4   An inkblot similar to those found on the Rorschach inkblot test.
What does this blot look like to you? What could it be? Rorschach assumed that people project their personalities into their responses to ambiguous inkblots as well as responding to the stimulus characteristics of the blot.

Lewis J Merrim/Science Source/Getty Images

FIGURE 2.5 The Thematic Apperception Test (TAT).
Psychologists ask test-takers to provide their impressions of what is happening in the scene depicted in the drawing. They ask test-takers what led up to the scene and how it will turn out. How might your responses reveal aspects of your own personality?

same Rorschach response differently. Attempts to develop a comprehensive scoring approach, such as the Exner system (Exner, 1991, 1993) and the Rorschach Performance Assessment System (R-PAS) (Meyer, Viglione, Mihura, Erard, & Erdberg, 2011) have advanced the effort to standardize scoring of responses. High interrater reliability has been documented by numerous studies when the evaluation is done by trained clinicians (Kivisalu, Lewey, Shaffer, & Canfield, 2016; Meyer, Mihura, & Smith, 2005). Yet even if a Rorschach response can be scored reliably, the interpretation of the response—what it means—remains an open question (Garb, Wood, Lilienfeld, & Nezworski, 2005).

The Thematic Apperception Test (TAT) was developed by psychologist Henry Murray (1943) at Harvard University in the 1930s. *Apperception* is a French word that can be translated as "interpreting (new ideas or impressions) on the basis of existing ideas (cognitive structures) and past experience." The TAT consists of a series of cards, like that shown in Figure 2.5, each of which depicts an ambiguous scene. Respondents are asked to construct stories about the cards. It is assumed that their tales reflect their experiences and outlooks on life—and, perhaps, also shed light on deep-seated needs and conflicts.

Respondents are asked to describe what is happening in each scene, what led up to it, what the characters are thinking and feeling, and what will happen next.

Psychodynamically oriented clinicians assume that respondents identify with the protagonists in their stories and project their psychological needs and conflicts into the events they apperceive. On a more superficial level, the stories suggest how respondents might interpret or behave in similar situations in their own lives. TAT results are also suggestive of clients' attitudes toward others, particularly family members and lovers.

One criticism of the TAT is that the stimulus properties of some of the cards, such as cues depicting sadness or anger, may exert too strong a "stimulus pull" on the subject. The pictures themselves may pull for certain types of stories. If so, clients' responses may represent reactions to the stimulus cues rather than projections of their personalities (Murstein & Mathes, 1996). The TAT, like the Rorschach, is open to criticism that the scoring and interpretation of responses largely depends on clinicians' subjective impressions. The validity of the TAT in eliciting deep-seated material or tapping underlying psychopathology also remains to be demonstrated.

Proponents of projective testing argue that in skilled hands, tests like the TAT and the Rorschach can yield meaningful material that might not be revealed in interviews or by self-rating inventories (Stricker & Gold, 1999). Moreover, allowing subjects freedom of expression through projective testing reduces the tendency of individuals to offer socially desirable responses. Despite the lack of direct evidence for the projective hypothesis, the appeal of projective tests among clinicians remains high (Basu, 2014; Camara, Nathan, & Puente, 2000).

Neuropsychological Assessment

neuropsychological assessment Methods of psychological assessment used to detect signs of underlying neurological damage or brain defects.

Neuropsychological assessment is used to evaluate whether or not psychological problems reflect underlying neurological damage or brain defects. Neuropsychological inventories may be used in conjunction with brain-imaging techniques, such as MRI and CT scans, not only to suggest whether clients are suffering from brain damage but also to determine which parts of the brain might be involved (Fiez, 2001). When neurological impairment is suspected, a neurological evaluation may be requested from a neurologist—a medical doctor who specializes in disorders of the nervous system. A clinical neuropsychologist may also be consulted to administer neuropsychological assessment techniques, such as behavioural observation and psychological testing, to reveal signs of possible brain damage.

One of the first neuropsychological tests to be developed and still one of the most widely used is the Bender Visual Motor Gestalt Test, now in its second edition, the Bender-Gestalt II (Brannigan & Decker, 2006). The test consists of geometric figures that illustrate various Gestalt principles of perception. The client is asked to copy geometric designs. Signs of possible brain damage include rotation of the figures, distortions in shape, and incorrect sizing of the figures in relation to one another. The examiner then asks the client to reproduce the designs from memory, because neurological damage can impair memory functioning. Although the Bender remains a convenient and economical means of uncovering possible organic impairment, more sophisticated tests have been developed for this purpose, including the Luria-Nebraska Neuropsychological Battery (LNNB) and the Halstead-Reitan Neuropsychological Battery (HRNB).

The LNNB is based on the work of the Russian neuropsychologist A. R. Luria (1902–1977) and was developed by psychologists at the University of Nebraska (Golden, Hammeke, & Purisch, 1980). The LNNB reveals patterns of skill deficits that are suggestive of particular sites of brain damage. A wide range of skills are assessed. Tests measure tactile, kinesthetic, and spatial skills; complex motor skills; auditory skills; receptive and expressive speech skills; reading, writing, and arithmetic skills; and general intelligence and memory functioning.

Psychologist Ralph Reitan (1922–2014) developed the HRNB by adapting tests used by his mentor, Ward Halstead (1908–1968), an experimental psychologist, to study brain–behaviour relationships in organically impaired individuals. The battery contains tests that measure perceptual, intellectual, and motor skills and performance. A battery of tests permits the psychologist to observe patterns of results, and various patterns of performance deficits are suggestive of certain kinds of brain defects, such as those occurring following head trauma (Allen, Thaler, Ringdahl, Barney, & Mayfield, 2012; Reitan & Wolfson, 2012).

Neuropsychological tests attempt to reveal brain dysfunctions without surgical procedures. We will later consider other contemporary techniques that allow us to probe the workings of the brain without surgery.

Behavioural Assessment

The traditional model of assessment, or **psychometric approach**, holds that psychological tests reveal signs of reasonably stable traits or dispositions that largely determine behaviour. The psychometric approach aims to classify people in terms of personality types according to traits such as anxiety, introversion–extroversion, obsessiveness, hostility, impulsivity, and aggressiveness. This model inspired development of trait-based tests such as the Rorschach, TAT, and MMPI.

The alternative model of **behavioural assessment** treats test results as samples of behaviour that occur in specific situations rather than signs of underlying personality types or traits. According to the behavioural approach, behaviour is primarily determined by environmental or situational factors, such as stimulus cues and reinforcements.

The examiner may conduct a *functional analysis* of the problem behaviour—an analysis of the problem behaviour in relation to antecedents, or stimulus cues that trigger it, and consequences, or reinforcements that maintain it. Knowledge of the environmental conditions in which a problem behaviour occurs may help the therapist work with the client and the family to change the conditions that trigger and maintain it.

The examiner may conduct a **behavioural interview** by posing questions to learn more about the history and situational aspects of problem behaviour. If a client seeks help because of panic attacks, the behavioural interviewer might ask how the client experiences these attacks—when, where, how often, and under what circumstances. The interviewer looks for precipitating cues, such as thought patterns (e.g., thoughts of dying or losing control) or situational factors (e.g., entering a department store) that may

psychometric approach Method of psychological assessment that seeks to use psychological tests to identify and measure the reasonably stable traits in an individual's personality that are believed to largely determine his or her behaviour.

behavioural assessment Approach to clinical assessment that focuses on the objective recording or description of problem behaviour rather than on inferences about personality traits.

behavioural interview Approach to clinical interviewing that focuses on relating problem behaviour to antecedent stimuli and reinforcement consequences.

provoke an attack. The interviewer also seeks information about reinforcers that may maintain the panic. Does the client flee the situation when an attack occurs? Is escape reinforced by relief from anxiety? Has the client learned to lessen anticipatory anxiety by avoiding exposure to situations in which attacks have occurred?

The examiner may also use observational methods to connect the problem behaviour to the stimuli and reinforcements that help maintain it. Consider the case of Kerry:

A seven-year-old boy, Kerry, is brought by his parents for evaluation. His mother describes him as a "royal terror." His father complains he won't listen to anyone. Kerry throws temper tantrums in the supermarket, screaming and stomping his feet if his parents refuse to buy him what he wants. At home, he breaks his toys by throwing them against the wall and demands new ones. Sometimes, though, he appears sullen and won't talk to anyone for hours. At school, he appears inhibited and has difficulty concentrating. His progress at school is slow and he has difficulty reading. His teachers complain he has a limited attention span and doesn't seem motivated.

The Authors' Files

The psychologist may use direct home observation to assess the interactions between Kerry and his parents. Alternatively, the psychologist may observe Kerry and his parents through a one-way mirror in the clinic. Such observations may suggest interactions that explain the child's noncompliance. For example, Kerry's noncompliance may follow parental requests that are vague (e.g., a parent says, "Play nicely now," and Kerry responds by throwing toys) or inconsistent (e.g., a parent says, "Go play with your toys but don't make a mess," to which Kerry responds by scattering the toys). Observation may suggest ways in which Kerry's parents can improve communication and cue and reinforce desirable behaviours.

There are advantages and disadvantages to direct observation. One advantage is that direct observation does not rely on a client's self-reports, which may be distorted by efforts to make a favourable or unfavourable impression. In addition to providing accurate measurements of problem behaviour, behavioural observation can suggest strategies for intervention. A mother might report that her son is so hyperactive he cannot sit still long enough to complete homework assignments. By using a one-way mirror, the clinician may discover that the boy becomes restless only when he encounters a problem he cannot solve right away. The child may thus be helped by being taught ways of coping with frustration and of solving certain kinds of academic problems.

Direct observation also has its drawbacks. One issue is the possible lack of consensus in defining problems in behavioural terms. In coding a child's behaviour for hyperactivity, clinicians must agree on which aspects of the behaviour represent hyperactivity. Another potential problem is a lack of reliability or inconsistency of measurement across time or between observers. Reliability is reduced when an observer is inconsistent in the coding of specific behaviours or when two or more observers code behaviour inconsistently.

Observers may also show response biases. An observer who has been sensitized to expect that a child is hyperactive may perceive normal variations in behaviour as subtle cues of hyperactivity and erroneously record them as instances of hyperactive behaviour. Such expectations are less likely to affect behavioural ratings when the target behaviours are defined concretely (Kazdin, 2003).

Behavioural clinicians may supplement behavioural observations with traditional forms of assessment, such as the MMPI, or perhaps even with projective tests, such as the Rorschach or TAT. However, they are likely to interpret test data as samples of clients' behaviour at a particular point in time, and not as signs of stable traits. Trait-oriented clinicians may similarly employ behavioural assessment to learn how personality "traits" are "revealed" in different settings and to see how particular traits affect clients' daily functioning.

In addition to behavioural interviews and direct observation, behavioural assessment may involve the use of other techniques, such as self-monitoring, contrived or analogue measures, and behavioural rating scales.

SELF-MONITORING Training clients to record or monitor the problem behaviour in their daily lives is another method of relating problem behaviour to the settings in which it occurs. In **self-monitoring**, clients assume the primary responsibility for assessing the problem behaviour.

Self-monitoring permits direct measurement of the problem behaviour when and where it occurs. Behaviours that can be easily counted, such as food intake, cigarette smoking, nail-biting, hair pulling, study periods, and social activities, are well suited for self-monitoring. Clients are usually best aware of the frequency of these behaviours and their situational contexts. Self-monitoring can also produce highly accurate measurement because the behaviour is recorded as it occurs, not reconstructed from memory.

Behavioural diaries can also help clients increase desirable but low-frequency behaviours, such as assertive behaviour and dating behaviour. Unassertive clients might track occasions that seem to warrant an assertive response and jot down their actual responses to each occasion. Clients and clinicians then review the log to highlight problematic situations and rehearse assertive responses. A client who is anxious about dating might record social contacts with potential dating partners. To measure the effects of treatment, clinicians may encourage clients to engage in a **baseline** period of self-monitoring before treatment is begun.

Self-monitoring, though, is not without its disadvantages. Some clients are unreliable and do not keep accurate records. They become forgetful or sloppy, or they underreport undesirable behaviours, such as overeating or smoking, because of embarrassment or fear of criticism. To offset these biases, clinicians may, with clients' consent, corroborate the accuracy of self-monitoring by gathering information from other parties, such as clients' spouses. Private behaviours such as eating or smoking alone cannot be corroborated in this way, however. Sometimes, other means of corroboration, such as physiological measures, are available. For example, biochemical analysis of the carbon monoxide in clients' breath samples or of nicotine metabolites in their saliva or blood can be used to corroborate reports of abstinence from smoking.

Self-monitoring may actually be an important, perhaps even necessary, feature of some behaviour change programs, such as weight management programs. A study showed that the more consistently participants monitored what they ate, the more weight they lost (Mockus et al., 2011). This is not to imply that self-monitoring alone is sufficient to produce a desired behaviour change. Motivation to change and skills needed to make behaviour changes are also important.

ANALOGUE OR CONTRIVED MEASURES Analogue or contrived measures are intended to simulate the setting in which a behaviour naturally takes place but are carried out in laboratory or controlled settings. Role-playing exercises are common analogue measures. Clinicians cannot follow clients who have difficulty expressing dissatisfaction to authority figures throughout the day. Instead, they may rely on role-playing exercises, such as having the clients enact challenging an unfair grade. A scene might be described to the client as follows: "You've worked very hard on a term paper and received a very poor grade, say a D or an F. You approach the professor, who asks, 'Is there some problem?' What do you do now?" The client's enactment of the scene may reveal deficits in self-expression that can be addressed in therapy or assertiveness training.

The behavioural approach task, or BAT (Lang & Lazovik, 1963), is a popular analogue measure of a phobic person's approach to a feared object, such as a snake. Approach behaviour is broken down into levels of response, such as looking in the direction of a snake from about six metres, touching a box holding a snake, and touching a snake. The BAT provides direct measurement of a response to a stimulus in a controlled situation. The subject's approach behaviour can be quantified by assigning a score to each level of approach. These types of measures tend to be part assessment and part treatment.

self-monitoring In behavioural assessment, the process of recording or observing one's own behaviour, thoughts, or emotions.

baseline Period of time preceding the implementation of a treatment. Used to gather data regarding the rate of occurrence of the target behaviour before treatment is introduced.

behavioural rating scale Method of behavioural assessment that involves the use of a scale to record the frequency of occurrence of target behaviours.

BEHAVIOURAL RATING SCALES A **behavioural rating scale** is a checklist that provides information about the frequency, intensity, and range of problem behaviours. Behavioural rating scales differ from self-report personality inventories in that items assess specific behaviours rather than personality characteristics, interests, or attitudes.

Behavioural rating scales are often used by parents to assess children's problem behaviours. The Child Behaviour Checklist (CBCL) (Achenbach & Rescorla, 2001), for example, asks parents to rate their children on more than 100 specific problem behaviours, including the following:

refuses to eat

is disobedient

hits

is uncooperative

destroys own things

The scale yields an overall problem behaviour score and subscale scores on dimensions such as delinquency, aggressiveness, and physical problems. A clinician can compare a child's score on these dimensions with norms based on samples of age-mates.

Cognitive Assessment

Cognitive assessment involves the measurement of cognitions—thoughts, beliefs, and attitudes. Cognitive therapists believe that people who hold self-defeating or dysfunctional cognitions are at greater risk of developing emotional problems, such as depression, in the face of stressful or disappointing life experiences. They help clients replace dysfunctional thinking patterns with self-enhancing, rational thought patterns.

THOUGHT RECORDS Several methods of cognitive assessment have been developed. One of the most straightforward is the thought record or diary. Depressed clients may carry such diaries to record dysfunctional thoughts as they arise. Aaron Beck (Beck, Rush, Shaw, & Emery, 1979) designed a thought diary or Daily Record of Dysfunctional Thoughts to help clients identify thought patterns connected with troubling emotional states. Each time a client experiences a negative emotion such as anger or sadness, entries are made to identify

1. the situation in which the emotional state occurred
2. the automatic or disruptive thoughts that passed through the client's mind
3. the type or category of disordered thinking that the automatic thought(s) represented (e.g., selective abstraction, overgeneralization, magnification, or absolutist thinking)
4. a rational response to the troublesome thought
5. the emotional outcome or final emotional response

A thought diary can become part of a treatment program in which a client learns to replace dysfunctional thoughts with rational alternative thoughts.

Cognitive assessment of a man's travel phobia might, for example, involve asking him to describe the thoughts that pass through his mind when he imagines himself approaching the fearful situation. He might also be asked to keep a diary of the thoughts he experiences while preparing for a drive or while driving toward a phobic stimulus, such as a bridge or an overpass. By examining thoughts, a therapist can help him identify styles of thinking that are linked to phobic episodes, such as catastrophizing ("I'm going to lose control of the car") and self-deprecation ("I'm just a jerk. I can't handle anything"). Several more formal methods of assessing cognitions have been developed, including those described next.

AUTOMATIC THOUGHTS QUESTIONNAIRE The Automatic Thoughts Questionnaire (ATQ-30) (Hollon & Kendall, 1980) has clients rate the weekly frequency of and degree

TABLE 2.3

Items Defining Factors on the Automatic Thoughts Questionnaire

Factor 1: Personal Maladjustment and Desire for Change	Something has to change. What's the matter with me? I wish I were a better person. What's wrong with me? I'm so disappointed in myself.
Factor 2: Negative Self-Concept and Negative Expectations	My future is bleak. I'm a failure. I'll never make it. My life's not going the way I wanted it to. I'm a loser. Why can't I ever succeed? I'm no good.
Factor 3: Low Self-Esteem	I'm worthless. I hate myself.
Factor 4: Giving Up/Helplessness	I can't finish anything. It's just not worth it.

Source: Republished with permission of Springer Science, from Cognitive self-statements in depression: Development of an automatic thoughts questionnaire. Cognitive therapy and research, Steven D Hollon & Philip C Kendall, 4(4), 1980; permission conveyed through Copyright Clearance Center, Inc.

of conviction associated with 30 automatic negative thoughts. (Automatic thoughts are thoughts that seem to just pop into our minds.) Sample items include the following:

I don't think I can go on.

I hate myself.

I've let people down.

A total score is obtained by summing the frequencies of occurrence of each item. Higher scores are considered typical of depressive thought patterns. The scale discriminates between subjects who attain high or low scores, with higher scores being more indicative of depressive symptoms (Blankstein & Segal, 2001). The 30-item ATQ has been statistically sorted into four categories or factors of related thoughts (see Table 2.3).

EVALUATING METHODS OF COGNITIVE ASSESSMENT Cognitive assessment has opened a new domain to the psychologist in understanding how disruptive thoughts are related to abnormal behaviour. Over the past three decades or so, cognitive and cognitive-behavioural therapists have been exploring what B. F. Skinner labelled the "black box"—people's internal states—to learn how thoughts and attitudes influence emotional states and behaviour.

The behavioural objection to cognitive techniques is that clinicians have no direct means of verifying clients' subjective experiences—their thoughts and beliefs. These are private experiences that can be reported but not observed and measured directly. Even though thoughts remain private experiences, reports of cognitions in the form of rating scales or checklists can be quantified and validated by reference to external criteria.

Physiological Measurement

We can also learn about abnormal behaviour by studying people's physiological responses. Anxiety, for example, is associated with arousal of the sympathetic division of the autonomic nervous system (see Chapter 3). Anxious people, therefore, show elevated heart rates and blood pressure, which can be measured directly by means of the pulse and a blood pressure cuff. People also sweat more heavily when they are anxious. When we sweat, our skin becomes wet, increasing its ability to conduct electricity. Sweating can be measured by means of the **electrodermal response** or **galvanic skin response** (GSR). (*Electrodermal* contains the Greek word *derma*, meaning "skin." The galvanic skin

electrodermal response Changes in the electrical conductivity of the skin following exposure to a stimulus.

galvanic skin response Measure of the change in electrical activity of the skin caused by increased activity of the sweat glands that accompanies states of sympathetic nervous system arousal, such as when a person is anxious. Abbreviated *GSR*.

response is named after the Italian physicist and physician Luigi Galvani, who was a pioneer in research in electricity.) Measures of the GSR assess the amount of electricity that passes through two points on the skin, usually on the hand. We assume that the person's anxiety level correlates with the amount of electricity conducted across the skin.

The GSR is just one example of a physiological response measured through probes or sensors connected to the body. Another example is the **electroencephalograph** (EEG), which measures brainwaves by attaching electrodes to the scalp.

Changes in muscle tension are also often associated with states of anxiety or tension. They can be detected through the **electromyograph** (EMG), which monitors muscle tension through sensors attached to targeted muscle groups. (*Myo-* derives from the Greek *mys*, meaning "mouse" or "muscle." The Greeks observed that muscles moved mouse-like beneath the skin.) Placement of EMG probes on the forehead can indicate muscle tension associated with tension headaches. Other probes are used to assess sexual arousal (see Chapter 9, "Gender Dysphoria, Paraphilic Disorders, and Sexual Dysfunctions").

Probing the Workings of the Brain

Advances in medical technology have made it possible to study the workings of the brain without the need for surgery (see Table 2.4).

Sociocultural Factors in Psychological Assessment

Researchers and clinicians must keep sociocultural and ethnic factors of clients in mind when assessing personality traits and psychological disorders. For example, in testing people from other cultures, careful translations are essential to capture the meaning of the original items. Clinicians also need to recognize that assessment techniques that may be reliable and valid in one culture may not be in another, even when they are translated accurately (Cheung, Kwong, & Zhang, 2003).

Researchers also need to disentangle psychopathology from sociocultural factors so as not to introduce cultural biases in assessment. Translations of assessment instruments should not only translate words, but also provide instructions that encourage examiners to address the importance of cultural beliefs, norms, and values, so that examiners will consider the client's background when making assessments of abnormal behaviour patterns. Examiners need to ensure they are not labelling cultural differences in beliefs or practices as evidence of abnormal behaviours.

Therapists must recognize the importance of considering clients' language preferences when conducting multicultural assessments. Meanings can get lost in translation, or worse, distorted. Therapists, too, may fail to appreciate the idioms and subtleties of different languages. We recall, for instance, one clinician, a foreign-born and -trained psychiatrist whose native language was not English, reporting that a patient had exhibited the delusional belief that he was outside his body. The clinician based this assessment on the patient's response when asked if he was feeling anxious. "Yes, doc," the patient had replied, "I feel like I'm jumping out of my skin at times."

In conclusion, people's psychological problems, which are no less complex than people themselves, are assessed in many ways. In hospital settings, for instance, clients are commonly reviewed by a multidisciplinary team that may include psychologists, psychiatrists, social workers, neuropsychologists, neuroimaging specialists, and other mental health experts as needed. Clients are generally asked to explain their problems as best they can. Psychologists can also draw on batteries of tests that assess anything from intelligence and personality to neuropsychological integrity. Many psychologists prefer to observe people's behaviour directly when possible, and sometimes devices that measure and record physiological markers of emotional states (e.g., changes in blood pressure, muscle tension, perspiration) are also used. Modern technology has provided several means of studying the structure and function of the brain. The methods of assessment selected by clinicians reflect the problems of their clients, the clinicians' theoretical orientations, and the clinicians' mastery of specialized technologies.

electroencephalograph Instrument for measuring the electrical activity of the brain (brainwaves). Abbreviated *EEG*.

electromyograph Instrument often used in biofeedback training for measuring muscle tension. Abbreviated *EMG*.

TABLE 2.4

Brain Activity and Imaging Techniques

Technique	How It Works
 Phanie/Science Source	The electroencephalograph (EEG) is a record of the electrical activity of the brain. The EEG detects minute amounts of electrical activity in the brain, or brainwaves, that are conducted between electrodes. Certain brainwave patterns are associated with mental states such as relaxation and with the different stages of sleep. The EEG is used to examine brainwave patterns associated with psychological disorders, such as schizophrenia, and with brain damage. It is also used to study various abnormal behaviour patterns. The EEG is also used by medical personnel to reveal brain abnormalities such as tumours.
 Stockbyte/Stockbyte/Getty Images	Computerized tomography (CT scan) consists of a narrow X-ray beam aimed at the head. The radiation that passes through is measured from multiple angles. The CT scan reveals abnormalities in shape and structure that may be suggestive of lesions, blood clots, or tumours. A computer enables scientists to integrate the measurements into a three-dimensional picture of the brain. Evidence of brain damage that was once detectable only by surgery may now be displayed on a monitor.
 Courtesy of Brookhaven National Laboratory	Positron emission tomography (the PET scan) is used to study the functioning of various parts of the brain. A small amount of a radioactive compound or tracer is mixed with glucose and injected into the bloodstream. When it reaches the brain, patterns of neural activity are revealed by measurement of the positrons—positively charged particles—emitted by the tracer. The glucose metabolized by parts of the brain generates a computer image of neural activity. Areas of greater activity metabolize more glucose. The PET scan has been used to learn which parts of the brain are most active (metabolize more glucose) when we are listening to music, solving a math problem, or using language. It can also be used to reveal differences in brain activity in people with schizophrenia.
 MriMan/Shutterstock	In magnetic resonance imaging (MRI), a person is placed in a doughnut-shaped tunnel that generates a strong magnetic field. Radio waves of certain frequencies are directed at the head. As a result, parts of the brain emit signals that can be measured from several angles. As with the CT scan, the signals are integrated into a computer-generated image of the brain, which can be used to investigate brain abnormalities associated with schizophrenia (see Chapter 10) and other disorders, such as obsessive-compulsive disorder (OCD).
 Copyright 2017 Dr Frank Gaillard. Image courtesy of Dr Frank Gaillard and Radiopaedia.org. Used under licence.	Functional magnetic resonance imaging (fMRI) is a form of resonance imaging that yields far more information than a basic MRI and produces static pictures of brain structure. In fMRI, computer-generated images show which regions of the brain are active during a specific mental activity, whether it is solving verbal riddles or visual puzzles, experiencing feelings, or initiating actions. The fMRI procedure has recently brought forth many intriguing discoveries in the neurobiology of stress.

(Continued)

TABLE 2.4   *(Continued)*

Technique	How It Works
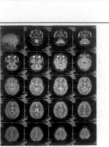 (a) (a) Marina Pousheva/ Shutterstock (b) (b) Haydenbird/iStock/ Thinkstock/Getty Images	Brain electrical activity mapping (BEAM) is a type of EEG in which electrodes are attached to the scalp (photo a) to measure electrical activity in various regions of the brain. The left column of photo b shows the average level of electrical activity in the brains of 10 normal people (controls) at four time intervals. The right-hand column shows the average level of activity of subjects with schizophrenia during the same intervals. Higher activity levels are represented in increasing order by yellows, reds, and whites. The computer-generated image in the bottom centre summarizes differences in activity levels between the brains of normal subjects and those with schizophrenia. Areas of the brain depicted in blue show small differences between the groups. White areas represent larger differences.
 Dr. Jurgen Scriba/ Science Source	Magnetoencephalography (MEG) measures brain activity in real time. In some cases, MEG can pinpoint the source of an epileptic seizure much more accurately than the traditional method of electroencephalography. Using a combination of MEG and MRI, neurosurgeons have a detailed brain map that allows them to remove just the damaged tissue while preserving healthy cells.

REVIEW IT

Methods of Assessment

- **What is a clinical interview?** A clinical interview involves the use of a set of questions designed to elicit relevant information from people seeking treatment. Interview formats include structured, semi-structured, and unstructured approaches.

- **What are psychological tests?** Psychological tests are structured methods of assessment used to evaluate reasonably stable traits, such as intelligence and personality.

- **What are the major types of psychological tests used by clinicians?** Tests of intelligence, such as the Stanford-Binet Intelligence Scale and the Wechsler Adult Intelligence Scale, are used for various purposes in clinical assessment, including determining evidence of intellectual disability or cognitive impairment and assessing strengths and weaknesses. Self-report personality inventories, such as the MMPI, use structured items to measure various personality traits, such as anxiety, depression, and masculinity–femininity. These tests are considered objective in the sense that they offer a limited range of possible responses to items and use an empirical or objective method of test construction. Projective personality tests, such as the Rorschach and TAT, ask subjects to interpret ambiguous stimuli in the belief that their answers may shed light on their unconscious processes. Concerns persist about the validity of these tests, however.

- **What is neuropsychological assessment?** Neuropsychological assessment involves the use of psychological tests to indicate possible neurological impairment or brain defects. Examples include the Bender Visual Motor Gestalt Test, the Luria-Nebraska Neuropsychological Battery, and the Halstead-Reitan Neuropsychological Battery.

- **What are some of the methods used in behavioural assessment?** In behavioural assessment, test responses are taken as samples of behaviour rather than as signs of underlying traits or dispositions. The behavioural examiner may conduct an assessment, which relates a problem behaviour to its antecedents and consequences. Methods of behavioural assessment include behavioural interviewing, self-monitoring, analogue or contrived measures, direct observation, and behavioural rating scales.

- **What is cognitive assessment?** Cognitive assessment focuses on the measurement of thoughts, beliefs, and attitudes to help identify distorted thinking patterns. Specific methods of assessment include the use of a thought record or diary and the use of rating scales such as the Automatic Thoughts Questionnaire (ATQ-30).

- **How do clinicians and researchers study physiological functioning?** Measures of physiological functioning include heart rate, blood pressure, galvanic skin response (GSR), muscle tension, and brainwave activity. Brain-imaging techniques such as EEG, CT scans, PET scans, MRI, fMRI, and BEAM probe the inner workings and structures of the brain.

CLASSIFICATION OF ABNORMAL BEHAVIOUR

Systems of Classification

The *Diagnostic and Statistical Manual of Mental Disorders* (DSM) is used widely in Canada and the United States. The DSM was introduced in 1952 and is now in its fifth edition (DSM-5). However, the most widely used diagnostic manual worldwide is the *International Statistical Classification of Diseases and Related Health Problems* (ICD) (Clay, 2012). Published by the World Health Organization (WHO), it is a compilation of both mental and physical disorders. The WHO first published an international mortality and morbidity diagnostic classification standards manual in 1893 (WHO, 2001). The series is now in its 10th edition (ICD-10) and is presently undergoing a revision scheduled for 2018. The Canadian Institute for Health Information (CIHI) petitioned the WHO for permission to make Canadian enhancements to the ICD-10, and the result was the ICD-10-CA, the Canadian modification (CIHI, 2001). The DSM is compatible with the ICD, so DSM diagnoses can be coded under the ICD system as well.

The Chinese Society of Psychiatry has published its own system of classification of mental disorders called the *Chinese Classification of Mental Disorders* (CCMD). Many Chinese psychiatrists believe the CCMD has special advantages over other manuals, such as simplicity, stability, the inclusion of culture-distinctive categories, and the exclusion of certain Western diagnostic categories. The Chinese translation of the ICD-10 was seen as linguistically complicated, containing very long sentences and awkward terms and syntax, and Chinese psychiatrists therefore developed their own classification (Lee, 2001).

We focus on the DSM as a method of classification because of its widespread adoption by mental health professionals in Canada. However, many psychologists and other professionals criticize the DSM on several grounds, such as relying too strongly on the medical model. Our focus on the DSM reflects recognition of its widespread use and should not be interpreted as a wholesale endorsement.

The *Diagnostic and Statistical Manual of Mental Disorders* (DSM)

FEATURES OF THE DSM   The DSM system, like the medical model, treats abnormal behaviours as signs or symptoms of underlying disorders or pathologies. However, the DSM does not assume that abnormal behaviours necessarily stem from biological causes or defects. It recognizes that the causes of most mental disorders remain unclear: Some disorders may have purely biological causes, whereas others may have psychological causes. Still others, probably most, are best explained within a multifactorial model that takes into account the interaction of biological, psychological, social (socioeconomic, sociocultural, and ethnic), and physical environmental factors.

In the DSM, abnormal behaviour patterns are classified as *mental disorders*. Mental disorders involve emotional distress (typically depression or anxiety) or significant impairment in psychological functioning. Impaired functioning involves difficulties in meeting responsibilities at work, within the family, or within society at large. It also includes behaviour that places people at risk for personal suffering, pain, or death. The developers of the DSM recognize that their use of the term *mental disorder* is problematic because it perpetuates a long-standing but dubious distinction between mental and physical disorders (American Psychiatric Association, 2000). They point out that there is much that is physical in mental disorders and much that is mental in physical disorders. The manual continues, however, to use the term *mental disorder* because its developers have not been able to agree on an appropriate substitute. In this text, we use the term *psychological disorder* in place of *mental disorder* because we believe it is more appropriate to place the study of abnormal behaviour squarely within a psychological context. Moreover, the term *psychological* has the advantage of encompassing behavioural patterns as well as strictly "mental" experiences, such as emotions, thoughts, beliefs, and attitudes.

Charles Sykes/AP Images

Science as quackery? Scientologists like actor Tom Cruise view psychiatry as a barbaric and corrupt profession and encourage alternative care based on spiritual healing. The Church of Scientology says psychiatry has had a long history of improper and abusive care. The group's views have been strongly disputed, criticized, and condemned by experts in the medical and scientific community and have been a source of public controversy.

The DSM classifies disorders people have, not the people themselves. Consequently, clinicians don't classify a person as a *schizophrenic* or a *depressive*. Rather, they refer to *an individual with schizophrenia* or *a person with major depression*. This difference in terminology is not simply a matter of semantics. To label someone a schizophrenic carries an unfortunate and stigmatizing implication that a person's identity is defined by the disorder the person has.

The DSM is *descriptive*, not *explanatory*. It describes the diagnostic features—or, in medical terms, symptoms—of abnormal behaviours; it does not attempt to explain their origins or adopt any particular theoretical framework, such as psychodynamic or learning theory. Abnormal behaviour patterns are categorized according to the clinical features they share. For example, abnormal behaviour patterns chiefly characterized by anxiety are classified as anxiety disorders (see Chapter 3, "Anxiety, Obsessive-Compulsive, and Trauma- and Stressor-Related Disorders").

The examining clinician determines whether a person's symptoms or problem behaviours match the DSM's criteria for a particular psychological disorder, such as major depressive disorder or schizophrenia. A diagnosis is given only when the minimum number of symptoms or features is present to meet the diagnostic criteria for the particular diagnosis. An example of diagnostic criteria for gambling disorder, a nonsubstance-related disorder, is shown in Table 2.5.

Diagnosis of mental disorders in the DSM system requires that the behaviour pattern not represent an expected or culturally appropriate response to a stressful event, such as the loss of a loved one. People who show signs of bereavement or grief following the death of loved ones are not considered disordered, even if their behaviour is significantly impaired. If their behaviour remains significantly impaired over an extended period of time, however, a diagnosis of a psychological disorder might become appropriate.

The DSM is based on a *categorical model of classification*, which means that clinicians need to make a categorical, or *yes–no*, type of judgment about whether the disorder is present in a given case. Categorical judgments are commonplace in modern medicine, such as in determining whether or not a person has cancer. One

TABLE 2.5

Diagnostic Criteria for Gambling Disorder

A. Persistent and recurrent problematic gambling behavior leading to clinically significant impairment or distress, as indicated by the individual exhibiting four (or more) of the following in a 12-month period:

1. Needs to gamble with increasing amounts of money in order to achieve the desired excitement.
2. Is restless or irritable when attempting to cut down or stop gambling.
3. Has made repeated unsuccessful efforts to control, cut back, or stop gambling.
4. Is often preoccupied with gambling (e.g., having persistent thoughts of reliving past gambling experiences, handicapping or planning the next venture, thinking of ways to get money with which to gamble).
5. Often gambles when feeling distressed (e.g., helpless, guilty, anxious, depressed).
6. After losing money gambling, often returns another day to get even ("chasing" one's losses).
7. Lies to conceal the extent of involvement with gambling.
8. Has jeopardized or lost a significant relationship, job, or educational or career opportunity because of gambling.
9. Relies on others to provide money to relieve desperate financial situations caused by gambling.

B. The gambling behavior is not better explained by a manic episode.

Source: Reprinted with permission from the *Diagnostic and Statistical Manual of Mental Disorders*, Fifth Edition (Copyright © 2013). American Psychiatric Association. p. 585.

limitation of the categorical model is that it does not directly provide a means of evaluating the severity of a disorder. Two people might have the same number of symptoms of a given disorder to warrant a diagnosis but differ markedly in the severity of the disorder.

EVALUATION OF THE DSM SYSTEM Many consider the major advantage of the DSM to be its designation of specific diagnostic criteria. The DSM permits a clinician to readily match a client's complaints and associated features with specific standards to see which diagnosis best fits a case.

The two basic criteria used in assessing the value of a diagnostic system such as the DSM are reliability and validity. A diagnostic system may be considered **reliable** or consistent if various diagnosticians using the system arrive at the same diagnoses when they evaluate the same cases.

The most appropriate test of the **validity** of the DSM is its correspondence with observed behaviour. Certain DSM classes, such as anxiety disorders, appear to have generally good validity in terms of grouping people who display similar behaviours (Brown, Di Nardo, Lehman, & Campbell, 2001; Turner, Beidel, Dancu, & Keys, 1986).

Another measure of validity, called *predictive validity*, is based on the ability of the diagnostic system to predict the course the disorder is likely to follow or its response to treatment. Evidence is accumulating that individuals classified in certain categories respond better to certain types of medication. Individuals with bipolar disorder, for example, respond reasonably well to lithium (see Chapter 4). Specific forms of psychological treatment may also be more effective with certain diagnostic groupings. For example, individuals who have specific phobias (such as fear of heights) are generally highly responsive to behavioural techniques for reducing fears (see Chapter 3).

Overall, evidence supports the reliability and validity of many DSM categories, including many anxiety disorders, depressive disorders, bipolar disorders, as well as substance use disorders (see, for example, Grant et al., 2006; Hasin, Hatzenbuehler, Keyes, & Ogburn, 2006). Yet questions about validity persist for some diagnostic categories (see Smith et al., 2011; Widiger & Simonsen, 2005).

Criticisms are also levelled against the DSM system. Critics challenge the utility of particular symptoms or features associated with a particular syndrome or of specified diagnostic criteria, such as the requirement that major depression be present for two weeks before a diagnosis is reached. Others challenge the reliance on the medical model. In the DSM system, problem behaviours are viewed as symptoms of underlying psychological disorders in much the same way that physical symptoms are seen as signs of underlying physical disorders. The very use of the term *diagnosis* presumes the medical model is an appropriate basis for classifying abnormal behaviours. But some clinicians feel that behaviour, abnormal or otherwise, is too complex and meaningful to be treated as merely symptomatic. They assert that the medical model focuses too much on what may happen within the individual and not enough on external influences on behaviour, such as social factors (socioeconomic, sociocultural, and ethnic) and physical environmental factors.

McGill University transcultural psychiatrists (e.g., Engelsmann, 2000; Kirmayer, 2001; Kirmayer & Minas, 2000; Prince, 2000) have argued that psychiatry in general and the DSM in particular should become more sensitive to diversity in culture and ethnicity. The behaviours included as diagnostic criteria in the DSM are determined by a consensus of mostly US- and Canadian-trained psychiatrists, psychologists, and social workers. Had the American Psychiatric Association asked Asian-trained or Latin American–trained professionals to develop the diagnostic manual, for example, there might have been some different or revised diagnostic categories.

In fairness to the DSM, however, the more recent editions place greater emphasis than earlier editions on weighing cultural factors when assessing abnormal behaviour. The DSM system recognizes that clinicians who are unfamiliar with an individual's cultural background may incorrectly classify that individual's behaviour as abnormal when in fact it falls within the normal spectrum in that individual's culture. The DSM also recognizes that abnormal behaviours may take different forms in different cultures and that some abnormal behaviour patterns are culture specific (see "Focus on Diversity: Culture-Bound Syndromes").

reliable In psychological assessment, the consistency of a measuring instrument, such as a psychological test or rating scale. There are various ways of measuring reliability, such as test-retest reliability, internal consistency, and interrater reliability. Also see *validity*.

validity (1) With respect to tests, the degree to which a test measures the traits or constructs that it purports to measure. (2) With respect to experiments, the degree to which an experiment yields scientifically accurate and defensible results

Culture-Bound Syndromes

Some patterns of psychological distress are limited to just one or a few cultures (Osborne, 2001). These **culture-bound disorders** are believed to be a manifestation, however exaggerated, of common folklore and belief patterns within the particular culture. For example, the psychiatric syndrome **taijin-kyofu-sho** (TKS) is common in Japan but rare elsewhere. TKS is characterized by excessive fear that one may behave in ways that will embarrass or offend other people (Kinoshita et al., 2008). People with TKS may dread blushing in front of others for fear of causing them embarrassment, not for fear of embarrassing themselves. In Western culture, an excessive fear of social embarrassment is called *social anxiety disorder* (see Chapter 3). Unlike people with TKS, however, people with social anxiety disorder have excessive concerns that they will be rejected by or embarrassed in front of others, not that they will embarrass other people. TKS primarily affects young Japanese men and is believed to be related to an emphasis in Japanese culture on not embarrassing others as well as deep concerns about issues of shame (Hofmann & Hinton, 2014).

Other examples include *koro*, found primarily in China and some other South and East Asian countries. The syndrome refers to an episode of acute anxiety involving the fear that one's genitals are shrinking and retracting into the body and that death may result. *Zār* is a term used in a number of countries in North Africa and the Middle East to describe the experience of spirit possession. Possession by spirits is often used in these cultures to explain dissociative episodes (sudden changes in consciousness or identity) that may be characterized by periods of shouting, banging the head against a wall, laughing, singing, or crying. Affected people may seem apathetic or withdrawn or refuse to eat or carry out their usual responsibilities (Dzokoto & Adams, 2005; Mianji & Semnani, 2015).

We generally think of culture-bound syndromes as abnormal behaviour patterns associated with folk cultures in non-Western societies. Yet some disorders, such as anorexia nervosa (discussed in Chapter 8, "Feeding and Eating Disorders and Sleep–Wake Disorders") and dissociative identity disorder (formerly called *multiple personality disorder*; discussed in Chapter 5, "Dissociative and Somatic Symptom and Related Disorders"), are recognized as culture-bound syndromes specific to industrialized or technological societies such as Canada (Hall, 2011). They occur rarely, if at all, in other societies.

---

culture-bound disorders Patterns of behaviour that are found within only one or a few cultural contexts.

taijin-kyofu-sho Psychiatric syndrome found in Japan that involves excessive fear of offending or causing embarrassment to others. Abbreviated *TKS*.

DSM-5

The latest revision of the DSM, the DSM-5, was years in the making and was published in 2013. It represents a major overhaul of the manual. The committees charged with revising the manual comprised experts in their fields. They closely examined the previous edition, the DSM-IV-TR, taking a careful look at what parts of the diagnostic system were working well and what parts needed to be revised to improve the manual's clinical utility (how it is used in practice) and to address concerns raised by clinicians and researchers.

The DSM-5 updated descriptive and background information on each disorder (APA, 2013). The definitions, diagnostic categories, and diagnostic criteria in DSM-5 remain similar to those in DSM-IV-TR. Some new disorders have sprung into being, and some existing disorders were reclassified or consolidated with other disorders under new diagnostic labels.

The DSM-5 classifies abnormal behaviour patterns, or psychological disorders, according to developmental models. This allows relevant lifespan information to be included in decisions regarding clinical diagnoses. Another major change in the DSM-5 was the adoption of a dimensional component in assessment and diagnosis. When a diagnosis of psychological disorder is made, other pertinent details are gathered from the individual, such as the psychosocial and environmental conditions that influence the persistence of the disorder. The impacts the disorder has on areas of the individual's life are also documented. For example, a diagnosis of depression may have a significant influence on a student's ability to fulfill his or her typical role functions. The DSM-5 did not abandon the categorical model, but expanded it to include a dimensional component for many disorders (Frances & Widiger, 2012; Shedler et al., 2010). This dimensional component gives the evaluator the opportunity to identify "shades of grey." For many disorders, the evaluator is charged not only with determining whether a disorder is present but also with rating the severity of the symptoms of a disorder along a scale ranging from "mild" to "severe."

Although every edition of the DSM has had its critics, the DSM-5 (as we see in "A Closer Look: DSM-5 Points of Controversy") has sparked a firestorm of criticism.

A CLOSER LOOK
DSM-5 Points of Controversy

Despite many years of debate, editing, and review, the final version of the DSM-5 remains steeped in controversy. Controversy has been a constant companion of the DSM system, in part because of difficulties involved in forging a consensus. Here are some points of controversy related to the DSM-5:

- *Expansion of diagnosable disorders.* One of the most common criticisms concerns the proliferation of new mental disorders—a problem dubbed *diagnostic inflation* (Frances & Widiger, 2012). Two disorders, *premenstrual dysphoric mood disorder* and *binge-eating disorder*, which had previously been placed in an appendix of the DSM containing proposed diagnoses in need of further study, became officially recognized mental disorders in the DSM-5. Other disorders are new to the diagnostic manual, including *mild neurocognitive disorder*. The result of diagnostic inflation may be to greatly expand the number of people labelled as suffering from a mental disorder or mental illness.
- *Changes in classification of mental disorders.* Another frequent criticism is that the DSM-5 changes the way in which many disorders are classified. A number of diagnoses were reclassified into broader categories, including Asperger's disorder. Many families of children who had an Asperger's diagnosis are concerned that their children's needs may not be met as effectively if Asperger's is no longer held to be a distinct diagnosis. Mental health professionals accustomed to using the earlier diagnostic categories have questioned whether changes in classification are justified and whether they will lead to more diagnostic confusion (e.g., Tanguay, 2011). The debate over classification will likely continue until the next edition of the DSM manual is developed.
- *Changes in diagnostic criteria for particular disorders.* Another criticism is that changes in the clinical definitions or diagnostic criteria for various disorders in the DSM-5 may change the number of cases in which these diagnoses are applied. Critics contend that many of the changes in the diagnostic criteria have not been sufficiently validated. Particular concerns have been raised about the substantial changes made in the set of symptoms or features used to diagnose autism spectrum

disorder, which may have profound effects on the number of children identified as suffering from autism and related disorders (Tanguay, 2011).
- *Process of development.* Other criticisms of the DSM-5 include the contention that the process of development was shrouded in secrecy, that it failed to incorporate input from many leading researchers and scholars in the field, and that changes to the diagnostic manual were not clearly documented on the basis of an adequate body of empirical research.

One significant change in the DSM-5 that has been generally well received is a greater emphasis on *dimensional assessment* across most categories of disorders. By conceptualizing disorders more broadly as representing dimensions of dysfunctional behaviour rather than simply as "present or absent" diagnostic categories, it allows clinicians to make judgments about the relative severity of disorders, such as by indicating the frequency of symptoms or the level of suicide risk or anxiety. Still, many psychologists believe that the developers of the DSM-5 did not go far enough in shifting from a categorical model of assessment to a dimensional model.

To sum up, let's reference the comments of a leading psychologist, Marsha Linehan, who remarked that the approval of the DSM-5 ended years of editing but began years of debate (Schwitzer, 2012). Ironically, the chairperson of the DSM-IV task force, psychiatrist Allen Frances, is now one of the leading critics of the DSM-5. Frances called the approval of the DSM-5 a "sad day for psychiatry" (cited in Schwitzer, 2012). In a scathing criticism, Frances argued that the introduction of new disorders and changes in the definition of existing disorders may medicalize behavioural problems like repeated temper tantrums in children (now classified as a new type of mental disorder called *disruptive mood dysregulation disorder*) and expectable life challenges, such as mild cognitive changes or everyday forgetting in older adults (now classified as a new disorder called *mild neurocognitive disorder*).

Why are these changes and controversies important to anyone other than psychologists and psychiatrists? The answer is that the diagnostic manual affects how clinicians identify, conceptualize, classify, and ultimately treat mental or psychological disorders. Changes in diagnostic practices can have far-reaching consequences. For example, Frances argues that bringing behaviour problems like recurrent temper tantrums under the umbrella of mental disorders will further increase the "excessive and inappropriate use of [psychiatric] medication in young children" (cited in Schwitzer, 2012). Under the best of circumstances, however, changes in diagnostic practices lead to improved patient care.

Time will tell how successful the DSM-5 will be and whether it will continue to be the most widely used diagnostic system in North America or be replaced by yet another revision or perhaps an alternative system, such as the ICD. All in all, the DSM-5 remains a work in progress, a document that will continue to be argued about and subjected to continuing scrutiny for the foreseeable future.

The DSM system, despite its critics, has become part of the everyday practice of most Canadian mental health professionals. It may be the one reference manual found on the bookshelves of nearly all such professionals, dog-eared from repeated use. Perhaps the DSM is best considered a work in progress, not a final product.

Now let's consider various ways of treating abnormal behaviour.

Classification of Abnormal Behaviour

- **What is the DSM and what are its major features?** The *Diagnostic and Statistical Manual of Mental Disorders* (DSM) is the most widely accepted system for classifying mental disorders in North America. The DSM uses specific diagnostic criteria to group patterns of abnormal behaviours that share common clinical features.

- **What are the major strengths and weaknesses of the DSM?** Strengths of the DSM include its use of specified diagnostic criteria and ratings to provide a comprehensive picture of an individual's functioning. Weaknesses may include the reliability and validity of certain diagnostic categories and, for some, the adoption of a medical model framework for classifying abnormal behaviour patterns.

METHODS OF TREATMENT

Carla, a 19-year-old undergraduate student, had been crying more or less continuously for several days. She felt that her life was falling apart, that her academic aspirations were in shambles, and that she was a disappointment to her parents. The thought of suicide had crossed her mind. She could not seem to drag herself out of bed in the morning and had withdrawn from her friends. Her misery seemed to descend on her from nowhere, although she could pinpoint some pressures in her life: a couple of poor grades at school, a recent breakup with a boyfriend, and some adjustment problems with roommates.

The psychologist who examined her arrived at a diagnosis of major depressive disorder. Had she broken her leg, her treatment from a qualified professional would have followed a fairly standard course. Yet the treatment that Carla or someone else with a psychological disorder receives is likely to vary not only with the type of disorder involved but also with the therapeutic orientation and professional background of the helping professional. A psychiatrist might recommend a course of antidepressant medication, perhaps in combination with some form of psychotherapy. A cognitively oriented psychologist might suggest a program of cognitive therapy to help Carla identify dysfunctional thoughts that may underlie her depression, whereas a psychodynamic therapist might recommend she begin psychodynamically oriented therapy to uncover inner conflicts originating in childhood that may lie at its root.

In these next sections, we focus on ways of treating psychological disorders. In later chapters, we see how these treatment approaches are applied to particular disorders. Here we focus on introducing the treatments themselves. We will see that the biological and psychological perspectives have spawned corresponding approaches to treatment. First, however, we consider the major types of mental health professionals who treat psychological or mental disorders and the different roles they play.

Types of Mental Health Professionals in Canada

Clinical psychologists, psychiatrists, and social workers constitute the majority of licensed mental health professionals in Canada. These three groups are regulated under provincial and territorial jurisdictions. But for the fourth broad cluster, psychotherapists and counsellors, there remains a lack of common pan-Canadian titles and clearly defined scopes of practice. Numerous provinces, including Quebec, Alberta, British Columbia, Nova Scotia, New Brunswick, and Ontario, have passed or are in the process of passing legislation that regulates the practices of psychotherapy and counselling. Distinguishing among the various helping professionals can be confusing to the public, and thus people seeking treatment are advised to inquire about the training and licensure of helping professionals.

Another reason for confusion is that all the different types of mental health providers, such as clinical psychologists, psychiatrists, clinical social workers, and a wide range of other mental health professionals, practise **psychotherapy** or "talk therapy"—a psychologically based method of treatment involving a series of verbal interchanges between clients and therapists taking place over a period of time, usually on a one-session-per-week basis. The particular approach used by individual psychotherapists reflects their theoretical orientation, such as psychodynamic, behavioural, humanistic, or cognitive. Some therapists adopt an **eclectic orientation**, which means they draw on the theories and techniques espoused by two or more theoretical orientations. We'll return to look at these different approaches to psychotherapy. But first, let's consider the different roles that the major types of mental health professionals play.

psychotherapy Method of helping involving a systematic interaction between a therapist and a client that brings psychological principles to bear on influencing the client's thoughts, feelings, or behaviours to help that client overcome abnormal behaviour or adjust to problems in living.

eclectic orientation Adoption of principles or techniques from various systems or theories.

CLINICAL PSYCHOLOGISTS   A clinical psychologist is a psychologist trained in the assessment, diagnosis, and treatment of psychological problems. All psychologists, including clinical psychologists, must have at least a master's degree. In most provinces, they must have a doctoral degree (PhD or PsyD) to be licensed to practise psychology independently (Edwards, 2000). Psychologists use various techniques to diagnose psychological problems, including clinical interviews, psychological tests, and behavioural observations (Canadian Psychological Association, 2002). They also use psychotherapy as a means of treating these problems. Psychologists often receive extensive training in research, which helps them conduct studies in clinical settings and critically evaluate the clinical literature.

PSYCHIATRISTS   Psychiatrists are licensed physicians who have earned medical degrees such as the Doctor of Medicine (MD). They have also completed a postdoctoral residency program in psychiatry that provides specialized training in diagnosing and treating psychological problems. Like psychologists, psychiatrists conduct psychotherapy and diagnostic interviews. Unlike psychologists, they can prescribe drugs and administer other biological treatments, such as electroconvulsive therapy (ECT). Psychiatrists often rely on psychologists for psychological testing to help determine a diagnosis or course of treatment.

SOCIAL WORKERS   Social workers earn a university degree in social work (Bachelor of Social Work, BSW; Master of Social Work, MSW; or Doctor of Social Work, DSW). They receive supervised training in helping people adjust and use social-support services and community agencies. Many social workers conduct psychotherapy or specialize in marital or family therapy.

Biological Therapies

psychopharmacology Field of study that examines the effects of drugs on behaviour and psychological functioning and explores the use of psychoactive drugs in the treatment of emotional disorders.

There is a growing emphasis in Canadian psychiatry on the biologically based treatment of abnormal behaviour, especially drug therapies (Gauthier, 1999). Biologically based approaches are generally administered by medical doctors, many of whom have specialized training in psychiatry or **psychopharmacology**. Many family physicians or general practitioners also prescribe psychotherapeutic or psychotropic drugs for their patients, however.

Although the biological or medical approaches have had dramatic success in treating some forms of abnormal behaviour, they also have their limitations. For one, biological therapies may have unwelcome or dangerous side effects. There is also the potential for abuse. One of the most commonly prescribed minor tranquillizers, Valium, has become a major drug of abuse among people who become psychologically and physiologically dependent on it. Psychosurgery has been all but eliminated as a form of treatment because of serious harmful effects of earlier procedures. There are, however, some new experimental biologically based techniques that show promise, such as transcranial magnetic stimulation, gene splicing, epigenetic therapy, and stem cell interventions.

Different classes of psychotropic drugs are used in the treatment of various types of mental health problems.

ANTI-ANXIETY DRUGS Anti-anxiety drugs (also called *anxiolytics*, from the Greek *anxietas*, meaning "anxiety," and *lysis*, meaning "bringing to an end") are drugs that combat anxiety and reduce states of muscle tension. They include mild tranquillizers, such as diazepam (Valium) and alprazolam (Xanax); barbiturates, such as meprobamate (Miltown); and sedative-hypnotics, such as triazolam (Halcion) and flurazepam (Dalmane). Clonazepam (Rivotril) and lorazepam (Ativan) are widely used in practice and fall into the category of mild tranquillizers like Valium.

Anti-anxiety drugs depress the level of activity in certain parts of the central nervous system (CNS). In turn, the CNS decreases the level of sympathetic nervous system activity, reducing the respiration rate and heart rate and lessening states of anxiety and tension. Minor tranquillizers such as Valium grew in popularity when physicians became concerned about the use of more potent sedatives, such as barbiturates, which are highly addictive and extremely dangerous when taken in overdoses or mixed with alcohol. Unfortunately, it has become clear that the minor tranquillizers also can, and often do, lead to physiological dependence (addiction). People who are dependent on Valium may go into convulsions when they abruptly stop taking it. Deaths have been reported among people who mix mild tranquillizers with alcohol or who are unusually sensitive to them. There are other less severe side effects, such as fatigue, drowsiness, and impaired motor coordination, which might reduce one's ability to function or to operate an automobile. Regular usage of benzodiazepines can also produce **tolerance**, a physiological sign of dependence: the need over time for increasing dosages of a drug to achieve the same effect. Quite commonly, patients become involved in tugs of war with their physicians as they demand increased dosages despite their physicians' concerns about the potential for abuse and dependence.

tolerance Physical habituation to a drug so that with frequent usage, higher doses are needed to attain similar effects.

When used on a short-term basis, anti-anxiety drugs can be safe and effective in treating anxiety and insomnia. Yet drugs by themselves do not teach people more adaptive ways of solving their problems and may encourage them to rely on a chemical agent to cope with stress rather than develop active means of coping. Drug therapy is thus often combined with psychotherapy to help people with anxiety complaints deal with the psychological and situational bases of their problems (Talbot & McMurray, 2004). However, combining drug therapy and psychotherapy may present special problems and challenges. For one, drug-induced relief from anxiety may reduce clients' motivation to try to solve their problems. For another, medicated clients who develop skills for coping with stress in psychotherapy may fail to retain what they have learned once the tranquillizers are discontinued, or find themselves too tense to employ their newly acquired skills.

Rebound anxiety is another problem associated with regular use of minor tranquillizers. Many people who regularly use anti-anxiety drugs report that anxiety or insomnia returns in a more severe form once they discontinue them. For some, this may represent a fear of not having the drugs to depend on. For others, rebound anxiety might reflect changes in biochemical processes that are not well understood at present.

ANTIPSYCHOTIC DRUGS   Antipsychotic drugs, also called **neuroleptics,** are commonly used to treat the more flagrant features of schizophrenia or other psychotic disorders, such as hallucinations, delusions, and states of confusion. Many of these drugs, including chlorpromazine (Thorazine), thioridazine (Mellaril), and fluphenazine (Prolixin), belong to the phenothiazine class of chemicals. Phenothiazines appear to control psychotic features by blocking the action of the neurotransmitter dopamine at receptor sites in the brain. Risperidone (Risperdal) and quetiapine (Seroquel) are also antipsychotics. Although the underlying causes of schizophrenia remain unknown, researchers suspect a dysregulation of the dopamine system in the brain may be involved (see Chapter 10). Clozapine (Clozaril), a neuroleptic of a different chemical class than the phenothiazines, has been shown to be effective in treating many people with schizophrenia whose symptoms were unresponsive to other neuroleptics (see Chapter 10). The use of clozapine must be carefully monitored, however, because of potentially dangerous side effects.

The use of neuroleptics has greatly reduced the need for more restrictive forms of treatment for severely disturbed patients, such as physical restraints and confinement in padded cells, and has lessened the need for long-term hospitalization. The introduction of major tranquillizers in the mid-1950s was one of the major factors that led to a massive exodus of chronic mental patients from institutions. Many ex-hospitalized patients have been able to resume family life and hold jobs while continuing to take their medications.

Neuroleptics are not without their problems, including potential side effects such as muscular rigidity and tremors. Although these side effects are generally controllable by the use of other drugs, long-term use of antipsychotic drugs (except possibly clozapine) can produce a potentially irreversible and disabling motor disorder called tardive dyskinesia (see Chapter 10), characterized by uncontrollable eye blinking, facial grimaces, lip smacking, and other involuntary movements of the mouth, eyes, and limbs. Researchers are experimenting with lowered dosages, intermittent drug regimens, and the use of new medications to reduce the risk of such complications.

ANTIDEPRESSANTS   Four major classes of **antidepressants** are used in treating depression: **tricyclics (TCAs), monoamine oxidase (MAO) inhibitors, selective serotonin-reuptake inhibitors (SSRIs),** and **serotonin-norepinephrine reuptake inhibitors (SNRIs).** Tricyclics and MAO inhibitors increase the availability of the neurotransmitters norepinephrine and serotonin in the brain. Some of the more common tricyclics are imipramine (Tofranil), amitriptyline (Elavil), and doxepin (Sinequan). The MAO inhibitors include such drugs as phenelzine (Nardil) and tranylcypromine (Parnate). Tricyclic antidepressants (TCAs) are commonly favoured over MAO inhibitors because of potentially serious side effects associated with MAO inhibitors.

SSRIs have more specific effects on serotonin function in the brain. Drugs in this class, which include fluoxetine (Prozac) and sertraline (Zoloft), increase the availability of serotonin in the brain by interfering with its reuptake by the transmitting neuron. SNRIs, such as venlafaxine (Effexor), work specifically on increasing levels of two neurotransmitters linked to mood states, serotonin and norepinephrine, by means of interfering with the reuptake of these chemicals by transmitting neurons.

The preferred antidepressant depends on individual patient characteristics, including the subtype and severity of depression, tolerance of side effects and safety, and interaction with other approaches such as psychotherapy (Kennedy, Lam, Cohen, Ravindran, & CANMAT Depression Work Group, 2001). Overall, the magnitude of the effect of antidepressant medication compared with a **placebo** increases with the severity of depression; for patients with very severe depression, the benefit of medications over a placebo is substantial (Elkin, 2010). A placebo—also referred to as a *sugar pill*—is an inert

rebound anxiety Occurrence of strong anxiety following withdrawal from a tranquillizer.

neuroleptics Group of antipsychotic drugs used in the treatment of schizophrenia, such as the phenothiazines (e.g., Thorazine).

antidepressants Types of drugs that act to relieve depression. Tricyclics, MAO inhibitors, selective serotonin-reuptake inhibitors, and serotonin-norepinephrine reuptake inhibitors are the major classes of antidepressants.

tricyclics Group of antidepressant drugs that increase the activity of norepinephrine and serotonin in the brain by interfering with the reuptake of these neurotransmitters by transmitting neurons. Also called *TCAs* (tricyclic antidepressants).

monoamine oxidase (MAO) inhibitors Antidepressants that act to increase the availability of neurotransmitters in the brain by inhibiting the actions of an enzyme, monoamine oxidase, that normally breaks down or degrades neurotransmitters (norepinephrine and serotonin) in the synaptic cleft.

selective serotonin-reuptake inhibitors (SSRIs) Type of antidepressant medication that prevents serotonin from being taken back up by the transmitting neuron, thus increasing its action.

serotonin-norepinephrine reuptake inhibitors (SNRIs) Type of antidepressant medication that works specifically on increasing levels of serotonin and norepinephrine by interfering with the reuptake of these chemicals by transmitting neurons.

placebo (*pluh-SEE-bo*) Inert medication or form of bogus treatment intended to control for the effects of expectancies. Sometimes referred to as a *sugar pill*.

Chris Pizzello/AP Images

Putting a public face on mental illness. Oscar-winning actress Catherine Zeta-Jones suffers from bipolar disorder and has previously checked herself into a mental health facility for treatment. Bipolar disorder can usually be controlled with a combination of medication and therapy. Lithium is one of the most common treatments.

electroconvulsive therapy Induction of a convulsive seizure by means of passing an electric current through the head; used primarily in the treatment of severe depression. Abbreviated *ECT*.

repetitive transcranial magnetic stimulation A procedure that uses strong magnetic pulses to stimulate the brain. Abbreviated *rTMS*.

substance that physically resembles an active drug. By comparing the effects of the active drug with those of the placebo, the experimenter can determine whether the drug has specific effects beyond those accounted for by expectations.

We shall see that antidepressants also have beneficial effects in treating a wide range of psychological disorders, including an array of anxiety disorders (see Chapter 3) and eating disorders (see Chapter 8). As research into the underlying causes of these disorders continues, we may find that dysregulation of neurotransmitters plays a key role in their development.

LITHIUM Lithium carbonate, a salt of the metal lithium in tablet form, has demonstrated remarkable effectiveness in stabilizing the dramatic mood swings associated with bipolar disorder (formerly called manic depression) (see Chapter 4). Because of its potential toxicity, the blood levels of patients maintained on lithium must be carefully monitored (Yatham et al., 2005). Like people with diabetes who must take insulin throughout their lifetimes to control their disease, people with bipolar disorder may have to continue using lithium indefinitely to control the disorder.

ELECTROCONVULSIVE THERAPY In 1939, the Italian psychiatrist Ugo Cerletti (1877–1963) introduced the technique of **electroconvulsive therapy** (ECT) in psychiatric treatment. Cerletti had observed in some slaughterhouses the practice of using electric shock to render animals unconscious. He saw that the shocks also produced convulsions. Cerletti incorrectly believed, as did other researchers in Europe at the time, that convulsions of the type found in epilepsy were incompatible with schizophrenia and that a method of inducing convulsions might be used to cure the disorder.

After the introduction of the phenothiazines in the 1950s, the use of ECT became generally limited to the treatment of severe depression. The introduction of antidepressants has further limited the use of ECT. Even though rates of ECT use are down from the 1960s, one Ontario study found that rates (roughly 12.5 per 100 000) have remained constant since the 1990s and are three times higher for elderly than for younger patients (Rapoport, Mamdani, & Herrmann, 2006).

Electroconvulsive therapy remains a source of controversy. For instance, many people, including many professionals, are uncomfortable about the idea of passing an electric shock through a person's head, even if the level of shock is closely regulated and the convulsions are controlled by drugs. Then there are the potential side effects. ECT often produces dramatic relief from severe depression, but concerns remain about its potential for inducing cognitive deficits, such as memory loss. A review of the evidence, however, finds memory losses following ECT to be temporary, except perhaps for some persistent loss of memory for events immediately around the time of the procedure itself (Devanand, Dwork, Hutchinson, Bolwig, & Sackeim, 1994).

A Canadian review found that up to 15% of depressive patients experience treatment-resistant depression (TRD) (Berlim & Turecki, 2007). Although controversies concerning the use of ECT persist, the facts support its effectiveness in helping people overcome severe depression that fails to respond to psychotherapy or antidepressant medication (Rabheru, 2001; Rapoport et al., 2006). However, ECT is usually considered a treatment of last resort, after less intrusive methods of treating TRD have been tried and have failed.

An alternative form of brain stimulation treatment for depression—**repetitive transcranial magnetic stimulation** (rTMS)—is now used in Canada. In rTMS, a strong magnetic field is directed through a coil held against the head for several daily hour-long sessions. Some early indications have shown rTMS to be an effective, painless, noninvasive procedure with zero to low side effects (Fitzgerald, Benitez, et al., 2006; Fitzgerald, Huntsman, Gunewardene, Kulkarni, & Daskalakis, 2006). In some cases, it can be a practical alternative to ECT, as it is a less costly treatment and is not associated with anaesthetic and other ECT risks (Rosa et al., 2006; Schulze-Rauschenbach et al., 2005). Find out more about the use of rTMS in the treatment of depression in Chapter 4.

DEEP BRAIN STIMULATION Deep brain stimulation involves implanting electrodes within the part of the brain that affects mood. During deep brain stimulation, electrical impulses transmitted through the electrodes deep within the brain affect brain cells and chemicals to relieve depression. The amount of stimulation delivered by the electrodes is controlled by a pacemaker-like device placed under the skin in the upper chest. A wire that travels under the skin connects the device, called a *pulse generator*, to the electrodes in the brain.

Although it's approved for other conditions, deep brain stimulation for depression hasn't been approved by the US Food and Drug Administration (FDA). It's still being studied as an experimental treatment. Most candidates for deep brain stimulation are participants in clinical trials.

Deep brain stimulation is an established treatment for essential tremor and Parkinson's disease. Some people with Parkinson's who underwent deep brain stimulation reported an improved mood. Because of those results, deep brain stimulation is being studied as a possible depression treatment to be used when standard treatments don't work. Standard treatments include antidepressants, psychological counselling (psychotherapy), and electroconvulsive therapy.

Sending electrical impulses to areas of the brain linked with mood affects brain cells and brain chemistry. While this can help ease depression symptoms, researchers are still investigating exactly how deep brain stimulation improves mood.

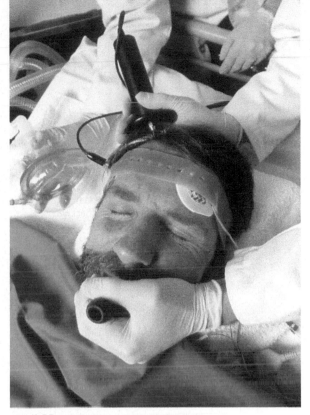

WILL & DENI MCINTYRE/Science Source/Getty Images

Electroconvulsive therapy (ECT). ECT is helpful in many cases of severe or prolonged depression that do not respond to other forms of treatment. Still, its use remains controversial.

Deep brain stimulation also shows some promise for some other mental illnesses. It has been approved by the FDA as a treatment for severe and debilitating OCD. It's also being investigated to see whether it may help with Tourette syndrome, chronic pain, and other disorders.

Although initial results are promising, more research is needed to determine whether deep brain stimulation can be considered a safe and effective treatment for depression. Researchers are still trying to identify the best locations for the electrode implants to help reduce symptoms while causing the fewest and least severe side effects.

In a systematic review of clinical trials of deep brain stimulation for OCD and TRD, Lakhan and Callaway (2010) found that about half of patients did show dramatic improvement. They caution that procedures differed from study to study, and the numbers of patients were usually too small to produce meaningful statistics or make valid inferences as to who will respond to treatment; however, deep brain stimulation is a promising technique for both OCD and TRD.

We now consider the major types of psychotherapy and their relationships to the theoretical models from which they derive.

Psychodynamic Therapies

Psychoanalysis is the form of psychodynamic therapy originated by Sigmund Freud. Practitioners of psychoanalysis, called *psychoanalysts*, view psychological problems as

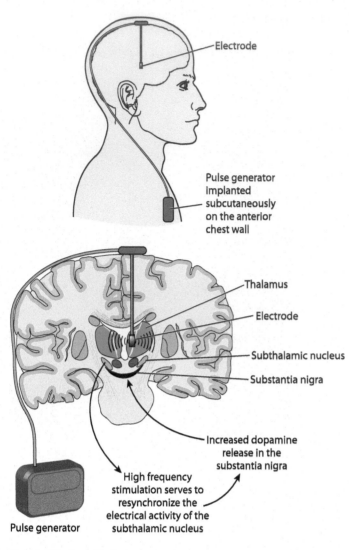

Blamb/Shutterstock

Stimulating the brain to improve mood? In deep brain stimulation, electrodes are inserted into the brain, transmitting impulses to brain cells. The method is already approved by the FDA as a treatment for obsessive-compulsive disorder and is showing promise for other mental illnesses.

Labels in figure:
Electrode

Pulse generator implanted subcutaneously on the anterior chest wall

Thalamus

Electrode

Subthalamic nucleus

Substantia nigra

Increased dopamine release in the substantia nigra

High frequency stimulation serves to resynchronize the electrical activity of the subthalamic nucleus

Pulse generator

rooted in early childhood experiences and unconscious conflicts. Freud used psychoanalysis to help clients gain insight into and resolve unconscious conflicts. Working through these conflicts, the ego would be freed of the need to maintain defensive behaviours—such as phobias, obsessive-compulsive behaviours, and hysterical complaints—that shield it from recognition of inner turmoil.

Freud summed up the goal of psychoanalysis by saying, "Where id was, there shall ego be." This meant, in part, that psychoanalysis could help shed the light of awareness, represented by the conscious ego, on the inner workings of the id. But Freud did not expect or intend that clients should seek to become conscious of all repressed material—of all their impulses, wishes, fears, and memories. The aim, rather, was to replace defensive behaviour with more adaptive behaviour. By so doing, clients could find gratification without incurring social or self-condemnation.

Through this process a man with a phobia of knives might become aware he had been repressing impulses to vent a murderous rage against his father. His phobia keeps him from having contact with knives, thereby serving a hidden purpose of keeping his homicidal impulses in check. A woman with a loss of sensation in her hand that could not be explained medically might come to see that she harboured guilt over urges to masturbate. The loss of sensation may have prevented her from acting on these urges. Through confronting hidden impulses and the conflicts they produce, clients learn to sort out their feelings and find more constructive and socially acceptable ways of handling their impulses and wishes. The ego is then freed to focus on more constructive interests.

The major methods that Freud used to accomplish these goals were free association, dream analysis, and analysis of the transference relationship.

FREE ASSOCIATION You are asked to lie down on a couch and to say anything that enters your mind. The psychoanalyst (or *analyst*, for short) sits in a chair behind you, out of direct view. For the next 45 or 50 minutes, you let your mind wander, saying whatever pops in, or saying nothing at all. The analyst remains silent most of the time, prompting you occasionally to utter whatever crosses your mind, no matter how seemingly trivial, no matter how personal. This process continues, typically for three or four sessions a week, for a period of several years. At certain points in the process, the analyst offers an interpretation, drawing your attention to connections between your disclosures and unconscious conflicts.

displacement In psychodynamic theory, a type of defence mechanism that involves the transferring of impulses toward threatening or unacceptable objects onto more acceptable or safer objects.

TRANSFERENCE Freud found that clients responded to him not only as an individual but also in ways that reflected their feelings and attitudes toward other important people in their lives. A young female client might respond to him as a father figure, transferring, in an act of **displacement**, onto Freud her feelings toward her own father. A man might also view him as a father figure, responding to him as a rival in a manner Freud believed might reflect the man's unresolved Oedipal complex.

The process of analyzing and working through the **transference relationship** is considered an essential component of psychoanalysis. Freud believed that the transference relationship provides a vehicle for the re-enactment of childhood conflicts with parents. Clients may react to the analyst with the same feelings of anger, love, or jealousy they felt toward their own parents. Freud termed the enactment of these childhood conflicts the *transference neurosis*. This "neurosis" had to be successfully analyzed and worked through for clients to succeed in psychoanalysis.

Childhood conflicts usually involve unresolved feelings of anger or rejection or needs for love. For example, a client may interpret any slight criticism by the therapist as a devastating blow, transferring feelings of self-loathing the client repressed from childhood experiences of parental rejection. Transferences may also distort or colour the client's relationships with others, such as a spouse or employer. Clients might relate to their spouse as they had to their parents, perhaps demanding too much from them or unjustly accusing them of being insensitive or uncaring. Or they might not give new friends or lovers the benefit of a fair chance if they had been mistreated by others who played similar roles in their past. The analyst helps the client recognize transference relationships, especially the therapy transference, and to work through the residues of childhood feelings and conflicts that lead to self-defeating behaviour in the present.

According to Freud, transference is a two-way street. Freud felt he transferred his underlying feelings onto his clients, perhaps viewing a young man as a competitor or a woman as a rejecting love interest. Freud referred to the feelings that he projected onto clients as **countertransference**. Psychoanalysts in training are expected to undergo psychoanalysis themselves to help them uncover motives that might lead to countertransferences in their therapeutic relationships. In their therapeutic training, psychoanalysts learn to monitor their own reactions in therapy so as to become better aware of when and how countertransferences intrude on the therapy process.

Although the analysis of the therapy transference is a crucial element of psychoanalytic therapy, it generally takes months or years for a transference relationship to develop and be resolved. This is one reason why psychoanalysis is typically a lengthy and expensive process.

MODERN PSYCHODYNAMIC APPROACHES   Although some psychoanalysts continue to practise traditional psychoanalysis in much the same manner as Freud, briefer and less intensive forms of psychodynamic treatment have emerged (Strupp, 1992). These newer approaches are often referred to as *brief psychodynamic therapies*. They are able to reach clients who are seeking more focused and less costly forms of treatment, perhaps once or twice a week.

Like Freudian psychoanalysis, the newer psychodynamic approaches aim to uncover unconscious motives and break down resistances and psychological defences, yet they focus more on the client's present relationships and encourage the client to make adaptive behaviour changes. As a result of the briefer format, therapy may entail a more open and direct exploration of the client's defences and transference relationships than was traditionally the case. Unlike the traditional approach, the client and therapist generally sit facing each other. Rather than offer an occasional interpretation, the therapist engages in more frequent verbal give-and-take with the client, as in the following vignette. Note how the therapist uses interpretation to help the client, Mr. Arianes, achieve insight into how his relationship with his wife involves a transference of his childhood relationship with his mother:

Mr. Arianes:	I think you've got it there, Doc. We weren't communicating. I wouldn't tell her [his wife] what was wrong or what I wanted from her. Maybe I expected her to understand me without saying anything.
Therapist:	Like the expectations a child has of its mother.
Mr. Arianes:	Not my mother!
Therapist:	Oh?
Mr. Arianes:	No, I always thought she had too many troubles of her own to pay attention to mine. I remember once I got hurt on my bike and came to her all bloodied up. When she saw me she got mad and yelled at

transference relationship In psychoanalysis, a client's transfer or generalization to the analyst of feelings and attitudes the client holds toward important figures in his or her life.

countertransference In psychoanalysis, the transfer of feelings that the analyst holds toward other persons in her or his life onto the client.

	me for making more trouble for her when she already had her hands full with my father.
Therapist:	Do you remember how you felt then?
Mr. Arianes:	I can't remember, but I know that after that I never brought my troubles to her again.
Therapist:	How old were you?
Mr. Arianes:	Nine. I know that because I got that bike for my ninth birthday. It was a little too big for me still, that's why I got hurt on it.
Therapist:	Perhaps you carried this attitude into your marriage.
Mr. Arianes:	What attitude?
Therapist:	The feeling that your wife, like your mother, would be unsympathetic to your difficulties. That there was no point in telling her about your experiences because she was too preoccupied or too busy to care.
Mr. Arianes:	But she's so different from my mother. I come first with her.
Therapist:	On one level you know that. On another, deeper level there may well be the fear that people—or maybe only women, or maybe only women you're close to—are all the same, and you can't take a chance at being rejected again in your need.
Mr. Arianes:	Maybe you're right, Doc, but all that was so long ago, and I should be over that by now.
Therapist:	That's not the way the mind works. If a shock or a disappointment is strong enough it can permanently freeze our picture of ourselves and our expectations of the world. The rest of us grows up—that is, we let ourselves learn about life from experience and from what we see, hear, or read of the experiences of others, but that one area where we really got hurt stays unchanged. So what I mean when I say you might be carrying that attitude into your relationship with your wife is that when it comes to your hopes of being understood and catered to when you feel hurt or abused by life, you still feel very much like that nine-year-old boy who was rebuffed in his need and gave up hope that anyone would or could respond to him.

Source: Republished with permission of Hachette Book Group USA, from Doing psychotherapy. New York, Michael Franz Basch, 1980; permission conveyed through Copyright Clearance Center, Inc.

Behaviour Therapy

Behaviour therapists apply the principles of learning to help clients make adaptive changes in their behaviour. Because the focus is on changing behaviour—not on personality change or deep probing into the past—behaviour therapy is relatively brief, lasting typically from a few weeks to a few months. Behaviour therapists, like other therapists, seek to develop warm therapeutic relationships with clients, but they believe the special efficacy of behaviour therapy derives from learning-based techniques rather than from the nature of the therapeutic relationship.

Behaviour therapy first gained widespread attention as a means of helping people overcome fears and phobias, problems that had proved resistant to insight-oriented therapies. Among these methods are systematic desensitization, gradual exposure, and modelling. **Systematic desensitization** involves a therapeutic program of exposure (in imagination or by means of pictures or slides) to progressively more fearful stimuli while one remains deeply relaxed.

In **gradual exposure**, also called *in vivo* ("in life") *exposure*, people troubled by phobias purposely expose themselves to the stimuli that evoke their fear. Like systematic desensitization, the person progresses at his or her own pace through a hierarchy of progressively more anxiety-evoking stimuli. A person with a fear of snakes, for example, might first look at a harmless, caged snake from across the room and then gradually approach and interact with the snake in a step-by-step process, progressing to each new step only when feeling completely

systematic desensitization
Behaviour therapy technique for overcoming phobias by means of exposure (in imagination or by means of pictures or slides) to progressively more fearful stimuli while one remains deeply relaxed.

gradual exposure In behaviour therapy, a method of overcoming fears through a stepwise process of direct exposure to increasingly fearful stimuli.

calm at the prior step. Gradual exposure is often combined with cognitive techniques that focus on replacing anxiety-arousing irrational thoughts with calming rational thoughts.

In modelling, clients first observe and then imitate others who approach or interact with fear-evoking situations or objects. After observing the model, the client may be assisted or guided by the therapist or the model in performing the target behaviour. The client receives ample reinforcement from the therapist for each attempt. Modelling approaches were pioneered by Albert Bandura and his colleagues, who had remarkable success using modelling techniques to treat various phobias, especially fears of animals, such as snakes and dogs (Bandura, Blanchard, & Ritter, 1969; Bandura, Jeffery, & Wright, 1974).

Behaviour therapists also use techniques based on operant conditioning, or systematic use of rewards and punishments, to shape desired behaviour. For example, parents and teachers may be trained to reinforce children systematically for appropriate behaviour by showing appreciation and to extinguish inappropriate behaviour by ignoring it. In institutional settings, **token economies** seek to increase adaptive behaviour by allowing patients to earn tokens for performing appropriate behaviours, such as self-grooming and making their beds. The tokens can eventually be exchanged for desired rewards. Token systems have also been used to treat children with conduct-disorder problems.

Other techniques of behaviour therapy discussed in later chapters include aversive conditioning (used in the treatment of substance use problems such as smoking and alcoholism), social-skills training (used in the treatment of social anxieties and skills deficits associated with schizophrenia), and self-control techniques (used in helping people reduce excess weight and quit smoking).

David Kilpatrick/Alamy Stock Photo

Modelling. Modelling techniques are often used to help people overcome phobic behaviours. Here, a child observes an adult handling a spider. As in phobia treatment, the client observes the harmless engagement with the phobic object and is then, with reinforcement from the therapist, more likely to imitate that behaviour.

token economies Behavioural treatment programs, in institutional settings, in which a controlled environment is constructed such that people are reinforced for desired behaviours by receiving tokens (such as poker chips) that may be exchanged for desired rewards or privileges.

A CLOSER LOOK

A New Vision of Stigma Reduction and Mental Health Support for Young Adults

A FAMILY INSPIRES COMPASSION AND CARE AFTER LOSING THEIR SON TO SUICIDE

Jack Windeler was a student at Queen's University who was struggling with mental illness. Partway through his first year, his grades started to fall and he became more and more withdrawn. Jack died by suicide in March 2010. Jack's note asked that no fuss be made of his passing, but to "help others." Jack's parents began the Jack Windeler Memorial Fund in partnership with Kids Help Phone, Canada's leading counselling service for youth aged 5–20. The tremendous outpouring of support inspired The Jack Project.

As an initiative of Kids Help Phone, and in partnership with the Mental Health Commission of Canada, the project seeks to promote mental health awareness and support for youth aged 15–20+ who are transitioning from high school to college, university, or independent living.

THE JACK PROJECT AT KIDS HELP PHONE

The Jack Project aligned with Canadian mental health organizations to implement a pilot program (2011–2012

Courtesy The Windeler Family

Jack Windeler died by suicide during his first year of studies at Queen's University. He asked that others be helped.

school year) at 36 schools across Ontario. Through this work, the team developed youth-led workshops with the goal of inspiring a national culture of informed compassion and care for youth impacted by mental health challenges. They also initiated an online chat service and mobile app so help would be more readily available to those in need. Through these integrated online efforts, they educated and supported youth and helped them find assistance in their community.

JACK.ORG

In October 2013, The Jack Project incorporated as a registered Canadian charity and later changed its name to Jack.org. They presently have chapters in 38 universities, 7 colleges, and 59 high schools throughout Canada. They continue to train youth to speak in schools about their own experiences with mental health and the challenges they have faced (Jack.org, 2016).

Humanistic-Existential Therapies

Psychodynamic therapists tend to focus on unconscious processes such as internal conflicts. By contrast, humanistic therapists focus on clients' subjective, conscious experiences. Like behaviour therapists, humanistic-existential therapists focus more on what clients are experiencing in the present—the here and now—than on the past. But there are also similarities between the psychodynamic and humanistic-existential therapies. Both assume that the past affects present behaviour and feelings, and both seek to expand clients' self-insight. The major form of humanistic therapy is **person-centred therapy** (formerly called **client-centred therapy**), which was developed by the psychologist Carl Rogers.

PERSON-CENTRED THERAPY   Rogers (1951) believed that people have natural motivational tendencies toward growth, fulfillment, and health. In Rogers's view, psychological disorders develop largely from the roadblocks that others place in the journey toward self-actualization. When others are selective in their approval of our childhood feelings and behaviour, we may come to disown the criticized parts of ourselves. To earn social approval, we may don social masks or facades. We learn "to be seen and not heard" and may become deaf even to our own inner voices. Over time, we may develop distorted self-concepts that are consistent with others' views of us but are not of our own making and design. As a result, we may become poorly adjusted, unhappy, and confused as to who and what we are.

Person-centred therapy creates conditions of warmth and acceptance in the therapeutic relationship—conditions that help clients become more aware and accepting of their true selves. Rogers was a major shaper of contemporary psychotherapy and was rated the single most influential psychotherapist in a survey of therapists (Smith, 1982). Rogers did not believe therapists should impose their own goals or values on their clients. His focus of therapy, as the name implies, is centred on the person.

Person-centred therapy is nondirective. The client, not the therapist, takes the lead and directs the course of therapy. The therapist uses reflection—the restating or paraphrasing of the client's expressed feelings without interpreting them or passing judgment on them. This encourages the client to further explore his or her feelings and get in touch with deeper feelings and parts of the self that have become disowned because of social condemnation.

Rogers stressed the importance of creating a warm therapeutic relationship that would encourage the client to engage in self-exploration and self-expression. The effective person-centred therapist should possess four basic qualities or attributes: **unconditional positive regard**, empathy, genuineness, and congruence between his or her thoughts, feelings, and behaviour. The therapist must be able to express unconditional positive regard for clients, in contrast to the conditional approval the client may have received from parents and others in the past. This provides clients with a sense of security that encourages them to explore their feelings without fear of disapproval.

person-centred therapy Carl Rogers's method of psychotherapy, emphasizing the establishment of a warm, accepting therapeutic relationship that frees clients to engage in a process of self-exploration and self-acceptance.

client-centred therapy Another name for Carl Rogers's *person-centred therapy.*

unconditional positive regard In Carl Rogers's view, the expression of unconditional acceptance of another person's basic worth as a person, regardless of whether one approves of all of the behaviour of the other person. The ability to express unconditional positive regard is considered a quality of an effective person-centred therapist.

Therapists serve as models of psychological integrity to their clients. Here, Rogers (C.R.) uses reflection to help a client, Jill, focus more deeply on her inner feelings:

Jill: I'm having a lot of problems dealing with my daughter. She's 20 years old; she's in college; I'm having a lot of trouble letting her go. . . . And I have a lot of guilt feelings about her; I have a real need to hang on to her.

C. R.: A need to hang on so you can kind of make up for the things you feel guilty about. Is that part of it?

Jill: There's a lot of that. . . . Also, she's been a real friend to me, and filled my life. . . . And it's very hard . . . a lot of empty places now that she's not with me.

C. R.: The old vacuum, sort of, when she's not there.

Jill: Yes. Yes. I also would like to be the kind of mother that could be strong and say, you know, "Go and have a good life," and this is really hard for me, to do that.

C. R.: It's very hard to give up something that's been so precious in your life, but also something that I guess has caused you pain when you mentioned guilt.

Jill: Yeah. And I'm aware that I have some anger toward her that I don't always get what I want. I have needs that are not met. And, uh, I don't feel I have a right to those needs. You know . . . she's a daughter; she's not my mother. Though sometimes I feel as if I'd like her to mother me . . . it's very difficult for me to ask for that and have a right to it.

C. R.: So, it may be unreasonable, but still, when she doesn't meet your needs, it makes you mad.

Jill: Yeah I get very angry, very angry with her.

C. R.: (Pause) You're also feeling a little tension at this point, I guess.

Jill: Yeah. Yeah. A lot of conflict . . . (C. R.: M-hm). A lot of pain.

C. R.: A lot of pain. Can you say anything more about what that's about?

Source: The Psychotherapy of Carl Rogers: Cases and Commentary (Psyche and Soul), Barry A. Farber, Debora C. Brink, Patricia M. Raskin, Guilford Press, ©1996. Reprinted with permission Guilford Press.

EMOTION-FOCUSED THERAPY Emotion-focused therapy (EFT) is based on the premise that "emotion, motivation, cognition, and action occur as an integrated response package" (Greenberg, 2002a, p. 26). From this perspective, there are multiple factors that contribute to maladaptive emotions, including our genetic makeup and temperament. Early in our development, reciprocal interpersonal relationships are formed with "significant others" and gradually we develop well-ingrained patterns of emotional responses. If our early emotional responses were intense, we may fall prey to "reliving" past hurts, fears, and rages in current situations. For example, "inattentiveness from a spouse can activate intense feelings of neglect from a loveless childhood. These feelings then become maladaptive responses to the present situation" (Greenberg, 2002a, p. 32).

An essential tenet of EFT is not to eliminate intense or uncomfortable feelings but to view them as a signal to take action—"emotion moves us and reason guides us" (Greenberg, 2002a, p. x). The challenge is to know "when to change emotion and when to be changed by it" (Greenberg, 2002a, p. xi). During a counselling session, for instance, an emotion-focused therapist acts as a coach who begins by helping people become more aware and accepting of their emotions. This is followed by helping them transform their negative emotions into more adaptive ones—for example, turning unproductive anger into adaptive sadness and then acceptance through the use of emotion-shifting techniques such as role play or guided imagery. This strategy is based on the premise that even though "thinking usually changes thoughts[;] only feeling can change emotions" (Greenberg, 2006, p. 91). Lastly, the emotional experiences are reflected upon and assimilated to allow a new meaning of self to emerge (Greenberg, 2006). This type of therapeutic collaboration between therapist and client promotes the development of the client's emotional intelligence (Elliot, Watson, Goldman, & Greenberg, 2004).

Cognitive-Behaviour Therapies

There is nothing either good or bad, but thinking makes it so.

—SHAKESPEARE, *HAMLET*

In these words, Shakespeare did not mean to imply that misfortunes or ailments are painless or easy to manage. His point, rather, is that the ways in which we evaluate upsetting events can heighten our discomfort and impair our ability to cope. Several hundred years later, cognitive therapists adopted this simple but elegant expression as a kind of motto for their approach to therapy.

Cognitive-behaviour therapists focus on helping clients identify and correct maladaptive beliefs, automatic types of thinking, and self-defeating attitudes that create or compound emotional problems and dysfunctional ways of behaving. They believe that negative emotions such as anxiety and depression are caused by the interpretations we place on troubling events, not by the events themselves. Canadian psychologists Keith Dobson (University of Calgary) and David Dozois (Western University) suggest that all cognitive-behavioural therapies share three fundamental propositions:

1. Cognitive activity affects behaviour.
2. Cognitive activity may be monitored and altered.
3. Desired behaviour change may be effected through cognitive change. (Dobson & Dozois, 2001, p. 4)

Here, we focus on the contributions of three prominent types of cognitive-behavioural therapy: Albert Ellis's rational-emotive behaviour therapy, Aaron Beck's cognitive therapy, and the cognitive-behavioural therapy of Donald Meichenbaum.

RATIONAL-EMOTIVE BEHAVIOUR THERAPY   Albert Ellis (1977, 1993, 2003) believed that the adoption of irrational, self-defeating beliefs gives rise to psychological problems and negative feelings. Consider the irrational belief that one must have the approval almost all the time of the people who are important to you. Ellis found it understandable to want other people's approval and love, but he argued that it is irrational to believe we cannot survive without it. Emotional difficulties such as anxiety and depression are directly caused not by negative events but rather by how we distort their meaning by viewing them through the dark-coloured glasses of irrational beliefs. Thinking irrationally transforms challenging events, such as forthcoming examinations, into looming disasters ("It would be so awful if I did poorly—I wouldn't be able to stand it"). Ellis's rational-emotive behaviour therapy (REBT) seeks to free people from such irrational beliefs and their consequences. In REBT, therapists actively dispute irrational beliefs and their premises and help clients develop more rational, adaptive beliefs.

Ellis and Dryden (1987) described the case of a 27-year-old woman, Jane, who was socially inhibited and shy, particularly with attractive men. Through REBT, Jane identified some of her underlying irrational beliefs, such as "I must speak well to people I find attractive" and "When I don't speak well and impress people as I should, I'm a stupid, inadequate person!" (p. 68). REBT helped her discriminate between these irrational beliefs and rational alternatives, such as "If people do reject me for showing them how anxious I am, that will be most unfortunate, but I can stand it" (p. 68). REBT encouraged her to debate or dispute irrational beliefs by posing challenging questions to herself: "Why must I speak well to people I find attractive?" and "When I don't speak well and impress people, how does that make me a stupid and inadequate person?" (p. 69). Jane learned to form rational responses to her self-questioning; for example, "There is no reason I must speak well to people I find attractive, but it would be desirable if I do so, so I shall make an effort—but not kill myself—to do so" and "When I speak poorly and fail to impress people, that only makes me a person who spoke unimpressively this time—not a totally stupid or inadequate person" (p. 69).

Ellis recognized that irrational beliefs may be formed on the basis of early childhood experiences. Changing those beliefs requires finding rational alternatives in the here and now, however. Rational-emotive behaviour therapists also help clients substitute more effective interpersonal behaviour for self-defeating or maladaptive behaviour.

BECK'S COGNITIVE THERAPY As formulated by psychiatrist Aaron Beck and his colleagues (Beck, 1976; Beck et al., 1979; Beck, Freeman, Davis, & Associates, 2004), cognitive therapy, like REBT, focuses on clients' maladaptive cognitions. Cognitive therapists encourage clients to recognize and change errors in their thinking, called *cognitive distortions*, that affect their moods and impair their behaviour, such as tendencies to magnify negative events and minimize personal accomplishments.

Cognitive therapists have clients record the thoughts that are prompted by upsetting events they experience and note the connections between their thoughts and their emotional responses. They then help them dispute distorted thoughts and replace them with rational alternatives. Therapists also use behavioural homework assignments, such as encouraging depressed clients to fill their free time with structured activities like gardening or completing work around the house. Carrying out such tasks serves to counteract the apathy and loss of motivation that tend to characterize depression and may also provide concrete evidence of competence, which helps combat self-perceptions of helplessness and inadequacy.

Another type of homework assignment involves reality testing. Clients are asked to test out their negative beliefs in the light of reality. For example, a depressed client who feels unwanted by everyone might be asked to call two or three friends on the phone to gather data about the friends' reactions to the calls. The therapist might then ask the client to report on the assignment: "Did they immediately hang up the phone? Or did they seem pleased you called? Did they express any interest at all in talking to you again or getting together sometime? Does the evidence support the conclusion that no one has any interest in you?" Such exercises help clients replace distorted beliefs with rational alternatives.

Consider this case, in which a depressed man was encouraged to test his belief that he was about to be fired from his job. The case also illustrates several cognitive distortions or errors in thinking, such as selectively perceiving only one's flaws (in this case, self-perceptions of laziness) and expecting the worst (expectations of being fired):

A 35-year-old man, a frozen-foods distributor, had suffered from chronic depression since his divorce six years earlier. During the past year, the depression had worsened and he found it increasingly difficult to call on customers or go to the office. Each day that he avoided working made it more difficult for him to go to the office and face his boss. He was convinced that he was in imminent danger of being fired because he had not made any sales calls for more than a month. Since he had not earned any commissions in a while, he felt he was not adequately supporting his two daughters and was concerned that he wouldn't have the money to send them to college. He was convinced that his basic problem was laziness, not depression. His therapist pointed out the illogic in his thinking. First of all, there was no real evidence that his boss was about to fire him. His boss had actually encouraged him to get help and was paying for part of the treatment. His therapist also pointed out that judging himself as lazy was unfair because it overlooked the fact that he had been an industrious, successful salesman before he became depressed. While not fully persuaded, the client agreed to a homework assignment in which he was to call his boss and also make a sales call to one of his former customers. His boss expressed support and reassured him that his job was secure. The customer ribbed him about "being on vacation" during the preceding six weeks but placed a small order. The client discovered that the small unpleasantness he experienced in facing the customer and being teased paled in comparison to the intense depression he felt at home while he was avoiding work. Within the next several weeks he gradually worked himself back to a normal routine, calling upon customers and making future plans. This process of viewing himself and the world from a fresh perspective led to a general improvement in his mood and behaviour.

David D Burns; Aaron T Beck; John Paul Foreyt; Diana P Rathjen, Modifications of Mood Disorders. In Cognitive behavior therapy: Research and application, Plenum. (pp. 124–126). 1978; "With permission of Springer Nature"

Rational-emotive behaviour therapy and Beck's cognitive therapy have much in common, especially the focus on helping clients replace self-defeating thoughts and beliefs with more rational ones. Perhaps the major difference between the two approaches is one of therapeutic style. REBT therapists tend to be more confrontational and forceful in their approach to disputing clients' irrational beliefs (Dryden, 1984; Ellis, Young, & Lockwood, 1987). Cognitive therapists tend to adopt a more gentle, collaborative approach in helping clients discover and correct the distortions in their thinking.

MEICHENBAUM'S COGNITIVE-BEHAVIOURAL THERAPY Today many, if not most, behaviour therapists identify with the broader cognitive-behavioural therapy. Donald Meichenbaum's cognitive-behavioural therapy developed from the attempt to integrate therapeutic techniques that focus not only on making overt behavioural changes but also on changing dysfunctional thoughts and cognitions (Meichenbaum, 1977). Cognitive-behavioural therapy draws on the assumptions that cognitions and information processing play important roles in the genesis and maintenance of maladaptive behaviour, and the impact of external events is filtered through thinking processes (Beidel & Turner, 1986).

Cognitive-behavioural therapists use an assortment of behavioural and cognitive techniques in therapy. The following case illustrates how behavioural techniques (exposure to fearful situations) and cognitive techniques (changing maladaptive thoughts) were used in the treatment of agoraphobia, a type of anxiety disorder characterized by excessive fears of venturing out in public:

Ms. X was a 41-year-old woman with a 12-year history of agoraphobia. She feared venturing into public places alone and required her husband or children to accompany her from place to place. In vivo (actual) exposure sessions were arranged in a series of progressively more fearful encounters—a fear-stimulus hierarchy. The first step in the hierarchy, for example, involved taking a shopping trip while accompanied by the therapist. After accomplishing this task, she gradually moved upward in the hierarchy. By the third week of treatment, she was able to complete the last step in her hierarchy—shopping by herself in a crowded supermarket. Cognitive restructuring was conducted along with the exposure training. Ms. X was asked to imagine herself in various fearful situations and to report the self-statements (self-talk) she experienced. The therapist helped her identify disruptive self-statements, such as "I am going to make a fool of myself." This particular self-statement was challenged by questioning whether it was realistic to believe that she would actually lose control and by disputing the belief that the consequences of losing control, were it to happen, would truly be disastrous.

She progressed rapidly with treatment and became capable of functioning more independently. But she still harboured concerns about relapsing in the future. The therapist focused at this point on deeper cognitive structures involving her fears of abandonment by the people she loved if she were to relapse and be unable to attend to their needs. In challenging these beliefs, the therapist helped her realize that she was not as helpless as she perceived herself to be and that she was loved for other reasons than her ability to serve others. She also explored the question "Who am I improving for?" She realized she needed to find reasons to overcome her phobia that were related to meeting her own personal needs, not simply the needs of her loved ones.

At a follow-up interview nine months after treatment, she was functioning independently, which allowed her to pursue her own interests, such as taking night courses and seeking a job.

Republished with permission of Springer Publishing Company, LLC, from Cognitive and exposure treatment for agoraphobia: Re-examination of the outcome research. Journal of Cognitive Psychotherapy: An International Quarterly, Mia Brain, 1988; permission conveyed through Copyright Clearance Center, Inc.

Donald Meichenbaum, co-founder of cognitive-behavioural therapy. Voted one of the 10 most influential therapists of the 20th century, Meichenbaum was a professor at University of Waterloo for 33 years. He is currently research director for the Melissa Institute for Violence Prevention and Treatment, an organization that uses psychological research to educate government and the public about violence and trauma.

It could be argued that any behavioural method involving imagination or mental imagery, such as systematic desensitization, bridges behavioural and cognitive domains. Cognitive therapies such as Ellis's rational-emotive behaviour therapy and Beck's cognitive therapy might also be regarded as forms of cognitive-behavioural therapy because they incorporate cognitive and behavioural treatment methods. The dividing lines between the psychotherapies may not be as clearly drawn as authors of textbooks—who are given the task of classifying them—might desire. Not only are traditional boundaries between the cognitive and behavioural therapies blurred, but many therapists endorse an eclectic orientation in which they incorporate principles and techniques derived from different schools of therapy.

Eclectic Therapy

Each of the major psychological models of abnormal behaviour—the psychodynamic, learning theory, humanistic-existentialist, and cognitive-behavioural approaches—has spawned its own approaches to psychotherapy. Although many therapists identify with one or another of these schools of therapy, an increasing number of therapists identify with an eclectic approach that draws on techniques and teachings of different therapeutic approaches. Eclectic therapists look beyond the theoretical barriers that divide one school of psychotherapy from another in an effort to define what is common among the schools of therapy and what is useful in each of them.

The largest percentage of clinical psychologists (31%) adopt a cognitive-behavioural approach, followed by those who draw from different schools of therapy (22%) (Norcross & Karpiak, 2012). Therapists who adopt an eclectic approach tend to be older and more experienced (Beitman, Goldfried, & Norcross, 1989). Perhaps they have learned through experience the value of drawing on diverse contributions to the practice of therapy.

Group, Family, and Marital Therapy

In group therapy, a group of clients meet together with a therapist or pair of therapists. Group therapy has several advantages over individual treatment. For one, group therapy is less costly because several clients are treated at the same time. Many clinicians also believe that group therapy may be more effective in treating groups of clients who have similar problems, such as complaints relating to anxiety, depression, lack of social skills, or adjustment to divorce or other life stresses. The group format provides clients with the opportunity to learn how people with similar problems cope with them and provides the social support of the group as well as the therapist. Group therapy also provides members with opportunities to work through their problems in relating to others. For example, the therapist or other members may point out to a particular member when he or she acts in a bossy manner or tends to withdraw when criticized, patterns of behaviour that may mirror the behaviour the client shows in relationships with others outside the group. Group members may also rehearse social skills with one another in a supportive atmosphere.

In family therapy, the family, not the individual, is the unit of treatment. Family therapy aims to help troubled families resolve their conflicts and problems so that they function better as a unit and individual members are subjected to less stress from family conflicts.

Faulty patterns of communication within the family often contribute to family problems. In family therapy, members of the family unit learn to communicate more effectively and to air their disagreements constructively. Family conflicts often emerge at transitional points in the life cycle when patterns are altered by changes in one or more members. Conflicts between parents and children, for example, often emerge when adolescent children seek greater independence or autonomy. Family members with low self-esteem may be unable to tolerate different attitudes or behaviours from other members of the family and may resist their efforts to change or become more independent.

One widely adopted approach to family therapy, called *conjoint family therapy*, was developed by Virginia Satir (1967). Satir conceptualized the family in terms of a pattern or system of communications and interactions that needs to be studied and changed to enhance family functioning as well as the growth of individual family members.

Another prominent approach to family therapy is structural family therapy (Minuchin, 1974). This approach also adopts a family system model of abnormal behaviour. It conceptualizes problem behaviours of individual members of the family as arising from dysfunctional relationship patterns within the family system, rather than as involving only the individuals themselves. Family members may develop psychological or physical problems in response to stressful role relationships in the family. The structural family therapist would help the family understand the hidden messages in a child's behaviour and assist the family to make changes in their relationships to meet the child's needs more adequately. In so doing, the therapist shows the family how the member with the identified problem is responding to wider problems in the family.

Marital therapy may be considered a subtype of family therapy in which the family unit is the marital couple. Like other forms of family therapy, marital therapy focuses on improving communication and analyzing role relationships to improve the marital relationship. For example, one partner may play a dominant role and resist any request to share power with the other. The marital therapist would help bring these role relationships into the open, so that alternative ways of relating to each other could be explored that would lead to a more satisfying relationship.

Indigenous Healing Perspective

Mainstream health-care approaches have not been readily accessible or reasonably successful at treating and preventing Indigenous peoples' physical and mental health problems (McCormick, 2000; Wieman, 2001). There were well-intentioned attempts to change the way that "experts" dealt with Indigenous health problems during the last decades of the 20th century, but, at best, medical and counselling professionals adopted as truth a range of overgeneralized, simplified, and underresearched beliefs about Indigenous cultural values and behaviours. Overreliance on Indigenous cultural stereotypes led to a cookie-cutter, one-size-fits-all, condescending approach to treatment and counselling that has netted few overall gains in health and well-being for Indigenous peoples. This lack of success creates a formidable challenge and opportunity, especially for the non-Indigenous health-care practitioner to become an effective partner in a meaningful healing process (Waldram, 2001, 2004).

Mental illness and mental disorders are concepts that do not exist among most First Nations, Inuit, and Métis communities. These terms reflect a dichotomy (either healthy or ill) and a focus on deficits rather than wellness. Mental wellness, in their view, comes from a balance of physical, mental, emotional, and spiritual aspects and is on a continuum from minimal to optimal (Mussell, 2014). Since all people are seen as interconnected, attaining optimal mental wellness requires the strengths of not only the individual but also the family and the community. As such, healing and wellness promotion are multilevelled, targeting the individual as well as the family and the community, while respecting both individual and group languages, customs, history, and environment (Smith & Morrissette, 2001). This perspective may ultimately evolve into a healing paradigm in which not only will Canadian health practitioners change the way they approach Indigenous peoples, but the Indigenous healing perspective will influence how practitioners approach members of any and all cultural minority groups. Ultimately, a holistic healing perspective may come to permeate and transform mainstream health, mental health, social services, and care practices in Canada (Menzies, 2014; Poonwassie & Charter, 2001) (see "Focus on Diversity: Traditional Indigenous Ceremonies and Practices").

Computer-Assisted Therapy

Computer-based interventions and therapy come in all forms, from online cognitive-behavioural therapy with a live therapist using a video-chat service to self-guided behaviour therapy for children with anxiety, in which they monitor their own progress. Support for this type of therapy, often to increase access to help for individuals, has been growing over the years. Evidence of its efficacy has been shown. One study (Wright et al., 2005) compared the efficacy of computer-assisted cognitive therapy against standard cognitive therapy and a control group without treatment for outpatients with nonpsychotic major depressive disorder. They found that computer-assisted cognitive therapy had more robust effects than standard cognitive therapy in reducing measures of cognitive distortion and in improving knowledge about cognitive therapy. Also, in a systematic review of computer-based interventions for substance use disorders, researchers from the Yale University School of Medicine found that, compared to treatment as usual, computer-based interventions led to less substance use and higher motivation to change, better retention, and greater knowledge of presented information (Moore, Fazzino, Garnet, Cutter, & Barry, 2011). Computer-based interventions for various disorders have the potential to dramatically expand and alter the landscape of treatment.

Does Psychotherapy Work?

What, then, of the effectiveness of psychotherapy? Does psychotherapy work? Are some forms of therapy more effective than others? Are some forms of therapy more effective for some types of clients or for some types of problems than for others? The effectiveness of psychotherapy receives strong support from the research literature. Reviews of the scientific literature often use a statistical technique called **meta-analysis**, which averages the results of a large number of studies to determine an overall level of effectiveness.

meta-analysis Statistical technique for combining the results of different studies into an overall average. In psychotherapy research, meta-analysis is used to compute the average benefit or size of effect associated with psychotherapy overall, or with different forms of therapy, in relation to control groups.

rSnapshotPhotos/Shutterstock

Computer-based interventions. Evidence for the efficacy of computer-assisted therapy, especially cognitive therapy, has been repeatedly found, and this treatment is a viable option for some.

Traditional Indigenous Ceremonies and Practices

Traditional healing strategies stem from Indigenous ways of understanding the world and incorporate community and spiritual connections. These practices are often facilitated by Elders who guide the individual on a personal journey through stories reflecting the values of the community (Menzies, 2014). Here are some important elements that form the foundation of these practices (Kirmayer & Valaskakis, 2009):

- *Balance.* The Indigenous medicine wheel represents the essential components in life (physical, spiritual, emotional, and mental) and the need for balance to attain optimal mental wellness.
- *Connectedness.* All individuals are seen as interconnected and, as such, relatives and community members are included in the healing process.
- *Spirituality.* Optimal mental wellness requires a strong spiritual identity.
- *Nature.* Land-based activities foster a spiritual connection with nature and a sense of being part of something larger.
- *Ceremony.* Ceremonies that have been passed on from generation to generation strengthen the individual's connection with his or her community.
- *Tradition/culture.* Strong culture identities and cultural values guide the individual in all aspects of their life.

The following is a sample of traditional ceremonies and practices (Hart, 2014):

- *Lodge ceremonies.* Lodge ceremonies, such as sweat lodges, incorporate elements of spirituality, community, and cultural identity.
- *Ceremonial dances.* The physical effort and time commitments involved in ceremonial dances promote healing and growth.
- *Pipe ceremonies.* Sacred pipes are included in ceremonies that promote healing through medication and prayer.
- *Fasting.* Periods of fasting, often lasting as long as four days, require immense sacrifice and helps the individual gain spiritual insights and self-awareness.

Fred Chartrand/CP Images

A Canadian Indigenous smudging ceremony. Smudging involves burning certain plants and allowing them to smoulder. The smoke helps to cleanse the mind, body, and spirit. Although there is no one thing that on its own leads to healing, a smudging ceremony is an important aspect of the larger Indigenous healing perspective. It serves to strengthen cultural identity, which builds self-respect. As the Indigenous person becomes aware of who he or she is, a sense of connectedness with nature and the Creator, healthier ways of living, and improved physical and mental well-being will follow (A. Magiskan, personal communication, February 10, 2004).

- *Feasting.* Feasting helps the individual form a connection with his or her ancestors.
- *Smudging.* Sacred medicinal plants such as sweetgrass, tobacco, sage, and cedar are ignited in a bowl or seashell and allowed to smoulder. Following ancient, traditional rituals, the smoke is used to purify, cleanse, and heal the mind, body, soul, and spirit.

Source: Ann Magiskan is of Ojibwa heritage and is responsible for the Native Heritage programs at Fort William Historical Park.

In the most frequently cited meta-analysis of psychotherapy research, Smith and Glass (1977) analyzed the results of some 375 controlled studies comparing various types of therapies (psychodynamic, behavioural, humanistic, etc.) against control groups. The results of their analyses showed that the average psychotherapy client in these studies was better off than 75% of the clients who remained untreated. In 1980, Smith and Glass and their colleague T. I. Miller reported the results of a larger analysis, based on 475 controlled outcome studies, that showed the average person who received therapy was better off at the end of treatment than 80% of people who did not (Smith,

Canadian Multicultural Issues in Psychotherapy

We live in a nation that has become increasingly multiethnic and multicultural. The 2011 census listed more than 200 ethnic groups living in Canada, of which 13 had reached the 1 million mark. Approximately one in five people are foreign-born (Statistics Canada, 2016b). From 2011 to 2016 the population of Canada increased by 1.7 million, and about two thirds of this growth was the result of migratory increase (the difference between the number of immigrants and emigrants) (Statistics Canada, 2017b).

In the past, the diagnosis and treatment of psychological disorders was heavily influenced by European and North American thought. But this Western perspective is not universally appropriate for people who hold different cultural beliefs. Cultural learning and values make a difference in what people bring to therapy (Beiser, 2003). Canada's substantial cultural diversity creates serious mental health issues that cannot be ignored, especially at a time when biomedical models of mental health care dominate (Macnaughton, 2000).

Mental health care practitioners in Canada have become increasingly responsive to the cultural factors that influence the delivery of mental health services. People from different cultural backgrounds often experience and express mental distress in ways that may be open to misinterpretation by someone from another culture. For example, expressions like "I am feeling blue," "I blew my top," "I feel out of sorts," "He's forever changing his mind," and "She is getting on my nerves" are common English idioms that can carry different meanings regarding a person's mental state in a different culture or language (Hamid, 2000). In addition, misunderstanding of nonverbal communication can lead to serious mistakes by therapists when a client and therapist have differing cultural traditions and customs (Singh, McKay, & Singh, 1998). This highlights the need to understand culture-specific idioms and nonverbal cues of distress when supporting a person's mental health needs, although the assumptions must be verified in each case to avoid erroneous stereotyping.

There are two broad approaches to the delivery of mental health-care services to Canada's culturally diverse groups. One model calls for the training of culturally skilled practitioners adept at working with clients from various cultural backgrounds (Arthur & Januszkowski, 2001; Lo & Fung, 2003; Macnaughton, 2000). To be culturally skilled, a counsellor must be able to demonstrate competency in self-awareness of how his or her personal worldview influences the counselling relationship, knowledge of the history and development of various Canadian cultural groups, intervention skills that address the need to vary the counselling relationship depending on the client's cultural expectations, and advocacy skills that promote cultural sensitivity of mental health problems in organizations and institutions (Arthur & Stewart, 2001).

In many Canadian settings, there are too few culturally skilled practitioners available to meet the high demand for culturally diverse mental health services. Additional methods of responding to the challenge presented by diverse populations are also needed within existing mental health-care settings. The cultural consultation services (CCS) model was designed by Laurence Kirmayer and others at McGill University to work within existing systems. This model made use of a culturally and professionally diverse team, including interpreters or culture brokers, community organizations, clinicians with generic cultural competency, and clinicians with expertise in a specific culture or ethnic group. Although the consultants were accessed as needed, there was a core cultural team consisting of psychiatrists, social workers, psychiatric nurses, medical anthropologists, a physician, and a full-time clinical psychologist. A database was used to track the specific skills of each cultural consultant. Benefits of the CCS model included the ability to avoid the pitfall of sweeping generalizations or cultural stereotypes while targeting mental health issues in the context of a person's particular cultural view of the problem. Moreover, there was a greatly reduced language barrier for assessment, diagnosis, and treatment, much-improved short- and long-term client functioning, decreased use of mental health services, and increased clinician satisfaction (Kirmayer, Groleau, Guzder, Blake, & Jarvis, 2003; Kirmayer, Jarvis, & Guzder, 2014).

Glass, & Miller, 1980). A meta-analysis of long-term psychoanalytic psychotherapy showed significantly higher outcomes in overall effectiveness, target problems, and personality functioning than shorter forms of psychotherapy (Leichsenring & Rabung, 2008). More recent meta-analyses also showed positive outcomes for particular types of therapy, including cognitive-behavioural therapy and psychodynamic therapy (Tolin, 2010; Town et al., 2012).

Andrey_Popov/Shutterstock

Nonspecific factors. Are the benefits of psychotherapy caused by nonspecific factors that various psychotherapists share in common, such as the mobilization of hope, the attention and support provided by the therapist, and the development of a good working alliance between the client and therapist? It appears that both specific and nonspecific factors are involved in accounting for therapeutic change.

nonspecific treatment factors Characteristics that are not specific to any one form of psychotherapy but tend to be shared by psychotherapies, such as the attention a client receives from a therapist and the therapist's encouragement of the client's sense of hope and positive expectancies.

Meta-analyses show only negligible differences overall in outcomes between the various therapies when the therapies are compared to control groups (Karyotaki et al., 2016; Wampold et al., 2011). Such minor differences suggest that the effectiveness of psychotherapy may have more to do with the features that different modes of therapy share than with the specific techniques that set them apart. These common features are called **nonspecific treatment factors**. Nonspecific or common factors in psychotherapy stem largely from the therapist–client relationship. These factors include empathy, support, and attention shown by the therapist; therapeutic alliance, or the attachment the client develops to the therapist and the therapy process; and the working alliance, or the development of an effective working relationship in which the therapist and client work together to identify and confront the important issues and problems the client faces (Crits-Christoph, Connolly Gibbons, Hamilton, Ring-Kurtz, & Gallop, 2011). The effectiveness of therapy may have more to do with the effectiveness of the therapists than with the particular form of therapy (Wampold, 2001).

Should we conclude that different therapies are about equally effective? One possibility is that different therapies are about equal in their effects overall but may not be equal in their effects with every patient (Wampold et al., 1997). Behaviour therapy, for example, has shown impressive results in treating various types of anxiety disorders, sleep–wake disorders, and sexual dysfunctions and in improving the adaptive functioning of people with schizophrenia and intellectual disability. Psychodynamic and humanistic approaches may be more effective in fostering self-insight and personality growth. Cognitive-behavioural therapy has demonstrated impressive results in treating depression and anxiety disorders. By and large, however, the process of determining which treatment, which type of practitioner, and what conditions are most effective for a given client remains a challenge.

REVIEW IT

Methods of Treatment

- **What are the major biological approaches to treating abnormal behaviour patterns?** Biological approaches include drug therapy, electroconvulsive therapy (ECT), repetitive transcranial magnetic stimulation (rTMS), and deep brain stimulation.
- **What is psychotherapy?** Psychotherapy involves a systematic interaction between a therapist and client that incorporates psychological principles to help the client overcome abnormal behaviour, solve problems in living, or develop as an individual.
- **What is psychodynamic therapy?** Psychodynamic therapy originated with psychoanalysis, the approach to treatment developed by Freud. Psychoanalysts use techniques such as free association and dream analysis to help people gain insight into their unconscious conflicts and work through them in the light of their adult personalities. More recent psychodynamic therapies are generally briefer and less intensive.

- **What is behaviour therapy?** Behaviour therapy applies the principles of learning to help people make adaptive behavioural changes. Behaviour therapy techniques include systematic desensitization, gradual exposure, modelling, operant conditioning approaches, and social-skills training.
- **What is humanistic-existential therapy?** Humanistic approaches focus on the client's subjective, conscious experience in the here and now. Rogers's person-centred therapy helps people increase their awareness and acceptance of inner feelings that had met with social condemnation and been disowned. The effective person-centred therapist possesses the qualities of unconditional positive regard, empathy, genuineness, and congruence. Greenberg's approach, emotion-focused therapy (EFT), aims not to eliminate intense or uncomfortable feelings but to transform them into more adaptive feelings.

- **What are three major approaches to cognitive-behavioural therapy?** Cognitive-behavioural therapies focus on modifying the maladaptive cognitions that are believed to underlie emotional problems and self-defeating behaviour. Ellis's rational-emotive behaviour therapy focuses on disputing the irrational beliefs that occasion emotional distress and substituting adaptive behaviour for maladaptive behaviour. Beck's cognitive therapy focuses on helping clients identify, challenge, and replace distorted cognitions, such as tendencies to magnify negative events and minimize personal accomplishments. Meichenbaum's cognitive-behavioural therapy integrates behavioural and cognitive approaches in treatment.
- **What are the general aims of group therapy, family therapy, and marital therapy?** Group therapy provides opportunities for mutual support and shared learning experiences within a group setting to help individuals overcome psychological difficulties and develop more adaptive behaviours. Family therapists work with conflicted families to help them resolve their differences. Family therapists focus on clarifying family communications, resolving role conflicts, guarding against scapegoating individual members, and helping members develop greater autonomy. Marital therapists focus on helping couples improve their communication and resolve their differences.
- **Does psychotherapy work?** Evidence from meta-analyses of psychotherapy outcome studies that compare psychotherapy with control groups supports the value of various approaches to psychotherapy.
- **How are multicultural issues involved in psychotherapy?** Therapists need to take cultural factors into account and become more aware of how their own biases may affect the therapeutic process. Western forms of psychotherapy may be inappropriate in treating members of cultural groups when conflicts in underlying cultural values emerge.

ABNORMAL PSYCHOLOGY AND SOCIETY

As a youngster, Edmond Yu showed he had the drive to achieve great things. He was an excellent student, leaving home early for classes and studying in his room late every night. Yet he balanced his rigorous academic work with a variety of hobbies. After emigrating from Hong Kong to Canada, Edmond spent two years at York University in pre-med classes, and later earned a scholarship to study medicine at the University of Toronto.

In his first term, Edmond's marks were excellent. But during the second term, he started to become reclusive; he began studying from home, avoiding campus except for exams or group projects. The initial signs that all was not well were detected an ocean away by his sister, Katherine Yu, who was living in Hong Kong. She got a phone call saying there had been a serious fight between Edmond and his elder brother. Edmond had been asked to leave the house. There were other calls from Edmond, too, in which he would ramble about someone stealing his wallet at the university. He sounded incoherent, illogical; not himself. "I realized at that point there was something wrong with him," his sister recalls. She flew to Canada.

Things began to quickly spiral downward. Katherine remembers going to his apartment to check up on him. "He said the people in his building, as well as in nearby buildings, were spies," she says. "He believed there were satellites planted in his building—even in his own apartment—watching him." Likely unaware he was suffering from an illness, Edmond rejected Katherine's attempts to get him to seek help.

Katherine went to Edmond, demanding he accept help, see a doctor, take medication. He refused. "I knew there was something wrong with him. He asked me to leave, but I insisted and kept on talking. And then he slapped me in the face." It was painful for Katherine to use the incident against her brother, but she felt his best interests were at stake. The police apprehended Edmond and he was taken to the Clarke Institute of Psychiatry, where he was diagnosed as having paranoid schizophrenia. He was persuaded that, if he accepted treatment, he might still be able to return to medical school. He consented.

At least initially, Edmond tried to stick with the treatment, which consisted of antipsychotic drugs to quell the delusions. Unfortunately, some people experience severe side effects with psychotropic drugs. Edmond was one of them. "When he was on medication, he seemed to be a totally different person," Katherine says. "All he could do was eat and sleep. He was completely non-communicative. His hands were so shaky he couldn't even hold a bowl of soup properly. The soup would always spill."

It was clear to Edmond he would not be able to attend school while on medication. It was equally clear he would not be able to attend school without it. Edmond requested that a doctor certify him fit for medical school. But because he would not take his medication, the doctor refused.

With no classes to attend, no career as a doctor, Edmond flew back to Hong Kong. Within a month, he was picked up by police on a charge of disturbing the peace. Edmond was sent to a psychiatric hospital. The hospital then decided to impose treatment on Edmond—to force medication. When he returned to Canada, he immediately stopped taking the drugs. His noncompliance marked the start of a long struggle with his family over treatment.

Edmond's illness deepened, and his behaviour worsened. He was overtaken by paranoia and suspicion. He would talk non-stop. He felt he had special influence over world affairs. He feared those around him were conspiring to harm him. On occasion, he would be verbally abusive. And he began burning things—clothes, books, photographs. He would take them out on to the driveway and put a match to them. Edmond also started to meditate in front of the family's Scarborough home, sometimes for hours. On two occasions, he threw a knife at a dartboard he set up outside the garage door. Neighbours called police both times. Other times, they just stared from their windows.

Edmond began to drift, from housing to hostels—where he says he was beaten and robbed—to the street. He made the occasional visit home, his deterioration more evident each time. His clothes were becoming ragged. The family later found him living in a public washroom in Grange Park, behind the Art Gallery of Ontario. His family managed to obtain a court order for him to be assessed by a psychiatrist. As a result, he was involuntarily committed to the Clarke Institute of Psychiatry for more than three months. Doctors declared him incapable of making his own treatment decisions, and his mother was appointed a substitute decision-maker. She had the power to authorize forced medication.

Over the next few years, a pattern set in: arrest, often for some form of assault, incarceration, release. The combination of winter, homelessness, and illness was beginning to wear Edmond down. Late one afternoon, he was at the bus loop at the foot of Spadina Avenue. Unaccountably, he struck a woman in the face, then boarded a bus. The police were called. The driver ordered everyone off the bus and left Edmond alone with the doors locked. Three police officers boarded the bus and tried to persuade Edmond to leave with them. At one point, he did agree to leave, but then took a hammer out of his jacket.

"I watched while he waggled his right wrist with the hammer in it," said a witness, who watched from an adjacent streetcar. "Then the movement of his wrist stopped, and seconds passed, when I heard what I thought initially was a cap gun. I could see the red flash of the gun, and the body slumped."

Constable Lou Pasquino fired six shots. One hit Edmond in the throat, his head twisting as the shots continued. A second hit his ear and entered the side of his head. The third hit the back of his skull. Edmond was dead before he hit the floor.

Scott Simmie, "Reality is sometimes painful," Toronto Star, October 3, 1998.
Reprinted courtesy of the Atkinson Foundation.

The case of Edmond Yu touches on many important issues, including the issue of balancing the rights of the individual with the rights of society. Do people have the right to live on the streets under unsanitary conditions? There are those who argue that a just and humane society has the right and responsibility to care for people who are perceived incapable of protecting their own best interests, even if "care" means involuntarily committing them to a psychiatric institution. Do people who are obviously mentally disturbed have the right to refuse treatment? Do psychiatric institutions have the right to inject them with antipsychotic and other drugs against their will? Should mental patients with a history of disruptive or violent behaviour be hospitalized indefinitely or permitted to live in supervised residences in the community once their conditions are stabilized? When severely disturbed people break the law, should society respond to them with the criminal justice system or with the mental health system?

Dick Loek/Toronto Star/Getty Images

Mandatory medication? A photograph of Edmond Yu taken at the Scott Mission on Christmas Day, 1996. Yu would be shot by police two months later. Should people suffering from serious mental illnesses, like Edmond Yu, be required to receive treatment?

Psychiatric Commitment and Patients' Rights

In Canada, legal placement of people in psychiatric institutions against their will is called civil or psychiatric commitment. Through civil commitment, individuals deemed to be mentally disordered and a threat to themselves or others may be involuntarily confined to psychiatric institutions to provide them with treatment and help ensure their own safety and that of others. Civil commitment should be distinguished from legal or criminal commitment, in which an individual who has been acquitted of a crime by reason of insanity—that is, found to be "not criminally responsible on account of a mental disorder"—is placed in a psychiatric institution for treatment. In **legal commitment**, a criminal's unlawful act is judged by a court of law to be the result of a mental disorder or defect that should be dealt with by having the individual committed to a psychiatric hospital where treatment can be provided rather than having the individual incarcerated in a prison.

Civil commitment should also be distinguished from voluntary hospitalization, in which a person voluntarily seeks treatment in a psychiatric institution and can, with adequate notice, leave the institution when she or he so desires. Even in such cases, however, when hospital staffers believe that a voluntary patient presents a threat to her or his own welfare or to others, the staff may petition the court to change the patient's legal status from voluntary to involuntary.

Involuntary placement of an individual in a psychiatric hospital usually requires that a petition be filed by a relative or a physician. Psychiatric review panels may be empowered by the court to evaluate the person in a timely fashion. In the event of commitment, the law usually requires periodic legal review and recertification of the patient's involuntary status. The legal process is intended to ensure that people are not indefinitely "warehoused" in psychiatric institutions. Hospital staff must demonstrate the need for continued inpatient treatment.

Legal safeguards are usually in place to protect people's civil rights in commitment proceedings. Defendants have the right to due process and to be assisted by a lawyer, for example. But when individuals are deemed to present a clear and imminent threat to themselves or others, the court may order immediate hospitalization until a more formal commitment hearing can be held. Such emergency powers are

civil commitment Legal process involved in placing an individual in a psychiatric institution, even against his or her will. Also called *psychiatric commitment.*

legal commitment Legal process involved in confining a person found "not criminally responsible on account of a mental disorder" in a psychiatric institution. Also called *criminal commitment.*

usually limited to a specific period, such as 72 hours. During this time, a formal commitment petition must be filed with the court or the individual has a right to be discharged.

Standards for psychiatric commitment have been tightened over the past generation, and the rights of individuals who are subject to commitment proceedings are more strictly protected. Civil commitment is based on standards that give greater weight to patients' rights. The current criteria for civil commitment differ to some extent across Canadian provinces and territories. However, all require that the person be mentally ill and pose an imminent risk of harm or danger to him- or herself or others (Schuller & Ogloff, 2000). Thus, people cannot be committed or forced to take medication because of their eccentricity. People must be judged mentally ill and as presenting a clear and present danger to themselves or others for them to be psychiatrically committed.

PREDICTING DANGEROUSNESS In order to be psychiatrically committed, a person must be judged to be at imminent risk of harming him- or herself or others. Professionals are thus responsible for making accurate predictions of dangerousness to determine whether someone should be involuntarily hospitalized or maintained involuntarily in a hospital. But how accurate are professionals in predicting dangerousness? Do professionals have special skills or clinical wisdom that renders their predictions accurate, or are their predictions no more accurate than those of laypeople?

Unfortunately, psychologists and other mental health professionals who rely on their clinical judgments are not very accurate when it comes to predicting the dangerousness of the people they treat. Mental health professionals tend to overpredict dangerousness—that is, to label many individuals as dangerous when they are not (Monahan, 1981). Clinicians tend to err on the side of caution in overpredicting the potential for dangerous behaviour, perhaps because they believe that failure to predict violence may have more serious consequences than overprediction. Clinicians may be more successful in predicting violence by basing predictions on a composite of factors, including evidence of past violent behaviour, than on any single factor. Still, it's fair to say that predicting future violent behaviour is difficult, and presently available methods are far from perfect (Yang, Wong, & Coid, 2010).

How likely is it that truly dangerous people will disclose their intentions to health professionals who are evaluating them or to their own therapists? The client in therapy is

Piotr Latacha/Shutterstock   Thakkura P/Shutterstock   Stuart Ramson/AP Images

Who is the most dangerous? Is it the apparently drunk driver (A)? Is it the institutionalized psychiatric patient (B)? Or is it the scheming corporate executive Bernie Madoff (C)? Critics of the mental health system, such as psychiatrist Thomas Szasz, point out that drunk drivers account for more injuries and deaths than do people with paranoid schizophrenia, although the latter are more likely to be committed. Others have suggested that corporate executives who knowingly make decisions that jeopardize the health of employees and consumers to maximize profits are guilty of corporate violence that accounts for more deaths and injuries than other types of crime.

not likely to inform a therapist of a clear threat, such as "I'm going to kill _____ next Wednesday morning." Threats are more likely to be vague and nonspecific, as in "I'm so sick of _____; I could kill her," or "I swear he's driving me to murder." In such cases, therapists must infer dangerousness from hostile gestures and veiled threats. Vague, indirect threats of violence are less reliable indicators of dangerousness than specific and direct threats.

As we explore in the Closer Look box, the problem of predicting dangerousness also arises when therapists need to evaluate the seriousness of threats made by their patients against others.

PATIENTS' RIGHTS   We have considered society's right to hospitalize involuntarily people who are judged to be mentally ill and who pose a threat to themselves or others. What

confidentiality The principle of safeguarding information so that it remains secret and is not disclosed to other parties.

duty to warn Obligation imposed on therapists to warn third parties of threats made against them by the therapists' clients. In the United States, the *Tarasoff* case established the legal basis for duty-to-warn provisions. Although US law does not apply in Canada, the Canadian Psychological Association states that, ethically, therapists have a duty to warn.

A CLOSER LOOK
The Duty to Warn

One of the most difficult dilemmas a therapist may face is whether or not to disclose confidential information that could protect third parties from harm. Part of the difficulty lies in determining whether the client has made a bona fide threat against another person.

The other part of the dilemma is that the information a client discloses in psychotherapy is generally considered to be confidential. But this right is not absolute. The therapist is obliged to breach **confidentiality** under certain conditions, such as when there is clear and compelling evidence that an individual poses a serious threat to him- or herself or others. Under such conditions, the therapist could, for example, call the police to prevent the patient from causing harm to him- or herself or others.

In addition, an important Californian case, *Tarasoff v. Regents of the University of California*, established a basis for the therapist's **duty to warn** the patient's potential victims. In 1969, a graduate student at the University of California at Berkeley, Prosenjit Poddar, a native of India, became depressed when his romantic overtures toward a young woman, Tatiana Tarasoff, were rebuffed. Poddar entered psychotherapy with a psychologist at a student health facility, during the course of which he informed the psychologist that he intended to kill Tatiana when she returned from her summer vacation. The psychologist, concerned about Poddar's potential for violence, first consulted with his colleagues and then notified campus police. He informed them that Poddar was dangerous and recommended he be taken to a facility for psychiatric treatment.

Poddar was subsequently interviewed by the campus police. They believed he was rational and released him after he promised to keep his distance from Tatiana. Poddar then terminated treatment with the psychologist, and shortly afterward killed Tatiana. He shot her with a pellet gun when she refused to allow him entry to her home and then repeatedly stabbed her as she fled into the street. Poddar was found guilty of the lesser sentence of voluntary manslaughter, rather than murder, based on testimony of three psychiatrists that Poddar suffered from diminished mental capacity and paranoid schizophrenia. Under California law, his diminished capacity prevented the finding of malice that was necessary for conviction on a charge of first- or second-degree murder.

Does the *Tarasoff* decision influence Canadian mental health practitioners? Since US court decisions do not apply in Canada, the *Tarasoff* ruling does not necessarily have sway in this country. Some Canadian civil lawsuits have raised arguments similar to those in the *Tarasoff* case, but there has yet to be a legal precedent like the *Tarasoff* ruling (Glancy & Chaimowitz, 2003; Schuller & Ogloff, 2000). Even so, it could be argued that it is ethical for mental health practitioners to warn third parties of impending harm. Accordingly, a duty to warn has been included in the code of ethics for the Canadian Psychological Association. The code states that psychologists should "do everything reasonably possible to stop or offset the consequences of actions by others when these actions are likely to cause serious physical harm or death. This may include reporting to appropriate authorities (e.g., the police) [or] an intended victim . . . and would be done even when a confidential relationship is involved" (Canadian Psychological Association, 2000, p. 19).

Although therapists have difficulty accurately predicting dangerousness, the duty-to-warn provision obliges them to judge whether their clients' disclosures indicate a clear intent to harm others. In the *Tarasoff* case, the threat was obvious enough to prompt the therapist to breach confidentiality by requesting the help of campus police. In most cases, however, threats are not so clear-cut. There remains a lack of clear criteria for determining whether a therapist "should have known" that a client was dangerous before a violent act occurs (Fulero, 1988). In the absence of guidelines that specify the criteria therapists should use to fulfill their duty to warn, they must rely on their best subjective judgments.

happens following commitment, however? Do involuntarily committed patients have the right to receive or demand treatment? Or can society just warehouse them in psychiatric facilities indefinitely without treating them? Consider the opposite side of the coin as well: Can people who are involuntarily committed refuse treatment? Such issues fall under the umbrella of patients' rights. Generally speaking, the history of abuses in the mental health system, as highlighted in such popular books and movies as *One Flew Over the Cuckoo's Nest*, have led to a tightening of standards of care and adoption of legal guarantees to protect patients' rights. The legal status of some issues, such as aspects of the right to treatment, remain unsettled, however.

Right to Treatment   We might assume that mental health institutions that accept people for treatment will provide them with treatment. However, it is only in the past three decades that Canada has adequately extended civil rights to people in psychiatric hospitals. Patient-advocacy groups and precedent-setting court cases have been required to establish important patient rights, such as the right to treatment in the least restrictive environment (Olley & Ogloff, 1995).

Treatment in the least restrictive environment involves, among other things, not hospitalizing a patient when he or she can be appropriately treated as an outpatient. This is important because it allows the person to continue living in the community. Thus, the state provides mandatory care when necessary, such as involuntary hospitalization, but care must not be unduly restrictive.

A problem in implementing this approach concerns the availability of treatment resources. A person might benefit from either inpatient treatment or a less restrictive alternative, such as treatment in a group home in the community. But what happens when the less restrictive alternatives are not available? Even in wealthy countries like Canada there are insufficient resources for treating patients in the community. Unfortunately, some patients are treated in psychiatric hospitals when they could be living in supervised accommodation in the community.

To make matters more complicated, patients have the right to be treated in the community even when they might be more appropriately treated in a psychiatric hospital. If community resources are unavailable, then the family sometimes assumes the onus of care, even though they may be ill prepared.

Right to Refuse Treatment   Consider the following scenario: A person, John Citizen, is involuntarily committed to a psychiatric hospital for treatment. The hospital staff determines that John suffers from a psychotic disorder, paranoid schizophrenia, and should be treated with antipsychotic medication. John, however, decides not to comply with treatment. He claims that the hospital has no right to treat him against his will. The hospital seeks a court order to mandate treatment, arguing it makes little sense to commit people involuntarily unless the hospital is empowered to treat them as the staff deems fit.

Does an involuntary patient like John have the right to refuse treatment? If so, does this right conflict with the rights of the state to commit people to mental institutions to receive treatment for their disorders? One might also wonder whether people who are judged in need of involuntary hospitalization are competent enough to make decisions about which treatments are in their best interests.

Some mental health professionals have raised the concern that involuntarily committed patients who refuse medications would be "rotting with their rights on"—incarcerated but untreated (Appelbaum & Gutheil, 1979). Fortunately, this does not often happen—at least not in Canada. Since the proclamation of the 1982 Canadian Charter of Rights and Freedoms, there has been increasing recognition across the provinces and territories of the right of competent, involuntary patients to refuse treatment (Gray & O'Reilly, 2005). Today, provincial mental health legislation generally does not allow for institutionalization and compulsory treatment of people who refuse treatment, unless that person poses a threat to him- or herself or to the general public (Canadian Centre for Justice Statistics, 2003). A person like Edmond Yu, from the case study on page 85, would not be involuntarily hospitalized and treated unless he was judged to be at imminent risk of harming himself or others. As we saw earlier, Edmond refused treatment and was generally allowed to do so, even though he was psychotic and would have benefited from treatment. Fortunately, most people in need of psychiatric treatment do not refuse. Fewer than 10% persistently refuse treatment (Gratzer & Matas, 1994).

Mental Illness and Criminal Responsibility

THE INSANITY DEFENCE   Our society has long held to the doctrine of free will as a basis for determining responsibility for wrongdoing. The doctrine of free will, as applied to criminal responsibility, requires that people can be held guilty of a crime only if they are judged to have been in control of their actions at the time of committing the crime. Not only must it be determined by a court of law that a defendant has committed a crime beyond a reasonable doubt, but the issue of the individual's state of mind must be considered as well in determining whether the person can be held accountable for his or her crime. Thus, the court must rule not only on whether a crime was committed, but also on whether an individual is held morally responsible and deserving of punishment. The **insanity defence** is based on the belief that when a criminal act derives from a distorted state of mind, and not from the exercise of free will, the individual should not be punished but rather treated for the underlying mental disorder. Historically, the consideration of the mental state of the individual at the time of the offence is a relatively recent consideration in cases of criminal behaviour. Changes to Canadian law actually had their inspiration in a famous case in England: the case of Daniel M'Naghten.

insanity defence Form of legal defence in which a defendant in a criminal case pleads guilty but not criminally responsible on the basis of having a mental disorder.

In early English law, which formed a basis for Canadian law, the insanity defence was also used. An important legal precedent for modern laws was set in the 1843 legal defence that led to the M'Naghten rule. This was based on a case in England of a Scotsman, Daniel M'Naghten, who had intended to assassinate the prime minister of England, Sir Robert Peel. Instead, he killed Peel's secretary, whom he had mistaken for the prime minister. M'Naghten claimed that the voice of God had commanded him to kill Lord Peel. The English court acquitted M'Naghten on the basis of insanity, finding that the defendant had been "labouring under such a defect of reason, from disease of the mind, as not to know the nature and quality of the act he was doing; or, if he did know it, that he did not know what he was doing was wrong." The M'Naghten rule, as it has come to be called, holds that people do not bear criminal responsibility if, by reason of a mental disease or defect, they either have no knowledge of their actions or are unable to tell right from wrong. A prominent Canadian case that exemplifies this rule of law is the attempted murder of former Prime Minister Jean Chrétien by André Dallaire, who was found guilty but not criminally responsible.

Armed with a knife, 34-year-old Dallaire, a thin, bespectacled former convenience-store worker, broke into the home of Prime Minister Chrétien. It was the early hours of November 5, 1995. Dallaire climbed the fence surrounding Chrétien's residence, smashed a window, and entered the house. He intended to cut the prime minister's throat. An inner voice commanded him to kill Chrétien, while another voice told him to stop. Dallaire believed he was a secret agent whose mission was to avenge the "No" side's victory in the Quebec referendum on independence (Fisher, 1996). He believed he would be glorified for liberating Canada from a "traitorous" prime minister.

Outside the bedroom where the prime minister was sleeping, Dallaire encountered Chrétien's wife, Aline. She fled to the bedroom, locked the door, and called the police. The RCMP arrived shortly afterward and took Dallaire into custody. A psychiatric assessment revealed that he was delusional and hallucinating. He had been suffering from paranoid schizophrenia since the age of 16. The judge ruled that Dallaire's intent to kill was the product of a severe mental disorder. Although Dallaire was found guilty of attempted murder, he was not held criminally responsible for his actions because he was suffering from hallucinations and delusions at the time, which prevented him from appreciating the nature and wrongfulness of his actions. Thus, Dallaire was judged to be "not criminally responsible on account of a mental disorder" (**NCRMD**). This is Canada's version of the insanity defence, and is similar to the "not guilty by reason of insanity" defence used in other countries.

NCRMD Not criminally responsible on account of a mental disorder.

How often is the NCRMD defence used? Do people using this defence really "get away with murder" or attempted murder? The defence is not often used, and even when it is used few people are judged to be NCRMD. From 1992 to 1998 in British Columbia, for example, an average of only 46 people per year were found NCRMD (Livingston, Wilson, Tien, & Bond, 2003). People found NCRMD are typically hospitalized until they can safely be released into the community, although some may not be hospitalized if they are no longer suffering from a serious mental disorder.

Before the NCRMD defence came into effect, the 1985 Criminal Code of Canada allowed a person to be found not guilty by reason of insanity (**NGRI**). People found NGRI were automatically placed in a secure psychiatric facility, indefinitely, "until the pleasure of the Lieutenant Governor is known"—meaning that a person was detained until the mental disorder had improved to an extent that would justify release. A person could be detained for longer than he or she would have served in prison if convicted for the crime (Gray & O'Reilly, 2005). Some people judged to be NGRI were held in psychiatric hospitals without receiving adequate treatment. Later changes to the Criminal Code rectified this problem.

Changes came with the case of *R. v. Swain* (1991), which challenged the insanity defence in a number of ways. Owen Swain was charged with aggravated assault after attacking his wife and two children. At the time, he was psychotic; he believed that his family was being attacked by devils and that he had to perform certain rituals to protect them, including physically assaulting them. Swain was hospitalized, successfully treated with antipsychotic medication, and then released on bail. At his trial, the Crown raised the issue of insanity, despite Swain's objections and those of his lawyer. Swain was judged NGRI, which meant he would be involuntarily placed in a psychiatric hospital. He appealed the decision, arguing that it violated his rights for the Crown to raise the issue of insanity and to automatically incarcerate people judged to be NGRI. Swain's appeal was successful, which led to important reforms in the Canadian version of the insanity defence.

As a result, the Canadian Criminal Code was amended to give the accused person greater procedural and civil rights. The amendment was an attempt to balance the goals of fair and humane treatment of the offender against the safety of the public (Schneider, Glancy, Bradford, & Seibenmorgen, 2000). Major changes included reductions in how long an accused person could be detained in a psychiatric facility and changes in the procedures for making appeals. The mental disorder defence was also changed, with NGRI being replaced with NCRMD. Thus, the Canadian Criminal Code now states that

> no person is criminally responsible for an act committed or an omission made while suffering from a mental disorder that rendered the person incapable of appreciating the nature and quality of the act or omission or of knowing that it was wrong.

Moreover,

> although personality disorders or psychopathic [antisocial] personalities are capable of constituting a disease of the mind, the defence of insanity is not made out where the accused has the necessary understanding of the nature, character and consequences of the act, but merely lacks appropriate feelings for the victim or lacks feelings of remorse or guilt for what he [or she] has done, even though such lack of feeling stems from a disease of the mind. (Greenspan, Rosenberg, & Henein, 1998, p. 50)

NGRI and NCRMD have many similarities, although there are some important differences. Under NCRMD, for example, the defendant is now considered to be "not criminally responsible" instead of "not guilty." This change more explicitly recognizes that the defendant committed the offence as opposed to being not guilty (Davis, 1993).

With the goal of increasing public safety, the government of Canada introduced Bill C-14, the Not Criminally Responsible Reform Act, which took effect on July 11, 2014. This legislation ensures that decisions regarding individuals found NCRMD place public safety as the primary consideration. As such, a high-risk designation process was created for individuals found NCRMD who pose a significant risk for future acts of violence.

Those evaluated as high risk are committed to a hospital and cannot be released until the courts remove the high-risk designation. In addition, victims now have the right to be advised as to when the accused is being discharged and where he or she will reside. They may also request a noncommunication order between them and the accused (Department of Justice Canada, 2014).

COMPETENCY TO STAND TRIAL   There is a basic rule of law that those who stand accused of crimes must be able to understand the charges and proceedings brought against them and be able to participate in their own defence. The concept of competency to stand trial should not be confused with the legal defence of insanity. A defendant can be held competent to stand trial but still be judged not criminally responsible on account of a mental disorder. A clearly delusional person, for example, may understand the court proceedings and be able to confer with defence counsel but still be held not criminally responsible. On the other hand, a person may be incapable of standing trial at a particular time but be tried and acquitted or convicted at a later time when competency is restored.

Billion Photos/Shutterstock

Criminal responsibility. According to the Canadian Criminal Code, no person is criminally responsible for an act committed or an omission made while suffering from a mental disorder that rendered the person incapable of appreciating the nature of the act or omission or of knowing that is was wrong.

In Canada, a judge can order compulsory treatment if the defendant in a criminal trial is found unfit to stand trial due to a mental disorder. It is presumed that every defendant is fit to stand trial unless the court is convinced otherwise. In order to verify the accused's fitness, a psychiatric assessment is needed. The issue of fitness is settled in a separate trial. A defendant is held unfit to stand trial when he or she meets one or more of the following criteria (Bal & Koenraadt, 2000):

- Is not capable of conducting his or her defence
- Can't distinguish between available pleas
- Doesn't understand the nature and purpose of the proceedings, including the respective roles of the judge, jury, and counsel
- Is unable to communicate with counsel rationally or make critical decisions on counsel's advice
- Is unable to take the stand to testify if necessary

An accused found unfit to stand trial can be committed to compulsory treatment in a psychiatric hospital. The case is adjourned until the accused has recovered to such an extent that he or she can be found fit. Mentally ill offenders can be committed to a psychiatric hospital on the verdict of unfitness to stand trial for an unlimited time without their criminal case being tried. Consequently, these accused offenders form a relatively large part of the population in psychiatric hospitals (Bal & Koenraadt, 2000).

REVIEW IT

Mental Illness and Criminal Responsibility

- **What are the legal bases of Canada's insanity defence?** The M'Naghten rule, based on a case in England in 1843, treated the failure to appreciate the wrongfulness of one's action as the basis of legal insanity. This rule was adapted and modified over the years to become "not guilty by reason of insanity" (NGRI) and, more recently, "not criminally responsible on account of a mental disorder" (NCRMD). A person found guilty of a crime is judged to be NCRMD if he or she was suffering from a mental disorder that rendered the person incapable of appreciating the nature and quality of the act or omission or of knowing that it was wrong.

- **What is meant by the legal concept of competency to stand trial?** People who are accused of crimes but are incapable of understanding the charges against them or assisting in their own defence can be found incompetent to stand trial and remanded to a psychiatric facility.

Define It

antidepressants, 67
baseline, 53
behavioural assessment, 51
behavioural interview, 51
behavioural rating scale, 54
civil commitment, 87
client-centred therapy, 74
confidentiality, 89
countertransference, 71
culture-bound disorders, 62
deviation IQ, 44
displacement, 70
duty to warn, 89
eclectic orientation, 65
electroconvulsive therapy, 68
electrodermal response, 55
electroencephalograph, 56
electromyograph, 56
forced-choice formats, 46
galvanic skin response, 55
gradual exposure, 72

insanity defence, 91
intelligence, 43
intelligence quotient, 44
legal commitment, 87
mental age, 44
mental status examination, 43
meta-analysis, 81
monoamine oxidase (MAO)
   inhibitors, 67
NCRMD, 91
neuroleptics, 67
neuropsychological
   assessment, 50
NGRI, 92
nonspecific treatment factors, 84
objective tests, 46
person-centred therapy, 74
placebo, 67
psychometric approach, 51
psychopharmacology, 66
psychotherapy, 65

rebound anxiety, 67
reliable, 61
repetitive transcranial magnetic
   stimulation, 68
selective serotonin-reuptake inhibitors (SSRIs), 67
self-monitoring, 53
semi-structured interview, 42
serotonin-norepinephrine reuptake
   inhibitors (SNRIs), 67
structured interview, 43
systematic desensitization, 72
taijin-kyofu-sho, 62
token economies, 73
tolerance, 66
transference relationship, 71
tricyclics, 67
unconditional positive regard, 74
unstructured interview, 42
validity, 61
validity scales, 46

Recall It

1. Which of the following is NOT considered a feature of a mental disorder in the DSM system?
   a. Emotional distress
   b. Difficulties meeting usual responsibilities
   c. Significant change in an underlying physical condition
   d. Impaired functioning

2. Cognitive therapists primarily focus on helping clients _____.
   a. actualize their unique potentials as individuals
   b. uncover deep-seated conflicts from childhood
   c. change maladaptive thinking patterns
   d. free themselves from unwanted impulses

3. Predictions of dangerousness by mental health professionals tend to be _____.
   a. biased in favour of underpredicting dangerousness
   b. biased in favour of overpredicting dangerousness
   c. accurate when predicting behaviour in the community based on behaviour observed in the hospital

   d. generally accurate except in cases of severe personality disorders

4. The *Tarasoff* case led to the establishment of _____.
   a. the duty of psychiatric hospitals to provide treatment to people in need
   b. minimum standards of care in psychiatric hospitals
   c. the duty of hospitals to release involuntarily held patients who are no longer considered dangerous
   d. the duty to warn

5. Stacy takes a personality test in which each item requires that she indicate which of two statements is more true for her. This test is a(n) _____ test.
   a. objective
   b. subjective
   c. projective
   d. comparison-based

Answers to Recall It

1. c,   2. c,   3. b,   4. d,   5. a

Think About It

- Can you think of other ways we might classify abnormal behaviour patterns? Which methods of assessment do you feel are most helpful in evaluating people with mental health problems? Explain.
- What type of therapy would you prefer if you were seeking treatment for a psychological disorder? Why? What problems do you see in taking pills to cope with anxiety or depression that may stem from academic or social difficulties?
- Do you think we should abolish the verdict of "not criminally responsible on account of mental disorder"? Should it be replaced with another type of verdict, like "not guilty by reason of insanity"? Why or why not?

Weblinks

CPA Code of Ethics
www.cpa.ca/aboutcpa/committees/ethics/codeofethics
Visit this page to read the Canadian Psychological Association's code of ethics for psychologists.

Mental Health Info Source
www.naccme.com/cme
A mental health education website. It contains access to e-journals and information on a wide range of mental disorders.

MentalHelp.net
www.mentalhelp.net
This site has articles and descriptions of psychological disorders. It also provides links to assessment tools and other mental health resources and services.

Psychiatry Online
www.priory.com/psych.htm
This site provides an international forum for psychiatry and has links to the latest articles, papers, and journals.

Clinical Psychology
www.cpa.ca/aboutcpa/cpasections/clinicalpsychology
This Canadian Psychological Association webpage is home to the section on Clinical Psychology. It is a central source for information about the clinical psychology profession in Canada.

Statistics Canada—Mental Health and the Criminal Justice System
www.statcan.gc.ca/pub/85-561-m/2009016/section-a-eng.htm
This site provides information on mental health and the Canadian criminal justice system, including statistics.

Assessment, Classification, and Treatment of Abnormal Behaviour

Test your understanding of the key concepts by filling in the blanks with the correct statements chosen from the list that follows. The answers are found at the end of the chapter.

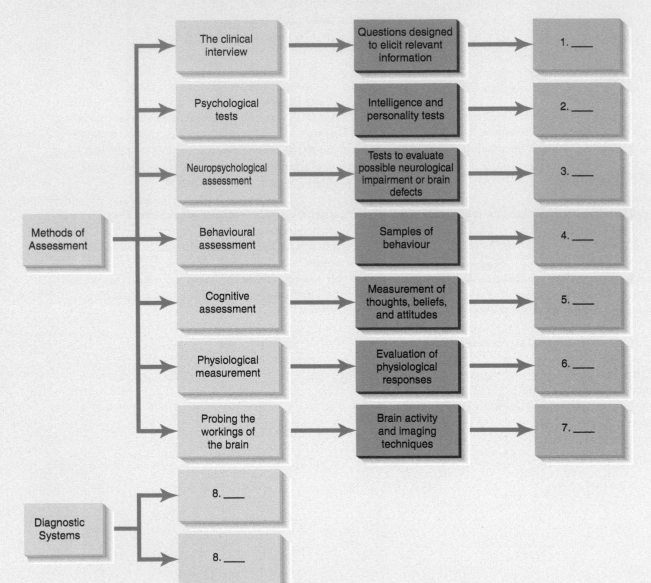

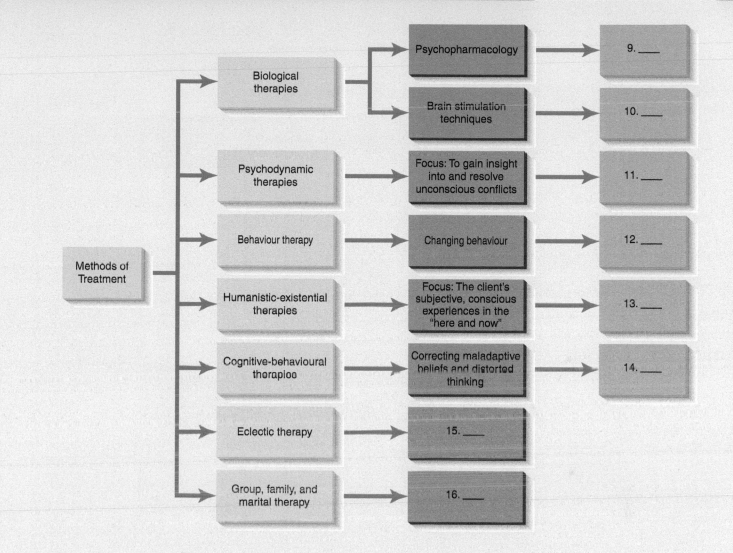

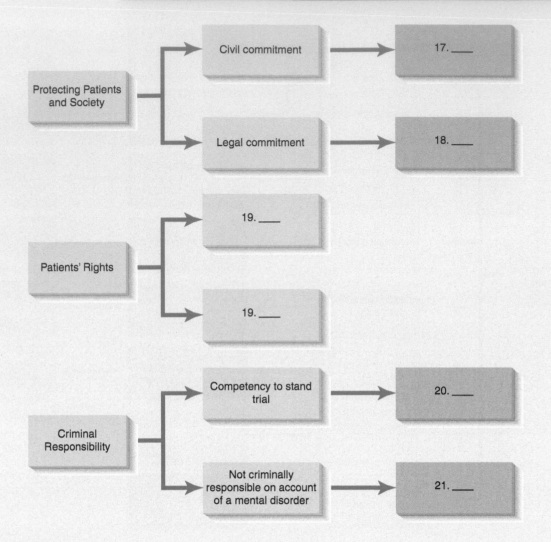

a. Examples: The Stanford-Binet, MMPI-2, Rorschach inkblot test

b. *International Statistical Classification of Diseases and Related Health Problems* (ICD-10)

c. Types: Self-monitoring, analogue or contrived measures, and behavioural rating scales

d. Examples: Heart rate, blood pressure, galvanic skin response (GSR), and muscle tension (EMG)

e. *Diagnostic and Statistical Manual of Mental Disorders* (DSM-5)

f. Methods: EEG, CT scan, PET scan, MRI, fMRI, BEAM, and MEG

g. Examples: The Bender Visual Motor Gestalt Test, Luria-Nebraska Neuropsychological Battery, and the Halstead-Reitan Neuropsychological Battery

h. Formats: Structured, semi-structured, and unstructured approaches

i. Examples: Thought record and the Automatic Thoughts Questionnaire (ATQ-30)

j. Methods: Rational-emotive behaviour therapy, Beck's cognitive therapy, and Meichenbaum's cognitive-behavioural therapy

k. Includes: Electroconvulsive therapy (ECT), repetitive transcranial magnetic stimulation (rTMS), and deep brain stimulation

l. Provides mutual support and shared learning experiences; goals are to improve communication and analyze roles to improve relationships

m. Methods: Systematic desensitization, gradual exposure, modelling, token economies, aversive conditioning, social-skills training, and self-control techniques

n. Methods: Person-centred therapy and emotion-focused therapy

o. Examples: Anti-anxiety drugs, antidepressants, antipsychotic drugs, and lithium

p. Draws upon techniques and teachings of different therapeutic approaches

q. Methods: Free association, dream analysis, and analysis of the transference relationship

r. Legal process of confining in a psychiatric institution a person found to be NCRMD

s. Although the individual is guilty of the crime, he or she is not being held accountable because the actions were due to a mental disorder

t. Legal process of confining in a psychiatric institution a person who has a mental disorder and is a threat to him- or herself or others

u. The right to refuse treatment

v. The ability of a defendant to understand the charges against him or her and to participate in their defence

w. The right to treatment

Answers: 1. h, 2. a, 3. g, 4. o, 5. l, 6. d, 7. f, 8. b, 9. v, 9. o, 10. k, 11. q, 12. m, 13. n, 14. j, 15. p, 16. i, 17. t, 18. r, 19. u, w, 20. v, 21. s

3

Anxiety, Obsessive-Compulsive, and Trauma- and Stressor-Related Disorders

Did You Know That...

- As many as 17% of people will suffer from an anxiety disorder at some point in their lives?

- People experiencing panic attacks are likely to believe they are having heart attacks, even though there is nothing wrong with their hearts?

- Although women are less likely to experience traumatic incidents than men, they are more likely to develop posttraumatic stress disorder (PTSD) at some point in their lives?

- According to one theory, humans may be genetically programmed to more readily acquire fears of snakes than of cuddly animals?

- The same drugs used to treat depression can also help treat anxiety disorders?

Pixabay.com

Fear is an unpleasant emotion caused by the belief that someone or something is dangerous, likely to cause pain, or a threat. Fear is associated with real or imagined immediate threat, and its manifestation is often fight or flight. Anxiety, on the other hand, involves an anticipated danger or misfortune resulting in a state of apprehension. There is much in our world to be anxious about—our health, social relationships, examinations, careers, international relations, and the condition of the environment are but a few sources of possible concern. It is normal, even adaptive, to be somewhat anxious about these aspects of life. Anxiety serves us when it prompts us to seek regular medical check-ups or motivates us to study for tests. Anxiety is an appropriate response to threats, but anxiety can be abnormal when its level is out of proportion to a threat or when it seems to come out of the blue—that is, when it is not in response to environmental changes. In extreme forms, anxiety can impair our daily functioning. Consider the case of Marius:

Slowly, trains snake their way through the city each morning. Most commuters pass the time reading a newspaper, sipping coffee, or catching a few last winks. For Marius, the morning commute was an exercise in terror. He noticed perspiration clinging to his shirt, but the air conditioning seemed to be working fine, for a change. So how then was he to account for the sweat? As the train entered the tunnel and darkness shrouded the windows, Marius was gripped by sheer terror. He sensed his heart beating faster, the muscles in his neck tightening. Queasiness soured his stomach. He felt as though he might pass out. Other commuters, engrossed in their morning papers or their private thoughts, paid no heed to Marius, nor did they seem concerned about the darkness that enveloped the train.

Marius had known these feelings all too well before. But now the terror was worse. Other days he could bear it. This time it seemed to start earlier than usual, before the train had entered the tunnel. "Just don't think about it," he told himself, hoping it would pass. "I must think of something to distract myself." He tried humming a song, but the panic grew worse. He tried telling himself that it would be all right, that at any moment the train would enter the station and the doors would open. Not this day, however. On this day, the train came to a screeching halt. The conductor announced a "signalling problem." Marius tried to calm himself: "It's only a short delay. We'll be moving soon." But the train did not start moving soon. More apologies from the conductor. A train had broken down farther ahead in the tunnel. Marius realized it could be a long delay, perhaps hours. Suddenly, he felt the urgent desire to escape. "But how?" he wondered.

Marius felt like he was losing control. Wild imaginings flooded his mind. He saw himself bolting down the aisles in a futile attempt to escape, bowling people over, trying vainly to pry open the doors. He was filled with a sense of doom. Something terrible was about to happen to him. "Is this the first sign of a heart attack?" he wondered anxiously. By now, perspiration had soaked his clothes. His once-neat tie hung awry. His breathing became heavy and laboured, drawing attention from other passengers. "What do they think of me?" he thought. "Will they help me if I need them?"

The train jerked into motion. He realized he would soon be free. "I'm going to be okay," he told himself. "The feelings will pass. I'm going to be myself again." The train pulled slowly into the station, 20 minutes late. The doors opened and the passengers hurried off. Stepping out himself, Marius adjusted his tie and readied himself to start the day. He felt as though he'd been in combat. Nothing that his boss could dish out could hold a candle to what he'd experienced on the 7:30 train.

The Authors' Files

Marius had suffered a panic attack, one of many he experienced before seeking treatment. The attacks varied in frequency. Sometimes they occurred daily, sometimes once a week or so. He never knew whether an attack would occur on a particular day. He knew, however, that he couldn't go on living that way. He feared that one day he would suffer a heart attack on the train. He pictured some passengers trying vainly to revive him while others stared blankly in the detached, distant way that people stare at traffic accidents. He pictured emergency workers rushing onto the train, bearing him on a stretcher to an ambulance. For a while, he considered changing jobs, accepting a less remunerative job closer to home, one that would free him of the need to take the train. He also considered driving to work, but the roads were too thick with traffic. No choice, he figured: either commute by train or switch jobs. His wife, Jill, was unaware of his panic attacks. She wondered why his shirts were heavily stained with perspiration and why he was talking about changing jobs. She worried about making ends meet on a lower income. She had no idea that it was the train ride, and not his job, that Marius was desperate to avoid.

panic disorder Type of anxiety disorder characterized by recurrent episodes of panic.

anxiety disorder Type of psychological disorder in which anxiety is the prominent feature.

Panic attacks, like the ones suffered by Marius, are a feature of **panic disorder**, a type of **anxiety disorder**. During a panic attack, one's level of anxiety can rise to a level of sheer terror.

Panic attacks are an extreme form of anxiety. Anxiety encompasses many physical features, cognitions, and behaviours, as shown in Table 3.1. Although anxious people need not experience all of them, it is easy to see why anxiety is distressing.

TABLE 3.1

Some Features of Anxiety

Physical Features of Anxiety	Behavioural Features of Anxiety	Cognitive Features of Anxiety
Jumpiness, jitteriness	Avoidance and escape behaviours	Worrying about something
Trembling or shaking of the hands or limbs	Clinging, dependent behaviours	A nagging sense of dread or apprehension about the future
Sensations of a tight band around the forehead	Agitated behaviours	Belief that something dreadful is going to happen, with no clear cause
Tightness in the pit of the stomach or chest	Seeking reassurance	Preoccupation with and keen awareness of bodily sensations
Heavy perspiration, sweaty palms	Repeatedly checking that something bad hasn't happened	Thinking things are getting out of hand
Heart pounding or racing		Feeling threatened by people or events that are normally of little or no concern
Light-headedness or faintness		Fear of losing control
Dryness in the mouth or throat		Fear of inability to cope with one's problems
Difficulty talking		Worrying about every little thing
Shortness of breath or shallow breathing		Finding one's thoughts jumbled or confused
Cold fingers or limbs		Thinking the same disturbing thought over and over
Upset stomach or nausea		Thinking that one must either flee crowded places or pass out
Difficulty swallowing, a "lump in the throat"		Not being able to shake off nagging thoughts

Continuum of Anxiety

Example: Social Anxiety Disorder

Does not meet criteria		Meets criteria		
NO SYMPTOMS	**STRUGGLING**	**MILD**	**MODERATE**	**SEVERE**
	Olga is uncomfortable in social situations and stays close to her best friend at parties where she doesn't know anyone.	Hiram is so nervous speaking in front of others that he throws up in the morning before each in-class oral presentation.	Stephanie eats alone in her car since she is too fearful of eating in front of others at the cafeteria.	Lee takes all his classes online. He rarely leaves his home to avoid all social encounters.

ANXIETY DISORDERS

According to a Simon Fraser University review of worldwide research on the **prevalence** of anxiety disorders, as many as 17% of adults will develop an anxiety disorder at some point in their lives (Somers, Goldner, Waraich, & Hsu, 2006) These disorders may persist for years or decades, especially if the person does not receive treatment.

The anxiety disorders, along with dissociative disorders and somatic symptom disorders (see Chapter 5, "Dissociative and Somatic Symptom and Related Disorders"), were classified as neuroses throughout most of the 19th century. The term *neurosis* derives from the root meaning "an abnormal or diseased condition of the nervous system." The Scottish physician William Cullen coined it in the 18th century. As the derivation implies, it was assumed that neuroses had biological origins. They were seen as an affliction of the nervous system.

At the beginning of the 20th century, Cullen's organic assumptions were largely replaced by Sigmund Freud's psychodynamic views. Freud maintained that neuroses stem from the threatened emergence of unacceptable, anxiety-evoking ideas into conscious awareness. Various neuroses—anxiety disorders, somatic symptom disorders, and dissociative disorders—might look different enough on the surface. According to Freud, however, they all represent ways in which the ego attempts to defend itself against anxiety. Freud's assumption of common **etiology**, in other words, united the disorders as neuroses. Freud's concepts were so widely accepted in the early 1900s that they formed the basis for the classification systems found in the first two editions of the *Diagnostic and Statistical Manual of Mental Disorders* (DSM).

Since 1980, the DSM has not contained a category termed *neuroses*. The present DSM is based on similarities in observable behaviour and distinctive features rather than on causal assumptions. Many clinicians continue to use the terms *neurosis* and *neurotic* in the manner in which Freud described them, however. Some clinicians use *neuroses* as a convenient means of grouping milder behavioural problems in which people maintain relatively good contact with reality. *Psychoses*, such as schizophrenia, are typified by loss of touch with reality and by the appearance of bizarre behaviour, beliefs, and hallucinations. Anxiety is not limited to the diagnostic categories traditionally termed *neuroses*, moreover. People with adjustment problems, depression, and psychotic disorders may also encounter problems with anxiety.

The DSM-5 recognizes the following specific types of anxiety disorders: panic disorder, agoraphobia, generalized anxiety disorder, specific phobia, and social anxiety disorder. These are not mutually exclusive—people frequently meet diagnostic criteria for more than one disorder.

prevalence Overall number of cases of a disorder existing in a population during a given period of time.

etiology Cause or origin; the study of causality.

Panic Disorder

Panic disorder involves the occurrence of repeated, unexpected panic attacks. Panic attacks are intense anxiety reactions accompanied by physical symptoms such as a pounding heart; rapid respiration, shortness of breath, or difficulty breathing; heavy perspiration; and weakness or dizziness. Panic attacks occur suddenly and quickly reach a peak of intensity, usually in 10 minutes or less. They typically last about 20 minutes. The attacks are accompanied by feelings of terror, a sense of imminent danger or impending doom, and an urge to escape the situation. They are usually accompanied by thoughts of losing control, going crazy, or dying. People who experience panic attacks tend to be keenly aware of changes in their heart rates (Taylor, 2000). They often believe they are having a heart attack even though there is nothing wrong with their heart.

Each year approximately 8–10% of the general population will experience a panic attack (Katzman et al., 2014). Fortunately, most of these individuals will not develop panic disorder. For a diagnosis of panic disorder to be made, there must be recurrent unexpected panic attacks—attacks that are not triggered by specific objects or situations. They seem to come out of the blue. Although the first attacks occur unexpectedly, over time they may become associated with certain situations or cues, such as entering a crowded department store or, like Marius, riding on a train.

Panic sufferers are sometimes unaware of subtle changes in their bodily sensations that may precipitate an attack, and so the panic may be perceived as spontaneous because these underlying changes are not detected. If panic sufferers are unable to identify the actual triggers, they may attribute their sensations to more serious causes, such as an impending heart attack or a break with reality ("going crazy").

After a panic attack, the person may feel exhausted, as if he or she has survived a truly traumatic experience, as in the following case:

> I was inside a very busy shopping mall and all of a sudden it happened; in a matter of seconds I was like a madwoman. It was like a nightmare, only I was awake: Everything went black and sweat poured out of me—my body, my hands, and even my hair got wet through. All of the blood seemed to drain out of me; I went white as a ghost. I felt as if I was going to collapse; it was as if I had no control over my limbs—my back and legs were very weak and I felt as though it was impossible to move. It was as if I had been taken over by some stronger force. I saw all the people looking at me—just faces, no bodies, all merged into one. My heart started pounding in my head and my ears. I thought that my heart was going to stop. I could see black and yellow lights. I could hear the voices of people but from a long way off. I could not think of anything except the way that I was feeling and how I had to get out and run quickly or I would die. I had to escape and get into fresh air. Outside it subsided a little but I felt limp and weak; my legs were like jelly, as though I had run a race and lost. I had a lump in my throat like a golf ball. The incident seemed to me to have lasted hours. I was absolutely drained when I got home and I just broke down and cried. It took until the next day to feel normal again.
>
> Based on Hawkrigg, 1975, Agoraphobia, pp. 1280–1282.
> Reprinted courtesy of nursingtimes.net.

People often describe panic attacks as the worst experiences of their lives. Their coping abilities are overwhelmed. They may feel they must flee. If flight seems useless, they may freeze. There is a tendency to cling to others for help or support. They worry so much about future attacks that they make changes to their daily behaviour in an attempt

Zdenka Darula/123RF

Panic. Panic attacks are associated with strong physical reactions, especially cardiovascular symptoms.

to prevent another attack or to be able to quickly escape if one does occur (e.g., sitting near the exit, not going out alone).

Recurrent panic attacks may become so difficult to cope with that sufferers can become suicidal. Table 3.2 outlines the diagnostic criteria for panic disorder according to DSM-5.

Panic disorder is known to occur in many countries, perhaps even universally. However, the specific features of panic attacks may vary from culture to culture. Some culture-bound syndromes have features similar to panic attacks, such as *ataque de nervios*. This syndrome, which occurs among Latin American and Latin Mediterranean groups, involves symptoms such as shouting uncontrollably, fits of crying, trembling, feelings of warmth or heat rising from the chest to the head, and aggressive verbal or physical behaviour. These episodes are usually precipitated by a stressful event affecting the family (e.g., receiving news of the death of a family member) and are accompanied by feelings of being out of control. A similar syndrome, *khyâl cap* ("wind attacks"), which is found among Cambodians in the United States and Cambodia, includes numerous physical symptoms typically found in panic attacks (palpitations, dizziness, shortness of breath) but is attributed to a fear that a wind-like substance (*khyâl*) will infiltrate the body causing serious consequences such as asphyxia, tinnitus, or loss of consciousness (APA, 2013).

National surveys in Canada and the United States reveal that 1–5% of people develop panic disorder at some point in their lives (Grant et al., 2006). The disorder usually begins in late adolescence or the early 20s. Women are twice as likely as men to develop panic

---

TABLE 3.2

Diagnostic Criteria for Panic Disorder

A. Recurrent unexpected panic attacks. A panic attack is an abrupt surge of intense fear or intense discomfort that reaches a peak within minutes, and during which time four (or more) of the following symptoms occur:

Note: The abrupt surge can occur from a calm state or an anxious state.

1. Palpitations, pounding heart, or accelerated heart rate.
2. Sweating.
3. Trembling or shaking.
4. Sensations of shortness of breath or smothering.
5. Feelings of choking.
6. Chest pain or discomfort.
7. Nausea or abdominal distress.
8. Feeling dizzy, unsteady, light-headed, or faint.
9. Chills or heat sensations.
10. Paresthesias (numbness or tingling sensations).
11. Derealization (feelings of unreality) or depersonalization (being detached from oneself).
12. Fear of losing control or "going crazy."
13. Fear of dying.

Note: Culture-specific symptoms (e.g., tinnitus, neck soreness, headache, uncontrollable screaming or crying) may be seen. Such symptoms should not count as one of the four required symptoms.

B. At least one of the attacks has been followed by 1 month (or more) of one or both of the following:

1. Persistent concern or worry about additional panic attacks or their consequences (e.g., losing control, having a heart attack, "going crazy").
2. A significant maladaptive change in behavior related to the attacks (e.g., behaviors designed to avoid having panic attacks, such as avoidance of exercise or unfamiliar situations).

C. The disturbance is not attributable to the physiological effects of a substance (e.g., a drug of abuse, a medication) or another medical condition (e.g., hyperthyroidism, cardiopulmonary disorders).

D. The disturbance is not better explained by another mental disorder (e.g., the panic attacks do not occur only in response to feared social situations, as in social anxiety disorder; in response to circumscribed phobic objects or situations, as in specific phobia; in response to obsessions, as in obsessive-compulsive disorder; in response to reminders of traumatic events, as in posttraumatic stress disorder; or in response to separation from attachment figures, as in separation anxiety disorder).

Source: Reprinted with permission from the *Diagnostic and Statistical Manual of Mental Disorders*, Fifth Edition, (Copyright © 2013). American Psychiatric Association. All Rights Reserved.

disorder (APA, 2013). What little we know about the long course of panic disorder suggests it tends to follow a chronic course that waxes and wanes in severity over time (Taylor, 2000).

Agoraphobia

agoraphobia A fear of places and situations from which it might be difficult or embarrassing to escape in the event of panicky symptoms or of situations in which help may be unavailable if such problems occur.

Agoraphobia involves fear of places and situations from which it might be difficult or embarrassing to escape in the event of panicky symptoms or of situations in which help may be unavailable if such problems occur (see Table 3.3). People with agoraphobia may fear shopping in crowded stores; walking through crowded streets; crossing bridges; travelling by bus, train, or car; eating in restaurants; or even just leaving the house. They may structure their lives around avoiding exposure to fearful situations and in some cases become housebound for months or even years. Although agoraphobia and panic disorder are classified as separate disorders, people who develop panic disorder often report agoraphobia before the onset of a panic disorder (APA, 2013).

Agoraphobia is more common in women than men (APA, 2013). It frequently begins in late adolescence or early adulthood. Approximately 2% of adults have experienced agoraphobia at some point in their lives (Grant et al., 2006; Kessler et al., 2006). People with agoraphobia may live in fear of recurrent attacks and avoid public places where attacks have occurred or might occur. Because panic attacks can occur unexpectedly, some people restrict their activities for fear of making public spectacles of themselves or finding themselves without help (Taylor, 2000). Others venture outside only with a companion. A diagnosis, however, would not be made without taking into consideration the sociocultural context. An individual living in a high-crime neighbourhood may have a valid reason to fear walking alone. In certain cultures, such as among orthodox Muslim women, it may be expected that women would not venture out of the house unaccompanied (APA, 2013).

TABLE 3.3

Diagnostic Criteria for Agoraphobia

A. Marked fear or anxiety about two (or more) of the following five situations:
  1. Using public transportation (e.g., automobiles, buses, trains, ships, planes).
  2. Being in open spaces (e.g., parking lots, marketplaces, bridges).
  3. Being in enclosed places (e.g., shops, theaters, cinemas).
  4. Standing in line or being in a crowd.
  5. Being outside of the home alone.

B. The individual fears or avoids these situations because of thoughts that escape might be difficult or help might not be available in the event of developing panic-like symptoms or other incapacitating or embarrassing symptoms (e.g., fear of falling in the elderly; fear of incontinence).

C. The agoraphobic situations almost always provoke fear or anxiety.

D. The agoraphobic situations are actively avoided, require the presence of a companion, or are endured with intense fear or anxiety.

E. The fear or anxiety is out of proportion to the actual danger posed by the agoraphobic situations and to the sociocultural context.

F. The fear, anxiety, or avoidance is persistent, typically lasting for 6 months or more.

G. The fear, anxiety, or avoidance causes clinically significant distress or impairment in social, occupational, or other important areas of functioning.

H. If another medical condition (e.g., inflammatory bowel disease, Parkinson's disease) is present, the fear, anxiety, or avoidance is clearly excessive.

I. The fear, anxiety, or avoidance is not better explained by the symptoms of another mental disorder—for example, the symptoms are not confined to specific phobia, situational type; do not involve only social situations (as in social anxiety disorder); and are not related exclusively to obsessions (as in obsessive-compulsive disorder), perceived defects or flaws in physical appearance (as in body dysmorphic disorder), reminders of traumatic events (as in posttraumatic stress disorder), or fear of separation (as in separation anxiety disorder).

Note: Agoraphobia is diagnosed irrespective of the presence of panic disorder. If an individual's presentation meets criteria for panic disorder and agoraphobia, both diagnoses should be assigned.

Source: Reprinted with permission from the *Diagnostic and Statistical Manual of Mental Disorders*, Fifth Edition, (Copyright © 2013). American Psychiatric Association. All Rights Reserved.

People with agoraphobia may experience mild panicky symptoms, such as dizziness, which lead them to avoid venturing away from places where they feel safe or secure. They tend to become dependent on others for support. The following case illustrates the dependencies often associated with agoraphobia:

Carmen, a 59-year-old widow, became increasingly agoraphobic after the death of her husband three years earlier. By the time she came for treatment, she was essentially housebound, refusing to leave her home except under the strongest urging of her daughter, Renata, age 32, and only if Renata accompanied her. Her daughter and 36-year-old son, Peter, did her shopping for her and took care of her other needs as best they could. Yet the burden of caring for their mother, on top of their other responsibilities, was becoming too great for them to bear. They insisted that Carmen begin treatment, and she begrudgingly acceded to their demands.

Carmen was accompanied to her evaluation session by Renata. The 59-year-old woman appeared frail when she entered the office clutching Renata's arm, and she insisted that Renata stay throughout the interview. Carmen recounted that she had lost her husband and mother within three months of each other; her father had died 20 years earlier. Although she had never experienced a panic attack, she always considered herself an insecure, fearful person. Even so, she had been able to function in meeting the needs of her family until the deaths of her husband and mother left her feeling abandoned and alone. She had now become afraid of "just about everything" and was terrified of being out on her own, lest something bad would happen and she wouldn't be able to cope. Even at home, she was fearful that she might lose Renata and Peter. She needed constant reassurance that they wouldn't abandon her.

The Authors' Files

NORMAL/ABNORMAL BEHAVIOUR

Anxiety: No Panic Disorder

Jennifer was a nursing student in her first year at university. She was taking a full course load and beginning some practical training at a local hospital. She had been assigned to work on the cancer unit for a rotation. One day on the unit she was shadowing her supervisor as she usually did. In their interaction with patients, they spent time talking to someone who had just learned that his cancer had spread throughout his body. All of a sudden, Jennifer felt like the room was spinning around her. She had trouble breathing and felt as if there was a heavy weight upon her chest. She asked the supervising nurse if she could take a break. She went to a quiet part of the unit and tried to focus on her breathing. After a few minutes, she rejoined her supervisor and finished her shift, although she felt physically uncomfortable for the rest of the day. Later that night, she told her roommate about the incident and chalked it up to being overwhelmed by her school demands and having interacted with someone who had been given a terminal diagnosis.

Anxiety: Panic Disorder

Sade was a second-year business student at a local university. She was physically healthy, having never had any major medical issues. Her second-year course load was demanding, such that Sade had little time to spend with friends or her boyfriend. The stress was beginning to get to her. She began to notice heart palpitations while studying, and tried to brush them off as stress. On the day her mid-term schedule was posted, Sade found out that she had three mid-terms in one day. She was already feeling behind in her work. Later that day, while studying, Sade began to have chest pains and felt a tingling sensation in her head and her fingers. Her body felt hot and cold, and she felt droplets of sweat down her back. These symptoms quickly escalated and Sade began feeling panicked that she was dying. She clutched her heart and tried to take her pulse. She felt as though she needed to bolt from the library and get fresh air as quickly as possible. Once she was outside, the symptoms did not abate, and so Sade called 911. Later, at the hospital, the ER doctor explained to her that she likely had a panic attack. Sade wasn't convinced, and began to avoid the library for fear that she would feel this way again.

Generalized Anxiety Disorder

generalized anxiety disorder Type of anxiety disorder characterized by general feelings of dread, foreboding, and heightened states of sympathetic arousal. Formerly referred to as *free-floating anxiety*. Abbreviated *GAD*.

Generalized anxiety disorder (GAD) is characterized by persistent feelings of anxiety that are not triggered by any specific object, situation, or activity but rather seem to be what Freud labelled "free floating." People with GAD are chronic worriers, and excessive, uncontrollable worrying is considered the key feature of the disorder (Behar & Borkovec, 2006). They may be excessively worried about life circumstances such as finances, the well-being of their children, social relationships, or even very minor things. Children with generalized anxiety are likely to be worried about academics, athletics, and social aspects of school life. Other related features include restlessness; feeling tense, "keyed up," or "on edge"; becoming easily fatigued; having difficulty concentrating or finding one's mind going blank; irritability; muscle tension; and disturbances of sleep such as difficulty falling asleep, staying asleep, or having restless and unsatisfying sleep (see Table 3.4) (APA, 2013). Not surprisingly, the features of GAD—anxiety, worry, and physical symptoms—cause a significant level of emotional distress or impaired functioning (Craske & Waters, 2005).

Generalized anxiety disorder tends to initially arise in the mid-teens to mid-20s and typically follows a lifelong course. The lifetime prevalence of GAD in the general population in Canada is estimated to be 8.7% (Pearson, Janz, & Ali, 2013). The disorder is more common in women. GAD frequently occurs (comorbidly) with other disorders, such as depressive disorders, anxiety disorders, or obsessive-compulsive disorder. The following case illustrates a number of features of GAD:

Rishad was a 52-year-old supervisor at an automobile plant. His hands trembled as he spoke. His cheeks were pale. His face was somewhat boyish, making his hair seem greyed with worry.

He was reasonably successful in his work, although he noted that he was not a "star." His marriage of nearly three decades was in "reasonably good shape," although sexual relations were "less than exciting—I shake so much that it isn't easy to get involved." The mortgage on his house was not a burden and would be paid off within five years, but, Rishad said, "I don't know what it is; I think about money all the time." His three children were doing well. One was employed, one was in college, and one was in high school. But "with everything going on these days, how can you help worrying about them? I'm up for hours worrying about them," Rishad said.

"But it's the strangest thing." Rishad shook his head. "I swear I'll find myself worrying when there's nothing in my head. I don't know how to describe it. It's like I'm worrying first and then there's something in my head to worry about. It's not like I start thinking about this or that and I see it's bad and then I worry. And then the shakes come, and then, of course, I'm worrying about worrying, if you know what I mean. I want to run away; I don't want anyone to see me. You can't direct workers when you're shaking."

Going to work had become a major chore. "I can't stand the noises of the assembly lines. I just feel jumpy all the time. It's like I expect something awful to happen. When it gets bad like that I'll be out of work for a day or two with shakes."

Rishad had been worked up "for everything; my doctor took blood, saliva, urine, you name it. He listened to everything; he put things inside me. He had other people look at me. He told me to stay away from coffee and alcohol. Then from tea. Then from chocolate and Coca-Cola, because there's a little bit of caffeine [in them]. He gave me Valium [a minor tranquillizer] and I thought I was in heaven for a while. Then it stopped working, and he switched me to something else. Then that stopped working, and he switched me back. Then he said he was 'out of chemical miracles' and I better see a shrink or something. Maybe it was something from my childhood."

The Authors' Files

TABLE 3.4

Diagnostic Criteria for Generalized Anxiety Disorder

A. Excessive anxiety and worry (apprehensive expectation), occurring more days than not for at least 6 months, about a number of events or activities (such as work or school performance).

B. The individual finds it difficult to control the worry.

C. The anxiety and worry are associated with three (or more) of the following six symptoms (with at least some symptoms having been present for more days than not for the past 6 months):

Note: Only one item is required in children.

1. Restlessness or feeling keyed up or on edge.

2. Being easily fatigued.

3. Difficulty concentrating or mind going blank.

4. Irritability.

5. Muscle tension.

6. Sleep disturbance (difficulty falling or staying asleep, or restless, unsatisfying sleep).

D. The anxiety, worry, or physical symptoms cause clinically significant distress or impairment in social, occupational, or other important areas of functioning.

E. The disturbance is not attributable to the physiological effects of a substance (e.g., a drug of abuse, a medication) or another medical condition (e.g., hyperthyroidism).

F. The disturbance is not better explained by another mental disorder (e.g., anxiety or worry about having panic attacks in panic disorder, negative evaluation in social anxiety disorder [social phobia], contamination or other obsessions in obsessive-compulsive disorder, separation from attachment figures in separation anxiety disorder, reminders of traumatic events in posttraumatic stress disorder, gaining weight in anorexia nervosa, physical complaints in somatic symptom disorder, perceived appearance flaws in body dysmorphic disorder, having a serious illness in illness anxiety disorder, or the content of delusional beliefs in schizophrenia or delusional disorder).

Phobic Disorders

The word *phobia* derives from the Greek *phobos,* meaning "fear." The concepts of fear and anxiety are closely related. We already know that **fear** is the feeling of anxiety and agitation in response to a threat. Phobic disorders are persistent fears of objects or situations that are disproportionate to the threats they pose. To experience a sense of gripping fear when your car is about to go out of control is normal because there is an objective basis to the fear. In phobic disorders, however, the fear exceeds any reasonable appraisal of danger. People with a driving phobia, for example, might become fearful even when they are driving well below the speed limit on a sunny day on an uncrowded highway. Or they might be so afraid they will not drive or even ride in a car. People with phobias are not out of touch with reality; they generally recognize that their fears are excessive or unreasonable.

A curious thing about phobias is that they usually involve fears of the ordinary things in life, not the extraordinary. People with phobias become frightened of ordinary experiences that most people take for granted, such as taking an elevator or driving on a highway. Phobias can become disabling when they interfere with daily tasks such as taking buses, planes, or trains; driving; shopping; or leaving the house. Different types of phobias usually appear at different ages, as noted in Table 3.5. The ages of onset appear to reflect levels of physical and cognitive development and life experiences. Fear of heights, for example, typically emerges when a child learns to crawl or walk and therefore is at risk for falling (Cox & Taylor, 1999). Let's consider the two types of phobic disorders classified within the DSM system: *specific phobia* and *social anxiety disorder.*

fear Unpleasant, negative emotion characterized by the perception of a specific threat, sympathetic nervous system activity, and tendencies to avoid the feared object.

TABLE 3.5
Typical Age of Onset for Various Phobias

	Mean Age of Onset
Animal phobia	7
Blood phobia	9
Injection phobia	8
Dental phobia	12
Social phobia	16
Claustrophobia	20
Agoraphobia	28

Source: Öst, 1987, pp. 223–229. Copyright the American Psychological Association. Reprinted with permission.

specific phobias Persistent but excessive fears of a specific object or situation, such as a fear of heights or of small animals.

acrophobia Excessive fear of heights.

claustrophobia Excessive fear of small, enclosed places.

SPECIFIC PHOBIAS **Specific phobias** are persistent, excessive fears of specific objects or situations, such as fear of heights (**acrophobia**), fear of enclosed spaces (**claustrophobia**), or fear of small animals such as mice or snakes and various other "creepy-crawlies." A person experiences high levels of fear and physiological arousal when encountering the phobic object, which prompts strong urges to escape the situation or avoid the feared stimulus. To rise to the level of a psychological disorder, the phobia must make a significant impact on a person's lifestyle or functioning or cause significant distress. You may have a fear of snakes, but unless your fear interferes with your daily life or causes you significant emotional distress, it would not warrant a diagnosis of phobic disorder.

According to the DSM-5, there are five diagnostic subtypes of specific phobia: (1) animal type (e.g., phobias of dogs or bugs); (2) natural environment type (e.g., phobias of storms, heights, or water); (3) blood-injection-injury type (e.g., phobias of seeing blood or receiving an injection); (4) situational type (e.g., phobias of specific situations, such as enclosed spaces or public transportation); and (5) other types (e.g., phobias of costumed characters).

Specific phobias often begin in childhood. Many children develop passing fears of specific objects or situations. Some, however, go on to develop chronic clinically significant phobias (Antony & Barlow, 2002). Claustrophobia seems to develop later than most other specific phobias, with a mean age of onset of 20 years (see Table 3.5).

Specific phobias are among the most common psychological disorders, affecting close to 1 in 10 people at some point in their lives (APA, 2013). They occur more frequently in women than men, perhaps because of cultural factors that socialize women to be dependent on men for protection from threatening objects in the environment (Antony & Barlow, 2002). Clinicians need to be aware of cultural factors when making diagnostic judgments. Fears of magic or spirits are common in some cultures and should not be considered a sign of a phobic disorder unless the fear is excessive in light of the cultural context in which it occurs and leads to significant emotional distress or impaired functioning. Table 3.6 (page 112) outlines the diagnostic criteria for specific phobia.

social anxiety disorder Excessive fear of engaging in behaviours that involve public scrutiny.

SOCIAL ANXIETY DISORDER (SOCIAL PHOBIA) It is not abnormal to experience some fear of social situations such as dating, attending parties or social gatherings, or giving a talk or presentation to a class or group. Yet people with **social anxiety disorder** have such an intense fear of social situations they may avoid them altogether or endure them only with great distress. Underlying social anxiety disorder is an excessive fear of negative evaluations from others. As noted by Lynn Alden and colleagues at the University of British Columbia, people with social anxiety disorder often worry about their social presentation ("Do I look foolish?") and are frightened of doing or saying something humiliating or embarrassing (Crozier & Alden, 2001; Mellings & Alden, 2000). Research by Martin Antony (from Ryerson University) shows that people with social anxiety disorder

(a) Sergey Fedenko/Hemera/Thinkstock/
Getty Images

(b) CC Studio/Science Source

(c) Jupiterimages/Stockbyte/Getty Images

(d) Charriau Pierre/The Image Bank/Getty Images

(e) Nomad_Soul/Shutterstock

Five diagnostic subtypes of specific phobias. Phobias fall into five subtypes: (a) animal type, (b) natural environment type, (c) blood-injection-injury type, (d) situational type, and (e) other types (e.g., phobias of costumed characters).

tend to see themselves as not being as good as others (Antony, Rowa, Liss, Swallow, & Swinson, 2005). They tend to be severely critical of their social skills and become absorbed in evaluating their own performance when interacting with others (Taylor & Alden, 2005). Some even experience full-fledged panic attacks in social situations.

Surveys conducted in Canada and the United States suggest that between 3% and 13% of people develop social anxiety disorder at some point in their lives (APA, 2013; Shields, 2004b).

According to McMaster University psychiatrist and anxiety expert Richard Swinson (2005), there is controversy about whether social anxiety disorder is overdiagnosed—that is, controversy about whether psychologists and psychiatrists are confusing ordinary shyness with a psychiatric disorder. Like all psychological disorders, social anxiety disorder is diagnosed only when it causes significant suffering or significantly impairs a person's level of functioning in important spheres of life, such as social

Diagnostic Criteria for Specific Phobia

A. Marked fear or anxiety about a specific object or situation (e.g., flying, heights, animals, receiving an injection, seeing blood).

   Note: In children, the fear or anxiety may be expressed by crying, tantrums, freezing, or clinging.

B. The phobic object or situation almost always provokes immediate fear or anxiety.

C. The phobic object or situation is actively avoided or endured with intense fear or anxiety.

D. The fear or anxiety is out of proportion to the actual danger posed by the specific object or situation and to the sociocultural context.

E. The fear, anxiety, or avoidance is persistent, typically lasting for 6 months or more.

F. The fear, anxiety, or avoidance causes clinically significant distress or impairment in social, occupational, or other important areas of functioning.

G. The disturbance is not better explained by the symptoms of another mental disorder, including fear, anxiety, and avoidance of situations associated with panic-like symptoms or other incapacitating symptoms (as in agoraphobia); objects or situations related to obsessions (as in obsessive-compulsive disorder); reminders of traumatic events (as in posttraumatic stress disorder); separation from home or attachment figures (as in separation anxiety disorder); or social situations (as in social anxiety disorder).

Source: Reprinted with permission from the *Diagnostic and Statistical Manual of Mental Disorders*, Fifth Edition, (Copyright © 2013). American Psychiatric Association. All Rights Reserved.

CREATISTA/Shutterstock

Not just shyness? People with social anxiety disorder sometimes experience such high levels of distress that they avoid social situations of all kinds.

relationships or performance at work or school. People with social anxiety disorder report lower levels of educational attainment, more employment difficulties, lower income, greater dependence on welfare and social assistance, lower likelihood of marriage, and greater social isolation (Shields, 2004b). In addition, they often turn to tranquillizers or try to "medicate" themselves with alcohol when preparing for social interactions.

Social anxiety disorder is more common among women than men (APA, 2013; Shields, 2004a), perhaps because of the greater social or cultural pressures placed on young women to please others and earn their approval. People with social anxiety disorder may find excuses for declining social invitations. They may eat lunch at their desks to avoid socializing with co-workers. Or they may find themselves in social situations and attempt a quick escape at the first sign of anxiety. Some people with social anxiety disorder are unable to order food in a restaurant for fear the server or their companions might make fun of the foods they order or how they pronounce them. Others fear meeting new people and dating (see Figure 3.1). Relief from anxiety negatively reinforces escape behaviour, and escape prevents people with phobias from learning to cope with fear-evoking situations more adaptively. Leaving the scene before anxiety dissipates only strengthens the association between the social situation and anxiety.

The roots of social anxiety disorder may begin in childhood. People with social anxiety disorder typically report that they were shy as children (Crozier & Alden, 2001; Stein & Walker, 2002). Consistent with the diathesis-stress model, shyness may represent a diathesis or predisposition that makes one more vulnerable to developing social anxiety disorder in the face of stressful experiences, such as traumatic social encounters (e.g., being embarrassed in front of others). Social anxiety disorder tends to begin in adolescence and typically follows a chronic and persistent course in life (Antony & Swinson, 2000).

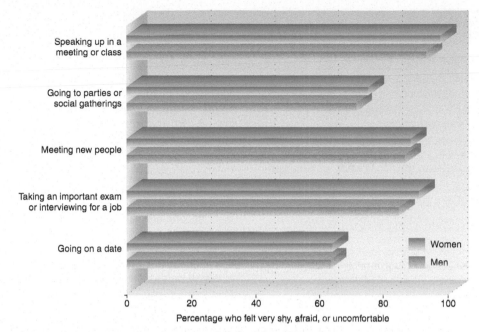

FIGURE 3.1 Percentage of people with social anxiety disorder reporting specific difficulties associated with their fears of social situations.
More than 90% of people with social anxiety disorder feel handicapped by anxiety in their jobs.

Source: Adapted from Statistics Canada (2004b). Social anxiety disorder—beyond shyness. This does not constitute an endorsement by Statistics Canada of this product.

OBSESSIVE-COMPULSIVE AND RELATED DISORDERS

Obsessive-Compulsive Disorder (OCD)

Individuals with obsessive-compulsive disorder are troubled by recurrent obsessions, compulsions, or both that occupy more than an hour a day and cause marked distress or significantly interfere with normal routines or occupational or social functioning.

An **obsession** is an intrusive, unwanted, and recurrent thought, image, or urge that seems beyond a person's ability to control. Obsessions can be potent and persistent enough to interfere with daily life and can cause significant distress or anxiety. Obsessions may involve persistent, unwanted doubts; the person may wonder endlessly whether he or she has locked the doors and shut the windows, for example. Some sufferers are plagued by personally repugnant images, such as the recurrent thought of a young mother that her children have been run over by traffic on the way home from school. The line between obsessions and the firmly held but patently false beliefs that are labelled *delusions*, which are found in schizophrenia, is sometimes less than clear. Obsessions, such as the belief that one is contaminating other people, can, like delusions, become almost unshakable. As noted by internationally recognized OCD expert David Clark (from the University of New Brunswick), although adults with OCD may be uncertain at a given time whether their obsessions or compulsions are unreasonable or excessive, they will eventually concede that their concerns are groundless or excessive (Clark, 2004). True delusions fail to be shaken. Children with OCD may not come to recognize that their concerns are groundless, however.

A **compulsion** is a repetitive behaviour (such as handwashing or checking door locks) or mental act (such as praying, repeating certain words, or counting) that a person feels compelled or driven to perform (APA, 2013). Compulsions often occur in response to obsessional

obsession An intrusive, unwanted, and recurrent thought, image, or urge that seems beyond a person's ability to control.

compulsion A repetitive behaviour or mental act that a person feels compelled or driven to perform.

hxdbzxy/Shutterstock

Compulsions often accompany obsessions and may temporarily relieve the anxiety created by obsessional thinking.

TABLE 3.7

Examples of Obsessive Thoughts and Compulsive Behaviours

Obsessive Thought Patterns	Compulsive Behaviour Patterns
Thinking that one's hands remain dirty despite repeated washing	Constantly washing one's hands to keep them clean and germ free
Difficulty shaking the thought that a loved one has been hurt or killed	Constantly checking with loved ones to be sure they are alive and well
Repeatedly thinking that one has left the door to the house unlocked; worrying constantly that the gas jets in the house were not turned off	Rechecking that doors are locked or gas jets are switched off before leaving home
Constant concerns with contamination (e.g., fear of dirt, germs, or illness)	Excessive cleaning (e.g., ritualized housecleaning)
Obsessive need for symmetry or exactness	Checking, ordering, and arranging rituals; counting; repeating routine activities (e.g., going in/out of a doorway)
Unacceptable sexual or religious thoughts (e.g., sacrilegious images of Christ)	Mental rituals (e.g., silent recitation of nonsense words to vanquish a horrific image)

thoughts and are frequent and forceful enough to interfere with daily life or cause significant distress. A compulsive handwasher, Corinne, engaged in elaborate handwashing rituals. She spent three to four hours daily at the sink and complained, "My hands look like lobster claws." Some people literally take hours checking and rechecking that all the appliances are off before they leave home, and even then doubts remain.

Most compulsions fall into two categories: checking rituals and cleaning rituals. Rituals can become the focal point of life. Checking rituals, like repeatedly checking that the gas jets are turned off or that doors are securely locked, cause delays and annoy companions; cleaning can occupy several hours a day. Table 3.7 shows some relatively common obsessions and compulsions.

Compulsions often appear to at least partially relieve the anxiety created by obsessional thinking (Clark, 2004). By washing one's hands 40 or 50 times in a row each time a public doorknob is touched, the compulsive handwasher may experience some relief from the anxiety engendered by the obsessive thought that germs or dirt still linger in the folds of skin. The person may believe the compulsive act will help prevent some dreaded event from occurring, even though there is no realistic basis to the belief or the behaviour far exceeds what is reasonable under the circumstances.

The case of Jack illustrates a checking compulsion:

Jack, a successful chemical engineer, was urged by his wife, Julie, a pharmacist, to seek help for "his little behavioural quirks," which she had found increasingly annoying. Jack was a compulsive checker. When they left the apartment, he would insist on returning to check that the lights or gas jets were off or that the refrigerator doors were shut. Sometimes he would apologize at the elevator and return to the apartment to carry out his rituals. Sometimes the compulsion to check struck him in the garage. He would return to the apartment, leaving Julie fuming. Going on vacation was especially difficult for Jack. The rituals occupied the better part of the morning of their departure. Even then, he remained plagued by doubts.

Julie had also tried to adjust to Jack's nightly routine of bolting out of bed to recheck the doors and windows. Her patience was running thin. Jack realized his behaviour was impairing their relationship as well as causing himself distress, yet he was reluctant to enter treatment. He gave lip service to wanting to be rid of his compulsive habits. However, he also feared that surrendering his compulsions would leave him defenceless against the anxieties they helped ease.

The Authors' Files

OCD affects slightly more than 1% of adults during their lifetimes and is typically chronic, waxing and waning in response to life stressors. The disorder seems to affect a greater number of females in adulthood and a greater number of males in childhood (APA, 2013).

TRAUMA- AND STRESSOR-RELATED DISORDERS

Adjustment Disorders

Adjustment disorders are among the mildest of psychological disorders. An adjustment disorder is a maladaptive reaction to an identified stressor that develops within a few months of the onset of the stressor. The maladaptive reaction is characterized by significant impairment in social, occupational, or academic functioning or by states of emotional distress that exceed those normally induced by the stressor. For the diagnosis to apply, the stress-related reaction must not be sufficient to meet the diagnostic criteria for other clinical syndromes, such as anxiety disorders or depressive disorders. The maladaptive reaction may be resolved if the stressor is removed or the individual learns to cope with it. If the maladaptive reaction lasts for more than six months after the stressor (or its consequences) have been removed, the diagnosis may be changed.

If your relationship with someone comes to an end (an identified stressor) and your grades are falling because you are unable to keep your mind on schoolwork, you may fit the bill for an adjustment disorder. If Uncle Harry has been feeling down and pessimistic since his divorce from Aunt Jane, he too may be diagnosed with an adjustment disorder. So, too, might Cousin Billy, if he has been cutting classes and spraying obscene words on school walls or showing other signs of disturbed conduct. Table 3.8 outlines the diagnostic criteria for adjustment disorders.

The concept of an adjustment disorder as a mental disorder highlights some of the difficulties in attempting to define what is normal and what is not. When something important goes wrong in life, we should feel bad about it. If there is a crisis in business,

Anna Yakimova/123RF

Difficulty concentrating or adjustment disorder? An adjustment disorder is a maladaptive reaction to a stressful event that may take the form of impaired functioning at school or work, such as having difficulties keeping one's mind on one's studies.

adjustment disorders
Maladaptive reactions to an identified stressor or stressors that occur shortly following exposure to the stressor(s) and result in impaired functioning or signs of emotional distress that exceed what would normally be expected in the situation. The reaction may be resolved if the stressor is removed or the individual learns to adapt to it successfully.

TABLE 3.8

Diagnostic Criteria for Adjustment Disorders

A. The development of emotional or behavioral symptoms in response to an identifiable stressor(s) occurring within 3 months of the onset of the stressor(s).

B. These symptoms or behaviors are clinically significant, as evidenced by one or both of the following:

    1. Marked distress that is out of proportion to the severity or intensity of the stressor, taking into account the external context and the cultural factors that might influence symptom severity and presentation.

    2. Significant impairment in social, occupational, or other important areas of functioning.

C. The stress-related disturbance does not meet the criteria for another mental disorder and is not merely an exacerbation of a preexisting mental disorder.

D. The symptoms do not represent normal bereavement.

E. Once the stressor or its consequences have terminated, the symptoms do not persist for more than an additional 6 months.

Source: Reprinted with permission from the *Diagnostic and Statistical Manual of Mental Disorders*, Fifth Edition, (Copyright © 2013). American Psychiatric Association. All Rights Reserved.

if we are victimized by a crime, if there is a flood or a devastating ice storm, it is understandable that we might become anxious or depressed. There might, in fact, be something more seriously wrong with us if we did not react in a "maladaptive" way, at least temporarily. However, if our emotional reaction exceeds an expectable response or our ability to function is impaired (e.g., avoidance of social interactions, difficulty getting out of bed, or falling behind in schoolwork), then a diagnosis of adjustment disorder may be indicated. Thus, if you are having trouble concentrating on your schoolwork following the breakup of a romantic relationship, you may have a mild type of psychological disorder—an adjustment disorder.

Acute and Posttraumatic Stress Disorders

In adjustment disorders, people have difficulty adjusting to life stressors—business or marital problems, chronic illness, or bereavement over a loss. Here, we focus on stress-related disorders that arise from exposure to traumatic events. Exposure to traumatic events can produce acute or prolonged stress-related disorders that are labelled, respectively, **acute stress disorder** (ASD) and **posttraumatic stress disorder** (PTSD). In these disorders, the traumatic event involves either actual or threatened death, or serious physical injury or threat to one's own or another's physical safety (APA, 2013). Both types of stress disorders have occurred among soldiers exposed to combat, rape survivors, victims of motor vehicle and other accidents, and people who have witnessed the destruction of their homes and communities by natural disasters such as floods, earthquakes, or tornadoes or who have witnessed or experienced technological disasters such as railroad or airplane crashes. The person's response to the threat involves feelings of intense fear, helplessness, or a sense of horror. Children with PTSD may respond to the threat differently, such as by showing confused or agitated behaviour.

The diagnosis of acute stress disorder is applied to a traumatic stress reaction that occurs during the days and weeks immediately following the traumatic experience. Many people with acute stress disorder go on to develop more persistent stress-related problems, leading to a diagnosis of PTSD (Harvey & Bryant, 2002). In PTSD, the symptoms have lasted at least one month and may persist for months, years, or even decades.

In acute and posttraumatic stress disorders, the traumatic event may be re-experienced in various ways. There can be intrusive memories, recurrent disturbing dreams, or the feeling that the event is indeed recurring (as in "flashbacks" to the event). Have you ever been awakened by a nightmare and been reluctant to return to sleep for fear of re-entering the dream? Nightmares that are part of traumatic stress reactions often involve the re-experiencing of the traumatic event, which can lead to abrupt awakenings and difficulty falling back to sleep because of fear associated with the nightmare and elevated levels of arousal. Other features of heightened arousal include irritability or anger outbursts, reckless or self-destructive behaviour, hypervigilance (being continuously on guard), difficulty concentrating, and an exaggerated startle response (jumping in response to sudden noises or other stimuli) (APA, 2013).

Exposure to events that resemble the traumatic experience can cause intense psychological distress. People with traumatic stress reactions tend to avoid stimuli that evoke recollections of the trauma. For example, they may not be able to handle a television account or a friend's wish to talk about it. They may have feelings of detachment or estrangement from other people. They may show less responsiveness to the external world after the traumatic event, losing the ability to enjoy previously preferred activities or to have loving feelings. In the case of ASD, there may be an inability to perform necessary tasks, such as obtaining needed medical or legal assistance, or a failure to mobilize one's resources to obtain support from family as the result of not informing family members about the traumatic experience (APA, 2013).

Acute stress disorder is further characterized by extreme anxiety and **dissociation**—feelings of detachment from oneself or one's environment. People with an acute stress disorder may feel they are "in a daze" or that the world seems unreal. A soldier may

acute stress disorder Traumatic stress reaction occurring in the days and weeks following exposure to a traumatic event. Abbreviated *ASD*.

posttraumatic stress disorder Disorder involving impaired functioning following exposure to a traumatic experience, such as combat, physical assault or rape, or natural or technological disasters, in which the person experiences, for at least one month, such problems as reliving or re-experiencing the trauma, intense fear, avoidance of event-related stimuli, generalized numbing of emotional responsiveness, and heightened autonomic arousal. Abbreviated *PTSD*.

dissociation Feelings of detachment from oneself or one's environment.

come through a horrific battle not remembering important features of the battle and feeling numb and detached from the environment. People who are injured or who nearly lose their lives in a hurricane, tsunami, or ice storm may walk around "in a fog" for days or weeks afterward. Those who have severe and persistent symptoms of dissociation are at greater risk of developing PTSD (Cardeña & Carlson, 2011). Surveys suggest that about 7–9% of Canadian and US adults are affected by PTSD at some point in their lives (Keane, Marshall, & Taft, 2006; Van Ameringen, Mancini, Pipe, & Boyle, 2004).

Exposure to trauma is quite common in the general population. More than three quarters of Canadians report having been exposed to a traumatic event (Katzman et al., 2014). The lifetime prevalence of traumatic stressors is illustrated in Table 3.9, which presents the results from a national survey of nearly 3000 Canadians (Van Ameringen, Mancini, Patterson, & Boyle, 2008). As in previous studies, the investigators found that men were generally more likely to experience traumatic stressors, although women were more likely to experience particular stressors such as sexual assault. Although men generally encounter more traumatic experiences, women are more likely to develop PTSD in response to trauma (Tolin & Foa, 2006). Olff and colleagues (Olff, Langeland, Draijer, & Gersons, 2007) propose that women's increased risk may be due to the type of trauma they experience, their younger age at the time of trauma exposure, their stronger perceptions of threat and loss of control, higher levels of dissociation, insufficient social support resources, and greater use of alcohol to manage trauma-related symptoms such as intrusive memories and psychobiological reactions to trauma.

TABLE 3.9

Lifetime Prevalence of Traumatic Events in a National Sample of 2991 Canadians Aged 18 and Over

Type of Traumatic Exposure	Men (%)	Women (%)
Assaultive violence		
Sexual assault	3.3	19.1
Sexual molestation	10.2	32.8
Being badly beaten	8.6	9.7
Mugged/threatened with a weapon	21.1	11.1
Kidnapped	1.2	1.6
Participated in combat	7.9	0.8
Other injury or shock		
Witnessed someone killed, dead, or badly injured	41.0	23.5
Witnessed physical domestic violence as a child	7.9	10.5
Life-threatening motor vehicle accident	22.9	13.1
Witnessed atrocities	4.8	2.1
Refugee	2.5	1.8
Involved in serious work related accident	13.6	2.5
Involved in major natural disaster	17.8	13.6
Exposed to toxic chemicals	15.4	5.1
Peacekeeper/relief worker	3.2	0.8
Other trauma	10.5	6.9
Learning about others		
Trauma experienced by someone else	15.7	17.8
Sudden unexpected death	39.9	42.2

Source: Van Ameringen, Mancini, Patterson, & Boyle, © 2008. *CNS Neuroscience & Therapeutics.* Blackwell Publishing Ltd. Reproduced with permission of John Wiley & Sons, Inc.

Christophe Ena/AP Images

Roméo Dallaire. Dallaire, the former head of the doomed United Nations peacekeeping mission in Rwanda, was discharged from the military for PTSD a few years after the 1994 mission, in which his force tried in vain to stop the slaughter of 800 000 to 1 million Tutsis and moderate Hutus. He attempted suicide several times before learning to cope thanks to medication and therapy. Dallaire says about the effects of PTSD, "Post-traumatic stress disorder hardwires events in your brain to the extent they will come back in digitally clear detail to your brain. You don't actually remember them. You relive them" (Canadian Press, 2007).

There are, unfortunately, many different examples of traumatic stressors leading to PTSD. Many Canadian Indigenous individuals were abused and developed PTSD after being removed from their communities and placed in residential schools (Söchting, 2004). An estimated 19% of US Vietnam War veterans developed PTSD (Dohrenwend et al., 2006). A Canadian government report acknowledged that PTSD is an important problem for the Canadian military and that more resources are needed to identify and treat people afflicted with this disorder (Marin, 2001). According to some estimates, as many as 10–20% of Canadian armed forces personnel, especially among those stationed in hot spots like Afghanistan, have developed PTSD (Wente, 2006). Some of the survivors of school shootings, such as the Columbine High School massacre (1999) and some survivors of the Montreal shootings at École Polytechnique (1989), Concordia University (1992), and Dawson College (2006), also may have developed PTSD, although the precise figures are unknown. After the September 11, 2001, terrorist attacks on New York's World Trade Center, about 8% of Manhattan residents developed PTSD (Galea et al., 2002). Most were traumatized because they were in the vicinity of the towers. The effect of this experience was apparently worsened when these residents saw television images of people falling or jumping from the towers (Ahern et al., 2002). To put a face to these tragedies, consider the following case:

Jennifer Charron, a Canadian-born graphic artist, had studios in World Trade Center's north tower, on the 91st and 92nd floors. Jennifer slept late on the morning of September 11, 2001, planning to go to her studios later in the afternoon. She heard about the first jet on the radio, and rushed to her apartment window just in time to see the unthinkable happen again. "I watched this big plane come across the sky and slam into the south tower," the 30-year-old recalls. "I close my eyes [today] and I can still see it." Jennifer spent the rest of September 11 on the phone trying to account for co-workers, numbed by the thought of how things might have been for her if the terrorists had struck in mid-afternoon. "You couldn't get away from it. You were constantly reminded," recalls Jennifer. Emotionally exhausted, she quit her job and returned to Ontario. "My favourite part of being back in Canada is that I don't think about it every day."

Not everyone who experiences trauma develops traumatic stress reactions. There are many important factors influencing a person's resiliency or vulnerability (Bonnano, 2005; Gabert-Quillen, Fallon, & Delahanty, 2011; Taylor, 2005). Vulnerability factors include a person's degree of neurobiological responsivity to traumatic experiences; the severity of the trauma and degree of exposure; the use of coping responses to stress; the availability of posttrauma social support; and perhaps perceptions of helplessness and leftover emotional effects, such as guilt and depression (Taylor, 2005). Cognitive factors also play a role. The individual's subjective rating of the severity of his or her injuries is a better predictor of PTSD than an objective evaluation (Gabert-Quillen et al., 2011).

The risk of being traumatized and developing PTSD is higher for people living in war-torn countries and for those engaging in hazardous activities or occupations. The latter was dramatically illustrated by a study of 100 women working as prostitutes in Vancouver (Farley, Lynne, & Cotton, 2005). Ninety percent of these women had been physically assaulted in prostitution. Many reported stabbings and beatings, concussions, and broken bones (e.g., jaws, ribs, collarbones, fingers), as well as cuts, black eyes, and other injuries—often incurred when they refused to perform specific sexual acts. Most of the women (72%) were classified as having PTSD, and 95% said they wanted to leave prostitution but felt unable to do so. Police officers and individuals who work in emergency services are also at greater risk for stress-related disorders. Cheryl Regehr (from the University of Toronto) and colleagues examined the prevalence of PTSD symptoms among emergency dispatchers and reported a rate of 31% in this population (Regehr, LeBlanc, Barath, Balch, & Birze, 2013).

Refugees have higher rates of PTSD and other mental disorders compared to other immigrants and the general population (Kirmayer et al., 2011). Recent refugees suffer from far more than the traumas they left behind. Although exposure to trauma certainly increases the risk of mental illness, those that end up displaced suffer a greater toll (Porter & Haslam, 2001). Their displacement, which occurred out of necessity rather than choice, forced them to leave behind their home, their community, their careers, as well as their vision of their future (Porter & Haslam, 2001). Only time will tell how the recent influx of refugees from Syria into Canada and other countries will adjust to the many stressors inherent in their relocation.

To learn more about the vulnerability of certain individuals, researchers have been focusing on the hippocampus in the brain. Researchers have also looked at the size of the hippocampus in people with and without PTSD. They have found that people who have severe, chronic cases of PTSD have smaller hippocampi. The researchers have taken this to suggest that the experience of constant stress as a result of severe and chronic PTSD may ultimately damage the hippocampus, making it smaller (Kolassa & Elbert, 2007).

On the other hand, it has also been proposed that the hippocampus may play a role in determining who is at risk for developing PTSD. Some people may be born with a smaller hippocampus, which could interfere with their ability to recover from a traumatic experience, putting them at risk for developing PTSD. In other words, a smaller hippocampus may be a sign that a person is vulnerable or more likely to develop PTSD after a traumatic experience (Gilbertson et al., 2002).

Although PTSD may wax and wane over time, it can last for years, even decades. Yet there is some good news: People who obtain treatment for PTSD typically recover sooner from its symptoms than those who do not seek help (Taylor, 2005).

REVIEW IT

Anxiety Disorders, Obsessive-Compulsive Disorder, and Trauma- and Stressor-Related Disorders

- **What is panic disorder?** Panic disorder is characterized by repeated panic attacks, which involve intense physical features, notably cardiovascular symptoms, and which may be accompanied by sheer terror and fears of losing control, losing one's mind, or dying. Panic disorder is often associated with agoraphobia.

- **What is agoraphobia?** Individuals with agoraphobia fear places or situations from which it might be difficult or embarrassing to escape or get assistance in the event of panic-like symptoms.

- **What is generalized anxiety disorder?** Generalized anxiety disorder is a type of anxiety disorder involving persistent anxiety and worry that seems to be "free floating" or not tied to specific situations.

- **What are phobic disorders?** Phobias are excessive fears of specific objects or situations. Phobias involve a behavioural component—avoidance of the phobic stimulus—in addition to physical and cognitive features. Specific phobias are excessive fears of particular

objects or situations, such as mice, spiders, tight places, or heights. Social anxiety disorder involves an intense fear of being judged negatively by others.

- **What is obsessive-compulsive disorder?** Obsessive-compulsive disorder, or OCD, involves recurrent patterns of obsessions, compulsions, or a combination of the two. Obsessions are nagging, persistent thoughts that create anxiety and seem beyond a person's ability to control. Compulsions are irresistible repetitious urges to perform certain behaviours, such as repeated elaborate handwashing after using a bathroom.

- **What are acute and posttraumatic stress disorders?** Both acute stress disorder (ASD) and posttraumatic stress disorder (PTSD) involve maladaptive stress reactions that follow exposure to traumatic events. ASD occurs in the days and weeks following exposure to a traumatic event. PTSD persists for months or even years or decades after the traumatic experience and may not begin until months or years after the event.

THEORETICAL PERSPECTIVES

The anxiety disorders and obsessive-compulsive disorders offer something of a theoretical laboratory. Many theories of abnormal behaviour were developed with these disorders in mind. Here, we consider the contributions of these theoretical perspectives to our understanding of these disorders.

Psychodynamic Perspectives

From the psychodynamic perspective, anxiety is a danger signal that threatening impulses of a sexual or aggressive (murderous) nature are nearing the level of awareness. To fend off these threatening impulses, the ego tries to stem or divert the tide by mobilizing its defence mechanisms. For example, with phobias, the defence mechanisms of **projection** and displacement come into play. A phobic reaction is believed to involve the projection of a person's own threatening impulses onto a phobic object. For instance, a fear of knives or other sharp instruments may represent the projection of one's own destructive impulses onto the phobic object. The phobia serves a useful function. Avoiding contact with sharp instruments prevents these destructive wishes from becoming consciously realized or acted on. The threatening impulses remain safely repressed. Similarly, people with acrophobia may harbour unconscious wishes to jump that are controlled by avoiding heights. The phobic object or situation symbolizes or represents these unconscious wishes or

projection In psychodynamic theory, a defence mechanism in which one's own impulses are attributed to another person.

desires. The person is aware of the phobia but not of the unconscious impulses that it symbolizes.

Freud's (1909/1959) historic case of "Little Hans," a five-year-old boy who feared he would be bitten by a horse if he left his house, illustrates his principle of displacement. Freud hypothesized that Hans's fear of horses represented the displacement of an unconscious fear of his father. According to Freud's conception of the Oedipus complex, boys have unconscious incestuous desires to possess their mothers and fears of retribution from their fathers, whom they see as rivals in love. Hans's fear of being bitten by horses thus symbolized an underlying fear of castration.

A learning theorist view of Hans's childhood fear would suggest that he "learned" it from being frightened by an accident involving a horse and a transport vehicle, which generalized to a fear of horses. The story of Little Hans has sparked a spirited debate in the psychological annals.

Applying the psychodynamic model to other anxiety disorders, we might hypothesize that in generalized anxiety disorder, unconscious conflicts remain hidden but anxiety leaks through to the level of awareness. The person is unable to account for the anxiety because its source remains shrouded in the unconscious. In panic disorder, unacceptable sexual or aggressive impulses approach the boundaries of consciousness and the ego strives desperately to repress them, generating high levels of conflict that bring on a full-fledged panic attack. Panic dissipates when the impulse has been safely repressed.

Obsessions are believed to represent the leakage of unconscious impulses into consciousness, and compulsions are acts that help keep these impulses repressed. Obsessive thoughts about contamination by dirt or germs may represent the threatened emergence of unconscious infantile wishes to soil oneself and play with feces. The compulsion (in this case, cleanliness rituals) helps keep such wishes at bay or partly repressed.

The psychodynamic model remains largely speculative, in large part because of the difficulty (some would say impossibility) of arranging scientific tests to determine the existence of the unconscious impulses and conflicts believed to lie at the root of these disorders.

Behavioural Perspectives

From the behavioural perspective, anxiety disorders are acquired through the process of conditioning. According to O. Hobart Mowrer's (1948) **two-factor model**, both classical and operant conditioning are involved in the development of phobias. The fear component of phobia is assumed to be acquired by means of classical conditioning. It is assumed that previously neutral objects and situations gain the capacity to evoke fear by being paired with noxious or aversive stimuli. A child who is frightened by a barking dog may acquire a phobia of dogs. A child who receives a painful injection may develop a phobia of hypodermic syringes. Consistent with this model, evidence shows that many cases of acrophobia, claustrophobia, and blood and injection phobias involve earlier pairings of the phobic object with aversive experiences (Cox & Taylor, 1999).

As Mowrer pointed out, the avoidance component of phobias is acquired and maintained by operant conditioning. That is, relief from anxiety negatively reinforces avoiding fear-inducing stimuli. A person with an elevator phobia learns to avoid anxiety over taking the elevator by opting for the stairs instead. Avoiding the phobic stimulus thus lessens anxiety, which negatively reinforces the avoidance behaviour. Yet there is a significant cost to avoiding the phobic stimulus. The person is not able to "unlearn" (extinguish) the fear via exposure to the phobic stimulus in the absence of any aversive consequences.

Learning theorists have also noted the role of observational learning in acquiring fears. Modelling (observing parents or others reacting fearfully to a stimulus) and receiving negative information (hearing from others or reading that particular stimuli—spiders, for example—are fearful or disgusting) may also lead to phobias (Field, 2006).

Some investigators suggest that people may be genetically prepared to acquire phobic responses more readily to certain classes of stimuli than to others (Mineka & Zinbarg,

two-factor model O. Hobart Mowrer's theory that both operant and classical conditioning are involved in the acquisition of phobic responses. The fear component of phobia is acquired by means of classical conditioning (pairing of a previously neutral stimulus with an aversive stimulus), and the avoidance component is acquired by means of operant conditioning (relief from anxiety negatively reinforces avoidance behaviour).

prepared conditioning Belief that people are genetically prepared to acquire fear responses to certain classes of stimuli, such as fears of large animals, snakes, heights, or strangers. Although the development of such phobias may have had survival value for prehistoric ancestors, such behaviour patterns may be less functional today.

2006). We're more likely to learn to fear spiders than rabbits, for example. This model, called **prepared conditioning**, suggests that evolutionary forces would have favoured the survival of human ancestors who were genetically predisposed to acquire fears of threatening objects, such as large animals, snakes, and other creepy-crawlies, and of heights, enclosed spaces, and strangers.

Posttraumatic stress disorder may also be explained from a conditioning framework. From a classical conditioning perspective, traumatic experiences function as unconditioned stimuli that become paired with neutral (conditioned) stimuli such as the sights, sounds, and smells associated with the trauma scene—for example, the battlefield or the neighbourhood in which a person has been raped or assaulted (Taylor, 2005). Subsequent exposure to similar stimuli evokes the anxiety (a conditioned emotional response) associated with PTSD. The conditioned stimuli that reactivate the conditioned response include visits to the scene and memories or dream images of the trauma. Consequently, the person avoids these stimuli. Avoidance is an operant response, which is reinforced by relief from anxiety. However, avoidance prolongs PTSD because sufferers do not have the opportunity to learn to manage their conditioned reactions. Extinction (gradual weakening or elimination) of conditioned anxiety may occur only when conditioned stimuli (i.e., cues associated with the trauma) are presented in a supportive therapeutic setting in the absence of the troubling unconditioned stimuli.

From a learning perspective, generalized anxiety is precisely that: a product of stimulus generalization. People concerned about broad life themes, such as finances, health, and family matters, are likely to experience their apprehensions in a variety of settings. Anxiety would thus become connected with almost any environment or situation. Similarly, agoraphobia would represent a kind of generalized fear triggered by cues associated with various situations in which it might be hazardous or embarrassing to have a panic attack (such as travelling far from home or being in a shopping mall). Some learning theorists assume that panic attacks, which appear to descend out of nowhere, are triggered by cues that are subtle and not readily identified.

There are challenges to the learning theory account of phobias. For example, many people with phobias insist that they cannot recall painful exposures to the dreaded stimuli. Learning theorists may assume that such memory failures are understandable because many phobias are acquired in early childhood. Yet many phobias, such as social anxiety disorder, develop at later ages and appear to involve cognitive processes relating to an exaggerated appraisal of threat in social situations (excessive fears of embarrassment or criticism) rather than the pairing of these situations with aversive experiences.

From the learning perspective, compulsive behaviours are operant responses that are negatively reinforced by relief of the anxiety engendered by obsessional thoughts. If a person obsesses that dirt or foreign bodies contaminate other people's hands, shaking hands or turning a doorknob may evoke powerful anxiety. Compulsive handwashing following exposure to a possible contaminant provides some relief from anxiety. The person thus becomes more likely to repeat the obsessive-compulsive cycle the next time he or she is exposed to anxiety-evoking cues such as shaking hands or touching doorknobs.

Cognitive Perspectives

Cognitive theorists and researchers focus on how dysfunctional patterns of thinking may set the stage for the disorders covered in this chapter. Here, we examine some of the most common thinking patterns associated with these disorders.

SELF-DEFEATING OR IRRATIONAL BELIEFS Self-defeating thoughts can heighten and perpetuate anxiety disorders. When faced with fear-evoking stimuli, a person may think "I've got to get out of here" or "My heart is going to burst out of my chest" (Antony & Swinson, 2000). Thoughts like these intensify autonomic arousal, disrupt planning, magnify the aversiveness of stimuli, prompt avoidance behaviour, and decrease one's confidence about controlling a situation.

Irrational beliefs may involve exaggerated needs to be approved of by everyone one meets and to avoid any situation in which negative appraisal from others might arise (Hofmann, 2008). The following is one such example: "What if I have an anxiety attack in front of other people? They might think I'm crazy!"

Cognitive theorists relate obsessive-compulsive disorder to tendencies to exaggerate the risk of unfortunate events (Clark, 2004). Because people with OCD expect terrible things to happen, they engage in rituals to prevent them. An accountant who imagines awful consequences for slight mistakes on a client's tax forms may feel compelled to repeatedly check her or his work. Other irrational beliefs, such as perfectionism, also enter the picture (Moretz & McKay, 2009; Taylor & Jang, 2011). The perfectionist exaggerates the consequences of turning in less-than-perfect work and may feel compelled to redo his or her efforts until every detail is flawless.

Cognitive theorists further argue that obsessions arise as a result of trying too hard to control one's thinking (Clark, 2004). All of us, from time to time, have unwanted, intrusive thoughts. These are the mental flotsam that drifts along the stream of consciousness, which some theorists have called "normal obsessions." Compared to obsessions in OCD, normal obsessions are easier to dismiss, are less frequent, cause less discomfort, and are less likely to lead to compulsions (Taylor, Abramowitz, & McKay, 2006). Normal obsessions are extremely common. Among a sample of 293 students from the University of New Brunswick, 99% acknowledged having at least one unwanted intrusive thought, impulse, or image. Women were more likely to have unwanted harm-related thoughts (e.g., leaving the stove on, running the car off the road), whereas men were more likely to have unwanted sexual thoughts (e.g., seeing strangers naked, having sex with an authority figure) (Purdon & Clark, 1993). Researchers at the University of Toronto and Northwestern University also reported evidence of normal compulsions; individuals are more likely to wash their hands if they believe that they might have behaved immorally (Zhong & Liljenquist, 2006). This suggests that people tend to associate moral impurity with physical dirtiness. This association may be particularly strong in people with OCD.

If nearly everyone experiences normal obsessions, then why do only some people develop more severe and frequent obsessions, such as those characterizing OCD? Part of the answer seems to lie in the way a person appraises his or her unwanted intrusive thoughts (Janeck, Calamari, Riemann, & Heffelfinger, 2003). Irrational beliefs about intrusive thoughts are likely to increase one's odds of developing clinical obsessions. According to Shams and Milosevic (from Concordia University), the thinking pattern that most differentiates individuals with OCD from those with a different anxiety disorder is the belief they can and should have total control over their thoughts (Shams & Milosevic, 2015). Research by University of Waterloo psychologist Christine Purdon suggests that people with OCD may become particularly upset about their failure to suppress their obsessions, which may make the person anxious and depressed and thereby worsen his or her OCD (Purdon, Rowa, & Antony, 2005). Similarly, research by Amy Janeck (from the University of British Columbia) and colleagues reveals that individuals with OCD are excessively preoccupied with their thoughts; they are highly aware of them and monitor them while engaging in "too much thinking about thinking" (Janeck et al., 2003). This may be because people with OCD regard their obsessions as unacceptable and repugnant. To add to the cognitive difficulties experienced by people with OCD, research by investigators including Sean Radomsky (from Concordia University) has shown that repeated checking undermines memory confidence (Radomsky, Gilchrist, & Dussault, 2006). For example, the more you check and recheck that a stove has been properly switched off by repeatedly turning it on and off, the more uncertain you will be later on about whether you finally did switch off the stove. This is apparently because repeated checking makes it more difficult to visually recall the last check as opposed to previous checks (Radomsky et al., 2006). It is not known whether the same applies to other compulsions such as repeated handwashing.

The distinction between normal and abnormal obsessions is illustrated by two examples from our case files:

Julia was carving a Halloween pumpkin for her young daughter. As she wielded the knife, she had the unwanted intrusive image of stabbing her daughter. This greatly frightened Julia—she believed that "the unwanted image means that, subconsciously, I must want to kill my daughter." Julia desperately tried to push the image out of her mind, and became greatly alarmed when it returned. Because she placed so much significance on it, the image became highly important to her, and therefore kept popping into her mind.

In comparison, one of our colleagues, Sandy, had a similar unwanted image of stabbing her daughter while carving a Halloween pumpkin. Sandy believed the image was "mental garbage." She ignored the image and continued carving. The image held no significance for Sandy and therefore did not return.

The Authors' Files

OVERSENSITIVITY TO THREAT An oversensitivity to threatening cues is a cardinal feature of anxiety disorders (Beck & Clark, 1997; Clark & Beck, 2010). People with phobias perceive danger in situations that most people consider safe, such as riding in elevators or driving over bridges. We all possess an internal alarm system that is sensitive to cues of threat. This system may have had evolutionary advantages to ancestral humans by increasing the chances of survival in a hostile environment (Beck & Clark, 1997). Ancestral humans who responded quickly to any sign of threat, such as a rustling sound in a bush that may have indicated a lurking predator about to pounce, may have been better prepared to take defensive action (to fight or flee) than those with less sensitive alarm systems. The emotion of fear is a key element in this alarm system and may have helped out ancestors survive. People today who have anxiety disorders may have inherited an acutely sensitive internal alarm that leads them to be overly responsive to cues of threat. Rather than helping them cope effectively with threats, it may lead to inappropriate anxiety reactions in response to a wide range of cues that actually pose no danger to them.

Research led by Michel Dugas from Concordia University suggests that the intolerance of uncertainty plays an important role in GAD (Buhr & Dugas, 2006). This intolerance is a special sort of sensitivity to threat that arises from the belief that it is unacceptable that threatening things occur. People who are intolerant of uncertainty become upset by the possibility of threatening events even when the probability of these events is very small. Considering that daily life is fraught with uncertainties, people who are intolerant of uncertainty are likely to frequently worry and become anxious about threats.

anxiety sensitivity A "fear of fear," or fear that one's emotions or states of bodily arousal will get out of control and lead to harmful consequences.

ANXIETY SENSITIVITY **Anxiety sensitivity** is a fear of fear. It refers to beliefs that internal emotions or bodily arousal will get out of control, leading to harmful consequences (Taylor, 2000; Ho et al., 2011). People with a high degree of anxiety sensitivity may be prone to panic when they experience bodily signs of anxiety, such as a racing heart or shortness of breath, because they take these symptoms to be signs of an impending catastrophe, such as a heart attack. Evidence collected at the University of British Columbia and elsewhere suggests that anxiety sensitivity is influenced by a combination of genetic factors and learning experiences. The latter teach people to be afraid of anxiety-related sensations—for example, observing one's parents becoming frightened of sensations such as rapid heartbeat or shortness of breath (Stewart et al., 2001).

Anxiety sensitivity is an important risk factor for panic attacks, as indicated by longitudinal research (Schmidt, Zvolensky, & Maner, 2006). As we will see next, panic-prone individuals also tend to misattribute changes in their bodily sensations to dire consequences.

MISATTRIBUTIONS OF PANIC SENSATIONS Cognitive models of panic disorder assume that panic attacks involve catastrophic misinterpretations of such bodily sensations as heart palpitations, dizziness, or light-headedness (Clark, 1986; Teachman, Smith-Janik, & Saporito, 2007). Rather than attribute changes in physical sensations to more neutral causes, panic-prone people believe they represent the first signs of an impending heart attack or other threatening event such as a loss of control or "going crazy." Changes in bodily sensations in otherwise healthy individuals may be induced by various factors such as unrecognized hyperventilation, temperature changes, or reactions to certain drugs or medications. Or they may be fleeting, normally occurring changes in bodily states that typically go unnoticed by most people.

A cognitive model of panic disorder involving an interaction of cognitive and physiological factors is depicted in Figure 3.2. The model suggests that people with a proneness to panic disorder perceive certain internal bodily cues or external stimuli as unduly threatening or dangerous, perhaps because they are overly sensitive to these cues or have associated them with earlier panic attacks. The sense of threat induces anxiety or feelings of apprehension, which intensify physical sensations by producing an accelerated heart rate, rapid breathing, and sweating, among other bodily symptoms. These changes in bodily sensations, in turn, are misinterpreted as signs of an impending panic attack or, worse, an imminent catastrophe ("I'm having a heart attack!"), which in either case reinforces perceptions of threat, which further heightens anxiety, leading to yet more anxiety-related bodily symptoms, and so on in a vicious cycle that can quickly spiral to a full-fledged panic attack. Thus, catastrophic misinterpretations of bodily cues may set into motion a vicious cycle that brings on panic attacks in panic-prone individuals.

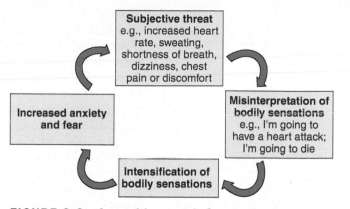

FIGURE 3.2   A cognitive model of panic disorder. This model involves the interaction of cognitive and physiological factors. In panic-prone people, perceptions of threat from internal or external cues lead to feelings of apprehension or anxiety, which lead to changes in body sensations (e.g., cardiovascular symptoms). These changes lead, in turn, to catastrophic interpretations, thereby intensifying the perception of threat, which further heightens anxiety, and so on in a vicious cycle that may culminate in a full-blown panic attack.

Source: Dozois, *Abnormal Psychology: Perspectives*, 6th edition, pg. 102. Pearson Canada, 2019. Reprinted with permission by Pearson Canada.

Mounting evidence points to the important role of cognitive factors in anxiety disorders. As the cognitive model would predict, for instance, people with panic disorder do have a greater tendency to misinterpret bodily sensations as signs of impending catastrophe than do people without anxiety disorders or those with other types of anxiety disorders (Mathews & MacLeod, 2005). Studies also show, as the cognitive model would predict, that panic-prone people have greater awareness of and sensitivity to their internal physiological cues, such as heart palpitations (Taylor, 1999, 2000). More research is needed, however, to determine the extent to which cognitive factors play a direct causal role in panic disorder or other anxiety disorders.

In addition to irrational beliefs and misinterpretations, other sorts of cognitive factors appear to play an important role in anxiety disorders. Research shows that people with anxiety disorders, compared to people without them, are more likely to selectively attend to threatening information, and there is some evidence that people with anxiety disorders are more likely to selectively remember threatening information (Mathews & MacLeod, 2005). These biases in attention and memory make intuitive sense; if you're anxious or frightened of something—say, spiders—then you're more likely to search for sources of potential threat (e.g., scanning a room for spiders) and you're more likely to recall where you've seen spiders in the past. The biases in attention and memory could be either vulnerability factors or a consequence of anxiety disorders, and they could worsen the disorders by increasing the chances that a person would notice or remember anxiety-provoking things.

Biological Perspectives

We also have a growing body of evidence that biological factors play a role in anxiety disorders. Many questions remain concerning the interactions of biological and other factors, however.

GENETIC FACTORS Increasing evidence points to the role of genetic factors in anxiety disorders. Consistent with a genetic contribution, studies of twin pairs reveal higher concordance (agreement) rates between MZ (monozygotic or identical twins) than between DZ (dizygotic or fraternal) twins for many anxiety disorders (Kendler & Prescott, 2006). Research conducted at the University of British Columbia, for example, suggests that social anxiety and PTSD symptoms are influenced, at least to some extent, by genes (Stein, Jang, & Livesley, 2002; Stein, Jang, Taylor, Vernon, & Livesley, 2002). Table 3.10, for example, shows the heritability coefficients for trauma exposure and PTSD symptoms. Findings from the Canadian civilian sample (Stein, Jang, Taylor, Vernon, & Livesley, 2002) are compared with results from a US Vietnam-era twin registry (Lyons et al., 1993). Heritability coefficients range from 0 to 1, with larger numbers indicating that genes make a greater contribution to the variability of the variable in question. The results in Table 3.10 show two important things: First, genes make a significant but modest contribution to PTSD symptoms in both civilian and Vietnam-era populations; and second, the risk of experiencing a traumatic event is also influenced by genes. For example, the chances of being mugged, beaten up in a bar fight, or sexually assaulted (examples of assaultive trauma) are all moderately heritable. Research from the University of British Columbia suggests that the genes that contribute to assaultive trauma are the same ones that contribute to antisocial personality traits (Jang, Stein, Taylor, Asmundson, & Livesley, 2003). In other words, if you have antisocial tendencies (as illustrated, for example, by a tendency to engage in criminal behaviour or to hang around with criminals in dangerous parts of town), then your risk increases for being exposed to certain types of traumatic events.

Many different genes are probably involved in the etiology of anxiety disorders, with each gene making a small, additive contribution to a person's risk of developing these disorders (Leonardo & Hen, 2006). There is no single gene for any of them. The process of "gene hunting" is a slow, laborious one, and many initial discoveries are not replicated in later research. So when you read a newspaper article announcing that researchers have discovered "the" gene for, say, panic disorder, you need to ask the all-important question of whether the findings have been replicated.

Research replicated in several studies suggests that some genes have narrow effects, influencing a person's risk for developing a particular anxiety disorder. For example, genetic factors for phobias may specifically influence fear conditioning. Other genes

---

TABLE 3.10

Heritability Coefficients for Trauma Exposure and PTSD Symptoms

Variable	Canadian Civilian Twin Sample (UBC Twin Study)	US Vietnam-Era Twin Sample
Trauma Exposure		
Assaultive trauma	0.20	—
Volunteered for SEA* service	—	0.36
SEA* service	—	0.35
Combat exposure	—	0.47
Received combat decoration	—	0.54
PTSD Symptoms		
Re-experiencing	0.36	0.25
Avoidance	0.28	0.00
Numbing	0.36	0.28
Hyperarousal	0.29	0.26

*SEA = Southeast Asia. Heritability coefficients range from 0 to 1. The larger the number, the greater the influence of genetic factors on the variability of the variable in question.

Source: Based on Data synthesized from Lyons et al., 1993, Stein et al., 2002, and True et al., 1993.

have broader effects, influencing the risk for many different types of anxiety disorders as well as the risk for other disorders (Kendler & Prescott, 2006). The genes with broad effects may be the ones linked to **neuroticism**. Neuroticism is not an anxiety disorder but a personality trait characterized by an enduring tendency to experience negative emotional states. People with high levels of neuroticism (also called *negative emotionality* or *internalizing*) tend to cope poorly with stress and frequently experience feelings of anxiety, anger, guilt, and depression. People high on this trait are at increased risk of developing anxiety disorders and other emotional problems (Krueger & Markon, 2006).

A growing body of research suggests that genes exert their influence by interacting with particular environmental events (Moffitt, Caspi, & Rutter, 2006). For example, people possessing a particular form of a gene involved in the serotonin neurotransmitter system (i.e., the "short" version of the serotonin-transporter gene) are more likely than people without this genetic variant to react to stressful life events by developing anxiety or depressive symptoms (Leonardo & Hen, 2006). In other words, both genes and the environment are important; people with genetic vulnerability for developing anxiety disorders appear to be at risk primarily when they experience particular sorts of environmental events.

neuroticism Trait describing a general neurotic quality involving such characteristics as anxious, worrisome behaviour; apprehension about the future; and avoidance behaviour.

NEUROTRANSMITTERS The neurotransmitter **gamma-aminobutyric acid (GABA)** is implicated in anxiety. GABA is an inhibitory neurotransmitter, which means it helps tone down excess activity in the nervous system by preventing neurons from overly exciting their neighbours. When the action of GABA is inadequate, neurons can fire excessively, possibly bringing about seizures. In less dramatic cases, inadequate action of GABA may contribute to states of anxiety. This view of the role of GABA is supported by the action of the family of anti-anxiety drugs referred to as **benzodiazepines**, which include the well-known Valium and Ativan. Benzodiazepines regulate GABA receptors, thus enhancing GABA's calming (inhibitory) effects (Lydiard, 2003).

Dysfunctions involving serotonin or norepinephrine receptors in the brain have also been implicated in anxiety disorders (Baldwin, 2006). This may explain why so-called antidepressant drugs that affect these neurotransmitter systems in the brain often have beneficial effects in treating some types of anxiety disorders. Investigators also suspect that genes involved in the regulation of serotonin may play a role in determining symptoms of anxiety and depression (Hariri & Brown, 2006).

gamma-aminobutyric acid An inhibitory neurotransmitter believed to play a role in regulating anxiety. Abbreviated *GABA*.

benzodiazepines Class of minor tranquillizers that includes Valium and Ativan.

BIOLOGICAL ASPECTS OF PANIC DISORDER The strong physical components of panic disorder have led some theorists to speculate that panic attacks have biological underpinnings, perhaps involving an underlying brain dysfunction (Gorman, Kent, Sullivan, & Coplan, 2000). Support for a biological basis of panic disorder is found in studies showing that people with panic disorder are more likely than people without to experience panicky symptoms in response to certain biological challenges, such as infusion of the chemical sodium lactate or manipulation of carbon dioxide (CO_2) levels in the blood either by intentional hyperventilation (which reduces levels of CO_2 in the blood) or inhalation of carbon dioxide (which increases CO_2 levels) (Barlow, 2002; Coryell, Pine, Fyer, & Klein, 2006).

There appears to be a similarity between (1) the physiological and behavioural consequences of response to a conditioned fear stimulus and (2) a panic attack. In animals, these responses are mediated by a "fear network" in the brain that is centred in the amygdala and involves its interaction with the hippocampus and medial prefrontal cortex. Projections from the amygdala to hypothalamic and brain stem sites explain many of the observed signs of conditioned fear responses. It is speculated that a similar network is involved in panic disorder. A convergence of evidence suggests that both inheritable factors and stressful life events,

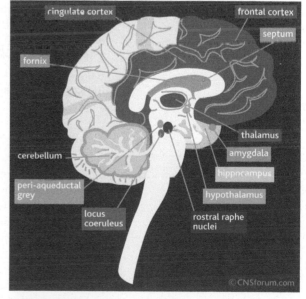

©CNS Forum.com

The fear network. In panic attacks, responses to fear are mediated by the "fear network" centred in the amygdala and involve interaction with the hippocampus and medial prefrontal cortex.

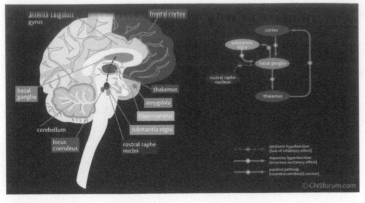

© CNS Forum.com

OCD and the brain. Patients with OCD exhibit increased activity in the neurotransmitter circuits between the cortex, basal ganglia, and thalamus. There seems to be a lack of inhibitory effect on the OCD pathway.

particularly in early childhood, are responsible for the onset of panic disorder (Gorman et al., 2000).

Cognitive theorists propose that cognitive factors may be involved in explaining these biological sensitivities. Theorists point out that biological challenges produce intense physical sensations that may be catastrophically misinterpreted by panic-prone people as signs of an impending heart attack or loss of control (Antony, Ledley, Liss, & Swinson, 2006). Perhaps these misinterpretations—not underlying biological sensitivities—may in turn induce panic.

Supportive evidence for the cognitive perspective comes from research showing that cognitive-behavioural therapy, which focuses on changing faulty interpretations of bodily sensations, eliminates CO_2-induced panic in panic disorder patients (Barlow, 2002).

The fact that panic attacks often seem to come out of the blue also seems to support the belief that the attacks are biologically triggered. However, it is possible the cues that set off many panic attacks may be internal, involving changes in bodily sensations, rather than external. Changes in physical cues combined with catastrophic thinking may lead to a spiralling of anxiety that culminates in a full-blown panic attack.

BIOLOGICAL ASPECTS OF OBSESSIVE-COMPULSIVE DISORDER Another biological model that receives attention suggests that obsessive-compulsive disorder may involve heightened arousal of a particular anxiety circuit, a neural network in the brain involved in signalling danger. In OCD, the brain may be constantly sending messages that something is wrong and requires immediate attention, leading to obsessional thoughts and repetitive compulsive behaviours. The compulsive aspects of OCD may also involve disturbances in other brain circuits that usually suppress repetitive behaviours, leading people to feel like they are "stuck in gear" and cannot seek the sense that a particular action (e.g., checking a door lock) has been performed correctly (Szechtman & Woody, 2004). The frontal cortex regulates brain centres in the lower brain that control bodily movement. Perhaps a disruption in these neural pathways is involved in the failure to inhibit the repetitive handwashing and compulsive checking behaviours seen in people with OCD. Evidence also points to differences in brain functioning of people with OCD compared to nonpatient controls (Friedlander & Desrocher, 2006). The significance of these differences in explaining OCD remains unclear, however, and the ability of such models to account for OCD has been called into question (Taylor, McKay, & Abramowitz, 2005).

Tying It Together

Unravelling the complex interactions of environmental, physiological, and psychological factors in explaining how anxiety disorders develop remains a challenge (see Figure 3.3). There may be different causal pathways at work. To illustrate, let's offer some possible causal pathways involved in phobic disorders and panic disorder.

Some people may develop phobias by way of classical conditioning—the pairing of a previously neutral stimulus with an unpleasant or traumatic experience. A person may develop a fear of small animals because of experiences in which he or she was bitten or nearly bitten. A fear of riding in elevators may arise from experiences of being trapped in elevators or other enclosed spaces.

Bear in mind that not all people who have traumatic experiences develop related phobias. Perhaps some people have a genetic predisposition that sensitizes them to more readily acquire conditioned responses to stimuli associated with aversive situations. Or perhaps people are more sensitized to these experiences because of an inherited

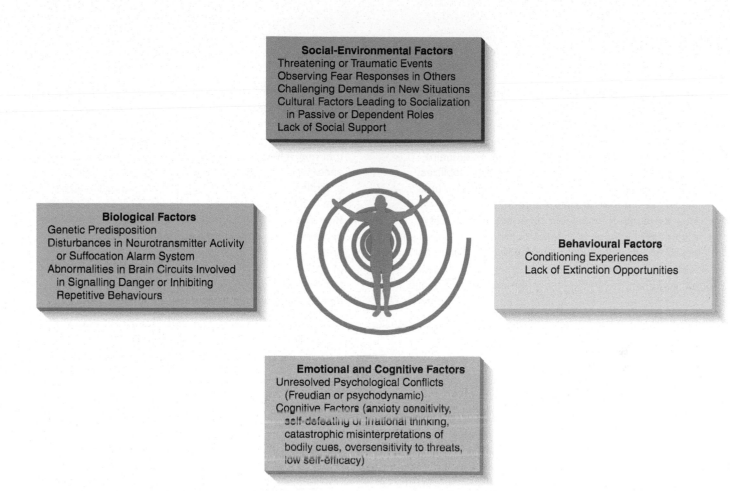

FIGURE 3.3 **Multiple factors in anxiety disorders.**

Source: Pearson Education

predisposition to respond with greater negative arousal to aversive situations. Whatever factors may be involved in the acquisition of a phobia, people with persistent phobias may have learned to avoid any further contact with the phobic stimulus and so do not avail themselves of opportunities to unlearn the phobia through repeated uneventful contacts with the feared object or situation. Then there are people who acquire phobias without any prior aversive experiences with the phobic stimulus, or at least none they can recall. We can conjecture that cognitive factors, such as observing other people's aversive responses, may play a contributing role in these cases.

Possible causal pathways in panic disorder highlight roles for biological, cognitive, and environmental factors. Some people may inherit a genetic predisposition or diathesis that makes them more likely to panic in response to changes in bodily sensations. This genetic predisposition may involve dysregulations in neurotransmitter systems that control emotional responding. Cognitive factors may also be involved. Bodily sensations such as dizziness, tingling, or numbness may be misconstrued as signs of impending death, insanity, or loss of control. This in turn may lead, like dominoes falling in line, to an anxiety reaction that quickly spirals into a full-fledged panic attack. Whether the anxiety reaction spirals into a state of panic may depend on another vulnerability factor: the individual's level of anxiety sensitivity. People with a high level of anxiety sensitivity (extreme fear of their own bodily sensations) may be more likely to panic in response to changes in their physical sensations. In some cases, anxiety sensitivity may be so high that panic ensues even in individuals without a genetic predisposition. Environmental factors may come into play as panic attacks come to be triggered by specific environmental cues, such as stimuli associated with situations (e.g., boarding a subway train or elevator) in which attacks have occurred in the past.

Theoretical Perspectives

- **How are anxiety disorders conceptualized within the psychodynamic perspective?** Psychodynamic theorists view anxiety disorders as attempts by the ego to control the conscious emergence of threatening impulses. Feelings of anxiety are warning signals that threatening impulses are nearing awareness. The ego mobilizes defence mechanisms to divert these impulses, thus leading to different anxiety disorders.

- **How do learning/behaviour theorists view anxiety disorders?** Learning and behaviour theorists explain anxiety disorders through conditioning and observational learning. Mowrer's two-factor model incorporates classical and operant conditioning in the explanation of phobias. Phobias, however, appear to be moderated by cognitive factors, such as irrational beliefs. The principles of reinforcement may help explain patterns of obsessive-compulsive behaviour. People may be genetically predisposed to acquire certain types of phobias that may have had survival value for our prehistoric ancestors. Cognitive factors, such as irrational beliefs and misattributions for panic attacks, may also play a role in anxiety disorders.

- **How does the biological perspective seek to inform our understanding of anxiety disorders?** The biological perspective seeks to uncover the biological underpinnings of anxiety disorders through studying the roles of genetic factors, neurotransmitters, and induction of panic by means of biological challenges.

TREATMENT

Each of the major theoretical perspectives has spawned approaches for treating anxiety disorders. Psychological approaches may differ from one another in their techniques and expressed aims, but they seem to have one thing in common: In one way or another, they encourage clients to face rather than avoid the sources of their anxieties. The biological perspective, by contrast, has focused largely on the use of drugs that quell anxiety.

Psychodynamic Approaches

From the psychodynamic perspective, anxieties reflect the energies attached to unconscious conflicts and the ego's efforts to keep them repressed. Traditional psychoanalysis fosters awareness of how clients' anxiety disorders symbolize their inner conflicts so that the ego can be freed from expending its energy on repression. The ego can thus attend to more creative and enhancing tasks.

More modern psychodynamic therapies also foster clients' awareness of inner sources of conflict. They focus more than traditional approaches on exploring sources of anxiety that arise from current rather than past relationships, however, and they encourage clients to develop more adaptive behaviours. Such therapies are briefer and more directive than traditional psychoanalysis.

Humanistic Approaches

Humanistic theorists believe that many of our anxieties stem from social repression of our genuine selves. Anxiety occurs when the incongruity between one's true inner self and one's social facade draws closer to the level of awareness. A person senses that something bad will happen but is unable to say what it is because the disowned parts of oneself are not directly expressed in consciousness. Because of the disapproval of others, people may fail to develop their individual talents and recognize their authentic feelings. Humanistic therapies thus aim at helping people get in touch with and express their genuine talents and feelings. As a result, clients become free to discover and accept their true selves, rather than reacting with anxiety whenever their true feelings and needs begin to surface.

Biological Approaches

A variety of drugs are used to treat anxiety disorders. Benzodiazepines such as clonazepam (brand name Rivotril) and alprazolam (Xanax) are often used. Although they tend to have a calming effect, physical dependence (addiction) can develop with chronic use of benzodiazepines, leading to withdrawal symptoms when use of the drugs is stopped abruptly. Withdrawal symptoms include rebound anxiety, insomnia, and restlessness (Joffe & Gardner, 2000). These symptoms prompt many patients to return to using the drugs.

Antidepressant drugs are effective not only in treating depression; they have also proven helpful in treating panic disorder, PTSD, social anxiety disorder, and obsessive-compulsive disorder (Taylor, 2005). Antidepressants may help counter anxiety by normalizing the activity of neurotransmitters in the brain. Antidepressants in common use for treating panic disorder include the tricyclics imipramine (Tofranil) and clomipramine (Anafranil) and the selective serotonin-reuptake inhibitors (SSRIs) paroxetine (Paxil) and sertraline (Zoloft). However, troublesome side effects may occur, such as heavy sweating and heart palpitations, which lead many patients to prematurely stop using the drugs. Alprazolam can also be helpful in treating panic disorder, social anxiety disorder, and generalized anxiety disorder (Cloos, 2005).

Research is ongoing to discover new-generation drugs that help reduce anxiety symptoms. For panic disorder, for example, a newer SNRI (serotonin-norepinephrine reuptake inhibitor) called venlafaxine (Effexor), one of the first and most commonly used, has shown promise during a study with outpatients who suffered from panic attacks. At week 10 of treatment, the percentage of patients who were free from full-symptom panic attacks was 52% in the venlafaxine group and 43% in the placebo group—not a massive difference, but worth further investigation (Liebowitz, Asnis, Mangano, & Tsanis, 2009).

Obsessive-compulsive disorder often responds to SSRI-type antidepressants—drugs such as fluoxetine (Prozac) and clomipramine (Anafranil) that work specifically on increasing the availability of the neurotransmitter serotonin in the brain (Dell'Osso, Nestadt, Allen, & Hollander, 2006). The effectiveness of these drugs leads researchers to suspect that a problem with serotonin transmission in the brain may be involved in the development of OCD in at least some people with the disorder (Denys, Van Nieuwerburgh, Deforce, & Westenberg, 2006). But as noted by University of Ottawa researchers, some patients fail to respond to these drugs, and among those who do respond, a complete remission of symptoms is uncommon (Blier, Habib, & Flament, 2006). In such cases, neurosurgery is sometimes performed in which connections between brain regions are severed. For example, in a cingulotomy, the cingulate gyrus—a small section of the brain that connects the limbic system and frontal lobes—is severed. Although some neurosurgical studies have found positive results, it is still too early to say whether neurosurgery is safe and effective for people with OCD who have failed to benefit from other treatments (Schruers, Koning, Luermans, Haack, & Griez, 2005).

A potential problem with drug therapy is that patients may attribute clinical improvement to the drugs and not to their own resources. Nor do such drugs produce cures. Relapses are common after patients discontinue medication (Antony & Swinson, 2000). Re-emergence of panic is likely unless cognitive-behavioural treatment is provided to help panic patients modify their cognitive overreactions to bodily sensations (Taylor, 2000). Drug therapy is sometimes combined with cognitive-behavioural therapy, although it is currently unclear whether combined treatment is more effective than either treatment alone (Pull, 2007).

Cognitive and Behaviour-Based Approaches

Cognitive-behavioural treatments are based on learning and cognitive approaches. These include a variety of techniques aimed at helping individuals confront the objects or situations that elicit their fears and anxieties and replacing their irrational or self-defeating thoughts.

TREATMENT OF PHOBIC DISORDERS

Sean has a phobia of receiving injections. His behaviour therapist treats him as he reclines in a comfortable padded chair. In a state of deep muscle relaxation, Sean observes slides projected on a screen. A slide of a nurse holding a needle has just been shown three times, 30 seconds at a time. Each time, Sean has shown no anxiety. So now a slightly more discomforting slide is shown: one of the nurse aiming the needle toward someone's bare arm. After 15 seconds, our armchair adventurer notices twinges of discomfort and raises a finger as a signal (speaking might disturb his relaxation). The projector operator turns off the light, and Sean spends a couple of minutes imagining his "safe scene"—lying on a beach beneath the tropical sun. Then the slide is shown again. This time Sean views it for 30 seconds before feeling anxiety.

Source: Psychology: Concepts & Connections, Brief Version, Cengage Learning, 2012.

Sean is undergoing systematic desensitization, a fear-reduction procedure originated by psychiatrist Joseph Wolpe (1958). Systematic desensitization is a gradual process. Clients learn to handle progressively more disturbing stimuli while they remain relaxed. About 10 to 20 stimuli are arranged in a sequence or hierarchy—called a **fear-stimulus hierarchy**—according to their capacity to evoke anxiety. By using their imagination or by viewing photos, clients are exposed to the items in the hierarchy, gradually imagining themselves approaching the target behaviour—be it the ability to receive an injection or to remain in an enclosed room or elevator—without undue anxiety.

fear-stimulus hierarchy Ordered series of increasingly fearful stimuli. Used in the behavioural techniques of *systematic desensitization* and *gradual exposure.*

Joseph Wolpe developed systematic desensitization on the assumption that maladaptive anxiety responses, like other behaviours, are learned or conditioned. He assumed they can be unlearned by counterconditioning. In counterconditioning, a response incompatible with anxiety is made to appear under conditions that usually elicit anxiety. Muscle relaxation is generally used as the incompatible response, and followers of Wolpe usually use the method of progressive relaxation to help clients acquire relaxation skills. For this reason, Sean's therapist is teaching Sean to experience relaxation in the presence of (otherwise) anxiety-evoking slides of needles.

Behaviourally oriented therapists, like Wolpe, explain the benefits of systematic desensitization and similar therapies in terms of principles of counterconditioning. Cognitively oriented therapists note, however, that remaining in the presence of phobic imagery, rather than running from it, is also likely to enhance one's confidence about being able to manage the phobic stimuli without anxiety.

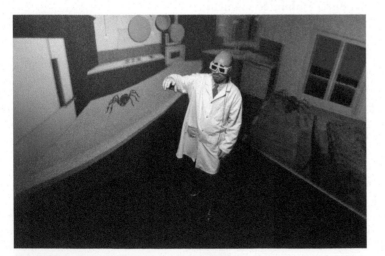

Thierry Berrod/Mona Lisa Production/Science Source

Virtual reality phobia therapy research. This researcher is testing a virtual reality therapy system to treat spider phobia (arachnophobia). The system contains eye-tracking software to study a person's response when exposed to virtual spiders in a virtual environment (onscreen).

Another exposure technique, gradual exposure, helps people overcome phobias through a stepwise approach of actual exposure to the phobic stimuli. The effectiveness of exposure therapy is well established, making it the treatment of choice for specific phobias (Antony & McCabe, 2005). Here exposure therapy was used in treating a case of claustrophobia:

Claustrophobia (fear of enclosed spaces) is quite common. Cho's claustrophobia took the form of a fear of riding in elevators. Interestingly, Cho worked as an elevator mechanic! He spent his workdays repairing elevators. Unless it was absolutely necessary, however, Cho managed to complete the repairs without riding in the elevator. He would climb the stairs to the floor where an elevator was stuck, make repairs, and hit the down button. He would then race downstairs to see that the elevator had operated correctly. When his work required an elevator ride, panic would seize him as the doors closed. Cho tried to cope by praying for divine intervention to prevent him from passing out before the doors opened.

Cho related the origin of his phobia to an accident three years earlier in which he had been pinned in his overturned car for nearly an hour. He remembered feelings of helplessness and suffocation and as a result developed claustrophobia. Cho's fear had become so incapacitating that he was seriously considering switching jobs, although the change would require considerable financial sacrifice. Each night, he lay awake wondering whether he would be able to cope the next day if he were required to test-ride an elevator.

Cho's therapy involved gradual exposure. Gradual exposure, like systematic desensitization, is a step-by-step procedure that involves a fear-stimulus hierarchy. In gradual exposure, however, the target behaviour is approached in actuality rather than symbolically. Moreover, the individual is active rather than relaxed in a recliner.

A typical hierarchy for overcoming a fear of riding in an elevator might include the following steps:

1. Standing outside the elevator
2. Standing in the elevator with the door open
3. Standing in the elevator with the door closed
4. Taking the elevator down one floor
5. Taking the elevator up one floor
6. Taking the elevator down two floors
7. Taking the elevator up two floors
8. Taking the elevator down two floors and then up two floors
9. Taking the elevator down to the basement
10. Taking the elevator up to the highest floor and down again

Clients begin at Step 1 and do not progress to Step 2 until they are able to remain calm for the first step. If they become bothered by anxiety, they remove themselves from the situation and regain calmness by practising muscle relaxation or focusing on soothing mental imagery. The encounter is then repeated as often as necessary to reach and sustain feelings of calmness. They then proceed to the next step, repeating the process.

Cho was also trained to practise self-relaxation and talk calmly and rationally to himself to help him remain calm during his exposure trials. Whenever he began to feel even slightly anxious, he would tell himself to calm down and relax. He was able to counter the disruptive belief that he was going to fall apart if he was trapped in an elevator with rational self-statements such as "Just relax. I may experience some anxiety, but it's nothing that I haven't been through before. In a few moments I'll feel relieved."

Cho gradually overcame his phobia but still occasionally experienced some anxiety, which he interpreted as a reminder of his former phobia. He did not exaggerate the importance of these feelings. Now and then it dawned on him that an elevator he was servicing had once occasioned fear. One day following his treatment, Cho was repairing an elevator that serviced a bank vault 30 metres underground. The experience of moving deeper and deeper underground aroused fear, but Cho did not panic. He repeated to himself, "It's only a couple of seconds and I'll be out." By the time he took his second trip down, he was much calmer.

The Authors' Files

flooding Type of exposure therapy in which subjects are exposed to intensely anxiety-provoking situations.

Gradual exposure is also an effective treatment for social anxiety disorder (Cottraux, 2005). Clients are instructed to enter increasingly stressful social situations and to remain in those situations until the urge to escape has lessened. The therapist may help guide them during exposure trials, gradually withdrawing direct support so that clients become capable of handling the situations on their own.

Flooding is a type of exposure therapy in which subjects are exposed to intensely anxiety-provoking situations. Why? It is believed that anxiety that has been conditioned to a phobic stimulus should extinguish if the individual remains in the phobic situation for a long enough period of time and nothing traumatic occurs. Typically, the phobic individual either avoids the phobic stimulus or beats a hasty retreat at the first opportunity for escape. Thus, no opportunity for unlearning (extinguishing) the fear response occurs. Flooding is just as effective as other forms of behavioural treatments but may work faster.

cognitive restructuring Cognitive therapy method that involves replacing irrational or self-defeating thoughts and attitudes with rational alternatives.

Behavioural techniques are often combined with cognitive therapy. Employing a technique called **cognitive restructuring**, therapists help clients pinpoint their self-defeating thoughts and generate rational alternatives so that they learn to cope with anxiety-provoking situations. For example, people with social anxiety disorder might think that no one at a party will want to talk with them and they will wind up lonely and isolated for the rest of their lives. Cognitive therapists help clients recognize the logical flaws in their thinking and assist them in viewing situations rationally. Clients may be asked to gather evidence to test out their beliefs, which may lead them to alter beliefs they find are not grounded in reality. Therapists may encourage clients with social anxiety disorder to test their beliefs that they are bound to be ignored, rejected, or ridiculed by others in social gatherings by attending a party, initiating conversations, and monitoring other people's reactions. Therapists may also help clients develop social skills to improve their interpersonal effectiveness and teach them how to handle social rejection, if it should occur, without catastrophizing. The cognitive-behavioural treatments for social anxiety disorder have been shown to be effective, and their benefits appear to be durable (Rowa & Antony, 2005).

These techniques are also beneficial for individuals with specific phobias. Cho learned to replace self-defeating thoughts with rational alternatives and to practise speaking rationally and calmly to himself during his exposure trials. Consider the case of Soraya, who also suffered from an elevator phobia:

Soraya, a 32-year-old writer and mother of two sons, had not been on an elevator in 16 years. Her life revolved around finding ways to avoid appointments and social events on high floors. She had suffered from a fear of elevators since the age of 8, when she had been stuck between floors with her grandmother.

To help overcome her fear of elevators, Soraya imagined herself getting stuck in an elevator and countering the self-defeating thoughts she might experience with rational self-statements. She closed her eyes and reported the thoughts that would come to mind. The psychologist encouraged her to create a rational counterpoint to each of them. She then repeated the exercise in her imagination and practised replacing the self-defeating thoughts with rational alternatives, as in the following examples:

Self-Defeating Thought	Rational Alternative
Uh-oh, I'm stuck. I'm going to lose control.	Relax. Just think coolly. What do I have to do next?
I can't take it. I'm going to pass out.	Okay, practise your deep breathing. Help will be coming shortly.
I'm having a panic attack. I can't stand it.	You've experienced all these feelings before. Just let them pass through.

Self-Defeating Thought	Rational Alternative
If it takes an hour, that would be horrible.	That would be annoying, but it wouldn't necessarily be horrible. I've been stuck in traffic longer than that.
I've got to get out of here.	Stay calm. There's no real danger. I can just sit down and imagine I'm somewhere else until someone comes to help.

The Authors' Files

TREATMENT OF AGORAPHOBIA Evidence shows gradual exposure to fear-inducing stimuli to be more effective than control conditions in reducing avoidance behaviour in people with agoraphobia (Taylor, 2000). Treatment is stepwise and gradually exposes the individual to increasingly fearful stimulus situations, such as walking through congested streets or shopping in department stores. A trusted companion or perhaps the therapist may accompany the person during the exposure trials. The eventual goal is for the person to be able to handle each situation alone and without discomfort or an urge to escape. The benefits of gradual exposure are typically enduring.

TREATMENT OF POSTTRAUMATIC STRESS DISORDER Exposure therapy has achieved good results in reducing symptoms of PTSD (National Institute for Clinical Excellence, 2005). Exposure to cues associated with a trauma may involve talking about the trauma, re-experiencing the trauma in one's imagination, viewing related slides or films, or visiting the scene of the event. For combat-related PTSD, homework assignments may involve visiting war memorials or viewing war movies. The person comes to gradually re-experience the traumatic event and accompanying anxiety in a safe setting that is free of negative consequences, which allows extinction to take its course. Exposure therapy is often supplemented with cognitive restructuring that focuses on replacing dysfunctional thoughts with rational alternatives. Training in stress-management skills, such as self-relaxation, may help enhance the client's ability to cope with the troubling features of PTSD, such as heightened arousal and the desire to run away from trauma-related stimuli. Training in anger-management skills may also be helpful, especially with combat veterans who have PTSD (Taylor, 2005).

Additional interventions may also be required. Specialist programs may be needed for people with two or more disorders, such as PTSD combined with substance use disorders (e.g., Najavits, 2002). Some of these programs cater to specific groups, such as the Tsow-Tun Le Lum residential program for Indigenous adults located in Nanaimo, British Columbia. Other programs need to be very broad in focus to address the needs of their clients. Survivors of torture, for example—many of whom have arrived in Canada as refugees—often have PTSD combined with a host of other practical problems, such as the need for housing, education in written and spoken English, and legal aid to help with refugee claims. Organizations such as the Canadian Centre for Victims of Torture, located in Toronto, provide important assistance in these areas.

TREATMENT OF OBSESSIVE-COMPULSIVE DISORDER Behaviour therapy has achieved impressive results in treating obsessive-compulsive disorder with a combination of exposure and response prevention (Clark, 2004; Franklin & Foa, 2011). Exposure involves purposefully placing oneself in situations that evoke obsessive thoughts. For many people, such situations are hard to avoid. Leaving the house, for example, can trigger obsessional thoughts about whether the gas jets are turned off or the windows and doors are locked. Response prevention involves the effort to physically prevent a compulsive behaviour from occurring. Through exposure with response prevention, people with OCD learn to tolerate the anxiety triggered by their obsessive thoughts while they are prevented from performing their compulsive rituals. With repeated exposure, the anxiety eventually subsides and the person feels less compelled to perform the ritual. Extinction, or the weakening of the anxiety response following repeated presentation of the obsessional

Virtual reality, a computer-generated simulated environment, has become a therapeutic tool. By donning a specialized helmet and gloves that are connected to a computer, a person with a fear of heights, for example, can encounter frightening stimuli in this virtual world, such as riding a glass-enclosed elevator to the 49th floor, peering over a railing on a balcony on the 20th floor, or flying in a helicopter (Pull, 2005). Findings from Canadian investigators suggest that virtual therapy is also useful for treating driving phobia (Wald & Taylor, 2003). Here, a client practises driving in a simulator under increasingly more challenging situations (e.g., on a quiet street, then in heavy traffic, then in the rain). By a process of exposure to a series of increasingly more frightening virtual stimuli, while progressing only when fears at each preceding step diminish, people learn to overcome fears in much the same way they would had they followed a program of graduated exposure to phobic stimuli in real-life situations. The advantage of virtual reality is that it provides an opportunity to experience situations that might be difficult or impossible to arrange in reality. Virtual therapy has been used successfully in helping people overcome many different kinds of phobias, including fears of heights, driving, flying, and spiders (Pull, 2005). It has also shown promising results in helping veterans with PTSD by exposing them to simulated war scenes (Reger & Gahm, 2008; Reger et al., 2011).

Therapists are experimenting with virtual therapy to help people overcome other types of fears, such as fear of public speaking and agoraphobia. In other applications, virtual therapy may help clients work through unresolved conflicts with significant figures in their lives by allowing them to confront these "people" in a virtual environment.

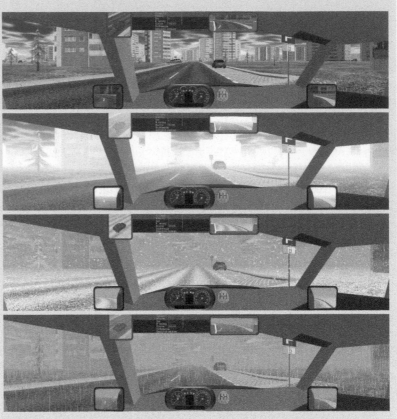

aplusbsoftware.com

Scene from a driving simulator (SimuRide by AplusB Software Corporation). Virtual reality therapy using a driving simulator can be useful in treating driving phobia.

cues in the absence of any aversive consequences, is believed to underlie the treatment effect. Overall, many people benefit from this treatment (Clark, 2004). Cognitive therapy is often combined with exposure therapy. The therapist focuses on helping the person correct cognitive distortions, such as tendencies to overestimate the likelihood and severity of feared consequences.

It appears that cognitive-behavioural therapy is at least as effective as drug therapy (use of SSRI-type antidepressants) and may produce more lasting results (Antony & Swinson, 2000; Franklin & Foa, 2011; Taylor, 2000). Yet it remains to be seen whether a combination of drugs and behaviour therapy is more effective than either approach alone.

Behavioural therapy may also change brain function as well as behaviour. People with obsessive-compulsive disorder who received cognitive-behavioural therapy show changes in their brain functioning, as measured by PET scans (Baxter et al., 2000). A part of the brain that is unusually active in people with OCD showed a lessening of activity—the same kind of change seen when OCD is treated with the antidepressant Prozac.

TREATMENT OF GENERALIZED ANXIETY Cognitive-behaviour therapists use a combination of techniques to treat generalized anxiety disorder, including relaxation training; substitution of adaptive thoughts for intrusive, anxiety-inducing thoughts; and decatastrophizing (avoiding tendencies to think the worst). Studies from Concordia University, Laval University, and elsewhere indicate that cognitive-behavioural approaches are superior to control conditions and yield effects equivalent to or better than alternative drug or psychological therapies (Mitte, 2005).

TREATMENT OF PANIC DISORDER The treatment components in cognitive-behavioural therapy for panic disorder include training in skills relating to handling panic attacks without catastrophizing, breathing retraining, exposure to situations linked to panic attacks and to bodily cues associated with panic, and training in relaxation (Taylor, 2000).

Therapists help clients think differently about their bodily cues, such as passing sensations of dizziness or heart palpitations. Receiving corrective information that these sensations will subside naturally and are not signs of an impending catastrophe helps clients learn to cope with them without panicking (Taylor, 2000). (Persons who complain of cardiovascular symptoms should also be evaluated medically to ensure they are physically healthy.) On a cognitive level, clients are taught to replace catastrophizing thoughts and self-statements ("I'm having a heart attack") with calming, rational alternatives ("Calm down. These are panicky feelings that will soon pass").

Breathing retraining aims at restoring a normal level of carbon dioxide in the blood by having clients breathe slowly and deeply from the abdomen to avoid the shallow, rapid breathing (hyperventilation) that leads to breathing off too much carbon dioxide. In some treatment programs, people with panic disorder purposefully hyperventilate in the controlled setting of the treatment clinic to discover for themselves the relationship between breathing off too much carbon dioxide and cardiovascular sensations. Through these first-hand experiences, they learn to calm themselves down and cope with these sensations rather than overreacting. Some of the common elements of cognitive-behavioural therapy for panic are shown in Table 3.11.

The efficacy of cognitive-behavioural therapy in treating panic disorder is well established (Antony & Swinson, 2000; Katon, 2006; Taylor, 2000). Investigators find that roughly two thirds to four fifths of panic patients treated with cognitive-behavioural therapy become panic-free by the end of treatment, and the gains from therapy appear to be long lasting (Barlow, 2002). Despite the common belief that panic disorder is best treated with psychiatric drugs, cognitive-behavioural therapy appears to produce even better results than drug treatment with imipramine or benzodiazepines (Schmidt & Keough, 2010; Taylor, 2000).

TABLE 3.11

Elements of Cognitive-Behavioural Programs for Treatment of Panic Disorder

Self-Monitoring	Keeping a log of panic attacks to help determine situational stimuli that might trigger them.
Exposure	A program of gradual exposure to situations in which panic attacks have occurred. During exposure trials, the person engages in self-relaxation and rational self-talk to prevent anxiety from spiralling out of control. In some programs, participants learn to tolerate changes in bodily sensations associated with panic attacks by experiencing these sensations within a controlled setting of the treatment clinic. The person may be spun around in a chair to induce feelings of dizziness, learning in the process that such sensations are not dangerous or signs of imminent harm.
Development of Coping Responses	Developing coping skills to interrupt the vicious cycle in which overreactions to anxiety cues or cardiovascular sensations culminate in panic attacks. Behavioural methods focus on deep, regular breathing and relaxation training. Cognitive methods focus on modifying catastrophic misinterpretations of bodily sensations. Breathing retraining may be used to help the individual avoid hyperventilation during panic attacks.

Coping with a Panic Attack

People who have panic attacks usually feel their hearts pounding such that they are overwhelmed and unable to cope. They typically feel an urge to flee the situation as quickly as possible. If escape is impossible, they may become immobilized and "freeze" until the attack dissipates. What can you do if you suffer a panic attack or an intense anxiety reaction? Here are a few coping responses:

- Don't let your breathing get out of hand. Breathe slowly and deeply.
- "Talk yourself down." Tell yourself to relax. Tell yourself you're not going to die. Tell yourself that no matter how painful the attack is, it is likely to pass soon.

- Find someone to help you through the attack. Telephone someone you know and trust. Talk about anything at all until you regain control.
- Don't fall into the trap of making yourself housebound to avert future attacks.
- If you are uncertain as to whether or not sensations such as pain or tightness in the chest have physical causes, seek immediate medical assistance. Even if you suspect your attack may "only" be one of anxiety, it is safer to have a medical evaluation than to diagnose yourself.

You need not suffer recurrent panic attacks and fears about loss of control. When in doubt, or if attacks are persistent or frightening, consult a professional.

Treatment of Anxiety, Obsessive-Compulsive, and Trauma- and Stressor-Related Disorders

- **How is the treatment of anxiety, obsessive-compulsive, and trauma- and stressor-related disorders approached from the major contemporary theoretical perspectives?** Traditional psychoanalysis helps people work through unconscious conflicts that are thought to underlie anxiety disorders. Modern psychodynamic approaches also focus on current disturbed relationships and encourage clients to assume more adaptive behaviour patterns. The biological perspectives have led to the development of various drug therapies to treat anxiety disorders. Learning perspectives encompass a broad range of behavioural and cognitive-behavioural techniques to help people overcome anxiety-related problems. Exposure methods help people with phobias overcome their fears through gradual exposure to the phobic stimuli. Obsessive-compulsive disorder is often treated with a combination of exposure and response prevention. Relaxation training is often used to help people overcome generalized anxiety. Behavioural treatment of PTSD incorporates progressive exposure to trauma-related cues and training in stress-management skills, such as self-relaxation. Cognitive approaches help people identify and correct cognitive errors that give rise to or maintain anxiety disorders. Cognitive-behavioural approaches to panic disorder focus on helping panic-prone people learn to use deep-breathing skills to tone down their bodily alarm in anxiety-inducing situations and to avoid catastrophizing changes in bodily sensations.

Define It

acrophobia, 110
acute stress disorder, 116
adjustment disorder, 115
agoraphobia, 106
anxiety disorder, 102
anxiety sensitivity, 124
benzodiazepines, 127
claustrophobia, 110
cognitive restructuring, 134

compulsion, 113
dissociation, 116
etiology, 103
fear, 109
fear-stimulus hierarchy, 132
flooding, 134
gamma-aminobutyric acid, 127
generalized anxiety disorder, 108
neuroticism, 127

obsession, 113
panic disorder, 102
posttraumatic stress disorder, 116
prepared conditioning, 122
prevalence, 103
projection, 120
social anxiety disorder, 110
specific phobias, 110
two-factor model, 121

Recall It

1. In panic disorder, the initial panic attacks occur _____.
   a. away from home
   b. in crowded situations
   c. unexpectedly
   d. when cued by particular stimuli

2. Which is NOT a feature of posttraumatic stress disorder?
   a. An exaggerated startle response
   b. Difficulty falling or remaining asleep
   c. Hypervigilance
   d. Delusions centring on the traumatic event

3. Anxiety sensitivity refers to _____.
   a. fear of future events
   b. fear of ambiguous situations
   c. fear of fear
   d. unusual sensitivity to external threats

4. The various psychological approaches to treating anxiety discussed in the text all share a common approach of encouraging clients to _____.
   a. use drugs to manage anxiety
   b. confront the sources of their anxieties
   c. distract themselves from their anxieties
   d. understand the childhood roots of their anxieties

5. John is seeking help for overcoming an anxiety disorder. His therapist helps him become aware of how his symptoms may be symbolizing inner conflicts of which he is unaware. The therapist is using a _____ approach to conceptualize John's disorder.
   a. psychodynamic
   b. humanistic
   c. behavioural
   d. cognitive

Answers to Recall It

1. c   2. d   3. c   4. b   5. a

Think About It

- Anxiety may be a normal emotional reaction in some situations, but not in others. Think of a situation in which you would consider anxiety to be a normal reaction and one in which you would consider it to be a maladaptive reaction. What are the differences? What criteria do you use to draw a line between normal and abnormal?

- Compare and contrast the psychodynamic and learning-based explanations of the classic case of Little Hans. How does this case illustrate the differences between the two models?

- Have you developed any specific phobias, such as fears of small animals, insects, heights, or enclosed spaces? What factors do you think contributed to the development of this phobia (or phobias)? How has the phobia made an impact on your life? How have you coped with it?

- What are the advantages and disadvantages of using anti-anxiety drugs?

Weblinks

Anxiety Treatment and Research Clinic at St. Joseph's Healthcare Hamilton
www.stjoes.ca/anxiety
Information on anxiety disorders, including Canadian treatment resources.

Anxiety Disorders Association of Canada
www.anxietycanada.ca
Information and links to provincial anxiety disorder associations.

Anxiety and Depression Association of America
www.adaa.org
The ADAA's website contains information on the nature and treatment of anxiety disorders, as well as links to self-help books and other resources.

International OCD Foundation
https://iocdf.org
This not-for-profit organization provides information on obsessive-compulsive disorder and its treatment.

National Center for PTSD
www.ptsd.va.gov
This organization's site contains a good deal of useful information on posttraumatic stress reactions and their treatment.

Anxiety, Obsessive-Compulsive, and Trauma- and Stressor-Related Disorders

Test your understanding of the key concepts by filling in the blanks with the correct statements chosen from the list that follows. The answers are found at the end of the chapter.

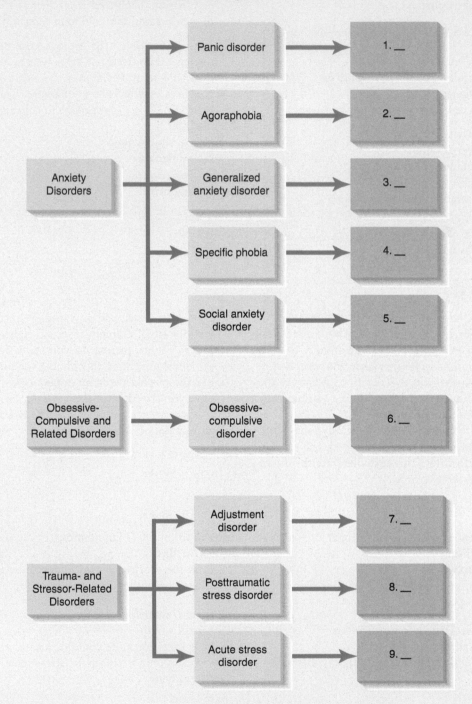

a. Excessive anxiety and worry about several situations

b. Severe fear of social or performance situations

c. Symptoms that last only days or weeks after exposure to a trauma

d. Recurrent obsessions and/or compulsions

e. Fear of places and situations from which it might be difficult to escape

f. Recurrent unexpected panic attacks

g. Severe fear of specific objects or situations

h. Persistent symptoms after exposure to a trauma

i. Maladaptive reaction to an identified stressor

CAUSES AND TREATMENTS ACCORDING TO VARIOUS THEORETICAL PERSPECTIVES

THEORETICAL PERSPECTIVES	CAUSES	TREATMENTS
PSYCHODYNAMIC	Anxiety is a signal that threatening sexual or aggressive impulses are nearing the level of awareness. The ego mobilizes defence mechanisms to ward off threatening impulses.	Traditional: Increase awareness of inner conflicts Modern: Focus on current relationships and coping skills
BEHAVIOURAL	Two-factor model: Fears are acquired by classical conditioning and maintained by operant conditioning Prepared conditioning: People might be biologically predisposed to fear certain types of stimuli	Systematic desensitization Gradual exposure Flooding
COGNITIVE	Dysfunctional thinking patterns	Challenging and replacing self-defeating or irrational beliefs
BIOLOGICAL	Genetic predisposition (diathesis) Dysfunctional neurotransmitter systems	Medications
HUMANISTIC	Anxiety stems from social repression of the genuine self	Help people to get in touch with and express their genuine talents

Answers: 1. f, 2. e, 3. a, 4. g, 5. b, 6. d, 7. i, 8. h, 9. c

4

Depressive Disorders, Bipolar and Related Disorders, and Suicide

Did You Know That...

- Feeling depressed is perfectly normal in some circumstances?

- Most people who become severely depressed will suffer additional episodes later in life?

- The bleak light of winter casts some people into a diagnosable state of depression?

- Some people ride an emotional roller coaster, swinging from the heights of elation to

the depths of depression without any external cause?

- The ancient Greeks and Romans used a chemical that is still used today to curb turbulent mood swings?

- The most widely used remedy for depression in Germany is not a drug but an herb?

- It is untrue that people who threaten suicide are only seeking attention?

Jack Spratt/The Image Works

Life has its ups and downs. Most of us feel elated when we have earned high grades, a promotion, or the affections of Ms. or Mr. Right. Most of us feel down or depressed when we are rejected by a date, flunk a test, or suffer financial losses. It is normal and appropriate to be happy about uplifting events. It is just as normal, just as appropriate, to feel depressed by dismal events. It might very well be "abnormal" if we were not depressed by life's miseries.

Our **moods** are enduring states of feeling that colour our psychological lives. Feeling down or depressed is not abnormal in the context of depressing events or circumstances. But people with depressive or bipolar disorders experience disturbances in mood that are unusually severe or prolonged and that impair their ability to function in meeting their normal responsibilities. Some people become severely depressed even when things appear to be going well or when they encounter mildly upsetting events that others take in stride. Still others experience extreme mood swings. They ride an emotional roller coaster with dizzying heights and abysmal depths when the world around them remains largely on an even keel.

In this chapter, we focus on several kinds of disorders involving mood, including two kinds of depressive disorders—major depressive disorder and persistent depressive disorder—and three kinds of mood swing disorders—bipolar I disorder, bipolar II disorder, and cyclothymic disorder. As displayed in Figure 4.1, moods are on a continuum from severe depression to severe mania. The depressive disorders are considered **unipolar** because the disturbance lies in only one emotional direction or pole—the downward part of the diagram. Disorders that involve mood swings are **bipolar**. They involve excesses of both depression and elation, usually in an alternating pattern, moving from the top of the diagram to the bottom, and usually passing through a period of normal, balanced mood in the middle.

moods Pervasive qualities of an individual's emotional experience, as in depressed mood, anxious mood, or elated mood.

unipolar Pertaining to a single pole or direction, as in unipolar (depressive) disorders. Contrast with *bipolar disorder*.

bipolar Characterized by opposites, as in *bipolar disorder*.

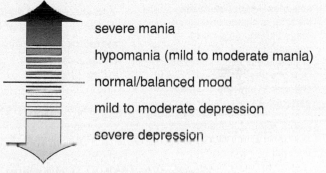

severe mania

hypomania (mild to moderate mania)

normal/balanced mood

mild to moderate depression

severe depression

FIGURE 4.1   A mood thermometer.
Mood states can be conceptualized as varying along a spectrum or continuum. One end represents severe depression and the other end severe mania, which is a cardinal feature of bipolar I disorder. Mild or moderate depression is often called "the blues" but is classified as dysthymia when it becomes chronic. In the middle of the spectrum is normal or balanced mood. Mild mania is called *hypomania*.

Source: Based on National Institutes of Mental Health.

Continuum of Depression

CHAPTER 4 · CONTINUUM CHART

Example: Major Depressive Disorder

Does not meet criteria		Meets criteria		
NO SYMPTOMS	**STRUGGLING**	**MILD**	**MODERATE**	**SEVERE**
	Jane broke up with her boyfriend and has not been herself lately. She has had bouts of crying and her mood is low.	Greg has 5 out of the 9 symptoms for major depression. Although he is distressed, he is managing to meet most of his social and occupational obligations.	Bianca is experiencing 7 symptoms of depression. Her grades and her relationships have suffered.	Osamu has all of the symptoms of depression, which have prevented him from working and taking care of many of his basic needs.

DEPRESSIVE DISORDERS

We all have periods of sadness from time to time. We may feel down in the dumps, cry, lose interest in things, find it hard to concentrate, expect the worst to happen, or even consider suicide. To illustrate the prevalence of sadness and depression, a survey of nearly 5000 high school students in Ontario found that 9.8% reported feeling depressed "most of the time" or "all of the time" in the preceding month. Female students were depressed more than twice as often as male students (14% versus 6%) (Boak, Hamilton, & Adlaf, 2014). For most of us, mood changes pass quickly or are not severe enough to interfere with our lifestyle or ability to function.

Among people with depressive disorders, mood changes are more severe or prolonged and affect daily functioning.

Major Depressive Disorder

major depressive disorder Severe depressive disorder characterized by the occurrence of major depressive episodes in the absence of a history of manic episodes. Major depressive disorder is characterized by a range of features such as depressed mood, lack of interest or pleasure in usual activities, lack of energy or motivation, and changes in appetite or sleep patterns. Abbreviated *MDD*.

manic Relating to mania, as in the manic phase of a bipolar disorder.

hypomanic episodes Mild manic episodes.

The diagnosis of **major depressive disorder** (MDD; also called *major depression*) is based on the occurrence of one or more major depressive episodes in the absence of a history of **manic** or **hypomanic episodes**. In a major depressive episode, the person experiences either a depressed mood (feeling sad, hopeless, or "down in the dumps") or loss of interest or pleasure in all or virtually all activities for a period of at least two weeks (APA, 2013). Table 4.1 lists some of the common features of depression. The diagnostic criteria for major depressive disorder are listed in Table 4.2.

People with major depressive disorder may also have poor appetite, lose or gain substantial amounts of weight, and become physically agitated or—at the other extreme—show a marked slowing down in their motor activity. They may lose interest in most of their usual activities and pursuits, have difficulty concentrating and making decisions, have pressing thoughts of death, and attempt suicide.

TABLE 4.1	
Common Features of Depression	
Changes in Emotional States	Changes in mood (persistent periods of feeling down, depressed, sad, or blue)
	Tearfulness or crying
	Increased irritability or loss of temper
Changes in Motivation	Feeling unmotivated, or having difficulty getting going in the morning or even getting out of bed
	Reduced level of social participation or interest in social activities
	Loss of enjoyment or interest in pleasurable activities
	Reduced interest in sex
	Failure to respond to praise or rewards
Changes in Functioning and Motor Behaviour	Moving about or talking more slowly than usual
	Changes in sleep habits (sleeping too much or too little, awakening earlier than usual and having trouble getting back to sleep in early morning hours—so-called *early morning awakening*)
	Changes in appetite (eating too much or too little)
	Changes in weight (gaining or losing weight)
	Functioning less effectively than usual at work or school
Cognitive Changes	Difficulty concentrating or thinking clearly
	Thinking negatively about oneself and one's future
	Feeling guilty or remorseful about past misdeeds
	Lack of self-esteem or feelings of inadequacy
	Thinking of death or suicide

TABLE 4.2

Diagnostic Criteria for Major Depressive Disorder

A. Five (or more) of the following symptoms have been present during the same 2-week period and represent a change from previous functioning; at least one of the symptoms is either (1) depressed mood or (2) loss of interest or pleasure.

   Note: Do not include symptoms that are clearly attributable to another medical condition.

   1. Depressed mood most of the day, nearly every day, as indicated by either subjective report (e.g., feels sad, empty, hopeless) or observation made by others (e.g., appears tearful). (**Note:** In children and adolescents, can be irritable mood.)

   2. Markedly diminished interest or pleasure in all, or almost all, activities most of the day, nearly every day (as indicated by either subjective account or observation).

   3. Significant weight loss when not dieting or weight gain (e.g., a change of more than 5% of body weight in a month), or decrease or increase in appetite nearly every day. (**Note:** In children, consider failure to make expected weight gain.)

   4. Insomnia or hypersomnia nearly every day.

   5. Psychomotor agitation or retardation nearly every day (observable by others, not merely subjective feelings of restlessness or being slowed down).

   6. Fatigue or loss of energy nearly every day.

   7. Feelings of worthlessness or excessive or inappropriate guilt (which may be delusional) nearly every day (not merely self-reproach or guilt about being sick).

   8. Diminished ability to think or concentrate, or indecisiveness, nearly every day (either by subjective account or as observed by others).

   9. Recurrent thoughts of death (not just fear of dying), recurrent suicidal ideation without a specific plan, or a suicide attempt or a specific plan for committing suicide.

B. The symptoms cause clinically significant distress or impairment in social, occupational, or other important areas of functioning.

C. The episode is not attributable to the physiological effects of a substance or to another medical condition.

Note: Criteria A–C represent a major depressive episode.

Note: Responses to a significant loss (e.g., bereavement, financial ruin, losses from a natural disaster, a serious medical illness or disability) may include the feelings of intense sadness, rumination about the loss, insomnia, poor appetite, and weight loss noted in Criterion A, which may resemble a depressive episode. Although such symptoms may be understandable or considered appropriate to the loss, the presence of a major depressive episode in addition to the normal response to a significant loss should also be carefully considered. This decision inevitably requires the exercise of clinical judgment based on the individual's history and the cultural norms for the expression of distress in the context of loss.[1]

D. The occurrence of the major depressive episode is not better explained by schizoaffective disorder, schizophrenia, schizophreniform disorder, delusional disorder, or other specified and unspecified schizophrenia spectrum and other psychotic disorders.

E. There has never been a manic episode or a hypomanic episode. Note: This exclusion does not apply if all of the manic-like or hypomanic-like episodes are substance-induced or are attributable to the physiological effects of another medical condition.

[1]In distinguishing grief from a major depressive episode (MDE), it is useful to consider that in grief the predominant affect is feelings of emptiness and loss, while in MDE it is persistent depressed mood and the inability to anticipate happiness or pleasure. The dysphoria in grief is likely to decrease in intensity over days to weeks and occurs in waves, the so-called pangs of grief. These waves tend to be associated with thoughts or reminders of the deceased. The depressed mood of MDE is more persistent and not tied to specific thoughts or preoccupations. The pain of grief may be accompanied by positive emotions and humor that are uncharacteristic of the pervasive unhappiness and misery characteristic of MDE. The thought content associated with grief generally features a preoccupation with thoughts and memories of the deceased, rather than the self-critical or pessimistic ruminations seen in MDE. In grief, self-esteem is generally preserved, whereas in MDE feelings of worthlessness and self-loathing are common. If self-derogatory ideation is present in grief, it typically involves perceived failings vis-à-vis the deceased (e.g., not visiting frequently enough, not telling the deceased how much he or she was loved). If a bereaved individual thinks about death and dying, such thoughts are generally focused on the deceased and possibly about "joining" the deceased, whereas in MDE such thoughts are focused on ending one's own life because of feeling worthless, undeserving of life, or unable to cope with the pain of depression.

Kevin Frayer/The Canadian Press

Major depression versus bereavement. Major depression is distinguished from a normal grief reaction to the death of a loved one, which is termed *bereavement*. But major depression may occur in people whose bereavement becomes prolonged or seriously interferes with normal functioning.

Although depression is a diagnosable psychological disorder, many people polled in surveys perceive it to be a sign of personal weakness (Jorm et al., 2006). Many people don't seem to understand that people who are clinically depressed can't simply "shake it off" or "snap out of it." This attitude may explain why, despite the availability of safe and effective treatments, many individuals who are clinically depressed remain untreated (Beck et al., 2005). Many people with untreated depression believe that they should be able to handle the problem themselves (Jorm et al., 2006). The truth is, it can be very difficult to handle major depression without receiving professional help.

Major depressive disorder affects—at some point in their lives—about 11% of Canadian adults (Pearson, Janz, & Ali, 2013). Depression may be even more prevalent in some other countries, such as the United States (Patten et al., 2006). At least 1 in 20 people can be diagnosed with major depression at any given time—it is so common that it's been dubbed the "common cold" of psychological problems. Effective treatment for depression is available and leads not only to psychological improvement but also to increased income, as people are able to return to a more productive level of functioning. In our clinical practices, we have seen college and university students who were on the verge of dropping out of school because of major depression receive effective treatment and become able to complete their degrees.

Major depression, particularly in more severe episodes, may be accompanied by psychotic features, such as delusions that one's body is rotting from illness (Meyers, 2006). People with severe depression may also experience hallucinations, such as "hearing" the voices of others or of demons condemning them for perceived misdeeds or telling them to kill themselves.

Sarah Hamid, an undergraduate at Simon Fraser University in Vancouver, provided the following illustration of some of the features of her unipolar depression:

The symptoms of mental illness crept over Sarah like a cold, damp fog. Cloaked in her dark world, Sarah was sleeping 12 to 16 hours a day. She would weep in class, so much that she'd sneak off to the bathroom so no one could see. "Almost like someone with an addiction," says Sarah, "I was finding places to hide my habit." She ate little and was losing weight. "It got to the point where I was driving home one day and I really wanted to drive the car over the yellow line into oncoming traffic," says Sarah. "I was like, Okay, I really have to tell someone." Her doctor diagnosed severe depression. Now 24, Sarah takes an effective antidepressant, and the crying fits that would overwhelm her for hours once or twice a day now happen only every few months or so and last only maybe 10 minutes.

A major depressive disorder, if left untreated, usually lasts for six months or longer and possibly even two or more years (APA, 2013). Some people experience a single episode with a full return to previous levels of functioning. However, the majority of people with major depression, at least 50%, have repeated occurrences (Monroe & Harkness, 2011). Given a pattern of repeated occurrences of major depressive episodes and prolonged symptoms, many professionals have come to view major depression as a chronic, indeed lifelong, disorder.

MAJOR DEPRESSIVE DISORDER WITH SEASONAL PATTERN Are you glum on gloomy days? Is your temper short during the brief days of winter? Are you dismal during the dark of long winter nights? Do you feel "up" when the long sunny days of spring and summer return?

Many people report that their moods vary with the weather. For some people, the changing of the seasons from summer into fall and winter leads to a type of depression called **major depressive disorder with seasonal pattern**.

The features of MDD with seasonal pattern, often referred to as *seasonal affective disorder*, include fatigue, excessive sleep, craving for carbohydrates, and weight gain. The depression tends to lift with the early buds of spring. It affects women more often than men and is most common among young adults (Magnusson & Partonen, 2005).

The seasonal pattern of MDD is more prevalent the farther one goes from the equator, because there are greater seasonal variations in daylight hours (Melrose, 2015). In a survey of a community sample in Toronto, for example, it was found that 11% of people with major depression had the seasonal subtype (Levitt, Boyle, Joffe, & Baumal, 2000).

Numerous explanations have been proposed to explain the cause of this type of depression. One possibility is that seasonal changes in light may alter the body's biological rhythms that regulate such processes as body temperature and

David De Lossy/Photodisc/Getty Images

When are changes in mood considered abnormal? Although changes in mood in response to the ups and downs of everyday life may be quite normal, persistent or severe changes in mood or cycles of extreme elation and depression may suggest the presence of a depressive or bipolar disorder.

major depressive disorder with seasonal pattern Major depressive disorder that occurs seasonally; also known as seasonal affective disorder.

NORMAL/ABNORMAL BEHAVIOUR

Sad Mood: No Disorder

Maira is a 28 year-old woman who works as a dental assistant. She had been dating her boyfriend, Brian, for three years when he abruptly broke off their relationship. Maira was shocked, having hoped that they would get married in the next few years. The couple fought periodically, but there were no signs for Maira that Brian was thinking of ending the relationship. For the week after the breakup, Maira constantly felt on the edge of tears, and would start crying if people asked her how she was doing. She had no interest in food and had to force herself to eat a few things through the day. At the end of the week, her pants were a little loose, as she had lost a few pounds. She called in sick to work for three days after the breakup, and spent the majority of the day in bed. She got herself up and dressed later that week when her best friend came over to take her out. Maira and her friend went to see a movie, but Maira was distracted by thoughts of Brian. A few weeks later, Maira still felt sad about the breakup and sometimes cried when things reminded her of Brian. However, she had returned to work and regained her appetite.

Depression: Disorder

Joaquin is a 39-year-old single man working full time as a mechanical engineer. He has never been married, though he has had several long-term relationships. His last relationship ended over a year ago, when the couple mutually decided to go their separate ways. A few months after that relationship ended, Joaquin began noticing that he was losing interest in his hobbies. He had to force himself to see his friends, and slowly, over the course of a few months, he stopped seeing his friends altogether. He just couldn't get up the energy to do anything but go to work. Work itself became a chore. While Joaquin had once been enthusiastic about his job and his colleagues, he began to have trouble focusing on his work and simply tried to get through the day. Joaquin also began to have trouble sleeping. He was able to get to sleep reasonably but found himself waking up through the night and waking up for the day at 3 or 4 a.m. without being able to get back to sleep. While lying in bed, Joaquin ruminated about how bad he felt and how these feelings were going to last forever. These problems continued for months until Joaquin began having upsetting thoughts about his own death. These thoughts prompted Joaquin to talk to his family doctor, who immediately suggested that Joaquin might be suffering from a clinical level of depression.

sleep–wake cycles (Kurlansik & Ibay, 2012; Sohn & Lam, 2005). Another possibility is that some parts of the central nervous system may have deficiencies in transmission of the mood-regulating neurotransmitter serotonin during the winter months (Sohn & Lam, 2005). A deficiency in vitamin D is also a possibility (Kerr et al., 2015). Whatever the underlying cause, a trial of intense light therapy, called *phototherapy*, often helps relieve depression (Lam et al., 2006; Rastad, Ulfberg, & Lindberg, 2011). Phototherapy typically consists of exposure to a range of 30 minutes to 3 hours of bright artificial light a day. The artificial light supplements the meagre sunlight the afflicted person otherwise receives. People can generally carry out some of their daily activities (e.g., eating, reading, writing) during their phototherapy sessions. Improvement typically occurs within several days of phototherapy, but treatment is likely required throughout the course of the winter season. Light directed at the eyes tends to be more successful than light directed at the skin.

We still don't know how phototherapy works. Mobilizing expectations of improvement (a placebo effect) may be involved in explaining at least part of the effect, although research has shown that phototherapy is more effective than a placebo (Golden et al., 2005; Lam et al., 2006). Phototherapy does not help all people with this type of depression. Fortunately, however, other treatments are effective. For example, a group of Canadian researchers led by Raymond Lam at the University of British Columbia has shown that the seasonal pattern of depression can be effectively treated with the antidepressant medication fluoxetine (trade name Prozac) (Lam et al., 2006).

MAJOR DEPRESSIVE DISORDER WITH PERIPARTUM ONSET   Many, perhaps even most, new mothers experience mood changes, periods of tearfulness, and irritability following the birth of a child. These mood changes are commonly called the "maternity blues," "postpartum blues," or "baby blues." They usually last for a couple of days and are believed to be a normal response to hormonal changes that accompany childbirth. Given these turbulent hormonal shifts, it would be "abnormal" for most women *not* to experience some changes in feeling states shortly following childbirth.

Some mothers, however, undergo severe mood changes that may persist for months or even a year or more. When these mood changes are so severe that they meet the criteria for major depressive disorder, they are referred to as **major depressive disorder with peripartum onset**. Previously known as postpartum depression (*postpartum* derives from the Latin roots *post*, meaning "after," and *papere*, meaning "to bring forth"), it is now recognized that 50% of these cases occur during pregnancy (APA, 2013). MDD with peripartum onset is often accompanied by disturbances in appetite and sleep, low self-esteem, and difficulties in maintaining concentration or attention. The prevalence of this type of depression is in the range of 10–15%, although there are considerable variations across different cultures (Halbreich & Karkun, 2006). This variation could be due to any of a number of factors, including cultural differences in the stigma associated with depression (which would influence the person's willingness to report depressive symptoms), along with further cultural differences in risk factors for depression, such as the prevalence of stressful life events and the availability of social support (Halbreich & Karkun, 2006). MDD with peripartum onset typically remits during the first three months after childbirth—although some cases persist for years (Verkerk, Pop, Van Son, & Van Heck, 2003). Tragically, some women with this disorder die by suicide. (Lindahl, Pearson, & Colpe, 2005).

In what is considered to be an especially severe case of peripartum onset depression, Dr. Suzanne Killinger-Johnson killed herself and her six-month-old baby, Cuyler, by jumping in front of an oncoming subway train. The night before—Thursday, August 10, 2000—Suzanne had been clutching her baby in a Toronto subway station. She stood by the platform for quite some time. Transit officials became concerned, so they called the police. Officers spoke with Suzanne and she left. About 90 minutes later, a similar thing happened at another subway station. This time the police drove her home, leaving her in

major depressive disorder with peripartum onset Major depressive disorder that occurs during pregnancy or following childbirth.

Screening tests for depression are offered annually by the organizers of the National Depression Screening Day (www.mentalhealthscreening.org). Tests like the one below can help you assess whether you are suffering from a serious depression. Such screening tests are not intended for you to diagnose yourself, but rather to raise your awareness of concerns you may want to discuss with a professional.

	Yes	No
1. I no longer find pleasure in the activities I used to enjoy.	____	____
2. On most days I feel sad or numb.	____	____
3. I am consumed by guilt or regret.	____	____
4. Even small decisions seem overwhelming.	____	____
5. The future seems bleak.	____	____
6. My appetite is not what it used to be.	____	____
7. On many mornings it seems pointless to get out of bed.	____	____
8. I often feel restless or on edge.	____	____
9. I do less than I used to yet I always seem tired.	____	____
10. I have thoughts about killing myself.	____	____

Rating your responses: If you agree with at least five of the statements, including either item 1 or 2, and if you have had these complaints for at least two weeks, professional help is strongly recommended. If you answered "yes" to statement 10, seek consultation with a professional immediately. If you don't know who to turn to, contact your college or university counselling centre, neighbourhood mental health centre, or health provider.

the care of her husband and relatives. During rush hour the next morning, Suzanne slipped out of the house with her baby and went to yet another subway station. Commuters watched in horror as Suzanne dived in front of an oncoming train, clutching her baby. The infant was killed instantly. Suzanne died several days later.

Although MDD with peripartum onset may involve chemical or hormonal imbalances brought on by pregnancy or childbirth (Bloch, Rotenberg, Koren, & Ehud, 2006), psychosocial factors such as financial problems, a troubled marriage, lack of social or emotional support from partners and family members, a history of depression, or an unwanted or sick baby all increase a woman's vulnerability to depression (Boyce & Hickey, 2005; Viguera et al., 2011). Having this type of depression also appears to increase a woman's risk of future depressive episodes (Bloch et al., 2006).

RISK FACTORS FOR MAJOR DEPRESSION Factors that place people at greater risk of developing major depression include age (initial onset is more common among younger adults than older ones), socioeconomic status (people on the lower rungs of the socioeconomic ladder are at greater risk than those who are better off), and marital status (people who are not in an intimate relationship tend to be at greater risk than those who are in such a relationship) (Afifi, Cox, & Enns, 2006).

Women are nearly twice as likely as men to develop major depression, although the difference becomes smaller with advancing age (Pearson et al., 2013) (see Figure 4.2). Although hormonal or other biologically linked gender differences may be involved, the gender difference may be caused by the greater amount of stress women encounter in contemporary life (Hammen, 2005). Women are more likely than men to encounter such stressful life factors as physical and sexual abuse, poverty, single parenthood, and sexism. According to Bohra, Srivastava, and Bhatia (2015), the high rate of depression among women in India may reflect the disadvantaged position of women, increased stressors related to multiple roles, and the effect of domestic violence.

Differences in coping styles may also help explain women's greater proneness to depression. Regardless of whether the initial precipitants of depression are biological, psychological, or social, one's coping responses may either worsen or reduce the severity and duration of depressive episodes. Nolen-Hoeksema and Corte (2004) have found that

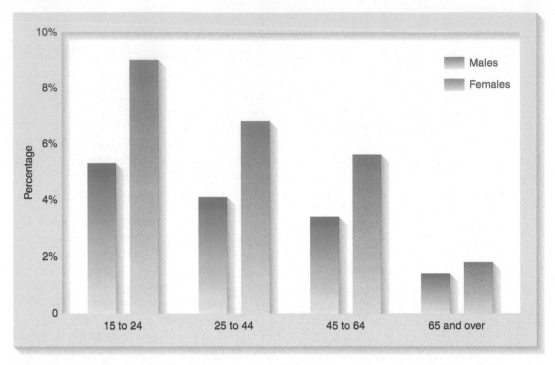

FIGURE 4.2 **Prevalence of major depressive disorder, by age (years) and gender, in the past 12 months in Canada.**

Source: Based on Statistics Canada (2013). Mental Health Profile, Canadian Community Health Survey - Mental Health (CCHS), by age group and sex, Canada and provinces, CANSIM Table 105-1101. This does not constitute an endorsement by Statistics Canada of this product.

men are more likely to distract themselves when they are depressed, whereas women are more likely to amplify depression by ruminating about their feelings and possible causes. Women may be more likely to sit at home when they are depressed and think about how they feel or try to understand the reasons they feel the way they do, whereas men may try to distract themselves by doing something they enjoy, such as going to a favourite hangout, to get their mind off their feelings. However, men often distract themselves by turning to alcohol as a form of self-medication, which can lead to another set of psychological and social problems (Nolen-Hoeksema & Corte, 2004).

Rumination is not limited to women, although they tend to ruminate more than men. Both men and women who repeatedly ruminate about the loss of loved ones or when feeling down or sad are more likely to become depressed and to suffer longer and more severe depression than those who ruminate less (Joormann, Levens, & Gotlib, 2011).

Although the gender gap in depression continues, more men are seeking help for depression. The male ego also seems to be battered by external assaults, from corporate downsizing to growing financial insecurity. While depression has long been viewed by men as a sign of personal weakness, the stigma associated with depression shows signs of lessening, although not disappearing.

Risks of major depression also vary with ethnicity. Indigenous Canadians (First Nations, Inuit, and Métis), compared to non-Indigenous groups, have higher rates of depression and suicide, although there is some fluctuation from one Indigenous community to another (Kirmayer, Brass, & Tait, 2000). According to a 2002 Health Canada report, there are several contributing factors: Because of conflicting messages about the value of their own culture, many Indigenous people do not have a strong sense of self.

atic12/123RF

Women and depression. Women are more likely to suffer from major depression than men. The higher rates of depression among women may be due to factors such as unhappy marriages, physical and sexual abuse, impoverishment, single parenthood, sexism, hormonal changes, childbirth, and the burden of being a primary caregiver to children.

Also, cultural instability has led to sexual abuse, family violence, and substance use disorders, which are associated with a high risk of depression and suicide. Childhood separation, poverty, and access to firearms are contributing factors as well (Health Canada, 2002a).

Major depression generally develops in young adulthood (people in their 20s and 30s) (APA, 2013). It can affect children, but depression is more common in adults (Costello, Erkanli, & Angold, 2006). A multinational study of nine countries[1] conducted in 1992 showed rising rates of major depression in Canada and elsewhere (Cross-National Collaborative Group, 1992). The increases were attributed to social and environmental changes, such as increasing fragmentation of families due to relocations, exposure to wars and civil conflicts, and increased rates of violent crimes, as well as possible exposure to toxins or infectious agents in the environment that might affect mental as well as physical health (Cross-National Collaborative Group, 1992).

One review study reported that the prevalence of MDD had more than doubled in the United States between 1991 and 2002 (Compton, Conway, Stinson, & Grant, 2006). An increase in depression from 7.3% in 2000 to 9.6% in 2011 was reported in a Finnish population (Markkula et al., 2015). Hidaka (2012) explains the historical trend of a rising prevalence of MDD to modernization, which has led to a more sedentary lifestyle as well as a more socially isolated population. Japan, a culture that values collectivism as opposed to individualism, has maintained a lower prevalence of major depression.

However, not all studies have revealed rising rates of depression. Patten and colleagues from the University of Calgary examined the trends in the rates of MDD in Canada from 1994 to 2012 and concluded that the prevalence of MDD has remained stable over the last 20 years (Patten et al., 2015). They report that the results of some prior studies may be a function of the different diagnostic instruments being used.

Persistent Depressive Disorder

Major depressive disorder is severe and marked by a relatively abrupt change from one's preexisting state and followed by periods of remission after a few weeks or months. The diagnosis of persistent depressive disorder is used to classify cases of chronic depression that last for at least two years. People with persistent depressive disorder may have either chronic major depressive disorder or a chronic but milder form of depression called *dysthymia*. Dysthymia often begins in childhood or adolescence and tends to follow a chronic course through adulthood (APA, 2013). The term *dysthymia* derives from the Greek roots *dys-*, meaning "bad" or "hard," and *thymos*, meaning "spirit."

persistent depressive disorder Chronic type of depressive disorder lasting at least two years.

Individuals with dysthymia feel "bad spirited" or "down in the dumps" most of the time, but they are not so severely depressed as those with major depressive disorder. Whereas major depressive disorder tends to be severe and time limited, dysthymia is relatively mild and nagging, typically lasting for years (Klein & Santiago, 2003).

About 3–6% of Canadian adults have dysthymia at some point in their lives (Health Canada, 2002b). Like major depressive disorder, dysthymia is more common in women than men. Similar findings have been reported in other Western countries (Klein & Santiago, 2003).

In persistent depressive disorder, complaints of depression may become such a fixture of people's lives that they seem to be part of their personality. The persistence of complaints may lead others to perceive them as whining and complaining. Although dysthymia is less severe than major depressive disorder, persistent depressed mood and low self-esteem can affect a person's occupational and social functioning.

We noted that major depressive disorder and persistent depressive disorder are unipolar disorders in the sense that the disturbance of mood is only in one direction—down. Yet some people may have fluctuations in mood in both directions that exceed the usual ups and downs of everyday life. These types of disorders are called bipolar disorders. Here, we focus on the three types of bipolar disorder: (1) bipolar I disorder, (2) bipolar II disorder, and (3) cyclothymic disorder.

[1]Canada, the United States, Puerto Rico, Italy, France, Germany, Lebanon, Taiwan, and New Zealand.

BIPOLAR AND RELATED DISORDERS

People with a bipolar disorder ride an emotional roller coaster, swinging from the heights of elation to the depths of depression without external cause.

Bipolar I Disorder

bipolar I disorder Bipolar disorder characterized by manic episodes.

manic episodes Periods of unrealistically heightened euphoria, extreme restlessness, and excessive activity characterized by disorganized behaviour and impaired judgment.

The essential feature of **bipolar I disorder** is the occurrence of one or more **manic episodes**. A disorder can thus be labelled "bipolar" even if it consists of manic episodes without any past or present major depressive episodes. In such cases, it is possible that a major depressive disorder will eventually appear or has been overlooked. In a few cases of bipolar I disorder, called the *mixed type*, a manic episode and a major depressive episode occur simultaneously (i.e., rapidly alternating between mania and depression) (Swann et al., 2013). More frequently, though, cycles of elated and depressed mood states alternate with intervening periods of normal mood. The first episode may be either manic or depressive.

Manic episodes, or periods of mania, typically begin abruptly, gathering force within days. These episodes, usually lasting from a few weeks to several months, are generally shorter in duration and end more abruptly than major depressive episodes. During a manic episode, the person experiences a sudden elevation or expansion of mood and feels unusually cheerful, euphoric, or optimistic. The full DSM-5 criteria are outlined in Table 4.3. The person seems to have boundless energy and is extremely sociable, although

---

TABLE 4.3

DSM-5 Criteria for Manic Episode

A. A distinct period of abnormally and persistently elevated, expansive, or irritable mood and abnormally and persistently increased goal-directed activity or energy, lasting at least 1 week and present most of the day, nearly every day (or any duration if hospitalization is necessary).

B. During the period of mood disturbance and increased energy or activity, three (or more) of the following symptoms (four if the mood is only irritable) are present to a significant degree and represent a noticeable change from usual behavior:

  1. Inflated self-esteem or grandiosity.

  2. Decreased need for sleep (e.g., feels rested after only 3 hours of sleep).

  3. More talkative than usual or pressure to keep talking.

  4. Flight of ideas or subjective experience that thoughts are racing.

  5. Distractibility (i.e., attention too easily drawn to unimportant or irrelevant external stimuli), as reported or observed.

  6. Increase in goal-directed activity (either socially, at work or school, or sexually) or psychomotor agitation (i.e., purposeless non-goal-directed activity).

  7. Excessive involvement in activities that have a high potential for painful consequences (e.g., engaging in unrestrained buying sprees, sexual indiscretions, or foolish business investments).

C. The mood disturbance is sufficiently severe to cause marked impairment in social or occupational functioning or to necessitate hospitalization to prevent harm to self or others, or there are psychotic features.

D. The episode is not attributable to the physiological effects of a substance (e.g., a drug of abuse, a medication, other treatment) or to another medical condition.
Note: A full manic episode that emerges during antidepressant treatment (e.g., medication, electroconvulsive therapy) but persists at a fully syndromal level beyond the physiological effect of that treatment is sufficient evidence for a manic episode and, therefore, a bipolar I diagnosis.

Note: Criteria A–D constitute a manic episode. At least one lifetime manic episode is required for the diagnosis of bipolar I disorder.

---

perhaps to the point of becoming overly demanding and overbearing toward acquaintances. Other people recognize the sudden shift in mood to be excessive in light of the person's circumstances. It's one thing to feel elated if you've just won the lottery; it is another to feel euphoric because it's Wednesday.

People in a manic phase are excited and may strike others as silly, by carrying jokes too far, for example. They tend to show poor judgment and to become argumentative, sometimes going so far as destroying property. Roommates may find manic people abrasive and avoid them. They tend to speak very rapidly (with **pressured speech**). Their thoughts and speech may jump from topic to topic (in a **rapid flight of ideas**). Others find it difficult to get a word in edgewise. Manic people may also become extremely generous and give away costly possessions or make large charitable contributions they can ill afford. They may not be able to sit still or sleep restfully. They almost always show less need for sleep. They tend to awaken early yet feel well rested and full of energy. They sometimes go for days without sleep and without feeling tired. Although they may have abundant stores of energy, they seem unable to organize their efforts constructively. Their elation impairs their ability to work and maintain normal relationships.

During a manic episode individuals generally experience an inflated sense of self-esteem that may range from extreme self-confidence to wholesale delusions of grandeur, believing, for example, that they have a special relationship with God. They may feel capable of solving the world's problems or of composing symphonies despite a lack of any special knowledge or talent. They may spout off about matters on which they know little, such as how to solve world hunger or how to prevent global warming. It soon becomes clear that they are disorganized and incapable of completing their projects. They become highly distractible. Their attention is easily diverted by irrelevant stimuli like the sounds of a ticking clock or of people talking in the next room. They tend to take on multiple tasks, more than they can handle. They may suddenly quit their jobs to enroll in art school, wait tables at night, organize charity drives on weekends, and work on a bestselling novel in their "spare time." They tend to exercise poor judgment and fail to weigh the consequences of their actions. They may get into trouble as a result of lavish spending, reckless driving, or sexual escapades.

The following case provides an account of a manic episode, documented by Toronto psychiatrist Dr. Virginia Edwards.

pressured speech Outpouring of speech in which words seem to surge urgently for expression, as in a manic state.

rapid flight of ideas A characteristic of manic behaviour involving rapid speech and changes of topic.

> Brian began acting quite strangely shortly after his brother's wife had a son. He told his wife, Wanda, he had invented a motor that could run on propane only, and he thought General Motors would buy his invention. He became more and more talkative, with monologues running far into the night, which Wanda found exhausting. Wanda called her father-in-law, who talked quietly to Brian. Brian then broke into tears, rocking back and forth and lamenting what a failure he was. They took Brian to the local hospital and he agreed to be admitted. After he calmed down, he said he felt great, as if his ideas were brilliant. He needed little sleep and his thoughts raced. Brian said that he had never felt so wonderful in his life but that he also felt he was on a roller coaster he couldn't get off.
>
> Used with the permission of Virginia Edwards.

More than 90% of people who experience manic episodes eventually experience a recurrence (APA, 2013). Some people with recurring bipolar disorder attempt suicide "on the way down" from the manic phase. They report they would do nearly anything to escape the depths of depression they know lie ahead.

Sometimes cases involve periods of "rapid cycling" in which the individual experiences two or more full cycles of mania and depression within a year without any intervening normal periods. Rapid cycling is associated with an earlier age of onset and is relatively uncommon (Miklowitz & Johnson, 2006).

Bipolar II Disorder

Bipolar II disorder is associated with a milder form of mania, called *hypomania*, from the Greek prefix *hypo-*, meaning "under" or "less than." In bipolar II, the person has experienced one or more major depressive episodes and at least one hypomanic episode, but never a full-blown manic episode. Hypomanic episodes are less severe than manic episodes and are not accompanied by the severe social or occupational problems associated with full-blown manic episodes. During hypomanic episodes, people may have an inflated sense of self-esteem, feel unusually charged with energy and alert, and be more restless and irritable than usual. They may be able to work long hours with little fatigue or need for sleep.

Bipolar disorders are relatively uncommon, with estimated lifetime prevalence rates in Canada of 0.87% for bipolar I and 0.57% for bipolar II (McDonald et al., 2015). Unlike major depression, rates of bipolar disorder appear about equal in men and women, although women tend to have more depressive episodes (Miklowitz & Johnson, 2006; McDonald et al., 2015). The typical age of onset of bipolar disorder is in the 20s (Schaffer, Cairney, Cheung, Veldhuizen, & Levitt, 2006), but sometimes the disorder does not appear until a person's 40s or 50s.

Whether bipolar I and bipolar II represent qualitatively different disorders or different points along a continuum of severity of bipolar disorder remains to be determined.

Cyclothymic Disorder

Cyclothymia is derived from the Greek *kyklos*, which means "circle," and *thymos*, "spirit." The notion of a circular-moving spirit is an apt description because this disorder involves a chronic cyclical pattern of mood disturbance characterized by mild mood swings of at least two years (one year for children and adolescents). The individual with **cyclothymic disorder** has numerous periods of hypomanic symptoms that are not severe enough to meet the criteria for a hypomanic episode and numerous periods of mild depressive symptoms that do not measure up to a major depressive episode (APA, 2013).

Cyclothymic disorder usually begins in late adolescence or early adulthood and persists for years. Few, if any, periods of normal mood last for more than a month or two. Neither the periods of elevated or depressed mood are severe enough to warrant a diagnosis of bipolar disorder, however. Estimates from community studies indicate lifetime prevalence rates for cyclothymic disorder of between 0.4% and 1% (4 to 10 people in 1000), with men and women about equally likely to be affected (APA, 2013).

When they are "up," people with cyclothymic disorder show elevated activity levels, which they direct toward accomplishing various professional or personal projects. However, their projects may be left unfinished when their moods reverse. When they enter a mildly depressed mood state they find it difficult to summon the energy or interest to persevere. They feel lethargic and depressed, but not to the extent typical of a major depressive episode.

Social relationships may become strained by shifting moods, and work may suffer. Social invitations, eagerly sought during hypomanic periods, may be declined during depressed periods. Phone calls may not be returned as the mood slumps. Sexual interest waxes and wanes with the person's moods.

The boundaries between bipolar disorder and cyclothymic disorder are not yet clearly established. Some forms of cyclothymic disorder may represent a mild, early type of bipolar disorder. About one third of people with cyclothymia go on to develop full-fledged bipolar disorder. People with cyclothymia, compared to other people in the general population, are more likely to have family members who suffer from bipolar disorder. Cyclothymia also responds to similar medications used to treat bipolar disorder. Findings such as these suggest that cyclothymia and bipolar disorder may have etiological factors in common (Akiskal, 2001).

Depressive and Bipolar and Related Disorders

- **What are the features associated with major depressive disorder?** People with major depressive disorder experience a profound change in mood that impairs their ability to function. There are many associated features of major depressive disorder, including downcast mood; changes in appetite; difficulty sleeping; reduced sense of pleasure in formerly enjoyable activities; feelings of fatigue or loss of energy; sense of worthlessness; excessive or misplaced guilt; difficulties concentrating, thinking clearly, or making decisions; repeated thoughts of death or suicide; attempts at suicide; and even psychotic behaviours (hallucinations and delusions).

- **What is persistent depressive disorder?** People with persistent depressive disorder may have either chronic major depressive disorder or a chronic but milder form of depression called *dysthymia*, which lasts at least two years.

- **What is bipolar I disorder?** Bipolar I disorder is defined by the occurrence of one or more manic episodes, which

generally but not necessarily occur in individuals who have experienced major depressive episodes.

- **What is bipolar II disorder?** In bipolar II disorder, depressive episodes occur along with hypomanic episodes but without the occurrence of a full-blown manic episode.

- **What characterizes manic episodes?** Manic episodes are characterized by sudden elevation or expansion of mood and sense of self-importance, feelings of almost boundless energy, hyperactivity, and extreme sociability, which often take a demanding and overbearing form. People in manic episodes tend to exhibit pressured or rapid speech, rapid "flight of ideas," and decreased need for sleep.

- **What characterizes hypomanic episodes?** Hypomanic episodes resemble manic episodes but are less severe and do not cause impairment in social or occupational functioning.

- **What is cyclothymic disorder?** Cyclothymic disorder is a type of bipolar disorder characterized by a chronic pattern of mild mood swings.

THEORETICAL PERSPECTIVES

Multiple factors—biological, psychological, social, and environmental—appear to be involved in the development of depressive and bipolar disorders. In this section, we first consider the impact of stress and the protective value of social support and particular coping styles. Then we consider the contributions of psychological and biological perspectives to our understanting of the depressive and bipolar disorders.

Stress

Research indicates that there is a robust and causal association between stressful life events and major depressive episodes (Colman et al., 2014; Hammen, 2005); major depression is often preceded by stressful events, although not everyone who experiences such events will become depressed. Stressors such as the loss of a loved one, prolonged unemployment, physical illness, marital or relationship problems, economic hardship, pressure at work, racism, and discrimination may all contribute to the development and recurrence of depressive disorders, especially major depressive disorder (Hammen, 2005; Kendler & Prescott, 2006). To illustrate with an example of a physical illness as a stressor, results from an Ontario study of 297 people with HIV/AIDS revealed that 54% were currently suffering from clinically significant depression (Williams et al., 2005). As we saw earlier, this is much higher than the rate of depression in the general population.

Although stress appears to contribute to the risk of becoming depressed, research indicates that not all cases of major depression are preceded by stressful life events (Kendler & Prescott, 2006). People are also more likely to become depressed when they hold themselves responsible for undesirable events, such as school problems, financial difficulties, unwanted pregnancy, interpersonal problems, and problems with the law (Hammen, 2005). Research by Kate Harkness at Queen's University in Ontario, as well as the work of other investigators, suggests that stressors may interact with one another to influence a person's risk of depression. For example, the experience of childhood abuse and neglect appears to increase the odds that future stressful events (e.g., in adolescence) will lead to depression (Harkness, Bruce, & Lumley, 2006).

People are also more likely to become depressed if they have a particular genetic makeup that leaves them vulnerable to stress. In such a case, a person might possess the short allele (variant) of a gene involved in the regulation of the neurotransmitter serotonin (Caspi & Moffitt, 2006).

To complicate matters, the relationship between stress and depression may cut both ways: Stressful life events may contribute to depression, and depressive symptoms in themselves may be stressful or lead to additional sources of stress, such as divorce or loss of employment. When you're depressed, for example, you may find it more difficult to keep up with your work at school or on the job, which can lead to more stress as your work piles up. The closer the stressful event taps the person's core concerns (failing at work or school, for instance), the more likely it is to precipitate a relapse in people who have a history of depression (Hammen, 2005). Stressful events may also play a role in triggering episodes of bipolar disorder (Miklowitz & Johnson, 2006).

Some people seem better able to withstand stress or recover from losses than others. Investigators find that psychosocial factors such as social support and coping styles may serve as buffers against depression in times of stress (Colman et al., 2014; Hammen, 2005). To illustrate, research conducted at the University of Manitoba and University of Calgary indicates that depression is more prevalent among people who live alone, such as women who are separated or divorced, or elderly men who never married (Afifi et al., 2006; Patten et al., 2006). Close relationships, such as with marital partners, may provide a source of support during times of stress. The availability of social support is also associated with quicker recoveries and better outcomes in cases of major depression (Nasser & Overholser, 2005).

Evidence also shows that people with major depression are less likely to use active problem-solving strategies to alleviate stress than are nondepressed people (Matheson & Anisman, 2003). People with major depression also show deficits in skills needed to solve interpersonal problems with friends, co-workers, or supervisors (Haugh, 2006). People who are better able to solve their problems in daily life are more likely to overcome their depression (Nezu, Wilkins, & Nezu, 2004).

Psychodynamic Perspectives

The classic psychodynamic theory of depression of Freud (1917/1957) and his followers (e.g., Abraham, 1916/1948) holds that depression represents anger directed inward rather than against significant others. Anger may become directed against the self following either the actual or threatened loss of these important others.

mourning Normal feelings or expressions of grief following a loss.

Freud believed that **mourning** or normal bereavement is a healthy process by which one eventually comes to psychologically separate oneself from a person who is lost through death, separation, divorce, or other reason. Pathological mourning, however, does not promote healthy separation. Rather, it fosters lingering depression. Pathological mourning is likely to occur in people who hold powerful ambivalent feelings—a combination of positive feelings (love) and negative ones (anger, hostility)—toward the person who has departed or whose departure is feared. Freud theorized that when people lose or even fear losing an important figure about whom they feel ambivalent, their feelings of anger toward the other person turn to rage. Yet rage triggers guilt, which in turn prevents the person from venting anger directly at the lost person (called an *object*).

To preserve a psychological connection to the lost object, people introject, or bring inward, a mental representation of the object. They thus incorporate the other person into the self. Now anger is turned inward, against the part of the self that represents the inward representation of the lost person. This produces self-hatred, which in turn leads to depression.

From a psychodynamic viewpoint, bipolar disorders represent shifting dominance of the individual's personality by the ego and superego. In the depressive phase, the superego is dominant, producing exaggerated notions of wrongdoings and flooding the individual with feelings of guilt and worthlessness. After a time, the ego rebounds and asserts supremacy, producing feelings of elation and self-confidence that come to characterize the manic phase. The excessive display of ego eventually triggers a return of guilt, once again plunging the individual into depression.

While also emphasizing the importance of loss in depression, more recent psychodynamic models focus on issues relating to the individual's sense of self-worth or self-esteem. One model, called the *self-focusing model*, considers how people allocate their attentional processes after a loss (death of a loved one, a personal failure, etc.) (Pyszczynski & Greenberg, 1992). According to this model, depression-prone people experience a period of intense self-examination (self-focusing) following a major loss or disappointment. They become preoccupied with thoughts about the lost object (loved one) or personal failure and remain unable to surrender hope of somehow regaining it.

Consider a person who must cope with the termination of a failed romantic relationship. It may be clear to all concerned that the relationship is beyond hope of revival. The self-focusing model proposes, however, that the depression-prone individual persists in focusing attention on restoring the relationship, rather than recognizing the futility of the effort and getting on with life. Moreover, the lost partner was someone who was a source of emotional support and upon whom the depression-prone individual had relied to maintain feelings of self-esteem. Following the loss, the depression-prone individual feels stripped of hope and optimism because these positive feelings that had depended on the other person are now lost. The loss of self-esteem and feelings of security, not the loss of the relationship itself, precipitate depression. Similarly, if depression-prone people peg their self-worth to a specific occupational goal, such as success in a modelling career, failure triggers self-focusing and consequent depression. Only by surrendering the object or lost goal and fostering alternative sources of identity and self-worth can the cycle be broken.

Psychodynamic theorists focus on the role of loss in depression. Research does show that the losses of significant others (e.g., through death or divorce) are often (but not invariably) associated with the onset of depression (Kendler & Prescott, 2006). Such losses may also lead to other psychological disorders, however. There is a lack of research to support Freud's view that repressed anger toward a departed loved one is turned inward in depression.

Research on the utility of the self-focusing model has been mixed. On one hand, evidence supports the view that a self-focusing style is associated with depression, especially in women (Mor & Winquist, 2002; Muraven, 2005). On the other hand, self-focused attention has been linked to disorders other than depression, including anxiety disorders, alcoholism, mania, and schizophrenia (Mor & Winquist, 2002; Muraven, 2005). The general linkage between self-focused attention and psychopathology may limit the model's value as an explanation of depression.

Learning Perspectives

Whereas psychodynamic perspectives focus on inner, often unconscious, determinants of mood disorders, learning perspectives dwell more on situational factors, such as the loss of positive reinforcement. We perform best when levels of reinforcement are commensurate with our efforts. Changes in the frequency or effectiveness of reinforcement can shift the balance so that life becomes unrewarding.

REINFORCEMENT AND DEPRESSION Peter Lewinsohn (e.g., Lewinsohn, Sullivan, & Grosscup, 1980) suggested that depression may result when a person's behaviour receives too little reinforcement from the environment. Lack of reinforcement can sap motivation and induce feelings of depression. A vicious cycle may ensue: Inactivity and social withdrawal deplete opportunities for reinforcement; lower levels of reinforcement exacerbate withdrawal. The low rate of activity typical of depression may also be a source of secondary reinforcement. Family members and other people may rally around people suffering from depression and release them from their responsibilities. Rather than help people who are struggling with depression regain normal levels of productive behaviour, sympathy may thus backfire and maintain depressed behaviour.

Reduction in reinforcement levels can occur for many reasons. A person who is recuperating at home from a serious illness or injury may find little that is reinforcing to do. Social reinforcement may plummet when people close to us, who were suppliers of reinforcement, die or leave us. People who suffer social losses are more likely to become depressed when they lack the social skills to form new relationships. Some first-year university students are homesick and depressed because they lack the skills to form rewarding new relationships. Widows and widowers may be at a loss as to how to ask someone for a date or start a new relationship.

Changes in life circumstances may also alter the balance of effort and reinforcement. A prolonged layoff may reduce financial reinforcements, which may in turn force painful cutbacks in lifestyle. A disability or an extended illness may also impair one's ability to ensure a steady flow of reinforcements.

Lewinsohn's model is supported by research findings that connect depression to a low level of positive reinforcement and by evidence that encouraging depressed individuals to participate in rewarding activities and goal-oriented behaviours can help alleviate depression (Hopko & Mullane, 2008; Ramnerö, Folke, & Kanter, 2016). It remains unclear, however, whether depression precedes or follows a decline in the level of reinforcement. It may be that people who become depressed lose interest in pleasant activities or withdraw from potentially reinforcing social interactions, and not that inactivity leads to depression.

INTERACTIONAL THEORY The interactions between depressed individuals and other people may help explain the former group's shortfall in positive reinforcement. Interactional theory (Coyne, 1999) proposes that the adjustment to living with a depressed person can become so stressful that the partner or family member becomes progressively less reinforcing toward the depressed person.

Interactional theory is based on the concept of reciprocal interaction. People's behaviour influences and is influenced by the behaviour of others. The theory holds that depression-prone people react to stress by demanding greater social support and reassurance. At first, people who become depressed may succeed in garnering support. Over time, however, their demands and behaviour begin to elicit anger or annoyance. Although loved ones may keep their negative feelings to themselves so as not to further upset the depressed person, these feelings may surface in subtle ways that spell rejection. Depressed people may react to rejection with deeper depression and greater demands, triggering a vicious cycle of further rejection and more profound depression. They may also feel guilty about distressing their family members, which can exacerbate negative feelings about themselves.

Evidence shows that people who become depressed tend to encounter rejection in long-term relationships (Schwartz-Mette & Rose, 2016; Starr & Davila, 2008). Family and friends may find it stressful to adjust to the behaviour of the person who is depressed, especially to such behaviours as withdrawal, lethargy, fretfulness, and despair. Similarly, evidence suggests that people with depressed spouses tend to have negative attitudes toward the spouse if the depressed person is constantly seeking reassurance about his or her self-worth (Van Orden & Joiner, 2006).

All in all, research evidence generally supports Coyne's belief that people who suffer from depression elicit rejection from others (Coyne, 1999), but there remains a lack of evidence to show that this rejection is mediated by negative emotions (anger and annoyance) that the depressed person induces in others. Rather, a growing body of literature suggests that depressed people may lack effective social skills, which may account for the fact that others often reject them. In some cases, these deficits in social skills may be long-standing (i.e., present even when the person is not depressed), while in other cases the deficits may be present only when the person is depressed (and perhaps a consequence of depression) (Petty, Sachs-Ericsson, & Joiner, 2004). People with major depression tend to be unresponsive, uninvolved, and even impolite when they interact with others. In conversation, for example, they tend to gaze very little at the other person, take an excessive amount of time to respond, show very little approval or validation of the other person, and dwell on their own problems and negative feelings. They dwell on negative feelings even when interacting with strangers. In effect, they turn other people off, setting the stage for rejection.

Whether social-skills deficits are a cause or a symptom of depression remains to be determined. Whatever the case, impaired social behaviour likely plays an important role in determining the persistence or recurrence of depression. As we shall see, some psychological approaches to treating depression (e.g., interpersonal psychotherapy and Lewinsohn's social-skills training approach, discussed later) focus on helping people with depression better understand and overcome their interpersonal problems. This may help, in turn, to alleviate depression or perhaps prevent future recurrences.

Cognitive Perspectives

Cognitive theorists relate the origin and maintenance of depression to the ways in which people see themselves and the world around them.

AARON BECK'S COGNITIVE THEORY One of the most influential cognitive theorists, psychiatrist Aaron Beck (Beck, Rush, Shaw, & Emery, 1979), relates the development of depression to the adoption early in life of a negatively biased or distorted way of thinking—the **cognitive triad of depression** (see Table 4.4). The cognitive triad includes negative beliefs about oneself (e.g., "I'm no good"), the environment or the world at large (e.g., "This school is awful"), and the future (e.g., "Nothing will ever turn out right for me"). Cognitive theory holds that people who adopt this negative way of thinking are at greater risk of becoming depressed in the face of stressful or disappointing life experiences, such as getting a poor grade or losing a job.

Beck views these negative concepts of the self and the world as mental templates, called *cognitive schemas*, that are adopted in childhood on the basis of early learning experiences. Children may find that nothing they do is good enough to please their parents or teachers. As a result, they may come to regard themselves as basically incompetent and to perceive their future prospects as dim. These beliefs may sensitize them later in life to interpret any failure or disappointment as a reflection of something basically wrong or inadequate about themselves. Minor disappointments and personal shortcomings become "blown out of proportion."

The tendency to magnify the importance of minor failures is an example of an error in thinking that Beck labels a *cognitive distortion*. He believes cognitive distortions set the stage for depression in the face of personal losses or negative life events. Psychiatrist David Burns (1980) enumerated a number of the cognitive distortions associated with depression:

1. *All-or-nothing thinking.* Seeing events in black and white, as either all good or all bad. For example, one may perceive a relationship that ended in disappointment

cognitive triad of depression In Aaron Beck's theory, the view that depression derives from the adoption of negative views of oneself, the world, and the future.

TABLE 4.4	
The Cognitive Triad of Depression	
Negative view of oneself	Perceiving oneself as worthless, deficient, inadequate, unlovable, and as lacking the skills necessary to achieve happiness.
Negative view of the environment	Perceiving the environment as imposing excessive demands or presenting obstacles that are impossible to overcome, leading continually to failure and loss.
Negative view of the future	Perceiving the future as hopeless and believing that one is powerless to change things for the better. All that one expects of the future is continuing failure and unrelenting misery and hardship.

According to Aaron Beck, depression-prone people adopt a habitual style of negative thinking—the so-called cognitive triad of depression.

Source: Based on Depression. In Clinical Handbook of Psychological Disorders (D.H. Barlow, ed.), 206–244; Beck et al. (1979) Cognitive Therapy of Depression.

as a totally negative experience, despite any positive feelings or experiences that may have occurred along the way. Perfectionism is an example of all-or-nothing thinking. Perfectionists judge any outcome other than perfect success to be complete failure. They may consider a grade of B+ or even A– to be tantamount to an F. They may feel like abject failures if they fall a few dollars short of their sales quotas or receive a very fine (but less than perfect) performance evaluation. Perfectionism is connected with an increased vulnerability to depression (Flett & Hewitt, 2002).

2. *Overgeneralization.* Believing that if a negative event occurs, it is likely to occur again in similar situations in the future. One may come to interpret a single negative event as foreshadowing an endless series of negative events. For example, receiving a letter of rejection from a potential employer leads one to assume that all other job applications will similarly be rejected.

3. *Mental filter.* Focusing only on negative details of events, thereby rejecting the positive features of one's experiences. Like a droplet of ink that spreads to discolour an entire beaker of water, focusing only on a single negative detail can darken one's vision of reality. Beck called this cognitive distortion **selective abstraction**, meaning the individual selectively abstracts the negative details from events and ignores their positive features. One's self-esteem is thus based on perceived weaknesses and failures rather than on positive features or on a balance of accomplishments and shortcomings. For example, a person receives a job evaluation that contains positive and negative comments but he or she focuses only on the negative.

4. *Disqualifying the positive.* The tendency to snatch defeat from the jaws of victory by neutralizing or denying your accomplishments. An example is dismissal of congratulations for a job well done by thinking and saying, "Oh, it's no big deal. Anyone could have done it." By contrast, taking credit where credit is due may help people overcome depression by increasing their belief that they can make changes that will lead to a positive future (Needles & Abramson, 1990).

5. *Jumping to conclusions.* Forming a negative interpretation of events, despite a lack of evidence. Two examples of this style of thinking are called *mind reading* and the *fortune teller error.* In mind reading, you arbitrarily jump to the conclusion that others don't like or respect you, as in interpreting a friend's not calling for a while as a rejection. The fortune teller error involves the prediction that something bad is always about to happen to oneself. The person believes that the prediction of calamity is factually based even though there is an absence of evidence to support it. For example, the person concludes that a passing tightness in the chest *must* be a sign of heart disease, discounting the possibility of more benign causes.

6. *Magnification and minimization.* Magnification, or *catastrophizing*, refers to the tendency to make mountains out of molehills—to exaggerate the importance of negative events, personal flaws, fears, or mistakes. Minimization is its mirror image, a type of cognitive distortion in which one minimizes or underestimates one's good points.

7. *Emotional reasoning.* Basing reasoning on emotions—thinking, for example, "If I feel guilty, it must be because I've done something really wrong." One interprets feelings and events on the basis of emotions rather than a fair consideration of evidence.

8. *Should statements.* Creating personal imperatives or self-commandments—*should*s or *must*s. For example, "I *should* always get my first serve in!" or "I *must* make Chris like me!" After creating unrealistic expectations, the person may become depressed when he or she falls short.

9. *Labelling and mislabelling.* Explaining behaviour by attaching negative labels to oneself and others. You may explain a poor grade on a test by thinking you were "lazy" or "stupid" rather than simply unprepared for the specific exam or, perhaps, ill. Labelling other people as "stupid" or "insensitive" can engender hostility toward them. Mislabelling involves the use of labels that are emotionally

selective abstraction In Beck's theory, a type of cognitive distortion involving the tendency to focus selectively only on the parts of one's experiences that reflect on one's flaws and to ignore those aspects that reveal one's strengths or competencies.

charged and inaccurate, such as calling yourself a "pig" because of a minor deviation from your usual diet.

10. *Personalization.* The tendency to assume you are responsible for other people's problems and behaviour. You may assume your partner or spouse is crying because of something you have done (or not done), rather than recognizing that other causes may be involved.

Consider the errors in thinking illustrated in the following case:

Christie was a 33-year-old real estate sales agent who suffered from frequent episodes of depression. Whenever a deal fell through, she would blame herself: "If only I had worked harder . . . negotiated better . . . talked more persuasively . . . the deal would have been done." After several successive disappointments, each one followed by self-recriminations, she felt like quitting altogether. Her thinking became increasingly dominated by negative thoughts, which further depressed her mood and lowered her self-esteem: "I'm a loser . . . I'll never succeed . . . It's all my fault . . . I'm no good and I'm never going to succeed at anything."

Christie's thinking included cognitive errors such as the following: (1) *personalization* (believing herself to be the sole cause of negative events); (2) *labelling and mislabelling* (labelling herself a loser); (3) *overgeneralization* (predicting a dismal future on the basis of a present disappointment); and (4) *mental filter* (judging her personality entirely on the basis of her disappointments). In therapy, Christie was helped to think more realistically about events and not to jump to conclusions that she was automatically at fault whenever a deal fell through, or to judge her whole personality on the basis of disappointments or perceived flaws within herself. In place of this self-defeating style of thinking, she began to think more realistically when disappointments occurred, such as telling herself, "Okay, I'm disappointed. I'm frustrated. I feel lousy. So what? It doesn't mean I'll never succeed. Let me discover what went wrong and try to correct it next time. I have to look ahead, not dwell on disappointments in the past."

The Authors' Files

Distorted thinking tends to be experienced as automatic, as if the thoughts had just popped into one's head. These **automatic thoughts** are likely to be accepted as statements of fact rather than opinions or habitual ways of interpreting events.

Supporting Beck's model is evidence linking cognitive distortions (including the magnification of one's shortcomings) and negative thinking to depressive symptoms and clinical depression (Beck & Perkins, 2001; Carson, Hollon, & Shelton, 2010). People who are depressed also tend to hold more pessimistic views of the future and are more critical of themselves and others (Beck & Perkins, 2001). Such pessimistic thinking predicts future development or worsening of depression (Alloy et al., 1999).

All in all, there is broad research support for many aspects of the theory, including Beck's concept of the cognitive triad of depression and his view that people with depression think more negatively than nondepressed people about themselves, the future, and the world in general. Although dysfunctional cognitions (negative, distorted, or pessimistic thoughts) are more common among people who are depressed, the causal pathways remain unclear. We can't yet say whether dysfunctional or negative thinking causes depression or is merely a feature of depression. Perhaps the causal linkages go both ways. Our thoughts may affect our moods and our moods may affect our thoughts. Think in terms of a vicious cycle. People who feel depressed may begin thinking in more negative, distorted ways (LaGrange et al., 2011). The more negative and distorted their thinking becomes, the more depressed they feel; the more depressed they feel, the more dysfunctional their thinking becomes. Alternatively, dysfunctional thinking may come first in

automatic thoughts Thoughts that seem to pop into one's mind. In Aaron Beck's theory, automatic thoughts that reflect cognitive distortions induce negative feelings such as anxiety or depression.

the cycle, perhaps in response to a disappointing life experience, which then leads to a downcast mood. This in turn may accentuate negative thinking, and so on. We are still faced with the old "chicken or egg" dilemma of determining which comes first in the causal sequence—distorted thinking or depression. Future research may help tease out these causal pathways. Even if it should become clear that distorted cognitions play no direct causal role in the initial onset of depression, the reciprocal interaction between thoughts and moods may play a role in maintaining depression and in determining the likelihood of recurrence. Fortunately, evidence shows that dysfunctional attitudes tend to decrease with effective treatment for depression (Clark & Beck, 1999; Hollon, 2011).

LEARNED HELPLESSNESS (ATTRIBUTIONAL) THEORY The **learned helplessness** model proposes that people may become depressed because they learn to view themselves as helpless to control the reinforcements in their environments—or to change their lives for the better. The originator of the learned helplessness concept, Martin Seligman (1975), suggests that people learn to perceive themselves as helpless because of their experiences. The learned helplessness model thus straddles the behavioural and the cognitive: Situational factors foster attitudes that lead to depression.

Seligman and his colleagues based the learned helplessness model on early laboratory studies of animals. In these studies, dogs exposed to an inescapable electric shock showed the "learned helplessness effect" by failing to learn to escape when the shock was later made escapable (Overmier & Seligman, 1967). Exposure to uncontrollable forces apparently taught the animals they were helpless to change their situation. Animals that developed learned helplessness showed behaviours that were similar to those of people with depression, including lethargy, lack of motivation, and difficulty acquiring new skills (Maier & Seligman, 1976).

Seligman (1975, 1991) proposed that some forms of depression in humans might result from exposure to apparently uncontrollable situations. Such experiences can instill the expectation that future reinforcements will also be beyond the individual's control. A vicious cycle may come into play in many cases of depression. A few failures may produce feelings of helplessness and expectations of further failure. Perhaps you know people who have failed certain subjects, such as mathematics. They may come to believe themselves incapable of succeeding in math. They may thus decide that studying for the quantitative section of the Graduate Record Examinations is a waste of time. They then do poorly, completing the self-fulfilling prophecy by confirming their expectations, which further intensifies feelings of helplessness, leading to lowered expectations, and so on, in a vicious cycle.

Although it stimulated much interest, Seligman's model failed to account for the low self-esteem typical of people who are depressed. Nor did it explain variations in the persistence of depression. Seligman and his colleagues (Abramson, Seligman, & Teasdale, 1978) offered a reformulation of the theory to meet these shortcomings. The revised theory held that perception of lack of control over reinforcement alone did not explain the persistence and severity of depression. It was also necessary to consider cognitive factors, especially the ways in which people explain their failures and disappointments to themselves.

Seligman and his colleagues recast the helplessness theory in terms of the social psychology concept of **attributional style**. An attributional style is a personal style of explanation. When disappointments or failures occur, we may explain them in various characteristic ways. We may blame ourselves (an **internal attribution**) or our circumstances (an **external attribution**). We may see bad experiences as typical events (a **stable attribution**) or as isolated events (an **unstable attribution**). We may see them as evidence of broader problems (a **global attribution**) or as evidence of precise and limited shortcomings (a **specific attribution**). The revised helplessness theory—called the *reformulated helplessness theory*—holds that people who explain the causes of negative events (such as failure in work, school, or romantic relationships) according to these three types of attributions are most vulnerable to depression:

1. *Internal factors* or beliefs that failures reflect their personal inadequacies, rather than external factors or beliefs that failures are caused by environmental factors.

learned helplessness In Martin Seligman's model, a behaviour pattern characterized by passivity and perceptions of lack of control that develops because of a history of failure to be able to exercise control over one's environment.

attributional style Personal style for explaining cause-and-effect relationships between events.

internal attribution In the reformulated helplessness theory, a type of attribution involving the belief that the cause of an event involved factors within oneself. Contrast with *external attribution*.

external attribution In the reformulated helplessness theory, a type of attribution involving the belief that the cause of an event involves factors outside the self. Contrast with *internal attribution*.

stable attribution In the reformulated helplessness theory, a type of attribution involving the belief that the cause of an event involved stable rather than changeable factors. Contrast with *unstable attribution*.

unstable attribution In the reformulated helplessness theory, a type of attribution involving the belief that the cause of an event involved changeable rather than stable factors. Contrast with *stable attribution*.

global attribution In the reformulated helplessness theory, a type of attribution involving the belief that the cause of an event involved generalized rather than specific factors. Contrast with *specific attribution*.

specific attribution In the reformulated helplessness theory, a type of attribution involving the belief that the cause of an event involved specific rather than generalized factors. Contrast with *global attribution*.

2. *Global factors* or beliefs that failures reflect sweeping flaws in personality, rather than specific factors or beliefs that failures reflect limited areas of functioning.
3. *Stable factors* or beliefs that failures reflect fixed personality factors, rather than unstable factors or beliefs that the factors leading to failures are changeable.

Let's illustrate these attributional styles with the example of a university student who goes on a disastrous date. Afterwards, he shakes his head in wonder and tries to make sense of his experience. An internal attribution for the calamity would involve self-blame, as in "I really messed it up." An external attribution would place the blame elsewhere, as in "Some couples just don't hit it off" or "She must have been in a bad mood." A stable attribution would suggest a problem that cannot be changed, as in "It's my personality." An unstable attribution, on the other hand, would suggest a transient condition, as in "It was probably the head cold." A global attribution for failure magnifies the extent of the problem, as in "I really have no idea what I'm doing when I'm with people." A specific attribution, in contrast, chops the problem down to size, as in "My problem is how to make small talk to get a relationship going."

The revised theory holds that each attributional dimension makes a specific contribution to feelings of helplessness. Internal attributions for negative events are linked to lower self-esteem. Stable attributions help explain the persistence—or, in medical terms, the *chronicity*—of helplessness cognitions. Global attributions are associated with the generality or pervasiveness of feelings of helplessness following negative events. Attributional style should be distinguished from negative thinking. You may think negatively (pessimistically) or positively (optimistically) but still hold yourself to blame for your perceived failures. An example of pessimistic self-blame for perceived failures would be "I messed up, and this is further evidence that I'm a loser." An example of more optimistic self-blame would be "I messed up, but I can learn from this experience so that it doesn't happen again."

Research is generally but not completely supportive of the reformulated helplessness (attributional) model. There is much evidence that people who are depressed are more likely than nondepressed people to attribute the causes of failures to internal, stable, and global factors (Alloy, Abramson, Walshaw, & Neeren, 2006). Longitudinal studies show that this attributional style, even in people who are currently not depressed, also predicts

Don Romero/Photolibrary/Getty Images

Is it me? According to reformulated helplessness theory, the kinds of attributions we make concerning negative events can make us more or less vulnerable to depression. Attributing the breakup of a relationship to internalizing ("It's me"), globalizing ("I'm totally worthless"), and stabilizing ("Things are always going to turn out badly for me") causes can lead to depression.

the person's future risk for the first onset or recurrence of future depressive episodes (Alloy et al., 2006). Further research, however, is needed to determine whether this attributional style truly causes depression. It could be that some other variable, correlated with depressive attributional style, is the actual causal agent. In addition, the theory may only be applicable to societies where freedom of choice and control are the norm and are culturally valued. The cultural context also needs to be considered when evaluating attributional styles. The impact of individual failures may not be as great in cultures that place greater emphasis on the success of the group (Kirmayer & Groleau, 2001).

Biological Perspectives

Evidence has accumulated pointing to the important role of biological factors, especially genetics and neurotransmitter functioning, in the development of depressive and bipolar disorders. Recent investigations are examining the biological roots of depression at the neurotransmitter level as well as at the genetic, molecular, and cellular levels.

GENETIC FACTORS A growing body of research implicates genetic factors in depressive and bipolar disorders (Jang, 2005; Kendler & Prescott, 2006; Lee, Woo, Greenwood, Kripke, & Kelsoe, 2013; Nes et al., 2013). For one thing, we know these disorders tend to run in families. Families, however, share environmental similarities as well as genes. Family members may share blue eyes (an inherited attribute) but also a common religion (a cultural attribute). Yet strengthening the genetic link are findings showing that the closer the genetic relationship one shares with a person with a major depressive or bipolar disorder, the greater the likelihood that one will also suffer from one of these disorders (Kendler & Prescott, 2006).

Twin studies and adoptee studies provide additional evidence of a genetic contribution. A higher concordance (agreement) rate among monozygotic (MZ) twins than among dizygotic (DZ) twins for a given disorder is taken as supportive evidence of genetic factors. Both types of twins share common environments, but MZ twins share 100% of their genes, as compared to approximately 50% for DZ twins. Twin studies suggest that major depression is moderately heritable (Kendler & Prescott, 2006; Nes et al., 2013). However, individual depressive symptoms vary widely in their heritabilities. Symptoms such as depressed mood or tearfulness do not appear to be heritable, whereas other symptoms (e.g., loss of libido and appetite) have a heritable basis (Jang, Livesley, Taylor, Stein, & Moon, 2004). Data from twin studies suggest that persistent depressive disorder may be relatively less influenced by genetic factors than either major depression or bipolar disorder. Genetic factors are particularly important in bipolar disorder, accounting for roughly 80% of the risk for developing this disorder, although the specific genes remain to be identified (Farmer, Elkin, & McGuffin, 2007).

All in all, researchers believe that heredity plays a contributing role in major depression in both men and women (Jang, 2005; Kendler & Prescott, 2006). However, genetics isn't the only, nor is it even the major, determinant of risk of major depression. Environmental factors, such as exposure to stressful life events, appear to play an important role in determining the risk of the disorder (Kendler & Prescott, 2006).

BIOCHEMICAL FACTORS AND BRAIN ABNORMALITIES If there is a genetic component to depression, just what is inherited? Perhaps the genetic vulnerability expresses itself in abnormalities in neurotransmitter activity. These malfunctions may involve either an overabundance or an oversensitivity of receptor sites on receiving (postsynaptic) neurons where neurotransmitters dock. Antidepressant drugs may work by gradually reducing the number and sensitivity of these receptors. Although early speculation focused mainly on the role of norepinephrine in depression, investigators today believe we also need to take into account irregularities in other neurotransmitters, especially serotonin, in explaining depression (Southwick, Vythilingam, & Charney, 2005).

One line of research uses brain imaging techniques such as the PET scan (to measure metabolic activity) and the MRI (to examine structural differences) that peer into the brains of people with depression. It turns out that the metabolic activity of the prefrontal cortex (the area of the frontal lobes lying in front of the motor areas) is typically lower in clinically depressed groups than in healthy controls (Duman & Aghajanian, 2012). The prefrontal cortex is involved in regulating neurotransmitters believed to be involved in depressive and bipolar disorders, including serotonin and norepinephrine, so it is not surprising that evidence points to irregularities in this region of the brain. Abnormalities in the emotional centres of the brain (the limbic system) have also been observed. Other investigators find that MRI scans of the brains of people with bipolar disorder show evidence of structural abnormalities in parts of the brain involved in regulating mood states, such as the limbic system (Miklowitz & Johnson, 2006).

Research, including work done at the University of Toronto, indicates that the brain abnormalities in depression can be corrected with either drugs and/or cognitive therapy. Both treatments can correct the abnormalities in activity in the prefrontal cortex and limbic system (Goldapple et al., 2004).

Tying It Together

Depressive disorders involve an interplay of multiple factors. Consistent with the diathesis-stress model (see Figure 4.3), depression may reflect an interaction of biological factors (such as genetic factors, neurotransmitter irregularities, or brain abnormalities), psychological factors (such as cognitive distortions or learned helplessness), and social and environmental stressors (such as divorce or loss of a job).

Consistent with this formulation, evidence suggests that genes interact with the environment; people with a particular genetic makeup (e.g., a particular version of a gene involved in serotonin regulation) are most likely to become depressed and suicidal in response to stressful life events (Caspi & Moffitt, 2006). In fact, there is a growing body of evidence that many forms of psychological disorder, including major depression, are the result of interactions between genes and the environment (Rutter, 2006). In other words, both genes and environmental events are important in shaping a person's risk for developing major depression and other psychological disorders.

Stressful life events, such as prolonged unemployment or a divorce, may have a depressing effect by reducing neurotransmitter activity in the brain. These biochemical effects may be more likely to occur or be more pronounced in people with a certain genetic predisposition, or *diathesis*, for depression. However, a depressive disorder may not develop, or may develop in a milder form, in people with more effective coping resources for handling stressful situations. For example, people who receive emotional support from others may be better able to withstand the effects of stress than those who attempt to deal with it on their own. So too may people who make active coping efforts to meet the challenges they face in life.

Sociocultural factors may be major sources of stress that affect the development of depressive disorders. These factors include poverty; overcrowding; exposure to racism,

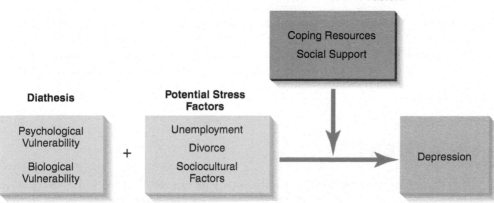

FIGURE 4.3   Diathesis-stress model of depression.
Source: © Pearson Education Canada

sexism, and prejudice; violence in the home or community; unequal stressful burdens placed on women; and family disintegration. These factors may figure prominently in either precipitating depressive disorders or accounting for their recurrence. Other sources of stress include negative life events such as the loss of a job, the development of a serious illness, the breakup of a romantic relationship, or the loss of a loved one.

The diathesis for depression may take the form of a psychological vulnerability involving a depressive thinking style, one characterized by tendencies to exaggerate the consequences of negative events, to heap blame on oneself, or to perceive oneself as helpless to effect positive change. This cognitive diathesis may increase the risk of depression in the face of negative life events. These cognitive influences may also interact with a genetically based diathesis to further increase the risk of depression following stressful life events. Then, too, the availability of social support from others may help bolster a person's resistance to stress during difficult times. People with more effective social skills may be better able to garner and maintain social reinforcement from others and thus be better able to resist depression than people lacking social skills.

REVIEW IT

Theoretical Perspectives on Depressive and Bipolar Disorders

- **How are depressive and bipolar disorders conceptualized within the psychodynamic model?** In classic psychodynamic theory, depression is viewed in terms of inward-directed anger. People who hold strongly ambivalent feelings toward people they have lost, or whose loss is threatened, may direct unresolved anger toward the inward representations of these people that they have incorporated or introjected within themselves, producing self-loathing and depression. Bipolar disorder is understood in psychodynamic theory in terms of the shifting balances between the ego and superego. More recent psychodynamic models, such as the self-focusing model, incorporate both psychodynamic and cognitive aspects in explaining depression in terms of the continued pursuit of lost love objects or goals that it would be more adaptive to surrender.

- **How do learning theorists view depression?** Learning perspectives focus on situational factors in explaining depression, such as changes in the level of reinforcement. When reinforcement is reduced, the person may feel unmotivated and depressed, which can occasion inactivity and further reduce opportunities for reinforcement. Coyne's interactional theory focuses on the negative interpersonal interactions that can lead family members and friends of people with depression to become less reinforcing toward them.

- **How do cognitive models view depression?** Beck's cognitive model focuses on the role of negative or distorted thinking in depression. Depression-prone people hold negative beliefs about themselves, the environment, and the future. This cognitive triad of depression leads to specific errors in thinking, or cognitive distortions, in response to negative events, which in turn lead to depression.

- **What is the learned helplessness model?** The learned helplessness model is based on the belief that people may become depressed when they come to view themselves as helpless to control the reinforcements in their environment or to change their lives for the better. A reformulated version of the theory holds that the ways in which people explain events—their attributions—determine their proneness toward depression in the face of negative events. The combination of internal, global, and stable attributions for negative events renders one most vulnerable to depression.

- **What role do biological factors play in depressive and bipolar disorders?** Genetic factors appear to play a role in explaining major depressive disorder and bipolar disorder. Imbalances in neurotransmitter activity in the brain appear to be involved in depression and mania. The diathesis-stress model is used as an explanatory framework to illustrate how biological or psychological diatheses may interact with stress in the development of depression.

TREATMENT

Just as theoretical perspectives suggest that many factors may be involved in the development of depressive and bipolar disorders, so too are there various approaches to treatment that derive from psychological and biological models. Here we focus on several of the leading contemporary approaches.

Psychodynamic Approaches

Traditional psychoanalysis aims to help people who become depressed understand their ambivalent feelings toward important people (objects) in their lives whom they have lost or whose loss was threatened. By working through feelings of anger toward these lost objects, they can turn anger outward—through verbal expression of feelings, for example—rather than leave it to fester and turn inward.

Traditional psychoanalysis can take years to uncover and deal with unconscious conflicts. Modern psychoanalytic approaches also focus on unconscious conflicts, but they are more direct, are relatively brief, and focus on present as well as past conflicted relationships. According to a recent review, patients treated with psychodynamic therapy tended to improve, although most of the research studies had important methodological problems, which makes it difficult to determine whether psychodynamic psychotherapy is any more effective than placebo (Bond, 2006). Eclectic psychodynamic therapists may also use behavioural methods to help clients acquire the social skills they need to develop a broader social network.

ESB Professional/Shutterstock

Interpersonal psychotherapy (IPT). IPT is a brief, psychodynamic form of therapy that focuses on issues in a person's current interpersonal relationships. Like traditional psychodynamic approaches, IPT assumes that early life experiences are key issues in adjustment, but IPT focuses on the present—the here and now.

Newer models of psychotherapy for depression have emerged from the interpersonal school of psychodynamic therapy derived from the work of neo-Freudians, such as Harry Stack Sullivan and Karen Horney. One contemporary example is **interpersonal psychotherapy (IPT)** (Weissman, Markowitz, & Klerman, 2000). IPT is a brief form of therapy (usually no more than 9 to 12 months) that focuses on the client's current interpersonal relationships. The developers of IPT believe that depression occurs within an interpersonal context and that relationship issues need to be emphasized in treatment. IPT has been shown to be an effective treatment for major depression and shows promise in treating other psychological disorders, including persistent depressive disorder and bulimia (Dietz, Weinberg, Brent, & Mufson, 2015; Markowitz, 2006a, 2006b). Although IPT shares some features with traditional psychodynamic approaches (principally the belief that early life experiences and persistent personality features are important issues in psychological adjustment), it differs from traditional psychodynamic therapy by focusing primarily on clients' current relationships, rather than helping them acquire insight into unconscious internal conflicts of childhood origins. Although unconscious factors and early childhood experiences are recognized, therapy focuses on the present—the here and now.

interpersonal psychotherapy A brief, psychodynamic form of therapy that focuses on helping people resolve interpersonal problems. Abbreviated *IPT*.

Interpersonal psychotherapy helps clients deal with unresolved or delayed grief reactions following the death of a loved one as well as role conflicts in present relationships (Weissman et al., 2000). The therapist helps clients express grief and come to terms with their loss while assisting them in developing new activities and relationships to help renew their lives. The therapist also helps clients identify areas of conflict in their present relationships, understand the issues that underlie them, and consider ways of resolving them. If the problems in a relationship are beyond repair, the therapist helps the client consider ways of ending it and establishing new relationships. In the case of Sal, a 31-year-old television repairman's assistant, depression was associated with marital conflict:

Sal began to explore his marital problems in the fifth therapy session, becoming tearful as he recounted his difficulty expressing his feelings to his wife because of feelings of being "numb." He felt that he had been "holding on" to his feelings, which was causing him to become estranged from his wife. The next

Behavioural Approaches

Behavioural treatment approaches presume that depressive behaviours are learned and can be unlearned. Behaviour therapists aim to directly modify behaviours rather than seeking to foster awareness of possible unconscious causes of these behaviours. Behaviour therapists generally focus on helping depressed patients develop more effective social or interpersonal skills and increasing their participation in pleasurable or rewarding activities.

One illustrative behavioural program was developed by Lewinsohn and colleagues (Hops & Lewinsohn, 1995; Lewinsohn, Antonuccio, Steinmetz Breckenridge, & Teri, 1984). It consists of a 12-session, 8-week group therapy program organized as a course—the Coping with Depression Course. The course helps clients acquire relaxation skills, increase pleasant activities, and build social skills that enable them to obtain social reinforcement. For example, students learn how to accept rather than deny compliments and how to ask friends to join them in activities to raise the frequency and quality of their social interactions. Participants are taught to generate a self-change plan, to think more constructively, and to develop a lifetime plan for maintaining treatment gains and preventing recurrent depression. The therapist is considered a teacher; the client, a student; the session, a class. Each participant is treated as a responsible adult who is capable of learning. The structure involves lectures, activities, and homework, and each session follows a structured lesson plan.

The most widely used behavioural treatment model, called *behavioural activation*, encourages patients to increase their frequency of rewarding or enjoyable activities (Chartier & Provencher, 2013; Kanter et al., 2010). Behaviour therapy has been shown to produce substantial benefits in treating depression in both adults and adolescents (Chartier & Provencher, 2013; Dimidjian et al., 2006).

Behavioural approaches are often used along with cognitive therapy in a broader treatment model called cognitive-behaviour therapy, which is perhaps the most widely used psychological treatment for depression today.

Cognitive Approaches

cognitive therapy A form of psychotherapy in which clients learn to recognize and change their dysfunctional thinking patterns.

Cognitive theorists believe that distorted thinking plays a key role in the development of depression. Aaron Beck and his colleagues have developed a multicomponent treatment approach called **cognitive therapy**, which focuses on helping people with depression learn to recognize and change their dysfunctional thinking patterns. Depressed people tend to focus on how they are feeling rather than on the thoughts that may underlie their feeling states. That is, they usually pay more attention to how bad they feel than to the thoughts that may trigger or maintain their depressed moods.

Cognitive therapy, like behaviour therapy, involves a relatively brief therapy format, frequently 14 to 16 weekly sessions. Therapists use a combination of behavioural and cognitive techniques to help clients identify and change dysfunctional thoughts and develop more adaptive behaviours (Dobson & Khatri, 2002). For example, they assist clients in connecting thought patterns to negative moods by having them monitor the automatic negative thoughts they experience throughout the day by means of a thought diary or daily record. Clients note when and where negative thoughts occur and how they feel at the time. Once these disruptive thoughts are identified, the therapist helps the client challenge their validity and replace them with more adaptive thoughts. The following case example shows how a cognitive therapist works with a client to dispute the validity of thoughts reflecting the cognitive distortion called *selective abstraction* (the tendency to judge oneself entirely on the basis of specific weaknesses or flaws in character). The client judged herself to be completely lacking in self-control because she ate a single piece of candy while she was on a diet.

Client: I don't have any self-control at all.

Therapist: On what basis do you say that?

C: Somebody offered me candy and I couldn't refuse it.

T: Were you eating candy every day?

C: No, I just ate it this once.

T: Did you do anything constructive during the past week to adhere to your diet?

C: Well, I didn't give in to the temptation to buy candy every time I saw it at the store. . . . Also, I did not eat any candy except that one time when it was offered to me and I felt I couldn't refuse it.

T: If you counted up the number of times you controlled yourself versus the number of times you gave in, what ratio would you get?

C: About 100 to 1.

T: So if you controlled yourself 100 times and did not control yourself just once, would that be a sign that you are weak through and through?

C: I guess not—not *through* and *through* (smiles).

Aaron T Beck , Cognitive therapy of depression, Used with permission.

Table 4.5 shows some common examples of automatic thoughts, the types of cognitive distortions they represent, and some rational alternative responses.

Research, such as studies conducted by Zindel Segal and colleagues at the University of Toronto, suggests that mindfulness-based cognitive therapy (MBCT) is a particularly useful way of preventing and prolonging time to relapse, regardless of whether the patient's depression was first treated with either medication or psychotherapy (Bondolfi et al., 2010; Carney & Segal, 2005). MBCT is a group-based psychosocial intervention that involves training the person in meditation exercises, including exercises that increase awareness of the things in the present (e.g., "What I am doing right now") instead of ruminating about bad things that happened in the past or might happen in the future. MBCT also teaches people to simply observe their unwanted thoughts as they float through the stream of consciousness, without attaching evaluative judgments (e.g., "I've just had the thought 'I'll always fail'—I don't need to get upset about the thought or believe it; all I need to do is to notice that the thought comes and goes") (Segal, Williams, & Teasdale, 2002).

There is ample evidence supporting the effectiveness of cognitive therapy in treating major depression and in preventing relapses (Hollon, 2011). Depressive symptoms often lift within 8 to 12 sessions. The benefits appear comparable to those of antidepressant medication in treating depression, even in treating moderate to severe depression (Beck &

TABLE 4.5

Cognitive Distortions and Rational Responses

Automatic Thought	Kind of Cognitive Distortion	Rational Response
I'm all alone in the world.	All-or-nothing thinking	It may feel like I'm all alone, but there are some people who care about me.
Nothing will ever work out for me.	Overgeneralization	No one can look into the future. Concentrate on the present.
My looks are hopeless.	Magnification	I may not be perfect looking, but I'm far from hopeless.
I'm falling apart. I can't handle this.	Magnification	Sometimes I just feel overwhelmed. But I've handled things like this before. Just take it a step at a time and I'll be okay.
I guess I'm just a born loser.	Labelling and mislabelling	Nobody is destined to be a loser. Stop talking yourself down.
I've lost only four kilograms on this diet. I should just forget it. I can't succeed.	Negative focusing/Minimization/Disqualifying the positive/Jumping to conclusions/All-or-nothing thinking	Four kilograms is a good start. I didn't gain all this weight overnight, and I have to expect that it will take time to lose it.
I know things must really be bad for me to feel this awful.	Emotional reasoning	Feeling something doesn't make it so. If I'm not seeing things clearly, my emotions will be distorted too.
I know I'm going to flunk this course.	Fortune teller error	Give me a break! Just focus on getting through this course, not jumping to negative conclusions.
I know John's problems are really my fault.	Personalization	Stop blaming yourself for everyone else's problems. There are many reasons why John has these problems that have nothing to do with me.
Someone my age should be doing better than I am.	Should statements	Stop comparing yourself to others. All anyone can be expected to do is their best. What good does it do to compare myself to others? It only leads me to get down on myself rather than getting me motivated.
I just don't have the brains for university.	Labelling and mislabelling	Stop calling yourself names like "stupid." I can accomplish a lot more than I give myself credit for.
Everything is my fault.	Personalization	There you go again. Stop playing this game of pointing blame at yourself. There's enough blame to go around. Better yet, forget placing blame and try to think through how to solve this problem.
It would be awful if Sue turns me down.	Magnification	It might be upsetting. But it needn't be awful unless I make it so.
If people really knew me, they would hate me.	Mind reader	What evidence is there for that? More people who get to know me like me than don't like me.
If something doesn't get better soon, I'll go crazy.	Jumping to conclusions/Magnification	I've dealt with these problems this long without falling apart. I just have to hang in there. Things are not as bad as they seem.
I can't believe I got another pimple on my face. This is going to ruin my whole weekend.	Mental filter	Take it easy. A pimple is not the end of the world. It doesn't have to spoil my whole weekend. Other people get pimples and seem to have a good time.

Dozois, 2011; Siddique, Chung, Brown, & Miranda, 2012). However, the combination of psychological treatment and antidepressant medication in some cases may be more effective than either treatment alone (Cuijpers et al., 2010). There is less research on the psychological treatment of dysthymia, although techniques used in treating major depression, such as cognitive therapy and interpersonal psychotherapy, have shown promising results (Dunner, 2005).

Biological Approaches

The most common biological approaches to treating mood disorders involve the use of antidepressant drugs and electroconvulsive therapy for depression and lithium carbonate for bipolar disorder.

ANTIDEPRESSANT DRUGS Drugs used to treat depression include several classes of antidepressants: tricyclic antidepressants (TCAs), monoamine oxidase (MAO) inhibitors, selective serotonin-reuptake inhibitors (SSRIs), and serotonin-norepinephrine reuptake inhibitors (SNRIs). All of these drugs increase levels and, perhaps, the actions of neurotransmitters in the brain. The increased availability of key neurotransmitters in the synaptic cleft may alter the sensitivity of postsynaptic neurons to these chemical messengers. It is not precisely known how antidepressant medications work in relieving depression. Given that there are many different types of these drugs working on various types (and subtypes) of neurotransmitters, it seems likely that there are several different ways in which the various antidepressant medications exert their therapeutic effects. Antidepressants tend to have a delayed effect, typically requiring several weeks of treatment before a therapeutic benefit is achieved. SSRIs not only lift mood, but in many cases also eliminate delusions that may accompany severe depression (Zanardi, Franchini, Gasperini, Perez, & Smeraldi, 1996). Antidepressant medication is clearly effective in helping relieve major depression in many cases (Wolf & Hopko, 2008). Evidence also shows that antidepressant medication is helpful in treating dysthymia as well (Dunner, 2005; Imel, Malterer, McKay, & Wampold, 2008).

The different classes of antidepressants increase the availability of neurotransmitters, but in different ways (see Figure 4.4). The tricylics, which include imipramine (trade name Tofranil), amitriptyline (Elavil), desipramine (Norpramin), and doxepin (Sinequan), are so named because of their three-ringed molecular structure. They increase levels in the brain of the neurotransmitters norepinephrine and serotonin by interfering with the reuptake (reabsorption by the transmitting cell) of these chemical messengers. As a result, more of these neurotransmitters remain available in the synapse, which induces the receiving cell to continue to fire, prolonging the volley of nerve impulses travelling through the neural highway in the brain.

The selective serotonin-reuptake inhibitors (SSRIs) (fluoxetine, trade name Prozac, is one) work in a similar fashion but have more specific effects on raising the levels of serotonin in the brain. The MAO inhibitors increase the availability of neurotransmitters by inhibiting the action of monoamine oxidase, an enzyme that normally breaks down or degrades neurotransmitters in the synaptic cleft. MAO inhibitors are used less widely than other antidepressants because of potentially serious interactions with certain foods and alcoholic beverages.

The potential side effects of tricyclics and MAO inhibitors include dry mouth, constipation, blurred vision, and, less frequently, urinary retention, paralytic ileus (a paralysis

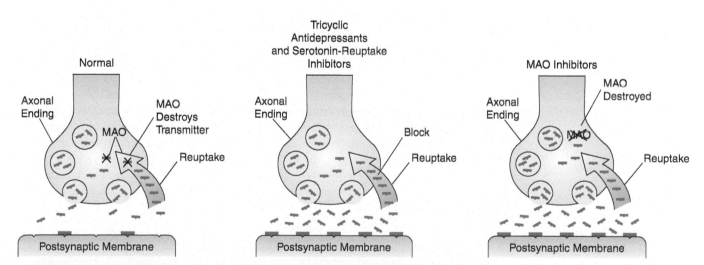

FIGURE 4.4   The actions of various types of antidepressants at the synapse.
Tricyclic antidepressants and selective reuptake inhibitors (SSRIs and SNRIs) increase the availability of neurotransmitters by preventing their reuptake by the presynaptic neuron. MAO inhibitors work by inhibiting the action of monoamine oxidase, an enzyme that normally breaks down neurotransmitters in the synaptic cleft.

of the intestines, which impairs the passage of intestinal contents), confusion, delirium, and cardiovascular complications such as reduced blood pressure. Tricyclics are also highly toxic in very high doses, which raises the prospect of suicidal overdoses if the drugs are used without close supervision.

Compared to the older generation of tricylics, SSRIs such as Prozac and Zoloft have two major advantages: First, they are less toxic and so are less dangerous when taken in very high doses (as in overdose); second, they have fewer of the common side effects (such as dry mouth, constipation, and weight gain) associated with the tricylics and MAO inhibitors. Still, Prozac and other SSRIs may produce side effects such as upset stomach, headaches, agitation, insomnia, lack of sexual drive, and delayed orgasm. Moreover, SSRIs are only moderately effective in treating depression (Taylor & Stein, 2006) and may be less effective than tricyclics (Montgomery, 2006).

Another promising class of medications are the serotonin-norepinephrine reuptake inhibitors (SNRIs), such as Effexor (venlafaxine). SNRIs are similar to tricyclics in that they increase the availability of both serotonin and norepinephrine. Although SNRIs have not been studied as extensively as SSRIs, the evidence so far suggests that in high doses SNRIs appear to be more effective than SSRIs, but not at low doses (Montgomery, 2006). SNRIs appear to be as effective as tricyclics but with milder side effects (Montgomery, 2006). Patients who fail to respond to a particular SNRI may benefit from another SNRI, or they may benefit from some other medication, such as an SSRI (Blier, 2006).

One issue we need to address in discussing drug therapy is the high rate of relapse following discontinuation of medication. A review of drug withdrawal studies showed relapse rates of 25–75% when antidepressants were withdrawn (Petersen, 2006). Continued (maintenance) medication can help reduce the rate of relapse. Psychologically based therapies appear to provide greater protection against a recurrence of depression following termination of treatment, presumably because the learning that occurs during therapy carries past the end of active treatment (Petersen, 2006).

One of the big challenges—and controversies—in recent years concerns the treatment of depressed children and adolescents. It is widely believed that SSRIs and SNRIs are associated with a worsening of suicidal thoughts and behaviours in children and adolescents. Drug-related suicidal ideation may emerge suddenly, without warning, even in people who have not had a previous episode of suicidal ideation. Agitation and restlessness may be early signs of danger (Simon, 2006). Health Canada and health agencies in other countries such as the United States and United Kingdom have issued warnings about the use of these drugs (Whittington, Kendall, & Pilling, 2005). Health Canada advises that patients (or their caregivers) should consult the treating physician to confirm that the benefits of the drug still outweigh its potential risks. According to a review by University of British Columbia psychiatrist E. Jane Garland (2004), there is also evidence suggesting that these medications may not be effective in children and adolescents.

Not all clinicians are convinced that these medications are ineffective and harmful, so the issue remains controversial (Simon, 2006). Adverse effects, when they do occur, appear to be rare. Alternatives to drugs are available, such as psychotherapies like cognitive-behavioural therapy. These treatments do not have the side effects associated with drugs. However, psychotherapies are only moderately effective in treating depression in children and adolescents (Weisz, McCarty, & Valeri, 2006). Clearly, much more research needs to be done to find ways of effectively helping depressed youth. Preliminary evidence suggests that the combination of psychotherapy and SSRIs may be both effective and protective against the increased risk of suicide-related thoughts and behaviours (Whittington et al., 2005).

LITHIUM   The drug lithium carbonate, a powdered form of the metallic element lithium, is the most widely used and one of the most recommended treatments for bipolar disorder (Yatham et al., 2006). It could be said that the ancient Greeks and Romans were among the first to use lithium as a form of chemotherapy. They prescribed mineral water that contained lithium for people with turbulent mood swings.

Lithium is effective in stabilizing moods in people with bipolar disorder and reducing recurrent episodes of mania and depression. People with bipolar disorder may need to use lithium indefinitely to control their mood swings, just as diabetics use insulin continuously to control their illness. Lithium is given orally in the form of a natural mineral salt, lithium carbonate. Despite more than 40 years of use, we still can't say how lithium works, although there is emerging evidence that it influences the communication between neurons (Miklowitz & Johnson, 2006). Lithium treatment must be closely monitored because of potential toxic effects and other side effects. Lithium is not a panacea; many patients fail to respond or cannot tolerate the side effects (e.g., stomach irritation, weight gain, increased thirst). Fortunately, there are other effective medications for bipolar disorder, including some antipsychotic and anticonvulsant medications that happen to have mood-stabilizing properties (e.g., Zyprexa, Tegretol) (Yatham et al., 2006). A meta-analysis of placebo-controlled studies revealed that the effect of the newer generation antipsychotics aripiprazole, olanzapine, quetiapine, risperidone, and ziprasidone was superior to placebo in the treatment of bipolar mania (Perlis, 2007). These alternative medications usually cause fewer or less severe side effects than lithium. However, some patients have only a partial response to lithium or other drugs and some fail to respond at all (Nierenberg et al., 2013). Thus, there remains a need for alternative treatments or drug strategies to be developed, perhaps involving a combination of these or other drugs.

ELECTROCONVULSIVE THERAPY   More commonly called *shock therapy*, electroconvulsive therapy (ECT) continues to evoke controversy. The idea of passing an electric current through someone's brain may seem barbaric. Yet ECT is a generally safe and effective treatment for severe depression and can help relieve depression in many cases in which alternative treatments have failed.

Electroconvulsive therapy involves the administration of an electrical current to the head. A current of between 70 to 130 volts is used to induce a convulsion that is similar to a grand mal epileptic seizure. ECT is usually administered in a series of 6 to 12 treatments over a period of several weeks. The patient is put to sleep with a brief-acting

A CLOSER LOOK

St. John's Wort—A Natural "Prozac"?

Might a humble herb be a remedy for depression? The herb, called St. John's wort, or *Hypericum perforatum*, has been used for centuries to help heal wounds. Now people are using it to relieve depression. Nowhere is it more popular than Germany, where high-strength versions of the herb are among the most widely used antidepressants on the market. The benefits of St. John's wort are currently unclear and have been the subject of much debate. Some studies provide support for the benefits of St. John's wort in treating major depressive disorder with fewer reported side effects than medications. For example, Alpert et al. (2005) found that the herb was more effective than fluoxetine (Prozac). Another study found that the herb was at least as effective as the SSRI drug paroxetine (Paxil) in moderate to severe major depression (Szegedi, Kohnen, Dienel, & Kieser, 2005). However, other studies have raised doubts about the herb's efficacy. According to a review of several recent placebo-controlled studies, St. John's wort has minimal beneficial effects on major depression but is useful in treating milder forms of depression (Apaydin et al., 2016; Linde, Berner, Egger, &

Mulrow, 2005). More promising treatments for major depression include cognitive-behaviour therapy or selective serotonin-reuptake inhibitors.

Regardless of the effects of St. John's wort on depressive symptoms, the herb appears to increase the levels of serotonin in the brain by interfering with its reabsorption, the same mechanism believed to account for Prozac's benefits. Yet we don't know about the herb's long-term safety. Evidence suggests that it should not be combined with conventional antidepressant medications such as Prozac because St. John's wort interacts with these drugs to produce an excess of serotonin in the brain. This is called the *serotonin syndrome*, and it can progress from dizziness, headaches, and vomiting to coma and death (Vermani, Milosevic, Smith, & Katzman, 2005). St John's wort also should be used with caution in patients receiving anticoagulants (blood thinners), oral contraceptives, or antiviral drugs because it can alter the levels of these medications in the blood by means of its effects on the liver (Vermani et al., 2005).

general anaesthetic and given a muscle relaxant to avoid wild convulsions that might result in injury. As a result, spasms may be barely perceptible to onlookers. The patient awakens soon after the procedure and generally remembers nothing. Although ECT was used earlier in the treatment of a wide variety of psychological disorders, including schizophrenia and bipolar disorder, it is typically used today only to treat major depressive disorder in people who do not respond to antidepressant medication (Pagnin, de Queiroz, Pini, & Cassano, 2004).

Evidence supports ECT as a generally safe and effective treatment for severe depression (Kellner et al., 2012). Although it often produces a dramatic relief of symptoms, no one knows exactly how ECT works. ECT produces such mammoth chemical and electrical changes in the body that it is difficult to pinpoint the mechanism of therapeutic action. It is possible that ECT may work by normalizing brain levels of certain neurotransmitters (Grover, Mattoo, & Gupta, 2005). Although ECT can be an effective short-term treatment of severe depression, it too is no panacea. Depression often returns at some later point, even among people who continue to be treated with antidepressant medication (Bourgon & Kellner, 2000).

Electroconvulsive therapy may be administered to either both sides of the head (*bilateral ECT*) or to only one (*unilateral ECT*). Unilateral ECT is applied to the nondominant hemisphere of the brain, which, for most people, is the right side. Bilateral ECT tends to produce a somewhat greater clinical benefit than unilateral ECT, but also greater short-term memory impairment (Reisner, 2003).

There is an understandable concern among patients, relatives, and professionals themselves concerning the possible risk of brain damage from ECT. Much of this concern has focused on potential memory loss. The evidence so far suggests that ECT does not result in structural damage to the human brain, and any memory losses suffered as the result of treatment are temporary except for events occurring shortly before or after ECT administration (Reisner, 2003). Earlier memories or those formed weeks after ECT do not appear to be affected. Still, many professionals view ECT as a treatment of last resort, to be used only after other treatment approaches have been tried and failed. Moreover, it is not possible to definitively rule out the possibility that ECT may cause brain damage in a small proportion of people (Reisner, 2003).

REPETITIVE TRANSCRANIAL MAGNETIC STIMULATION Another promising treatment approach is called *repetitive transcranial magnetic stimulation* (rTMS). This is a noninvasive way of stimulating particular regions of the brain. It involves the use of a device containing a powerful electromagnet, which is placed next to the person's head to induce weak electric currents in particular regions of the brain at particular frequencies for a few minutes per day for several days or weeks. It is thought that this can induce enduring changes (i.e., stimulating or calming down) in the activity of particular brain regions (Fitzgerald, Fountain, & Daskalakis, 2006). When used in the treatment of depression, brain regions that are thought to play a role in depression are repeatedly stimulated, typically the left prefrontal cortex. Although there is some preliminary evidence for the benefits of rTMS, more research is needed to evaluate the magnitude of its effects (Mitchell & Loo, 2006). Research suggests that rTMS is as effective as ECT for severe depression without causing deficits in memory (Hadley et al., 2011).

Other innovative methods have also been developed for the treatment of depression, such as deep brain stimulation (involving the placement of electrodes deep within the brain) and vagus nerve stimulation (stimulating the vagus nerve with electrical signals). These methods show promise in the treatment of severely depressed people who have not benefited from other treatments. In one study, for example, 10 patients suffering from very resistant forms of depression (treatment-resistant depression) were given deep brain stimulation. These patients were not responding to pharmacotherapy, psychotherapy, or ECT. Twelve months following initiation of deep brain stimulation treatment, five patients reached 50% reduction in depressive symptoms and reported significant increases in pleasurable activities (Bewernick et al., 2010).

In summing up, let's note that experts have described clinical practice guidelines for depression. The guidelines are based on evidence from controlled studies showing the following treatments to be effective in treating depression (APA, 2010):

- Antidepressant medication (tricyclics, SSRIs, SNRIs)
- Three specific forms of psychotherapy: cognitive therapy, behaviour therapy, and interpersonal psychotherapy
- A combination of one of the recommended forms of psychotherapy and antidepressant medication
- Other specified forms of treatment, including ECT for severe depression and phototherapy for seasonal depression

Overall, evidence shows that most people with major depressive disorder will respond favourably to cognitive therapy, cognitive-behavioural therapy, or interpersonal psychotherapy, or to antidepressant medications (Cuijpers et al., 2012; Hollon & Shelton, 2001). It is currently a matter of debate whether drugs or psychotherapy is most appropriate for severe depression (Hollon, 2006), although drugs would be indicated if the depressed person is experiencing delusions and hallucinations. Some people who fail to respond to drug therapy may respond favourably to psychotherapy, and vice versa.

Treatments for depression are continually evolving, and researchers have been seeking to identify and investigate new treatments. Combinations of particular medications have been examined. As noted by depression researchers Sidney Kennedy (University of Toronto) and Raymond Lam (University of British Columbia), for patients who have failed to respond to conventional depression treatments, it may be useful to add drugs that are used in the treatment of schizophrenia, such as risperidone (Kennedy & Lam, 2003).

Other interventions can also be useful as adjuncts or alternatives to medication or psychotherapy. For example, research indicates that physical exercise is useful for alleviating depressive symptoms in people with mild to moderate depression (Colman et al. 2014; Hallgren et al., 2015; Martinsen, 2005; Mata et al., 2012).

REVIEW IT

Treatment of Depression

- **What are the approaches taken by the major theoretical perspectives in treating depressive and bipolar disorders?** Psychodynamic treatment of depression has traditionally focused on helping the depressed person uncover and work through ambivalent feelings toward the lost object, thereby lessening the anger directed inward. Modern psychodynamic approaches tend to be more direct and briefer, and they focus more on developing adaptive means of achieving self-worth and resolving interpersonal conflicts. Learning theory approaches focus on helping people with depression increase the frequency of reinforcement in their lives through such means as increasing the rates of pleasant activities in which they participate and assisting them in developing more effective social skills to increase their ability to obtain social reinforcements from others. Cognitive therapists focus on helping the person identify and correct distorted or dysfunctional thoughts and learn more adaptive behaviours. Biological approaches focus on the use of antidepressant drugs and other biological treatments, such as electroconvulsive therapy (ECT). Antidepressant drugs may help normalize neurotransmitter functioning in the brain. Bipolar disorder is commonly treated with lithium.

SUICIDE

Suicidal thoughts are common enough. According to University of Waterloo psychologist Donald Meichenbaum (2005), a practising clinical psychologist will see an average of five patients per month who have suicidal thoughts. Under great stress, many, if not most, people have considered suicide. One Canadian survey found that 10% of men and 13% of women had contemplated suicide at some point in their lives, and 2% of men and 6% of women had attempted suicide (Weissman et al., 1999). Thus, most people who

FIGURE 4.5 Suicide rates according to age (years) and gender. Although adolescent suicides may be more widely publicized, adults, especially middle-aged and elderly men, tend to have high suicide rates.

Source: Data from Statistics Canada (2017). Suicide and suicide rate, by sex and age group. CANSIM, Table 102-0551.

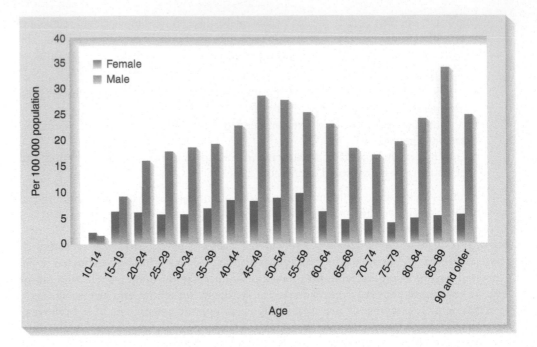

have suicidal thoughts do not act on them. Even so, far too many people kill themselves. In 2012, for example, nearly 4000 Canadians took their lives (Statistics Canada, 2015b). The rates of deaths by suicide, according to the most recent data, are shown in Figure 4.5, where it can be seen that men are more likely than women to actually kill themselves in suicide attempts.

Who Dies By Suicide?

Suicide is one of the leading causes of death in both men and women from adolescence to middle age (Spirito & Esposito-Smythers, 2006; Statistics Canada, 2015b). Disturbingly, suicide rates among Canadian adolescents doubled between 1969 and 1999 (Stewart, Manion, & Davidson, 2002) and have continued to rise. Suicide accounts for 25% of all deaths among 15- to 24-year-olds, and 16% among 25- to 44-year-olds (Statistics Canada, 2015b). Although the problem of teenage suicide often grabs the headlines, suicide rates are higher in middle-aged and elderly men (see Figure 4.5) (Statistics Canada, 2017a).

Despite life-extending advances in medical care, some older adults may find the quality of their lives is less than satisfactory. With longer life, older people are more susceptible to diseases such as cancer and Alzheimer's disease, which can leave them with feelings of helplessness and hopelessness that can give rise to suicidal thinking. Many older adults also suffer a mounting accumulation of losses of friends and loved ones as time progresses, leading to social isolation. These losses, as well as the loss of good health and of a responsible role in the community, may wear down the will to live. Not surprisingly, the highest suicide rates in older men are among those who are widowed or lead socially isolated lives. Whatever the causes, suicide has become an increased risk for elderly people (Mills, Watts, Huh, Boar, & Kemp, 2013). Perhaps society should focus its attention as much on the quality of life that is afforded our elderly as on providing them the medical care that helps make longer life possible.

Although more women than men, by a ratio of 1.5 to 1, attempt suicide, men are three times more likely to actually die by suicide—in large part because they tend to choose quicker-acting and more lethal means, such as firearms or hanging, whereas women are more likely to overdose on pills (Navaneelan, 2012).

Gender differences in suicide risk may mask underlying factors. One explanation for these gender differences is that men are more likely to have a history of alcohol and drug abuse and less likely to have children in the home. Another possibility, according to John Oliffe from the University of British Columbia, is that the stigma associated with male depression and suicide prevent men from seeking help and confiding in others (Oliffe et al., 2016).

Suicide rates are also higher among Indigenous populations. Eduardo Chachamovich, from McGill University, reported a significant increase in suicides among Inuit, which have led to overall rates that are 10 times higher than the rest of Canada. This increase is predominately among the youth of this population (Chachamovich et al., 2015). On April 9, 2016, the First Nation of Attawapiskat in northern Ontario declared a state of emergency following the attempted suicides of 11 youth.

Why Do People Choose to Die By Suicide?

To many lay observers, suicide seems so extreme an act that they believe only "insane" people (meaning people who are out of touch with reality) would choose to die by suicide. However, suicidal thinking does not necessarily imply loss of touch with reality, deep-seated unconscious conflict, or a personality disorder. Having thoughts about suicide generally reflects a narrowing of the range of options people think are available to them to deal with their problems (Brent & Mann, 2006). That is, they are discouraged by their problems and see no other way out. This is illustrated by the following example:

> Sue Goodwin left work one day with a simple, spontaneous plan: She intended to die. Midway through a regular shift at a regular office, she walked calmly into a Toronto subway station. "I remember standing on the platform, thinking, 'This will show all the people who've hurt me. This will show them what they've done to me.'" The rush of air was coming. The train hurtled toward the station. "And then I jumped." The coma lasted five weeks. "I tried to commit suicide because I thought nobody loved me."
>
> Nunes, J. & Simmie, S. (2002). Beyond crazy:
> Journeys through mental illness, McClelland & Stewart.

Many suicides are associated with major depression or bipolar disorder (Gonda et al., 2012; Hawton, Casañas i Comabella, Haw, & Saunders, 2013; Miklowitz & Johnson, 2006), which is why we include the topic in this chapter. Attempted or death by suicide is also connected with other psychological disorders such as alcoholism and drug dependence, schizophrenia, and personality disorders, including antisocial personality disorder and borderline personality disorder (Joiner, Brown, & Wingate, 2005).

Stress is also implicated in many suicides (Renaud, Chagnon, Turecki, & Marquette, 2005). Suicide attempts often occur following highly stressful life events, especially "exit events" such as the death of a spouse, close friend, or relative; divorce or separation; or a family member leaving home. People who consider taking their lives in response to stressful events appear to have poorer problem-solving skills than those who do not consider suicide (Brent & Mann, 2006). People who consider suicide in times of stress may be less able to find alternative ways of coping with the stressors they face.

Theoretical Perspectives on Suicide

The classic psychodynamic model views depression as the turning inward of anger against the internal representation of a lost love object. Suicide thus represents inward-directed anger that

Shutterstock

What happens when we lose our sense of direction?
According to the humanistic-existential perspective, depression may result from the inability to find meaning and purpose in one's life.

Concussions, Depression, and Suicide among NHLers

The summer of 2011 was a tough time for hockey fans, with the untimely deaths of three players, Derek Boogaard, Rick Rypien, and Wade Belak. While fans still question the link between concussions, depression, and suicide, the medical field has confirmed this connection time and again. Dr. Robert Cantu, a neurosurgeon and co-director of the Chronic Trauma Encephalopathy Center at Boston University, explains that depression, anxiety, and substance use disorders are all common in athletes with CTE (chronic traumatic encephalopathy) (Aubry et al., 2009). Sadly, players often fail to report concussive-type injuries and aren't aware that feelings of depression are common in individuals who have suffered a concussion.

Dr. Alain Ptito, neuropsychologist and researcher at the Montreal Neurological Institute at McGill University, has confirmed the connection between depression and concussions:

> Researchers at the Montreal Neurological Institute of McGill University have identified the neurological basis of depression in male athletes with persisting post-concussion symptoms. The study . . . has important clinical implications for the treatment of individuals who have suffered a cerebral concussion. Depression is one of a number of persisting symptoms experienced by athletes following sports concussion. The prevalence of depression in the general population is around 5%, whilst the prevalence of depression in head trauma patients can reach an astounding 40%. "Until now, very little was known about the neurological basis of the depression frequently reported by athletes following concussion," says Dr. Alain Ptito, . . . lead investigator for the study. ("Neurological Basis," 2008)

Source: MNI researchers locate neurological basis of depression frequently reported by athletes following sports concussion, 17 Jan 2008. Used with the Permission of McGill University.

David Zalubowski/AP Images

Concussions, depression, and suicide? Former Toronto Maple Leafs and Calgary Flames tough guy Wade Belak took his own life after suffering with severe depression.

turns murderous. Suicidal people, then, do not seek to destroy themselves. Instead, they seek to vent their rage against the internalized representation of the love object. In so doing, they destroy themselves as well, of course. In his later writings, Freud (1920/1987) speculated that suicide may be motivated by the "death instinct," a tendency to return to the tension-free state that preceded birth. Existential and humanistic theorists relate suicide to the perception that life is meaningless and hopeless.

In the 19th century, sociologist Émile Durkheim (1897/1958) noted that people who experience **anomie**—who feel lost, without identity, rootless—are more likely to die by suicide. Sociocultural theorists likewise believe that alienation in today's society may play a role in suicide. In our modern, mobile society, people frequently move hundreds or thousands of kilometres for school and jobs. Executives and their families may be relocated every two years or so. Military personnel and their families may be shifted about yet more rapidly. Many people are thus socially isolated or cut off from their support

anomie Lack of purpose or identity; aimlessness.

groups. Moreover, city dwellers tend to limit or discourage informal social contacts because of crowding, overstimulation, and fear of crime. It is thus understandable that many people find few sources of support in times of crisis. In some cases, the availability of family support may not be helpful. Family members may be perceived as part of the problem, not part of the solution.

Learning theorists point to the reinforcing effects of prior suicide threats and attempts and to the effects of stress, especially when combined with inability to solve personal problems. People who threaten or attempt suicide may also receive sympathy and support from loved ones and others, perhaps making future—and more lethal—attempts more likely. This is not to suggest that suicide attempts or gestures should be ignored. It is not the case that people who threaten suicide are merely seeking attention. Although people who threaten suicide might not carry out the act, their threats should be taken seriously. People who die by suicide often tell others of their intentions or leave clues beforehand (Joiner, 2006).

Social-cognitive theorists suggest that suicide may be motivated by positive expectancies and by approving attitudes toward the legitimacy of suicide (Joiner, 2006). People who kill themselves may expect they will be missed or eulogized after death, or that survivors will feel guilty for mistreating them. Suicidal psychiatric patients hold more positive expectancies concerning suicide than do nonsuicidal psychiatric samples. They more often expressed the belief that suicide would solve their problems, for example (Linehan, Camper, Chiles, Strosahl, & Shearin, 1987). Suicide may represent a desperate attempt to deal with one's problems in one fell swoop rather than piecemeal.

Social-cognitive theorists also focus on the potential modelling effects of observing suicidal behaviour in others, especially among teenagers who feel overwhelmed by academic and social stressors. A *social contagion*, or spreading of suicide in a community, may occur in the wake of suicides that receive widespread publicity. Teenagers, who seem to be especially vulnerable to these modelling effects, may even romanticize the suicidal act as one of heroic courage, and may expect their demise to have a profound impact on their community. A suicide of a close friend or sibling does not usually increase the risk of a suicide attempt; such imitation is more likely to be triggered by a suicidal model who is not personally known to the imitator, such as a famous musician, actor, or other celebrity (Brent & Mann, 2006).

Biological factors also appear to be involved in suicide. Evidence shows reduced serotonin activity in people who die, or attempt to die, by suicide (Brent & Mann, 2006). Serotonin deficits have been implicated in depression, so the relationship with suicide is not surprising. Yet serotonin acts to curb or inhibit nervous system activity, so perhaps decreased serotonin function leads to a disinhibition, or release, of impulsive behaviour that takes the form of a suicidal act in vulnerable individuals. Consistent with this, serotonin deficits have also been linked to impulsive aggression (Brent & Mann, 2006).

Genetic factors influence, to some extent, the risk of suicidal behaviour (Brent et al., 2015; Joiner, 2006). Suicidal behaviour that occurs before 25 years of age is highly familial; the greater the number of family members with a history of suicidal behaviour, the earlier the age of the appearance of suicidal acts in offspring (Brent & Mann, 2006).

Suicide is connected with a complex web of factors, and its prediction is not simple. There are, however, common risk factors such as family discord, poor coping skills, and bullying, and protective factors, such as social competence and achievement in school (see Table 4.6). Yet it is clear that many suicides could be prevented if people with suicidal feelings would receive treatment for the disorders that underlie suicidal behaviour, including depression, schizophrenia, and alcohol and substance use disorders (Brent & Mann, 2006; Joiner, 2006).

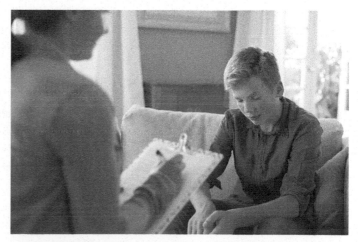

Cathy Yeulet/123RF

Teen suicide. Suicidal teenagers may see no other way of handling their life problems. The availability of counselling and support services may help prevent suicide by assisting troubled teens in learning alternative ways of reducing stress and resolving conflicts with others.

TABLE 4.6

Suicide Risk and Protective Factors

Key Context	Predisposing Factors	Contributing Factors	Precipitating Factors	Protective Factors
Individual	• previous suicide attempt • depression or other mental disorder (e.g., substance use disorder, schizophrenia) • hopelessness • suicidal thoughts	• rigid cognitive style • poor coping skills • gay, lesbian, bisexual, or transgendered sexual orientation • impulsivity • aggression • hypersensitivity/anxiety	• personal failure • humiliation • trauma • health crisis	• individual coping and problem-solving skills • willingness to seek help • good physical and mental health • strong cultural identity and spiritual beliefs
Family	• family history of suicidal behaviour/suicide • family history of childhood neglect, sexual or physical abuse • family history of mental disorder • early childhood loss/ separation or deprivation	• family discord • impaired parent–child relationships	• loss of a significant family member • death of a family member, especially by suicide • recent conflict	• family cohesion and warmth • adults modelling healthy adjustment • high and realistic expectations
Peers	• social isolation and alienation	• negative youth attitudes toward seeking adult assistance • peer modelling of maladaptive behaviours	• teasing/cruelty/bullying • interpersonal loss or conflict • rejection • peer death, especially by suicide	• social competence • healthy peer modelling • acceptance and support
School	• long-standing history of negative school experience • lack of meaningful connection to school	• disruption during key transitional periods at school • reluctance/uncertainty among school staff about how to help	• failure • expulsion • disciplinary crisis	• success at school • interpersonal connectedness/belonging
Community	• multiple suicides • community marginalization • political disenfranchisement • socioeconomic deprivation	• sensational media portrayal of suicide • access to firearms or other lethal methods • reluctance/uncertainty among key gatekeepers about how to help • inaccessible community resources	• high-profile/celebrity death, especially by suicide • conflict with the law/ incarceration	• opportunities for youth participation • community self-determination • availability of resources • community control over local services

Source: Copyright © Province of British Columbia. All rights reserved. Reproduced with permission of the Province of British Columbia.

Predicting Suicide

"I don't believe it. I saw him just last week and he looked fine."
"She sat here just the other day, laughing with the rest of us.
How were we to know what was going on inside her?"
"I knew he was depressed, but I never thought he'd do something like this.
I didn't have a clue."
"Why didn't she just call me?"

Friends and family members often respond to news of a suicide with disbelief or with guilt that they failed to pick up signs of the impending act. Yet even trained professionals find it difficult to predict who is likely to die by suicide.

Evidence points to the role of hopelessness as an important predictor or perhaps contributor to suicidal thinking and behaviour (Brent & Mann, 2006; Joiner, 2006; Marco, Pérez, & Garcia-Alandete, 2016). In one study, psychiatric outpatients with hopelessness scores above a certain cut-off were 11 times more likely to die by suicide than those with scores below the cut-off (Beck, Brown, Berchick, Stewart, & Steer, 1990). But *when* does hopelessness lead to suicide?

People who die by suicide tend to signal their intentions, often quite explicitly, such as by telling others about their suicidal thoughts. Some attempt to cloak their intentions. Behavioural clues may still reveal suicidal intent, however. Edwin Shneidman (1994), a leading researcher on suicide, found that 90% of the people who died by suicide had left clear clues, such as disposing of their possessions. People contemplating suicide may also suddenly try to sort out their affairs, as in drafting a will or buying a cemetery plot. They may purchase guns despite lack of prior interest in firearms. When troubled people decide to die by suicide, they may seem to be suddenly at peace; they feel relieved of having to contend with life problems. This sudden calm may be misinterpreted as a sign of hope.

The prediction of suicide is not an exact science, even for experienced professionals. Many observable factors, such as hopelessness, do seem to be connected with suicide, but we cannot predict *when* a hopeless person will attempt suicide, if at all.

A CLOSER LOOK

Suicide Prevention

Imagine yourself having an intimate conversation with a close campus friend, Chris. You know that things have not been good. Chris's grandfather died six weeks ago, and the two were very close. Chris's grades have been going downhill, and his romantic relationship also seems to be coming apart at the seams. Still, you are unprepared when he says very deliberately, "I just can't take it anymore. Life is just too painful. I don't feel like I want to live anymore. I've decided that the only thing I can do is to kill myself."

When somebody discloses that he or she is contemplating suicide, you may feel bewildered and frightened, as if a great burden has been placed on your shoulders. It has. If someone confides suicidal thoughts to you, your goal should be to persuade him or her to see a professional or to get the advice of a professional yourself as soon as you can. But if the suicidal person declines to talk to another person and you sense you can't break away for such a conference, there are some things you can do then and there (Shneidman, Farberow, & Litman, 1994):

1. *Draw the person out.* Frame questions like "What's going on?" "Where do you hurt?" "What would you like to see happen?" Such questions may prompt people to verbalize thwarted psychological needs and offer some relief. They also grant you the time to appraise the risk and contemplate your next move.
2. *Be sympathetic.* Show that you fathom how troubled the person is. Don't say something like "You're just being silly. You don't really mean it."
3. *Suggest that means other than suicide can be discovered to work out the person's problems, even*

if they are not apparent at the time. Suicidal people can usually see only two solutions to their predicaments—either suicide or some kind of magical resolution. Professionals try to broaden the available alternatives of people who are suicidal.

4. *Ask how the person expects to die by suicide.* People with explicit methods who also possess the means (e.g., a gun or drugs) are at greater risk. Ask if you may hold on to the gun, drugs, or whatever for a while. Sometimes the person will agree.
5. *Propose that the person accompany you to consult a professional right now.* Many campuses have hotlines that you or the suicidal individual can call. Many towns and cities have such hotlines and they can be called anonymously. Other possibilities include the emergency room of a general hospital, a campus health centre or counselling centre, or the campus or local police. If you are unable to maintain contact with the suicidal person, get professional assistance as soon as you separate.
6. *Don't say something like "You're talking crazy."* Such comments are degrading and injurious to the individual's self-esteem.
7. *Don't press the suicidal person to contact specific people, such as parents or a spouse.* Conflict with them may have given rise to the suicidal thoughts.

Above all, keep in mind that your primary goal is to confer with a helping professional. Don't go it alone any longer than you have to.

Suicide

- **What are some of the factors linked to suicide?**
Depressive and bipolar disorders are often linked to suicide. Although women are more likely to attempt suicide, more men actually succeed, probably because they select more lethal means. The elderly—not the young—are more likely to die by suicide, and the rate of suicide among the elderly appears to be increasing. People who attempt suicide are often depressed, but they are generally in touch with reality. They may,

however, lack effective problem-solving skills and see no way to deal with their life stress other than suicide. A sense of hopelessness figures prominently in suicides.

- **Why should you never ignore a person's suicide threat?**
Although certainly not all people who threaten suicide follow through, many do. People who die by suicide often signal their intentions, by telling others about their suicidal thoughts, for example.

Define It

anomie, 178
attributional style, 162
automatic thoughts, 161
bipolar, 143
bipolar I disorder, 152
bipolar II disorder, 154
cognitive therapy, 168
cognitive triad of depression, 159
cyclothymic disorder, 154
external attribution, 162
global attribution, 162

hypomanic episodes, 144
internal attribution, 162
interpersonal psychotherapy, 167
learned helplessness, 162
major depressive disorder, 144
major depressive disorder with peripartum onset, 148
major depressive disorder with seasonal pattern, 147
manic, 144
manic episodes, 152

moods, 143
mourning, 156
persistent depressive disorder, 151
pressured speech, 153
rapid flight of ideas, 153
selective abstraction, 160
specific attribution, 162
stable attribution, 162
unipolar, 143
unstable attribution, 162

Recall It

1. In the classic psychodynamic formulation, depression represents _____.
   a. loss of self-worth or self-esteem
   b. perceptions of existence lacking in meaning
   c. failure of the ego to dominate the id
   d. anger turned inward

2. Behavioural theorists emphasize the role of _____ in explaining depression.
   a. person variables
   b. unconscious conflicts
   c. reinforcement
   d. self-esteem factors

3. A depressed patient who blows negative events out of proportion shows a type of cognitive distortion called _____.
   a. labelling
   b. magnification

   c. overgeneralization
   d. dismissing the positives

4. Which of the following drugs (or drug groups) is used in the treatment of bipolar disorder?
   a. selective serotonin-reuptake inhibitors
   b. MAO inhibitors
   c. lithium
   d. tricyclics

5. Which of the following is NOT true of people who attempt or commit suicide?
   a. People who die by suicide usually have deep-seated personality disorders.
   b. People who die by suicide often leave clues beforehand.
   c. Suicide often follows exit events in people's lives.
   d. Many people who take their own lives have problems with alcohol or substance abuse.

Answers to Recall It

1. d, 2. c, 3. b, 4. c, 5. a

Think About It

- Where would you draw the line between a person with a naturally exuberant personality and someone with a bipolar disorder?
- What are the advantages and disadvantages of drug therapy for depression? If you were to become clinically depressed, which course of treatment would you prefer—medication, psychotherapy, or a combination? Explain.
- Did your reading of the text change your ideas about how you might deal with a suicidal threat by a friend or loved one? If so, how?

Weblinks

Mood Disorders Society of Canada
https://mdsc.ca
The Mood Disorders Society of Canada is a national, not-for-profit organization that is committed to improving the quality of life for people affected by depression, bipolar disorder, and other related disorders. The site provides information and treatment resources for mood disorders, including major depression and bipolar disorder.

Internet Mental Health
www.mentalhealth.com
A good source of information with numerous links on major depression and bipolar disorder.

Depressive Disorders, Bipolar and Related Disorders, and Suicide

Test your understanding of the key concepts by filling in the blanks with the correct statements chosen from the list that follows. The answers are found at the end of the chapter.

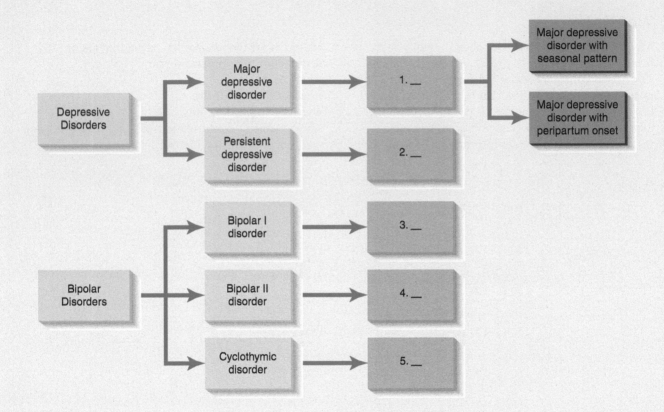

a. One or more manic episodes

b. Chronic depression lasting at least two years

c. One or more major depressive episodes with no history of manic or hypomanic episodes

d. Chronic pattern of mood swings between depression and hypomania that are not severe enough to qualify for either a depressive episode or a hypomanic episode

e. One or more major depressive episodes and at least one hypomanic episode; no history of manic episodes

Causes and Treatments According to Various Theoretical Perspectives

THEORETICAL PERSPECTIVES	CAUSES	TREATMENTS
	Stress: Major life stressors increase the risk of depressive and bipolar disorders	
PSYCHODYNAMIC	Anger directed inward rather than against significant others can lead to depression Bipolar disorders represent shifting dominance of the individual's personality by the ego and superego **Self-focusing model:** Self-examination following a major loss that affects the individual's self-esteem and feelings of security	Working through feelings of anger toward others **Interpersonal psychotherapy:** Focuses on helping people resolve interpersonal problems
LEARNING/BEHAVIOURAL	Lack of reinforcement from the environment can induce feelings of depression **Interactional theory:** The individual's increased need for social support and reassurance elicits anger, annoyance, and eventually rejection from others	Increase the amount of reinforcement in an individual's life by increasing his or her participation in pleasurable activities and improving social skills
COGNITIVE	**Aaron Beck's cognitive theory:** Depression results from the adoption early in life of a negatively biased or distorted way of thinking **Learned helplessness:** Depression results when the individual feels helpless to control the reinforcements in his or her environment **Reformulated helplessness theory:** Individuals who explain the causes of negative events according to internal, global, and stable attributions are more vulnerable to depression	Challenging and replacing self-defeating or irrational beliefs
BIOLOGICAL	Genetic predisposition (diathesis) Dysfunctional neurotransmitter systems Brain abnormalities	Antidepressants Electroconvulsive therapy Repetitive transcranial magnetic stimulation Lithium (for bipolar disorders)

Answers: 1. c, 2. b, 3. a, 4. e, 5. d

5

Dissociative Disorders and Somatic Symptom and Related Disorders

CHAPTER OUTLINE

Did You Know That...

- The term *split personality* is a lay term that refers to dissociative identity disorder, not schizophrenia?

- At some time or another, the majority of adults have episodes of feeling detached from their own bodies or thought processes?

- The great majority of people with multiple personalities were physically or sexually abused as children?

- Some people undergo operations even though they know nothing is medically wrong with them?

- Some people who have lost their ability to see or move their legs have displayed a strangely indifferent attitude toward their physical condition?

- There was an epidemic in China in the 1980s affecting more than 3000 people who fell prey to the belief that their genitals were shrinking and retracting into their bodies?

Pixabay.com

n the Middle Ages, the clergy used rites of exorcism to bring forth demons from people believed to be possessed. Curious incantations were heard during the contests for victims' souls between the exorcist and the demons believed to lurk within.

Curious phrasings were also heard more recently in 20th-century Los Angeles. They were intended to elicit another sort of demon from Kenneth Bianchi, a suspect in an investigation.

At one point, a question was put to Bianchi: "Part, are you the same thing as Ken or are you different?" The interviewer was not a member of the clergy, but a police psychiatrist. The interviewee had been dubbed the "Hillside strangler" by the press. He had terrorized the city, leaving prostitutes dead in the mountains that bank the metropolis.

Under hypnosis—not religious incantations—Bianchi claimed that a hidden personality or "part" named "Steve" had committed the murders. "Ken" knew nothing of them. Bianchi claimed to be suffering from multiple personality disorder (now called *dissociative identity disorder*), one of the intriguing but perplexing psychological disorders we explore in this chapter. Dissociative identity disorder is classified as a dissociative disorder, a type of psychological disorder involving a change or disturbance in the functions of self-identity, memory, or consciousness that make the personality whole. Normally speaking, we know who we are. We may not be certain of ourselves in an existential, philosophical sense, but we know our names, where we live, and what we do for a living. We also tend to remember the salient events of our lives. We may not recall every detail, and we may confuse what we ate for dinner on Tuesday with what we had on Monday, but we generally know what we have been doing for the past days, weeks, and years. Normally speaking, there is a unity to consciousness that gives rise to a sense of self. We perceive ourselves as progressing through space and time. In the dissociative disorders, one or more of these aspects of daily living is disturbed—sometimes bizarrely so.

This chapter also focuses on *somatic symptom and related disorders*, a class of psychological disorders involving complaints of physical symptoms that are believed to reflect underlying psychological issues. In some cases there is no apparent medical basis to the physical symptoms, such as in hysterical blindness or numbness (now called *conversion disorder*). In other cases, people may hold an exaggerated view of the meaning of their physical symptoms, believing them to be signs of underlying serious illnesses despite reassurances from their physicians to the contrary.

The dissociative and conversion disorders were grouped with the anxiety disorders in earlier versions of the DSM under the more general category of "neurosis." The common grouping was based on the psychodynamic model, which held that these various disorders involve maladaptive ways of managing anxiety. In the anxiety disorders, the appearance of disturbing levels of anxiety was expressed directly in behaviour, such as in a phobia where a person would avoid a feared object or situation. But the role of anxiety in the dissociative and somatic symptom and related disorders was inferred from rather than expressed in behaviour. Individuals with dissociative disorders may show no signs of overt anxiety. However, they manifest other psychological problems, such as loss of memory or changes in identity, that are theorized within the psychodynamic model to serve the purpose of keeping the underlying sources of anxiety out of awareness. Likewise, people with conversion disorder often show a strange indifference to physical problems (e.g., loss of vision). Here, too, it was theorized that the "symptoms" mask unconscious sources of anxiety. Some theorists interpret indifference to symptoms to mean there is an underlying benefit to them; that is, they help prevent anxiety from intruding into consciousness. But, as we will see later, this interpretation has been recently challenged.

The DSM now separates the anxiety disorders from the other categories of neuroses—the dissociative disorders and somatic symptom and related disorders—with which they were historically linked. Yet many practitioners continue to use the broad conceptualization of neuroses as a framework for classifying the anxiety, dissociative, and somatic symptom disorders.

Continuum of Somatic Concerns

Example: Illness Anxiety Disorder

Does not meet criteria | Meets criteria →

NO SYMPTOMS	STRUGGLING	MILD	MODERATE	SEVERE
	Marco worries about health issues. He changes the subject whenever someone brings up the topic of illnesses and avoids medical types of television shows.	Massimo is preoccupied with concerns about getting ill. He visits his doctor on a monthly basis.	Greg checks his body daily for signs of illness and rarely goes a week without visiting a health professional.	Shahda is consumed with fears of having a serious illness. She does not believe her doctor when she reassures her that nothing is wrong and will seek out the advice of other physicians.

DISSOCIATIVE DISORDERS

The major dissociative disorders include dissociative identity disorder, dissociative amnesia, and depersonalization/derealization disorder. In each case, there is a disruption or dissociation ("splitting off") of the functions of identity, memory, or consciousness—functions that normally combine to make us whole.

Dissociative Identity Disorder

In response to a newspaper inquiry, Nancy came forth to tell her story about her struggles with a dissociative identity disorder. Nancy, who resides in Ontario, gave the following account of her problems, how they arose, and how she has worked to overcome them:

> The piano has a place of honour in Nancy's living room. It's a red mahogany Lesage made in Quebec. But Nancy fears that piano. She will play it only if the doors are locked or if her husband, Hugh, is around. When she was a girl, she loved to play the classics every day—sonatinas, rondos, and allegros by Mozart. She concentrated so hard. She shut herself off from her surroundings. "I felt I was inside the music." And while Nancy played, her father and sometimes other men molested her. Her father touched her; he masturbated. From the time she was a toddler, he had abused her. It could happen anywhere in the house. At the piano, she had the music to take her away. But wherever she was, Nancy had grown skilled at using her mind to float away from her father's grasp. She could peel off a piece of herself, so she hardly felt the pain. That ability saved her then. But now it's a problem.

She got therapy and soon even started a self-help group. "I found out it's okay to talk about what happened, to say it out loud. I realized it really wasn't my fault." After a few years, she left the group. "I thought I was doing quite well. I'd learned to handle the flashbacks and the memories." But she started getting sick a lot again. There was something that had bothered Nancy for years—the voices inside her. And by this point, they seemed awfully persistent. "There's a saying that it's okay to talk to yourself and as long as you don't answer, you're not crazy." But Nancy noticed she was waking up at night, hearing herself talking and answering. She had said something to her husband years before: "Hughie, I think I'm going crazy. I hear all these voices. They're talking, fighting, arguing." The arguments that rattled through her head could be about something as simple as whether to serve a chicken dinner with baked potatoes or rice. Or whether to go to the mall. "It was like Siamese twins who constantly talk back and forth because they can't do anything without each other." And there was amnesia, confusion, lost time. Nancy was sure she had invited that couple to dinner. They were puzzled why she got angry when they didn't show up.

We all dissociate. We all daydream; we cruise along a straight stretch of highway and later we don't really remember the details at all. But for someone like Nancy, those moments of lost time were deeper, more frequent. Her earliest memory of abuse is from when she was about three years old. The abuse continued until she was 18, when she got married. Hugh showed up in Nancy's life and helped her. She told him about some of the past. "You need to talk about this," he told her. Nancy said she was fine. She was married, to the right man. And she was a nurse, which she'd always wanted to be. But that fell apart one night at work. Nancy went to walk into the medication room and walked into the wall instead. She collapsed. She was sick for months. She couldn't drive, couldn't climb stairs. She vomited and had severe headaches. Nancy underwent many tests. Maybe it was a brain tumour. Or an inner-ear problem. Finally, a neurologist said, "Nancy, is it possible you've been under stress?" "It was like a light being turned on," she says. "And I said, 'Yes, I'm 36 and I've been under stress for 33 years.'"

She was then sent to two psychiatrists. Both made the diagnosis of dissociative identity disorder. There appear to be eight different parts to Nancy's personality. In her mind, each has its own physical appearance. She pictures them with different hair, different glasses. There is Malveen. She's shy, introverted, overwhelmed with guilt. This part of Nancy stopped growing when she was a teenager and met Hugh. There's Dorothy, well organized, able to do 10 things at once. There's another part that's all anger. And there is Just Me, that persistent part she always argued with. Good therapy and the right medication sent that personality away. Nancy continues to work on her recovery.

Six years earlier, one of the men who abused her was convicted of assault, gross indecency, and sexual intercourse with a female under 14. The judge called the crimes abhorrent. But because of the way that the judge addressed the jury, the man was granted a new trial. He died before it took place. Nancy's mother and father, both abused as children, are gone now. Mother, a nurse, died 13 years ago in Nancy's home. Father, a postal worker then city employee, died seven years ago. Nancy had been looking after him, cleaning his apartment, getting his groceries. She had confronted him and wrung out an apology. He was about to be charged when he died.

Therapy has been hard and slow, but Nancy is not discouraged. "Each of these parts of me was beneficial. They helped me to survive. But it would be good for me now to merge these parts. It would be good to become one healthy person."

Keeping pain at a distance, May 16, 2000. Reprinted courtesy of *The Hamilton Spectator*.

Nancy was diagnosed with multiple personality disorder, which is now called **dissociative identity disorder**. In this disorder, sometimes referred to as *split personality*, two or more personalities—each with well-defined traits and memories—"occupy" one person. They may or may not be aware of one another. There are many variations. Sometimes two personalities vie for control. Sometimes there is one dominant or core personality and several subordinate ones. Themes of sexual ambivalence (sexual openness versus inhibition) and shifting sexual orientations are particularly common. It is as if conflicting internal impulses cannot coexist or achieve dominance. As a result, each is expressed as the cardinal or steering trait of an alternate personality. The clinician can sometimes bring forth alternate personalities by inviting them to make themselves known, as in asking, "Is there another part of you that wants to say something to me?"

The transformation from one personality into another is described by some cultures as a form of possession. In fact, the individual's cultural background can influence the form that the alter personalities take (spirits, demons, or even mythical figures). In non-Western societies, the occurrence of nonepileptic seizures and other conversion symptoms such as paralysis and sensory loss are common (APA, 2013). The norms of the culture or religion must also be taken into consideration when making a diagnosis. Experiences of possession that are culturally accepted would not be considered as dissociative identity disorder. An example is *zār*, a term used in North African and Middle Eastern countries to describe spirit possession in people who experience dissociative states during which they engage in unusual behaviour, ranging from shouting to banging their heads against a wall. The behaviour itself is not deemed abnormal, because it is believed to be controlled by spirits (Mianji & Semnani, 2015).

The case of Margaret illustrates the purported emergence of an alternate personality:

[Margaret explained that] she often "heard a voice telling her to say things and do things." It was, she said, "a terrible voice" that sometimes threatened to "take over completely." When it was finally suggested to [Margaret] that she let the voice "take over," she closed her eyes, clenched her fists, and grimaced for a few moments during which she was out of contact with those around her. Suddenly she opened her eyes and one was in the presence of another person. Her name, she said, was "Harriet." Whereas Margaret had been paralyzed, and complained of fatigue, headache and backache, Harriet felt well, and she at once proceeded to walk unaided around the interviewing room. She spoke scornfully of Margaret's religiousness, her invalidism, and her puritanical life, professing that she herself liked to drink and "go partying" but that Margaret was always going to church and reading the Bible. "But," she said impishly and proudly, "I make her miserable—I make her say and do things she doesn't want to." At length, at the interviewer's suggestion, Harriet reluctantly agreed to "bring Margaret back," and after more grimacing and fist clenching, Margaret reappeared, paralyzed, complaining of her headache and backache, and completely amnesiac for the brief period of Harriet's release from prison.*

*I am indebted to Dr. F. H. Frankel for permission to use these observations.

THE HARVARD GUIDE TO MODERN PSYCHIATRY, edited by Armand M. Nicholi, Jr., M.D., Cambridge, Mass.: The Belknap Press of Harvard University Press, Copyright © 1978 by the President and Fellows of Harvard College.

As with Margaret, the dominant personality is often unaware of the existence of the alternate personalities. This seems to suggest that the mechanism of dissociation is controlled by unconscious processes. Although the dominant personality lacks insight into the existence of the other personalities, she or he may vaguely sense that something is amiss. There may even be interpersonality rivalry, in which one personality aspires to do away with another, usually in blissful ignorance of the fact that this would result in the death of all.

Celebrated cases of multiple personality have been depicted in the popular media. One became the subject of the film *The Three Faces of Eve*. In the film, Eve White is a timid housewife who harbours two other personalities: Eve Black, a sexually provocative, antisocial personality, and Jane, a balanced, developing personality who can reconcile her sexual needs with the demands of social acceptability. The three faces eventually merge into one—Jane, providing a "happy ending." The real-life Eve, whose name was Chris Sizemore, failed to maintain this integrated personality. Her personality split into 22 subsequent personalities, purportedly after she learned that another famous case—Sybil—had 16 personalities (Kihlstrom, 2005). As for the celebrated case of Sybil, which was also made into a movie, recent evidence, including tape recordings of sessions with a psychiatrist who claimed to have elicited Sybil's multiple personalities, indicates that Sybil was highly suggestible to the psychiatrist's suggestions that there were multiple personalities but is unlikely to have had genuine multiple personality disorder (Rieber, Takoosian, & Iglesias, 2002).

The diagnostic criteria for dissociative identity disorder are listed in Table 5.1.

The 1970s witnessed an "epidemic" of dissociative identity disorder cases. The number of alter egos reported by patients has also risen over time. It was almost as if there was some kind of contest to determine who could have (or be) the patient with the greatest number of alternate personalties (Kihlstrom, 2005). In the 1980s and 1990s, it also became common for multiple-personality patients to talk with their therapists about previously unheard-of phenomena: alters of races or sexes different from the hosts; alters of different species, including cats, dogs, panthers, gorillas, and lobsters; and alters of demons, angels, and even God (Piper & Merskey, 2004).

Although dissociative identity disorder is generally considered rare, the very existence of the disorder continues to arouse debate. Increased public attention paid to the disorder in recent years may also account for the perception that its prevalence is greater than was previously believed.

The disorder as defined in prior editions of the DSM was largely restricted to North America (Spanos, 2001). Very few cases had been reported elsewhere (Piper & Merskey, 2004). Now with the inclusion of an experience of possession (except those that are culturally accepted) in the diagnostic criteria, the disorder is more applicable to other cultural groups. Even in North America, few psychologists and psychiatrists have ever encountered a case of multiple personality. Most cases of multiple personality are reported by a relatively small number of investigators and clinicians who strongly believe in the existence of the disorder. Surveys in Canada and the United States reveal that many mental health professionals are skeptical of the validity of the concept of dissociative identity disorder (e.g., Lalonde, Hudson, Gigante, & Pope, 2001). Critics such as Western University's Harold Merskey and colleagues wonder whether some overzealous clinicians might be helping to manufacture that which they are seeking (Piper & Merskey, 2004).

Some other leading authorities agree, most notably the late psychologist Nicholas Spanos, who worked at Carleton University. To Spanos and other psychologists (e.g., Lilienfeld & Lynn, 2003), multiple personality is not a distinct disorder but a form of role playing in which individuals first come to construe themselves as having multiple selves and then begin to act in ways that are consistent with their conception of the disorder. Eventually,

Moviestore collection Ltd/Alamy Stock Photo

The three faces of Eve. In the film *The Three Faces of Eve*, a timid housewife, Eve White, harbours two alternate personalities: Eve Black, an antisocial personality, and Jane, an integrated personality who can accept her sexual and aggressive urges but still engage in socially appropriate behaviour. The 1957 film is reportedly based on the life of Christine Costner Sizemore, who suffered with dissociative identity disorder and was a patient of Hervey M. Cleckley and Corbett H. Thigpen.

TABLE 5.1
Diagnostic Criteria for Dissociative Identity Disorder (Formerly Multiple Personality Disorder)

A. Disruption of identity characterized by two or more distinct personality states, which may be described in some cultures as an experience of possession. The disruption in identity involves marked discontinuity in sense of self and sense of agency, accompanied by related alterations in affect, behavior, consciousness, memory, perception, cognition, and/or sensory-motor functioning. These signs and symptoms may be observed by others or reported by the individual.

B. Recurrent gaps in the recall of everyday events, important personal information, and/or traumatic events that are inconsistent with ordinary forgetting.

C. The symptoms cause clinically significant distress or impairment in social, occupational, or other important areas of functioning.

D. The disturbance is not a normal part of a broadly accepted cultural or religious practice. **Note:** In children, the symptoms are not better explained by imaginary playmates or other fantasy play.

E. The symptoms are not attributable to the physiological effects of a substance (e.g., blackouts or chaotic behavior during alcohol intoxication) or another medical condition (e.g., complex partial seizures).

Source: Reprinted with permission from the *Diagnostic and Statistical Manual of Mental Disorders*, Fifth Edition, (Copyright © 2013). American Psychiatric Association. All Rights Reserved.

their role playing becomes so ingrained that it becomes a reality to them. Perhaps their therapists or counsellors, maybe unintentionally, first planted the idea in their minds that their confusing welter of emotions and behaviours may represent different personalities at work. Impressionable people may have learned how to enact the role of someone with the disorder by watching others perform the role on television and in the movies. Films like *The Three Faces of Eve* and *Sybil* have given detailed examples of the behaviours that characterize multiple personalities (Spanos, 2001). Or perhaps therapists provided cues about the features of multiple personality, enough for clients to enact the role convincingly.

Many reinforcers may become contingent on enacting the role of a multiple-personality type. Receiving attention from others and evading accountability for unacceptable behaviour are two possible sources of reinforcement (Spanos, 2001). This is not to suggest that people with multiple personalities are "faking" any more than it would be to suggest you are faking your behaviour when you perform daily roles as a student, spouse, or worker. You may enact the role of a student (sitting attentively in class, raising your hand when you wish to talk, etc.) because you have learned to organize your behaviour according to the nature of the role and because you have been rewarded for doing so. People with multiple personalities may have come to identify so closely with the role that it becomes real for them.

In support of their belief that dissociative identity disorder represents a form of role playing, Spanos and his colleagues showed that with proper cues, college students in a laboratory simulation of the Bianchi-type interrogation could easily enact a multiple-personality role, even attributing the blame to an alternate personality for a murder they were accused of committing (Spanos, 2001). Perhaps the manner in which the Bianchi interrogation was conducted had cued Bianchi to enact the multiple-personality role to evade criminal responsibility. (It didn't work, as he was eventually convicted.)

Relatively few cases of dissociative identity disorder involve criminal behaviour, in which enactment of a multiple-personality role might relieve individuals of criminal responsibility for their

POOL/AP Images

Kenneth Bianchi, the so-called Hillside strangler. Did the police psychiatrist who interviewed Bianchi suggest to him that he could role play a person with multiple personalities?

behaviour. But even in more typical cases, there may be more subtle incentives for enacting the role of a multiple personality, such as a therapist's expression of interest and excitement at discovering a multiple personality. People with multiple personalities were often highly imaginative during childhood. Accustomed to playing games of "make believe," they may readily adopt alternate identities—especially if they learn how to enact the multiple-personality role and there are external sources of validation such as a clinician's interest and concern.

The social-reinforcement model may help to explain why some clinicians seem to "discover" many more cases of multiple personality than others. These clinicians may be "multiple-personality magnets." They may unknowingly cue clients to enact the multiple-personality role and may reinforce the performance with extra attention and concern. With the right set of cues, certain clients may adopt the role of a multiple personality to please their clinicians.

The role-playing model has been challenged by some researchers (e.g., Gleaves, Hernandez, & Warner, 2003), and it remains to be seen how many cases of the disorder in clinical practice the model can explain. Whether multiple personality is a real phenomenon or a form of role playing, there is no question that people who display this behaviour have serious emotional and behavioural difficulties. Ninety percent of cases in Canada, the United States and Europe report histories of physical and sexual abuse, and over 70% have attempted suicide (APA, 2013).

Dissociative identity disorder, which is often called *split personality* by laypeople, should not be confused with schizophrenia. The term *split personality* refers to multiple personality, not schizophrenia. *Schizophrenia* (which comes from roots that mean "split brain") occurs much more commonly than multiple personality and involves the "splitting" of cognition, affect, and behaviour (see Chapter 10). Thus, there may be little agreement between thoughts and emotions or between the individual's perception of reality and what is truly happening. The person with schizophrenia may become giddy when told of disturbing events or may experience hallucinations or delusions. In people with dissociative identity disorder, the personality apparently divides into two or more personalities, but each of them usually shows more integrated functioning on cognitive, emotional, and behavioural levels than is true of people with schizophrenia.

Dissociative Amnesia

Dissociative amnesia is another controversial diagnostic category (Kihlstrom, 2005). *Amnesia* derives from the Greek roots *a-*, meaning "not," and *mnasthai*, meaning "to remember." In **dissociative amnesia** (formerly called *psychogenic amnesia*), a person becomes unable to recall important personal information usually involving material relating to traumatic or stressful experiences that cannot be accounted for by simple forgetfulness. Nor can the memory loss be attributed to a particular organic cause, such as a blow to the head or a particular medical condition, or to the direct effects of drugs or alcohol. Unlike some progressive forms of memory impairment (such as dementia associated with Alzheimer's disease), the memory loss in dissociative amnesia is reversible, although it may last for days, weeks, or even years. Recall of dissociated memories may happen gradually but often occurs suddenly and spontaneously, as when a soldier who has no recall of a battle for several days afterward suddenly recalls the experience after being transported to a hospital away from the battlefield.

Most types of dissociative amnesia involve localized amnesia, which means that events occurring during a specific time period are lost to memory. For example, a person cannot recall events for a number of hours or days after a stressful or traumatic incident, as in warfare or a case where there's an uninjured survivor of an accident. Other forms of dissociative amnesia include selective amnesia and generalized amnesia. In selective amnesia, people forget only the disturbing particulars that take place during a certain time period. Some people may recall the period of life during which they conducted an extramarital affair, but not the guilt-arousing affair itself. A soldier may recall most of a

dissociative amnesia Type of dissociative disorder in which a person experiences memory losses in the absence of any identifiable organic cause. General knowledge and skills are usually retained.

Dmytro Hurnytskiy/Hemera/Getty Images

Derealization. Episodes of derealization are characterized by the sense that one's surroundings have become strange or unreal—for example, colours may seem washed out or very bright—and time may seem to be oddly slowed down or sped up.

battle, but not the death of his or her compatriot. In generalized amnesia, people forget their entire lives—who they are, what they do, where they live, and with whom they live. This form of amnesia is very rare, although you wouldn't think so if you watch daytime soap operas. Persons with generalized amnesia cannot recall personal information but tend to retain their habits, tastes, and skills. If you had generalized amnesia, you would still know how to read, although you would not recall your elementary school teachers. You would still prefer french fries to broccoli, or vice versa. People with dissociative amnesia usually forget events or periods of life that were traumatic—ones that generated strong negative emotions such as horror or guilt.

Some researchers argue that true dissociative amnesia is exceedingly rare, and that many cases of so-called dissociative amnesia are actually caused by brain injury or disease (Kihlstrom, 2005). In some cases, this explanation is quite plausible. For example, forgetting what happened during a severe motor vehicle accident may not be dissociative amnesia; it may simply reflect the fact that you had a mild brain injury (concussion) that temporarily disrupted the brain's ability to form and retain memories. However, other cases, particularly dissociative amnesia purportedly involving the loss of one's identity (as the person's only problem), are typically very different from the memory problems caused by brain damage or disease. People with this type of amnesia have seemingly lost the most deeply ingrained of all their memories—those of who they are—while they are able to readily recall other more recent things, such as what they had for breakfast in the hospital that morning. Other cognitive functions such as reasoning skills are also unaffected. In comparison, people with brain damage or disease often have difficulty recalling recent events—even for patients with dementia associated with Alzheimer's disease, one of the last things they forget is who they are

(Lezak, Howieson, & Loring, 2004). A simple concussive blow to the head might wipe out your memory of events in the hours or days before the concussion, but you'll likely still remember who you are and recognize friends and family.

People sometimes claim they cannot recall certain events of their lives, such as criminal acts, promises made to others, and so forth. Falsely claiming amnesia as a way of escaping responsibility is called **malingering** and involves the attempt to fake symptoms or make false claims for personal gain. It can be sometimes be difficult to determine whether a person's reported memory loss is dissociative amnesia, malingering, or some other problem.

malingering Faking illness to avoid or escape work or other duties, or to obtain benefits.

depersonalization Feelings of unreality or detachment from one's self or one's body, as if one were a robot or functioning on automatic pilot or observing oneself from outside.

Depersonalization/Derealization Disorder

Depersonalization involves a temporary loss or change in the usual sense of our own reality. In a state of depersonalization, people may feel detached from their minds or bodies. They may have the sense of living in a dream or a movie, or acting like a robot (Holmes et al., 2005).

Derealization—a sense of unreality about the external world involving strange changes in perception of surroundings or in the sense of the passage of time—may also be present. People and objects may seem to change in size or shape; they may sound different. All these feelings can be associated with feelings of anxiety, including dizziness and fears of going insane, or with depression.

Although these sensations are strange, people with depersonalization maintain contact with reality. They can distinguish reality from unreality, even during the depersonalization episode. In contrast to people experiencing generalized amnesia, they know who they are. Their memories are intact and they know where they are—even if they do not like their present state. Feelings of depersonalization usually come on suddenly and fade gradually.

What is even more unusual about all this is that we have thus far described only normal feelings of depersonalization. According to the DSM, single brief episodes of depersonalization are experienced by about half of all adults, usually during times of extreme stress. People will often describe them as having an "out of body" experience. Consider Dimitry's experience:

> "We went to Orlando with the children after school let out. I had also been driving myself hard, and it was time to let go. We spent three days 'doing' Disney World, and it got to the point where we were all wearing shirts with mice and ducks on them and singing Disney songs like 'Yo ho, yo ho, a pirate's life for me.' On the third day, I began to feel unreal and ill at ease while we were watching these teenagers singing and dancing in front of Cinderella's Castle. The day was finally cooling down, but I broke into a sweat. I became shaky and dizzy and sat down on the cement next to the four-year-old's stroller without giving [my wife] an explanation. There were strollers and kids and [adults'] legs all around me, and for some strange reason I became fixated on the pieces of popcorn strewn on the ground. All of a sudden it was like the people around me were all silly mechanical creatures, like the dolls in the It's a Small World [exhibit] or the animals on the Jungle Cruise. Things sort of seemed to slow down, the way they do when you've smoked marijuana, and there was this invisible wall of cotton between me and everyone else.
>
> "Then the concert was over and my wife was like, 'What's the matter?' and did I want to stay for the Electrical Parade and the fireworks or was I sick? Now I was beginning to wonder if I was going crazy and I said I was sick, that my wife would have to take me by the hand and drive us back to the Sonesta Village [motel]. Somehow, we got back to the monorail and turned in the strollers. I waited in the herd [of people] at the station like a dead person, my eyes glazed over, looking out over kids with Mickey Mouse ears and Mickey Mouse balloons. The mechanical voice on the monorail almost did me in and I got really shaky.
>
> "I refused to go back to the Magic Kingdom. I went with the family to Sea-World, and on another day I dropped [my wife] and the kids off at the Magic Kingdom and picked them up that night. My wife thought I was goldbricking or something, and we had a helluva fight about it, but we had a life to get back to and my sanity had to come first."
>
> The Authors' Files

Dimitry's depersonalization experience was limited to the one episode and would not qualify for a diagnosis of depersonalization disorder. **Depersonalization/derealization disorder** is diagnosed only when such experiences are persistent or recurrent and cause

derealization Loss of the sense of reality of one's surroundings, experienced in terms of strange changes in one's environment (e.g., people or objects changing size or shape) or in the sense of the passage of time.

depersonalization/derealization disorder Disorder characterized by persistent or recurrent episodes of depersonalization.

> **TABLE 5.2**
>
> **Diagnostic Criteria for Depersonalization/Derealization Disorder**
>
> A. The presence of persistent or recurrent experiences of depersonalization, derealization, or both:
>
> 1. **Depersonalization:** Experiences of unreality, detachment, or being an outside observer with respect to one's thoughts, feelings, sensations, body, or actions (e.g., perceptual alterations, distorted sense of time, unreal or absent self, emotional and/or physical numbing).
>
> 2. **Derealization:** Experiences of unreality or detachment with respect to surroundings (e.g., individuals or objects are experienced as unreal, dreamlike, foggy, lifeless, or visually distorted).
>
> B. During the depersonalization or derealization experiences, reality testing remains intact.
>
> C. The symptoms cause clinically significant distress or impairment in social, occupational, or other important areas of functioning.
>
> D. The disturbance is not attributable to the physiological effects of a substance (e.g., a drug of abuse, medication) or another medical condition (e.g., seizures).
>
> E. The disturbance is not better explained by another mental disorder, such as schizophrenia, panic disorder, major depressive disorder, acute stress disorder, posttraumatic stress disorder, or another dissociative disorder.
>
> *Source:* Reprinted with permission from the *Diagnostic and Statistical Manual of Mental Disorders*, Fifth Edition, (Copyright © 2013). American Psychiatric Association. All Rights Reserved.

marked distress (APA, 2013). Religious and spiritual practices that induce meditative states would also not qualify. The DSM diagnoses depersonalization disorder according to the criteria shown in Table 5.2.

Commonalities exist between the Western concept of dissociative disorders and certain culture-bound syndromes found in other parts of the world. For example, *amok* is a culture-bound syndrome occurring primarily in Southeast Asian and Pacific Island cultures that involves a trance-like state in which a person suddenly becomes highly excited and violently attacks other people or destroys objects. People who "run amok" may later claim to have no memory of the episode or recall feeling as if they were acting like a robot (Flaskerud, 2012).

In terms of observable behaviour and associated features, depersonalization/derealization may be more closely related to disorders such as phobias and panic than to dissociative disorders (Holmes et al., 2005). Unlike other forms of dissociative disorders that seem to protect the self from anxiety, depersonalization can lead to anxiety and in turn to avoidance behaviour, as we saw in the case of Dimitry.

Theoretical Perspectives

The dissociative disorders are fascinating and perplexing phenomena. How can one's sense of personal identity become so distorted that one develops multiple personalities, blots out large chunks of personal memory, or develops a new self-identity? Although these disorders remain in many ways mysterious, clues have emerged that provide insights into their origins.

Psychodynamic theorists believe that dissociative disorders involve the massive use of repression, which leads to the "splitting off" from consciousness of unacceptable impulses and painful memories, especially sexual abuse (Ross & Ness, 2010). It is possible that in some cases severely abused children may retreat into alter personalities as a psychological defence against unbearable abuse. The construction of alter personalities may allow these children to escape psychologically or distance themselves from their suffering; dissociation may offer a means of escape when no other means is available. In the face of repeated abuse, these alter personalities may become stabilized, making it difficult for the person to maintain a unified personality.

Depersonalization: No Disorder

Alex is a 44-year-old man who had worked in the bank industry for over 15 years. Recently, he was laid off and found himself needing to go back on the job market. His strong résumé and job experience made him a good candidate for several jobs, and he began going on job interviews. At his first interview, he was mildly nervous, being out of practice at job interviews. It went fairly well, but he wasn't interested in the job. At his second interview, several weeks later, Alex quickly realized that this was a desirable position for him and he felt his anxiety about doing well in the interview increase. During the interview, Alex met with two of the company's staff members. They were friendly and encouraging and seemed to feel that Alex might be a good fit with their staff. During one conversation, Alex noticed that the room appeared strange around him. It was as if things were moving a bit slower than normal and people were talking slower than usual. He also felt the odd sensation that his arms and legs did not belong to him. Although he felt unusual, he was able to answer questions. After the interview he returned home and told his wife about his experience. By dinner, these strange feelings had gone away.

Depersonalization: Disorder

Cheng is a 30-year-old man who works as a bus driver. Through the years, he has had ups and downs with some anxiety, but nothing that kept him from working or managing his responsibilities. He is married with two small children and is very involved with their activities. About a year ago, Cheng began having periods in which he felt "spaced out," especially during times of anxiety. These episodes became progressively worse, to the point that he now feels "spacey" almost all day. He began to question whether he was really alive or not, or if what he was experiencing was a dream. He described watching the world as if there were a layer of Saran Wrap between him and reality. He constantly did things to "check" if things around him were real. This included touching objects that looked odd and asking his wife whether he was really alive or not. These feelings were very upsetting for Cheng, to the point that he began to withdraw from his family and call in sick to work on a regular basis. Driving had become a great source of stress for Cheng, as he constantly wondered if he was capable of driving a bus with these symptoms. He wondered, "How can I be responsible for a bus full of people when I don't even know if things around me are real?" After six months of these symptoms, Cheng stopped going to work and spent most of the day in bed. He still feels like there is something between him and "reality."

In adulthood, people with multiple personalities may use their alter personalities to block out traumatic childhood memories and their emotional reactions to them—wiping the slate clean and beginning life anew in the guise of alter personalities (Ross, 2001). The alter identities or personalities may also serve as a way of coping with stressful situations or of expressing deep-seated resentments that the individual is unable to integrate within his or her primary personality. Although this theory is popular with many clinicians, the evidence comes largely from methodologically weak studies (Kihlstrom, 2005).

In dissociative amnesia, the ego protects itself from becoming flooded with anxiety by blotting out disturbing memories or by dissociating threatening impulses of a sexual or aggressive nature. In dissociative identity disorder, people may express these unacceptable impulses through the development of alternate personalities. In depersonalization, people stand outside themselves—safely distanced from the emotional turmoil within.

Learning and cognitive theorists view dissociation as a learned response that involves *not thinking* about disturbing acts or thoughts to avoid feelings of guilt and shame evoked by such experiences. The habit of not thinking about these matters is negatively reinforced by relief from anxiety or by removal of feelings of guilt or shame. Some social cognitive theorists, such as Spanos (2001) and others (e.g., Lilienfeld & Lynn, 2003), propose that dissociative identity disorder is a form of role playing acquired by means of observational learning and reinforcement. This is not quite the same as pretending or malingering; people can honestly come to organize their behaviour patterns according to particular roles they have observed. They might also become so absorbed in role playing that they "forget" they are enacting a role.

An Inventory of Dissociative Experiences

Brief dissociative experiences, such as momentary feelings of depersonalization, are quite common. The great majority of us experience them at least some of the time (Simeon & Abugel, 2006). Dissociative disorders, by contrast, involve more persistent and severe dissociative experiences.

The following is a sampling of dissociative experiences similar to those experienced by many people in the general population. If these experiences become persistent or commonplace, or cause you concern or distress, it might be worthwhile to discuss them with a professional.

Have you ever experienced the following?

1. Realized after reading a page of text that you had no recollection of what you just read.
2. Found yourself driving somewhere and forgot where you were going.
3. Had a memory that you weren't sure actually happened or was just a dream.
4. Found yourself somewhere and had no recollection of how you got there.
5. Felt like you were outside of yourself watching your actions.
6. Realized that you were talking to yourself out loud.
7. Were so absorbed in your thoughts that you didn't notice what was going on around you.
8. Been in a familiar place and yet felt disoriented.
9. Caught a glimpse of yourself in the mirror and didn't realize it was you.
10. Wondered whether you were awake or in a dream.
11. Been uncertain whether you had just done something or had merely thought of it.
12. Felt like you were in a fog and other people seemed unreal.
13. Became so absorbed in a daydream that you thought it was actually happening.
14. Behaved so differently at times that you felt you were two different people.

Source: Nevid, Jeffrey S, Essentials of Abnormal Psychology in a Changing World; Fourth Canadian Edition; © 2019, Pearson Education, Inc., New York, NY.

The great majority of people with dissociative identity disorder report being physically or sexually abused as children, although most people abused as children do not develop multiple personalities (Piper & Merskey, 2004). Similarly, the vast majority of people exposed to trauma do not develop dissociative disorders (Kihlstrom, 2005).

Consistent with the diathesis-stress model, only certain individuals may be predisposed to develop dissociative disorders when exposed to severe stress. Certain personality traits, such as a proneness to fantasize, a high ability to be hypnotized, and an openness to altered states of consciousness, may predispose individuals to develop dissociative experiences in the face of extreme stress caused by events such as traumatic abuse (Dalenberg et al., 2012; Isaac & Chand, 2006). These personality traits themselves do not lead to dissociative disorders, but they might increase the risk that people who experience severe trauma will develop dissociative phenomena as a survival mechanism.

Perhaps most of us can divide our consciousness so that we become unaware—at least temporarily—of those events we normally focus on. Perhaps most of us can thrust the unpleasant from our minds and enact various roles—parent, child, lover, businessperson, soldier—that help us meet the requirements of our situations. Perhaps the marvel is *not* that attention can be splintered, but that human consciousness is normally integrated into a meaningful whole.

Treatment of Dissociative Disorders

Dissociative amnesia is usually a fleeting experience that ends abruptly. Episodes of depersonalization can be recurrent and persistent, and they are most likely to occur when people are undergoing periods of mild anxiety or depression. In such cases, clinicians usually focus on managing the anxiety or the depression. Much of the attention in the research literature has focused on dissociative identity disorder and specifically on bringing together an integration of the alter personalities into a cohesive personality structure.

Traditional psychoanalysis aims at helping people with dissociative identity disorder uncover and learn to cope with early childhood traumas. The analyst can work with whatever personality dominates the therapy session. Any and all personalities can be asked to talk about their memories and dreams as best they can and can be assured that the therapist will help them make sense of their anxieties and safely "relive" traumatic experiences and make them conscious. If therapy is successful, the self will be able to work through the traumatic memories and will no longer need to escape into alternate "selves" to avoid the anxiety associated with the trauma. Thus, reintegration of the personality becomes possible.

Does this sort of therapy work? Coons (1986) followed 20 "multiples" aged 14 to 47 at time of intake for an average of 39 months. Only five of the subjects showed a complete reintegration of their personalities. Other therapists report significant improvement in measures of dissociative and depressive symptoms in treated patients (Ellason & Ross, 1997), but these studies have been criticized for methodological problems (Kihlstrom, 2005). Reports of the effectiveness of other forms of therapy, such as cognitive-behavioural therapy, rely largely on uncontrolled case studies. Nor do we have evidence showing psychiatric drugs or other biological approaches to be effective in bringing about an integration of various alternate personalities. Accordingly, it is not possible to draw firm conclusions about the safety and efficacy of psychoanalytic or other treatments for dissociative identity disorder.

Little is known about the treatment of other forms of dissociative disorder. The relative infrequency of these disorders has hampered efforts to conduct controlled experiments that compare different forms of treatment with one another and with control groups. However, preliminary evidence suggests that cognitive-behavioural therapy and some types of medication may be helpful in treating depersonalization disorder (Hunter, Baker, Phillips, Sierra, & David, 2005; Simeon & Abugel, 2006).

A CLOSER LOOK

A Recovered-Memory Controversy

A high-level business executive's comfortable life fell apart one day when his 19-year-old daughter accused him of having repeatedly molested her throughout her childhood. He lost his marriage as well as his $400 000-a-year job. But he fought back against the allegations that he insisted were untrue. He sued his daughter's therapists who had assisted her in recovering these memories. A jury sided with the father, awarding him $500 000 in damages from the two therapists.

In the Canadian case of *R. v. François* (1994), Lorne François was convicted of repeatedly raping a 13-year-old girl in 1985. The only evidence was the girl's testimony. She said that she had repressed memories of the sexual assaults but that the recollections returned in 1990. At the time of the recollections, the police suggested that if she thought long enough about her past, she might recall something in a "flashback." The girl reported that the flashbacks occurred while doing this. The conviction was later overturned by the Supreme Court of Canada.

These are just two of many cases involving allegations made by adults who claim to have only recently become aware of memories of being sexually abused during childhood. Hundreds of people throughout North America have been brought to trial on the basis of recovered memories of childhood abuse, with many of these cases resulting in convictions and long jail sentences, even in the absence of any corroborating evidence. Recovered memories of sexual abuse in childhood may occur following suggestive probing

by a therapist or hypnotist (Loftus & Davis, 2006). The issue of recovered memories continues to be hotly debated in psychology and the broader community (Laney & Loftus, 2013). At the heart of the debate is the question, "Are recovered memories believable?" No one doubts that child sexual abuse is a major problem confronting our society. But should recovered memories be taken at face value?

Several lines of evidence lead us to question the validity of recovered memories. Research evidence shows, for example, that under some circumstances, people who are given plausible but false information about their childhoods may come to believe the information to be true. To illustrate, consider the research by psychologist Stephen Porter, who with his colleagues at the University of British Columbia demonstrated that some people can create false memories of emotional childhood events (Porter, Birt, Yuille, & Lehman, 2000; Porter, Yuille, & Lehman, 1999). Participants in this research were university students. The parents of the students were asked to provide information about six emotional events (e.g., serious accidents, medical procedures, animal attacks) that the student may or may not have experienced as a child. This information enabled the researchers to construct, for a given student, a fabricated childhood event that could form the basis of a false memory. The experiment consisted of three interviews over two weeks. In the first interview, students were interviewed about a real and a false event, with both introduced to the student as true. In the second and third interviews, students were re-interviewed about the false event. Interviewers attempted to elicit a false memory in each student, using methods such as guided imagery (e.g., asking the student to repeatedly imagine the fictitious event), mild social pressure that the event actually occurred, and the encouragement of repeated attempts to recover the memory. Porter, Yuille, and Lehman (1999) found that 26% of students created a false memory, 30% created a partial false memory (e.g., the student was unsure about whether the false event had occurred), and 44% created no false memory. Further results suggested that false memories are most likely to occur in people with dissociative tendencies (i.e., high scores on the Dissociative Experiences Scale) and when the interviewer is engaging, persuasive, and confident (Porter et al., 2000).

Underscoring the importance of findings such as these, a leading memory expert, psychologist Elizabeth Loftus, wrote of the dangers of taking recovered memories at face value:

> After developing false memories, innumerable "patients" have torn their families apart, and more than a few innocent people have been sent to prison. This is not to say that people cannot forget horrible things that have happened to them; most certainly they can. But there is virtually no support for the idea that clients presenting for therapy routinely have extensive histories of abuse of which they are completely unaware, and that they can be helped only if the alleged abuse is resurrected from their unconscious. (Loftus, 1996, p. 356)

Should we conclude, then, that all recovered memories are bogus? Not necessarily. It is possible for people in adulthood to recover memories of childhood, including memories of abuse (Erdleyi, 2010). There is little doubt that abuse can be forgotten and later remembered, although ordinary forgetting and remembering—rather than a special mechanism such as repression—seem more than adequate to account for this (Loftus & Davis, 2006). Some recovered memories may be true; others may not. Unfortunately, we don't have the tools to distinguish the true memory from the false one. A "memory" report being detailed or a person expressing it with confidence and emotion does not mean the event actually happened (Loftus & Davis, 2006).

We shouldn't think of the brain as a kind of mental camera that stores snapshots of events as they actually happened in the form of memories. Memory is more of a reconstructive process, in which bits of information are pieced together in ways that can sometimes lead to a distorted recollection of events, even though the person may be convinced the memory is accurate.

REVIEW IT

Dissociative Disorders

- **What are dissociative disorders?** Dissociative disorders involve changes or disturbances in identity, memory, or consciousness that affect the ability to maintain an integrated sense of self. They include dissociative identity disorder, dissociative amnesia, and depersonalization/ derealization disorder.
- **What is the major feature of dissociative identity disorder?** In dissociative identity disorder, two or more distinct personalities, each possessing well-defined traits and memories, exist within a person and repeatedly take control of the person's behaviour.
- **What are the clinical features associated with dissociative amnesia and depersonalization/derealization disorder?** Dissociative amnesia involves loss of memory for personal information that cannot be accounted for by organic causes. Depersonalization/derealization disorder involves persistent or recurrent episodes of depersonalization that are of sufficient severity to cause significant distress or impairment in functioning.
- **How do psychodynamic theorists conceptualize dissociative disorders?** Psychodynamic theorists view dissociative disorders as involving a form of psychological defence by which the ego defends itself against troubling memories and unacceptable impulses by blotting them out of consciousness.
- **How do learning and cognitive theorists account for these disorders?** To learning and cognitive theorists, dissociative experiences involve ways of learning not to think about certain troubling behaviours or thoughts that might lead to feelings of guilt or shame. Relief from anxiety negatively reinforces this pattern of dissociation. Some social cognitive theorists suggest that multiple personality may represent a form of role-playing behaviour.
- **How has dissociative identity disorder been treated?** Most therapeutic approaches help the person with dissociative identity disorder uncover and cope with dissociated painful experiences from childhood. Biological approaches focus on the use of drugs to treat the anxiety and depression often associated with the disorder, but drugs have not been able to bring about reintegration of the personality.

SOMATIC SYMPTOM AND RELATED DISORDERS

The word *somatic* derives from the Greek *soma*, meaning "body." In the **somatic symptom and related disorders**, people have physical symptoms suggestive of physical disorders, but no organic abnormalities can be found to account for them. Moreover, there is evidence or some reason to believe that the symptoms reflect psychological factors. Some people complain of problems in breathing or swallowing or of a "lump in the throat." Problems such as these can reflect overactivity of the sympathetic branch of the autonomic nervous system, which can be related to anxiety. Sometimes the symptoms take more unusual forms, as in a "paralysis" of a hand or leg that is inconsistent with the workings of the nervous system. In yet other cases, people are preoccupied with the belief that they have a serious disease yet no evidence of a physical abnormality can be found. We consider several forms of somatic symptom and related disorders, including *conversion disorder*, *illness anxiety disorder*, *somatic symptom disorder*, and *factitious disorder*.

somatic symptom and related disorders Disorders in which people complain of physical (somatic) problems although no physical abnormality can be found. See *conversion disorder*, *illness anxiety disorder*, *somatic symptom disorder*, and *factitious disorder*.

Conversion Disorder (Functional Neurological Symptom Disorder)

Conversion disorder (functional neurological symptom disorder) is characterized by symptoms or deficits that affect the ability to control voluntary movements (e.g., an inability to walk or move an arm) or that impair sensory functions, such as an inability to see, hear, or feel tactile stimulation (touch, pressure, warmth, or pain). The individual may experience tremors, have difficulty articulating, or may not be able to raise their voice. What qualifies these problems as a psychological disorder is that the loss or impairment of physical functions is either inconsistent or incompatible with known medical conditions or diseases. (The diagnostic criteria for conversion disorder can be found in Table 5.3.) The symptoms are not intentionally produced; the person is not malingering. The physical symptoms usually come on suddenly in stressful situations. A soldier's hand may become "paralyzed" during intense combat, for example. The fact that conversion symptoms first appear in the context of or are aggravated by conflicts or stressors the individual encounters gives credence to the view that they relate to psychological factors (APA, 2013).

Conversion disorder is so named because of the psychodynamic belief that it represents the channelling, or *conversion*, of repressed sexual or aggressive energies into physical symptoms. Conversion disorder was formerly called *hysteria* or *hysterical neurosis* and played an important role in Freud's development of psychoanalysis (see Chapter 1). Hysterical or conversion disorders seem to have been more common in Freud's day but are relatively rare today.

conversion disorder (functional neurological symptom disorder) A disorder characterized by symptoms or deficits that affect the ability to control voluntary movements or that impair sensory functions and that are inconsistent or incompatible with known medical conditions or diseases. Formerly called *hysteria* or *hysterical neurosis*.

TABLE 5.3

Diagnostic Criteria for Conversion Disorder (Functional Neurological Symptom Disorder)

A. One or more symptoms of altered voluntary motor or sensory function.

B. Clinical findings provide evidence of incompatibility between the symptom and recognized neurological or medical conditions.

C. The symptom or deficit is not better explained by another medical or mental disorder.

D. The symptom or deficit causes clinically significant distress or impairment in social, occupational, or other important areas of functioning or warrants medical evaluation.

Coding note: The ICD-9-CM code for conversion disorder is 300.11, which is assigned regardless of the symptom type. The ICD-10-CM code depends on the symptom type.

Source: Reprinted with permission from the *Diagnostic and Statistical Manual of Mental Disorders*, Fifth Edition, (Copyright © 2013). American Psychiatric Association. All Rights Reserved.

According to the DSM, conversion symptoms mimic neurological or general medical conditions involving problems with voluntary motor (movement) or sensory functions. Some of the "classic" symptom patterns involve paralysis, epilepsy, problems in coordination, blindness and tunnel vision, loss of the sense of hearing or of smell, or loss of feeling in a limb (anaesthesia). The bodily symptoms found in conversion disorders do not match the medical conditions they suggest. For example, conversion epileptics, unlike true epileptic patients, may maintain control over their bladders during an attack. People whose vision is supposedly impaired may move through the physician's office without bumping into the furniture. People who become "incapable" of standing or walking may nevertheless perform other leg movements normally. Nonetheless, there are some cases in which hysteria or conversion disorder has been incorrectly diagnosed in people who turned out to have underlying medical conditions that went unrecognized and untreated.

If you suddenly lost your vision, or if you could no longer move your legs, you would probably be very upset. But some people with conversion disorders, like those with dissociative amnesia, show a remarkable indifference to their symptoms, a phenomenon termed *la belle indifférence* ("beautiful indifference"). This was once thought to be an important feature that distinguished conversion disorders from real physical disorders. However, accumulating evidence shows that many people cope with real physical disorders by denying their pain or concern, which provides the semblance of indifference and relieves anxieties—at least temporarily. In fact, people with conversion disorder are no more likely than people with real physical disorders to display *la belle indifférence*, suggesting that this feature is of little diagnostic value (Stone, Smyth, Carson, Warlow, & Sharpe, 2006).

la belle indifférence French term describing the lack of concern over one's symptoms displayed by some people with conversion disorder but also by people with real physical disorders.

Illness Anxiety Disorder

illness anxiety disorder A disorder characterized by a preoccupation with the fear of having or the belief that one has a serious medical illness, but no medical basis for the complaints can be found.

The core feature of **illness anxiety disorder** is a preoccupation or fear that relatively minor or mild symptoms are signs of a serious undiagnosed illness. It is not the symptoms that the person finds troubling but the fear of what these symptoms might mean. In some cases there are no reported symptoms at all, but the person still expresses serious concerns about having a serious undiagnosed illness. In other cases the person has a family history of a serious disease (e.g., Alzheimer's disease) and becomes preoccupied with an exaggerated concern that he or she is suffering from the disease or is slowly developing it. The person may become preoccupied with checking his or her body for signs of the feared disease (see Table 5.4).

There are two general subtypes of the disorder. One subtype, the *care-avoidant subtype*, applies to people who postpone or avoid medical visits or lab tests because of high levels of anxiety about what might be discovered. The second subtype, called the *care-seeking subtype*, describes people who go doctor shopping, basically jumping from doctor to doctor in the hope of finding the one medical professional who might confirm their worst fears. These individuals may get angry at doctors who try to convince them that their fears are unwarranted.

The disorder appears to be about equally common in men and women but is rare in children. It most often begins in early and middle adulthood, although it can begin at any age (APA, 2013).

People who develop illness anxiety disorder have more health worries, have more psychiatric symptoms, and perceive their health to be worse than do other people. They are also more likely than other psychiatric patients to report being sick as children, having missed school because of health reasons, and having experienced childhood trauma, such as sexual abuse or

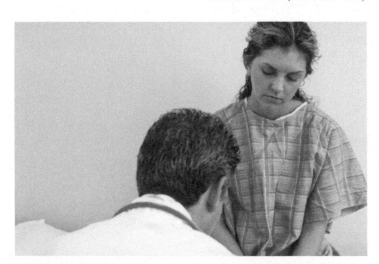

Michele Constantini/PhotoAlto/Getty Images

Faking or real? People with illness anxiety do not consciously fake their symptoms but fear their symptoms are due to a real illness. Feeling resentful toward their own doctor, they often go "doctor shopping."

TABLE 5.4

Diagnostic Criteria for Illness Anxiety Disorder

A. Preoccupation with having or acquiring a serious illness.

B. Somatic symptoms are not present or, if present, are only mild in intensity. If another medical condition is present or there is a high risk for developing a medical condition (e.g., strong family history is present), the preoccupation is clearly excessive or disproportionate.

C. There is a high level of anxiety about health, and the individual is easily alarmed about personal health status.

D. The individual performs excessive health-related behaviors (e.g., repeatedly checks his or her body for signs of illness) or exhibits maladaptive avoidance (e.g., avoids doctor appointments and hospitals).

E. Illness preoccupation has been present for at least 6 months, but the specific illness that is feared may change over that period of time.

F. The illness-related preoccupation is not better explained by another mental disorder, such as somatic symptom disorder, panic disorder, generalized anxiety disorder, body dysmorphic disorder, obsessive-compulsive disorder, or delusional disorder, somatic type.

Source: Reprinted with permission from the *Diagnostic and Statistical Manual of Mental Disorders*, Fifth Edition, (Copyright © 2013). American Psychiatric Association. All Rights Reserved.

physical violence. Illness anxiety disorder may fluctuate in severity over time or it may persist in a severe form for many years (Strassnig, Stowell, First, & Pincus, 2006; Taylor & Asmundson, 2004). Many people with this disorder also have other psychological disorders, especially major depression and anxiety disorders (Taylor & Asmundson, 2004).

Somatic Symptom Disorder

Most people have the occasional physical symptom indicating something might be wrong. It is normal to feel concerned about one's physical symptoms and to seek medical attention. However, people with **somatic symptom disorder** not only have troubling physical symptoms, but they are excessively concerned about their symptoms to the extent that it affects their thoughts, feelings, and behaviours in daily life. Thus, the diagnosis emphasizes the psychological features of physical symptoms, not whether the underlying cause or causes of the symptoms can be medically explained. The diagnosis of somatic symptom disorder requires that physical symptoms be persistent, lasting typically for a period of six months or longer (though any one symptom may not be continuously present), and that they are associated with either significant personal distress or interference with daily functioning. The symptoms may include such complaints as gastric (stomach) distress and various aches and pains.

somatic symptom disorder A disorder involving one or more somatic symptoms which cause excessive concern to the extent that it affects the individual's thoughts, feelings, and behaviours in daily life.

People with somatic symptom disorder may have excessive concerns about the seriousness of their symptoms. Or they may be bothered by nagging anxiety about what their symptoms might mean and spend a great deal of time running from doctor to doctor seeking a cure or confirmation that their worries are valid (Strassnig et al., 2006). Their concerns may last for years and become a source of continuing frustration for themselves, as well as for their families and physicians (Kurlansik & Maffei, 2016).

In some cases, somatic symptom disorder is characterized by a preoccupation with pain in cases in which a physical cause cannot adequately explain the persistence of the person's pain. Psychological factors are judged to play an important role in creating or intensifying the person's chronic pain. For example, receiving sympathy and attention from others can motivate the person to focus on and complain excessively of pain. In other cases, complaints of pain may be reinforced because they enable the person to get out of arduous or boring tasks (e.g., household chores).

Somatic symptom disorder usually begins in adolescence or young adulthood and appears to be a lifelong disorder involving major disability (Kirmayer & Looper, 2006).

It usually occurs in the context of other psychological disorders, especially anxiety disorders and depressive disorders (APA, 2013). The individual's cultural or ethnic background may influence the types of symptoms reported (APA, 2013). Estimates are that 5–7% of the population is affected by somatic symptom disorder, with 10 times as many cases found among women as among men (Kurlansik & Maffei, 2016). Not much is known of the childhood background of people with somatic symptom disorder. Although a number of studies found high rates of childhood sexual abuse among patients with somatic symptom disorders, several recent studies found that other aspects of negative parenting style have a stronger association with somatic symptom disorder, such as childhood physical and emotional abuse and an unsupportive (e.g., hostile and rejecting/neglectful) family environment (Kirmayer & Looper, 2006; Kurlansik & Maffei, 2016).

The essential feature of illness anxiety disorder is fear of disease, of what bodily symptoms may portend. People with somatic symptom disorder, by contrast, are also pestered by the symptoms themselves. Both diagnoses may be given to the same individual if the diagnostic criteria for both disorders are met.

Factitious Disorder

factitious disorder Type of psychological disorder characterized by the intentional fabrication of psychological or physical symptoms for no apparent gain.

Individuals diagnosed with **factitious disorder** fake or manufacture physical or psychological symptoms, but without any apparent motive. Sometimes they are outright faking, claiming they cannot move an arm or a leg or claiming a pain that doesn't exist. Sometimes they injure themselves or take medication that causes troubling, even life-threatening symptoms. The puzzlement involves the lack of a motive for these deceitful behaviours. Factitious disorder is not the same as malingering. Because malingering is motivated by external rewards or incentives, it is not considered a mental disorder within the DSM framework. People who feign physical illness to avoid work or to qualify for disability benefits may be deceitful and even dishonest, but they are not deemed to be suffering from a psychological disorder. But in factitious disorder, the symptoms do not bring about obvious gains or external rewards. Thus, factitious disorder serves an underlying psychological need involved in assuming a sick role; hence, it is classified as a type of mental or psychological disorder.

The two major subtypes of factitious disorder are (1) *factitious disorder on self* (characterized by faking or inducing symptoms in oneself) and (2) *factitious disorder imposed on another* (characterized by inducing symptoms in others).

Factitious disorder imposed on onseself is the most common form of the disorder and is popularly referred to as Munchausen syndrome. The syndrome is a form of feigned illness in which the person either fakes being ill or makes him- or herself ill (e.g., by ingesting toxic substances such as rat poison or injecting themselves with bacteria). Although people with somatic symptom disorder may reap some benefits from having physical symptoms (e.g., drawing sympathy from others), they do not purposefully produce them. They do not set out to deceive others. But Munchausen syndrome is a type of factitious disorder in which there is deliberate fabrication or inducement of seemingly plausible physical complaints for no obvious gain, apart from assuming the role of a medical patient and receiving sympathy and support from others. Munchausen syndrome was named after Baron Karl von Münchhausen, one of history's great fibbers. The good baron, an 18th-century German army officer, entertained friends with tales of outrageous adventures. People who have Munchausen syndrome usually suffer deep anguish as they bounce from hospital to hospital and subject themselves to unnecessary, painful, and sometimes risky medical treatments, even surgery.

Factitious disorder imposed on another, referred to as Munchausen by proxy syndrome (MBPS), often involves a parent who feigns or induces illness in a child (Ayoub, 2006). For example, the parent may attempt to poison the child in order for the child (and, by proxy, the parent) to receive medical attention. Thus, MBPS can be associated with severe and sometimes deadly child abuse.

Why do patients with factitious disorder feign illness or sometimes put themselves at grave risk by causing themselves to be sick or injured? This syndrome represents an extreme need for nurturance or attention (Slovenko, 2006), although the underlying reasons for this need are unclear. Perhaps enacting the sick role in the protected hospital environment provides a sense of security that was lacking in childhood. Perhaps the hospital becomes a stage on which patients can act out resentments against doctors and parents, resentments that have been brewing since childhood. Perhaps they are trying to identify with a parent who was often sick. Or perhaps they learned to enact a sick role in childhood to escape repeated sexual abuse or other traumatic experiences and continue to enact the role to escape stressors in their adult lives (Trask & Sigmon, 1997). No one is really sure, and the disorder remains one of the more puzzling forms of abnormal behaviour.

Theoretical Perspectives

Conversion disorder, or *hysteria*, was known to Hippocrates, who attributed the strange bodily symptoms to a wandering uterus, which created internal chaos. The term *hysterical* derives from the Greek *hystera*, meaning "uterus." Hippocrates noticed that these complaints were less common among married women. He prescribed marriage as a "cure" on the basis of these observations, and also on the theoretical assumption that pregnancy would satisfy uterine needs and fix the organ in place. Pregnancy fosters hormonal and structural changes that are of benefit to some women with menstrual complaints, but Hippocrates's belief in the "wandering uterus" has contributed throughout the centuries to degrading interpretations of complaints by women of physical problems. Despite Hippocrates's belief that hysteria is exclusively a female concern, it also occurs in men.

Photos.com/Thinkstock/Getty Images

Tall Tales. Baron Münchhausen, who, according to the fictional accounts published by Rudolf Erich Raspe, regaled his friends with tales of his incredible feats. In one of his tall tales, depicted here, he claimed that he had fallen asleep inside a cannon and was inadvertently shot across the Thames River.

Modern theoretical accounts of the somatic symptom and related disorders, like those of the dissociative disorders, have most often sprung from psychodynamic and learning theories. Although not much is known about the biological underpinnings of somatic symptom and related disorders, evidence indicates that somatic symptom disorder tends to run in families. A twin study conducted at the University of British Columbia indicates that hypochondriacal features—such as excessive health-related worry and the unfounded belief that one has a serious, undiagnosed disease—are caused by a combination of environmental and genetic factors (Taylor, Thordarson, Jang, & Asmundson, 2006). Environmental factors include learning experiences such as episodes of childhood illness that teach the child that he or she is sickly and frail (Taylor & Asmundson, 2004). Such experiences can give rise to unrealistic beliefs (e.g., "My health is in constant jeopardy"), which can cause people to focus their attention on their bodies and thereby notice and misinterpret the significance of minor bodily aches and pains or other bodily changes (Marcus, Gurley, Marchi, & Bauer, 2007). Such factors also appear to play a role in illness anxiety disorder (Brown, 2004). Thus, an accumulating body of research supports learning theories of illness anxiety disorder and other somatic symptom disorders, although the results indicate that biological factors such as genes also play a role (Kirmayer & Looper, 2006; Rief & Barsky, 2005; Taylor et al., 2006).

Hysterical disorders provided an arena for some of the debate between the psychological and biological theories of the 19th century. The alleviation—albeit often temporary—of hysterical symptoms through hypnosis by Jean-Martin Charcot, Josef Breuer, and Freud contributed to the belief that hysteria was rooted in psychological rather than physical causes and led Freud to the development of a theory of the unconscious mind. Freud held that the ego manages to control unacceptable or threatening sexual and aggressive impulses arising from the id through defence mechanisms such as repression. Such control prevents the outbreak of anxiety that would occur if the person were to become aware of these impulses. In some cases, the leftover emotion or energy that is "strangulated" or cut off from the threatening impulses becomes converted into a physical symptom, such as hysterical paralysis or blindness. Although the early psychodynamic formulation of hysteria is still widely held, empirical evidence has been lacking. One problem with the Freudian view is that it does not explain how energies left over from unconscious conflicts become transformed into physical symptoms (Miller, 1987). A further problem is that psychodynamic theory does not consider the role of learning factors (e.g., sympathy or other forms of positive reinforcement for expressing symptoms) or biological factors in the disorder (Stonnington, Barry, & Fisher, 2006; Wald, Taylor, & Scamvougeras, 2004).

According to psychodynamic theory, hysterical symptoms are functional: They allow the person to achieve primary gains and secondary gains. The primary gains consist of allowing the individual to keep internal conflicts repressed. The person is aware of the physical symptom, but not of the conflict it represents. In such cases, the "symptom" is symbolic of, and provides the person with a "partial solution" of, the underlying conflict. For example, the hysterical paralysis of an arm might symbolize and also prevent the individual from acting on repressed unacceptable sexual (e.g., masturbatory) or aggressive (e.g., murderous) impulses. Repression occurs automatically, so the individual remains unaware of the underlying conflicts. *La belle indifférence*, first noted by Charcot, is believed to occur because the physical symptoms help relieve rather than cause anxiety. From the psychodynamic perspective, conversion disorders, like dissociative disorders, serve a purpose.

nyul/123RF

What to take? Illness anxiety disorder involves persistent concerns or fears that one is seriously ill, although no organic basis can be found to account for the person's physical complaints. People with this disorder frequently medicate themselves with over-the-counter preparations and find little, if any, reassurance in doctors' assertions that their health is not in jeopardy.

Secondary gains may allow the individual to avoid burdensome responsibilities and to gain the support—rather than condemnation—of those around them. For example, soldiers sometimes experience sudden "paralysis" of their hands, which prevents them from firing their guns in battle. They may then be sent to recuperate at a hospital rather than face enemy fire. The symptoms in such cases are not considered contrived, as would be the case in malingering. A number of World War II bomber pilots suffered hysterical "night blindness" that prevented them from carrying out dangerous nighttime missions. In the psychodynamic view, their "blindness" may have achieved a primary gain of shielding them from guilt associated with dropping bombs on civilian areas. It may also have achieved a secondary purpose of helping them avoid dangerous missions.

Psychodynamic theory and learning theory concur that the symptoms in conversion disorders relieve anxiety, but psychodynamic theorists seek the causes of anxiety in unconscious conflicts. However, there is little evidence to support psychodynamic theories that propose that medically unexplained symptoms such as those found in somatic symptom and related disorders are the expression of unconscious psychological conflicts (Brown, 2004).

Learning theorists focus on the more direct reinforcing properties of the symptom and its secondary role in helping the individual avoid or escape uncomfortable or anxiety-evoking situations. From the learning perspective, the symptoms in conversion and other somatic symptom disorders may also carry the benefits or reinforcing properties of the "sick role" (Speed & Mooney, 1997). People with conversion disorders may be relieved of chores and responsibilities such as going to work or performing household tasks. Being sick also usually earns sympathy and support. People who received such reinforcers during past illnesses are likely to learn to adopt a sick role even when they are not ill. We are not suggesting that people with conversion disorders are fakers. We are merely pointing out that people may learn to adopt roles that lead to reinforcing consequences, regardless of whether they deliberately seek to enact these roles.

A leading cognitive explanation of illness anxiety disorder focuses on the role of distorted thinking (Fulton, Marcus, & Merkey, 2011; Marcus et al., 2007; Taylor & Asmundson, 2004). People who develop illness anxiety disorder have a tendency to "make mountains out of molehills" by exaggerating the importance of their physical complaints. They misinterpret relatively minor physical complaints as signs of a serious illness, creating anxiety and leading them to chase down one doctor after another in an attempt to uncover the dreaded disease they fear they have. The anxiety itself may lead to unpleasant physical symptoms, which are likewise exaggerated in importance, leading to more worrisome thoughts.

Cognitive theorists have speculated that illness anxiety disorder and panic disorder, which often occur concurrently, may share a common cause, namely a cognitive bias to misinterpret changes in bodily cues or sensations as signs of catastrophic harm (Gropalis, Bleichhardt, Hiller, & Witthöft, 2013). Differences between the two disorders may hinge on whether the misinterpretation of bodily cues carries a perception of imminent threat, leading to a rapid spiralling of anxiety (panic disorder), or of a longer-range threat in the form of an underlying disease process (illness anxiety disorder). Research into cognitive processes involved in illness anxiety disorder deserves further study. Given the linkages that may exist between illness anxiety disorder and anxiety disorders such as panic disorder and obsessive-compulsive disorder, it remains unclear whether illness anxiety disorder should be classified as a somatic symptom disorder or an anxiety disorder (Gropalis, Bleichhardt, Witthöft, & Hiller, 2012).

Treatment of Somatic Symptom and Related Disorders

The treatment approach that Freud pioneered—psychoanalysis—began with the treatment of hysteria, which is now termed *conversion disorder*. Psychoanalysis seeks to uncover and bring unconscious conflicts that originated in childhood into conscious awareness. Once the conflict is aired and worked through, the symptom is no longer needed as a "partial solution" to the conflict and should disappear. The psychoanalytic method is supported by case studies, some reported by Freud and others by his followers. However, the infrequency of conversion disorders in contemporary times has made it difficult to mount controlled studies of the psychoanalytic technique.

The behavioural approach to treating conversion disorders and other somatic symptom disorders may focus on removing sources of secondary reinforcement (or secondary gain) that may become connected with physical complaints. Family members and others, for example, often perceive individuals with somatic symptom disorder as sickly and infirm and as incapable of carrying normal responsibilities. Other people may be unaware of how they reinforce dependent and complaining behaviours when they relieve the sick person of responsibilities. The behaviour therapist may teach family members to reward attempts to assume responsibility and ignore nagging and complaining. The behaviour therapist may also work more directly with the person who has a somatic symptom and related disorder, for example, helping the person to learn more adaptive ways of handling stress or anxiety through relaxation and cognitive restructuring (e.g., Wald et al., 2004). A lack of controlled studies in this area limits any general conclusions about the effectiveness of behavioural methods. A growing number of studies, however, indicate that cognitive-behavioural therapy (CBT) is effective in treating illness anxiety and somatic symptom disorders (Greeven et al., 2007; Janca, 2005; Taylor, Asmundson, & Coons, 2005). CBT is used to help modify the exaggerated illness-related beliefs of patients with the disorder.

Some studies support the use of antidepressants, especially SSRI medications such as fluoxetine (Prozac) and paroxetine (Paxil), in treating some types of somatic symptom and related disorders (Fallon, 2004; Rief & Sharpe, 2004). Interestingly, both

Koro and *Dhat* Syndromes: Asian Somatic Symptom Disorders?

In Canada, it is common for people who develop illness anxiety disorder to be troubled by the idea that they have serious illnesses, such as cancer. The *koro* and *dhat* syndromes of East Asia and India, respectively, share some clinical features with illness anxiety disorder. Although these syndromes may seem strange to most North American readers, they are each connected through folklore within their cultures.

KORO SYNDROME

Koro syndrome is a culture-bound syndrome found primarily in China and some other East Asian countries, although *koro*-like cases have also been described in Africa, India, and Western countries, including Canada (Dzokoto & Adams, 2005). People with *koro* fear that their genitals are shrinking and retracting into the body and believe that this will result in death (Cheng, 1996). The syndrome, which tends to be short-lived, has been identified mainly in young men, although some cases have also been reported in women, who fear that their genitals or breasts are shrinking or retracting into the body (Chowdhury, 1996; Dzokoto & Adams, 2005). Physiological signs of anxiety that approach panic proportions are common, including profuse sweating, breathlessness, and heart palpitations. Men who suffer from *koro* have been known to use mechanical devices such as chopsticks to try to prevent the penis from retracting into the body (Cheng, 1996).

Epidemics involving hundreds or thousands of people have been reported in parts of Asia, including China, Singapore, Thailand, and India (Dzokoto & Adams, 2005). For example, in southern China an epidemic of *koro* involving more than 3000 people occurred during 1984–1985, with incidence in the most severely afflicted villages ranging from 6% to 19% (Cheng, 1996). People who fall victim to *koro* tend to be poorly educated, lacking in proper sex information, and accepting of *koro*-related folk beliefs (such as the belief that shrinkage of the penis will be lethal) (Cheng, 1996; Chowdhury, 1996; Dzokoto & Adams, 2005). Medical reassurance that such fears are unfounded often quell *koro* episodes. Similar reassurance generally fails to dent the concerns of Westerners who develop illness anxiety disorder, however (Taylor & Asmundson, 2004). *koro* episodes among those who do not receive corrective information tend to pass with time but may recur.

Koro has been classified in various ways—as a form of anxiety disorder, depersonalization, body-image disturbance, or an atypical somatic symptom disorder (Chowdhury, 1996; Dzokoto & Adams, 2005).

DHAT SYNDROME

Dhat[1] syndrome is found among young males in India and involves excessive fears over the loss of seminal fluid during nocturnal emissions (Ranjith & Mohan, 2006). Some men with this syndrome also believe (incorrectly) that semen mixes with urine and is excreted through urination. Men with *dhat* syndrome may roam from physician to physician seeking help to prevent nocturnal emissions or the (imagined) loss of semen mixed with excreted urine. There is a widespread belief within Indian culture (and in other Eastern cultures) that the loss of semen is harmful because it depletes the body of physical and mental energy (Ranjith & Mohan, 2006). Like other culture-bound syndromes, *dhat* must be understood within its cultural context. Based on the cultural belief in the life-preserving nature of semen, it is not surprising that some Indian males experience extreme anxiety over the involuntary loss of the fluid through nocturnal emissions.

According to Ranjith and Mohan (2006), *dhat* is a form of health anxiety similar to illness anxiety disorder: Under stress, people who are predisposed to worry about their health may focus their attention on bodily products or changes, such as turbidity of urine and tiredness. And, in light of widely held beliefs in their community, they may misattribute these bodily products or changes to loss of semen.

Culture-bound disorders such as *koro* and *dhat* are unlikely to remain static. The prevalence and features of such disorders probably shift along with changes in the pertinent cultures. In recent years, there have been several reports of cases of *dhat* in various countries, including Western countries, which raise doubt about whether we should still consider *koro* and *dhat* to be culture-bound syndromes (Chandrashekar & Math, 2006).

Tukaram.Karve/Shutterstock

Dhat syndrome. Found principally in India, *dhat* syndrome afflicts young men with an intense fear or anxiety over the loss of semen.

---

[1]The word *dhat* can be loosely translated as "the elixir of life."

CBT and paroxetine were similarly effective for illness anxiety disorder in an 18-month follow-up study (Greeven et al., 2007). Although we lack specific drug therapies for conversion disorder, several studies suggest that illness anxiety can be successfully treated with SSRI medications (Greeven et al., 2007; Taylor et al., 2005). We lack any systematic studies of approaches to treating factitious disorder (Munchausen syndrome) and are limited to a few isolated case examples; for the most part, Munchausen syndrome is extremely difficult to treat and the prognosis is poor (Huffman & Stern, 2003; Slovenko, 2006).

The dissociative and somatic symptom and related disorders remain among the most intriguing and least-understood patterns of abnormal behaviour.

Koro syndrome Culture-bound somatoform disorder, found primarily in China, in which people fear that their genitals are shrinking and retracting into the body.

Dhat syndrome Usually diagnosed among young Indian men who describe an intense fear or anxiety over the loss of semen.

REVIEW IT

Somatic Symptom and Related Disorders

- **What are somatic symptom and related disorders?** In somatic symptom and related disorders, people have physical symptoms suggestive of physical disorders, but no organic abnormalities can be found to account for them. Moreover, there is evidence or some reason to believe that the symptoms reflect psychological factors. Four types of disorders are considered: conversion disorder, illness anxiety disorder, somatic symptom disorder, and factitious disorder.

- **What are the major features of conversion disorder, illness anxiety disorder, somatic symptom disorder, and factitious disorder?** In conversion disorder, symptoms or deficits in voluntary motor or sensory functions occur that suggest an underlying physical disorder, but no apparent medical basis for the condition can be found. Illness anxiety disorder is a preoccupation with the fear of having or the belief that one has a serious medical illness, but no medical basis for the complaints can be found and fears of illness persist despite medical reassurances. Somatic symptom disorder is a disorder involving one or more somatic symptoms that cause excessive concern to the extent that it affects the individual's thoughts, feelings, and behaviours in daily life. Factitious disorder is characterized by the intentional fabrication of psychological or physical symptoms for no apparent gain.

- **How are somatic symptom and related disorders conceptualized by the various theoretical perspectives?** The psychodynamic view holds that conversion disorders represent the conversion into physical symptoms of the leftover emotion or energy resulting from unacceptable or threatening impulses that the ego has prevented from reaching awareness. The symptom is functional, allowing the person to achieve both primary gains and secondary gains. Learning theorists focus on reinforcements that are associated with conversion disorders, such as the reinforcing effects of adopting a "sick role." Cognitive factors in illness anxiety disorder include unrealistic beliefs about health and disease.

- **How is the treatment of conversion disorder approached by the various theoretical perspectives?** Psychodynamic therapists attempt to uncover and bring to the level of awareness the unconscious conflicts, originating in childhood, that are believed to be at the root of the problem. Once the conflict is uncovered and worked through, the symptoms should disappear because they are no longer needed as a partial solution to the underlying conflict. Behavioural approaches focus on removing underlying sources of reinforcement that may be maintaining the abnormal behaviour pattern. More generally, behaviour therapists assist people with somatic symptom and related disorders to learn to handle stressful or anxiety-arousing situations more effectively.

Define It

conversion disorder (functional neurological symptom disorder), 201
depersonalization, 194
depersonalization/derealization disorder, 195

derealization, 195
dhat syndrome, 209
dissociative amnesia, 193
dissociative identity disorder, 190
factitious disorder, 204
illness anxiety disorder, 202

koro syndrome, 209
la belle indifférence, 202
malingering, 194
somatic symptom and related disorders, 201
somatic symptom disorder, 203

Recall It

1. Harry has experiences in which he feels like he is walking through a fog and is strangely detached from his own body. This type of experience is most likely to occur in the context of _____.
   a. dissociative identity disorder
   b. depersonalization/derealization disorder
   c. dissociative amnesia
   d. split personality

2. Psychodynamic theorists believe that dissociative disorders are caused by _____.
   a. a form of role playing acquired by means of observational learning and reinforcement
   b. repression, which leads to the "splitting off" from consciousness of unacceptable impulses and painful memories
   c. malingering
   d. the physiological effects of a substance

3. Which of the following is NOT a classic symptom of conversion disorder?
   a. paranoia
   b. epilepsy
   c. blindness
   d. paralysis

4. Amir is preoccupied with the idea that he has cancer even though he does not have any symptoms and he has been reassured by his doctors that his fears are unfounded. He is most likely to be diagnosed with _____.
   a. conversion disorder
   b. factitious disorder
   c. somatic symptom disorder
   d. illness anxiety disorder

5. In treating people with a somatic symptom or related disorder, behaviour therapists often focus on _____.
   a. rewarding sources of primary gain
   b. punishing hysterical complaints
   c. removing sources of secondary gain
   d. restricting the stimulus field

Answers to Recall It

1. b,   2. b,   3. a,   4. d,   5. c.

Think About It

- Why is conversion disorder considered a treasure trove in the annals of abnormal psychology? What role did the disorder play in the development of psychological models of abnormal behaviour?

- How might you apply the diathesis-stress model in accounting for the development of dissociative identity disorder?
- Do you believe that people with dissociative identity disorder are playing a role? Why or why not?

Weblinks

Sidran Institute
www.sidran.org
The Sidran Institute's website contains information on dissociative disorders, including links to books and educational materials.

Recovered Memories
http://psych.athabascau.ca/html/aupr/psyclaw.shtml#Recovered_Memories
This webpage from Athabasca University contains useful links on recovered memories.

False Memory Syndrome Foundation
www.fmsfonline.org
This organization provides useful information on repressed and recovered memories and dissociative disorders.

Psychology Works for Intense Illness Concern (Hypochondriasis)
www.cpa.ca/cpasite/UserFiles/Documents/factsheets/hypo.pdf
This fact sheet from the Canadian Psychological Association provides information and links on hypochondriasis.

Dissociative and Somatic Symptom and Related Disorders

Test your understanding of the key concepts by filling in the blanks with the correct statements chosen from the list that follows. The answers are found at the end of the chapter.

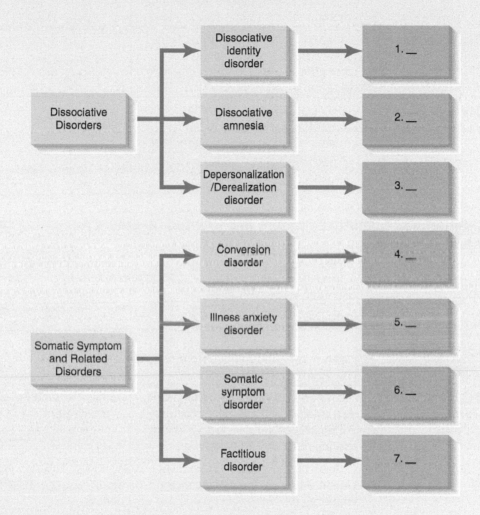

a. Falsification of physical symptoms in the absence of obvious external rewards

b. Symptoms of altered voluntary motor or sensory function that are incompatible with recognized neurological or medical conditions

c. Memory losses in the absence of any identifiable organic cause

d. Preoccupation with having or acquiring a serious illness

e. Disruption of identity characterized by two or more distinct personality states

f. Feelings of unreality or detachment from one's self or one's body or a loss of the sense of reality of one's surrounding

g. Somatic symptoms that cause excessive concern to the extent that it affects the individual's thoughts, feelings, and behaviours

Causes and Treatments of Dissociative Disorders According to Various Theoretical Perspectives

THEORETICAL PERSPECTIVES	CAUSES	TREATMENTS
PSYCHODYNAMIC	Repression that leads to the "splitting off" from consciousness of unacceptable impulses and painful memories.	Uncover and cope with early childhood trauma
BEHAVIOURAL/LEARNING	Learned response that involves not thinking about disturbing acts or thoughts to avoid feelings of guilt or shame.	
SOCIAL COGNITIVE	Dissociative identity disorder is a form of role playing acquired by means of observational learning and reinforcement.	

Causes and Treatments of Somatic Symptom and Related Disorders According to Various Theoretical Perspectives

THEORETICAL PERSPECTIVES	CAUSES	TREATMENTS
PSYCHODYNAMIC	Somatic symptoms allow the individual to keep internal conflicts repressed and may provide increased sympathy and attention from others and release from ordinary responsibilities.	Uncover and bring unconscious conflicts that originated in childhood into conscious awareness
BEHAVIOURAL/LEARNING	Somatic symptoms help the individual avoid or escape uncomfortable or anxiety-evoking situations as well as provide relief from chores and responsibilities.	Remove sources of secondary reinforcement Coping skills to deal with anxiety or stress
COGNITIVE	Misinterpreting the significance of minor bodily aches and pains or bodily changes	Modify exaggerated illness-related beliefs
BIOLOGICAL	Genetic predisposition (diathesis)	Antidepressants

Answers: 1. e, 2. c, 3. f, 4. b, 5. d, 6. g, 7. a

Personality Disorders

Did You Know That...

- Warning signs of personality disorders may begin appearing in childhood, even during the preschool years?

- People with schizoid personalities may develop stronger attachments to animals than to people?

- Not all people with antisocial personalities are lawbreakers; some are very successful in their chosen, lawful occupations?

- Adults with dependent personalities may have such difficulty making independent decisions that they allow their parents to decide whom they will or will not marry?

- It is often difficult to draw the line between normal variations in behaviour and personality disorders?

- The conceptualization of certain types of personality disorders may be sexist?

- Despite a veneer of self-importance, people with narcissistic personalities may harbour deep feelings of insecurity?

- Identical twins reared apart show remarkable similarity in psychopathic traits?

Paul Taylor/Photodisc/Getty Images

All of us have particular styles of behaviour and ways of relating to others. Some of us are orderly; others, sloppy. Some of us prefer solitary pursuits; others are more social. Some of us are followers; others, leaders. Some of us seem immune to rejection by others, whereas others avoid social initiatives for fear of getting shot down. When behaviour patterns become so inflexible or maladaptive they cause significant personal distress or impair people's social or occupational functioning, they may be diagnosed as personality disorders.

Continuum of Personality Disorders

Example: Borderline Personality

Does not meet criteria		Meets criteria		
NO SYMPTOMS	**STRUGGLING**	**MILD**	**MODERATE**	**SEVERE**
	Madison is undecided about her future goals and has changed programs at school numerous times. In relationships she is jealous and suspicious without reason and can alienate others as a result.	Manuela's temper quickly flares into an angry outburst when others disappoint her. She feels empty inside and inflicts superficial cuts on her arms to fill the void.	Sofia panics at the thought of being alone and attempts to manipulate others by threatening suicide. She often becomes enamoured with men she has just met, impulsively having sex with them and making unreasonable demands.	Felicia's fears of abandonment have resulted in numerous suicide attempts. Sometimes she has overwhelming feelings of paranoia, and at other times she feels outside herself, as if she does not exist.

TYPES OF PERSONALITY DISORDERS

In most of us by the age of thirty, the character has set like plaster, and will never soften again.

—WILLIAM JAMES

personality disorders Types of enduring patterns of inner experience and behaviour that deviate markedly from the expectations of the individual's culture, are pervasive and inflexible, and lead to distress or impairment.

ego syntonic Behaviour or feelings that are perceived as natural or compatible parts of the self.

ego dystonic Behaviour or feelings that are perceived to be foreign or alien to one's self-identity.

Personality disorders are pervasive and inflexible patterns of behaviour or ways of relating to others. Their rigidity prevents people from adjusting to external demands; thus, they ultimately become self-defeating. Disordered personality traits become evident by adolescence or early adulthood and continue through much of adult life, becoming so deeply ingrained they are highly resistant to change. The warning signs of personality disorders may be detected during childhood, even in the troubled behaviour of preschoolers. Children with childhood behaviour problems such as conduct disorder, depression, anxiety, hyperactivity, impulsivity, and attention problems are at greater-than-average risk of developing personality disorders (De Clercq & De Fruyt, 2007).

Despite the self-defeating consequences of their behaviour, people with personality disorders do not generally perceive a need to change. Using psychodynamic terms, the DSM notes that people with personality disorders tend to perceive their traits as **ego syntonic**—as natural parts of themselves. As a result, individuals with personality disorders are more likely to be brought to the attention of mental health professionals by others than to seek services themselves. In contrast, individuals with anxiety disorders or depressive disorders tend to view their disturbed behaviour as **ego dystonic**. They do not see their behaviour as parts of their self-identities and are thus more likely to seek help to relieve the distress caused by it.

The DSM groups personality disorders into three clusters:

Cluster A: People who are perceived as odd or eccentric. This cluster includes paranoid, schizoid, and schizotypal personality disorders.

Cluster B: People whose behaviour is overly dramatic, emotional, or erratic. This grouping consists of antisocial, borderline, histrionic, and narcissistic personality disorders.

Cluster C: People who often appear anxious or fearful. This cluster includes avoidant, dependent, and obsessive-compulsive personality disorders.

Personality Disorders Characterized by Odd or Eccentric Behaviour

This group of personality disorders includes paranoid, schizoid, and schizotypal disorders. People with these disorders often have difficulty relating to others, or may show little or no interest in developing social relationships.

PARANOID PERSONALITY DISORDER The defining trait of **paranoid personality disorder** is pervasive suspiciousness—the tendency to interpret other people's behaviour as deliberately threatening or demeaning. People with the disorder are excessively mistrustful of others, and their relationships suffer for it. They may be suspicious of co-workers and supervisors but can generally maintain employment.

People who have paranoid personalities tend to be overly sensitive to criticism, whether real or imagined. They take offence at the smallest slight. They are readily angered and hold grudges when they think they have been mistreated. They are unlikely to confide in others because they believe that personal information may be used against them. They question the sincerity and trustworthiness of friends and associates. A smile or a glance may be viewed with suspicion. As a result, they have few friends and intimate relationships. When they do form an intimate relationship, they may suspect infidelity, although there is no evidence to back up their suspicions. They tend to remain hypervigilant, as if they must be on the lookout against harm. They deny blame for misdeeds, even when warranted, and are perceived by others as cold, aloof, scheming, devious, and humourless. They tend to be argumentative and may launch repeated lawsuits against those who they believe have mistreated them.

Clinicians need to weigh cultural and sociopolitical factors when arriving at a diagnosis of paranoid personality disorder. They may find members of immigrant or ethnic minority groups, political refugees, or people from other cultures to be guarded or defensive in their behaviour. This behaviour may, however, reflect unfamiliarity with the language, customs, or rules and regulations of the majority culture or a cultural mistrust arising from a history of neglect or oppression. Such behaviour should not be confused with paranoid personality disorder (APA, 2013).

Although the suspicions of people with paranoid personality disorder are exaggerated and unwarranted, there is an absence of the outright paranoid delusions that characterize the thought patterns of some people with schizophrenia (e.g., believing the RCMP are out to get them). People who have paranoid personalities are unlikely to seek treatment for themselves; they see others as causing their problems. The reported prevalence of paranoid personality disorder in the general population ranges from 2.3% to 4.4% (APA, 2013). The disorder is diagnosed in clinical samples more often in men than women.

SCHIZOID PERSONALITY DISORDER Social isolation is the cardinal feature of **schizoid personality disorder**. Often described as a loner or an eccentric, the person with a schizoid personality lacks interest in social relationships. The emotions of people with schizoid personalities appear shallow or blunted, but not to the degree found in schizophrenia (see Chapter 10, "Schizophrenia Spectrum and Other Psychotic Disorders").

paranoid personality disorder
Type of personality disorder characterized by persistent distrust and suspiciousness of the motives of others.

schizoid personality disorder
Type of personality disorder characterized by detachment from social relationships and a restricted range of emotional expression.

Able Images/Photodisc/Getty Images

Schizoid personality. It is normal to be reserved about displaying one's feelings, especially when one is among strangers, but people with schizoid personalities rarely express emotions and are distant and aloof. Yet the emotions of people with schizoid personalities are not as shallow or blunted as they are in people with schizophrenia.

People with this disorder seem to rarely, if ever, experience strong anger, joy, or sadness. They look distant and aloof. Their faces tend to show no emotional expression, and they rarely exchange social smiles or nods. They seem indifferent to criticism or praise and appear to be wrapped up in abstract ideas rather than in thoughts about people. Although they prefer to remain distant from others, they maintain better contact with reality than do people with schizophrenia. The prevalence of the disorder in the general population is estimated to be 3.1–4.9% (APA, 2013). Men with schizoid personality disorder rarely date or marry. Women who have it are more likely to accept romantic advances passively and marry, but they seldom initiate relationships or develop strong attachments to their partners. Triebwasser and colleagues claim that the reclusiveness typical of individuals with schizoid personality disorder may be attributed to other disorders commonly found among this population, such as a depressive or anxiety disorder (Triebwasser, Chemerinski, Roussos, & Siever, 2012).

Akhtar (1987, 2003) claims there may be discrepancies between outer appearances and the inner lives of people with schizoid personalities. Although they may appear to have little appetite for sex, for example, they may harbour voyeuristic wishes and become attracted to pornography. Akhtar also suggests that the distance and social aloofness of people with schizoid personalities could be somewhat superficial. They may also harbour exquisite sensitivity, deep curiosities about people, and wishes for love they cannot express. In some cases, sensitivity is expressed in deep feelings for animals rather than people.

schizotypal personality disorder Type of personality disorder characterized by acute discomfort in close relationships, cognitive or perceptual distortions, and eccentricities of behaviour.

SCHIZOTYPAL PERSONALITY DISORDER Schizotypal personality disorder usually becomes evident by early adulthood. The diagnosis applies to people who have difficulties forming close relationships and whose behaviour, mannerisms, and thought patterns are peculiar or odd but not disturbed enough to merit a diagnosis of schizophrenia. They may be especially anxious in social situations, even when interacting with familiar people. Their social anxieties seem to be associated with paranoid thinking (e.g., fears that others mean them harm) rather than concerns about being rejected or evaluated negatively by others (APA, 2013).

Schizotypal personality disorder is believed to be slightly more common in males and is thought to affect about 3% of the general population (APA, 2013). Clinicians need to be careful not to label certain behaviour patterns that reflect culturally determined beliefs or religious rituals as schizotypal, such as beliefs in voodoo and other magical beliefs.

The eccentricity associated with the schizoid personality is not limited to a lack of interest in social relationships. Schizotypal personality disorder refers to a wider range of odd behaviour, beliefs, and perceptions. Individuals with the disorder may experience unusual perceptions or illusions, such as feeling the presence of a deceased family member in the room. They realize, however, that the person is not actually there. They may become unduly suspicious of others or paranoid in their thinking. They may develop **ideas of reference**, such as the belief that other people are talking about them. They may engage in "magical thinking," such as believing they possess a "sixth sense" (i.e., can foretell the future) or that others can sense their feelings. They may attach unusual meanings to words. Their own speech may be vague or unusually abstract, but not so much that it becomes incoherent or filled with the loose associations that characterize schizophrenia. They may appear unkempt, display unusual mannerisms, and engage in unusual behaviour such as talking to themselves in the presence of others. Their faces may register little emotion. Like people with schizoid personalities, they may fail to exchange smiles

ideas of reference Form of delusional thinking in which a person reads personal meaning into the behaviour of others or external events that are completely independent of the person.

with or nod at others. They may appear silly and smile and laugh at the wrong times. They tend to be socially withdrawn and aloof, with few if any close friends or confidants. They seem to be especially anxious around unfamiliar people.

Some of these features are found in the case of Nisar:

> Nisar, a 27-year-old auto mechanic, had few friends and preferred science fiction novels to socializing with other people. He seldom joined in conversations. At times, he seemed to be lost in his thoughts, and his co-workers would have to whistle to get his attention when he was working on a car. He often showed a "queer" expression on his face. Perhaps the most unusual feature of his behaviour was his reported intermittent experience of "feeling" his deceased mother standing nearby. These illusions were reassuring to him, and he looked forward to their occurrence. Nisar realized they were not real. He never tried to reach out to touch the apparition, knowing it would disappear as soon as he drew closer. It was enough, he said, to feel her presence.
>
> The Authors' Files

Despite the DSM's grouping of schizotypal behaviour with personality disorders, the schizotypal behaviour pattern may fall within a spectrum of schizophrenia-related disorders that also includes schizoaffective disorder (discussed in Chapter 10) and schizophrenia itself. Schizotypal personality disorder may actually share a common genetic basis with schizophrenia (Siever & Davis, 2004). Let us note, however, that schizotypal personality disorder tends to follow a chronic course, and relatively few people diagnosed with the disorder go on to develop schizophrenia or other psychotic disorders (APA, 2013). Perhaps the emergence of schizophrenia in people with this shared genetic predisposition is determined by such factors as stressful early family relationships.

Personality Disorders Characterized by Dramatic, Emotional, or Erratic Behaviour

This cluster of personality disorders includes the antisocial, borderline, histrionic, and narcissistic types. The behaviour patterns of these types are excessive, unpredictable, or self-centred. People with these disorders have difficulty forming and maintaining relationships.

Much of our attention in this section focuses on antisocial personality disorder. Historically, it is the personality disorder that has been most extensively studied by scholars and researchers.

ANTISOCIAL PERSONALITY DISORDER People with **antisocial personality disorder** (APD) persistently violate the rights of others and often break the law. They disregard social norms and conventions, are impulsive, and fail to live up to interpersonal and vocational commitments. Yet they often show a superficial charm and are at least average in intelligence. Perhaps the features that are most striking about them are their low levels of anxiety in threatening situations and their lack of guilt or remorse following wrongdoing (Bandelow & Wedekind, 2015). Punishment seems to have little if any effect on their behaviour. Although parents and others have usually punished them for their misdeeds, they persist in leading irresponsible and impulsive lives.

Men are more likely than women to receive diagnoses of APD (Sher et al., 2015). The prevalence rate for the disorder is estimated to be about about 4.3% (Goldstein et al., 2017) but is much higher among offenders. In a survey of psychiatric disorders in incoming Canadian male offenders, antisocial personality disorder was the second most frequent disorder (44.1%), following substance disorders (66%). Rates are even higher among Indigenous offenders, at 60.4% (Beaudette & Stewart, 2016). Researchers report greater rates among male offenders (47%) than among female offenders (21%) (Fazel & Danesh, 2002) (see Figure 6.1).

antisocial personality disorder Type of personality disorder characterized by a chronic pattern of disregard for, and violation of, the rights of others. Abbreviated *APD*.

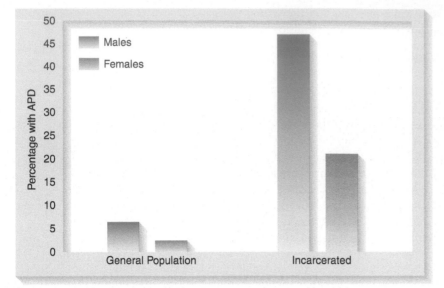

FIGURE 6.1 **Estimates of lifetime prevalence rates of antisocial personality disorder in general and incarcerated populations.**

Sources: Based on Beaudette, J. N. & Stewart, L. A. (2016) National prevalence of mental disorders among incoming Canadian male offenders. The Canadian Journal of psychiatry, 61, 624-632. and Offord, D.R., Boyle, M.H., Campbell, D., Goering, P, Lin, E., Wong, M., & Racine, Y. A. (1996). One-year prevalence of psychiatric disorders in Ontarians 15 to 64 years of age. Canadian Journal of Psychiatry, 41 (9), 559–563.

psychopathy Type of personality pattern characterized by affective and interpersonal traits, such as shallow emotions, selfishness, arrogance, superficial charm, deceitfulness, manipulativeness, irresponsibility, sensation seeking, and a lack of empathy, anxiety, and remorse, combined with persistent violations of social norms, a socially deviant and nomadic lifestyle, and impulsiveness.

Frank Gunn/CP Images

Antisocial personality. Serial killer Paul Bernardo killed without feeling or remorse and displayed some of the superficial charm seen in some people with antisocial personality disorder.

For a diagnosis of APD to be applied, the person must be at least 18 years of age. The alternative diagnosis of conduct disorder is used for younger people (see Chapter 11, "Abnormal Behaviour across the Lifespan"). Many children with conduct disorders do not continue to show antisocial behaviour as adults.

We once used terms like *psychopath* and *sociopath* to refer to the type of people who are commonly classified as having antisocial personalities—people whose behaviour is amoral and asocial, impulsive, and lacking in remorse and shame. The roots of the word *psychopath* focus on the idea that something is amiss (pathological) in the individual's psychological functioning. The roots of sociopathy centre on the person's social deviance. The DSM criteria for APD focus more on elements of criminal actions (e.g., those that involve antisocial behaviour and social deviance) than on the traditional elements of **psychopathy**, which emphasize emotional (e.g., callousness and a lack of the normal pangs of guilt, anxiety, and remorse) and interpersonal traits (e.g., superficial charm and manipulative behaviour). The pattern of behaviour that characterizes both APD and psychopathic personality begins in childhood or adolescence and extends into adulthood (Black, 2015).

Profile of the Antisocial Personality   Common features of people with APD include failure to conform to social norms, irresponsibility, aimlessness and lack of long-term goals or plans, impulsive behaviour, outright lawlessness, violence, chronic unemployment, marital problems, lack of remorse or empathy, substance use disorder, a history of alcoholism, and a disregard for the truth and for the feelings and needs of others (APA, 2013; Bandelow & Wedekind, 2015; Thylstrup, Schröder, & Hesse, 2015). Irresponsibility may be seen in a personal history dotted by repeated, unexplained absences from work, abandonment of jobs without having other job opportunities to fall back on, or long stretches of unemployment despite available job opportunities. Irresponsibility extends to financial matters, where there may be repeated failure to repay debts, pay child support, or meet other financial responsibilities to one's family and dependants. The diagnostic features of APD, as defined in the DSM, are shown in Table 6.1.

Antisocial Behaviour and Criminality   We may tend to think of antisocial personality disorder as synonymous with criminal behaviour. Although there is a strong relationship between the two, not all criminals have antisocial personality disorder and not everyone with APD becomes a criminal (Sinnamon, 2017). Some individuals with APD are quite successful in their chosen occupations, yet they possess a personality style characterized by a callous disregard of the interests and feelings of others.

We should also note that people may become criminals or delinquents not because of a disordered personality but because they were reared in environments or subcultures that encouraged and rewarded criminal behaviour. The criminal behaviour of a professional thief or drug pusher, although antisocial, does not in itself justify a diagnosis of APD (APA, 2013). Canadian studies indicate that criminal and aggressive behaviour have multiple causes and represent many personality styles in both male and female offenders (Laishes, 2002). Although the

TABLE 6.1

Diagnostic Criteria for Antisocial Personality Disorder

A. A pervasive pattern of disregard for and violation of the rights of others, occurring since age 15 years, as indicated by three (or more) of the following:

   1. Failure to conform to social norms with respect to lawful behaviors, as indicated by repeatedly performing acts that are grounds for arrest.

   2. Deceitfulness, as indicated by repeated lying, use of aliases, or conning others for personal profit or pleasure.

   3. Impulsivity or failure to plan ahead.

   4. Irritability and aggressiveness, as indicated by repeated physical fights or assaults.

   5. Reckless disregard for safety of self or others.

   6. Consistent irresponsibility, as indicated by repeated failure to sustain consistent work behavior or honor financial obligations.

   7. Lack of remorse, as indicated by being indifferent to or rationalizing having hurt, mistreated, or stolen from another.

B. The individual is at least age 18 years.

C. There is evidence of conduct disorder with onset before age 15 years.

D. The occurrence of antisocial behavior is not exclusively during the course of schizophrenia or bipolar disorder.

Source: Reprinted with permission from the *Diagnostic and Statistical Manual of Mental Disorders*, Fifth Edition, (Copyright © 2013). American Psychiatric Association. p. 659.

behaviour of criminals is deviant to society at large, it may be normal by the standards of their subcultures. We should also recognize that lack of remorse, a cardinal feature of APD, does not characterize all criminals. Some criminals regret their crimes, and evidence of remorse is considered when a sentence is passed.

Sociocultural Factors and Antisocial Personality Disorder   Antisocial personality disorder cuts across all racial and ethnic groups. Researchers find no evidence of ethnic or racial differences in the rates of the disorder (Veen et al., 2011). The disorder is more common, however, among people with lower socioeconomic status (SES). One explanation is that people with APD may drift downward occupationally, perhaps because their antisocial behaviour makes it difficult for them to hold steady jobs or progress upward. It is possible, too, that people from lower SES levels are more likely to have been reared by parents who themselves modelled antisocial behaviour. However, it is also possible that the diagnosis is misapplied to people living in hard-pressed communities who may engage in seemingly antisocial behaviour as a type of defence strategy in order to survive (APA, 2013).

Psychophysiological and Biological Factors Associated with Antisocial Personality and Psychopathy   There are several psychophysiological and biological factors that are related to antisocial personality and psychopathy:

   1. *Lack of emotional responsiveness.* People with antisocial personalities can maintain their composure in stressful situations that would induce anxiety in most people (Thompson, Ramos, & Willett, 2014). Lack of anxiety in response to threatening situations may help explain the failure of punishment to induce antisocial people to relinquish their behaviour. For most of us, the fear of getting caught and being punished is sufficient to inhibit antisocial impulses. People with antisocial personalities, however, often fail to inhibit behaviour that has led to punishment in the past (Arnett, Smith, & Newman, 1997). They may not learn to inhibit antisocial or aggressive behaviour because they experience little if any fear or anticipatory anxiety about being caught and punished.

   2. *The craving-for-stimulation model.* Other investigators have attempted to explain the antisocial personality's lack of emotional response in terms of the levels of stimulation necessary to maintain an **optimum level of arousal**. Our

optimum level of arousal Level of arousal associated with peak performance and maximum feelings of well-being.

optimum levels of arousal are the degrees of arousal at which we feel best and function most efficiently.

Individuals with APD appear to have exaggerated cravings for stimulation (Bandelow & Wedekind, 2015). Perhaps they require a higher-than-normal threshold of stimulation to maintain an optimum state of arousal. That is, they may need more stimulation than other people to function normally.

A need for higher levels of stimulation may explain why people with psychopathic traits tend to become bored more easily than other people and more often gravitate to more stimulating but potentially dangerous activities, such as the use of intoxicants (such as drugs or alcohol), motorcycling, skydiving, high-stakes gambling, or sexual adventures. A higher-than-normal threshold for stimulation would not directly cause antisocial or criminal behaviour; after all, part of the "right stuff" of respected astronauts includes sensation seeking. However, threat of boredom and inability to tolerate monotony may influence some sensation seekers to drift into crime or reckless behaviour.

3. *Lack of restraint on impulsivity.* Other research on brainwave functions shows lower levels of activity in the frontal lobes of the cerebral cortex in men with APD (Liu, Liao, Jiang, & Wang, 2014; Yang & Raine, 2009). The frontal cortex plays a key role in inhibiting impulsive behaviour, which may help explain why people with antisocial personalities have difficulty controlling impulsive or aggressive behaviour.

4. *Limbic abnormalities.* As described above, one of the distinguishing features of antisocial personalities is a dysfunctional processing of emotional information. A study of the brain's limbic system using magnetic resonance imaging compared both criminal nonpsychopaths and noncriminal control participants with criminal psychopaths while they performed an affective memory task (Kiehl et al., 2001). Results revealed that criminal psychopaths showed significantly less brain activity in the emotional parts of the brain found within the limbic system but showed overstimulation in areas of the frontal-temporal lobes that are associated with processing and regulating emotional information. This suggests that the emotional irregularities found in psychopathic offenders may be tied to diminished input from brain structures within the limbic system.

borderline personality disorder
Type of personality disorder characterized by instability in interpersonal relationships, self-image, and affects and marked impulsivity. Abbreviated *BPD*.

BORDERLINE PERSONALITY DISORDER Borderline personality disorder (BPD) is primarily characterized by a pervasive pattern of instability in relationships, self-image, and mood and a lack of control over impulses. People with BPD tend to be uncertain about their values, goals, loyalties, careers, choices of friends, and perhaps even sexual orientations. This instability in self-image or identity leaves them with persistent feelings of emptiness and boredom. They cannot tolerate being alone and will make desperate attempts to avoid feelings of abandonment (APA, 2013). Fear of abandonment renders them clinging and demanding in their social relationships, but their clinging often pushes away the people on whom they depend. Signs of rejection may enrage them, straining their relationships further. Their feelings toward others are consequently intense and shifting. They alternate between extremes of adulation (when their needs are met) and loathing (when they feel neglected). They tend to view other people as all good or all bad, shifting abruptly from one extreme to the other. As a result, they may flit from partner to partner in a series of brief and stormy relationships. People they had idealized are treated with contempt when relationships end or when they feel the other person fails to meet their needs (APA, 2013).

Borderline personality disorder is estimated to occur in about 1.6–5.9% of the general population and about 20% of psychiatric inpatients (APA, 2013). Although it is diagnosed more often (about 75% of the time) in women, gender differences in prevalence rates for BPD in the general population remain undetermined. A review of 43 studies involving college students revealed prevalence rates of 0.5–32.1% with a lifetime prevalence of 9.7%. No gender differences were detected (Meany, Hasking, & Reupert, 2016). Tadić and colleagues reported a gender difference in their clinical population with a greater incidence among women (70%). They also revealed that men with BPD had a greater incidence of substance use disorders while women had higher rates of mood, anxiety, and eating disorders (Tadić et al., 2009).

The term *borderline personality* was originally used to refer to individuals whose behaviour appeared to be on the border between neuroses and psychoses. People with BPD generally maintain better contact with reality than people with psychoses, although they may show transient psychotic behaviour during times of stress. Generally speaking, they seem to be more severely impaired than most people with neuroses but not as dysfunctional as those with psychotic disorders.

Borderline personality disorder may actually lie closer to mood disorders than psychotic disorders. Many individuals diagnosed with BPD also meet diagnostic criteria for mood disorders, such as major depression and bipolar disorder (Tomko, Trull, Wood, & Sher, 2014). Many people with BPD also meet criteria for other personality disorders. University of Toronto researcher Paul Links and his colleagues conducted a seven-year follow-up study of a Canadian sample of BPD patients. They found that those patients with persistent symptoms of the disorder were more likely to have coexisting personality disorders than those patients who were in remission for BPD, including avoidant (59.2%), self-defeating (40.7%), passive-aggressive (37%), dependent (33.3%), and histrionic (25.9%) symptoms (Links, Heslegrave, & van Reekum, 1998). Zimmerman and colleagues also found high rates of coexisting personality disorders in their sample, other than schizoid, histrionic, and obsessive-compulsive (Zimmerman, Rothschild, & Chelminski, 2005). In addition to meeting the DSM criteria for a variety of personality disorders, patients with BPD share the personality dimensions of neuroticism, impulsivity, anxiousness, affective liability, and insecure attachment (Skodol, Gunderson, et al., 2002; Skodol, Siever, et al., 2002).

Instability of moods is a central characteristic of borderline personality disorder. Moods run the gamut from anger and irritability to depression and anxiety and may shift frequently and abruptly (Weissman, 2011). Other features of BPD are ongoing anger, loneliness, boredom, a deep sense of emptiness, and impulsivity. Patients with BPD tend to view their relationships as rife with hostility and to perceive others as rejecting and abandoning (Berenson, Downey, Rafaeli, Coifman, & Paquin, 2011). They have difficulty controlling anger and are prone to fights or smashing things. They often act on impulse, like eloping with someone they have just met (Gvirts et al., 2012). This impulsive and unpredictable behaviour can often be self-destructive and is linked to a risk of suicidal attempts and gestures (Gunderson, 2011; Zimmerman et al., 2014); approximately 10% of people diagnosed with BPD will die from suicide (Meany, Hasking, & Reupert, 2016). It may also involve spending sprees, gambling, drug abuse, engaging in unsafe sexual activity, reckless driving, binge eating, or shoplifting. People with BPD sometimes partake in impulsive acts of self-mutilation, such as scratching their wrists or burning cigarettes on their arms, as in this young woman's case:

> **Client:** I've got such repressed anger in me; what happens is . . . I can't feel it; I get anxiety attacks. I get very nervous, smoke too many cigarettes. So what happens to me is I tend to explode. Into tears or hurting myself or whatever . . . because I don't know how to contend with all those mixed up feelings.
>
> **Interviewer:** What was the more recent example of such an explosion?
>
> **Client:** I was alone at home a few months ago; I was frightened! I was trying to get in touch with my boyfriend and I couldn't. . . . He was nowhere to be found. All my friends seemed to be busy that night and I had no one to talk to. . . . I just got more and more nervous and more and more agitated. Finally, bang!—I took out a cigarette and lit it and stuck it into my forearm. I don't know why I did it because I didn't really care for him all that much. I guess I felt I had to do something dramatic. . . .
>
> The borderline syndromes: Constitution, personality, and adaptation. (007061685X) P. 400. 1980. The McGraw-Hill Education. Used with permission.

Self-mutilation is sometimes carried out as an expression of anger or a means of manipulating others. Such acts may be intended to counteract self-reported feelings of "numbness," particularly in times of stress. Not surprisingly, frequent self-mutilation among people with BPD is associated with an increased risk of suicidal thinking (Dulit, Fyer, Leon, Brodsky, & Frances, 1994).

Individuals with BPD tend to have very troubled relationships with their families of origin and others. Commonly, BPD patients remember traumatic childhood experiences, ranging from their parents being neglectful or abusive to parental losses or separations (Karamanolaki et al., 2016; Laporte, Paris, Guttman, Russell, & Correa, 2012). Additionally, there is an association between documented childhood sexual abuse and the later development of BPD (Hernandez, Arntz, Gaviria, Labad, & Gutiérrez-Zotes, 2012). Kuo and colleagues from Ryerson University report that emotional abuse, not physical or sexual abuse, is at the root of this disorder. Since other types of childhood abuse often include emotional abuse, they controlled for other types of abuse in their study. They claim that emotional abuse prevents children from developing emotional regulation (awareness, acceptance, and

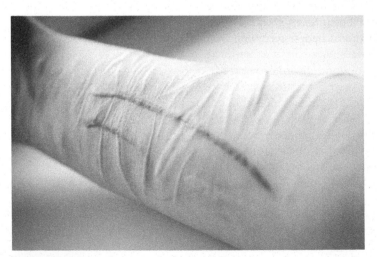

Olga Sapegina/Shutterstock

Cutting. People with borderline personality disorder may engage in impulsive acts of self-mutilation, such as cutting themselves, perhaps as a means of temporarily blocking or escaping from deep, emotional pain.

control of emotions), which in turn can lead to borderline personality disorder (Kuo, Khoury, Metcalfe, Fitzpatrick, & Goodwill, 2015). Other studies have also demonstrated a link between childhood abuse, difficulties in emotional regulation, and borderline personality disorder (Gratz, Tull, Baruch, Bornovalova, & Lejuez, 2008; Hughes, Crowell, Uyeji, & Coan, 2012). Similarly, researchers from the University of British Columbia reported an association between a lack of emotional support and features of borderline personality disorder (Kealy, Sierra-Hernandez, & Ogrodniczuk, 2016).

From the modern psychodynamic perspective, borderline individuals cannot synthesize positive and negative elements of personality into complete wholes. They therefore fail to achieve fixed self-identities or images of others. Rather than viewing important figures in their lives as sometimes loving, sometimes rejecting, they shift back and forth between viewing them as all good or all bad, between idealization and abhorrence. These abrupt shifts in feelings are interpreted by psychoanalysts as signs of "**splitting**," or an inability to reconcile the positive and negative aspects of one's experiences of oneself and others.

As a result, individuals with BPD tend to be difficult to work with in psychotherapy, demanding a great deal of support from therapists and calling them at all hours or acting suicidal to elicit support. Their behaviour toward therapists, as toward other people, undergoes rapid alterations between adulation and outrage, often leading them to end therapy prematurely (Paris, 2015). According to a leading BPD researcher, psychiatrist Joel Paris of McGill University, not all individuals with BPD will follow a chronic course, and most will benefit from treatments specifically designed for BPD, which include support, problem solving, and emotional regulation (Paris, 2015). Follow-up studies on the long-term outcomes of patients with BPD at 15- and 27-year time periods demonstrated that in the long term, a slight majority of BPD patients no longer met the full criteria for the disorder. Moreover, most BPD patients showed improvement leading up to and beyond the ages of 40 and 50 (Gunderson et al., 2011; Paris, 2015).

HISTRIONIC PERSONALITY DISORDER Histrionic personality disorder involves excessive emotionality and the necessity to be the centre of attention. The term is derived from the Latin *histrio*, which means "actor." People with histrionic personality disorder tend to be dramatic and emotional, but their emotions seem shallow, exaggerated, and volatile. The disorder was formerly called *hysterical personality*. The supplanting of hysterical with histrionic and the associated exchange of the roots *hystera* (meaning "uterus") and *histrio* allow professionals to distance themselves from the notion that the disorder is intricately bound up with being female. The disorder is diagnosed more frequently in women than men, however. Some studies, using structured interview methods, find similar rates of occurrence among men and women (APA, 2013). Whether the gender discrepancy in clinical practice reflects true differences in the underlying rates of the disorder, diagnostic biases, or other unseen factors remains something of an open question.

People with histrionic personalities may become unusually upset by news of a sad event and cancel plans for the evening, inconveniencing their friends. They may exude exaggerated delight when they meet someone or become enraged when someone fails to notice their new hairstyle. They may faint at the sight of blood or blush at a slight faux pas. They tend to demand that others meet their needs for attention and play the victim when others fall short. If they feel a touch of fever, they may insist that others drop everything to rush them to a doctor. They tend to be self-centred and intolerant of delays of gratification—they want what they want when they want it. They grow restless quickly with routine and crave novelty and stimulation. They are drawn to fads. Others may see them as putting on airs or play acting, although they may show a certain charm. They may enter a room with a flourish and embellish their experiences with flair. When pressed for details, however, they fail to colour in the specifics of their tales. They tend to be flirtatious and seductive but are too wrapped up in themselves to develop intimate relationships or have deep feelings toward others. As a result, their associations tend to be stormy and ultimately ungratifying. They tend to use their physical appearance as a means of drawing attention to themselves. Men with the disorder may act and dress in an overly "macho" manner to draw attention to themselves; women may choose very frilly, feminine clothing. Glitter supersedes substance.

splitting Term describing the inability of some people (especially people with borderline personalities) to reconcile the positive and negative aspects of themselves and others into a cohesive integration, resulting in sudden and radical shifts between strongly positive and strongly negative feelings.

histrionic personality disorder Type of personality disorder characterized by excessive need to be the centre of attention and to receive reassurance, praise, and approval from others. Such individuals often appear overly dramatic and emotional in their behaviour.

People with histrionic personalities may be attracted to professions like modelling or acting, where they can hog the spotlight. Despite outward successes, they may lack self-esteem and strive to impress others to boost their self-worth. If they suffer setbacks or lose their place in the limelight, depressing inner doubts may emerge. The case of Marcella shows some of these features:

Marcella was a 36-year-old attractive but overly made-up woman who was dressed in tight pants and high heels. Her hair was in a style that had been popular when she was a teenager. Her social life seemed to bounce from relationship to relationship, from crisis to crisis. Marcella sought help from a psychologist at this time because her 17-year-old daughter, Natasha, had just been hospitalized for cutting her wrists. Natasha lived with Marcella and her mother's current boyfriend, Morris, and there were constant arguments in the apartment. Marcella recounted the disputes that took place with high drama, waving her hands, clanging the bangles that hung from her wrists, and clutching her breast. It was difficult having Natasha live at home, because Natasha had expensive tastes, was "always looking for attention," and flirted with Morris as a way of "flaunting her youth." Marcella saw herself as a doting mother and denied any possibility that she was in competition with her daughter.

Marcella came for a handful of sessions, during which she basically vented her feelings and was encouraged to make decisions that might lead to a reduction of some of the pressures on her and her daughter. At the end of each session, she said, "I feel so much better," and thanked the psychologist profusely. At termination of "therapy," she took the psychologist's hand and squeezed it endearingly. "Thank you so much, doctor," she said, and made her exit.

The Authors' Files

narcissistic personality disorder Type of personality disorder characterized by grandiosity, need for admiration, and lack of empathy.

G. Nimatallah/DEA/De Agostini/Getty Images

Narkissos. According to one version of the Greek myth, Narkissos fell in love with his reflection in a spring. Because of his excessive self-love, the gods transformed him into a flower—the narcissus.

Marcella also showed a number of features of narcissism, which we discuss next.

NARCISSISTIC PERSONALITY DISORDER Narkissos was a handsome youth who, according to Greek myth, fell in love with his reflection in a spring. Because of his excessive self-love, in one version of the myth, he was transformed by the gods into the flower we know as the narcissus.

People with **narcissistic personality disorder** have an inflated or grandiose sense of themselves and an extreme need for admiration. They brag about their accomplishments and expect others to shower them with praise and notice their special qualities, even when their accomplishments are ordinary. Narcissists enjoy basking in the light of adulation; they are self-absorbed and tend to lack empathy for others. Although they share certain features with histrionic personalities, such as demanding to be the centre of attention, they have a much more inflated view of themselves and are less melodramatic than people with histrionic personality disorder. The label of borderline personality disorder is sometimes applied to them, but people with narcissistic personality disorder are generally better able to organize their thoughts and actions. They tend to be more successful in their careers and better able to rise to positions of status and power. Their relationships tend to be more stable than those of people with BPD.

The occurrence of narcissistic personality disorder ranges from 0% to 6.2% in community samples (APA, 2013). Although more than half of the people diagnosed with the disorder are men, we cannot say whether there is an underlying gender difference in the prevalence rates of the general population. A certain degree of narcissism or

TABLE 6.2

Healthy Narcissism and Destructive Narcissism

Healthy Narcissism	Destructive Narcissism
Has healthy confidence and self-esteem but does not value him- or herself more than others	Tends to exaggerate achievements or talents; believes he or she is special
Is assertive yet takes into consideration others' perspectives	Expects constant praise and admiration from others
Shares in the emotional lives of others	Has great difficulty receiving any sort of criticism; has fragile self-esteem
May enjoy positions of power but does not think he or she is better than others	Believes he or she is better than others; relationships are self-serving
After failure, feels dissatisfied but not worthless	Experiences of failure are felt as extremely degrading
Being criticized prompts self-evaluation but does not shake emotional stability	Criticism produces excessive aggravation and self-focus

self-aggrandizement may represent a healthful adjustment to insecurity, a shield from criticism and failure, or a motive for achievement (Goleman, 1988). Excessive narcissistic qualities can become unhealthy, especially when cravings for adulation are insatiable. Table 6.2 compares "normal" self-interest with self-defeating extremes of narcissism. Up to a point, self-interest fosters success and happiness. In more extreme cases, as with narcissism, it can compromise relationships and careers.

People with narcissistic personalities tend to be preoccupied with fantasies of success and power, ideal love, or recognition for brilliance or beauty. They, like people with histrionic personalities, may gravitate toward careers in which they can receive adulation, such as modelling, acting, or politics. Although they tend to exaggerate their accomplishments and abilities, many people with narcissistic personalities are quite successful in their occupations but envy those who achieve even greater success. Insatiable ambition may prompt them to devote themselves tirelessly to work. They are driven to succeed, not so much for money as for the adulation that attends success.

Their interpersonal relationships are invariably strained by the demands they impose on others and by their lack of empathy with and concern for other people. They seek the company of flatterers and are often superficially charming and friendly and able to draw people to them. But their interest in people is one-sided: They seek people who will serve their interests and nourish their sense of self-importance (APA, 2013). They have a sense of entitlement that leads them to exploit others. They treat sex partners as devices for their own pleasure or to brace their self-esteem.

The case of Devon illustrates several features of the narcissistic personality:

Most people agreed that Devon, a 35-year-old investment banker, had a certain charm. He was bright, articulate, and attractive. He possessed a keen sense of humour that drew people to him at social gatherings. He would always position himself in the middle of the room, where he could be the centre of attention. The topics of conversation invariably focused on his "deals," the "rich and famous" people he had met, and his outmanoeuvring of opponents. His next project was always bigger and more daring than the last. Devon loved an audience. His face would light up when others responded to him with praise or admiration for his business successes, which were always inflated beyond their true measure. But when the conversation shifted to other people, he would lose interest and excuse himself to make a drink or to call his answering machine. When hosting a party, he would urge guests to stay late and feel hurt if they had to leave early; he showed no sensitivity to or awareness of the needs of his friends.

The few friends he had maintained over the years had come to accept Devon on his own terms. They recognized that he needed to have his ego fed or that he would become cool and detached.

Devon had also had a series of romantic relationships with women who were willing to play the adoring admirer and make the sacrifices that he demanded—for a time. But they inevitably tired of the one-sided relationship or grew frustrated by Devon's inability to make a commitment or feel deeply toward them. Lacking empathy, Devon was unable to recognize other people's feelings and needs. His demands for constant attention from willing admirers derived not from selfishness but from a need to ward off underlying feelings of inadequacy and diminished self-esteem. It was sad, his friends thought, that Devon needed so much attention and adulation from others and that his many achievements were never enough to calm his inner doubts.

The Authors' Files

Personality Disorders Characterized by Anxious or Fearful Behaviour

This cluster of personality disorders includes the avoidant, dependent, and obsessive-compulsive types. Although the features of these disorders differ, they share a component of fear or anxiety.

avoidant personality disorder
Type of personality disorder characterized by avoidance of social relationships due to fears of rejection.

AVOIDANT PERSONALITY DISORDER People with **avoidant personality disorder** are so terrified of rejection and criticism that they are generally unwilling to enter relationships without ardent reassurances of acceptance. As a result, they may have few close relationships outside their immediate families. They also tend to avoid group occupational or recreational activities for fear of rejection. They prefer to eat lunch alone at their desks. They shun company picnics and parties, unless they are perfectly sure of acceptance. Avoidant personality disorder, which appears to be equally common in men and women, is believed to affect 2.4% of the general population (APA, 2013).

Unlike people with schizoid qualities, with whom they share the feature of social withdrawal, individuals with avoidant personalities have interest in and feelings of warmth toward other people. However, fear of rejection prevents them from striving to meet their needs for affection and acceptance. In social situations, they tend to hug the walls and avoid conversing with others. They fear public embarrassment—the thought that others might see them blush, cry, or act nervously. They tend to stick to their routines and exaggerate the risks or effort involved in trying new things. They may refuse to attend a party that is an hour away on the pretext that the late drive home would be too taxing.

The case of Jamie illustrates several of the features of the avoidant personality:

Jamie, a 24-year-old accounting clerk, had dated only a few women, and he had met them through family introductions. He never felt confident enough to approach a woman on his own. Perhaps it was his shyness that first attracted Loren. A 22-year-old secretary, she worked alongside Jamie and asked him if he would like to get together some time after work. At first Jamie declined, claiming some excuse, but when Loren asked again a week later, Jamie agreed, thinking she must really like him if she were willing to pursue him. The relationship developed quickly, and soon they were dating virtually every night. The relationship was strained, however. Jamie interpreted any slight hesitation in her voice as a lack of interest. He repeatedly requested reassurance that she cared about him and evaluated every word and gesture for evidence of her feelings. If Loren said she could not see him because of fatigue or illness, Jamie assumed she was rejecting him and sought reassurance. After several months, Loren decided she could no longer accept Jamie's nagging, and the relationship ended. Jamie assumed that Loren had never truly cared for him.

The Authors' Files

There is a good deal of overlap between avoidant personality disorder and social anxiety disorder (Friborg, Martinussen, Kaiser, Øvergårda, & Rosenvinge, 2013). It may well turn out that avoidant personality disorder is a more severe form of social anxiety disorder and not a distinct diagnosis. Some research has lent support to this hypothesis (Carmichael, Sellbom, Liggett, & Smith, 2016; Chambless, Fydrich, & Rodebaugh, 2008).

DEPENDENT PERSONALITY DISORDER Dependent personality disorder describes people who have an excessive need to be taken care of by others. This leads them to be overly submissive and clinging in their relationships and extremely fearful of separation. People with this disorder find it difficult to do things on their own. They seek advice in making even the smallest decision. Children or adolescents with the problem may look to their parents to select their clothes, diets, schools or universities, even their friends. Adults with the disorder allow others to make important decisions for them. Sometimes, they are so dependent on others for making decisions that they allow their parents to determine whom they will or will not marry.

After marriage, people with dependent personality disorder may rely on their spouses to make decisions such as where they should live, which neighbours they should befriend, how they should discipline their children, what jobs they should take, how they should budget money, and where they should vacation. Individuals with dependent personality disorder avoid positions of responsibility. They turn down challenges and promotions and work beneath their potential. They tend to be overly sensitive to criticism and are preoccupied with fears of rejection and abandonment. They may be devastated by the end of a close relationship or by the prospect of living on their own. Because of a fear of rejection, they often subordinate their wants and needs to those of others. They may agree with outlandish statements about themselves and do degrading things to please others.

Dependence needs to be examined through the lens of culture. Arranged marriages are the norm in some traditional cultures, so people from those cultures who let their parents decide whom they will marry would not be classified as having dependent personality disorder. Similarly, in strongly patriarchal cultures, women may be expected to defer to their fathers and husbands in making many life decisions, even small everyday decisions.

We needn't look beyond our own society to consider the role of culture. Evidence shows that dependent personality disorder is diagnosed more frequently in women (APA, 2013). The diagnosis is often applied to women who, for fear of abandonment, tolerate husbands who openly cheat on them, abuse them, or gamble away family resources. Underlying feelings of inadequacy and helplessness discourage them from taking effective action. In a vicious circle, their passivity encourages further abuse, leading them to feel yet more inadequate and helpless. The diagnosis of women with this disorder is controversial and may be seen as unfairly "blaming the victim" because some women in our society are socialized into more dependent roles. Women typically encounter greater stress than men in contemporary life as well as greater social pressures to be passive, demure, or deferential. Therefore, dependent behaviours in women may reflect cultural influences rather than an underlying personality disorder.

Dependent personality disorder has been linked to other psychological disorders, including major depression, bipolar disorder, and social anxiety disorder, and to physical problems such as hypertension, cancer, and gastrointestinal disorders such as ulcers and colitis (Bornstein, 1999; Samuels, 2011). There also appears to be a link between dependent personality and what psychodynamic theorists refer to as "oral" behaviour

dependent personality disorder Type of personality disorder characterized by difficulties making independent decisions and by overly dependent behaviour.

Adam Gault/Photodisc/Getty Images

"A place for everything, and everything in its place"? People with obsessive-compulsive personalities may have invented this maxim. Many such people have excessive needs for orderliness in their environment.

obsessive-compulsive personality disorder Type of personality disorder characterized by rigid ways of relating to others, perfectionistic tendencies, lack of spontaneity, and excessive attention to details.

problems, such as smoking, eating disorders, and alcoholism (Bornstein, 1999; Fernández del Río, López-Durán, Martínez, & Becoña, 2016). Psychodynamic theorists trace dependent behaviour to the utter dependence of a newborn baby and the baby's seeking of nourishment through oral means (suckling). From infancy, they suggest, people associate provision of food with love. Food may come to symbolize love, and people with dependent personalities may overeat to symbolically ingest love. People with dependent personalities often attribute their problems to physical rather than emotional causes and seek support and advice from medical experts rather than psychologists or counsellors (Greenberg & Bornstein, 1988).

OBSESSIVE-COMPULSIVE PERSONALITY DISORDER

The defining features of **obsessive-compulsive personality disorder** involve an excessive degree of orderliness, perfectionism, rigidity, difficulty coping with ambiguity, difficulties expressing feelings, and meticulousness in work habits. Between 2.1% and 7.9% of people in community samples are diagnosed with the disorder (APA, 2013). The disorder is about twice as common in men as in women. Unlike obsessive-compulsive anxiety disorder, people with obsessive-compulsive personality disorder do not necessarily experience outright obsessions or compulsions. If they do, both diagnoses may be deemed appropriate.

People with obsessive-compulsive personality disorder are so preoccupied with perfection they cannot complete things in a timely fashion. Their efforts inevitably fall short of their expectations and they force themselves to redo their work. Or they may ruminate about how to prioritize their assignments and never seem to get started working. They focus on details that others perceive as trivial. As the saying goes, they often fail to see the forest for the trees. Their rigidity impairs their social relationships; they insist on doing things their way rather than compromising. Their zeal for work keeps them from participating in or enjoying social and leisure activities. They tend to be stingy with money. They find it difficult to make decisions and postpone or avoid them for fear of making the wrong choice. They tend to be overly rigid in issues of morality and ethics because of inflexibility in personality rather than deeply held convictions. They tend to be overly formal in relationships and find it difficult to express feelings. It is hard for them to relax and enjoy pleasant activities; they worry about the costs of such diversions.

Consider the case of Andrew:

Andrew, a 34-year-old systems analyst, was perfectionistic, overly concerned with details, and rigid in his behaviour. Andrew was married to Teja, a graphic artist. He insisted on scheduling their free time hour by hour and became unnerved when they deviated from his agenda. He would circle a parking lot repeatedly in search of just the right parking spot to ensure that another car would not scrape his car. He refused to have the apartment painted for over a year because he couldn't decide on the colour. He had arranged all the books on their bookshelf alphabetically and insisted that every book be placed in its proper position.

Andrew never seemed to be able to relax. Even on vacation, he was bothered by thoughts of work that he had left behind and by fears that he might lose his job. He couldn't understand how people could lie on a beach and let all their worries evaporate in the summer air. Something can always go wrong, he figured, so how can people let themselves go?

The Authors' Files

Normal Perfectionism: No Disorder	OCPD: Disorder
Carley had always been a high achiever. She got straight A's in high school, played on several sports teams, and was student council president. Her parents told her stories of how she had been a high achiever even as a small child. For example, if she went out of the lines while colouring, she would start the picture over. She always spent a lot of time on her school work, making sure she had completed it properly and had done her best. Her quality of work was rewarded—teachers were always thrilled to have Carley in their classes and regularly praised her neat and thorough work. At university, Carley continued to have high expectations for herself. She often prioritized her school work and readings over socializing, making sure that her assignments were done before she went out. At the beginning of university, Carley would often rewrite lecture notes to make them neater, but soon realized that she did not have enough time to do this for all lectures. Instead, she decided to bring her laptop to lectures so that her notes would be neatly typed. Her room in residence was the neatest room on the floor, and her friends in residence often teased her about how everything in her room was "perfect." Carley was able to laugh at herself and identified with being a "perfectionist."	Danish is a 50-year-old divorced man who lives in a small house by himself. He works as an accountant. He and his former wife divorced 15 years ago after having years of relationship stress. The couple would constantly fight about their different styles—Julia being laid back and relaxed, Danish being uptight and perfectionistic. At first, Julia would tease Danish about his stubbornness and need for things to be done "his way." However, this gentle teasing soon gave way to real frustration and resentment. Danish would often start projects around the house but was unable to finish them after getting stuck on a detail. For example, it took Danish two months to install a closet organization system because he wanted to ensure that all the screws were even and installed "properly." "Properly" to Danish meant that things were done his way. A huge source of frustration between the two was Danish's judgmental style. He had a strict moral code, and often made snide judgmental remarks about things Julia had said or done. Since the couple divorced, Danish continued to have difficulty in relationships, and so had stopped dating. He had few friends, as many of his old friends found him to be inflexible and judgmental toward them.

Problems With the Classification of Personality Disorders

Questions remain about the reliability and validity of the diagnostic categories for personality disorders. There may be too much overlap among the diagnoses to justify so many different categories. Agreement between raters on personality disorder diagnoses remains modest at best (Clark, 2007; Coolidge & Segal, 1998). The classification system also seems to blur the distinctions between normal and abnormal variations in personality. Moreover, some categories of personality disorder may be based on sexist presumptions.

OVERLAP AMONG DISORDERS   Psychologists Brian O'Connor of Lakehead University and Jamie Dyce of Concordia University of Edmonton contend that not only are the diagnostic criteria for any given category of personality disorder broader than they are for other psychological disorders, but there is also a high degree of overlap among the personality disorders. Moreover, a person does not have to satisfy all the diagnostic criteria to be diagnosed with a personality disorder (O'Connor & Dyce, 2001). Overlap undermines the DSM's conceptual clarity or purity by increasing the number of cases that seem to fit two or more diagnostic categories (Skodol, 2012). Although some personality disorders have distinct features, many appear to share common traits. For example, the same person may have traits suggestive of dependent personality disorder (inability to make decisions or initiate activities independently) and of avoidant personality disorder (extreme social anxiety and heightened sensitivity to criticism). One study found that among individuals with a personality disorder, as many as 60% met the criteria for another personality disorder and 25% could be diagnosed with two or more (Zimmerman et al., 2005). Another study reported that in a sample of people with borderline personality disorder, nearly one in four (23%) also met the criteria for APD (Hudziak et al., 1996). The high degree of overlap suggests that the personality disorders included in the DSM system may not be sufficiently distinct from one another (Clark, 2007; Westen & Shedler, 1999). Some so-called disorders may thus represent different aspects of the same disorder, not separate diagnostic categories. To address the problem of overlap of diagnoses, the DSM-5 proposed a research model for personality disorder diagnosis and conceptualization. This model emphasizes functional impairments in personality *and* traits with underlying pathology. Six personality disorders are derived from the model and include antisocial, avoidant, borderline, narcissistic, obsessive-compulsive, and schizotypal personality disorders (APA, 2013). Since the model includes both traits and disorders, it would allow a clinician to take into account the antisocial traits of a person without diagnosing APD (See "A Closer Look: Personality Disorders—Categories or Dimensions?").

DIFFICULTY IN DISTINGUISHING BETWEEN VARIATIONS IN NORMAL BEHAVIOUR AND ABNORMAL BEHAVIOUR   Another problem with the diagnosis of personality disorders is that they involve traits that, in lesser degrees, describe the behaviour of most normal individuals. Feeling suspicious now and then does not mean you have a paranoid personality disorder. The tendency to exaggerate your own importance does not mean you are narcissistic. You may avoid social interactions for fear of embarrassment or rejection without having an avoidant personality disorder, and you may be especially conscientious in your work without having an obsessive-compulsive personality disorder. Because the defining attributes of these disorders are commonly occurring personality traits, clinicians should apply these diagnostic labels only when the patterns are so pervasive that they interfere with the individual's functioning or cause significant personal distress. Yet it can be difficult to know where to draw the line between normal variations in behaviour and personality disorders. We continue to lack the data to more precisely determine the point at which a trait becomes sufficiently inflexible or maladaptive to justify a personality disorder diagnosis (Livesley, 2001).

SEXIST BIASES   The construction of certain personality disorders may have sexist underpinnings. For example, diagnostic criteria for personality disorders label stereotypical feminine behaviour as pathological with greater frequency than is the case with stereotypical masculine behaviour. The concept of the histrionic personality seems a caricature of the traditional stereotype of the feminine personality: flighty, emotional, shallow, seductive, attention seeking. But if the feminine stereotype corresponds to a mental disorder, shouldn't we also have a diagnostic category that reflects the masculine stereotype of the "macho male"? It may be possible to show that overly masculinized traits are associated with significant distress or impairment in social or occupational functioning in certain males. Highly masculinized males often get into fights and experience difficulties working for female bosses. There is no personality disorder that corresponds to the macho male stereotype, however.

The diagnosis of dependent personality disorder may also unfairly stigmatize women who are socialized into dependent roles as having a "mental disorder." Women may be at a greater risk of receiving diagnoses of histrionic or dependent personality disorders because clinicians perceive these patterns as existing more commonly among women or because women are more likely than men to be socialized into these behaviour patterns. Clinicians may also be biased in favour of perceiving women as having histrionic personality disorder and men as having antisocial personality disorder even when the men and women in question do not differ in symptomatology (Garb, 1997).

Clinicians may also have a gender bias when it comes to diagnosing borderline personality disorder (Boggs et al., 2005). In one study, researchers presented a hypothetical case example to a sample of 311 psychologists, social workers, and psychiatrists (Becker & Lamb, 1994). Half of the sample was presented with a case identified as a female; the other half read the identical case except that it was identified as male. Clinicians more often diagnosed the case identified as female as having borderline personality disorder. Studies using similar methodologies have also found a gender bias in diagnosing histrionic personality disorder (Flanagan & Blashfield, 2005; Samuel & Widiger, 2009).

All in all, personality disorders are convenient labels for identifying common patterns of ineffective and ultimately self-defeating behaviour, but labels do not explain their causes. Still, the development of an accurate descriptive system is an important step toward scientific explanation. The establishment of reliable diagnostic categories sets the stage for valid research into causation and treatment.

Personality Disorders—Categories or Dimensions?

Are personality disorders best understood as distinct categories of psychological disorders marked by particular symptoms or behavioural features? Or should we think of them as extreme variations of common personality dimensions found in the general population? The DSM adopts a categorical model for classifying abnormal behaviour patterns into specific diagnostic categories based on particular diagnostic criteria.

Let's use antisocial personality disorder as an example. To warrant a diagnosis of antisocial personality disorder, a person must show a range of clinical features, as seen in Table 6.1. Three or more of the listed symptoms need to be present. Why *three*? Basically, this determination represents a consensus of the authors of the DSM. A person may exhibit two of these features in abundance but still not be diagnosed with antisocial personality disorder, whereas someone showing three of the features in a milder form would merit a diagnosis. The problem of where to draw the line when applying diagnostic categories ripples throughout the DSM system, raising concerns of many critics that the system relies too heavily on an arbitrary set of cut-offs or diagnostic criteria.

Another concern with the categorical model is that many of the features associated with personality disorders and with many other diagnostic categories (e.g., depressive disorders, anxiety disorders) are found to some degree in the general population. Thus, it may be difficult to distinguish between normal variations of these features (or traits) and abnormal variations (Skodol, 2012). People with antisocial personality disorder, for example, may fail to plan ahead, show impulsive behaviour, or lie for personal gain. But so do many people without antisocial personality disorder. The dimensional model of personality disorders offers an alternative to the traditional categorical model of the DSM (e.g., Widiger, Livesley, & Clark, 2009).

The dimensional model depicts personality disorders as maladaptive and extreme variations along a continuum of personality traits found within the general population. Widiger and his colleagues propose that personality disorders can be represented as extreme variations of the following five basic traits of personality that make up the five-factor model of personality (the so-called "Big Five"): (1) *neuroticism* or emotional instability, (2) *extraversion*, (3) *openness to experience*, (4) *agreeableness* or friendliness, and (5) *conscientiousness* (Widiger & Costa, 2012; Widiger & Mullins-Sweat, 2005). In the dimensional model, a disorder like antisocial personality disorder might be characterized in part by extremely low levels of conscientiousness and agreeableness (Widiger & Lowe, 2008). People with this combination of traits are often described as aimless and unreliable, as well as manipulative and exploitive of others. In a similar way, other personality disorders can

be mapped onto extreme ends of the Big Five dimensions. A growing body of evidence shows links between the dimensions underlying personality disorders and the Big Five personality traits (e.g., Miller, Morse, Nolf, Stepp, & Pilkonis, 2012; Tackett, Silberschmidt, Krueger, & Sponheim, 2008).

An advantage of the dimensional component in assessment and diagnosis is that it allows the examiner to make a judgment of the severity of the problem based on the degree of extremity of pathological traits, as opposed to merely a yes/no or dichotomous judgment of whether a particular disorder is present or not. One limitation of the dimensional model is that we lack clear guidelines for setting cut-off scores on personality scales to determine just how extreme a trait needs to be for it to be deemed clinically meaningful (Skodol, 2012).

The DSM-5 does offer an alternate model for diagnosing personality disorders, based on impairments in personality functioning (self and interpersonal) and pathological personality traits (APA, 2013). Elements of personality functioning, which encompass self identity, self-direction, empathy, and intimacy, are each evaluated on a continuum from little or no impairment to extreme impairment. A diagnosis of a personality disorder requires that the individual be exhibiting a moderate or greater level of impairment in two or more areas of personality functioning and possess a certain number of pathological traits. Twenty-five pathological traits, falling within five categories (negative affectivity, detachment, antagonism, disinhibition, and psychotism) are identified. A specific number of designated traits are required for each personality disorder. For example, a diagnosis of antisocial personality disorder requires at least six of the following traits: manipulativeness, callousness, deceitfulness, hostility, risk taking, impulsivity, and irresponsibility. The pathological traits associated with borderline personality disorder include emotional lability, anxiousness, separation insecurity, depressivity, impulsivity, risk taking, and hostility. Four are required, one of which must be impulsivity, risk taking, or hostility (APA, 2013).

Although this alternate model for diagnosing personality disorders incorporates some elements of the dimensional approach, some believe that it does not go far enough in representing dysfunctional personality in a dimensional framework and that it is too complicated for practical use (Shedler et al., 2010). One study, however, found that clinicians favoured this alternate model over the categorical approach adopted in DSM-5 (Morey, Skodol, & Oldham, 2014). We hope that as the debate continues to unfold about whether the DSM should be categorical, dimensional, or a kind of hybrid of the two models, it will be informed by evidence pertaining to the utility and validity of different models of classification.

Types of Personality Disorders

- **What are personality disorders?** Personality disorders are maladaptive or rigid behaviour patterns or personality traits associated with states of personal distress that impair a person's ability to function in social or occupational roles. People with personality disorders do not generally recognize a need to change themselves.

- **What are the classes of personality disorders within the DSM system?** The DSM categorizes personality disorders according to the following clusters of characteristics: odd or eccentric behaviour; dramatic, emotional, or erratic behaviour; anxious or fearful behaviour.

- **What are the features associated with personality disorders characterized by odd or eccentric behaviour?** People with paranoid personality disorder are unduly suspicious and mistrustful of others, to the point that their relationships suffer. But they do not hold the more flagrant paranoid delusions typical of schizophrenia. Schizoid personality disorder describes people who have little if any interest in social relationships, show a restricted range of emotional expression, and appear distant and aloof. People with schizotypal personalities appear odd or eccentric in their thoughts, mannerisms, and behaviour, but not to the degree found in schizophrenia.

- **What are the features associated with personality disorders characterized by dramatic, emotional, or erratic behaviour?** Antisocial personality disorder describes people who persistently engage in behaviour that violates social norms and the rights of others and who tend to show no remorse for their misdeeds. Borderline personality disorder is defined in terms of instability in self-image, relationships, and mood. People with borderline personality disorder often engage in impulsive acts, which are frequently self-destructive. People with histrionic personality disorder tend to be highly dramatic and emotional in their behaviour, whereas people diagnosed with narcissistic personality disorder have an inflated or grandiose sense of self and, like those with histrionic personalities, demand to be the centre of attention.

- **What are the features associated with personality disorders characterized by anxious or fearful behaviour?** Avoidant personality disorder describes people who are so terrified of rejection and criticism that they are generally unwilling to enter relationships without unusually strong reassurances of acceptance. People with dependent personality disorder are overly dependent on others and have extreme difficulty acting independently or making even the smallest decisions on their own. People with obsessive-compulsive personality disorder have various traits such as orderliness, perfectionism, rigidity, and excessive attention to detail but are without the true obsessions and compulsions associated with obsessive-compulsive disorder.

- **What are some problems associated with the classification of personality disorders?** Various controversies and problems attend the classification of personality disorders, including a lack of demonstrated reliability and validity, too much overlap among the categories, difficulty in distinguishing between variations in normal behaviour and abnormal behaviour, and underlying sexist biases in certain categories.

THEORETICAL PERSPECTIVES

In this section we consider the theoretical perspectives on personality disorders. Many of the theoretical accounts of disturbed personality derive from the psychodynamic model. We thus begin with a review of traditional and modern psychodynamic models.

Psychodynamic Perspectives

Traditional Freudian theory focused on problems arising from the Oedipus complex as the foundation for many abnormal behaviours, including personality disorders. Freud (1905/1962) believed that children normally resolve the Oedipus complex by forsaking incestuous wishes for the parent of the opposite gender and identifying with the parent of the same gender. As a result, they incorporate the parent's moral principles in the form of a personality structure called the *superego*. Many factors may interfere with appropriate identification, however, such as having a weak or absent father or an antisocial parent. These factors may sidetrack the normal developmental process, preventing children from developing the moral constraints that prevent antisocial behaviour and the feelings of guilt or remorse that normally follow behaviour that is hurtful to others.

More recent psychodynamic theories have generally focused on the earlier, pre-Oedipal period of about 18 months to 3 years of age, during which infants are theorized to begin to develop their identities as separate from those of their parents. These recent advances in psychodynamic theory focus on the development of the sense of self in explaining such disorders as narcissistic and borderline personality disorders.

HEINZ KOHUT One of the principal shapers of modern psychodynamic concepts was Heinz Kohut (1913–1981), whose views are labelled **self psychology**. Kohut focused much of his attention on the development of the narcissistic personality.

Kohut (1966) believed that people with narcissistic personalities may mount a facade of self-importance to cover up deep feelings of inadequacy. Kohut maintained that early childhood is characterized by a normal stage of "healthful narcissism." Infants feel powerful, as though the world revolves around them. Infants also normally perceive older people, especially parents, as idealized towers of strength and wish to be one with them to share their power. Empathic parents reflect their children's inflated perceptions by making them feel that anything is possible and by nourishing their self-esteem (e.g., telling them how terrific and precious they are). Even empathic parents are critical from time to time, however, and puncture their children's grandiose sense of self. Or they fail to measure up to their children's idealized views of them. Gradually, unrealistic expectations dissolve and are replaced by more realistic appraisals. This process of childhood narcissism that eventually gives way to more realistic appraisals of self and others is perfectly normal. Earlier grandiose self-images form the basis for assertiveness later in childhood and set the stage for ambitious striving in adulthood. In adolescence, childhood idealization is transformed into realistic admiration for parents, teachers, and friends. In adulthood, these ideas develop into a set of internal ideals, values, and goals.

Lack of parental empathy and support, however, sets the stage for pathological narcissism in adulthood. Children who are not prized by their parents may fail to develop a sturdy sense of self-esteem. They may be unable to tolerate even slight blows to their self-worth. They develop damaged self-concepts and feel incapable of being loved and admired because of perceived inadequacies or flaws. Pathological narcissism involves the construction of a grandiose facade of self-perfection that is merely a shell to cloak perceived inadequacies. The facade always remains on the brink of crumbling, however, and must be continually shored up by a constant flow of reassurance that one is special and unique. This leaves the person vulnerable to painful blows to self-esteem following failure to achieve social or occupational goals. Being so needy of constant approval, a person with a narcissistic personality may fly into a rage when he or she feels slighted in any way.

OTTO KERNBERG Modern psychodynamic views of the borderline personality also trace the disorder to difficulties in the development of the self in early childhood. Otto Kernberg (1975), a leading psychodynamic theorist (born 1928), views borderline personality in terms of a pre-Oedipal failure to develop a sense of constancy and unity in one's image of the self and others. Kernberg proposes that childhood failure to synthesize these contradictory images of good and bad results in a failure to develop a consistent self-image and in tendencies toward splitting—shifting back and forth between viewing oneself and other people as "all good" or "all bad."

In Kernberg's view, parents, even excellent parents, invariably fail to meet all their children's needs. Infants therefore face the early developmental challenge of reconciling images of the nurturing, comforting "good mother" with those of the withholding, frustrating "bad mother." Failure to reconcile these opposing images into a realistic, unified, and stable parental image may fixate children in the pre-Oedipal period. As adults, then, they may retain these rapidly shifting attitudes toward their therapists and others.

MARGARET MAHLER Margaret Mahler (1897–1985), another influential modern psychodynamic theorist, explained borderline personality disorder in terms of childhood separation from the mother figure. Mahler and her colleagues (Mahler & Kaplan, 1977) believed that during the first year, an infant develops a **symbiotic** attachment to his or her mother. *Symbiosis* is a biological term derived from the Greek root meaning "to live

self psychology Heinz Kohut's theory that describes processes that normally lead to the achievement of a cohesive sense of self or, in narcissistic personality disorder, to a grandiose but fragile sense of self.

symbiotic (1) In biology, the living together of two different but interdependent organisms. (2) In Margaret Mahler's object-relations theory, the term used to describe the state of oneness that normally exists between a mother and infant in which the infant's identity is fused with the mother's.

together"; it describes life patterns in which two species lead interdependent lives. In psychology, symbiosis is likened to a state of oneness in which a child's identity is fused with his or her mother's. Normally, children gradually differentiate their own identities or senses of self from their mothers. The process is called **separation-individuation**. Separation involves developing a separate psychological and biological identity from the mother. Individuation involves recognizing the personal characteristics that define one's self-identity. Separation-individuation may be a stormy process. Children may vacillate between seeking greater independence and moving closer to, or "shadowing," their mother, which is seen as a wish for reunion. The mother may disrupt normal separation-individuation by refusing to let go of the child or by too quickly pushing the child toward independence. The tendencies of people with borderline personalities to react to others with ambivalence and to alternate between love and hate are suggestive to Mahler of earlier ambivalences during the separation-individuation process. Borderline personality disorder may arise from a failure to master this developmental challenge.

Further on in this chapter, we underscore the links between abuse in childhood and the later development of personality disorders. These linkages suggest that failure to form close-bonding relationships with parental caregivers in childhood plays a critical role in developing many of the maladaptive personality patterns classified as personality disorders.

Learning Perspectives

Learning theorists tend to focus more on the acquisition of behaviour than on the notion of enduring personality traits. Similarly, they think more in terms of maladaptive behaviour than of disorders of "personality" or "personality traits." Trait theorists believe that personality traits steer behaviour, providing a framework for consistent behaviour in diverse situations. Many critics (e.g., Mischel, 1979), however, argue that behaviour is actually less consistent across situations than trait theorists would suggest. Behaviour may depend more on situational demands than on inherent traits. For example, we may describe a person as lazy and unmotivated. But is this person always lazy and unmotivated? Aren't there some situations in which the person may be energetic and ambitious? What differences in these situations may explain differences in behaviour? Learning theorists are generally interested in defining the learning histories and situational factors that give rise to maladaptive behaviour and the reinforcers that maintain them.

Learning theorists suggest that in childhood, many important experiences occur that shape the development of the maladaptive habits of relating to others that constitute personality disorders. For example, children who are regularly discouraged from speaking their minds or exploring their environments may develop a dependent personality behaviour pattern. Obsessive-compulsive personality disorder may be connected with excessive parental discipline or overcontrol in childhood. Theodore Millon (1981) suggests that children whose behaviour, even slight transgressions, is rigidly controlled and punished by parents may develop inflexible, perfectionistic standards. As these children mature, they may strive to develop in an area in which they excel, such as school work or athletics, as a way of avoiding parental criticism or punishment. But excessive attention to a single area of development may prevent them from becoming well rounded. They may thus squelch spontaneity and avoid new challenges or risks. They may also place perfectionistic demands on themselves to avoid any risk of punishment or rebuke and develop other behaviour associated with the obsessive-compulsive personality pattern.

Millon suggests that histrionic personality disorder may be rooted in childhood experiences in which social reinforcers, such as parental attention, are connected to a child's appearance and willingness to perform for others, especially in cases where reinforcers are dispensed inconsistently. Inconsistent attention teaches children not to take approval for granted and to strive for it continually. People with histrionic personalities may also have identified with parents who are dramatic, emotional, and attention seeking. Extreme sibling rivalry would further heighten motivation to perform for attention from others.

separation-individuation In Margaret Mahler's theory, the process by which young children come to separate psychologically from their mothers and to perceive themselves as separate and distinct persons.

Benis Arapovic/Hemera/Thinkstock/Getty Images

What are the origins of antisocial personality disorder? Are youth who develop antisocial personalities largely unsocialized because early learning experiences lack the consistency and predictability that help other children connect their behaviour with rewards and punishments? Or are they very "socialized"—but socialized to imitate the behaviour of other antisocial youth? Are we confusing antisocial behaviour with antisocial personality disorder? To what extent does criminal behaviour or membership in gangs overlap with antisocial personality disorder? Can environmental factors explain how people with antisocial personality disorder maintain their composure (their relatively low levels of arousal) under circumstances that would induce anxiety in most of us?

Behaviour theories emphasize the role of reinforcement in explaining the origins of antisocial behaviour. Ullmann and Krasner (1975) proposed, for example, that people with antisocial personalities may have failed to learn to respond to other people as potential reinforcers. Most children learn to treat others as reinforcing agents because others reinforce them with praise when they behave appropriately and punish them for misbehaviour. Reinforcement and punishment provide feedback (information about social expectations) that helps children modify their behaviour to maximize the chances of future rewards and minimize the risks of future punishment. As a consequence, children become socialized. They become sensitive to the demands of powerful others, usually parents and teachers, and learn to regulate their behaviour accordingly. They thus adapt to social expectations. They learn what to do and what to say, how to dress and how to act to obtain social reinforcement or approval from others.

People with antisocial personalities, by contrast, may not have become socialized because their early learning experiences lacked the consistency and predictability that help other children connect their behaviour with rewards and punishments (Kazdin, 2005). Perhaps they were sometimes rewarded for doing the "right thing," but just as often they were not. They may have borne the brunt of harsh physical punishments that depended more on parental whims than on their own conduct. As adults they may not place much value on what other people expect because there was no clear connection between their own behaviour and reinforcement in childhood. They may have learned as children that there was little they could do to prevent punishment and so perhaps lost the motivation to try. Although Ullmann and Krasner's views may account for some features of antisocial personality disorder, they may not adequately address the development of the "charming" type of antisocial personality, which describes people who are skilful at reading social cues produced by other people and using them for personal advantage.

Family Perspectives

Many theorists have argued that disturbances in family relationships underlie the development of personality disorders. Researchers find that people with borderline personality disorder remember their parents as having been more controlling and less caring than do reference subjects with other psychological disorders (Zweig-Frank & Paris, 1991), which is consistent with psychodynamic formulations. When people with borderline personality disorder recall their earliest memories, they are more likely than other people to paint significant others as malevolent or evil. They portray their parents and others close to them as having been more likely to injure them deliberately or to fail to help them escape injuries by others (Nigg, Lohr, Western, Gold, & Silk, 1992).

A number of researchers have linked a history of physical or sexual abuse or neglect in childhood to the development of personality disorders in adulthood, including borderline personality disorder (e.g., Infurna et al., 2016). Perhaps the "splitting" observed in people with the disorder is a function of having learned to cope with unpredictable and harsh behaviour from parental figures or other caregivers.

Again consistent with psychodynamic theory, family factors such as parental overprotection and authoritarianism have been implicated in the development of dependent personality traits that may hamper the development of independent behaviour (Bornstein, 1992). Extreme fears of abandonment may also be involved, perhaps resulting from a failure to develop secure bonds with parental attachment figures in childhood because of parental neglect, rejection, or death. Subsequently, a chronic fear of being abandoned by other people with whom one has close relationships may develop, leading to the clinginess that typifies dependent personality disorder. Theorists also suggest that obsessive-compulsive personality disorder may emerge within a strongly moralistic and rigid family environment, which does not permit even minor deviations from expected roles or behaviour (e.g., Oldham, 1994).

As in the case of borderline personality disorder, researchers find that childhood abuse or neglect is a risk factor in the development of antisocial personality disorder in adulthood (Lee, Brook, Finch, & Brook, 2016; Luntz & Widom, 1994). In a view that straddles the psychodynamic and learning theories, the McCords (McCord & McCord, 1964) focus on the role of parental rejection or neglect in the development of antisocial personality disorder. They suggest that children normally learn to associate parental approval with conformity to parental practices and values, and disapproval with disobedience. When tempted to transgress, children feel anxious for fear of losing parental love. Anxiety serves as a signal that encourages a child to inhibit antisocial behaviour. Eventually, the child identifies with parents and internalizes these social controls in the form of a conscience. When parents do not show love for their children, this identification does not occur. Children do not fear loss of love because they have never had it. The anxiety that might have served to restrain antisocial and criminal behaviour is absent.

Children who are rejected or neglected by their parents may not develop warm feelings of attachment to others. They may lack the ability to empathize with the feelings and needs of others, developing instead an attitude of indifference. Or perhaps they still retain a wish to develop loving relationships but lack the ability to experience genuine feelings.

Although family factors may be implicated in some cases of antisocial personality disorder, many neglected children do not later show antisocial or other abnormal behaviour. We are left to develop other explanations to predict which deprived children will develop antisocial personalities or other abnormal behaviour and which will not.

Cognitive-Behavioural Perspectives

Social-cognitive theorist Albert Bandura (1973, 1986) has studied the role of observational learning in aggressive behaviour, which is one of the common components of antisocial behaviour. He and his colleagues (e.g., Bandura, Ross, & Ross, 1963) have shown that children acquire skills, including aggressive skills, by observing the behaviour of others. Exposure to aggression may come from watching violent television programs or observing parents who act violently toward one another. Bandura does not believe that children and adults display aggressive behaviour in a mechanical way, however. Rather, people usually do not imitate aggressive behaviour unless they are provoked and believe they are more likely to be rewarded than punished for it. When models get their way with others by acting aggressively, children may be more likely to imitate them. Children may also acquire antisocial behaviour such as cheating, bullying, or lying by direct reinforcement if they find such behaviour helps them avoid blame or manipulate others.

Cognitive-behaviour–oriented psychologists have shown that the ways in which people with personality disorders interpret their social experiences influence their behaviour (Herpertz & Bertsch, 2014). Antisocial adolescents, for example, tend to incorrectly interpret other people's behaviour as threatening (Dodge, Laird, Lochman, & Zelli, 2002). Perhaps because of family and community experiences, they tend to presume that others intend them ill when they do not. In a cognitive therapy method based on such findings—**problem-solving therapy**—antisocial adolescent boys have been encouraged to reconceptualize their social interactions as problems to be solved rather than as threats to be responded to with aggression (Kazdin & Whitley, 2003). They then generate nonviolent solutions to social confrontations and, like scientists, test out the most promising ones. In the section on biological perspectives, we also see that the antisocial personality's failure to profit from punishment is connected with a cognitive factor: the meaning of the aversive stimulus.

problem-solving therapy Form of therapy that focuses on helping people develop more effective problem-solving skills.

Biological Perspectives

Our knowledge about biological factors in most personality disorders has progressed rapidly in recent years with advances in genetics and neuroimaging technologies. We have suggestive evidence of genetic factors based in part on findings that the first-degree biological relatives (parents and siblings) of people with certain personality disorders, especially antisocial, schizotypal, and borderline types, are more likely to be diagnosed with these disorders than are members of the general population (APA, 2013). Studies using fMRI technology have also provided evidence for neurological differences in personality traits (Gray & Braver, 2002; Reuter et al., 2004).

GENETIC FACTORS Evidence points to genetic factors playing a role in the development of several types of personality disorders, including antisocial, narcissistic, paranoid, and borderline types (Gunderson, 2011; Meier, Slutske, Heath, & Martin, 2011). Parents and siblings of people with personality disorders, such as antisocial, schizotypical, and borderline types, are more likely to be diagnosed with these disorders themselves than are members of the general population (APA, 2013). Genetic factors also appear to be involved in the development of personality traits that underlie antisocial personality disorder, such as poor cognitive functioning, antisocial behaviour, emotional reactivity, impulsivity, and hyperactivity (Tuvblad, Narusyte, Grann, Sarnecki, & Lichtenstein, 2011; Werner, Few, & Bucholz, 2015). Although some investigators report finding genetic indicators in particular chromosomes linking to features of borderline personality disorder (e.g. Distel, Hottenga, Trull, & Boomsma, 2008), an overall review of the research to date is inconclusive (Amad, Ramoz, Thomas, Jardri, & Gorwood, 2014; Calati, Gressier, Balestri, & Serretti, 2013).

Studies of familial transmission are limited because family members share common environments as well as genes. Hence, researchers have turned to twin and adoptee studies to tease out genetic and environmental effects. Evidence from twin studies suggests that dimensions of personality associated with particular personality disorders have an inherited component (Reichborn-Kjennerud, 2010; Reichborn-Kjennerud et al., 2013). Researchers examined the genetic contribution to 18 dimensions that underlie various personality disorders, including callousness, identity problems, anxiousness, insecure attachment, narcissism, social avoidance, self-harm, and oppositionality (negativity) (Livesley, Jang, Jackson, & Vernon, 1993). Genetic influences were suggested by findings of greater correlations of a given trait among identical (monozygotic, or MZ) twins than among fraternal (dizygotic, or DZ) twins. A statistical measure of heritability, reflecting the percentage of variability in a given trait that is accounted for by genetics, was computed for each personality dimension. The results showed that 12 of the 18 dimensions had heritabilities in the range of 40–60%, indicating a substantial genetic contribution to these characteristics. The highest heritabilities were for narcissism (64%) and identity problems (59%), and the lowest were for conduct problems (0%) and submissiveness (25%).

The findings suggest that genetics play a role in varying degrees in the development of the traits that underlie personality disorders. Certainly, not all people possessing these traits develop personality disorders. It is possible, however, that people with a genetic predisposition for these traits may be more vulnerable to developing personality disorders if they encounter certain environmental influences, such as being reared in a dysfunctional family.

In fact, it may be the case that genetically based behaviour dictates what environments and situations a person will seek out (Jang, Vernon, & Livesley, 2001). Jang and his colleagues at the University of British Columbia argue that people do not just passively respond to nor are merely shaped by their environment, but that personality plays a role in the kinds of environments that will be actively sought out. For instance, a person with a genetic predisposition for sensation seeking may gravitate toward exhilarating situations such as bungee jumping, heli-skiing/boarding, or street racing. In this regard, genetic personality traits and the environment act cyclically (e.g., thrill seekers gravitate to thrilling environments and thrilling environments serve to reinforce the thrill seeking), and thus the person's personality becomes self-reinforcing and well ingrained. The question remains: To what extent is the influence of the environment dependent upon preexisting genetic factors?

Evidence from adoption studies shows that biological and adopted children of people with antisocial personality disorder are more likely to develop the disorder themselves, which is consistent with the view that both genetics and environment play a role in its development (APA, 2013). Consistent with a genetic contribution, evidence shows striking similarities between identical twins reared apart on some personality dimensions, including a psychopathic personality dimension (DiLalla, Carey, Gottesman, & Bouchard, 1996). Environmental influences also contribute to antisocial behaviour. Evidence from adoption studies links criminal behaviour to genetics, although environmental factors also play a role (Carey, 1992; DiLalla & Gottesman, 1991; Hopwood et al., 2011).

NEUROPSYCHOLOGICAL FACTORS The neuroscience theory of personality can be traced back to physiologist Ivan Pavlov, who introduced the concept of nervous system excitation (e.g., a conditioned pleasure response) and inhibition (e.g., a conditioned fear response) (Corr, 2004; Corr & Perkins, 2005). Later, personality theorist Hans Eysenck (Eysenck & Eysenck, 1985) incorporated Pavlov's ideas of excitatory and inhibitory processes into his theory of personality and suggested that extroverts—active, socially outgoing people—differ from introverts—socially withdrawn, introspective people—with respect to differences in cortical arousal sensitivity. Eysenck believed that extroverts have a lower level of arousal and seek out stimulating activity to increase their arousal. In contrast, introverts have higher levels of arousal and are more easily aroused, and thus seek to avoid sensory stimulation. Because social behaviour is arousing, in social situations you may expect an extrovert to be the "life of the party," whereas an introvert may prefer to avoid parties altogether.

Over a 40-year period, theorist Jeffrey Gray (1934–2004) wove the theories of Pavlov and Eysenck into what is now known as reinforcement sensitivity theory (RST) (Corr, 2004). Gray's RST has evolved into a biological personality theory that focuses on three distinct neuropsychological systems: (1) the behavioural approach system (BAS), (2) the fight-flight-freeze system (FFFS), and (3) the behavioural inhibition system (BIS) (Gray, 1970; Gray & McNaughton, 2003). New evidence supporting the neurological basis of personality comes from a growing body of molecular genetics (Canli et al., 2006; Caspi et al., 2003; Ebstein, Benjamin, & Belmaker, 2003) as well as neuroimaging research studies (Reuter et al., 2004; Schaefer et al., 2006).

Gray suggests that each neuropsychological system functions in a unique way. The BAS, for instance, is sensitive to and anticipates rewards; it acts to seek out pleasure (Aluja, Blanch, Blanco, & Balada, 2015). It has been linked with personality traits characterized by positive affect, extroversion, and impulsivity, but it may also underlie addictive behaviours, hypomania, and mania (Segarra et al., 2007; Smits & Boeck, 2006). The FFFS is a fear response to punishing stimuli; it acts to avoid pain. The FFFS is tied to defensive escape (panic) and avoidance (fear) behaviours and is linked to panic disorders and phobias (Corr, 2004). The BIS is sensitive to potential conflicts caused by the expected rewards and punishments in a situation. When there is a goal conflict, the BIS is activated to resolve any potential or anticipated threat and to bring the person back to a nonconflict state.

Let's say, for example, that you and your friends are vacationing in a foreign country and you are excited (BAS activation) about going to a raucous nightclub that is quite a distance from your hotel. Although you are out to have a fun time, you may initially tend to be alert to your surroundings, looking for potential danger in this novel situation (BIS activation). If all goes well, the BIS relaxes and you and your extroverted friends are free to enjoy the evening's events (BAS activity). If someone were actually to threaten you, however, the FFFS would immediately kick in and you would be ready to respond to the danger. As for any introverted friends among your group, chances are they'd be on high alert before, during, and even after your night out on the town. Thus, as you can see from this illustration, the BIS acts as an alarm signal and is characterized by risk assessment, worry, rumination, and vigilance. Traits associated with the BIS include negative affect, neuroticism, low self-esteem, and anxiety (Segarra et al., 2007) and conditions such as generalized anxiety, obsessive-compulsive disorder, and personality disorders (Bijttebier, Beck, Claes, & Vandereycken, 2009; Corr & Perkins, 2006; Johnson, Sellbom, & Phillips, 2014).

Sociocultural Views

The sociocultural perspective leads us to examine the social conditions that may contribute to the development of the behaviour patterns identified as personality disorders. Socioeconomic status (SES) risk factors, such as low family income, teenage-parent family, lone-parent family, low parental education, and family dysfunction, are associated with an increased vulnerability to one or more behavioural problems in young children, especially when the children are exposed to hostile or ineffective parenting (Granic & Patterson, 2006; Landy & Tam, 1998). Because antisocial personality disorder is reported more frequently among people from lower socioeconomic classes, we might examine the role that the kinds of stressors encountered by disadvantaged families play in developing problem behaviour patterns. Some Canadian neighbourhoods and communities are beset by social problems such as alcohol and drug abuse, teenage pregnancy, and disorganized and disintegrating families. These stressors are associated with an increased likelihood of child abuse and neglect, which may in turn contribute to lower self-esteem and breed feelings of anger and resentment in children. Neglect and abuse may be translated into the lack of empathy and callous disregard for the welfare of others that are associated with antisocial personalities.

Little information is available about the rates of personality disorders outside North America. One initiative in this direction involved a joint program sponsored by the World Health Organization and the Alcohol, Drug Abuse, and Mental Health Administration of the US government. The goal of the program was to develop and standardize diagnostic instruments that could be used to arrive at psychiatric diagnoses worldwide. The result of this effort was the development of the International Personality Disorder Examination (IPDE), a semi-structured interview protocol for diagnosing personality disorders (Loranger et al., 1994). The IPDE was pilot-tested by psychiatrists and clinical psychologists in 11 countries (India, Switzerland, the Netherlands, the United Kingdom,

Luxembourg, Germany, Kenya, Norway, Japan, Austria, and the United States). The interview protocol had reasonably good reliability for diagnosing personality disorders among the different languages and cultures that were sampled. Later studies also obtained good reliability in Pakistan, India, and Greece (Fountoulakis et al., 2002; Haider et al., 2014; Sharan, Kulhara, Verma, & Mohanty, 2002). Although more research is needed to determine the rates of particular personality disorders in other parts of the world, investigators found borderline and avoidant types to be the most frequently diagnosed. Perhaps the characteristics associated with these personality disorders reflect some dimensions of personality disturbance that are commonly encountered throughout the world.

REVIEW IT

Theoretical Perspectives

- **How do traditional Freudian concepts of disturbed personality development compare with more recent psychodynamic approaches?** Traditional Freudian theory focused on unresolved Oedipal conflicts in explaining normal and abnormal personality development. More recent psychodynamic theorists have focused on the pre-Oedipal period in explaining the development of such personality disorders as narcissistic and borderline personality.

- **How do learning theorists view personality disorders?** Learning theorists view personality disorders in terms of maladaptive patterns of behaviour rather than personality traits. Learning theorists seek to identify the early learning experiences and present reinforcement patterns that may explain the development and maintenance of personality disorders.

- **What is the role of family relationships in personality disorders?** Many theorists have argued that disturbed family relationships play a formative role in the development of many personality disorders. For example, theorists have connected antisocial personality to parental rejection or neglect and parental modelling of antisocial behaviour.

- **How do cognitive encoding strategies of antisocial adolescents differ from those of their peers?** Antisocial

adolescents are more likely to interpret social cues as provocations or intentions of ill will. This cognitive bias may lead them to be confrontative in their relationships with peers.

- **What roles might biological factors play in personality disorders?** To varying degrees, genetics play a role in the development of traits that underlie personality disorders. Some people with a genetic predisposition for these traits may be more vulnerable to developing personality disorders if they encounter certain environmental influences. In others, genetically based behaviour can dictate what environments a person will seek out. Reinforcement sensitivity theory (RST), backed up by genetic and neuropsychological evidence, helps explain and describe the psychophysiological basis of personality differences.

- **What role do sociocultural factors play in the development of personality disorders?** The effects of poverty, urban blight, and drug abuse can lead to family disorganization and disintegration, making it less likely that children will receive the nurturance and support they need to develop more socially adaptive behaviour patterns. Sociocultural theorists believe that such factors may underlie the development of personality disorders, especially antisocial personality disorder.

TREATMENT

We began the chapter with a quotation from the eminent psychologist William James (1842–1910), who suggested that people's personalities seem to be "set in plaster" by a certain age. His view may be especially applicable to many people with personality disorders, who are typically highly resistant to change.

People with personality disorders usually see their behaviour, even maladaptive, self-defeating behaviour, as natural parts of themselves. Although they may be unhappy and distressed, they are unlikely to perceive their own behaviour as causative. Like Marcella on page 224, whom we described as showing features of a histrionic personality disorder, they may condemn others for their problems and believe that others, not themselves, need to change. Thus, they usually do not seek help on their own. Or, they begrudgingly acquiesce to treatment at the urging of others but drop out or fail to cooperate with a therapist. Or they may go for help when they feel overwhelmed by anxiety or depression and terminate treatment as soon as they find some relief rather than probing more deeply for the underlying causes of their problems. Despite these obstacles, evidence supports the effectiveness of psychotherapy in treating personality disorders, as we shall see in the following sections (Ali & Findlay, 2016; Muran, Eubanks-Carter, & Safran, 2010).

Psychodynamic Approaches

Psychodynamic approaches are often used to help people with personality disorders become more aware of the roots of their self-defeating behaviour patterns and learn more adaptive ways of relating to others. Progress in therapy may be hampered by difficulties in working therapeutically with people who have personality disorders, especially clients with borderline and narcissistic personality disorders. Psychodynamic therapists often report that people with borderline personality disorder tend to have turbulent relationships with them, sometimes idealizing them, sometimes denouncing them as uncaring. Case studies suggest that therapists feel manipulated and exploited by borderline clients' needs to test their approval, such as by calling them at all hours or threatening suicide. Such clients can be exhausting and frustrating, although some successes have been reported among therapists who can handle clients' demands.

Promising results have been reported using structured forms of psychodynamically oriented therapies in treating personality disorders (e.g., Gunderson, 2011; Leichsenring & Leibing, 2003; Vermote et al., 2015). These therapies raise clients' awareness of how their behaviours cause problems in their close relationships. The therapist takes a more direct, confrontational approach that addresses the client's defences than would be the case in traditional psychoanalysis. With borderline personality disorder, the psychodynamic therapist helps clients better understand their own and other people's emotional responses in the context of their close relationships.

Cognitive-Behavioural Approaches

Behaviour therapists see their task as changing clients' behaviour rather than their personality structures. Many behaviour theorists do not think in terms of clients' "personalities" at all, but rather in terms of acquired maladaptive behaviour that is maintained by reinforcement contingencies. Behaviour therapists therefore focus on attempting to replace maladaptive behaviour with adaptive behaviour through techniques such as extinction, modelling, and reinforcement. If clients are taught behaviour likely to be reinforced by other people, the new behaviour may well be maintained.

Behavioural marital therapists, for example, may encourage clients not to reinforce their spouse's histrionic behaviour. Techniques for treating social anxiety disorder, such as those described in Chapter 3, have also been beneficial in treating people with avoidant personality disorder (Renneberg, Goldstein, Phillips, & Chambless, 1990). This may include social-skills training to help clients function more effectively in social situations, such as dating and meeting new people. Cognitive methods may be incorporated to help socially avoidant individuals offset catastrophizing beliefs, such as the exaggerated fear of being shot down or rejected by dates.

Despite the difficulties in treating borderline personality disorder, two groups of therapists headed by Aaron Beck (e.g., Beck, Freeman, Davis, & Associates, 2004) and Marsha Linehan (Koerner & Linehan, 2002; Linehan, 1993) report promising results using cognitive-behavioural techniques specifically adapted to the problems encountered in working with clients with borderline personality disorder. Beck's approach focuses on helping the individual correct cognitive distortions that underlie tendencies to see oneself and others as either all good or all bad. Linehan's technique, called dialectical behaviour therapy (DBT), combines behaviour therapy and supportive psychotherapy.

DBT involves several modules, including (1) mindfulness techniques, through which individuals are taught to pay attention to the present moment in a nonjudgmental way; (2) distress tolerance, where individuals learn to tolerate strong emotions and their decisions; (3) emotion regulation strategies, which include identifying and labelling emotions, taking opposite action from what the emotion is telling you, and being mindful of current emotions; and (4) interpersonal effectiveness.

One component of distress tolerance is

IMPROVE the Moment

This skill is used in moments of distress to help one relax. The acronym stands for

Imagery: Imagine relaxing scenes, things going well, or other things that please you.

Meaning: Find some purpose or meaning in what you are feeling.

Prayer: Either pray to whomever you worship or, if not religious, chant a personal mantra.

Relaxation: Relax your muscles, breathe deeply; use with self-soothing.

One thing in the moment: Focus your entire attention on what you are doing right now. Keep yourself in the present.

Vacation (brief): Take a break from it all for a short period of time.

Encouragement: Cheer-lead yourself. Tell yourself you can make it through this.

DBT seems to help the lives of those with borderline personality disorder (Ali & Findlay, 2016; Pistorello, Fruzzetti, MacLane, Gallop, & Iverson, 2012). A study led by a psychologist with Toronto's Centre for Addiction and Mental Health (CAMH), Shelley McMain, found that DBT and active psychiatric management were similarly helpful in reducing suicidal and self-injurious episodes, reducing health-care use, and improving BPD symptoms (McMain et al., 2009).

Behaviour techniques are used to help clients develop more effective social skills and problem-solving skills, which can help improve their relationships with others and their ability to cope with negative events. Because people with borderline personality disorder tend to be overly sensitive to even the slightest cues of rejection, therapists provide continuing acceptance and support, even when clients push the limits by becoming manipulative or overly demanding.

Biological Approaches

Drug therapy does not directly treat personality disorders. Antidepressants or anti-anxiety drugs are sometimes used to treat the emotional distress that individuals with personality disorders may encounter, however. Drugs do not alter the long-standing patterns of maladaptive behaviour that may give rise to distress. However, antidepressants of the selective serotonin-reuptake inhibitor class (e.g., Prozac) can reduce aggressive behaviour and irritability in impulsive and aggressive individuals with personality disorders (Gunderson, 2011; Rivas-Vazquez & Blais, 2002). Researchers suspect that impulsive aggressive behaviour may be related to serotonin deficiencies. Prozac and similar drugs act to increase the availability of serotonin in the synaptic connections in the brain. Atypical antipsychotics may also have benefits in controlling aggressive and self-destructive behaviour in people with borderline personality disorder, but the effects are modest and the drugs carry serious potential side effects (Ali & Findlay, 2016; Gunderson, 2011).

Canadian Treatment Services

Paris (2008, 2015) takes the approach that personality disorders are clusters of traits that can be viewed as amplifications of normal personality traits. The therapy implications of this premise are as follows: First, psychotherapy should focus on reducing the extremeness of the traits in part by identifying maladaptive behavioural patterns and bringing them to the attention of the patient. Second, the maladaptive behaviours should be given some historical perspective so that the patient can see how his or her behaviour is shaped by past experiences more than current realities and how this leads to inappropriate consequences. Third, treatment involves change. Patients are given the skills to practise alternative and more adaptive behaviour patterns. Still, the treatment goals for patients with personality disorders remain modest, and therapy sessions should be spaced out because these disorders' chronic nature precludes quick change.

Because of the diversity of problems associated with personality disorders, no single therapy modality works with all patients. Added to this are the cost-containment constraints on mental health services across Canada and the need for service-delivery mechanisms that must be comprehensive and flexible yet efficient and effective. Livesley (2005) suggests that just such a system of care for personality-disordered patients needs to be grounded in evidence-based therapies and requires an integrated and systematic approach. Treatment phases would focus on safety and crisis support (e.g., telephone and mobile crisis support and hospital emergency support), containment of psychological distress through continuing care (e.g., outpatient treatment, daycare, and community-based care), control and regulation (e.g., improving self-management skills, coping skills, and problem-solving skills), exploration and change (e.g., changing maladaptive beliefs and interpersonal behaviours), and long-term treatment that focuses on the integration of clear boundaries between self and others (e.g., through goal-setting and experimenting with new behaviours).

Paris (2015) recommends a *stepped care model* in which all patients are initially offered short-term interventions followed by intermittent follow-ups. Only those who do not benefit from brief interventions should be provided with a more long-term, resource-intensive treatment. He believes that all programs should be time limited to free up resources for other patients.

Much remains to be learned about working with people who have personality disorders. The major challenges involve recruiting people who do not see themselves as being disordered into treatment and prompting them to develop insight into their self-defeating or injurious behaviour. Current efforts to help such people are too often reminiscent of an old couplet:

> *He that complies against his will,*
> *Is of his own opinion still.*

SAMUEL BUTLER, *HUDIBRAS*

In this chapter, we have considered a number of problems in which people act out on maladaptive impulses yet fail to see how their behaviour is disrupting their lives. In the next chapter, we explore other maladaptive behaviours that are frequently connected with lack of self-insight: behaviours involving substance use disorders.

REVIEW IT

Treatment of Personality Disorders

- **How do therapists approach the treatment of personality disorders?** Experts from different schools of therapy try to assist people with personality disorders to gain better awareness of their self-defeating behaviour patterns and learn more adaptive ways of relating to others. Despite the difficulties in working therapeutically with these clients, promising results are emerging from the use of relatively short-term psychodynamic therapy and cognitive-behaviour treatment approaches. The delivery of mental health services across Canada needs to be comprehensive and flexible yet efficient and effective.

Define It

Recall It

1. The major characteristic of schizoid personality disorder is _____.
   a. bizarre thinking
   b. social isolation
   c. the flagrant disregard for others' rights
   d. obsessive thinking

2. From the DSM perspective, each personality disorder is a distinct category. Other theorists contend that personality consists of dimensions that are based on _____ between normal and abnormal traits.
   a. an axis
   b. the boundary
   c. a pendulum
   d. a continuum

3. Harriet is very sensitive to criticism, even to the point of taking offence at the most trivial slight, whether real or imagined. She angers easily and doesn't trust anyone. She has few friends and holds grudges for years. Her pattern of behaviour most closely resembles _____ personality disorder.
   a. avoidant
   b. antisocial
   c. histrionic
   d. paranoid

4. Researchers report links between borderline personality disorder and _____.
   a. birth trauma
   b. death of a parent during early adolescence
   c. childhood trauma
   d. rejection by peers in early adolescence

5. _____ is a technique that combines behaviour therapy and supportive psychotherapy in the treatment of borderline personality disorder.
   a. Object-relations therapy
   b. Cognitive restructuring
   c. Attachment therapy
   d. Dialectical behaviour therapy

Answers to Recall It

1. b,   2. d,   3. d,   4. c,   5. d

Think About It

- Have you known people whose personality traits or styles caused continuing difficulties in their relationships with others? Did their personalities relate to any one of the types of personality disorders discussed in this chapter? Did they ever seek help from a mental health professional? If so, what was the outcome? If not, why not?
- Have you known anyone who you believe might fit the profile of an antisocial personality? What factors do you believe may have shaped this individual's personality development? How did the individual's personality affect his or her relationships with others?
- What factors make it difficult to treat people with personality disorders? If you were a therapist, how might you attempt to overcome these difficulties?

Key for Sensation-Seeking Scale (page 221)

Answers that agree with the following key are suggestive of sensation seeking:

1. A	4. B	7. A	10. A
2. A	5. A	8. A	11. A
3. A	6. B	9. B	12. A

Weblinks

Personality Disorders
www.phac-aspc.gc.ca/publicat/miic-mmac/pdf/chap_5_e.pdf
A chapter on personality disorders from Health Canada's *A Report on Mental Illness in Canada* (Health Canada, 2002b).

Internet Mental Health
http://mentalhealth.com/p20-grp.html
This site includes a list of personality disorders linked to relevant information about description, diagnosis, treatment, and research.

MentalHelp.Net
www.mentalhelp.net/articles/personality-disorders
This site includes a list of personality disorders linked to information about symptoms and treatment.

Borderline Personality Disorder Clinic, CAMH
www.camh.ca/en/hospital/care_program_and_services/specialty_clinics/Pages/Borderline-Personality-Disorder-(BPD)-Clinic.aspx
This is an example of a treatment program for borderline personality disorder, run through the Centre for Addiction and Mental Health.

Personality Disorders

Test your understanding of the key concepts by filling in the blanks with the correct statements chosen from the list that follows. The answers are found at the end of the chapter.

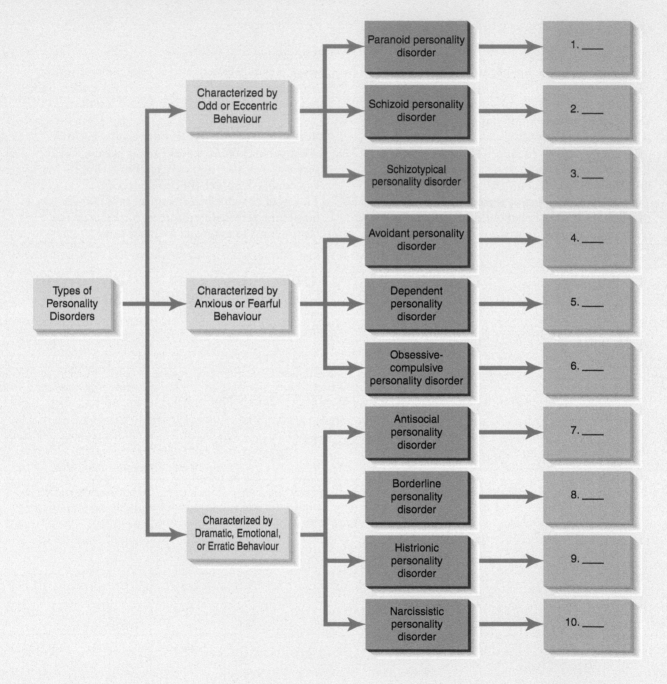

a. Avoidance of social relationships due to fears of rejection

b. Abrupt shifts in mood, lack of a coherent sense of self, and unpredictable, impulsive behaviour

c. Persistent lack of interest in social relationships, flattened affect, and social withdrawal

d. Persistent suspiciousness of the motives of others, but not to the point of having delusions

e. Difficulty making independent decisions; overly dependent behaviour

f. Chronic pattern of antisocial and irresponsible behaviour and lack of remorse

g. Adoption of an inflated self-image and demands for constant attention and admiration

h. Eccentricities or oddities of thought and behaviour but without psychotic features

i. Rigid ways of relating to others, perfectionistic tendencies, lack of spontaneity, and excessive attention to details

j. Excessive need to be the centre of attention and to receive reassurance, praise, and approval from others

Causes and Treatments According to Various Theoretical Perspectives

THEORETICAL PERSPECTIVE	CAUSES	TREATMENT
PSYCHODYNAMIC PERSPECTIVES	Self psychology: Heinz Kohut's theory that describes processes that normally lead to the achievement of a cohesive sense of self. Object relations theory: Disruptions in the normal separation-individuation process.	Help people with personality disorders become more aware of the roots of their self-defeating behaviour patterns and learn more adaptive ways of relating to others.
LEARNING PERSPECTIVES	Focus on the acquisition of behaviour. Many important experiences occur in childhood that shape the development of maladaptive habits of relating to others.	Focus on replacing maladaptive behaviour with adaptive behaviour through techniques such as extinction, modelling, and reinforcement. If clients are taught behaviours that are likely to be reinforced by other people, the new behaviour may be maintained.
COGNITIVE-BEHAVIOURAL PERSPECTIVES	Albert Bandura noted that children acquire behaviours by observing the behaviour of others. The ways in which people with personality disorders interpret their social experiences influence their behaviour.	Dialectical behaviour therapy: Includes mindfulness techniques, distress tolerance, emotion regulation strategies, and interpersonal effectiveness.
FAMILY PERSPECTIVES	Disturbances in family relationships	
BIOLOGICAL PERSPECTIVES	Genetics Jeffrey Gray's reinforcement sensitivity theory	Antidepressants or anti-anxiety drugs are sometimes used to treat emotional distress.
SOCIOCULTURAL PERSPECTIVES	Social conditions contribute to the development of maladaptive behaviour patterns.	

Answers: 1. d, 2. c, 3. h, 4. a, 5. e, 6. i, 7. f, 8. b, 9. j, 10. g

7

Substance-Related and Addictive Disorders

Did You Know That...

- You can become psychologically dependent on a drug without becoming physically addicted?

- Alcohol "goes to women's heads" more rapidly than men's?

- Light to moderate alcohol intake is associated with a reduced risk of heart disease and lower death rates?

- Coca-Cola originally contained cocaine?

- Habitual smoking is a form of physical addiction, not just a bad habit?

- Being able to "hold your liquor" better than most people may put you at risk of developing a drinking problem?

- A widely used treatment for heroin addiction involves the substitution of another addictive drug?

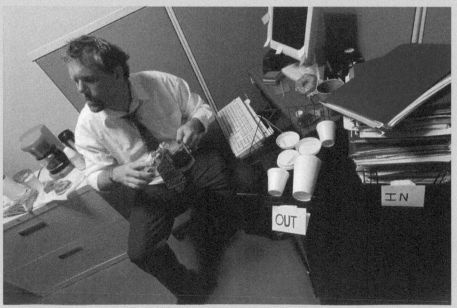

Stockbyte/Thinkstock/Getty Images

The planet is a supermarket of psychoactive chemicals or drugs. The Western world is flooded with substances that alter the mood and twist perceptions—substances that lift you up, calm you down, and turn you upside down. Many people use these substances because their friends do. Some adolescents use them because their parents and authority figures tell them not to. Some users are seeking pleasure or temporary relief from emotional pain. Others are searching for inner truth.

Throughout North America, psychoactive drugs are widely used. An Ontario survey revealed that 45% of people aged 15 and older had used marijuana at some point in their lives, and 79% had used alcohol (Adlaf, Begin, & Sawka, 2005). According to the survey, compared to marijuana and alcohol, the lifetime use of other substances is less common: hallucinogens, 11%; cocaine, 11%; amphetamines (speed), 6%; MDMA (ecstasy), 4%; and heroin, 1%. Some people consume multiple substances, which is called *polydrug use*. To illustrate, consider the following study conducted by members of Robert Pihl's research group at McGill University (Barrett, Gross, Garand, & Pihl, 2005). Pihl is an internationally acclaimed substance use researcher. He and his colleagues conducted a survey of drug use of 186 people who attended "raves" in Montreal. Most participants were in their early 20s. About 80% reported using multiple psychoactive substances (excluding tobacco) at the most recent rave they attended. Cannabis, alcohol, ecstasy, amphetamines, cocaine, ketamine (special K), and GHB (gamma-hydroxybutyrate) were the most frequently used. Frequent rave attendees tended to use more of these substances than infrequent attendees. Later in this chapter we will discuss the brain damage and other harmful effects of these drugs, especially when used repeatedly and in large quantities.

The old standby, alcohol, is the most popular drug on campus—whether the campus is a high school or a university. In fact, 85% of Canadian students report having consumed alcohol as compared to an estimated 50% who report having used any illicit drug (Leyton & Stewart, 2014). Under certain conditions, the use of substances that affect mood and behaviour is normal enough, at least as gauged by statistical frequency and social standards. It is normal to start the day with caffeine in the form of coffee or tea, to take wine or coffee with meals, to meet friends for a drink after work, and to end the day with a nightcap. Many of us take prescription drugs that calm us down or ease our pain. Flooding the bloodstream with nicotine by means of smoking is normal in the sense that about one in five Canadians smoke (Statistics Canada, 2016c). Some psychoactive substances are illegal and are used illicitly, such as cocaine and heroin. Others are available by prescription, such as minor tranquillizers, amphetamines, and opiate analgesics. Still others are available without prescription or over the counter, such as tobacco (which contains nicotine, a mild stimulant) and alcohol (which is a depressant). The most widely and easily accessible substances—tobacco and alcohol—cause more deaths through sickness and accidents than all other illicit drugs combined.

Table 7.1 shows results, separated by gender, from the Canadian Alcohol and Drug Use Monitoring Survey. Such surveys suggest that the prevalence of illicit drug use has remained roughly stable over the past two decades (Health Canada, 2014), although the prevalence of marijuana use may increase once the drug is legalized.

TABLE 7.1

Drug Use among Canadian Men and Women 15 Years and Older (Percentages)

	Men	Women
Alcohol—past 12 months	82.7	74.4
Alcohol—lifetime	92.9	89.3
Cannabis—past 12 months	13.7	7
Cannabis—lifetime	47.9	35.5
Cocaine/Crack—past 12 months	1.5	N/A
Cocaine/Crack—lifetime	9.9	4.7
Speed—lifetime	5.7	2.5
Methamphetamine/Crystal meth—lifetime	0.9	0.5
Hallucinogens—past 12 months	1.5	N/A
Hallucinogens—lifetime	16.6	8.6
Ecstasy—lifetime	5.6	3.2
Heroin—lifetime	0.7	N/A

Note: N/A indicates reliable data was not available.

© All rights reserved. Canadian Alcohol and Drug Use Monitoring Survey. Health Canada, 2014. Adapted and reproduced with permission from the Minister of Health, 2017.

The prevalence of tobacco use has declined to some extent over the past few decades (Canadian Centre on Substance Abuse & Centre for Addiction and Mental Health, 1999; Health Canada, 2001). To illustrate, in 1965 a total of 61% of men and 38% of women were smokers. In 2001, these figures dropped to 25% and 20%, respectively (Health Canada, 2001). From 1999 to 2014 we saw a further overall decline, to 18% (Statistics Canada, 2016c). The decline is likely because of a range of factors, including government legislation banning smoking in various public places, restrictions on the sale of tobacco to minors, warnings on tobacco packages, and public health campaigns emphasizing the harmful effects of smoking.

Although there has been some decline in overall alcohol consumption over the years (e.g., CCSA & CAMH, 1999), problem drinking, especially binge drinking, remains widespread on university campuses and elsewhere in society. A binge drinker is someone who reports consuming five or more drinks (for men) or four or more drinks (for women) on one occasion during the preceding two-week period. A 2004 survey of Canadian universities (the sample of 6282 undergraduates averaged 22 years of age and included 2248 men and 4034 women) found that undergraduates display diverse drinking patterns.

Two drinking types represent more than half of students: light-infrequent drinking (indicated by the usual consumption of fewer than five drinks daily and less than weekly drinking), reported by 35.8%, and light-frequent drinking (indicated by the usual consumption of fewer than five drinks on the days they drink and weekly drinking), reported by 22.1%.

Almost one third of students reported a heavy pattern of drinking, including 16.1% who reported heavy-frequent drinking (indicated by the usual consumption of more than five drinks on the days they drink and weekly drinking) and 11.7% who reported heavy-infrequent drinking (indicated by the usual consumption of more than five drinks on the days they drink and less than weekly drinking). The prevalence of binge drinking is higher in men than women (Statistics Canada, 2016d).

Example: Alcohol Use Disorder

Does not meet criteria		Meets criteria		

NO SYMPTOMS	STRUGGLING	MILD	MODERATE	SEVERE
	Jun has a tendency to drink too much at social gatherings.	Stuart has two symptoms of alcohol use disorder, which has affected his performance at work.	Esther has four symptoms of alcohol use disorder and both her relationships and her grades have suffered.	Myrna has six symptoms of alcohol use disorder, which have caused her significant distress and impairment.

CLASSIFICATION OF SUBSTANCE-RELATED AND ADDICTIVE DISORDERS

The DSM-5 classifies substance-related disorders into two major categories: **substance use disorders** and **substance-induced disorders**. Substance use disorders involve maladaptive use of **psychoactive** substances. Substance-induced disorders involve disorders that can be induced by using psychoactive substances, such as intoxication, withdrawal syndromes, mood disorders, delirium, dementia, amnesia, psychotic disorders, anxiety disorders, sexual dysfunctions, and sleep disorders. Different substances have different effects, so some of these disorders may apply to one, a few, or nearly all substances.

Substance-Induced Disorders

Substance **intoxication** is a disorder characterized by clinically significant problematic behavioural or psychological changes caused by the recent ingestion of a substance (a state of drunkenness or "being high"). These effects largely reflect the chemical actions of the psychoactive substances. The particular features of intoxication depend on which drug is ingested, the dose, the user's biological reactivity, and—to some degree—the user's expectations. Signs of intoxication often include confusion, belligerence, impaired judgment, inattention, and impaired motor and spatial skills. Extreme intoxication from the use of alcohol, cocaine, opiates, and PCP (phencyclidine) can even result in death (yes, you can die from an alcohol overdose), either because of the substance's biochemical effects or because of behaviour patterns—such as suicide—that are connected with psychological pain or impaired judgment brought on by use of the drug.

A **withdrawal syndrome** (also called an *abstinence syndrome*) involves a characteristic cluster of symptoms that occur when a person abruptly stops using a particular substance following a prolonged period of heavy use. People who experience a withdrawal syndrome often return to using the substance to relieve the discomfort associated with withdrawal, which serves to maintain the addictive pattern. Withdrawal symptoms vary with the particular type of drug. With alcohol use disorder, typical withdrawal symptoms include dryness in the mouth, nausea or vomiting, weakness, **tachycardia**, anxiety and depression, headaches, insomnia, elevated blood pressure, and fleeting hallucinations.

In some cases of chronic alcoholism, withdrawal produces a state of **delirium tremens**, or "the DTs." The DTs are usually limited to chronic, heavy users of alcohol who dramatically lower their intake of alcohol after many years of steady drinking. The DTs involve intense autonomic hyperactivity (profuse sweating and tachycardia) and

substance use disorders Patterns of maladaptive behaviour involving the use of a psychoactive substance.

substance-induced disorders Disorders induced by the use of psychoactive substances, including intoxication, withdrawal syndromes, mood disorders, delirium, and amnesia.

psychoactive Describing chemical substances or drugs that have psychological effects.

intoxication Substance-induced disorder characterized by clinically significant problematic behavioural or psychological changes caused by the recent ingestion of a substance (state of drunkenness or "being high").

withdrawal syndrome Characteristic cluster of withdrawal symptoms following the sudden reduction or abrupt cessation of use of a psychoactive substance after physiological dependence has developed.

tachycardia Abnormally rapid heartbeat.

delirium tremens Withdrawal syndrome that often occurs following a sudden decrease or cessation of drinking in chronic alcoholics that is characterized by extreme restlessness, sweating, disorientation, and hallucinations. Abbreviated *DTs*.

delirium—a state of mental confusion characterized by incoherent speech, disorientation, and extreme restlessness. Terrifying hallucinations—frequently of creepy-crawly animals (worms, snakes, etc.)—may also be present. Substances that tend to lead to withdrawal syndromes include alcohol, cannabis, opiates, cocaine, amphetamines, sedatives and barbiturates, nicotine, and anti-anxiety agents (minor tranquillizers).

Substance Use Disorders

According to the DSM, substance use disorders involve a pattern of recurrent use that leads to damaging consequences. Damaging consequences may involve failing to meet one's major role responsibilities (e.g., as a student, worker, or parent), putting oneself in situations where substance use is physically dangerous (e.g., combining driving with substance use), encountering repeated problems with the law arising from substance use (e.g., multiple arrests for substance-related behaviour), or having recurring social or interpersonal problems because of substance use (e.g., repeatedly getting into fights when drinking).

When people repeatedly miss school or work because they are drunk or "sleeping it off," their behaviour may fit the definition of substance use disorder. A single incident of excessive drinking at a friend's wedding would not qualify. Nor would regular consumption of low to moderate amounts of alcohol be considered abusive, so long as it is not connected with any impairment in functioning. Neither the amount nor the type of drug ingested, nor whether the drug is illicit, is key to defining a substance use disorder according to the DSM. Rather, the determining feature of substance use disorder is whether a pattern of drug-using behaviour becomes repeatedly linked to damaging consequences.

The diagnostic criteria for an example of a substance use disorder—alcohol use disorder—are listed in Table 7.2. The severity of the disorder is reflected in the number

---

TABLE 7.2

Diagnostic Criteria for Alcohol Use Disorder

A. A problematic pattern of alcohol use leading to clinically significant impairment or distress, as manifested by at least two of the following, occurring within a 12-month period:

1. Alcohol is often taken in larger amounts or over a longer period than was intended.

2. There is a persistent desire or unsuccessful efforts to cut down or control alcohol used.

3. A great deal of time is spent in activities necessary to obtain alcohol, use alcohol, or recover from its effects.

4. Craving, or a strong desire or urge to use alcohol.

5. Recurrent alcohol use resulting in a failure to fulfill major role obligations at work, school, or home.

6. Continued alcohol use despite having persistent or recurrent social or interpersonal problems caused or exacerbated by the effects of alcohol.

7. Important social, occupational, or recreational activities are given up or reduced because of alcohol use.

8. Recurrent alcohol use in situations in which it is physically hazardous.

9. Alcohol use is continued despite knowledge of having a persistent or recurrent physical or psychological problem that is likely to have been caused or exacerbated by alcohol.

10. Tolerance, as defined by either of the following:

    a. A need for markedly increased amounts of alcohol to achieve intoxication or desired effect.

    b. A markedly diminished effect with continued use of the same amount of alcohol.

11. Withdrawal, as manifested by either of the following:

    a. The characteristic withdrawal syndrome for alcohol (refer to Criteria A and B of the criteria set for alcohol withdrawal, pp. 499–500).

    b. Alcohol (or a closely related substance, such as a benzodiazepine) is taken to relieve or avoid withdrawal symptoms.

Source: Reprinted with permission from the *Diagnostic and Statistical Manual of Mental Disorders*, Fifth Edition, (Copyright © 2013). American Psychiatric Association. All Rights Reserved.

of symptoms the individual has. Only two symptoms are required for a diagnosis. The presence of four or five symptoms would signify a moderate level of severity, and six or more symptoms would be considered severe. Substance use disorder may continue for a long period of time or progress to a more severe level of substance use disorder in which use is associated with physiological signs of dependence (tolerance or withdrawal) and/or compulsive use of a substance. People who are compulsive users lack control over their drug use. They may be aware of how their drug use is disrupting their lives or damaging their health but feel helpless or powerless to stop using drugs, even though they may want to. By the time they become dependent on a given drug, they've given over much of their lives to obtaining and using it.

Repeated use of a substance may alter the body's physiological reactions, leading to the development of tolerance or a physical withdrawal syndrome. Tolerance is a state of physical habituation to a drug such that with frequent use, higher doses are needed to achieve the same effect. Tolerance and withdrawal syndromes are often, but not necessarily, associated with substance use disorders. Substance use disorders sometimes involve a pattern of compulsive use without the development of the physiological features of dependence (tolerance or a withdrawal syndrome). For example, people may become compulsive users of marijuana, especially when they come to rely on the drug to help them cope with the stresses of daily life. Yet they may not require larger amounts of the substance to get "high" or experience distressing withdrawal symptoms when they cease using it. In most cases, however, substance use disorders and physiological features of dependence occur together.

People can abuse or become dependent on more than one psychoactive substance at the same time. People who abuse or become dependent on heroin, for instance, may also abuse or become dependent on other drugs, such as alcohol, cocaine, or stimulants—simultaneously or successively. In fact, surveys from Canada and elsewhere indicate that most illicit users of opioids such as heroin are polydrug users involved in the intensive co-use of crack or cocaine (or both) (Fischer & Rehm, 2006). People who engage in these patterns of polydrug abuse face increased potential of harmful overdoses when drugs are used in combination. Moreover, "successful" treatment of one form of abuse may not affect, and in some cases could even exacerbate, abuse of other drugs.

John Lamb/Taxi/Getty Images

Scott T. Baxter/Photodisc/Getty Images

Alcohol use and alcohol use disorder. Alcohol is our most widely used—and overused—drug. Many people use alcohol to celebrate achievements and happy occasions, as in the photograph on the left. Unfortunately, like the man in the photograph on the right, some people use alcohol to drown their sorrows, which may only worsen their problems. Where does substance use end and disorder begin? According to the DSM, use becomes a disorder when it leads to damaging consequences.

Addiction, Physiological Dependence, and Psychological Dependence

The DSM uses the term *substance use disorder* to classify people whose use of these substances impairs their functioning. It does not use the term *addiction* to describe these problems, yet the concept of addiction is widespread among professionals and laypeople alike. But what is meant by *addiction*?

People define **addiction** in different ways. For our purposes, we define it as the habitual or compulsive use of a drug accompanied by evidence of physiological dependence. **Physiological dependence** means that one's body has changed as a result of the regular use of a psychoactive drug such that it comes to depend on a steady supply of the substance. The major signs of physiological dependence involve the development of tolerance or an abstinence syndrome. A **psychological dependence** involves a pattern of compulsive use associated with impaired control over the use of a drug.

Although physical addiction is generally associated with substance use disorder, some cases of substance use disorder involve compulsive patterns of using drugs without physical signs of addiction (Schuckit et al., 1999). You can become psychologically dependent on a drug without developing a physiological dependence or addiction.

On the other hand, people may become physiologically dependent on a drug but not become compulsive users or psychologically dependent. For example, people recuperating from surgery are often given narcotics derived from opium as painkillers. Some may develop signs of physiological dependence—such as tolerance and a withdrawal syndrome—but they likely will not become habitual users or show a lack of control over the use of these drugs.

In recent years, the concept of addiction has been extended beyond the abuse of chemical substances to apply to many habitual forms of maladaptive behaviour, such as pathological gambling (Ladouceur, 2002). In the vernacular, we hear of people being "addicted to" love or shopping or almost anything. There have even been suggestions that people can become addicted to the Internet (Beard, 2005), whereby people (usually males) lose sleep, miss meals, experience social isolation, and fail to attend classes or neglect work responsibilities because of excessive use of the Internet, such as for the purpose of using chat rooms, playing online games, or visiting gambling or sexual websites (Chou, Condron, & Belland, 2005). These people are excessively preoccupied with using the Internet, to the exclusion of everything else in their lives, and they seem to experience symptoms of withdrawal (anxiety, depression) when they are separated from it (Niemz, Griffiths, & Banyard, 2005).

DSM-5 also includes *gambling addiction* as a nonsubstance-related disorder (see the diagnostic criteria on page 60 in Chapter 2). Problem gambling behaviour was considered an impulse control disorder in former editions of the DSM. Gambling disorder has commonalities in expression, etiology, comorbidity, and treatment with substance use disorders (APA, 2013). Similar to other substance use disorders, the patterns of gambling disorder prevalence tend to emerge in younger male populations (APA, 2013). Older individuals are also affected, but their gambling behaviour tends to involve slot machines and bingo games, whereas younger and middle-aged individuals often become involved in many different forms of gambling (APA, 2013). Typically, males have higher rates of gambling disorder than females, although there is a trend toward increased rates of gambling disorder among females (APA, 2013).

Preoccupation with the Internet and other so-called addictions do not involve physiological dependence on a chemical substance. In this chapter, we limit the term *addiction* to the habitual use of substances that produce physiological dependence.

Pathways to Substance Use Disorder

Although the progression to substance use disorder varies from person to person, some common pathways can be described according to the following stages (Weiss, Mirin, & Bartel, 1994):

---

addiction Impaired control over the use of a chemical substance accompanied by physiological dependence.

physiological dependence State of physical dependence on a drug in which the user's body comes to depend on a steady supply.

psychological dependence Reliance, as on a substance, although one may not be physiologically dependent.

1. *Experimentation.* During the stage of experimentation, or occasional use, the drug temporarily makes users feel good, even euphoric. Users feel in control and believe they can stop at any time.

2. *Routine use.* During the next stage, a period of routine use, people begin to structure their lives around the pursuit and use of drugs. Denial plays a major role at this stage, as users mask the negative consequences of their behaviour to themselves and others. Values change. What had formerly been important, such as family and work, comes to matter less than the drugs.

   As routine drug use continues, problems mount. Users devote more of their resources to drugs. Family bank accounts are emptied, "temporary" loans are sought from friends and relatives for trumped-up reasons, and family heirlooms and jewellery are sold to pawnbrokers for a fraction of their value. Lying and manipulation become a way of life to cover up the drug use. The husband sells the television set to a pawnbroker and forces the front door open to make it look like a burglary. The wife claims to have been robbed at knifepoint to explain the disappearance of a gold chain or engagement ring. Family relationships become strained as the mask of denial shatters and the consequences of drug abuse become apparent: days lost from work, unexplained absences from home, rapid mood shifts, depletion of family finances, failure to pay bills, stealing from family members, and absence from family gatherings or children's birthday parties.

3. *Addiction or dependence.* Routine use becomes addiction or dependence when users feel powerless to resist drugs, either because they want to experience their effects or to avoid the consequences of withdrawal. Little or nothing else matters at this stage, as seen in the case of Eugene, a 41-year old architect, who related the following conversation with his wife: "She had just caught me with cocaine again after I had managed to convince her that I hadn't used in over a month. Of course I had been tooting (snorting) almost every day, but I had managed to cover my tracks a little better than usual. So she said to me that I was going to have to make a choice—either cocaine or her. Before she finished the sentence, I knew what was coming, so I told her to think carefully about what she was going to say. It was clear to me that there wasn't a choice. I love my wife, but I'm not going to choose anything over cocaine. It's sick, but that's what things have come to. Nothing and nobody comes before my coke." (Weiss et al., 1994, p. 55)

REVIEW IT

Classification of Substance-Related Disorders

- **How does the DSM describe substance use disorders?** According to the DSM, substance use disorders involve a pattern of recurrent use of a substance that repeatedly leads to damaging consequences and impaired control over the use of a substance and often include features of physiological dependence on the substance, as manifested by the development of tolerance or an abstinence syndrome.

- **How does the DSM describe substance-induced disorders?** Substance-induced disorders involve disorders that can be induced by using psychoactive substances, such as intoxication, withdrawal syndromes, mood disorders, delirium, dementia, amnesia, psychotic disorders, anxiety disorders, sexual dysfunctions, and sleep disorders.

DRUGS OF ABUSE

Drugs of abuse are generally classified into three major groupings: (1) depressants, such as alcohol and opiates; (2) stimulants, such as amphetamine and cocaine; and (3) hallucinogens.

Depressants

depressant Drug that lowers the
level of activity of the central
nervous system.

A **depressant** is a drug that slows down or curbs the activity of the central nervous system. It reduces feelings of tension and anxiety, causes our movements to become sluggish, and impairs our cognitive processes. In high doses, depressants can arrest vital functions and cause death. The most widely used depressant, alcohol, can lead to death when taken in large amounts because of its depressant effects on respiration (breathing). Other effects are specific to the particular kind of depressant. For example, some depressants, such as heroin, produce a "rush" of pleasure. Here we will consider several of the major types of depressants.

ALCOHOL You may not have thought of alcohol as a drug, perhaps because it is so popular, or maybe because it is ingested by drinking rather than by smoking or injection. But alcoholic beverages such as wine, beer, and hard liquor contain a depressant called *ethyl alcohol* (or *ethanol*). The concentration of the drug varies with the type of beverage (wine and beer have less pure alcohol per ounce than distilled spirits such as whisky, gin, or vodka). Alcohol is classified as a depressant drug because it has biochemical effects similar to those of a class of minor tranquillizers, the benzodiazepines, which include the well-known drugs diazepam (Valium) and chlordiazepoxide (Librium). We can think of alcohol as a type of over-the-counter tranquillizer.

Alcohol is used in many ways. It is our mealtime relaxant, our party social facilitator, our bedtime sedative. We observe holy days, laud our achievements, and express joyful wishes with alcohol. Adolescents assert their maturity with alcohol. Pediatricians used to swab the painful gums of teething babies with alcohol. Alcohol even deals the death blow to germs on surface wounds and is the active ingredient in some antiseptic mouthwashes. In Western countries such as Canada, most adults drink alcohol at least occasionally. Most people who drink do so in moderation, but many develop significant problems with alcohol use (Adlaf et al., 2005). Alcohol is the most widely abused substance in the world. Many lay and professional people use the term *alcoholism* to refer to problems of alcohol dependence. Although definitions of alcoholism vary, we use the term to refer to alcohol use disorder as defined by DSM-5 (see Table 7.2, page 252).

The personal and social costs of alcoholism are considerable. In Canada, the economic costs of alcoholism—based on days lost from work, health problems associated with alcoholism, and costs resulting from motor vehicle accidents involving alcohol use—are staggering, amounting to more than $14.6 billion annually according to a 2002 estimate (Public Health Agency of Canada, 2016). Alcohol abuse is connected with lower productivity, loss of jobs, and downward movement in socioeconomic status. Estimates are that over 20% of homeless people suffer from alcohol use disorder (Farrell et al., 2003). Alcohol also plays a part in about 27% of all male suicides and 17% of all female suicides in Canada (Dingle, Samtani, Kraatz, & Solomon, 2002). It is a leading cause of death of young people. Approximately 40% of Canadian teens killed in motor vehicle accidents have alcohol in their systems (Centre for Addictions Research, BC, 2006).

Alcohol, not cocaine or other drugs, is the drug of choice among young people today, and the leading drug of abuse (Health Canada, 2014). Drinking is so integrated into university life that it has become essentially normative, as much a part of the experience as attending a weekend hockey or basketball game.

Despite the popular image of alcoholics as skid-row drunks, the truth is that only a small minority of people with alcoholism fit that stereotype. The great majority of alcoholics are the type of people you're likely to see every day—your neighbours, co-workers, friends, and members of your own family. They are found in all walks of life and every social and economic class. Many have families, hold good jobs, and live fairly comfortably. Yet alcoholism can have just as devastating an effect on the well-to-do as the indigent, leading to wrecked careers and ruined marriages, motor vehicle and other accidents, and severe, life-threatening physical disorders, as well as exacting an enormous emotional toll.

No single drinking pattern is exclusively associated with alcoholism. Some people with alcoholism drink heavily every day; others binge only on weekends. Still others can abstain for lengthy periods of time but periodically "go off the wagon" and engage in episodes of binge drinking that may last for days, weeks, or months.

Risk Factors for Alcoholism   Investigators have identified a number of factors that place people at increased risk for developing alcoholism and alcohol-related problems:

1. *Gender.* The lifetime prevalence of alcohol dependence among women and men is similar, according to some studies. For example, a Canadian survey reported that the lifetime prevalence among women and men was 11% and 12%, respectively (Lukassen & Beaudet, 2005). However, other studies have found that alcohol use disorder is more common in men (APA, 2013). The conflicting results may have to do with when the studies were conducted; the gender gap in the prevalence of alcoholism is narrowing, with women catching up to men (Zilberman, Tavares, & el-Guebaly, 2003). This seems to be partly because social drinking has become more acceptable for women. In general, women start drinking several years later than men, but once alcohol use disorder develops in women, the disorder progresses somewhat more rapidly. But in general, the clinical course of alcohol use disorder is more similar than different (APA, 2013).

   Alcohol seems to "go to women's heads" more rapidly than men's. This is apparently because women metabolize less alcohol in the stomach than men do. Why? It appears that women have less of an enzyme that metabolizes alcohol in the stomach (Frezza et al., 1990). Alcohol then reaches women's circulatory systems and brains relatively intact. This means that gram for gram, women drinkers absorb more alcohol into their bloodstreams than their male counterparts. It is almost as if women were injecting alcohol intravenously. It is not a substance to be trifled with.

2. *Age.* The great majority of cases of alcohol use disorder develop in young adulthood, before age 40. The typical age of onset is late adolescence (Sher, Grekin, & Williams, 2005). Although alcohol use disorder tends to develop somewhat later in women than men, women who develop these problems experience health, social, and occupational problems by middle age just as their male counterparts do. Although many people who develop alcohol problems "grow out" of them, a significant number of people have lifelong problems (Sher et al., 2005).

QUESTIONNAIRE

How Do You Know If You're Hooked?

Are you dependent on alcohol? If you shake and shiver and feel tormented when you go without a drink for a while, the answer is clear enough. Sometimes the clues are more subtle, however.

The following self-test can shed some light on the question. Simply place a check mark in the yes or no column for each item. Then refer to the key on page 289.

	Yes	No
1. Do you often find yourself drinking more than you had intended?	___	___
2. Do you prefer drinking alone?	___	___
3. Do you drink and drive?	___	___
4. Have friends and family members voiced concerns about your drinking?	___	___

5. Have you tried to cut down on your drinking but have been unable to? ___ ___
6. Do you crave alcohol throughout the day? ___ ___
7. Do you find excuses to miss social or recreational activities so that you can stay home and drink? ___ ___
8. Do you ever skip meals to conserve calories or save money in order to drink? ___ ___
9. Do you often miss school or work because of hangovers? ___ ___
10. Do you often regret your actions following an incident of drinking? ___ ___

Striking cultural differences in alcohol use and abuse have long been evident. Chinese and Jewish populations, for example, are considerably less susceptible to alcohol problems than Irish people and some Indigenous groups (Prince, 2000). In Canada, the Indigenous population consists of three broad groups: First Nations, Métis, and Inuit people. They encompass a diverse range of smaller groups, differing from one another in history, culture, and traditions (Tjepkema, 2002). Surveys of people living in First Nations communities reveal that more than 80% of respondents believe alcohol abuse is an important problem in their community (Health Canada, 2011). Alcohol abuse in Indigenous communities is often associated with other forms of drug abuse, such as inhalant abuse (Gfellner & Hundelby, 1995). Alcohol-related health problems, such as liver disease, are also significantly higher in Indigenous populations (Scott, 1994).

Taken as a group, Indigenous Canadians, compared to their non-Indigenous counterparts, do not have more of a tendency to drink alcohol. But those who do consume alcohol are likely to drink more heavily, even when socio-economic status is taken into consideration (First Nations Information Governance Centre, 2012; Haggarty, Cernovsky, Kermeen, & Merskey, 2000; Lavallée & Bourgault, 2000; Tjepkema, 2002). Tjepkema (2002), for example, assessed "heavy drinking" (defined as five or more drinks in a single sitting) among off-reserve Indigenous and non-Indigenous Canadians. Fewer Indigenous than non-Indigenous people were weekly drinkers (27% versus 38%). The groups did not differ in the proportion of people who were light or abstinent drinkers (both 50%), but the Indigenous group had more heavy drinkers (23% versus 16%). The same pattern was found regardless of whether the respondents lived in urban or rural areas. Similar findings were obtained in a study of women in northern Quebec: Alcohol consumption was less frequent among Indigenous women, but those who

did drink consumed higher quantities of alcohol (Lavallée & Bourgault, 2000).

Group differences in alcohol use and abuse have been attributed to psychosocial factors such as cultural or religious attitudes toward drinking. The cultural traditions concerning the use of alcohol in family, religious, and social settings, particularly during childhood, can influence the risk for later alcohol problems (APA, 2013). Jewish people, for example, tend to expose children to the ritual use of wine within a religious context and to impose strong cultural restraints on excessive and underage drinking.

Psychosocial factors within cultures also may influence drinking patterns. To illustrate, Gfellner and Hundelby (1990) investigated the predictors of drug and alcohol use in a small urban community in Manitoba. The number of a person's friends who used alcohol or drugs was the strongest predictor of alcohol or drug use for both Indigenous and non-Indigenous students. Peer attitudes about drug or alcohol use was also a predictor for Indigenous students (Gfellner & Hundelby, 1990).

Many writers see the prevalence of alcoholism among Indigenous peoples as a consequence of the forced attempt by European colonists to eradicate tribal language and culture, leading to a loss of cultural identity that sets the stage for alcoholism, drug abuse, and depression. The greater incidence of psychopathology among Indigenous peoples can be attributed to the disruption in traditional culture caused by the appropriation of their lands by European powers and the attempts to sever them from their cultural traditions while denying them full access to the dominant Western culture. Indigenous peoples have since lived in severe cultural and social disorganization that has resulted in high rates of psychopathology and substance abuse. Beset by such problems, Indigenous adults are prone to child abuse and neglect. Abuse and neglect contribute to feelings of hopelessness and

3. *Antisocial personality disorder.* Antisocial behaviour in adolescence or adulthood increases the risk of later alcoholism (Sher et al., 2005).
4. *Family history.* The best predictor of problem drinking in adulthood appears to be a family history of alcohol abuse. Family members who drink may act as models and "set a poor example." Moreover, the biological relatives of people with alcohol use disorder may also inherit a predisposition that makes them more likely to develop problems with alcohol (Söderpalm Gordh & Söderpalm, 2011).
5. *Sociodemographic factors.* Alcohol problems are more common among people of lower income and educational levels and among people living alone (Kahn, Murray, & Barnes, 2002; PHAC, 2016). In Canada, alcohol and drug dependence are more common among Indigenous than non-Indigenous people (Tjepkema, 2002). We further examine ethnic group differences in alcohol use and abuse in the accompanying feature, "Focus on Diversity: Ethnicity and Alcohol Abuse."

depression among adolescents, who then seek to escape their feelings through alcohol and other drugs (Health Canada, 2011).

Research into the acculturation hypothesis suggests that alcohol and drug abuse is greatest among Indigenous youths who identify least closely with traditional values. Bicultural youth, consisting of those who felt comfortable within both their traditional culture and the larger society, showed the lowest levels of abuse of alcohol and other drugs ("Acculturation," 2004). These findings would suggest that the best adjustment (meaning the lowest levels of culture-related stress) is found among youth who have adapted to both cultures. Other factors, such as the poverty faced by many Indigenous peoples, may also contribute to stress and alcohol and drug abuse.

Biological factors also appear to contribute to ethnic differences in alcohol use and abuse. The low rates of alcohol problems in Asian countries appear to be related to a lack in some Asians of the enzyme aldehyde dehydrogenase, which is involved in metabolizing alcohol in the body. Roughly 50% of Asians are at least partially missing the enzyme, compared to only 5–15% of White individuals (APA, 2013; Prince, 2000). The enzyme may be partially or totally absent—an estimated 10% of Asian people completely lack the enzyme. When they drink alcohol, they experience a flushed face and palpitations, and sometimes nausea, dizziness, and headaches. This reaction can be so intense that it sometimes leads the person to abstain from drinking altogether. The other 40% of Asian people with a relative deficiency of the enzyme have less intense reactions but still are less likely to develop an alcohol problem (APA, 2013). The flushing response is evident even in infants (Prince, 2000) and can be a deterrent to alcohol use and abuse. However, the flushing response provides only a modest defence against excessive drinking. Among the Japanese, for example, alcohol abuse has increased considerably in recent years, despite their susceptibility to the flushing response (Prince, 2000).

Noam Armonn/Hemera/Thinkstock/Getty Images

Paul Chesley/Stone/Getty Images

Alcohol and ethnic diversity. The damaging effects of alcohol abuse appear to be taking the heaviest toll on Canada's First Nations peoples. Jewish people have relatively low incidences of alcohol-related problems, perhaps because they tend to expose children to the ritual use of wine in childhood and impose strong cultural restraints on excessive drinking. Asian people tend to drink less heavily than most other Canadians, in part because of cultural constraints and possibly because they have less biological tolerance of alcohol, as shown by a greater flushing response.

Conceptions of Alcoholism: Disease, Moral Defect, or Behaviour Pattern?   According to the medical perspective, alcoholism is a disease. E. M. Jellinek (1960), a leading proponent of the disease model, believed that alcoholism is a permanent, irreversible condition. Jellinek believed that once a person with alcoholism takes a drink, the biochemical effects of the drug on the brain create an irresistible physical craving for more. Jellinek's ideas have contributed to the view that "once an alcoholic, always an alcoholic." Alcoholics Anonymous (AA), which adopted Jellinek's concepts, views people who suffer from alcoholism as either drinking or "recovering." In other words, alcoholism is never cured. Jellinek's concepts have also supported the idea that "just one drink" will cause the person with alcoholism to "fall off the wagon." In this view, the sole path to recovery is abstinence.

Although the disease model has achieved prominence and gained wide public acceptance, the nature of alcoholism continues to be debated. For most of history, immoderate drinking was seen as a moral defect. Alcoholism was first considered a disease in the 1960s. Since that time, the campaign to instill this view has been so pervasive that most people now endorse it.

Yet not all professionals regard alcoholism as a medical disease. To some, the term is used as a label to describe a harmful pattern of alcohol ingestion and related behaviours. In this view, the "just-one-drink" hypothesis is not a biochemical inevitability. For these observers, it is instead a common self-fulfilling prophecy, as we see later in the chapter.

Psychological Effects of Alcohol   The effects of alcohol or other drugs vary from person to person. By and large, they reflect the interaction of (1) the physiological effects of the substances and (2) our interpretations of those effects. What do most people expect from alcohol? People frequently hold stereotypical expectations that alcohol will reduce states of tension, enhance pleasurable experiences, wash away their worries, and enhance their social skills. But what does alcohol actually do?

At a physiological level, alcohol, like the benzodiazepines, appears to heighten the sensitivity of the gamma-aminobutyric acid (GABA) receptor sites (Suzdak et al., 1986). Because GABA is an inhibitory neurotransmitter, increasing the action of GABA reduces overall nervous system activity, producing feelings of relaxation. As people drink, their senses become clouded, and balance and coordination suffer. Still higher doses act on the parts of the brain that regulate involuntary vital functions such as heart rate, respiration rate, and body temperature.

People may do many things when drinking that they would not do when sober, in part because of expectations concerning the drug and in part because of the drug's effects on the brain. For example, they may become more flirtatious or sexually aggressive or say or do things they later regret. Their behaviour may reflect their expectation that alcohol has liberating effects and provides an external excuse for questionable behaviour. Later they can claim, "It was the alcohol, not me." The drug may impair the brain's ability to curb impulsive behaviour, perhaps by interfering with information-processing functions (Abbey, Zawackia, Bucka, Clinton, & McAuslan, 2004). Although alcohol may make them feel more relaxed and self-confident, it may prevent them from exercising good judgment, which can lead to choices they would ordinarily reject, such as engaging in risky sex (Orchowski, Mastroleo, & Borsari, 2012). One of the lures of alcohol is that it induces short-term feelings of euphoria and elation that can drown self-doubts and self-criticism. Alcohol may also make people less capable of perceiving the unfortunate consequences of their behaviour. Chronic use, however, may deepen feelings of depression. Alcohol and other substance use disorders are strongly correlated with depression (Currie et al., 2005; Lukassen & Beaudet, 2005). This correlation exists for various reasons, as described later in this chapter.

Alcohol in increasing amounts can dampen sexual arousal or excitement and impair our ability to perform sexually. As an intoxicant, alcohol also hampers coordination and motor ability and slurs speech. These effects help explain why alcohol use is implicated in so many road fatalities, other accidents, and violent crimes (see Figure 7.1).

In a more general sense, Health Canada reports that in 2010, 14.6% of Canadians reported experiencing at least one harm in their lifetime as a result of their alcohol use. The prevalence of lifetime harm due to alcohol use for males (20.4%) was double that reported by females (9.2%). *Harm* is defined by Health Canada as problems occurring in any of the following eight areas: physical health; friendships and social life; financial position; home life or marriage; work, studies, or employment opportunities; legal issues; learning ability; and housing (Health Canada, 2014).

Physical Health and Alcohol   Chronic, heavy alcohol use affects virtually every organ and body system either directly or indirectly. Heavy alcohol use is linked to a higher risk of various forms of cancer, such as cancer of the throat, esophagus, larynx, stomach, colon, liver, and possibly cancer of the bowel and breast as well as coronary heart disease, ulcers, hypertension, gout, and pancreatitis (painful inflammation of the pancreas) (CCSA & CAMH, 1999; Grønbæk, 2009). The linkages noted here are based on a statistical association or correlation between heavy drinking on the one hand and health problems on the other. These linkages are strongly suggestive of the damaging effects of heavy

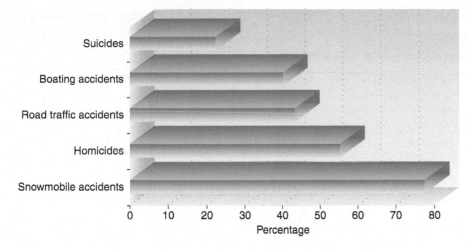

FIGURE 7.1 **Estimated percentages of deaths in Canada from various causes connected with the use of alcohol.**
Alcohol is a factor in over half of the homicides in Canada.
Source: Based on Dingle, Samtani, Kraatz, & Solomon (2002). *The real facts on alcohol use, injuries and deaths*. MADD.

drinking. However, because they are based on correlational evidence, we cannot conclude they are necessarily causal.

Heavy drinking clearly does damage the liver, the organ that serves as the primary site of alcohol metabolism. Chronic, heavy consumption of alcohol is a leading cause of illness and death from liver disease (US Department of Health and Human Services, 2001). Two of the major forms of alcohol-related liver disease are alcoholic hepatitis, a serious and potentially life-threatening inflammation of the liver, and cirrhosis of the liver, a potentially fatal liver disease in which healthy liver cells are replaced with scar tissue. To a great extent, the health risks of alcohol consumption depend on the amount and duration of use. Some people may also be genetically more susceptible to the harmful effects of heavy alcohol use than others.

Habitual drinkers tend to be malnourished, which can put them at risk of complications arising from nutritional deficiencies. Chronic drinking is thus associated with nutritionally linked disorders such as cirrhosis of the liver (linked to protein deficiency) and alcohol-induced persisting amnestic disorder (connected with vitamin B deficiency). Alcohol-induced persisting amnestic disorder (also known as **Korsakoff's syndrome**) is characterized by glaring confusion, disorientation, and memory loss regarding recent events.

All told, it is estimated that in 2002 over 4200 Canadians lost their lives as a result of alcohol consumption, with motor vehicle accidents, liver cirrhosis, and suicide as the primary causes (Rehm et al., 2006). Each year, it is estimated that thousands of Canadians die because of alcohol. After tobacco, alcohol is the second leading cause of premature death in our society. Alcohol is responsible for 50% of deaths caused by liver disease. The number of deaths in Canada from alcoholic liver disease increased from 1104 in 2000 to 1535 in 2011 (PHAC, 2016).

Mothers who drink during pregnancy put their fetuses at risk for infant mortality, birth defects, central nervous system dysfunctions, and later academic problems (Jones, 2006). Many children whose mothers drank during pregnancy develop fetal alcohol syndrome (FAS), a syndrome characterized by facial features such as a flattened nose, widely spaced eyes, an underdeveloped upper jaw, and mental retardation. Research from all over the world suggests FAS is disturbingly common, affecting 1 in 100 babies (Mukherjee, Hollins, & Turk, 2006).

Studies have shown that there is no established "safe" limit for alcohol use by pregnant women (Feldman et al., 2012). The safest course for women who know or suspect they are pregnant is to not drink. Period. The fact remains that FAS is an entirely preventable birth defect. The same applies, of course, to other substances, such as cocaine and heroin. Even tobacco smoking during pregnancy can have harmful effects, including low birth weight and sudden infant death syndrome (SIDS) (Jones, 2006).

Korsakoff's syndrome Form of brain damage associated with chronic thiamine deficiency. The syndrome is associated with chronic alcoholism and characterized by memory loss, disorientation, and the tendency to invent memories to replace lost ones (confabulation). Also called *alcohol-induced persisting amnestic disorder.*

Alcohol Use: No Disorder

Navleen is a 25-year-old manager of a retail store. She recently moved into an apartment with a roommate after living with her parents through university. She is enjoying her new-found freedom, especially the freedom to stay out late with her friends. Her closest friends are all single and they enjoy going to nightclubs to dance. Navleen goes out at least three nights per week and often has several glasses of wine when out. Her friends also drink when they are out, and they plan ahead to share taxis home. Every once in a while, Navleen has more than a few glasses of wine. For example, a few weeks ago, Navleen was celebrating a friend's birthday and ended up drinking several cocktails and shooters. She hadn't intended to drink that much but got caught up in the celebration. The next morning, she could not get out of bed and ended up calling in sick. Once she felt better, she reminded herself to drink less at the next birthday celebration. At the next outing, she stuck with a few glasses of wine and felt much better the next day.

Alcohol Abuse: Disorder

Jenelle lives on her own and works at a local bank. She is single and enjoys partying with her other single friends. She goes out two or three nights per week and often consumes a number of drinks when out. Although she goes out regularly, Jenelle does not plan for how she will get home. On numerous occasions, she has accepted a ride home from men she has just met who have also been drinking. Fortunately, she has not been in a car accident yet, though she recognizes, after the fact, that she has put herself in danger a number of times. Recently, Jenelle had a very frightening experience. After a night of partying and drinking, she accepted a ride home from a man she met that evening. Instead of taking her home, he began driving toward a remote end of the city. Jenelle did not realize this immediately, but when she did she became fearful about what this man might do to her. She began to cry and beg him to take her home. Luckily, he turned around and took her home, but Jenelle realized she had narrowly escaped a horrible situation. She realized that her judgment was grossly impaired by her drinking.

Moderate Drinking: Is There a Health Benefit?   According to the Canadian guidelines for low-risk drinking, weekly intake should not exceed 14 drinks for men and 9 for women, and daily consumption should not exceed 2 drinks for both women and men (Adlaf et al., 2005). Despite the above list of adverse effects associated with heavy drinking, growing evidence links light to moderate use of alcohol with reduced risk of heart attacks and lower death rates (PHAC, 2016). Researchers suspect that alcohol may help prevent blood clots from forming that can clog arteries and lead to heart attacks. Alcohol also appears to increase the levels of HDL cholesterol—the so-called good cholesterol—that sweeps away fatty deposits along artery walls (Ochs, 1998). Although light to moderate use of alcohol (about one drink per day) may have a protective effect on the heart, public health officials caution that promoting the possible health benefits of alcohol may backfire by increasing the risks of alcohol use disorder (PHAC, 2016).

BARBITURATES   Estimates indicate that almost 1% of the adult population meet the criteria for a substance use disorder involving the use of barbiturates, sleep medication (hypnotics), or anti-anxiety agents at some point in their lives (APA, 2013; Russell, Newman, & Bland, 1994). **Barbiturates** such as amobarbital, pentobarbital, phenobarbital, and secobarbital are depressants or **sedatives** with several medical uses, including alleviation of anxiety and tension, anaesthetization of pain, treatment of epilepsy and high blood pressure, and short-term treatment of insomnia. Barbiturate use quickly leads to psychological dependence and physiological dependence in the form of both tolerance and the development of a withdrawal syndrome.

In contrast to the profiles of young cocaine or narcotic abusers, most barbiturate addicts are middle-aged people who initially used sedatives to combat anxiety or insomnia and then got hooked. Because of concerns about abuse, physicians today prescribe other drugs for the temporary relief of anxiety and tension, such as minor tranquillizers like Valium and Librium. However, it is now recognized that minor tranquillizers can also create physiological dependence. Moreover, regular use of these drugs fails to help people alter the sources of stress in their lives.

Barbiturates are also popular street drugs because they are relaxing and produce a mild state of euphoria or "high." High doses of barbiturates, like alcohol, produce drowsiness, slurred speech, motor impairment, irritability, and poor judgment—a

barbiturates Types of depressant drugs that are sometimes used to relieve anxiety or induce sleep but that are highly addictive.

sedatives Types of depressant drugs that reduce states of tension and restlessness and induce sleep.

particularly deadly combination of effects when their use is combined with the operation of a motor vehicle. The effects of barbiturates last from three to six hours.

Because of synergistic effects, a mixture of barbiturates and alcohol is about four times as powerful as either drug used by itself (Aston & Cullumbine, 1959). A combination of barbiturates and alcohol was implicated in the deaths of the entertainers Marilyn Monroe and Judy Garland. Even such widely used anti-anxiety drugs as Valium and Librium, which have a wide margin of safety when used alone, can be dangerous and lead to overdose when their use is combined with alcohol (APA, 2013).

Physiologically dependent people need to be withdrawn from sedatives, barbiturates, and anti-anxiety agents carefully and only under medical supervision. Abrupt withdrawal can produce states of delirium that can be life-threatening (APA, 2013). Delirium may involve visual, tactile, or auditory hallucinations and disturbances in thinking processes and consciousness. The longer the period of use and the higher the doses used, the greater the risk of severe withdrawal effects. Grand mal epileptic seizures and even death may occur if the individual undergoes untreated, abrupt withdrawal.

OPIATES Opiates are narcotics, a term applied to addictive drugs that have pain-relieving and sleep-inducing properties. They are derived from the poppy plant and include such derivatives as morphine, heroin, and codeine. Synthetic opiates such as Demerol, Percodan, and fentanyl are manufactured in a laboratory to have effects similar to natural opiates. The major medical application of opiates—natural or synthetic—is the relief of pain; that is, analgesia. Opiates produce a rush or intense feelings of pleasure, which is the primary reason for their popularity as street drugs. They also dull awareness of one's personal problems, which is attractive to people seeking a mental escape from stress.

The medical use of opiates is carefully regulated because overdoses can lead to comas and even death, although prescription opiates are, unfortunately, readily available on the street—and through the Internet. Street use of these drugs is associated with many fatal overdoses and accidents. Estimates are that about 0.7% of the adult population (7 people in 1000) currently have or have had an opiate use disorder (APA, 2013; Russell et al., 1994). Once dependence sets in, it usually follows a chronic course, although periods of temporary abstinence are frequent (APA, 2013).

Opiates become drugs of abuse because they are capable of producing a euphoric state of pleasure or rush. They produce pleasurable effects because they stimulate brain centres that regulate sensations of pleasure and pain (Levinger, 2011). It appears that the brain has its own natural opiate system. Two revealing discoveries were made in the 1970s. One was that neurons in the brain have receptor sites into which opiates fit—like a key in a lock. The second was that the human body produces substances similar to opiates in chemical structures that dock at those same receptor sites (Goldstein, 1976). Some of these natural substances are labelled **endorphins**, which is short for *endogenous morphine*—that is, morphine coming from within. Endorphins appear to play a role in regulating states of pleasure and pain. Opiates mimic the actions of endorphins by docking at receptor sites intended for them, which in turn stimulates the brain centres that produce pleasurable sensations.

The opiate heroin is usually injected either directly beneath the skin ("skin popping") or into a vein ("mainlining"). You may be surprised to learn that heroin is not the most widely abused opiate. Studies from Canada and the United States indicate that prescription opiates, often illicitly obtained, such as oxycodone (OxyContin) and hydrocodone (Vicodin), are more widely abused than heroin (Kuehn, 2007).

The positive effects of opiates are immediate. In the case of heroin, there is a powerful rush that lasts for 5 to 15 minutes and a state of satisfaction, euphoria, and well-being that lasts for 3 to 5 hours. In this state, all positive drives seem satisfied. All negative feelings of guilt, tension, and anxiety disappear. With prolonged usage, addiction can develop. Many physiologically dependent people support their habits through dealing (selling heroin), prostitution, or selling stolen goods. Heroin is a depressant, however, and its chemical effects do not directly stimulate criminal or aggressive behaviour.

The withdrawal syndrome associated with dependence on opiates can be severe. It begins within four to six hours after the last dose. Flu-like symptoms are accompanied

opiates Types of depressant drugs with strong addictive properties that are derived from the opium poppy; provide feelings of euphoria and relief from pain.

narcotics Drugs, such as opiates, that are used for pain relief and treatment of insomnia, but which have strong addictive potential.

analgesia State of relief from pain without loss of consciousness.

endorphins Natural substances that function as neurotransmitters in the brain and are similar in their effects to morphine.

by anxiety, feelings of restlessness, irritability, and cravings for the drug. Within a few days, symptoms progress to rapid pulse, high blood pressure, cramps, tremors, hot and cold flashes, fever, vomiting, insomnia, and diarrhea, among other symptoms. Although these symptoms can be uncomfortable, they are usually not devastating, especially when other drugs are prescribed to relieve them. Moreover, unlike withdrawal from barbiturates, the withdrawal syndrome rarely results in death.

Stimulants

Stimulants such as amphetamines and cocaine are psychoactive substances that increase the activity of the nervous system. Effects vary somewhat from drug to drug, but some stimulants contribute to feelings of euphoria and self-confidence. Stimulants such as amphetamines, cocaine, and even caffeine (the stimulant found in coffee) increase the availability in the brain of the neurotransmitters norepinephrine and dopamine. High levels of these neurotransmitters, therefore, remain available in the synaptic gaps between neurons, which maintains high levels of nervous system activity and states of high arousal.

amphetamines Types of synthetic stimulants, such as Dexedrine and Benzedrine. Abuse can trigger an amphetamine psychosis that mimics acute episodes of schizophrenia.

AMPHETAMINES The **amphetamines** are a class of synthetic stimulants. Street names for stimulants include speed, uppers, bennies (for amphetamine sulphate; trade name Benzedrine), dexies (dextroamphetamine; trade name Dexedrine), and meth (for methamphetamine, a street drug).

Amphetamines are used in high doses for their euphoric rush. They are often taken in pill form or smoked in a relatively pure form called "ice" or "crystal meth." The most potent form of amphetamine, liquid methamphetamine, is injected directly into the veins and produces an intense and immediate rush. Some users inject methamphetamine for days on end to maintain an extended high. Eventually, such highs come to an end. People who have been on extended highs sometimes "crash" and fall into a deep sleep or depression, and may suffer from brain damage (Maxwell, 2005). Some people die by suicide on the way down. High doses can cause restlessness, irritability, hallucinations, paranoid delusions, loss of appetite, and insomnia.

Physiological dependence can develop, leading to an abstinence syndrome characterized most often by depression and fatigue as well as unpleasant, vivid dreams, insomnia or hypersomnia (excessive sleeping), increased appetite, and either a slowing down of motor behaviour or agitation (APA, 2013). Psychological dependence is seen most often in people who use amphetamines as a way of coping with stress or depression.

amphetamine psychosis Psychotic state induced by ingestion of amphetamines.

Violent behaviour may occur in the context of amphetamine dependence, especially when the drug is smoked or injected intravenously (APA, 2013). The hallucinations and delusions of the **amphetamine psychosis** mimic the features of schizophrenia, which has encouraged researchers to study the chemical changes induced by amphetamines as possible causes of schizophrenia.

cocaine Stimulant derived from coca leaves.

COCAINE It might surprise you to learn that the original formula for Coca-Cola contained an extract of **cocaine**. In 1906, however, the company withdrew cocaine from its secret formula. The beverage was originally described as a "brain tonic and intellectual beverage," in part because of its cocaine content. Cocaine is a natural stimulant extracted from the leaves of the coca plant—the plant from which the soft drink obtained its name. Coca-Cola is still flavoured with an extract from the coca plant, but one that is not known to be psychoactive.

It was long believed that cocaine was not physically addicting. However, evidence supports the addictive properties of the drug in producing a tolerance effect and an identifiable withdrawal syndrome, consisting of depression, inability to experience pleasure, and intense cravings for the drug (APA, 2013). Withdrawal symptoms are usually brief in duration and may involve a "crash" or period of intense depression and exhaustion following a cocaine binge.

crack Hardened, smokable form of cocaine.

Cocaine is brewed from coca leaves as a "tea," breathed in ("snorted") in powder form, or injected ("shot up") in liquid form. The rise in the use of **crack**, a hardened form of cocaine suitable for smoking that may contain more than 75% pure cocaine, has made cocaine—once the toy of the well-to-do—available to adolescents. Crack "rocks"—so called because they look like small white pebbles—are available in small ready-to-smoke amounts and are considered the most habit-forming street drug available. Crack produces a prompt and potent rush that wears off in a few minutes. The rush from snorting cocaine is milder and takes a while to develop, but it tends to linger longer than the rush of crack.

Freebasing also intensifies the effects of cocaine. Cocaine in powder form is heated with ether, freeing the psychoactive chemical base of the drug, and then smoked. Ether, however, is highly flammable.

Cocaine is most commonly used by young adults, although even in Canada it is not widely used—a 2012 survey found that 5.5% of young adults had tried cocaine (Health Canada, 2014). Approximately 1% of Canadians reported using cocaine in the previous 12 months (Health Canada, 2014).

Cocaine abuse is characterized by periodic binges lasting perhaps 12 to 36 hours, which are then followed by 2 to 5 days of abstinence, during which time the abuser may experience cravings that prompt another binge. An individual can develop a cocaine use disorder in as little as one week (APA, 2013). According to one estimate, between 10% and 15% of people who try snorting cocaine eventually develop cocaine abuse or dependence (Gawin, 1991).

Cocaine increases the availability in the brain of the neurotransmitter dopamine, producing a pleasurable "high" (Berridge & Kringelbach, 2015; Volkow et al., 1997). The drug produces a sudden rise in blood pressure, constricts blood vessels (with associated reduction of the oxygen supply to the heart), and accelerates the heart rate. Overdoses can produce restlessness, insomnia, headaches, nausea, convulsions, tremors, hallucinations, delusions, and even sudden death. Death may result from respiratory or cardiovascular collapse. Although intravenous use of cocaine carries the greatest risk of a lethal overdose, other forms of use can also be fatal. Table 7.3 summarizes a number of the health risks of cocaine use.

Exposure to cocaine in utero can also affect the cognitive abilities of infants, as revealed in a study by Susan Potter from McGill University and colleagues (Potter, Zelazo, Stack, & Papageorgiou, 2000). Infants exposed to cocaine showed impaired auditory information processing, which may lead to subsequent language deficits. Repeated and high dose use of cocaine can lead to depression and anxiety (Weiss et al., 1994). Depression may be severe enough to prompt suicidal behaviour. Both initial and routine users report episodes of "crashing" (feelings of depression after a binge), although crashing is more common among long-term high-dose users. Psychotic behaviours, which can be induced by cocaine use as well as by use of amphetamines, tend to become more severe with continued use. Cocaine psychosis is usually preceded by a period of heightened suspiciousness, depressed mood, compulsive behaviour, fault finding, irritability, and increasing paranoia (APA, 2013). Psychosis may also include visual and auditory hallucinations and delusions of persecution.

NICOTINE Habitual smoking is not just a bad habit. It is also a form of physical addiction to a stimulant drug, nicotine, found in tobacco products including cigarettes, cigars, and smokeless tobacco. Smoking (or other tobacco use) is the means of administering the drug to the body.

More than 30 000 lives in Canada are lost each year from smoking-related causes, mostly from lung cancer, cardiovascular disease, and chronic obstructive lung disease (CCSA & CAMH, 1999). Smoking is implicated in one in three cancer deaths (American Cancer Society, 2003). Smokers overall stand twice the risk of dying from cancer as nonsmokers; among heavy smokers, the risk is four times as great (Bartecchi, MacKenzie, & Schrier, 1994; Peto, Lopez, Boreham, & Thun, 2006).

freebasing Method of ingesting cocaine by means of heating the drug with ether to separate its most potent component (its "free base") and then smoking the extract.

Pixabay.com

E-cigarette. The popularity of e-cigarettes is increasing among youth despite concerns they may encourage smoking.

TABLE 7.3

Health Risks of Cocaine Use

Physical Effects and Risks

Effects	Risks
Increased heart rate	Accelerated heart rate may give rise to heart irregularities that can be fatal, such as ventricular tachycardia (extremely rapid contractions) or ventricular fibrillation (irregular, weakened contractions).
Increased blood pressure	Rapid or large changes in blood pressure may place too much stress on a weak-walled blood vessel in the brain, which can cause it to burst, producing cerebral hemorrhage or stroke.
Increased body temperature	Can be dangerous to some individuals.
Possible grand mal seizures (epileptic convulsions)	Some grand mal seizures are fatal, particularly when they occur in rapid succession or while driving a car.
Respiratory effects	Overdoses can produce gasping or shallow, irregular breathing that can lead to respiratory arrest.
Dangerous effects in special populations	Various special populations are at greater risk from cocaine use or overdose. People with coronary heart disease have died because their heart muscles were taxed beyond the capacity of their arteries to supply oxygen.

Medical Complications of Cocaine Use

Nasal problems	When cocaine is administered intranasally (snorted), it constricts the blood vessels serving the nose, decreasing the supply of oxygen to these tissues, leading to irritation and inflammation of the mucous membranes, ulcers in the nostrils, frequent nosebleeds, and chronic sneezing and nasal congestion. Chronic use may lead to tissue death of the nasal septum, the part of the nose that separates the nostrils, requiring plastic surgery.
Lung problems	Freebase smoking may lead to serious lung problems within three months of initial use.
Malnutrition	Cocaine suppresses the appetite so that weight loss, malnutrition, and vitamin deficiencies may accompany regular use.
Seizures	Grand mal seizures, typical of epileptics, may occur due to irregularities in the electrical activity of the brain. Repeated use may lower the seizure threshold, described as a type of "kindling" effect.
Sexual problems	Despite the popular belief that cocaine is an aphrodisiac, frequent use can lead to sexual dysfunctions, such as impotence and failure to ejaculate among males, and decreased sexual interest in both sexes. Although some people report initial increased sexual pleasure with cocaine use, they may become dependent on cocaine for sexual arousal or lose the ability to enjoy sex for extended periods following long-term use.
Other effects	Cocaine use may increase the risk of miscarriage among pregnant women. Sharing of infected needles is associated with transmission of hepatitis, endocarditis (infection of the heart valve), and HIV. Repeated injections often lead to skin infections as bacteria are introduced into the deeper levels of the skin.

Source: Based on Weiss & Mirin, Cocaine (2nd ed.). Washington, DC: American Psychiatric Press. 1994.

The World Health Organization estimates that a billion people worldwide smoke, and more than 3 million die each year from smoking-related causes. Smoking is expected to become the world's leading cause of death by the year 2020 ("Smoking," 1996).

Largely because of health concerns, the percentage of Canadians who smoke declined from 61% of men and 38% of women in 1965 to 18.1% overall in 2014 (Statistics Canada, 2016c). Teenage smoking has not decreased as dramatically. Young adults aged 20 to 34 still have the highest smoking rate of any age group, at 29.6% for men and 19.4% for women (Statistics Canada, 2016c). The younger that people start to smoke, the more difficulty they have in quitting (Health Canada, 2001). The use of e-cigarettes among high school students has now surpassed tobacco cigarettes. Among students in Grades 7 to 12, 9% reported using regular cigarettes in the past 12 months as compared to 12% who used e-cigarettes (Boak, Hamilton, Adlaf, & Mann, 2015). Although e-cigarettes were initially marketed as an aid to quit smoking, studies have shown that they have not served this purpose and may in fact encourage smoking (Beal, 2016; Dutra & Glantz, 2014).

Cigarette smoking causes cancer of the larynx, oral cavity, esophagus, and lungs and may contribute to cancer of the bladder, pancreas, and kidneys. Pregnant women who smoke risk miscarriage, premature birth, and birth defects in their offspring. Smokers have twice the risk of developing Alzheimer's disease and other forms of dementia as nonsmokers ("Extinguishing Alzheimer's," 1998). Lung cancer, which in 90% of cases is caused by smoking, has now surpassed breast cancer as the leading killer of women. Approximately 50% of long-term smokers will die from a tobacco-related illness (APA, 2013). Although quitting smoking clearly has health benefits, it unfortunately does not reduce the risks to normal (nonsmoking) levels. The lesson is clear: If you don't smoke, don't start. But if you do smoke, quit.

Indigenous peoples have the highest rates of smoking (42.7%) compared to other ethnic groups in Canada (see Figure 7.2). Smoking is also more pronounced among the poorer and less well-educated segments of the population (Corsi et al., 2012).

Nicotine is delivered to the body through the use of tobacco products. As a stimulant, it increases alertness but can also give rise to cold, clammy skin, nausea and vomiting, dizziness and faintness, and diarrhea—all of which account for the discomforts of novice smokers. Nicotine also stimulates the release of epinephrine, a hormone that generates a rush of autonomic activity, including rapid heartbeat and release of stores of sugar into the blood. Nicotine quells the appetite and provides a sort of psychological "kick" (Grunberg, 1991). Nicotine also leads to the release of endorphins, opiate-like hormones produced in the brain. This may account for the pleasurable feelings associated with tobacco use.

Habitual use of nicotine leads to a physiological dependence on the drug (APA, 2013). Nicotine dependence is associated with both tolerance (intake rises to a level of a pack or two a day before levelling off) and a characteristic withdrawal syndrome. The withdrawal syndrome for nicotine includes such features as lack of energy, depressed mood,

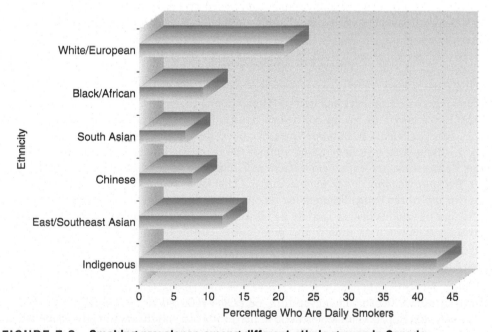

FIGURE 7.2 Smoking prevalence among different ethnic groups in Canada.

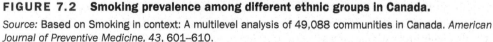

Source: Based on Smoking in context: A multilevel analysis of 49,088 communities in Canada. *American Journal of Preventive Medicine, 43,* 601–610.

irritability, frustration, nervousness, impaired concentration, light-headedness and dizziness, drowsiness, headaches, fatigue, irregular bowels, insomnia, cramps, lowered heart rate, heart palpitations, increased appetite, weight gain, sweating, tremors, and craving for cigarettes (APA, 2013; Klesges et al., 1997). It is tobacco use disorder, not cigarette smoking per se, that is classifiable as a psychological disorder in the DSM system.

Hallucinogens

hallucinogens Substances that give rise to sensory distortions or hallucinations.

psychedelics Class of drugs that induce sensory distortions or hallucinations. Also called *hallucinogens*.

Hallucinogens, also known as **psychedelics**, are a class of drugs that produce sensory distortions or hallucinations. Hallucinations involve major alterations in colour perception and hearing. Hallucinogens may also have additional effects, such as relaxation and euphoria or, in some cases, panic. The hallucinogens include such drugs as lysergic acid diethylamide (LSD), psilocybin, and mescaline. Psychoactive substances that are similar in effect to psychedelic drugs are marijuana (cannabis) and phencyclidine (PCP). Mescaline is derived from the peyote cactus and has been used for centuries by Native Americans in the southwest United States, Mexico, and Central America in religious ceremonies, as has psilocybin, which is derived from certain mushrooms. LSD, PCP, and marijuana are more commonly used in North America.

Although tolerance to hallucinogens may develop, we lack evidence of a consistent or characteristic withdrawal syndrome associated with their use (APA, 2013). Cravings following withdrawal may occur, however. One exception is cannabis, for which DSM-5 has identified diagnostic criteria for withdrawal.

LSD A powerful hallucinogenic drug. LSD is the acronym for *lysergic acid diethylamide*.

LSD   LSD is the acronym for *lysergic acid diethylamide*, a synthetic hallucinogenic drug. In addition to the vivid parade of colours and visual distortions produced by LSD, users have claimed that it "expands consciousness" and opens new worlds—as if they were looking into some reality beyond the usual reality. Sometimes they believe they have achieved great insights during an LSD "trip," but when it wears off they usually cannot follow through on or even summon up these discoveries.

LSD apparently decreases the action of serotonin, a neurotransmitter that inhibits neural firing. It may also increase utilization of dopamine. Because LSD curbs the action of an inhibiting neurotransmitter and increases dopamine activity, brain activity escalates, in this case giving rise to a flurry of colourful sensations or hallucinations.

The effects of LSD are unpredictable and depend on the amount taken as well as the user's expectations, personality, mood, and surroundings (US Department of Health and Human Services, 1992). The user's prior experiences with the drug may also play a role, as users who have learned to handle the effects of the drug through past experience may be better prepared than new users.

flashbacks (1) Vivid re-experiencings of a past event, which may be difficult to distinguish from current reality. (2) Experiences of sensory distortions or hallucinations occurring days or weeks after use of LSD or another hallucinogenic drug that mimic the drug's effects.

Some users have unpleasant experiences or "bad trips" with the drug. Feelings of intense fear or panic may occur (US Department of Health and Human Services, 1992). Users may fear losing control or sanity. Some experience terrifying fears of death. Fatal accidents have sometimes occurred during LSD trips. **Flashbacks**, typically involving a re-experiencing of some of the perceptual distortions of the trip, may occur days, weeks, or even years afterward. Flashbacks tend to occur suddenly and often without warning. They may stem from chemical changes in the brain caused by the prior use of the drug. Triggers for flashbacks include entry into darkened environments, use of various drugs, anxiety or fatigue states, and stress (APA, 2000). Psychological factors, such as underlying personality problems, may also be involved in explaining why some users experience flashbacks. In some cases, a flashback may involve an imagined re-enactment of the LSD experience (Baggott, Coyle, Erowid & Robertson, 2011).

PHENCYCLIDINE (PCP)   Phencyclidine, or PCP—referred to as "angel dust" on the street—was developed as an anaesthetic in the 1950s but was discontinued as such when its hallucinatory side effects were discovered. A smokable form of PCP became popular as a street drug in the 1970s because it was readily manufactured and relatively inexpensive. By the mid-1980s, more than one in five young people in the 18- to 25-year-old age range had used PCP (US Department of Health and Human Services, 1986). However, its popularity has since waned, largely because of its unpredictable effects.

The effects of PCP, like most drugs, are dose related. In addition to causing hallucinations, PCP accelerates the heart rate and blood pressure and causes sweating, flushing, and numbness. PCP is classified as a deliriant—a drug capable of producing states of delirium. It also has dissociating effects, causing users to feel as if there is some sort of invisible barrier or wall between themselves and their environments. Dissociation can be experienced as pleasant, engrossing, or frightening, depending on the user's expectations, mood, setting, and so on. Overdoses can give rise to drowsiness and a blank stare, convulsions, and, now and then, coma; paranoia and aggressive behaviour; and tragic accidents resulting from perceptual distortion or impaired judgment during states of intoxication.

MARIJUANA   **Marijuana** is produced from the *Cannabis sativa* plant. Marijuana sometimes produces mild hallucinations, so it is regarded as a minor hallucinogen. The psychoactive substance in marijuana is **delta-9-tetrahydrocannabinol**, or THC, which is found in the plant's branches and leaves but is highly concentrated in the resin of the female plant. **Hashish**, or "hash," is also derived from the resin. Although it is more potent than marijuana, hashish has similar effects.

Marijuana dependence is the most common form of dependence on illicit drugs in North America, affecting an estimated 5–6% of the adult population at some point in their lives (APA, 2013). Males are more likely than females to develop a marijuana use disorder, and the rates of these disorders are greatest among young people aged 18 to 30 (APA, 2013). One third of Canadian young adults between the age of 18 and 24 reported using marijuana in the past 12 months (41.1% of males and 25.2% of females). The second-highest prevalence rates are among youth between the ages of 15 and 17 at 20% (Rotermann & Langlois, 2015).

Low doses of the drug can produce relaxing feelings similar to drinking a highball of liquor. Some users report that at low doses the drug makes them feel more comfortable in social gatherings. Higher doses, however, often lead users to withdraw into themselves. Some users believe the drug increases their capacity for self-insight or creative thinking, although the insights or thoughts achieved under its influence may not seem so insightful or creative once the drug's effects have passed. People may turn to marijuana, as to other drugs, to help them cope with life problems or to help them function when

marijuana A mild or minor hallucinogen derived from the *Cannabis sativa* plant.

delta-9-tetrahydrocannabinol Major active ingredient in marijuana. Abbreviated *THC*.

hashish Drug derived from the resin of the marijuana plant, *Cannabis sativa*.

Shutterstock

Marijuana. The proportion of marijuana users in Canada is much higher among young adults than in the population as a whole.

they are under stress. Strongly intoxicated people perceive time as passing more slowly; a song of a few minutes may seem to last an hour. There is increased awareness of bodily sensations, such as heartbeat. Smokers also report that strong intoxication heightens sexual sensations. Visual hallucinations may occur.

Strong intoxication can cause smokers to become disoriented. If their moods are euphoric, disorientation may be construed as harmony with the universe. Yet some smokers find strong intoxication disturbing. An accelerated heart rate and sharpened awareness of bodily sensations cause some smokers to fear their hearts will "run away" from them. Marijuana elevates the heart rate to about 140 to 150 beats per minute and, in some people, raises blood pressure. These changes may be especially dangerous to people with heart conditions or hypertension. Finally, marijuana smoke contains carcinogenic hydrocarbons, so chronic users risk lung cancer and other respiratory diseases.

Marijuana use disorder is associated more with patterns of compulsive use or psychological dependence than with physiological dependence. Although tolerance to many of the drug's effects may occur with chronic use, some users report reverse tolerance or sensitization. A withdrawal syndrome has been identified in DSM-5. Symptoms of cannabis withdrawal include mood, anxiety, sleep, and appetite disturbances. Allsop and colleagues studied the withdrawal symptoms experienced in a nonclinical population of individuals who smoked marijuana at least five days a week for over three months. Most individuals reported mild symptoms, similar to tobacco withdrawal. The symptoms that interfered most with everyday functioning included sleep problems, anger, irritability, loss of appetite, and nightmares (Allsop et al., 2012). Some withdrawal symptoms may last for weeks or even months (Mason et al., 2012).

Marijuana use has also been shown to impair cognitive abilities and increase experiences of paranoia as well as psychotic symptoms (Freeman et al., 2015; Turnbridge et al., 2015). University students who are heavy users of marijuana show evidence of cognitive impairment, including diminished ability in tasks requiring attention, abstraction, mental flexibility, and working memory (Freeman et al., 2015; Pope & Yurgelun-Todd, 1996). Shrivastava, from Western University, and colleagues reviewed the research examining the link between cannabis abuse and schizophrenia. Although some findings appear to support a causal link, the neurobiological evidence at this time is weak (Shrivastava, Johnston, Terpstra, & Bureau, 2015).

The use of marijuana has been shown to precede the use of harder drugs such as heroin and cocaine (Kandel, 2003). Whether marijuana use is a causal factor leading to use of harder drugs remains unclear. We do know that marijuana impairs perception and motor coordination and thus makes driving and the operation of other machines dangerous. Asbridge and colleagues from Dalhousie University reported that drivers who use marijuana within three hours of driving are nearly twice as likely to cause a crash as those who were unimpaired by drug use (Asbridge, Hayden, & Cartwright, 2012).

Inhalants

inhalants Substances that produce chemical vapours that are inhaled for their psychoactive effect.

Inhalants are substances that produce chemical vapours that are inhaled for its psychoactive effect. Many different kinds of substances fall into the category of inhalants. Substances commonly used in inhalant abuse include adhesives, aerosols, anaesthetics, benzene, carbon dioxide, cleaning fluids, correction fluid, deodorants and deodorizers, disinfectants, ether, fingernail polish, refrigeration and air conditioner coolant, lighter fluid, fuels, whiteboard markers, paint and paint removers, styrene, toluene, and transmission fluid. In cases of inhalant abuse, these substances are typically used by soaking a cloth with the substance and then either holding the cloth near the face to inhale fumes or putting the cloth in a bag and inhaling from the bag. An alternative is to pour the substance into a bag or balloon and then inhale the fumes. Inhalants can induce feelings of intoxication and euphoria. The reinforcing effects of inhalants occur mainly through their effects on GABA and dopamine neurotransmitter systems. Inhalant abuse is a serious and dangerous problem—it is associated with impairments in learning and memory. The use of inhalants, even on a single occasion, increases the risk of serious medical illness and even death (Ridenour, 2005).

Drugs of Abuse

- **What are depressants?** Depressants are drugs that depress or slow nervous system activity. They include alcohol, sedatives and minor tranquillizers, and opiates. Their effects include intoxication, impaired coordination, slurred speech, and impaired intellectual functioning. Chronic alcohol abuse is linked to alcohol-induced persisting amnestic disorder (Korsakoff's syndrome), cirrhosis of the liver, fetal alcohol syndrome, and other physical health problems. Barbiturates are depressants or sedatives that have been used medically for relief of anxiety and short-term insomnia, among other uses. Opiates such as morphine and heroin are derived from the opium poppy. Others are synthesized. Used medically for relief of pain, they are strongly addictive.
- **What are stimulants?** Stimulants increase the activity of the nervous system. Amphetamines and cocaine are stimulants that increase the availability of neurotransmitters in the brain, leading to heightened states of arousal and pleasurable feelings. High doses can produce psychotic reactions that mimic features of schizophrenia. Habitual cocaine use can lead to a variety of health problems, and an overdose can cause sudden death. Repeated use of nicotine, a mild stimulant found in cigarettes, leads to physiological dependence.
- **What are hallucinogens?** Hallucinogens are drugs that distort sensory perceptions and can induce hallucinations. They include lysergic acid diethylamide (LSD), psilocybin, and mescaline. Other drugs with similar effects are cannabis (marijuana) and phencyclidine (PCP). There is little evidence that these drugs induce physiological dependence, although psychological dependence may occur.

THEORETICAL PERSPECTIVES

People begin using psychoactive substances for various reasons. Some adolescents start using drugs because of peer pressure or because they believe drugs make them seem more sophisticated or grown up. Some use drugs as a way of rebelling against their parents or society at large. Regardless of why people get started with drugs, they continue to use them because of their pleasurable effects or because they find it difficult to stop. Most adolescents drink alcohol to "get high," not to establish that they are adults. Many people smoke cigarettes for the pleasure they provide. Others smoke to help them relax when they are tense and, paradoxically, to give them a kick or a lift when they are tired. Many would like to quit but find it difficult to break their addiction.

People who are anxious about their jobs or social lives may be drawn to the calming effects of alcohol, marijuana (in certain doses), tranquillizers, and sedatives. People with low self-confidence and self-esteem may be drawn to the ego-boosting effects of amphetamines and cocaine. Many poor young people attempt to escape the poverty, anguish, and tedium of inner-city life through using heroin and similar drugs. More well-to-do adolescents may rely on drugs to manage the transition from dependence on their parents to independence and major life changes concerning jobs, university, and lifestyles. In the next sections, we consider several major theoretical perspectives on substance use disorders.

Biological Perspectives

We are beginning to learn more about the biological underpinnings of addiction. Much of the recent research has focused on neurotransmitters, especially dopamine, and on the role of genetic factors.

NEUROTRANSMITTERS A common pathway in the brain involving the neurotransmitter dopamine may explain the pleasure-inducing effects of many drugs. Researchers suspect that drugs such as nicotine, alcohol, heroin, cocaine, and even marijuana produce pleasurable effects by increasing the levels of the neurotransmitter dopamine—the brain's "reward and reinforcing" agent (Chang & Haning, 2006).

We know that laboratory rats will work for injections of cocaine by repetitively pressing a lever. They will continue to work for cocaine injections even if the neural pathways that use norepinephrine are destroyed. Their work effort plummets when the neural pathways for dopamine are destroyed (Weiss et al., 1994). With repeated drug use over time, the brain's ability to make dopamine on its own can diminish, leading to cravings for drugs that will provide a steady supply of dopamine (Dubovsky, 2006; Martinez et al., 2009). This may explain the intense cravings and anxiety that accompany drug withdrawal and the difficulty people with chemical dependencies have maintaining abstinence.

Other neurotransmitters are also believed to be involved in drug use and abuse (Addolorato, Leggio, Abenavoli, & Gasbarrini, 2005; Buchert et al., 2004). Evidence points to the neurotransmitter serotonin playing a role in activating the brain's pleasure or reward circuits in response to the use of cocaine and other drugs. We also know that a group of neurotransmitters called *endorphins* have pain-blocking properties similar to opiates such as heroin. Endorphins and opiates dock at the same receptor sites in the brain. Normally, the brain produces a certain level of endorphins that maintains a sort of psychological steady state of comfort and potential to experience pleasure. However, when the body becomes habituated to a supply of opiates, it may stop producing endorphins. This makes the user dependent on opiates for feelings of comfort, relief from pain, and feelings of pleasure. When the habitual user stops using heroin or other opiates, feelings of discomfort and little aches and pains may be magnified until the body resumes adequate production of endorphins. This discomfort might account, at least in part, for the unpleasant withdrawal symptoms experienced by opiate addicts when they attempt to quit using. However, this model remains speculative, and more research is needed to document direct relationships between endorphin production and withdrawal symptoms.

GENETIC FACTORS Increasing evidence points to genetic factors in substance use disorders. We know that alcoholism runs in families. People with a family history of alcoholism are about three or four times more likely to develop problems of alcohol abuse or dependence than others (APA, 2000; Urbanoski & Kelly, 2012). The closer the genetic relationship, the greater the risk. Familial patterns provide only suggestive evidence of genetic factors because families share common environments as well as common genes. More definitive evidence comes from twin and adoptee studies.

Monozygotic (MZ) twins have identical genes, whereas fraternal or dizygotic (DZ) twins share only half of their genes. If genetic factors are involved, we would expect MZ twins to have higher concordance (agreement) rates for alcoholism than DZ twins. The evidence for higher concordance rates for alcoholism among MZ twins than DZ twins is stronger for male twin pairs than female twin pairs, which indicates that genetic factors may be more strongly involved in alcoholism in males than females (Jang, Livesley, & Vernon, 1997; Kendler & Prescott, 2006). To illustrate, research conducted at the University of British Columbia found that alcohol and drug problems were due to a combination of environmental and genetic factors in men but were entirely due to environmental factors in women (Jang et al., 1997). Future research may help clarify these apparent gender differences.

Other evidence points to a genetic contribution in other forms of substance abuse, including opiate, marijuana, cocaine, and nicotine dependence (Ducci et al., 2011; Frahm et al., 2011; Hartz et al., 2012; Kendler & Prescott, 2006; Kendler et al., 2012; Ray, 2012). An emerging body of research suggests the importance of gene–environment interactions in the development of substance use disorders, where people with a particular genetic makeup are most likely to develop substance use disorders when exposed to substances such as alcohol, cocaine, or nicotine under particular environmental conditions (e.g., highly stressful conditions) (Caspi & Moffitt, 2006).

If alcoholism or other forms of substance use disorders are influenced by genetic factors, what is it that is inherited? Some clues have begun to emerge (e.g., Corbett et al., 2005; Radel et al., 2005). Researchers have linked alcoholism, tobacco use disorder, and opiate addiction to genes involved in determining the structure of dopamine receptors in the brain (Kotler et al., 1997). We've mentioned that dopamine is involved in regulating states of pleasure, which leads researchers to suspect that genetic factors enhance feelings of pleasure derived from alcohol, which in turn may increase cravings for the drug. In all likelihood there is not one "alcoholism gene" but a set of genes that interact with each other and with environmental factors to increase the risk of alcoholism (Kendler & Prescott, 2006).

Evidence also suggests that a genetic vulnerability to alcoholism may involve a combination of at least two factors (Sher et al., 2005). First, genetic factors influence the ability to rapidly metabolize alcohol. (Some people, such as many people from Asian backgrounds, are genetically predisposed to have difficulty metabolizing alcohol, thereby leading to flushing and nausea when they drink.) People who metabolize alcohol relatively quickly can tolerate larger doses and are less likely to develop upset stomachs, dizziness, and headaches when they drink. Unfortunately, a lower sensitivity to the unpleasant effects of alcohol may make it difficult to know when to say "when." Thus, people who are better able to "hold their liquor" may be at greater risk of developing drinking problems. They may need to rely on other cues, such as counting their drinks, to learn to limit their drinking. People whose bodies more readily "put the brakes" on excess drinking may be less likely to develop problems in moderating their drinking than those with better tolerance. Second, genetic factors influence the degree of reinforcement (enjoyment) obtained from consuming alcohol (Sher et al., 2005).

Despite the role of genetic factors in alcoholism, environmental factors are also important. For example, there is evidence that some types of family experiences, such as drinking at home and particular types of parenting, promote the development of alcohol problems, especially in genetically vulnerable individuals (Sher et al., 2005).

Learning Perspectives

Learning theorists propose that substance-related behaviours are largely learned and can, in principle, be unlearned. They focus on the roles of operant and classical conditioning and observational learning. Substance use problems are regarded not as symptoms of diseases but rather as problem habits. Although learning theorists do not deny that genetic or biological factors may be involved in the genesis of substance use problems, they place a greater emphasis on the role of learning in the development and maintenance of these problem behaviours.

Drug use may become habitual because of the pleasure or positive reinforcement that drugs produce. In the case of drugs like cocaine, which appear capable of directly stimulating pleasure mechanisms in the brain, the reinforcement is direct and powerful.

OPERANT CONDITIONING In animal studies, injection of psychoactive drugs like cocaine has been made contingent on the performance of various tasks, such as pressing a lever (Weiss et al., 1994). Laboratory animals will learn to press a lever repeatedly for cocaine. Researchers can estimate the reinforcing power of drugs by comparing the rates at which animals perform operant responses such as pressing a lever to receive them. Animals will perform to receive a wide range of drugs, including amphetamines, nicotine, barbiturates, opiates, alcohol, and PCP. Performance rates are most dramatic for cocaine, however. Rhesus monkeys will work continuously for cocaine until they die (Weiss et al., 1994).

People may initially use a drug because of social influence, trial and error, or social observation. In the case of alcohol, they learn that the drug can produce reinforcing effects, such as feelings of euphoria and reductions in states of anxiety and tension. Alcohol may also release behavioural inhibitions. Alcohol can thus be reinforcing when it is used to combat depression (by producing euphoric feelings, even if short-lived), to combat tension (by functioning as a tranquillizer), or to help people sidestep moral conflicts (e.g., by dulling awareness of moral prohibitions against sexual behaviour or aggression). Social reinforcers are also made available by substance use, such as the approval of drug-abusing companions and, in the cases of depressants and stimulants, the (temporary) overcoming of social shyness.

ALCOHOL AND TENSION REDUCTION Learning theorists have long maintained that one of the primary reinforcers for using alcohol is relief from states of tension. The tension-reduction theory proposes that the more often one drinks to reduce tension or anxiety, the stronger or more habitual the habit becomes. Viewed in this way, alcohol use can be likened to a form of self-medication—a way of easing psychological pain, at least temporarily (Robinson, Sareen, Cox, & Bolton, 2009).

Laboratory studies have provided inconsistent support for the tension-reduction theory (Pihl & Smith, 1983), although the stressors induced in those studies tended to be mild (for ethical reasons). The occurrence of more severe stressful events, such as physical or sexual assault, is associated with an increased risk of alcohol abuse (Stewart, 1996). These effects are more pronounced among individuals who have a tendency to behave impulsively in stressful situations (Menary et al., 2015). Thus, there is some support for the tension-reduction theory, although many other factors aside from tension reduction appear to play a role in alcohol use and abuse.

Drugs, including nicotine from cigarette smoking, may also be used as a form of self-medication for depression (Breslau, Peterson, Schultz, Chilcoat, & Andreski, 1998). Stimulants such as nicotine temporarily elevate the mood, whereas depressants such as alcohol quell anxiety. Although nicotine, alcohol, and other drugs may temporarily alleviate emotional distress, they cannot resolve underlying personal or emotional problems. Rather than learning to resolve these problems, people who use drugs as forms of self-medication often find themselves facing additional substance-related problems.

NEGATIVE REINFORCEMENT AND WITHDRAWAL Once people become physiologically dependent, negative reinforcement comes into play in maintaining a drug habit. In other words, people may resume using drugs to gain relief from unpleasant withdrawal symptoms. In operant conditioning terms, the resumption of drug use is negatively reinforced by relief from unpleasant withdrawal symptoms that occur following cessation of drug use. For example, the addicted smoker who quits cold turkey may shortly return to smoking to fend off the discomfort of withdrawal. Smokers who are able to quit and maintain abstinence are occasionally bothered by urges to smoke but have learned to manage them.

THE CONDITIONING MODEL OF CRAVINGS Principles of classical conditioning may help explain the cravings for drugs experienced by people with drug dependencies. Repeated exposure to cues associated with drug use (such as the sight or aroma of an alcoholic beverage or the sight of a needle and syringe) may elicit conditioned responses in the form of alcohol or drug cravings (Kilts, Gross, Ely, & Drexler, 2004; Potenza et al., 2012). Although drug cravings may have a biological basis involving a bodily need to restore levels of the addictive substance, they may also become conditioned responses triggered by a wide range of cues (conditioned stimuli) that were previously associated with use of the substance. For example, socializing with certain companions (drinking buddies) or even passing a liquor store may elicit conditioned cravings for alcohol. Sensations of anxiety or depression that were paired with use of alcohol or drugs may also elicit cravings.

Similarly, some people are primarily "stimulus smokers." They reach for a cigarette in the presence of smoking-related stimuli such as seeing someone smoke or smelling smoke. Smoking becomes a strongly conditioned habit because it is paired repeatedly with many situational cues—watching television, finishing dinner, driving in the car, studying, drinking or socializing with friends, sex, and, for some, using the bathroom. Environmental stimuli associated with substance use (e.g., being in a bar or seeing someone smoke) can influence tolerance, elicit withdrawal symptoms, and trigger relapse of substance use (Siegel, 2005). The conditioning model of craving is strengthened by research showing that people with alcoholism tend to salivate more than others to the sight and smell of alcohol (Monti et al., 1994). In Pavlov's classic experiment, a salivation response was conditioned in dogs by repeatedly pairing the sound of a bell (a neutral or conditioned stimulus) with the presentation of food powder (an unconditioned stimulus). Salivation among people who develop alcoholism can also be viewed as a conditioned response to alcohol-related cues. Whereas salivating to a bell may be harmless, salivating at a bottle of scotch or at a picture of a bottle in a magazine ad can throw the person who suffers from alcoholism and is trying to remain abstinent into a tailspin. People with drinking problems who show the greatest salivary response to alcohol cues may be at the highest risk of relapse. They may also profit from treatments designed to extinguish their responses to alcohol-related cues.

OBSERVATIONAL LEARNING Modelling or observational learning plays an important role in determining risk of drug-related problems. Parents who model inappropriate or excessive drinking or use of illicit drugs may set the stage for maladaptive drug use in their children (Kirisci, Vanyukov, & Tarter, 2005). Evidence shows that adolescents who have a parent who smokes face a substantially higher risk of smoking than do their peers in families where neither parent smokes (Peterson et al., 2006). Other investigators find that having friends who smoke influences adolescents to begin smoking (Bricker et al., 2006).

Cognitive Perspectives

Evidence supports the role of various cognitive factors in substance abuse and dependence, including expectancies, attitudes, beliefs, decision-making processes, and self-awareness.

OUTCOME EXPECTANCIES, DECISION MAKING, AND SUBSTANCE ABUSE The beliefs and expectancies you hold concerning the effects of alcohol and other drugs clearly influence your decision to use them or not. People who hold positive expectancies about the effects of a drug not only are more likely to use the drug (Doran, Schweizer, & Meyers, 2011; Schmits, Mathys, & Quertemont, 2016) but are also more likely to use larger quantities of it (Baldwin, Oei, & Young, 1994). One of the key factors in predicting problem alcohol use in adolescents is the degree to which their friends hold positive attitudes toward alcohol use (Scheier, Botvin, & Baker, 1997). Similarly, students in Grades 5 and 7 who hold more positive impressions of smokers (e.g., seeing them as cool, independent, or good looking) were more likely than their peers to become smokers by the time they reached Grade 9 (Dinh, Sarason, Peterson, & Onstad, 1995). Positive expectancies have also been shown to influence the use of e-cigarettes (Harrell et al., 2015). Smoking prevention programs may need to focus on changing the image that young people hold of smokers long before they ever light up a cigarette themselves. Positive alcohol expectancies also appear in children even before drinking begins.

Among the most widely held positive expectancies concerning alcohol is that it reduces tension, helps divert attention from one's problems, heightens pleasure, lessens anxiety in social situations, and makes one more socially adept (MacLatchy-Gaudet & Stewart, 2001). In one study, alcohol expectancies were stronger predictors of the likelihood of drinking among adolescents than family drinking history (Christiansen & Goldman, 1983). The belief that alcohol helps make a person more socially adept (more relaxed, outgoing, assertive, and carefree in social interactions) appears to be an especially important factor in prompting drinking in adolescents and university students (Burke & Stephens, 1999; Smith, Goldman, Greenbaum, & Christiansen, 1995).

From a decision-making perspective, people choose whether to use drugs according to their weighing of the expected positive and negative consequences. Consider people with drinking problems who face the choice to drink or not to drink every day. They may be aware of the eventual negative consequences of drinking (e.g., getting fired or divorced or incurring serious health troubles), but expectations of immediate relief from anxiety and feelings of pleasure may be more prominent at a given moment (Sawyer & Stevenson, 2008). They may well decide, then, to drink. The person with a drinking problem may or may not be aware of such decisions, or of decisions to engage in the chain of behaviours that lead to problem drinking—such as whether to take a route from work that runs past a favourite watering hole.

SELF-EFFICACY EXPECTANCIES Part of the appeal of substances like alcohol lies in their ability to enhance self-efficacy expectancies (beliefs in our ability to accomplish tasks) either directly (by enhancing feelings of energy, power, and well-being) or indirectly (by reducing stressful states of arousal, such as anxiety). Cocaine also enhances self-efficacy expectancies, an outcome sought in particular by performance-conscious athletes. People may therefore come to rely on substances in challenging situations in which they doubt their abilities. Alcohol can also help protect one's sense of self-efficacy by shunting criticism for socially unacceptable behaviour from the self to the alcohol. People who "screw up" while drinking can maintain their self-esteem by attributing their misdeeds to alcohol.

CAN YOU HAVE JUST ONE DRINK?   According to the disease model of alcoholism, abstainers who binge after just one drink do so largely for biochemical reasons. Experimental research, however, suggests that cognitive factors may be more important. In fact, the one-drink hypothesis may be explained by the drinker's expectancies rather than the biochemical properties of alcohol.

Studies of the one-drink hypothesis, like many other studies on alcohol, are made possible by the fact that the taste of vodka can be cloaked by tonic water. In a classic study by Marlatt, Demming, and Reid (1973), subjects were led to believe they were participating in a taste test. Alcohol-dependent subjects and social drinkers who were informed they were sampling an alcoholic beverage (vodka) drank significantly more than counterparts who were informed they were sampling a nonalcoholic beverage. The expectations of the alcohol-dependent subjects and the social drinkers alike turned out to be the crucial factors that predicted the amount consumed (see Figure 7.3). The actual content of the beverages was immaterial.

Marlatt (1978) explains the one-drink effect as a self-fulfilling prophecy. If people with alcohol-related problems believe just one drink will cause a loss of control, they perceive the outcome as predetermined when they drink. Their drinking—even taking one drink—may thus escalate into a binge. When individuals who were formerly

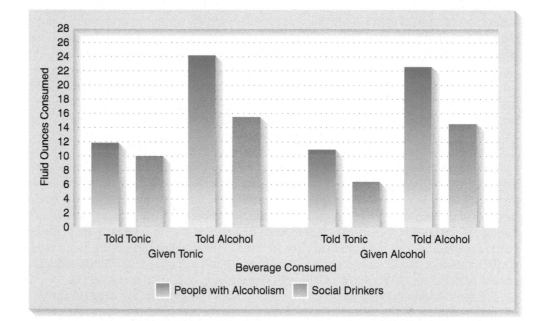

FIGURE 7.3   Must people who develop alcoholism fall off the wagon if they have one drink?
It is widely believed that people who develop alcoholism will "lose control" if they have just one drink. Will they? If so, why? Laboratory research by Marlatt and his colleagues (1973) suggests that the tendency of people who suffer from alcoholism to drink to excess following a first drink may be the result of a self-fulfilling prophecy rather than a craving. Like the dieter who eats a piece of chocolate, people who develop alcoholism may assume they have lost control because they have fallen off the wagon, and then go on a binge. This figure shows that people with alcoholism who participated in the Marlatt study drank more when they were led to believe that the beverage contained alcohol, regardless of its actual content. It remains unclear, however, whether binge drinking by people with alcohol-related problems in real-life settings can be explained as a self-fulfilling prophecy.

Source: Marlatt, G. Alan, and Demming, Barbara. Loss of control drinking in alcoholics: An experimental analogue, *Journal of Abnormal Psychology*, Vol 81(3), Jun 1973, 233–241.

physiologically dependent on alcohol share this belief—which is propounded by many groups, including AA—they may interpret "just one drink" as "falling off the wagon." Marlatt's point is that the "mechanism" of falling off the wagon due to one drink is cognitive, reflecting one's expectations about the effects of the drink, and not physiological. This expectation is an example of what Aaron Beck refers to as *absolutist thinking* (Beck, Rush, Shaw, & Emery, 1979). When we insist on seeing the world in black and white rather than shades of grey, we may interpret one bite of dessert as proof we are off our diets, or one cigarette as proof we are hooked again. Rather than telling ourselves, "Okay, I goofed, but that's it—I don't have to have more," we encode our lapses as catastrophes and transform them into full-blown relapses. Still, alcohol-dependent people who believe they may go on a drinking binge if they have just one drink are well advised to abstain rather than place themselves in situations they feel they may not be able to manage.

Psychodynamic Perspectives

According to traditional psychodynamic theory, alcoholism reflects certain features of what is termed an *oral-dependent personality*. Alcoholism is, by definition, an oral behaviour pattern. Psychodynamic theory also associates excessive alcohol use with other oral traits, such as dependence and depression, and traces the origins of these traits to fixation in the oral stage of psychosexual development. Excessive drinking in adulthood symbolizes efforts to attain oral gratification.

Psychodynamic theorists also view smoking as an oral fixation, although they have not been able to predict who will or will not smoke. Sigmund Freud smoked upward of 20 cigars a day despite several attempts to desist. Although he contracted oral cancer and had to have painful jaw surgery, he would still not surrender his "oral fixation." He eventually succumbed to cancer of the mouth in 1939 at the age of 83, after years of agony.

Research support for these psychodynamic concepts is mixed. Although people who develop alcoholism often show dependent traits, it is unclear whether dependence contributes to or stems from problem drinking. Chronic drinking, for example, is connected with loss of employment and downward movement in social status, both of which would render drinkers more reliant on others for support. Moreover, an empirical connection between dependence and alcoholism does not establish that alcoholism represents an oral fixation that can be traced to early development.

Sociocultural Perspectives

Cultural and religious factors are also related to consumption of alcohol and drugs. Rates of alcohol abuse vary across ethnic and religious groups (see the earlier "Focus on Diversity" box, pages 258–259). Let's note some other sociocultural factors. Church attendance, for example, is generally connected with abstinence from alcohol. Perhaps people who are more willing to engage in culturally sanctioned activities, such as church going, are also more likely to adopt culturally sanctioned prohibitions against excessive drinking. Rates of alcohol use also vary across cultures. For example, alcohol use is greater in Germany than in Canada, apparently because of a cultural tradition that makes the consumption of alcohol, especially beer, normative in German society (Cockerham, Kunz, & Lueschen, 1989).

Use of alcohol and drugs often occurs within a group or social setting. We go drinking with friends or entertain over drinks at home. A good wine list is a sign of class in a restaurant. Drinking is determined, in part, by where we live, with whom we worship, and the social or cultural norms that regulate our behaviour. Cultural attitudes can encourage or discourage problem drinking.

Peer pressure and peer drug use play important roles in the use of alcohol and drugs among adolescents (Dishion & Owen, 2002). Montreal researchers Poulin, Denault, and

Pedersen (2011) discovered that these pressures are especially prominent among girls when they transition from an age where they have only same-sex friends to having friendships of both sexes. Conversely, support from family members can reduce the negative influence of drug-using peers on an adolescent's use of tobacco and other drugs (Farrell & White, 1998).

Tying It Together

Substance use disorders are complex patterns of behaviour that involve an interplay of biological, psychological, and environmental factors. Genetic factors and the early home environment may give rise to predispositions (diatheses) to abuse and dependence. In adolescence and adulthood, positive expectations concerning drug use, together with social pressures and a lack of cultural constraints, affect drug-use decisions and tendencies toward abuse. When physiological dependence occurs, people may use a substance to avoid withdrawal symptoms.

Genetic factors may create an inborn tolerance for certain drugs, such as alcohol, which can make it difficult to regulate usage or to know "when to say when." Some individuals may have genetic tendencies that lead them to become unusually tense or anxious. Perhaps they turn to alcohol or other drugs to quell their nervousness. Genetic predispositions may interact with environmental factors that increase the potential for drug abuse and dependence—factors such as pressure from peers to use drugs, parental modelling of excessive drinking or drug use, and family disruption that results in a lack of effective guidance or support. Cognitive factors, especially positive drug expectancies (e.g., beliefs that using drugs will enhance one's social skills or sexual prowess), may also raise the potential for alcohol or drug problems.

Sociocultural factors need to be taken into account in this matrix of factors, such as the availability of alcohol and other drugs, presence or absence of cultural constraints that might curb excessive or underage drinking, the glamorizing of drug use in popular media, and inborn tendencies (such as among Asians) to flush more readily following alcohol intake.

Learning factors also play important roles. Drug use may be positively reinforced by the pleasurable effects associated with its use (mediated perhaps by release of dopamine in the brain or by activation of endorphin receptors). It may also be negatively reinforced by the reduction of states of tension and anxiety that depressant drugs such as alcohol, heroin, and tranquillizers can produce. Sadly, people who become dependent on drugs often continue to use them solely because of the relief from withdrawal symptoms and cravings they encounter when they go without the drug.

Problems of substance use disorders are best approached by investigating the distinctive constellation of factors that apply to each individual case. No single model or set of factors will explain each case, which is why we need to understand each individual's unique characteristics and personal history.

REVIEW IT

Theoretical Perspectives

- **How are problems of substance use disorders conceptualized within the major theoretical perspectives?** Biological perspectives focus on uncovering the biological pathways that may explain the mechanisms of physiological dependence. The disease model is a prominent biological perspective that treats problems of substance use disorders as disease processes. Learning perspectives view substance use disorders as learned patterns of behaviour, with roles for classical and operant conditioning and observational learning. Cognitive perspectives focus on the roles of attitudes, beliefs, and expectancies in accounting for substance use and abuse. Sociocultural perspectives emphasize the cultural, group, and social factors that underlie drug-use patterns, including the role of peer pressure in determining adolescent drug use. Psychodynamic theorists view problems of substance abuse, such as excessive drinking and habitual smoking, as signs of an oral fixation.

TREATMENT

There have been and remain a vast array of nonprofessional, biological, and psychological approaches to substance use disorders. However, treatment has often been a frustrating endeavour. In many, perhaps most, cases, people with drug dependencies really do not want to discontinue the substances they are abusing. Most people who use cocaine, for example, like most users of alcohol and other drugs, do not seek treatment on their own. Those who do not seek treatment tend to be heavy abusers who deny the negative impact of cocaine on their lives and dwell within a social milieu that fails to encourage them to get help. When people do come for treatment, helping them through a withdrawal syndrome is usually straightforward enough, as we shall see. However, helping them pursue a life devoid of their preferred substances is more problematic. Moreover, treatment takes place in a setting—such as a therapist's office, support group, residential centre, or hospital—in which abstinence is valued and encouraged. Then the individual returns to the work, family, or street settings in which the substance use was instigated and maintained. The problem of returning to abuse and dependence following treatment—that is, of relapse—can thus be more troublesome than the problems involved in initial treatment. For this reason, recent treatment efforts have focused on relapse prevention (Brandon, Vidrine, & Litvin, 2007). Given the difficulties encountered in treating people with substance use problems, it is no wonder there is much variability in the outcomes achieved in treatment, regardless of the types of clients, treatments, or measures of outcome used (McLellan et al., 1994). One consistent finding that does emerge is that people with more severe alcohol- and drug-use problems preceding treatment tend to have poorer outcomes in controlling their substance use following treatment.

Another complication is that many people with substance use problems also have psychological disorders and vice versa (APA, 2013; Currie et al., 2005). Most clinics and treatment programs focus on either the drug or alcohol problem or the other psychological disorders, rather than treating all these problems simultaneously. This narrow focus results in poorer treatment outcomes, including more frequent rehospitalizations among those with these dual diagnoses.

Biological Approaches

An increasing range of biological approaches is used in treating problems of substance use disorders. For people with chemical dependencies, biological treatment typically begins with **detoxification**—that is, helping them through withdrawal from addictive substances.

DETOXIFICATION Detoxification is often carried out in a hospital setting to provide the support needed to help the person withdraw safely from the addictive substance. In the case of addiction to alcohol or barbiturates, hospitalization allows medical personnel to monitor the development of potentially dangerous withdrawal symptoms, such as convulsions. The tranquillizing agents called benzodiazepines, such as Valium, may help block more severe withdrawal symptoms such as seizures and delirium tremens (Mayo-Smith, 1997). Detoxification from alcohol takes about a week. When tranquillizers are used to cope with subsequent urges to drink, however, people can be caught up in a game of "musical drugs."

Next, we consider other drugs used to treat people with chemical dependencies.

DISULFIRAM The drug disulfiram (brand name Antabuse) discourages alcohol consumption because the combination of the two produces a strong aversive reaction consisting of nausea, sweating, flushing, rapid heart rate, reduced blood pressure, and vomiting. In some extreme cases, drinking alcohol while taking disulfiram can lead to such a dramatic drop in blood pressure that the individual goes into shock and may even die. The benefits of disulfiram extend beyond the aversive effects of the substance. With each dose, the patient reaffirms his or her commitment to remain abstinent. Also, patients are no longer tormented by an internal dialogue pulling them in both directions as to

detoxification Process of ridding the system of alcohol or drugs under supervised conditions in which withdrawal symptoms can be monitored and controlled.

Stockbyte/Getty Images

Is the path to abstinence from smoking skin deep? Forms of nicotine replacement therapy—such as nicotine transdermal (skin) patches and chewing gum that contains nicotine—allow people to continue to receive nicotine when they quit smoking. Though nicotine replacement therapy is more effective than a placebo in helping people quit smoking, it does not address the behavioural components of addiction to nicotine, such as the habit of smoking while drinking alcohol. For this reason, nicotine replacement therapy may be more effective if it is combined with behaviour therapy that focuses on changing smoking habits.

whether or not they should consume. Since ingesting alcohol is no longer an option, it permits them to implement coping strategies (Newton-Howes, Levack, McBride, Gilmor, & Tester, 2016). Although disulfiram has been used widely in alcoholism treatment, its effectiveness is limited because many patients who want to continue drinking simply stop using the drug. Others stop taking the drug in the belief they can maintain abstinence without it. Unfortunately, many return to uncontrolled drinking.

ANTIDEPRESSANTS Antidepressants have shown some promise in reducing cravings for cocaine following withdrawal from the drug. These drugs may stimulate neural processes that regulate feelings of pleasure derived in everyday experiences. If pleasure can be more readily derived from non-drug-related activities, cocaine-addicted patients may be less likely to return to using the drug to induce pleasurable feelings. However, antidepressants have thus far failed to produce consistent results in reducing relapse rates for cocaine dependence (O'Brien, 1996). Of all the medications tested to date, disulfiram (Antabuse) has demonstrated the most consistent effect in reducing cocaine use (Vocci & Elkashef, 2005). Other medications that look promising according to controlled studies include baclofen, modafinil, tiagabine, and topiramate. All pharmacotherapy trials in cocaine-dependent patients include behaviour therapy. Therefore, these trials essentially evaluate whether the medications add to the effect of behavioural interventions (Vocci & Elkashef, 2005).

Researchers suspect that deficiencies of the neurotransmitter serotonin may underlie alcohol desires or cravings (Anton, 1994). Research is underway focusing on whether the appetite for alcohol can be curbed by using serotonin-reuptake inhibitors (e.g., Prozac), which increase the availability of serotonin in the brain. The use of these drugs in the early stages of abstinence may help people who are alcohol dependent to maintain sobriety and continue in treatment. Although some studies showed positive results with the use of serotonin-reuptake inhibitors with heavy drinkers, others showed an increase in alcohol consumption (Atigari, Kelly, Jabeen, & Healy, 2013). The actions of another neurotransmitter, dopamine, may account for the pleasurable or euphoric effects of alcohol. Drugs that mimic dopamine may be helpful in blocking the pleasurable reinforcing effects of alcohol.

NICOTINE REPLACEMENT THERAPY Many regular smokers, perhaps the great majority, have tobacco use disorder. The use of nicotine replacements in the form of prescription gum (brand name Nicorette), transdermal (skin) patches, and nasal sprays can help smokers avert withdrawal symptoms following smoking cessation (Strasser et al., 2005). After quitting smoking, ex-smokers can gradually wean themselves from the nicotine replacement.

Evidence supports the therapeutic benefits of nicotine replacement therapy, although men seem to benefit more then women (Japuntich, Piper, Leventhal, Bolt, & Baker, 2011; Strasser et al., 2005). Although nicotine replacement may help quell the physiological components of withdrawal, they have no effect on the behavioural components of the addiction, such as the habit of smoking while drinking alcohol. As a result, nicotine replacement may be ineffective in promoting long-term changes unless it is combined with behaviour therapy that focuses on changing smoking habits.

A non-nicotine-based antismoking drug, an antidepressant called bupropion (trade name Zyban), has been shown to be effective in helping smokers quit (McDonough, 2015). This is the first drug that works on reducing cravings for nicotine, in much the same way that other antidepressants are being used to treat cocaine cravings. Side effects may include insomnia and reduced levels of concentration.

METHADONE MAINTENANCE PROGRAMS Methadone, a synthetic opiate, is widely used in treating heroin addiction. Although methadone treatment for opioid use disorder gained its popularity through studies in the United States, it was first experimentally

methadone Artificial narcotic that lacks the rush associated with heroin and is used to help people addicted to heroin abstain without incurring an abstinence syndrome.

practised in the late 1950s by Dr. Robert Halliday and his addiction-treatment team in Vancouver (Fischer & Rehm, 2006). Methadone satisfies cravings for heroin and prevents the intense withdrawal symptoms that people addicted to heroin suffer upon withdrawal (O'Brien, 1996). Methadone does not produce the intense high or the stuporous state associated with heroin use, so people using it can hold jobs (O'Brien & McKay, 1998). However, like other opiates, methadone is highly addictive. For this reason, people treated with methadone can be conceptualized as swapping dependence on one drug for dependence on another. Yet methadone programs are usually publicly financed and so relieve people who are addicted to heroin of the need to engage in criminal activity to support their opioid use disorder. Although methadone is safer than heroin, its use needs to be strictly monitored because overdoses can be lethal, and it may become abused as a street drug (Veilleux, Colvin, Anderson, York, & Heinz, 2010).

For maximum effectiveness, methadone treatment must be combined with psychosocial treatments (Veilleux et al., 2010). Although methadone treatment produces clear benefits in improved daily functioning, not everyone succeeds with methadone, even with counselling (O'Brien & McKay, 1998). Some addicts turn to other drugs such as cocaine to get high, or they return to using heroin.

Buprenorphine, another synthetic opiate drug that is chemically similar to morphine, blocks withdrawal symptoms and cravings without producing a strong narcotic high (Ling et al., 2011; Veilleux et al., 2010). Many treatment providers prefer buprenorphine to methadone because it produces less of a sedative effective and can be taken in pill form only three times a week, whereas methadone is given in liquid form daily. Levomethadyl, another synthetic anti-opiate, also lasts longer than methadone and can be dispensed three times a week.

NALOXONE AND NALTREXONE   Naloxone and naltrexone are sister drugs that block the high produced by heroin and other opiates. By blocking the opiate's effects, they may be useful in helping addicts avoid relapsing following opiate withdrawal.

Naltrexone (brand name ReVia) blocks the high from alcohol as well as from opiates and has been approved in Canada for the treatment of alcoholism (Gianoulakis, 2001). Naltrexone doesn't prevent the person from taking a drink, but seems to blunt cravings for the drug (Anton, 2008; Myrick et al., 2008). By blocking the pleasure produced by alcohol, the drug can help break the vicious cycle in which one drink creates a desire for another, leading to episodes of binge drinking. A systematic review of 122 randomized controlled trials concluded that naltrexone was effective at controlling alcohol consumption (Jonas et al., 2014).

Naloxone is also used in emergency situations to reduce the risk of death in the case of an overdose since it can temporarily reverse the effects of opioids. In March 2016, following a drastic rise in the number of overdoses from fentanyl, Health Canada removed naloxone from the prescription drug list in order to increase its availability (Canadian Centre on Substance Abuse, 2016).

A nagging problem with drugs such as naltrexone, naloxone, disulfiram, and methadone is that people with substance use problems may simply stop using them and return to their substance using behaviour. Nor do such drugs provide alternative sources of positive reinforcement that can replace the pleasurable states produced by drugs of abuse. Drugs such as these are effective only in the context of a broader treatment program, consisting of psychological counselling and other treatment components such as job training and stress-management training—treatments designed to help people with substance use problems attain the skills they need to embark on a life in the mainstream culture (Fouquereau, Fernandez, Mullet, & Sorum, 2003).

Nonprofessional Support Groups

Despite the complexity of the factors contributing to substance use disorders, these problems are frequently handled by laypeople or nonprofessionals. Such people often have or had the problems themselves. For example, self-help group meetings are sponsored by organizations such as Alcoholics Anonymous, Narcotics Anonymous, and

naloxone Drug that prevents users from becoming high if they subsequently take heroin. Some people are placed on naloxone after being withdrawn from heroin to prevent return to heroin.

naltrexone Chemical cousin of naloxone that blocks the high from alcohol as well as opiates and is now approved for use in treating alcoholism.

Cocaine Anonymous. These groups promote abstinence and provide members with an opportunity to discuss their feelings and experiences in a supportive group setting. More experienced group members ("sponsors") support newer members during periods of crisis or potential relapse. The meetings are sustained by nominal voluntary contributions.

The most widely used nonprofessional program, Alcoholics Anonymous, is based on the belief that alcoholism is a disease, not a sin. AA assumes that people who suffer from alcoholism are never "cured," regardless of how long they abstain from alcohol or how well they control their drinking. Instead of being cured, people who suffer from alcoholism are seen as "recovering." It is also assumed that people who suffer from alcoholism cannot control their drinking and need help to stop. There are more than 65 000 chapters of AA in North America (Alcoholics Anonymous, 2016). AA is so deeply embedded in the consciousness of health-care professionals that many of them automatically refer newly detoxified people to AA as a follow-up agency. About half of AA members have problems with illicit drugs as well as alcohol.

The AA experience is part spiritual, part group-supportive, part cognitive. AA follows a 12-step approach in which the beginning steps deal with acceptance of one's powerlessness over alcohol and turning one's will and life over to a higher power. This spiritual component may be helpful to some participants but not to others who prefer not to appeal to divine support. (Other lay organizations, such as Rational Recovery, do not adopt a spiritual approach.) The later steps focus on examining one's character flaws, admitting one's wrongdoings, being open to God's help in overcoming character defects, making amends to others, and, at the 12th step, bringing the AA message to other people suffering from alcoholism (Alcoholics Anonymous, 2016). Prayer and meditation are urged on members to help them get in touch with their higher power. The meetings themselves provide group support. So does the buddy or sponsoring system, which encourages members to call each other for support when they feel tempted to drink.

The success rate of AA remains in question, in large part because AA does not keep records of its members, but also because of an inability to conduct randomized clinical trials in AA settings. However, evidence exists that participation in AA is linked to lower frequency and intensity of drinking (Ilgen, Wilbourne, Moos, & Moos, 2008). Many people drop out of AA, as well as from other treatment programs. People who are more likely to do well with AA tend to be those who make a commitment to abstinence, who express intentions to avoid high-risk situations associated with alcohol use, and who stay longer with the program (e.g., McKellar, Stewart, & Humphreys, 2003; Moos & Moos, 2004).

Al-Anon, begun in 1951, is a spin-off of AA that supports the families and friends of people suffering from alcoholism. Another spin-off of AA, Alateen, provides support to children whose parents have alcoholism, helping them see they are not to blame for their parents' drinking and are thus undeserving of the guilt they may feel.

Al-Anon Organization sponsoring support groups for family members of people with alcoholism.

Residential Approaches

A residential approach to treatment involves a stay in a hospital or therapeutic residence. Hospitalization may be recommended when substance abusers cannot exercise self-control in their usual environments or cannot tolerate withdrawal symptoms, and when their behaviour is self-destructive or dangerous to others. Outpatient treatment is less costly and often indicated when withdrawal symptoms are less severe, clients are committed to changing their behaviour, and environmental support systems, such as families, strive to help clients make the transition to a drug-free lifestyle. The great majority (nearly 90%) of people treated for alcoholism are helped on an outpatient basis (McCaul & Furst, 1994).

Most inpatient programs use an extended 28-day detoxification or drying-out period. Clients are helped through withdrawal symptoms in a few days. Then the emphasis shifts to counselling about the destructive effects of alcohol and combating distorted ideas or rationalizations. Consistent with the disease model, the goal of abstinence is urged.

Researchers find that most people with alcohol use disorders do not require hospitalization, although some certainly do. A classic review article comparing outpatient and inpatient programs reveal no overall difference in relapse rates (Miller & Hester, 1986). However, medical insurance may not cover outpatient treatment, which may encourage many people who may benefit from outpatient treatment to admit themselves for inpatient treatment.

A number of residential therapeutic communities are also in use. Some of them have part- or full-time professional staffs. Others are run entirely by laypeople. Residents are expected to remain free of drugs and take responsibility for their actions. They are often confronted about their excuses for failing to take responsibility for themselves and about their denial of the damage being done by their drug abuse. They share their life experiences to help one another develop productive ways of handling stress. As with AA, we lack evidence from controlled studies demonstrating the efficacy of residential treatment programs. Also like AA, therapeutic communities have high numbers of early dropouts. Moreover, many former members of residential treatment programs who remain substance free during their time in residence relapse upon returning to the world outside. Evidence suggests that a day-treatment therapeutic community may be as effective as a residential treatment facility (Guydish, Werdegar, Sorensen, Clark, & Acampora, 1998).

Psychodynamic Approaches

Psychoanalysts view substance abuse and dependence as symptomatic of conflicts that are rooted in childhood experiences. Focusing on substance use disorders per se is seen to offer, at most, a superficial type of therapy. It is assumed that if the underlying conflicts are resolved, abusive behaviour will also subside as more mature forms of gratification are sought. Traditional psychoanalysts also assume that programs directed solely at abusive behaviour will be of limited benefit because they fail to address the underlying psychological causes of abuse. Although there are many reports of successful psychodynamic case studies of people with substance use problems, there is a dearth of controlled and replicable research studies. The effectiveness of psychodynamic methods for treating substance use disorders thus remains unsubstantiated.

Cognitive-Behavioural Approaches

The use of cognitive-behaviour therapy in treating substance use disorders focuses on modifying abusive and dependent behaviour patterns. The issue to many behaviourally oriented therapists is not whether substance use disorders are diseases but whether individuals can learn to change their behaviour when they are faced with temptation.

SELF-CONTROL STRATEGIES Self-control training focuses on helping users develop skills they can use to change their abusive behaviour. Behaviour therapists focus on three components of substance abuse:

1. The antecedent cues or stimuli (A's) that prompt or trigger abuse,
2. The abusive behaviours (B's) themselves, and
3. The reinforcing or punishing consequences (C's) that maintain or discourage abuse.

Table 7.4 shows the kinds of strategies used to modify the "ABCs" of substance abuse.

SOCIAL-SKILLS TRAINING Social-skills training helps people develop effective interpersonal responses in social situations that prompt substance use. Assertiveness training, for example, may be used to teach people with alcohol-related problems how to fend off social pressures to drink. Behavioural marital therapy seeks to improve marital communication and a couple's problem-solving skills to relieve marital stresses that can

TABLE 7.4

Self-Control Strategies for Modifying the "ABCs" of Substance Abuse

1. Controlling the A's (Antecedents) of Substance Abuse

People who use psychoactive substances become conditioned to a wide range of external (environmental) and internal stimuli (body states). They may begin to break these stimulus-response connections by

- Removing drinking and smoking paraphernalia from the home—all alcoholic beverages, beer mugs, carafes, ashtrays, matches, cigarette packs, lighters, etc.

- Restricting the stimulus environment in which drinking or smoking is permitted. Using the substance only in a stimulus-deprived area of the home, such as the garage, bathroom, or basement. All other stimuli that might be connected to using the substance are removed—there is no television, reading material, radio, or telephone. In this way, substance use becomes detached from many controlling stimuli.

- Not socializing with others with substance use problems by avoiding situations linked to use—bars, the street, bowling alleys, etc.

- Frequenting substance-free environments—lectures or concerts, gyms, museums, evening classes—by socializing with nonusers, sitting in nonsmoking cars of trains, eating in restaurants without liquor licences.

- Managing the internal triggers for use. By practising self-relaxation or meditation and not taking the substance when tense; by expressing angry feelings by writing them down or self-assertion, not by taking the substance; and by seeking counselling for prolonged feelings of depression, not alcohol, pills, or cigarettes.

2. Controlling the B's (Behaviours) of Substance Abuse

People can prevent and interrupt substance use by

- Using response prevention—breaking abusive habits by physically preventing them from occurring or making them more difficult—by not bringing alcohol home or cigarettes to the office.

- Using competing responses when tempted, by being prepared to handle substance-related situations with appropriate ammunition—mints, sugarless chewing gum, etc.—and by taking a bath or shower, walking the dog, walking around the block, taking a drive, calling a friend, spending time in a substance-free environment, practising meditation or relaxation, or exercising when tempted rather than using the substance.

- Making use more laborious—buying one can of beer at a time; storing matches, ashtrays, and cigarettes far apart; wrapping cigarettes in foil to make smoking more cumbersome; pausing for 10 minutes when struck by the urge to drink, smoke, or use another substance and asking oneself, "Do I really need this one?"

3. Controlling the C's (Consequences) of Substance Abuse

Substance use has immediate positive consequences such as pleasure, relief from anxiety and withdrawal symptoms, and stimulation. People can counter these intrinsic rewards and alter the balance of power in favour of nonabuse by

- Rewarding themselves for nonuse and punishing themselves for use.

- Switching to brands of beer or cigarettes they don't like.

- Setting gradual substance-reduction schedules and rewarding themselves for sticking to them.

- Punishing themselves for failing to meet substance-reduction goals. People with substance use problems can assess themselves at, say, 10 cents for each slip, and donate the cash to an unpalatable cause, such as a brother-in-law's birthday present.

- Rehearsing motivating thoughts or self-statements—like writing reasons for quitting smoking on index cards. For example,

    Each day I don't smoke adds another day to my life.

    Quitting smoking will help me breathe deeply again.

    Foods will smell and taste better when I quit smoking.

    Think how much money I'll save by not smoking.

    Think how much cleaner my teeth and fingers will be by not smoking.

    I'll be proud to tell others that I kicked the habit.

    My lungs will become clearer each and every day I don't smoke.

    Smokers can carry a list of 20 to 25 such statements and read several of them at various times throughout the day. The statements can become a part of their daily routine, a constant reminder of their goals.

trigger abuse. Couples may learn how to use written behavioural contracts. One such contract might stipulate that the person with a substance use problem agrees to abstain from drinking or to start taking Antabuse, and his or her spouse agrees to refrain from making comments about past drinking and the probability of future lapses. The available evidence supports the utility of social-skills training and behavioural marital therapy approaches in treating alcoholism (Finney & Monahan, 1996; O'Farrell et al., 1996).

CUE-EXPOSURE TRAINING Cue-exposure training is a treatment designed to extinguish the individual's responses to substance-related cues. In this treatment, a person is repeatedly seated in front of drug- or alcohol-related cues, such as open alcoholic beverages, while being prevented from using the drug. This pairing of the cue (alcohol bottle) with nonrein-forcement (by preventing drinking) may lead to extinction of the conditioned craving. Cue-exposure treatment may be combined with coping-skills training to help people with substance-related problems learn to cope with drug-use urges without resorting to drug use (Monti et al., 1994). Cue-exposure training holds promise in the treatment of alcohol dependence and other forms of addictive behaviour (Dawe, Rees, Mattick, Sitharthan, & Heather, 2002; Drummond & Glautier, 1994; Monti et al., 1994). It has also been applied to helping problem drinkers learn to stop drinking after two or three drinks (Sitharthan, Sitharthan, Hough, & Kavanagh, 1997). More recent studies are exploring the benefits of adding virtual reality to cue-exposure therapy so clients can practise coping skills when faced with high-risk situations (Giovancarli et al., 2016; Hone-Blanchet, Wensing, & Fecteau, 2014).

MOTIVATIONAL ENHANCEMENT THERAPY (MET) One of the greatest challenges in the treatment of individuals with a substance use disorder is helping them realize that treatment is in their best interest. The goal of motivational enhancement therapy, also referred to as motivational interviewing, is to address the client's ambivalence toward change and create an intrinsic motivation. Unless the individual is willing to change, change will not occur. This brief, client-centred, directive approach can be used in conjunction with other treatment modalities. The role of the therapist is to guide the individual to recognize the discrepancy between their behaviour (substance use) and their personal goals (Miller & Rollnick, 2013). The available evidence supports the utility of motivational enhancement therapy in treating substance use disorders (Barnett, Sussman, Smith, Rohrbach, & Spruijt-Metz, 2012; Bertrand et al., 2015; D'Amico, Hunter, Miles, Ewing, & Osilla, 2013; Macgowan & Engle, 2010).

Relapse-Prevention Training

The word **relapse** derives from Latin roots meaning "to slide back." From 80% to 95% of people who are successfully treated for substance use problems eventually relapse (Hendershot, Witkiewitz, George, & Marlatt, 2011). Relapses often occur in response to negative mood states such as depression or anxiety, to interpersonal conflict, or to social pressures to resume drinking (Cooney, Litt, Morse, Bauer, & Gaupp, 1997). People with drinking problems who relapse are more likely than those who do not to have encountered stress, such as the loss of a loved one or economic problems. They are also more likely than those who maintain sobriety to rely on avoidance methods of coping, such as denial. Successful abstainers from alcohol tend to have more social and family resources and support to draw on in handling stress (Chung & Maisto, 2006).

Because of the prevalence of relapse, behaviourally oriented therapists have devised a number of methods referred to as **relapse-prevention training**. Such training helps people with substance use problems cope with temptations and high-risk situations to prevent lapses—that is, slips—from becoming full-blown relapses (Witkiewicz & Marlatt, 2004). High-risk situations include negative mood states, such as depression, anger, or anxiety; interpersonal conflict, such as marital problems or conflicts with employers; and socially conducive situations, such as "the guys getting together." Participants learn to cope with these situations by, for example, learning self-relaxation skills to counter anxiety and learning to resist social pressures to resume use of the substance. Trainees are also taught to avoid practices that might prompt a relapse, such as keeping alcohol on hand for friends.

Although it contains many behavioural strategies, relapse-prevention training is a cognitive-behavioural technique in that it also focuses on the person's interpretations of any lapses or slips that may occur, such as smoking a first cigarette or taking a first drink following quitting. Clients are taught how to avoid the so-called **abstinence-violation effect** (AVE)—the tendency to overreact to a lapse—by learning to reorient their thinking about lapses and slips. People who have a slip may be more likely to relapse if they attribute their slip to personal weakness and experience shame and guilt rather than to an external or transient event (Witkiewicz & Marlatt, 2004). For example, consider a skater who slips on the ice. Whether or not the skater gets back up and continues to perform depends largely on whether he or she sees the slip as an isolated and correctable event or as a sign of complete failure. Evidence shows that the best predictor of progression from a first to a second lapse among ex-smokers was the feeling of giving up after the first lapse (Shiffman et al., 1996). But those who responded to a first lapse by using coping strategies were more likely to succeed in averting a subsequent lapse on the same day.

A reformulated relapse-prevention training, called *mindfulness-based relapse prevention (MBRP)* includes a mindfulness component whereby clients are taught to attend to their

controlled social drinking
Controversial approach to treating problem drinkers in which the goal of treatment is the maintenance of controlled social drinking in moderate amounts, rather than total abstinence.

A CLOSER LOOK

The Controlled Social Drinking Controversy

The disease model of alcoholism contends that people who suffer from alcoholism who have just one drink will lose control and go on a binge. Some professionals, however, such as Linda and Mark Sobell, have argued that behaviour modification self-control techniques can teach many people who have alcohol use disorder to engage in **controlled social drinking**—to have a drink or two without necessarily falling off the wagon.

The contention that people who develop alcoholism can learn to drink moderately remains controversial. The proponents of the disease model of alcoholism, who have wielded considerable political strength, stand strongly opposed to attempts to teach controlled social drinking.

To support their contention, the Sobells, who did a good deal of their research at Toronto's Addiction Research Foundation, published the results of an experiment in which people who suffered from alcoholism were either taught to control their drinking or encouraged to abstain from alcohol. The Sobells (Sobell & Sobell, 1973, 1976, 1984) reported that 85% of their 20 controlled drinking subjects remained in control of their drinking at a two-year follow-up. However, a research group critical of the Sobells (Pendery, Maltzman, & West, 1982) published its own 10-year follow-up of the Sobells' subjects. The group claimed that only 1 in 20 people remained successful at controlled social drinking. Most had returned to uncontrolled drinking on many occasions, and four of the group had died from alcohol-related causes.

Despite the controversy it caused, Pendery et al.'s study was flawed. The researchers reported results for only the controlled drinking group without reporting data for the Sobells' control group (the abstinence-based treatment condition). Without some kind of control group, it is impossible to assess the effects of controlled drinking. A 10-year follow-up of the Sobells' study reported by Dickens, Doob, Warwick, and Winegard (1982) found that there were more deaths in the abstinence group (30%) than in the controlled drinking group (20%).

Other investigators have found that controlled social drinking is a reasonable treatment goal for younger people with less severe problem drinking but are headed on the road toward chronic alcoholism (e.g., Miller & Muñoz, 1983; Sanchez-Craig, Annis, Bornet, & MacDonald, 1984; Sanchez-Craig & Wilkinson, 1986/1987). Evidence supporting controlled social drinking programs for people with chronic alcoholism, however, remains lacking. Interest in controlled social drinking programs has also waned, largely because of strong opposition from professionals and lay organizations committed to the abstinence model. Nevertheless, as noted by University of Calgary psychologist David Hodgins (2006), controlled drinking is feasible for some people, so we should consider how best to integrate it into our treatment systems. Controlled drinking programs may be best suited for younger people with early-stage alcoholism or problem drinking, those who reject goals of total abstinence or have failed in programs requiring abstinence, and those who do not show severe withdrawal symptoms (Marlatt, Larimer, Baer, & Quigley, 1993; McMurran, 2006; Rosenberg, 1993; Sobell, Toneatto, & Sobell, 1990). Researchers also find that women tend to do better than men in controlled drinking programs (Marlatt et al., 1993). By offering moderation as a treatment goal, controlled drinking programs may also reach many people with alcohol use disorders who might otherwise go untreated because they refuse to participate in abstinence-only treatment programs (Marlatt et al., 1993; McMurran, 2006).

Controlled drinking programs may actually represent a pathway to abstinence for people who would not otherwise enter abstinence-only treatment programs (Marlatt et al., 1993; Sobell & Sobell, 2011). That is, treatment in a controlled drinking program may be the first step in the direction of giving up drinking completely. A large percentage—about one out of four in one study (Miller, Leckman, Delaney, & Tinkcom, 1993)—enter with the goal of achieving controlled drinking but become abstinent by the end of treatment. Heather (2006) adds that the goal of any treatment program should be harm reduction, that is, the reduction of problems as a result of alcohol, and not merely the reduction of alcohol itself.

thoughts and urges while recognizing that they are transient and will subside (Witkiewitz, Bowen, Douglas, & Hsu, 2013). Numerous studies obtained lower relapse rates in subjects assigned to MBRP versus those assigned to traditional relapse-prevention training (Amaro, Spear, Vallejo, Conron, & Black, 2014; De Souza et al., 2015; Witkiewitz et al., 2014).

In contrast to the disease model, which contends that people who suffer from alcoholism automatically lose control if they take a single drink, the relapse-prevention model assumes that whether a lapse becomes a relapse depends on the person's interpretation of the lapse (Witkiewicz & Marlatt, 2004). Self-defeating attributions such as "What's the use? I'm just doomed to fail" trigger depression, resignation, and resumption of problem drinking. Participants in relapse-prevention training programs are encouraged to view lapses as temporary setbacks that provide opportunities to learn what kinds of situations lead to temptation and how they can avoid or cope with such situations. If they can learn to think "Okay, I had a slip, but that doesn't mean all is lost unless I believe it is," they are less likely to catastrophize lapses and subsequently relapse. Other relapse-prevention techniques focus on training smokers' spouses or partners to be more helpful in maintaining abstinence. Social support appears to play a key role in determining relapse in abstinence-based programs for alcoholism, drug abuse, and cigarette smoking (e.g., Nides et al., 1995).

All in all, efforts to treat people with substance use problems have been mixed at best. Many users really do not want to discontinue use of these substances, although they would prefer, if possible, to avoid their negative consequences. The more effective substance use treatment programs involve intensive, multiple treatment approaches that address the wide range of problems that people with substance use disorders frequently present, including co-occurring (comorbid) psychiatric problems such as depression (Grant et al., 2004; Watkins et al., 2011). Comorbidity of substance use disorders and other psychiatric disorders has become the rule in treatment facilities rather than the exception (Pettinati, O'Brien, & Dundon, 2013). Substance users who have comorbid disorders or more severe psychological problems typically fare more poorly in treatment for their drug or alcohol problems (Simpson, Joe, Fletcher, Hubbard, & Anglin, 1999). Although effective treatment programs are available, only a minority of people with alcohol use disorder ever receive treatment, even when treatment is defined broadly enough to include AA (Kranzler, 2006). A Canadian study echoed these findings. In a sample of more than 1000 people in Ontario with alcohol use disorder, only about one in three had ever received any treatment for their disorder (Cunningham & Breslin, 2004). Clearly, more needs to be done in helping people with drug-related problems.

In the case of inner-city youth who have become trapped in a milieu of street drugs and hopelessness, the availability of culturally sensitive counselling and job-training opportunities would be of considerable benefit in helping them assume more productive social roles. The challenge is clear: to develop cost-effective ways of helping people recognize the negative effects of substances and forgo the powerful and immediate reinforcements they provide.

REVIEW IT

Treatment

- **What treatment approaches are used to help people overcome substance use disorders?** Biological approaches to substance use disorders include detoxification; the use of drugs such as disulfiram, methadone, naloxone, naltrexone, and antidepressants; and nicotine replacement therapy. Residential treatment approaches include hospitals and therapeutic residences. Nonprofessional support groups, such as Alcoholics Anonymous, promote abstinence within a supportive group setting. Psychodynamic therapists focus on uncovering the inner conflicts, originating in childhood, that are believed to be at the root of substance use problems. Behavioural therapists focus on helping people with substance-related problems change problem behaviours through such techniques as self-control training, aversive conditioning, and skills training. Regardless of the initial success of a treatment technique, relapse remains a pressing problem in treating people with substance use problems. Relapse-prevention training employs cognitive-behavioural techniques to help ex-abusers cope with high-risk situations and to prevent lapses from becoming relapses by helping participants interpret lapses in less damaging ways.

Define It

abstinence-violation effect, 285
addiction, 254
Al-Anon, 282
amphetamine psychosis, 264
amphetamines, 264
analgesia, 263
barbiturates, 262
cocaine, 264
controlled social drinking, 286
crack, 264
cue-exposure training, 285
delirium, 252
delirium tremens, 251
delta-9-tetrahydrocannabinol, 269
depressant, 256

detoxification, 279
disorientation, 252
endorphins, 263
flashbacks, 268
freebasing, 265
hallucinogens, 268
hashish, 269
inhalants, 270
intoxication, 251
Korsakoff's syndrome, 261
LSD, 268
marijuana, 269
methadone, 280
naloxone, 281
naltrexone, 281

narcotics, 263
opiates, 263
physiological dependence, 254
psychedelics, 268
psychoactive, 251
psychological dependence, 254
relapse, 285
relapse-prevention training, 285
sedatives, 262
substance-induced
     disorders, 251
substance use disorders, 251
tachycardia, 251
withdrawal syndrome, 251

Recall It

1. _____ involves a process of physical habituation to the repeated use of a drug such that higher and higher dosages of the drug are needed to achieve a similar effect.
   a. Tolerance
   b. Dependence
   c. Potentiation
   d. Reverse tolerance

2. Drugs that increase the activity of the central nervous system are called _____.
   a. stimulants
   b. narcotics
   c. hallucinogens
   d. depressants

3. Whenever Cynthia walks by a local bar where she often had drinks with her friends, she experiences cravings for alcohol. In classical conditioning terms, her cravings represent _____.
   a. unconditioned stimuli
   b. unconditioned responses

   c. conditioned stimuli
   d. conditioned responses

4. The initial step in treating problems of chemical dependence generally involves _____.
   a. insight-oriented therapy
   b. detoxification
   c. behavioural counselling
   d. relapse-prevention training

5. Hasim has been fighting his addiction to heroin. He has been given an alternative drug to help him withdraw from heroin without experiencing unpleasant withdrawal symptoms. The alternative drug is also an opiate, but it doesn't produce the rush provided by heroin. The drug he is taking is _____.
   a. naloxone
   b. methadone
   c. disulfiram
   d. diazepam

Answers to Recall It

1. a,   2. a,   3. d,   4. b,   5. b

Think About It

- Many teenagers today have parents who themselves smoked marijuana or used other drugs when they were younger. If you were one of those parents, what would you tell your kids about drugs?
- What do you think of the concept of using methadone, a narcotic drug, to treat problems of addiction to another narcotic drug, heroin? What are the advantages and disadvantages of this approach?

Do you believe the government should support methadone maintenance programs? Why or why not?

- Do you use alcohol? How does it affect you physically and mentally? Have you consumed alcohol and driven? How do you feel about that? Have you ever done anything under the influence of alcohol that you later regretted? What? Why?

Key for "How Do You Know If You're Hooked?" Questionnaire (page 257)

Any "yes" answer suggests you may have alcohol use disorder. If you have answered any of these questions in the affirmative, we suggest you seriously examine what your drinking means to you.

Weblinks

Centre for Addiction and Mental Health (CAMH)
www.camh.ca
This is a public hospital providing direct patient care for people with mental health and addiction problems. CAMH is also a research facility, an education and training institute, and a community-based organization providing health promotion and prevention services across Ontario.

Canadian Centre on Substance Use and Addiction
www.ccsa.ca
This website provides statistics and other information on substance use disorders.

Alcoholics Anonymous
www.aa.org
AA's website provides information on the nature and treatment of alcohol problems.

Mothers Against Drunk Driving (MADD)
www.madd.ca
MADD's Canadian site provides information on the prevalence and cost of alcohol abuse.

National Council on Alcoholism and Drug Dependence
www.ncadd.org
This site contains numerous links providing information on the nature and treatment of substance use disorders.

FASworld
www.fasworld.com
FASworld is a Canadian-based organization providing information about fetal alcohol spectrum (FAS) disorders.

Substance-Related and Addictive Disorders

Test your understanding of the key concepts by filling in the blanks with the correct statements chosen from the list that follows. The answers are found at the end of the chapter.

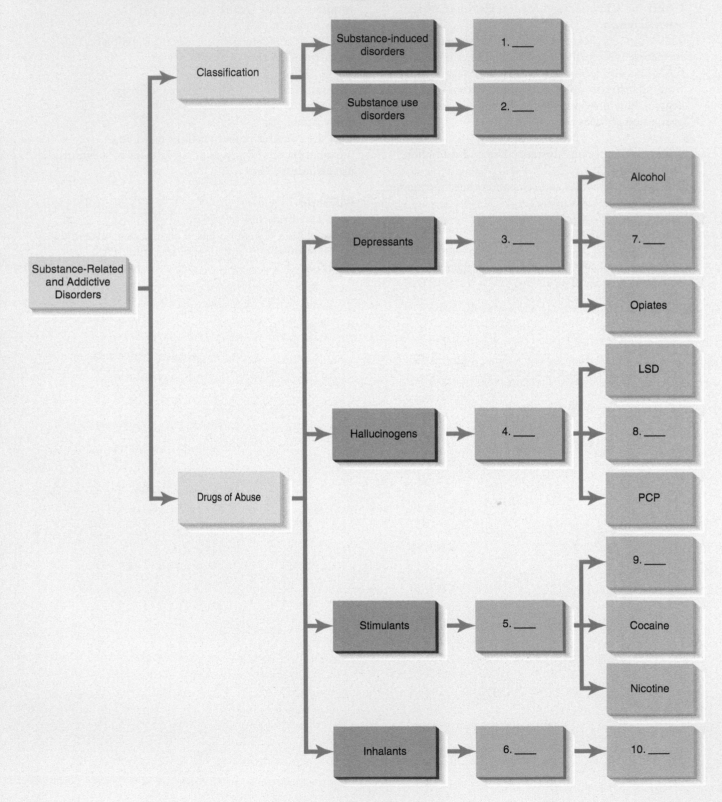

a. Pattern of repeated drug-using behaviour that has damaging consequences

b. Amphetamines

c. Drugs that lower the level of activity of the central nervous system

d. Substances that produce chemical vapours that are inhaled for their psychoactive effect

e. Marijuana

f. Substances that cause sensory distortions or hallucinations

g. Psychoactive substances that increase the activity of the central nervous system

h. Diverse group of substances such as aerosols, paint, and cleaning fluids

i. Disorders induced by the use of psychoactive substances

j. Barbiturates

Causes and Treatments According to Various Theoretical Perspectives

THEORETICAL PERSPECTIVE	CAUSES	TREATMENT
BIOLOGICAL PERSPECTIVES	Neurotransmitters Genetic factors	Detoxification Disulfiram Antidepressants Nicotine replacement therapy Methadone maintenance programs Naxolone and naltrexone
LEARNING PERSPECTIVES	**Operant conditioning** Positive reinforcement: Feelings of euphoria Negative reinforcement: Tension reduction, relief from withdrawal symptoms **Classical Conditioning** Cues associated with drug use lead to cravings **Observational Learning** Exposure to others who model drug use	Self-control strategies Social-skills training Cue-exposure training Motivational enhancement therapy Relapse-prevention training
COGNITIVE PERSPECTIVES	Outcome expectancies Decision making Self-efficacy expectancies	
PSYCHODYNAMIC PERSPECTIVES	Fixation in the oral stage of psychosexual development	Resolving underlying conflicts rooted in childhood experiences
SOCIOCULTURAL PERSPECTIVES	Cultural and religious factors Peer drug use	
		Nonprofessional support groups: AA, NA, Al-Anon

Answers: 1. i, 2. a, 3. c, 4. f, 5. g, 6. d, 7. j, 8. e, 9. b, 10. h

Feeding and Eating Disorders and Sleep–Wake Disorders

Did You Know That...

- Although others see them as "skin and bones," young women with anorexia nervosa still see themselves as too fat?

- Some individuals with bulimia force themselves to vomit after every meal?

- Drugs used to treat depression may also help curb bulimic binges?

- Nutrition management and psychoeducational programs are important in the treatment of eating disorders?

- Some people have sleep attacks in which they suddenly fall asleep without any warning?

- Some people literally gasp for breath hundreds of times during sleep without realizing it?

- Sleeping pills are only a short-term solution for the treatment of sleeping disorders and can actually worsen insomnia?

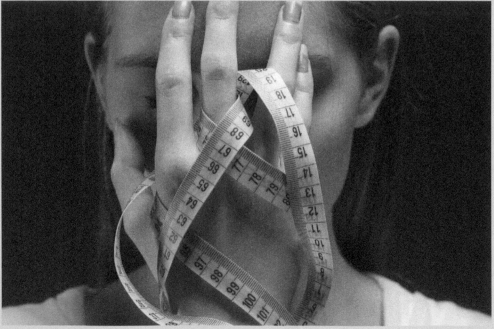

Photographee.eu/Shutterstock

J essica was a 20-year-old communications major when she consulted a psychologist for the first time. For years she had kept a secret from everyone, including her fiancé, Ken. She and Ken were planning to get married in three months. She had decided that it was time to finally confront her problem. She told the psychologist she didn't want to bring the problem into the marriage with her, that it wouldn't be fair to Ken. She said, "I don't want him to have to deal with this. I want to stop this before the marriage." Jessica went on to describe her problem: "I go on binges and then throw it all up. It makes me feel like I'm in control, but really I'm not." To conceal her secret, she would lock herself in the bathroom, run the water in the sink to mask the sounds, and induce vomiting. She would then clean up after herself and spray an air freshener to mask any odours. "The only one who suspects," she said with embarrassment, "is my dentist. He said my teeth are beginning to decay from stomach acid."

Jessica had bulimia nervosa, an eating disorder characterized by recurrent cycles of bingeing and purging. Eating disorders such as bulimia nervosa and anorexia nervosa often affect young people of high school or university age, especially young women. Although rates of diagnosable eating disorders in college and university students are not as high as you might think, chances are you have known people with anorexia or bulimia or with disturbed eating patterns that fall within a spectrum of eating-related disorders, such as repeated binge eating or excessive dieting.

Another class of psychological disorders that commonly affects young adults is sleep–wake disorders. The most common form of sleep–wake disorder, insomnia disorder, affects many young people who are making their way in the world and tend to bring their worries and concerns to bed with them.

Continuum of Eating Disorders

CHAPTER 8 · CONTINUUM CHART

Example: Bulimia Nervosa

Does not meet criteria		Meets criteria		
NO SYMPTOMS	**STRUGGLING**	**MILD**	**MODERATE**	**SEVERE**
	Sorina worries about her weight and is constantly dieting. Her self-esteem fluctuates in relation to the numbers on the scale.	Madison is desperate to lose weight and follows a very restrictive diet. At some point during the week she breaks a dietary rule, which leads to an episode of binge eating and purging.	In an attempt to control her weight, Ansia always skips breakfast and lunch. By the afternoon, she is so hungry that she loses control and binge eats. She then panics and makes herself throw up.	Shaneal binges several times a day and can't eat anything without purging afterwards.

FEEDING AND EATING DISORDERS

In a nation of plenty, some people literally starve themselves—sometimes to death. They are obsessed with their weight and desire to achieve an exaggerated image of thinness. Others engage in repeated cycles in which they binge on food, and some attempt to purge their excess eating afterward, such as by inducing vomiting. These dysfunctional

feeding and eating disorders
Psychological disorders involving
disturbed eating patterns and
maladaptive ways of controlling
body weight.

anorexia nervosa Eating disorder,
primarily affecting young women,
characterized by maintenance of
an abnormally low body weight,
distortions of body image, and
intense fears of gaining weight.

bulimia nervosa Eating disorder
characterized by a recurrent
pattern of binge eating followed
by inappropriate compensatory
behaviours to prevent weight gain
and accompanied by persistent
overconcern with body weight
and shape.

binge-eating disorder Eating
disorder characterized by
repeated episodes in which binge
eating occurs but is not followed
by purging.

patterns characterize the major types of **feeding and eating disorders: anorexia nervosa, bulimia nervosa,** and **binge-eating disorder.** Eating disorders involve disturbed patterns of eating and maladaptive ways of controlling body weight. Like many other psychological disorders, eating disorders are often accompanied by other forms of psychopathology, including mood, anxiety, impulse-control, and substance use disorders (Hudson, Hiripi, Pope, & Kessler, 2007; Jenkins, Hoste, Meyer, & Blissett, 2011).

Anorexia nervosa and bulimia nervosa were once considered rare, but they have become increasingly common in Canada and other developed countries. Estimates are that about 0.4% of the Canadian population (aged 15 years and older) is currently diagnosed with an eating disorder (Statistics Canada, 2013b). The great majority of cases (about 80%) occur among women, especially young women (LeBlanc, 2014). Since many cases go undiagnosed, higher rates are found in community samples. Canadian researchers reported that approximately 4.5% of female high school students and 2.2% of male students met the DSM-5 criteria for an eating disorder (Flament et al., 2015). Hospitalization rates for men with eating disorders in Canada is 0.8 per 100 000, while for women it is 15 times greater, at 11.7 per 100 000 (Bushnik, 2016). Although these disorders may develop in middle or even late adulthood, they typically begin during adolescence or early adulthood, when the pressures to be thin are the strongest (Jilek, 2001; National Institute of Nutrition, 2001). As these social pressures have increased, so too have the rates of eating disorders. The rates among Canadian females between the ages of 10 to 19 years increased by 42% from 2006 to 2013 (Bushnik, 2016).

A much larger percentage of young women show bulimic behaviours (occasional bingeing and purging) or excessive dieting but not to the point that they would warrant a diagnosis of an eating disorder. In one large study, researchers found that almost one quarter of Ontario high school females were dieting to lose weight and 27% showed symptoms of an eating disorder along with reported bingeing and purging. It was also found that disordered eating attitudes and behaviours increased significantly with age. Among younger females (aged 12 to 15), 18.8% had binged or purged, while the reported incidence increased to 26.3% in females aged 15 and older (Jones, Bennett, Olmsted, Lawson, & Rodin, 2001). These figures are disturbing because these eating attitudes and behaviours put females at risk for developing full-blown eating disorders (Fairburn, Cooper, Doll, & Davies, 2005; Flament et al., 2015).

Anorexia Nervosa

Nairi was the 22-year-old daughter of a renowned English professor. She had begun her college career full of promise at the age of 17, but two years ago, after "social problems" occurred, she returned to live at home and took progressively lighter course loads at a local college. Nairi had never been overweight, but about a year ago her mother noticed that she seemed to be gradually "turning into a skeleton."

Nairi spent literally hours every day shopping at the supermarket, butcher, and bakeries, conjuring up gourmet treats for her parents and younger siblings. Arguments over her lifestyle and eating habits divided the family into two camps. The camp led by her father called for patience; that headed by her mother demanded confrontation. Her mother feared that Nairi's father would "protect her right into her grave" and wanted Nairi placed in residential treatment "for her own good." The parents finally compromised on an outpatient evaluation.

At an even five feet, Nairi looked like a prepubescent 11-year-old. Her nose and cheekbones protruded crisply. Her lips were full, but the redness of her lipstick was unnatural, as if too much paint had been dabbed on a corpse for a funeral. Nairi weighed only 78 pounds, but she dressed in a stylish silk blouse, scarf, and baggy pants so that not one inch of her body was revealed.

Nairi vehemently denied that she had a problem. Her figure was "just about where I want it to be" and she engaged in aerobic exercise daily. A deal was struck in which outpatient treatment would be tried as long as Nairi lost no more weight and showed steady gains back to at least 90 pounds. Treatment included a day hospital with group therapy and two meals a day. But word came back that Nairi was artfully toying with her food—cutting it up, sort of licking it, and moving it about her plate—rather than eating it. After three weeks Nairi had lost another pound. At that point, her parents were able to persuade her to enter a residential treatment program, where her eating behaviour could be more carefully monitored.

The Authors' Files

Anorexia derives from the Greek roots *an-*, meaning "without," and *orexis*, meaning "a desire for." Thus, *anorexia* means "without desire for [food]," which is something of a misnomer because loss of appetite is rare among people with anorexia nervosa. However, they may be repelled by food and refuse to eat more than is absolutely necessary to maintain a minimal weight for their ages and heights. Often, they starve themselves to the point where they become dangerously emaciated. By and large, anorexia nervosa develops in early to late adolescence, between the ages of 12 and 18, although earlier and later onsets are sometimes found.

The clinical features listed in Table 8.1 are used to diagnose anorexia nervosa. Although reduced body weight is the most obvious sign, the most prominent clinical feature is an intense fear of obesity. One common pattern of anorexia begins after menarche, when a girl notices added weight and insists it must come off. Extreme dieting and, often, excessive exercise continue unabated after the initial weight loss goal is achieved, however—even after the girls' families and others express concern. Another common pattern occurs among young women when they leave home to attend university

---

TABLE 8.1

Diagnostic Criteria for Anorexia Nervosa

A. Restriction of energy intake relative to requirements, leading to a significantly low body weight in the context of age, sex, developmental trajectory, and physical health. *Significantly low weight* is defined as a weight that is less than minimally normal or, for children and adolescents, less than that minimally expected.

B. Intense fear of gaining weight or of becoming fat, or persistent behavior that interferes with weight gain, even though at a significantly low weight.

C. Disturbance in the way in which one's body weight or shape is experienced, undue influence of body weight or shape on self-evaluation, or persistent lack of recognition of the seriousness of the current low body weight.

Coding note: The ICD-9-CM code for anorexia nervosa is 307.1, which is assigned regardless of the subtype. The ICD-10-CM code depends on the subtype (see below).

Specify whether:

(F50.01) Restricting type: During the last 3 months, the individual has not engaged in recurrent episodes of binge eating or purging behavior (i.e., self-induced vomiting or the misuse of laxatives, diuretics, or enemas). This subtype describes presentations in which weight loss is accomplished primarily through dieting, fasting, and/or excessive exercise.

(F50.02) Binge-eating/purging type: During the last 3 months, the individual has engaged in recurrent episodes of binge eating or purging behavior (i.e., self-induced vomiting or the misuse of laxatives, diuretics, or enemas).

Source: Reprinted with permission from the *Diagnostic and Statistical Manual of Mental Disorders*, Fifth Edition, (Copyright © 2013). American Psychiatric Association. All Rights Reserved.

Jupiterimages/Goodshoot/Getty Images

Who's at risk? Competitive activities that emphasize endurance, aesthetics, and weight levels put athletes at risk for developing an eating disorder. Runners, wrestlers, swimmers, and dancers are among the athletes who have a high occurrence of eating disorders.

or college and encounter difficulties adjusting to the demands of college life and independent living. Anorexia is also more common among young women involved in ballet or modelling, in which there is often a strong emphasis on maintaining an unrealistically thin body shape.

Adolescent girls and women with anorexia almost always deny they are losing too much weight or wasting away. They may argue that their ability to engage in stressful exercise demonstrates their fitness. Women with eating disorders are more likely than normal women to view themselves as heavier than they are. Others may see them as nothing but "skin and bones," but anorexic women have a distorted body image and may still see themselves as too fat (Boehm et al., 2016). Although they literally starve themselves, they may spend much of the day thinking and talking about food, and even preparing elaborate meals for others (Rock & Curran-Celentano, 1996).

Although anorexia is far more common in women than in men, an increasing number of young men are presenting with anorexia. Many are involved in sporting activities, such as wrestling and gymnastics, in which they have experienced pressure to maintain a lower weight classification. In this regard, it seems that young men and women experience similar pressures to achieve weight loss and leanness (Ricciardelli & McCabe, 2004).

SUBTYPES OF ANOREXIA Due to the earlier work of Canadian eating disorder authorities Garfinkel, Moldofsky, and Garner (1980), the DSM diagnosis of anorexia includes two general subtypes of anorexia: a binge-eating/purging type and a restrictive type. The first type is characterized by frequent episodes of binge eating and purging; the second type is not. Although repeated cycles of binge eating and purging occur in bulimia, bulimic individuals do not reduce their weight to anorexic levels. The distinction between the subtypes of anorexia is supported by differences in personality patterns. Individuals with the eating/purging type tend to have problems related to impulse control, which, in addition to binge-eating episodes, may involve substance abuse or stealing (Garner, 1993). They tend to alternate between periods of rigid control and impulsive behaviour. Those with the restrictive type tend to be rigidly, even obsessively, controlled about their diet and appearance.

MEDICAL COMPLICATIONS OF ANOREXIA Anorexia can lead to serious medical complications that in extreme cases can be fatal. Approximately 10% will die within 10 years of receiving a diagnosis (LeBlanc, 2014). Weight losses of as much as 35% of body weight may occur, and anemia may develop. Females suffering from anorexia are also likely to encounter dermatological problems such as dry, cracking skin; fine, downy hair; even a yellowish discoloration that may persist for years after weight is regained. Cardiovascular complications include heart irregularities, hypotension (low blood pressure), and associated dizziness upon standing, sometimes causing blackouts. Decreased food ingestion can cause gastrointestinal problems such as constipation, abdominal pain, and obstruction or paralysis of the bowels or intestines. Menstrual irregularities are common, and **amenorrhea** (absence or suppression of menstruation) is possible. Muscular weakness and abnormal growth of bones may occur, causing loss of height and **osteoporosis**.

The death rate from anorexia is among the highest of all the mental disorders, with most deaths caused by suicide or medical complications associated with severe weight loss (LeBlanc, 2014). Researchers reported an 8.6% prevalence rate of suicide attempts in women with the restrictive subtype of anorexia nervosa and a prevalence rate of 25% in those with the binge-eating/purge subtype (Forcano et al., 2011).

amenorrhea Absence of menstruation—a possible sign of anorexia nervosa.

osteoporosis Physical disorder caused by calcium deficiency that is characterized by extreme brittleness of the bones (from the Greek *osteon*, meaning "bone," and the Latin *porus*, meaning "pore").

Bulimia Nervosa

I remember receiving a box of chocolates for Valentine's Day from a man I had been dating for a few weeks. I knew his intentions were good, but I felt so angry. How could he torment me this way? Throughout the evening, my thoughts kept returning to the chocolates. I had been following my diet perfectly for the last few days and knew this would send me over the edge. I debated all evening whether I should give the chocolates away or just throw them out. I decided that I would bring them to work the next day and share them with my co-workers. However, once I got home from my date the anxiety of having them in the house became too much. So I decided to throw them out. I knew I would have to pour cleaning fluids over them or the temptation to retrieve them from the garbage would haunt me. When I opened the box, I sampled one and before I knew it, I had finished the whole box. They went down so quickly that I felt cheated for not having enjoyed them. Since my diet was obviously ruined, I foraged through the pantry consuming whatever I could find that might be off limits once my diet resumed the next day. Hours later, I felt so full and disgusted in myself that I resorted to a behaviour that I promised myself I wouldn't do again: I made myself throw up. Maybe tomorrow would be different.

Bulimia derives from the Greek roots *bous*, meaning "ox" or "cow," and *limos*, meaning "hunger." The unflattering picture inspired by the origin of the term is one of continuous eating, like a cow chewing its cud. Bulimia nervosa is an eating disorder characterized by recurrent episodes of gorging on large quantities of food followed by use of inappropriate ways to prevent weight gain, such as purging by means of self-induced vomiting or by using laxatives, diuretics, or enemas; fasting; or engaging in excessive exercise (see Table 8.2). Two or more strategies may be used for purging, such as both vomiting and use of laxatives (APA, 2013). Although people with anorexia are extremely thin, bulimic individuals are usually of normal weight. However, they have an excessive concern about their shape and weight.

Bulimic individuals typically gag themselves to induce vomiting. Most attempt to conceal their behaviour. Fear of gaining weight is a constant factor. Although an

TABLE 8.2

Diagnostic Criteria for Bulimia Nervosa

A. Recurrent episodes of binge eating. An episode of binge eating is characterized by both of the following:

1. Eating, in a discrete period of time (e.g., within any 2-hour period), an amount of food that is definitely larger than what most individuals would eat in a similar period of time under similar circumstances.

2. A sense of lack of control over eating during the episode (e.g., a feeling that one cannot stop eating or control what or how much one is eating).

B. Recurrent inappropriate compensatory behaviors in order to prevent weight gain, such as self-induced vomiting; misuse of laxatives, diuretics, or other medications; fasting; or excessive exercise.

C. The binge eating and inappropriate compensatory behaviors both occur, on average, at least once a week for 3 months.

D. Self-evaluation is unduly influenced by body shape and weight.

E. The disturbance does not occur exclusively during episodes of anorexia nervosa.

Source: Reprinted with permission from the *Diagnostic and Statistical Manual of Mental Disorders*, Fifth Edition, (Copyright © 2013). American Psychiatric Association. All Rights Reserved.

overconcern with body shape and weight is a cardinal feature of both bulimia and anorexia, bulimic individuals do not pursue the extreme thinness characteristic of anorexia. Their ideal weights are similar to those of women who do not suffer from eating disorders (Lowe, Witt, & Grossman, 2013).

The binge itself usually occurs in secret and most commonly at home during unstructured afternoon or evening hours (Guertin, 1999). A binge typically lasts from 30 to 60 minutes and involves consumption of forbidden foods that are generally sweet and rich in fat. Binge eaters typically feel they lack control over their bingeing and may consume 5000 to 10000 calories at a sitting. One young woman described eating everything available in the refrigerator, even to the point of scooping out margarine from its container with her finger (Guertin, 1999). The episode continues until the binger is spent or exhausted, suffers painful stomach distension, induces vomiting, or runs out of food. Drowsiness, guilt, and depression usually ensue, but bingeing is initially pleasant because of release from dietary constraints.

The age range for onset of bulimia is the late teens, when concerns about dieting and dissatisfaction with bodily shape or weight are at their height (APA, 2013).

MEDICAL COMPLICATIONS OF BULIMIA   Bulimia is also associated with many medical complications. Many of these stem from repeated vomiting. There may be irritations of the skin around the mouth (due to frequent contact with stomach acid), blockage of salivary ducts, decay of tooth enamel, and dental cavities (Westmoreland, Krantz, & Mehler, 2016). The acid from the vomit may damage taste receptors on the palate, which may make the person less sensitive to the taste of vomit with repeated purgings. Decreased sensitivity to the aversive taste of vomit may play a role in maintaining the purging

NORMAL/ABNORMAL BEHAVIOUR

Eating Issues: No Disorder

Sophia is a beautiful 41-year-old woman who has struggled with her weight for over 20 years. At five foot six inches, she weighs 140 pounds, and this has fluctuated plus or minus 10 pounds over these last 20 years. She is unhappy with her body shape, feeling that her hips are too big and her stomach is not flat enough. When she was in her 20s, she tried a bunch of fad diets but was never able to sustain any weight loss. She now eschews diets but is always trying to be "careful" about what she eats. She reads food labels and tries not to eat takeout or fast food too often. When she does feel like she's indulged too much, she is a bit stricter with her food intake the following day. For example, she recently had two helpings of dinner at a friend's dinner party and compensated the following day with a smaller breakfast and lunch, and also made sure to go on a brisk walk. Although Sophia still thinks about her weight and shape more than she'd like, it doesn't consume her. She is able to wear a bathing suit in front of others, she doesn't mind clothes shopping, and she still enjoys desserts now and then.

Eating Issues: Eating Disorder

Jiao has always struggled with eating and body image. She was an athlete in high school, excelling in track and cross-country running. Although her body type was not that of a typical runner, she kept herself in excellent condition and trained extensively. Once Jiao graduated from high school, she did not run as often as before and noticed that this led to changes in her body shape and a weight gain of about five pounds. She was annoyed with the change in her weight, and became obsessed with the small folds of skin on her stomach, calling them "disgusting" even when her friends told her they couldn't even see what she was talking about. Though not competing as a runner anymore, Jiao picked up her training schedule again to match what she used to do. After several weeks, she could not see any changes in the shape of her stomach, so she upped her efforts. She began training even more vigorously, running 10 kilometres or more daily. She also reduced her food intake, gradually getting her intake down to 900 calories per day. She refused to eat before she'd exercised. Jiao's weight dropped dramatically. After a few months of this, she became obsessed with food. She dreamed about food, watched cooking shows, and thought about food all day long. Finally, one afternoon she gave in and ate everything she had been denying herself—cookies, chocolate, peanut butter, french fries. . . . She ate until she couldn't eat anymore. Afterwards, she felt disgusted with herself and vowed to run even more the next day. This began a cycle of starvation and bingeing for Jiao.

behaviour. Cycles of bingeing and vomiting may cause abdominal pain, hiatal hernia, and other abdominal complaints. Stress on the pancreas may produce pancreatitis (inflammation), which is a medical emergency. Disturbed menstrual function is found in as many as 50% of normal-weight women with bulimia (Weltzin, Cameron, Berga, & Kaye, 1994; Westmoreland et al., 2016). Excessive use of laxatives may cause bloody diarrhea and laxative dependency, so the person cannot have normal bowel movements without laxatives. In the extreme, the bowel can lose its reflexive eliminatory response to pressure from waste material. Bingeing on large quantities of salty food may cause convulsions and swelling. Repeated vomiting or abuse of laxatives can lead to potassium deficiency, producing muscular weakness, cardiac irregularities, even sudden death—especially when diuretics are used. As with anorexia, menstruation may come to a halt.

Causes of Anorexia and Bulimia

Like other psychological disorders, anorexia and bulimia involve a complex interplay of a host of biopsychosocial factors. Increasingly, researchers are finding that eating disorders arise when underlying genetic and neurobiological vulnerabilities interact with the social pressures felt by young people that lead them to put a high value on their physical appearance, especially their weight (Steiger, 2007).

SOCIOCULTURAL FACTORS Sociocultural theorists point to societal pressures and expectations placed on young men and, to an even greater extent, women in our society as contributing to the development of eating disorders (Ricciardelli, McCabe, Williams, & Thompson, 2007). The pressure to achieve an unrealistic standard of thinness, combined with the importance attached to appearance in defining the female role in our society, can lead young women to strive toward an unrealistically thin ideal and to develop an overriding fear of gaining weight that can put them at risk of developing eating disorders. Additionally, University of Toronto psychologists Janet Polivy and Peter Herman (2002) suggest that in our culture, thinness acts as a point of focus for women's dissatisfaction and distress, and its pursuit serves as an ineffective problem-solving strategy.

The media plays an important role in promoting cultural values and has been shown to exert its influence on both women's and men's reactions to thinness. For example, Canadian female university students participated in a study that examined how they responded to pictures of fashion models who represented the thin ideal. The researchers discovered that the women who viewed the pictures of models were significantly more depressed and angry than the women who viewed pictures that did not contain human figures. This study demonstrates that viewing idealized female models has an immediate negative emotional impact and arguably gives credence to the role media images play in the development of disordered eating attitudes and behaviours (Pinhas, Toner, Ali, Garfinkel, & Stuckless, 1999).

Evidence shows that eating disorders are less common, even rare, in non-Western countries (Ricciardelli et al., 2007). Although the prevalence rate of eating disorders has historically been lower in China, one study reported increased rates of disordered eating cognitions among Chinese women exposed to Western ideals through Internet or television use (Peat et al., 2014). Researchers from the University of Ontario Institute of Technology claim that increased rates of eating disorders among second-generation Canadian South Asian women may reflect an internalized conflict between traditional South Asian values and beliefs and the desire to assimilate into Western society (Mustafa, Zaidi, & Weaver, 2017).

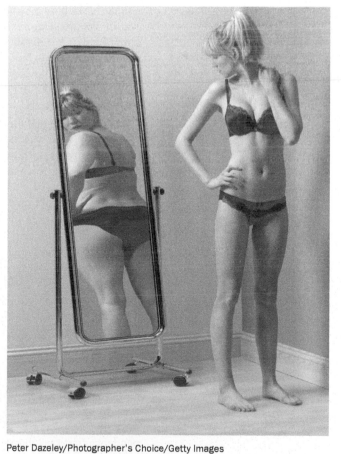

Peter Dazeley/Photographer's Choice/Getty Images

How do I see myself? A distorted body image is a key component of eating disorders.

Studies have found that the more time adolescent girls spend on Facebook and other social media sites, the greater their chances of developing a negative body image and various eating disorders, such as anorexia, bulimia, and exaggerated dieting (Cohen & Blaszczynski, 2015; Sidani, Shensa, Hoffman, Hanmer, & Primack, 2016). A similar direct link was found between viewing gossip- and leisure-related television programs (the likes of *Gossip Girl*) and eating disorders in adolescent girls. It was also revealed that the level of personal empowerment in these girls is negatively linked to eating disorders, such that the higher level of empowerment, the more positive the physical self-image and the lower the chances of developing an eating disorder.

Men, too, are experiencing greater dissatisfaction with their body image. They are under increasing media influence to look leaner and more muscular (Leit, Gray, & Pope, 2002). The authors of one Canadian study, for example, have suggested that more males are participating in weight training and bodybuilding in an attempt to achieve the media-endorsed image of the ideal body shape (Goldfield, Blouin, & Woodside, 2006). One side effect of this trend is that male bodybuilders exhibit many eating-related characteristics of men with bulimia nervosa. Competitive bodybuilders show even higher rates of unhealthy eating and weight-control practices than do recreational bodybuilders and may be at risk of developing bulimia nervosa.

Despite the widespread belief that eating disorders, especially anorexia nervosa, are more common among affluent people, Canadian research (Jones et al., 2001) supports evidence that shows no strong linkage between socioeconomic status and eating disorders (Gard & Freeman, 1996). Beliefs that eating disorders are associated with high socioeconomic status may reflect the likelihood that affluent patients find treatment more accessible. Alternatively, it may be that the social pressures on young women to strive to achieve an ultra-thin ideal have now generalized across all socioeconomic levels.

PSYCHOSOCIAL FACTORS Although cultural pressures to conform to an ultra-thin female ideal play a major role in eating disorders, the great majority of young women exposed to these pressures do not develop the disorders. Other factors must be involved. One likely factor involved in bulimic cases is a history of rigid dieting (Anderson, Reilly, Schaumberg, Dmochowski, & Anderson, 2016; Lowe, Thomas, Safer, & Butryn, 2007). Women with bulimia typically engage in extreme dieting characterized by strict rules about what they can eat, how much they can eat, and how often they can eat (Drewnowski, Yee, Kurth, & Krahn, 1994). Not surprisingly, they tend to spend more time thinking about their weight than nonbulimic women (Zotter & Crowther, 1991).

Bulimic women tend to have been slightly overweight preceding the development of bulimia, and the initiation of the binge–purge cycle usually follows a period of strict dieting to lose weight. In a typical scenario, the rigid dietary controls fail, which prompts initial bingeing. This sets in motion a chain reaction in which bingeing leads to fear of weight gain, which prompts self-induced vomiting or excessive exercise to reduce any added weight. Some bulimic women become so concerned about possible weight gain they resort to vomiting after every meal (Thomas & Lovell, 2015). Purging is negatively reinforced by producing relief, or at least partial relief, from anxiety over gaining weight.

Body dissatisfaction is another important factor in eating disorders (Naumann, Tuschen-Caffier, Voderholzer, Schäfer, & Svaldi, 2016). Body dissatisfaction may lead to maladaptive attempts—through self-starvation and purging—to attain a desired body weight or shape. Bulimic and anorexic women tend to be extremely concerned about their body weight and shape (Jacobi, Hayward, de Zwaan, Kraemer, & Agras, 2004).

Cognitive factors are also involved. University of Toronto researchers have found that women with anorexia often have significantly higher perfectionistic attitudes in comparison to healthy controls, and the higher the perfectionism score, the poorer the outcome (Sutandar-Pinnock, Woodside, Carter, Olmsted, & Kaplan, 2003). Perfectionists tend to get down on themselves when they fail to meet the high standards they set, including their rigid dieting standards. Their extreme dieting may give them a sense of control and independence that they may feel they lack in other aspects of their lives. Bulimic women tend to be both perfectionistic and dichotomous ("black or white") in their thinking patterns (Lavender et al., 2016). Thus, they expect themselves to adhere perfectly to their rigid dietary rules and judge themselves as complete failures when they deviate even slightly.

They also judge themselves harshly for episodes of binge eating and purging. These cognitive factors influence each other, as illustrated in Figure 8.1. In addition, women with bulimic tendencies tend to have a dysfunctional cognitive style that may lead to exaggerated beliefs about the negative consequences of gaining weight (Morrison, Waller, & Lawson, 2006).

Researchers have also noted linkages between bulimia and problems in interpersonal relationships. Bulimic women tend to be shy and to have few, if any, close friends (Krug et al., 2013). One study of 21 college women with bulimia and a matched control group of 21 nonbulimic women found that those with bulimia had more social problems. They believed that less social support was available to them and reported more social conflict, especially with family members (Grissett & Norvell, 1992). They also rated themselves, and were judged by others, as less socially skilful than the control group. Although causal links between a lack of social skills and eating disorders remain to be substantiated fully, it is possible that enhancing the social skills of women with bulimia may increase the quality of their relationships and perhaps reduce their tendencies to use food in maladaptive ways.

Young women with bulimia also tend to have more psychological problems and lower self-esteem than other dieters (Jacobi et al., 2004). Canadian researchers have found that close to half of individuals with eating problems also have depressive or anxiety disorders (Meng & D'Arcy, 2015). Perhaps some forms of binge eating involve attempts at

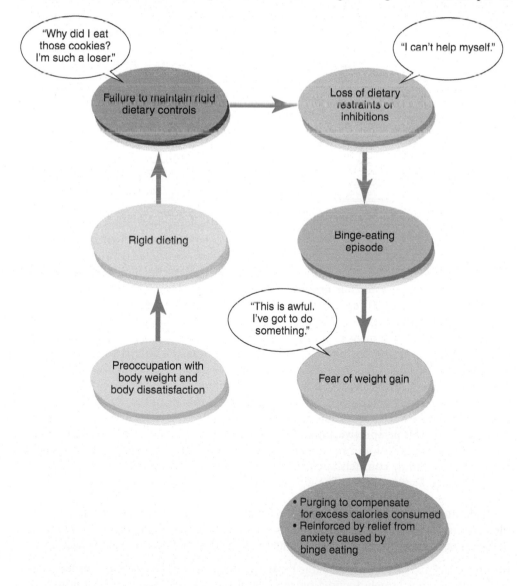

FIGURE 8.1 A potential causal pathway in bulimia nervosa.

Source: Nevid, Jeffrey S., Rathus, Spencer A., Greene, Beverly S. (2014). Abnormal Psychology in a Changing World, 9th Ed. Reprinted and electronically reproduced by permission of Pearson Education, Inc., New York, NY.

Digital Vision/Photodisc/Getty Images

Bingeing. People with bulimia nervosa may cram in thousands of calories during a single binge and then attempt to purge what they have consumed by forcing themselves to vomit.

systems perspective View that problems reflect the systems (family, social, school, ecological, etc.) in which they are embedded.

self-medication for emotional problems. Consistent with this view is evidence that bulimic women are more likely than other women to have experienced childhood sexual and physical abuse (Kent & Waller, 2000). Bulimia may develop in some cases as an ineffective means of coping with abuse (Gonçalves et al., 2016).

What we have gained from this research is the understanding that bulimia often develops within a context of extreme, rigid dieting overlying psychological, interpersonal, and cognitive factors.

FAMILY FACTORS AND EATING DISORDERS Eating disorders frequently develop against a backdrop of family conflicts (Blodgett Salafia, Schaefer, & Haugen, 2014). Some theorists focus on the brutal effect of self-starvation on parents. They suggest that some adolescents use their refusal to eat to punish parents for feelings of loneliness and alienation they experience in the home. One related study compared the mothers of adolescent girls with eating disorders to the mothers of other girls. Mothers of the adolescents with eating disorders were more likely to be unhappy about their families' functioning, to have their own problems with eating and dieting, to believe their daughters ought to lose weight, and to regard their daughters as unattractive (Pike & Rodin, 1991). Moreover, mothers of daughters with eating disorders showed high levels of perfectionism and an overconcern about shape and weight (Woodside et al., 2002). Is binge eating, as suggested by Humphrey (1986), a metaphoric effort to gain the nurturance and comfort that the mother is denying her daughter? Does purging represent the symbolic upheaval of negative feelings toward the family?

Families of young women with eating disorders tend to be more often conflicted while at the same time less cohesive and nurturing and more overprotective and critical than reference groups (Fairburn, Welch, Doll, Davies, & O'Connor, 1997). The parents seem less capable of promoting independence in their daughters (Strober & Humphrey, 1987). Conflicts with parents over issues of autonomy are often implicated in the development of both anorexia nervosa and bulimia (Ratti, Humphrey, & Lyons, 1996). Yet it remains uncertain whether these family patterns contribute to the initiation of eating disorders or whether eating disorders go on to disrupt family life. The truth probably lies in an interaction between the two.

From the **systems perspective**, families are systems that regulate themselves in ways that minimize the open expression of conflict and reduce the immediate need for overt change. Within this perspective, girls who develop anorexia may be seen as helping maintain the shaky balances and harmonies found in dysfunctional families by displacing attention from family conflicts and marital tensions onto themselves (George, Fairchild, Cummings, & Davies, 2014). The girl may become the identified patient although the family unit is actually dysfunctional.

Regardless of the factors that initiate eating disorders, social reinforcers may maintain them. Young women with eating disorders may quickly become the focus of attention of their families and receive attention from their parents that might otherwise be lacking.

BIOLOGICAL FACTORS Interest in the biological underpinnings of eating disorders, especially bulimia, has largely focused on the role of the neurotransmitter serotonin. Serotonin is involved in regulating mood and appetite, especially appetite for carbohydrates. Decreased serotonin activity or responsivity may be involved in prompting binge eating in bulimic individuals, especially carbohydrate bingeing (Levitan, Kaplan, Joffe, Levitt, & Brown, 1997). This line of thinking is buttressed by evidence that antidepressants like Prozac, which increase serotonin activity, can decrease binge-eating episodes in bulimic women (Walsh, Fairburn, Mickley, Sysko, & Parides, 2004). We also know that many women with eating disorders are depressed or have a history of depression, and imbalances of serotonin are implicated in depressive disorders. It may be that bulimia is related to depression, perhaps at a genetic level.

Research has also implicated another common neurotransmitter, dopamine, and the reward circuitry in the brain with bulimia. Dopamine helps regulate behaviour such as learning and motivation. Frank, Reynolds, Shott, and O'Reilly (2011) found that weakened responses in the brain regions implicated in reward were related to the frequency of binge/purge episodes. This might indicate that overeating and purging episodes cause this weaker response and set off a vicious cycle of altered brain function.

Before now, the dopamine–bulimia connection had not been fully explored. The research described here confirms that bulimic behaviour affects the brain's reward function; however, at this point it is uncertain whether these alterations return to normal with recovery. Future developments might include specific medication to alter brain dopamine action.

Another interesting finding related to brain function in those with bulimia was that individuals with bulimia were more impulsive than others during psychological testing. Rachel Marsh and her colleagues at Columbia University and the New York State Psychiatry Institute compared the performance on a task by 20 women with bulimia nervosa with that by 20 healthy women who served as controls (Marsh et al., 2009). During the testing, the women's brain functioning was monitored by means of functional magnetic resonance imaging (fMRI). The task was the Simon Spatial Incompatibility task, in which participants must indicate the direction an arrow is pointing regardless of where it appears on a screen. The task is easier when the arrow direction matches the side of the screen but more difficult when, for instance, an arrow that points left appears on the right-hand side of the screen. Ignoring the side of the screen to focus on the arrow direction requires regulating behaviour, by fighting the tendency to respond automatically and resolving conflicting messages.

Marsh and colleagues (2009) found differences in how the two groups responded. The women with bulimia responded faster and made more errors on conflict trials that required self-regulatory control to respond correctly. They responded faster on congruent trials following incorrect conflict trials, suggesting impulsive responding even immediately after having committed an error. When patients with bulimia did respond correctly on trials in which the arrow side and direction did not match, their frontostriatal circuits did not activate (as should happen) to the same degree as did those of women in the control group.

> These group differences in performance and patterns of brain activity suggest that individuals with bulimia nervosa do not activate frontostriatal circuits appropriately, perhaps contributing to impulsive responses to conflict stimuli that normally require both frontostriatal activation and the exercise of self-regulatory control to generate a correct response. . . . We speculate that this inability to engage frontostriatal systems also contributes to their inability to regulate binge-type eating and other impulsive behaviors. (Marsh et al., 2009, p. 57)

Evidence also supports a genetic link with eating disorders (Baker et al., 2009; Lamberg, 2003). A large-scale study of more than 2000 female twins showed a much higher concordance rate for bulimia nervosa—23% versus 9%—among monozygotic (MZ) twins than among dizygotic (DZ) twins (Kendler et al., 1991). Greater concordance for anorexia is also found among MZ than DZ twins—50% versus 5%—suggesting that genetics plays a role in anorexia as well (Holland, Sicotte, & Treasure, 1988). Eating disorders also tend to run in families, which is further suggestive of a genetic component. However, genetic factors cannot fully account for the development of eating disorders. Eating disorder researchers Howard Steiger and Kenneth Bruce (2007) of the McGill University–affiliated Douglas Hospital Research Centre propose that, as in the diathesis-stress model, a genetic predisposition involving a dysfunction of neurotransmitter activity interacts with family, social, cultural, and environmental pressures, thereby leading to the development of eating disorders.

Canadian studies have also shown that adolescent girls with type 1 diabetes were twice as likely to develop eating disorders as their nondiabetic peers (Frankenfield, 2000). A long-term follow-up of young diabetic women with eating disorders found they had a threefold higher risk of developing diabetic retinopathy (a potentially blinding complication of diabetes that damages the eye's retina) compared to other diabetic women (Rodin et al., 2002). It was recommended that young women with diabetes who have poor metabolic control and who are concerned about their shape and weight should be monitored for a potential eating disorder.

Treatment of Anorexia Nervosa and Bulimia Nervosa

Eating disorders are difficult to treat, and treatment efforts are often met with ongoing denial and resistance by patients with such disorders, especially anorexia (Kaplan & Garfinkel, 1999). People with anorexia may be hospitalized, especially when weight loss is severe or body weight is falling rapidly. In a hospital, they are usually placed on a closely monitored re-feeding regimen. Dalhousie University philosopher Chris MacDonald (2002) alerts us to the ethical dilemma that results when caregivers are confronted with patients who resist treatment. It forces caregivers to decide which interventions, such as tube feeding or chemical restraints, justify a violation of the patient's autonomy and right to refuse treatment, especially when the patient's well-being is at stake.

Allan Kaplan (2002) contends that psychotherapy is still a common treatment for anorexia, but by itself its efficacy remains in question. The best outcomes result from treatment that involves psychotherapy combined with nutritional management and family interventions (Kaplan, 2002). Cognitive analytic therapy has been shown to benefit anorexic patients (Treasure & Ward, 1997). Behaviour therapy has also been shown to be effective in promoting weight gain in anorexic patients (Johnson, Tsoh, & Varnado, 1996). Behaviour therapy is commonly used with rewards made contingent on adherence to the re-feeding protocol (Rock & Curran-Celentano, 1996). Individual or family therapy following hospitalization has also shown favourable long-term benefits (Eisler et al., 1997). Family therapy may also be employed to help resolve underlying family conflicts. Family group psychoeducation (FGP) has been shown to be a cost-effective alternative to family therapy during the first months of treatment for severely

---

QUESTIONNAIRE

The Body Shape Questionnaire

The fear of becoming fat is a prime factor underlying eating disorders such as anorexia and bulimia. The Body Shape Questionnaire (Cooper, Taylor, Cooper, & Fairburn, 1987) measures the degree to which people are concerned about weight and shape and can assist in the diagnosis of an eating disorder. The questionnaire has been adapted for several countries, and numerous studies have confirmed its validity and reliability (e.g. da Silva, Dias, Maroco, & Campos, 2014; Lentillon-Kaestner, Berchtold, Rousseau, & Ferrand, 2014; Welch, Lagerström, & Ghaderi, 2012).

Here is a sample of items from this 34-item questionnaire:

1. Have you been so worried about your shape that you have been feeling that you ought to diet?

2. Have you been afraid that you might become fat (or fatter)?

3. Has being with thin women made you feel self-conscious about your shape?

4. Has thinking about your shape interfered with your ability to concentrate?

5. Have you not gone out to social occasions because you have felt bad about your shape?

6. Have you felt ashamed of your body?

7. Have you thought that you are the shape you are because you lack self-control?

8. Have you vomited in order to feel thinner?

9. Have you taken laxatives in order to feel thinner?

10. Have you avoided wearing clothes which make you particularly aware of the shape of your body?

Source: International Journal of eating disorders, Christopher G Fairburn, © 1987. Reproduced with permission of John Wiley & Sons, Inc.

anorexic teens (Geist, Heinmaa, Stephens, Davis, & Katzman, 2000). FGP provides patients and parents with information about the nature of eating disorders, developmental issues, and weight-regulation issues, and also provides them with opportunities to discuss the information.

Hospitalization may also be used to help break the binge–purge cycle in bulimia, but it appears to be necessary only in cases in which eating behaviours are clearly out of control and outpatient treatment has failed or where there is evidence of severe medical complications, suicidal thoughts or attempts, or substance abuse (APA, 2013).

Cognitive-behavioural therapy (CBT) is useful in helping bulimic individuals challenge self-defeating thoughts and beliefs, such as unrealistic, perfectionistic expectations regarding dieting and body weight (Byrne, Fursland, Allen, & Watson, 2011; Fairburn et al., 2015). Another common dysfunctional thinking pattern is dichotomous (all-or-nothing) thinking, which predisposes bulimic individuals to purge when they slip even a little from their rigid diets. CBT also challenges tendencies to overemphasize appearance in determining self-worth. To eliminate self-induced vomiting, therapists may use the behavioural technique of exposure with response prevention, developed for treatment of people with obsessive-compulsive disorder. In this technique, the bulimic patient is exposed to eating forbidden foods while the therapist stands by to prevent vomiting until the urge to purge passes. Bulimic individuals thus learn to tolerate violations of their dietary rules without resorting to purging.

Another psychologically based treatment, interpersonal psychotherapy, has also shown good success and may be used as an alternative treatment in cases where CBT proves unsuccessful (Murphy, Straebler, Basden, Cooper, & Fairburn, 2012). Interpersonal therapy focuses on resolving interpersonal problems in the belief that more effective interpersonal functioning will lead to healthier food habits and attitudes.

A Canadian study also found that brief therapy interventions are effective for reducing symptoms in bulimic patients. As a first step in their treatment, Carter et al. (2003) found that bulimic patients who were not well informed about bulimia had more problems with intimacy, and those with higher compulsivity scores benefited from self-help manuals that provided information about the disorder or focused on self-assertion skills. In another study, it was shown that group psychoeducation by itself provided therapeutic benefits in six sessions (Hilker et al., 2016).

The pharmacological treatment of eating disorders has generally been disappointing (Zhu & Walsh, 2002). Antidepressant drugs have been shown to provide short-term therapeutic benefits in treating bulimia but have not been very successful in treating anorexia (Walsh et al., 2006). They are believed to work by decreasing the urge to binge through normalizing serotonin—the brain chemical involved in regulating appetite.

A review of the available evidence suggests that CBT is more effective than antidepressant medication in treating bulimia nervosa and carries a lower rate of relapse (Zhu & Walsh, 2002). It appears that CBT should be the first treatment choice for bulimia, followed by use of antidepressant medication if psychological treatment is not successful (Compas, Haaga, Keefe, Leitenberg, & Williams, 1998; Wilson & Fairburn, 1998). Studies examining whether a combined CBT–medication treatment approach is more effective than either treatment component alone have thus far produced inconsistent results (Brown & Keel, 2012).

Treatment of eating disorders in Canada has moved away from relying on long-term hospitalization, psychotherapy, and drugs that have risky side effects. Treatment has progressed toward a team approach that focuses on nutritional stabilization along with brief forms of psychotherapy, group and family psychoeducation, and outpatient care that is tailored to different stages of recovery (LeBlanc, 2014).

Although progress has been made in treating eating disorders, there is considerable room for improvement. Even with CBT, about half of treated patients show continued evidence of bulimic behaviour (Compas et al., 1998; Wilson & Fairburn, 1998). Eating disorders can be a tenacious and enduring problem, especially when excessive fears of body weight and distortions of body image are maintained. One study reported that 10 years after an initial presentation with bulimia, approximately 30% of women still showed recurrent binge-eating or purging behaviours (Keel, Mitchell, Miller, Davis, & Crow, 1999). Recovery from anorexia also tends to be a long process. A study of 88 German patients with anorexia showed that 50% of the patients did not recover sooner than

Many other disordered conditions that involve food, eating, and body image have been identified. Some have a formal diagnosis, while others are somewhat controversial.

Feeding and eating problems associated with infancy and childhood include the following:

- *Pica.* The persistent craving or eating of items that are not food, such as clay, dirt, stones, feces, paint chips, or plastic.
- *Rumination disorder.* Characterized by repeated eating, regurgitation, and then re-chewing and re-eating of food.
- *Feeding disorder of infancy or early childhood.* Persistent failure to consume foods that provide adequate nutrition, which results in weight loss or a failure to gain weight appropriately for development.
- *Prader-Willi syndrome.* A disorder of chromosome 15 characterized by a severe loss of muscle tone and feeding difficulties in early infancy, followed in later childhood by an insatiable appetite, excessive eating, and gradual development of life-threatening obesity.
- *Cyclic vomiting syndrome* (also known as *abdominal migraine*). Characterized by recurrent bouts of severe nausea and vomiting that last for hours or even days and alternate with longer periods without symptoms.

Eating and body image disorders associated with adolescents and adults include the following:

- *Anorexia athletica.* Exercising for an amount of time or at an intensity that is well beyond normal (in association with an obsessive preoccupation with diet and weight).
- *Muscle dysmorphia* (also known as *bigorexia* or *reverse anorexia nervosa*). Common in bodybuilders, a chronic preoccupation with the belief and insecurity that one is not muscular enough, accompanied by a variety of muscle-bulking strategies.

ALL best fitness is HERE/Shutterstock

Bigorexia. People with muscle dysmorphia, also known as *reverse anorexia nervosa*, are preoccupied with the belief that they are not muscular enough and will go to extreme lengths to build muscle.

- *Orthexia nervosa.* Obsession with eating "pure" or "superior" foods and with "proper" food preparation to the point that it interferes with a person's life.
- *Night-eating syndrome.* A form of compulsive eating whereby more than half the person's daily food intake is consumed after dinner and before breakfast, accompanied by feelings of anxiety and guilt.
- *Nocturnal sleep-related eating disorder.* A rare type of sleepwalking disorder characterized by recurrent episodes of eating during sleep; it can lead to significant weight gain.
- *Gourmand syndrome.* An eating disorder linked to damage of the right hemisphere of the brain that results in the person becoming obsessed with shopping for specialty foods and engaging in elaborate food preparation and dining rituals associated with gourmet food.

6 years after their first hospitalization (Herzog, Schellberg, & Deter, 1997). Unfortunately, relapses are common, and upward of 50% of inpatients treated for anorexia nervosa are rehospitalized within a year of discharge (Haynos & Fruzzetti, 2011). Individuals with a premorbid depression have a lesser chance of recovering than those who were not depressed prior to the onset of anorexia (Keski-Rahkonen et al., 2014).

On a more positive note, research has shown that involving parents in treatment of bulimia doubles the success rate. The first randomized controlled study of those dealing with bulimia nervosa took place in 2007 and was run by a team based at the University of Chicago Medical Center ("Involving Parents," 2011). They found that, immediately following treatment, almost 40% of individuals who included their family in the treatment stopped bingeing and purging, while only about 18% of those who participated in the usual treatment, psychotherapy, stopped. Even more encouraging was that six months after the end of their treatment, about 30% of the family-included treatment group were still abstinent (not bingeing and purging), compared to only 10% of the group that received only psychotherapy.

Binge-Eating Disorder

People with binge-eating disorder (BED) have recurrent eating binges but do not purge themselves of the excess food afterwards. Binge eating is accompanied by a sense of lack of control. Typically, binge eating is associated with feelings of shame and attempts to conceal binge-eating behaviour.

Binge-eating disorder is more common than either anorexia or bulimia, affecting about 2.6% of women and 1.4% of men at some point in their lives (Cossrow et al., 2016). Binge-eating disorder tends to develop later in life, often in the person's 30s or 40s. Many, but not all, individuals with BED are either overweight or obese (Bulik, Marcus, Zerwas, Levine, & La Via, 2012). The disorder is frequently associated with people suffering from depression who have a history of unsuccessful attempts at losing excess weight and keeping it off. Like other eating disorders, BED is found more frequently among women, although of all the eating disorders, men are most likely to experience BED (Mason & Heron, 2016).

People with BED are often described as "compulsive overeaters." During a binge, they feel a loss of control over their eating. BED may fall within a broader domain of compulsive behaviours characterized by impaired control over maladaptive behaviours, such as pathological gambling and substance use disorders. A history of dieting may play a role in some cases of BED, although it appears to be a less important factor in BED than in bulimia (Howard & Porzelius, 1999).

Cognitive-behavioural techniques have shown some positive effects in treating binge-eating disorder (Grilo, Crosby, Wilson, & Masheb, 2012). Antidepressants, especially antidepressants of the SSRI family, may also reduce the frequency of binge-eating episodes by helping regulate serotonin levels in the brain (Wilfley et al., 2008).

REVIEW IT

Eating Disorders

- **What are the major types of eating disorders?** There are three major types of eating disorders included in the DSM: anorexia nervosa, bulimia nervosa, and binge-eating disorder. Anorexia nervosa involves maintenance of an abnormally low body weight, intense fears of becoming overweight, and a distorted body image. In comparison, people with bulimia nervosa are usually of normal weight, but because of a preoccupation with weight control and body shape, they engage in repeated binges and regular purging to keep weight down. Another type of eating disorder, binge-eating disorder, involves recurrent episodes of binge eating and feelings of distress.

- **What are some of the factors involved in these types of eating disorders?** They tend to begin in adolescence and affect many more females than males. Both anorexia and bulimia involve preoccupations with weight control and maladaptive ways of trying to keep weight down. Many factors have been implicated in their development, including social pressures on young women to adhere to unrealistic standards of thinness, issues of control, underlying psychological problems, and conflict within the family—especially over issues of autonomy. People with binge-eating disorder tend to be older than those with anorexia or bulimia and to suffer from obesity.

SLEEP–WAKE DISORDERS

Sleep is a biological function that remains in many ways a mystery. We know that sleep is restorative and that most of us need at least seven or more hours of sleep a night to function at our best. Yet we cannot identify the specific biochemical changes occurring during sleep that account for its restorative function. We also know that many of us are troubled by sleep problems, although the causes of some of these problems remain

sleep–wake disorders Diagnostic category representing persistent or recurrent sleep-related problems that cause significant personal distress or impaired functioning.

polysomnographic (PSG) recording The simultaneous measurement of multiple physiological responses during sleep or attempted sleep.

insomnia Term applying to difficulties falling asleep, remaining asleep, or achieving restorative sleep.

obscure. Sleep problems of sufficient severity and frequency that lead to significant personal distress or impaired functioning in social, occupational, or other roles are classified in the DSM system as **sleep–wake disorders**.

Highly specialized diagnostic facilities, called *sleep disorders centres*, have been established throughout Canada to provide a more comprehensive assessment of sleep problems. The Canadian Sleep Society provides a list of about 130 sleep centres across Canada (see https://css-scs.ca). People with sleep–wake disorders typically spend a few nights at a sleep centre, where they are wired to devices that track their physiological responses during sleep or attempted sleep—brainwaves, heart and respiration rates, and so on. This form of assessment is called **polysomnographic (PSG) recording**, because it involves simultaneous measurement of diverse physiological response patterns, including brainwaves, eye movements, muscle movements, and respiration. Information obtained from physiological monitoring of sleep patterns is combined with that obtained from medical and psychological evaluations, subjective reports of sleep disturbance, and sleep diaries (daily logs compiled by the problem sleeper that track the length of time between retiring to bed and falling asleep, number of hours slept, nightly awakenings, daytime naps, etc.). Multidisciplinary teams of physicians and psychologists in sleep centres sift through this information to arrive at a diagnosis and suggest treatment approaches to address the presenting problem.

There are a number of different types of sleep–wake disorders, including the major types we discuss here: insomnia disorder, hypersomnolence disorder, narcolepsy, breathing-related sleep disorders, circadian rhyhm sleep–wake disorders, and parasomnias.

Insomnia Disorder

The word **insomnia** derives from the Latin *in-*, meaning "not" or "without," and, of course, *somnus*, meaning "sleep." Occasional bouts of insomnia, especially during times of stress, are not abnormal. All the same, more than an estimated 3.3 million Canadians aged 15 and older suffer from insomnia, averaging just 6.5 hours of sleep a night—a full hour less than those who don't have insomnia (Tjepkema, 2005). Although chronic insomnia affects older people in greater numbers, young people usually complain that it takes too long to get to sleep whereas older people are more likely to complain of waking frequently during the night or of waking too early in the morning. Many seniors also have more chronic health problems that interfere with their sleep patterns (Tjepkema, 2005). A diagnosis of insomnia disorder requires that the problem occurs at least three nights per week for at least three months (APA, 2013). Overall, there are a host of factors that can have a negative impact on the odds of Canadians getting a good night's sleep, including, for example, high levels of life stress; shift work; heavy drinking or cannabis use; obesity; being divorced, separated, or widowed; being female; and lower levels of education and income (Tjepkema, 2005).

Chronic insomnia may also be a feature of an underlying physical problem or of a psychological disorder such as depression. If the underlying problem is treated successfully, chances are that normal sleep patterns will be restored. Insomnia disorder cannot be accounted for by another psychological or physical disorder or by the effects of drugs or medications. People with insomnia disorder have persistent difficulty falling asleep, remaining asleep, or achieving restorative sleep (sleep that leaves the person feeling refreshed and alert). The sleep disturbance or associated daytime fatigue causes significant levels of personal distress or difficulties performing usual social, occupational, student, or other roles. Not surprisingly, there is a high rate of comorbidity (co-occurrence) between insomnia disorder and other psychological problems, especially anxiety and depression (Morin, LeBlanc, Daley, Gregoire, & Mérette, 2006; Toward Optimized Practice, 2007). The prevalence of insomnia disorder is estimated to be about 6–10% of the population and is considered the most common form of sleep disturbance (APA, 2013). Canadian researchers from Université Laval in Quebec surveyed 2000 adults across Canada and found that almost 20% were dissatisfied with their sleep and that 13.4% met the diagnostic criteria for insomnia disorder. Greater prevalence rates were found among women (15.6%) than men (11%) (Morin et al., 2011). A review of studies reporting on the prevalence rates of insomnia disorder in university students obtained a mean prevalence rate of 18.5% (Jiang et al., 2015).

There's a price to be paid for sleep deprivation associated with insomnia. Research shows the sleep-deprived brain is less able to concentrate, pay attention, respond quickly, solve problems, and remember recently acquired information (Florian, Vecsey, Halassa, Haydon, & Abel, 2011; Lim & Dinges, 2010). Chronic sleep deprivation—regularly getting too little sleep—is linked to a range of serious physical health problems, including poorer immune system functioning (Carpenter, 2013). The immune system protects the body against disease, so it is not surprising that researchers report that people who sleep less than seven hours a night had a threefold higher risk of developing the common cold after exposure to cold viruses than those who sleep eight or more hours nightly (Cohen, Doyle, Alper, Janicki-Deverts, & Turner, 2009).

Psychological factors play a prominent role in insomnia. For example, University of Ottawa psychologists found that high levels of anxiety were associated with moderate to severe sleep-onset chronic insomnia (Viens, De Koninck, Mercier, St-Onge, & Lorrain, 2003). People troubled by insomnia tend to bring their anxieties and worries to bed with them, which raises their bodily arousal to a level that prevents natural sleep. Then they worry about not getting enough sleep, which only compounds their sleep difficulties. They may try to force themselves to sleep, which tends to backfire by creating more anxiety and tension, making sleep even less likely to occur. Sleep cannot be forced. Trying to make yourself fall asleep is likely to backfire. We can set the scene for sleep only by retiring when we are tired and relaxed and allowing sleep to occur naturally.

Hypersomnolence Disorder

The word *hypersomnolence* is derived from the Greek *hyper*, meaning "over" or "more than normal," and the Latin *somnus*, meaning "sleep." Hypersomnolence disorder involves a pattern of excessive sleepiness during the day occurring at least three days a week for a period of at least three months (APA, 2013). People with hypersomnolence disorder may sleep nine or more hours a night but still not feel refreshed upon awakening. Or there may be a pattern of daytime sleep episodes occurring virtually every day in the form of intended or unintended napping (such as inadvertently falling asleep while watching television). Despite the fact that daytime naps often last an hour or more, the person does not feel refreshed after the nap. The disorder cannot be accounted for by inadequate amounts of sleep during the night due to insomnia, by another psychological or physical disorder, by drug or medication use, or by other factors (such as loud neighbours keeping the person up).

Although many of us feel sleepy during the day from time to time, and may even drift off occasionally while reading or watching television, the person with hypersomnolence disorder has more persistent and severe periods of sleepiness that typically lead to difficulties in daily functioning, such as missing important meetings because of difficulty awakening. Although the prevalence of the disorder is unknown, 5–10% of those who present at sleep disorder clinics are given a diagnosis of hypersomnolence disorder (APA, 2013).

hypersomnolence disorder Sleep–wake disorder involving a persistent pattern of excessive sleepiness during the day.

Narcolepsy

The word **narcolepsy** derives from the Greek *narke*, meaning "stupor," and *lepsis*, meaning "an attack." People with narcolepsy experience sleep attacks in which they suddenly fall asleep without any warning at various times during the day. They remain asleep for an average period of about 15 minutes. The person can be in the midst of a conversation at one moment and slump to the floor fast asleep a moment later. The diagnosis is made when sleep attacks occur at least three times per week for a period of three months or longer and are combined with the presence of one of the following conditions: (1) **cataplexy** (a sudden loss of muscular control), (2) deficiency of hypocretin (a protein-like molecule

narcolepsy Sleep–wake disorder characterized by sudden, irresistible episodes of sleep (sleep attacks).

cataplexy Brief, sudden loss of muscular control, typically lasting from a few seconds to as long as two minutes.

REM sleep REM (rapid eye movement) sleep is the stage of sleep associated with dreaming that is characterized by the appearance of rapid eye movements under closed eyelids. Hypocretin neurotransmitter is involved in arousal and wakefulness.

neuropeptide An amino acid found in cerebrospinal fluid that plays a role in neuronal transmission and the modulation of brain circuits or regions.

breathing-related sleep disorders Sleep disorders in which sleeping is repeatedly disrupted due to difficulties breathing normally.

obstructive sleep apnea hypopnea Type of breathing-related disorder involving repeated episodes of either complete or partial obstruction of breathing during sleep.

apnea Temporary cessation of breathing.

produced by the hypothalamus that plays an important role in regulating the sleep–wake cycle), and (3) intrusions of **REM sleep** in the transitional state between wakefulness and sleep. REM, or rapid eye movement, sleep is the stage of sleep associated with dreaming. It is so named because the sleeper's eyes tend to dart about rapidly under his or her closed lids. Narcoleptic attacks are associated with an almost immediate transition into REM sleep from a state of wakefulness. In normal sleep, REM typically follows several stages of non-REM sleep.

Cataplexy typically follows a strong emotional reaction such as joy or anger. It can range from a mild weakness in the legs to a complete loss of muscle control that results in the person suddenly collapsing (Siegel, 2004). People with narcolepsy may also experience sleep paralysis, a temporary state following awakening in which the person feels incapable of moving or talking. The person may also report frightening hallucinations, called *hypnagogic hallucinations*, which occur just before the onset of sleep and tend to involve visual, auditory, tactile, and kinesthetic (body movement) sensations.

Narcolepsy affects men and women equally and is a relatively uncommon disorder, affecting an estimated 0.02% (2 in 10 000) to 0.04% (4 in 10 000) people within the general adult population (APA, 2013). Unlike hypersomnolence disorder, in which daytime sleep episodes follow a period of increasing sleepiness, narcoleptic attacks occur abruptly, without prior sleepiness. The attacks can be dangerous and frightening, especially if they occur when the person is driving or using heavy equipment or sharp implements. About two out of three people with narcolepsy have fallen asleep while driving, and four out of five have fallen asleep on the job (Aldrich, 1992). Household accidents resulting from falls are also common (Cohen, Ferrans, & Eshler, 1992). Not surprisingly, the disorder is associated with a lower quality of life in terms of general health and daily functioning (Ferrans, Cohen, & Smith, 1992). Scientists have discovered that narcolepsy with cataplexy is related to low levels of a **neuropeptide**, hypocretin, in the cerebrospinal fluid in the brain (Baumann, Khatami, Werth, & Bassetti, 2006). The hypocretin deficiency is due to a loss of hypocretin-producing neurons, but the exact cause of that loss remains unknown.

Breathing-Related Sleep Disorders

People with a **breathing-related sleep disorder** experience repeated disruptions of sleep due to respiratory problems (APA, 2013). These frequent disruptions of sleep result in insomnia or excessive daytime sleepiness.

The subtypes of the disorder are distinguished in terms of the underlying causes of the breathing problem. The most common type is **obstructive sleep apnea hypopnea**, which involves repeated episodes of either complete or partial obstruction of breathing during sleep (APA, 2013). The word **apnea** derives from the Greek prefix *a-*, meaning "not" or "without," and *pneuma*, meaning "breath." The breathing difficulty results from the blockage of airflow in the upper airways, often due to a structural defect, such as an overly thick palate or enlarged tonsils or adenoids. In cases of complete obstruction, the sleeper may literally stop breathing for periods of 15 to 90 seconds as many as 30 times an hour, or more in severe cases (APA, 2013; Fleetham et al., 2006). When these lapses of breathing occur, the sleeper may suddenly sit up, gasp for air, take a few deep breaths, and fall back asleep without awakening or realizing that breathing was interrupted. The narrowing of the air passages also produces loud snoring, which alternates with these momentary silences when breathing is suspended (APA, 2013).

Although a biological reflex kicks in to force a gasping breath after these brief interruptions of breathing, the frequent disruptions of normal sleep resulting from apneas can leave people feeling sleepy the following day, making it more difficult for them to function effectively. Obstructive sleep apnea hypopnea is a relatively common problem, affecting an estimated 2–15% of middle-aged adults and 20% of older adults (APA, 2013). The disorder is more common in younger men than women, but the rates increase and become more similar in both men and women as they approach age 50 (Bardwell, Moore, Ancoli-Israel, & Dimsdale, 2003). It is also much more common among people who are obese (e.g., because of a narrowing of the upper airways caused by an enlargement of soft tissue); along with rising obesity rates in people across North America, we are now seeing an associated rise in the incidence of sleep apnea (Banno, Walld, & Kryger, 2005). Alcohol use before bedtime can also cause snoring from a narrowing of the breathing passageways that sometimes turns into outright blockages, resulting in sleep apneas (Kitamura et al., 2016).

People with sleep apnea may gasp for breath hundreds of times during the night without realizing it. They may become aware of the problem only when it is diagnosed or when their bed partners point it out to them. The person's bed partner is usually very aware of the problem because the loudness of the person's snoring can reach levels associated with industrial noise pollution (Caffier et al., 2007). Bed partners commonly look for other sleeping places to obtain a good night's sleep. Not surprisingly, people who have sleep apnea report a poorer quality of life than unaffected people; they are vulnerable to excessive daytime sleepiness, impaired intellectual and memory functioning, and depression—factors that can contribute to the loss of employment, marriage breakups, and accidents at work and on the road (Banno & Kryger, 2007). Sleep apnea is also associated with an increased risk of high blood pressure, heart attacks, strokes, cancer, and even sudden death (Campos-Rodriguez et al., 2012; Marin et al., 2012; Martinez-Garcia, Campos-Rodriguez, Almendros, & Farré, 2015).

Wavebreakmedia/Shutterstock

Obstructive sleep apnea hypopnea. Loud snoring may be a sign of obstructive sleep apnea hypopnea, a breathing-related sleep disorder in which a person may temporarily stop breathing as many as 500 times during a night's sleep. Loud snoring, described by bed partners as reaching levels of industrial noise pollution, may alternate with momentary silences when breathing is suspended.

Not only does obstructive sleep apnea result in personal suffering, there is also a high cost to the health-care system when it goes undiagnosed. Meir Kryger and others at Winnipeg's St. Boniface Hospital Research Centre, North America's first sleep disorder breathing lab, tracked medical system usage by sleep apnea patients before and after treatment (Kryger, 2001). In studies that looked at the two-year and ten-year time spans preceding diagnosis, it was shown that sleep apnea patients used about two times the medical resources as the general population (Ronald et al., 1999). Prior to diagnosis for apnea, patients were being treated for cardiovascular diseases, chronic obstructive airways disease, and depression, which accounted for most of the increased medical resource utilization (Smith et al., 2002). The good news is that once apnea patients are diagnosed and they follow a treatment regime, there is a significant reduction in medical care costs (Bahammam et al., 1999). Toronto Western Hospital psychiatrists conducted a review of the sleep apnea literature and concluded that the disorder has serious medical, socioeconomic, and psychological consequences, although it remains largely undiagnosed (Chung, Jairam, Hussain, & Shapiro, 2002). They contend that by detecting and treating obstructive sleep apnea, morbidity and mortality rates and health-care costs associated with the disorder will be reduced. Consequently, they strongly recommend that primary-care physicians be prepared to screen patients who have symptoms of obstructive sleep apnea and refer them for an overnight (polysomnographic) assessment at a sleep clinic.

Circadian Rhythm Sleep–Wake Disorders

Most bodily functions follow a cycle or an internal rhythm—called a circadian rhythm—that lasts about 24 hours. Even when people are relieved of scheduled activities and work duties and placed in environments that screen the time of day, they usually follow relatively normal sleep–wake schedules. Our circadian rhythm appears to be partially genetically based—we tend to be either morning people (early risers who are more alert early in the day) or evening people (late risers who are more alert at night) (Hur, 2007).

In **circadian rhythm sleep–wake disorders**, this rhythm becomes grossly disturbed because of a mismatch between the sleep schedule demands imposed on the person and the person's internal sleep–wake cycle. The disruption in normal sleep patterns can lead to insomnia or hypersomnia. The disorder must be persistent and severe enough to cause significant levels of distress or impair one's ability to function in social, occupational, or other roles. The jet lag that can accompany travel between time zones does not qualify because it is usually transient. However, frequent changes of time zones and frequent changes of work shifts (as encountered, for example, by nursing personnel) can induce more persistent or recurrent problems adjusting sleep patterns to scheduling demands, resulting in a circadian rhythm sleep–wake disorder. Treatment may involve a program of making gradual adjustments in the sleep schedule to allow the person's circadian system to become aligned with changes in the sleep–wake schedule (Dahl, 1992).

Parasomnias

Sleep typically runs in cycles of about 90 minutes each that progress from light sleep to deep sleep and then to REM sleep, when most dreams occur. For some people, however, sleep is interrupted by partial or incomplete arousals during sleep. During these partial arousals, the person may appear confused, detached, or disconnected from the environment. The sleeper may be unresponsive to attempts by other people to awaken or comfort him or her. The individual typically gets up the next day without any memory of these episodes of partial arousal.

DSM-5 characterizes abnormal behaviour patterns associated with partial or incomplete arousals as **parasomnias**, a category of sleep–wake disorders that is further divided into disorders associated with REM sleep and those associated with non-REM sleep. The word *parasomnia* literally means "around sleep" and signifies that abnormal behaviours involving partial or incomplete arousals occur around the boundary between wakefulness and sleep. As with other sleep–wake disorders, parasomnias cause significant levels of personal distress or interfere with the person's ability to perform expected social, occupational, or other important life roles. Here we consider the major types of parasomnias associated with REM sleep (nightmare disorder) and non-REM sleep (non-rapid eye movement sleep arousal disorders).

NIGHTMARE DISORDER **Nightmare disorder** involves recurrent awakenings from sleep because of frightening dreams (nightmares). The nightmares are typically lengthy, story-like dreams that involve threats of imminent physical danger to the individual, such as being chased, attacked, or injured. The nightmare is usually recalled vividly upon awakening.

Although alertness is regained quickly after awakening, anxiety and fear may linger and prevent a return to sleep. In a major poll, nearly one in five Canadians reported that they often (3.6%) or sometimes (14.7%) have nightmares that disturb their sleep (Leger Marketing, 2002). The prevalence of frequent nightmares in adults is 1–2% (APA, 2013).

Nightmares are often associated with traumatic experiences and are generally more frequent when the individual is under stress. Supporting the general link between trauma and nightmares, researchers report that the incidence of nightmares was greater among survivors of the 1989 San Francisco earthquake in the weeks following the quake than among comparison groups (Wood, Bootzin, Rosenham, Nolen-Hoeksema, & Jourden, 1992). An increased frequency of nightmares was also observed among children who were exposed to the 1994 Los Angeles earthquake (Kolbert, 1994).

circadian rhythm sleep–wake disorders Sleep disorders characterized by disruption of sleep caused by a mismatch in sleep schedules between the body's internal sleep–wake cycle and the demands of the environment.

parasomnias Category of sleep–wake disorders involving the occurrence of abnormal behaviours or physiological events during sleep or at the transition between wakefulness and sleep.

nightmare disorder Sleep–wake disorder characterized by recurrent awakenings from sleep because of frightening nightmares. Formerly called *dream anxiety disorder*.

Alby851/Shutterstock

Nightmares. Although frightening dreams are common in people of all ages, they occur more frequently during times of stress.

Nightmares generally occur during REM sleep. REM tends to become longer and the dreams occurring during REM more intense in the latter half of sleep, so nightmares usually occur late at night or toward morning. Although nightmares may contain great motor activity, as in fleeing from an assailant, dreamers show little muscle activity. The same biological processes that activate dreams—including nightmares—inhibit body movement, causing a type of paralysis. This is indeed fortunate, as it prevents the dreamer from jumping out of bed and running into a dresser or a wall in an attempt to elude the pursuing assailants from a dream.

NON-RAPID EYE MOVEMENT SLEEP AROUSAL DISORDERS Non-rapid eye movement **sleep arousal disorders** involve recurrent episodes of incomplete arousals from sleep that are accompanied by either *sleep terrors* or *sleepwalking* of sufficient severity to cause significant levels of personal distress or impaired functioning. Sleep terrors typically begin with a loud, piercing cry or scream in the night. Even the most soundly asleep parent will be summoned to their child's bedroom as if shot from a cannon. The child (most cases involve children) may be sitting up, appear frightened, and show signs of extreme arousal—profuse sweating with rapid heartbeat and respiration. The child may start talking incoherently or thrash about wildly but remain asleep. If the child awakens fully, he or she will usually appear confused and disoriented for a few minutes and may not recognize the parent or may attempt to push the parent away. The person may feel a vague sense of terror and be able to report some fragmentary dream images, but not the sort of detailed dreams typical of nightmares. After a few minutes, the child falls back into a deep sleep and upon awakening in the morning remembers nothing of the experience. These terrifying attacks are more intense than ordinary nightmares. Unlike nightmares, sleep terrors tend to occur during the first third of nightly sleep and during deep non-REM sleep (Dahl, 1992).

Sleep terrors in children are typically outgrown during adolescence. More boys than girls are affected by sleep terrors, but among adults the gender ratio is about even. In adults, the disorder tends to follow a chronic course during which the frequency and intensity of the episodes waxes and wanes over time. Episodes of sleep terrors occur in 2.2% of adults and appropriately 36.9% of 18-month-old children and 19.7% of 30-month-old children (APA, 2013). The cause of sleep terrors remains a mystery.

Sleepwalking involves episodes in which the sleeper arises from bed and walks about the house while remaining fully asleep. Because these episodes tend to occur during the deeper stages of sleep, when there is an absence of dreaming, it does not appear that a sleepwalking episode involves the enactment of a dream. Sleepwalking is more common in children, with 2–3% prevalence (APA, 2013). Between 10% and 30% of children are believed to have had at least one episode of sleepwalking. A systematic review of 51 studies revealed a prevalence rate of 1.5% in adults and 5% in children (Stallman & Kohler, 2016). However, perhaps as many as 29.2% of adults have experienced sleepwalking episodes in their lifetime (APA, 2013). The causes of sleepwalking remain obscure, although both genetic and environmental factors are believed to be involved (Zadra, Desautels, Petit, & Montplaisir, 2013).

Although sleepwalkers typically avoid walking into things, accidents occasionally happen. Sleepwalkers tend to have a blank stare on their faces during these episodes. They are generally unresponsive to others and difficult to awaken. When they do awaken the following morning, they typically have little if any recall of the experience. If they are awakened during the episode, they may be disoriented or confused for a few minutes (as is the case with sleep terrors), but full alertness is soon restored. There is no basis to the belief that it is harmful to sleepwalkers to awaken them during episodes.

Isolated incidents of violent behaviour have been associated with sleepwalking, but these are rare occurrences and may well involve other forms of psychopathology. For instance, Canadian psychiatrists describe a type of sleepwalking (*sexsomnia*) that can include sexual activity with other people, while asleep (Shapiro, Trajanovic, & Fedoroff, 2003). Look at the case of D. W.:

non-rapid eye movement sleep arousal disorders Sleep–wake disorders involving recurrent episodes of incomplete arousals during sleep that are accompanied by sleep terrors or sleepwalking.

D. W. is a 43-year-old divorced police officer. He has an extensive sleep history of parasomnias. A few years earlier, he had stood trial for impaired driving and driving under the influence of alcohol. His defence was parasomnia, based on a previous history of sleepwalking and sleep talking that had intensified in the two years prior to his offence. Many features surrounding the case supported the parasomnia (sleepwalking) claim.

Subsequently, it was discovered that Mr. W. had another manifestation of his parasomnia, namely sexsomnia. This emerged at a "routine" follow-up in which the [interviewer] commented to Mr. W. that his "sleep-driving" was being rivalled as the most unusual of parasomnias. A description of sexsomnia was given, and Mr. W. responded by saying, "Oh, but I do that." The disingenuous response by the interviewer—"But you never told me"—was followed by Mr. W. saying, "But you never asked." Mr. W.'s two current girlfriends independently confirmed that he frequently engages in sexual behaviour while asleep. One described him as a "different person" during these activities—apparently, he is a more amorous and gentle lover and more oriented toward satisfying his partner when he is asleep.

Republished with permission of Sage Publications (US), from Sexsomnia: A new parasomnia? Canadian Journal of Psychiatry, Colin M Shapiro; Nikola N Trajanovic; J Paul Fedoroff, 48, 2003; permission conveyed through Copyright Clearance Center, Inc.

Treatment of Sleep–Wake Disorders

The most common pharmacologic method for treating sleep–wake disorders in Canada is the use of sleep medications called **anxiolytics**. However, because of problems associated with these drugs, nonpharmacological treatment approaches, principally cognitive-behavioural therapy, have come to the fore.

BIOLOGICAL APPROACHES Various anxiolytic (anti-anxiety) drugs are frequently used to treat insomnia, including a class of minor tranquillizers called benzodiazepines (e.g., Valium, Ativan, Dalmane, Halcion, and Restoril) and, to a lesser extent, barbiturates (e.g., Seconal, Nembutal, and Amytal) (Szabadi, 2014). (These drugs are also widely used in the treatment of anxiety disorders, as we saw in Chapter 3.) When Canadians were polled in 2002, the results indicated that nearly 1 in 10 takes a sleeping pill to help with sleep (Leger Marketing, 2002). The use of sleeping pills by Canadians increases with age, and two thirds more women than men use them (Health Canada, 1995). However, McMaster University researchers caution that the overall benefit of anxiolytic drugs in comparison to a placebo is relatively minor (Holbrook, Crowther, Lotter, Cheng, & King, 2000). Prudent use of these drugs is recommended, as they can produce adverse side effects as well as dependence if used regularly over time.

When used for the short-term treatment of insomnia, anxiolytics are generally effective in reducing the time it takes to get to sleep, increasing total length of sleep, and reducing nightly awakenings (Nowell, Buysse, Morin, Reynolds, & Kupfer, 1998). They work by reducing arousal and inducing feelings of calmness, thereby making the person more receptive to sleep. However, as many as 10% of sleep disorder patients take sleeping pills for months or years, despite a lack of evidence from controlled studies supporting their long-term efficacy.

A number of problems are associated with using drugs to combat insomnia (Ramakrishnan & Scheid, 2007). Sleep-inducing drugs tend to suppress REM sleep, which may interfere with some of the restorative functions of sleep. They can also lead to a carryover or "hangover" the following day, which is associated with daytime sleepiness and reduced performance. Rebound insomnia can follow discontinuation of the drug, causing worse insomnia than was originally the case. Rebound insomnia may be lessened, however, by tapering off the drug rather than abruptly discontinuing it. These drugs quickly lose their effectiveness at a given dosage level, so progressively larger doses must be used to achieve the same effect. High doses can be dangerous, especially if they

anxiolytics Drugs, such as sedatives and anaesthetics, that induce partial or complete unconsciousness and are commonly used in the treatment of sleep–wake disorders.

are mixed with alcoholic beverages at bedtime. Regular use can also lead to physical dependence (addiction). Once dependence is established, withdrawal symptoms following cessation of use may occur, including agitation, tremors, nausea, headaches, and in severe cases delusions or hallucinations.

Users can also become psychologically dependent on sleeping pills. That is, they can develop a psychological need for the medication and assume they will not be able to get to sleep without it. Because worry about going without drugs heightens bodily arousal, such self-doubts are likely to become self-fulfilling prophecies. Moreover, users may attribute their success in falling asleep to the pill and not to themselves, which strengthens reliance on the drugs and makes it harder to forgo using them.

Not surprisingly, there is little evidence of long-term benefits of drug therapy after withdrawal (Morin & Wooten, 1996). Relying on sleeping pills does nothing to resolve the underlying cause of the problem nor help the person learn more effective ways of coping with it. If anxiolytic drugs like benzodiazepines are to be prescribed at all for sleep problems, they should be used only for a brief period of time (a few weeks at most) and at the lowest possible dose (Holbrook et al., 2000). The aim should be to provide a temporary respite so that the clinician can help the client find effective ways of handling the sources of stress and anxiety that contribute to insomnia.

Minor tranquillizers of the benzodiazepine family and tricyclic antidepressants are also used to treat non-REM sleep arousal disorders—sleep terrors and sleepwalking. They seem to have a beneficial effect by decreasing the length of deep sleep and reducing partial arousals between sleep stages (Dahl, 1992). Use of sleep medications for these disorders, as for insomnia disorder, also incurs the risk of physiological and psychological dependence and thus should be used only in severe cases and only as a temporary means of breaking the cycle.

Narcolepsy is predominantly a neurological disorder, and sleep apnea involves physiological factors. Thus, both disorders are commonly treated using medical interventions. The excessive daytime sleepiness that accompanies narcolepsy is commonly treated with psychostimulants, such as Modafinil, but prospective new therapies are emerging (e.g., hypocretin gene therapy and stem cell transplantation) (Thorpy, 2007). Treatments for sleep apnea range from the use of medical assistive devices (e.g., continuous positive airway pressure—a technique of delivering pressurized air via a face mask to prevent the airway from collapsing—or oral appliances that expand the size of the upper airway) to lifestyle changes (e.g., weight loss, avoiding alcohol and sleeping pills, and a regular sleep routine) to, in some cases, surgery (e.g., to expand the upper airway by removing excess tissue from inside the roof of the mouth) (Banno & Kryger, 2007; Canadian Lung Association, 2006).

PSYCHOLOGICAL APPROACHES Psychological approaches have by and large been limited to treatment of insomnia disorder. Overall, cognitive-behavioural treatment approaches have produced substantial benefits in treating chronic insomnia, as measured by both reductions in sleep latency and improvement of perceived sleep quality (Viens et al., 2003). As many as 60–80% of patients respond favourably. Still, only about a third become good sleepers.

Cognitive-behavioural techniques are short term in emphasis and focus on directly lowering states of physiological arousal, modifying maladaptive sleeping habits, and changing dysfunctional thoughts. Cognitive-behavioural therapists typically use a combination of techniques, including stimulus control, relaxation training, and anxiety-management training. Stimulus control involves changing the stimulus environment associated with sleeping. Under normal conditions, we learn to associate stimuli relating to lying down in bed with sleeping, so exposure to these stimuli comes to induce feelings of sleepiness. But when people use their beds for many other activities—such as eating, reading, and watching television—the bed may lose its association with sleepiness. Moreover, the longer the person with insomnia lies in bed tossing and turning, the more the bed becomes associated with cues related to anxiety and frustration. Stimulus control techniques attempt to strengthen the connection between the bed and sleep by restricting as much as possible the activities spent in bed to sleeping and by limiting the time spent in bed trying to fall asleep to 10 or 20 minutes at a time. If sleep does not occur within the designated time period, the person is instructed to leave the bed and go to another room to restore a relaxed frame of mind before returning to bed, such as by sitting quietly, reading, watching television, or practising relaxation exercises.

Cognitive restructuring involves substituting rational alternatives for self-defeating, maladaptive thoughts or beliefs (see the Closer Look box for examples). The belief that failing to get a good night's sleep will lead to unfortunate, even disastrous, consequences the next day reduces the chances of falling asleep because it raises the level of anxiety and can lead the person to try unsuccessfully to force sleep to happen. Most of us do reasonably well if we lose sleep or even miss a night of sleep, even though we might like more.

Cognitive-behavioural therapy yields substantial therapeutic benefits, as measured by reductions in the time it takes to get to sleep and by improved quality of sleep (Schwartz & Carney, 2012; Vincent & Walsh, 2013). Research supports the use of a cognitive-behavioural intervention for insomnia delivered online that can significantly improve insomnia in adults (Ritterband et al., 2009; Seyffert et al., 2016). Ritterband and colleagues at the American Academy of Sleep Medicine found that sleep improved significantly for those who received a cognitive-behavioural intervention for insomnia via the Internet over a period of six weeks, whereas control participants showed no change during the treatment period. Ritterband reports that all patients with improved sleep after using the Internet intervention maintained these improvements six months after the study's completion. This potentially opens up help to a much wider group of individuals dealing with this difficult problem.

A CLOSER LOOK

To Sleep, Perchance to Dream

Many of us have difficulty from time to time falling asleep or remaining asleep. Although sleep is a natural function and cannot be forced, we can develop more adaptive sleep habits that help us become more receptive to sleep. However, if insomnia or other sleep-related problems persist or become associated with difficulties functioning during the day, it would be worthwhile to have the problem checked out by a professional. Here are some techniques to help you acquire more adaptive sleep habits:

1. Retire to bed only when you feel sleepy.
2. Limit your activities in bed as much as possible to sleeping. Avoid watching television or reading in bed.
3. If after 10 to 20 minutes of lying in bed you are unable to fall asleep, get out of bed, leave the bedroom, and put yourself in a relaxed mood by reading, listening to calming music, or practising self-relaxation.
4. Establish a regular routine. Sleeping late to make up for lost sleep can throw off your body clock. Set your alarm for the same time each morning and get up, regardless of how many hours you have slept.
5. Avoid naps during the daytime. You'll feel less sleepy at bedtime if you catch Z's during the afternoon.
6. Avoid ruminating in bed. Don't focus on solving your problems or organizing the rest of your life as you're attempting to sleep. Tell yourself that you'll think about tomorrow tomorrow. Help yourself enter a more sleepful frame of mind by engaging in a mental

Dougal Waters/Photodisc/Getty Images

Is your bed a cue for sleeping? People who use their beds for many activities, including eating, reading, and watching television, may find that lying in bed loses its association with sleeping. Behaviour therapists use stimulus control techniques to help people with insomnia create a stimulus environment associated with sleeping.

>

fantasy or mind trip, or just let all thoughts slip away from consciousness. If an important idea comes to you, don't rehearse it in your mind. Jot it down on a handy pad of paper so you won't lose it. But if thoughts persist, get up and follow them elsewhere.

7. Put yourself in a relaxed frame of mind before sleep. Some people unwind before bed by reading; others prefer watching television or just resting quietly. Do whatever you find most relaxing. You may find it helpful to incorporate into your regular bedtime routine techniques for lowering your level of arousal, such as meditation or progressive relaxation.

8. Establish a regular daytime exercise schedule. Regular exercise during the day (not directly before bedtime) can help induce sleepiness upon retiring.

9. Avoid use of caffeinated beverages, such as coffee and tea, in the evening or late afternoon. Also, avoid drinking alcoholic beverages. Alcohol can interfere with normal sleep patterns (reduced total sleep, REM sleep, and sleep efficiency) even when consumed six hours before bedtime.

10. Practise rational restructuring. Substitute rational alternatives for self-defeating thoughts. Here are some examples:

Self-Defeating Thoughts	Rational Alternatives
"I must fall asleep right now or I'll be a wreck tomorrow."	"I may feel tired, but I've been able to get by with little sleep before. I can make up for it tomorrow by getting to bed early."
"What's the matter with me that I can't seem to fall asleep?"	"Stop blaming yourself. You can't control sleep. Just let whatever happens happen."
"If I don't get to sleep right now, I won't be able to concentrate tomorrow on the exam (conference, meeting, etc.)."	"My concentration may be off a bit, but I'm not going to fall apart. There's no point blowing things out of proportion. I might as well get up for a while and watch a little television rather than lie here ruminating."

REVIEW II

Sleep–Wake Disorders

- **What are the major types of sleep–wake disorders?** The major types of sleep–wake disorders include insomnia disorder, hypersomnolence disorder, narcolepsy, breathing-related sleep disorders, circadian rhythm sleep–wake disorders, and parasomnias. Parasomnias involve disturbed behaviours or abnormal physiological responses occurring either during sleep or at the threshold between wakefulness and sleep. They include nightmare disorder and non-rapid eye movement sleep arousal disorders (sleep terror type and sleepwalking type).

- **What are the major forms of treatment for sleep–wake disorders?** The most common form of treatment for sleep disorders involves the use of anxiolytic drugs. However, use of these drugs should be time limited because of the potential for psychological or physical dependence, among other problems associated with their use. Cognitive-behavioural interventions have produced substantial benefits in helping people with chronic insomnia.

Define It

amenorrhea, 296
anorexia nervosa, 294
anxiolytics, 314
apnea, 310
binge-eating disorder, 294
breathing-related sleep disorders, 310
bulimia nervosa, 294
cataplexy, 309
circadian rhythm sleep–wake disorders, 312

feeding and eating disorders, 294
hypersomnolence disorder, 309
insomnia, 308
narcolepsy, 309
neuropeptide, 310
nightmare disorder, 312
non-rapid eye movement sleep arousal disorders, 313
obstructive sleep apnea hypopnea, 310
osteoporosis, 296

parasomnias, 312
polysomnographic (PSG) recording, 308
REM sleep, 310
sleep–wake disorders, 308
systems perspective, 302

Recall It

1. Deaths associated with anorexia nervosa most commonly result from _____.
   a. cancer
   b. suicide or direct complications from severe weight loss
   c. pancreatic disorders caused by calcium deficiencies
   d. thrombosis

2. The behaviour technique of _____ is used to help people with bulimia nervosa tolerate eating forbidden foods without resorting to purging.
   a. relapse-prevention training
   b. cognitive restructuring
   c. exposure with response prevention
   d. response-contingent reinforcement

3. The diagnosis of binge-eating disorder is applied most often to _____.
   a. young women with a history of anorexia
   b. young women without a history of anorexia
   c. women who are typically older than those with anorexia or bulimia
   d. men and women in about equal proportions

4. People who suddenly fall asleep without any warning at various times during the day suffer from _____.
   a. apnea
   b. hypersomnia
   c. circadian rhythm sleep disorder
   d. narcolepsy

5. Parasomnias involve _____.
   a. abnormal behaviours or physiological events that occur during sleep or during the threshold between wakefulness and sleep
   b. difficulties falling asleep or remaining asleep
   c. disturbances in the body's regulation of the sleep–wake cycle
   d. excessive sleepiness during the day

Answers to Recall It

1. b,   2. c,   3. c,   4. d,   5. a

Think About It

- How are sociocultural factors related to the development of eating disorders? How might we as a society change the social influences that lead many young women to develop disordered eating habits?
- Do you believe that high-risk anorexic patients who resist or refuse treatment should be forced to accept medical intervention? Why or why not?
- Do your sleep habits help or hinder your sleeping patterns? Explain.
- What are the drawbacks of relying on sleep medications to combat chronic insomnia? Do you get enough sleep? If not, what can you do about it?

Weblinks

Eating Disorders
www.phac-aspc.gc.ca/publicat/miic-mmac/pdf/chap_6_e.pdf
This webpage links to the chapter on eating disorders from Health Canada's *A Report on Mental Illness in Canada* (2002b).

Internet Mental Health
http://mentalhealth.com/home/dx/anorexia.html
The Internet Mental Health site has links to information about anorexia nervosa and bulimia.

Bulimia Anorexia Nervosa Association
www.bana.ca
This site offers Canadian-focused information and support for eating disorders.

National Eating Disorder Information Centre (NEDIC)
www.nedic.ca
This site provides Canadian information and resources on eating disorders and weight preoccupation.

Canadian Sleep Society (CSS)
https://css-scs.ca
The CSS's website has information on research and links to treatment centres.

Eating Disorders and Sleep–Wake Disorders

Test your understanding of the key concepts by filling in the blanks with the correct statements chosen from the list that follows. The answers are found at the end of the chapter.

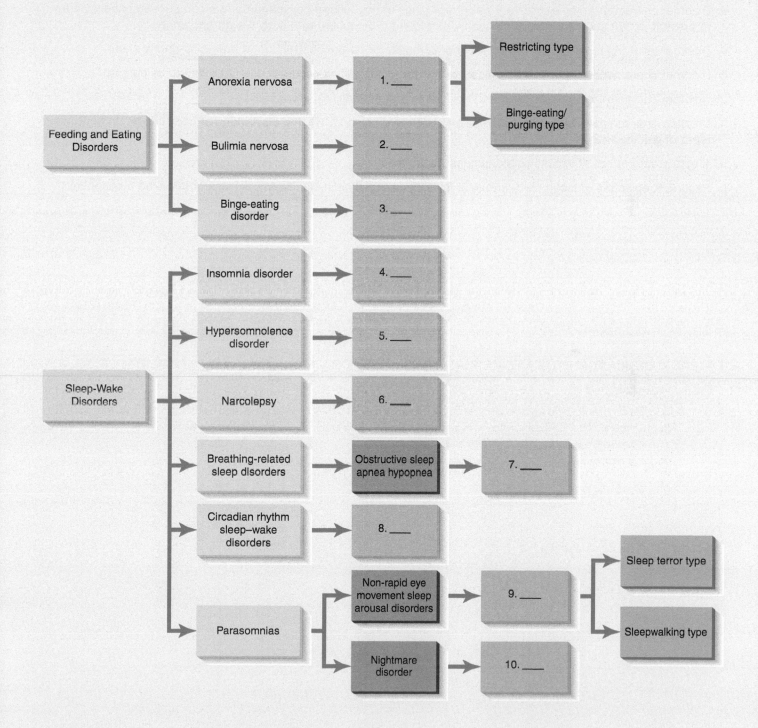

a. Individuals with this disorder have persistent difficult falling asleep, remaining asleep, or achieving restorative sleep

b. Disruption of sleep due to a mismatch in sleep schedules between the body's internal sleep–wake cycle and the demands of the environment

c. Recurrent awakenings from sleep because of frightening nightmares

d. Disorder characterized by a recurrent pattern of binge eating followed by inappropriate compensatory behaviours to prevent weight gain, and accompanied by persistent overconcern with body weight and shape

e. Disorder involving repeated episodes of either complete or partial obstruction of breathing during sleep

f. Disorder characterized by repeated episodes in which binge eating occurs but is not followed by purging

g. Disorder characterized by sudden, irresistible episodes of sleep

h. Disorder characterized by maintenance of an abnormally low body weight, distortions of body image, and intense fears of gaining weight

i. A persistent pattern of excessive sleepiness during the day

j. Recurrent episodes of incomplete arousals from sleep resulting in significant distress or impaired functioning

Answers: 1. h, 2. d, 3. f, 4. a, 5. i, 6. g, 7. e, 8. b, 9. j, 10. c

9

Gender Dysphoria, Paraphilic Disorders, and Sexual Dysfunctions

CHAPTER OUTLINE

Did You Know That...

- Unlike people with gender dysphoria, gay and lesbian people do not perceive themselves as members of the opposite sex?

- Homosexuality was once considered a psychological disorder?

- Professional strippers are not classified as exhibitionists?

- Becoming sexually aroused by watching your partner disrobe or viewing an X-rated movie is not a form of voyeuristic disorder?

- Some people cannot become sexually aroused unless others subject them to pain or humiliation?

- In most cases of sexual assault, the woman was acquainted with the assailant?

- Orgasm is a reflex?

- Premature ejaculation affects about one out of three men?

- Both men and women have the male sex hormone testosterone circulating in their bodies?

- The drug Viagra, used in the treatment of erectile dysfunction, became the fastest-selling drug in history when it was introduced?

Ballyscanlon/Photodisc/Getty Images

Ballyscanlon/Photodisc/Getty Images

Ballyscanlon/Photodisc/Getty Images

Off the fog-bound shore of Ireland lies the isle of Inis Beag.[1] From the air it is an emerald jewel, warm and enticing. From the ground, the perspective is different.

The inhabitants of Inis Beag believe that normal women do not have orgasms and that those who do must be deviant (Messenger, 1971). Premarital sex is virtually unknown. Women participate in sexual relations to conceive children and pacify their husbands' lustful urges. They need not be concerned about being called on for frequent performances because the men of Inis Beag believe, groundlessly, that sex saps their strength. Relations on Inis Beag take place in the dark—literally and figuratively—and with night-clothes on. Consistent with local standards of masculinity, the man ejaculates as quickly as he can. Then he rolls over and goes to sleep, without concern for his partner's satisfaction. Women do not complain, however, as they are reared to believe it is abnormal for them to experience sexual pleasure.

If Inis Beag is not your cup of tea, perhaps the ambience of the island of Mangaia will strike you as more congenial. Mangaia is a Polynesian pearl; languidly, it lifts out of the azure waters of the Pacific. Inis Beag and Mangaia are on opposite sides of the world— literally and figuratively.

From childhood, Mangaian children are expected to explore their sexuality through masturbation (Marshall, 1971). Mangaian teenagers are encouraged by their elders to engage in sexual relations. They are often found on hidden beaches or beneath the sheltering fronds of palms, industriously practising skills acquired from their elders. Mangaian women usually reach orgasm numerous times before their partners do. Young men vie to see who is more skilful in helping their partner attain multiple orgasms.

The inhabitants of Mangaia and Inis Beag have identical anatomic features and the same hormones pulsing through their bodies. Their attitudes and cultural values about what is normal and abnormal differ vastly, however. Their attitudes affect their sexual behaviour and the enjoyment they attain—or do not attain—from sex. In sex, as in other areas of behaviour, the lines between normal and abnormal are not always drawn precisely. Sex, like eating, is a natural function. Yet this natural function has been profoundly affected by cultural, religious, and moral beliefs, customs, folklores, and superstitions.

Even in Canada today we find attitudes as diverse as those on Inis Beag and Mangaia. Some people feel guilty about any form of sexual activity and thus reap little if any pleasure from sex. Others, who see themselves as sexually liberated, may worry about whether they have become free enough or skilful enough in their sexual activity.

In the realm of sexual behaviour, our conceptions of what is normal and what is not are clearly influenced by sociocultural factors. Various patterns of sexual behaviour that might be considered abnormal in Inis Beag, such as masturbation, premarital intercourse, and oral-genital sex, are normal in Western society from the standpoint of statistical frequency. For example, a survey of a representative sample of 3432 males and females between the ages of 18 and 59 found that 63% of adult men and 42% of adult women questioned reported that they had masturbated during the previous year (Laumann, Gagnon, Michael, & Michaels, 1994). It is likely that many more practised masturbation but were hesitant to admit so to interviewers.

Behaviour may be labelled abnormal because it deviates from the norms of one's society. For example, kissing is a highly popular form of mild petting in Western cultures but is considered

---

[1] "Inis Beag" is a pseudonym for an actual small Irish community studied by cultural anthropologist John Cowan Messenger between 1958 and 1966.

deviant behaviour in some societies, such as among the Sirionó of Bolivia and the Thonga of Africa. The Thonga tribesmen were shocked when they first observed European visitors kissing, and one man exclaimed, "Look at them—they eat each other's saliva and dirt."

Sexual behaviour may also be considered abnormal if it is self-defeating, harms others, causes personal distress, or interferes with one's ability to function. The disorders we feature in this chapter—gender dysphoria, paraphilic disorders, and sexual dysfunctions—meet one or more of the criteria of abnormality. In exploring these disorders, we touch on questions that probe the boundaries between abnormality and normality. For example, is gay or lesbian sexual orientation a psychological disorder? Are some instances of voyeurism or exhibitionism normal and others abnormal? When is it considered abnormal to have difficulty becoming sexually aroused or reaching orgasm?

Continuum of Sexual Dysfunctions

Example: Erectile Disorder

Does not meet criteria		Meets criteria		
NO SYMPTOMS	**STRUGGLING**	**MILD**	**MODERATE**	**SEVERE**
	It upsets Brad on the few occasions when he is unable to achieve an erection.	Reginald is mildly distressed that he has difficulty maintaining an erection during most sexual encounters.	Frank reports moderate distress by his inability to obtain an erection in the majority of occasions of sexual activity.	Bruce is extremely distressed that he has never been able to sustain an erection throughout a sexual encounter.

GENDER DYSPHORIA

Our **gender identity** is our sense of being male or female. Gender identity is normally based on anatomic gender, and in the normal run of things, our gender identity is consistent with our anatomic gender. In **gender dysphoria,** the individual experiences significant personal distress or impaired functioning as a result of a discrepancy between his or her anatomic sex and gender identity. The word *dysphoria* (from the Greek *dysphoros,* meaning "difficult to bear") refers to feelings of dissatisfaction or discomfort.

People with a **transgender identity** have the psychological sense of belonging to one gender while possessing the sexual organs of the other. Not all people with transgender identity have gender dysphoria or any other diagnosable disorder. A disorder exists only if a condition causes significant distress or disability. A good portion of transgendered people do not find their gender distressing. Finding the necessary support to express their gender identity and minimize discrimination is their focus, not a mental disorder. It should also be noted that the diagnosis of gender dysphoria is not without controversy, as some contend it inappropriately pathologizes gender noncongruence.

Gender is a psychosocial concept distinguishing maleness from femaleness, as in *gender roles* (societal expectations of behaviours appropriate for men and women) and *gender identity*—our psychological sense of ourselves as females or males. Conceptions of gender differ both across and within cultures, and they also vary across time in a given culture. Most assumptions we make about gender identity are based on the social construction of gender as a dichotomous, mutually exclusive category in which people are either male or female. Yet this assumption is challenged by studies of cultures that have a

gender identity One's psychological sense of being female or being male.

gender dysphoria Disorder in which an individual experiences significant personal distress or impaired functioning as a result of a discrepancy between his or her anatomic sex and gender identity.

transgender identity A type of gender identity in which the individual has the psychological sense of belonging to one gender while possessing the sexual organs of the other.

recognized social identity for individuals who do not fit typical male or female roles or gender identities (Dunham & Olson, 2016). These individuals have an accepted role in their societies and are not deemed to be disordered or undesirable.

For example, in India the term *Hijra* refers to a group of individuals who are considered to be of a third gender, being neither male nor female but having traits of both. A similar concept also exists in Samoa, where they refer to these individuals as *fa'afafine* (Dunham & Olson, 2016). Many Indigenous peoples of North and Central America believe that all human beings have both male and female elements. In many tribes, the term *two-spirit* is used for people who embody a higher level of integration of their male and female spirits (O'Brien-Teengs & Monette, 2014).

These cultural variations highlight the importance of taking cultural contexts into account when making judgments about disordered behaviour. Given the malleability of gender roles and identities we observe across cultures, we may question the validity of conceptualizing a transgender identity as a type of psychological disorder.

Gender dysphoria often begins in childhood. Children with the disorder find their anatomic gender to be a source of persistent and intense distress. The diagnosis is not used simply to label "tomboyish" girls and "sissyish" boys. It is applied to children who persistently repudiate their anatomic traits (girls might insist on urinating standing up or assert that they do not want to grow breasts; boys may find their penis and testes revolting) or who are preoccupied with clothing or activities that are stereotypic of the other gender (see Table 9.1).

TABLE 9.1

Diagnostic Criteria for Gender Dysphoria

Gender Dysphoria in Children

A. A marked incongruence between one's experienced/expressed gender and assigned gender, of at least 6 months' duration, as manifested by at least six of the following (one of which must be Criterion A1):

(1) A strong desire to be of the other gender or an insistence that one is the other gender (or some alternative gender different from one's assigned gender).

(2) In boys (assigned gender), a strong preference for cross-dressing or simulating female attire; or in girls (assigned gender), a strong preference for wearing only typical masculine clothing and a strong resistance to the wearing of typical feminine clothing.

(3) A strong preference for cross-gender roles in make-believe play or fantasy play.

(4) A strong preference for the toys, games, or activities stereotypically used or engaged in by the other gender.

(5) A strong preference for playmates of the other gender.

(6) In boys (assigned gender), a strong rejection of typically masculine toys, games, and activities and a strong avoidance of rough-and-tumble play; or in girls (assigned gender), a strong rejection of typically feminine toys, games, and activities.

(7) A strong dislike of one's sexual anatomy.

(8) A strong desire for the primary and/or secondary sex characteristics that match one's experienced gender.

B. The condition is associated with clinically significant distress or impairment in social, school, or other important areas of functioning.

Coding note: Code the disorder of sex development as well as gender dysphoria.

Gender Dysphoria in Adolescents and Adults

A. A marked incongruence between one's experienced/expressed gender and assigned gender, of at least 6 months' duration, as manifested by at least two of the following:

(1) A marked incongruence between one's experienced/expressed gender and primary and/or secondary sex characteristics (or in young adolescents, the anticipated secondary sex characteristics).

(Continued)

TABLE 9.1 *(Continued)*

Gender Dysphoria in Adolescents and Adults

(2) A strong desire to be rid of one's primary and/or secondary sex characteristics because of a marked incongruence with one's experienced/expressed gender (or in young adolescents, a desire to prevent the development of the anticipated secondary sex characteristics).

(3) A strong desire for the primary and/or secondary sex characteristics of the other gender.

(4) A strong desire to be of the other gender (or some alternative gender different from one's assigned gender).

(5) A strong desire to be treated as the other gender (or some alternative gender different from one's assigned gender).

(6) A strong conviction that one has the typical feelings and reactions of the other gender (or some alternative gender different from one's assigned gender).

B. The condition is associated with clinically significant distress or impairment in social, occupational, or other important areas of functioning.

Source: Reprinted with permission from the Diagnostic and Statistical Manual of Mental Disorders, Fifth Edition, (Copyright ©2013). American Psychiatric Association. All Rights Reserved.

The prevalence of gender dysphoria is greater in males than in females, although the exact ratios vary across studies. With an estimated worldwide lifetime prevalence of 0.001–0.003%, gender dysphoria is rare (Zucker, Lawrence, & Kreukels, 2016). The disorder takes many paths. It can come to an end or abate markedly by adolescence, with the child becoming more accepting of her or his gender identity. It may persist into adolescence or adulthood. The child may also develop a gay or lesbian sexual orientation at about the time of adolescence (Steensma, McGuire, Kreukels, Beekman, & Cohen-Kettenis, 2013).

Gender identity should not be confused with sexual orientation. Gay and lesbian individuals have erotic interest in members of their own gender, but their gender identity (sense of being male or female) is consistent with their anatomic sex. They do not desire to become members of the opposite gender or despise their own genitalia, as we may find in people with gender dysphoria. Nor is homosexuality any longer considered a psychological disorder. In 1973, it was dropped from the DSM listing of psychological disorders. We refer to *gay* and *lesbian* people rather than *homosexuals*. There are several problems with the label *homosexual:* (1) Since it has been historically associated with concepts of deviance and mental illness, it may perpetuate negative stereotypes of gay men and lesbians; (2) the term is often used to refer to men only, thus rendering lesbians

Lacy Atkins/AP Images

Paul Smith/Featureflash Photo Agency/Shutterstock

Gender reassignment. Chastity Bono, left; Chaz Bono, right, in 2011. Bono has gender dysphoria and has undergone hormone and surgical procedures to transition from female to male.

invisible; and (3) it is often ambiguous in meaning—that is, does it refer to sexual behaviour or to sexual orientation?

Unlike a gay or lesbian sexual orientation, gender dysphoria is rare. People with gender dysphoria who are sexually attracted to members of their own anatomic gender are unlikely to consider themselves gay or lesbian, however. Nature's gender assignment is a mistake in their eyes. From their perspective, they are trapped in bodies of the wrong gender.

Theoretical Perspectives

No one knows what causes gender dysphoria (Zucker, 2005). Psychodynamic theorists point to extremely close mother–son relationships, parents with empty relationships, and fathers who were absent or detached (Stoller, 1969). These family circumstances may foster strong identification with the mother in young males, leading to a reversal of expected gender roles and identity. Girls with weak, ineffectual mothers and strong, masculine fathers may overly identify with their fathers and develop a psychological sense of themselves as "little men."

Learning theorists similarly point to father absence in the case of boys—to the unavailability of a strong male role model. Socialization patterns might have affected children who were reared by parents who had wanted children of the other gender and who strongly encouraged cross-gender dressing and patterns of play.

Learning history or childhood rearing experiences are probably insufficient by themselves to shape gender identity or to produce gender dysphoria. This point is underscored by the case of a Winnipeg boy, originally known as Bruce, who was raised as a girl (Colapinto, 2000). When he was eight months old, his doctor badly botched a circumcision, resulting in the loss of Bruce's penis. The family was persuaded by the

NORMAL/ABNORMAL BEHAVIOUR

Gender Dissatisfaction: No Disorder

Maya had always been a tomboy. Her mother remembers Maya gravitating toward her older brother's toys even as a small child. While Maya's sister was playing "house," Maya preferred to smash cars into each other and run around outside. When Maya turned seven, she asked her mother if she could cut her hair more like a boy's. Maya's mother complied, and Maya wore her hair short for several years. She dressed in jogging pants and T-shirts, which she found much more comfortable than dresses and tights. These clothes also made it easier for her to play with the boys at recess, climbing and horsing around. A few times, she complained to her mother that it would be easier to be a boy—boys don't ever have to wear dresses, and they can pee standing up. Other than this, Maya never complained about being a girl. She identified as a girl, and ended up having both female and male friends throughout school. Even as a teenager, however, Maya still liked sports and wearing comfortable clothes, but she found that lots of other girls felt the same way she did.

Gender Dissatisfaction: Gender Dysphoria

From a very young age, Renato's mother felt that Renato was different from other little boys. At first, she thought it was cute that he preferred dolls and liked to play dress-up with his older sister and her friends. In fact, when they were older, his sister's friends always asked if Renato would come to play with them, and they loved dressing him up, putting makeup on him, and having him do a "show" for his parents. But Renato's mom started to worry when Renato was four years old. At that point, Renato expressed a strong preference for dresses and girls' clothes. Renato's mother didn't want to make a big deal of this, so would let him dress in girls' clothes at home. But when it came time for Renato to start school, she was concerned about what the teacher and other kids would say. She told Renato that he would have to wear pants to school, and that sent him into a tantrum. He also told his mother than he hated his penis and wished that he could cut it off. He began refusing to stand when urinating, and said that he wanted to go to the bathroom like a girl. This continued for the next several years, and Renato never wavered in his desire to be a girl. In fact, he began to talk about feeling that he really was a girl and that there'd been a mistake when he was born.

leading sexologist John Money to raise Bruce as a girl. Even though Bruce received hormones to promote a female appearance, the results were disastrous. Renamed Brenda and wearing a dress, he was clearly masculine in his appearance, interests, and behaviour, and he always felt that he was really a boy. "She" was teased at school because of his masculine appearance and behaviour, and life was miserable. At age 14, he was told of the botched operation, and shortly thereafter he changed his name to David and began living in the male role. He later married and adopted three children. Thus, years of socialization into the female gender role were unsuccessful in altering his gender identity. But even life as a male was not easy for him. David suffered from marital difficulties and bouts of depression. Tragically, he died by suicide in 2004, at age 38.

The great majority of people with the type of family histories described here by psychodynamic and learning theorists do not develop gender dysphoria. Perhaps family factors play a role in combination with a biological predisposition. We know that people with gender dysphoria often showed cross-gender preferences in toys, games, and clothing very early in childhood. If there are critical early learning experiences in gender dysphoria, they may occur very early in life. Prenatal hormonal imbalances may also be involved. Perhaps the brain is "masculinized" or "feminized" by sex hormones during certain stages of prenatal development. The brain could become differentiated as to gender identity in one direction while the genitals develop in the other. Gender dysphoria may develop as the result of an interaction in utero between the developing brain and the release of sex hormones (Zucker et al., 2016). Yet speculations about the origins of gender dysphoria remain unsubstantiated by hard evidence.

Treatment of Gender Dysphoria

The World Professional Association for Transgender Health has developed guidelines for the treatment of individuals with gender dysphoria, *The Standards of Care for the Health of Transsexual, Transgender, and Gender-Nonconforming People, Version 7* outlines treatment options with the goal of optimizing psychological health and self-fulfillment. Recommended treatments include hormone therapy, real-life experience (living as the identified gender), sex reassignment surgery, and psychotherapy (Coleman et al., 2012).

Not all people with gender dysphoria seek sex reassignment surgery. For those who do, surgeons attempt to construct external genitalia that are as close as possible to those of the opposite gender. People who undergo these operations can engage in sexual activity, even achieve orgasm, yet they are incapable of conceiving or bearing children because they lack the internal reproductive organs of their reconstructed gender.

Hormone treatments promote the development of secondary sex characteristics of the reassigned sex, such as growth of fatty tissue in the breasts in male-to-female cases and the growth of facial and body hair in female-to-male cases.

Men seeking gender reassignment outnumber female applicants. Clinical studies show generally favourable psychological outcomes following gender reassignment surgery, especially when safeguards are taken to restrict surgical treatment to the most appropriate candidates (Keo-Meier et al., 2015). In one study of 162 postoperative transsexuals, the majority were found to be functioning well socially and psychologically, with only two expressing regrets about the procedure (Smith, Van Goozen, Kuiper, & Cohen-Kettenis, 2005). Unfavourable outcomes were predicted in these cases by being nonhomosexual male-to-female transsexuals who also had other significant psychological problems.

In regards to the treatment of gender dysphoria in children, Olson and colleagues recommend supporting these children in their identified genders. They reported that children who were allowed to socially transition (wearing the clothing and using a name of the identified gender) had lower rates of depression and anxiety than is typical among this population (Olson, Durwood, DeMeules, & McLaughlin, 2016).

Gender Dysphoria

- **What is gender dysphoria?** People with gender dysphoria find their anatomic gender to be a source of persistent and intense distress. People with the disorder may seek to change their sex organs to resemble those of the opposite gender, and many undergo gender reassignment surgery to accomplish this purpose.
- **How is gender dysphoria different from sexual orientation?** Gender dysphoria involves a mismatch between

one's psychological sense of being male or female and one's anatomic sex. Sexual orientation relates to the direction of one's sexual attraction—toward members of one's own or the opposite gender. Unlike people with gender dysphoria, people with a gay or lesbian sexual orientation have a gender identity consistent with their anatomic gender.

PARAPHILIC DISORDERS

The word *paraphilia* was coined from the Greek roots *para*, meaning "to the side of," and *philos*, meaning "loving." Paraphilias involve strong and recurrent sexual arousal to atypical stimuli as evidenced by fantasies, urges, or behaviours (acting upon the urges) for a period of six months or longer. The range of atypical stimuli include nonhuman objects such as underwear, shoes, leather, or silk; humiliation or experience of pain in oneself or one's partner; or children or other individuals who do not or cannot grant consent.

In the DSM-5, there is a separation between a paraphilia (according to the nature of the urges, fantasies, or behaviours) and a diagnosed **paraphilic disorder** (on the basis of distress and impairment). In other words, having a paraphilia is a necessary but not a sufficient condition for having a paraphilic disorder (APA, 2013), and the addition of "disorder" to the diagnosis confirms this separation of non-normal and pathological. This approach assumes the possibility of non-normal sexual behaviour that is not pathological.

Some people who receive the diagnosis of paraphilic disorder can function sexually in the absence of paraphilic stimuli or fantasies. Others resort to paraphilic stimuli under stress. Still others cannot become sexually aroused unless these stimuli are used, in actuality or in fantasy. For some individuals, the paraphilia is their exclusive means of attaining sexual gratification.

The majority of people with paraphilic disorders are men (APA, 2013). However, studies in Canada, England, and the United States have identified women who have paraphilic disorders (Litman, 2003) and raise the possibility that paraphilic disorders in women may have been previously overlooked by researchers and clinicians. Little is known about the prevalence of paraphilic disorders in women, although they are probably rare. According to the Canadian Centre for Justice Statistics (1999), in 1999 only 2% of convicted sex offenders were women.

Some paraphilic disorders are relatively harmless and victimless. Among these are fetishistic and transvestic disorders. Others, such as exhibitionism and pedophilia, have unwilling victims. A most harmful paraphilic disorder is sexual sadism when acted out with a nonconsenting partner. Voyeurism falls somewhere in between because the "victim" does not typically know he or she is being watched.

Types of Paraphilic Disorders

EXHIBITIONISTIC DISORDER **Exhibitionistic disorder** involves recurrent, powerful urges to expose one's genitals to an unsuspecting stranger to surprise, shock, or sexually arouse the victim. The person may masturbate while fantasizing about or actually exposing himself. Almost all cases involve men (Baur et al., 2016), and the victims are almost always women.

paraphilic disorders Types of sexual disorders in which a person experiences recurrent sexual urges and sexually arousing fantasies involving nonhuman objects (such as articles of clothing), inappropriate or nonconsenting partners (e.g., children), or situations producing humiliation or pain to oneself or one's partner. The person has either acted on such urges or is strongly distressed by them.

exhibitionistic disorder Type of paraphilic disorder almost exclusively occurring in males in which the man experiences persistent and recurrent sexual urges and sexually arousing fantasies involving the exposure of his genitals to a stranger and either has acted on these urges or feels strongly distressed by them.

Although most exhibitionists are married, they tend to report unsatisfactory relationships with women (Hopkins, Green, Carnes, & Campling, 2016). The person diagnosed with exhibitionistic disorder is typically not interested in actual sexual contact with the victim and therefore is not usually dangerous. Nevertheless, some progress to more serious crimes of sexual aggression (McLawsen, Scalora, & Darrow, 2012). Whether or not the exhibitionist seeks physical contact, victims may believe themselves to be in great danger and may be traumatized by the act. Victims are probably best advised to show no reaction to people who expose themselves but to just continue on their way, if possible. It would be unwise to insult the person who exposed himself, lest it provoke a violent reaction. Nor do we recommend an exaggerated show of shock or fear—it tends to reinforce the person for the act of exposing himself.

Some researchers view exhibitionistic disorder as a means for perpetrators to indirectly express hostility toward women, perhaps because of perceptions of having been wronged by women in the past or of not being noticed or taken seriously by them (Lee, Jackson, Pattison, & Ward, 2002). Men with this disorder tend to be shy, dependent, and lacking in social and sexual skills—even socially inhibited (Allen et al., 2004). Some doubt their masculinity and harbour feelings of inferiority (Murphy & Page, 2012). Their victims' revulsion or fear boosts their sense of mastery of the situation and heightens their sexual arousal. Consider the case of Devon:

Couperfield/Shutterstock

Exhibitionistic disorder. Exhibitionistic disorder is a type of paraphilic disorder that characterizes people who seek sexual arousal or gratification by exposing themselves to unsuspecting victims. People with this disorder are usually not interested in actual sexual contact with their victims.

Devon was a 26-year-old, handsome, boyish-looking married male with a 3-year-old daughter. He had spent about a quarter of his life in reform schools and prison. As an adolescent, he had been a fire-setter. As a young adult, he had begun to expose himself. He came to the clinic without his wife's knowledge because he was exposing himself more and more often—up to three times a day—and was afraid he would eventually be arrested and thrown into prison again.

Devon said he liked sex with his wife, but it wasn't as exciting as exposing himself. He couldn't prevent his exhibitionism, especially now, when he was between jobs and worried about where the family's next month's rent was coming from. He loved his daughter more than anything and couldn't stand the thought of being separated from her.

Devon's method of operation was as follows: He would look for slender adolescent females, usually near the junior and senior high schools. He would take his penis out of his pants and play with it while he drove up to a girl or a small group of girls. He would lower the car window, continuing to play with himself, and ask them for directions. Sometimes the girls didn't see his penis. That was okay. Sometimes they saw it and didn't react. That was okay, too. When they saw it and became flustered and afraid, that was best of all. He would start to masturbate harder, and now and then he managed to ejaculate before the girls had departed.

Devon's history was unsettled. His father had left home before he was born, and his mother had drunk heavily. He was in and out of foster homes throughout his childhood. Before he was 10 years old he was involved in sexual activities with neighbourhood boys. Now and then, the boys forced neighbourhood girls into petting, and Devon had mixed feelings when the girls got upset. He felt bad for them, but he also enjoyed it. A couple of times girls seemed horrified at the sight of his penis, and it made him "really feel like a man. To see that look, you know, with a girl, not a woman, but a girl—a slender girl—that's what I'm after."

The Authors' Files

Wearing revealing bathing suits is not a form of exhibitionistic disorder in the clinical sense of the term. Nearly all people diagnosed with exhibitionistic disorder are men, and they are motivated by the wish to shock and dismay unsuspecting observers, not to show off the attractiveness of their bodies. Nor do professional strippers typically meet the clinical criteria for exhibitionism. Although they may seek to show off the attractiveness of their bodies, they are generally not motivated by the desire to become aroused by exposing themselves to unsuspecting strangers. The chief motive of the stripper, of course, may simply be to earn a living.

FETISHISTIC DISORDER   The French *fetiche* is thought to derive from the Portuguese *feitico*, referring to a "magic charm." In this case, the "magic" lies in the object's or situation's ability to sexually arouse. The object or situation of interest is called the *fetish*, the person a *fetishist* who has a *fetish* for that object or situation. The chief feature of **fetishistic disorder** is recurrent, powerful sexual urges and arousing fantasies involving inanimate objects, such as an article of clothing (bras, panties, hosiery, boots, shoes, leather, silk, and the like) or a nongenital body part (e.g., feet), referred to as *partialism*. It is normal for men to like the sight, feel, and smell of their lovers' undergarments. Men with fetishism, however, may prefer the object to the person and may not be able to become sexually aroused without it. They often experience sexual gratification by masturbating while fondling the object, rubbing or smelling it, or by having their partners wear it during sexual activity.

The origins of fetishistic disorder can sometimes be traced to early childhood experiences; fetishism is thought to be a type of conditioning or imprinting, like a pathological association. But although research suggests that early learning experiences may be important, the origin of fetishes is likely to be more complex, involving an interplay of learning experiences and various biological (e.g., hormonal) factors (Quinsey, 2003). Winnicott (1953) described a fetish as a specific object or type of object, dating from an experience during the period in which the mother gradually pulls back as an immediate provider of satisfaction of the child's desires, that persists as a characteristic in adult sexual life. Another, newer possible explanation comes from the field of neuroscience. The neuroscientists Ramachandran and Hubbard (2001) state that the region processing sensory input from the feet lies immediately next to the region processing sexual stimulation and could possibly be an explanation for certain types of fetishes of the feet.

TRANSVESTIC DISORDER   The chief feature of **transvestic disorder** is recurrent, powerful urges and related fantasies involving cross-dressing for purposes of sexual arousal. Other people with fetishes can be satisfied by handling objects such as women's clothing while they masturbate; people with transvestic disorder want to wear them. They may wear full feminine attire and makeup or favour one particular article of clothing, such as women's stockings. Men with transvestic disorder are usually heterosexual. Typically, the man cross-dresses in private and imagines himself to be a woman whom he is stroking as he masturbates. Some men frequent transvestite clubs or become involved in transvestic subcultures.

Gay men may cross-dress to attract other men or because it is fashionable to masquerade as women in some social circles, not because they are sexually aroused by cross-dressing. Males with gender dysphoria cross-dress because of gender discomfort associated with wearing men's clothing. Transvestic disorder sometimes develops into gender dysphoria, if the individual is already predisposed toward gender dysphoria and show signs of *autogynephilia* (sexual arousal associated with the fantasy of being a woman) (Blanchard, 2010).

Because cross-dressing among gay men and men with gender dysphoria is usually performed for reasons other than sexual arousal or gratification, it is not considered a form of transvestic disorder. Nor are female impersonators who cross-dress for theatrical purposes considered to have a form of transvestic disorder. For reasons such as these, the diagnosis is usually limited to heterosexuals.

Most men with transvestic disorder are married and engage in sexual activity with their wives, but they seek additional sexual gratification through dressing as women, as in the case of Mario:

fetishistic disorder Type of paraphilic disorder in which a person uses an inanimate object or a nongenital body part (*partialism*) as a focus of sexual interest and as a source of arousal.

transvestic disorder Type of paraphilic disorder characterized by recurrent sexual urges and sexually arousing fantasies involving cross-dressing, in which the person has either acted on these urges or is strongly distressed by them. Also termed *transvestism*.

Mario was a 55-year-old plumber who had been cross-dressing for many years. There was a time when he would go out in public as a woman, but as his prominence in the community grew, he became more afraid of being discovered in public. His wife, Myrna, knew of his "peccadillo," especially since he borrowed many of her clothes, and she also encouraged him to stay at home, offering to help him with his "weirdness." For many years, his paraphilia had been restricted to the home.

The couple came to the clinic at the urging of the wife. Myrna described how Mario had imposed his will on her for 20 years. Mario would wear her undergarments and masturbate while she told him how disgusting he was. (The couple also regularly engaged in "normal" sexual intercourse, which Myrna enjoyed.) The cross-dressing situation had come to a head because a teenaged daughter had almost walked into the couple's bedroom while they were acting out Mario's fantasies.

With Myrna out of the consulting room, Mario explained that he had grown up in a family with several older sisters. He described how underwear had been perpetually hanging all around the one bathroom to dry. As an adolescent, Mario experimented with rubbing against articles of underwear, then with trying them on. On one occasion a sister walked in while he was modelling panties before the mirror. She told him he was one of the "dregs of society" and he straightaway experienced unparalleled sexual excitement. He masturbated when she left the room, and his orgasm was the strongest of his young life.

Mario did not think that there was anything wrong with wearing women's undergarments and masturbating. He was not about to give it up, regardless of whether his marriage was destroyed as a result. Myrna's main concern was finally separating herself from Mario's "sickness." She didn't care what he did anymore, so long as he did it by himself. "Enough is enough," she said.

That was the compromise the couple worked out in marital therapy. Mario would engage in his fantasies by himself. He would choose times when Myrna was not at home, and she would not be informed of his activities. He would also be very, very careful to choose times when the children would not be around.

Six months later the couple was together and content. Mario had replaced Myrna's input into his fantasies with transvestic-sadomasochistic magazines. Myrna said, "I see no evil, hear no evil, smell no evil." They continued to have sexual intercourse. After a while, Myrna even forgot to check to see which underwear had been used.

The Authors' Files

VOYEURISTIC DISORDER   The chief feature of **voyeuristic disorder** is either acting on or being strongly distressed by recurrent, powerful sexual urges and related fantasies involving watching unsuspecting people, generally strangers, who are undressed, disrobing, or engaging in sexual activity. The purpose of watching or "peeping" is to attain sexual excitement. The person who engages in voyeurism does not typically seek sexual activity with the person or persons being observed.

Are the acts of watching one's partner disrobe or viewing sexually explicit films forms of voyeuristic disorder? The answer is no. The people who are observed know they are being observed by their partners or will be observed by film audiences. Voyeuristic acts involve watching unsuspecting people disrobing or engaging in sexual activities. Note that feelings of sexual arousal while watching our partners undress or observing sex scenes in R- or X-rated films fall within the normal spectrum of human sexuality.

During voyeuristic acts, the person usually masturbates while watching or fantasizing about watching. Peeping may be the person's exclusive sexual outlet. Voyeurs are often lacking in sexual experiences and may harbour deep feelings of inferiority or inadequacy (Leue, Borchard, & Hoyer, 2004). Some people engage in voyeuristic acts in

voyeuristic disorder Type of paraphilic disorder characterized by recurrent sexual urges and sexually arousing fantasies involving the act of watching unsuspecting others who are naked, in the act of undressing, or engaging in sexual activity, in which the person has either acted on these urges or is strongly distressed by them.

which they place themselves in risky situations—the prospect of being found out or injured apparently heightens the excitement.

FROTTEURISTIC DISORDER   The French word *frottage* refers to the artistic technique of making a drawing by rubbing against a raised object. The chief feature of **frotteuristic disorder** is recurrent, powerful sexual urges and related fantasies involving rubbing against or touching a nonconsenting person. Frotteurism, or "mashing," generally occurs in crowded places, such as subway cars, buses, or elevators. It is the rubbing or touching, not the coercive aspect of the act, that is sexually arousing. Almost all people diagnosed with frotteuristic disorder are male. The man may imagine himself enjoying an exclusive, affectionate sexual relationship with the victim. Because the physical contact is brief and furtive, people who commit frotteuristic acts stand only a small chance of being caught by authorities. Even the victims may not realize at the time what has happened or register much protest (Patra et al., 2013).

PEDOPHILIC DISORDER   The word *pedophilia* derives from the Greek *paidos*, meaning "child." The chief feature of **pedophilic disorder** is recurrent, powerful sexual urges and related fantasies involving sexual activity with prepubescent children (typically 13 years old or younger). Some people with pedophilic disorder may not have actually molested children, because the diagnosis can be made on the basis of recurrent fantasies or sexual urges without the person necessarily acting on them (APA, 2013). To be diagnosed with pedophilic disorder, the person must be at least 16 years of age and at least five years older than the child or children toward whom he or she is sexually attracted or whom he or she has victimized. In some cases of pedophilic disorder, the person is attracted only to children. In other cases, the person is attracted to adults as well.

Although some people with pedophilic disorder restrict their pedophilic activity to looking at or undressing children, others engage in exhibitionism, kissing, fondling, oral sex, anal intercourse, and, in the case of girls, vaginal intercourse (Knudsen, 1991). Not being worldly wise, children are often exploited by molesters who inform them that they are "educating" them, "showing them something," or doing something they will "like." Some men with pedophilic disorder limit their sexual activity with children to incestuous relations with family members; others molest children only outside the family. Not all child molesters have pedophilic disorder, however. The clinical definition of pedophilic disorder is brought to bear only when sexual attraction to children is recurrent and persistent. Some molesters engage in these acts or experience pedophilic urges only occasionally or during times of opportunity. A relevant diagnostic indicator is the extensive use of child pornography (APA, 2013).

Despite the stereotype, most cases of pedophilic disorder do not involve "dirty old men" who hang around schoolyards in raincoats. Men with this disorder are usually (otherwise) law-abiding, respected citizens in their 30s or 40s. Most are married or divorced and have children of their own. They are usually well acquainted with their victims, who are typically either relatives or friends of the family. Many cases of pedophilic disorder are not isolated incidents. They may be a series of acts that begin when children are very young and continue for many years until they are discovered or the relationship is broken off (Finkelhor, Hotaling, Lewis, & Smith, 1990).

Nearly all pedophiles are men, although the disorder is occasionally seen in women (Seto, 2009). In recent years, there have been a number of widely publicized newspaper and television reports of female high school teachers in their late 20s, 30s, or older having affairs with adolescent students (e.g., Denov, 2001). Such reports have come from schools in British Columbia, Ontario, and elsewhere. Some of these may be cases of pedophilic disorder, especially where the female teacher persistently seeks sexual encounters with young students.

The origins of pedophilic disorder are complex and varied. Some cases fit the stereotype of a weak, shy, socially inept, and isolated person who is threatened by mature relationships and turns to children for sexual gratification because children are less critical and demanding (Ames & Houston, 1990). In other cases, it may be that childhood sexual experiences with other children were so enjoyable that the person, as an adult, is attempting to recapture the excitement of earlier years. Or perhaps in some cases of

frotteuristic disorder Type of paraphilic disorder characterized by recurrent sexual urges or sexually arousing fantasies involving bumping and rubbing against nonconsenting victims for sexual gratification. The person has either acted on these urges or is strongly distressed by them.

pedophilic disorder Type of paraphilic disorder characterized by recurrent sexual urges or sexually arousing fantasies involving sexual activity with prepubescent children.

pedophilic disorder, people who were sexually abused in childhood by adults may now be reversing the situation in an effort to establish feelings of mastery. Consistent with the latter possibility, research indicates that pedophilic men, compared to other kinds of sex offenders, are more likely to have been sexually abused as children (Marshall, Serran, & Cortoni, 2000; Seto, 2004). According to researchers at Carleton University, sexual offenders who were sexually abused as children prey on younger victims than those who were not victimized as a child (Nunes, Hermann, Malcom, & Lavoie, 2013). This suggests that early sex related experiences may be somehow linked to pedophilic disorder. Michael Seto's developmental theory of persistent sexual offending against children proposes two pathways: antisociality, stemming from psychopathy or adverse disadvantages, and sexual attraction to prepubescent children (pedophilic disorder). When both are present, offending against children is especially likely (Seto, 2008). (See Figure 9.1 for details.) Men whose pedophilic acts involve incestuous relationships with their own children tend to fall at one extreme or the other on the dominance spectrum, either being very dominant or very passive (Ames & Houston, 1990).

Effects of Child Sexual Abuse   Child survivors of sexual abuse are more likely than non-abused children to develop psychological problems, including anxiety, depression, anger issues and aggressive behaviour, eating disorders, premature sexual behaviour or promiscuity, drug abuse, self-destructive behaviour such as suicide attempts, lack of trust, low self-esteem, social withdrawal, psychosomatic problems such as stomach aches and headaches, and symptoms of posttraumatic stress disorder (PTSD) (Stoltenborgh, van Ijzendoorn, Euser, & Bakermans-Kranenburg, 2011). Regressive behaviours in the form of thumb

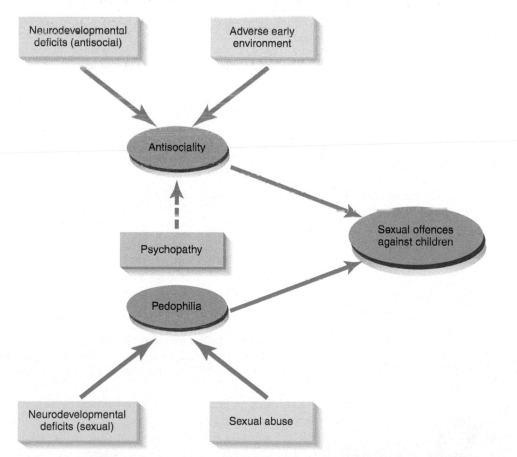

FIGURE 9.1   Developmental theory of persistent sexual offending against children.
The developmental theory proposes two pathways: antisociality, stemming from psychopathy or adverse disadvantages, and sexual attraction to prepubescent children (pedophilic disorder). When both are present, offending against children is especially likely (Seto, 2008).

Source: Psychology of Criminal Behaviour: A Canadian Perspective, Adelle Forth et al, 2010, 112–113, Pearson Education Canada. Reprinted with permission by Pearson Canada Inc.

sucking or recurrences of childhood fears, such as fear of the dark or of strangers, are not uncommon. Although the effects of child sexual abuse are more similar than not between boys and girls (e.g., both genders tend to experience fears and sleep disturbances), there are some important differences. The clearest gender difference is that boys tend to develop "externalized" behaviour problems, such as excessive aggressive behaviour, whereas girls tend to experience "internalized" problems, such as depression (Finkelhor et al., 1990).

Late adolescence and early adulthood is a particularly difficult time for survivors of child sexual abuse because unresolved feelings of anger and guilt and a deep sense of mistrust can prevent survivors from developing intimate relationships (Jackson, Calhoun, Amick, Maddever, & Habif, 1990). Research and scientific reviews conducted throughout the world, including at universities in Ontario and Manitoba, indicate that there are many serious long-term consequences of childhood sexual abuse (Abdulrehman & De Luca, 2001). Adult survivors of childhood sexual abuse, compared to people who were never abused, are more likely to have psychological disorders (e.g., anxiety disorders, mood disorders, suicidal behaviour, substance abuse, and antisocial behaviour), relationship problems, fewer friends, more social adjustment problems, and greater problems in sexual functioning. Martin Kruze is a tragic case in point. He, along with many other young hockey players, was sexually abused by men working in Toronto's Maple Leaf Gardens from the 1970s to the 1990s (Vine & Challen, 2002). Many boys were traumatized. Kruze, who as an adult blew the whistle on the abuse, later died by suicide.

SEXUAL MASOCHISM DISORDER Sexual masochism disorder derives its name from the Austrian novelist Leopold von Sacher-Masoch (1836–1895), who wrote stories and novels about men who sought sexual gratification from women by having the women inflict pain on them, often in the form of flagellation (being beaten or whipped). Sexual masochism disorder involves strong, recurrent urges and fantasies relating to sexual acts that involve being humiliated, bound, flogged, or made to suffer in other ways. The urges are either acted on or cause significant personal distress. In some cases of sexual masochism, the person cannot attain sexual gratification in the absence of pain or humiliation.

In some cases, sexual masochism involves binding or mutilating oneself during masturbation or sexual fantasies. In others, a partner is engaged to restrain (bondage), blindfold (sensory bondage), paddle, or whip the person. Some partners are prostitutes; others are consensual partners who are asked to perform the sadistic role. In some cases, the person may desire, for purposes of sexual gratification, to be urinated or defecated on or subjected to verbal abuse.

A most dangerous expression of masochism is **hypoxyphilia** (also known as *autoerotic asphyxiation*), in which participants are sexually aroused by being deprived of oxygen— for example, by using a noose, plastic bag, chemical, or pressure on the chest during a sexual act, such as masturbation. The oxygen deprivation is usually accompanied by fantasies of asphyxiating or being asphyxiated by a lover. People who engage in this activity generally discontinue it before they lose consciousness, but occasional deaths due to suffocation have resulted from miscalculations (Coluccia et al., 2016).

To illustrate the nature of this paraphilic disorder, an Alberta study of 19 cases of death due to hypoxyphilia revealed that the person is often a single male aged 15 to 29 years who performed the act repetitively and when alone. Accidental death typically occurred when there was a failure of the "safety" mechanism designed to restore oxygen (Tough, Butt, & Sanders, 1994). According to Stephen Hucker, a Toronto psychiatrist and expert on paraphilic disorders, people who engage in hypoxyphilia often report other paraphilias, such as fetishism and transvestism (Hucker, 2011).

SEXUAL SADISM DISORDER Sexual sadism disorder is named after the infamous Marquis de Sade, the 18th-century Frenchman who wrote stories about the pleasures of achieving sexual gratification by inflicting pain or humiliation on others. Sexual sadism disorder is the flip side of sexual masochism disorder. It involves recurrent, powerful urges and

sexual masochism disorder Type of paraphilic disorder characterized by sexual urges and sexually arousing fantasies involving receiving humiliation or pain, in which the person has either acted on these urges or is strongly distressed by them.

hypoxyphilia Paraphilic disorder in which a person seeks sexual gratification by being deprived of oxygen by means of using a noose, plastic bag, chemical, or pressure on the chest.

sexual sadism disorder Type of paraphilic disorder or sexual deviation characterized by recurrent sexual urges and sexually arousing fantasies involving inflicting humiliation or physical pain on sex partners, in which the person has either acted on these urges or is strongly distressed by them.

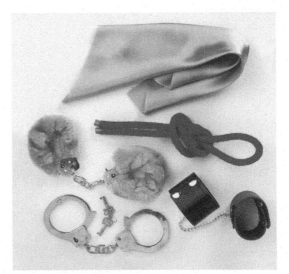

Dorling Kindersley/Getty Images

S & M paraphernalia. Some of the devices used by people who engage in sadomasochism.

related fantasies of engaging in acts in which the person is sexually aroused by inflicting physical suffering or humiliation on another person. People with this paraphilic disorder either act out their fantasies or are disturbed by them. They may recruit consenting partners, who may be lovers or wives with a masochistic streak or prostitutes. Still others— known as *sadistic rapists*—stalk and assault nonconsenting victims and become aroused by inflicting pain or suffering on them. Most rapists, however, do not seek to become sexually aroused by inflicting pain on their victims; they may even lose sexual interest when they see their victims in pain (Seto, Lalumière, Harris, & Chivers, 2012).

Many people have occasional sadistic or masochistic fantasies or engage in sex play involving simulated or mild forms of **sadomasochism** with their partners. *Sadomasochism* describes a mutually gratifying sexual interaction involving both sadistic and masochistic acts. Simulation may take the form of using a feather brush to strike one's partner, so that no actual pain is administered. People who engage in sadomasochism frequently switch roles during their encounters or from one encounter to another. The clinical diagnosis of sexual masochism disorder or sadism disorder is not usually brought to bear unless such people become distressed by their behaviour or fantasies or act them out in ways that are harmful to themselves or others.

sadomasochism Sexual activities between consenting partners involving the attainment of gratification by means of inflicting and receiving pain and humiliation.

OTHER PARAPHILIC DISORDERS   There are many other paraphilic disorders. These include making obscene phone calls (telephone scatologia); necrophilia (sexual urges or fantasies involving sexual contact with corpses); zoophilia (sexual urges or fantasies involving sexual contact with animals); and sexual arousal associated with feces (coprophilia), enemas (klismaphilia), and urine (urophilia).

Theoretical Perspectives

Psychodynamic theorists see many paraphilic disorders as defences against leftover castration anxiety from the Oedipal period. The thought of the penis disappearing into the vagina is unconsciously equated with castration.

The man who develops a paraphilic disorder may avoid this threat of castration anxiety by displacing sexual arousal into other activities—for example, undergarments, children, or watching others. By sequestering his penis under women's clothes, the man with transvestic disorder engages in a symbolic act of denial that women do not have penises, which eases castration anxiety by unconsciously providing evidence of women's (and his own) safety. The shock and dismay shown by the victim of a man who exposes himself provides unconscious reassurance that he does, after all, have a penis. Sexual sadism disorder involves an unconscious identification with the man's father— the "aggressor" of his Oedipal fantasies—and relieves anxiety by giving him the opportunity to enact the role of the castrator. Some psychoanalytic theorists see sexual masochism disorder as a way of coping with conflicting feelings about sex. Basically, the man feels guilty about sex but is able to enjoy it so long as he is being punished for it. Others view sexual masochism disorder as the redirection inward of aggressive impulses originally aimed at the powerful, threatening father. Like the child who is relieved when his inevitable punishment is over, the man gladly accepts bondage and flagellation in place of castration. These views remain speculative and controversial. We lack any direct evidence that men with paraphilic disorders are handicapped by unresolved castration anxiety.

Learning theorists explain paraphilic disorders in terms of conditioning and observational learning (Pfaus, Kippin, & Centeno, 2001; Seto, 2004). Some object or activity becomes inadvertently associated with sexual arousal. The object or activity then gains the capacity to elicit sexual arousal. For example, a boy who glimpses his mother's stockings on the towel rack while he is masturbating may go on to develop a fetish for stockings (Breslow, 1989). Orgasm in the presence of the object reinforces the erotic connection, especially when it occurs repeatedly. Yet if fetishes were acquired by mechanical association, we would expect people to develop fetishes for stimuli that are inadvertently and repeatedly connected with sexual activity, such as bedsheets, pillows, even ceilings (Breslow, 1989; Marshall & Eccles, 1993). Such is not the case. The meaning of the stimulus also apparently plays a role. Perhaps the development of fetishes depends on people's ability to eroticize certain types of stimuli (like women's undergarments) and incorporate them into their erotic and masturbatory fantasies. Fetishistic disorders can often be traced to experiences in early childhood.

Like other patterns of abnormal behaviour, paraphilic disorders may involve multiple biological, psychological, and sociocultural factors. Money and Lamacz (1990) hypothesize a multifactorial model that traces the development of paraphilic disorders to childhood. They suggest that childhood experiences etch a pattern, or "lovemap," that can be likened to a software program in the brain that determines the kinds of stimuli and behaviours that come to arouse people sexually. In the case of paraphilic disorders, lovemaps become "vandalized" by early traumatic experiences. Evidence does tie early childhood emotional or sexual trauma, such as incest, physical abuse, or neglect to later development of paraphilias (Barbaree & Blanchard, 2008). Yet not all children who undergo such experiences develop paraphilic disorders. Nor do all people with paraphilic disorders have such traumatic experiences. Perhaps some children are more vulnerable to developing distorted lovemaps than others. The precise nature of such vulnerability remains to be defined.

Treatment of Paraphilic Disorders

Thinkstock Images/Stockbyte/Getty Images

Origins of fetishistic disorder? The conditioning model of the origins of fetishistic disorder suggests that men who develop fetishistic disorders involving women's undergarments may have had experiences in childhood in which sexual arousal was repeatedly paired with exposure to their mother's undergarments. The developing fetish may have been strengthened by the boy incorporating the object into his erotic fantasies or masturbatory activity.

Therapists of various theoretical persuasions have attempted to treat clients with paraphilic disorders. Psychoanalysts, for example, attempt to bring childhood sexual conflicts (typically of an Oedipal nature) into awareness so they can be resolved in the light of the individual's adult personality. Favourable results from individual case studies appear in the literature from time to time, but there is a dearth of controlled investigations to support the efficacy of psychodynamic treatment of paraphilic disorders.

Behaviour therapists have used aversive conditioning to induce a negative emotional reaction to paraphilic stimuli or fantasies. In aversive conditioning, the stimulus that elicits sexual arousal (e.g., panties) is paired repeatedly with an aversive stimulus (e.g., electric shock) in the belief that the stimulus will acquire aversive properties. A basic limitation of aversive conditioning is that it does not help the individual acquire more adaptive behaviours in place of maladaptive response patterns. This may explain why researchers find that a broad-based, cognitive-behavioural program for treating exhibitionistic disorder that emphasizes the development of adaptive thoughts, the building of social skills, and the development of stress-management skills is more effective than an alternative program based on aversion therapy (Marshall, Marshall, Serran, & O'Brien, 2008; Seto, 2009). Marshall and Marshall (2015) also reported that treatment is more successful when the therapist is warm, empathic, nonjudgmental and supportive, as opposed to a more confrontational approach.

Maletzky (1991, 1998; Maletzky & Steinhauser, 2002) reported on the success rates of the largest treatment program study to date, based on more than 7000 cases of rapists and sex offenders with paraphilic disorders. Treatment procedures incorporated a variety of behavioural techniques, including aversive and nonaversive methods, tailored to the particular type of paraphilic disorders. Success rates for treatment of various paraphilic disorders ranged from 78.6% for transvestic disorder to 95.6% for situational pedophilia (heterosexual). Success rates above 90% were also obtained for situational pedophilia (homosexual), exhibitionist disorder, voyeuristic disorder, and fetishistic disorder. Two cautions are advised in interpreting these data, however. First, criteria for success were at least partly dependent on self-reports of an absence of deviant sexual interests or behaviour, and self-reports may be biased, especially in offender groups. Second, with the lack of a control group, we cannot

Correctional Service Canada's National Sex Offender Programs

The National Sex Offender Programs are cognitive-behavioural interventions that are designed to be a therapeutic rather than solely a didactic or psychoeducational program. They are based on empirical research and best practice in the provision of services to sex offenders and on the principles of social learning, adult learning, group processes, therapeutic rapport and alliance, motivational enhancement, overlearning, and skills development.

HIGH INTENSITY NATIONAL SEX OFFENDER PROGRAM

This program is designed for individuals who are at high risk of reoffending sexually. The program incorporates both group and individual sessions in which the offender gains an awareness of the dynamics and motivations of his sexual offending behaviour and learns skills to control his behaviour and his emotions. The program also targets known risk factors and teaches the offender coping strategies and the importance of healthy relationships.

MODERATE INTENSITY NATIONAL SEX OFFENDER PROGRAM

This program is similar to the High Intensity National Sex Offender Program but is geared for individuals who are at

a moderate risk of reoffending sexually. The same treatments are offered, but it consists of fewer sessions (55 group sessions and 6 individual sessions versus 75 group sessions and 7 individual sessions).

NATIONAL SEX OFFENDER MAINTENANCE PROGRAM

The National Sex Offender Maintenance Program is a follow-up program for those who have completed either the High or Moderate Intensity National Sex Offender Programs. The goal of this program is to reinforce the skills taught in the treatment programs and to help the offender cope with high-risk situations.

TUPIQ PROGRAM

The Tupiq Program is a sex offender treatment and maintenance program for Inuit men who have either a moderate or high risk of reoffending sexually. This program incorporates a healing component in addition to the treatments offered in the previously mentioned programs.

Source: Based on Correctional Services Canada, National Sex Offender Programs, http://www.csc-scc.gc.ca/correctional-process/002001-2008-eng.shtml#s. Accessed 19/01/17.

discount the possibility that other factors, such as fears of legal consequences or nonspecific factors unrelated to the specific behavioural techniques used, influenced the outcome. Nonetheless, these data are among the strongest sources of evidence supporting the effectiveness of behavioural techniques in treating paraphilic disorders. Abracen and colleagues reported recidivism rates of approximately 10% over a nine-year period among sexual offenders treated at the Regional Treatment Centre (Ontario) Sex Offender Treatment Program (Abracen, Looman, Ferguson, Harkins, & Mailloux, 2011).

Some promising results are also reported in using selective serotonin-reuptake inhibitors (SSRIs) like Prozac in treating exhibitionism, voyeurism, and fetishism (Thibaut, 2011, 2016). Why SSRIs? These medications have been used effectively in treating obsessive-compulsive disorder (see Chapter 3), and researchers speculate that paraphilic disorders may fall within an obsessive-compulsive spectrum (Kruesi, Fine, Valladares, Phillips, & Rapoport, 1992). Many people with paraphilic disorders report feeling compelled to carry out paraphilic acts in much the same way that people with obsessive-compulsive disorder feel driven to perform compulsive acts. Paraphilic disorders also tend to have an obsessional quality. The person experiences intrusive, repetitive urges to engage in paraphilic acts or thoughts that relate to the paraphilic object or situation. However, these drugs may act to reduce sexual drives rather than specifically target deviant sexual fantasies (Baratta, Javelot, Morali, Halleguen, & Weiner, 2012).

Sexual Assault

Although **sexual assault** is not a diagnosable psychological disorder, it certainly meets several of the criteria used to define abnormal behaviour. Sexual assault, like pedophilia, is socially unacceptable, violates social norms, and is grievously harmful to its victims.

sexual assault Nonconsensual bodily contact for a sexual purpose.

Sexual assault may also be associated with some clinical syndromes, especially some forms of sexual sadism.

The term *sexual assault* has particular legal meaning:

> *Sexual assault* has replaced *rape* as the term used in the Canadian legal system. There are three levels of sexual assault. Level 1 encompasses any non-consensual bodily contact for a sexual purpose, including touching, kissing, and oral, vaginal, and anal sex. Bodily contact can involve any part of the accused's body or an object. Level 2 is sexual assault with a weapon, in which the weapon is used to threaten or injure the victim. Level 3 is **aggravated sexual assault**, in which the victim is maimed or disfigured or has her or his life endangered. The central issue in determining whether an assault has occurred is whether consent was freely given. The person has to be capable of giving consent; therefore a person who is drunk, under the influence of drugs, unconscious, fearful, or underage is unable to give consent. (Adapted from Nevid, J. S., Fichner-Rathus, L. & Rathus, S. A. (1995). Human Sexuality in a World of Diversity (2nd ed.) p. 336. Reprinted and electronically reproduced by permission of Pearson Education, Inc., Upper Saddle River, New Jersey.)

aggravated sexual assault
Sexual assault in which the victim is maimed or disfigured or has his or her life endangered.

INCIDENCE OF SEXUAL ASSAULT Sexual assault is disturbingly common. To illustrate, a Winnipeg survey of 551 women revealed that "about a quarter of all women in North America" reported being sexually assaulted (e.g., unwanted touching) at some point in their lives (Brickman & Briere, 1984). In a later and larger survey of students from colleges and universities across Canada, 28% of women reported being sexually abused in the previous year and 11% of men reported having victimized a female dating partner in this way during the same period (DeKeseredy, 1997). Similar results have been reported from campuses in the United States (e.g., Gross, Winslett, Roberts, & Gohm, 2006; Jordan, Combs, & Smith, 2014). In 2002, 8800 sexual assaults against children and youth were reported to a subset of 94 police departments in Canada. This included 2863 sexual assaults against children and youth by family members. In the Canadian population in general, it has been estimated that more than 30% of men and over 50% of women have been sexually assaulted (Committee on Sexual Offences Against Children and Youth, 1984).

In over 80% of sexual assault cases overall, the woman is acquainted with the assailant (Cole, 2006). Sexual assault is the most common violent crime on campus. Most sexual assaults occur in social situations, such as at a party or when students study together in a dormitory room, and roughly half of perpetrators and sexual assault survivors are drinking alcohol at the time of the assault (Cole, 2006). Some men may use alcohol intoxication as an excuse for sexual assault, and some men perceive women who drink alcohol to be more sexually available and therefore appropriate targets for sexual aggression. Regardless of the motives or perceptions of a man or a woman, sexual assault is never justified. Although sexual assaults on males do occur, especially in prisons, the great majority of cases involve women as the victim.

THEORETICAL PERSPECTIVES There is no single kind of perpetrator of sexual assault. Sexual assailants are no more likely than other offenders to have psychological disorders (Polaschek, Ward, & Hudson, 1997). Sexual assault has more to do with violent impulses and issues of power and control than with sexual gratification. According to DeKeseredy's (1997) survey of Canadian undergraduates, men who had sexually abused tended to hold beliefs that women should be obedient, respectful, dependent, and sexually submissive toward men. Such beliefs may increase the odds that a man will become sexually abusive. Many sex offenders were sexually abused themselves as children (Seto, 2004). Some rapists who were abused as children may humiliate women as a way of expressing anger and power over them and of taking revenge. For still other rapists, violent cues appear to enhance sexual arousal, so they are motivated to combine sex with aggression (Marshall & Moulden, 2001). Sadistic sexual assaults frequently employ torture and bondage, merging sex and aggression. Sadistic rapists are most likely to mutilate their victims.

William L. Marshall, a psychologist at Queen's University and an expert on paraphilic disorders, argues that the risk of committing sexual offences is increased by early learning experiences that cause the person to have low self-confidence and poor social skills.

Possessing poor social skills means that the person has difficulty attracting dating partners. Sexual offences involve the domination or humiliation of victims, and thereby may give a sense of power to men who are otherwise lacking in power and self-confidence. Offensive sexual behaviours are maladaptive attempts to achieve intimacy through sex. These efforts are invariably unsuccessful and self-defeating; they merely serve to isolate the person further from society. Paradoxically, the pattern may become deeply ingrained because it results in the momentary pleasure associated with orgasm and because it offers the illusory hope of eventually achieving intimacy with another person. These and other factors are implicated in Marshall's theory (see, for example, Marshall, 2001).

Marshall and others emphasize the role of attachment problems in sexual offenders (Beech & Mitchell, 2005; Marshall, 2001). Many sexual offenders report having had sexually or physically abusive childhood experiences; they also in many cases did not have safe, loving relationships (bondings) with one or both parents, because the parents were abusive, rejecting, or emotionally cold. These experiences are thought to increase the chances that a child will as an adult either seek out intimate, sexual attachments with children, perhaps confusing sex with intimacy, or become sexually aggressive with women (Beech & Mitchell, 2005).

Does pornography lead to sexual aggression? Given the seriousness of sexual assault and the growing size of the pornography industry, it is important to understand the role of pornography and sex offending. Psychologist Michael Seto and colleagues from the Centre for Addiction and Mental Health in Toronto reviewed the evidence regarding this important question (Seto, Maric, & Barbaree, 2001). They concluded that the existing evidence suggests that people who are already predisposed to sexually offend are most likely to show an effect of pornography exposure (e.g., to be stimulated or encouraged by violent pornography or more likely to engage in sexual violence). Subsequent research lends support for this conclusion (e.g., Carr & VanDeusen, 2004). According to Kingston and Bradford (2013) from the University of Ottawa Institute of Mental Health Research, sex offenders who show features of hypersexuality (excessive sexual fantasies and urges) are at greater risk of reoffending.

Sociocultural factors also need to be considered. Although many rapists show evidence of psychopathology on psychological tests, especially psychopathic traits (Beech & Mitchell, 2005), many do not (Brown & Forth, 1997). The normality of many rapists on psychological instruments suggests that socialization factors play an important role. Some sociocultural theorists argue that our culture actually breeds rapists by socializing men into sexually dominant and aggressive roles associated with stereotypical concepts of masculinity (Hall & Barongan, 1997). Sexually coercive college men tend to have an excessively masculinized personality orientation, adhere more strictly to traditional gender roles, view women as adversaries in the "mating game," and hold more accepting attitudes toward the use of violence against women than do noncoercive men (Polaschek et al., 1997). They are also more prone to blame sexual assault survivors over rapists and to become sexually aroused by portrayals of sexual assault than are men who hold less rigid stereotypes. Sociocultural influences also reinforce themes that may underlie sexual assault, such as the cultural belief that a masculine man is expected to be sexually assertive and overcome a woman's resistance until she "melts" in his arms (Davies, Gilston, & Rogers, 2012).

Date sexual assault is a form of acquaintance sexual assault. College and university men on dates frequently perceive their dates' protests as part of an adversarial sex game. One male undergraduate said, "Hell, no," when asked whether a date had consented to sex. He added, "But she didn't say no, so she must have wanted it, too. It's the way it works" (Celis, 1991). Consider the case of William, a man who sexually assaulted a woman he had met online:

William met Sarah two months ago in a chat room on the Internet. They were drawn to each other's comments and quickly began talking just between the two of them. After a few weeks of online chatting, William called Sarah. They hit it off on the phone as well and planned to meet up for dinner. Sarah seemed really interested in William—she laughed at all his jokes and complimented him throughout dinner. After dinner, he invited her to his apartment. He was thrilled that she said yes. They started watching a movie, but soon began kissing instead. When William went to remove Sarah's dress, she hesitated. He thought she was just being shy, so he tried again. This time she pulled his hand away. But William knew that she really liked him, and had come to his apartment, so she must want to have sex as much as he did. He ignored her protests, thinking that sometimes women had to resist a bit to protect their reputations. Afterwards, he couldn't understand why she was crying. She'd given him all the right signs that she was into him, and it wasn't like they'd just met. He was surprised when Sarah didn't return his calls in the following days.

Let's rebut these beliefs: Accepting a date is not the equivalent of consenting to intercourse. Accompanying a man to his room or apartment is not the equivalent of consenting to intercourse. Kissing and petting are not the equivalent of consenting to intercourse. When a woman fails to consent or says no, the man must take no for an answer.

EFFECTS OF SEXUAL ASSAULT Women who are sexually assaulted suffer more than the assault itself. They report loss of appetite, headaches, irritability, anxiety and depression, and menstrual irregularity in the wake of a sexual assault. Some become sullen, withdrawn, and mistrustful. In some cases, women show an unrealistic composure, which often gives way to venting of feelings later on. Because of society's tendency to blame the victim for the assault, some survivors also have misplaced feelings of guilt, shame, and self-blame. Survivors often develop sexual dysfunctions such as lack of sexual desire and difficulty becoming sexually aroused (Postma, Bicanic, van der Vaart, & Laan, 2013). Many survivors show signs of PTSD, including intrusive memories of the sexual assault, nightmares, emotional numbing, and heightened autonomic arousal as well as increased rates of problem drinking, self-harm, and suicidal attempts (Creighton & Jones, 2011; Taylor, 2005; Ullman, 2016).

A CLOSER LOOK

Sexual Assault Prevention

Given the incidence of sexual assault, it is important to be aware of strategies that may prevent it. By listing strategies for sexual assault prevention, we do not mean to imply that sexual assault survivors are somehow responsible for falling prey to an attack. The responsibility for any act of sexual violence lies with the perpetrator, not with the person who is assaulted, and also with society for fostering attitudes that underlie sexual violence. On a societal level, we need to do a better job of socializing young men to acquire prosocial and respectful attitudes toward women. Exposing them to feminist, egalitarian, and multicultural education, as well as educating them about the often devastating impact of sexual assault on the person who is assaulted, may help promote more respectful attitudes in young men (Foubert & Perry, 2007; Hall & Barongan, 1997; Kershner, 1996).

PREVENTING STRANGER SEXUAL ASSAULT

- Establish signals and plans with other women in the building or neighbourhood.
- List only first initials in the phone directory and on the mailbox.
- Use deadbolt locks.
- Lock windows and install iron grids on first-floor windows.
- Keep doorways and entries well lit.
- Have keys handy for the car or the front door.
- Do not walk by yourself after dark.
- Avoid deserted areas.
- Do not allow strange men into the apartment or the house without checking their credentials.
- Keep the car door locked and the windows up.
- Check out the back seat of the car before getting in.

- Don't live in a risky building.
- Don't give rides to hitchhikers (that includes female hitchhikers).
- Don't converse with strange men on the street.
- Shout "Fire!" not "Rape!" People flock to fires but circumvent scenes of violence.

PREVENTING DATE RAPE

- Avoid getting into secluded situations until you know your date very well.
- Be wary when a date attempts to control you in any way, such as frightening you by driving rapidly or taking you some place you would rather not go.
- Stay sober. We often do things we would not otherwise do—including engaging in sexual activity with people we might otherwise reject—when we have had too many drinks. Be aware of your limits. And if you do drink, don't leave your drink unattended. Many women have been sexually assaulted as a result of their drinks being spiked with drugs.

- Be assertive and clear concerning your sexual intentions. Some rapists, particularly date rapists, tend to misinterpret women's wishes. If their dates begin to implore them to stop during kissing or petting, they construe pleading as "female game playing." So if kissing or petting is leading where you don't want it to go, speak up.
- When dating a person for the first time, try to date in a group.
- Encourage your college or university to offer educational programs about date sexual assault.
- Talk to your date about his attitudes toward women. If you get the feeling that he believes men are in a war with women, or that women try to "play games" with men, you may be better off dating someone else.

Source: From Human Sexuality in a World of Diversity, Rathus et al., © 1995. Reprinted and electronically reproduced by permission of Pearson Education, Inc

Psychological problems experienced by sexual assault survivors often continue through at least the first year following the sexual assault (Kimerling & Calhoun, 1994). About one in four sexual assault survivors continues to encounter psychological problems such as depression and anxiety for a number of years after the attack (Calhoun & Atkeson, 1991; Koss et al., 1994).

TREATMENT OF SEXUAL ASSAULT SURVIVORS Treatment of sexual assault survivors is often a two-phase process that first assists women in coping with the immediate aftermath of sexual assault and then helps them with their long-term adjustment. Crisis intervention provides women with emotional support and information to help them see to their immediate needs as well as to help them develop strategies for coping with the trauma (Taylor, 2005). Longer-term treatment may be designed to help sexual assault survivors cope with undeserved feelings of guilt and shame, lingering feelings of anxiety and depression, and the interpersonal and sexual problems they may develop with the men in their lives. Unfortunately, most sexual assault survivors do not seek help from mental health professionals, sexual assault crisis centres, or sexual assault survivor assistance programs (Kimerling & Calhoun, 1994). The cultural stigma associated with seeking help for mental health problems may discourage a fuller utilization of psychological services.

REVIEW IT

Paraphilic Disorders

- **What are paraphilic disorders?** Paraphilic disorders are sexual deviations involving patterns of arousal to stimuli such as nonhuman objects (e.g., shoes or clothes), humiliation, the experience of pain in oneself or one's partner, or children.
- **What are the major types of paraphilic disorders?** Paraphilic disorders include exhibitionistic disorder, fetishistic disorder, transvestic disorder, voyeuristic disorder,

frotteuristic disorder, pedophilic disorder, sexual masochism disorder, and sexual sadism disorder. Although some paraphilic disorders are essentially harmless (such as fetishistic disorder), others, such as pedophilic disorders and sexual sadism disorder, often harm nonconsenting victims.
- **What causes paraphilic disorders, and what makes them so difficult to treat?** Paraphilic disorders may be

caused by the interaction of biological, psychological, and social factors. Efforts to treat paraphilic disorders are compromised by the fact that most people with these disorders do not wish to change.

- **What factors underlie tendencies to sexually assault?** The desires to dominate women or express hatred toward them may be more prominent motives for sexual assault than is sexual desire. Although some men

who sexually assault show clear evidence of underlying psychopathology, many do not. Sexual assault has more to do with violent impulses and issues of power than with pursuit of sexual gratification. From a socio-cultural perspective, we should examine cultural attitudes, such as stereotypes of male aggressiveness and social dominance, that underlie propensities to sexually assault.

SEXUAL DYSFUNCTIONS

sexual dysfunctions
Psychological disorders involving persistent difficulties with sexual interest, arousal, or response.

Sexual dysfunctions involve problems with sexual interest, arousal, or response. Sexual dysfunctions are widespread in our society, affecting over 40% of women and 20–30% of men (Hayes, Bennett, Fairley, & Dennerstein, 2006; Lewis et al., 2010). They are often significant sources of distress to the affected person and his or her partner. Nicolosi and colleagues conducted a survey of the sexual behaviour of nearly 6000 individuals aged 40 to 80 years in five anglophone countries (United States, Canada, United Kingdom, Australia, and New Zealand). Prevalence rates among sexually active individuals reporting at least one sexual dysfunction were the lowest in Canada (18% of men and 28% of women) and the highest in New Zealand (51% of men and 57% of women) (Nicolosi et al., 2006). There are various types of sexual dysfunctions, but they tend to share some common features, as outlined in Table 9.2.

Sexual dysfunctions are classified according to two general categories: lifelong versus acquired, and situational versus generalized. Cases of sexual dysfunction that have existed throughout the individual's lifetime are labelled lifelong dysfunctions. In the case of acquired dysfunctions, the problem begins following a period (or at least one occurrence) of normal functioning. In situational dysfunctions, the problem occurs in some situations (e.g., with one's spouse) but not in others (e.g., with a lover or when masturbating), or at some times but not others. Generalized dysfunctions occur in all situations and every time the individual engages in sexual activity.

Types of Sexual Dysfunctions

Sexual dysfunctions can be grouped into the following categories:

1. Disorders involving problems with sexual interest or arousal
2. Disorders involving problems with orgasmic response
3. Problems involving pain during sexual intercourse or penetration (in women)

TABLE 9.2	
Common Features of Sexual Dysfunction	
Fear of failure	Fears relating to failure to achieve or maintain erection or failure to reach orgasm
Assumption of a spectator role rather than a performer role	Monitoring and evaluating your body's reactions during sex
Diminished self-esteem	Thinking less of yourself for failure to meet your standard of normality
Emotional effects	Guilt, shame, frustration, depression, anxiety
Avoidance behaviour	Avoiding sexual contact for fear of failure to perform adequately; making excuses to your partner

Source: Human Sexuality in a World of Diversity, 2nd ed., Rathus et al., 1995. Reprinted and electronically reproduced by permission of Pearson Education, Inc

In making a diagnosis of a sexual dysfunction, the clinician must determine that the problem is not related to the use of drugs or medications, other medical conditions, severe relationship distress, or other serious stressors. The disorders must cause significant personal distress or impairment in daily functioning and have lasted at least six months.

DISORDERS OF SEXUAL INTEREST OR AROUSAL   These disorders involve deficiencies in either sexual interest or arousal. Men with **male hypoactive sexual desire disorder** persistently have little, if any, desire for sexual activity or may lack sexual or erotic thoughts or fantasies.

Women with **female sexual interest/arousal disorder** experience either a lack of or greatly reduced level of sexual interest, drive, or arousal. Women with problems becoming sexually aroused may lack feelings of sexual pleasure or excitement that normally accompany sexual arousal. Or they may experience little or no sexual interest or pleasure. They may also have few if any genital sensations during sexual activity.

However, clinicians have not reached any universally agreed upon criteria for determining the level of sexual desire that is considered normal. Individual clinicians must weigh various factors in reaching a diagnosis in cases of low sexual desire, such as the client's lifestyle (e.g., a lack of sexual energy or interest in parents contending with the demands of infants or young children is to be expected), sociocultural factors (e.g., culturally restrictive attitudes may restrain sexual desire or interest), the quality of the relationship between the client and her or his partner (declining sexual interest or activity may reflect relationship problems rather than diminished drive), and the client's age (desire normally declines but does not disappear with increasing age). Couples usually seek help when one or both partners recognize that the level of sexual activity in the relationship is deficient or has waned to the point that little desire or interest remains. Sometimes the lack of desire is limited to one partner. In other cases, both partners may feel sexual urges but anger and conflict concerning other issues inhibit sexual interaction. Female sexual interest/arousal disorder is the most commonly diagnosed sexual dysfunction in women (Hayes et al., 2006). Although lack of sexual desire is more common among women than men, the belief that men are always ready for sex is a myth (Géonet, De Sutter, & Zech, 2013).

Problems with sexual arousal in men typically take the form of failure to achieve or maintain an erection sufficient to engage in sexual activity through completion. Almost all men have occasional difficulty achieving or maintaining erection during sex. But men with persistent erectile difficulties may be diagnosed with **erectile disorder**. They may have difficulty achieving an erection or maintaining an erection to the completion of sexual activity, or have erections that lack the rigidity needed to perform effectively. The diagnosis requires the problem be present for a period of six months or longer and that it occurs on all or almost all (approximately 75–100%) occasions of sexual activity.

ORGASM DISORDERS   Orgasm, or sexual climax, is an involuntary reflex that results in rhythmic contractions of the pelvic muscles and is usually accompanied by feelings of intense pleasure. In men, these contractions are accompanied by expulsion of semen. There are three specific types of orgasm disorders: **female orgasmic disorder**, **delayed ejaculation**, and **premature ejaculation**.

In female orgasmic disorder and delayed ejaculation, there is a marked delay in reaching orgasm (in women) or ejaculation (in men), or an infrequency or absence of orgasm or ejaculation. The clinician needs to make a judgment about whether there is an "adequate" amount and type of stimulation to achieve an orgasmic response. There is a broad range of normal variation in sexual response that needs to be considered. Many women, for example, require direct clitoral stimulation (by means of stimulation by her own hand or her partner's) to achieve orgasm during vaginal intercourse. This should not be considered abnormal, because the clitoris, not the vagina, is the woman's most erotically sensitive organ.

Delayed ejaculation has received little attention in the clinical literature. Men with this problem are generally able to ejaculate through masturbation but have difficulty achieving ejaculation during intercourse with a partner, or may be unable to do so. Although the disorder may allow the man to prolong the sexual act, the experience is usually one of frustration for both partners (Althof, 2012).

male hypoactive sexual desire disorder A type of sexual dysfunction in men involving a persistent or recurrent lack of sexual interest or sexual fantasies.

female sexual interest/arousal disorder A type of sexual dysfunction in women involving either a lack of or greatly reduced level of sexual interest, drive, or arousal. Women with problems becoming sexually aroused may lack feelings of sexual pleasure or excitement that normally accompany sexual arousal, or they may experience little or no sexual interest or pleasure.

erectile disorder Sexual dysfunction in males characterized by difficulty in achieving or maintaining erection during sexual activity.

female orgasmic disorder Type of sexual dysfunction in women involving difficulties achieving orgasm.

delayed ejaculation Type of sexual dysfunction in men involving persistent difficulties achieving orgasm.

premature ejaculation Type of sexual dysfunction involving a persistent or recurrent pattern of ejaculation occurring during sexual activity at a point before the man desires it.

A New View of Women's Sexual Dysfunctions?

Leonore Tiefer, a clinical psychologist and activist, convened a group of feminist social scientists in 2000 to propose a new diagnostic system [for women's sexual dysfunctions] that was intended to be free of the pharmaceutical conflicts of interest and the medical model on which they are based. Specifically, there was concern over the creation of a "Female Sexual Dysfunction" diagnosis by pharmaceutical companies that would then be in a profitable position to develop and market a drug to treat this "disease." Thus, the "New View Campaign" was formed.

The New View classification system . . . is based on feminist theories attributing women's sexual problems to cultural and relational factors (Tiefer, 2001). The system deliberately avoids specifying any particular "normal" pattern of sexual response. Instead, the resulting four-part classification system focuses on the causes of sexual problems, defined as "discontent or dissatisfaction with any emotional, physical, or relational aspect of sexual experience." It does not differentiate among the problematic symptoms of desire, arousal, orgasm, or other sexual complaints.

The causes of women's sexual problems are classified by Tiefer (2001) into four main groupings:

- Sexual problems due to sociocultural, political, or economic factors
- Sexual problems relating to a partner or a relationship
- Sexual problems due to psychological factors
- Sexual problems due to medical factors

The New View classification [was] an improvement over the DSM's perspective on sexual response, which [was] was based on a medical model of men's sexuality. However, empirical data supporting the usefulness and validity of the new classification system has not been collected. . . . Also, an overriding question exists: Is it useful to diagnose sexual dysfunction on the basis of causes rather than on the basis of symptoms? Moreover, with a new system, we need to start all over again in determining the prevalence of sexual difficulties. What we previously knew about the rates of sexual desire, arousal, orgasm, and genital pain complaints would thus be lost.

Lori A. Brotto, PhD, is an assistant professor in the Department of Obstetrics and Gynaecology at the University of British Columbia.

Source: Human Sexuality in a World of Diversity, 3Ce, Rathus et al, 2010, Pearson Canada. Reprinted with permission by Pearson Canada Inc.

Premature ejaculation is characterized by a recurrent pattern of ejaculation occurring within about one minute of vaginal penetration and before the man desires it (APA, 2013). In some cases, rapid ejaculation occurs prior to penetration or following only a few penile thrusts. Occasional experiences of rapid ejaculation, such as when the man is with a new partner, has had infrequent sexual contacts, or is very highly aroused, fall within the normal spectrum. More persistent patterns of premature ejaculation would occasion a diagnosis of the disorder. About one in three men experience premature ejaculation (Hellstrom, Nehra, Shabsigh, & Sharlip, 2006).

genito-pelvic pain/penetration disorder Persistent or recurrent pain experienced during vaginal intercourse or penetration attempts.

vaginismus The involuntary spasm of the muscles surrounding the vagina when vaginal penetration is attempted, making sexual intercourse difficult or impossible.

GENITO-PELVIC PAIN/PENETRATION DISORDER This disorder applies to women who experience sexual pain or difficulty engaging in vaginal intercourse or penetration. Approximately 15% of North American women report recurrent pain during intercourse (APA, 2013). According to the DSM-5, **genito-pelvic pain/penetration disorder** comprises one or more of the following symptoms: (1) difficulty with vaginal penetration during intercourse, (2) genito-pelvic pain during vaginal intercourse or penetration attempts, (3) fear of pain in anticipation of vaginal penetration, and (4) tension of the pelvic floor muscles during attempted vaginal penetration. The pain cannot be explained by an underlying medical condition. Some cases of genito-pelvic pain/penetration disorder involve **vaginismus,** a condition in which the muscles surrounding the vagina involuntarily contract whenever vaginal penetration is attempted, making sexual intercourse painful or impossible. Genito-pelvic pain/penetration disorder tends to appear during the postpartum, perimenopausal, and postmenopausal periods (APA, 2013). Because many cases of pain during intercourse are traceable to an underlying medical condition that may go undiagnosed, such as insufficient lubrication or urinary tract infection, controversy persists over whether sexual pain during intercourse or penetration should be classified as a mental disorder (Van Lankveld et al., 2010).

Theoretical Perspectives

As emphasized by internationally renowned University of British Columbia sexologist Rosemary Basson (2001, 2005), sexual dysfunctions, like most psychological disorders, reflect a complex interplay of biological, psychological, and other factors.

Frenk Kaufmann/Hemera/Thinkstock/Getty Images

When a source of pleasure becomes a source of anxiety. Sexual dysfunctions can be a source of intense personal distress and lead to friction between partners. Problems in communication can give rise to or exacerbate sexual dysfunctions.

BIOLOGICAL PERSPECTIVES Deficient testosterone production and thyroid overactivity or underactivity are among the many biological conditions that can lead to impaired sexual desire (Davis & Braunstein, 2012; Maggi, 2012). Medical conditions can also impair sexual arousal in both men and women. Diabetes, for instance, is the most common organic cause of erectile disorder, with estimates indicating that half of diabetic men eventually suffer some degree of erectile dysfunction (Eardley et al., 2010). Diabetes also impairs sexual response in women, resulting in decreased vaginal lubrication and sexual pain (Celik, Golbasi, Kelleci, & Satman, 2015).

Biological factors may play a prominent role in as many as 70–80% of cases of erectile disorder (Brody, 1995). Other biological factors that can impair sexual desire, arousal, and orgasm include nerve-damaging conditions such as multiple sclerosis, lung disorders, kidney disease, circulatory problems, damage caused by sexually transmitted diseases, and side effects of various drugs (Koehler et al., 2012). Yet even in cases of sexual dysfunction that are traced to physical causes, emotional problems such as anxiety, depression, and marital conflict can compound the problem.

The male sex hormone testosterone plays a pivotal role in sexual interest and functioning in women as well as men (both genders produce testosterone in varying amounts) (Meston & Bradford, 2006). Men with deficient production of testosterone may lose sexual interest and the capacity for erections (Montorsi et al., 2010). The adrenal glands and ovaries are the sites of testosterone production in women. Women who have these organs surgically removed because of invasive disease no longer produce testosterone and may gradually lose sexual interest and the capacity for sexual response (Davis & Braunstein, 2012). Although hormonal deficiencies may play a role in sexual dysfunction in such cases, researchers find that most men and women with sexual dysfunctions have normal hormone levels (Schreiner-Engel, Schiavi, White, & Ghizzani, 1989; Stuart, Hammond, & Pett, 1987).

Many temporary physical conditions can lead to problems in desire, arousal, and orgasm—even to sexual pain. Fatigue impairs sexual response and can lead to genital pain if the couple persists in attempting intercourse. Depressants such as tranquillizers, alcohol, and narcotics can lessen sexual response (IsHak, Bokarius, Jeffrey, Davis, & Bakhta, 2010). These effects are normally isolated unless people do not recognize their causes and attach too much meaning to them. That is, if you are intoxicated and do not know that alcohol can suppress your sexual response, you may wonder whether there is something wrong with you. Biological factors may thus interact with psychological factors in leading to the development of a persistent problem. Because of your concern, you may be more anxious during your next sexual opportunity, causing further interference with normal sexual response. A second failure may strengthen self-doubts, creating more anxiety, which in turn stems performance, which may lead to a vicious cycle resulting in repeated failure experiences.

LEARNING PERSPECTIVES Learning theorists focus on the role of conditioned anxiety in the development of sexual dysfunctions. The occurrence of physically or psychologically painful experiences associated with sexual activity may cause a person to respond to sexual encounters with anxiety that is strong enough to counteract sexual pleasure and performance. A history of sexual abuse or sexual assault plays a role in many cases in women with sexual interest/arousal disorder or orgasmic disorder. People who were sexually traumatized earlier in life may find it difficult to respond sexually when they develop intimate relationships. They may be flooded with feelings of helplessness, unresolved anger, or misplaced guilt, or experience flashbacks of the abusive experiences when they engage in sexual relations with their partners, preventing them from becoming sexually aroused or achieving orgasm.

Sexual fulfillment is also based on learning sexual skills. Sexual skills or competencies, like other types of skills, are acquired through opportunities for new learning. We learn about how our bodies and our partners' bodies respond sexually in various ways, including trial and error with our partners, learning about our own sexual response through self-exploration (as in masturbation), reading about sexual techniques, and perhaps by talking to others or viewing sex films or videos. Yet those who have been raised to feel guilty or anxious about sex may have lacked such opportunities to develop sexual knowledge and skills. Consequently, they may respond to sexual opportunities with feelings of anxiety and shame rather than arousal and pleasure.

COGNITIVE PERSPECTIVES Irrational beliefs and attitudes may contribute to sexual dysfunctions (Meston & Bradford, 2006). Consider the irrational beliefs that we must have the approval at all times of everyone who is important to us and we must be thoroughly competent at everything we do. If we cannot accept the occasional disappointment of others, we may catastrophize the significance of a single frustrating sexual episode. If we insist that every sexual experience be perfect, we set the stage for inevitable failure.

Most people respond to sexual arousal with positive emotions, such as joy and warmth. But for men with sexual dysfunctions, sexual arousal becomes disconnected from positive emotions (Rowland, Cooper, & Slob, 1996). Psychologist David Barlow (1986) proposed that anxiety may have inhibiting or arousing effects on sexual response depending on the man's thought processes (see Figure 9.2). For men with sexual dysfunctions, anxiety has inhibiting effects. Perhaps because they expect to fail in sexual encounters, their thoughts are focused on anticipated feelings of shame and embarrassment rather than on erotic stimuli. Concerns about failing increase autonomic arousal or anxiety, which leads men to focus even more attention on the consequences of failure, which in turn leads to dysfunctional performance. Failure experiences in turn lead to avoidance of sexual encounters because these situations have become encoded as opportunities for repeated failure, frustration, and self-defeat. Functional men, by contrast, expect to succeed and focus their attention on erotic stimuli, not on fears of failure. Their erotic attentional focus increases autonomic arousal or anxiety, but not to the point that it interferes with their sexual response. Mild anxiety may actually enhance their sexual arousal. By focusing on erotic cues, functional men become more aroused, successfully engage in sexual activity, and heighten their expectations of a future successful performance—all leading to increased approach tendencies. Although the model was derived from research on men, it may also help explain sexual dysfunctions in women (Géonet et al., 2013).

performance anxiety Fear relating to the threat of failing to perform adequately.

The cognitive model formulated by Barlow highlights the role of interfering cognitions in sexual dysfunctions. Interfering cognitions include **performance anxiety**, a type of anxiety that involves an excessive concern about whether we will be able to perform successfully. People troubled by performance anxiety become spectators during sex rather than performers. Their attention is focused on how their bodies are responding (or not responding) to sexual stimulation and on concerns they have about the negative consequences of failing to perform adequately, rather than absorbing themselves in their erotic experiences. Men with performance anxiety may have difficulty achieving or maintaining an erection or may ejaculate prematurely; women may fail to become adequately aroused or have difficulty achieving orgasm. A vicious cycle may ensue in which each failure experience instills deeper doubts, which leads to more anxiety during sexual encounters, which occasions repeated failure, and so on.

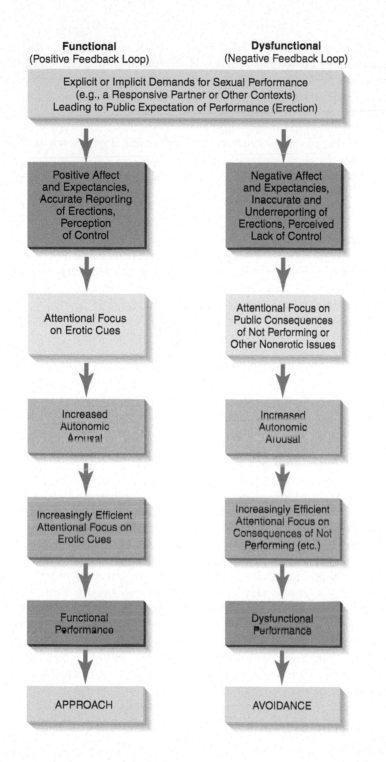

Functional
(Positive Feedback Loop)

Dysfunctional
(Negative Feedback Loop)

Explicit or Implicit Demands for Sexual Performance
(e.g., a Responsive Partner or Other Contexts)
Leading to Public Expectation of Performance (Erection)

Positive Affect
and Expectancies,
Accurate Reporting
of Erections,
Perception
of Control

Negative Affect
and Expectancies,
Inaccurate and
Underreporting of
Erections, Perceived
Lack of Control

Attentional Focus
on Erotic Cues

Attentional Focus on
Public Consequences
of Not Performing or
Other Nonerotic Issues

Increased
Autonomic
Arousal

Increased
Autonomic
Arousal

Increasingly Efficient
Attentional Focus on
Erotic Cues

Increasingly Efficient
Attentional Focus on
Consequences of Not
Performing (etc.)

Functional
Performance

Dysfunctional
Performance

APPROACH

AVOIDANCE

FIGURE 9.2   Barlow's model of erectile dysfunction.

In this model, past experience with erectile dysfunction leads men to expect they will fail again. They consequently focus on anticipated feelings of shame and embarrassment when they engage in sexual relations rather than on erotic stimuli. These concerns heighten their anxiety, impairing their performance and distracting them from erotic cues. Functional men, by contrast, expect to succeed and focus more of their attention on erotic stimuli, which heightens their sexual response. Although they too may experience anxiety, it is not severe enough to distract them from erotic cues or impair their performance.

Source: Barlow, D.H. Causes of sexual dysfunction: The role of anxiety and cognitive interference, *Journal of Consulting and Clinical Psychology*, Vol 54(2), Apr 1986, 140–148.

One man described how performance anxiety led him to prepare for sexual relations as though he were psyching himself up for a big game:

> At work I have control over what I do. With sex, you don't have control over your sex organ. I know that my mind can control what my hands do. But the same is not true of my penis. I had begun to view sex as a basketball game. I used to play in college. When I would prepare for a game, I'd always be thinking, "Who was I guarding that night?" I'd try to psych myself up, sketching out in my mind how to play this guy, thinking through all possible moves and plays.

I began to do the same thing with sex. If I were dating someone, I'd be thinking the whole evening about what might happen in bed. I'd always be preparing for the outcome. I'd sketch out in my mind how I was going to touch her, what I'd ask her to do. But all the time, right through dinner or the movies, I'd be worrying that I wouldn't get it up. I kept picturing her face and how disappointed she'd be. By the time we did go to bed, I was paralyzed with anxiety.

The Authors' Files

SOCIOCULTURAL PERSPECTIVES At around the turn of the last century, an English-woman was quoted as saying she would "close her eyes and think of England" when her husband engaged her in sexual relations. This old-fashioned stereotype suggests how sexual pleasure was once considered exclusively a male preserve—for women, sex was primarily a duty. Mothers usually informed their daughters of the conjugal duties before the wedding, and girls encoded sex as just one of the ways in which women serviced the needs of others. Women who harbour such stereotypical attitudes toward female sexuality may be unlikely to become aware of their sexual potential. In addition, sexual anxieties may transform negative expectations into self-fulfilling prophecies. Sexual dysfunctions in men, too, may be linked to severely restricted sociocultural beliefs and sexual taboos. Other negative beliefs about sexuality may interfere with sexual desire, such as the belief that sexual desire is not appropriate for older adults past childbearing age (Géonet et al., 2013).

According to the World Health Organization (2016), women who have undergone female genital mutilation (FGM) are at increased risk for sexual dysfunctions such as sexual pain and decreased sexual satisfaction and desire. Despite strong advocacy for the abandonment of FGM, this procedure (partial or total removal of external female genitalia for nonmedical reasons) continues to be reported in 30 countries in Africa as well as in some countries in Asia and the Middle East, and among some ethnic groups in Central and South America. The procedure is performed for a variety of reasons, which include safeguarding virginity before marriage, ensuring fidelity after marriage, aesthetics, and a rite of passage into adulthood.

Sociocultural factors also play an important role in erectile disorder. Investigators find a greater incidence of erectile disorder in cultures with more restrictive sexual attitudes toward premarital sex among females, sex in marriage, and extramarital sex (Welch & Kartub, 1978). Men in these cultures may be prone to developing sexual anxiety or guilt that may interfere with sexual performance. In India, some men may develop erectile disorder because of the cultural belief that the loss of semen drains a man's life energy (Rajkumar, 2016).

In Western cultures, the connection between a man's sexual performance and his sense of manhood is deeply ingrained. The man who repeatedly fails to perform sexually may suffer a loss of self-esteem, become depressed, or feel he is no longer a man (Carey, Wincze, & Meisler, 1998). He may see himself as a total failure, despite other accomplishments in life. Sexual opportunities are construed as tests of his manhood, and he may respond to them by trying to will (force) an erection. Willing an erection may backfire, because erection is a reflex that cannot be forced. With so much of his self-esteem riding on the line whenever he makes love, it is little wonder that anxiety about the quality of his performance—performance anxiety—may mount to a point that it inhibits erection. The erectile reflex is controlled by the parasympathetic branch of the autonomic nervous system. Activation of the sympathetic nervous system, which occurs when we are anxious, can block parasympathetic control, preventing the erectile reflex from occurring. Ejaculation, in contrast, is under sympathetic nervous system control, so heightened levels of arousal, as in the case of performance anxiety, can trigger premature ejaculation.

One client who suffered erectile disorder described his feelings of sexual inadequacy this way:

> I always felt inferior, like I was on probation, having to prove myself. I felt like I was up against the wall. You can't imagine how embarrassing this was. It's like you walk out in front of an audience that you think is a nudist convention and it turns out to be a tuxedo convention.
>
> The Authors' Files

Women, too, may equate their self-esteem with their ability to reach frequent and intense orgasms. Yet when men and women try to will arousal or lubrication or to force an orgasm, they may find that the harder they try, the more these responses elude them. Forty years ago the pressures concerning sex often revolved around the issue "Should I or shouldn't I?" Today, however, the pressures for both men and women are often based more on achieving performance goals relating to proficiency at reaching orgasm and satisfying one's partner's sexual needs.

Treatment of Sexual Dysfunctions

Until the groundbreaking work of sex researchers William Masters and Virginia Johnson in the 1960s, there was no effective treatment for most sexual dysfunctions. Psychoanalytic forms of therapy approached sexual dysfunctions indirectly, for example. It was assumed that sexual dysfunctions represented underlying conflicts and that the dysfunctions might abate if the underlying conflicts—the presumed causes of the dysfunctions—were resolved through psychoanalysis. A lack of evidence that psychoanalytic approaches reversed sexual dysfunctions led clinicians and researchers to develop other approaches that would focus more directly on the sexual problems themselves.

Most contemporary sex therapists assume that sexual dysfunctions can be treated by directly modifying a couple's sexual interactions. Pioneered by Masters and Johnson (1970), sex therapy employs a variety of relatively brief, cognitive-behavioural techniques that centre on enhancing self-efficacy expectancies, improving a couple's ability to communicate, fostering sexual competencies (sexual knowledge and skills), and reducing performance anxiety. Therapists may also work with couples to help them resolve problems in their relationship that may impede sexual functioning. When feasible, both sex partners are involved in therapy. In some cases, however, individual therapy may be preferable, as we shall see.

Significant changes have occurred in the treatment of sexual dysfunctions in the past 20 years. There is greater emphasis now on the role of biological or organic factors in the development of sexual problems and greater use of medical treatments, such as the use of the drugs Viagra, Cialis, and Levitra, in treating male erectile disorder. But even men whose erectile problems can be traced to physical causes can benefit from sex therapy along with medical intervention (Bach, Barlow, & Wincze, 2004).

Let's briefly survey some of the more common treatments for particular types of disorders.

DISORDERS OF SEXUAL INTEREST OR AROUSAL Sex therapists may try to help people with low sexual desire kindle their sexual appetite through the use of self-stimulation (masturbation) exercises together with erotic fantasies (Leiblum, 2006). Or, in working with couples, the therapist

Bettmann/Getty Images

Masters and Johnson. Sex therapists William Masters and Virginia Johnson.

might prescribe mutual pleasuring exercises the couple could perform at home or encourage them to expand their sexual repertoire to add novelty and excitement to their sex life. Mutual pleasuring, beginning with partner stimulation in nongenital areas and gradually progressing to genital stimulation, may also help desensitize fears about sexual contact. When a lack of sexual desire is connected with depression, the treatment would probably focus on relieving the underlying depression in the hope that sexual interest would rebound when the depression lifts. Some cases of hypoactive sexual desire involve hormonal deficiencies, especially lack of testosterone. Testosterone replacement is effective only in the relatively few cases in which production of the hormone is truly deficient (Simpkins & Van Meter, 2005). A lack of sexual desire may also reflect relationship problems that may need to be addressed through couples therapy (McCarthy & Bodnar, 2005).

Women who have difficulty becoming sexually aroused and men with erectile problems are first educated to the fact that they need not "do" anything to become aroused. As long as their problems are psychological, not organic, they need only experience sexual stimulation under relaxed, nonpressured conditions, so that disruptive cognitions and anxiety do not inhibit reflexive responses. Mindfulness-based therapies, which help the individual stay focused in the present moment, have been shown to be beneficial (Brotto & Basson, 2014).

Masters and Johnson have the couple counter performance anxiety by engaging in **sensate focus exercises**. These are nondemand sexual contacts—sensuous exercises that do not demand sexual arousal in the form of vaginal lubrication or erection. Partners begin by massaging each other without touching the genitals. The partners learn to "pleasure" each other and to "be pleasured" by means of following and giving verbal instructions and by guiding each other's hands. The method fosters both communication and sexual skills and countermands anxiety because there is no demand for sexual arousal. After several sessions, direct massage of the genitals is included in the pleasuring exercise. Even when obvious signs of sexual excitement are produced (lubrication or erection), the couple does not straightaway engage in intercourse, because intercourse might create performance demands. After excitement is achieved consistently, the couple engages in a relaxed sequence of other sexual activities, culminating eventually in intercourse.

A number of similar sex therapy methods were employed in the case of Victor P.:

sensate focus exercises In sex therapy, mutual pleasuring activities between partners that are focused on the partners taking turns giving and receiving physical pleasure.

Victor P., a 44-year-old concert violinist, was eager to show the therapist reviews of his concert tour. A solo violinist with a distinguished orchestra, Victor's life revolved around practice, performances, and reviews. He dazzled audiences with his technique and the energy of his performance. As a concert musician, Victor had exquisite control over his body, especially his hands. Yet he could not control his erectile response in the same way. Since his divorce seven years earlier, Victor had been troubled by recurrent episodes of erectile failure. Time and time again he had become involved in a new relationship, only to find himself unable to perform sexually. Fearing repetition, he would sever the relationship. He was unable to face an audience of only one. For a while, he dated casually, but then he met Michelle.

Michelle was a writer who loved music. They were a perfect match because Victor, the musician, loved literature. Michelle, a 35-year-old divorcée, was exciting, earthy, sensual, and accepting. The couple soon grew inseparable. He would practise while she would write—poetry mostly, but also short magazine pieces. Unlike some women Victor met who did not know Bach from Bartok, Michelle held her own in conversations with Victor's friends and fellow musicians over a late-night dinner. They kept their own apartments; Victor needed his own space and solitude for practice.

In the nine months of their relationship, Victor was unable to perform on the stage that mattered most to him—his canopied bed. It was just so frustrating. He said, "I would become erect and then just as I approach her to penetrate, pow! It collapses on me." Victor's history of nocturnal erections and erections during light petting suggested that he was basically suffering from performance anxiety. He was attempting to force an erection, much as he might try to learn the fingering of a difficult violin piece. Each night became a command performance in which Victor served as his own harshest critic. Victor became a spectator to his own performance, a role that Masters and Johnson refer to as **self-spectatoring**. Rather than focusing on his partner, his attention was riveted on the size of his penis. As noted by the late great pianist Vladimir Horowitz, the worst thing a pianist can do is watch his fingers. Perhaps the worst thing a man with erectile problems can do is watch his penis.

To break the vicious cycle of anxiety, erectile failure, and more anxiety, Victor and Michelle followed a sex therapy program (Rathus & Nevid, 1977) modelled after the Masters and Johnson–type treatment. The aim was to restore the pleasure of sexual activity, unfettered by anxiety. The couple was initially instructed to abstain from attempts at intercourse to free Victor from any pressure to perform. The couple progressed through a series of steps:

1. Relaxing together in the nude without any touching, such as when reading or watching television together.
2. Sensate focus exercises.
3. Genital stimulation of each other manually or orally to orgasm.
4. Nondemand intercourse (intercourse performed without any pressure on the man to satisfy his partner). The man may afterward help his partner achieve orgasm by using manual or oral stimulation.
5. Resumption of vigorous intercourse (intercourse involving more vigorous thrusting and use of alternative positions and techniques that focus on mutual satisfaction). The couple is instructed not to catastrophize occasional problems that may arise.

The therapy program helped Victor overcome his erectile disorder. Victor was freed of the need to prove himself by achieving erection on command. He surrendered his post as critic. Once the spotlight was off the bed, he became a participant and not a spectator.

The Authors' Files

self-spectatoring Tendency to observe one's behaviour as if one were a spectator of oneself. People with sexual dysfunctions often become self-spectators in the sense of focusing their attention during sexual activity on the response of their sex organs rather than on their partners or the sexual stimulation itself.

Sexual arousal in both men and women depends on engorgement of blood in the genitals. Drugs that increase blood flow to the penis, such as Viagra and Cialis, are safe and effective in helping men with erectile disorder achieve more reliable erections. However, evidence also indicates that combining psychotherapy with medications like Viagra can be more effective than medication alone (Montorsi et al., 2010). When taking pills is ineffective, alternatives such as self-injection in the penis of a drug that increases penile blood flow, or use of a vacuum erection device that works like a penis pump, may prove more helpful (Montorsi et al., 2010). Surgery may be effective in rare cases in which blocked blood vessels prevent blood flow to the penis, or in which the penis is structurally defective (Rowland et al., 2010).

DISORDERS OF ORGASM Women with orgasmic disorder often harbour underlying beliefs that sex is dirty or sinful. They may have been taught not to touch themselves. They are often anxious about sex and have not learned, through trial and error, what kinds of sexual stimulation will arouse them and help them reach orgasm. Treatment in these cases includes modification of negative attitudes toward sex. When orgasmic disorder reflects the woman's feelings about, or relationship with, her partner, treatment requires working through these feelings or enhancing the relationship.

In either case, Masters and Johnson work with the couple and first use sensate focus exercises to lessen performance anxiety, open channels of communication, and help the couple acquire pleasuring skills. Then during genital massage and later during intercourse, the woman directs her partner to use caresses and techniques that stimulate her. By taking charge, the woman becomes psychologically freed from the stereotype of the passive, submissive female role.

Many researchers find that a program of directed masturbation is most effective in helping preorgasmic women—women who have never achieved orgasm through any means (Baucom, Shoham, Mueser, Daiuto, & Stickle, 1998; IsHak et al., 2010). Masturbation provides a chance to learn about one's own body and give oneself pleasure without reliance on a partner or need to attend to a partner's needs. Directed masturbation programs educate women about their sexual anatomy and encourage them to experiment with self-caresses in the privacy of their own homes. Women proceed at their own pace and are encouraged to incorporate sexual fantasies and imagery during self-stimulation exercises designed to heighten their level of sexual arousal. They gradually learn to bring themselves to orgasm, sometimes with the help of a vibrator. Once women can masturbate to orgasm, additional couples-oriented treatment can facilitate but does not guarantee transference to orgasm with a partner (Heiman & LoPiccolo, 1987; LoPiccolo & Stock, 1986).

Delayed ejaculation has received less attention in the clinical literature, but may involve psychological factors such as fear, anxiety, hostility, and relationship difficulties. The standard treatment, barring any underlying organic problem, focuses on increasing sexual stimulation and reducing performance anxiety (Althof, 2012; Shin & Spitz, 2014).

The most widely used approach to treating premature ejaculation, called the *stop–start* or *stop-and-go technique*, was introduced in 1956 by the urologist James Semans. The man and his partner just suspend sexual activity when he is about to ejaculate and then resume stimulation when his sensations subside. Repeated practice enables the man to regulate ejaculation by sensitizing him to the cues that precede the ejaculatory reflex (making him more aware of his "point of no return," the point at which the ejaculatory reflex is triggered).

A CLOSER LOOK

How Do You Find a Qualified Sex Therapist?

How would you locate a sex therapist if you had a sexual dysfunction? Since provinces do not regulate use of the term sex *therapist*, it is essential to determine that a sex therapist is a member of a recognized profession (such as psychology, social work, medicine, or marriage and family counselling) and has had training and supervision in sex therapy. Professionals are usually licensed or certified by their provinces. (All provinces require licensing of psychologists and physicians, but some provinces do not license social workers or marriage counsellors.) Only physicians are permitted to bill their provincial health plans for providing sex therapy services.

If you are uncertain how to locate a qualified sex therapist in your area, try your university or college psychology department, health department, or counselling centre; a medical or psychological association; a marriage and family therapy association; a family physician; or your instructor.

Relatively few people in Canada have been trained as specialists in sex therapy. The only Canadian organization that certifies sex therapists is the Board of Examiners in Sex Therapy and Counselling in Ontario (BESTCO), comprising professionals from diverse backgrounds with clinical expertise in human sexual concerns.

Some Canadian therapists are also certified by American-based organizations such as the American Association of

Sexuality Educators, Counselors, and Therapists and the Society for Sex Therapy and Research.

Ethical professionals are not annoyed or embarrassed if you ask them (1) what their profession is, (2) where they earned their advanced degree, and (3) whether they are licensed or certified, or if you inquire about (4) their fees, (5) their plans for treatment, and (6) their training in human sexuality and sex therapy. These questions are important because there is such a wide diversity in the professional background and training of sex therapists. Accordingly, the type of treatments and services that are available vary enormously (Kleinplatz, 2003). If the therapist becomes uncomfortable, asks why you are asking such questions, or fails to provide a direct answer, beware.

Professionals are also prohibited, by the ethical principles of their professions, from engaging in unethical practices, such as sexual relations with their clients. Any therapist who makes a sexual overture toward a client or tries to persuade a client to engage in sexual relations is acting unethically.

Source: Human Sexuality in a World of Diversity, 3Ce, Rathus et al, 2010, Pearson Canada. Reprinted with permission by Pearson Canada Inc.

SSRIs, such as the antidepressants fluoxetine (Prozac), paroxetine (Paxil), and sertraline (Zoloft), work by increasing the action of the neurotransmitter serotonin. Increased availability of serotonin in the brain can have the side effect of delaying ejaculation, which can help men with early ejaculation problems (Mohee & Eardley, 2011; Rowland et al., 2010).

Investigators are exploring biomedical therapies for female sexual dysfunctions, including use of erectile dysfunction drugs such as Viagra. Research on the effectiveness of these drugs in treating female orgasmic dysfunction has yielded mixed results, but the drugs may be helpful in some cases (IsHak et al., 2010).

GENITO-PELVIC PAIN/PENETRATION DISORDER Vaginismus is a conditioned reflex involving the involuntary constriction of the vaginal opening. It involves a psychologically based fear of penetration, rather than a physical defect or disorder (Graziottin, 2008). Treatment for vaginismus involves a combination of cognitive-behavioural exercises, such as relaxation techniques, and the use of vaginal dilators to gradually desensitize the vaginal musculature. The woman herself regulates the insertion of dilators (plastic rods) of increasing diameter, always proceeding at her own pace to avoid any discomfort (Graziottin, 2008). The method is generally successful as long as it is unhurried. Because women with vaginismus often have histories of sexual molestation or sexual assault, psychotherapy may be part of the treatment program to deal with the psychological consequences of traumatic experiences (LoPiccolo & Stock, 1986). In cases of painful intercourse, treatment focuses on attempting to resolve the underlying psychological or medical conditions that give rise to the pain (Bergeron, Corsini-Munt, Aerts, Rancourt, & Rosen, 2015). Al-Abbadey and colleagues recommend a couples therapy approach geared toward finding mutually pleasurable sexual activities with less emphasis on intercourse as the goal of treatment (Al-Abbadey, Liossi, Curran, Schoth, & Graham, 2016).

REVIEW IT

Sexual Dysfunctions

- **What are the major types of sexual dysfunctions?** Sexual dysfunctions include sexual interest/arousal disorders (female sexual interest/arousal disorder, male hypoactive sexual desire disorder, erectile disorder), orgasm disorders (female orgasmic disorder, delayed ejaculation, premature ejaculation), and genito-pelvic pain/penetration disorder.

- **What causes sexual dysfunctions?** Sexual dysfunctions can stem from biological factors (such as disease or the effects of alcohol and other drugs), psychological factors (such as performance anxiety, unresolved conflicts, or lack of sexual competencies), and sociocultural factors (such as sexually restrictive cultural learning).

- **What are the major goals of sex therapy?** Sex therapists help people overcome sexual dysfunctions by enhancing self-efficacy expectancies, teaching sexual competencies, improving sexual communication, and reducing performance anxiety.

Define It

aggravated sexual assault, 338

delayed ejaculation, 343

erectile disorder, 343

exhibitionistic disorder, 328

female orgasmic disorder, 343

female sexual interest/arousal disorder, 343

fetishistic disorder, 330

frotteuristic disorder, 332

gender dysphoria, 323

gender identity, 323

genito-pelvic pain/penetration disorder, 344

hypoxyphilia, 334

male hypoactive sexual desire disorder, 343

paraphilic disorders, 328

pedophilic disorder, 332

performance anxiety, 346

premature ejaculation, 343

sadomasochism, 335

self-spectatoring, 351

sensate focus exercises, 350

sexual assault, 337

sexual dysfunctions, 342

sexual masochism disorder, 334

sexual sadism disorder, 334

transgender identity, 323

transvestic disorder, 330

vaginismus, 344

voyeuristic disorder, 331

Recall It

1. People with _____ have a basic conflict between their anatomical gender and their gender identity.
   a. a bisexual orientation
   b. gender dysphoria
   c. a gay or lesbian sexual orientation
   d. transvestic fetishim

2. Which of the following is considered a form of voyeurism?
   a. using binoculars to watch a person undress through a bedroom window
   b. becoming aroused while watching a sexually explicit movie
   c. becoming aroused while observing your partner undress in front of you
   d. All three of the above acts are considered forms of voyeurism.

3. Jamie has strong, recurrent sexual urges and fantasies involving desires to caress women's undergarments. This pattern of behaviour most closely resembles _____.
   a. frotteurism
   b. voyeurism

c. fetishism
d. pedophilia

4. A sexual dysfunction that begins following a period (or at least one occurrence) of normal functioning is labelled _____.
   a. acquired
   b. situational
   c. lifelong
   d. generalized

5. Jim rarely has any interest in sexual activity or experiences sexual fantasies or desires. He doesn't find sexual relations revolting. Nor does he have trouble performing sexually. Yet he doesn't understand why people seem so interested in sex. When he consults a psychologist at the urging of his wife, the most likely diagnosis would be _____.
   a. sexual aversion disorder
   b. male hypoactive sexual desire disorder
   c. erectile disorder
   d. delayed ejaculation

Answers to Recall It

1. b,   2. a,   3. c,   4. a,   5. b

Think About It

- Do you believe that how children are reared by their parents plays a causative role in the development of gender dysphoria? Why or why not?
- Do you think our culture is to blame for socializing boys and young men into sexually aggressive roles? Why or why not?

- Do you believe that exhibitionists, voyeurs, and pedophiles should be punished, treated, or both? Explain.
- When does a sexual problem become a sexual dysfunction?

Weblinks

Sex & U
www.sexandu.ca
This is one of the best sources of sexuality information for young adults in Canada. This site includes information for young people, parents, and physicians, including current research.

Notes on Gender Role Transition
www.avitale.com
This website contains information on gender dysphoria and some paraphilic disorders.

The Lesbian, Gay, Bisexual, and Transgender Community Center
www.gaycenter.org
This site provides information on gender dysphoria.

Gender Identity Clinic
www.camh.ca/en/hospital/care_program_and_services/hospital_services/Pages/gid_guide_to_camh.aspx
This site describes treatment options for gender dysphoria from Toronto's Centre for Addiction and Mental Health.

Board of Examiners in Sex Therapy & Counselling in Ontario
www.bestco.info
The BESTCO organization sets standards for the granting of registered status in sex therapy. It also identifies clinicians who have expertise in sex therapy.

Gender Dysphoria, Paraphilic Disorders, and Sexual Dysfunctions

Test your understanding of the key concepts by filling in the blanks with the correct statements chosen from the list that follows. The answers are found at the end of the chapter.

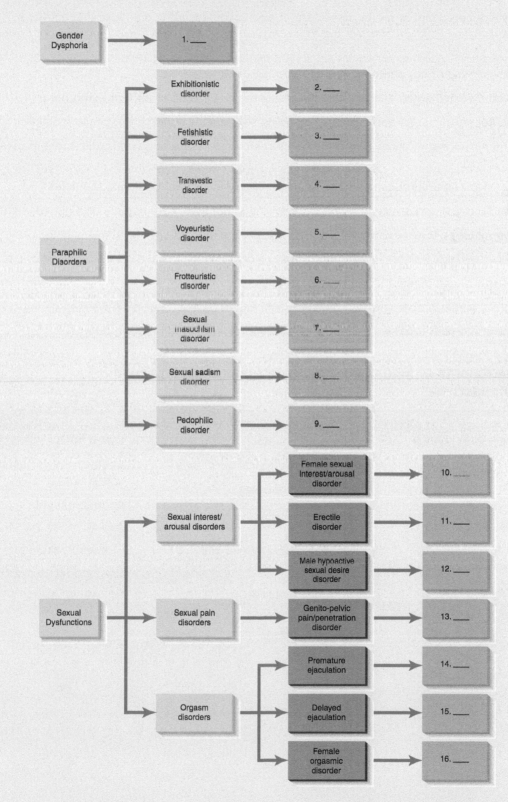

a. Disorder in women involving difficulties achieving orgasm

b. Acting on or being strongly distressed by recurrent, powerful sexual urges and fantasies about watching unsuspecting people undressing or engaging in sex

c. Recurrent, powerful sexual urges and fantasies involving rubbing against or touching a nonconsenting person

d. Recurrent, powerful sexual urges and fantasies about sexual acts involving humiliation or suffering

e. Disorder involving a persistent or recurrent pattern of ejaculation occurring during sexual activity at a point before the man desires it

f. Disorder in which an individual experiences significant personal distress or impaired functioning as a result of a discrepancy between his or her anatomic sex and gender identity

g. Recurrent, powerful sexual urges and fantasies involving the humiliation or suffering of others

h. Recurrent, powerful sexual urges and fantasies involving sexual activity with prepubescent children

i. Disorder in women involving difficulty becoming sexually aroused or lack of sexual excitement or pleasure during sexual activity

j. Disorder in men involving a persistent or recurrent lack of sexual interest or sexual fantasies

k. Recurrent, powerful urges and arousing fantasies involving either inanimate objects or a nongenital body part

l. Recurrent, powerful urges to expose genitals to unsuspecting strangers

m. Disorder in men involving persistent difficulties achieving orgasm

n. Recurrent, powerful sexual urges and fantasies involving cross-dressing

o. Sexual dysfunction in males characterized by difficulty in achieving or maintaining erection during sexual activity

p. Persistent or recurrent pain experienced during vaginal intercourse or penetration attempts

Causes and Treatments of Sexual Dysfunctions According to Various Theoretical Perspectives

THEORETICAL PERSPECTIVE	CAUSES	TREATMENT
BIOLOGICAL PERSPECTIVES	Deficient testosterone production Medical and physical conditions Side effects of drugs	Drugs such as Viagra and Cialis Resolving physical and medical conditions Antidepressants
LEARNING PERSPECTIVES	Conditioned anxiety Lack of sexual knowledge and skills	Self-stimulation Mutual pleasuring Sensate focus exercises
COGNITIVE PERSPECTIVES	Performance anxiety	Relaxation exercises
SOCIOCULTURAL PERSPECTIVES	Restricted sociocultural beliefs and sexual taboos	Couples therapy

Answers: 1. f, 2. l, 3. k, 4. n, 5. b, 6. c, 7. d, 8. g, 9. h, 10. i, 11. o, 12. j, 13. p, 14. e, 15. m, 16. a

10

Schizophrenia Spectrum and Other Psychotic Disorders

Did You Know That...

- You cannot be diagnosed with schizophrenia until months have passed, even though you show all the signs of the disorder?

- Despite wide differences in cultures, the rates of schizophrenia are similar in both developed and developing nations throughout the world?

- Auditory hallucinations may be a form of inner speech?

- Some people with schizophrenia maintain unusual, seemingly uncomfortable positions for hours during which they will not respond to questions or communicate with others?

- Even if you have two parents with schizophrenia, your chances of developing the disorder are less than 1 in 2?

- Living in a family environment that is hostile, critical, and unsupportive increases the risk of relapse among people with schizophrenia?

- Drugs can help control but cannot cure schizophrenia?

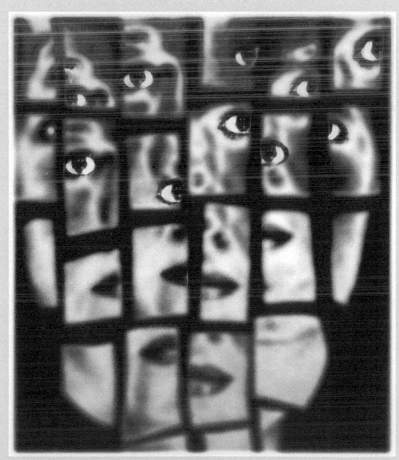

Lisa Valder/The Image Bank/Getty Images

Schizophrenia is perhaps the most puzzling and disabling clinical syndrome. It is the psychological disorder that best corresponds to popular conceptions of madness or lunacy. It often elicits fear, misunderstanding, and condemnation rather than sympathy and concern. Accordingly, social stigma is an important problem associated with schizophrenia. The disorder strikes at the heart of a person, stripping the mind of the intimate connections between thoughts and emotions and filling it with distorted perceptions, false ideas, and illogical conceptions, as in the case of Marilyn:

It was the second time this month Marilyn had called the police. She was fed up with all the noise and the harassment. "Why are they targeting me? What have I done to them?" Marilyn stated. Marilyn lived in a small, one-bedroom apartment that was in much need of repair. Garbage littered the floors and dust bunnies could be spotted in most corners of the main living area. She sat on a dirty, worn sofa and recounted to the police how the neighbours on both sides were constantly tormenting her. "I hear them day and night, telling me that I am no good and that I don't deserve to live." John, the neighbour on the right, was the worst. She could hear him screaming profanities and calling her all sorts of degrading names. She could hear Anne, in the apartment on the left, mumbling but had trouble making out what she was saying. At times, she heard her speak her name and could sense hostility by the tone of her voice.

Steve, her older brother, visits her about once a month. No one else comes. She never had many friends and those that she had have long since disappeared from her life. There was a time when she had great hopes and dreams. When she was at university, she aspired to be a writer. It was after she spoke up about what she uncovered that her life took a turn for the worst. But what could she do? Someone had to stop them. The government was transmitting high-frequency radiowaves through the university's computers. People couldn't hear them, but it changed their thoughts and influenced their behaviour. She had heard of mind control but never imagined it would happen in Canada. When she reported it to the head of the department and later to the press, she was asked to leave the university.

Now she is beginning to wonder if Steve can be trusted. Every time he visits he claims not to hear John and Anne despite their constant ranting. When she agreed to go to a restaurant with him last week, he must have informed them of her whereabouts because she could hear them even there. When will it end?

Finally the landlord arrived and spoke to the police. She overhears him saying, "The apartments on both sides have been vacant for over three months."

Schizophrenia touches every facet of an affected person's life. Acute episodes of schizophrenia are characterized by delusions, hallucinations, illogical thinking, incoherent speech, and bizarre behaviour. Between acute episodes, people with schizophrenia may still be unable to think clearly and may lack appropriate emotional responses to people and events in their lives. They may speak in a flat tone and show little if any facial expressiveness. Although researchers are immersed in probing the psychological and biological foundations of schizophrenia, the disorder remains in many ways a mystery. In this chapter, we examine how research has illuminated our understanding of schizophrenia.

Continuum of Psychotic Disorders

Example: Schizophrenia

Does not meet criteria		Meets criteria →		
NO SYMPTOMS	**STRUGGLING**	**MILD**	**MODERATE**	**SEVERE**
	Lyne has started to withdraw socially and has been neglecting her appearance. Her family has noticed changes in her behaviour.	Sadhika hears voices but is not bothered by them and only occasionally displays bizarre motor behaviour.	Aamir feels some pressure to act upon his delusions, and his speech is often difficult to follow.	Richard responds to his auditory hallucinations and his speech is impossible to comprehend.

CLINICAL FEATURES OF SCHIZOPHRENIA

Although various forms of "madness" have afflicted people throughout the course of history, no one knows how long the behaviour pattern we now label schizophrenia existed before it was first described as a medical syndrome by Emil Kraepelin in 1893. Modern conceptualizations of schizophrenia have been largely shaped by the contributions of Kraepelin, Eugen Bleuler, and Kurt Schneider.

Historical Contributions to Concepts of Schizophrenia

Emil Kraepelin (1856–1926), one of the fathers of modern psychiatry, called the disorder we recognize today as schizophrenia *dementia praecox*. The term was derived from the Latin *dementis*, meaning "out" (*de-*) of one's "mind" (*mens*), and the roots that form the word *precocious*, meaning "before" one's level of "maturity." *Dementia praecox* thus refers to premature impairment of mental abilities. Kraepelin believed that dementia praecox was a disease process caused by specific, although unknown, pathology in the body.

Kraepelin wrote that dementia praecox involves the "loss of the inner unity of thought, feeling, and acting." The syndrome begins early in life, and the course of deterioration eventually results in complete "disintegration of the personality" (Kraepelin, 1909–1913, p. 943). Kraepelin's description of dementia praecox includes delusions, hallucinations, and odd motor behaviours—things that typically characterize the disorder today.

In 1911, the Swiss psychiatrist Eugen Bleuler (1857–1939) renamed dementia praecox *schizophrenia*, from the Greek *schistos*, meaning "cut" or "split," and *phren*, meaning "brain." In doing so, Bleuler focused on the major characteristic of the syndrome: the splitting of the brain functions that give rise to cognition, feelings or affective responses, and behaviour. A person with schizophrenia, for example, might giggle inappropriately when discussing an upsetting event, or might show no emotional expressiveness in the face of tragedy.

Although Bleuler accepted Kraepelin's description of the symptoms of schizophrenia, he did not accept Kraepelin's views that schizophrenia necessarily begins early in life and inevitably follows a deteriorating course. Bleuler proposed that schizophrenia follows a more variable course. In some cases, acute episodes occur intermittently. In others, there might be limited improvement rather than inevitable deterioration. Bleuler believed that schizophrenia could be recognized on the basis of four primary features or symptoms. Today, we refer to them as the **four A's**:

schizophrenia A chronic psychotic disorder characterized by acute episodes involving a break with reality, as manifested by such features as delusions, hallucinations, illogical thinking, incoherent speech, and bizarre behaviour.

four A's In Bleuler's view, the primary characteristics of schizophrenia: loose *associations*, blunted or inappropriate *affect*, *ambivalence*, and *autism*.

loeseness of associations Ideas are strung together with little or no relationship among them.

affect The behavioural expression of emotions. Pronounced *AF-fect*.

first-rank symptoms In Kurt Schneider's view, the primary features of schizophrenia, such as hallucinations and delusions, that distinctly characterize the disorder.

second-rank symptoms In Schneider's view, symptoms associated with schizophrenia that also occur in other psychological disorders.

1. *Associations*. Associations or relationships among thoughts become disturbed. We now call this type of disturbance *thought disorder* or **looseness of associations**. Looseness of associations means that ideas are strung together with little or no relationship among them, and the speaker does not appear to be aware of the lack of connectedness. The person's speech appears to others to become rambling and confused.
2. *Affect*. **Affect** or emotional response becomes flattened or inappropriate. The individual may show a lack of response to upsetting events or burst into laughter upon hearing that a family member or friend has died.
3. *Ambivalence*. People with schizophrenia hold ambivalent or conflicting feelings toward others, such as loving and hating them at the same time.
4. *Autism*. Autism is withdrawal into a private fantasy world that is not bound by principles of logic. (Note that autism, as a feature of schizophrenia, is different from the disorder of childhood known as autism, which is discussed in Chapter 11.)

In Bleuler's view, hallucinations and delusions represent "secondary symptoms" that accompany the primary symptoms but do not define the disorder.

Another influential developer of modern concepts of schizophrenia was German psychiatrist Kurt Schneider (1887–1967). Schneider believed that Bleuler's criteria (his four A's) were too vague for diagnostic purposes and that they failed to distinguish schizophrenia adequately from other disorders. Schneider (1957) distinguished between two sets of symptoms: **first-rank symptoms**, which he believed are central to diagnosis, and **second-rank symptoms**, which he believed are found not only in schizophrenia but also in other psychoses and in some nonpsychotic disorders, such as personality disorders. In contrast to Bleuler, Schneider proposed that hallucinations and delusions are key or first-rank features of schizophrenia (Schneider, 1957). He considered disturbances in mood and confused thinking to be second-rank symptoms because they are also found in other disorders. Although Schneider's ranking of disturbed behaviours helped distinguish schizophrenia from other disorders, we now know that first-rank symptoms are sometimes found among people with other disorders, especially bipolar disorder. Although first-rank symptoms are clearly associated with schizophrenia, they are not unique to it.

Today, the contributions of Kraepelin, Bleuler, and Schneider are expressed in modified form in the present DSM diagnostic system. However, the diagnostic code for schizophrenia is not limited, as Kraepelin had proposed, to cases in which there is a course of progressive deterioration. The present code is also tighter than earlier conceptualizations; it separates into other diagnostic categories cases in which there are disturbances of mood combined with psychotic behaviour (schizoaffective disorder) or that involve schizophrenic-like thinking but without overt psychotic behaviour (schizotypal personality disorder). The DSM-5 criteria for schizophrenia also require that psychotic behaviours be present at some point during the course of the disorder and that signs of the disorder be present for at least six months. People with briefer forms of psychosis are placed in diagnostic categories that may be connected with more favourable outcomes. Table 10.1 outlines the diagnostic criteria for schizophrenia.

Paul Prescott/Shutterstock

Hallucinations. According to Kurt Schneider, hallucinations and delusions are numbered among the first-rank symptoms of schizophrenia—that is, the symptoms of schizophrenia that are central to the diagnosis. So-called second-rank symptoms are found in other disorders as well. Schneider considered confusion and disturbances in mood to be second-rank symptoms.

Prevalence and Costs of Schizophrenia

According to the best estimates, about 1% of the adult Canadian population suffers from schizophrenia at some point in their lives (Statistics Canada, 2012a). The rates of schizophrenia appear to be

TABLE 10.1
Diagnostic Criteria for Schizophrenia

A. Two (or more) of the following, each present for a significant portion of time during a 1-month period (or less if successfully treated). At least one of these must be (1), (2), or (3):

   (1) Delusions.

   (2) Hallucinations.

   (3) Disorganized speech (e.g., frequent derailment or incoherence).

   (4) Grossly disorganized or catatonic behavior.

   (5) Negative symptoms (i.e., diminished emotional expression or avolition).

B. For a significant portion of the time since the onset of the disturbance, level of functioning in one or more major areas, such as work, interpersonal relations, or self-care, is markedly below the level achieved prior to the onset (or when the onset is in childhood or adolescence, there is failure to achieve expected level of interpersonal, academic, or occupational functioning).

C. Continuous signs of the disturbance persist for at least 6 months. This 6-month period must include at least 1 month of symptoms (or less if successfully treated) that meet Criterion A (i.e., active-phase symptoms) and may include periods of prodromal or residual symptoms. During these prodromal or residual periods, the signs of the disturbance may be manifested by only negative symptoms or by two or more symptoms listed in Criterion A present in an attenuated form (e.g., odd beliefs, unusual perceptual experiences).

D. Schizoaffective disorder and depressive or bipolar disorder with psychotic features have been ruled out because either 1) no major depressive or manic episodes have occurred concurrently with the active-phase symptoms, or 2) if mood episodes have occurred during active-phase symptoms, they have been present for a minority of the total duration of the active and residual periods of the illness.

E. The disturbance is not attributable to the physiological effects of a substance (e.g., a drug of abuse, a medication) or another medical condition.

F. If there is a history of autism spectrum disorder or a communication disorder of childhood onset, the additional diagnosis of schizophrenia is made only if prominent delusions or hallucinations, in addition to the other required symptoms of schizophrenia, are also present for at least 1 month (or less if successfully treated).

similar in both developed and developing countries (Saha, Welham, Chant, & McGrath, 2006). Schizophrenia is the fifth leading cause of disability worldwide and the most common diagnosis of people who are involuntarily hospitalized (Bland, 1998; Health Canada, 2006a). Although some people with schizophrenia have healthy relationships, most (60–70%) do not marry, and most have limited social contacts (Health Canada, 2006a; Hooley, 2010). The chronic course of the disorder contributes to ongoing social problems. As a result, people with schizophrenia are greatly overrepresented in prison and homeless populations. The unemployment rate among this population is very high at 79% (Shean, 2007). In addition, up to 80% of people with schizophrenia abuse substances at some point in their lives. Substance abuse in people with schizophrenia is associated with poorer functional adjustment, suicidal behaviour, and violence (Health Canada, 2006a). About 40–60% of people with schizophrenia attempt suicide, and about 10% die from suicide. They are between 15 and 25 times more likely than the general population to die from a suicide attempt (Health Canada, 2006a).

Because of their behavioural problems (such as odd or socially inappropriate behaviour), people with schizophrenia are more often the victims than the perpetrators of violence (Health Canada, 2006a). Public misunderstanding and fear contribute to the serious stigma associated with schizophrenia. Contrary to popular opinion, most people with the disorder are withdrawn and not violent. In fact, when adequately treated, people with the disorder are no more violent than the general population. Even so, the stigma of violence interferes with their ability to acquire housing, employment, and treatment, and also makes it difficult for them to make friends or enter intimate relationships. The stigma associated with schizophrenia also adds to the burden of the people caring for the person with the disorder, such as families and caregivers (Health Canada, 2006a; Hooley, 2010; Sartorius & Schulze, 2005). Public education about the nature of schizophrenia is an important step toward reducing the stigma associated with the disorder.

Phases of Schizophrenia

Schizophrenia usually afflicts young people and often does so at the very time they are making their way from the family into the outside world (APA, 2013). People who develop schizophrenia become increasingly disengaged from society. They fail to function in the expected roles of student, worker, or spouse, and their families and communities grow intolerant of their deviant behaviour. The disorder typically develops in the late teens or early 20s, a time at which the brain is reaching full maturation (Dobbs, 2010). In about three quarters of cases, the first signs of schizophrenia appear by the age of 25 (Keith, Regier, & Rae, 1991). Men have a slightly higher risk of developing schizophrenia than women and also tend to develop the disorder at an earlier age (APA, 2013).

In some cases, the onset of the disorder is acute. It occurs suddenly, within a few weeks or months. The individual may have been well adjusted and may have shown few if any signs of behavioural disturbance. Then a rapid transformation in personality and behaviour leads to an acute psychotic episode.

In most cases, however, there is a slower, more gradual decline in functioning. It may take years before psychotic behaviours emerge, although early signs of deterioration may be observed. This period of deterioration is called the **prodromal phase**. It is characterized by waning interest in social activities and increasing difficulty in meeting the responsibilities of daily living. At first, such people seem to take less care of their appearance. They fail to bathe regularly or they wear the same clothes repeatedly. Over time, their behaviour may become increasingly odd or eccentric. There are lapses in job performance or schoolwork. Their speech may become increasingly vague and rambling. These changes in personality may start out so gradually that they raise little concern among friends and families. They may be attributed to a "phase" that the person is passing through. But as behaviour becomes more bizarre—like hoarding food, collecting garbage, or talking to oneself on the street—the **acute phase** of the disorder begins. Finally, psychotic symptoms such as wild hallucinations, delusions, and increasingly bizarre behaviour develop.

Following acute episodes, people who develop schizophrenia may enter the **residual phase,** in which their behaviour returns to the level that was characteristic of the prodromal phase. Although flagrant psychotic behaviours may be absent during the residual phase, the person may continue to be impaired by a deep sense of apathy, difficulties in thinking or speaking clearly, and the harbouring of unusual ideas, such as beliefs in telepathy or clairvoyance. Such patterns of behaviour make it difficult for the person to meet expected social roles as wage earners, marital partners, or students. Full return to normal behaviour is uncommon but may occur. More commonly, a chronic pattern characterized by occasional relapses and continued impairment between acute episodes may develop (Heilbronner, Samara, Leucht, Falkai, & Schulze, 2016). Newman and colleagues at the University of Alberta followed 128 individuals with schizophrenia over 34 years. Over the course of this time period, patients experienced severe symptoms 50% of the time and moderate symptoms 25% of the time. Most of these individuals did not show any improvement in the severity of their symptoms over the course of their life (Newman, Bland, & Thompson, 2012).

Major Features of Schizophrenia

Schizophrenia is a pervasive disorder that affects a wide range of psychological processes involving cognition, affect, and behaviour. People with schizophrenia show a marked decline in occupational and social functioning. They may have difficulty holding a conversation, forming friendships, holding a job, or taking care of their personal hygiene. Yet no single behaviour pattern is unique to schizophrenia, nor is any one behaviour

prodromal phase (1) Stage in which the early features or signs of a disorder become apparent. (2) In schizophrenia, the period of decline in functioning that precedes the development of the first acute psychotic episode.

acute phase In schizophrenia, the phase in which psychotic symptoms develop, such as hallucinations, delusions, and disorganized speech and behaviour.

residual phase In schizophrenia, the phase of the disorder that follows an acute phase, characterized by a return to a level of functioning typical of the prodromal phase.

pattern invariably present among all people with schizophrenia. People with schizophrenia may exhibit delusions, problems with associative thinking, and hallucinations at one time or another, but not necessarily all at once. Although schizophrenia occurs across cultures, the course of the disorder and how symptoms are expressed can vary. For example, the themes conveyed in delusions or hallucinations, such as particular religious or racial themes, vary across cultures (Whaley & Hall, 2009).

Let's consider how schizophrenia affects thinking, speech, attentional and perceptual processes, emotional processes, and voluntary behaviour.

DELUSIONS The most prominent disturbance in the content of thought involves delusions, or false beliefs that remain fixed in the person's mind despite their illogical bases and lack of supporting evidence. They tend to remain unshakable even in the face of disconfirming evidence. Delusions may take many forms, including delusions of persecution (e.g., "The police are out to get me"), delusions of reference ("People on the bus are talking about me," or "People on television are making fun of me"), delusions of being controlled (believing that one's thoughts, feelings, impulses, or actions are controlled by external forces, such as agents of the devil), and delusions of grandeur (believing oneself to be Jesus or to be on a special mission, or having grand but illogical plans for saving the world). People with delusions of persecution may think they are being pursued by the Mafia, terrorists, the RCMP, or some other group. A woman we treated who had delusions of reference believed that television news correspondents were broadcasting coded information about her. A man with delusions of this type expressed the belief that his neighbours had bugged the walls of his house. Other delusions include beliefs that one has committed unpardonable sins or is rotting from some horrible disease. Common delusions include thought broadcasting (believing that one's thoughts are somehow transmitted to the external world so that others can overhear them), thought insertion (believing that one's thoughts have been planted in one's mind by an external source), and thought withdrawal (believing that thoughts have been removed from one's mind).

Mellor (1970) offers the following examples of thought broadcasting, thought insertion, and thought withdrawal:

Thought Broadcasting: A 21-year-old student reported, "As I think, my thoughts leave my head on a type of mental ticker-tape. Everyone around has only to pass the tape through their mind and they know my thoughts" (p. 17).

Thought Insertion: A 29-year-old housewife reported that when she looks out of the window, she thinks, "The garden looks nice and the grass looks cool, but the thoughts of [a man's name] come into my mind. There are no other thoughts there, only his. . . . He treats my mind like a screen and flashes his thoughts on it like you flash a picture" (p. 17).

Thought Withdrawal: A 22-year-old woman experienced the following: "I am thinking about my mother, and suddenly my thoughts are sucked out of my mind by a phrenological vacuum extractor, and there is nothing in my mind, it is empty" (pp. 16–17).

DISORGANIZED SPEECH Unless we are engaged in daydreaming or purposefully letting our thoughts wander, our thoughts tend to be tightly knit together. The connections (or associations) between our thoughts tend to be logical and coherent. People with schizophrenia, however, tend to think in a disorganized, illogical fashion, which is reflected in their speech patterns. In schizophrenia, the form or structure of thought processes as well as their content is often disturbed. Clinicians label this type of disturbance a **thought disorder**.

Thought disorder is recognized by a breakdown in the organization, processing, and control of thoughts. As a result, the speech pattern of people with schizophrenia is often disorganized or jumbled, with parts of words combined incoherently or words strung together to make meaningless rhymes. Looseness of associations, which we now regard as a chief sign of thought disorder, was one of Bleuler's four A's. Speech may jump from one topic to another but show little interconnectivity between the ideas or thoughts that are expressed. People with thought disorder are usually unaware that their thoughts and behaviour appear abnormal. In severe cases, their speech may become completely incoherent or incomprehensible.

thought disorder Disturbances in thinking characterized by various features, especially a breakdown in logical associations between thoughts.

neologisms Type of disturbed thinking associated with schizophrenia involving the coining of new words.

perseveration Persistent repetition of the same thought or train of thought.

clanging In people with schizophrenia, the tendency to string words together because they rhyme or sound alike.

blocking (1) Disruption of self-expression of threatening or emotionally laden material. (2) In people with schizophrenia, a condition of suddenly becoming silent with loss of memory for what they have just discussed.

Another common sign of thought disorder is poverty of speech; that is, speech that is coherent but is so limited in production or vague that little informational value is conveyed. Less commonly occurring signs include **neologisms** (words made up by the speaker that have little or no meaning to others), **perseveration** (inappropriate but persistent repetition of the same words or train of thought), **clanging** (stringing together words or sounds on the basis of rhyming, such as, "I know who I am but I don't know Sam"), and **blocking** (involuntary abrupt interruption of speech or thought).

Many but not all people with schizophrenia show evidence of thought disorder. Some appear to think and speak coherently but have disordered content of thought, as seen by the presence of delusions. Nor is disordered thought unique to schizophrenia; it has even been found in milder form among people without psychological disorders (Bachman & Cannon, 2005), especially when they are tired or under stress. Disordered thought is also found among other diagnostic groups, such as people with mania. Thought disorders in people experiencing a manic episode tend to be short-lived and reversible, however. In those with schizophrenia, thought disorder tends to be more persistent or recurrent—it occurs most often during acute episodes but may linger into residual phases. Thought disorders that persist beyond acute episodes are connected with poorer prognoses, perhaps because lingering thought disorders reflect more severe disorders (Marengo & Harrow, 1997).

HALLUCINATIONS

Every so often during the interview, Sara would look over her right shoulder in the direction of the office door and smile gently. When asked why she kept looking at the door, she said that the voices were talking about the two of us just outside the door and she wanted to hear what they were saying. "Why the smile?" Sara was asked. "They were saying funny things," she replied, "like maybe you thought I was cute or something."

Alex was flailing his arms wildly in the hall of the psychiatric unit. Sweat seemed to pour from his brow, and his eyes darted about with agitation. He was subdued and injected with haloperidol (brand name Haldol) to reduce his agitation. When he was about to be injected he started shouting, "Father, forgive them for they know not . . . forgive them . . . father . . ." His words became jumbled. Later, after he had calmed down, he reported that the ward attendants had looked to him like devils or evil angels. They were red and burning, and steam issued from their mouths.

The Authors' Files

Hallucinations, the most common form of perceptual disturbance in schizophrenia, are perceptions that occur in the absence of an external stimulus. They are difficult to distinguish from reality. For Sara, the voices coming from outside the consulting room were real enough, even though no one was there. Hallucinations may involve any of the senses. Auditory hallucinations ("hearing voices") are most common. Tactile hallucinations (such as tingling, electrical, or burning sensations) and somatic hallucinations (feeling like snakes are crawling inside one's belly) are also common. Visual hallucinations (seeing things that are not there), gustatory hallucinations (tasting things that are not present), and olfactory hallucinations (sensing odours that are not present) are rarer.

Auditory hallucinations occur in 60–80% of cases of schizophrenia (Bauer et al., 2011; Lim et al., 2016). In auditory hallucinations, the voices may be experienced as female or male and as originating inside or outside one's head (APA, 2013). When hallucinating, people with schizophrenia may hear voices conversing about them in the third person, debating their virtues or faults.

Some people with schizophrenia experience command hallucinations, voices that instruct them to perform certain acts, such as harming themselves or others. Joanne, for example, was instructed by "devils" to kill herself, so she attempted to jump from a bridge. People with schizophrenia who experience command hallucinations are often hospitalized for fear they may harm themselves or others. There is a good reason for this. One study found that 62% of people with command hallucinations reported obeying benign commands and 30% reported they had obeyed commands to harm themselves during the past month (Bucci et al., 2013). Yet command hallucinations often go undetected by professionals because command hallucinators deny them or are unwilling to discuss them.

Hallucinations of Other Types   Hallucinations are not unique to schizophrenia. People with major depression and mania sometimes experience hallucinations. Nor are hallucinations invariably a sign of psychopathology. Cross-cultural evidence shows they are common and socially valued in some developing countries (Bentall, 1990). Even in developed countries, about 5% of respondents in nonpatient samples reported experiencing hallucinations during the preceding year, mostly auditory hallucinations (Vellante et al., 2012). Hallucinations in people without psychiatric conditions are often triggered by unusually low levels of sensory stimulation (lying in the dark in a soundproof room for an extended time) or low levels of arousal (Teunisse, Cruysberg, Hoefnagels, Verbeek, & Zitman, 1996). Unlike psychotic individuals, these people realize their hallucinations are not real and feel in control of them.

People who are free of psychological disorders sometimes experience hallucinations during the course of a religious experience or ritual (APA, 2013). Participants in such experiences may report fleeting trance-like states with visions or other perceptual aberrations. All of us hallucinate nightly, if we consider dreams to be a form of hallucination (perceptual experience in the absence of external stimuli).

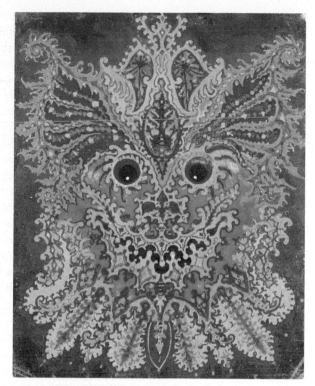

Lebrecht Music and Arts Photo Library/Alamy Stock Photo

***The Cat* by Louis Wain (1860–1939).** This is one of the later paintings by a Victorian artist who developed schizophrenia. The painting depicts his withdrawal from reality to fantasy, a hallmark of schizophrenia.

Hallucinations may occur in response to hallucinogenic drugs, such as LSD. They may also occur during grief reactions, when images of the deceased may appear, and in other stressful conditions. In most cases, grief-induced hallucinations can be differentiated from psychotic ones in that the individual can distinguish the former type from reality. Psychiatric patients, however, tend to confuse real and imaginary (hallucinatory) events.

Drug-induced hallucinations tend to be visual and often involve abstract shapes, such as circles or stars, or flashes of light. Schizophrenic hallucinations, in contrast, tend to be more fully formed and complex. Hallucinations (e.g., of bugs crawling on one's skin) are common during delirium tremens, which often occurs as part of the withdrawal syndrome for chronic alcoholism. Hallucinations may also occur as side effects of medications or in neurological disorders, such as Parkinson's disease.

Causes of Hallucinations   The causes of psychotic hallucinations remain unknown, but speculations abound. Disturbances in brain chemistry are suspected of playing a role. The neurotransmitter dopamine has been implicated because antipsychotic drugs that block dopamine activity also tend to reduce hallucinations. Conversely, drugs that lead to increased production of dopamine tend to induce hallucinations. Because hallucinations resemble dream-like states, it is also possible that hallucinations are types of daytime dreams connected with a failure of brain mechanisms that normally prevent dream images from intruding on waking experiences.

Hallucinations may also represent a type of subvocal inner speech (Arguedas, Stevenson, & Langdon, 2012; Stephane, Barton, & Boutros, 2001). Many of us talk to ourselves from time to time, although we usually keep our mutterings beneath our breath (subvocal) and recognize the voice as our own. Might auditory hallucinations that occur among people with schizophrenia be projections of their own internal voices or self-speech onto external sources? In one experiment, individuals who suffered from schizophrenia reported that the voices disappeared when they engaged in a procedure that prevented them from talking to themselves under their breath (Turkington & Morrison, 2012). Researchers found that activity in Broca's area, a part of the brain involved in controlling speech, was greater in people with schizophrenia when they were hearing voices than at a later time when they were no longer hallucinating (McGuire, Shah, & Murray, 1993). This same area is known to become active when people engage in inner speech (Paulesu, Frith, & Frackowiak, 1993). Researchers have also found evidence of similar electrical activity in the auditory cortex of the brain during auditory hallucinations and in response to hearing real sounds (Stephane et al., 2001). This evidence supports the view that auditory hallucinations may be a form of inner speech (silent self-talk) that for some unknown reason is attributed to external sources rather than to one's own thoughts (Johns, Gregg, Allen, & McGuire, 2006).

Even if theories linking subvocal speech to auditory hallucinations stand up to further scientific inquiry, however, they cannot account for hallucinations in other sensory modalities, such as visual, tactile, and olfactory hallucinations (Larøi, 2006).

The brain mechanisms responsible for hallucinations are likely to involve a number of interconnected brain systems. One intriguing possibility is that defects in deeper brain structures may lead the brain to create its own reality, which goes unchecked because of a failure of the higher thinking centres in the brain, located in the frontal lobes of the cerebral cortex, to perform a reality check on these images to determine whether they are real, imagined, or hallucinated (Collerton, Perry, & McKeith, 2005).

Consequently, people may misattribute their own internally generated voices to outside sources. As we'll see later, evidence from other brain-imaging studies points to abnormalities in the frontal and temporal lobes in at least some people with schizophrenia.

GROSSLY DISORGANIZED OR CATATONIC BEHAVIOUR

Grossly disorganized behaviour may manifest itself in a variety of ways, ranging from child-like "silliness" to unpredictable agitation. The emotional responses of individuals with schizophrenia may be inappropriate, like giggling at bad news. Problems may be noted in any form of goal-directed behaviour, leading to difficulties in performing activities of daily living.

In some cases, individuals with schizophrenia may show catatonic behaviours, which involve severely impaired cognitive and motor functioning. People with **catatonia** may become unaware of the environment and maintain a fixed or rigid posture—even bizarre, apparently strenuous positions for hours as their limbs become stiff or swollen. They may exhibit odd gestures and bizarre facial expressions or become unresponsive and curtail spontaneous movement. They may show highly excited or wild behaviour or slow to a state of **stupor**. A striking but less common feature of catatonia is **waxy flexibility**, which involves adopting a fixed posture into which they have been positioned by others. They will not respond to questions or comments during these periods, which can last for hours. Later, however, they may report they heard what others were saying at the time.

As we have just seen, schizophrenia is associated with a wide range of symptoms that involve thinking, speech, emotional and perceptual processes, and voluntary behaviour. One way of grouping the features of schizophrenia is to distinguish between positive and negative symptoms. **Positive symptoms** are characterized by the *presence* of abnormal behaviour, such as hallucinations, delusions, thought disorder, disorganized speech, and disorganized behaviour.

NEGATIVE SYMPTOMS

The **negative symptoms** of schizophrenia are characterized by the absence of normal behaviour and represent the more enduring or persistent characteristics of the disorder. Negative symptoms are deficits or behavioural deficiencies, such as social-skills deficits, social withdrawal, flattened or blunted affect, poverty of speech and thought, psychomotor retardation, or failure to experience pleasure in pleasant activities.

People with schizophrenia tend to show significant impairment in their interpersonal relationships. They tend to withdraw from social interactions and become absorbed in

catatonia Gross disturbances in motor activity and cognitive functioning.

stupor State of relative or complete unconsciousness in which a person is not generally aware of or responsive to the environment, as in a catatonic stupor.

waxy flexibility Feature of catatonia involving adopting a fixed posture into which people with schizophrenia have been positioned by others.

positive symptoms The more flagrant features of schizophrenia characterized by the *presence* of abnormal behaviour, such as hallucinations, delusions, thought disorder, disorganized speech, and disorganized behaviour.

negative symptoms Features of schizophrenia characterized by the *absence* of normal behaviour. Negative symptoms are deficits or behavioural deficiencies, such as social-skills deficits, social withdrawal, flattened affect, poverty of speech and thought, psychomotor retardation, or failure to experience pleasure in pleasant activities.

private thoughts and fantasies. Or they cling so desperately to others they make them uncomfortable. They may become so dominated by their own fantasies they essentially lose touch with the outside world. They also tend to have been introverted and peculiar even before the appearance of psychotic behaviour (Metsänen et al., 2004). These early signs may be associated with a vulnerability to schizophrenia, at least in people with a genetic risk of developing the disorder.

Individuals with schizophrenia may not experience a normal range of emotional response to people and events. Disturbances of affect or emotional response are typified by **blunted affect** or **flat affect**. Blunted affect is a reduction in emotional expression, whereas flat affect is inferred from the absence of emotional expression in the face and voice. People with schizophrenia may speak in a monotone and maintain an expressionless face, or "mask."

It is not fully clear, however, whether emotional blunting in people with schizophrenia is a disturbance in their ability to express emotions, to report the presence of emotions, or to actually experience emotions (Berenbaum & Oltmanns, 2005). They may, in other words, experience emotions even if their experiences are not communicated to the world outside through such means as facial expression. Support along these lines is found in research showing that people with schizophrenia displayed less facial expression of positive and negative emotions when viewing emotion-eliciting films than did control subjects but reported experiencing as much positive or negative emotion (Kring, Kerr, Smith, & Neale, 1993). It may be that people with schizophrenia experience emotions internally but lack the capacity to express them outwardly (Kring & Neale, 1996).

blunted affect Significant reduction in emotional expression.

flat affect Absence of emotional expression.

NORMAL/ABNORMAL BEHAVIOUR

Unusual Experiences: No Disorder

Ahmed is a 17-year-old high school student. He does not drink or do drugs. With his family, Ahmed belongs to a local church that holds very particular views about religion and Christianity. He has been attending this church since he was a baby. Most members of the church hold strong beliefs about spirits and the afterlife. It is a commonplace experience at church for people to talk about communicating with spirits, and no one finds this unusual or frightening. In fact, the congregation values these experiences, and the stories are told and retold to other members. Ahmed has had a few experiences that he's shared with his congregation. For example, while falling asleep he sometimes feels a "presence" near him. He never sees anything, but he has a very strong sensation of someone being near him. He feels that this is the presence of a spirit, and he welcomes these experiences. When he told a friend outside of the congregation, the friend thought this sounded "weird." Ahmed realized that other people do not share his beliefs about spirits, so he decided to share these experiences only with his fellow churchgoers from now on rather than his school friends.

Unusual Experiences: Psychotic Disorder

Dejuan is a 20-year-old college student studying marketing. He has a family history of mental illness, with his paternal uncle having been diagnosed with schizophrenia when he was a young man. Dejuan has been having a series of unusual experiences for a few years that he has not told anyone about. It started with hearing sounds and words that other people could not hear. Dejuan would be standing in a room and feel as though he heard someone calling his name. When he would look, no one would be there. He chalked this up as an unusual experience, and didn't think about it much further. However, these experiences had begun to intensify more recently. Dejuan began hearing a voice talking to him even when no one was around. This voice would comment on what he was doing and give him suggestions for things he should do. At first, the voice was pleasant and simply made observations. More recently, the voice had become more critical and demanding. Although Dejuan felt a lot of anxiety about the voice, he began to take it more seriously, trying to appease it in the way he acted. Dejuan's family became increasingly worried about him, as they noticed odd expressions on his face, his seeming distraction from others, and his beginning to withdraw from his friends and family. At one point, Dejuan began talking back to the voices, and his parents overheard. They immediately took him to the emergency room at their local hospital.

Jodi Cobb/National Geographic/Getty Images

On the run? People with schizophrenia may hold systematized delusions that involve themes of persecution and grandeur.

Disturbances of volition are most often seen in the residual or chronic state and are characterized by loss of initiative to pursue goal-directed activities. People with schizophrenia may be unable to carry out plans and may lack interest or drive. Apparent ambivalence toward choosing courses of action may block goal-directed activities.

Negative symptoms tend to persist even when positive symptoms have abated and often have a greater effect on the person's functioning than positive symptoms. They are also less responsive than positive symptoms to treatment with antipsychotic drugs (Barch, 2013).

OTHER TYPES OF IMPAIRMENT People who suffer from schizophrenia may become confused about their personal identities—the cluster of attributes and characteristics that define them as individuals and give meaning and direction to their lives. They may fail to recognize themselves as unique individuals and be unclear as to how much of what they experience is part of themselves. In psychodynamic terms, this phenomenon is sometimes referred to as *loss of ego boundaries*. They may also have difficulty adopting a third-party perspective and fail to perceive their own behaviour and verbalizations as socially inappropriate in a given situation because they are unable to see things from another person's point of view (Penn, Combs, & Mohamed, 2001).

To read this book, you must screen out background noises and other environmental stimuli. The ability to focus on relevant stimuli is basic to learning and thinking. Kraepelin and Bleuler suggested that schizophrenia involves a breakdown in the processes of attention. People with schizophrenia appear to have difficulty filtering out irrelevant, distracting stimuli, a deficit that makes it nearly impossible for them to focus their attention and organize their thoughts (Wang et al., 2007).

The mother of a son who had schizophrenia provided the following illustration of her son's difficulties in filtering out extraneous sounds:

> [H]is hearing is different when he's ill. One of the first things we notice when he's deteriorating is his heightened sense of hearing. He cannot filter out anything. He hears each and every sound around him with equal intensity. He hears the sounds from the street, in the yard, and in the house, and they are all much louder than normal. (Schizophrenia-a Mother's Agony Over Her Son's Pain, 1985 by Orlando Sentinel)

People with schizophrenia also appear to be hypervigilant or acutely sensitive to extraneous sounds, especially during the early stages of the disorder. During acute episodes, they may become flooded by these stimuli, overwhelming their ability to make sense of their environment. Through measuring involuntary brainwave responses to auditory stimuli, researchers have found that the brains of people with schizophrenia are less able than those of other people to inhibit or screen out responses to distracting sounds (Bergida & Lenzenweger, 2006).

Investigators suspect that attentional deficits associated with schizophrenia are, to a certain extent, inherited (Goldberg et al., 2006). Although the underlying mechanism is not entirely clear, attentional deficits may be related to dysfunction in the subcortical parts of the brain that regulate attention to external stimuli, such as the basal ganglia (Cornblatt & Keilp, 1994). Scientists suspect there may be a "gating" mechanism in the brain responsible for filtering extraneous stimuli, much like how the closing of a gate in a road can stem the flow of traffic (de Bruin, Van Luijtelaar, Cools, & Ellenbroek, 2003). Evidence suggests that training in attention skills may help reduce attentional deficits in schizophrenia patients (Medalia, Aluma, Tryon, & Merriam, 1998).

Clinical Features of Schizophrenia

- **What is schizophrenia, and how prevalent is it?** Schizophrenia is a chronic psychotic disorder characterized by acute episodes involving a break with reality, as manifested by such features as delusions, hallucinations, illogical thinking, incoherent speech, and bizarre behaviour. Residual deficits in cognitive, emotional, and social areas of functioning persist between acute episodes. Schizophrenia is believed to affect about 1% of the population.
- **What key historical figures in psychiatry influenced our conceptions of schizophrenia?** Emil Kraepelin was the first to describe the syndrome we identify as schizophrenia. He labelled the disorder *dementia praecox* and believed that it was a disease that develops early in life and follows a progressively deteriorating course. Eugen Bleuler renamed the disorder *schizophrenia* and believed that its course is more variable. He also distinguished between primary symptoms (the four A's) and secondary symptoms. Kurt Schneider distinguished between first-rank symptoms that define the

disorder and second-rank symptoms that occur in schizophrenia and other disorders.
- **What are the major phases of schizophrenia?** Schizophrenia usually develops in late adolescence or early adulthood. Its onset may be abrupt or gradual. The period of deterioration preceding the onset of acute symptoms is called the prodromal phase. An acute episode involves the emergence of clear psychotic features. A level of functioning that was typical of the prodromal phase characterizes the residual phase.
- **What are the most prominent features of schizophrenia?** Among the more prominent features of schizophrenia are disorders in the content of thought (delusions) and form of thought (thought disorder), as well as the presence of perceptual distortions (hallucinations) and emotional disturbances (flattened or inappropriate affect). There are also dysfunctions in the brain processes that regulate attention to the external world.

THEORETICAL PERSPECTIVES

The understanding of schizophrenia has been approached from each of the major theoretical perspectives. Although the underlying causes of schizophrenia have not been identified, they are presumed to involve biological abnormalities in combination with psychosocial and environmental influences.

Psychodynamic Perspectives

According to the psychodynamic perspective, schizophrenia represents the overwhelming of the ego by primitive sexual or aggressive drives or impulses arising from the id. These impulses threaten the ego and give rise to intense intrapsychic conflict. Under such a threat, the person regresses to an early period in the oral stage, referred to as *primary narcissism*. In this period, the infant has not yet learned that it and the world are distinct entities. Because the ego mediates the relationship between the self and the outer world, this breakdown in ego functioning accounts for the detachment from reality that is typical of schizophrenia. Input from the id causes fantasies to become mistaken for reality, giving rise to hallucinations and delusions. Primitive impulses may also carry more weight than social norms and be expressed in bizarre, socially inappropriate behaviour.

Freud's followers, such as Erik Erikson and Harry Stack Sullivan, placed more emphasis on interpersonal than intrapsychic factors. Sullivan (1962), for example, who devoted much of his life's work to schizophrenia, emphasized the importance of impaired mother–child relationships, arguing they can set the stage for gradual withdrawal from other people. In early childhood, anxious and hostile interactions between the child and parent lead the child to take refuge in a private fantasy world. A vicious cycle ensues: The more the child withdraws, the less opportunity there is to develop a sense of trust in others and the social skills necessary to establish intimacy. Then the weak bonds between the child and others prompt social anxiety and further withdrawal. This cycle continues until young adulthood. Then, faced with increasing demands at school or work and in intimate relationships, the person becomes overwhelmed with anxiety and withdraws completely into a world of fantasy.

Critics of Freud's views point out that schizophrenic behaviour and infantile behaviour are not much alike, so schizophrenia cannot be explained by regression. Freud's detractors and modern psychodynamic theorists note that psychodynamic explanations are post hoc, or retrospective. Early child–adult relationships are recalled from the vantage point of adulthood rather than observed longitudinally. Psychoanalysts have not been able to demonstrate that hypothesized early childhood experiences or family patterns lead to schizophrenia.

Learning Perspectives

Although learning theory may not account for schizophrenia, the principles of conditioning and observational learning may play a role in the development of some forms of schizophrenic behaviour. From this perspective, people may learn to "emit" schizophrenic behaviours when they are more likely to be reinforced than normal behaviour.

Ullmann and Krasner (1975) focused on the reinforcement value of social stimulation. Children who later develop schizophrenia may grow up in nonreinforcing environments because of disturbed family patterns or other environmental influences. Thus, they never learn to respond appropriately to social stimuli. Instead, as Sullivan (1962) also argued, they increasingly attend to private or idiosyncratic stimuli. Other people perceive them as strange, and they suffer social rejection. In a vicious cycle, rejection spurs feelings of alienation; alienation, in turn, engenders more bizarre behaviour. Patterns of bizarre behaviour may be maintained by the unintentional reinforcement they receive from some people in the form of attention and expressions of sympathy.

Support for this view is found in operant conditioning studies in which bizarre behaviour is shaped by reinforcement. Experiments involving people with schizophrenia show, for example, that reinforcement affects the frequency of bizarre versus normal verbalizations and that hospital patients can be shaped into performing odd behaviours. In a classic case example, Haughton and Ayllon (1965) conditioned a 54-year-old woman with chronic schizophrenia to cling to a broom. A staff member gave her the broom to hold, and when she did, another staff member gave her a cigarette. This pattern was repeated several times. Soon, the woman could not be parted from the broom. But the fact that reinforcement can influence people to engage in peculiar behaviour does not demonstrate that bizarre behaviours characterizing schizophrenia are learned behaviours determined by reinforcement.

There are other shortcomings to these behavioural explanations. For example, many of us grow up in harsh or punishing circumstances but do not retreat into private worlds of fantasy or display bizarre behaviour. Also, many people with schizophrenia grow up in homes that are supportive and socially reinforcing. Moreover, schizophrenic behaviours fall into patterns that are unlikely to occur by chance and then be reinforced to the point they become learned habits.

Social-cognitive theorists suggest that modelling of schizophrenic behaviour can occur within mental hospitals. In that setting, patients may begin to model themselves after fellow patients who act strangely. Hospital staff may inadvertently reinforce schizophrenic behaviour by paying more attention to those patients who exhibit more bizarre behaviour. This understanding is consistent with the observation that schoolchildren who disrupt class garner more attention from their teachers than do well-behaved children.

Perhaps some forms of schizophrenic behaviour can be explained by the principles of modelling and reinforcement. However, many people come to display schizophrenic behaviour patterns without prior exposure to other people with schizophrenia. In fact, the onset of schizophrenic behaviour patterns is more likely to lead to hospitalization than to result from it.

Biological Perspectives

Although we still have much to learn about the biological underpinnings of schizophrenia, most investigators today recognize that biological factors play a determining role.

GENETIC FACTORS We now have compelling evidence that schizophrenia is strongly influenced by genetic factors (DeLisi & Fleischhaker, 2007; Grant, Fathalli, Rouleau, Joober, & Flores, 2012; Pogue-Geile & Yokley, 2010). One source of evidence of genetic factors is based on familial studies. Schizophrenia, like many other disorders, tends to run in families. Overall, people with biological relatives with schizophrenia have about a tenfold greater risk of developing the disorder than do members of the general population (APA, 2000).

Further supporting a genetic linkage, evidence shows that the closer the genetic relationship between people diagnosed with schizophrenia and their family members, the greater the likelihood (or concordance rate) of schizophrenia in their relatives. Figure 10.1 shows the pooled results of European studies on family incidence of schizophrenia conducted from 1920 to 1987. However, the fact that families share common environments as well as common genes requires that we dig deeper to examine the genetic underpinnings of schizophrenia.

More support for a genetic contribution to schizophrenia is found in twin studies, which show the concordance rate for the disorder among identical or monozygotic (MZ) twins to be more than twice the rate found among fraternal or dizygotic (DZ) twins (Kendler & Prescott, 2006; Pogue-Geile & Yokley, 2010).

We should be careful, however, not to overinterpret the results of twin studies. MZ twins not only share 100% genetic similarity, they may also be treated more alike than

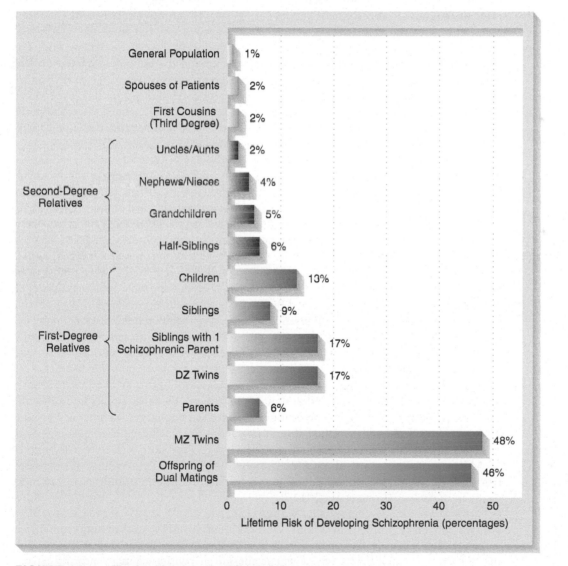

FIGURE 10.1 The familial risk of schizophrenia.
Generally speaking, the more closely one is related to people who have developed schizophrenia, the greater the risk of developing the disorder oneself. Monozygotic (MZ) twins, whose genetic heritages overlap fully, are much more likely than dizygotic (DZ) twins, whose genes overlap by 50%, to be concordant for schizophrenia.

Source: Based on Gottesman, I.I., McGuffin, P., & Farmer, A.E. (1987). Clinical genetics as clues to the "real" genetics of schizophrenia. *Schizophrenia Bulletin, 13,* 23–47.

DZ twins. Thus, environmental factors may play a role in explaining the higher concordance rates found among MZ twins. To help sort out environmental from genetic factors, investigators have turned to adoption studies in which high-risk (HR) children (children of one or more biological parents with schizophrenia) were adopted away shortly after birth and reared apart from their biological parents.

Adoption studies provide stronger evidence for a genetic contribution to schizophrenia (Wicks, Hjern, & Dalman, 2010). In perhaps the best-known example, researchers in Denmark examined official registers and found 39 HR adoptees who had been reared apart from their biological mothers who had schizophrenia (Rosenthal et al., 1968, 1975). Three of the 39 HR adoptees (8%) were diagnosed with schizophrenia, as compared to none of a reference group of 47 adoptees whose biological parents had no psychiatric history.

Other investigators have approached the question of heredity in schizophrenia from the opposite direction. Kety and colleagues (Kety, Rosenthal, Wender, & Schulsinger, 1968; Kety, Rosenthal, Wender, Schulsinger, & Jacobsen, 1975, 1978) used official records to find 33 index cases of children in Copenhagen, Denmark, who had been adopted early in life and were later diagnosed with schizophrenia. They compared the rates of diagnosed schizophrenia in the biological and adoptive relatives of the index cases with those of the relatives of a matched reference group that consisted of adoptees with no psychiatric history. The results strongly supported the genetic explanation. The incidence of diagnosed schizophrenia was greater among the biological relatives of the adoptees who had schizophrenia than among the biological relatives of the control adoptees. Adoptive relatives of both the index and control cases showed similar low rates of schizophrenia. Similar results were found in later research that extended the scope of the investigation to the rest of Denmark (Kety et al., 1994). It thus appears that family linkages in schizophrenia follow shared genes, not shared environments.

Still another approach, the **cross-fostering study**, has yielded additional evidence of genetic factors in schizophrenia. In this approach, investigators compare the incidence of schizophrenia among children whose biological parents either had or didn't have schizophrenia and who were reared by adoptive parents who either had or didn't have schizophrenia. Another Danish study, by Wender and colleagues (Wender, Rosenthal, Kety, Schulsinger, & Welner, 1974), found that the incidence of schizophrenia related to the presence of the disorder in the children's biological parents but not in their adoptive parents. High-risk children (children whose biological parents had schizophrenia) were almost twice as likely to develop schizophrenia as children of nonschizophrenic biological parents, regardless of whether they were reared by a parent with schizophrenia. It is also notable that adoptees whose biological parents did not suffer from schizophrenia were at no greater risk of developing the disorder if reared by an adoptive parent with schizophrenia than if reared by a nonschizophrenic parent. In sum, a genetic relationship with a person with schizophrenia seems to be the most prominent risk factor for developing the disorder.

Although it is recognized that genetic factors play an important role in schizophrenia, the mode of genetic transmission remains unknown. Evidence points to an interaction of multiple genes involved in determining risk for schizophrenia (Kendler & Prescott, 2006). Researchers have identified several chromosomes, including chromosomes 6, 8, 13, 15, and 22, that appear to contain genes linked to the disorder (Detera-Wadleigh & McMahon, 2006; Vazza et al., 2007). The offspring of older fathers have an increased risk of developing schizophrenia, presumably because the sperm of older men are more prone to mutations (Kong et al., 2012).

York University psychologist R. Walter Heinrichs (2001, 2005) argued that *schizophrenia* may be an umbrella term for several different disorders, each arising from different mechanisms manifesting themselves primarily in cognitive disturbances. It is possible that there are several different sets of genetic aberrations, with each independently causing schizophrenia. Preliminary findings support this idea. For example, Anne Bassett and her colleagues at the University of Toronto have found that one form of schizophrenia seems to be associated with abnormalities specifically on chromosome 22 (Bassett & Chow, 1999; Chow, Watson, Young, & Bassett, 2006). About 25% of people with this genetic abnormality develop a psychotic disorder such as schizophrenia. These people also tend to have unusual facial features (e.g., long, narrow face, prominent nose, small ears and

cross-fostering study Method of determining heritability of a trait or disorder by examining differences in prevalence among adoptees reared by either adoptive parents or biological parents who possessed the trait or disorder in question. Evidence that the disorder followed biological rather than adoptive parentage favours the heritability of the trait or disorder.

mouth) and congenital defects (e.g., heart defects). Genetics alone does not determine risk of schizophrenia. For one thing, people may carry a high genetic risk of schizophrenia and not develop the disorder. For another, the rate of concordance among MZ twins, as noted earlier, is well below 100%, even though identical twins carry identical genes. The prevailing view today, which we discuss later, is the diathesis-stress model, which holds that schizophrenia involves a complex interplay of genetic and environmental factors.

BIOCHEMICAL FACTORS Contemporary biological investigations of schizophrenia have focused on the role of the neurotransmitter dopamine. The **dopamine theory** posits that schizophrenia involves an overreactivity of dopamine receptors in the brain—the receptor sites on postsynaptic neurons into which molecules of dopamine lock (Abi-Dargham, 2004; Howes et al., 2012).

dopamine theory Biochemical theory of schizophrenia that proposes schizophrenia involves the action of dopamine.

People with schizophrenia do not appear to produce more dopamine. Instead, they appear to use more of it. But why? Research suggests that people with schizophrenia may have a greater than normal number of dopamine receptors in their brains or have receptors that are overly sensitive to dopamine (Grace, 2010; Seeman & Kapur, 2001).

The major source of evidence for the dopamine model is found in the effects of anti-psychotic drugs called *major tranquillizers* or *neuroleptics*. The most widely used neuroleptics belong to a class of drugs called *phenothiazines*, which includes such drugs as Largactil and Mellaril. Neuroleptic drugs block dopamine receptors, thereby reducing the level of dopamine activity (Kane, 1996). As a consequence, neuroleptics inhibit excessive transmission of neural impulses that may give rise to schizophrenic behaviour.

Another source of evidence supporting the role of dopamine in schizophrenia is based on the actions of amphetamines, a class of stimulant drugs. These drugs increase the concentration of dopamine in the synaptic cleft by blocking its reuptake by presynaptic neurons. When given in large doses to normal people, these drugs can lead to abnormal behaviour states that mimic paranoia in schizophrenia.

Overall, evidence points to irregularities in schizophrenia patients in the neural pathways in the brain that use dopamine (Meador-Woodruff et al., 1997; Seeman & Kapur, 2001). The specific nature of this abnormality remains under study. One possibility is that overreactivity of dopamine receptors may be involved in producing more flagrant behaviour patterns (positive symptoms) but not the negative symptoms or deficits associated with schizophrenia. Decreased rather than increased dopamine reactivity may be connected with some of the negative symptoms of schizophrenia (Earnst & Kring, 1997). We should also note that other neurotransmitters, such as norepinephrine, serotonin, and GABA, also appear to be involved in the disorder (Dobbs, 2010; Walker, Shapiro, Esterberg, & Trotman, 2010).

VIRAL INFECTIONS Might schizophrenia be caused by a slow-acting virus that attacks the developing brain of a fetus or newborn child? Prenatal rubella (German measles), a viral infection, is a cause of later intellectual disability. Could another virus give rise to schizophrenia?

Viral infections are more prevalent in the winter months. Viral infection during pregnancy or infancy could account for findings of an excess number of people with schizophrenia being born in the winter (King, St-Hilaire, & Heidkamp, 2010; Müller, 2004). However, we have yet to find an identified viral agent we can link to schizophrenia. Moreover, there is some evidence to suggest that many different sorts of infectious agents—not just viruses—are linked to schizophrenia, raising the possibility that some cases of schizophrenia are the result of a reaction by the immune system of a developing child (Müller, 2004). But such infections probably account for only a fraction of the number of cases of schizophrenia (Müller, 2004).

BRAIN ABNORMALITIES Despite the widely held belief that schizophrenia is a brain disease, researchers are still asking, "Where is the pathology?" They are trying to find an answer by using modern brain-imaging techniques, including PET scans, EEGs, CT scans, and MRIs, to probe the inner workings of the brains of people with schizophrenia. Evidence from these types of studies shows various abnormalities in the brains of people with schizophrenia.

The most prominent finding involves enlargements of brain ventricles (the hollow spaces in the brain) (Arango et al., 2012; Keshavan, Nasrallah, & Tandon, 2011). Ventricular enlargement is a sign of structural damage involving loss of brain cells. It is found in about three out of four schizophrenia patients (Coursey, Alford, & Safarjan, 1997). Still, not all people with schizophrenia show evidence of enlarged ventricles or other signs of brain damage. Research conducted at the University of Toronto and York University, for example, shows that only some people with schizophrenia seem to have abnormalities in the frontal or temporal lobes (Zakzanis, Poulin, Hansen, & Jolic, 2000). This leads researchers to suspect there may be several forms of schizophrenia that have different causal processes. Perhaps one form involves a degenerative loss of brain tissue (Kempton, Stahl, Williams, & DeLisi, 2010).

Structural damage to the brains of some schizophrenia patients may have occurred long before the initial onset of the disorder, most probably either prenatally or very early in life (King et al., 2010; Walker et al., 2010). One theory points to prenatal complications occurring during the period of 13 to 15 weeks in fetal development, when certain brain structures are forming (Davis & Bracha, 1996). Consistent with this possibility, a cross-national group of Canadian investigators have found that schizophrenia tends to be associated with poor fetal growth, premature birth, and low birth weight (Smith et al., 1999).

The source of brain damage in schizophrenia remains an open question. Among the suspected causes are prenatal infections, birth complications such as anoxia (oxygen deprivation), brain traumas suffered early in life or during prenatal development, environmental influences in childhood, or genetic defects leading to abnormal brain development (Van Os, Krabbendam, Myin-Germeys, & Delespaul, 2005).

Another line of research points to possible neurotransmitter disturbances. By tracking blood flow in the brain and using brain-imaging techniques such as PET scans, EEGs, and MRIs, researchers find evidence that some people with schizophrenia have reduced brain activity in the frontal lobes, specifically in the prefrontal cortex, the area of the frontal lobes in the cerebral cortex that lies in front of the motor cortex (Zakzanis & Heinrichs, 1999) (see Figure 10.2). The prefrontal cortex is involved in performing

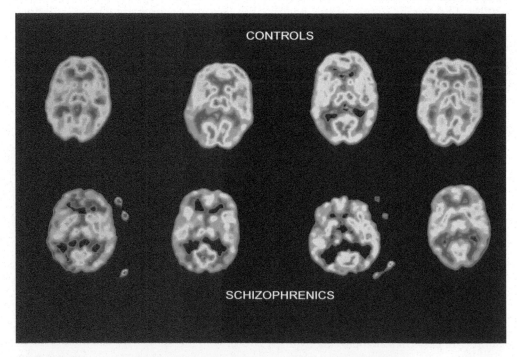

FIGURE 10.2 PET scans of people with and without schizophrenia.
Positron emission tomography (PET scan) evidence of the metabolic processes of the brain shows relatively less metabolic activity (indicated by less yellow and red) in the frontal lobes of the brains of people with schizophrenia. PET scans of the brains of four people without schizophrenia are shown in the top row, and PET scans of the brains of four people with schizophrenia are shown below.

Monte S. Buchsbaum, M.D., Mount Sinai School of Medicine, New York, NY.

various cognitive and emotional functions, the kinds of functions that are often impaired in people with schizophrenia. One function of the prefrontal cortex is to serve as a kind of mental clipboard for holding information needed to guide organized behaviour (Hahn et al., 2012). Abnormalities in the complex circuitry of the frontal lobes may explain why people with schizophrenia have difficulty organizing their thoughts and behaviour and performing higher-level cognitive tasks, such as formulating concepts, prioritizing information, and formulating goals and plans (Barch, 2005). Imbalances in neurotransmitter functioning in these neural pathways may be involved in explaining disturbed brain circuitry (Goldman-Rakic & Selemon, 1997). The prefrontal cortex is also involved in regulating attention, so findings of reduced activity coincide with research evidence of deficits in attention among people with schizophrenia. These are intriguing findings that may provide clues as to the biological bases of schizophrenia.

Other evidence points to defects in brain circuitry involving brain regions lying below the cortex, especially the **hippocampus** and **amygdala,** two structures in the limbic system (Boos, Aleman, Cahn, Hulshoff Pol, & Kahn, 2007). The limbic system plays a key role in regulating emotions and higher mental functions, including memory. These structures send projections to the prefrontal cortex, which interprets information received from lower brain centres. Imbalances in neurotransmitter function may also be involved in disrupting these brain circuits.

hippocampus One of a pair of structures in the limbic system involved in processes of memory.

amygdala One of a pair of structures in the limbic system involved in emotion and memory.

The Diathesis-Stress Model

In 1962, psychologist Paul Meehl proposed an integrative model that led to the development of the diathesis-stress model. Meehl suggested that certain people possess a genetic predisposition to schizophrenia that is expressed behaviourally only if they are reared in stressful environments (Meehl, 1962, 1972).

Later, Zubin and Spring (1977) formulated the diathesis-stress model, which views schizophrenia in terms of the interaction or combination of a diathesis in the form of a genetic predisposition to develop the disorder with environmental stress that exceeds the individual's stress threshold or coping resources. Environmental stressors may include psychological factors such as family conflict, child abuse, emotional deprivation, or loss of supportive figures, as well as physical environmental influences, such as early brain trauma or injury. On the other hand, if environmental stress remains below the person's stress threshold, schizophrenia may never develop—even in individuals at genetic risk (see Figure 10.3).

More recently, Western University psychologist Richard W. J. Neufeld developed a comprehensive dynamic vulnerability model, which posits that genetic factors and environmental stressors interact in complex, mutually reinforcing ways (Neufeld, Vollick,

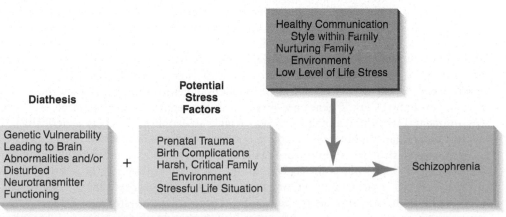

FIGURE 10.3   Diathesis-stress model of schizophrenia.

Source: Based on Diagnostic and Statistical Manual of Mental Disorders (DSM-5®), 2013, Published by American Psychiatric Association.

Carter, Boksman, & Jetté, 2002). According to this model, genetic vulnerability to schizophrenia influences the person's ability to cope and affects the way she or he appraises (interprets) stressful events. In turn, coping is said to influence the genetically mediated vulnerability to developing schizophrenia symptoms. To illustrate, a genetic predisposition leads to odd behaviour and thinking problems, which leads to environmental stress (e.g., school failure, rejection by peers). This then creates distress for the person, which impairs coping and worsens schizophrenic symptoms.

What is the biological basis for the diathesis? No one has yet been able to find any specific brain abnormality present in all individuals who receive a schizophrenia diagnosis (Jablensky, 2006). Perhaps it shouldn't surprise us that a "one-size-fits-all" model doesn't apply. Schizophrenia is a complex disorder characterized by complex symptoms. There may be different causal processes in the brain explaining different patterns of symptoms.

We noted two possible causal processes, with one involving structural damage to brain tissue and the other involving disturbed neurotransmitter functioning that disrupts complex brain circuits involved in thought, perception, emotions, and attention. The wealth of confusing thoughts and perceptions, social withdrawal, and bizarre behaviour that characterizes schizophrenia may be the result of this disturbed neurotransmitter functioning in brain circuits involving the prefrontal cortex and its connections to lower brain regions (Barch, 2005; Weinberger, 1997). These neural networks are involved in processing information efficiently and turning it into meaningful thoughts and behaviour. A defect in this circuitry may be involved in explaining the more flagrant, positive features of schizophrenia such as hallucinations, delusions, and thought disorder.

Another potential causal process involves structural damage to the brain, as evidenced by the presence of enlarged ventricles. Ventricular enlargement may play a greater role in explaining negative symptoms and chronic cognitive impairment than the more flagrant features of the disorder (Antonova, Sharma, Morris, & Kumari, 2004).

RESEARCH EVIDENCE SUPPORTING THE DIATHESIS-STRESS MODEL Several lines of evidence support the diathesis-stress model. Evidence suggests that stress predicts the initial onset of schizophrenia occurring in genetically vulnerable individuals (Van Os et al., 2005). Sources of stress may involve sociocultural factors associated with poverty, such as overcrowding, poor diet and sanitation, impoverished housing, and inadequate health care (Selten, Cantor-Graae, & Kahn, 2007). Research from several countries, including Canada, has shown that the incidence of schizophrenia is higher among immigrants than among those who are native-born. The high rate of schizophrenia among immigrants is thought to be a result of the stress that is often associated with immigration, such as discrimination, difficulty coping because of language problems, and feeling isolated within one's new community (Smith et al., 2006). Such stressors appear to trigger schizophrenia in genetically vulnerable individuals.

Research on gene–environment interactions provides further support for the diathesis-stress model. To illustrate, consider the research on cannabis use and schizophrenia (Caspi & Moffitt, 2006). Here, cannabis use can be considered an environmental stimulus. People who possess particular forms of the COMT gene are liable to develop psychotic symptoms (delusions and hallucinations) when they use cannabis, and sometimes these symptoms persist to the point that the person develops schizophrenia. In comparison, people with other forms of the COMT gene do not experience these reactions to cannabis. COMT genes are involved in the regulation of dopamine. Thus, an environmental stimulus (cannabis use) may trigger schizophrenia only in genetically vulnerable individuals. In other words, there is a gene–environment interaction.

Perhaps the strongest support for the diathesis-stress model comes from longitudinal studies of HR (high-risk) children who are at increased genetic risk of developing the disorder by virtue of having one or more parents with schizophrenia. Longitudinal studies of HR children support the central tenet of the diathesis-stress model that heredity interacts with environmental influences in determining vulnerability to schizophrenia. Longitudinal studies track individuals over extended periods of time. Ideally, they begin before the emergence of the disorder or behaviour pattern in question and follow its course. In this way, investigators can identify early characteristics that predict the later development of a particular disorder, such as schizophrenia. These studies require a commitment of many years and substantial cost. Because schizophrenia occurs in only about 1% of the general population, researchers have focused on HR children, who are more likely to develop the disorder. Children with one schizophrenic parent have about a 10–25% chance of developing schizophrenia, and those with two schizophrenic parents have about a 45% risk (Erlenmeyer-Kimling et al., 1997). Still, children who have two biological parents with schizophrenia stand a better than even chance of not developing the disorder themselves. Supporting the view that both genetics and environment play a part in schizophrenia, HR children who were adopted but raised in economically disadvantaged homes (single-parent homes or families with parental unemployment) were at a much greater risk than HR children raised in more comfortable circumstances (Wicks et al., 2010).

Finnish researchers followed 112 HR children, index cases who were adopted away at birth (Tienari et al., 1987, 1990; Tienari, Wahlberg, & Wynne, 2006). These index cases, who were compared with a reference group of 135 cases, matched adopted children of nonschizophrenic biological parents. Evidence showed a much higher rate of schizophrenia in the index cases than the control cases, 5% versus 1%, respectively (Tienari, 1991, 1992).

Consistent with the diathesis-stress model, environmental factors appear to have played a role in the Finnish study. Disturbed rearing in adoptive families predicted the development of schizophrenia (Tienari et al., 2006). Moreover, index children reared by disturbed adoptive families were more likely to have developed other serious psychological problems, such as borderline personality, than those reared by more functional families. Some of the disturbed families were rigid and tended to cope with family conflict by denying it. Others were chaotic; they showed low levels of trust and high levels of anxiety. The evidence from the Finnish study indicates that a combination of genetic factors and a disruptive family environment increases the risk of schizophrenia. A drawback of the Finnish study, however, was that it was not possible to determine whether disturbed family relationships represented the reaction of the families to the emergence of behavioural problems in their troubled offspring or, instead, were a contributing factor in their own right (Kendler & Prescott, 2006; Miklowitz, 2004).

Researchers have also compared HR children and other children to search for factors or markers that may predispose HR children to schizophrenia (e.g., Szymanski, Kane, & Lieberman, 1991). If we understand these early indicators, we may be able to understand the processes that lead to schizophrenia. We may also be able to identify children at greatest risk and devise intervention programs that might prevent the development of the disorder.

The best-known longitudinal study of HR children was undertaken by Sarnoff Mednick and his colleagues in Denmark. In 1962, the Mednick group identified 207 HR children (those whose mothers had schizophrenia) and 104 reference subjects who were matched for factors such as gender, social class, age, and education but whose mothers did not have schizophrenia (Mednick, Parnas, & Schulsinger, 1987). The children from both groups ranged in age from 10 to 20 years, with a mean of 15 years. None showed signs of disturbance when first interviewed.

Later, at an average age of 20, the children were re-examined. By then, 20 of the HR children were found to have demonstrated abnormal behaviour, although not necessarily a schizophrenic episode (Mednick & Schulsinger, 1968). The children who showed abnormal behaviour, referred to as the HR "sick" group, were then compared with a matched group of 20 HR children from the original sample who remained well functioning (an HR "well" group) and a matched group of 20 low-risk (LR) subjects. It turned out that the mothers of the HR "well" offspring had experienced easier pregnancies and deliveries than those of the HR "sick" group or the LR group. Seventy percent of the mothers of the HR "sick" children had serious complications during pregnancy or delivery. Consistent with the diathesis-stress model, perhaps complications during pregnancy or childbirth or shortly after birth cause brain damage (a stress factor) that in combination with a genetic vulnerability leads to severe psychological disorders in later life. A study in Finland provided a supportive link in showing an association between fetal and postnatal abnormalities and the development of

Stockbyte/Getty Images

Protective factors in high-risk children. A supportive and nurturing environment may reduce the likelihood of developing schizophrenia among high-risk children.

schizophrenia in adulthood (Jones, Rantakallio, Hartikainen, Isohanni, & Sipila, 1998). The low rate of complications during pregnancy and birth in the HR "well" group in the Danish study suggests that normal pregnancies and births may actually help protect HR children from developing abnormal behaviour patterns (Mednick et al., 1987).

Evaluation of these same HR subjects in the late 1980s, when they averaged 42 years of age and had passed through the period of greatest risk for development of schizophrenia, showed a significantly higher percentage of schizophrenia in the HR group than the LR comparison group—16% versus 2% respectively (Parnas et al., 1993). These results, like those of the Finnish study, show a strong familial association for schizophrenia between mothers and their children. An Israeli study paralleled the Danish and Finnish studies in finding a significantly greater risk of schizophrenia in a sample of HR children (8% with diagnosed schizophrenia) as compared to LR controls (0%) by the age of 30 (Ingraham, Kugelmass, Frenkel, Nathan, & Mirsky, 1995).

Evidence from longitudinal studies of HR children indicates that environmental factors, including quality of parenting and possible complications occurring prenatally or shortly after birth, may interact with genetic factors in the causal pathway leading to schizophrenia. Certain environmental factors, such as good parenting, may actually have a protective role in preventing the development of the disorder in people at increased genetic risk. In support of the role of early environmental influences, Mednick and his colleagues found that HR children who developed schizophrenia had poorer relationships with their parents than did HR children who did not go on to develop the disorder (Mednick et al., 1987). The presence of childhood behaviour problems may also be a marker for the later development of schizophrenia-related disorders in HR children (Amminger et al., 1999).

In the next section, we go on to consider the role of family factors in schizophrenia.

Family Theories

schizophrenogenic mother Type of mother, described as cold but also overprotective, who was believed to be capable of causing schizophrenia in her children. Research has failed to support the validity of this concept.

Disturbed family relationships have long been regarded as playing a role in the development and course of schizophrenia (Miklowitz, 2004). Early family theories of schizophrenia focused on the role of a "pathogenic" family member, such as the **schizophrenogenic mother** (Fromm-Reichmann, 1948, 1950). In what some feminists view as historical psychiatric sexism, the schizophrenogenic mother was described as cold, aloof, overprotective, and domineering. She was characterized as stripping her children of self-esteem, stifling their independence, and forcing them into dependency on her. Children reared by such mothers were believed to be at special risk for developing schizophrenia if their fathers were passive and failed to counteract the pathogenic influences of the mother. Despite extensive research, however, mothers of people who develop schizophrenia do not fit the stereotypical picture of the schizophrenogenic mother (Neill, 1990).

double-bind communications Pattern of communication involving the transmission of contradictory or mixed messages without acknowledgment of the inherent conflict; posited by some theorists to play a role in the development of schizophrenia.

In the 1950s, family theorists began to focus on the role of disturbed communications in the family. One of the more prominent theories, put forth by Gregory Bateson and his colleagues (Bateson, Jackson, Haley, & Weakland, 1956), was that **double-bind communications** contributed to the development of schizophrenia. A double-bind communication transmits two mutually incompatible messages. In a double-bind communication with a child, a mother might freeze up when the child approaches her and then scold the child for keeping a distance. Whatever the child does, she or he is wrong. With repeated exposure to such double binds, the child's thinking may become disorganized and chaotic. The double-binding mother prevents discussion of her inconsistencies because she cannot admit to herself that she is unable to tolerate closeness. Note this vignette:

Perhaps double-bind communications serve as a source of family stress that increases the risk of schizophrenia in genetically vulnerable individuals. In more recent years, investigators have broadened the investigation of family factors in schizophrenia by viewing the family in terms of a system of relationships among the members, rather than singling out mother–child or father–child interactions. Research has begun to identify stressful factors in the family that may interact with a genetic vulnerability in leading to the development of schizophrenia. Two principal sources of family stress that have been studied are patterns of deviant communications and negative emotional expression in the family.

COMMUNICATION DEVIANCE Communication deviance describes a pattern characterized by unclear, vague, disruptive, or fragmented parental communication and by parental inability to focus in on what the child is saying (Kymalainen, Weisman, Resales, & Armesto, 2006). Parents high in communication deviance tend to attack their children personally rather than offer constructive criticism and may subject them to double-bind communications. They also tend to interrupt the child with intrusive, negative comments. They are prone to telling the child what she or he "really" thinks rather than allowing the child to formulate her or his own thoughts and feelings. Parents of people with schizophrenia show higher levels of communication deviance than parents of people without schizophrenia (Kymalainen et al., 2006; Kymalainen & Weisman, 2008).

Communication deviance may be one of the stress-related factors that increase the risk of development of schizophrenia in genetically vulnerable individuals (Kymalainen et al., 2006). Then, too, the causal pathway may work in the opposite direction. Perhaps communication deviance is a parental reaction to the behaviour of disturbed children. Parents may learn to use odd language as a way of coping with children who continually interrupt and confront them (Miklowitz, 2004). Or perhaps parents and children share genetic traits that become expressed as disturbed communications and increased vulnerability toward schizophrenia, without there being a causal link between the two.

EXPRESSED EMOTION Another measure of disturbed family communications is called **expressed emotion** (EE). EE involves the tendency of family members to be hostile, critical, and unsupportive of their family member with schizophrenia. People with schizophrenia whose families are high in EE tend to show poorer adjustment and have higher rates of relapse following release from the hospital than those with more supportive families (Hooley, 2010; Kymalainen & Weisman, 2008; Miklowitz, 2004).

Low-EE families may actually serve to protect or buffer the family member with schizophrenia from the adverse impact of outside stressors and help prevent recurrent episodes (Cechnicki, Bielańska, Hanuszkiewicz, & Daren, 2013) (see Figure 10.4). Yet family interactions are a two-way street. Family members and patients influence each other and are influenced in turn. Disruptive behaviours by the schizophrenic family member frustrate other members of the family, prompting them to respond to the person in a less supportive and more critical and hostile way. This in turn can exacerbate the patient's disruptive behaviour (Miklowitz, 2004).

We need to take a close look at cultural differences in both the frequency of expressed emotion in family members of patients with schizophrenia and the effects these behaviours have on patients. Investigators find high-EE families to be more common in

expressed emotion A form of disturbed family communication in which the family members of the individual with schizophrenia have a tendency to be hostile, critical, and unsupportive.

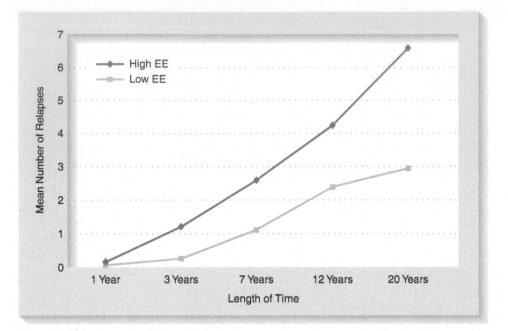

FIGURE 10.4 **Mean number of relapses of people with schizophrenia in high- and low-EE families.**
People with schizophrenia whose families are high in expressed emotion (EE) are at greater risk of relapse than those whose families are low in EE. Whereas low-EE families may help protect the family member with schizophrenia from environmental stressors, high-EE families may impose additional stress.

Source: Republished with permission of Elsevier Ltd., from The predictive validity of expressed emotions (EE) in schizophrenia, Andrzej Cechnicki, 47, 2013; permission conveyed through Copyright Clearance Center, Inc.

industrialized countries, such as the United States and Canada, than in developing countries, such as India (Barrowclough & Hooley, 2003). Cross-cultural evidence shows that Mexican American, Anglo American, and Chinese families with high levels of EE are more likely than low-EE families to view the psychotic behaviour of a family member with schizophrenia as within the person's control (Weisman, Nuechterlein, Goldstein, & Snider, 1998; Yang, Phillips, Licht, & Hooley, 2004). The anger and criticism of high-EE family members may stem from the perception that patients can and should exert greater control over their aberrant behaviour.

In a study of cultural differences in EE, investigators found that high levels of EE in family members were linked to more negative outcomes in patients with schizophrenia among Anglo American families but not among Mexican American families (López et al., 2004). Rather, for Mexican American families, the degree of family warmth, not EE per se, was related to a more positive course of schizophrenia in the affected family members, whereas for Anglo American patients, family warmth did not relate to such outcomes. In another study, investigators reported that among African American patients, high levels of EE were actually associated with better outcomes (Rosenfarb, Bellack, & Aziz, 2006). What might be the reason for this apparent contradiction? The study investigators suggested that for African Americans, intrusive critical comments during family interactions may be perceived as signs of caring and concern rather than rejection. Other investigators concur, finding relationships between how much relatives criticize patients and patients' perceptions of their relatives' criticism only among White European and Latino patients, but not among African American patients (Kymalainen & Weisman, 2008). These studies underscore the importance of looking at abnormal behaviour patterns through a cultural lens.

Families of people with schizophrenia tend to have little if any preparation or training for coping with the stressful demands of caring for them. Rather than focusing so much on the negative influence of high-EE family members, we should learn to better understand the negative day-to-day interactions between people with schizophrenia and their family members that lead to high levels of expressed emotion. Fortunately, families can be helped to reduce the level of expressed emotion (Miklowitz, 2004).

Research on expressed emotion and family stress factors helps focus attention on the need for family-intervention programs that help prepare families for the burdens of caregiving and assist them in learning more adaptive ways of relating to one another. This, in turn, may reduce the stress imposed on the family member with schizophrenia and improve family harmony.

FAMILY FACTORS IN SCHIZOPHRENIA: CAUSES OR SOURCES OF STRESS?   No evidence supports the belief that family factors, such as negative family interactions, lead to schizophrenia in children who do not have a genetic vulnerability. What, then, is the role of family factors in schizophrenia? In the diathesis-stress model, disturbed patterns of emotional interaction and communication in the family represent a source of potential stress that may increase the risks of developing schizophrenia among people with a genetic predisposition for the disorder. Perhaps these increased risks can be minimized or eliminated if families are taught to handle stress and to be less critical and more supportive of the members of their families with schizophrenia. Counselling programs that help family members of people with chronic schizophrenia learn to express their feelings without attacking or criticizing the person with the disorder may prevent family conflicts that damage the person's adjustment (Miklowitz, 2004). The family member with schizophrenia may also benefit from efforts to reduce the level of contact with relatives who fail to respond to family interventions.

REVIEW IT

Theoretical Perspectives

- **How is schizophrenia conceptualized in traditional psychodynamic theory and learning perspectives?** In the traditional psychodynamic model, schizophrenia represents a regression to a psychological state corresponding to early infancy in which the proddings of the id produce bizarre, socially deviant behaviour and give rise to hallucinations and delusions. Learning theorists propose that some forms of schizophrenic behaviour may result from a lack of social reinforcement, which leads to gradual detachment from the social environment and increased attention to an inner world of fantasy. Modelling and selective reinforcement of bizarre behaviour may explain some schizophrenic behaviours in a hospital setting.

- **What do we know about the biological bases of schizophrenia?** Compelling evidence for a strong genetic component in schizophrenia comes from studies of family patterns of schizophrenia, twin studies, and adoption studies. The mode of genetic transmission remains

unknown. Most researchers believe the neurotransmitter dopamine plays a role in schizophrenia, especially in the more flagrant features of the disorder. Viral factors may also be involved, but definite proof of viral involvement is lacking. Evidence of brain dysfunctions and structural damage in schizophrenia is accumulating, but researchers are uncertain about causal pathways.

- **How is schizophrenia conceptualized in the diathesis-stress model?** The diathesis-stress model posits that schizophrenia results from an interaction of a genetic predisposition (the diathesis) and environmental stressors (e.g., family conflict, child abuse, emotional deprivation, loss of supportive figures, and early brain trauma).

- **How are family factors related to the development and course of schizophrenia?** Family factors such as communication deviance and expressed emotion (EE) may act as sources of stress that increase the risk of development or recurrence of schizophrenia among people with a genetic predisposition.

TREATMENT

There is no cure for schizophrenia. Treatment of schizophrenia is generally multifaceted, incorporating pharmacological, psychological, and rehabilitative approaches. Most people treated for schizophrenia in organized mental health settings receive some form of antipsychotic medication, which is intended to control more flagrant behaviour patterns such as hallucinations and delusions and decrease the risk of recurrent episodes.

Biological Approaches

The advent in the 1950s of antipsychotic drugs—also referred to as *major tranquillizers* or *neuroleptics*—revolutionized the treatment of schizophrenia and provided the impetus for large-scale releases of mental patients into the community (deinstitutionalization). The first of these drugs, chlorpromazine (Largactil), was introduced to North America by McGill University psychiatrist Heinz Lehmann (Lehmann & Hanrahan, 1954). Antipsychotic medication helped control the more flagrant behaviour patterns of schizophrenia and reduced the need for long-term hospitalization when taken on a maintenance basis (Sheitman, Kinon, Ridgway, & Lieberman, 1998). Yet for many chronic patients with schizophrenia today, entering a hospital is like going through a revolving door. That is, they are repeatedly admitted and discharged within a relatively brief time frame. Many are simply discharged to the streets once they are stabilized on medication and receive little if any follow-up care or available housing. This often leads to a pattern of chronic homelessness punctuated by brief stays in the hospital. Only a small proportion of people with schizophrenia who are discharged from long-term care facilities are successfully reintegrated into the community (Bellack & Mueser, 1990).

Commonly used antipsychotic drugs include the phenothiazines chlorpromazine (Largactil), thioridazine (Mellaril), trifluoperazine (Stelazine), and fluphenazine (Moditen), as well as haloperidol (Haldol), which is chemically distinct from the phenothiazines but produces similar effects.

Although we can't say with certainty how these drugs work, it appears they derive their therapeutic effect from blocking dopamine receptors in the brain. This reduces dopamine activity, which seems to quell the more flagrant signs of schizophrenia, such as hallucinations and delusions. The effectiveness of antipsychotic drugs has been repeatedly demonstrated in double-blind, placebo-controlled studies (Kane, 1996). Yet a substantial minority of people with schizophrenia receive little benefit from traditional neuroleptics, and no clear-cut factors determine who will best respond (Kane & Marder, 1993).

tardive dyskinesia Movement disorder characterized by involuntary movements of the face, mouth, neck, trunk, or extremities caused by long-term use of antipsychotic medications. Abbreviated *TD*.

The major risk of long-term treatment with neuroleptic drugs (possibly excluding clozapine and other new-generation drugs) is a potentially disabling side effect called **tardive dyskinesia** (TD). TD is an involuntary movement disorder that can affect any body part (Hansen, Casey, & Hoffman, 1997). It is irreversible in many cases, even when the neuroleptic medication is withdrawn. It occurs most often in patients who are treated with neuroleptics for six months or longer. TD can take different forms, the most common of which is frequent eye blinking. Common signs of the disorder include involuntary chewing and eye movements, lip smacking and puckering, facial grimacing, and involuntary movements of the limbs and trunk. In some cases, the movement disorder is so severe that patients have difficulties breathing, talking, or eating. Overall, about one in four people receiving long-term treatment with neuroleptics eventually develop TD (Sarró et al., 2013).

Tardive dyskinesia is more common among older people and women (Hansen et al., 1997). Unfortunately, we lack a safe and effective treatment for TD (Sheitman et al., 1998). Although TD tends to improve gradually or stabilize over a period of years, many people with TD remain persistently and severely disabled.

The risk of these potentially disabling side effects requires physicians to carefully weigh the risks and benefits of long-term treatment with these drugs. Investigators have altered drug regimens in an attempt to reduce the risk of TD, such as by stopping medication in stable outpatients and starting it again when early symptoms reappear. However, intermittent medication schedules are associated with a twofold increase in the risk of relapse and have not been shown to lower the risk of TD (Kane, 1996).

A second generation of drugs, called *atypical antipsychotic drugs* (clozapine, risperidone, and olanzapine are examples), have largely replaced the earlier generation of antipsychotics. Atypical antipsychotics are at least as effective as the first-generation antipsychotics but have the advantage of fewer neurological side effects and a lower risk of TD (Crespo-Facorro et al., 2011). Atypical antipsychotics also carry risks of significant side effects, including such serious medical complications as sudden cardiac death, substantial weight gain, and metabolic disorders associated with increased risks of death due to heart disease and stroke (Stroup et al., 2011). In addition, the atypical antipsychotic drug clozapine carries a risk of a potentially lethal disorder in which the body produces inadequate supplies of white blood cells. Because of the seriousness of this risk, patients receiving the drug need to have their blood checked regularly. Research has shown olanzapine to be helpful, but most people with schizophrenia show only a partial response to this drug (Stauffer et al., 2011). In sum, doctors face a difficult choice, having to balance the benefits of treatment with the attendant risks.

A panel of Canadian experts on schizophrenia (psychologists and psychiatrists) published a set of clinical practice guidelines on the treatment of the disorder (Working Group for the Canadian Psychiatric Association and Canadian Alliance for Research on Schizophrenia, 1998). The guidelines, based on the current state of knowledge, are similar to those of other countries. According to the guidelines, antipsychotic medications are the most effective treatment available, especially when combined with psychoeducational interventions. Antipsychotic drugs help control the more flagrant or bizarre features of schizophrenia, but they are not a cure. Updates to the original guidelines reemphasize the use of antipsychotics as an essential part of the treatment plan and emphasize that the medication must be individualized due to the wide range of responses ("Clinical Practice Guidelines," 2005).

People with chronic schizophrenia typically receive maintenance doses of antipsychotic drugs once their flagrant symptoms abate. The working group notes that the relapse rate may be as high as 90% in the first year after hospital discharge if the patient discontinues medication. Staying on medication can reduce the relapse rate to about 40% (see Figure 10.5) (Haro, Novick, Suarez, Ochoa, & Roca, 2008; Hogarty, 1993). Still, not all people with schizophrenia require antipsychotic medication to maintain themselves in the community. Unfortunately, no one can yet predict which patients can manage effectively without continued medication.

Drug therapy needs to be supplemented with psychoeducational programs that help schizophrenia patients develop better social skills and adjust to the demands of community living. A wide array of treatment components are needed within a comprehensive model of care, including such elements as antipsychotic medication, medical care, family therapy, social-skills training, crisis intervention, rehabilitation services, and housing and other social services (Hooker et al., 2012; LeVine, 2012). Programs also need to ensure a continuity of care between the hospital and the community.

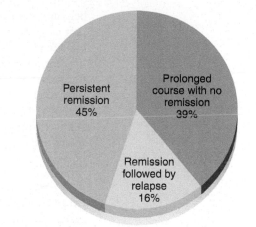

FIGURE 10.5 Course of illness in 5950 patients with schizophrenia treated with antipsychotic medication.
This figure shows the outcome of a three-year follow-up study of 5950 patients with schizophrenia who were being treated with antipsychotic medication in an outpatient setting.

Source: Based on Haro, J.M., Novick, D., Suarez, D., Ochoa, S., Roca, M. (2008). Predictors of the course of illness in outpatients with schizophrenia: A prospective three year study. Progress in Neuro-Psychopharmocology and Biological Psychiatry. 32, 1287–1292.

Psychoanalytic Approaches

Freud did not believe traditional psychoanalysis to be well suited to the treatment of schizophrenia. The withdrawal into a fantasy world that typifies schizophrenia prevents the individual with schizophrenia from forming a meaningful relationship with the psychoanalyst. The techniques of classical psychoanalysis, Freud wrote, must "be replaced by others; and we do not know yet whether we shall succeed in finding a substitute" (Arieti, 1974, p. 532).

Other psychoanalysts, such as Harry Stack Sullivan and Frieda Fromm-Reichmann, adapted psychoanalytic techniques specifically for the treatment of schizophrenia. However, research has failed to demonstrate the effectiveness of psychoanalytic or psychodynamic therapy for schizophrenia. In light of negative findings, some critics have argued that further research on the use of psychodynamic therapies for treating schizophrenia is not warranted (e.g., Klerman, 1984).

Learning-Based Approaches

Although few behaviour therapists believe that faulty learning causes schizophrenia, learning-based interventions have been shown to be effective in modifying schizophrenic behaviour and assisting people with the disorder in developing more adaptive behaviours that can help them adjust more effectively to living in the community. Therapy methods include techniques such as (1) selective reinforcement of behaviour (e.g., providing attention for appropriate behaviour while extinguishing bizarre verbalizations through withdrawal of attention); (2) the token economy, in which individuals on inpatient units are rewarded for appropriate behaviour with tokens, such as plastic chips, that can be exchanged for tangible reinforcers such as desirable goods or privileges; and (3) social-skills training, in which clients are taught conversational skills and other appropriate social behaviours through coaching, modelling, behaviour rehearsal, and feedback.

TOKEN ECONOMY SYSTEMS Promising results emerged from early studies applying intensive learning-based approaches in hospital settings. A classic study by Paul and Lentz (1977) showed that a psychosocial treatment program based on a token economy system improved adaptive behaviour in the hospital, decreased need for medication, and lengthened community tenure following release in relation to a traditional, custodial-type treatment condition with a milieu approach that emphasized patient participation in decision making.

Overall, token economies have proven to be more effective than intensive milieu treatment and traditional custodial treatment in improving social functioning and reducing psychotic behaviour (Mueser & Liberman, 1995). However, the many prerequisites may limit the applicability of this approach. Such programs require strong administrative support, skilled treatment leaders, extensive staff training, and continuous quality control. As a result, they have largely fallen out of favour in psychiatric hospitals in recent years (Dickerson, Tenhula, & Green-Paden, 2005).

SOCIAL-SKILLS TRAINING Social-skills training (SST) involves programs that help individuals acquire a range of social and vocational skills. People with schizophrenia are often deficient in basic social skills, including skills involving assertiveness, interview skills, and general conversational skills—skills that may be needed to adjust successfully to community living. Controlled studies have shown that SST can improve a wide range of social skills, increase social adjustment, reduce psychiatric symptoms in people with schizophrenia, and improve community functioning (Hooley, 2010). Social-skills training has also been shown to reduce relapse rates during the first year following treatment (Hooley, 2010).

Although different approaches to skills training have been developed, the basic model uses role-playing exercises in a group format. Participants practise skills such as starting or maintaining conversations with new acquaintances and receive feedback and reinforcement from the therapist and other group members. The first step might be a dry run in which the participant role plays the targeted behaviour, such as asking strangers for bus directions. The therapist and other group members then praise the effort and provide constructive feedback. Role playing is augmented by techniques such as modelling (observation of the therapist or other group members enacting the desired behaviour), direct instruction (specific directions for enacting the desired behaviour), shaping (reinforcement for successive approximations to the target behaviour), and coaching (therapist's use of verbal or nonverbal prompts to elicit a particular desired behaviour in the role play). Participants are given homework assignments to practise the behaviours in the settings in which they live, such as on the hospital ward or in the community. The aim is to enhance generalization or transfer of training to other settings. Training sessions may also be run in stores, restaurants, schools, and other real-life settings.

COGNITIVE-BEHAVIOURAL THERAPY WITH SOCIAL-SKILLS TRAINING Multifaceted cognitive-behavioural interventions, which can include social-skills training and other techniques, appear to be helpful (Addington, Piskulic, & Marshall, 2010; Rector & Beck, 2012). Cognitive-behavioural interventions can include teaching patients skills for managing the stress in their lives and showing them ways of managing their symptoms. For example, they can include helping patients identify triggers that make their symptoms worse (e.g., anxiety, family conflicts) and teaching them skills for dealing with the triggers (e.g., relaxation training, cognitive restructuring, skills training for conflict negotiating). Recently, cognitive-behavioural interventions have been targeted to reduce particular symptoms, such as hallucinations, along with improving social functioning. Cognitive-behavioural therapy combined with social-skills training has shown significant long-term improvements on psychotic effects and social functioning. Researchers at the University of Calgary reviewed various psychosocial treatments that have been used with patients with schizophrenia, including cognitive-behavioural therapy, social-skills training, family interventions, and supported employment. Beneficial results were found among all of them that extended beyond the use of pharmacology. Individuals partaking in these programs had improvements in social functioning and coping skills and reduced levels of relapse (Addington et al., 2010).

In a naturalistic study (Wiersma, Jenner, van de Willige, Spakman, & Nienhuis, 2001), patients were assessed at two and four years post-treatment. The combined treatments improved the overall burden of "hearing voices"; 60% of the individuals showed improvement with regard to fear, loss of control, disturbance of thought, and interference with thinking. Complete disappearance of hallucinations occurred in 18% of the patients. It appears that cognitive-behavioural therapy with coping training can improve both overall symptomatology and quality of life, even over longer periods of time.

Psychosocial Rehabilitation

People with schizophrenia typically have difficulties functioning in social and occupational roles. These problems limit their ability to adjust to community life even in the absence of overt psychotic behaviour. Many older, long-hospitalized individuals who have been resettled in the community are particularly ill prepared to handle the tasks of daily living, such as cooking, shopping, or travelling around town. Many younger individuals with schizophrenia have markedly deficient social skills. As a result, a number of self-help groups and more structured psychosocial rehabilitation centres have sprung up to help people with schizophrenia find a place in society. Many centres were launched by nonprofessionals or by people with schizophrenia themselves, largely because mental health agencies often failed to provide comparable services. This, combined with family-intervention programs and community programs, can reduce the risk of relapse (Rathod & Turkington, 2005).

Community programs typically offer services such as housing and job and educational opportunities. These programs often make use of skills-training approaches to help clients learn how to handle money, resolve disputes with family members, develop friendships, take buses, cook their own meals, shop, and so on.

The rehabilitation model teaches that people with emotional or physical disabilities can achieve their potentials if they are given the support and structure they need and if the expectations and demands placed on them are consistent with their capabilities. Both the client and the family should be helped to adjust their expectations to attainable levels (Addington et al., 2010).

Family-Intervention Programs

Family conflicts and negative family interactions can heap stress on family members with schizophrenia, increasing the risk of recurrent episodes (Addington et al., 2010; Guo et al., 2010). Researchers and clinicians have worked with families of people with schizophrenia to help them cope with the burdens of care and assist them in developing more cooperative, less confrontational ways of relating to others. The specific components involved in family interventions vary from program to program, but they tend to share certain common features, such as a focus on the practical aspects of everyday living, educating family members about schizophrenia, teaching them how to relate in a less hostile way to family members with schizophrenia, improving communication in the family, and fostering effective problem-solving and coping skills for handling family problems and disputes.

Structured family-intervention programs have been shown to reduce rates of relapse among schizophrenia patients (Addington et al., 2010; Guo et al., 2010). However, the benefits appear to be modest, and questions remain about whether recurrences are prevented or merely delayed. We should also note that not all people with schizophrenia live with their families. Perhaps similar psychoeducational programs can be applied to non-family environments in which people live with schizophrenia, such as foster-care homes or board-and-care homes.

In sum, no single treatment approach meets all the needs of people with schizophrenia. The conceptualization of schizophrenia as a lifelong disability underscores the need for long-term treatment interventions involving antipsychotic medication, family interventions, psychological interventions, vocational training, and social-system support such as provision of decent housing. These interventions should be coordinated and integrated within a comprehensive model of treatment to be most effective in helping the individual achieve maximal social adjustment (Addington et al., 2010).

Early-Intervention Programs

The treatment approaches described so far in this chapter were all intended for people with full-blown schizophrenia. More recently, there have been important developments in treating symptoms before they become severe. Such programs are important because the earlier a person receives treatment, the better the outcome in terms of reducing symptoms and improving daily functioning (Killackey & Yung, 2007; Norman et al., 2011). There are two main forms of early intervention. The first is to initiate treatment as early as possible once the person has developed schizophrenia, using the treatments described

A CLOSER LOOK

Psychosis Sucks! Early Psychosis Intervention Programs

Have you experienced unusual sensitivity to noise, light, and colour? Appetite changes, loss of energy, and withdrawal from friends? Do you hear voices that no one else hears? Do your thoughts seem to be sped up or slowed down? Do you feel just generally confused? Do you have periods of feeling spacey or disoriented, difficulty concentrating or remembering things? Are you suspicious of others? If you were experiencing any of these things, would you seek help? Often friends and family members are the first to notice these changes. And some might say these signs are just typical teenage experiences, when in fact these are potentially early signs of psychosis.

You can understand why, out of fear, a young person might not seek help, but early intervention makes a difference.

While the whole field of early intervention for psychosis is still growing, there is good research that shows intervention can help prevent the full development of acute psychosis (Norman et al., 2011; Perkins, Gu, Boteva, & Lieberman, 2005). In addition, it seems that the duration of time before intervention influences how well the person responds to medication and other forms of treatment. It's important to treat these early symptoms—within the first three to five years—with medication, psychosocial interventions, stress management, and family support (Norman et al., 2011). According to the Canadian Mental Health Association (2000), "in most cases, psychosis will not go away on its own. Early detection and appropriate treatment offer the best chance for full recovery and reduction in relapse rates" (Bertelsen et al., 2008).

WHY GET HELP EARLY?

According to the Canadian Mental Health Association, the benefits of early intervention can include

- reduced disruption of activities
- reduced disruption of family and social relationships
- reduced likelihood of hospitalization
- reduced disability and fewer relapses
- reduced risk of suicide
- improved capacity to maintain self-identity and self-esteem
- faster and more complete recovery

At this point Canada has well-established early psychosis intervention clinics. However, many communities still lack ready access to comprehensive services, so the type of treatment really does depend on where your family lives.

RESOURCE WORTH NOTING

PEPP: Prevention and Early Intervention Program for Psychoses
www.lhsc.on.ca/About_Us/PEPP
Support for friends and family members of those suffering with psychosis.

above. The second is to intervene before the onset of schizophrenia (i.e., prevention programs). This involves accurately identifying people at high risk for schizophrenia, as suggested by (1) a high-risk age (late teens or early 20s), (2) recent deterioration in social functioning, and (3) a family history of psychosis. Such high-risk people are then offered treatment—typically cognitive-behavioural therapy or antipsychotic medication (Killackey & Yung, 2007).

Research suggests that treating the symptoms as early as possible is important in improving outcomes (Malla, Norman, & Joober, 2005). However, further studies are needed to fully evaluate the benefits of treatments aimed at preventing schizophrenia (Killackey & Yung, 2007; Malla et al., 2005; Norman et al., 2011).

REVIEW IT

Treatment Approaches

- **How does the treatment of schizophrenia involve a multifaceted approach?** Contemporary treatment approaches tend to be multifaceted, incorporating pharmacological and psychosocial approaches. Antipsychotic medication is not a cure, but it tends to stem the more flagrant aspects of the disorder and to reduce the need for hospitalization and the risk of recurrent episodes.
- **What types of psychosocial interventions have shown promising results?** These are principally learning-based approaches, such as token economy systems and social-skills training. They help increase the adaptive behaviour of patients with schizophrenia. Psychosocial rehabilitation approaches help people with schizophrenia adapt more successfully to occupational and social roles in the community. Family-intervention programs help families cope with the burdens of care, communicate more clearly, and learn helpful ways of relating to the patient.

Define It

acute phase, 362
affect, 360
amygdala, 375
blocking, 364
blunted affect, 367
catatonia, 366
clanging, 364
cross-fostering study, 372
dopamine theory, 373
double-bind communications, 378

expressed emotion, 379
first-rank symptoms, 360
flat affect, 367
four A's, 359
hippocampus, 375
looseness of associations, 360
negative symptoms, 366
neologisms, 364
perseveration, 364
positive symptoms, 366

prodromal phase, 362
residual phase, 362
schizophrenia, 359
schizophrenogenic mother, 378
second-rank symptoms, 360
stupor, 366
tardive dyskinesia, 382
thought disorder, 363
waxy flexibility, 366

Recall It

1. To receive a diagnosis of schizophrenia, signs of the disorder must be present for a period of at least _____.
   a. two weeks
   b. one month
   c. six months
   d. one year

2. People with schizophrenia who adopt a fixed posture, into which they have been positioned by others, are said to demonstrate _____.

   a. perseveration
   b. waxy flexibility
   c. loosening of associations
   d. autistic paralysis

3. A family factor linked to an increased risk of relapse in people with schizophrenia is _____.
   a. communication deviance
   b. family size
   c. sibling rivalry
   d. expressed emotion

4. The most common treatment for people with schizophrenia involves _____.
   a. electroconvulsive therapy
   b. antipsychotic medication
   c. psychosurgery
   d. insight-oriented therapy

5. The neurological disorder caused by exposure to antipsychotic drugs and characterized by involuntary movements such as eye blinking, lip smacking, and facial grimacing is called _____.
   a. tardive dyskinesia
   b. Wernicke's syndrome
   c. institutionalization syndrome
   d. Huntington's chorea

Answers to Recall It

1. c,   2. b,   3. d,   4. b,   5. a

Think About It

- The authors state that schizophrenia is perhaps the most disabling type of mental or psychological disorder. What makes it so?
- What are the relative risks and benefits of antipsychotic medication? Do you believe that people with schizophrenia should be treated indefinitely with these drugs? Why or why not?
- What might you say to critics who claim that schizophrenia is not a disease because no one has yet found any specific disease process in the brain that accounts for it?

Weblinks

Schizophrenia Society of Canada
www.schizophrenia.ca
This site offers information in English and French about the causes and treatments of schizophrenia. It contains a number of useful links.

Schizophrenia
www.nimh.nih.gov/health/topics/schizophrenia/index.shtml
The National Institute of Mental Health's schizophrenia page provides useful information on the disorder.

Schizophrenia.com
www.schizophrenia.com
Another informationally rich website containing many links and discussion forums concerning schizophrenia.

Schizoaffective Disorder
www.nami.org/Learn-More/Mental-Health-Conditions/Schizoaffective-Disorder
This webpage provides information on schizoaffective disorder.

Schizophrenia Spectrum and Other Psychotic Disorders

Test your understanding of the key concepts by filling in the blanks with the correct statements chosen from the list that follows. The answers are found at the end of the chapter.

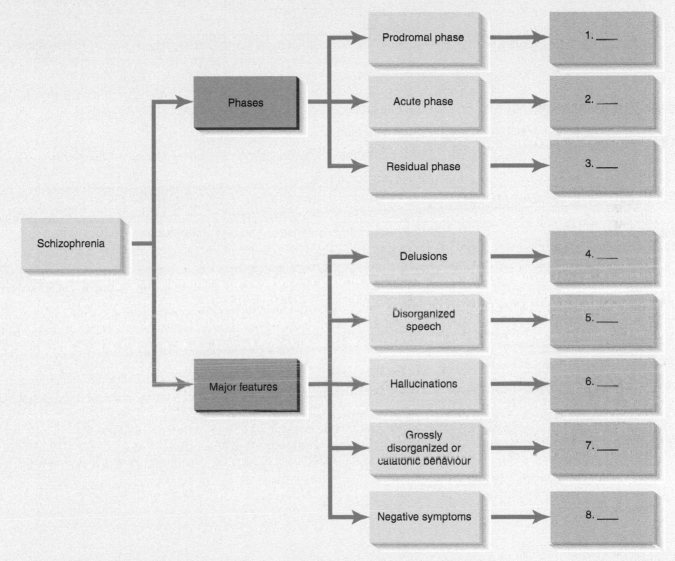

a. Examples include neologisms, perseveration, clanging, and blocking

b. Deficits or behavioural deficiencies, such as social-skills deficits, social withdrawal, flattened affect, poverty of speech and thought, psychomotor retardation, and failure to experience pleasure in pleasant activities

c. In schizophrenia, the phase in which psychotic symptoms develop, such as hallucinations, delusions, and disorganized speech and behaviour

d. Examples include stupor, unpredictable agitation, inappropriate affect, and waxy flexibility

e. In schizophrenia, the phase of the disorder that follows an acute phase, characterized by a return to a level of functioning typical of the prodromal phase

f. Firmly held but inaccurate beliefs that persist despite evidence they have no basis in reality

g. The period of decline in functioning that precedes the development of the first acute psychotic episode

h. Perceptions that occur in the absence of external stimulus that are confused with reality

Causes and Treatments According to Various Theoretical Perspectives

THEORETICAL PERSPECTIVES	CAUSES	TREATMENT
PSYCHODYNAMIC PERSPECTIVES	The overwhelming of the ego by the id, producing intrapsychic conflict and regression to an early period called primary narcissism	
LEARNING PERSPECTIVES	Operant conditioning: Bizarre behaviour is shaped by reinforcement	Assisting the individual to develop more adaptive behaviours: token economies, cognitive-behavioural interventions, and social-skills training
BIOLOGICAL PERSPECTIVES	Genetic factors Dopamine theory Viral infections Brain abnormalities	Antipsychotic medication
THE DIATHESIS-STRESS MODEL	The interaction of genetic and environmental influences	
FAMILY THEORIES	Communication deviance Expressed emotion	Family-intervention programs

Answers: 1. g, 2. c, 3. e, 4. f, 5. a, 6. h, 7. d, 8. b

11

Abnormal Behaviour across the Lifespan

CHAPTER OUTLINE

Neurodevelopmental Disorders

Autism Spectrum Disorder

Intellectual Disability (Intellectual Developmental Disorder)

Specific Learning Disorder

Attention-Deficit/Hyperactivity Disorder

Disruptive, Impulse-Control, and Conduct Disorders

Conduct Disorder

Oppositional Defiant Disorder

Anxiety and Depression in Childhood and Adolescence

Separation Anxiety Disorder

Perspectives on Anxiety Disorders in Childhood

Depression in Childhood and Adolescence

Suicide among Children and Adolescence

Neurocognitive Disorders

Delirium

Major Neurocognitive Disorder (Dementia)

Did You Know That...

- Many behaviour patterns considered normal for children would be considered abnormal in adults?
- Maternal smoking during pregnancy may contribute to the development of attention-deficit/hyperactivity disorder (ADHD) in children?
- Some people can recall verbatim every story they read in a newspaper?
- Most children with ADHD are given stimulants to help calm them down?
- Major depression can occur in young children?
- In the elderly, delirium-like symptoms can sometimes occur as early signs of infection or heart problems, making accurate delirium diagnosis problematic?

Nacivet/Photographer's Choice/Getty Images

P sychological problems in childhood and adolescence often have a special poignancy. They affect children at ages when they have little capacity to cope. The same could be said for some diseases that are more likely to occur later in life. Contrary to images and messages we get from our current culture that aging is equated with disease and decline, most older people are physically and mentally healthy, living happy and productive lives. In fact, psychological disorders in general are lower among older people than younger people. Here we'll focus on the 10–20% of people over the age of 65 who have psychological problems that could be severe enough to warrant diagnosis and treatment, such as delirium and major neurocognitive disorders (dementia). We'll come to these at the end of this chapter.

Some psychological problems in childhood and adolescence mirror the types of problems found in adults—problems such as depressive and anxiety disorders. In some cases, such as separation anxiety, the problems are unique to childhood; in others, such as attention-deficit/hyperactivity disorder (ADHD), the problems manifest differently in childhood than in adulthood.

To determine what is normal and abnormal among children and adolescents, not only do we consider the criteria outlined in earlier chapters, we also weigh what is to be expected given a child's age, gender, and family and cultural background, as well as the sundry developmental transformations that are taking place. Many problems are first identified when a child enters school. They may have existed earlier but were tolerated or unrecognized as problematic in the home. Sometimes the stress of starting school contributes to their onset. Keep in mind, however, that what is socially acceptable at one age, such as intense fear of strangers at about nine months, may be socially unacceptable at more advanced ages. Many behaviour patterns that would be considered abnormal among adults—such as intense fear of strangers and lack of bladder control—are perfectly normal for children at certain ages.

Just how common are mental health problems among Canada's children and adolescents? According to the Canadian Institute for Health Information (CIHI), 10–20% of Canadian children will develop a mental disorder (CIHI, 2015). The four most common categories—anxiety disorders, conduct disorders, ADHD, and depressive disorders—account for nearly 90% of those mental disorders (Public Health Agency of Canada, 2009; Waddell, McEwan, Shepherd, Offord, & Hua, 2005; Waddell & Shepherd, 2002). Findings from the Ontario Student Drug Use and Health Survey revealed that 34% of high school students reported moderate to serious levels of anxiety and depressive symptoms, and 12% admitted to having serious suicidal thoughts in the past year (Boak, Hamilton, Adlaf, Henderson, & Mann, 2016).

The number of Canadian children and youth who received inpatient treatment for a mental disorder increased by 37% from 2006–2007 to 2013–2014 (CIHI, 2015). This increase likely reflects a shortage of community services. Despite the prevalence of psychological disorders among the young, fewer than a quarter of children and youth with mental disorders receive specialized clinical services (CIHI, 2015; PHAC, 2009). Children who have internalized problems, such as anxiety and depression, are at higher risk of going untreated than are children with externalized problems (problems involving acting out or aggressive behaviour), which tend to be disruptive or annoying to others.

In this chapter we first examine a number of psychological disorders affecting children and adolescents, and then focus on two of the most frequent neurocognitive disorders found among the elderly: delirium and major neurocognitive disorders (dementia). Delirium develops quickly and can be described as a confused state, while dementia is the gradual worsening of memory and cognitive function. We examine the features of these disorders, their causes, and the treatments used.

Continuum of Disruptive Behaviour among Children and Youth

Example: Conduct Disorder

Does not meet criteria		Meets criteria		→
NO SYMPTOMS	**STRUGGLING**	**MILD**	**MODERATE**	**SEVERE**
	Brendon has been skipping school and lying to his parents.	Not only is Arielle frequently truant from school, she has been staying out at night without her parents' permission and on two occasions she did not come home at all.	Sebastien has been caught numerous times for shoplifting and doing graffiti. His teachers describe him as a bully who verbally intimidates others to get his way.	Nathan has been charged with breaking and entering. He often initiates physical fights and has forced girls from his school into sexual activity.

NEURODEVELOPMENTAL DISORDERS

Neurodevelopmental disorders are disorders that begin in the developmental period. These disorders generally become evident in the first few years of life and are associated with personal, social, or academic impairments (APA, 2013). The DSM-5 includes the following neurodevelopmental disorders: autism spectrum disorder, intellectual disability, communication disorders, attention-deficit/hyperactivity disorder, specific learning disorder, and motor disorders.

Autism Spectrum Disorder

Autism spectrum disorder (ASD) is one of the severest disorders of childhood. It is a chronic, lifelong condition. Children with autism, like Mahin, who is described in the following case study, seem utterly alone in the world. Despite parental efforts to bridge the gulf that divides them, children with ASD remain in their private worlds.

Mahin nursed eagerly, sat, and walked at the expected ages. Yet some of his behaviour made us vaguely uneasy. He never put anything in his mouth. Not his fingers nor his toys—nothing. . . . More troubling was the fact that Mahin didn't look at us, or smile, and wouldn't play the games that seemed as much a part of babyhood as diapers. He rarely laughed, and when he did, it was at things that didn't seem funny to us. He didn't cuddle, but sat upright in my lap, even when I rocked him. But children differ and we were content to let Mahin be himself. We thought it hilarious when my brother, visiting us when Mahin was eight months old, observed, "That kid has no social instincts whatsoever." Although Mahin was a first child, he was not isolated. I frequently put him in his playpen in front of the house, where the schoolchildren stopped to play with him as they passed. He ignored them, too.

It was Natasha, a personality kid, born two years later, whose responsiveness emphasized the degree of Mahin's difference. When I went into her room for the late feeding, her little head bobbed up and she greeted me with a smile that reached from her head to her toes. And the realization of that difference chilled me more than the wintry bedroom. Mahin's babbling had not turned into speech by the time he was three. His play was solitary and repetitious. He tore paper into long thin strips, bushel baskets of it every day. He spun the lids from my canning jars and became upset if we tried to divert him. Only rarely could I catch his eye, and then saw his focus change from me to the reflection in my glasses. . . .

[Mahin's] adventures in our suburban neighbourhood had been unhappy. He had disregarded the universal rule that sand is to be kept in sandboxes, and the children themselves had punished him. He walked around a sad and solitary figure, always carrying a toy airplane, a toy he never played with. At that time, I had not heard the word that was to dominate our lives, to hover over every conversation, to sit through every meal beside us. That word was autism.

From Journal of Child Psychology and Psychiatry, Franges Eberhardy, © 1967. Reproduced with permission of John Wiley & Sons, Inc.

autistic thinking The tendency to view oneself as the centre of the universe, to believe that external events somehow refer to oneself.

autism spectrum disorder Disorder characterized by pervasive deficits in the ability to relate to and communicate with others, and by a restricted range of activities and interests. Children with autism spectrum disorder lack the ability to relate to others and seem to live in their own private worlds. Abbreviated *ASD*.

Autism derives from the Greek *autos*, meaning "self." The term *autism* was first used in 1906 by Swiss psychiatrist Eugen Bleuler to refer to a peculiar style of thinking among people with schizophrenia. (Autism is one of Bleuler's four A's.) **Autistic thinking** is the tendency to view oneself as the centre of the universe, to believe that external events somehow refer to oneself. In 1943, another psychiatrist, Leo Kanner, applied the diagnosis "early infantile autism" to a group of disturbed children who seemed unable to relate to others, as if they lived in their own private worlds. Unlike children suffering from intellectual disability, children with **autism spectrum disorder** seemed to shut out any input from the outside world, creating a kind of "autistic aloneness" (Kanner, 1943).

ASD is a lifelong condition that spans all socioeconomic levels (Fombonne, 2005). It typically becomes evident in toddlers between 18 and 30 months of age (Rapin, 1997) and is four times more common in boys (Fombonne, 2005).

FEATURES OF AUTISM SPECTRUM DISORDER The DSM-5 identifies autism spectrum disorder on the basis of a set of behaviours representing persistent deficits in social communication and social interactions, and restricted or fixated interests and repetitive behaviours (see Table 11.1). Clinicians rate the severity of ASD (severe, moderate, or mild) and whether or not there is an intellectual or language impairment.

The diagnostic term Asperger's disorder was used in the previous edition of the DSM to describe a distinct disorder within the autism spectrum but is now classified as a form of autism spectrum disorder if diagnostic criteria for ASD are met. Asperger's disorder refers to a pattern of abnormal behaviour involving social awkwardness and stereotyped or repetitive behaviours or fixated interests but without the significant language or cognitive deficits associated with more severe forms of ASD.

Perhaps the most poignant feature of ASD is the child's utter aloneness. Children at the severe range of the spectrum may be mute, or if some language skills are present, they may be characterized by peculiar usage, as in echolalia (parroting back what the child has heard in a high-pitched monotone); pronoun reversals (using "you" or "he" instead of "I"); use of words that have meaning only to those who have intimate knowledge of the child; and tendencies to raise the voice at the end of sentences, as if asking a question. Nonverbal communication may

Tatyana Dzemileva/Shutterstock

Autism spectrum disorder. One of the most severe childhood disorders, autism spectrum disorder is characterized by pervasive deficits in the ability to relate to and communicate with others, and by a restricted range of activities and interests. Children with autism spectrum disorder lack the ability to relate to others and seem to live in their own private worlds.

TABLE 11.1

Diagnostic Criteria for Autism Spectrum Disorder

A. Persistent deficits in social communication and social interaction across multiple contexts, as manifested by the following, currently or by history (examples are illustrative, not exhaustive; see text):

1. Deficits in social-emotional reciprocity, ranging, for example, from abnormal social approach and failure of normal back-and-forth conversation; to reduced sharing of interests, emotions, or affect; to failure to initiate or respond to social interactions.

2. Deficits in nonverbal communicative behaviors used for social interaction, ranging, for example, from poorly integrated verbal and nonverbal communication; to abnormalities in eye contact and body language or deficits in understanding and use of gestures; to a total lack of facial expressions and nonverbal communication.

3. Deficits in developing, maintaining, and understanding relationships, ranging, for example, from difficulties adjusting behavior to suit various social contexts; to difficulties in sharing imaginative play or in making friends; to absence of interest in peers.

B. Restricted, repetitive patterns of behavior, interests, or activities, as manifested by at least two of the following, currently or by history (examples are illustrative, not exhaustive; see text):

1. Stereotyped or repetitive motor movements, use of objects, or speech (e.g., simple motor stereotypies, lining up toys or flipping objects, echolalia, idiosyncratic phrases).

2. Insistence on sameness, inflexible adherence to routines, or ritualized patterns of verbal or nonverbal behavior (e.g., extreme distress at small changes, difficulties with transitions, rigid thinking patterns, greeting rituals, need to take same route or eat same food every day).

3. Highly restricted, fixated interests that are abnormal in intensity or focus (e.g., strong attachment to or preoccupation with unusual objects, excessively circumscribed or perseverative interests).

4. Hyper- or hyporeactivity to sensory input or unusual interest in sensory aspects of the environment (e.g., apparent indifference to pain/temperature, adverse response to specific sounds or textures, excessive smelling or touching of objects, visual fascination with lights or movement).

C. Symptoms must be present in the early developmental period (but may not become fully manifest until social demands exceed limited capacities, or may be masked by learned strategies in later life).

D. Symptoms cause clinically significant impairment in social, occupational, or other important areas of current functioning.

E. These disturbances are not better explained by intellectual disability (intellectual developmental disorder) or global developmental delay. Intellectual disability and autism spectrum disorder frequently co-occur; to make comorbid diagnoses of autism spectrum disorder and intellectual disability, social communication should be below that expected for general developmental level.

Note: Individuals with a well established DSM-IV diagnosis of autistic disorder, Asperger's disorder, or pervasive developmental disorder not otherwise specified should be given the diagnosis of autism spectrum disorder. Individuals who have marked deficits in social communication, but whose symptoms do not otherwise meet criteria for autism spectrum disorder, should be evaluated for social (pragmatic) communication disorder.

Specify if:
  With or without accompanying intellectual impairment
  With or without accompanying language impairment

Source: Reprinted with permission from the *Diagnostic and Statistical Manual of Mental Disorders*, Fifth Edition, (Copyright © 2013). American Psychiatric Association. All Rights Reserved.

also be impaired or absent. For example, children with ASD may not engage in eye contact or display facial expressions. Although these children may be unresponsive to others, researchers find them to be capable of displaying strong emotions, especially strong negative emotions such as anger, sadness, and fear (Capps, Kasari, Yirmiya, & Sigman, 1993).

A primary feature of ASD is interminable, repeated, purposeless, stereotyped movements—twirling, flapping the hands, or rocking back and forth with the arms around the knees. Some children with ASD mutilate themselves, even as they cry out in pain. They may bang their head, slap their face, bite their hands and shoulders, or pull out their hair. They may also throw sudden tantrums or panics. Another feature of ASD is an aversion to environmental changes—a feature termed "preservation of sameness." When familiar objects are moved even slightly from their usual places, children may throw tantrums or cry continually until their placement is restored. They may also insist on eating the same food every day.

Children with ASD are bound by ritual. The teacher of one five-year-old girl with ASD learned to greet her every morning by saying, "Good morning, Lily, I am very, very glad to see you" (Diamond, Balvin, & Diamond, 1963). Although Lily would not respond to the greeting, she would shriek if the teacher omitted even one of the *very*s.

Children who develop ASD appear to have failed to develop a differentiated self-concept—a sense of themselves as distinct individuals (Toichi et al., 2002). Despite their unusual behaviour, children with ASD are often quite attractive and can have an "intelligent look" about them. However, as measured by scores on standardized tests, their intellectual development tends to lag below the norm. International studies indicate that 30% of ASD subjects have mild to moderate levels of intellectual disability, and 40% have severe to profound levels (Fombonne, 2005). Even those who function at an average level of intelligence show deficits in activities requiring the ability to symbolize, such as recognize emotions, engage in symbolic play, and problem solve conceptually (Yirmiya & Sigman, 1991). They also display difficulty in attending to tasks that involve interacting with other people.

THEORETICAL PERSPECTIVES   An early and now discredited belief held that the autistic child's aloofness was a reaction to parents who were cold and detached and who lacked the ability to establish warm relationships with their children.

Psychologist O. Ivar Løvaas and his colleagues (Løvaas, Koegel, & Schreibman, 1979) offer a cognitive-behavioural perspective on autism spectrum disorder. They suggest that children with ASD have perceptual deficits that limit them to processing only one stimulus at a time. As a result, they are slow to learn by means of classical conditioning (association of stimuli). From the learning theory perspective, children become attached to their primary caregivers because they are associated with primary reinforcers such as food and hugging. Children with ASD, however, attend either to the food or to the cuddling and do not connect it with the parent.

Cognitive theorists have focused on the kinds of cognitive deficits shown by children with ASD and the possible relationships among these deficits. Children with ASD appear to have difficulty integrating information from various senses (Russo et al., 2010). At times, they seem hypersensitive to stimulation. At other times they are so insensitive that an observer might wonder whether they are deaf. Perceptual and cognitive deficits seem to diminish their capacity to make use of information—to comprehend and apply social rules. This may impede the development of what psychologists call a **theory of mind**. Theory of mind is the ability to appreciate that other people have a mental state that is different from one's own. Children with ASD show deficits in their ability to infer beliefs, intentions, and emotions in others (Baron-Cohen, 1995, 1998). Not being able to readily see the world from another person's perspective interferes with the normal give and take of social relationships.

But what is the basis of these perceptual and cognitive deficits? We don't yet know what causes autism, but mounting evidence points to a neurological basis involving brain abnormalities, perhaps involving prenatal influences leading to abnormal wiring in the circuitry of the developing brain (Norton, 2012; Wolff et al., 2012). Evidence of brain abnormalities comes more directly from brain-imaging studies showing malfunctions in complex circuitry in networks of brain cells and structural damage involving loss of brain tissue (e.g., Cortese et al., 2012; Ecker et al., 2013). Scientists suspect that the brain of the child with ASD develops abnormally because of a combination of genetic factors and (presently unknown) environmental influences, possibly involving exposure to certain toxins or viruses or prenatal influences (Dawson, 2013; Szatmari, 2011). Even before symptoms emerge, we see evidence of abnormal brain development in infant children who go on to develop ASD (Wolff et al., 2012).

MRI scans show that compared to normal children, children with ASD have a period of overgrowth of brain size early in postnatal development, especially in the frontal regions. This period is followed by significantly slowed growth resulting in a brain volume smaller than average for children aged 5 to 16 (Hua et al., 2013). The brain tissue that connects the two halves of the brain, the corpus callosum, is smaller than normal in patients with ASD, which may affect **lateralization** of brain function. The area of the brain that regulates motor function, the cerebellum, also shows abnormal development in individuals with ASD.

Evidence links a greater risk of ASD to certain prenatal risk factors, including influenza infection or prolonged fevers in the mother during pregnancy (Atladóttir, Henriksen,

theory of mind The ability to appreciate that other people have a mental state that is different from one's own.

lateralization The developmental process by which the left hemisphere specializes in verbal and analytic functions and the right hemisphere specializes in nonverbal, spatial functions.

Schendel, & Parner, 2012). These factors may adversely affect the developing brain in the fetus. Nicolson and Szatmari's review of the research indicates there is substantial support for the suggestion that genetics plays a significant role in the neurodevelopment of children with ASD, with susceptible genes on chromosomes 2 and 7 in particular (Nicolson & Szatmari, 2003). It is suspected that multiple genes are involved and that they interact with other factors, possibly environmental or biological in origin, leading to ASD (Nauert, 2011; Sanders et al., 2011; Santini et al., 2013).

Researchers have found that the mirror neurons—circuits that activate in similar ways when we perform actions or watch other people perform the same actions—in those with ASD are not as fully developed and may be the reason for social deficits (Bastiaansen et al., 2011). Also, brain scans are revealing the disorder's characteristic signature. Researchers from Yale University have identified three distinct neural signatures: trait markers, which are brain regions with reduced activity in children with ASD and their unaffected siblings; state markers, which are brain areas with

Sergey Novikov/Shutterstock

Establishing contact. One of the principal therapeutic tasks in working with children with autism spectrum disorder is the establishment of interpersonal contact. Behaviour therapists use reinforcers to increase adaptive social behaviours, such as paying attention to the therapist and playing with other children. Behaviour therapists may also use punishments to suppress self-mutilative behaviour.

reduced activity found only in children with ASD; and compensatory activity, which is enhanced activity seen only in unaffected siblings. The enhanced brain activity may reflect a developmental process by which these children overcome a genetic predisposition to develop ASD (Kaiser et al., 2010). This discovery may lead to earlier diagnosis of ASD. Early diagnosis tools are crucial to early intervention programs ("Children with Autism," 2011; "New Research Tool," 2008).

The Early Autism Study, led by Mel Rutherford at McMaster University, is developing an early diagnosis tool using eye-tracker technology that measures eye direction while babies look at faces, eyes, and bouncing balls on a computer screen. These researchers are finding they can distinguish between a group of siblings with the disorder from a group without the disorder at 9 months and 12 months ("New Research Tool," 2008).

Still, the cause of ASD remains unknown, and some recent controversial but scientifically plausible ideas are being examined. Some ideas point to the immune system, to viruses, and to an overload of hormones.

TREATMENT   Although there is no cure for ASD, structured treatment programs have yielded the best results. The most effective treatment programs focus on behavioural, educational, and communication deficits and are highly intensive and structured, offering a great deal of individual instruction (Eikeseth, Klintwall, Jahr, & Karlsson, 2012). In a classic study conducted by Løvaas (1987) at UCLA, children suffering from ASD received more than 40 hours of one-to-one behaviour modification each week for at least two years. Significant intellectual and educational gains were reported for 9 of the 19 children (47%) in the program. The children who improved achieved normal IQ scores and were able to succeed in Grade 1. Only 2% of a control group that did not receive the intensive treatment achieved similar gains. Treatment gains were well maintained at the time of a follow-up when the children were 11 years old (McEachin, Smith, & Løvaas, 1993).

These psychological intervention programs are effective for many children with ASD, but the key point is that any intervention must begin early. Research continues to support the necessity of early intervention programs; the more intense or comprehensive the therapy, the better it is in terms of helping children improve social and communication skills. Those who received therapy, including behavioural, speech, and occupational therapy, had the best outcomes in a recent study of over 1000 children with ASD (Mazurek, Kanne, & Miles, 2012). Children who are better functioning at the start of treatment typically gain the most.

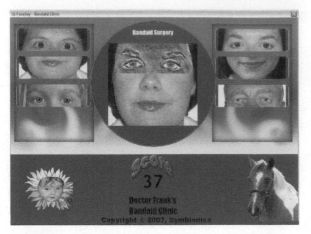

FaceSay images provided courtesy of Symbionica, LLC. All rights reserved.

Learning to recognize emotions through computer programs. An interactive computer game called FaceSay™, by Symbionica, helps children with ASD learn where to look for clues to emotions on faces and thereby learn how to recognize emotions in others.

Biological approaches have had only limited impact in the treatment of ASD. One line of research has focused on drugs normally used to treat schizophrenia, such as Haldol, which blocks dopamine activity. Several controlled studies show Haldol to be helpful in many cases in reducing social withdrawal and repetitive motor behaviour (such as rocking), aggression, hyperactivity, and self-injurious behaviour (McCracken et al., 2002). Investigators found that antipsychotic drugs work better when treatment includes parents in a training program that teaches them how to respond to the child's disruptive behaviour (Scahill et al., 2012).

An interactive computer program called FaceSay™, by Symbionica, LLC, has been shown to improve the ability of children with ASD to recognize faces, facial expressions, and emotions, according to the results of a study conducted by psychologists at the University of Alabama at Birmingham (Hopkins et al., 2011). FaceSay™ features interactive games that let children with ASD practise recognizing the facial features and expressions of an avatar, or software "puppet." Specifically, the computer program teaches the children where to look for facial cues, such as an eye gaze or a facial expression.

Traits in ASD generally continue into adulthood to one degree or another. Yet some children with ASD do go on to achieve college and university degrees and are able to function independently (Rapin, 1997). Others need continuing treatment throughout their lives, even institutionalized care. Even the highest-functioning adults with the disorder manifest deficient social and communication skills and a highly limited range of interests and activities (APA, 2013).

Autism Spectrum Disorder

- **What is autism spectrum disorder?** Autism spectrum disorder is characterized by pervasive deficits in the ability to relate to and communicate with others, and by a restricted range of activities and interests.
- **What are the clinical features of autism spectrum disorder?** Children with autism spectrum disorder shun affectionate behaviour, engage in stereotyped behaviour, attempt to preserve sameness, and tend to have peculiar speech habits such as echolalia, pronoun reversals, and idiosyncratic speech. The causes of the disorder remain unknown, but gains in academic and social functioning have been obtained through the use of early intensive behaviour therapy.

Intellectual Disability (Intellectual Developmental Disorder)

Intellectual disability, also called *intellectual developmental disorder*, involves a broad delay in the development of cognitive and social functioning. The course of development of children with intellectual disability is variable. Many improve over time, especially if they receive support, guidance, and enriched educational opportunities. Children with intellectual disability who are reared in impoverished environments may fail to improve or may deteriorate further in relation to other children.

Intellectual disability is generally assessed by a combination of formal intelligence tests and observation of adaptive functioning. The DSM-5 uses three criteria in diagnosing intellectual disability: (1) deficits in intellectual functions as indicated by clinicians and standardized testing, (2) evidence of impaired functioning in adaptive behaviour, and (3) onset of the disorder in the developmental period. People whose behaviour is impaired fail to meet the standards of behaviour that are expected of someone of the same age within a given cultural setting. They do not develop comparable social and communication skills or become adequately independent and self-sufficient. For infants,

TABLE 11.2

Classifications of Developmental Delay

Classification	Range of IQ Scores	Adaptive Limitations	Percentage of Developmentally Delayed Population
Mild	55–70	Can reach Grade 6 skill level. Capable with training of living independently and being self-supporting.	90%
Moderate	40–55	Can reach Grade 2 skill level. Can work and live in sheltered environments with supervision.	6%
Severe	25–40	Can learn to talk and perform basic self-care, but needs constant supervision.	3%
Profound	Below 25	Very limited ability to learn; may only be able to learn very simple tasks; poor language skills and limited self-care.	1%

Source: Psychology: An Exploration, Ciccarelli, Harrigan, & Fritzley, 2010, p. 339. Reprinted with permission by Pearson Canada Inc.

task-related judgments of subaverage intellectual functioning may be used in place of IQ scores because tests of infant intelligence either do not yield reliable IQ scores or do not yield any IQ scores at all.

The DSM-5 classifies intellectual disability according to level of severity. Table 11.2 provides a description of the deficits and abilities associated with various degrees of intellectual disability. Children with mild intellectual disability are generally capable of meeting basic academic demands, such as learning to read simple passages. As adults, they are generally capable of independent functioning, although they may require some guidance and support.

Approximately 1–3% of the Canadian population has an intellectual disability. The majority (85%) of these individuals fall within the mild range (Statistics Canada, 2015a). Not all systems of classification of intellectual disability are based on level of severity. The American Association on Intellectual and Developmental Disabilities (AAIDD), an organization comprising leading professionals in the field, classifies intellectual disability according to the intensity of support needed by the individual in various areas of functioning (AAIDD, 2010). Some individuals need only intermittent support that varies in intensity from time to time on an as-needed basis, whereas others require more constant or pervasive support involving extensive commitment of staff and resources. This system of classification attempts to match the level of support needed to the individual's ability to function in work, school, and home environments.

CAUSES OF INTELLECTUAL DISABILITY In many cases, intellectual disability can be traced to biological causes, including chromosomal and genetic disorders, infectious diseases, and brain damage. Specifically, where the intellectual disability is due to genes, geneticists have uncovered several genes that have been identified to cause this disorder. However, it is not one or two genes that cause intellectual disability but spontaneous mutations in the genes, as demonstrated in research by Dutch geneticists. The majority of intellectual disability is caused by spontaneous mutations in paternal sperm or maternal egg cells (Vissers et al., 2010). To be clear, intellectual disability is not transmitted from one generation to the next but occurs through spontaneous genetic changes such as deletions and duplications (Webber et al., 2009). The gene in which the child has a defect still shows a normal function in both parents.

Unexplained cases might involve cultural or familial causes, such as being raised in an impoverished home environment, or perhaps they involve an interaction of environmental and genetic factors, the nature of which remains poorly understood (Thapar, Gottesman, Owen, O'Donovan, & McGuffin, 1994).

Down syndrome Condition caused by a chromosomal abnormality involving an extra chromosome on the 21st pair (trisomy 21); it is characterized by intellectual disability and various physical abnormalities. Formerly called *mongolism* and *Down's syndrome* in Canada.

Down Syndrome and Other Chromosomal Abnormalities   The most common chromosomal abnormality resulting in intellectual disability is **Down syndrome**, which is characterized by an extra or third chromosome on the 21st pair of chromosomes, resulting in 47 chromosomes rather than the normal complement of 46. Down syndrome occurs in about 1 in 800 births. It usually occurs when the 21st pair of chromosomes in either the egg or the sperm fails to divide normally, resulting in an extra chromosome. Chromosomal abnormalities become more likely as parents age, so expectant couples in their mid-30s or older often undergo prenatal genetic tests to detect Down syndrome and genetic abnormalities. Down syndrome can be traced to a defect in the mother's chromosomes in about 90% of cases (Stern, Biron, & Moses, 2016), with the remainder attributable to defects in the father's sperm.

People with Down syndrome are recognizable by certain physical features, such as a round face; broad, flat nose; and small, downward-sloping folds of skin at the inside corners of the eyes that give the impression of slanted eyes. Children with Down syndrome are also characterized by a protruding tongue; small, squarish hands and short fingers; a curved fifth finger; and disproportionately small arms and legs in relation to their bodies. Nearly all of these children have intellectual disability, and many suffer from physical problems, such as malformations of the heart and respiratory difficulties. Sadly, most die by middle age. In their later years, they tend to suffer memory losses and experience childish emotions that represent a form of senility.

Children with Down syndrome suffer various deficits in learning and development. They tend to be uncoordinated and to lack proper muscle tone, which makes it difficult for them to carry out physical tasks and engage in play activities like other children. Down syndrome children suffer memory deficits, especially for information presented verbally, which makes it difficult for them to learn in school. They also have difficulty following instructions from teachers and expressing their thoughts or needs clearly in speech. Despite their disabilities, most can learn to read, write, and perform simple arithmetic if they receive appropriate schooling and the right encouragement.

Although less common than Down syndrome, chromosomal abnormalities on the sex chromosome may also result in intellectual disability, such as in Klinefelter syndrome and Turner syndrome. Klinefelter syndrome, which occurs only in males, is characterized by the presence of an extra X sex chromosome, resulting in an XXY sex chromosomal pattern rather than the XY pattern that men normally have. Estimates of the prevalence of Klinefelter syndrome range from one to two cases per 1000 male births (Morris, Alberman, Scott, & Jacobs, 2008). Men with this XXY pattern fail to develop appropriate secondary sex characteristics, resulting in small, underdeveloped testes; low sperm production; enlarged breasts; poor muscular development; and infertility. Mild intellectual disability or learning disabilities frequently occur among these men. Men with Klinefelter syndrome often don't discover they have the condition until they undergo tests for infertility.

Turner syndrome is found exclusively in females and is characterized by the presence of a single X sex chromosome instead of the normal two. Although such girls develop normal external genitals, their ovaries remain poorly developed, producing reduced amounts of estrogen. As women, they tend to be shorter than average and infertile. They also tend to show evidence of mild intellectual disability, especially in skills relating to math and science.

Fragile X Syndrome and Other Genetic Abnormalities   Fragile X syndrome is the most common type of inherited (genetic) intellectual disability (Grigsby, 2016). It is the second most common form of intellectual disability overall after Down syndrome (Dean, Muthuswamy, & Agarwal, 2016). The disorder is believed to be caused by a mutated gene on the X sex chromosome (Huber, Gallagher, Warren, & Bear, 2002). The defective gene is located in an area of the chromosome that appears fragile, hence the name *fragile X syndrome*. Fragile X syndrome occurs in about 1 in 4000 males and 1 in 8000 females (Dean et al., 2016). The effects of fragile X syndrome range from mild learning disabilities to intellectual disability so profound that those affected can hardly speak or function.

Females normally have two X sex chromosomes, whereas males have only one. For females, having two X sex chromosomes seems to provide some protection against the disorder if the defective gene turns up on one of the two chromosomes (Dean et al., 2016).

This may explain why the disorder usually has more profound effects on males than on females. Yet the mutation does not always manifest itself. Many males and females carry the fragile X mutation but show no clinical evidence of it. Nevertheless, they can pass along the syndrome to their offspring.

A genetic test can detect the presence of the mutation by direct DNA analysis and may help prospective parents who seek out genetic counselling. Prenatal testing of the fetus is also available. Although there is no treatment for fragile X syndrome, identifying the defective gene is the first step toward understanding how the protein produced by the gene functions to create the disability—which may lead to the development of treatments (Healy, Rush, & Ocain, 2011).

Phenylketonuria (PKU) is a genetic disorder that occurs in 1 in 10 000 to 15 000 births (Widaman, 2009). It is caused by a recessive gene that prevents the child from metabolizing the amino acid phenylalanine (Phe), which is found in many foods. Consequently, phenylalanine and its derivative, phenylpyruvic acid, accumulate in the body, causing damage to the central nervous system that results in intellectual disability and emotional disturbance. PKU can be detected in newborns by analyzing blood or urine samples. Although there is no cure for PKU, children with the disorder may suffer less damage or develop normally if they are placed on a diet low in phenylalanine soon after birth (Giżewska et al., 2016). Such children receive protein supplements that compensate for their nutritional loss.

University of Toronto researchers Mary Lou Smith and her colleagues tested children with PKU who had either high or low levels of Phe (Smith, Klim, & Hanley, 2000). They found that PKU children with low Phe levels were indistinguishable from non-PKU controls on several cognitive tasks. In contrast, however, the higher the levels of Phe in school aged children with PKU, the greater the impairment in cognitive performance on specific problem-solving and verbal memory tasks.

Tay-Sachs disease is caused by recessive genes on chromosome 15. A fatal degenerative disease of the central nervous system, it mostly afflicts Jews of Eastern European ancestry and French Canadians of the Gaspé region of Quebec (Triggs-Raine, Richard, Wasel, Prence, & Natowicz, 1995). About 1 in 14 French Canadians in Eastern Quebec is a carrier of the recessive gene responsible for the disorder (Chodirker et al., 2001; Kaback et al., 1993). Children afflicted by Tay-Sachs suffer gradual loss of muscle control, deafness and blindness, intellectual disability, and paralysis, and usually die before the age of five.

Today, various prenatal diagnostic tests can detect the presence of chromosomal abnormalities and genetic disorders. In amniocentesis, which is usually conducted about 14 to 15 weeks following conception, a sample of amniotic fluid is drawn with a syringe from the amniotic sac that contains the fetus. With chorionic villus sampling (CVS), cells are extracted from the placenta outside the sac where the fetus develops. CVS is best performed between 10 and 12 weeks into a woman's pregnancy. Depending upon the procedure, cells from the fetus or the placenta can then be examined for abnormalities, including Down syndrome, X-linked disorders, PKU, Smith-Lemli-Opitz syndrome, and Tay-Sachs disease.

In the future, it may be possible to control the impact of defective genes during prenatal development. For now, expectant couples rely on genetic counselling. It offers a complete and accurate view of the options available and can assist couples in making informed decisions about terminating a pregnancy or, alternatively, help them prepare for a baby who has congenital defects.

Prenatal Factors   Some cases of intellectual disability are caused by maternal infections or substance abuse during pregnancy. Rubella (German measles) in the mother, for example, can be passed along to the unborn child, causing brain damage that results in intellectual disability, and may play a role in autism spectrum disorder. Although the mother might experience only mild symptoms or none at all, the effects on the fetus can be tragic. Other maternal diseases that can cause intellectual disability in the child include syphilis, **cytomegalovirus**, and genital herpes.

Widespread programs that immunize women against rubella before pregnancy and tests for syphilis during pregnancy have reduced the risk of transmission of these infections to children. Most children who contract genital herpes from their mothers do so

phenylketonuria Genetic disorder that prevents the metabolization of phenylpyruvic acid, leading to intellectual disability. Abbreviated *PKU*.

Tay-Sachs disease Disease of lipid metabolism that is genetically transmitted and usually results in death in early childhood.

cytomegalovirus Maternal disease of the herpes virus group that carries a risk of intellectual disability to the unborn child.

during delivery by coming into contact with the herpes simplex virus that causes the disease in the birth canal. Caesarean sections (C-sections) reduce the risk of the baby's coming into contact with the virus during outbreaks.

Drugs the mother ingests during pregnancy are able to pass through the placenta to the child. Some can cause severe birth deformities and intellectual disability. Children whose mothers drink alcohol during pregnancy are often born with fetal alcohol syndrome (FAS). FAS is among the most prominent causes of intellectual disability.

Birth complications, such as oxygen deprivation or head injuries, place children at increased risk for neurological disorders, including intellectual disability. Prematurity also places children at risk of intellectual disability and other developmental problems. Brain infections, such as encephalitis and meningitis, or traumas during infancy and early childhood can cause intellectual disability and other health problems. Children who ingest toxins, such as paint chips containing lead, may also suffer brain damage that produces intellectual disability.

Cultural/Familial Causes Children with intellectual disability fall mainly into the mild range of severity, and there is no apparent biological cause or distinguishing physical feature that sets these children apart from other children. Psychosocial factors, such as an impoverished home, a social environment that is not intellectually stimulating, or parental neglect or abuse, may play a causal or contributing role in the development of intellectual disability in such children. Supporting a family linkage is evidence from a study in Atlanta in which mothers who failed to finish high school were four times more likely than better-educated mothers to have children with mild intellectual disability (Drews, Yeargin-Allsopp, Decouflé, & Murphy, 1995).

These cases are considered **cultural/familial intellectual disability**. Children in impoverished families may lack toys, books, or opportunities to interact with adults in intellectually stimulating ways. Consequently, they may fail to develop appropriate language skills or become unmotivated to learn the skills that are valued in contemporary society. Economic burdens, such as the need to hold multiple jobs, may prevent the parents from spending time reading to them, talking to them at length, and exposing them to creative play or trips to museums and parks. Children may spend most of their days glued to the television set. The parents, most of whom were also reared in poverty, may lack the reading or communication skills to help shape the development of these skills in their children. A vicious cycle of poverty and impoverished intellectual development may be repeated from generation to generation.

Children with this form of developmental delay may respond dramatically when provided with enriched learning experiences, especially at earlier ages. For example, the Health Canada–funded Aboriginal Head Start (AHS) program was instituted in 134 urban centres and northern communities across Canada to promote education and school readiness, Indigenous culture and language, parental involvement, health, nutrition, and social support (PHAC, 2012). To date, the AHS program has been highly successful and has exceeded program expectations as major gains have been achieved in all areas of children's development (PHAC, 2012).

INTERVENTIONS FOR CHILDREN WITH INTELLECTUAL DISABILITY The services that children with intellectual disability require to meet the developmental challenges they face depend in part on the type of intellectual disability and the level of severity (Dykens & Hodapp, 1997; Snell, 1997). With appropriate training, children with mild intellectual disability may approach a Grade 6 level of competence. They can acquire vocational skills that allow them to support themselves minimally through meaningful work. In Canada, most mildly intellectually disabled children are integrated into the regular classroom, typically with a modified curriculum. Children with more severe forms of intellectual disability, on the other hand, may be placed in special schools or classes if the caregiver prefers (Bradley, Thompson, & Bryson, 2002).

Controversy remains over the **mainstreaming** of children with intellectual disability into regular classes. Although some children with mild intellectual disability may achieve better when they are mainstreamed, others may not do so well in regular classes. Some of these children find regular classes overwhelming, and they withdraw

cultural/familial intellectual disability Milder form of intellectual disability that is believed to result, or at least be influenced by, impoverishment in the child's home environment.

mainstreaming The practice of having all students with disabilities included in the regular classroom. Also referred to as *integration* or *inclusion*.

Savant Syndrome

Got a minute? Try the following:

1. Without referring to a calendar, calculate the day of the week that March 15, 2079, will fall on.
2. List the prime numbers between 1 and 1 billion. (Hint: The list starts 1, 2, 3, 5, 7, 11, 13, 17 . . .)
3. Repeat verbatim the newspaper stories you read over coffee this morning.
4. Sing accurately every note played by the first violin in Beethoven's *Ninth Symphony*.

These tasks are impossible for all but a very few. Ironically, people who are most likely to be able to accomplish these feats suffer from autism spectrum disorder, intellectual disability, or both. Such a person is commonly called an idiot savant. The term *savant* is derived from the French *savoir*, meaning "to know." The label *savant syndrome* is preferable to the pejorative *idiot savant* in referring to someone with severe mental deficiencies who possesses some remarkable mental abilities. The prevalence of savant syndrome among people with intellectual disability is estimated at about 1 oooo in 200 (Mottron et al., 2013). Most people with savant syndrome, like most people with ASD, are male (Treffert, 1988). Among a sample of 5400 people with ASD, 531 cases (9.8%) were reported by parents to have savant syndrome (Rimland, 1978). Because they want to think of their children as special, however, parents might overreport the incidence of savant syndrome.

The savant syndrome phenomenon occurs more frequently in males by a ratio of roughly 6 to 1. The special skills of people with savant syndrome tend to appear out of the blue and may disappear as suddenly. Some people with the syndrome engage in lightning calculations. Thomas Fuller, a 19th-century enslaved man in Virginia, "was able to calculate the number of seconds in 70 years, 17 days, and 12 hours in a minute and one half, taking into account the 17 leap years that would have occurred in the period" (Smith, 1983). There are also cases of people with the syndrome who were blind but could play back any musical piece, no matter how complex, or repeat long passages of foreign languages without losing a syllable.

Various theories have been presented to explain savant syndrome (Treffert, 1988). Some experts believe that children with savant syndrome have unusually well-developed memories that allow them to record and scan vast amounts of information. It has been suggested that people with savant syndrome may inherit two sets of hereditary factors, one for intellectual disability and the other for special abilities. Perhaps it is coincidental that their special abilities and their mental handicaps were inherited in common. Other theorists suggest that the left and right hemispheres of their cerebral cortex are organized in an unusual way. This latter belief is supported by research suggesting that the special abilities these individuals possess often involve skills associated with right hemisphere functioning. Still other theorists suggest they learn special skills to compensate for their lack of more general skills, perhaps as a means of coping with their environment or of earning social reinforcements. It could be that their skills in concrete functions, such as calculation, compensate for their lack of abstract thinking ability. Perhaps, as the neurologist Oliver Sacks speculates, the brain circuits of some people with savant syndrome are wired with a "deep arithmetic"—an innate structure for perceiving mathematical relationships that is analogous to the prewiring that allows people to perceive and produce language.

Some earlier research has pointed to possible gender-linked left hemisphere damage occurring prenatally or congenitally. Compensatory right hemisphere development might then take place, establishing specialized brain circuitry that processes concrete and narrowly defined kinds of information (Treffert, 1988). An environment that reinforces savant abilities and provides opportunities for practice and concentration would give further impetus to the development of these unusual abilities. As it stands, savant syndrome remains a mystery.

United Archives GmbH/Alamy Stock Photo

Savant syndrome. Dustin Hoffman won the Best Actor Oscar for his portrayal in the 1988 film *Rain Man* of a man with autism who showed a remarkable capacity for numerical calculation. Hoffman was able to capture a sense of emotional detachment and isolation in his character.

Shutterstock

Inclusion. Across Canada, most children with special learning needs remain in regular classrooms and are provided with educational programs that meet their individual needs.

from their schoolmates. There has also been a trend in Canada and the United States toward deinstitutionalization of people with more severe intellectual disability, a policy shift motivated in large part by public outrage over the appalling conditions that existed in many institutions serving this population.

People with intellectual disability who are capable of functioning in the community have the right to receive less restrictive care than is provided in large institutions. Many are capable of living outside an institution and have been placed in supervised group homes. Residents typically share household responsibilities and are encouraged to participate in meaningful daily activities, such as training programs or sheltered workshops. Others live with their families and attend structured day programs. Adults with intellectual disability often work in outside jobs and live in their own apartments or share apartments with other individuals who have mild intellectual disability. Behavioural approaches can be used to teach people with more severe intellectual disability such basic hygienic behaviours as toothbrushing, self-dressing, and hair combing. In demonstrating toothbrushing, the therapist might first define the component parts of the targeted behaviour (picking up the toothbrush, wetting the toothbrush, taking the cap off the tube, putting the paste on the brush, etc.) (Kissel, Whitman, & Reid, 1983). The therapist might then shape the desired behaviour by using such techniques as verbal instruction (e.g., "Jim, pick up the toothbrush"), physical guidance (physically guiding the client's hand in performing the desired response), and reward (use of positive verbal reinforcement) for successful completion of the desired response ("That's really good, Jim"). Such behavioural techniques have been shown to be effective in teaching a simple but remunerative vocational skill (e.g., stamping return addresses on envelopes) to a group of adult women with such severe intellectual disability they were essentially nonverbal (Schepis, Reid, & Fitzgerald, 1987). These techniques may also help people with severe intellectual disability develop adaptive capacities that can enable them to perform more productive roles.

Other behavioural treatment techniques include social-skills training, which focuses on increasing the individual's ability to relate cooperatively with others, and anger-management training to help individuals develop more effective ways of handling conflicts than aggressively acting out (Huang & Cuvo, 1997).

Children with intellectual disability stand perhaps a three to four times greater chance of developing other psychological disorders, such as attention-deficit/hyperactivity disorder (ADHD), depression, or anxiety disorders (Lakhan, 2013; McGillivray & Kershaw, 2013). Canadian researchers reported that up to 50% of adults with an intellectual disability also have a psychiatric disorder (Durbin, Sirotich, Lunsky, & Durbin, 2017). Mental health professionals have been slow to recognize the prevalence of mental health problems among people with intellectual disability, perhaps because of a long-held conceptual distinction between emotional impairment on the one hand and intellectual deficits on the other (Nezu, 1994). Many professionals even assumed (wrongly) that people with intellectual disability were worry free and somehow immune to psychological problems (Nezu, 1994). Given these commonly held beliefs, it is perhaps not surprising that many of the psychological problems of people with intellectual disability have gone unrecognized and untreated (Havercamp, Scandlin, & Roth, 2004).

Children and adults with intellectual disability may need psychological counselling to help them adjust to life in the community. Many have difficulty making friends and may become socially isolated. Problems with self-esteem are also common, especially because people who have intellectual disability are often demeaned and ridiculed. Supportive counselling may be supplemented with behavioural techniques to help those with developmental disabilities acquire skills in areas such as personal hygiene, work, and social relationships.

Intellectual Disability

- **What is intellectual disability, and how is it assessed?** Intellectual disability is a general delay in the development of intellectual and adaptive abilities. It is assessed through evaluation of performance on intelligence tests and measures of functional ability. Most cases fall in the range of mildly intellectually disabled.
- **What are the causes of intellectual disability?** There are many causes of intellectual disability, including chromosomal abnormalities such as Down syndrome; genetic disorders such as fragile X syndrome, phenylketonuria, and Tay-Sachs disease; prenatal factors such as maternal diseases and alcohol (and other drug) use; and cultural/familial factors associated with intellectually impoverished home environments.

Specific Learning Disorder

Many famous scientists, leaders, and celebrities have been thought to have what are now considered a specific learning disorder. Among their number are Albert Einstein, Alexander Graham Bell, Winston Churchill, Agatha Christie, and Tom Cruise. These highly creative and successful people suffered from **dyslexia** and related disorders. The term *dyslexia* is derived from the Greek roots *dys-*, meaning "bad," and *lexikon*, meaning "of words." Dyslexia is the most common type of specific learning disorder (Shaywitz, 1998). It accounts for roughly 80% of learning disability cases. People with a specific learning disorder have average or higher intelligence, and may even be gifted, but show inadequate development in reading, math, or writing skills that impairs school performance or daily activities. (See the A Closer Look box for a Canadian definition of *learning disabilities*.)

Among Canadian children aged 5–14 years, 4.1% of boys and 2.2% of girls are identified as having a learning disability (Statistics Canada, 2008). Learning disorders tend to run a chronic course and are the most common long-term conditions of children up to age 14 (Cossette & Duclos, 2002). The more severe the problem is in childhood, the more likely it is to affect adult development (Spreen, 1988). Children with learning disorders tend to perform poorly in school; about half of all children who received remedial education were identified as having a learning disability (Lipps & Frank, 1997).

DSM-5 classifies specific learning disorder as a single disorder with three subtypes: impairment in mathematics, impairment in written expression, and impairment in reading.

IMPAIRMENT IN MATHEMATICS Impairment in mathematics is a specific learning disorder characterizing children with deficiencies in arithmetic skills. They may have problems understanding basic mathematical terms or operations, such as addition or subtraction; decoding mathematical symbols (+, =, etc.); or learning sequential facts, such as multiplication tables, by rote memory. The problem may become apparent as early as Grade 1 (age 6) but is not generally recognized until about Grade 3 (age 8).

IMPAIRMENT IN WRITTEN EXPRESSION Impairment in written expression—dysgraphia—characterizes children with grossly deficient writing skills and occurs regardless of the ability to read. It is not related to intellectual impairment. The deficiency may be characterized by errors in spelling, grammar, or punctuation or by difficulty in composing sentences and paragraphs. Severe writing difficulties generally become apparent by age 7 (Grade 2), although milder cases may not be recognized until age 10 (Grade 5) or later. Dysgraphia often overlaps with other neurodevelopmental disorders such as speech impairment, ADHD, or developmental coordination disorder (Nicolson & Fawcett, 2011; Nicolson & Szatmari, 2003).

dyslexia Type of specific learning disorder characterized by impaired reading ability that may involve difficulty with the alphabet or spelling.

specific learning disorder Deficiency in a specific learning ability noteworthy because of the individual's general intelligence and exposure to learning opportunities.

A Canadian Definition of Learning Disabilities

On January 30, 2002, after years of deliberation, the Learning Disabilities Association of Canada (LDAC) adopted an official definition of learning disabilities that is the culmination of a thorough review of learning disabilities research and input from hundreds of individuals in all provinces and territories by the LDAC National Legal Committee and the LDAC "Think Tank." The definition was re-endorsed on March 2, 2015 (Learning Disabilities Association of Canada, 2015):

> Learning Disabilities refer to a number of disorders that may affect the acquisition, organization, retention, understanding or use of verbal or nonverbal information. These disorders affect learning in individuals who otherwise demonstrate at least average abilities essential for thinking and/or reasoning. As such, learning disabilities are distinct from global intellectual deficiency.
>
> Learning disabilities result from impairments in one or more processes related to perceiving, thinking, remembering, or learning. These include but are not limited to: language processing; phonological processing; visual spatial processing; processing speed; memory and attention; and executive functions (e.g., planning and decision-making).
>
> Learning disabilities range in severity and may interfere with the acquisition and use of one or more of the following:
>
> - oral language (e.g., listening, speaking, understanding);
> - reading (e.g., decoding, phonetic knowledge, word recognition, comprehension);
> - written language (e.g., spelling and written expression); and
> - mathematics (e.g., computation, problem solving).
>
> Learning disabilities may also involve difficulties with organizational skills, social perception, social interaction, and perspective taking.

> Learning disabilities are lifelong. The way in which they are expressed may vary over an individual's lifetime, depending on the interaction between the demands of the environment and the individual's strengths and needs. Learning disabilities are suggested by unexpected academic under-achievement or achievement that is maintained only by unusually high levels of effort and support.
>
> Learning disabilities [occur] due to genetic and/or neurobiological factors or injury that alters brain functioning in a manner that affects one or more processes related to learning. These disorders are not due primarily to hearing and/or vision problems, socio-economic factors, cultural or linguistic differences, lack of motivation or ineffective teaching, although these factors may further complicate the challenges faced by individuals with learning disabilities. Learning disabilities may co-exist with various conditions including attentional, behavioural and emotional disorders, sensory impairments or other medical conditions.
>
> For success, individuals with learning disabilities require early identification and timely specialized assessments and interventions involving home, school, community, and workplace settings. The interventions need to be appropriate for each individual's learning disability subtype and, at a minimum, include the provision of:
>
> - specific skill instruction;
> - accommodations;
> - compensatory strategies; and
> - self-advocacy skills.

Source: Learning Disabilities Association of Canada, 2015. Reprinted with the kind permission of the Learning Disabilities Association of Canada.

IMPAIRMENT IN READING Impairment in reading—dyslexia—characterizes children who have poorly developed skills in recognizing letters and words and comprehending written text. Children with dyslexia may read slowly, with difficulty, and may distort, omit, or substitute words when reading aloud. They may have trouble decoding letters. They may perceive letters upside down (*w* for *m*) or reversed (*b* for *d*). Dyslexia is usually apparent by the age of 7, coinciding with Grade 2, but it is sometimes recognized in 6-year-olds. Although it was earlier believed that the problem affected mostly boys, more recent studies find similar rates among boys and girls (Hawke, Wadsworth, Olson, & DeFries, 2007). Yet boys with dyslexia are more likely than girls to exhibit disruptive behaviour and so are more likely to be referred for evaluation. Children and adolescents with dyslexia tend to be more prone than their peers to depression, to have lower self-worth and feelings of competence in their academic work, and to have signs of ADHD (Boetsch, Green, & Pennington, 1996; Stegemann, 2016).

THEORETICAL PERSPECTIVES Canadian neuropsychologists contend that learning disorders originate primarily from neurobiological factors (Fiedorowicz, 1999; Fiedorowicz, Benezra, MacDonald, McElgunn, & Wilson, 1999; Fiedorowicz et al., 2002). Many children with learning disorders have problems with visual or auditory sensation and perception. They may lack the capacity to copy words or to discriminate geometric shapes. Other children have short attention spans or show hyperactivity, which is also suggestive of an underlying brain abnormality.

Much of the research on learning disorders has focused on dyslexia. Mounting evidence points to underlying brain dysfunctions (Nicolson & Fawcett, 2008). Cross-cultural language research has now shown that dyslexia is a universal neuroanatomical disorder that causes the same reading disabilities (Paulesu et al., 2001). There is evidence of impaired visual processing in people with dyslexia that would be consistent with a defect in a major visual relay station in the brain involved in sequencing the flow of visual information from the retina to the visual cortex (Livingstone, Rosen, Drislane, & Galaburda, 1991). Inspection of the autopsied brains of people who had dyslexia showed that this relay station was smaller and less well organized than in other people. As a result, the brains of people with dyslexia are not likely to be able to decipher a rapid succession of visual stimuli, such as those involved in decoding letters and words. Words may thus become blurry, fuse together, or seem to jump off the page—all problems reported by people with dyslexia (Ziegler, Pech-Georgel, Dufau, & Grainger, 2010).

Peter Dazeley/Photographer's Choice/Getty Images

Dyslexia. Children with dyslexia have difficulty decoding words. Note the mispelled words in this person's message.

Dysfunctions in other sensory pathways involving the sense of hearing and even the sense of touch may also be involved in learning disorders. For example, research suggests that some forms of dyslexia may be traceable to an abnormality in the brain circuits responsible for processing rapidly flowing auditory information (Blakeslee, 1994). This flaw in brain circuitry may make it difficult to understand rapidly occurring speech sounds, such as the sounds corresponding to the letters *b* and *p* in syllables like *ba* and *pa*. Problems discerning the differences between many basic speech sounds can make it difficult for people with dyslexia to learn to speak correctly and later, perhaps, to learn to read. They continue to have problems distinguishing between words like *boy* and *toy* or *pet* and *bet* in rapid speech. If defects in brain circuitry responsible for relaying and processing sensory data are involved in learning disorders, as the evidence suggests, it may lead the way to the development of specialized treatment programs to help children adjust to their sensory capabilities.

Genetic factors appear to be involved in brain abnormalities associated with dyslexia (Mueller et al., 2014). People whose parents have dyslexia are at greater risk themselves (Thompson et al., 2015). Moreover, higher rates of concordance (agreement) for dyslexia are found between identical (MZ) than fraternal (DZ) twins—70% versus 40% (Plomin, Owen, & McGuffin, 1994). Suspicion has focused on the role that particular genes may play in causing subtle defects in the brain circuitry involved in reading.

INTERVENTIONS With the growing recognition of the neurobiological nature of learning disabilities, our approach to treatment in Canada now involves support and intervention strategies that focus on a child's information processing style and academic strengths. The support aspect focuses on bolstering the child's self-esteem and increasing motivation, developing close teacher–parent partnerships, and, in older children, developing effective self-advocacy skills. Strategies need to be tailored to each child's particular type of disability and educational needs (Schiff & Joshi, 2016). Once an **individual education plan** (IEP) is in place, intervention can be accomplished through language re-education;

individual education plan
A contractual document that contains learning and behavioural outcomes for a student, a description of how the outcomes will be achieved, and a description of how the outcomes will be evaluated. Abbreviated *IEP*.

a variety of mixed-ability teaching methods; academic accommodations such as alternative learning and testing methods; development of compensatory skills; and the use of assistive technologies such as computers, spell checkers, and calculators (Learning Disabilities Association of Canada, 2003a, 2003b).

REVIEW IT

Specific Learning Disorder

- **What is specific learning disorder?** Specific learning disorder is characterized by specific deficits in the development of arithmetic, writing, or reading skills.
- **What are the causes of specific learning disorder and approaches to treatment?** The causes remain under study but most probably involve underlying neurobiological brain dysfunctions that make it difficult to process or decode visual and auditory information. Intervention focuses mainly on the remediation and accommodation of specific skill deficits.

Attention-Deficit/Hyperactivity Disorder

attention-deficit/hyperactivity disorder Neurodevelopmental disorder characterized by excessive motor activity, impulsivity, and/or an inability to focus one's attention. Abbreviated *ADHD*.

hyperactivity Abnormal behaviour pattern found most often in young boys that is characterized by extreme restlessness and difficulty maintaining attention.

Many parents believe their children are not attentive toward them—that they run around on whim and do things in their own way. Some inattention, especially in early childhood, is normal enough. In **attention-deficit/hyperactivity disorder** (ADHD), however, children display degrees of impulsivity, inattention, and **hyperactivity** that are considered inappropriate to their developmental levels.

ADHD is divided into three subtypes: a predominantly inattentive type, a predominantly hyperactive or impulsive type, and a combination type characterized by high levels of both inattention and hyperactivity-impulsivity (APA, 2013) (see Table 11.3).

The disorder is usually first diagnosed during elementary school, when problems with attention or hyperactivity-impulsivity make it difficult for the child to adjust to school. Although signs of hyperactivity are often observed earlier, many overactive toddlers do not go on to develop ADHD.

ADHD is far from rare. Canadian studies have found the prevalence rates of ADHD to be between 5% and 10% in children aged 6 to 14 (Romano, Baillargeon, & Tremblay, 2002; Wade, Prime, & Madigan, 2015). Boys were two to three times more likely than girls to be identified as having ADHD, and 6- to 8-year-olds had higher rates than 12- to 14-year-olds. In addition to inattention, associated problems include an inability to sit still for more than a few moments, bullying, temper tantrums, stubbornness, and failure to respond to punishment.

Activity and restlessness impair the ability of children with ADHD to function in school. They seem incapable of sitting still. They fidget and squirm in their seats, butt into other children's games, have outbursts of temper, and may engage in dangerous behaviour, such as running into the street without looking. All in all, they can drive parents and teachers to despair.

Where does "normal" age-appropriate overactivity end and hyperactivity begin? Assessment of the degree of hyperactive behaviour is crucial, because many normal children are called "hyper" from time to time. Some critics of the ADHD diagnosis argue that it merely labels children who are difficult to control as mentally disordered or sick. Most children, especially boys, are highly active during the early school years. Proponents of the diagnosis counter that there is a difference in quality between normal overactivity and ADHD. Normally overactive children are goal directed and can exert voluntary control over their own behaviour. But children with ADHD appear hyperactive without reason and do not seem to be able to conform their behaviour to the demands of teachers and parents. Put another way, most children can sit still and concentrate for a while when they want to; children with ADHD seemingly cannot.

Children with ADHD tend to do more poorly in school than their peers despite being, for the most part, of average or above average intelligence. They may fail to follow or

Diagnostic Criteria for Attention-Deficit/Hyperactivity Disorder (ADHD)

A. A persistent pattern of inattention and/or hyperactivity-impulsivity that interferes with functioning or development, as characterized by (1) and/or (2):

1. **Inattention:** Six (or more) of the following symptoms have persisted for at least 6 months to a degree that is inconsistent with developmental level and that negatively impacts directly on social and academic/occupational activities:

   Note: The symptoms are not solely a manifestation of oppositional behavior, defiance, hostility, or failure to understand tasks or instructions. For older adolescents and adults (age 17 and older), at least five symptoms are required.

   a. Often fails to give close attention to details or makes careless mistakes in schoolwork, at work, or during other activities (e.g., overlooks or misses details, work is inaccurate).

   b. Often has difficulty sustaining attention in tasks or play activities (e.g., has difficulty remaining focused during lectures, conversations, or lengthy reading).

   c. Often does not seem to listen when spoken to directly (e.g., mind seems elsewhere, even in the absence of any obvious distraction).

   d. Often does not follow through on instructions and fails to finish schoolwork, chores, or duties in the workplace (e.g., starts tasks but quickly loses focus and is easily sidetracked).

   e. Often has difficulty organizing tasks and activities (e.g., difficulty managing sequential tasks; difficulty keeping materials and belongings in order; messy, disorganized work; has poor time management; fails to meet deadlines).

   f. Often avoids, dislikes, or is reluctant to engage in tasks that require sustained mental effort (e.g., schoolwork or homework; for older adolescents and adults, preparing reports, completing forms, reviewing lengthy papers).

   g. Often loses things necessary for tasks or activities (e.g., school materials, pencils, books, tools, wallets, keys, paperwork, eyeglasses, mobile telephones).

   h. Is often easily distracted by extraneous stimuli (for older adolescents and adults, may include unrelated thoughts).

   i. Is often forgetful in daily activities (e.g., doing chores, running errands; for older adolescents and adults, returning calls, paying bills, keeping appointments).

2. **Hyperactivity and Impulsivity:** Six (or more) of the following symptoms have persisted for at least 6 months to a degree that is inconsistent with developmental level and that negatively impacts directly on social and academic/occupational activities:

   Note: The symptoms are not solely a manifestation of oppositional behavior, defiance, hostility, or a failure to understand tasks or instructions. For older adolescents and adults (age 17 and older), at least five symptoms are required.

   a. Often fidgets with or taps hands or feet or squirms in seat.

   b. Often leaves seat in situations when remaining seated is expected (e.g., leaves his or her place in the classroom, in the office or other workplace, or in other situations that require remaining in place).

   c. Often runs about or climbs in situations where it is inappropriate. (Note: In adolescents or adults, may be limited to feeling restless.)

   d. Often unable to play or engage in leisure activities quietly.

   e. Is often "on the go," acting as if "driven by a motor" (e.g., is unable to be or uncomfortable being still for extended time, as in restaurants, meetings; may be experienced by others as being restless or difficult to keep up with).

   f. Often talks excessively.

   g. Often blurts out an answer before a question has been completed (e.g., completes people's sentences; cannot wait for turn in conversation).

   h. Often has difficulty waiting his or her turn (e.g., while waiting in line).

   i. Often interrupts or intrudes on others (e.g., butts into conversations, games, or activities; may start using other people's things without asking or receiving permission; for adolescents and adults, may intrude into or take over what others are doing).

B. Several inattentive or hyperactive-impulsive symptoms were present prior to age 12 years.

C. Several inattentive or hyperactive-impulsive symptoms are present in two or more settings (e.g., at home, school, or work; with friends or relatives; in other activities).

D. There is clear evidence that the symptoms interfere with, or reduce the quality of, social, academic, or occupational functioning.

E. The symptoms do not occur exclusively during the course of schizophrenia or another psychotic disorder and are not better explained by another mental disorder (e.g., mood disorder, anxiety disorder, dissociative disorder, personality disorder, substance intoxication or withdrawal).

Source: Reprinted with permission from the *Diagnostic and Statistical Manual of Mental Disorders*, Fifth Edition, (Copyright © 2013). American Psychiatric Association. All Rights Reserved.

remember instructions and complete assignments. They are more likely than their peers to have learning disabilities, to repeat grades, and to be placed in special education classes. Inattention in elementary school leads to poorer educational outcomes in adolescence and early adulthood, including increased risk of failing to complete high school by

Attention Issues: No Disorder

Kai is a seven-year-old boy in Grade 2. His parents describe him as an active and energetic boy who sometimes seems like he has "ants in his pants." He is especially excitable in new situations that are full of stimulation. For example, his teacher has had to talk to him a few times because of his excitability during gym class. He sometimes gets too rough when playing games with his classmates, though his intentions are never aggressive. When he's excited about something, Kai has trouble focusing on anything else. His mom says that it's virtually impossible to get his attention when he's waiting for a friend to come over or just before a birthday party. Sometimes she worries about leaving him at a friend's house in case he gets out of hand. Luckily, this hasn't happened, and Kai continues to be invited on playdates and to parties. Kai's teacher has remarked that he has the ability to focus on lots of things at school, especially activities where he has something to do with his hands. Kai's parents also note that he is able to sit and listen to stories or watch kids' movies.

Attention Issues: ADHD

Behzad is a nine-year-old boy who lives with his parents and two younger siblings. He is in Grade 4 at school and is struggling. He has been identified by his teacher as having attention and behaviour problems at school. On a regular basis, Behzad is removed from the regular classroom because of disruptive behaviour. He constantly interrupts the teacher and other children, he has trouble staying in his seat, and he cannot finish classroom assignments. Behzad's parents have had similar concerns at home. Behzad is very physical with his siblings and sometimes accidentally hurts them. He is especially aggressive when he's frustrated, and it seems that he is increasingly frustrated even when doing things he likes. He has trouble sitting through television shows and is not able to sit and read books. He can sometimes focus on a video game for a sustained period of time, but this seems to be one of the only activities that can consume his attention. Behzad's parents are very worried because his disruptive behaviour and trouble focusing appears to be having a negative impact on his achievement at school. They are also worried that the teachers are beginning to think of him as a "problem" and are removing him from the classroom rather than looking at ways of helping him focus.

early adulthood (Uchida, Spencer, Faraone, & Biederman, 2015). Children with ADHD also stand a greater risk of having depressive disorders, anxiety disorders, and problems getting along with family members. Investigators find that boys with ADHD tend to lack empathy, or awareness of other people's feelings (Braaten & Rosén, 2000). They are frequently disruptive in the classroom and tend to get into fights (especially the boys). Not surprisingly, they are frequently unpopular with their classmates. Although ADHD symptoms tend to decline with age, the disorder often persists into adolescence and adulthood (Uchida et al., 2015). ADHD in adulthood usually takes the form of inattention, problems with working memory, and distractibility rather than hyperactivity (Finke et al., 2011; Gonzalez-Gadea et al., 2013).

THEORETICAL PERSPECTIVES Although the causes of ADHD are not known, both biological and environmental influences are believed to be involved (Wade et al., 2015). Increasing evidence points to a complex genetic vulnerability to ADHD wherein multiple genes have a singularly small, albeit additive, impact (Chang, Lichtenstein, Asherson, & Larsson, 2013; Faraone & Khan, 2006). Hereditary evidence comes from findings of higher concordance rates for ADHD among monozygotic (MZ) twins than dizygotic (DZ) twins, supporting a genetic linkage (Wade et al., 2015).

Neuropsychological testing, EEG studies, and MRI studies of children and adolescents with ADHD point to abnormalities in the areas of the brain involved in regulating the processes of attention, inhibition of motor (movement) behaviour, and executive control (i.e., the ability to focus, plan, and act) (Bush, Valera, & Seidman, 2005; Castellanos, Glaser, & Gerhardt, 2006; Seidman, Valera, & Makris, 2005; Serene, Ashtari, Szeszko, & Kumra, 2007). We shall also see that the effects of stimulants on children with ADHD offer some support to the hypothesis of organic causes. Despite evidence suggestive of biological factors, we lack a definitive biological explanation of ADHD. In fact, some theorists suggest that the mounting evidence from neuropsychological studies challenges the long-held belief that ADHD is a single coherent clinical entity (Stefanatos & Baron, 2007).

ADHD has also been linked with exposure to environmental toxins. Children who have ADHD were found to be 2.5 times more likely than other children to have had prenatal exposure to environmental tobacco smoke (ETS) (Braun, Kahn, Froehlich, Auinger, & Lanphear, 2006). Moreover, a significant dose–response relationship was found: The greater the exposure to ETS, the higher the risk of ADHD, especially for girls. Canadian researchers confirmed the association between prenatal exposure to smoking and also linked ADHD symptoms to lead exposure in children (Arbuckle, Davis, Boylan, Fisher, & Fu, 2016).

TREATMENT It seems odd that the drugs used to help ADHD children calm down and attend better in school belong to a class of stimulants that include Ritalin (methylphenidate) and longer-acting variants, such as Ritalin SR and Concerta. These stimulants have a paradoxical effect of calming down children with ADHD and increasing their attention spans. Although the use of stimulant medication is not without criticism, it is clear that these drugs can help many children with ADHD calm down and concentrate better on tasks and schoolwork, perhaps for the first time in their lives (Van der Oord, Prins, Oosterlaan, & Emmelkamp, 2008). These drugs not only improve attention in ADHD children but also reduce impulsivity, overactivity, and disruptive, annoying, or aggressive behaviour. Stimulant medication appears to be safe and effective when carefully monitored, and it is successful in helping about three out of four children with ADHD ("Attention Deficit Disorder," 1995; Hinshaw, 1992; Spencer et al., 1996). Improvements are noted at home as well as in school. The normal (voluntary) high activity levels shown in physical education classes and on weekends are not disrupted, however.

Annabella Bluesky/Science Source

Attention-deficit/hyperactivity disorder (ADHD).
ADHD is more common in boys than girls and is characterized by attentional difficulties, restlessness, impulsivity, excessive motor behaviour (continuous running around or climbing), and temper tantrums.

It is believed that these drugs work by heightening dopamine and norepinephrine activity in the prefrontal cortex of the brain, the area that regulates attention and control of impulsive behaviour (Storebø et al., 2015). Thus, the drugs may help ADHD children focus their attention and avoid acting out impulsively. Stimulant medication has become so popular that its use increased more than sevenfold during the 1990s (Gibbs, 1998). Currently, an estimated 82 in 1000 Canadian children are using these types of drugs as treatment for ADHD (Romano et al., 2005). The rate of usage climbs from 0.58% in 4- to 5-year-old boys to a peak of 6.31% in 10- to 11-year-old boys. By comparison, girls are much less likely to use these drugs; their highest usage is at age 8 to 9 (1.09%).

Although stimulant medication can help reduce restlessness and increase attention, it is hardly a panacea. Canadian pediatric researchers caution that although Ritalin has a significant short-term effect on the symptoms of ADHD, there is a lack of evidence that demonstrates its usefulness beyond four weeks of treatment. Research is needed to determine its long-term effectiveness (Schachter, Pham, King, Langford, & Moher, 2001). Moreover, no solid evidence has shown that stimulant medication improves academic performance. Uchida and colleagues reported on a longitudinal study that found significant benefits to stimulant treatment. Children with ADHD who received stimulant treatment in childhood had less disruptive behaviour and addictive disorders and were less likely to develop depressive and anxiety disorders than children with ADHD who had not received stimulant treatments (Uchida et al., 2015).

Then there is the question of side effects. Although short-term side effects (e.g., loss of appetite or insomnia) usually subside within a few weeks of treatment or may be eliminated by lowering the dose, concerns have been raised about whether stimulants might retard a child's growth. Although these drugs do slow growth for a few years, researchers found that the drug delays but does not stunt a youngster's growth (Uchida et al., 2015). Health Canada (2006b) posted a drug advisory warning Canadians with high blood pressure, heart disease, and cardiovascular conditions or an overactive thyroid to avoid any stimulant drugs to manage symptoms of ADHD. In rare cases, these drugs can result in cardiac arrest, stroke, or sudden death. A subsequent Health Canada (2006c) information update also indicated the potential for adverse psychiatric effects, such as agitation and hallucinations in children who use ADHD drugs. A more recent advisory (Health Canada, 2015b) warns about the possibility of suicidal thoughts and behaviours with the use of stimulant drugs.

With so many children on Ritalin and similar drugs, critics claim we are too ready to seek a "quick fix" for problem behaviour in children rather than examining other factors contributing to the child's problem, such as dysfunctions in the family (Gibbs, 1998). As one pediatrician put it, "It takes time for parents and teachers to sit down and talk to kids. . . . It takes less time to get a child a pill" (Hancock, 1996, p. 52). Whatever the benefits of stimulant medication, medication alone typically fails to bring the social and academic behaviour of children with ADHD into a normal range (Van der Oord et al., 2008). Drugs cannot teach new skills. Thus, attention has focused on whether a combination of stimulant medication and behavioural or cognitive-behavioural techniques can produce greater benefits than either approach alone. Cognitive-behavioural treatment of ADHD combines behaviour modification, typically based on the use of reinforcement (e.g., a teacher praising the child with ADHD for sitting quietly) and cognitive modification (e.g., training the child to silently talk himself or herself through the steps involved in solving challenging academic problems). Thus far, the evidence favours a combination approach. A McMaster University–based review of 14 studies involving nearly 1400 participants found that a combination of medication and behavioural interventions yielded better outcomes than either type of treatment alone (Schachar et al., 2002).

REVIEW IT

Attention-Deficit/Hyperactivity Disorder

- **What is attention-deficit/hyperactivity disorder?** ADHD is divided into three subtypes: a predominantly inattentive type, a predominantly hyperactive or impulsive type, and a combination type characterized by high levels of both inattention and hyperactivity-impulsivity.

- **How is this disorder treated?** Stimulant medication is generally effective in reducing hyperactivity, but it has not led to general academic gains. Cognitive-behavioural treatments help children with ADHD adapt better to school.

DISRUPTIVE, IMPULSE-CONTROL, AND CONDUCT DISORDERS

Conduct Disorder

conduct disorder Pattern of abnormal behaviour in childhood characterized by disruptive, antisocial behaviour. Abbreviated CD.

Children with **conduct disorder** (CD) purposefully engage in patterns of antisocial behaviour that violate social norms and the rights of others. The symptoms of conduct disorder fall into four categories of behaviours: aggression to people and animals, destruction of property, deceitfulness or theft, and serious violation of rules. Whereas children with ADHD throw temper tantrums, children diagnosed as conduct disordered are intentionally aggressive and cruel. Like antisocial adults, many conduct-disordered children are callous and apparently do not experience guilt or remorse for their misdeeds.

The DSM-5 lists two types of conduct disorder: childhood-onset type (symptoms appear before age 10) and adolescent-onset type. The prevalence of conduct disorder in

Canadian children and youth is estimated to be 4.2% (PHAC, 2009). Conduct disorders are much more common among boys than girls, especially the childhood-onset type (APA, 2013). Conduct disorder typically takes a somewhat different form in boys than girls. In boys, it is more likely to be manifested in stealing, fighting, vandalism, or disciplinary problems at school, whereas in girls the disorder is more likely to involve lying, truancy, running away, substance use, and prostitution (APA, 2013). Although there are differences between ADHD and conduct disorder, some children with conduct disorder also display a pattern of short attention span and hyperactivity that may justify a double diagnosis.

Children with conduct disorder often present with other disorders aside from ADHD, such as major depression and substance use disorders (Conner & Lochman, 2010). Other commonly found traits include callousness (being uncaring, mean, and cruel), an unemotional way of relating to others, and a lack of empathy (Kostić, Nešić, Stanković, Žikić, & Marković, 2016). Conduct disorder is typically a chronic or persistent disorder (Lahey et al., 1995). Longitudinal studies show that Canadian elementary schoolchildren with conduct disorders are more likely than other children to engage in delinquent acts as early adolescents (Lacourse, 2012). Childhood-onset conduct disorder is also linked to antisocial behaviour and the development of antisocial personality disorder in adulthood (Burke, Waldam, & Lahey, 2010).

oppositional defiant disorder Disorder in childhood or adolescence characterized by excessive oppositionality or tendencies to refuse requests from parents and others.

Oppositional Defiant Disorder

Children with **oppositional defiant disorder** (ODD) display a pattern of behaviours that fall into three categories of symptoms: angry/irritable mood, argumentative/defiant behaviour, and vindictiveness (APA, 2013). In comparison to conduct disorder, ODD is more closely related to nondelinquent (negativistic) conduct disturbance, whereas conduct disorder involves more outright delinquent behaviour in the form of truancy, stealing, lying, and aggressiveness (Rey, 1993). University of British Columbia researchers have found a strong association between oppositional defiant disorder symptoms and generalized anxiety symptoms in preadolescent children (Garland & Garland, 2001). More recent Canadian research found that ODD symptoms in the angry/irritable mood category predicted higher levels of depression and anxiety in children at a two-year follow-up. This association was not found with ODD symptoms in the argumentative/defiant behaviour and vindictiveness categories (Déry et al., 2017).

Children with ODD tend to be negativistic or oppositional. They are defiant of authority, which is exhibited by their tendency to argue with parents and teachers and refuse to follow requests or directives from adults. They may deliberately annoy other people, become easily angered or lose their temper, become touchy or easily annoyed, blame others for their mistakes or misbehaviour, feel resentful toward others, or act in spiteful or vindictive ways toward others (Angold & Costello, 1996; APA, 2013). The disorder typically begins before age eight and develops gradually over a period of months or years. It typically starts in the home environment but may extend to other settings, such as school.

ODD is one of the most common diagnoses among children (Doll, 1996). Studies show that among children diagnosed with a psychological disorder, about one in three are judged to meet the criteria for ODD (Rey, 1993). An

Eric Larrayadieu/The Image Bank/Getty Images

Oppositional defiant disorder (ODD). A common childhood disorder that engenders a "no-win" situation for everyone concerned.

estimated 6–12% of school-aged children display ODD (Frick & Silverthorn, 2001). ODD is more common overall among boys than girls. However, this overall effect masks a gender shift over age. Among children 12 years of age or younger, ODD appears to be more than twice as common among boys; yet among adolescents, a higher prevalence is reported in girls (Rey, 1993). By contrast, most studies find conduct disorder to be more common in boys than girls across all age groups. A meta-analysis of the literature across a wide range of countries (including Spain, Ethiopia, the United States, Great Britain, India, Germany, Korea, and others) revealed that gender differences in rates of ODD only occur in Western cultures (Demmer, Hooley, Sheen, McGillivray, & Lum, 2017). The authors speculate that cultures with more traditional sex roles may be less tolerant of girls who display ODD behaviours, which may result in increased diagnosis of girls compared to Western cultures.

THEORETICAL PERSPECTIVES   The causal factors in ODD remain obscure. Some theorists believe that oppositionality is an expression of an underlying child temperament described as the "difficult-child" type (Rey, 1993). Learning theorists view oppositional behaviours as arising from parental use of inappropriate reinforcement strategies. In this view, parents may inappropriately reinforce oppositional behaviour by "giving in" to the child's demands whenever the child refuses to comply with the parents' wishes, which can become a pattern.

McMaster University researchers have found that family and parenting factors are implicated in the development of disruptive behaviour disorders such as oppositional defiant disorder and conduct disorder (Cunningham & Boyle, 2002). Some forms of disruptive behaviour disorders appear to be linked to unassertive and ineffective parenting styles, such as failure to provide positive reinforcement for appropriate behaviour and use of harsh and inconsistent discipline for misbehaviour. Families of children with conduct disorder tend to be characterized by negative, coercive interactions (Lacourse, 2012). Children with conduct disorder are often demanding and noncompliant in relating to their parents and other family members. Family members often reciprocate by using negative behaviours, such as threatening or yelling at the child or using physical means of coercion. Parental aggression against children with conduct behaviour problems is common, including pushing, grabbing, slapping, spanking, hitting, or kicking (Jouriles, Mehta, McDonald, & Francis, 1997). Parents of children with oppositional defiant disorder or severe conduct disorder display high rates of antisocial personality disorder and substance abuse (Frick et al., 1992). It's not too much of a stretch to speculate that parental modelling of antisocial behaviours can lead to antisocial conduct in their children. Other risk factors that have been identified include hyperactivity/inattention, nonintact family, family mobility, coercive/ineffective parenting, and affiliation with deviant peers (Lacourse, 2012; Lacourse et al., 2010).

Some investigations focus on the ways in which children with disruptive behaviour disorders process information (Crozier et al., 2008). For example, children who are overly aggressive in their behaviour tend to be biased in their processing of social information: They may assume that others intend them ill when they do not. They usually blame others for the scrapes they get into. They believe they are misperceived and treated unfairly and that aggression will lead to favourable results (Dodge, Lochman, Hamish, Bates, & Pettit, 1997). They are also less able than their peers to generate alternative (nonviolent) responses to social conflicts (Lochman & Dodge, 1994).

Genetic factors may interact with family or other environmental factors in the development of conduct disorder in children and antisocial behaviour in adolescence (Kendler, Aggen, & Patrick, 2013). Genetic factors may also be involved in the development of oppositional defiant disorder.

TREATMENT   The treatment of conduct disorders remains a challenge. Although there is not an established pharmacological treatment approach, Toronto psychiatrist Lindley Bassarath (2003) reviewed studies that indicate that certain antipsychotic and stimulant drugs may be effective in reducing antisocial behaviour in children and adolescents with conduct disorder. However, according to Canadian guidelines that have been developed on pharmacotherapy for these disorders, stimulant medication should only be prescribed if psychosocial interventions have not been successful (Gorman et al., 2015). Evidence supports the use of these medications in cases where the disruptive and aggressive behaviours occur in children who also meet the diagnositic criteria for ADHD (Gorman et al., 2015). In children without ADHD, the recommended treatments are psychosocial interventions such as parent training, affect regulation, interpersonal and social-skills training, family therapy, and cognitive-behaviour therapy (Scotto Rosato et al., 2012).

Many children with conduct disorders, especially boys, display aggressive behaviour and have problems controlling their anger. Many can benefit from programs designed to help them learn anger-coping skills they can use to handle conflict situations without resorting to violent behaviour. Cognitive-behavioural therapy has been used to teach boys who engage in antisocial and aggressive behaviour to reconceptualize social provocations as problems to be solved rather than as challenges to their manhood that must be answered with violence. They have been trained to use calming self-talk to inhibit impulsive behaviour and control anger whenever they experience social taunts or provocations and to generate and try out nonviolent solutions to social conflicts (Lochman & Lenhart, 1993; Scotto Rosato et al., 2012). Other programs present child models on video demonstrating skills of anger control. The results of these programs appear promising (Kazdin & Weisz, 1998; Webster-Stratton & Hammond, 1997).

The following example illustrates the involvement of the parents in the behavioural treatment of a case of oppositional defiant disorder:

Dimitry was a seven-year-old second-grader referred by his parents. The family relocated frequently because the father was in the navy. Dimitry usually behaved when his father was taking care of him, but he was noncompliant with his mother and yelled at her when she gave him instructions. His mother was incurring great stress in the effort to control Dimitry, especially when her husband was at sea.

Dimitry had become a problem at home and in school during Grade 1. He ignored and violated rules in both settings. Dimitry failed to carry out his chores and frequently yelled at and hit his younger brother. When he acted up, his parents would restrict him to his room or the yard, take away privileges and toys, and spank him. But all of these measures were used inconsistently. He also played on the railroad tracks near his home and twice the police had brought him home after he had thrown rocks at cars.

A home observation showed that Dimitry's mother often gave him inappropriate commands. She interacted with him as little as possible and showed no verbal praise, physical closeness, smiles, or positive facial expressions or gestures. She paid attention to him only when he misbehaved. When Dimitry was noncompliant, she would yell back at him and then try to catch him to force him to comply. Dimitry would then laugh and run from her.

Dimitry's parents were informed that the child's behavior was a product of inappropriate cueing techniques (poor directions), a lack of reinforcement for appropriate behavior, and lack of consistent sanctions for misbehavior. They were taught the appropriate use of reinforcement, punishment, and **time out**. The parents then charted Dimitry's problem behaviors to gain a clearer idea of what triggered and maintained them. They were shown how to reinforce acceptable behavior and use time out as a contingent punishment for misbehavior. Dimitry's mother was also taught relaxation training to help desensitize her to Dimitry's disruptions. Biofeedback was used to enhance the relaxation response.

During a 15-day baseline period, Dimitry behaved in a noncompliant manner about four times per day. When treatment was begun, Dimitry showed an immediate drop to about one instance of noncompliance every two days. Follow-up data showed that instances of noncompliance were maintained at a bearable level of about one per day. Fewer behavioral problems in school were also reported, even though they had not been addressed directly.

Republished with permission of Springer Science & Business Media, from *The Private Practice of Behavior Therapy: A Guide for Behavioral Practitioners*, Sheldon J. Kaplan, 1986; permission conveyed through Copyright Clearance Center, Inc.

time out Behavioural technique in which an individual who emits an undesired behaviour is removed from an environment in which reinforcers are available and placed in an unreinforcing environment for a period of time as a form of punishment. Time out is frequently used in behavioural programs for modifying behaviour problems in children, in combination with positive reinforcement for desirable behaviour.

In Canada, as in most other industrialized nations, the emphasis is more on treatment than prevention. This usually means that by the time a conduct-disordered youth gets into care, his or her problem behaviour is well established and therefore more resistant and more expensive to treat. A failure to implement effective prevention programs may have more to do with short-sighted political agendas and rigid service-delivery systems than it does with program costs or a lack of desire to serve long-term needs to prevent future conduct-disordered youth (Moretti et al., 1997).

REVIEW IT

Disruptive, Impulse-Control, and Conduct Disorders

- **What are disruptive, impulse-control, and conduct disorders?** Children with conduct disorder intentionally engage in antisocial behaviour. Children with oppositional defiant disorder (ODD) show negativistic or oppositional behaviour but not the outright delinquent or antisocial behaviour that is characteristic of conduct

disorder. However, ODD may represent an early stage of development of conduct disorder.

- **How are these disorders treated?** Behaviour therapy and other psychosocial interventions may be helpful in modifying behaviours of children with conduct disorder or oppositional defiant disorder.

Stockfour/Shutterstock

Separation anxiety disorder. It is common for young children to have difficulty separating from a parent, but extreme fears of separation in school-aged children may be problematic.

ANXIETY AND DEPRESSION IN CHILDHOOD AND ADOLESCENCE

Anxieties and fears are a normal feature of childhood, just as they are a normal feature of adult life. Childhood fears—of the dark or of small animals—are commonplace and are usually outgrown naturally. Anxiety is considered abnormal, however, when it is excessive and interferes with normal academic or social functioning or becomes troubling or persistent. Children, like adults, may suffer from different types of diagnosable anxiety disorders, including specific phobias, social phobias, and generalized anxiety disorder. Although these disorders may develop at any age, we will consider a type of anxiety disorder that typically develops during early childhood: separation anxiety disorder.

Despite the stereotype of a happy childhood, clinical depression is found in children and adolescents. Among Canadian children aged 12 to 17 years, 5% of girls and 2.8% of boys report having a diagnosed depressive disorder (Hudon, 2017). Major depression has even been found, although rarely, among preschoolers. Although there is no discernible gender difference in the risk of depression in childhood, a prominent gender difference appears after the age of 15, with adolescent girls becoming about twice as likely to become depressed as adolescent boys (Bilginer & Kandil, 2016; Pearson, Janz, & Ali, 2013). Nationwide surveys have revealed that, of Canadian youth aged 15 to 18 years, 6.5% have had a major depression and 11.2% have had suicidal thoughts (Findlay, 2017).

Separation Anxiety Disorder

It is normal for children to show anxiety when they are separated from their caregivers (Ainsworth & Bowlby, 1991). Mary Ainsworth (1989), who has chronicled the development of attachment behaviours, notes that separation anxiety is a normal feature of the child–caregiver relationship and begins during the first year of life. The sense of security normally provided by bonds of attachment apparently encourages children to explore their environments and become progressively independent of their caregivers (Bowlby, 1988).

Separation anxiety disorder is diagnosed when separation anxiety is persistent and excessive or inappropriate for the child's developmental level. That is, three-year-olds ought to be able to attend preschool without nausea and vomiting brought on by anxiety. Six-year-olds ought to be able to attend Grade 1 without persistent dread that something awful will happen to themselves or their parents. Children with this disorder tend to cling to their parents and follow them around the house. They may voice concerns about death and dying and insist that someone stay with them while they are falling asleep. Other features of the disorder include nightmares, stomach aches, nausea and vomiting when separation is anticipated (as on school days), pleading with parents not to leave, or throwing tantrums when parents are about to depart. Children may refuse to attend school for fear that something will happen to their parents while they are away. The disorder affects about 4% of children and young adolescents and occurs more frequently, according to community-based studies, among females (APA, 2013). The disorder may persist into adulthood, leading to an exaggerated concern about the well-being of one's children and spouse and difficulty tolerating any separation from them.

The development of separation anxiety disorder frequently follows a stressful life event, such as illness, the death of a relative or pet, or a change of schools or homes. Richa's problems followed the death of her grandmother:

separation anxiety disorder
Childhood disorder characterized by extreme fears of separation from parents or others on whom the child is dependent.

Richa's grandmother died when Richa was seven years old. Her parents decided to permit her request to view her grandmother in the open coffin. Richa took a tentative glance from her father's arms across the room, then asked to be taken out of the room. Her five-year-old sister took a leisurely close-up look, with no apparent distress.

Richa had been concerned about death for two or three years by this time, but her grandmother's passing brought on a new flurry of questions: "Will I die?" "Does everybody die?" and so on. Her parents tried to reassure her by saying, "Grandma was very, very old, and she also had a heart condition. You are very young and in perfect health. You have many, many years before you have to start thinking about death."

Richa also could not be alone in any room in her house. She pulled one of her parents or her sister along with her everywhere she went. She also reported nightmares about her grandmother and, within a couple of days, insisted on sleeping in the same room with her parents. Fortunately, Richa's fears did not extend to school. Her teacher reported that Richa spent some time talking about her grandmother, but her academic performance was apparently unimpaired.

Richa's parents decided to allow Richa time to "get over" the loss. Richa gradually talked less and less about death, and by the time three months had passed, she was able to go into any room in her house by herself. She wanted to continue to sleep in her parents' bedroom, however, so her parents "made a deal" with her. They would put off the return to her own bedroom until the school year had ended (a month away) if Richa would agree to return to her own bed at that time. As a further incentive, a parent would remain with her until she fell asleep for the first month. Richa overcame the anxiety problem in this fashion with no additional delays.

The Authors' Files

Perspectives on Anxiety Disorders in Childhood

Theoretical understandings of excessive anxiety in children to some degree parallel explanations of anxiety disorders in adults. Psychoanalytic theorists argue that childhood anxieties and fears, like their adult counterparts, symbolize unconscious conflicts. Cognitive theorists focus on the role of cognitive biases underlying anxiety reactions. In support of the cognitive model, investigators find that highly anxious children show cognitive biases in processing information, such as interpreting ambiguous situations as threatening, expecting negative outcomes, thinking poorly of themselves and of their ability to cope, and engaging in negative self-talk (Micco, Hirshfeld-Becker, Henin, & Ehrenreich-May, 2013). Expecting the worst, combined with low self-confidence, encourages avoidance of feared activities—with friends, in school, and elsewhere. Negative expectations may also heighten feelings of anxiety to the point where they impede performance. Learning theorists suggest that the occurrence of generalized anxiety may touch on broad themes, such as fears of rejection or failure, that carry across situations. Underlying fears of rejection or self-perceptions of inadequacy may generalize to most areas of social interaction and achievement.

Depression in Childhood and Adolescence

The basic features of depression in children and adolescents are similar to those in adults. Depressed children and adolescents typically show a greater sense of hopelessness, display more cognitive errors and negative attributions (e.g., blaming themselves for negative events), have lower perceived competence or self-efficacy, and have lower self-esteem than do their nondepressed peers (Maughan, Collishaw, & Stringaris, 2013). They often report episodes of sadness, crying, and apathy as well as insomnia, fatigue, and poor appetite. They may refuse to attend school, express fears of their parents' dying, and cling to their parents or retreat to their rooms. They may have suicidal thoughts or attempt suicide.

Moderate levels of depression may persist for years, severely impacting school performance and social functioning (Bilginer & Kandil, 2016). Adolescent depression is associated with an increased risk of future major depressive episodes and suicide attempts in adulthood (Maughan et al., 2013). About 50–70% of children who become depressed from age 8 to 13 have a recurrence later in life (Maughan et al., 2013).

Children who experience depression may also lack skills in various domains, including academic performance, social acceptance by peers, and athletic performance (Seroczynski, Cole, & Maxwell, 1997). They may find it hard to concentrate in school and may suffer from impaired memory, making it difficult for them to keep their grades up (Goleman, 1994).

Childhood depression rarely occurs by itself. Depressed children typically experience other psychological disorders, especially anxiety disorders and conduct or oppositional defiant disorders (Bilginer & Kandil, 2016). Eating disorders are also common among depressed adolescents, at least among females (Ackard, Fulkerson, & Neumark-Sztainer, 2011; Stankovska, Osmani, Pandilovska, & Dimitrovski, 2015). Overall, childhood depression increases the chances that a child will develop another psychological disorder by at least twentyfold (Angold & Costello, 1993).

Shyamalamuralinath/Shutterstock

Is this child too young to be depressed? Although we tend to think of childhood as the happiest and most carefree time of life, depression is actually quite common among children and adolescents. Depressed children may report feelings of sadness and lack of interest in previously enjoyable activities. Many, however, do not report or are not aware of feelings of depression, even though they may look depressed to observers. Depression may also be masked by other problems, such as conduct/school-related problems, physical complaints, and overactivity.

We should recognize that depressed children or adolescents may fail to label what they are feeling as depression. Further, conduct disorders, academic problems, physical complaints, and even hyperactivity may stem now and then from unrecognized depression (Bilginer & Kandil, 2016). Among adolescents, aggressive and sexual acting out may also be signs of underlying depression.

CORRELATES AND TREATMENT OF DEPRESSION IN CHILDHOOD AND ADOLESCENCE
As children mature and their cognitive abilities increase, however, cognitive factors, such as attributional styles, appear to play a stronger role in the development of depression (Chan, 2012). Older children (aged 12 to 15 years) who adopt a more helpless or pessimistic explanatory style (attributing negative events to internal, stable, and global causes and attributing positive events to external, unstable, and specific causes) are more likely than children with a more optimistic explanatory style to develop depression (Rueger & George, 2017). Researchers also find that adolescents who are depressed tend to hold more dysfunctional attitudes and to adopt a more helpless explanatory style than their nondepressed peers. Genetic factors also appear to play a role in explaining depressive symptoms in children and adolescents (Michalek et al., 2017).

Adolescent girls tend to show greater levels of depressive symptoms than adolescent boys, a finding that mirrors the gender gap in depression among adults (Hudon, 2017; Stewart et al., 2004). Girls who adopt a more passive, ruminative style of coping (brooding and obsessing about their problems) may be at a greater risk of developing depression.

Evidence supports the effectiveness of cognitive-behavioural therapy (CBT) in treating depression in childhood and adolescence (Chorpita et al., 2011; Ebert et al., 2015). Although individual approaches vary, CBT usually involves a coping-skills model in which children or adolescents receive social-skills training (e.g., learning how to start a conversation or make friends) to increase the likelihood of obtaining social reinforcement (Kazdin & Weisz, 1998). In addition, family therapy may be useful in helping families resolve underlying conflicts and reorganize their relationships so that members can become more supportive of each other.

Studies reviewing the benefits of antidepressants for the treatment of depression in youth have yielded mixed results (Cheung, Emslie, & Mayes, 2005; Spielmans & Gerwig, 2014). We cannot assume drugs that may be effective with adults will work as well or be as safe when used with children. Canadian researcher Garland and colleagues recommend caution in the use of antidepressants with children and youth in light of the limited evidence of their effectiveness and the risk of serious side effects. Their use, however, may be warranted for moderate to severe depression with stringent monitoring (Garland, Kutcher, Virani, & Elbe, 2016).

Suicide among Children and Adolescents

Suicide is relatively uncommon among children under the age of 10 in Canada. However, for youth aged 10 to 19 years, suicide is the second leading cause of death following traffic fatalities, accounting for almost one in five deaths (Butler & Pang, 2014). The rates of suicide climb with age, rising from 1.9 in 100 000 between the ages of 10 and 14 years to 7.7 in 100 000 between the ages of 15 and 19 (Statistics Canada, 2017a). Among youth aged 15 years and over, the rates are greater for males than females. It is estimated that the rates are five to seven times greater for First Nations youth, at 30 per 100 000 for males and 25.5 per 100 000 for females (Statistics Canada, 2016a). These official statistics account only for reported suicide; some apparently accidental deaths may be suicides as well. The Organisation for Economic Co-operation and Development (OECD) ranked the rate of suicide for youth aged 15 to 19 years per 100 000 population across 33 countries. Canada had the sixth highest rate of suicide, following Poland, Slovenia, Finland, Ireland, and New Zealand. The country with the lowest rate of teenage suicide was Greece (see Figure 11.1) (OECD, 2016).

Despite the commonly held view that children and adolescents who talk about suicide are only venting their feelings, young people who do intend to kill themselves may very well talk about it beforehand (Bongar, 2002). In fact, those who discuss their plans are

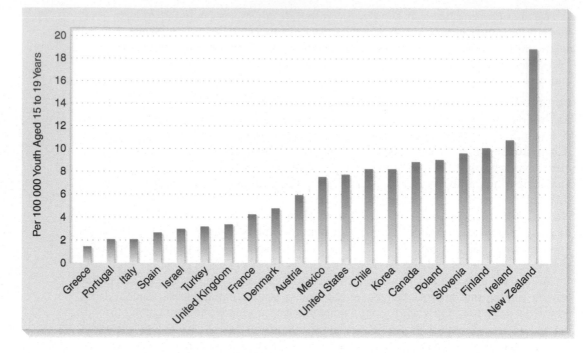

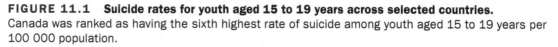

FIGURE 11.1 Suicide rates for youth aged 15 to 19 years across selected countries.
Canada was ranked as having the sixth highest rate of suicide among youth aged 15 to 19 years per 100 000 population.

Source: Based on data from OECD Family Database http://www.oecd.org/els/family/database.htm (01 Sep, 2017)

the ones most likely to carry them out. Moreover, children and adolescents who have survived suicide attempts are most likely to try again (Brody, 1992). Unfortunately, parents tend not to take their children's suicidal talk seriously. They often refuse treatment for their children or terminate treatment prematurely.

Several factors are associated with an increased risk of suicide among children and adolescents:

1. *Gender.* Girls, like women, are three times more likely than boys to attempt suicide. Boys, like men, are more likely to succeed, however, perhaps because boys, like men, are more apt to use lethal means, such as guns. The presence of a loaded handgun in the house turns out to be the greatest risk factor for suicide deaths among children, even those as young as five (Wolfe, Foxwell, & Kennard, 2014).
2. *Age.* Young people in late adolescence or early adulthood (ages 15 to 24) are at greater risk than younger adolescents (Statistics Canada, 2017a).
3. *Ethnicity.* The suicide rate for Canadian Indigenous youth is five to seven times higher than for youth in the general population (Statistics Canada, 2016a). The rates of suicide in some First Nations communities are among the highest in the world ("Federal Paternalism," 1999).
4. *Depression and hopelessness.* Depression and hopelessness, especially when combined with low self-esteem, are major risk factors for suicide among adolescents, as for adults (Wolfe et al., 2014).
5. *Previous suicidal behaviour.* A quarter of adolescents who attempt suicide are repeaters. More than 80% of adolescents who take their lives have talked about it before doing so. Suicidal teenagers may carry lethal weapons, talk about death, make suicide plans, or engage in risky or dangerous behaviour. A family history of suicide also increases risk of teenage suicide (Mann, Underwood, & Arango, 1996).
6. *Family problems.* Family problems are present among about 75% of adolescent suicide attempters. Problems include family instability and conflict, physical or sexual abuse, loss of a parent because of death or separation, and poor parent–child communication (Castellvi et al., 2017; Rice & Tan, 2017).

7. *Stressful life events.* Many suicides among young people are directly preceded by stressful or traumatic events, such as the breakup of a relationship, unwanted pregnancy, getting arrested, having problems at school, moving to a new school, or having to take an important test (Wolfe et al., 2014).

8. *Substance abuse.* Addiction in the adolescent's family or by the adolescent is a factor in suicide (Pompili et al., 2012; Thompson, Alonzo, Hu, & Hasin, 2017).

9. *Social contagion.* Adolescent suicides sometimes occur in clusters, especially when a suicide or a group of suicides receives widespread publicity (Easson, Agarwal, Duda, & Bennett, 2014; Zimmerman, Rees, Posick, & Zimmerman, 2016). Adolescents may romanticize suicide as a heroic act of defiance. There are often suicides or attempts among the siblings, friends, parents, or adult relatives of suicidal adolescents. Note the case of Alexandra:

Alexandra was an exceptionally attractive 17-year-old who was hospitalized after cutting her wrists.

"Before we moved to [an upper-middle-class US town in Westchester County]," she told the psychologist, "I was the brightest girl in the class. Teachers loved me. If we had had a yearbook, I'd have been the most likely to succeed. Then we moved, and suddenly I was hit with it. Everybody was bright, or tried to be. Suddenly I was just another ordinary student planning to go to college.

"Teachers were good to me, but I was no longer special, and that hurt. Then we all applied to college. Do you know that 90% of the kids in the high school go on to college? I mean four-year colleges? And we all knew—or suspected—that the good schools had quotas on kids from here. I mean you can't have 30 kids from our senior class going to Yale or Princeton or Wellesley, can you? You're better off applying from Utah.

"Then Carmen got her early-acceptance rejection from Brown. Carmen was number one in the class. Nobody could believe it. Her father had gone to Brown and Carmen had scored almost 1500 on her SATs. Carmen was out of commission for a few days—I mean she didn't come to school or anything—and then, boom, she was gone. She offed herself, kaput, no more, the end. Then Brian was rejected from Cornell. A few days later, he was gone, too. And I'm like, 'These kids were better than me.' I mean their grades and their SATs were higher than mine, and I was going to apply to Brown and Cornell. I'm like, 'What chance do I have? Why bother?'"

The Authors' Files

You can identify how catastrophizing cognitions can play a role in such tragic cases. Consistent with the literature on suicide among adults, suicidal children and adolescents make less use of active problem-solving strategies in handling stressful situations. They may see no other way out of their perceived failures or stresses. As with adults, one approach to working with suicidal children and adolescents involves helping them challenge distorted thinking and generate alternative strategies for handling the problems and stressors they face.

REVIEW IT

Anxiety, Depression, and Suicide

- **What types of anxiety disorders affect children?** Anxiety disorders that occur commonly among children and adolescents include specific phobias, social anxiety disorder, and generalized anxiety disorder. Children may also show separation anxiety disorder, which involves excessive anxiety at times when they are separated from their parents. Cognitive biases such as expecting negative outcomes, negative self-talk, and interpreting ambiguous situations as threatening figure prominently in anxiety disorders in children and adolescents, as they often do among adults.

(Continued)

- **What are the distinguishing features of depression in childhood and adolescence?** Depressed children, especially younger children, may not report or be aware of feeling depressed. Depression may also be masked by seemingly unrelated behaviours, such as conduct disorders. Depressed children also tend to show cognitive biases associated with depression in adulthood, such as adoption of a pessimistic explanatory style and distorted thinking. Although rare, suicide in children does occur and threats should be taken seriously. Risk factors for adolescent suicide include gender, age, geography, race, depression, past suicidal behaviour, strained family relationships, stress, substance abuse, and social contagion.

NEUROCOGNITIVE DISORDERS

Neurocognitive disorders are diagnosed based on deficits in cognitive functioning that represent a marked change from the individual's prior level of functioning. Neurocognitive disorders are not psychologically based; they are caused by physical or medical diseases, or drug use or withdrawal that affects the brain's functioning. These disorders arise when the brain is either damaged or impaired in its ability to function because of injury, illness, exposure to toxins, or use or abuse of psychoactive drugs. The more widespread the damage to the brain, the greater and more extensive the impairment in functioning. The extent and location of brain damage largely determine the range and severity of impairment. The location of the damage is also critical because many brain structures or regions perform specialized functions. In some cases, the specific cause of the neurocognitive disorder can be pinpointed; in others, it cannot. Although these disorders are biologically based, psychological and environmental factors play key roles in determining the impact and range of disabling symptoms as well as the individual's ability to cope with them. DSM-5 classifies neurocognitive disorders into three types: delirium, major neurocognitive disorders, and mild neurocognitive disorders.

Delirium

The word *delirium* derives from the Latin roots *de-*, meaning "from," and *lira*, meaning "line" or "furrow." It means straying from the line or the norm in perception, cognition, and behaviour. Delirium is a state of extreme mental confusion in which people have difficulty focusing their attention, speaking clearly and coherently, and orienting themselves to the environment (see Table 11.4). People suffering from delirium may find it difficult to tune out irrelevant stimuli or to shift their attention to new tasks. They may speak excitedly, but their speech conveys little—if any—meaning. Disorientation as to time (not knowing the current date, day of the week, or time) and place (not knowing where one is) is common. Disorientation to person (the identities of oneself and others) is not. People in a state of delirium may experience terrifying hallucinations, especially visual hallucinations. The severity of symptoms tends to fluctuate during the course of the day (APA, 2013).

Disturbances in perceptions often occur, such as misinterpretations of sensory stimuli (e.g., confusing an alarm clock for a fire bell) or illusions (e.g., feeling as if the bed has an electrical charge passing through it). There can be a dramatic slowing down of movement into a state resembling catatonia. There may be rapid fluctuations between restlessness and stupor. Restlessness is characterized by insomnia and agitated, aimless movements, even bolting out of bed or striking out at nonexistent objects. This may alternate with periods in which the person has to struggle to stay awake.

There are many causes of delirium, including head trauma; metabolic disorders, such as hypoglycemia (low blood sugar); underlying medical conditions such as severe infections or heart failure; drug abuse or withdrawal; fluid or electrolyte imbalances; seizure disorders (epilepsy); deficiencies of the B vitamin thiamine; brain lesions; stroke and diseases affecting the central nervous system, including Parkinson's disease; viral

A. A disturbance in attention (i.e., reduced ability to direct, focus, sustain, and shift attention) and awareness (reduced orientation to the environment).

B. The disturbance develops over a short period of time (usually hours to a few days), represents a change from baseline attention and awareness, and tends to fluctuate in severity during the course of a day.

C. An additional disturbance in cognition (e.g., memory deficit, disorientation, language, visuospatial ability, or perception).

D. The disturbances in Criteria A and C are not better explained by another preexisting, established, or evolving neurocognitive disorder and do not occur in the context of a severely reduced level of arousal, such as coma.

E. There is evidence from the history, physical examination, or laboratory findings that the disturbance is a direct physiological consequence of another medical condition, substance intoxication or withdrawal (i.e., due to a drug of abuse or to a medication), or exposure to a toxin, or is due to multiple etiologies.

Source: Reprinted with permission from the *Diagnostic and Statistical Manual of Mental Disorders*, Fifth Edition, (Copyright © 2013). American Psychiatric Association. All Rights Reserved.

---

encephalitis (a type of brain infection); liver disease; and kidney disease (Bondi & Lange, 2000; Oldenbeuving et al., 2011).

The prevalence of delirium is estimated at about 1–2% in the general community, but rises to 14% among people over the age of 85 (Inouye, 2006). Delirium most often affects hospitalized patients, especially elderly hospitalized patients following surgical operations (Choi et al., 2012; Day et al., 2012). Between 15% and 50% of elderly patients experience delirium following major surgery (Marcantonio, 2012). Delirium may also occur because of exposure to toxic substances (such as eating certain poisonous mushrooms), as a side effect of using certain medications, or during states of drug or alcohol intoxication. Among young people, delirium is most commonly the result of abrupt withdrawal from psychoactive drugs, especially alcohol. However, among older patients, it is often a sign of a life-threatening medical condition (Inouye, 2006).

People with chronic alcoholism who abruptly stop drinking may experience a form of delirium called *delirium tremens*, or DTs (see Chapter 7). During an acute episode of the DTs, the person may be terrorized by wild and frightening hallucinations, such as "bugs crawling down walls" or on the skin. The DTs can last for a week or more and are best treated in a hospital, where the patient can be carefully monitored and the symptoms treated with mild tranquillizers and environmental support. Although there are many known causes of delirium, in many cases the specific cause cannot be identified.

Whatever the cause may be, delirium involves a widespread disruption of brain activity, possibly resulting from imbalances in the levels of certain neurotransmitters (Inouye, 2006). As a result, the person may be unable to process incoming information, leading to a state of general confusion. The person may not be able to speak or think clearly or to make sense of his or her surroundings. States of delirium may occur abruptly, as in cases resulting from seizures or head injuries, or gradually over hours or days, as in cases involving infections, fever, or metabolic disorders. During the course of delirium, the person's mental state often fluctuates between periods of clarity ("lucid intervals"), which are most common in the morning, and periods of confusion and disorientation. Delirium is generally worse in the dark and following sleepless nights.

Unlike dementia or other forms of major neurocognitive disorder (discussed below) in which there is a gradual deterioration of mental functioning, delirium develops rapidly, generally in a few hours to a few days and involves more clearly disturbed processes of attention and awareness (Wong, Holroyd-Leduc, Simel, & Straus, 2010).

DIAGNOSIS In order to properly diagnose delirium, several measures are typically used. Initially, cognitive impairment is identified with instruments such as the Mini–Mental

TABLE 11.6

Distinguishing Features of Depression, Dementia, and Delirium

Features	Depression	Delirium	Dementia
Onset	Weeks to months (rapid)	Hours to days (acute)	Months to years (slow, indefinite)
Duration	Short	Variable	Long/lifetime
Mood	Consistent	Labile	Fluctuation
Disabilities	Recognizes	New disabilities appear (acute)	May conceal deficits
Answers	"Don't know"	May be incoherent (acute)	Offers response but not correct, but may be close to correct
MMSE	Performance fluctuates	Acute fluctuations	Fairly stable with downward trajectory over time
Progression	Resolves with treatment	Resolves with treatment	Ongoing

Source: From Deciphering the four D's: cognitive decline, delerium, dementia and depression. J of Advanced Nursing, Michel Hersen,Terry A Badger, © 2002 Reproduced with permission of John Wiley & Sons, Inc.

State Examination (MMSE) (Folstein, Folstein, & McHugh, 1975) (see Table 11.5 for sample questions used in this exam). Following this, a rating scale is used to determine the actual symptoms experienced and the type of onset of these symptoms. Formal delirium diagnosis requires documentation of acute onset and fluctuant course. The Delirium Rating Scale (DRS) (Trzepacz, Baker, & Greenhouse, 1998) is the most widely used scale to date, and although it requires interpretation by a skilled clinician, it has the significant advantage of distinguishing between the disturbances of depression, delirium, and dementia (see Table 11.6 for further details on distinguishing among these three diagnoses). The DRS is performed by a skilled clinician, who then also applies the DSM or ICD criteria for the full picture of dysfunction.

TREATMENT AND OUTCOMES Since most cases of delirium are reversible, the underlying causes, whether medical or injury, must be identified immediately. Treatment typically involves medication, environment changes, and family support (APA, 2013). The medications most widely used are neuroleptics (Fricchione et al., 2008).

In some cases the individual recovers naturally, without intervention. In others, treatment is effective or the individual develops a progressive neurological deficit or dies from an underlying physical condition.

REVIEW IT

Delirium

- **What is delirium?** Delirium is a state of extreme mental confusion in which people have difficulty focusing their attention, speaking clearly and coherently, and orienting themselves to the environment. People in a state of delirium may experience terrifying hallucinations, especially visual hallucinations. The severity of symptoms tends to fluctuate during the course of the day.

Major Neurocognitive Disorder (Dementia)

Major neurocognitive disorder (commonly called **dementia**) represents a profound decline or deterioration in mental functioning characterized by significant impairment of memory, thinking processes, attention, and judgment and by specific cognitive deficits. It is estimated that over 35 million people worldwide are afflicted with dementia, and this number is expected to double in the next two decades (Wong, Gilmour, & Ramage-Morin, 2016). The number of individuals in Canada living with dementia in 2016 is believed to be approximately 564 000 (Chambers, Bancej, & McDowell, 2016).

There are at least 50 disorders known to cause dementia (Bondi & Lange, 2001), including degenerative diseases such as Huntington's and Parkinson's. Other causes are severe head injury; inhalation of toxic substances; oxygen deprivation; strokes; infectious diseases such as syphilis, meningitis, and AIDS; intracranial tumours; and certain dietary deficiencies, especially of the B vitamins. However, the most frequent cause is the disabling and degenerative brain disease called *Alzheimer's disease (AD)*.

AD is a degenerative brain disease that leads to progressive and irreversible dementia, characterized by memory loss and deterioration of other cognitive functions, including judgment and ability to reason. The risk of AD increases dramatically with advancing age (Kocahan & Doğan, 2017). AD accounts for more than half of the cases of dementia in the general population. Alzheimer's disease that strikes earlier in life appears to involve a more severe form of the disease.

People with AD may become depressed, confused, or even delusional when they sense their mental ability is slipping away but do not understand why. They may experience hallucinations and other psychotic features. Bewilderment and fear may lead to paranoid delusions or beliefs that their loved ones have betrayed them, robbed them, or don't care about them. They may forget the names of their loved ones or fail to recognize them. They may even forget their own names.

AD was first described in 1907 by the German physician Alois Alzheimer (1864–1915). During an autopsy of a 56-year-old woman who had suffered from severe dementia, he found two brain abnormalities now regarded as characteristic signs of the disease: amyloid plaques (deposits of fibrous protein fragments composed of a material called *beta amyloid*) and neurofibrillary tangles (twisted bundles of fibres of a protein called *tau*) (Carrillo et al., 2013; Han et al., 2012).

NEUROPATHY **Amyloid plaques** are made largely of protein, called *beta amyloid*, or *A-beta*, and are split from a much larger protein molecule known as APP. Both APP and A-beta are present in normal brains. The key problem in Alzheimer's disease is that abnormally high amounts of A-beta accumulate in the brain, overwhelming the enzymes and other molecules whose job it is to clear it away (Cummings, 2004). As well, the clearing away process itself appears to be defective.

The **neurofibrillary tangles** are made of a protein called *tau*, which, like amyloid, occurs in normal nerve cells. In Alzheimer's disease, tau becomes chemically altered and piles up as thread-like tangles, impairing the protein's key roles in nerve cells. One of these roles is in nerve sprouting, an important feature of self-repair in the nervous system.

The third important alteration in the brain concerns the neurotransmitter *acetylcholine* (Ach), which is important in memory. It seems that one of the areas affected the earliest and most severely is in the base of the forebrain involved in Ach release. The depletion of Ach contributes significantly to the memory deficits characteristic of AD (Schliebs & Arendt, 2006). Drugs that inhibit the breakdown of the already-reduced levels of Ach can be beneficial for patients.

Another common characteristic of the disease is inflammation of the brain. Whenever and wherever the body suffers trauma or is attacked by some kind of potentially threatening influence, such as an infection or a toxin, it defends itself in part by mounting an inflammatory response. This immune response also occurs in the Alzheimer's brain.

DIAGNOSIS The diagnosis of dementia involves a thorough physical and psychological assessment to evaluate symptoms such as aphasia (difficulty remembering words or being

dementia Profound deterioration of cognitive functioning, characterized by deficits in memory, thinking, judgment, and language use.

amyloid plaques The accumulation of protein fragments, normally broken down in healthy brains, that accumulate to form hard, insoluble plaques between nerve cells (neurons) in the brain. A hallmark of Alzheimer's disease.

neurofibrillary tangles Pathological protein aggregates (or brain lesions) found within brain cells (in the cerebral cortex and hippocampus) in patients with Alzheimer's disease and thought to contribute to the degradation of neurons in the brain.

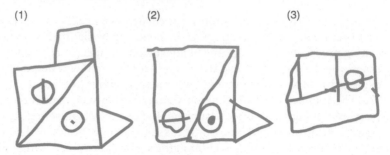

(1)   (2)   (3)

FIGURE 11.2 Neuropsychological test performance.
These drawings represent part of the neuropsychological test performance of a 59-year-old woman with a diagnosis of Alzheimer's disease. The figure at the left (1) was drawn by the psychologist, who then handed the piece of paper to the patient and asked her to make an exact copy of the figure next to the original. After the patient had completed her replica (2), the piece of paper was turned over and she was asked to draw the figure again, this time from memory. The figure that she drew based on memory is presented at the right (3).

Source: Oltmanns, Thomas F. & Emery, Robert E. *Abnormal Psychology*, 6th ed. © 2010. Reprinted and electronically reproduced by permission of Pearson Education, Inc., Upper Saddle River, New Jersey

completely unable to speak, read, or write), apraxia (loss of the ability to execute or carry out learned, purposeful movements), and other memory loss.

The diagnosis of Alzheimer's is often given only after all other potential causes of dementia are ruled out. Only in the past decade have reliable screening and diagnostic tools been available. Researchers have discovered a previously unknown substance in spinal fluid that can be used to diagnose Alzheimer's disease: a beta-amyloid protein called Abeta16 ("New Marker," 2009). Independent studies show that patients with AD have higher levels of the protein in their spinal fluid than do healthy individuals (Fukumoto et al., 2010). Researchers are proposing that the discovery of the new protein could be used to diagnose patients with Alzheimer's and also help determine which medications are most effective for the disease.

Detecting Alzheimer's disease early in the process is ideal. Brain scanning techniques have shown promising results in diagnosing AD by showing plaques associated with the disease together with clinical evidence of memory loss (Harada et al., 2015; Sabri et al., 2015; Zwan et al., 2017). Memory tests, like the neuropsychological memory test in Figure 11.2, can aid in the evaluation of memory loss.

In 2010, the American Academy of Neurology reported on tests performed on 85 people with mild cognitive impairment who were part of a larger study called the Alzheimer's Disease Neuroimaging Initiative (Landau et al., 2010). Several techniques were used in assessing the subjects in the study, including MRI brain scans to measure the size of a participant's hippocampus, the part of the brain responsible for learning and memory; measurement of amyloid proteins (such as those discussed above); and PET brain scans to detect metabolic abnormalities in the brain that might signal Alzheimer's disease. People who showed abnormal results on both PET scans and episodic memory tests were nearly 12 times more likely to develop Alzheimer's disease than those who scored normally on both measures (Landau et al., 2010). In other words, the PET scans and the memory tests best predicted later development of Alzheimer's disease.

Various medical and psychological conditions sometimes mimic symptoms of AD, such as severe depression resulting in memory loss. Consequently, misdiagnoses may occur, especially in the early stages of the disease, so doctors need to be careful in making a diagnosis of this dreadful disease.

SYMPTOMS OF ALZHEIMER'S DISEASE The early stages of AD are marked by limited memory problems and subtle personality changes. People may at first have trouble managing their finances; remembering recent events or basic information such as telephone numbers, area codes, postal codes, and the names of their grandchildren; and performing numerical computations. A business executive who once managed millions of dollars may become unable to perform simple arithmetic. There may be subtle personality changes, such as signs of withdrawal in people who had been outgoing or irritability in people who had been gentle. In these early stages, people with AD generally appear neat and well groomed and are usually cooperative and socially appropriate.

Some people with AD are not aware of their deficits. Others deny them. At first, they may attribute their problems to other causes, such as stress or fatigue. Denial may protect people with AD in the early or mild stages of the disease from recognizing their intellectual abilities are declining. Or the recognition that their mental abilities are slipping away may lead to depression.

In moderately severe AD, people require assistance in managing everyday tasks. At this stage, patients with AD may be unable to select appropriate clothes or recall their addresses or names of family members. When they drive, they begin making mistakes, such as failing to stop at stop signs or accelerating when they should be braking. They may encounter difficulties in toileting and bathing themselves. They often make mistakes in recognizing themselves in mirrors. They may no longer be able to speak in full sentences; verbal responses may become limited to a few words.

Movement and coordination functions deteriorate further. People with AD at the moderately severe level may begin walking in shorter, slower steps. They may no longer be able to sign their names, even when assisted by others. They may have difficulty handling a knife and fork. Agitation becomes a prominent feature at this stage, and patients may act out in response to the threat of having to contend with an environment that no longer seems controllable. They may pace or fidget or display aggressive behaviour such as yelling, throwing, or hitting. Patients may wander off because of restlessness and be unable to find their way back.

People with advanced AD may start talking to themselves or experience visual hallucinations or paranoid delusions. They may believe that someone is attempting to harm them or is stealing their possessions or that their spouses are unfaithful to them. They may even believe that their spouses are actually other people.

At the most severe stage, cognitive functions decline to the point where people become essentially helpless. They may lose the ability to speak or control body movement. They become incontinent; are unable to communicate, walk, or even sit up; and require assistance in toileting and feeding. In the end state, seizures, coma, and death result.

CAUSAL FACTORS We don't yet know what causes AD, but clues may lie in understanding the process by which steel-wool-like plaques and tangled nerve fibres form in the brain in AD patients. We don't yet know whether the accumulation of plaques and tangles accounts for memory loss and other symptoms in AD or is merely a symptom of the disease (Herrup, 2010; Karran, Mercken, & De Strooper, 2011).

Scientists are exploring the underlying processes involved in AD, focusing on the loss of synapses in the brain—the tiny gaps between neurons through which neurons communicate (Guerreiro et al., 2013; Hongpaisan, Sun, & Alkon, 2011; Jonsson et al., 2011; Kocahan & Doğan, 2017). The hope is that a better understanding of the biological bases of AD may lead to specific therapies to treat or perhaps even prevent the disease (Orešič et al., 2011).

Scientists have identified a number of genes linked to AD, raising hopes that we may one day find ways of counteracting their adverse effects (e.g., Braskie et al., 2011; Lane-Donovan & Herz, 2017; Naj et al., 2011; Pottier et al., 2012; Ramanan et al., 2012). Different combinations of genes may be involved in different forms of the disease. Some forms of AD are associated with particular genes linked to the production of beta amyloid or to abnormal buildup of amyloid plaques and neurofibrillary tangles associated with AD (Bookheimer & Burggren, 2009). People with a genetic variant called the *ApoE4* gene stand a much higher risk of developing AD, perhaps as much as three times greater than average (Lane-Donovan & Herz, 2017).

Environmental factors may also be involved in the development of AD (Sotiropoulos et al., 2011). We don't yet know which environmental factors may be involved, but stress is a possible culprit. Scientists are working to develop a better understanding of how genes and environmental factors interact in the development of the disease.

TREATMENT AND PREVENTION Presently available drugs for AD offer at best only modest benefits in slowing cognitive decline and boosting cognitive functioning. None is a cure. One widely used drug, *donepezil* (brand name Aricept), increases levels of the neurotransmitter acetylcholine (Ach). AD patients show lower levels of Ach, possibly because of the death of brain cells in Ach-producing areas of the brain. However, the drug produces only small or modest improvements in cognitive functioning in people with moderate to severe AD (Howard et al., 2012). Antipsychotic medication may also be used to help control the aggressive or agitated behaviour of dementia patients, but these drugs carry significant safety risks (Corbett & Ballard, 2012; Devanand et al., 2012).

Inflammation in the brain appears to play a key role in the development of AD. Hence, investigators are evaluating the potential preventive effects of anti-inflammatory drugs, such as the common pain reliever *ibuprofen* (brand name Advil). Medical experts caution against widespread use of these drugs until it becomes clear whether they can reduce the risk of AD or delay its onset (Rogers, 2009). Unfortunately, we lack any drugs that can prevent or delay the development of AD. Scientists suspect that the biological process involved in AD may begin more than 20 years before dementia develops (Bateman et al., 2012). Consequently, investigators are calling for greater attention to developing drugs that target the early stages of the disease rather than its end stage (Buchhave et al., 2012).

Engaging in stimulating cognitive activities—solving puzzles, reading newspapers, playing word games, and so on—can help boost cognitive performance in people with mild to moderate AD (Woods, Spector, Prendergast, & Orrell, 2012). Patients with AD may also benefit from memory training programs to help them make optimal use of their remaining abilities. Hopes for the future lie in the development of an effective vaccine to prevent this devastating disease (Michaud et al., 2013; Winblad et al., 2012).

On the prevention front, there is some evidence that lifestyle factors such as maintaining a regular exercise program and following a healthy diet low in animal fat and rich in vegetables and fish can reduce the risk of AD (Buchman et al., 2012). That said, links between lifestyle factors such as diet and exercise and the risk of AD need to be more fully tested. Encouraging findings along these lines showed that physical fitness in middle adulthood was associated with a lower risk of dementia in later adulthood (DeFina et al., 2013). This study was based on observational methods that cannot demonstrate cause-and-effect relationships, but it does suggest that physical fitness programs may help prevent dementia. We also need other research to test whether regular mental exercises of the type involved in completing mentally challenging tasks can delay or perhaps even prevent the development of AD.

REVIEW IT

Dementia

- **Is memory impairment the only indication that a person is developing dementia?** No, memory impairment is not the only sign. Decline in executive functioning is another sign that is often revealed through difficulty performing familiar tasks. There might also be problems with language and difficulties with orientation of time and space as well as decreased judgment and changes in mood or behaviour.

Define It

Recall It

1. All of the following are diagnostic features of attention-deficit/hyperactivity disorder *except* _____.
   a. lack of attention
   b. impulsivity
   c. intentional cruelty
   d. hyperactivity

2. Conduct disorder in boys is more likely to be shown by behaviours such as _____ and ____, whereas in girls it is more likely to involve ____ and ____.
   a. vandalism and disciplinary problems; lying and substance abuse
   b. truancy and running away; stealing and fighting
   c. hyperactivity and distractibility; suicidal behaviour and panic attacks
   d. lying and substance abuse; vandalism and disciplinary problems

3. Each of the following is a feature of separation anxiety disorder *except* _____.
   a. clingingness to parents
   b. concerns about death and dying
   c. physical symptoms such as stomach aches, nausea, and vomiting
   d. involuntary soiling of clothes

4. The factor most strongly linked to the risk of death by suicide among children is _____.
   a. physical abuse
   b. relocation to another part of the country
   c. the presence of a loaded handgun in the house
   d. the occurrence of suicide in classmates

5. Which of the following is a state of extreme mental confusion in which people have difficulty focusing their attention, speaking clearly and coherently, and orienting themselves to the environment?
   a. dementia
   b. delirium
   c. Alzheimer's disorder
   d. autism spectrum disorder

Answers to Recall It

1. c,   2. a,   3. d,   4. c,   5. b

Think About It

- Have you known anyone with autism spectrum disorder or worked with children who have the disorder? What were the most prominent features of the disorder? What, if any, interventions were helpful?
- Do you think children with intellectual disabilities should be mainstreamed into regular classes? Why or why not?
- Do you think people with learning disorders should be given special consideration when given standardized tests (e.g., provincial achievement tests), such as having extra time? Why or why not?
- What are the risks and benefits of using stimulant medication such as Ritalin in treating ADHD in children?
- Do you know someone with Alzheimer's disease? Were there signs of memory loss early on? What interventions are helpful?

Weblinks

Autism Canada
www.autismcanada.org
This website is a primary source for Canadian information about autism spectrum disorder, including the services and resources available.

Canadian Association for Community Living
www.cacl.ca
This site provides information about Canadian community supports and services for people of all ages who have intellectual disabilities.

Special Olympics Canada
www.specialolympics.ca
Special Olympics Canada is a not-for-profit organization dedicated to enriching the lives of Canadians with intellectual disabilities.

Learning Disabilities Association of Canada (LDAC)
www.ldac-acta.ca
This site is Canada's central repository for information about learning disabilities, including the resources and supports available.

**Children and Adults with Attention-Deficit/
Hyperactivity Disorder (CHADD)**
www.chadd.org
This Canadian site is dedicated to the support,
education, and betterment of the lives of children and
adults with ADHD.

Children and Youth
https://ontario.cmha.ca/mental-health/child-and-
youth-mental-health
This page from the Canadian Mental Health
Association provides information about a wide range
of mental and emotional problems of children and
youth.

Alzheimer Society Canada
www.alzheimer.ca
The Alzheimer Society is a leading national not-for-
profit health organization. Its aim is to improve the
quality of life for Canadians affected by Alzheimer's
disease and related dementias and advance the search
for the cause and cure.

Canadian Dementia Action Network
www.cdan.ca/aboutus.html
CDAN brings together Canada's world-class
biomedical researchers and clinicians for the purpose
of quickly identifying promising treatments for
Alzheimer's disease and related dementias.

Abnormal Behaviour across the Lifespan

Test your understanding of the key concepts by filling in the blanks with the correct statements chosen from the list that follows. The answers are found at the end of the chapter.

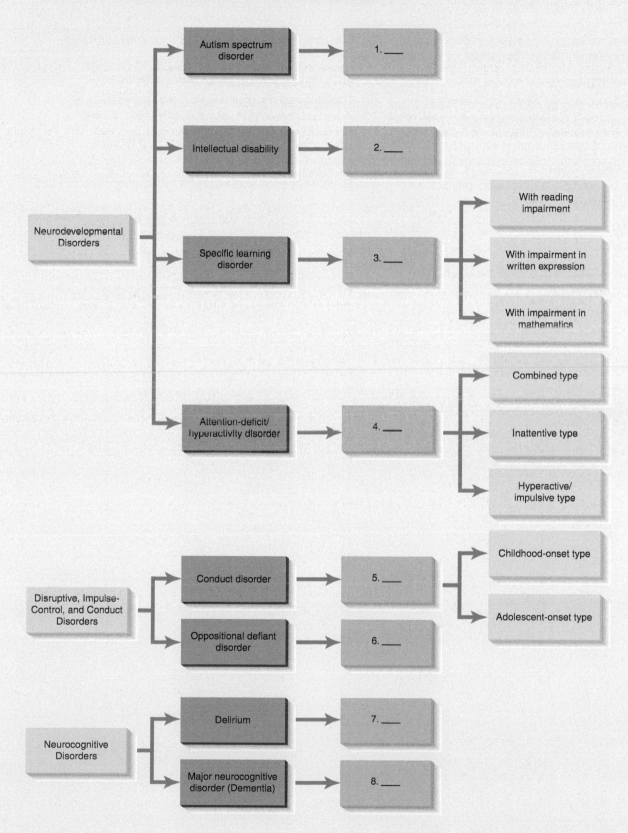

a. State of extreme mental confusion in which people have difficulty focusing their attention, speaking clearly and coherently, and orienting themselves to the environment

b. Broad delay in the development of intellectual and adaptive functioning

c. Profound deterioration of cognitive functioning characterized by deficits in memory, thinking, judgment, and language use

d. Disorder characterized by a pattern of behaviours that fall into three categories of symptoms: angry/irritable mood, argumentative/defiant behaviour, and vindictiveness

e. Disorder characterized by excessive motor activity, impulsivity, or an inability to focus one's attention

f. Disorder characterized by pervasive deficits in social communication and social interactions and restricted or fixated interests and repetitive behaviours

g. The symptoms of this disorder fall into four categories of behaviours: aggression to people and animals, destruction of property, deceitfulness or theft, and serious violation of rules

h. Deficiency in a specific learning ability despite average or higher intelligence and exposure to learning opportunities

Answers: 1. f, 2. b, 3. h, 4. e, 5. g, 6. d, 7. a, 8. c

APPENDIX

RESEARCH METHODS IN ABNORMAL PSYCHOLOGY

Abnormal psychology is a branch of the scientific discipline of psychology, which means that the pursuit of knowledge in the field is based on the application of the scientific method. Here we examine how researchers apply the scientific method in investigating abnormal behaviour.

Let's begin by asking you to imagine that you're in your first psychology class and the professor enters the room carrying a small wire-mesh cage with a white rat. She smiles and sets the cage on her desk. The professor removes the rat from the cage and places it on the desk. She asks the class to observe its behaviour. As a serious student, you attend closely. The animal moves to the edge of the desk, pauses, peers over, and seems to jiggle its whiskers at the floor below. It manoeuvres along the edge, tracking the perimeter. Now and then it pauses and vibrates its whiskers downward in the direction of the floor.

The professor picks up the rat and returns it to the cage. She asks the class to describe the animal's behaviour.

A student responds, "The rat seems to be looking for a way to escape."

The professor writes each response on the blackboard. Another student raises her hand: "The rat is making a visual search of the environment," she says. "Maybe it's looking for food."

The professor prompts other students for their descriptions.

"It's looking around," says one.

"Trying to escape," says another.

Your turn arrives. Trying to be scientific, you say, "We can't say what its motivation might be. All we know is that it's scanning its environment."

"How so?" the professor asks.

"Visually," you reply, confidently.

The professor writes the response and then turns to the class, shaking her head. "Each of you observed the rat," she said, "but none of you described its behaviour. Each of you made certain inferences, that the rat was 'looking for a way down' or 'scanning its environment' or 'looking for food,' and the like. These are not unreasonable inferences, but they are inferences, not descriptions. They also happen to be wrong. You see, the rat is blind. It's been blind since birth. It couldn't possibly be looking around, at least not in a visual sense."

Description, Explanation, Prediction, and Control: The Objectives of Science

Description is one of the primary objectives of science. To understand abnormal behaviour, we must first learn to describe it. Description allows us to recognize abnormal behaviour and provides the basis for explaining it.

description In science, the representation of observations without interpretation or inferences as to their nature or meaning. Contrast with *inference*, which is the process of drawing conclusions based on observations.

433

inference Conclusion that is drawn from data.

theories (1) Plausible or scientifically defensible explanations of events. (2) Formulations of the relationships underlying observed events. Theories are helpful to scientists because they provide a means of organizing observations and lead to predictions about future events.

Descriptions should be clear, unbiased, and based on careful observation. Our anecdote about the blind rat illustrates that our observations and our attempts to describe them can be influenced or biased by our expectations. Our expectations reflect our models of behaviour, and they may incline us to perceive events—such as the rat's movements and other people's behaviour—in certain ways. Describing the rat in the classroom as "scanning" and "looking" for something is an **inference** or conclusion we draw from our observations based on our model of how animals explore their environments. Description would involve a precise accounting of the animal's movements around the desk, measuring how far in each direction it moves, how long it pauses, how it bobs its head from side to side, and so on.

Inference is also important in science, however. Inference allows us to jump from the particular to the general—to suggest laws and principles of behaviour that can be woven into models and **theories** of behaviour. In Chapter 1, we considered the major theoretical perspectives or models of abnormal behaviour. Let's note here that without a way of organizing our descriptions of phenomena in terms of models and theories, we would be left with a buzzing confusion of unconnected observations. The crucial issue is to distinguish between description and inference—to recognize when we jump from a description of events to an inference based on an interpretation of events. For example, we do not describe a person's behaviour as "schizophrenic"; rather, we interpret behaviour as schizophrenic on the basis of our model of schizophrenia. To do otherwise would be to affix ourselves to a given label or model and lose the intellectual flexibility needed to revise our inferences in the light of new evidence or ways of conceptualizing information.

Theories help scientists explain puzzling behaviour and predict future behaviour. Prediction entails the discovery of factors that anticipate the occurrence of events. Geology, for example, seeks clues in the forces affecting the earth that can forecast natural events such as earthquakes and volcanic eruptions. Scientists who study abnormal behaviour seek clues in overt behaviour, biological processes, family interactions, and so forth to predict the development of abnormal behaviours as well as factors that might predict response to various treatments. It is not sufficient for theoretical models to help us explain or make sense of events or behaviours that have already occurred. Useful theories must allow us to predict the occurrence of particular behaviours.

The idea of controlling human behaviour—especially the behaviour of people with serious problems—is controversial. The history of societal response to abnormal behaviours, including abuses such as exorcism and cruel forms of physical restraint, render the idea particularly distressing. Within science, however, the word *control* need not imply that people are coerced into doing the bidding of others like puppets dangling on strings. Psychologists, for example, are committed to the dignity of the individual, and the concept of human dignity requires that people be free to make decisions and exercise choices. Within this context, controlling behaviour means using scientific knowledge to help people shape their own goals and more efficiently use their resources to accomplish them. Today, in Canada, even when helping professionals restrain people who are violently disturbed, their goal is to assist them to overcome their agitation and regain the ability to exercise meaningful choices in their lives.[1] Ethical standards prohibit the use of injurious techniques in research or practice.

Psychologists and other scientists use the scientific method to advance the description, explanation, prediction, and control of abnormal behaviour.

The Scientific Method

The scientific method involves systematic attempts to test our assumptions and theories about the world through gathering objective evidence. Various means are used in

---

[1]Here we are talking about violently confused and disordered behaviour, not criminal behaviour. Both criminals and disturbed people may be dangerous to others, but with criminals the intention of restraint is usually limited to protecting society.

applying the scientific method, including observational and experimental methods. Here, let's focus on the basic steps involved in using the scientific method in experimentation:

1. *Formulating a research question.* Scientists derive research questions from their observations and theories of events and behaviour. For instance, based on their clinical observations and understandings of the underlying mechanisms in depression, they may formulate questions about whether certain experimental drugs or particular types of psychotherapy can help people overcome depression.

2. *Framing the research question in the form of a hypothesis.* A **hypothesis** is a precise prediction about behaviour examined through research. For example, scientists might hypothesize that people who are clinically depressed will show greater improvement on measures of depression if they are given an experimental drug than if they receive an inert placebo ("sugar pill").

3. *Testing the hypothesis.* Scientists test hypotheses through carefully controlled observation and experimentation. They might test the hypothesis about the experimental drug by setting up an experiment in which one group of people with depression is given the experimental drug and another group is given the placebo. They would then administer tests to see if the people who received the active drug showed greater improvement over a period of time than those who received the placebo.

4. *Drawing conclusions about the hypothesis.* In the final step, scientists draw conclusions from their findings about the correctness of their hypotheses. Psychologists use statistical methods to determine the likelihood that differences between groups are **significant** as opposed to chance fluctuations. Psychologists are reasonably confident that group differences are significant—that is, not due to chance—when the probability that chance alone can explain the difference is less than 5%. When well-designed research findings fail to bear out hypotheses, scientists can modify the theories from which the hypotheses are derived. Research findings often lead to modifications in theory, new hypotheses, and, in turn, subsequent research.

hypothesis Assumption that is tested through experimentation.

significant In statistics, a magnitude of difference that is taken as indicating meaningful differences between groups because of the low probability that it occurred by chance.

We will consider the major research methods used by psychologists and others in studying abnormal behaviour: the naturalistic-observation, correlational, experimental, epidemiological, kinship, and case study methods. Before we do so, however, let's consider some of the principles that guide ethical conduct in research.

Ethics in Research

Ethical principles are designed to protect the rights of people, respect the dignity and integrity of the individual, impart responsible caring, protect human welfare, and preserve scientific integrity. Psychological practitioners, researchers, and scientists follow ethical standards that address the following major concerns: Psychologists are prohibited from using methods that cause psychological or physical harm to subjects or clients; they must inform participants and obtain a signed consent form stating they are aware of the risks of participation; they must ensure confidentiality; and they must aim to maximize what is of benefit to subjects or clients (Canadian Psychological Association, 2016). Psychologists also must follow ethical guidelines that protect animal subjects in research.

Institutions such as universities and hospitals have review committees, often called research ethics boards, that review proposed research studies in light of ethical guidelines (National Council on Ethics in Human Research, 2002). Investigators must receive approval before they are permitted to begin their studies. Two of the major principles on which ethical research guidelines are based are (1) informed consent and (2) confidentiality.

The principle of **informed consent** requires that people be free to choose whether they wish to participate in research studies. They must be given sufficient information in advance about the study's purposes, methods, risks, and benefits to allow them to make an informed decision about their participation. Subjects must also be free to withdraw from a study at any time without penalty. In some cases, researchers may withhold certain information until all the data are collected. For instance, subjects in placebo-control

informed consent Agreement by individuals to participate in research based on a prior disclosure of information about the study's purposes, methods, risks, and benefits sufficient to allow subjects to make informed decisions about their participation.

studies of experimental drugs are told they may receive an inert placebo rather than the active drug. After the study is concluded, participants who received the placebo are given the option of receiving the active treatment. In studies in which information was withheld or deception was used, subjects must be **debriefed** afterwards. That is, they must receive an explanation of the true methods and purposes of the study and why it was necessary to keep them in the dark.

Subjects also have a right to expect that their identities will not be revealed. Investigators are required to protect their confidentiality by keeping the records of their participation secure and by not disclosing their identities to others.

The Naturalistic-Observation Method

The **naturalistic-observation method** is used to observe behaviour in the field, where it happens. Anthropologists have lived in preliterate societies in order to study human diversity. Sociologists have followed the activities of adolescent gangs in inner cities. Psychologists have spent weeks observing the behaviour of homeless people in train stations and bus terminals. They have even observed the eating habits of slender and overweight people in fast-food restaurants, searching for clues to obesity.

Scientists take every precaution to ensure their naturalistic observations are **unobtrusive** to prevent any interference with the behaviour they observe. Otherwise, the presence of the observer may distort the observed behaviour. Over the years, naturalistic observers have sometimes found themselves in controversial situations. For example, they have allowed sick or injured apes to die when medicine could have saved them. Observers of substance abuse and other criminal behaviour have allowed illicit behaviour to go unreported to authorities. In such cases, the ethical trade-off is that unobtrusive observation can yield information of benefit to all.

Naturalistic observation provides a good deal of information on how subjects behave, but it does not necessarily reveal why they behave as they do. Men who frequent bars and drink, for example, are more likely to get into fights than men who do not. But such observations do not show that alcohol causes aggression. As we see in the following pages, questions of cause and effect are best approached by means of controlled experiments.

Correlation

Correlation is a statistical measure of the relationship between two factors or **variables**. In the naturalistic-observation study that occurred in the fast-food restaurant, eating behaviours were related—or correlated—to patrons' weights. They were not directly manipulated. In other words, the investigators did not manipulate the weights or eating rates of their subjects, but merely measured the two variables in some fashion and examined whether they were statistically related to each other. When one variable (weight level) increases as the second variable (rate of eating) increases, there is a **positive correlation** between them. If one variable decreases as the other increases, there is a **negative correlation** between the variables.

Although correlational research reveals whether there is a statistical relationship between variables, it does not prove the variables are causally related. Causal connections sometimes work in unexpected directions, and sometimes there is no causal connection between variables that are merely correlated. There are correlations between depression and negative thoughts, and it may seem logical that depression is caused by such thoughts. However, it is also possible that feelings of depression give rise to negative thoughts. Perhaps the direction of causality works both ways, with negative thinking contributing to depression and depression in turn influencing negative thinking. Moreover, depression and negative thinking may both reflect a common causative factor, such as stress, and not be causally related to each other at all.

Although correlational research does not reveal cause and effect, it can be used to serve the scientific objective of prediction. When two variables are correlated, we can use one to predict the other. Knowledge of correlations among alcoholism, family history, and attitudes toward drinking helps us predict which adolescents are at great risk of developing problems with alcohol, although causal connections are complex and somewhat nebulous. But knowing which factors predict future problems may help us direct preventive efforts toward these high-risk groups to help prevent problems from developing.

THE LONGITUDINAL STUDY One type of correlational study is the **longitudinal study**, in which subjects are studied at periodic intervals over lengthy periods, perhaps for decades. By studying people over time, researchers can investigate the events associated with the onset of abnormal behaviour and, perhaps, learn to identify factors that predict the development of such behaviour. However, such research is time-consuming and costly. It requires a commitment that may literally outlive the original investigators. Therefore, long-term longitudinal studies are relatively uncommon. In Chapter 10, "Schizophrenia Spectrum and Other Psychotic Disorders," we examine one of the best-known longitudinal studies, the Danish high-risk study that has tracked since 1962 the development of a group of children whose mothers had schizophrenia and so were at increased risk of developing the disorder (Mednick, 1970).

Prediction is based on the correlation between events or factors that are separated in time. As in other forms of correlational research, we must be careful not to infer causation from correlation. A **causal relationship** between two events involves a time-ordered relationship in which the second event is the direct result of the first. We need to meet two strict conditions to posit a causal relationship between two factors:

1. The effect must follow the cause in a time-ordered sequence of events.
2. Other plausible causes of the observed effects (rival hypotheses) must be eliminated.

Through the experimental method, scientists seek to demonstrate causal relationships by first manipulating the causal factor and then measuring its effects under controlled conditions that minimize the risk of possible rival hypotheses.

The Experimental Method

The term *experiment* can cause some confusion. Broadly speaking, an experiment is a trial or test of a hypothesis. From this vantage point, any method that actually seeks to test a hypothesis could be considered experimental—including naturalistic observation and correlational studies. But investigators usually limit the use of the term **experimental method** to refer to studies in which researchers seek to uncover cause-and-effect relationships by manipulating possible causal factors directly.

The factors or variables hypothesized to play a causal role are manipulated or controlled by the investigator in experimental research. A manipulated or controlled factor is called an **independent variable**. The observed effects are labelled **dependent variables**, because changes in them are believed to depend on the independent or manipulated variable. Dependent variables are observed and measured, not manipulated, by the experimenter. Examples of independent and dependent variables of interest to investigators of abnormal behaviour are shown in Table A.1.

In an experiment, subjects are exposed to an independent variable, for example, the type of beverage (alcoholic versus nonalcoholic) they consume, in a laboratory setting. They are

longitudinal study Research study in which subjects are followed over time. Longitudinal studies have helped researchers identify factors in early life that may predict the later development of disorders such as schizophrenia.

causal relationship Relationship between two factors or events in which one is necessary and sufficient to bring about the other. Also called a *cause-and-effect relationship*.

experimental method Scientific method that aims to discover cause-and-effect relationships by means of manipulating the independent variable(s) and observing their effects on the dependent variable(s).

independent variable Factor in an experiment that is manipulated so that its effects can be measured or observed.

dependent variable Measure of outcome in a scientific study that is assumed to be dependent on the effects of the independent variable.

TABLE A.1

Examples of Independent and Dependent Variables in Experimental Research

Independent Variables	Dependent Variables
Type of treatment: for example, different types of drug treatments or psychological treatments	Behavioural variables: for example, measures of adjustment, activity levels, eating behaviour, smoking behaviour
Treatment factors: for example, brief vs. long-term treatment, inpatient vs. outpatient treatment	Physiological variables: for example, measures of physiological responses such as heart rate, blood pressure, and brainwave activity
Experimental manipulations: for example, type of beverage consumed (alcoholic vs. nonalcoholic)	Self-report variables: for example, measures of anxiety, mood, or marital or life satisfaction

then observed or examined to determine whether the independent variable makes a difference in their behaviour, or, more precisely, whether the independent variable affects the dependent variable—in this case, whether they behave more aggressively if they consume alcohol.

EXPERIMENTAL AND CONTROL SUBJECTS Well-controlled experiments assign subjects to experimental and control groups at random. **Experimental subjects** are given the experimental treatment. **Control subjects** are not. Care is taken to hold other conditions constant for each group. By using random assignment and holding other conditions constant, experimenters can be reasonably confident that the experimental treatment, and not uncontrolled factors such as room temperature or differences between the types of subjects in the experimental and control groups, brought about the differences in outcome between the experimental and control groups.

When experimenters use random assignment to ensure that subject characteristics are randomly distributed across groups, it is reasonable to assume that differences between groups involve the treatments they receive, rather than differences in the types of subjects making up the groups. Still, it is possible that apparent treatment effects stem from subjects' expectancies about the treatments they receive rather than from the active components in the treatments themselves. For example, knowing you are being given an alcoholic beverage to drink might affect your behaviour, quite apart from the alcoholic content of the beverage itself.

CONTROLLING FOR SUBJECT EXPECTANCIES In order to control for subject expectancies, experimenters rely on procedures that render subjects **blind,** or uninformed, as to what treatments they are receiving. For example, the taste of an alcoholic beverage such as vodka may be masked by mixing it with tonic water in certain amounts to keep subjects blind as to whether the drinks they receive contain alcohol or tonic water only. In this way, subjects who truly receive alcohol should have no expectations different from those receiving the nonalcoholic control beverage. Similarly, drug-treatment studies are often designed to control for subjects' expectations by keeping subjects in the dark as to whether they are receiving the experimental drug or an inert placebo control.

The term *placebo* derives from the Latin for "I shall please," referring to the fact that belief in the effectiveness of a treatment (its pleasing qualities) may inspire hopeful expectations that help people mobilize themselves to overcome their problems, regardless of whether the substance they receive is chemically active or inert. In medical research, a placebo—also referred to as a "sugar pill"—is an inert substance that physically resembles an active drug. By comparing the effects of the active drug with those of the placebo, the experimenter can determine whether the drug has specific effects beyond those accounted for by expectations.

In a single-blind placebo-control study, subjects are randomly assigned to treatment conditions in which they receive an active drug (experimental condition) or a placebo (placebo-control condition) but are kept blind, or uninformed, about which drug they are receiving. It is also helpful to keep the dispensing researchers blind as to which substances the subjects are receiving, lest the researchers' expectations come to affect the results. So in the case of a double-blind placebo design, neither the researcher nor the subject is told whether an active drug or a placebo is being administered. Of course, this approach assumes that the subjects and the experimenters cannot "see through" the blind. In some cases, however, telltale side effects or obvious drug effects may break the blind (Basoglu, Marks, Livanou, & Swinson, 1997). Still, the double-blind placebo control is among the strongest and most popular experimental designs, especially in drug-treatment research.

Placebo-control groups have also been used in psychotherapy research to control for subject expectancies. Assume you want to study the effects of therapy method A on mood. It would be inadequate to assign the experimental group to therapy method A randomly and the control group to a no-treatment waiting list. The experimental group might show improvement because of group participation, not because of therapy method A. Participation might raise expectations of success, and these expectations might be sufficient to engender improvement. Changes in control subjects placed on the "waiting list" would help to account for effects due to the passage of time, but they would not account for placebo effects, such as the benefits of therapy that result from instilling a sense of hope.

experimental subjects (1) In an experiment, subjects receiving a treatment or intervention, in contrast to *control subjects*. (2) More generally, people who participate in an experiment.

control subjects Subjects who do not receive the experimental treatment or manipulation but for whom all other conditions are held constant.

blind In the context of research design, a state of being unaware of whether or not one has received a treatment.

An attention-placebo *control group design* can be used to separate the effects of a particular form of psychotherapy from placebo effects. In an attention-placebo group, subjects are exposed to a believable or credible treatment that contains the nonspecific factors that therapies share—such as the attention and emotional support of a therapist—but not the specific ingredients of therapy represented in the active treatment. Attention-placebo treatments commonly substitute general discussions of participants' problems for the specific ingredients of therapy contained in the experimental treatment. Unfortunately, although attention-placebo subjects may be kept blind as to whether they are receiving the experimental treatment, the therapists themselves are generally aware of which treatment is being administered. Therefore, the attention-placebo method may not control for therapists' expectations.

The Epidemiological Method

The **epidemiological method** studies the rates of occurrence of abnormal behaviour in various settings or population groups. One type of epidemiological study is the **survey method,** which relies on interviews or questionnaires. Surveys are used to ascertain the rates of occurrence of various disorders in the population as a whole and in various subgroups classified according to such factors as race, ethnicity, gender, or social class. Rates of occurrence of a given disorder are expressed in terms of **incidence,** or the number of new cases of a disorder occurring during a specific period of time, and prevalence, which refers to the overall number of cases of a disorder existing in a population during a given period of time. Prevalence rates, then, include both new and continuing cases.

Epidemiological studies may point to potential causal factors in illnesses and disorders, even though they lack the power of experiments. By finding that illnesses or disorders cluster in certain groups or locations, researchers may be able to identify certain distinguishing characteristics that place these groups or regions at higher risk. Yet such epidemiological studies cannot control for selection factors—that is, they cannot rule out rival hypotheses that other unrecognized factors might play a causal role in putting a certain group at greater risk. Therefore, they must be considered suggestive of possible causal influences that must be tested further in experimental studies.

SAMPLES AND POPULATIONS   In the best of possible worlds, we would conduct surveys in which every member of the **population** of interest would participate. In that way, we could be sure the survey results accurately represent the population we wish to study. In reality, unless the population of interest is rather narrowly defined (e.g., designating the population of interest as the students living on your dormitory floor), chances are it is extremely difficult, if not impossible, to survey every member of a given population. Even census takers can't count every head in the general population. Consequently, most surveys are based on a **sample** or subset of a population. Researchers take steps when constructing a sample to ensure that it represents the target population. A researcher who sets out to study smoking rates in a local community by interviewing people drinking coffee in late-night cafés will probably overestimate its true prevalence.

One method of obtaining a representative sample is **random sampling.** A random sample is drawn in such a way that each member of the population of interest has an equal probability of selection. Epidemiologists sometimes construct random samples by surveying at random a given number of households within a target community. By repeating this process in a random sample of Canadian communities, the overall sample can approximate the general Canadian population, based on even a tiny percentage of the overall population. In fact, a representative nationwide sample of about 1500 eligible voters may be more accurate in predicting an election result than a haphazard sample of millions.

Random sampling is often confused with random assignment. *Random sampling* refers to the process of randomly choosing individuals within a target population to participate in a survey or research study. By contrast, *random assignment* refers to a process by which members of a research sample are assigned at random to different experimental conditions or treatments.

epidemiological method Method of research involved in tracking the rates of occurrence of particular disorders among different groups.

survey method Method of scientific research in which large samples of people are questioned by the use of a survey instrument.

incidence Number of new cases of a disorder occurring within a specific period of time.

population Total group of people, other organisms, or events.

sample Part of a population.

random sampling Drawing samples in such a way that every member of a population has an equal probability of being selected.

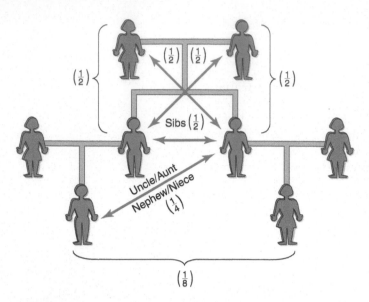

FIGURE A.1 A family tree showing the proportion of shared inheritance among relatives.
The more closely people are related, the more genes they have in common. Kinship studies, including twin studies and adoptee studies, afford researchers insight into the heritability of various patterns of abnormal behaviour.

proband Initial diagnosed case of a given disorder. Also called an *index case*.

monozygotic (MZ) twins Twins who develop from the same fertilized egg and therefore share identical genes. Also called *identical twins*. Abbreviated *MZ twins*. Contrast with fraternal or *dizygotic (DZ) twins*.

dizygotic (DZ) twins Twins who develop from separate fertilized eggs. Also called *fraternal twins*. Abbreviated *DZ twins*. Often contrasted with *monozygotic (MZ) twins* in studies of heritability of particular traits or disorders.

concordance Agreement.

Kinship Studies

Kinship studies attempt to disentangle the roles of heredity and environment in determining behaviour. Heredity plays a critical role in determining a wide range of traits. The structures we inherit make our behaviour possible (humans can walk and run) and at the same time place limits on us (humans cannot fly without artificial equipment). Heredity plays a role in determining not only our physical characteristics (hair colour, eye colour, height, etc.) but also many of our psychological characteristics. The science of heredity is called *genetics*. Human behavioural genetics is the study of the interactive effect of genetic and environmental factors on behaviour, especially personality patterns and psychological disorders.

The more closely people are related, the more genes they have in common. Children receive half their genes from each parent. There is thus a 50% overlap in genetic heritage between each parent and his or her offspring. Siblings (brothers and sisters) similarly share half their genetic heritage. Aunts and uncles related by blood to their nephews and nieces have a 25% overlap; first cousins, a 12.5% overlap (see Figure A.1).

To determine whether a pattern of abnormal behaviour has a genetic basis, researchers locate one case of a person with the disorder and then study how the disorder is distributed among that person's family members. The case first diagnosed is referred to as the *index case*, or **proband**. If the distribution of the disorder among family members of the proband approximates their degree of kinship, there may be a genetic involvement in the disorder. However, the closer their kinship, the more likely people also are to share environmental backgrounds. For this reason, twin and adoptee studies are of particular value.

TWIN STUDIES Sometimes a fertilized egg cell (or *zygote*) divides into two cells that separate, so that each develops into a separate person. In such cases, there is a 100% overlap in genetic makeup, and the offspring are known as identical or **monozygotic (MZ) twins**. Sometimes a woman releases two egg cells, or ova, in the same month, and they are both fertilized. In such cases, the zygotes (fertilized egg cells) develop into fraternal or **dizygotic (DZ) twins**. DZ twins overlap 50% in their genetic heritage, just as other siblings do.

Identical or MZ twins are important in the study of the relative influences of heredity and environment because differences between MZ twins are the result of environmental rather than genetic influences. MZ twins look more alike and are closer in height than DZ twins. In twin studies, researchers identify probands for a given disorder who are members of MZ or DZ twin pairs and then study the other twins in the pairs. A role for genetic factors is suggested when MZ twins are more likely than DZ twins to share a disorder. Differences in the rates of **concordance** (agreement for the given trait or disorder) for MZ versus DZ twins are found for some forms of abnormal behaviour, such as schizophrenia and bipolar disorder. Even among MZ twins, though, environmental influences cannot be ruled out. Parents and teachers, for example, often encourage MZ twins to behave in similar ways. Put another way, if one twin does *x*, everyone expects the other to do *x* also. Expectations have a way of influencing behaviour and making for self-fulfilling prophecies. We should also note that twins might not be typical of the general population, so we need to be cautious when generalizing the results of twin studies to the larger population. Twins tend to have had shorter gestational periods, lower birth weights, and a greater frequency of congenital malformations than nontwins (Kendler & Prescott, 2006). Perhaps differences in prenatal experiences influence their later development in ways that set them apart from nontwins.

ADOPTEE STUDIES Adoptee studies can provide powerful arguments for or against genetic factors in the appearance of psychological traits and disorders. Assume that children are reared by adoptive parents from a very early age—perhaps from birth. The children share environmental backgrounds with their adoptive parents but not their genetic heritages. Then assume we compare the traits and behaviour patterns of these children to those of their biological parents and their adoptive parents. If the children show a greater similarity to their biological parents than their adoptive parents on certain traits or disorders, we have strong evidence indeed for genetic factors in these traits and disorders.

Although adoptee studies may represent the strongest source of evidence for genetic factors in explaining abnormal behaviour patterns, we should recognize that adoptees, like twins, may not be typical of the general population. In this text we explore how adoptee and other kinship studies add to our understanding of genetic and environmental influences in many psychological disorders.

The Case-Study Method

Case studies have been important influences in the development of theories and treatment of abnormal behaviour. Freud developed his theoretical model primarily on the basis of case studies, such as that of Anna O. Therapists representing other theoretical viewpoints have also reported cases studies.

TYPES OF CASE STUDIES Case studies involve intensive studies of individuals. Some case studies are based on historical material, involving subjects who have been dead for hundreds of years. Freud, for example, conducted a case study of the Renaissance artist and inventor Leonardo da Vinci. More commonly, case studies reflect an in-depth analysis of an individual's course of treatment. They typically include detailed histories of the subject's background and response to treatment. The therapist attempts to glean information from a particular client's experience in therapy that may be of help to other therapists treating similar clients.

Despite the richness of clinical material that case studies can provide, they are much less rigorous as research designs than experiments. There are bound to be distortions or gaps in memory when people discuss historical events, especially those of their childhoods. Some people may intentionally colour events to make a favourable impression on the interviewer; others aim to shock the interviewer with exaggerated or fabricated recollections. Interviewers themselves may unintentionally guide subjects into slanting the histories they report in ways that are compatible with their own theoretical perspectives.

SINGLE-CASE EXPERIMENTAL DESIGNS The lack of control available in the traditional case-study method led researchers to develop more sophisticated methods, called **single-case experimental designs**, in which subjects are used as their own controls. One of the most common forms of the single-case experimental design is the A-B-A-B, or **reversal design** (see Figure A.2). The reversal design consists of the repeated measurement of clients' behaviour across four successive phases:

1. *A baseline phase (A).* The baseline phase, which occurs prior to the inception of treatment, is characterized by repeated measurement of the target problem behaviours at periodic intervals. This measurement allows the experimenter to establish a baseline rate for the behaviour before treatment begins.
2. *A treatment phase (B).* Now the target behaviours are measured as the client undergoes treatment.
3. *A second baseline phase (A, again).* Treatment is now temporarily withdrawn or suspended. This is the reversal in the reversal design, and it is expected that the positive effects of treatment should now be reversed because the treatment has been withdrawn.
4. *A second treatment phase (B, again).* Treatment is reinstated and the target behaviours are reassessed.

adoptee studies Studies of adopted-away children that examine whether their behaviour patterns and psychological functioning more closely resemble those of their biological parents or adoptive parents.

case studies Carefully drawn biographies that are typically constructed on the basis of clinical interviews, observations, psychological tests, and, in some cases, historical records.

single-case experimental design Type of case study in which the subject (case) is used as his or her own control by varying the conditions to which the subject is exposed (by use of a reversal phase) or by means of a multiple-baseline design.

reversal design An A-B-A-B type of experimental single-subject design in which treatment is instituted following a baseline phase and then withdrawn (reversal phase) so as to examine effects on behaviour.

FIGURE A.2   **Diagram of an A-B-A-B reversal design.**

Clients' target behaviours or response patterns are compared from one phase to the next to determine the effects of treatment. The experimenter looks for evidence of a correspondence between the subject's behaviour and the particular phase of the design to determine whether the independent variable (i.e., the treatment) has produced the intended effects. If the behaviour improves whenever treatment is introduced (during the first and second treatment phases) but returns (or is reversed) to baseline levels during the reversal phase, the experimenter can be reasonably confident that the treatment had the intended effect.

The method is illustrated by a case in which Azrin and Peterson (1989) used a controlled blinking treatment to eliminate a severe eye tic—a form of squinting in which the subject's eyes shut tightly for a fraction of a second—in a nine-year-old girl. The tic occurred about 20 times a minute when the girl was at home. In the clinic, the rate of eye tics or squinting was measured for 5 minutes during a baseline period (A). Then the girl was prompted to blink her eyes softly every 5 seconds (B). The experimenters reasoned that voluntary "soft" blinking would activate motor (muscle) responses incompatible with those producing the tic, thereby suppressing it. As seen in Figure A.3, the tic was virtually eliminated in just a few minutes of practising the incompatible or competing response ("soft" blinking), but returned to near baseline levels during the reversal phase (A) when the competing response was withdrawn. The positive effects were quickly reinstated during the second treatment period (B). The child was also taught to practise the blinking response at home during scheduled three-minute practice periods and whenever the tic occurred or she felt an urge to squint. The tic was completely eliminated during the first six weeks of the treatment program and remained absent at a follow-up evaluation two years later.

modelling In behaviour therapy, a technique for helping a client acquire new behaviour by means of having the therapist or members of a therapy group demonstrate a target behaviour that is then imitated by a client.

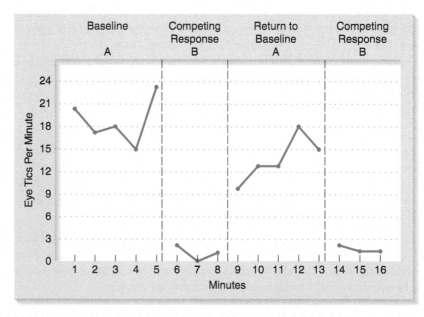

FIGURE A.3   **Treatment results from the Azrin and Peterson study.**
Notice how the target response, eye tics per minute, decreased when the competing response was introduced in the first "B" phase. It then increased to near baseline levels when the competing response was withdrawn during the second "A" phase. It decreased again when the competing response was reinstated in the second "B" phase.

Source: Republished with permission of Elsevier Inc., from Reduction of an eye tic controlled by blinking. Behavior Therapy, Nathan H. Azrin; Alan L. Peterson, 1989; permission conveyed through Copyright Clearance Center, Inc.

Although reversal designs offer better controls than traditional treatment case studies, it is not always possible or ethical to reverse certain behaviours or treatment effects. For example, participants in a stop-smoking program who reduce or quit smoking during treatment are not advised to revert to their baseline smoking rates when treatment is temporarily withdrawn during a reversal phase.

The multiple-baseline design is a type of single-case experimental design that does not require a reversal phase. In a multiple-baseline design across behaviours, treatment is applied, in turn, to two or more behaviours following a baseline period. A treatment effect is inferred if changes in each of these behaviours corresponded to the time at which each was subjected to treatment. Because no reversal phase is required, many of the ethical and practical problems associated with reversal designs are avoided.

A multiple-baseline design was used to evaluate the effects of a social-skills training program in the treatment of a shy, unassertive seven-year-old girl named Jane (Bornstein, Bellack, & Hersen, 1977). The program taught Jane to maintain eye contact, speak more loudly, and make requests of other people through **modelling** (therapist demonstration of the target behaviour), **rehearsal** (practice), and therapist **feedback** regarding the effectiveness of practice. However, the behaviours were taught sequentially, not simultaneously. Measurement of each behaviour and an overall rating of assertiveness were obtained during a baseline period from observations of Jane's role playing of social situations with other children, such as playing social games at school and conversing in class. As shown in Figure A.4, Jane's performance of each behaviour improved following treatment. The rating of overall assertiveness showed more gradual improvement as the number of behaviours included in the program increased. Treatment gains were generally maintained at a follow-up evaluation.

To show a clear-cut treatment effect, changes in target behaviours should occur only when those behaviours are subjected to treatment. In some cases, however, changes in the treated behaviours may lead to changes in the yet untreated behaviours, apparently because of generalization of the effect. Fortunately, though, generalization effects have tended to be the exception, rather than the rule, in experimental research (Kazdin, 1992).

No matter how tightly controlled the design or how impressive the results, single-case designs suffer from weak external validity because they do not show whether a treatment effective for one person is effective for others. Replication with other individuals can help strengthen external validity. If these results prove encouraging, they may lead to controlled experiments to provide even more convincing evidence of treatment effectiveness.

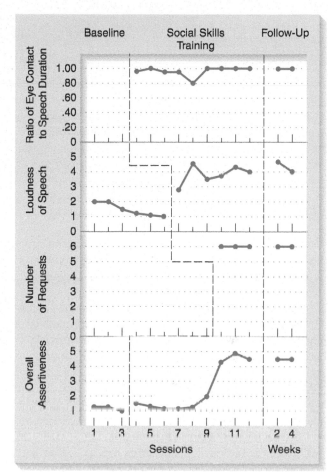

FIGURE A.4 Treatment results from the study by Bornstein, Bellack, and Hersen.
The blue dotted line shows the point at which social-skills training was applied to each of the targeted behaviours. Here we see that the targeted behaviours (eye contact, loudness of speech, and number of requests) improved only when they were subject to the treatment approach (social-skills training). We thus have evidence that the treatment—and not another, unidentified factor—accounted for the results. The section on the bottom shows ratings of Jane's overall level of assertiveness during the baseline assessment period, the social-skills training program, and the follow-up period.

Source: From *Journal of Applied Behavior Analysis*, Mitchell R. Bornstein, Alan S. Bellack, and Michel Hersen, © 1977. Reproduced with permission of John Wiley & Sons, Inc.

rehearsal In behaviour therapy, a practice opportunity in which a person enacts a desired response and receives feedback from others.

feedback Information about one's behaviour.

critical thinking A style of thinking characterized by the adoption of a questioning attitude and careful weighing of available evidence to determine if claims made by others stand up to scrutiny.

Critical Thinking

Scientists may use different methods to study phenomena of interest to them, but they have in common a skeptical, hard-nosed way of thinking called **critical thinking**. Critical thinking involves a willingness to challenge the conventional wisdom and common knowledge that many of us take for granted. It also means finding reasons to support beliefs, rather than relying on feelings or gut impressions. When people think critically, they maintain open minds. They suspend their beliefs until they have obtained and evaluated evidence that either supports or refutes them. In "A Closer Look: Thinking Critically about Abnormal Psychology" we examine the features of critical thinking and how they can be applied in our study of abnormal psychology.

Thinking Critically about Abnormal Psychology

We are exposed to a flood of information about our mental health that comes streaming down to us through a variety of media—television, radio, Internet, and print media including books, magazines, and newspapers. We may hear a news report touting a new drug as a *"breakthrough"* in the treatment of anxiety, depression, or obesity only to learn some time later that the so-called breakthrough doesn't live up to expectations or carries serious side effects. Some reports in the media are accurate and reliable; others are misleading, biased, or contain half-truths, exaggerated claims, or unsupported conclusions. The situation is compounded when even reputed experts disagree with one another. How are we to know what to believe?

To sort through the high volume of sometimes confusing information, we need to arm ourselves with skills of critical thinking, which involves adopting a questioning attitude toward information we hear and read. Critical thinkers carefully weigh available evidence to see if claims people make can stand up to scrutiny. Becoming a critical thinker means never taking claims at face value. It means looking carefully at both sides of an argument. Sad to say, most of us take certain "truths" for granted. Critical thinkers, however, never say, "This is true because so-and-so says it is true." They seek to evaluate assertions and claims for themselves.

We encourage you to apply critical thinking skills to questions posed in the "Think About It" sections in each chapter. We will now review some general principles of critical thinking.

FEATURES OF CRITICAL THINKING

Critical thinkers adopt a skeptical attitude toward information they receive. They carefully examine the definitions of terms, evaluate the logical bases of arguments, and evaluate claims in light of available evidence. Here are some key features of critical thinking:

1. Maintain a skeptical attitude. Don't take anything at face value, not even claims made by respected scientists or textbook authors. Consider evidence yourself and seek additional information to help you evaluate claims made by others.

2. Consider the definitions of terms. Statements may be true or false depending on how the terms used are defined. Consider the statement "Stress is bad for you." If we define stress in terms of hassles and work or family pressures that stretch our ability to cope to the max, then there is perhaps substance to the statement. However, if we define stress more broadly to include any factors that impose a demand on us to adjust, including events such as a new marriage or the birth of a child, then perhaps certain types of stress can be positive, even if they are stressful. Perhaps we all need some amount of stress to be active and alert.

3. Weigh the assumptions or premises on which arguments are based. Consider a case in which we are comparing differences in the rates of psychological disorders across racial or ethnic groups in our society. Assuming we find differences, should we conclude that ethnicity or racial identity accounts for these differences? This conclusion might be valid if we can assume all other factors that distinguish one racial or ethnic group from another are held constant. However, ethnic or racial minorities in Canada and the United States are disproportionately represented among the poor, and the poor are more apt to develop more severe psychological disorders. Differences among racial or ethnic groups may thus be a function of poverty, not race or ethnicity per se. These differences may also be due to negative stereotyping of racial minorities by clinicians in making diagnostic judgments, rather than to differences in underlying rates of the disorder.

4. Bear in mind that correlation is not causation. Consider the relationship between depression and stress. Evidence shows a positive correlation between these variables, which means depressed people tend to have higher levels of stress in their lives (Hammen, 2005; Pianta & Egeland, 1994). But does stress cause depression? Perhaps it does. Or perhaps depression leads to greater stress. After all, depressive symptoms may be stressful in themselves and may lead to additional stress as the person finds it increasingly difficult to meet life responsibilities, such as keeping up with work at school or on the job. It is also possible that the two variables are not causally linked at all but are linked through a third variable, perhaps an underlying genetic factor. It is conceivable that people inherit clusters of genes that make them more prone to encounter both depression and stress.

5. Consider the kinds of evidence on which conclusions are based. Some conclusions, even seemingly "scientific" conclusions, are based on anecdotes and personal endorsements. They are not founded on sound research. For example, there is much controversy today about so-called recovered memories that may suddenly arise in adulthood, usually during the course of psychotherapy or hypnosis, and usually involving incidents of sexual abuse committed during

>

childhood by the person's parents or family members. Are such memories accurate? Or might they be tales spun of imaginary thread? (See Chapter 5, "Dissociative and Somatic Symptom and Related Disorders.")

6. Do not oversimplify. Consider the statement "Alcoholism is inherited." In Chapter 7, "Substance-Related and Addictive Disorders," we review evidence suggesting that genetic factors may create a predisposition to alcoholism, at least in males. But the origins of alcoholism, as well as of schizophrenia, depression, and physical health problems such as cancer and heart disease, are more complex, reflecting a complicated interplay of biological and environmental factors. In only a few cases are diseases the direct result of a single defective gene or genes. People may even inherit a predisposition to the development of a particular psychological or physical disorder but avoid developing it if they are raised in a supportive family environment and learn to manage stress effectively.

7. Do not overgeneralize. In Chapter 5, we consider evidence showing that a history of severe abuse in childhood figures prominently in the great majority of cases of people who later develop multiple personalities. Does this mean that all (or even most) abused children go on to develop multiple personalities? Actually, very few do.

THINKING CRITICALLY ABOUT ONLINE INFORMATION

With today's online services, a world of information is literally at your fingertips. If you have access to the Internet, you can obtain information relating to the following:

- Listings and abstracts (brief descriptions) of scientific studies published in leading psychology journals. Much of this information is provided free of charge
- Do-it-yourself psychology quizzes and questionnaires
- Online encyclopedias containing hundreds if not thousands of entries relating to psychological issues
- Homepages of leading psychology organizations, such as the Canadian Psychological Association, the Canadian Mental Health Association (CMHA), and the Canadian Alliance on Mental Illness and Mental Health, that provide information about professional psychology and topics in psychology of general interest to the lay public
- Forums and chat lines that bring together people who share similar concerns, such as people who have suffered loss of loved ones and people with family members who have psychological disorders
- Topics relating to psychology provided by federal health agencies, including Health Canada's Mental Health Site and the Canadian Health Network (CHN)

The Internet holds a vast repository of health-related information. Anyone can post information online, so the casual browser may not know how to distinguish accurate, scientifically based information from misinformation. The beauty— and the risk—of the Internet is that it is freely available to anyone to post just about anything, from credible scientific information to advertising hype to complete malarkey. Don't believe everything you read online: Think critically!

1. Check out the credentials of the source. Who is posting the material? Is it a well-respected medical or scientific institution, or is it an individual or group of individuals with no scientific credentials or perhaps even with a grudge against the scientific establishment? The most reliable sources are scientific journals that are subject to peer review, a process by which other scientists carefully scrutinize each potential contributor's work before publication. In addition to scientific journals, the more reliable sources of health and medical information are those that are frequently updated, such as websites maintained by government agencies such as Health Canada and its many divisions, as well as those sponsored by leading psychology organizations, including the Canadian Psychological Association and the Canadian Psychiatric Association.

2. Look for citations. Scientists back up what they say with citations of original scientific sources. The references listed at the end of this text, for example, represent the sources your authors used in preparing these chapters. If online authors cite findings from scientific literature, you should expect them to supply some of the references they use, such as noting the journals or other periodicals in which the studies were published (including the year, volume, and page numbers). Having this information allows the reader to check the original sources to see if the statements made are accurate. In some cases, however, scientific organizations such as the CMHA and scholarly organizations such as the Canadian Psychological Association prepare information for the general public that is no less reliable, although it may not be annotated with source notes or references.

3. Beware of any product claims. Many commercial organizations use the Internet to tout or sell services and products. Don't assume that product claims are scientifically valid. Think of them as electronic advertising—basically an Internet version of a television commercial. Be skeptical (and keep a tight grip on your wallet). Don't be misled by the offer of a money-back guarantee. These are not guarantees that the product will work as advertised. Rather, they guarantee you'll get your money back if they don't succeed (although often there are strings attached).

Research Methods in Abnormal Psychology

- **What are the basic objectives of the scientific method and the steps involved in applying it?** The scientific approach focuses on four general objectives: description, explanation, prediction, and control. There are four steps to the scientific method: formulating a research question, framing the research question in the form of a hypothesis, testing the hypothesis, and drawing conclusions about the correctness of the hypothesis.

- **How are ethical standards applied in conducting research?** Psychologists follow the ethical principles of the profession that govern research with human and nonhuman subjects. Two of the key ethical provisions in research with humans are informed consent and confidentiality. Psychologists conducting research in institutional settings are required to obtain approval from institutional review boards to ensure their methods meet ethical standards.

- **What are the methods used by psychologists to study abnormal behaviour?** The naturalistic-observation method allows scientists to measure behaviour under naturally occurring conditions. Correlational research explores the relationship between variables, which may help predict future behaviour and suggest possible underlying causes. But correlational research does not directly test cause-and-effect relationships. Longitudinal research is a type of correlational design that involves the study of selected subjects at periodic intervals over long periods of time, sometimes spanning decades. Research samples need to be representative of a target population.

In the experimental method, the investigator directly controls or manipulates the independent variable under controlled conditions to demonstrate cause-and-effect relationships. Experiments use random assignment as the basis for determining which subjects (called *experimental subjects*) receive an experimental treatment and which others (called *control subjects*) do not. Researchers use various methods to attempt to control for subjects' and researchers' expectations, including single-blind placebo-control, double-blind placebo-control, and attention-placebo control group designs.

The epidemiological method examines the rates of occurrence of abnormal behaviour in various population groups or settings. Evidence of how disorders cluster in certain groups or geographic areas may reveal underlying causes. Kinship studies attempt to disentangle the contributions of environment and heredity.

Case-study methods can provide a richness of clinical material, but they are limited by the difficulties of obtaining accurate and unbiased client histories, by possible therapist biases, and by a lack of control groups. Single-case experimental designs are intended to help researchers overcome some of the limitations of the case-study method.

Define It

adoptee studies, 441
blind, 438
case studies, 441
causal relationship, 437
concordance, 440
control subjects, 438
correlation, 436
critical thinking, 443
debriefed, 436
dependent variable, 437
description, 433
dizygotic (DZ) twins, 440
epidemiological method, 439
experimental method, 437

experimental subjects, 438
feedback, 443
hypothesis, 435
incidence, 439
independent variable, 437
inference, 434
informed consent, 435
longitudinal study, 437
modelling, 442
monozygotic (MZ) twins, 440
naturalistic-observation method, 436
negative correlation, 436
population, 439
positive correlation, 436

proband, 440
random sampling, 439
rehearsal, 443
reversal design, 441
sample, 439
significant, 435
single-case experimental designs, 441
survey method, 439
theories, 434
unobtrusive, 436
variables, 436

Think About It

- Why should we not assume that because two variables are correlated they are causally linked?
- Why should experimenters assign subjects to experimental and control groups at random?

- How do investigators attempt to separate out the effects of heredity and environment?
- What are the limitations of the case study in drawing cause-and-effect relationships?

GLOSSARY

A

abnormal psychology Branch of psychology that deals with the description, causes, and treatment of abnormal behaviour patterns, p. 2.

abstinence-violation effect Tendency in people trying to maintain abstinence from a substance, such as alcohol or cigarettes, to overreact to a lapse with feelings of guilt and a sense of resignation that may then trigger a full-blown relapse. Abbreviated *AVE*, p. 285.

acetylcholine A neurotransmitter important in memory. Abbreviated *Ach*, p. 11.

acrophobia Excessive fear of heights, p. 110.

acute phase In schizophrenia, the phase in which psychotic symptoms develop, such as hallucinations, delusions, and disorganized speech and behaviour, p. 362.

acute stress disorder Traumatic stress reaction occurring in the days and weeks following exposure to a traumatic event. Abbreviated *ASD*, p. 116.

addiction Impaired control over the use of a chemical substance accompanied by physiological dependence, p. 254.

adjustment disorders Maladaptive reactions to an identified stressor or stressors that occur shortly following exposure to the stressor(s) and result in impaired functioning or signs of emotional distress that exceed what would normally be expected in the situation. The reaction may be resolved if the stressor is removed or the individual learns to adapt to it successfully, p. 115.

adoptee studies Studies of adopted-away children that examine whether their behaviour patterns and psychological functioning more closely resemble those of their biological parents or adoptive parents, p. 141.

affect The behavioural expression of emotions. Pronounced *AF-fect*, p. 360.

aggravated sexual assault Sexual assault in which the victim is maimed or disfigured or has his or her life endangered, p. 338.

agoraphobia A fear of places and situations from which it might be difficult or embarrassing to escape in the event of panicky symptoms or of situations in which help may be unavailable if such problems occur, pp. 5, 106.

Al-Anon Organization sponsoring support groups for family members of people with alcoholism, p. 282.

Alzheimer's disease Progressive brain disease characterized by gradual loss of memory and intellectual functioning, personality changes, and eventual loss of ability to care for oneself, p. 22.

amenorrhea Absence of menstruation—a possible sign of anorexia nervosa, p. 296.

amphetamine psychosis Psychotic state induced by ingestion of amphetamines, p. 264.

amphetamines Types of synthetic stimulants, such as Dexedrine and Benzedrine. Abuse can trigger an amphetamine psychosis that mimics acute episodes of schizophrenia, p. 264.

amygdala One of a pair of structures in the limbic system involved in emotion and memory, p. 375.

amyloid plaques The accumulation of protein fragments, normally broken down in healthy brains, that accumulate to form hard, insoluble plaques between nerve cells (neurons) in the brain. A hallmark of Alzheimer's disease, p. 425.

analgesia State of relief from pain without loss of consciousness, p. 263.

anomie Lack of purpose or identity; aimlessness, p. 178.

anorexia nervosa Eating disorder, primarily affecting young women, characterized by maintenance of an abnormally low body weight, distortions of body image, and intense fears of gaining weight, p. 294.

antidepressants Types of drugs that act to relieve depression. Tricyclics, MAO inhibitors, selective seotonin-reuptake inhibitors, and serotonin-norepinephrine reuptake inhibitors are the major classes of antidepressants, p. 67.

antisocial personality disorder Type of personality disorder characterized by a chronic pattern of disregard for, and violation of, the rights of others. Abbreviated *APD*, p. 217.

anxiety disorder Type of psychological disorder in which anxiety is the prominent feature, p. 102.

anxiety sensitivity A "fear of fear," or fear that one's emotions or states of bodily arousal will get out of control and lead to harmful consequences, p. 124.

anxiolytics Drugs, such as sedatives and anaesthetics, that induce partial or complete unconsciousness and are commonly used in the treatment of sleep–wake disorders, p. 314.

apnea Temporary cessation of breathing, p. 310.

attention-deficit/hyperactivity disorder Neurodevelopmental disorder characterized by excessive motor activity, impulsivity, and/or an inability to focus one's attention. Abbreviated *ADHD*, p. 408.

attributional style Personal style for explaining cause-and-effect relationships between events, p. 162.

autism spectrum disorder Disorder characterized by pervasive deficits in the ability to relate to and communicate with others, and by a restricted range of activities and interests. Children with autism spectrum disorder lack the ability to relate to others and seem to live in their own private worlds. Abbreviated *ASD*, p. 394.

autistic thinking The tendency to view oneself as the centre of the universe, to believe that external events somehow refer to oneself, p. 394.

automatic thoughts Thoughts that seem to pop into one's mind. In Aaron Beck's theory, automatic thoughts that reflect cognitive distortions induce negative feelings such as anxiety or depression, p. 161.

avoidant personality disorder Type of personality disorder characterized by avoidance of social relationships due to fears of rejection, p. 226.

axon Long, thin part of a neuron along which nervous impulses travel, p. 20.

B

barbiturates Types of depressant drugs that are sometimes used to relieve anxiety or induce sleep but that are highly addictive, p. 262.

baseline Period of time preceding the implementation of a treatment. Used to gather data regarding the rate of occurrence of the target behaviour before treatment is introduced, p. 53.

behaviour therapy A learning-based model of therapy, p. 28.

behavioural assessment Approach to clinical assessment that focuses on the objective recording or description of problem behaviour rather than on inferences about personality traits, p. 51.

behavioural interview Approach to clinical interviewing that focuses on relating problem behaviour to antecedent stimuli and reinforcement consequences, p. 51.

behavioural rating scale Method of behavioural assessment that involves the use of a scale to record the frequency of occurrence of target behaviours, p. 54.

behaviourism School of psychology that defines psychology as the study of observable or overt behaviour and focuses on investigating the relationships between stimuli and responses, p. 26.

benzodiazepines Class of minor tranquillizers that includes Valium and Ativan, p. 127.

binge-eating disorder Eating disorder characterized by repeated episodes in which binge eating occurs but is not followed by purging, p. 294.

biopsychosocial model A conceptual model emphasizing that human behaviour is linked to complex interactions among biological, psychological, and sociocultural factors, p. 35.

bipolar Characterized by opposites, as in *bipolar disorder*, p. 143.

bipolar I disorder Bipolar disorder characterized by manic episodes, p. 152.

bipolar II disorder Bipolar disorder characterized by periods of major depressive episodes and hypomanic episodes, p. 154.

blind In the context of research design, a state of being unaware of whether or not one has received a treatment, p. 438.

blocking (1) Disruption of self-expression of threatening or emotionally laden material. (2) In people with schizophrenia, a condition of suddenly becoming silent with loss of memory for what they have just discussed, p. 364.

blunted affect Significant reduction in emotional expression, p. 367.

borderline personality disorder Type of personality disorder characterized by instability in interpersonal relationships, self-image, and affects and marked impulsivity. Abbreviated *BPD*, p. 220.

breathing-related sleep disorders Sleep disorders in which sleeping is repeatedly disrupted due to difficulties breathing normally, p. 310.

bulimia nervosa Eating disorder characterized by a recurrent pattern of binge eating followed by inappropriate compensatory behaviours to prevent weight gain and accompanied by persistent overconcern with body weight and shape, p. 294.

C

case studies Carefully drawn biographies that are typically constructed on the basis of clinical interviews, observations, psychological tests, and, in some cases, historical records, p. 441.

cataplexy Brief, sudden loss of muscular control, typically lasting from a few seconds to as long as two minutes, p. 309.

catastrophize To exaggerate or magnify the negative consequences of events; to "blow things out of proportion", p. 30.

catatonia Gross disturbances in motor activity and cognitive functioning, p. 366.

causal relationship Relationship between two factors or events in which one is necessary and sufficient to bring about the other. Also called a *cause-and-effect relationship*, p. 437.

choleric Having or showing bad temper, p. 9.

chromosomes Structures found in the nuclei of cells that carry the units of heredity, or *genes*, p. 18.

circadian rhythm sleep–wake disorders Sleep disorders characterized by disruption of sleep caused by a mismatch in sleep schedules between the body's internal sleep–wake cycle and the demands of the environment, p. 312.

civil commitment Legal process involved in placing an individual in a psychiatric institution, even against his or her will. Also called *psychiatric commitment*, p. 87.

clanging In people with schizophrenia, the tendency to string words together because they rhyme or sound alike, p. 364.

claustrophobia Excessive fear of small, enclosed places, p. 110.

client-centred therapy Another name for Carl Rogers's *person-centred therapy*, p. 74.

clinical psychologist Person with graduate training in psychology who specializes in abnormal behaviour. He or she must be registered and licensed with a provincial psychological regulatory body in order to provide psychological services in that province, p. 2.

cocaine Stimulant derived from coca leaves, p. 264.

cognitive restructuring Cognitive therapy method that involves replacing irrational or self-defeating thoughts and attitudes with rational alternatives, p. 134.

cognitive therapy A form of psychotherapy in which clients learn to recognize and change their dysfunctional thinking patterns, p. 168.

cognitive triad of depression In Aaron Beck's theory, the view that depression derives from the adoption of negative views of oneself, the world, and the future, p. 159.

compulsion A repetitive behaviour or mental act that a person feels compelled or driven to perform, p. 113.

concordance Agreement, p. 440.

conditioned response (1) In classical conditioning, a learned or acquired response to a previously neutral stimulus. (2) A response to a conditioned stimulus. Abbreviated *CR*, p. 26.

conditioned stimulus Previously neutral stimulus that comes to evoke a conditioned response following repeated pairings with a stimulus (unconditioned stimulus) that had already evoked that response. Abbreviated *CS*, p. 26.

conduct disorder Pattern of abnormal behaviour in childhood characterized by disruptive, antisocial behaviour. Abbreviated *CD*, p. 412.

confidentiality The principle of safeguarding information so that it remains secret and is not disclosed to other parties, p. 89.

conscious In psychodynamic theory, the part of the mind that corresponds to our present awareness, p. 23.

control subjects Subjects who do not receive the experimental treatment or manipulation but for whom all other conditions are held constant, p. 438.

controlled social drinking Controversial approach to treating problem drinkers in which the goal of treatment is the maintenance of controlled social drinking in moderate amounts, rather than total abstinence, p. 286.

conversion disorder (functional neurological symptom disorder) A disorder characterized by symptoms or deficits that affect the ability to control voluntary movements or that impair sensory functions and that are inconsistent or incompatible with known medical conditions or diseases. Formerly called *hysteria* or *hysterical neurosis*, p. 201.

correlation Relationship or association between two or more variables. A correlation between variables may suggest, but does not prove, that a causal relationship exists between them, p. 436.

countertransference In psychoanalysis, the transfer of feelings that the analyst holds toward other persons in her or his life onto the client, p. 71.

crack Hardened, smokable form of cocaine, p. 264.

critical thinking A style of thinking characterized by the adoption of a questioning attitude and careful weighing of available evidence to determine if claims made by others stand up to scrutiny, p. 443.

cross-fostering study Method of determining heritability of a trait or disorder by examining differences in prevalence among adoptees reared by either adoptive parents or biological parents who possessed the trait or disorder in question. Evidence that the disorder followed biological rather than adoptive parentage favours the heritability of the trait or disorder, p. 372.

cue-exposure training Treatment used for people with substance-related disorders; it involves exposure to cues associated with ingestion of drugs or alcoholic beverages in a controlled situation in which the person is prevented from using the drug, p. 285.

cultural/familial intellectual disability Milder form of intellectual disability that is believed to result, or at least be influenced by, impoverishment in the child's home environment, p. 402.

culture-bound disorders Patterns of behaviour that are found within only one or a few cultural contexts, p. 62.

cyclothymic disorder Disorder characterized by a chronic pattern of mild mood swings between depression and hypomania that are not of sufficient severity to be classified as bipolar disorder, p. 154.

cytomegalovirus Maternal disease of the herpes virus group that carries a risk of intellectual disability to the unborn child, p. 401.

D

debriefed Providing research participants with a fuller accounting of a study's aims and purposes after their participation, including information about any deception that may have been used or other information that may have been withheld, p. 436.

defence mechanisms In psychodynamic theory, the reality-distorting strategies used by the ego to shield itself from conscious awareness of anxiety-evoking or troubling material, p. 24.

deinstitutionalization Practice of discharging large numbers of hospitalized mental patients to the community and reducing the need for new admissions through the development of alternative treatment approaches such as halfway houses and crisis intervention services, p. 12.

delayed ejaculation Type of sexual dysfunction in men involving persistent difficulties achieving orgasm, p. 343.

delirium (1) State of mental confusion, disorientation, and extreme difficulty in focusing attention. (2) A syndrome occurring among the elderly that typically involves confusion, problems with concentration, and cognitive dysfunction, p. 252.

delirium tremens Withdrawal syndrome that often occurs following a sudden decrease or cessation of drinking in chronic alcoholics that is characterized by extreme restlessness, sweating, disorientation, and hallucinations. Abbreviated *DTs*, p. 251.

delta-9-tetrahydrocannabinol Major active ingredient in marijuana. Abbreviated *THC*, p. 269.

delusions Firmly held but inaccurate beliefs that persist despite evidence that they have no basis in reality, p. 4.

dementia Profound deterioration of cognitive functioning, characterized by deficits in memory, thinking, judgment, and language use, p. 425.

dementia praecox Term used by Emil Kraepelin to describe the disorder we now call *schizophrenia*, p. 14.

demonological model The model that explains abnormal behaviour in terms of supernatural forces, p. 4.

dendrites Root-like structures at the end of a neuron that receive nerve impulses from other neurons, p. 20.

dependent personality disorder Type of personality disorder characterized by difficulties making independent decisions and by overly dependent behaviour, p. 227.

dependent variable Measure of outcome in a scientific study that is assumed to be dependent on the effects of the independent variable, p. 437.

depersonalization Feelings of unreality or detachment from one's self or one's body, as if one were a robot or functioning on automatic pilot or observing oneself from outside, p. 195.

depersonalization/derealization disorder Disorder characterized by persistent or recurrent episodes of depersonalization, p. 196.

depressant Drug that lowers the level of activity of the central nervous system, p. 256.

derealization Loss of the sense of reality of one's surroundings, experienced in terms of strange changes in one's environment (e.g., people or objects changing size or shape) or in the sense of the passage of time, p. 195.

description In science, the representation of observations without interpretation or inferences as to their nature or meaning. Contrast with *inference*, which is the process of drawing conclusions based on observations, p. 433.

detoxification Process of ridding the system of alcohol or drugs under supervised conditions in which withdrawal symptoms can be monitored and controlled, p. 279.

deviation IQ Intelligence quotient derived by determining the deviation between the individual's score and the norm (mean), p. 44.

dhat **syndrome** Usually diagnosed among young Indian men who describe an intense fear or anxiety over the loss of semen, p. 209.

diathesis A predisposition or vulnerability, p. 34.

diathesis-stress model Model of abnormal behaviour positing that abnormal behaviour patterns, such as schizophrenia, involve the interaction of genetic and environmental influences. In this model, a genetic or acquired predisposition, or *diathesis*, increases an individual's vulnerability to developing the disorder in response to stressful life circumstances. If, however, the level of stress is kept under the person's particular threshold, the disorder may never develop, even among people with the predisposition, p. 34.

disorientation State of mental confusion or lack of awareness with respect to time, place, or the identity of oneself or others, p. 262.

displacement In psychodynamic theory, a type of defence mechanism that involves the transferring of impulses toward threatening or unacceptable objects onto more acceptable or safer objects, p. 70.

dissociation Feelings of detachment from oneself or one's environment, p. 116.

dissociative amnesia Type of dissociative disorder in which a person experiences memory losses in the absence of any identifiable organic cause. General knowledge and skills are usually retained, p. 193.

dissociative identity disorder Dissociative disorder in which a person has two or more distinct or alternate personalities, p. 190.

dizygotic (DZ) twins Twins who develop from separate fertilized eggs. Also called *fraternal twins*. Abbreviated *DZ twins*. Often contrasted with *monozygotic (MZ) twins* in studies of heritability of particular traits or disorders, p. 440.

DNA Deoxyribonucleic acid is a double-strand complex molecule of helical structure that contains the genetic instructions for building and maintaining living organisms, p. 18.

dopamine Neurotransmitter of the catecholamine class that is believed to play a role in schizophrenia, p. 22.

dopamine theory Biochemical theory of schizophrenia that proposes schizophrenia involves the action of dopamine, p. 373.

double-bind communications Pattern of communication involving the transmission of contradictory or mixed messages without acknowledgment of the inherent conflict; posited by some theorists to play a role in the development of schizophrenia, p. 378.

Down syndrome Condition caused by a chromosomal abnormality involving an extra chromosome on the 21st pair (trisomy 21); it is characterized by intellectual disability and various physical abnormalities. Formerly called *mongolism* and *Down's syndrome* in Canada, p. 400.

downward drift hypothesis The belief that people with psychological problems may drift downward in socioeconomic status, p. 33.

duty to warn Obligation imposed on therapists to warn third parties of threats made against them by the therapists' clients. In the United States, the *Tarasoff* case established the legal basis for duty-to-warn provisions. Although US law does not apply in Canada, the Canadian Psychological Association states that, ethically, therapists have a duty to warn, p. 89.

dyslexia Type of specific learning disorder characterized by impaired reading ability that may involve difficulty with the alphabet or spelling, p. 405.

E

eclectic orientation Adoption of principles or techniques from various systems or theories, p. 65.

ego In psychodynamic theory, the psychic structure corresponding to the concept of the self. The ego is governed by the reality principle and is responsible for finding socially acceptable outlets for the urgings of the id. The ego is characterized by the capacity to tolerate frustration and delay gratification, p. 24.

ego dystonic Behaviour or feelings that are perceived to be foreign or alien to one's self-identity, p. 214.

ego ideal In Freud's view, the configuration of higher social values and moral ideals embodied in the superego, p. 25.

ego syntonic Behaviour or feelings that are perceived as natural or compatible parts of the self, p. 214.

electroconvulsive therapy Induction of a convulsive seizure by means of passing an electric current through the head; used primarily in the treatment of severe depression. Abbreviated *ECT*, p. 68.

electrodermal response Changes in the electrical conductivity of the skin following exposure to a stimulus, p. 55.

electroencephalograph Instrument for measuring the electrical activity of the brain (brainwaves). Abbreviated *EEG*, p. 56.

electromyograph Instrument often used in biofeedback training for measuring muscle tension. Abbreviated *EMG*, p. 56.

emotional intelligence "Involves the ability to monitor one's own and others' feelings and emotions, to discriminate among them, and to use this information to guide one's thinking and actions" (Salovey, 2008, p. vii), p. 29.

endorphins Natural substances that function as neurotransmitters in the brain and are similar in their effects to morphine, p. 263.

epidemiological method Method of research involved in tracking the rates of occurrence of particular disorders among different groups, p. 439.

epigenetics The study of the heritable and acquired changes in gene regulation (phenotype) that occur without affecting DNA sequence (genotype), p. 19.

epigenome The sum total of inherited and acquired molecular variations to the genome that lead to changes in gene regulation without changing the DNA sequence of the genome itself, p. 19.

erectile disorder Sexual dysfunction in males characterized by difficulty in achieving or maintaining erection during sexual activity, p. 343.

etiology Cause or origin; the study of causality, p. 103.

exhibitionistic disorder Type of paraphilic disorder almost exclusively occurring in males in which the man experiences persistent and recurrent sexual urges and sexually arousing fantasies involving the exposure of his genitals to a stranger and either has acted on these urges or feels strongly distressed by them, p. 328.

exorcism Ritual intended to expel demons or evil spirits from a person believed to be possessed, p. 9.

expectancies In social-cognitive theory, a personal variable describing people's predictions of future outcomes, p. 32.

experimental method Scientific method that aims to discover cause-and-effect relationships by means of manipulating the independent variable(s) and observing their effects on the dependent variable(s), p. 437.

experimental subjects (1) In an experiment, subjects receiving a treatment or intervention, in contrast to *control subjects*. (2) More generally, people who participate in an experiment, p. 438.

expressed emotion A form of disturbed family communication in which the family members of the individual with schizophrenia have a tendency to be hostile, critical, and unsupportive, p. 379.

external attribution In the reformulated helplessness theory, a type of attribution involving the belief that the cause of an event involves factors outside the self. Contrast with *internal attribution*, p. 162.

F

factitious disorder Type of psychological disorder characterized by the intentional fabrication of psychological or physical symptoms for no apparent gain, p. 204.

fear Unpleasant, negative emotion characterized by the perception of a specific threat, sympathetic nervous system activity, and tendencies to avoid the feared object, p. 109.

fear-stimulus hierarchy Ordered series of increasingly fearful stimuli. Used in the behavioural techniques of *systematic desensitization* and *gradual exposure*, p. 132.

feedback Information about one's behaviour, p. 443.

feeding and eating disorders Psychological disorders involving disturbed eating patterns and maladaptive ways of controlling body weight, p. 294.

female orgasmic disorder Type of sexual dysfunction in women involving difficulties achieving orgasm, p. 343.

female sexual interest/arousal disorder A type of sexual dysfunction in women involving either a lack of or greatly reduced level of sexual interest, drive, or arousal. Women with problems becoming sexually aroused may lack feelings of sexual pleasure or excitement that normally accompany sexual arousal, or they may experience little or no sexual interest or pleasure, p. 343.

fetishistic disorder Type of paraphilic disorder in which a person uses an inanimate object or a nongenital body part (*partialism*) as a focus of sexual interest and as a source of arousal, p. 330.

first-rank symptoms In Kurt Schneider's view, the primary features of schizophrenia, such as hallucinations and delusions, that distinctly characterize the disorder, p. 360.

flashbacks (1) Vivid re-experiencings of a past event, which may be difficult to distinguish from current reality. (2) Experiences of sensory distortions or hallucinations occurring days or weeks after use of LSD or another hallucinogenic drug that mimic the drug's effects, p. 268.

flat affect Absence of emotional expression, p. 367.

flooding Type of exposure therapy in which subjects are exposed to intensely anxiety-provoking situations, p. 134.

forced-choice formats Method of structuring test questions that requires respondents to select among a set number of possible answers, p. 46.

four A's In Bleuler's view, the primary characteristics of schizophrenia: loose *associations*, blunted or inappropriate *affect*, *ambivalence*, and *autism*, p. 359.

freebasing Method of ingesting cocaine by means of heating the drug with ether to separate its most potent component (its "free base") and then smoking the extract, p. 265.

frotteuristic disorder Type of paraphilic disorder characterized by recurrent sexual urges or sexually arousing fantasies involving bumping and rubbing against nonconsenting victims for sexual gratification. The person has either acted on these urges or is strongly distressed by them, p. 332.

G

galvanic skin response Measure of the change in electrical activity of the skin caused by increased activity of the sweat glands that accompanies states of sympathetic nervous system arousal, such as when a person is anxious. Abbreviated *GSR*, p. 55.

gamma-aminobutyric acid An inhibitory neurotransmitter believed to play a role in regulating anxiety. Abbreviated *GABA*, p. 127.

gender dysphoria Disorder in which an individual experiences significant personal distress or impaired functioning as a result of a discrepancy between his or her anatomic sex and gender identity, p. 323.

gender identity One's psychological sense of being female or being male, p. 323.

gene expression The process by which a gene sequence becomes activated ("turned on") and is translated into the proteins that determine the structure and functions of body cells, p. 19.

gene silencing The process of preventing or suppressing ("switching off") a gene sequence from being translated into proteins, p. 19.

general paresis Degenerative brain disorder that occurs during the final stage of syphilis, p. 14.

generalized anxiety disorder Type of anxiety disorder characterized by general feelings of dread, foreboding, and heightened states of sympathetic arousal. Formerly referred to as *free-floating anxiety*. Abbreviated *GAD*, p. 108.

genes Units found on chromosomes that carry heredity, p. 18.

genetics Science of heredity, p. 18.

genito-pelvic pain/penetration disorder Persistent or recurrent pain experienced during vaginal intercourse or penetration attempts, p. 344.

genotype The set of traits specified by our genetic code, p. 18.

global attribution In the reformulated helplessness theory, a type of attribution involving the belief that the cause of an event involved generalized rather than specific factors. Contrast with *specific attribution*, p. 162.

gradual exposure In behaviour therapy, a method of overcoming fears through a stepwise process of direct exposure to increasingly fearful stimuli, p. 72.

H

hallucinations Perceptions that occur in the absence of an external stimulus that are confused with reality, p. 3.

hallucinogens Substances that give rise to sensory distortions or hallucinations, p. 268.

hashish Drug derived from the resin of the marijuana plant, *Cannabis sativa*, p. 269.

hippocampus One of a pair of structures in the limbic system involved in processes of memory, p. 375.

histrionic personality disorder Type of personality disorder characterized by excessive need to be the centre of attention and to receive reassurance, praise, and approval from others. Such individuals often appear overly dramatic and emotional in their behaviour, p. 223.

humours Four fluids in the body: phlegm, black bile, blood, and yellow bile. Hippocrates believed the health of the body and mind depended on their balance, p. 9.

hyperactivity Abnormal behaviour pattern found most often in young boys that is characterized by extreme restlessness and difficulty maintaining attention, p. 408.

hypersomnolence disorder Sleep–wake disorder involving a persistent pattern of excessive sleepiness during the day, p. 309.

hypnosis Trance-like state, induced by suggestion, in which one is generally passive and responsive to the commands of the hypnotist, p. 15.

hypomanic episodes Mild manic episodes, p. 144.

hypothesis Assumption that is tested through experimentation, p. 435.

hypoxyphilia Paraphilic disorder in which a person seeks sexual gratification by being deprived of oxygen by means of using a noose, plastic bag, chemical, or pressure on the chest, p. 334.

hysteria Former term for *conversion disorder*, p. 15.

I

id In psychodynamic theory, the unconscious psychic structure present at birth. The id contains instinctual drives and is governed by the pleasure principle, p. 24.

ideas of persecution A form of delusional thinking characterized by false beliefs that one is being persecuted or victimized by others, p. 4.

ideas of reference Form of delusional thinking in which a person reads personal meaning into the behaviour of others or external events that are completely independent of the person, p. 216.

identification (1) In psychodynamic theory, the process of incorporating the personality or behaviour of others. (2) In social learning theory, a process of imitation by which children acquire behaviours similar to those of role models, p. 25.

illness anxiety disorder A disorder characterized by a preoccupation with the fear of having or the belief that one has a serious medical illness, but no medical basis for the complaints can be found, p. 202.

incidence Number of new cases of a disorder occurring within a specific period of time, p. 439.

independent variable Factor in an experiment that is manipulated so that its effects can be measured or observed, p. 436.

individual education plan A contractual document that contains learning and behavioural outcomes for a student, a description of how the outcomes will be achieved, and a description of how the outcomes will be evaluated. Abbreviated *IEP*, p. 407.

inference Conclusion that is drawn from data, p. 434.

informed consent Agreement by individuals to participate in research based on a prior disclosure of information about the study's purposes, methods, risks, and benefits sufficient to allow subjects to make informed decisions about their participation, p. 435.

inhalants Substances that produce chemical vapours that are inhaled for their psychoactive effect, p. 270.

insanity defence Form of legal defence in which a defendant in a criminal case pleads guilty but not criminally responsible on the basis of having a mental disorder, p. 91.

insomnia Term applying to difficulties falling asleep, remaining asleep, or achieving restorative sleep, p. 308.

intelligence (1) Global capacity to understand the world and cope with its challenges. (2) Trait or traits associated with successful performance on intelligence tests, p. 43.

intelligence quotient Measure of intelligence derived on the basis of scores on an intelligence test. Called a *quotient* because it was originally derived by dividing a respondent's mental age by her or his actual age. Abbreviated *IQ*, p. 44.

internal attribution In the reformulated helplessness theory, a type of attribution involving the belief that the cause of an event involved factors within oneself. Contrast with *external attribution*, p. 162.

interpersonal psychotherapy A brief, psychodynamic form of therapy that focuses on helping people resolve interpersonal problems. Abbreviated *IPT*, p. 167.

intoxication Substance-induced disorder characterized by clinically significant problematic behavioural or psychological changes caused by the recent ingestion of a substance (state of drunkenness or "being high"), p. 251.

K

knobs Swollen endings of axon terminals, p. 20.

koro syndrome Culture-bound somatoform disorder, found primarily in China, in which people fear that their genitals are shrinking and retracting into the body, p. 209.

Korsakoff's syndrome Form of brain damage associated with chronic thiamine deficiency. The syndrome is associated with chronic alcoholism and characterized by memory loss, disorientation, and the tendency to invent memories to replace lost ones (confabulation). Also called *alcohol-induced persisting amnestic disorder*, p. 261.

L

la belle indifférence French term describing the lack of concern over one's symptoms displayed by some people with conversion disorder but also by people with real physical disorders, p. 202.

lateralization The developmental process by which the left hemisphere specializes in verbal and analytic functions and the right hemisphere specializes in nonverbal, spatial functions, p. 396.

learned helplessness In Martin Seligman's model, a behaviour pattern characterized by passivity and perceptions of lack of control that develops because of a history of failure to be able to exercise control over one's environment, p. 162.

legal commitment Legal process involved in confining a person found "not criminally responsible on account of a mental disorder" in a psychiatric institution. Also called *criminal commitment*, p. 87.

longitudinal study Research study in which subjects are followed over time. Longitudinal studies have helped researchers identify factors in early life that may predict the later development of disorders such as schizophrenia, p. 437.

looseness of associations Ideas are strung together with little or no relationship among them, p. 360.

LSD A powerful hallucinogenic drug. LSD is the acronym for *lysergic acid diethylamide*, p. 268.

M

mainstreaming The practice of having all students with disabilities included in the regular classroom. Also referred to as *integration* or *inclusion*, p. 402.

major depressive disorder Severe depressive disorder characterized by the occurrence of major depressive episodes in the absence of a history of manic episodes. Major depressive disorder is characterized by a range of features such as depressed mood, lack of interest or pleasure in usual activities, lack of energy or motivation, and changes in appetite or sleep patterns. Abbreviated *MDD*, p. 144.

major depressive disorder with peripartum onset Major depressive disorder that occurs during pregnancy or following childbirth, p. 148.

major depressive disorder with seasonal pattern Major depressive disorder that occurs seasonally; also known as *seasonal affective disorder*, p. 147.

male hypoactive sexual desire disorder A type of sexual dysfunction in men involving a persistent or recurrent lack of sexual interest or sexual fantasies, p. 343.

malingering Faking illness to avoid or escape work or other duties, or to obtain benefits, p. 194.

manic Relating to mania, as in the manic phase of a bipolar disorder, p. 144.

manic episodes Periods of unrealistically heightened euphoria, extreme restlessness, and excessive activity characterized by disorganized behaviour and impaired judgment, p. 152.

marijuana A mild or minor hallucinogen derived from the *Cannabis sativa* plant, p. 269.

medical model Biological perspective in which abnormal behaviour is viewed as symptomatic of underlying illness, p. 2.

melancholia State of severe depression, p. 9.

mental age Age equivalent that corresponds to the person's level of intelligence, as measured by performance on the Stanford-Binet Intelligence Scale. Abbreviated *MA*, p. 44.

mental status examination Structured clinical evaluation to determine various aspects of a client's mental functioning, p. 43.

meta-analysis Statistical technique for combining the results of different studies into an overall average. In psychotherapy research, meta-analysis is used to compute the average benefit or size of effect associated with psychotherapy overall, or with different forms of therapy, in relation to control groups, p. 81.

methadone Artificial narcotic that lacks the rush associated with heroin and is used to help people addicted to heroin abstain without incurring an abstinence syndrome, p. 280.

modelling In behaviour therapy, a technique for helping a client acquire new behaviour by means of having the therapist or members of a therapy group demonstrate a target behaviour that is then imitated by a client, p. 443.

monoamine oxidase (MAO) inhibitors Antidepressants that act to increase the availability of neurotransmitters in the brain by inhibiting the actions of an enzyme, monoamine oxidase, that normally breaks down or degrades neurotransmitters (norepinephrine and serotonin) in the synaptic cleft, p. 67.

monozygotic (MZ) twins Twins who develop from the same fertilized egg and therefore share identical genes. Also called *identical twins*. Abbreviated *MZ twins*. Contrast with fraternal or *dizygotic (DZ) twins*, p. 440.

moods Pervasive qualities of an individual's emotional experience, as in depressed mood, anxious mood, or elated mood, p. 143.

moral principle In psychodynamic theory, the principle that governs the superego to set moral standards and enforce adherence to them, p. 25.

moral therapy A 19th-century treatment philosophy emphasizing that hospitalized mental patients should be treated with care and understanding in a pleasant environment, not shackled in chains, p. 11.

mourning Normal feelings or expressions of grief following a loss, p. 156.

N

naloxone Drug that prevents users from becoming high if they subsequently take heroin. Some people are placed on naloxone after being withdrawn from heroin to prevent return to heroin, p. 281.

naltrexone Chemical cousin of naloxone that blocks the high from alcohol as well as opiates and is now approved for use in treating alcoholism, p. 281.

narcissistic personality disorder Type of personality disorder characterized by grandiosity, need for admiration, and lack of empathy, p. 224.

narcolepsy Sleep–wake disorder characterized by sudden, irresistible episodes of sleep (sleep attacks), p. 309.

narcotics Drugs, such as opiates, that are used for pain relief and treatment of insomnia, but which have strong addictive potential, p. 263.

naturalistic-observation method Method of scientific research in which the behaviour of subjects is carefully and unobtrusively observed and measured in their natural environments, p. 436.

NCRMD Not criminally responsible on account of a mental disorder, p. 91.

negative correlation Statistical relationship between two variables such that increases in one variable are associated with decreases in the other, p. 436.

negative reinforcers Reinforcers whose removal increases the frequency of an operant behaviour. Anxiety, pain, and social disapproval often function as negative reinforcers; that is, their removal tends to increase the rate of the immediately preceding behaviour. Contrast with *positive reinforcer*, p. 27.

negative symptoms Features of schizophrenia characterized by the *absence* of normal behaviour. Negative symptoms are deficits or behavioural deficiencies, such as social-skills deficits, social withdrawal, flattened affect, poverty of speech and thought, psychomotor retardation, or failure to experience pleasure in pleasant activities, p. 366.

neo-Freudians Term used to describe the "second generation" of theorists who followed in the Freudian tradition. On the whole, neo-Freudians (such as Jung, Adler, Horney, and Sullivan) placed greater emphasis on the importance of cultural and social influences on behaviour and lesser importance on sexual impulses and the functioning of the id, p. 25.

neologisms Type of disturbed thinking associated with schizophrenia involving the coining of new words, p. 364.

neurofibrillary tangles Pathological protein aggregates (or brain lesions) found within brain cells (in the cerebral cortex and hippocampus) in patients with Alzheimer's disease and thought to contribute to the degradation of neurons in the brain, p. 425.

neuroleptics Group of antipsychotic drugs used in the treatment of schizophrenia, such as the phenothiazines (e.g., Thorazine), p. 67.

neurons Nerve cells, p. 20.

neuropeptide An amino acid found in cerebrospinal fluid that plays a role in neuronal transmission and the modulation of brain circuits or regions, p. 310.

neuropsychological assessment Methods of psychological assessment used to detect signs of underlying neurological damage or brain defects, p. 50.

neuroticism Trait describing a general neurotic quality involving such characteristics as anxious, worrisome behaviour; apprehension about the future; and avoidance behaviour, p. 127.

neurotransmitters Chemical substances that serve as a type of messenger by transmitting neural impulses from one neuron to another, p. 29.

NGRI A person found not guilty by reason of insanity, p. 92.

nightmare disorder Sleep–wake disorder characterized by recurrent awakenings from sleep because of frightening nightmares. Formerly called *dream anxiety disorder*, p. 312.

non-rapid eye movement sleep arousal disorders Sleep–wake disorders involving recurrent episodes of incomplete arousals during sleep that are accompanied by sleep terrors or sleepwalking, p. 313.

nonspecific treatment factors Characteristics that are not specific to any one form of psychotherapy but tend to be shared by psychotherapies, such as the attention a client receives from a therapist and the therapist's encouragement of the client's sense of hope and positive expectancies, p. 84.

norepinephrine Type of neurotransmitter of the catecholamine class, p. 22.

O

objective tests Tests that allow a limited, specified range of response options or answers so that they can be scored objectively, p. 46.

obsession An intrusive, unwanted, and recurrent thought, image, or urge that seems beyond a person's ability to control, p. 113.

obsessive-compulsive personality disorder Type of personality disorder characterized by rigid ways of relating to others, perfectionistic tendencies, lack of spontaneity, and excessive attention to details, p. 228.

obstructive sleep apnea hypopnea Type of breathing-related disorder involving repeated episodes of either complete or partial obstruction of breathing during sleep, p. 319.

opiates Types of depressant drugs with strong addictive properties that are derived from the opium poppy; provide feelings of euphoria and relief from pain, p. 263.

oppositional defiant disorder Disorder in childhood or adolescence characterized by excessive oppositionality or tendencies to refuse requests from parents and others, p. 413.

optimum level of arousal Level of arousal associated with peak performance and maximum feelings of well-being, p. 219.

osteoporosis Physical disorder caused by calcium deficiency characterized by extreme brittleness of the bones (from the Greek *osteon*, meaning "bone," and the Latin *porus*, meaning "pore"), pp. 21, 86.

P

panic disorder Type of anxiety disorder characterized by recurrent episodes of panic, p. 102.

paranoid Having irrational suspicions, p. 4.

paranoid personality disorder Type of personality disorder characterized by persistent distrust and suspiciousness of the motives of others, p. 215.

paraphilic disorders Types of sexual disorders in which a person experiences recurrent sexual urges and sexually arousing fantasies involving nonhuman objects (such as articles of clothing), inappropriate or nonconsenting partners (e.g., children), or situations producing humiliation or pain to oneself or one's partner. The person has either acted on such urges or is strongly distressed by them, p. 328.

parasomnias Category of sleep–wake disorders involving the occurrence of abnormal behaviours or physiological events during sleep or at the transition between wakefulness and sleep, p. 312.

pedophilic disorder Type of paraphilic disorder characterized by recurrent sexual urges or sexually arousing fantasies involving sexual activity with prepubescent children, p. 332.

performance anxiety Fear relating to the threat of failing to perform adequately, p. 346.

perseveration Persistent repetition of the same thought or train of thought, p. 364.

persistent depressive disorder Chronic type of depressive disorder lasting at least two years, p. 151.

person-centred therapy Carl Rogers's method of psychotherapy, emphasizing the establishment of a warm, accepting therapeutic relationship that frees clients to engage in a process of self-exploration and self-acceptance, p. 74.

personality disorders Types of enduring patterns of inner experience and behaviour that deviate markedly from the expectations of the individual's culture, are pervasive and inflexible, and lead to distress or impairment, p. 214.

phenothiazines Group of antipsychotic drugs or "major tranquillizers" used in the treatment of schizophrenia, p. 11.

phenotype Representation of the total array of traits of an organism, as influenced by the interaction of nature (genetic factors) and nurture (environmental factors), p. 18.

phenylketonuria Genetic disorder that prevents the metabolization of phenylpyruvic acid, leading to intellectual disability. Abbreviated *PKU*, p. 401.

phlegmatic Slow and stolid, p. 9.

physiological dependence State of physical dependence on a drug in which the user's body comes to depend on a steady supply, p. 254.

placebo (*pluh-SEE-bo*) Inert medication or form of bogus treatment intended to control for the effects of expectancies. Sometimes referred to as a "sugar pill", p. 67.

pleasure principle In psychodynamic theory, the governing principle of the id, involving the demands for immediate gratification of instinctual needs, p. 24.

polygenic Traits or characteristics that are determined by more than one gene, p. 18.

polysomnographic (PSG) recording The simultaneous measurement of multiple physiological responses during sleep or attempted sleep, p. 308.

population Total group of people, other organisms, or events, p. 439.

positive correlation Statistical relationship between two variables such that increases in one variable are associated with increases in the other, p. 436.

positive reinforcers Types of reinforcers that increase the frequency of a behaviour when they are presented. Food and social approval are generally, but not always, positive reinforcers. Contrast with *negative reinforcer*, p. 27.

positive symptoms The more flagrant features of schizophrenia characterized by the *presence* of abnormal behaviour, such as hallucinations, delusions, thought disorder, disorganized speech, and disorganized behaviour, p. 366.

possession In demonology, a type of superstitious belief in which abnormal behaviour is taken as a sign that the individual has become possessed by demons or the devil, usually as a form of retribution or the result of making a pact with the devil, p. 8.

posttraumatic stress disorder Disorder involving impaired functioning following exposure to a traumatic experience, such as combat, physical assault or rape, or natural or technological disasters, in which the person experiences, for at least one month, such problems as reliving or re-experiencing the trauma, intense fear, avoidance of event-related stimuli, generalized numbing of emotional responsiveness, and heightened autonomic arousal. Abbreviated *PTSD*, p. 116.

preconscious In psychodynamic theory, descriptive of material that lies outside of present awareness but can be brought into awareness by focusing attention. See also *unconscious*, p. 23.

premature ejaculation Type of sexual dysfunction involving a persistent or recurrent pattern of ejaculation occurring during sexual activity at a point before the man desires it, p. 343.

prepared conditioning Belief that people are genetically prepared to acquire fear responses to certain classes of stimuli, such as fears of large animals, snakes, heights, or strangers. Although the development of such phobias may have had survival value for prehistoric ancestors, such behaviour patterns may be less functional today, p. 122.

pressured speech Outpouring of speech in which words seem to surge urgently for expression, as in a manic state, p. 153.

prevalence Overall number of cases of a disorder existing in a population during a given period of time, p. 103.

primary process thinking In psychodynamic theory, the mental process in infancy by which the id seeks gratification of primitive impulses by means of imagining it possesses what it desires. Thinking that is illogical and magical and fails to discriminate between reality and fantasy, p. 24.

primary reinforcers Natural reinforcers or stimuli that have reinforcement value without learning. Water, food, warmth, and relief from pain are examples of primary reinforcers. Contrast with *secondary reinforcers*, p. 28.

proband Initial diagnosed case of a given disorder. Also called an *index case*, p. 440.

problem-solving therapy Form of therapy that focuses on helping people develop more effective problem-solving skills, p. 237.

prodromal phase (1) Stage in which the early features or signs of a disorder become apparent. (2) In schizophrenia, the period of decline in functioning that precedes the development of the first acute psychotic episode, p. 362.

projection In psychodynamic theory, a defence mechanism in which one's own impulses are attributed to another person, p. 120.

proteins Organic compounds consisting of amino acids that perform most life functions and make up the majority of cellular structures, p. 18.

psychedelics Class of drugs that induce sensory distortions or hallucinations. Also called *hallucinogens*, p. 268.

psychiatrist Physician who specializes in the diagnosis and treatment of mental disorders, p. 2.

psychic (1) Relating to mental phenomena. (2) A person who claims to be sensitive to supernatural forces, p. 23.

psychoactive Describing chemical substances or drugs that have psychological effects, p. 251.

psychoanalytic theory Theoretical model of personality developed by Freud. Also called *psychoanalysis*, p. 23.

psychodynamic model Theoretical model of Freud and his followers in which behaviour is viewed as the product of clashing forces within the personality, p. 15.

psychological dependence Reliance, as on a substance, although one may not be physiologically dependent, p. 254.

psychological disorders Disturbances of psychological functioning or behaviour associated with states of personal distress or impaired social, occupational, or interpersonal functioning. Also called *mental disorders*, p. 2.

psychometric approach Method of psychological assessment that seeks to use psychological tests to identify and measure the reasonably stable traits in an individual's personality that are believed to largely determine his or her behaviour, p. 51.

psychopathy Type of personality pattern characterized by affective and interpersonal traits, such as shallow emotions, selfishness, arrogance, superficial charm, deceitfulness, manipulativeness, irresponsibility, sensation seeking, and a lack of empathy, anxiety, and remorse, combined with persistent violations of social norms, a socially deviant and nomadic lifestyle, and impulsiveness, p. 218.

psychopharmacology Field of study that examines the effects of drugs on behaviour and psychological functioning and explores the use of psychoactive drugs in the treatment of emotional disorders, p. 66.

psychosis A severe form of disturbed behaviour in which people show impaired ability to interpret reality and difficulties in meeting the demands of daily life. Schizophrenia is a prominent example of a psychotic disorder. Plural: *psychoses*, p. 25.

psychotherapy Method of helping involving a systematic interaction between a therapist and a client that brings psychological principles to bear on influencing the client's thoughts, feelings, or behaviours to help that client overcome abnormal behaviour or adjust to problems in living, p. 65.

punishments Unpleasant stimuli that suppress the frequency of the behaviours they follow, p. 28.

R

random sampling Drawing samples in such a way that every member of a population has an equal probability of being selected, p. 439.

rapid flight of ideas A characteristic of manic behaviour involving rapid speech and changes of topics, p. 153.

reality principle In psychodynamic theory, the governing principle of the ego that involves consideration of what is socially acceptable and practical in gratifying needs, p. 24.

rebound anxiety Occurrence of strong anxiety following withdrawal from a tranquillizer, p. 67.

receptor site Part of a dendrite on the receiving neuron that is structured to receive a neurotransmitter, p. 22.

reciprocal determinism The ongoing process of two-way interactions among personal factors (cognitive abilities—expectancies, values, attitudes, and beliefs—as well as affective and biological characteristics), behaviours (skills, talents, habits, and interpersonal relations), and environmental factors (physical surroundings and other people), p. 32.

rehearsal In behaviour therapy, a practice opportunity in which a person enacts a desired response and receives feedback from others, p. 443.

reinforcement Stimulus that increases the frequency of the response it follows. See *positive reinforcers*, *negative reinforcers*, *primary reinforcers*, and *secondary reinforcers*, p. 27.

relapse Recurrence of a problem behaviour or disorder, p. 285.

relapse-prevention training Cognitive-behavioural technique used in the treatment of addictive behaviours that involves the use of behavioural and cognitive strategies to resist temptations and prevent lapses from becoming relapses, p. 285.

reliable In psychological assessment, the consistency of a measuring instrument, such as a psychological test or rating scale. There are various ways of measuring reliability, such as test-retest reliability, internal consistency, and interrater reliability. Also see *validity*, p. 61.

REM sleep REM (rapid eye movement) sleep is the stage of sleep associated with dreaming that is characterized by the appearance of rapid eye movements under closed eyelids. Hypocretin neurotransmitter is involved in arousal and wakefulness, p. 310.

repetitive transcranial magnetic stimulation A procedure that uses strong magnetic pulses to stimulate the brain. Abbreviated *rTMS*, p. 68.

repression In psychodynamic theory, a type of defence mechanism involving the ejection from awareness of anxiety-provoking ideas, images, or impulses without the conscious awareness that one has done so, p. 25.

residual phase In schizophrenia, the phase of the disorder that follows an acute phase, characterized by a return to a level of functioning typical of the prodromal phase, p. 362.

reversal design An A-B-A-B type of experimental single-subject design in which treatment is instituted following a baseline phase and then withdrawn (reversal phase) so as to examine effects on behaviour, p. 441.

S

sadomasochism Sexual activities between consenting partners involving the attainment of gratification by means of inflicting and receiving pain and humiliation, p. 335.

sample Part of a population, p. 439.

sanguine Cheerful, p. 9.

schizoid personality disorder Type of personality disorder characterized by detachment from social relationships and a restricted range of emotional expression, p. 215.

schizophrenia A chronic psychotic disorder characterized by acute episodes involving a break with reality, as manifested by such features as delusions, hallucinations, illogical thinking, incoherent speech, and bizarre behaviour, p. 359.

schizophrenogenic mother Type of mother, described as cold but also overprotective, who was believed to be capable of causing schizophrenia in her children. Research has failed to support the validity of this concept, p. 378.

schizotypal personality disorder Type of personality disorder characterized by acute discomfort in close relationships, cognitive or perceptual distortions, and eccentricities of behaviour, p. 216.

second-rank symptoms In Schneider's view, symptoms associated with schizophrenia that also occur in other psychological disorders, p. 360.

secondary process thinking In psychodynamic theory, the reality-based thinking processes and problem-solving activities of the ego, p. 24.

secondary reinforcers Stimuli that gain reinforcement value through their association with established reinforcers. Money and social approval are typically secondary reinforcers. Contrast with *primary reinforcers*, p. 28.

sedatives Types of depressant drugs that reduce states of tension and restlessness and induce sleep, p. 262.

selective abstraction In Beck's theory, a type of cognitive distortion involving the tendency to focus selectively only on the parts of one's experiences that reflect on one's flaws and to ignore those aspects that reveal one's strengths or competencies, p. 160.

selective serotonin-reuptake inhibitors (SSRIs) Type of antidepressant medication that prevents serotonin from being taken back up by the transmitting neuron, thus increasing its action, p. 67.

self Centre of consciousness that organizes sensory impressions and governs one's perceptions of the world. The sum total of a person's thoughts, sensory impressions, and feelings, p. 24.

self psychology Heinz Kohut's theory that describes processes that normally lead to the achievement of a cohesive sense of self or, in narcissistic personality disorder, to a grandiose but fragile sense of self, p. 233.

self-monitoring In behavioural assessment, the process of recording or observing one's own behaviour, thoughts, or emotions, p. 53.

self-spectatoring Tendency to observe one's behaviour as if one were a spectator of oneself. People with sexual dysfunctions often become self-spectators in the sense of focusing their attention during sexual activity on the response of their sex organs rather than on their partners or the sexual stimulation itself, p. 351.

semi-structured interviews Type of clinical interview in which interviewers are guided by a general outline but are free to modify the order in which questions are asked and to branch off in other directions, p. 42.

sensate focus exercises In sex therapy, mutual pleasuring activities between partners that are focused on the partners taking turns giving and receiving physical pleasure, p. 350.

separation anxiety disorder Childhood disorder characterized by extreme fears of separation from parents or others on whom the child is dependent, p. 417.

separation-individuation In Margaret Mahler's theory, the process by which young children come to separate psychologically from their mothers and to perceive themselves as separate and distinct persons, p. 234.

serotonin Type of neurotransmitter, imbalances of which have been linked to depressive and bipolar disorders and anxiety, p. 22.

serotonin-norepinephrine reuptake inhibitors (SNRIs) Type of antidepressant medication that works specifically on increasing levels of serotonin and norepinephrine by interfering with the reuptake of these chemicals by transmitting neurons, p. 67.

sexual assault Nonconsensual bodily contact for a sexual purpose, p. 337.

sexual dysfunctions Psychological disorders involving persistent difficulties with sexual interest, arousal, or response, p. 342.

sexual masochism disorder Type of paraphilic disorder characterized by sexual urges and sexually arousing fantasies involving receiving humiliation or pain, in which the person has either acted on these urges or is strongly distressed by them, p. 334.

sexual sadism disorder Type of paraphilic disorder or sexual deviation characterized by recurrent sexual urges and sexually arousing fantasies involving inflicting humiliation or physical pain on sex partners, in which the person has either acted on these urges or is strongly distressed by them, p. 334.

significant In statistics, a magnitude of difference that is taken as indicating meaningful differences between groups because of the low probability that it occurred by chance, p. 435.

single-case experimental design Type of case study in which the subject (case) is used as his or her own control by varying the conditions to which the subject is exposed (by use of a reversal phase) or by means of a multiple-baseline design, p. 441.

sleep–wake disorders Diagnostic category representing persistent or recurrent sleep-related problems that cause significant personal distress or impaired functioning, p. 308.

social anxiety disorder Excessive fear of engaging in behaviours that involve public scrutiny, p. 110.

social-cognitive theory A broader view of learning theory that emphasizes both situational determinants of behaviour (reinforcements and punishments) and cognitive factors (expectancies, values, attitudes, beliefs, etc.), p. 32.

soma Cell body, p. 20.

somatic symptom disorder A disorder involving one or more somatic symptoms which cause excessive concern to the extent that it affects the individual's thoughts, feelings, and behaviours in daily life, p. 203.

somatic symptom and related disorders Disorders in which people complain of physical (somatic) problems although no physical abnormality can be found. See *conversion disorder, illness anxiety disorder, somatic symptom disorder,* and *factitious disorder*, p. 201.

specific attribution In the reformulated helplessness theory, a type of attribution involving the belief that the cause of an event involved specific rather than generalized factors. Contrast with *global attribution*, p. 162.

specific learning disorder Deficiency in a specific learning ability noteworthy because of the individual's general intelligence and exposure to learning opportunities, p. 405.

specific phobias Persistent but excessive fears of a specific object or situation, such as a fear of heights or of small animals, p. 110.

splitting Term describing the inability of some people (especially people with borderline personalities) to reconcile the positive and negative aspects of themselves and others into a cohesive integration, resulting in sudden and radical shifts between strongly positive and strongly negative feelings, p. 223.

stable attribution In the reformulated helplessness theory, a type of attribution involving the belief that the cause of an event involved stable rather than changeable factors. Contrast with *unstable attribution*, p. 162.

structural hypothesis In Freud's theory, the belief that the clashing forces within the personality could be divided into three psychic structures: the id, the ego, and the superego, p. 23.

structured interviews Means by which an interviewer obtains clinical information from a client by asking a fairly standard series of questions concerning such issues as the client's presenting complaints or problems, mental state, life circumstances, and psychosocial or developmental history, p. 43.

stupor State of relative or complete unconsciousness in which a person is not generally aware of or responsive to the environment, as in a catatonic stupor, p. 366.

substance-induced disorders Disorders induced by the use of psychoactive substances, including intoxication, withdrawal syndromes, mood disorders, delirium, and amnesia, p. 251.

substance use disorders Patterns of maladaptive behaviour involving the use of a psychoactive substance, p. 251.

superego In psychodynamic theory, the psychic structure that represents the incorporation of the moral values of parents and important others and floods the ego with guilt and shame when it falls short of meeting those standards. The superego is governed by the moral principle and consists of two parts: the conscience and the ego ideal, p. 24.

survey method Method of scientific research in which large samples of people are questioned by the use of a survey instrument, p. 439.

symbiotic (1) In biology, the living together of two different but interdependent organisms. (2) In Margaret Mahler's object-relations theory, the term used to describe the state of oneness that normally exists between a mother and infant in which the infant's identity is fused with the mother's, p. 233.

synapse Junction between the terminal knob of one neuron and the dendrite or soma of another, through which nerve impulses pass, p. 21.

systematic desensitization Behaviour therapy technique for overcoming phobias by means of exposure (in imagination or by means of pictures or slides) to progressively more fearful stimuli while one remains deeply relaxed, p. 72.

systems perspective View that problems reflect the systems (family, social, school, ecological, etc.) in which they are embedded, p. 302.

T

tachycardia Abnormally rapid heartbeat, p. 251.

taijin-kyofu-sho Psychiatric syndrome found in Japan that involves excessive fear of offending or causing embarrassment to others. Abbreviated *TKS*, p. 62.

tardive dyskinesia Movement disorder characterized by involuntary movements of the face, mouth, neck, trunk, or extremities caused by long-term use of antipsychotic medications. Abbreviated *TD*, p. 382.

Tay-Sachs disease Disease of lipid metabolism that is genetically transmitted and usually results in death in early childhood, p. 401.

terminals In neuropsychology, the small branching structures found at the tips of axons, p. 20.

theories (1) Plausible or scientifically defensible explanations of events. (2) Formulations of the relationships underlying observed events. Theories are helpful to scientists because they provide a means of organizing observations and lead to predictions about future events, p. 434.

theory of mind The ability to appreciate that other people have a mental state that is different from one's own, p. 396.

thought disorder Disturbances in thinking characterized by various features, especially a breakdown in logical associations between thoughts, p. 363.

time out Behavioural technique in which an individual who emits an undesired behaviour is removed from an environment in which reinforcers are available and placed in an unreinforcing environment for a period of time as a form of punishment. Time out is frequently used in behavioural programs for modifying behaviour problems in children, in combination with positive reinforcement for desirable behaviour, p. 415.

token economies Behavioural treatment programs, in institutional settings, in which a controlled environment is constructed such that people are reinforced for desired behaviours by receiving tokens (such as poker chips) that may be exchanged for desired rewards or privileges, p. 73.

tolerance Physical habituation to a drug so that with frequent usage, higher doses are needed to attain similar effects, p. 66.

transference relationship In psychoanalysis, a client's transfer or generalization to the analyst of feelings and attitudes the client holds toward important figures in his or her life, p. 71.

transgender identity A type of gender identity in which the individual has the psychological sense of belonging to one gender while possessing the sexual organs of the other, p. 323.

transvestic disorder Type of paraphilic disorder characterized by recurrent sexual urges and sexually arousing fantasies involving cross-dressing, in which the person has either acted on these urges or is strongly distressed by them. Also termed *transvestism*, p. 330.

trephining Harsh prehistoric practice of cutting a hole in a person's skull, possibly as an ancient form of surgery for brain trauma, or possibly as a means of releasing the demons prehistoric people may have believed caused abnormal behaviour in the afflicted individuals, p. 8.

tricyclics Group of antidepressant drugs that increase the activity of norepinephrine and serotonin in the brain by interfering with the reuptake of these neurotransmitters by transmitting neurons. Also called *TCAs* (tricyclic antidepressants), p. 67.

two-factor model O. Hobart Mowrer's theory that both operant and classical conditioning are involved in the acquisition of phobic responses. The fear component of phobia is acquired by means of classical conditioning (pairing of a previously neutral stimulus with an aversive stimulus), and the avoidance component is acquired by means of operant conditioning (relief from anxiety negatively reinforces avoidance behaviour), p. 121.

U

unconditional positive regard In Carl Rogers's view, the expression of unconditional acceptance of another person's basic worth as a person, regardless of whether one approves of all of the behaviour of the other person. The ability to express unconditional positive regard is considered a quality of an effective person-centred therapist, p. 74.

unconditioned response Unlearned response or a response to an unconditioned stimulus. Abbreviated *UR* or *UCR*, p. 26.

unconditioned stimulus Stimulus that elicits an instinctive or unlearned response from an organism. Abbreviated *US* or *UCS*, p. 26.

unconscious (1) In psychodynamic theory, pertaining to impulses or ideas that are not readily available to awareness, in many instances because they are kept from awareness by means of *repression*. (2) Also in psychodynamic theory, the part of the mind that contains repressed material and primitive urges of the id. (3) More generally, a state of unawareness or loss of consciousness, p. 23.

unipolar Pertaining to a single pole or direction, as in unipolar (depressive) disorders. Contrast with *bipolar disorder*, p. 143.

unobtrusive Not interfering, p. 436.

unstable attribution In the reformulated helplessness theory, a type of attribution involving the belief that the cause of an event involved changeable rather than stable factors. Contrast with *stable attribution*, p. 162.

unstructured interviews Type of clinical interview in which interviewers determine which questions to ask rather than following a standard interview format, p. 42.

V

vaginismus The involuntary spasm of the muscles surrounding the vagina when vaginal penetration is attempted, making sexual intercourse difficult or impossible, p. 344.

validity (1) With respect to tests, the degree to which a test measures the traits or constructs that it purports to measure. (2) With respect to experiments, the degree to which an experiment yields scientifically accurate and defensible results, p. 61.

validity scales Groups of test items that serve to detect whether the results of a particular test are valid or whether a person responded in a random manner or in a way intended to create a favourable or unfavourable impression, p. 46.

variables Conditions that are measured (dependent variables) or manipulated (independent variables) in scientific studies, p. 436.

voyeuristic disorder Type of paraphilic disorder characterized by recurrent sexual urges and sexually arousing fantasies involving the act of watching unsuspecting others who are naked, in the act of undressing, or engaging in sexual activity, in which the person has either acted on these urges or is strongly distressed by them, p. 331.

W

waxy flexibility Feature of catatonia involving adopting a fixed posture into which people with schizophrenia have been positioned by others, p. 366.

withdrawal syndrome Characteristic cluster of withdrawal symptoms following the sudden reduction or abrupt cessation of use of a psychoactive substance after physiological dependence has developed, p. 251.

worldview Prevailing view of the times (English translation of the German *Weltanschauung*), p. 8.

REFERENCES

A

Abbey, A., Zawackia, T., Bucka, O., Clinton, A. M., & McAuslan, P. (2004). Sexual assault and alcohol consumption: What do we know about their relationship and what types of research are still needed? *Aggression and Violent Behavior, 9,* 271–303.

Abdulrehman, R. Y., & De Luca, R. V. (2001). The implications of childhood sexual abuse on adult social behavior. *Journal of Family Violence, 16,* 193–203.

Abi-Dargham, A. (2004). Do we still believe in the dopamine hypothesis? New data bring new evidence. *International Journal of Neuropsychopharmacology, 7*(Suppl. 1), S1–S5.

Aboriginal Planet. (2002). Aboriginal Planet—who are we? Retrieved from http://www.dfait-maeci.gc.ca/foreign policy/aboriginal/talk/talk-en.asp

Abracen, J., Looman, J., Ferguson, M., Harkins, L., & Mailloux, D. (2011). Recidivism among treated sexual offenders and comparison subjects: Recent outcome data from the Regional Treatment Centre (Ontario) high-intensity sex offender treatment programme. *Journal of Sexual Aggression, 17,* 142–152.

Abraham, K. (1948). The first pregenital stage of the libido. In D. Bryan & A. Strachey (Trans.), *Selected papers of Karl Abraham, M.D.* (pp. 248–279). London: Hogarth Press. (Original work published 1916)

Abramson, L. T., Seligman, M. E. P., & Teasdale, J. D. (1978). Learned helplessness in humans: Critique and reformulation. *Journal of Abnormal Psychology, 87,* 49–74.

Acculturation increases risk for substance use by foreign-born youth. (2004, January–February). *SAMHSA News, 12*(1). Retrieved from http://www.samhsa.gov/samhsa_news/VolumeXII_1/article2.htm

Achenbach, T. M., & Rescorla, L. A. (2001). *Manual for the ASEBA school-age forms and profiles: An integrated system multi-informant assessment.* Burlington: University of Vermont, Research Center for Children, Youth, and Families.

Ackard, D. M., Fulkerson, J. A., & Neumark-Sztainer, D. M. (2011). Psychological and behavioral risk profiles as they relate to eating disorder diagnoses and symptomatology among a school-based sample of youth. *International Journal of Eating Disorders, 44,* 440–446.

Addington, J., Piskulic, D., & Marshall, C. (2010). Psychosocial treatments for schizophrenia. *Current Directions in Psychological Science, 19,* 260–263.

Addolorato, G., Leggio, L., Abenavoli, L., & Gasbarrini, G. (2005). Neurobiochemical and clinical aspects of craving in alcohol addiction: A review. *Addictive Behaviors, 30,* 1209–1224.

Adewuya, A. O., & Makanjuola, R. O. A. (2008). Lay beliefs regarding causes of mental illness in Nigeria: Pattern and correlates. *Social Psychiatry and Psychiatric Epidemiology, 43,* 336–341.

Adlaf, E. M., Begin, P., & Sawka, E. (Eds.). (2005). *Canadian Addiction Survey (CAS): A national survey of Canadians' use of alcohol and other drugs.* Ottawa: Health Canada, Canadian Executive Council on Addictions, & Canadian Centre on Substance Abuse.

Afifi, T. O., Cox, B. J., & Enns, M. W. (2006). Mental health profiles among married, never-married, and separated/divorced mothers in a nationally representative sample. *Social Psychiatry and Psychiatric Epidemiology, 41,* 122–129.

Ahern, J., Galea, S., Resnick, H., Kilpatrick, D., Bucuvalas, M., Gold, J., & Vlahov, D. (2002). Television images and psychological symptoms after the September 11 terrorist attacks. *Psychiatry: Interpersonal and Biological Processes, 65,* 289–300.

Ainsworth, M. D. (1989). Attachments beyond infancy. *American Psychologist, 44,* 709–716.

Ainsworth, M. D. S., & Bowlby, J. (1991). An ethological approach to personality development. *American Psychologist, 46,* 333–341.

Akhtar, S. (1987). Schizoid personality disorder: A synthesis of developmental, dynamic, and descriptive features. *American Journal of Psychotherapy, 41,* 499–518.

Akhtar, S. (2003). Things: Developmental, psychopathological, and technical aspects of inanimate objects. *Canadian Journal of Psychoanalysis, 11*(1), 1–44.

Akiskal, H. S. (2001). Dysthymia and cyclothymia in psychiatric practice a century after Kraepelin. *Journal of Affective Disorders, 62,* 17–31.

Al-Abbadey, M., Liossi, C., Curran, N., Schoth, D. E., & Graham, C. A. (2016). Treatment of sexual pain disorders: A systematic review. *Journal of Sex & Marital Therapy, 42,* 99–142.

Alcoholics Anonymous. (2016). Estimates of AA groups and members as of January 1, 2016. Service material from the general service office. Retrieved from http://www.aa.org/assets/en_US/smf-53_en.pdf

Aldrich, M. S. (1992). Narcolepsy. *Neurology, 42*(7, Suppl. 6), 34–43.

Ali, S., & Findlay, C. (2016). A review of NICE guidelines on the management of borderline personality disorders. *British Journal of Medical Practitioners, 9,* a909.

Allderidge, P. (1979). Hospitals, madhouses and asylums: Cycles in the care of the insane. *British Journal of Psychiatry, 134,* 321–324.

Allen, D. N., Thaler, N. S., Ringdahl, E. N., Barney, S. J., & Mayfield, J. (2012). Comprehensive trail making test performance in children and adolescents with traumatic brain injury. *Psychological Assessment, 24,* 556–564.

Allen, M., Bourhis, J., Sahlstein, E., Laskowski, K., Falato, W. L., Ackerman, J., . . . Cashman, L. (2004). A meta-analysis of the relationship between social skills and sexual offenders. *Communication Reports, 17,* 1–10.

Alloy, L. B., Abramson, L. Y., Walshaw, P. D., & Neeren, A. M. (2006). Cognitive vulnerability to unipolar and bipolar mood disorders. *Journal of Social and Clinical Psychology, 25,* 726–754.

Alloy, L. B., Abramson, L. Y., Whitehouse, W. G., Hogan, M. E., Panzarella, C., & Rose, D. T. (2006). Prospective incidence of first onsets and recurrences of depression in individuals at high and low cognitive risk for depression. *Journal of Abnormal Psychology, 115,* 145–156.

Alloy, L. B., Abramson, L. Y., Whitehouse, W. G., Hogan, M. E., Tashman, N. A., Steinberg, D. L., . . . Donovan, P. (1999). Depressogenic cognitive styles: Predictive validity, information processing and personality characteristics, and developmental origins. *Behaviour Research and Therapy, 37,* 503–531.

Alpert, J., Nierenberg, A. A., Mischoulon, D., Otto, M. W., Zajecka, J., Murck, H., & Rosenbaum, J. F. (2005). A double-blind, randomized trial of St John's wort, fluoxetine, and placebo in major depressive disorder. *Journal of Clinical Psychopharmacology, 25,* 441–447.

Allsop, D. J., Copeland, J., Norberg, M. M., Fu, S., Molnar, A., Lewis, J., & Budney, A. J. (2012). Quantifying the clinical significance of cannabis withdrawal. *PLoS ONE, 7*(9), e44864.

Althof, S. E. (2012). Psychological interventions for delayed ejaculation/orgasm. *International Journal of Impotence Research, 24,* 131–136.

Aluja, A., Blanch, A., Blanco, E., & Balada, F. (2015). Affective modulation of the startle reflex and the reinforcement sensitivity theory of personality: The role of sensitivity to reward. *Physiology & Behavior, 138,* 332–339.

Amad, A., Ramoz, N., Thomas, P., Jardri, R., & Gorwood, P. (2014). Genetics of borderline personality disorder: systematic review and proposal of an integrative model. *Neuroscience and Biobehavioral Reviews, 40,* 6–19.

Amaro, H., Spear, S., Vallejo, Z., Conron, K., & Black, D. S. (2014). Feasibility, acceptability, and preliminary outcomes of a mindfulness-based relapse prevention intervention for culturally-diverse, low-income women in substance use disorder treatment. *Substance Use & Misuse, 49,* 547–559.

American Association on Intellectual and Developmental Disabilities. (2010). *Intellectual Disability: Definition, classification, and systems of supports* (11th ed.). Washington, DC: Author.

American Cancer Society. (2003). *Cancer facts and figures 2003.* Atlanta: Author.

American Psychiatric Association. (2000). *Diagnostic and statistical manual of mental disorders* (4th ed., text revision). Washington, DC: Author.

American Psychiatric Association. (2010). *Practice guideline for the treatment of patients with major depressive disorder* (3rd ed.). Washington, DC: Author.

American Psychiatric Association. (2013). *Diagnostic and statistical manual of mental disorders* (DSM-5) (5th ed.). Washington, DC: Author.

Ames, M. A., & Houston, D. A. (1990). Legal, social, and biological definitions of pedophilia. *Archives of Sexual Behavior, 19,* 333–342.

Amminger, G. P., Pape, S., Rock, D., Roberts, S. A., Ott, S. L., Squires-Wheeler, E., . . . Erlenmeyer-Kimling, L. (1999). Relationship between childhood behavioral disturbance and later schizophrenia in the New York High-Risk Project. *American Journal of Psychiatry, 156,* 525–530.

Anderson, L. M., Reilly, E. E., Schaumberg, K., Dmochowski, S., & Anderson, D. A. (2016). Contributions of mindful eating, intuitive eating, and restraint to BMI, disordered eating, and meal consumption in college students. *Eating and Weight Disorders, 21,* 83–90.

Angold, A., & Costello, E. J. (1993). Depressive comorbidity in children and adolescents: Empirical, theoretical, and methodological issues. *American Journal of Psychiatry, 150,* 1779–1791.

Angold, A., & Costello, E. J. (1996). Toward establishing an empirical basis for the diagnosis of oppositional defiant disorder. *Journal of the American Academy of Child and Adolescent Psychiatry, 35,* 1205–1212.

Anton, R. F. (1994). Medications for treating alcoholism. *Alcohol Health and Research World, 18,* 265–271.

Anton, R. F. (2008). Naltrexone for the management of alcohol dependence. *New England Journal of Medicine, 359,* 715–721.

Antonova, E., Sharma, T., Morris, R., & Kumari, V. (2004). The relationship between brain structure and neurocognition in schizophrenia: A selective review. *Schizophrenia Research, 70,* 117–145.

Antony, M. M., & Barlow, D. H. (2002). Specific phobias. In D. H. Barlow, *Anxiety and its disorders: The nature and treatment of anxiety and panic* (2nd ed., pp. 380–417). New York: Guilford.

Antony, M. M., Ledley, D. R., Liss, A., & Swinson, R. P. (2006). Responses to symptom induction exercises in panic disorder. *Behaviour Research and Therapy, 44,* 85–98.

Antony, M. M., & McCabe, R. E. (2005). *Overcoming animal and insect phobias: How to conquer fear of dogs, snakes, rodents, bees, spiders, and more.* Oakland, CA: New Harbinger.

Antony, M. M., Rowa, K., Liss, A., Swallow, S. R., & Swinson, R. P. (2005). Social comparison processes in social phobia. *Behavior Therapy, 36,* 65–75.

Antony, M. M., & Swinson, R. P. (2000). *Phobic disorders and panic in adults: A guide to assessment and treatment.* Washington, DC: American Psychological Association.

Apaydin, E. A., Maher, A. R., Shanman, R., Booth, M. S., Miles, J. N. V., Sorbero, M. E., & Hempel, S. (2016). A systematic review of St. John's wort for major depressive disorder. *Systematic Reviews, 5,* 1–25.

Appelbaum, P. S., & Gutheil, T. G. (1979). "Rotting with their rights on": Constitutional theory and clinical reality in drug refusal by psychiatric patients. *Bulletin of the American Academy of Psychiatry and the Law, 7,* 306–315.

Arango, C., Rapado-Castro, M., Reig, S., Castro-Fornieles, J., González-Pinto, A., Otero, S., . . . Desco, M. (2012). Progressive brain changes in children and adolescents with first-episode psychosis. *Archives of General Psychiatry, 69,* 16–26.

Arbuckle, T. E., Davis, K., Boylan, K., Fisher, M., & Fu, J. (2016). Bisphenol A, phthalates and lead and learning and behavioral problems in Canadian children 6–11 years of age: CHMS 2007–2009. *NeuroToxicology, 54,* 89–98.

Arguedas, D., Stevenson, R. J., & Langdon, R. (2012). Source monitoring and olfactory hallucinations in schizophrenia. *Journal of Abnormal Psychology, 121,* 936–943.

Arieti, S. (1974). *Interpretation of schizophrenia* (2nd ed.). New York: Basic Books.

Arnett, J. L. (2006). Psychology and health. *Canadian Psychology, 47*(1), 19–32.

Arnett, P. A., Smith, S. S., & Newman, J. P. (1997). Approach and avoidance motivation in psychopathic criminal offenders during passive avoidance. *Journal of Personality and Social Psychology, 72,* 1413–1428.

Arthur, N., & Januszkowski, T. (2001). The multicultural counselling competencies of Canadian counsellors. *Canadian Journal of Counselling, 35*(1), 36–48.

Arthur, N., & Stewart, J. (2001). Multicultural counselling in the new millennium: Introduction to the special theme issue. *Canadian Journal of Counselling, 35*(1), 3–14.

Asbridge, M., Hayden, J. A., & Cartwright, J. L. (2012). Acute cannabis consumption and motor vehicle collision risk: Systematic review of observational studies and meta-analysis. *British Medical Journal, 344,* e536.

Aston, R., & Cullumbine, H. (1959). Studies on the nature of the joint action of ethanol and barbiturates. *Toxicology and Applied Pharmacology, 1,* 65–72.

Atigari, O. V., Kelly, A. M., Jabeen, Q., & Healy, D. (2013). New onset alcohol dependence linked to treatment with selective serotonin reuptake inhibitors. *International Journal of Risk and Safety in Medicine, 25*(2), 105–109

Atladóttir, H. O., Henriksen, T. B., Schendel, D. E., & Parner, E. T. (2012). Autism after infection, febrile episodes, and antibiotic use during pregnancy: An exploratory study. *Pediatrics, 130,* e1447–e1454.

Attention deficit disorder—Part II. (1995, May). *The Harvard Mental Health Letter, 11*(11), 1–3.

Aubry, M., Cantu, R., Dvorak, J., Johnston, K., McCrory, P., Meeuwisse, W., & Molloy, M. (2009). Consensus statement on concussion in sport: The 3rd International Conference on Concussion in Sport held in Zurich, November 2008. *British Journal of Sports Medicine, 43,* i76–i84.

Ayoub, C. C. (2006). Munchausen by proxy. In T. G. Plante (Ed.), *Mental disorders of the new millennium: Vol. 3. Biology and function* (pp. 173–193). Westport, CT: Praeger.

Azrin, N. H., & Peterson, A. L. (1989). Reduction of an eye tic by controlled blinking. *Behavior Therapy, 20,* 467–473.

B

Bach, A. K., Barlow, D. H., & Wincze, J. P. (2004). The enhancing effects of manualized treatment for erectile dysfunction among men using sildenafil: A preliminary investigation. *Behavior Therapy, 35,* 55–73.

Bachman, P., & Cannon, T. D. (2005). Cognitive and neuroscience aspects of thought disorder. In K. J. Holyoak & R. G. Morrison (Eds.), *Cambridge handbook of thinking and reasoning* (pp. 493–526). New York: Cambridge University Press.

Baggott, M. J., Coyle, J. R., Erowid, E., & Robertson, L. C. (2011). Abnormal visual experiences in individuals with histories of hallucinogen use: A web-based questionnaire. *Drug and Alcohol Dependence, 114,* 61–67.

Bahammam, A., Delaive, K., Ronald, J., Manfreda, J., Roos, L., & Kryger, M. H. (1999). Health care utilization in males with obstructive sleep apnea syndrome two years after diagnosis and treatment. *Sleep, 22,* 740–747.

Baker, J. H., Maes, H. H., Lissner, L., Aggen, S. H., Lichtenstein, P., & Kendler, K. S. (2009). Genetic risk factors for disordered eating in adolescent males and females. *Journal of Abnormal Psychology, 118,* 576–578.

Bal, P., & Koenraadt, F. (2000). Criminal law and mentally ill offenders in comparative perspective. *Psychology, Crime and Law, 6,* 219–250.

Baldwin, A. R., Oei, T. P. S., & Young, R. (1994). To drink or not to drink: The differential role of alcohol expectancies and drinking refusal self-efficacy in quantity and frequency of alcohol consumption. *Cognitive Therapy and Research, 17,* 511–530.

Baldwin, D. S. (2006). Serotonin noradrenaline reuptake inhibitors: A new generation of treatment for anxiety disorders. *International Journal of Psychiatry in Clinical Practice, 67*(Suppl. 6), 9–15.

Bandelow, B., & Wedekind, D. (2015). Possible role of a dysregulation of the endogenous opioid system in antisocial personality disorder. *Human Psychopharmacology: Clinical and Experimental, 30,* 393–415.

Bandura, A. (1973). *Aggression: A social learning analysis.* Englewood Cliffs, NJ: Prentice-Hall.

Bandura, A. (1986). *Social foundations of thought and action: A social cognitive theory.* Englewood Cliffs, NJ: Prentice-Hall.

Bandura A. (1989). Social cognitive theory. In R. Vasta (Ed.), *Annals of child development. Vol. 6. Six theories of child development* (pp. 1–60). Greenwich, CT: JAI Press.

Bandura, A. (2001). Social cognitive theory: An agentic perspective. *Annual Review of Psychology, 52*(2), 1–26.

Bandura, A., Blanchard, E. B., & Ritter, B. (1969). The relative efficacy of desensitization and modeling approaches for inducing behavioral, affective, and cognitive changes. *Journal of Personality and Social Psychology, 13,* 173–199.

Bandura, A., Jeffery, R. W., & Wright, C. L. (1974). Efficacy of participant modeling as a function of response induction aids. *Journal of Abnormal Psychology, 83,* 56–64.

Bandura, A., Ross, D., & Ross, S. A. (1963). Imitation of film-mediated aggressive models. *Journal of Abnormal and Social Psychology, 66,* 3–11.

Banno, K., & Kryger, M. H. (2007). Sleep apnea: Clinical investigations in humans. *Sleep Medicine, 8*(4), 402–426.

Banno, K., Walld, R., & Kryger, M. H. (2005). Increasing obesity trends in patients with sleep-disordered breathing referred to a sleep disorders center. *Journal of Clinical Sleep Medicine, 1,* 364–366.

Baratta, A., Javelot, H., Morali, A., Halleguen, O., & Weiner, L. (2012). The role of antidepressants in treating sex offenders. *Sexologies, 21,* 106–108.

Barbaree, H. E., & Blanchard, R. (2008) Sexual deviance over the lifespan. In D. R. Laws & W. T. O'Donohue (Eds.), *Sexual deviance: Theory, assessment, and treatment* (pp. 37–60). New York: Guilford Press.

Barch, D. M. (2005). The cognitive neuroscience of schizophrenia. *Annual Review of Clinical Psychology, 1,* 321–353.

Barch, D. M. (2013). The CAINS: Theoretical and practical advances in the assessment of negative symptoms in schizophrenia. *American Journal of Psychiatry, 170,* 133–135.

Bardwell, W. A., Moore, P., Ancoli-Israel, S., & Dimsdale, J. E. (2003). Fatigue in obstructive sleep apnea: Driven by depressive symptoms instead of apnea severity? *The American Journal of Psychiatry, 160,* 350–355.

Barlow, D. H. (1986). Causes of sexual dysfunction: The role of anxiety and cognitive interference. *Journal of Consulting and Clinical Psychology, 54,* 140–148.

Barlow, D. H. (2002). *Anxiety and its disorders: The nature and treatment of anxiety and panic* (2nd ed.). New York: Guilford.

Barnett, E., Sussman, S., Smith, C., Rohrbach, L. A., & Spruijt-Metz, D. (2012). Motivational interviewing for adolescent substance use: A review of the literature. *Addictive Behaviors, 37,* 1325–1334.

Baron-Cohen, S. (1995). *Mindblindness: An essay on autism and theory of mind.* Cambridge, MA: MIT Press.

Baron-Cohen, S. (1998). Autism and "theory of mind": An introduction and review. International Symposium on Autism 1998. Toronto. Geneva Centre for Autism. Retrieved from http://www.autism.net/html/baron-cohen.html

Barrett, S. P., Gross, S. R., Garand, I., & Pihl, R. O. (2005). Patterns of simultaneous polysubstance use in Canadian rave attendees. *Substance Use & Misuse, 40,* 1525–1537.

Barrowclough, C., & Hooley, J. M. (2003). Attributions and expressed emotion: A review. *Clinical Psychology Review, 23,* 849–880.

Bartecchi, C. E., MacKenzie, T. D., & Schrier, R. W. (1994). The human costs of tobacco use. *New England Journal of Medicine, 330,* 907–912.

Basch, M. F. (1980). *Doing psychotherapy.* New York: Basic Books.

Basoglu, M., Marks, I., Livanou, M., & Swinson, S. (1997). Double-blindness procedures, rater blindness, and ratings of outcome. *Archives of General Psychiatry, 54,* 744–748.

Bassarath, L. (2003). Medication strategies in childhood aggression: A review. *Canadian Journal of Psychiatry, 48,* 367–373.

Bassett, A. S., & Chow, E. W. C. (1999). 22q11 deletion syndrome: A genetic subtype of schizophrenia. *Biological Psychiatry, 46,* 882–891.

Basson, R. (2001). Human sex-response cycles. *Journal of Sex & Marital Therapy, 27,* 33–43.

Basson, R. (2005). Women's sexual dysfunction: Revised and expanded definitions. *Canadian Medical Association Journal, 172,* 1327–1333.

Bastiaansen, J. A., Thioux, M., Nanetti, L., Van der Gaag, C., Ketelaars, C., Minderaa, R., & Keysers, C. (2011). Age-related increase in inferior frontal gyrus activity and social functioning in autism spectrum disorder. *Biological Psychiatry, 69,* 832–838.

Basu, J. (2014). Psychologists' ambivalence toward ambiguity: Relocating the projective test debate for multiple interpretative hypotheses. *SIS Journal of Projective Psychology & Mental Health, 21,* 25–36.

Bateman, R. J., Xiong, C., Benzinger, T. L. S., Fagan, A. M., Goate, A., Fox, N. C., . . . Morris, J. C. (2012). Clinical and biomarker changes in dominantly inherited Alzheimer's disease. *New England Journal of Medicine, 367,* 795–804.

Bateson, G. D., Jackson, D., Haley, J., & Weakland, J. (1956). Toward a theory of schizophrenia. *Behavioral Science, 1,* 251–264.

Baucom, D. H., Shoham, V., Mueser, K. T., Daiuto, A. D., & Stickle, T. (1998). Empirically supported couple and family interventions for marital distress and adult mental health problems. *Journal of Consulting and Clinical Psychology, 66,* 53–88.

Bauer, S. M., Schanda, H., Karakula, H., Olajossy-Hilkesberger, L., Rudaleviciene, P., Okribelashvili, N., . . . Stompe, T. (2011). Culture and the prevalence of hallucinations in schizophrenia. *Comprehensive Psychiatry, 52,* 319–325.

Baumann, C. R., Khatami, R., Werth, E., & Bassetti, C. L. (2006). Hypocretin (orexin) deficiency predicts severe objective excessive daytime sleepiness in narcolepsy with cataplexy. *Journal of Neurology, Neurosurgery, and Psychiatry, 77,* 402–404.

Baur, E., Forsman, M., Santtila, P., Johansson, A., Sandnabba, K., & Långström, N. (2016). Paraphilic sexual interests and sexually coercive behaviors: A population-based twin study. *Archives of Sexual Behavior, 45,* 1163–1172.

Baxter, L. R., Ackerman, R. F., Swerdlow, N. R., Brody, A., Saxena, S., Schwartz, J. M., . . . Phelps, M. E. (2000). Specific brain system mediation of obsessive-compulsive disorder responsive to either medication or behavior therapy. In W. K. Goodman, M. V. Rudorfer, & J. D. Maser (Eds.), *Obsessive-compulsive disorder: Contemporary issues in treatment* (pp. 573–609). Mahwah, NJ: Erlbaum.

Baylis, P. J. (2002). Promoting resilience: A review of the literature. Alberta Mental Health Board. Retrieved from http://www.amhb.ab.ca/chmh/resources/page.cfm?pg=Promoting%20Resilience%20

Beal, J. A. (2016). Adolescent use of e-cigarettes: What are the risks? *American Journal of Maternal Child Nursing, 41,* 310.

Beard, K. W. (2005). Internet addiction: A review of current assessment techniques and potential assessment questions. *Cyber Psychology & Behavior, 8,* 7–14.

Beaudette, J. N., & Stewart, L. A. (2016). National prevalence of mental disorders among incoming Canadian male offenders. *Canadian Journal of Psychiatry, 61,* 624–632.

Beck, A. T. (1976). *Cognitive therapy and the emotional disorders.* New York: International Universities Press.

Beck, A. T., Brown, G., Berchick, R. J., Stewart, B. L., & Steer, R. A. (1990). Relationship between hopelessness and ultimate suicide: A replication with psychiatric outpatients. *American Journal of Psychiatry, 147*, 190–195.

Beck, A. T., & Clark, D. A. (1997). An information processing model of anxiety: Automatic and strategic processes. *Behaviour Research and Therapy, 35*, 49–58.

Beck, A. T., & Dozois, D. J. A. (2011). Cognitive therapy: Current status and future directions. *Annual Review of Medicine, 62*, 397–409.

Beck, A. T., Freeman, A., Davis, D. D., & Associates. (2004). *Cognitive therapy of personality disorders* (2nd ed.). Guilford Clinical Psychology and Psychopathology Series. New York: Guilford Press.

Beck, A. T., Rush, A. J., Shaw, B. F., & Emery, G. (1979). *Cognitive therapy of depression*. New York: Guilford.

Beck, A. T., & Young, J. E. (2001). Depression. In D. H. Barlow (Ed.), *Clinical handbook of psychological disorders: A step-by-step treatment manual* (pp. 206–244). New York: Guilford.

Beck, C. A., Patten, S. B., Williams, J. V. A., Wang, J. L., Currie, S. R., Maxwell, C. J., & el-Guebaly, N. (2005). Antidepressant utilization in Canada. *Social Psychiatry and Psychiatric Epidemiology, 40*, 799–807.

Beck, R., & Perkins, T. S. (2001). Cognitive content-specificity for anxiety and depression: A meta-analysis. *Cognitive Therapy and Research, 25*, 651–663.

Becker, D., & Lamb, S. (1994). Sex bias in the diagnosis of borderline personality disorder and posttraumatic stress disorder. *Professional Psychology: Research and Practice, 25*, 55–61.

Beech, A. R., & Mitchell, I. J. (2005). A neurobiological perspective on attachment problems in sexual offenders and the role of selective serotonin re-uptake inhibitors in the treatment of such problems. *Clinical Psychology Review, 25*, 153–182.

Behar, E., & Borkovec, T. D. (2006). The nature and treatment of generalized anxiety disorder. In B. O. Rothbaum (Ed.), *Pathological anxiety: Emotional processing in etiology and treatment* (pp. 181–196). New York: Guilford.

Beidel, D. C., & Turner, S. M. (1986). A critique of the theoretical bases of cognitive behavioral theories and therapy. *Clinical Psychology Review, 6*, 177–199.

Beiser, M. (2003). Culture and psychiatry, or "the tale of the hole and the cheese." *Canadian Journal of Psychiatry, 48*(3), 143–144.

Beitman, B. D., Goldfried, M. R., & Norcross, J. C. (1989). The movement toward integrating the psychotherapies: An overview. *American Journal of Psychiatry, 146*, 138–147.

Bellack, A. S., & Mueser, K. T. (1990). Schizophrenia. In A. S. Bellack, M. Hersen, & A. E. Kazdin (Eds.), *International handbook of behavior modification and therapy* (2nd ed., pp. 353–370). New York: Plenum.

Bentall, R. P. (1990). The illusion of reality: A review and integration of psychological research on hallucinations. *Psychological Bulletin, 107*, 82–95.

Berenbaum, H., & Oltmanns, T. F. (2005). Emotional experience and expression in schizophrenia and depression. In P. Ekman & E. L. Rosenberg (Eds.), *What the face reveals: Basic and applied studies of spontaneous expression using the Facial Action Coding System (FACS)* (2nd ed., pp. 441–458). New York: Oxford University Press.

Berenson, K., R., Downey, G., Rafaeli, E., Coifman, K. G., & Paquin, N. L. (2011). The rejection–rage contingency in borderline personality disorder. *Journal of Abnormal Psychology, 120*, 681–690.

Bergeron, S., Corsini-Munt, S., Aerts, L., Rancourt, K., & Rosen, N. O. (2015). Female sexual pain disorders: A review of the literature on etiology and treatment. *Current Sexual Health, 7*, 159–169.

Bergida, H., & Lenzenweger, M. F. (2006). Schizotypy and sustained attention: Confirming evidence from an adult community sample. *Journal of Abnormal Psychology, 115*, 545–551.

Berlim, M. T., & Turecki, G. (2007). Definition, assessment, and staging of treatment-resistant refractory major depression: A review of current concepts and methods. *Canadian Journal of Psychiatry, 52*, 46–54.

Berridge, K. C., & Kringelbach, M. L. (2015). Pleasure systems in the brain. *Neuron, 86*, 646–664.

Bertelsen, M., Jeppesen, P., Petersen, L., Thorup, A., Øhlenschlaeger, J., le Quach, P., . . . Nordentoft, M. (2008). Five-year follow-up of a randomized multicenter trial of intensive early intervention vs. standard treatment for patients with a first episode of psychotic illness: The OPUS trial. *Archives of Geneneral Psychiatry, 65*, 762–771.

Bertrand, K., Roy, E., Vaillancourt, E., Vandermeerschen, J., Berbiche, D., & Boivin, J. F. (2015). Randomized controlled trial of motivational interviewing for reducing injection risk behaviours among people who inject drugs. *Addiction, 110*, 832–841.

Bewernick, B. H., Hurlemann, R., Matusch, A., Kayser, S., Grubert, C., Hadrysiewicz, B., . . . Schlaepfer, T. E. (2010). Nucleus accumbens deep brain stimulation decreases ratings of depression and anxiety in treatment-resistant depression. *Biological Psychiatry, 67*, 110–116.

Bibby, R. W. (2006). *The boomer factor: What Canada's most famous generation is leaving behind*. Toronto: Bastian Books.

Bijttebier, P., Beck, I., Claes, L., & Vandereycken, W. (2009). Gray's reinforcement sensitivity theory as a framework for research on personality-psychopathology associations. *Clinical Psychology Review, 29*, 421–430.

Bilginer, C., & Kandil, S. (2016). Emotional and behavioral characteristics of childhood depression. *Journal of Experimental and Clinical Medicine, 33*, 85–92.

Biran, M. (1988). Cognitive and exposure treatment for agoraphobia: Reexamination of the outcome research. *Journal of Cognitive Psychotherapy: An International Quarterly, 2*(3), 165–178.

Black, D. W. (2015). The natural history of antisocial personality disorder. *Canadian Journal of Psychiatry, 60*(7), 309–314.

Blakeslee, S. (1994, August 16). New clue to cause of dyslexia seen in mishearing of fast sounds. *The New York Times*, pp. C1, C10.

Blanchard, R. (2010). The DSM diagnostic criteria for transvestic fetishism. *Archives of Sexual Behavior, 39*, 363–372.

Bland, R. C. (1998). Psychiatry and the burden of mental illness. *Canadian Journal of Psychiatry, 43*, 801–810.

Blankstein, K. R., & Segal, Z. V. (2001). Cognitive assessment: Issues and methods. In K. S. Dobson (Ed.), *Handbook of cognitive-behavioral therapies* (2nd ed., pp. 40–85). New York: Guilford.

Blier, P. (2006). Dual serotonin and noradrenaline reuptake inhibitors: Focus on their differences. *International Journal of Psychiatry in Clinical Practice, 10*(Suppl. 2), 22–32.

Blier, P., Habib, R., & Flament, M. F. (2006). Pharmacotherapies in the management of obsessive-compulsive disorder. *Canadian Journal of Psychiatry, 51*, 417–430.

Bloch, M., Rotenberg, N., Koren, D., & Ehud, K. (2006). Risk factors for early postpartum depressive symptoms. *General Hospital Psychiatry, 28*, 3–8.

Blodgett Salafia, E. H., Schaefer, M. K., & Haugen, E. C. (2014). Connections between marital conflict and adolescent girls'disordered eating: Parent–adolescent relationship quality as a mediator. *Journal of Child and Family Studies, 23*, 1128–1138.

Boak, A., Hamilton, H. A., & Adlaf, E. M. (2014). The mental health and well-being of Ontario students, 1991–2013: Detailed OSDUHS findings. *CAMH Research Document Series, 38*. Toronto: Centre for Addiction and Mental Health.

Boak, A., Hamilton, H., Adlaf, E., Henderson, J. and Mann, R. (2016). The mental health and well-being of Ontario students, 1991–2015: Detailed OSDUHS findings *CAMH Research Document Series, 43*. Toronto: Centre for Addiction and Mental Health.

Boak, A., Hamilton, H. A., Adlaf, E. M., & Mann, R. E. (2015). Drug use among Ontario students, 1977–2015: Detailed OSDUHS findings. *CAMH Research Document Series, 41*. Toronto: Centre for Addiction and Mental Health.

Boehm, I., Finke, B., Tam, F. I., Fittig, E., Scholz, M., Gantchev, K., . . . Ehrlich, S. (2016). Effects of perceptual body image distortion and early weight gain on long-term outcome of adolescent anorexia nervosa. *European Child & Adolescent Psychiatry, 25*, 1319–1326.

Boetsch, E. A., Green, P. A., & Pennington, B. F. (1996). Psychosocial correlates of dyslexia across the lifespan. *Development and Psychopathology, 8*, 539–562.

Boggs, C. D., Morey, L. C., Skodol, A. E., Shea, M. T., Sanislow, C. A., Grilo, C. M., . . . Gunderson, J. G. (2005). Differential impairment as an indicator of sex bias in DSM-IV criteria for four personality disorders. *Psychological Assessment, 4,* 492–496.

Bohra, N., Srivastava, S., & Bhatia, M. S. (2015). Depression in women in Indian context. *Indian Journal of Psychiatry, 57,* 239–245.

Bond, M. (2006). Psychodynamic psychotherapy in the treatment of mood disorders. *Current Opinion in Psychiatry, 19,* 40–43.

Bondi, M. W., & Lange, K. L. (2001). Alzheimer's disease. In H. S. Friedman (Ed.), *The disorders: Specialty articles from the encyclopedia of mental health.* San Diego, CA: Academic Press.

Bondolfi, G., Jermann, F., Van der Linden, M., Gex-Fabry, M., Bizzini, L., Rouget, B. W., . . . Bertschy, G. (2010). Depression relapse prophylaxis with mindfulness-based cognitive therapy: Replication and extension in the Swiss health care system. *Journal of Affective Disorders, 122,* 224–231.

Bongar, B. (2002). *The suicidal patient: Clinical and legal standards of care.* Washington, DC: American Psychological Association.

Bonnano, G. A. (2005). Resilience in the face of potential trauma. *Current Directions in Psychological Science, 14,* 135–138.

Booij, L., Casey, K. F., Antunes, J. M., Szyf, M., Joober, R., Israël, M., & Steiger, H. (2015). DNA methylation in individuals with anorexia nervosa and in matched normal-eater controls: A genome-wide study. *International Journal of Eating Disorders, 48,* 874–882.

Bookheimer, S., & Burggren, A. (2009). APOE-4 genotype and neurophysiological vulnerability to Alzheimer's and cognitive aging. *Annual Review of Clinical Psychology, 5,* 343–362.

Boos, H. B., Aleman, A., Cahn, W., Hulshoff Pol, H., & Kahn, R. S. (2007). Brain volumes in relatives of patients with schizophrenia: A meta-analysis. *Archives of General Psychiatry, 64,* 297–304.

Bornstein, M. R., Bellack, A. S., & Hersen, M. (1977). Social-skills training for unassertive children: A multiple-baseline analysis. *Journal of Applied Behavior Analysis, 10,* 183–195.

Bornstein, R. F. (1992). The dependent personality: Developmental, social, and clinical perspectives. *Psychological Bulletin, 112,* 3–23.

Bornstein, R. F. (1999). Dependent and histrionic personality disorders. In T. Millon & P. H. Blaney (Eds.), *Oxford textbook of psychopathology* (pp. 535–554). New York: Oxford University Press.

Bourgon, L. N., & Kellner, C. H. (2000). Relapse of depression after ECT: A review. *Journal of ECT, 16,* 19–31.

Bowlby, J. (1988). *A secure base: Clinical applications of attachment theory.* New York: Basic Books.

Boyce, P., & Hickey, A. (2005). Psychosocial risk factors to major depression after childbirth. *Social Psychiatry and Psychiatric Epidemiology, 40,* 605–612.

Braaten, E. B., & Rosén, L. E. (2000). Self-regulation of affect in attention deficit–hyperactivity disorder (ADHD) and non-ADHD boys: Differences in empathic responding. *Journal of Consulting and Clinical Psychology, 68,* 313–321.

Bradley, E. A., Thompson, A., & Bryson, S. E. (2002). Mental retardation in teenagers: Prevalence data from the Niagara Region, Ontario. *Canadian Journal of Psychiatry, 47,* 652–659.

Brandon, T. H., Vidrine, J. I., & Litvin, E. B. (2007). Relapse and relapse prevention. *Annual Review of Clinical Psychology, 3,* 258–284.

Brannigan, G. G., & Decker, S. L. (2006). The Bender-Gestalt II. *American Journal of Orthopsychiatry, 76,* 10–12.

Braskie, M. N., Jahanshad, N., Stein, J. L., Barysheva, M., McMahon, K. L., de Zubicaray, G. I., . . . Thompson, P. M. (2011). Common Alzheimer's disease risk variant within the CLU gene affects white matter microstructure in young adults. *Journal of Neuroscience, 31,* 6764–6770.

Braun, J. M., Kahn, R. S., Froehlich, T., Auinger, P., & Lanphear, B. P. (2006). Exposures to environmental toxicants and attention deficit hyperactivity disorder in U.S. children. *Environmental Health Perspectives, 114,* 1904–1909.

Braxton, L. E., Calhoun, P. S., Williams, J. E., & Boggs, C. D. (2007). Validity rates of the Personality Assessment Inventory and the Minnesota Multiphasic Personality Inventory–2 in a VA medical center setting. *Journal of Personality Assessment, 88*(1), 5–15.

Brennand, K. J., Simone, A., Jou, J., Gelboin-Burkhart, C., Tran, N., Sangar, S., . . . Gage, F. H. (2011). Modelling schizophrenia using human induced pluripotent stem cells. *Nature, 473,* 221–225.

Brent, D. A., & Mann, J. J. (2006). Familial pathways to suicidal behavior—Understanding and preventing suicide among adolescents. *New England Journal of Medicine, 355,* 2719–2721.

Brent, D. A., Melhem, N. M., Oquendo, M., Burke, A., Birmaher, B., Stanley, B., . . . Mann, J. J. (2015). Familial pathways to early-onset suicide attempt. *JAMA Psychiatry, 72,* 160–168.

Breslau, N., Peterson, E. L., Schultz, L. R., Chilcoat, H. D., & Andreski, P. (1998). Major depression and stages of smoking: A longitudinal investigation. *Archives of General Psychiatry, 55,* 161–166.

Breslow, N. (1989). Sources of confusion in the study and treatment of sadomasochism. *Journal of Social Behavior and Personality, 4,* 263–274.

Bricker, J. B., Peterson, A. V., Jr., Andersen, M. R., Rajana, K. B., Leroux, B. G., & Sarasona, I. G. (2006). Childhood friends who smoke: Do they influence adolescents to make smoking transitions? *Addictive Behaviors, 31,* 889–900.

Brickman, J., & Briere, J. (1984). Incidence of rape and sexual assault in an urban Canadian population. *International Journal of Women's Studies, 7,* 195–206.

Brody, J. E. (1992, June 16). Suicide myths cloud efforts to save children. *The New York Times,* pp. C1, C3.

Brody, J. E. (1995, August 2). With more help available for impotence, few men seek it. *The New York Times,* p. C9.

Brotto, L. A., & Basson, R. (2014). Group mindfulness-based therapy significantly improves sexual desire in women. *Behaviour Research and Therapy, 57,* 43–54.

Brown, R. J. (2004). Psychological mechanisms of medically unexplained symptoms: An integrative conceptual model. *Psychological Bulletin, 130,* 793–812.

Brown, S. L., & Forth, A. E. (1997). Psychopathy and sexual assault: Static risk factors, emotional precursors, and rapist subtypes. *Journal of Consulting and Clinical Psychology, 65,* 848–857.

Brown, T. A., Di Nardo, P. A., Lehman, C. L., & Campbell, L. A. (2001). Reliability of DSM-IV anxiety and mood disorders: Implications for the classification of emotional disorders. *Journal of Abnormal Psychology, 110*(1), 49–58.

Brown, T. A., & Keel, P. K. (2012). Current and emerging directions in the treatment of eating disorders. *Substance Abuse: Research and Treatment, 6,* 33–61.

Bucci, S., Birchwood, M., Twist, L., Tarrier, N., Emsley, R., & Haddock, G. (2013). Predicting compliance with command hallucinations: Anger, impulsivity and appraisals of voices' power and intent. *Schizophrenia Research, 147,* 163–168.

Buchert, R., Thomasius, R., Wilke, F., Petersen, K., Nebeling, B., Obrocki, J., . . . Clausen, M. (2004). A voxel-based PET investigation of the long-term effects of "ecstasy" consumption on brain serotonin transporters. *American Journal of Psychiatry, 161,* 1181–1189.

Buchhave, P., Minthon, L., Zetterberg, H., Wallin, A. K., Blennow, K., & Hansson, O. (2012). Cerebrospinal fluid levels of b-Amyloid 1–42, but not of tau, are fully changed already 5 to 10 years before the onset of Alzheimer dementia. *Archives of General Psychiatry, 69,* 98–106.

Buchman, A. S., Boyle, P. A., Yu, L., Shah, R. C., Wilson, R. S., & Bennett, D. A. (2012). Total daily physical activity and the risk of AD and cognitive decline in older adults. *Neurology, 78,* 1323–1329.

Buhr, K., & Dugas, M. J. (2006). Investigating the construct validity of intolerance of uncertainty and its unique relationship with worry. *Journal of Anxiety Disorders, 20,* 222–236.

Bulik, C. M., Marcus, M. D., Zerwas, S., Levine, M. D., & La Via, M. (2012). The changing "weightscape" of bulimia nervosa. *American Journal of Psychiatry, 169,* 1031–1036.

Burke, J. D., Waldman, I., & Lahey, B. B. (2010). Predictive validity of childhood oppositional defiant disorder and conduct disorder: Implications for the DSM-V. *Journal of Abnormal Psychology, 119,* 739–751.

Burke, R. S., & Stephens, R. S. (1999). Social anxiety and drinking in college students: A social cognitive theory analysis. *Clinical Psychology Review, 19,* 513–530.

Burns, D. D. (1980). *Feeling good: The new mood therapy.* New York: Morris.

Burns, D. D., & Beck, A. T. (1978). Modification of mood disorders. In J. P. Foreyt & D. P. Rathjen (Eds.), *Cognitive behavior therapy: Research and application* (pp. 109–134). New York: Plenum Press.

Bush, G., Valera, E. M., & Seidman, L. J. (2005). Functional neuroimaging of attention-deficit/hyperactivity disorder: A review and suggested future directions. *Biological Psychiatry, 57,* 1273–1284.

Bushnik, T. (2016). The health of girls and women. *Women in Canada: A gender-based statistical report.* Catalogue no. 89-503-X. Ottawa: Statistics Canada.

Butcher, J. N. (2011). *A beginner's guide to the MMPI-2* (3rd ed.). Washington, DC: American Psychological Association.

Butler, M., & Pang, M. (2014). Current issues in mental health in Canada: Child and youth mental health. Retrieved from www.lop.parl.gc.ca/Content/LOP/ResearchPublications/2014-13-e.pdf

Byrne, S. M., Fursland, A., Allen, K. L., & Watson, H. (2011). The effectiveness of enhanced cognitive behavioural therapy for eating disorders: An open trial. *Behaviour Research and Therapy, 49,* 219–226.

C

Caffier, P. P., Berl, J. C., Muggli, A., Reinhardt, A., Jakob, A., Möser, M., . . . Hölzl, M. (2007). Snoring noise pollution— the need for objective quantification of annoyance, regulatory guidelines and mandatory therapy for snoring. *Physiological Measurement, 28,* 25–40.

Calati, R., Gressier, F., Balestri, M., & Serretti, A. (2013). Genetic modulation of borderline personality disorder: Systematic review and meta-analysis. *Journal of Psychiatric Research, 47,* 1275–1287.

Calhoun, K. S., & Atkeson, B. M. (1991). *Treatment of rape victims: Facilitating psychosocial adjustment.* New York: Pergamon.

Callinan, P. A., & Feinberg, A. P. (2006). The emerging science of epigenomics. *Human Molecular Genetics, 15*(Suppl. 1), R95–R101.

Camara, W. J., Nathan, J. S., & Puente, A. E. (2000). Psychological test usage: Implications in professional psychology. *Professional Psychology: Research and Practice, 31*(2), 141–154.

Campos-Rodriguez, F., Martinez-Garcia, M. A., de la Cruz-Moron, I., Almeida-Gonzalez, C., Catalan-Serra, P., & Montserrat, J. M. (2012). Cardiovascular mortality in women with obstructive sleep apnea with or without continuous positive airway pressure treatment: A cohort study. *Annals of Internal Medicine, 156,* 115–122.

Canadian Centre for Justice Statistics. (1999). Crime statistics in Canada. *Juristat, 20*(5).

Canadian Centre for Justice Statistics. (2003). *Special study on mentally disordered accused in the criminal justice system* (Catalogue No. 85-559-XIE). Ottawa: Statistics Canada.

Canadian Centre on Substance Abuse. (2016). *CCENDU Bulletin: The availability of take-home naloxone in Canada.* Ottawa: Author.

Canadian Centre on Substance Abuse & Centre for Addiction and Mental Health. (1999). *Canadian profile: Alcohol, tobacco and other drugs.* Ottawa: Author.

Canadian Institute for Health Information. (2001). The Canadian enhancement of ICD-10 (*International Statistical Classification of Diseases and Related Health Problems,* tenth revision): Final report. Ottawa: Author.

Canadian Institute for Health Information. (2015). *Care for children and youth with mental disorders.* Ottawa: Author.

Canadian Lung Association. (2006). Sleep apnea. Retrieved from http://www.lung.ca/diseases-maladies/apnea-apnee_e.php

Canadian Mental Health Association. (2000). Early psychosis intervention. Retrieved from http://www.cmha.ca/bins/content_page.asp?cid=3-105-107

Canadian Press. (2007, October 3). Dallaire says PTSD seared genocide in his memory. *CBC News.* Retrieved from http://www.cbc.ca/news/canada/montreal/story/2007/10/03/qc-dallaire1003.html

Canadian Psychological Association. (2000). *Canadian Code of Ethics for Psychologists.* Retrieved from: http://www.cpa.ca/aboutcpa/committees/ethics/codeofethics/

Canadian Psychological Association. (2002). The clinical psychologist in Canada: How can we help? Retrieved October 2, 2011, from http://www.cpa.ca/cpasite/userfiles/Documents/sections/clinical/brochureE.pdf

Canadian Psychological Association. (2016). *Canadian code of ethics for psychologists* (4th ed.). Ottawa: Author.

Canli, T., Qiu, M., Omura, K., Congdon, E., Haas, B. W., Amin, Z., . . . Lesch, K. P. (2006). Neural correlates of epigenesis. *Proceedings of the National Academy of Sciences of the United States of America, 103,* 16033–16038.

Capps, L., Kasari, C., Yirmiya, N., & Sigman, M. (1993). Parental perception of emotional expressiveness in children with autism. *Journal of Consulting and Clinical Psychology, 61,* 475–484.

Cardeña, E., & Carlson, E. (2011). Acute stress disorder revisited. *Annual Review of Clinical Psychology, 7,* 245–267.

Carey, G. (1992). Twin imitation for antisocial behavior: Implications for genetic and family environment research. *Journal of Abnormal Psychology, 101,* 18–25.

Carey, M. P., Wincze, J. P., & Meisler, A. W. (1998). Sexual dysfunction: Male erectile disorder. In D. H. Barlow (Ed.), *Clinical handbook for psychological disorders: A step-by-step treatment manual* (pp. 442–480). New York: Guilford.

Carmichael, K. L. C., Sellbom, M., Liggett, J., & Smith, A. (2016). A personality and impairment approach to examine the similarities and differences between avoidant personality disorder and social anxiety disorder. *Personality and Mental Health, 10,* 337–347.

Carney, C. E., & Segal, Z. V. (2005). Mindfulness-based cognitive therapy for depression. In L. VandeCreek (Ed.), *Innovations in clinical practice: Focus on adults* (pp. 5–17). Sarasota, FL: Professional Resource Press.

Carpenter, S. (2013, January). Awakening to sleep. *Monitor on Psychology, 44,* 40–45.

Carr, J. L., & VanDeusen, K. M. (2004). Risk factors for male sexual aggression on college campuses. *Journal of Family Violence, 19,* 279–289.

Carrillo, M. C., Blennow, K., Soares, H., Lewczuk, P., Mattsson, N., Oberoi, P., . . . Zetterberg, H. (2013). Global standardization measurement of cerebral spinal fluid for Alzheimer's disease: An update from the Alzheimer's Association Global Biomarkers Consortium. *Alzheimer's & Dementia, 9,* 137–140.

Carson, R. C., Hollon, S. D., & Shelton, R. C. (2010). Depressive realism and clinical depression. *Behaviour Research and Therapy, 48,* 257–265.

Carter, J. C., Olmsted, M. P., Kaplan, A. S., McCabe, R. E., Mills, J. S., & Aimé, A. (2003). Self-help for bulimia nervosa: A randomized control trial. *American Journal of Psychiatry, 160,* 973–978.

Caspi, A., & Moffitt, T. E. (2006). Gene– environment interactions in psychiatry: Joining forces with neuroscience. *Nature Reviews: Neuroscience, 7,* 583–590.

Caspi, A., Sugden, K., Moffitt, T. E., Taylor, A., Craig, I. W., Harrington, H., . . . Poulton, R. (2003). Influence of life stress on depression: Moderation by a polymorphism in the 5-HTT gene. *Science, 301,* 386–389.

Castellanos, F. X., Glaser, P. E., & Gerhardt, G. A. (2006). Towards a neuroscience of attention-deficit/hyperactivity disorder: Fractionating the phenotype. *Journal of Neuroscience Methods, 151*(1), 1–4.

Castellvi, P., Miranda-Mendizábal, A., Parés-Badell, O., Almenara, J., Alonso, I., Blasco, M. J., . . . Alonso, J. (2017). Exposure to violence, a risk for suicide in youths and young adults. A meta-analysis of longitudinal studies. *Acta Psychiatrica Scandinavica, 135,* 195–211.

Cechnicki, A., Bielańska, A., Hanuszkiewicz, I., & Daren, A. (2013). The predictive validity of expressed emotions (EE) in schizophrenia: A 20-year prospective study. *Journal of Psychiatric Research, 47,* 208–214.

Celik, S., Golbasi, Z., Kelleci, M., & Satman, I. (2015). Sexual dysfunction and sexual quality of life in women with diabetes: The study based on a diabetic center. *Sexual Disabilities, 33,* 233–241.

Celis, W. (1991, January 2). Students trying to draw line between sex and an assault. *The New York Times,* pp. 1, B8.

Centre for Addictions Research, BC. (2006). *Responding to your teen's alcohol use.* Victoria, BC: Author.

Chachamovich, E., Kirmayer, L. J., Haggarty, J. M., Cargo, M., McCormick, R., & Turecki, G. (2015). Suicide among Inuit: Results from a large, epidemiologically representative follow-back study in Nunavut. *Canadian Journal of Psychiatry, 60,* 268–275.

Chambers, L. W., Bancej, C., & McDowell, I. (2016). *Prevalence and monetary costs of dementia in Canada.* Toronto: Alzheimer Society of Canada.

Chambless, D. L., Fydrich, T., & Rodebaugh, T. L. (2008). Generalized social phobia and avoidant personality disorder: Meaningful distinction or useless duplication? *Depression and Anxiety, 25,* 8–19.

Chan, S. M. (2012). Early adolescent depressive mood: Direct and indirect effects on attributional styles and coping. *Child Psychiatry and Human Development, 43,* 455–470.

Chandrashekar, C. R., & Math, S. B. (2006). Psychosomatic disorders in developing countries: Current issues and future challenges. *Current Opinion in Psychiatry, 19,* 201–206.

Chang, L., & Haning, W. (2006). Insights from recent positron emission tomographic studies of drug abuse and dependence. *Current Opinion in Psychiatry, 19,* 246–252.

Chang, Z., Lichtenstein, P., Asherson, P. J., & Larsson, H. (2013). Developmental twin study of attention problems: High heritabilities throughout development. *JAMA Psychiatry, 70,* 311–318.

Chartier, I. S., & Provencher, M. D. (2013). Behavioral activation for depression: Efficacy, effectiveness and dissemination. *Journal of Affective Disorders, 145,* 292–299.

Cheng, S. T. (1996). A critical review of Chinese koro. *Culture, Medicine and Psychiatry, 20,* 67–82.

Cheung, A. H., Emslie, G. L., & Mayes, T. L. (2005). Review of the efficacy and safety of antidepressants in youth depression. *Journal of Child Psychology and Psychiatry, 46,* 735–754.

Cheung, F. M., Kwong, J. Y. Y., & Zhang, J. (2003). Clinical validation of the Chinese Personality Assessment Inventory. *Psychological Assessment, 15,* 89–100.

Children with autism benefit from early, intensive therapy. (2011, September 28). *ScienceDaily.* Retrieved from http://www.sciencedaily.com/releases/2011/09/110928125418.htm

Chodirker, B. N., Cadrin, C., Davies, G. A. L., Summers, A. M., Wilson, R. D., Winsor, E. J. T., & Young, D. (2001). Canadian guidelines for prenatal diagnosis: Genetic indications for prenatal diagnosis. *Journal of Obstetrics and Gynaecology Canada, 105*(6), 1–7.

Choi, S.-H., Lee, H., Chung, T.-S., Park, K. M., Jung, Y. C., Kim, S. I., . . . Kim, J.-J. (2012). Neural network functional connectivity during and after an episode of delirium. *American Journal of Psychiatry, 169,* 498–507.

Chorpita, B. F., Daleiden, E. L., Ebesutani, C., Young, J., Becker, K. D., Nakamura, B. J., . . . Starace, N. (2011). Evidence-based treatments for children and adolescents: An updated review of indicators of efficacy and effectiveness. *Clinical Psychology: Science and Practice, 18,* 154–172.

Chou, C., Condron, L., & Belland, J. C. (2005). A review of the research on Internet addiction. *Educational Psychology Review, 17,* 363–388.

Chow, E. W. C., Watson, M., Young, D. A., & Bassett, A. S. (2006). Neurocognitive profile in 22q11 deletion syndrome and schizophrenia. *Schizophrenia Research, 87,* 270–278.

Chowdhury, A. N. (1996). The definition and classification of koro. *Culture, Medicine and Psychiatry, 20,* 41–65.

Christiansen, B. A., & Goldman, M. S. (1983). Alcohol-related expectancies versus demographic/background variables in the prediction of adolescent drinking. *Journal of Consulting and Clinical Psychology, 52,* 249–257.

Chung, S. A., Jairam, S., Hussain, M. R., & Shapiro, C. M. (2002). How, what, and why of sleep apnea. Perspectives for primary care physicians. *Canadian Family Physician, 48,* 1073–1080.

Chung, T., & Maisto, S. A. (2006). Relapse to alcohol and other drug use in treated adolescents: Review and reconsideration of relapse as a change point in clinical course. *Clinical Psychology Review, 26,* 149–161.

Ciccarelli, S. K., Harrigan, T. R., & Fritzley, V. H. (2010). *Psychology* (Canadian ed.). Toronto: Pearson Education Canada.

Clark, D. A. (2004). *Cognitive-behavioral therapy for OCD.* New York: Guilford.

Clark, D. A., & Beck, A. T. (with Alford, B. A.). (1999). *Scientific foundations of cognitive theory and therapy of depression.* New York: Wiley.

Clark, D. A., & Beck, A. T. (2010). *Cognitive therapy of anxiety disorders: Science and practice.* New York: Guilford Press.

Clark, D. M. (1986). A cognitive approach to panic. *Behaviour Research and Therapy, 24*(4), 461–470.

Clark, L. A. (2007). Assessment and diagnosis of personality disorder: Perennial issues and an emerging reconceptuatization. *Annual Review of Psychology, 58,* 227–257.

Clay, R. A. (2012, February). Improving disorder classification, worldwide. *Monitor on Psychology, 43*(2), 40.

Clinical practice guidelines: Treatment of schizophrenia [Special issue]. (2005). *Canadian Journal of Psychiatry, 50*(Suppl. 1).

Cloos, J.-M. (2005). The treatment of panic disorder. *Current Opinion in Psychiatry, 18,* 45–50.

Cockerham, W. C., Kunz, G., & Lueschen, G. (1989). Alcohol use and psychological distress: A comparison of Americans and West Germans. *International Journal of the Addictions, 24,* 951–961.

Cohen, F. L., Ferrans, C. E., & Eshler, B. (1992). Reported accidents in narcolepsy. *Loss, Grief and Care, 5*(3/4), 71–80.

Cohen, R., & Blaszczynski, A. (2015). Comparative effects of Facebook and conventional media on body image dissatisfaction. *Journal of Eating Disorders, 3,* 23.

Cohen, S., Doyle, W. J., Alper, C. M., Janicki-Deverts, D., & Turner, R. B. (2009). Sleep habits and susceptibility to the common cold. *Archives of Internal Medicine, 169,* 62–66.

Colapinto, J. (2000). *As nature made him: The boy who was raised as a girl.* New York: HarperCollins.

Cole, T. B. (2006). Rape at US colleges often fueled by alcohol. *JAMA: Journal of the American Medical Association, 296,* 504–505.

Coleman, E., Bockting, W., Botzer, M., Cohen-Kettenis, P., DeCuypere, G., Feldman, J., . . . Zucker, K. (2012). Standards of care for the health of transsexual, transgender, and gender-nonconforming people, version 7. *International Journal of Transgenderism, 13,* 165–232.

Collerton, D., Perry, E., & McKeith, I. (2005). Why people see things that are not there: A novel perception and attention deficit model for recurrent complex visual hallucinations. *Behavioral and Brain Sciences, 28,* 737–794.

Colman, I., Zeng, Y., McMartin, S. E., Naicker, K., Ataullahjan, A., Weeks, M., . . . Galambos, N. L. (2014). Protective factors against depression during the transition from adolescence to adulthood: Findings from a national Canadian cohort. *Preventive Medicine, 65,* 28–32.

Coluccia, A., Gabbrielli, M., Gualtieri, G., Ferretti, F., Pozza, A., & Fagiolini, A. (2016). Sexual masochism disorder with asphyxiophilia: A deadly yet underrecognized disease. Hindawi Publishing Corporation, Article ID 5474862.

Committee on Sexual Offences Against Children and Youths (Canada). (1984). *Sexual offences against children: Report of the Committee on Sexual Offences Against Children and Youths.* Ottawa: Ministry of Supply and Services Canada.

Compas, B. E., Haaga, D. A., Keefe, F. J., Leitenberg, H., & Williams, D. A. (1998). Sampling of empirically supported psychological treatments from health psychology: Smoking, chronic pain, cancer, and bulimia nervosa. *Journal of Consulting and Clinical Psychology, 66,* 89–112.

Compton, W. M., Conway, K. P., Stinson, F. S., & Grant, B. F. (2006). Changes in the prevalence of major depression and comorbid substance use disorders in the United States between 1991–1992 and 2001–2002. *American Journal of Psychiatry, 163,* 2141–2147.

Conner, B. T., & Lochman, J. E. (2010). Comorbid conduct disorder and substance use disorders. *Clinical Psychology: Science and Practice, 17,* 337–349.

Coolidge, F. L., & Segal, D. L. (1998). Evolution of personality disorder diagnosis in the Diagnostic and Statistical Manual of Mental Disorders. *Clinical Psychology Review, 18,* 585–599.

Cooney, N. L., Litt, M. D., Morse, P. A., Bauer, L. O., & Gaupp, L. (1997). Alcohol cue reactivity, negative-mood reactivity, and relapse in treated alcoholic men. *Journal of Abnormal Psychology, 106,* 243–250.

Coons, P. M. (1986). Treatment progress in 20 patients with multiple personality disorder. *Journal of Nervous and Mental Disease, 174,* 715–721.

Cooper, P. J., Taylor, M. J., Cooper, Z., & Fairburn, C. G. (1987). The development and validation of the Body Shape Questionnaire. *International Journal of Eating Disorders, 6,* 485–494.

Corbett, A., & Ballard, C. (2012). Antipsychotics and mortality in dementia. *American Journal of Psychiatry, 169,* 7–9.

Corbett, J., Saccone, N. L., Foroud, T., Goate, A., Edenberg, H., Nurnberger, J., . . . Rice, J. P. (2005). Sex adjusted and age adjusted genome screen for nested alcohol dependence diagnoses. *Psychiatric Genetics, 15,* 25–30.

Cornblatt, B. A., & Keilp, J. G. (1994). Impaired attention, genetics, and the pathophysiology of schizophrenia. *Schizophrenia Bulletin, 20,* 31–46.

Corr, P. J. (2004). Reinforcement sensitivity theory and personality. *Neuroscience and Biobehavioral Reviews, 28,* 317–332.

Corr, P. J., & Perkins, A. M. (2006). The role of theory in the psychophysiology of personality: From Ivan Pavlov to Jeffrey Gray. *International Journal of Psychophysiology, 62,* 367–376.

Correctional Services Canada. (2014). National sex offender programs. Retrieved from http://www.csc-scc.gc.ca/correctional-process/002001-2008-eng.shtml

Corsi, D. J., Chow, C. K., Lear, S. A., Subramanian, S. V., Teo, K. K., & Boyle, M. H. (2012). Smoking in context: A multilevel analysis of 49,088 communities in Canada. *American Journal of Preventive Medicine, 43,* 601–610.

Cortese, S., Kelly, C., Chabernaud, C., Proal, E., Di Martino, A., Milham, M. P., & Castellanos, F. X. (2012). Toward systems neuroscience of ADHD: A meta-analysis of 55 fMRI studies. *American Journal of Psychiatry, 169,* 1038–1055.

Coryell, W., Pine, D., Fyer, A., & Klein, D. (2006). Anxiety responses to CO2 inhalation in subjects at high risk for panic disorder. *Journal of Affective Disorders, 92,* 63–70.

Cossette, L., & Duclos, E. (2002). A profile of disability in Canada, 2001 (Catalogue No. 89-577-XIE). Ottawa: Statistics Canada. Retrieved from http://www.statcan.gc.ca/english/freepub/89-577-XIE/pdf/89-577-XIE01001.pdf

Cossrow, N., Pawaskar, M., Witt, E. A., Ming, E. E., Victor, T. W., Herman, B. K., . . . Erder, M. H. (2016). Estimating the prevalence of binge eating disorder in a community sample from the United States: Comparing DSM-IV-TR and DSM-5 criteria. *Journal of Clinical Psychiatry, 77,* e968–e974.

Costello, E. J., Erkanli, A., & Angold, A. (2006). Is there an epidemic of child or adolescent depression? *Journal of Child Psychology and Psychiatry, 47,* 1263–1271.

Cottraux, J. (2005). Recent developments in research and treatment for social phobia (social anxiety disorder). *Current Opinion in Psychiatry, 18,* 51–54.

Coursey, R. D., Alford, J., & Safarjan, B. (1997). Significant advances in understanding and treating serious mental illness. *Professional Psychology: Research and Practice, 28,* 205–216.

Cox, B. J., & Taylor, S. (1999). Anxiety disorders: Panic and phobias. In T. Millon & P. Blaney (Eds.), *Oxford textbook of psychopathology* (pp. 81–113). Oxford: Oxford University Press.

Coyne, J. C. (1999). Thinking interactionally about depression: A radical restatement. In T. Joiner & J. C. Coyne (Eds.), *The interactional nature of depression: Advances in interpersonal approaches* (pp. 365–392). Washington, DC: American Psychological Association.

Craske, M. G., & Waters, A. M. (2005). Panic disorder, phobias, and generalized anxiety disorder. *Annual Review of Clinical Psychology, 1,* 197–225.

Creighton, C. D., & Jones, A. C. (2012). Psychological profiles of adult sexual assault victims. *Journal of Forensic and Legal Medicine, 19,* 35–39.

Crespo-Facorro, B., Pérez-Iglesias, R.-O., Mata, I., Ramirez-Bonilla, M., Martínez-Garcia, O., Pardo-Garcia, G., . . . Vázquez-Barquero, J. L. (2011). Effectiveness of haloperidol, risperidone and olanzapine in the treatment of first-episode non-affective psychosis: Results of a randomized, flexible-dose, open-label 1-year follow-up comparison. *Journal of Psychopharmacology, 219,* 225–233.

Crits-Christoph, P., Connolly Gibbons, M. B., Hamilton, J., Ring-Kurtz, S., & Gallop, R. (2011). The dependability of alliance assessments: The alliance-outcome correlation is larger than you might think. *Journal of Consulting and Clinical Psychology, 79,* 267–278.

Cross-National Collaborative Group. (1992). The changing rate of major depression: Cross-national comparisons. *JAMA: Journal of the American Medical Association, 268,* 3098–3105.

Crozier, J. C., Dodge, K. A., Fontaine, R. G., Lansford, J. E., Bates, J. E., Pettit, G. S., & Levenson, R. W. (2008). Social information processing and cardiac predictors of adolescent antisocial behavior. *Journal of Abnormal Psychology, 117,* 253–267.

Crozier, W. R., & Alden, L. E. (Eds.). (2001). *International handbook of social anxiety: Concepts, research, and interventions relating to the self and shyness.* New York: Wiley.

Cuijpers, P. (2014). Towards a dimensional approach to common mental disorders in the ICD-11? *Australian & New Zealand Journal of Psychiatry, 48,* 481–485.

Cuijpers, P., Reynolds, C. F., Donker, T., Li, J., Andersson, G., & Beekman, A. (2012). Personalized treatment of adult depression: Medication, psychotherapy, or both? A systematic review. *Depression and Anxiety, 29,* 855–864.

Cuijpers, P., Van Straten, A., Schuurmans, J., Van Oppen, P., Hollon, S. D., & Andersson, G. (2010). Psychotherapy for chronic major depression and dysthymia: A meta-analysis. *Clinical Psychology Review, 30,* 51–62.

Cummings, J. L. (2004). Alzheimer's disease. *New England Journal of Medicine, 351,* 56–67.

Cunningham, C. E., & Boyle, M. H. (2002). Preschoolers at risk for attention-deficit hyperactivity disorder and oppositional defiant disorder: Family, parenting, and behavioral correlates. *Journal of Abnormal Child Psychology, 30,* 555–569.

Cunningham, J. A., & Breslin, F. C. (2004). Only one in three people with alcohol abuse or dependence ever seek treatment. *Addictive Behaviors, 29,* 221–223.

Currie, S. R., Patten, S. B., Williams, J. V. A., Wang, J., Beck, C. A., el-Guebaly, N., & Maxwell, C. (2005). Comorbidity of major depression with substance use disorders. *Canadian Journal of Psychiatry, 50,* 660–666.

D

Dahl, R. E. (1992). The pharmacologic treatment of sleep disorders. *Psychiatric Clinics of North America, 15,* 161–178.

Dalenberg, C. J., Brand, B. L., Gleaves, D. H., Dorahy, M. J., Loewenstein, R. J., Cardeña, E., . . . Spiegel, D. (2012). Evaluation of the evidence for the trauma and fantasy models of dissociation. *Psychological Bulletin, 138,* 550–588.

D'Amico, E. J., Hunter, S. B., Miles, J. N. V., Ewing, B. A., & Osilla, K. C. (2013). A randomized controlled trial of a group motivational interviewing intervention for adolescents with a first time alcohol or drug offense. *Journal of Substance Abuse Treatment, 45,* 400–408.

da Silva, W. R., Dias, J. C., Maroco, J., & Campos, J. A. (2014). Confirmatory factor analysis of different versions of the Body Shape Questionnaire applied to Brazilian university students. *Body Image, 11,* 384–390.

Davies, M., Gilston, J., & Rogers, P. (2012). Examining the relationship between male rape myth acceptance, female rape myth acceptance, victim blame, homophobia, gender roles, and ambivalent sexism. *Journal of Interpersonal Violence, 27,* 2807–2823.

Davis, J. O., & Bracha, H. S. (1996). Prenatal growth markers in schizophrenia: A monozygotic co-twin control study. *American Journal of Psychiatry, 153,* 1166–1172.

Davis, S. (1993). Changes to the Criminal Code provisions for mentally disordered offenders and their implications for Canadian psychiatry. *Canadian Journal of Psychiatry, 38,* 122–126.

Davis, S. R., & Braunstein, G. D. (2012). Efficacy and safety of testosterone in the management of hypoactive sexual desire disorder in menopausal women. *Journal of Sexual Medicine, 9,* 1134–1148.

Dawe, S., Rees, V. W., Mattick, R., Sitharthan, T., & Heather, N. (2002). Efficacy of moderation-oriented cue exposure for problem drinkers: A randomized controlled trial. *Journal of Consulting and Clinical Psychology, 70,* 1045–1050.

Dawson, G. (2013). Dramatic increase in autism prevalence parallels explosion of research into its biology and causes. *JAMA Psychiatry, 70,* 9–10.

Day, H. R., Perencevich, E. N., Harris, A. D., Gruber-Baldini, A. L., Himelhoch, S. S., Brown, C. H., . . . Morgan, D. J. (2012). The association between contact precautions and delirium at a tertiary care center. *Infection Control and Hospital Epidemiology, 33,* 34–39.

Dean, D. D., Muthuswamy, S., & Agarwal, S. (2016). Fragile X syndrome: Current insight. *Egyptian Journal of Medical Human Genetics, 17,* 303–309.

de Bruin, N. M., Van Luijtelaar, E. L., Cools, A. R., & Ellenbroek, B. A. (2003). Filtering disturbances in schizophrenic patients: Gating of auditory evoked potentials and prepulse inhibition of the acoustic startle response compared. Emphasis on the role of dopamine. *Current Neuropharmacology, 1,* 47–87.

De Clercq, B., & De Fruyt, F. (2007). Childhood antecedents of personality disorder. *Current Opinion in Psychiatry, 20,* 57–61.

DeFina, L. F., Willis, B. L., Radford, N. B., Gao, A., Leonard, D., Haskell, W. L., . . . Berry, J. D. (2013). The association between midlife cardiorespiratory fitness levels and later-life dementia: A cohort study. *Annals of Internal Medicine, 158,* 162–168.

DeKeseredy, W. S. (1997). Measuring sexual abuse in Canadian university/college dating relationships: The contributions of a national representative sample survey. In M. D. Schwartz (Ed.), *Researching sexual violence against women* (pp. 43–53). Thousand Oaks, CA: Sage.

DeLisi, L. E., & Fleischhaker, W. (2007). Schizophrenia research in the era of the genome, 2007. *Current Opinion in Psychiatry, 20,* 109–110.

Dell'Osso, B., Nestadt, G., Allen, A., & Hollander, E. (2006). Serotoin-norepinephrine reuptake inhibitors in the treatment of obsessive-compulsive disorder: A critical review. *Journal of Clinical Psychiatry, 67,* 600–610.

Demmer, D. H., Hooley, M., Sheen, J., McGillivray, J. A., Lum, J. A. G. (2017). Sex differences in the prevalence of oppositional defiant disorder during middle childhood: A meta-analysis. *Journal of Abnormal Child Psychology, 45,* 313–325.

Denov, M. S. (2001). A culture of denial: Exploring professional perspectives on female sex offending. *Canadian Journal of Criminology, 43,* 303–329.

Denys, D., Van Nieuwerburgh, F., Deforce, D., & Westenberg, H. G. M. (2006). Association between serotonergic candidate genes and specific phenotypes of obsessive compulsive disorder. *Journal of Affective Disorders, 91,* 39–44.

Department of Justice Canada. (2014). Bill C-14, Not Criminally Responsible Reform Act. Retrieved from laws-loi.justice.gc.ca/eng/annualStatutes/2014_6/page-1.html

Déry, M., Lapalme, M., Jagiellowicz, J., Poirier, M., Temcheff, C., & Toupin, J. (2017). Predicting depression and anxiety from oppositional defiant disorder symptoms in elementary school-age girls and boys with conduct problems. *Child Psychiatry and Human Development, 48,* 53–62.

De Souza, I. C. W., De Barros, V. V., Gomide, H. P., Miranda, T. C., Menezes Vde, P., Kozasa, E. H. & Noto, A. R. (2015). Mindfulness-based interventions for the treatment of smoking: A systematic literature review. *Journal of Alternative and Complementary Medicine, 21,* 129–140.

Detera-Wadleigh, S. D., & McMahon, F. J. (2006). G72/G30 in schizophrenia and bipolar disorder: Review and meta-analysis. *Biological Psychiatry, 60,* 106–114.

Devanand, D. P., Dwork, A. J., Hutchinson, E. R., Bolwig, T. G., & Sackeim, H. A. (1994). Does ECT alter brain structure? *American Journal of Psychiatry, 151,* 957–970.

Devanand, D. P., Mintzer, J., Schultz, S. K., Andrews, H. F., Sultzer, D. L., de la Pena, D., . . . Levin, B. (2012). Relapse risk after discontinuation of risperidone in Alzheimer's disease. *New England Journal of Medicine, 367,* 1497–1507.

Diamond, S., Balvin, R., & Diamond, F. R. (1963). *Inhibition and choice: A neurobehavioral approach to problems of plasticity in behavior.* New York: Harper & Row.

Dickens, B. M., Doob, A. N., Warwick, O. H., & Winegard, W. C. (1982). *Report of the Committee of Enquiry into Allegations Concerning Drs. Linda and Mark Sobell.* Toronto: Addiction Research Foundation.

Dickerson, F. B., Tenhula, W. N., & Green-Paden, L. D. (2005). The token economy for schizophrenia: Review of the literature and recommendations for future research. *Schizophrenia Research, 75,* 405–416.

Dietz, L. J., Weinberg, R. J., Brent, D. A., & Mufson, L. (2015). Family-based interpersonal psychotherapy for depressed preadolescents: Examining efficacy and potential treatment mechanisms. *Journal of the American Academy of Child & Adolescent Psychiatry, 54,* 191–199.

DiLalla, D. L., Carey, G., Gottesman, I. I., & Bouchard, T. J., Jr. (1996). Heritability of MMPI personality indicators of psychopathology in twins reared apart. *Journal of Abnormal Psychology, 105,* 491–499.

DiLalla, L. F., & Gottesman, I. I. (1991). Biological and genetic contributors to violence: Widom's untold tale. *Psychological Bulletin, 109,* 125–129.

Dimidjian, S., Hollon, S. D., Dobson, K. S., Schmaling, K. B., Kohlenberg, R. J., Addis, M. E., . . . Jacobson, N. S. (2006). Randomized trial of behavioral activation, cognitive therapy, and antidepressant medication in the acute treatment of adults with major depression. *Journal of Consulting and Clinical Psychology, 74,* 658–670.

Dingle, G., Samtani, P., Kraatz, J., & Solomon, R. (2002). *The real facts on alcohol use, injuries and deaths.* Mississauga, ON: MADD.

Dinh, K. T., Sarason, I. G., Peterson, A. V., & Onstad, L. E. (1995). Children's perceptions of smokers and nonsmokers: A longitudinal study. *Health Psychology, 14,* 32–40.

Dishion, T. J., & Owen, L. D. (2002). A longitudinal analysis of friendships and substance use: Bidirectional influence from adolescence to adulthood. *Developmental Psychology, 38,* 480–491.

Distel, M. A., Hottenga, J.-J., Trull, T. J., & Boomsma, D. I. (2008). Chromosome 9: Linkage for borderline personality disorder features. *Psychiatric Genetics, 18,* 302–307.

Dix, D. L. (1999). *Asylum, prison, and poorhouse: The writings and reform of Dorothea Dix in Illinois.* (D. L. Lightner, Ed.) Carbondale: Southern Illinois University Press.

Dobbs, D. (2010). Schizophrenia appears during adolescence. But where does one begin and the other end? *Nature, 468,* 154–156.

Dobson, K. S., & Dozois, D. J. A. (2001). Historical and philosophic bases of the cognitive-behavioral therapies. In K. S. Dobson (Ed.), *Handbook of cognitive-behavioral therapies* (2nd ed., pp. 3–39). New York: Guilford.

Dobson, K. S., & Khatri, N. (2002). Major depressive disorder. In M. Hersen (Ed.), *Clinical behavior therapy: Adults and children* (pp. 37–51). New York: Wiley.

Dodge, K. A., Laird, R., Lochman, J. E., & Zelli, A. (2002). Multidimensional latent-construct analysis of children's social information processing patterns: Correlations with aggressive behavior problems. *Psychological Assessment, 14*(1), 60–73.

Dodge, K. A., Lochman, J. E., Hamish, J. D., Bates, J. E., & Pettit, G. S. (1997). Reactive and proactive aggression in school children and psychiatrically impaired chronically assaultive youth. *Journal of Abnormal Psychology, 106,* 37–51.

Dohrenwend, B. P., Turner, J. B., Turse, N. A., Adams, B. G., Koenen, K. C., & Marshall, R. (2006). The psychological risks of Vietnam for U.S. veterans: A revisit with new data and methods. *Science, 313,* 979–982.

Doll, B. (1996). Prevalence of psychiatric disorders in children and youth: An agenda for advocacy by school psychology. *School Psychology Quarterly, 11,* 20–46.

Doran, N., Schweizer, C. A., & Myers, M. G. (2011). Do expectancies for reinforcement from smoking change after smoking initiation? *Psychology of Addictive Behaviors, 25,* 101–107.

Donoin, D., & Firestone, P. (2010) *Abnormal psychology: Perspectives* (4th ed.). Toronto: Pearson.

Drewnowski, A., Yee, D. K., Kurth, C. L., & Krahn, D. D. (1994). Eating pathology and DSM-III-R bulimia nervosa: A continuum of behavior. *American Journal of Psychiatry, 151,* 1217–1219.

Drews, C. D., Yeargin-Allsopp, M., Decouflé, P., & Murphy, C. C. (1995). Variation in the influence of selected sociodemographic risk factors for mental retardation. *American Journal of Public Health, 85,* 329–334.

Drummond, D. C., & Glautier, S. (1994). A controlled trial of cue exposure treatment in alcohol dependence. *Journal of Consulting and Clinical Psychology, 62,* 809–817.

Dryden, J., Johnson, B. R., Howard, S., & McGuire, A. (1998, April 13–17). Resiliency: A comparison arising from conversations with 9 year old–12 year old children and their teachers. Paper presented at the Annual Meeting of the American Educational Research Association, San Diego.

Dryden, W. (1984). *Rational-emotive therapy: Fundamentals and innovations.* London: Croom Helm.

Dubovsky, S. (2006). Reviews of note: An update on the neurobiology of addiction. *Journal Watch. Psychiatry.*

Ducci, F., Kaakinen, M., Pouta, A., Hartikainen, A.-L., Veijola, J., Isohanni, M., . . . Järvelin, M.-R. (2011). TTC12-ANKK1-DRD2 and CHRNA5-CHRNA3-CHRNB4 influence different pathways leading to smoking behavior from adolescence to mid-adulthood. *Biological Psychiatry, 69,* 650–660.

Dulit, R. A., Fyer, M. R., Leon, A. C., Brodsky, B. S., & Frances, A. J. (1994). Clinical correlates of self-mutilation in borderline personality disorder. *American Journal of Psychiatry, 151,* 1305–1311.

Duman, R. S., & Aghajanian, G. K. (2012). Synaptic dysfunction in depression: Potential therapeutic targets. *Science, 338,* 68–72.

Dunham, Y., & Olson, K. R. (2016). Beyond discrete categories: Studying multiracial, intersex, and transgender children will strengthen basic developmental science. *Journal of Cognition and Development, 17,* 642–665.

Dunner, D. L. (2005). Dysthymia and double depression. *International Review of Psychiatry, 17,* 3–8.

Durbin, A., Sirotich, F., Lunsky, Y., & Durbin, J. (2017). Unmet needs of adults in community mental health care with and without intellectual and developmental disabilities: A cross-sectional study. *Community Mental Health Journal, 53,* 15–26.

Durkheim, E. (1958). *Suicide: A study in sociology* (J. A. Spaulding & G. Simpson, Trans.). New York: Free Press. (Original work published 1897)

Dutra, L. M., & Glantz, S. A. (2014). Electronic cigarettes and conventional cigarette use among US adolescents. *JAMA Pediatrics, 168,* 610–617.

Dykens, E. M., & Hodapp, R. M. (1997). Treatment issues in genetic mental retardation syndromes. *Professional Psychology: Research and Practice, 28,* 263–270.

Dzokoto, V. A., & Adams, G. (2005). Understanding genital-shrinking epidemics in West Africa: *Koro, juju,* or mass psychogenic illness? *Culture, Medicine and Psychiatry, 29,* 53–78.

E

Eardley, I., Donatucci, C., Corbin, J., El-Meliegy, A., Hatzimouratidis, K., McVary, K., . . . Lee, S. W. (2010). Pharmacotherapy for erectile dysfunction. *Journal of Sexual Medicine, 7,* 524–540.

Earnst, K. S., & Kring, A. M. (1997). Construct validity of negative symptoms: An empirical and conceptual review. *Clinical Psychology Review, 17,* 167–189.

Easson, A., Agarwal, A., Duda, S., & Bennett, K. (2014). Portrayal of youth suicide in Canadian news. *Journal of the Canadian Academy of Child and Adolescent Psychiatry, 23,* 167–173.

Eberhardy, F. (1967). The view from "the couch." *Journal of Child Psychology and Psychiatry, 8(3–4),* 257–263.

Ebert, D. D., Zarski, A., Christensen, H., Stikkelbroek, Y., Cuijpers, P., Berking, M., & Riper, H. (2015). Internet and computer-based cognitive behavioral therapy for anxiety and depression in youth: A meta-analysis of randomized controlled outcome trials. *PLoS ONE, 10,* e0119895.

Ebstein, R. H., Benjamin, J., & Belmaker, R. H. (2003). Behavioral genetics, genomics, and personality. In R. Plomin, J. C. DeFries, I. W. Craig, & P. McGuffin (Eds.), *Behavioral genetics in the postgenomic era.* Washington, DC: American Psychological Association.

Ecker, C., Ginestet, C., Feng, Y., Johnston, P., Lombardo, M. V., Lai, M.-C., . . . MRC AIMS Consortium. (2013). Brain surface anatomy in adults with autism: The relationship between surface area, cortical thickness, and autistic symptoms. *JAMA Psychiatry, 70,* 59–70.

Edman, J. L., & Johnson, R. C. (1999). Filipino American and Caucasian American beliefs about the causes and treatment of mental problems. *Cultural Diversity and Ethnic Minority Psychology, 5,* 380–386.

Edwards, H. P. (2000, January 4). Regulatory requirements for registration in psychology across Canada: A comparison of acts, regulations, by-laws and guidelines in view of the AIT. Ottawa. Retrieved August 15, 2011, from http://www.cpa.ca/documents/PSWAIT%20Report.pdf

Edwards, V. (2002). *Depression and bipolar disorders: Everything you need to know.* Toronto: Key Porter.

Eikeseth, S., Klintwall, L., Jahr, E., & Karlsson, P. (2012). Outcome for children with autism receiving early and intensive behavioral intervention in mainstream preschool and kindergarten settings. *Research in Autism Spectrum Disorders, 6,* 829–835.

Eisler, I., Dare, C., Russell, G. F., Szmukler, G., le Grange, D., & Dodge, E. (1997). Family and individual therapy in anorexia nervosa: A 5-year follow-up. *Archives of General Psychiatry, 54,* 1025–1030.

Elkin, I. (2010). Depression severity and effect of antidepressant medications. *JAMA: Journal of the American Medical Association, 303,* 1596.

Ellason, J. W., & Ross, C. A. (1997). Two-year follow-up of inpatients with dissociative identity disorder. *American Journal of Psychiatry, 154,* 832–839.

Elliot, R., Watson, J. C., Goldman, R. N., & Greenberg, L. S. (2004). *Learning emotion-focused therapy: The process-experiential approach to change.* Washington, DC: American Psychological Association.

Ellis, A. (1977). *How to live with—and without—anger.* New York: Reader's Digest.

Ellis, A. (1993). Reflections on rational-emotive therapy. *Journal of Consulting and Clinical Psychology, 61,* 199–201.

Ellis, A. (2003). Early theories and practices of rational-emotive behavior theory and how they have been augmented and revised during the last three decades. *Journal of Rational-Emotive & Cognitive-Behavior Therapy, 21(3/4),* 219–243.

Ellis, A., & Dryden, W. (1987). *The practice of rational emotional therapy (RET).* New York: Springer.

Ellis, A., Young, J., & Lockwood, G. (1987). Cognitive therapy and rational-emotive therapy: A dialogue. *Journal of Cognitive Psychotherapy, 1,* 205–255.

Employment and Social Development Canada. (2016). National shelter study, 2005–2014. Retrieved from http://www.esdc.gc.ca/eng/communities/homelessness/reports/shelter_study_2014.shtml

Employment and Social Development Canada. (2017). 2016 coordinated point-in-time count of homelessness in Canadian communities. Retrieved from https://www.canada.ca/content/dam/canada/employment-social-development/programs/communities/homelessness/reports/highlights/PiT-Doc.pdf

Engelsmann, F. F. (2000). Transcultural psychiatry: Goals and challenges. *Canadian Journal of Psychiatry, 45,* 429–430.

Erdleyi, M. H. (2010). The ups and downs of memory. *American Psychologist, 65,* 622–633.

Erlenmeyer-Kimling, L., Adamo, U. H., Rock, D., Roberts, S. A., Bassett, A. J., Squires-Wheeler, E., . . . Gottesman, I. I. (1997). The New York High-Risk Project: Prevalence and comorbidity of Axis I disorders in offspring of schizophrenic parents at 25-year follow-up. *Archives of General Psychiatry, 54,* 1096–1102.

Everett, B. (2006). Stigma: The hidden killer: Background paper and literature review. Mood Disorders Society of Canada. Retrieved from http://www.mooddisorderscanada.ca/documents/Publications/Stigma%20the%20hidden%20killer.pdf

Exner, J. E. (1991). *The Rorschach: A comprehensive system: Vol. 2. Interpretation* (2nd ed.). New York: Wiley.

Exner, J. E. (1993). *The Rorschach: A comprehensive system: Vol. 1. Basic foundations* (3rd ed.). New York: Wiley.

Extinguishing Alzheimer's. (1998, June 23). *The New York Times*, p. F7.

Eysenck, H. J., & Eysenck, M. W. (1985). *Personality and individual differences: A natural science approach*. New York: Plenum.

F

Fairburn, C. G., Bailey-Straebler, S., Basden, S., Doll, H. A., Jones, R., Murphy, R., . . . Cooper, Z. (2015). A transdiagnostic comparison of enhanced cognitive behavioral therapy (CBT-E) and interpersonal psychotherapy in the treatment of eating disorders. *Behaviour Research and Therapy, 70*, 64e71.

Fairburn, C. G., Cooper, Z., Doll, H. A., & Davies, B. A. (2005). Identifying dieters who will develop an eating disorder: A prospective, population-based study. *American Journal of Psychiatry, 162*(12), 2249-2255.

Fairburn, C. G., Welch, S. L., Doll, H. A., Davies, B. A., & O'Connor, M. E. (1997). Risk factors for bulimia nervosa: A community-based case-control study. *Archives of General Psychiatry, 54*, 509-517.

Fallon, B. A. (2004). Pharmacotherapy of somatoform disorders. *Journal of Psychosomatic Research, 56*, 455-460.

Faraone, S. V., & Khan, S. A. (2006). Candidate gene studies of attention-deficit/hyperactivity disorder. *Journal of Clinical Psychiatry, 67*(Suppl. 8), 13-20.

Farber, B. A., Brink, D. C., & Raskin, P. M. (Eds.). (1996). *The psychotherapy of Carl Rogers: Cases and commentary*. New York: Guilford.

Farley, M., Lynne, J., & Cotton, A. J. (2005). Prostitution in Vancouver: Violence and the colonization of First Nations women. *Transcultural Psychiatry, 42*, 242-271.

Farmer, A., Elkin, A., & McGuffin, P. (2007). The genetics of bipolar affective disorder. *Current Opinion in Psychiatry, 20*, 8-12.

Farrell, A. D., & White, K. S. (1998). Peer influences and drug use among urban adolescents: Family structure and parent adolescent relationship as protective factors. *Journal of Consulting and Clinical Psychology, 66*, 248-258.

Farrell, M., Howes, S., Taylor, C., Lewis, G., Jenkins, R., Bebbington, P., . . . Meltzer, H. (2003). Substance misuse and psychiatric comorbidity: An overview of the OPCS National Psychiatric Morbidity Survey. *International Review of Psychiatry, 15*, 43-49.

Fazel, S., & Danesh, J. (2002). Serious mental disorder in 23 000 prisoners: A systematic review of 62 surveys. *The Lancet, 359*, 545-550.

Federal paternalism angers Pikangikum. (1999). *Canadian Aboriginal News*. Retrieved from http://www.canadian aboriginal.com/news/news131a.html

Feldman, H. S., Jones, K. L., Lindsay, S., Slymen, D., Klonoff-Cohen, H., Kao, K., . . . Chambers, C. (2012). Prenatal alcohol exposure patterns and alcohol-related birth defects and growth deficiencies: A prospective study. *Alcoholism: Clinical and Experimental Research, 36*, 670-676.

Fernández del Río, E., López-Durán, A., Martínez, Ú., & Becoña, E. (2016). Personality disorders and smoking in Spanish general and clinical population. *Psicothema, 28*, 278-283.

Ferrans, C. E., Cohen, F. L., & Smith, K. M. (1992). The quality of life of persons with narcolepsy. *Loss, Grief and Care, 5*, 23-32.

Fiedorowicz, C. (1999). Neurobiological basis of learning disabilities: An overview. In E. Lowe (Ed.), *Linking research to practice: Second Canadian forum: November 25-27, 1999: Proceedings report* (pp. 64-67). Ottawa: Canadian Child Care Federation.

Fiedorowicz, C., Benezra, E., MacDonald, G. W., McElgunn, B., & Wilson, A. (1999). *Neurobiological basis of learning disabilities*. Ottawa: Learning Disabilities Association of Canada.

Fiedorowicz, C., Benezra, E., MacDonald, G. W., McElgunn, B., Wilson, A., & Kaplan, B. (2002). The neurobiological basis of learning disabilities: An update. *Learning Disabilities: A Multidisciplinary Focus, 11*(2), 61-73.

Field, A. P. (2006). Is conditioning a useful framework for understanding the development and treatment of phobias? *Clinical Psychology Review, 26*, 857-875.

Fiez, J. A. (2001). Bridging the gap between neuroimaging and neuropsychology: Using working memory as a case-study. *Journal of Clinical & Experimental Neuropsychology, 23*(1), 19-31.

Findlay, L. (2017). Depression and suicidal ideation among Canadians aged 15 to 24. *Health Reports*. Statistics Canada, catalogue no. 82-003-X.

Finke, K., Schwarzkopf, W., Müller, U., Frodl, T., Müller, H. J., Schneider, W. X., . . . Hennig-Fast, K. (2011). Disentagling the adult attention-deficit hyperactivity disorder endophenotype: Parametric measurement of attention. *Journal of Abnormal Psychology, 120*(4), 890-901.

Finkelhor, D., Hotaling, G., Lewis, I. A., & Smith, C. (1990). Sexual abuse in a national survey of adult men and women: Prevalence, characteristics, and risk factors. *Child Abuse and Neglect, 14*, 19-28.

Finney, J. W., & Monahan, S. C. (1996). The cost-effectiveness of treatment for alcoholism: A second approximation. *Journal of Studies on Alcohol, 57*, 229-243.

First Nations Information Governance Centre. (2012). First Nations regional health survey (RHS) 2008/10: National report on adults, youth and children living in First Nations communities. Retrieved from http://fnigc.ca/sites/default/files/docs/first_nations_regional_health_survey_rhs_2008-10_-_national_report_child_2.pdf

Fischer, B., & Rehm, J. (2006). Illicit opioid use and treatment for opioid dependence: Challenges for Canada and beyond. *Canadian Journal of Psychiatry, 51*, 621-623.

Fisher, L. (1996). Bizarre right from Day 1. *Maclean's*, p. 14.

Fitzgerald, P. B., Benitez, J., de Castella, A., Daskalakis, Z. J., Brown, T. L., & Kulkarni, J. (2006). A randomized, controlled trial of sequential bilateral repetitive transcranial magnetic stimulation for treatment-resistant depression. *American Journal of Psychiatry, 163*, 88-94.

Fitzgerald, P. B., Fountain, S., & Daskalakis, Z. J. (2006). A comprehensive review of the effects of rTMS on motor cortical excitability and inhibition. *Clinical Neurophysiology, 117*, 2584-2596.

Fitzgerald, P. B., Huntsman, S., Gunewardene, R., Kulkarni, J., & Daskalakis, Z. J. (2006). A randomized trial of low-frequency right-prefrontal-cortex transcranial magnetic stimulation as augmentation in treatment-resistant major depression. *International Journal of Neuropsychopharmacology, 9*, 655-666.

Flament, M. F., Henderson, K., Buchholz, A., Obeid, N., Nguyen, H. N. T., Birmingham, M., & Goldfield, G. (2015). Weight status and DSM-5 diagnoses of eating disorders in adolescents from the community. *Journal of the American Academy of Child & Adolescent Psychiatry, 54*, 403-411.

Flanagan, E. H., & Blashfield, R. K. (2005). Gender acts as a context for interpreting diagnostic criteria. *Journal of Clinical Psychology, 61*, 1485-1498.

Flaskerud, J. H. (2012). Case studies in amok? *Issues in Mental Health Nursing, 33*, 898-900.

Fleetham, J., Ayas, N., Bradley, D., Ferguson, K., Fitzpatrick, M., George, C., . . . CTS Sleep Disordered Breathing Committee. (2006). Canadian Thoracic Society guidelines: Diagnosis and treatment of sleep disordered breathing in adults. *Canadian Respiratory Journal: Journal of the Canadian Thoracic Society, 13*(7), 387-392.

Flett, G. L., & Hewitt, P. L. (Eds.). (2002). *Perfectionism: Theory, research, and treatment*. Washington, DC: American Psychological Association.

Florian, C., Vecsey, C. G., Halassa, M. M., Haydon, P. G., & Abel, T. (2011). Astrocyte-derived adenosine and a1 receptor activity contribute to sleep loss-induced deficits in hippocampal synaptic plasticity and memory in mice. *Journal of Neuroscience, 31*, 6956-6962.

Folstein, M. F., Folstein, S. E., & McHugh, P. R. (1975). "Mini-Mental State": A practical method for grading the cognitive state of patients for the clinician. *Journal of Psychiatric Research, 12*, 189-198.

Fombonne, E. (2005). Epidemiology of autistic disorder and other pervasive developmental disorders. *Journal of Clinical Psychiatry, 66*(Suppl. 10), 3-8.

Forcano, L., Alvarez, E., Santamaria, J. J., Jimenez-Murcia, S., Granero, R., Penelo, E., . . . Fernández-Aranda, F. (2011). Suicide attempts in anorexia nervosa subtypes. *Comprehensive Psychiatry, 52,* 352–358.

Foubert, J. D., & Perry, B. C. (2007). Creating lasting attitude and behavior change in fraternity members and male student athletes: The qualitative impact of an empathy-based rape prevention program. *Violence Against Women, 13,* 70–86.

Fountoulakis, K. N., Iacovides, A., Ioannidou, C., Bascialla, F., Nimatoudis, I., Kaprinis, G., . . . Dahl, A. (2002). Reliability and cultural applicability of the Greek version of the International Personality Disorders Examination. *BMC Psychiatry, 2,* 6.

Fouquereau, E., Fernandez, A., Mullet, E., & Sorum P. C. (2003). Stress and the urge to drink. *Addictive Behaviors, 28,* 669–685.

Frahm, S., Ślimak, M. A., Ferrarese, L., Santos-Torres, J., Antolin-Fontes, B., Auer, S., . . . Ibañez-Tallon, I. (2011). Aversion to nicotine is regulated by the balanced activity of β4 and α5 nicotinic receptor subunits in the medial habenula. *Neuron, 70,* 522–535.

Frances, A. J., & Widiger, T. (2012). Psychiatric diagnosis: Lessons from the DSM-IV past and cautions for the DSM-5 future. *Annual Review of Clinical Psychology, 8,* 109–130.

Frank, G. K. W., Reynolds, J. R., Shott, M. E., & O'Reilly, M. E. (2011). Altered temporal difference learning in bulimia nervosa. *Biological Psychiatry, 70,* 728–735.

Frankenfield, G. (2000). Eating disorders more likely in diabetic girls. *WebMD.* Retrieved from http://my.webmd.com/content/Article/26/1728_58622.htm

Franklin, M. E., & Foa, E. B. (2011). Treatment of obsessive compulsive disorder. *Annual Review of Clinical Psychology, 7,* 229–243.

Freedman, R., Adler, L. E., Gerhardt, G. A., Waldo, M., Baker, N., Rose, G. M., . . . Franks, R. (1987). Neurobiological studies of sensory gating in schizophrenia. *Schizophrenia Bulletin, 13,* 669–678.

Freeman, D., Dunn, G., Murray, R. M., Evans, N., Lister, R., Antley, A., . . . Morrison, P. D. (2015). How cannabis causes paranoia: Using the intravenous administration of Δ9-tetrahydrocannabinol (THC) to identify key cognitive mechanisms leading to paranoia. *Schizophrenia Bulletin, 41,* 391–399.

Freud, S. (1957). Mourning and melancholia. In J. Rickman (Ed.), *A general selection from the works of Sigmund Freud.* Garden City, NY: Doubleday. (Original work published 1917)

Freud, S. (1959). Analysis of a phobia in a 5-year-old boy. In A. Strachey & J. Strachey (Ed. & Trans.), *Collected papers* (Vol. 3). New York: Basic Books. (Original work published 1909)

Freud, S. (1962). *Three essays on the theory of sexuality* (J. Strachey, Trans.). New York: Basic Books. (Original work published 1905)

Freud, S. (1964). New introductory lectures. In J. Strachey (Ed. and Trans.), *Standard edition of the complete psychological works of Sigmund Freud: Vol. 22.* London: Hogarth Press. (Original work published 1933)

Freud, S. (1987). Beyond the pleasure principle. In J. Strachey (Trans.), *On metapsychology: The theory of psychoanalysis.* Middlesex, UK: Penguin. (Original work published 1920)

Frezza, M., di Padova, C., Pozzato, G., Terpin, M., Baraona, E., & Lieber, C. S. (1990). High blood alcohol levels in women: The role of decreased gastric alcohol dehydrogenase activity and first-pass metabolism. *New England Journal of Medicine, 322,* 95–99.

Friborg, O., Martinussen, M., Kaiser, S., Øvergårda, K. T., & Rosenvinge, J. H. (2013). Comorbidity of personality disorders in anxiety disorders: A meta-analysis of 30 years of research. *Journal of Affective Disorders, 45,* 143–155.

Fricchione, G. L., Nejad, S. H., Esses, J. A., Cummings, T. J., Querques, J., Cassem, N. H., & Murray, G. B. (2008). Post-operative delirium. *American Journal of Psychiatry, 165,* 803–812.

Frick, P. J., Lahey, B. B., Loeber, R., Stouthamer-Loeber, M., Christ, M. A., & Hanson, K. (1992). Familial risk factors to oppositional defiant disorder and conduct disorder: Parental psychopathology and maternal parenting. *Journal of Consulting and Clinical Psychology, 60,* 49–55.

Frick, P. J., & Silverthorn, P. (2001). Psychopathology in children. In H. E. Adams & P. B. Sutker (Eds.), *Comprehensive handbook of psychopathology* (3rd ed., pp. 881–919). New York: Plenum.

Friedlander, L., & Desrocher, M. (2006). Neuroimaging studies of obsessive-compulsive disorder in adults and children. *Clinical Psychology Review, 26,* 32–49.

Fromm-Reichmann, F. (1948). Notes on the development of treatment of schizophrenics by psychoanalytic psychotherapy. *Psychiatry, 11,* 263–273.

Fromm-Reichmann, F. (1950). *Principles of intensive psychotherapy.* Chicago: University of Chicago Press.

Fukumoto, H., Tokuda, T., Kasai, T., Ishigami, N., Hidaka, H., Kondo, M., . . . Nakagawa, M. (2010). High-molecular-weight beta-amyloid oligomers are elevated in cerebrospinal fluid of Alzheimer patients. *FASEB Journal: The Journal of the Federation of American Societies for Experimental Biology, 24,* 2716–2726.

Fulero, S. M. (1988). *Tarasoff:* 10 years later. *Professional Psychology: Research and Practice, 19,* 184–190.

Fulton, J. J., Marcus, D. K., & Merkey, T. (2011). Irrational health beliefs and health anxiety. *Journal of Clinical Psychology, 67,* 527–538.

G

Gabert-Quillen, C. A., Fallon, W., & Delahanty, D. L. (2011). PTSD after traumatic injury: An investigation of the impact of injury severity and peritraumatic moderators. *Journal of Health Psychology, 16,* 678–687.

Galea, S., Ahern, J., Resnick, H., Kilpatrick, D., Bucuvalas, M., Gold, J., . . . Vlahov, D. (2002). Psychological sequelae of the September 11 terrorist attacks in New York City. *New England Journal of Medicine, 346,* 982–987.

Garb, H. N. (1997). Race bias, social class bias, and gender bias in clinical judgment. *Clinical Psychology: Science and Practice, 4,* 99–120.

Garb, H. N., Wood, J. M., Lilienfeld, S. O., & Nezworski, M. T. (2005). Roots of the Rorschach controversy. *Clinical Psychology Review, 25,* 97–118.

Gard, M. C., & Freeman, C. P. (1996). The dismantling of a myth: A review of eating disorders and socioeconomic status. *International Journal of Eating Disorders, 20,* 1–12.

Garfinkel, P. E., Moldofsky, H., & Garner, D. M. (1980). The heterogeneity of anorexia nervosa: Bulimia as a distinct subgroup. *Archives of General Psychiatry, 37,* 1036–1040.

Garland, E. J. (2004). Facing the evidence: Antidepressant treatment in children and adolescents. *Canadian Medical Association Journal, 170,* 490–491.

Garland, E. J., & Garland, O. M. (2001). Correlation between anxiety and oppositionality in a children's mood and anxiety disorder clinic. *Canadian Journal of Psychiatry, 46,* 953–958.

Garland, E. J., & Kutcher, S., Virani, A., & Elbe, D. (2016). Update on the use of SSRIs and SNRIs with children and adolescents in clinical practice. *Journal of the Canadian Academy of Child and Adolescent Psychiatry, 25,* 4–10.

Garner, D. M. (1993). Binge eating in anorexia nervosa. In C. G. Fairburn & G. T. Wilson (Eds.), *Binge eating: Nature, assessment, and treatment* (pp. 50–76). New York: Guilford.

Gatehouse, J. (2002, September 16). The echoes of terror. *Maclean's,* p. 18.

Gauthier, J. G. (1999). Bridging the gap between biological and psychological perspectives in the treatment of anxiety disorders. *Canadian Psychology, 40*(1), 1–11.

Gawin, F. H. (1991). Cocaine addiction: Psychology and neurophysiology. *Science, 251,* 1580–1586.

Geist, R., Heinmaa, M., Stephens, D., Davis, R., & Katzman, D. K. (2000). Comparison of family therapy and family group psychoeducation in adolescents with anorexia nervosa. *Canadian Journal of Psychiatry, 45,* 173–178.

Géonet, M., De Sutter, P., & Zech, E. (2013). Cognitive factors in women hypoactive sexual desire disorder. *Sexologies, 22,* e9–e15.

George, M. W., Fairchild, A. J., Cummings, E. M., & Davies, P. T. (2014). Marital conflict in early childhood and adolescent disordered eating: Emotional insecurity about the marital relationship as an explanatory mechanism. *Eating Behaviors, 15*, 532–539.

Gfellner, B. M., & Hundelby, J. D. (1990). Family and peer predictors of substance use among Aboriginal and non-Aboriginal adolescents. *Canadian Journal of Native Studies, 10*, 267–294.

Gfellner, B. M., & Hundelby, J. D. (1995). Patterns of drug use among Native and white adolescents: 1990–1993. *Canadian Journal of Public Health, 86*, 95–97.

Gianoulakis, C. (2001). Influence of the endogenous opioid system on high alcohol consumption and genetic predisposition to alcoholism. *Journal of Psychiatry and Neuroscience, 26*, 304–318.

Gibbs, N. (1998, November 30). The age of Ritalin. *Time*, pp. 84–94.

Gilbertson, M. W., Shenton, M. E., Ciszewski, A., Kasai, K., Lasko, N. B., Orr, S. P., & Pitman, R. K. (2002). Smaller hippocampal volume predicts pathologic vulnerability to psychological trauma. *Nature Neuroscience, 5*, 1242–1247.

Giovancarli, C., Malbos, E., Baumstarck, K., Parola, N., Pélissier, M.-F., Lançon, C., . . . Boyer, L. (2016). Virtual reality cue exposure for the relapse prevention of tobacco consumption: a study protocol for a randomized controlled trial. *Clinical Trials, 17*, 96.

Giżewska, M., MacDonald, A., Bélanger-Quintana, A., Burlina, A., Cleary, M., Coşkun, . . . Blau, N. (2016). Diagnostic and management practices for phenylketonuria in 19 countries of the South and Eastern European region: Survey results. *European Journal of Pediatrics, 175*, 261–272.

Glancy, G. D., & Chaimowitz, G. (2003). [Letter]. *Journal of the American Academy of Psychiatry and the Law, 31*, 524–525.

Glaskin, K. (2011). Dreams, memory, and the ancestors: Creativity, culture, and the science of sleep. *Journal of the Anthropological Institute, 17*, 44–62.

Gleaves, D. H., Hernandez, E., & Warner, M. S. (2003). The etiology of dissociative identity disorder: Reply to Gee, Allen and Powell (2003). *Professional Psychology: Research and Practice, 34*, 116–118.

Goering, P., Veldhuizen, S., Watson, A., Adair, C., Kopp, B., Latimer, E., Nelson, G., MacNaughton, E., Streiner, D., & Aubry, T. (2014). National At Home/Chez Soi final report. Mental Health Commission of Canada. Retrieved from http://www.mentalhealthcommission.ca

Goldapple, K., Segal, Z., Garson, C., Lau, M., Bieling, P., Kennedy, S., & Mayberg, H. (2004). Modulation of cortical-limbic pathways in major depression. *Archives of General Psychiatry, 61*, 34–41.

Goldberg, T. E., Straub, R. E., Callicott, J. H., Hariri, A., Mattay, V. S., Bigelow, L., . . . Weinberger, D. R. (2006). The G72/G30 gene complex and cognitive abnormalities in schizophrenia. *Neuropsychopharmacology, 31*, 2022–2032.

Golden, C. J., Hammeke, T. A., & Purisch, A. D. (1980). *The Luria-Nebraska Neuropsychological Battery: Manual*. Los Angeles: Western Psychological Services.

Golden, R. N., Gaynes, B. N., Ekstrom, R. D., Hamer, R. M., Jacobsen, F. M., Suppes, T., . . . Nemeroff, C. B. (2005). The efficacy of light therapy in the treatment of mood disorders: A review and meta-analysis of the evidence. *American Journal of Psychiatry, 162*, 656–662.

Goldfield, G. S., Blouin, A. G., & Woodside, D. B. (2006). Body image, binge eating, and bulimia nervosa in male bodybuilders. *Canadian Journal of Psychiatry, 51*(3), 160–168.

Goldman-Rakic, P. S., & Selemon, L. D. (1997). Functional and anatomical aspects of prefrontal pathology in schizophrenia. *Schizophrenia Bulletin, 23*, 437–458.

Goldstein, A. (1976). Opioid peptides (endorphins) in pituitary and brain. *Science, 193*, 1081–1086.

Goldstein, R., Chou, P., Saha, T. D., Smith, S. M., Jung, J., Zhang, H., . . . Grant, B. F. (2017). The epidemiology of antisocial behavioral syndromes in adulthood: Results from the National Epidemiologic Survey of Alcohol and Related Conditions-III. *Journal of Clinical Psychiatry, 78*, 90–98.

Goleman, D. (1988, November 1). Narcissism looming larger as root of personality woes. *The New York Times*, pp. C1, C16.

Goleman, D. (1994, January 11). Childhood depression may herald adult ills. *The New York Times*, pp. C1, C10.

Gonçalves, S., Machado, B., Silva, C., Crosby, R. D., Lavender, J. M., Cao, L., & Machado, P. P. P. (2016). The moderating role of purging behavior in the relationship between sexual/physical abuse and non-suicidal self-injury in eating disorder patients. *European Eating Disorders Review, 24*, 164–168.

Gonda, X., Pompili, M., Serafini, G., Montebovi, F., Campi, S., Dome, P., . . . Rihmer, Z. (2012). Suicidal behavior in bipolar disorder: Epidemiology, characteristics and major risk factors. *Journal of Affective Disorders, 143*, 16–26.

Gonzalez-Gadea, M. L., Baez, S., Torralva, T., Castellanos, F. X., Rattazzi, A., Bein, V., . . . Ibanez, A. (2013). Cognitive variability in adults with ADHD and AS: Disentangling the roles of executive functions and social cognition. *Research in Developmental Disabilities, 34*, 817–830.

Gorman, D. A., Gardner, D. M., Murphy, A. L., Feldman, M., Bélanger, S. A., Steele, M. M., . . . Pringsheim, T. (2015). Canadian guidelines on pharmacotherapy for disruptive and aggressive behaviour in children and adolescents with attention-deficit hyperactivity disorder, oppositional defiant disorder, or conduct disorder. *Canadian Journal of Psychiatry, 60*, 62–76.

Gorman, J., Kent, J. M., Sullivan, G. M., & Coplan, J. D. (2000). Neuroanatomical hypothesis of panic disorder, revised. *American Journal of Psychiatry, 157*, 493–505.

Gottesman, I. I., McGuffin, P., & Farmer, A. E. (1987). Clinical genetics as clues to the "real" genetics of schizophrenia (A decade of modest gains while playing for time). *Schizophrenia Bulletin, 13*(1), 23–47.

Grace, A. A. (2010). Ventral hippocampus, interneurons, and schizophrenia: A new understanding of the pathophysiology of schizophrenia and its implications for treatment and prevention. *Current Directions in Psychological Science, 19*, 232–237.

Graham, J. R. (2011). *MMPI-2: Assessing personality and psychopathology* (5th ed.). New York: Oxford University Press.

Granic, I., & Patterson, G. R. (2006). Toward a comprehensive model of antisocial development: A dynamic systems approach. *Psychological Review, 113*, 101–131.

Grant, A., Fathalli, G., Rouleau, G., Joober, R., Flores, C. (2012). Association between schizophrenia and genetic variation in DCC: A case-control study. *Schizophrenia Research, 137*, 26–31.

Grant, B. F., Hasin, D. S., Stinson, F. S., Dawson, D. A., Goldstein, R. B., Huang, B., & Saha, T. D. (2006). The epidemiology of DSM-IV panic disorder and agoraphobia in the United States: Results from the National Epidemiologic Survey on alcohol and related conditions. *Journal of Clinical Psychiatry, 67*, 363–374.

Grant, B. F., Stinson, F. S., Dawson, D. A., Chou, S. P., Ruan, J., & Pickering, R. P. (2004). Co-occurrence of 12-month alcohol and drug use disorders and personality disorders in the United States. *Archives of General Psychiatry, 61*, 361–368.

Gratz, K. L., Tull, M. T., Baruch, D. E., Bornovalova, M. A., & Lejuez, C. W. (2008). Factors associated with co-occurring borderline personality disorder among inner-city substance users: The roles of childhood maltreatment, negative affect intensity/reactivity, and emotion dysregulation. *Comprehensive Psychiatry, 49*, 603–615.

Gratzer, T. G., & Matas, M. (1994). The right to refuse treatment: Recent Canadian developments. *Bulletin of the American Academy of Psychiatry and Law, 22*, 249–256.

Gray, J. A. (1970). The psychophysiological basis of introversion-extraversion. *Behaviour Research & Therapy, 8*, 249–266.

Gray, J. A., & McNaughton, N. (2003). *The neuropsychology of anxiety: An enquiry into the functions of the septo-hippocampal system* (2nd ed.). Oxford: Oxford University Press.

Gray, J. E., & O'Reilly, R. L. (2005). Canadian compulsory community treatment laws: Recent reforms. *International Journal of Law and Psychiatry, 28*, 13–22.

Gray, J. R., & Braver, T. S. (2002). Personality predicts working-memory-related activation in the caudal anterior cingulate cortex. *Cognitive and Affective Behavioral Neuroscience, 2*(1), 64–75.

Graziottin, A. (2008). Dyspareunia and vaginismus: Review of the literature and treatment. *Current Sexual Health Reports, 5*, 43–50.

Greenberg, L. S. (2002a). *Emotion-focused therapy: Coaching clients to work through their feelings*. Washington, DC: American Psychological Association.

Greenberg, L. S. (2002b). Integrating an emotion-focused approach to treatment into psychotherapy integration. *Journal of Psychotherapy Integration, 12*(2), 154–189.

Greenberg, L. S. (2006). Emotion-focused therapy: A synopsis. *Journal of Contemporary Psychotherapy, 36*(2), 87–93.

Greenberg, R. P., & Bornstein, R. F. (1988). The dependent personality: II. Risk for psychological disorders. *Journal of Personality Disorders, 2*, 136–143.

Greenspan, E. L., Rosenberg, M., & Henein, M. (Annotators). (1998). *Martin's Criminal Code*. Aurora, ON: Canada Law Book.

Greeven, A., Van Balkom, A. J., Visser, S., Merkelbach, J. W., Van Rood, Y. R., Van der Does, A. J., . . . Spinhoven, P. (2007). Cognitive behavior therapy and paroxetine in the treatment of hypochondriasis: A randomized controlled trial. *American Journal of Psychiatry, 164*, 91–99.

Griffin, J. D. (1993, December). A historical oversight. *Newsletter of the Ontario Psychiatric Association*, pp. 9–10.

Grilo, C. M., Crosby, R. D., Wilson, G. T., & Masheb, R. (2012). 12-month follow-up of fluoxetine and cognitive behavioral therapy for binge eating disorder. *Journal of Consulting and Clinical Psychology, 80*, 1108–1113.

Grigsby, J. (2016). The fragile X mental retardation 1 gene (FMR1): Historical perspective, phenotypes, mechanism, pathology, and epidemiology. *Clinical Neuropsychologist, 30*, 815–833.

Grissett, N. I., & Norvell, N. K. (1992). Perceived social support, social skills, and quality of relationships in bulimic women. *Journal of Consulting and Clinical Psychology, 60*, 293–299.

Grønbæk, M. (2009). The positive and negative health effects of alcohol and the public health implications. *Journal of Internal Medicine, 265*, 407–420.

Gropalis, M., Bleichhardt, G., Hiller, W., & Witthöft, M. (2013). Specificity and modifiability of cognitive biases in hypochondriasis. *Journal of Consulting and Clinical Psychology, 81*, 558–565.

Gropalis, M., Bleichhardt, G., Witthöft, M., & Hiller, W. (2012). Hypochondriasis, somatoform disorders, and anxiety disorders: Sociodemographic variables, general psychopathology, and naturalistic treatment effects. *Journal of Nervous & Mental Disease, 200*, 406–412.

Gross, A. M., Winslett, A., Roberts, M., & Gohm, C. L. (2006). An examination of sexual violence against college women. *Violence Against Women, 12*, 288–300.

Grover, S., Mattoo, S. K., & Gupta, N. (2005). Theories on mechanism of action of electroconvulsive therapy. *German Journal of Psychiatry, 8*, 70–84.

Grunberg, N. E. (1991). Smoking cessation and weight gain. *New England Journal of Medicine, 324*, 768–769.

Guerreiro, R., Wojtas, A., Bras, J., Carrasquillo, M., Rogaeva, E., Majounie, E., . . . Alzheimer Genetic Analysis Group. (2013). TREM2 variants in Alzheimer's disease. *New England Journal of Medicine, 368*, 117–127.

Guertin, T. L. (1999). Eating behavior of bulimics, self-identified binge eaters, and non-eating disordered individuals: What differentiates these populations? *Clinical Psychology Review, 19*, 1–24.

Gunderson, J. G. (2011). Borderline personality disorder. *New England Journal of Medicine, 364*, 2037–2042.

Gunderson, J. G., Stout, R. L., McGlashan, T. H., Shea, M. T., Morey, L. C., Grilo, C. M., . . . Skodol, A. E. (2011). Ten-year course of borderline personality disorder: Psychopathology and function from the Collaborative Longitudinal Personality Disorders Study. *Archives of General Psychiatry, 68*, 827–837.

Guo, X., Zhai, J., Liu, Z., Fang, M., Wang, B., Wang, C., . . . Zhao, J. (2010). Effect of antipsychotic medication alone vs. combined with psychosocial intervention on outcomes of early-stage schizophrenia: A randomized, 1-year study. *Archives of General Psychiatry, 67*, 895–904.

Guydish, J., Werdegar, D., Sorensen, J. L., Clark, W., & Acampora, A. (1998). Drug abuse day treatment: A randomized clinical trial comparing day and residential treatment programs. *Journal of Consulting and Clinical Psychology, 66*, 280–289.

Gvirts, H. Z., Harari, H., Braw, Y., Shefet, D., Shamay-Tsoory, S. G., & Levkovitz, Y. (2012). Executive functioning among patients with borderline personality disorder (BPD) and their relatives. *Journal of Affective Disorders, 143*, 261–264.

H

Hadley, D., Anderson, B. S., Borckardt, J. J., Arana, A., Li, X., Nahas, Z., & George, M. S. (2011). Safety, tolerability, and effectiveness of high doses of adjunctive daily left prefrontal repetitive transcranial magnetic stimulation for treatment-resistant depression in a clinical setting. *Journal of ECT, 27*, 18–25.

Haggarty, J., Cernovsky, Z., Kermeen, P., & Merskey, H. (2000). Psychiatric disorders in an Arctic community. *Canadian Journal of Psychiatry, 45*, 357–362.

Hahn, B., Hollingworth, A., Robinson, B. M., Kaiser, S. T., Leonard, C. J., Beck, V. M., . . . Gold, J. M. (2012). Control of working memory content in schizophrenia. *Schizophrenia Research, 134*, 70–75.

Haider, I. I., Bukharie, F., Hamid, F., Ayub, M., Irfan, M., & Naeem, F. (2014). Reliability of the ICD-10 International Personality Disorder Examination (Urdu translation): A preliminary study. *Pakistan Journal of Medical Sciences, 30*, 1372–1376.

Halbreich, U., & Karkun, S. (2006). Cross-cultural and social diversity of prevalence of postpartum depression and depressive symptoms. *Journal of Affective Disorders, 91*, 97–111.

Hallgren, M., Kraepelien, M., Öjehagen, A., Lindefors, N., Zeebari, Z., Kaldo, V., & Forsell, Y. (2015). Physical exercise and Internet-based cognitive-behavioural therapy in the treatment of depression: Randomised controlled trial. *British Journal of Psychiatry, 207*, 227–234.

Hall, G. C., & Barongan, C. (1997). Prevention of sexual aggression: Sociocultural risk and protective factors. *American Psychologist, 52*, 5–14.

Hall, T. M. (2011). *Index of culture-bound syndromes: By culture*. Retrieved November 22, 2011, from http://homepage.mac.com/mccajor/cbs_cul.html

Hamid, S. (2000). Culture-specific syndromes: It's all relative. *Visions: BC's Mental Health Journal, 9*(Winter), 5–8.

Hammen, C. (2005). Stress and depression. *Annual Review of Clinical Psychology, 1*, 293–319.

Han, J., Kesner, P., Metna-Laurent, M., Duan, T., Xu, L., Georges, G., . . . Ren, W. (2012). Acute cannabinoids impair working memory through astroglial CB1 receptor modulation of hippocampal LTD. *Cell, 148*(5), 1039–1050.

Hancock, L. (1996, March 18). Mother's little helper. *Newsweek*, pp. 51–56.

Hansen, T. E., Casey, D. E., & Hoffman, W. F. (1997). Neuroleptic intolerance. *Schizophrenia Bulletin, 23*, 567–582.

Harada, R., Okamura, N., Furumoto, S., Furukawa, K., Ishiki, A., Tomita, N., . . . Kudo, Y. (2015). [18F]THK-5117 PET for assessing neurofibrillary pathology in Alzheimer's disease. *European Journal of Nuclear Medicine and Molecular Imaging, 42*, 1052–1061.

Hariri, A. R., & Brown, S. M. (2006). Images in neuroscience: Serotonin. *American Journal of Psychiatry, 163*, 12.

Harkness, K. L., Bruce, A. E., & Lumley, M. N. (2006). The role of childhood abuse and neglect in the sensitization to stressful life events in adolescent depression. *Journal of Abnormal Psychology, 115*, 730–741.

Haro, J. M., Novick, D., Suarez, D., Ochoa, S., & Roca, M. (2008). Predictors of the course of illness in outpatients with schizophrenia: A prospective three year study. *Progress in Neuro-Psychopharmocology and Biological Psychiatry, 32*, 1287–1292.

Harrell, P. T., Simmons, V. N., Piñeiro, B., Correa, J. B., Menzie, N. S., Meltzer, L. R., . . . Brandon, T. H. (2015). E-cigarettes and expectancies: Why do some users keep smoking? *Addiction, 110*, 1833–1843.

Harris, S., Davies, M. F., & Dryden, W. (2006). An experimental test of a core REBT hypothesis: Evidence that irrational beliefs lead to physiological as well as psychological arousal. *Journal of Rational-Emotive & Cognitive-Behaviour Therapy, 24*(2), 101–111.

Hart, M. A. (2014). Indigenous ways of helping. In V. Harper, P. Menzies, & L. Lavallée (Eds.), *Journey to healing: Aboriginal people with addiction and mental health issues: What health, social* service and justice workers need to know (pp. 73–86). Toronto: Centre for Addiction & Mental Health.

Hartz, S. M., Short, S. E., Saccone, N. L., Culverhouse, R., Chen, L., Schwantes-An, T.-H., . . . Bierut, L. J. (2012). Increased genetic vulnerability to smoking at CHRNA5 in early-onset smokers. *Archives of General Psychiatry, 69*, 854–860.

Harvey, A. G., & Bryant, R. A. (2002). Acute stress disorder: A synthesis and critique. *Psychological Bulletin, 128*, 886–902.

Hasin, D., Hatzenbuehler, M. L., Keyes, K., & Ogburn, E. (2006). Substance use disorders: *Diagnostic and Statistical Manual of Mental Disorders*, fourth edition (DSM-IV) and *International Classification of Diseases*, tenth edition (ICD-10). *Addiction, 101*(Suppl. 1), 59–75.

Haugh, J. A. (2006). Specificity and social problem-solving: Relation to depressive and anxious symptomatology. *Journal of Social and Clinical Psychology, 25*, 392–403.

Haughton, E., & Ayllon, T. (1965). Production and elimination of symptomatic behavior. In L. P. Ullmann & L. Krasner (Eds.), *Case studies in behavior modification*. New York: Holt, Rinehart and Winston.

Havercamp, S. M., Scandlin, D., & Roth, M. (2004). Health disparities among adults with developmental disabilities, adults with other disabilities, and adults not reporting disability in North Carolina. *Public Health Reports, 119*, 418–426.

Hawaleshka, D. (2002, October 21). New national survey data shows that many health problems are getting worse. *Maclean's*, p. 38.

Hawke, J. L., Wadsworth, S. J., Olson, R. K., & DeFries, J. C. (2007). Etiology of reading difficulties as a function of gender and severity. *Reading and Writing, 20*, 13–25.

Hawkrigg, J. J. (1975). Agoraphobia. *Nursing Times, 71*, 1280–1282.

Hawton, K., Casañas i Comabella, C., Haw, C., & Saunders, K. (2013). Risk factors for suicide in individuals with depression: A systematic review. *Journal of Affective Disorders, 47*, 17–28.

Hayes, R. D., Bennett, C. M., Fairley, C. K., & Dennerstein, L. (2006). What can prevalence studies tell us about female sexual difficulty and dysfunction? *Journal of Sexual Medicine, 3*, 589–595.

Haynos, A. F., & Fruzzetti, A. E. (2011). Anorexia nervosa as a disorder of emotion dysregulation: Evidence and treatment implications. *Clinical Psychology: Science and Practice, 18*, 183–202.

Health Canada. (1995). Canada's alcohol and other drugs survey (Catalogue No. H39-338/1995E). Retrieved from http://dsp-psd.pwgsc.gc.ca/Collections/H39-338-1995E.pdf

Health Canada. (2001). Canadian Tobacco Use Monitoring Survey (CTUMS) 2001. Retrieved from http://www.hc-sc.gc.ca/hc-ps/tobac-tabac/research-recherche/stat/_ctums-esutc_2001/ar-rpa-2001-eng.php

Health Canada. (2002a). Aboriginal Head Start in urban and northern communities. Retrieved from http://www.hc-sc.gc.ca/dca-dea/programs-mes/ahs_overview_e.html#top

Health Canada. (2002b). *A report on mental illnesses in Canada* (Catalogue No. 0-662-32817-5). Ottawa: Health Canada Editorial Board Mental Illnesses in Canada. Retrieved from http://www.phac-aspc.gc.ca/publicat/miic-mmac/pdf/men_ill_e.pdf

Health Canada. (2003). Mental health promotion: Frequently asked questions. Retrieved from http://www.hc-sc.gc.ca/hppb/mentalhealth/mhp/faq.html

Health Canada. (2006a). *The human face of mental health and mental illness in Canada 2006* (Catalogue No. HP5-19/2006E). Ottawa: Minister of Public Works and Government Services. Retrieved from http://www.phac-aspc.gc.ca/publicat/human-humain06/

Health Canada. (2006b). New cautions regarding rare heart-related risks for all ADHD drugs: Advisory. Retrieved from http://www.hc-sc.gc.ca/ahc-asc/media/advisories-avis/2006/2006_35_e.html

Health Canada. (2006c). New information regarding uncommon psychiatric adverse events for all ADHD drugs: Advisory. Retrieved from http://www.hc-sc.gc.ca/ahc-asc/media/advisories-avis/2006/2006_91_e.html

Health Canada. (2011). *Honouring our strengths: A renewed framework to address substance use issues among First Nations people in Canada*. Assembly of First Nations, National Native Addiction Partnership Foundation. Retrieved from http://publications.gc.ca/collections/collection_2011/sc-hc/H14-63-2011-eng.pdf

Health Canada. (2014). Canadian Alcohol and Drug Use Monitoring Survey. Retrieved from http://www.hc-sc.gc.ca/hc-ps/drugs-drogues/stat/_2012/tables-tableaux-eng.php#t1

Health Canada. (2015a). Indian residential schools health supports. Retrieved from http://www.hc-sc.gc.ca/fniah-spnia/services/indiresident/index-eng.php

Health Canada. (2015b). Summary safety review—methylphenidate—suicidal thoughts and behaviour (suicidality). Retrieved from http://www.hc-sc.gc.ca/dhp-mps/medeff/reviews-examens/methylphenidate-eng.php

Healy, A., Rush, R., & Ocain, T. (2011). Fragile X syndrome: An update on developing treatment modalities. *ACS Chemical Neuroscience, 2*, 402–410.

Heather, N. (2006). Controlled drinking, harm reduction and their roles in the response to alcohol-related problems. *Addiction Research & Theroy, 14*, 7–18.

Hebb, D. O. (2002). *The organization of behavior: A neuropsychological theory*. Mahwah, NJ: Erlbaum. (Original work published 1949)

Heilbronner, U., Samara, M., Leucht, S., Falkai, P., & Schulze, G. (2016). The longitudinal course of schizophrenia across the lifespan: Clinical, cognitive, and neurobiological aspects. *Harvard Review of Psychiatry, 24*, 118–128.

Heiman, J. R., & LoPiccolo, J. (1987). *Becoming orgasmic: A sexual and personal growth program for women* (2nd ed.). Englewood Cliffs, NJ: Prentice Hall.

Heinrichs, R. W. (2001). *In search of madness: Schizophrenia and neuroscience*. Oxford: Oxford University Press.

Heinrichs, R. W. (2005). The primacy of cognition in schizophrenia. *American Psychologist, 60*, 229–242.

Hellstrom, W. J. G., Nehra, A., Shabsigh, R., & Sharlip, I. D. (2006). Premature ejaculation: The most common male sexual dysfunction. *Journal of Sexual Medicine, 3*(Suppl. S1), 1–3.

Hendershot, C. S., Witkiewitz, K., George, W. H., & Marlatt, G. A. (2011). Relapse prevention for addictive behaviors. *Substance Abuse Treatment, Prevention, and Policy, 6*, 17.

Hernandez, A., Arntz, A., Gaviria, A. M., Labad, A., & Gutiérrez-Zotes, J. A. (2012). Relationships between childhood maltreatment, parenting style, and borderline personality disorder criteria. *Journal of Personality Disorders, 26*, 727–736.

Herpertz, S. C., & Bertsch, K. (2014). The social-cognitive basis of personality disorders. *Current Opinion in Psychiatry, 27*, 73–77.

Herrup, K. (2010). Reimagining Alzheimer's disease—An age-based hypothesis. *Journal of Neuroscience, 30*, 16755–16762.

Herzog, W., Schellberg, D., & Deter, H. C. (1997). First recovery in anorexia nervosa patients in the long-term course: A discrete-time survival analysis. *Journal of Consulting and Clinical Psychology, 65*, 169–177.

Hidaka, B. H. (2012). Depression as a disease of modernity: Explanations for increasing prevalence. *Journal of Affective Disorders, 140*, 205–214.

Hilker, I., Sánchez, I., Steward, T., Jiménez-Murcia, S., Granero, R., Gearhardt, A. N., . . . Fernández-Aranda, F. (2016). Food addiction in bulimia nervosa: Clinical correlates and association with response to a brief psychoeducational intervention. *European Eating Disorders Review, 24*, 482–488.

Hinshaw, S. P. (1992). Academic underachievement, attention deficits, and aggression: Comorbidity and implications for intervention. *Journal of Consulting and Clinical Psychology, 60*, 893–903.

Ho, M.-H. R., Auerbach, R. P., Jun, H. L., Abela, J. R. Z., Zhu, X., & Yao, S. (2011). Understanding anxiety sensitivity in the development of anxious and depressive symptoms. *Cognitive Therapy and Research, 35*, 232–240.

Hodgins, D. (2006). Can patients with alcohol use disorders return to social drinking? Yes, so what should we do about it? *Canadian Journal of Psychiatry, 50*, 264–265.

Hofmann, S. G. (2008). Cognitive processes during fear acquisition and extinction in animals and humans: Implications for exposure therapy of anxiety disorder. *Clinical Psychology Review, 28,* 199–210.

Hofmann, S. G., & Hinton, D. E. (2014). Cross-cultural aspects of anxiety disorders. *Current Psychiatry Reports, 16,* 450.

Hogarty, G. E. (1993). Prevention of relapse in chronic schizophrenic patients. *Journal of Clinical Psychiatry, 54*(Suppl.), 18–23.

Holbrook, A. M., Crowther, R., Lotter, A., Cheng, C., & King, D. (2000). The diagnosis and management of insomnia in clinical practice: A practical evidence-based approach. *CMAJ: Canadian Medical Association Journal, 162,* 216–220.

Holland, A. J., Sicotte, N., & Treasure, J. (1988). Anorexia nervosa: Evidence for a genetic basis. *Journal of Psychosomatic Research, 32,* 561–571.

Hollon, S. D. (2006). Cognitive therapy in the treatment and prevention of depression. In T. E. Joiner, J. S. Brown, & J. Kistner (Eds.), *The interpersonal, cognitive, and social nature of depression* (pp. 133–151). Mahwah, NJ: Erlbaum.

Hollon, S. D. (2011). Cognitive and behavior therapy in the treatment and prevention of depression. *Depression and Anxiety, 28,* 263–266.

Hollon, S. D., & Kendall, P. C. (1980). Cognitive self-statements in depression: Development of an Automatic Thoughts Questionnaire. *Cognitive Therapy and Research, 4*(4), 383–395.

Hollon, S. D., & Shelton, R. C. (2001). Treatment guidelines for major depressive disorder. *Behavior Therapy, 32,* 235–258.

Holmes, E. A., Brown, R. J., Mansell, W., Fearon, R. P., Hunter, E. C. M., Frasquilho, F., & Oakley, D. A. (2005). Are there two qualitatively distinct forms of dissociation? A review and some clinical implications. *Clinical Psychology Review, 25,* 1–23.

Hone-Blanchet, A., Wensing, T., & Fecteau, S. (2016). The use of virtual reality in craving assessment and cue-exposure therapy in substance use disorders. *Frontiers in Human Neuroscience, 8,* 1–15.

Hongpaisan, J., Sun, M.-K., & Alkon, D. L. (2011). PKC ε activation prevents synaptic loss, Aβ elevation, and cognitive deficits in Alzheimer's disease transgenic mice. *Journal of Neuroscience, 31,* 630–643.

Hooker, C. I., Bruce, L., Fisher, M., Verosky, S. C., Miyakawa, A., & Vinogradov, S. (2012). Neural activity during emotion recognition after combined cognitive plus social cognitive training in schizophrenia. *Schizophrenia Research, 39,* 53–59.

Hooley, J. M. (2010). Social factors in schizophrenia. *Current Directions in Psychological Science, 19,* 238–242.

Hopkins, I. M., Gower, M. W., Perez, T. A., Smith, D. S., Amthor, F. R., Wimsatt, F. C., & Biasini, F. J. (2011). Avatar assistant: Improving social skills in students with an ASD through a computer-based intervention. *Journal of Autism and Developmental Disorders, 41,* 1443–1455.

Hopkins, T. A., Green, B. A., Carnes, P. J., & Campling, S. (2016). Varieties of intrusion: Exhibitionism and voyeurism. *Sexual Addiction & Compulsivity, 23,* 4–33.

Hopko, D. R., & Mullane, C. M. (2008). Exploring the relation of depression and overt behavior with daily diaries. *Behaviour Research and Therapy, 46,* 1085–1089.

Hops, H., & Lewinsohn, P. M. (1995). A course for the treatment of depression among adolescents. In K. D. Craig & K. S. Dobson (Eds.), *Anxiety and depression in adults and children* (pp. 230–245). Thousand Oaks, CA: Sage.

Hopwood, C. J., Donnellan, M. B., Blonigen, D. M., Krueger, R. F., McGue, M., Iacono, W. G., & Burt, S. A. (2011). Genetic and environmental influences on personality trait stability and growth during the transition to adulthood: A three-wave longitudinal study. *Journal of Personality and Social Psychology, 100,* 545–556.

Howard, C. E., & Porzelius, L. K. (1999). The role of dieting in binge eating disorder: Etiology and treatment implications. *Clinical Psychology Review, 19,* 25–44.

Howard, R., McShane, R., Lindesay, J., Ritchie, C., Baldwin, A., Barber, R., . . . Phillips, P. (2012). Donepezil and memantine for moderate-to-severe Alzheimer's disease. *New England Journal of Medicine, 66,* 893–903.

Howes, O. D., Kambeitz, J., Kim, E., Stahl, D., Slifstein, M., Abi-Dargham, A., & Kapur, S. (2012). The nature of dopamine dysfunction in schizophrenia and what this means for treatment: Meta-analysis of imaging studies. *Archives of General Psychiatry, 69,* 776–786.

Hua, X., Thompson, P. M., Leow, A. D., Madsen, S. K., Caplan, R., Alger, J. R., . . . Levitt, J. G. (2013). Brain growth rate abnormalities visualized in adolescents with autism. *Human Brain Mapping, 34,* 425–436.

Huang, W., & Cuvo, A. J. (1997). Social skills training for adults with mental retardation in job-related settings. *Behavior Modification, 21,* 3–44.

Huber, K. M., Gallagher, S. M., Warren, S. T., & Bear, M. F. (2002). Altered synaptic plasticity in a mouse model of fragile X mental retardation. *Proceedings of the National Academy of Sciences of the United States of America, 99,* 7746–7750.

Hucker, S. J. (2011). Hypoxyphilia. *Archives of Sexual Behavior, 40,* 1323–1326.

Hudon, T. (2017). The girl child. In *Women in Canada: A gender-based statistical report*. Catalogue no. 89-503-X. Ottawa: Statistics Canada.

Hudson, C. G. (2005). Socioeconomic status and mental illness: Tests of the social causation and selection hypotheses. *American Journal of Orthopsychiatry, 75*(1), 3–18.

Hudson, J. I., Hiripi, E., Pope, H. G., Jr., & Kessler, R. C. (2007). The prevalence and correlates of eating disorders in the National Comorbidity Survey Replication. *Biological Psychiatry, 61*(3), 348–358.

Hudziak, J. J., Boffeli, T. J., Kreisman, J. J., Battaglia, M. M., Stanger, C., & Guze, S. B. (1996). Clinical study of the relation of borderline personality disorder to Briquet's syndrome (hysteria), somatization disorder, antisocial personality disorder, and substance abuse disorders. *American Journal of Psychiatry, 153,* 1598–1606.

Huffman, J. C., & Stern, T. A. (2003). The diagnosis and treatment of Munchausen's syndrome. *General Hospital Psychiatry, 25,* 358–363.

Hughes, A. E., Crowell, S. E., Uyeji, L., & Coan, J. A. (2012). A developmental neuroscience of borderline pathology: Emotion dysregulation and social baseline theory. *Journal of Abnormal Child Psychology, 40*(1), 21–33.

Humphrey, L. L. (1986). Family dynamics in bulimia. *Adolescent Psychiatry, 13,* 315–332.

Hunter, E. C., Baker, D., Phillips, M. L., Sierra, M., & David, A. S. (2005). Cognitive-behaviour therapy for depersonalization disorder: An open study. *Behaviour Research and Therapy, 43,* 1121–1130.

Hur, Y.-M. (2007). Stability of genetic influence on morningness-eveningness: A cross-sectional examination of South Korean twins from preadolescence to young adulthood. *Journal of Sleep Research, 16*(1), 17–23.

Hurd, H. M., Drewry, W. F., Dewey, R., Pilgrim, C. W., Blumer, G. A., & Burgess, T. J. W. (1916). *The institutional care of the insane in the United States and Canada* (Vols. 1–3). Baltimore, MD: The Johns Hopkins Press.

I

Ilgen, M. A., Wilbourne, P. L., Moos, B. S., & Moos, R. H. (2008). Problem-free drinking over 16 years among individuals with alcohol use disorders. *Drug and Alcohol Dependence, 92,* 116.

Imel, Z. E., Malterer, M. B., McKay, K. M., & Wampold, B. E. (2008). A meta-analysis of psychotherapy and medication in unipolar depression and dysthymia. *Journal of Affective Disorders, 110,* 197–206.

Infurna, M. R., Brunner, R., Holz, B., Parzer, P., Giannone, F., Reichl, C., . . . Kaess, M. (2016). The specific role of childhood abuse, parental bonding, and family functioning in female adolescents with borderline personality disorder. *Journal of Personality Disorders, 30,* 177–192.

Ingraham, L. J., Kugelmass, S., Frenkel, E., Nathan, M., & Mirsky, A. F. (1995). Twenty-five year follow-up of the Israeli High-Risk Study: Current and lifetime psychopathology. *Schizophrenia Bulletin, 21,* 183–192.

Inouye, S. K. (2006). Delirium in older persons. *New England Journal of Medicine, 354,* 1157–1165.

Insel, K. C., and Badger, T. A. (2002). Deciphering the 4 D's: Cognitive decline, delirium, depression and dementia—A review. *Journal of Advanced Nursing, 38*(4), 360–368.

Involving parents in therapy doubles success rates for bulimia treatment. (2007, September 7). *ScienceDaily*. Retrieved from http://www.sciencedaily.com/releases/2007/09/070903204931.htm

Isaac, M., & Chand, P. K. (2006). Dissociative and conversion disorders: Defining boundaries. *Current Opinion in Psychiatry, 19,* 61–66.

IsHak, W. W., Bokarius, A., Jeffrey, J. K., Davis, M. C., & Bakhta, Y. (2010). Disorders of orgasm in women: A literature review of etiology and current treatments. *Journal of Sexual Medicine, 7,* 3254–3268.

J

Jablensky, A. (2006). Subtyping schizophrenia: Implications for genetic research. *Molecular Psychiatry, 11,* 815–836.

Jablensky, A., Sartorius, N., Ernberg, G., & Anker, M. (1992). Schizophrenia: Manifestations, incidence and course in different cultures: A World Health Organization ten-country study. *Psychological Medicine, 20* (Monograph Suppl.), 1–97.

Jack.org. (2016). About. Retrieved from https://www.jack.org/about

Jackson, J., Calhoun, K. S., Amick, A. E., Maddever, H. M., & Habif, V. L. (1990). Young adult women who report childhood intrafamilial sexual abuse: Subsequent adjustment. *Archives of Sexual Behavior, 19,* 211–221.

Jacobi, C., Hayward, C., de Zwaan, M., Kraemer, H. C., & Agras, W. S. (2004). Coming to terms with risk factors for eating disorders: Application of risk terminology and suggestions for a general taxonomy. *Psychological Bulletin, 130,* 19–65.

Janca, A. (2005). Rethinking somatoform disorders. *Current Opinion in Psychiatry, 18,* 65–71.

Janeck, A. S., Calamari, J. E., Riemann, B. C., & Heffelfinger, S. K. (2003). Too much thinking about thinking? Metacognitive differences in obsessive-compulsive disorder. *Journal of Anxiety Disorders, 17,* 181–195.

Jang, K. L. (2005). *The behavioral genetics of psychopathology: A clinical guide.* Mahwah, NJ: Erlbaum.

Jang, K. L., Livesley, W. J., Taylor, S., Stein, M. B., & Moon, E. C. (2004). Heritability of individual depressive symptoms. *Journal of Affective Disorders, 80,* 125–133.

Jang, K. L., Livesley, W. J., & Vernon, P. A. (1997). Gender-specific etiological differences in alcohol and drug problems: A behavioural genetic analysis. *Addiction, 92,* 1265–1276.

Jang, K. L., Stein, M. B., Taylor, S., Asmundson, G. J., & Livesley, W. J. (2003). Exposure to traumatic events and experiences: Aetiological relationships with personality function. *Psychiatry Research, 120,* 61–69.

Jang, K. L., Vernon, P. A., & Livesley, W. J. (2001). Behavioural-genetic perspectives on personality function. *Canadian Journal of Psychiatry, 46,* 234–244.

Japuntich, S. J., Piper, M. E., Leventhal, A. M., Bolt, D. M., & Baker, T. B. (2011). The effect of five smoking cessation pharmacotherapies on smoking cessation milestones. *Journal of Consulting and Clinical Psychology, 79,* 34–42.

Jellinek, E. M. (1960). *The disease concept of alcoholism.* New Haven, CT: Hillhouse.

Jenkins, P. E., Hoste, R. R., Meyer, C., & Blissett, M. M. (2011). Eating disorders and quality of life: A review of the literature. *Clinical Psychology Review, 31,* 113–121.

Jiang, X. L., Zheng, X. Y., Yang, J., Ye, C. P., Chen, Y. Y., Zhang, Z. G., & Xiao, Z. J. (2015). A systematic review of studies on the prevalence of insomnia in university students. *Public Health, 129,* 1579–1584.

Jilek, W. G. (2001, July). Anorexia nervosa: Cultural factors in psychiatric disorders. Paper presented at the 26th Congress of the World Federation for Mental Health, Vancouver, BC. Retrieved from http://www.mentalhealth.com/mag1/wolfgangex.html

Joffe, R. T., & Gardner, D. M. (2000). *The Canadian psychotropic handbook.* Mississauga, ON: Sudler & Hennessey.

Johns, L. C., Gregg, L., Allen, P., & McGuire, P. K. (2006). Impaired verbal self-monitoring in psychosis: Effects of state, trait and diagnosis. *Psychological Medicine, 36,* 465–474.

Johnson, A. K., Sellbom, M., & Phillips, T. R. (2014). Elucidating the associations between psychopathy, Gray's reinforcement sensitivity theory constructs, and externalizing behavior. *Personality and Individual Differences, 71,* 1–8.

Johnson, P. A. (1989). *Wellness behaviour specialist program proposal for the Ontario Ministry of Colleges and Universities.* Unpublished manuscript. Confederation College, Thunder Bay, ON.

Johnson, W. G., Tsoh, J. Y., & Varnado, P. J. (1996). Eating disorders: Efficacy of pharmacological and psychological interventions. *Clinical Psychology Review, 16,* 457–478.

Joiner, T. E. (2006). *Why people die by suicide.* Cambridge, MA: Harvard University Press.

Joiner, T. E., Jr., Brown, J. S., & Wingate, L. R. (2005). The psychology and neurobiology of suicidal behavior. *Annual Review of Psychology, 56,* 287–314.

Jonas, D. E., Amick, H. R., Feltner, C., Bobashev, G., Thomas, K., Wines, R., . . . Garbutt, J. C. (2014). Pharmocotherapy for adults with alcohol use disorders in outpatient settings: A systematic review and meta-analysis. *JAMA: Journal of the American Medical Association, 311,* 1889–1900.

Jones, E. (1953). *The life and work of Sigmund Freud.* New York: Basic Books.

Jones, H. E. (2006). Drug addiction during pregnancy: Advances in maternal treatment and understanding child outcomes. *Current Directions in Psychological Science, 15,* 126–130.

Jones, J. M., Bennett, S., Olmsted, M. P., Lawson, M. L., & Rodin, G. (2001). Disordered eating attitudes and behaviours in teenaged girls: A school-based study. *CMAJ: Canadian Medical Association Journal, 165,* 547–552.

Jones, P. B., Rantakallio, P., Hartikainen, A.-L., Isohanni, M., & Sipila, P. (1998). Schizophrenia as a long-term outcome of pregnancy, delivery, and perinatal complications: A 28-year follow-up of the 1966 North Finland general population birth cohort. *American Journal of Psychiatry, 155,* 355–364.

Jonsson, T., Stefansson, H., Steinberg, S., Jonsdottir, I., Jonsson, P. V., Snaedal, J., . . . Stefansson, K. (2013). Variant of TREM2 associated with the risk of Alzheimer's disease. *New England Journal of Medicine, 368,* 107–116.

Joormann, J., & Levens, S. M., & Gotlib, I. H. (2011). Depression and rumination are associated with difficulties manipulating emotional material in working memory. *Psychological Science, 22,* 979–983.

Jordan, C. E., Combs, J. L., & Smith, G. T. (2014). An exploration of sexual victimization and academic performance among college women. *Trauma, Violence, & Abuse, 15,* 191–200.

Jorm, A. F., Kelly, C. M., Wright, A., Parslow, R. A., Harris, M. G., & McGorry, P. D. (2006). Belief in dealing with depression alone: Results from community surveys of adolescents and adults. *Journal of Affective Disorders, 96,* 59–65.

Jouriles, E. N., Mehta, P., McDonald, R., & Francis, D. J. (1997). Psychometric properties of family members' reports of parental physical aggression toward clinic-referred children. *Journal of Consulting and Clinical Psychology, 65,* 309–318.

K

Kaback, M., Lim-Steele, J., Dabholkar, D., Brown, D., Levy, N., & Zeiger, K. (1993). Tay-Sachs disease: Carrier screening, prenatal diagnosis, and the molecular era. *JAMA: Journal of the American Medical Association, 270,* 2307–2315.

Kahan, B., & Goodstadt, M. (2002, April). The IDM manual for using the Interactive Domain Model approach to health promotion. Centre for Health Promotion, University of Toronto. Retrieved from http://www.utoronto.ca/chp/download

Kahn, S., Murray, R. P., & Barnes, G. E. (2002). A structural equation model of the effect of poverty and unemployment on alcohol abuse. *Addictive Behaviors, 27*(3), 405–423.

Kaiser, M. D., Hudac, C. M., Shultz, S., Lee, S. M., Cheung, C., Berken, A. M., . . . Pelphrey, K. A. (2010). Neural signatures of autism. *Proceedings of the National Academy of Sciences of the United States of America, 107,* 21223–21228.

Kandel, D. B. (2003). Does marijuana use cause the use of other drugs? *JAMA: Journal of the American Medical Association, 289,* 482–483.

Kane, J. M. (1996). Drug therapy: Schizophrenia. *New England Journal of Medicine, 334,* 34–41.

Kane, J. M., & Marder, S. R. (1993). Psycho-pharmalogic treatment of schizophrenia. *Schizophrenia Bulletin, 19,* 287–302.

Kanner, L. (1943). Autistic disturbances of affective content. *Nervous Child, 2,* 217–240.

Kanter, J. W., Manos, R. C., Bowe, W. M., Baruch, D. E., Busch, A. M., & Rusch, L. C. (2010). What is behavioral activation? A review of the empirical literature. *Clinical Psychology Review, 30,* 608–620.

Kaplan, A. S. (2002). Psychological treatments for anorexia nervosa: A review of published studies and promising new directions. *Canadian Journal of Psychiatry, 47,* 235–242.

Kaplan, A. S., & Garfinkel, P. E. (1999). Difficulties in treating patients with eating disorders: A review of patient and clinical variables. *Canadian Journal of Psychiatry, 44,* 665–670.

Kaplan, S. J. (1986). *The private practice of behavior therapy: A guide for behavioral practitioners.* New York: Plenum Press.

Karamanolaki, H., Spyropoulou, A. C., Iliadou, A., Vousoura, E., Vondikaki, S., Pantazis, N., & Vaslamatzis, G. (2016). Birth order and memories of traumatic and family experiences in Greek patients with borderline personality disorder versus patients with other personality disorders. *Bulletin of the Menninger Clinic, 80,* 234–254.

Karran, E., Mercken, M., & De Strooper, B. (2011). The amyloid cascade hypothesis for Alzheimer's disease: An appraisal for the development of therapeutics. *Nature Reviews Drug Discovery, 10,* 698–712.

Karyotaki, E., Smit, Y., de Beurs, D. P., Henningsen, K. H., Robays, J., Huibers, M. J. H., . . . Cuijpers, P. (2016). The long-term efficacy of acute-phase psychotherapy for depression: A meta-analysis of randomized trials. *Depression and Anxiety, 33,* 370–383.

Katon, W. J. (2006). Panic disorder. *New England Journal of Medicine, 354,* 2360–2367.

Katzman, M. A., Bleau, P., Blier, P., Chokka, P., Kjernisted, K., & Van Ameringen, M. (2014). Canadian clinical practice guidelines for the management of anxiety, posttraumatic stress and obsessive-compulsive disorders. *BMC Psychiatry,* 14(Suppl. 1):S1. http://www.biomedicalcentral.com/1471-244X/14/S1/S1

Kazdin, A. E. (1992). *Research design in clinical psychology* (2nd ed.). Boston: Allyn & Bacon.

Kazdin, A. E. (2003). *Research design in clinical psychology* (4th ed.). Boston: Allyn & Bacon.

Kazdin, A. E. (2005). *Parent management training: Treatment for oppositional, aggressive, and antisocial behavior in children and adolescents.* New York: Oxford University Press.

Kazdin, A. E., & Weisz, J. R. (1998). Identifying and developing empirically supported child and adolescent treatments. *Journal of Consulting and Clinical Psychology, 66,* 19–36.

Kazdin, A. E., & Whitley, M. K. (2003). Treatment of parental stress to enhance therapeutic change among children referred for aggressive and antisocial behavior. *Journal of Consulting and Clinical Psychology, 71,* 504–515.

Kealy, D., Sierra-Hernandez, C. A., & Ogrodniczuk, J. S. (2016). Childhood emotional support and borderline personality features in a sample of Canadian psychiatric outpatients. *International Journal of Social Psychiatry, 62,* 452–454.

Keane, T. M., Marshall, A. D., & Taft, C. T. (2006). Posttraumatic stress disorder: Etiology, epidemiology, and treatment outcome. *Annual Review of Clinical Psychology, 2,* 161–197.

Kearins, J. M. (1981). Visual spatial memory in Australian Aboriginal children in desert regions. *Cognitive Psychology, 13,* 434–460.

Keel, P. K., Mitchell, J. E., Miller, K. B., Davis, T. L., & Crow, S. J. (1999). Long-term outcome of bulimia nervosa. *Archives of General Psychiatry, 56,* 63–69.

Keith, S. J., Regier, D. A., & Rae, D. S. (1991). Schizophrenic disorders. In L. N. Robins & D. A. Regier (Eds.), *Psychiatric disorders in America: The Epidemiologic Catchment Area Study* (pp. 33–52). New York: Free Press.

Kellner, C. H., Greenberg, R. M., Murrough, J. W., Bryson, E. O., Briggs, M. C., & Pasculli, R. M. (2012). ECT in treatment-resistant depression. *American Journal of Psychiatry, 169,* 1238–1244.

Kempton, M. J., Stahl, D., Williams, S. C. R., & DeLisi, L. E. (2010). Progressive lateral ventricular enlargement in schizophrenia: A meta-analysis of longitudinal MRI studies. *Schizophrenia Research, 120,* 54–62.

Kendler, K. S., Aggen, S. H., & Patrick, C. J. (2013). Familial influences on conduct disorder reflect 2 genetic factors and 1 shared environmental factor. *JAMA Psychiatry, 70,* 78–86.

Kendler, K. S., MacLean, C., Neale, M., Kessler, R., Heath, A., & Eaves, L. (1991). The genetic epidemiology of bulimia nervosa. *American Journal of Psychiatry, 148,* 1627–1637.

Kendler, K. S., & Prescott, C. A. (2006). *Genes, environment, and psychopathology: Understanding the causes of psychiatric and substance use disorders.* New York: Guilford.

Kendler, K. S., Sundquist, K., Ohlsson, H., Palmér, K., Maes, H., Winkleby, M. A., & Sundquist, J. (2012). Genetic and familial environmental influences on the risk for drug abuse: A National Swedish Adoption Study. *Archives of General Psychiatry, 69,* 690–697.

Kennedy, S. H., & Lam, R. W. (2003). Enhancing outcomes in the management of treatment resistant depression: A focus on atypical antipsychotics. *Bipolar Disorders,* 5(Suppl. 2), 36–47.

Kennedy, S. H., Lam, R. W., Cohen, N. L., Ravindran, A. V., & CANMAT Depression Work Group. (2001). Clinical guidelines for the treatment of depressive disorders: IV. Medications and other biological treatments. *Canadian Journal of Psychiatry,* 46(Suppl. 1), 38S–58S.

Kent, A., & Waller, G. (2000). Childhood emotional abuse and eating psychopathology. *Clinical Psychology Review, 20,* 887–903.

Keo-Meier, C. L., Herman, L. I., Reisner, S. L., Pardo, S. T., Sharp, C., & Babcock, J. C. (2015). Testosterone treatment and MMPI-2 improvement in transgender men: A prospective controlled study. *Journal of Consulting and Clinical Psychology, 83,* 143–156.

Kernberg, O. F. (1975). *Borderline conditions and pathological narcissism.* New York: Aronson.

Kerr, D. C. R., Zava, D. T., Piper, W. T., Saturn, S. R., Frei, B., & Gombart, A. F. (2015). Associations between vitamin D levels and depressive symptoms in healthy young adult women. *Psychiatry Research, 227,* 46–51.

Kershner, R. (1996). Adolescent attitudes about rape. *Adolescence, 31,* 29–33.

Keshavan, M. S., Nasrallah, H. A., & Tandon, R. (2011). Schizophrenia, "Just the Facts" 6. Moving ahead with the schizophrenia concept: From the elephant to the mouse. *Schizophrenia Research, 127,* 3–13.

Keski-Rahkonen, A., Raevuori, A., Bulik, C. M., Hoek, H. W., Rissanen, A., & Kaprio, J. (2014). Factors associated with recovery from anorexia nervosa: A population-based study. *International Journal of Eating Disorders, 47,* 117–123.

Kessler, R. C., Chiu, W. T., Jin, R., Ruscio, A. M., Shear, K., & Walters, E. E. (2006). The epidemiology of panic attacks, panic disorder, and agoraphobia in the National Comorbidity Survey Replication. *Archives of General Psychiatry, 63,* 415–424.

Kety, S. S., Rosenthal, D., Wender, P. H., & Schulsinger, F. (1968). The types and prevalence of mental illness in the biological and adoptive families of adopted schizophrenics. In D. Rosenthal & S. S. Kety (Eds.), *The transmission of schizophrenia: Proceedings of the second research conference of the Foundations' Fund for Research in Psychiatry, Dorado, Puerto Rico, 26 June to 1 July 1967.* Oxford: Pergamon.

Kety, S. S., Rosenthal, D., Wender, P. H., Schulsinger, F., & Jacobsen, B. (1975). Mental illness in the biological and adoptive families of adoptive individuals who have become schizophrenic: A preliminary report based on psychiatric interviews. In R. R. Fieve, D. Rosenthal, & H. Brill (Eds.), *Genetic research in psychiatry: Proceedings of the sixty-third annual meeting of the American Psychopathological Association.* Baltimore, MD: Johns Hopkins University Press.

Kety, S. S., Rosenthal, D., Wender, P. H., Schulsinger, F., & Jacobsen, B. (1978). The biological and adoptive families of adopted individuals who become schizophrenic. In L. C. Wynne, R. L. Cromwell, & S. Mathysse (Eds.), *The nature of schizophrenia: New approaches to research and treatment* (pp. 25–37). New York: Wiley.

Kety, S. S., Wender, P. H., Jacobsen, B., Ingraham, L. J., Jansson, L., Faber, B., & Kinney, D. K. (1994). Mental illness in the biological and adoptive relatives of schizophrenic adoptees: Replication of the Copenhagen Study to the rest of Denmark. *Archives of General Psychiatry, 51*, 442–455.

Kiehl, K. A., Smith, A. M., Hare, R. D., Mendrek, A., Forster, B. B., Brink, J., & Liddle, P. F. (2001). Limbic abnormalities in affective processing by criminal psychopaths as revealed by functional magnetic resonance imaging. *Biological Psychiatry, 50*, 678–684.

Kielland, N., & Simeone, T. (2014). *Current issues in mental health in Canada: The mental health of First Nations and Inuit communities.* Ottawa: Library of Parliament.

Kihlstrom, J. K. (2005). Dissociative disorders. *Annual Review of Clinical Psychology, 1*, 227–253.

Killackey, E., & Yung, A. R. (2007). Effectiveness of early intervention in psychosis. *Current Opinion in Psychiatry, 20*, 121–125.

Kilts, C. D., Gross, R. E., Ely, T. D., & Drexler, K. P. G. (2004). The neural correlates of cue-induced craving in cocaine-dependent women. *American Journal of Psychiatry, 161*, 233–241.

Kimerling, R., & Calhoun, K. S. (1994). Somatic symptoms, social support, and treatment seeking among sexual assault victims. *Journal of Consulting and Clinical Psychology, 62*, 333–340.

King, S., St-Hilaire, A., & Heidkamp, D. (2010). Prenatal factors in schizophrenia. *Current Directions in Psychological Science, 19*, 209–213.

Kingston, D. A., & Bradford, J. M. (2013). Hypersexuality and recidivism among sexual offenders. *Sexual Addiction & Compulsivity, 20*, 91–105.

Kinoshita, Y., Chen, J., Rapee, R. M., Bogels, S., Schneier, F. R., Choy, Y., . . . Furukawa, T. A. (2008). Cross-cultural study of conviction subtype *taijin kyofu*: Proposal and reliability of Nagoya-Osaka diagnostic criteria for social anxiety disorder. *The Journal of Nervous and Mental Disease, 196*, 307–313.

Kirby, M. J. L., & Keon, W. J. (2004). *Mental health, mental illness and addiction: Overview of policies and programs in Canada.* Interim report of the Standing Senate Committee on Social Affairs, Science and Technology. Ottawa: Senate of Canada. Retrieved from http://www.parl.gc.ca/Content/SEN/Committee/381/soci/rep/report1/repintnov04vol1-e.pdf

Kirby, M. J. L., & Keon, W. J. (2006). *Out of the shadows at last: Transforming mental health, mental illness and addiction services in Canada.* Report of the Standing Senate Committee on Social Affairs, Science and Technology. Ottawa: Senate of Canada. Retrieved from http://www.parl.gc.ca/Content/SEN/Committee/391/soci/rep/rep02may06-e.htm

Kirisci, L., Vanyukov, M., & Tarter, R. (2005). Detection of youth at high risk for substance use disorders: A longitudinal study. *Psychology of Addictive Behaviors, 19*, 243–252.

Kirmayer, L. J. (2001). Cultural variations in the clinical presentation of depression and anxiety: Implications for diagnosis and treatment. *Journal of Clinical Psychiatry, 62*(Suppl. 13), 22–28.

Kirmayer, L. J., Brass, G. M., & Tait, C. L. (2000). The mental health of Aboriginal peoples: Transformations of identity and community. *Canadian Journal of Psychiatry, 45*, 607–616.

Kirmayer, L. J., & Groleau, D. (2001). Affective disorders in cultural context. *The Psychiatric Clinics of North America, 24*, 465–478.

Kirmayer, L. J., Groleau, D., Guzder, J., Blake, C., & Jarvis, E. (2003). Cultural consultation: A model of mental health service for multicultural societies. *Canadian Journal of Psychiatry, 48*, 145–153.

Kirmayer, L. J., Jarvis, G. E., & Guzder, J. (2014). The process of cultural consultation. In L. J. Kirmayer, J. Guzder, & C. Rouseau (Eds.), *Cultural consultation: Encountering the other in mental health care* (pp. 47–70). New York: Springer.

Kirmayer, L. J., & Looper, K. J. (2006). Abnormal illness behaviour: Physiological, psychological and social dimensions of coping with distress. *Current Opinion in Psychiatry, 19*, 54–60.

Kirmayer, L. J., & Minas, H. (2000). The future of cultural psychiatry: An international perspective. *Canadian Journal of Psychiatry, 45*, 438–446.

Kirmayer, L. J., Narasiah, L., Munoz, M., Rashid, M., Ryder, A. G., Guzder, J., . . . Canadian Collaboration for Immigrant and Refugee Health (CCIRH). (2011). Common mental health problems in immigrants and refugees: General approach in primary care. *Canadian Medical Association Journal, 183*(12), E959–67.

Kirmayer, L., J. & Valaskakis, G. G. (2009). *Healing traditions: The mental health of Aboriginal peoples in Canada.* Vancouver: University of British Columbia Press.

Kissel, R. C., Whitman, T. L., & Reid, D. H. (1983). An institutional staff training and self-management program for developing multiple self-care skills in severely/profoundly retarded individuals. *Journal of Applied Behavior Analysis, 16*, 395–415.

Kitamura, T., Miyazaki, S., Koizumi, H., Takeuchi, S., Tabata, T., & Suzuki, H. (2016). Sleep hygiene education for patients with obstructive sleep apnea. *Sleep & Biological Rhythms, 14*, S101–S106.

Kivisalu, T. M., Lewey, J. H., Shaffer, T. W., & Canfield, M. L. (2016). An investigation of interrater reliability for the Rorschach Performance Assessment System (R-PAS) in a nonpatient U.S. sample. *Journal of Personality Assessment, 98*, 382–390.

Klein, D. N., & Santiago, N. J. (2003). Dysthymia and chronic depression: Introduction, classification, risk factors, and course. *Journal of Clinical Psychology, 59*, 807–816.

Kleinplatz, P. J. (2003). What's new in sex therapy? From stagnation to fragmentation. *Sexual and Relationship Therapy, 18*, 95–106.

Klerman, G. L. (1984). Ideology and science in the individual psychotherapy of schizophrenia. *Schizophrenia Bulletin, 10*, 608–612.

Klerman, G. L., Weissman, M. M., Rounsaville, B. J., & Chevron, E. S. (1984). *Interpersonal psychotherapy of depression.* New York: Basic Books.

Klesges, R. C., Winders, S. E., Meyers, A. W., Eck, L. H., Ward, K. D., Hultquist, C. M., . . . Shadish, W. R. (1997). How much weight gain occurs following smoking cessation? A comparison of weight gain using both continuous and point prevalence abstinence. *Journal of Consulting and Clinical Psychology, 65*, 286–291.

Knudsen, D. D. (1991). Child sexual coercion. In E. Grauerholz & M. A. Koralewski (Eds.), *Sexual coercion: A sourcebook on its nature, causes, and prevention* (pp. 17–28). Lexington, KY: Lexington Books.

Kocahan, S., & Doğan, Z. (2017). Mechanisms of Alzheimer's disease pathogenesis and prevention: The brain, neural pathology, N-methyl-D-aspartate receptors, tau protein and other risk factors. *Clinical Psychopharmacology and Neuroscience, 15*, 1–8.

Koehler, N., Holze, S., Gansera, L., Rebmann, U., Roth, S., Scholz, H.-J., . . . Braehler, E. (2012). Erectile dysfunction after radical prostatectomy: The impact of nerve-sparing status and surgical approach. *International Journal of Impotence, 24*, 155–160.

Koerner, K., & Linehan, M. M. (2002). Research on dialectical behavior therapy for patients with borderline personality disorder. *Psychiatric Clinics of North America, 23*(1), 151–167.

Kohut, H. (1966). Forms and transformations of narcissism. *Journal of the American Psychoanalytic Association, 14*, 243–272.

Kolassa, I.-T., & Elbert, T. (2007). Structural and functional neuroplasticity in relation to traumatic stress. *Current Directions in Psychological Science, 16*, 321–325.

Kolbert, E. (1994, January 21). Demons replace dolls and bicycles in world of children of the quake. *The New York Times*, p. A19.

Kong, A., Frigge, M. L., Masson, G., Besenbacher, S., Sulem, P., Magnusson, G., . . . Stefansson, K. (2012). Rate of *de novo* mutations and the importance of father's age to disease risk. *Nature, 488*, 471–475.

Koss, M. P., Goodman, L. A., Browne, A., Fitzgerald, L. F., Keita, G. P., & Russo, N. F. (1994). *No safe haven: Male violence against women at home, at work, and in the community.* Washington, DC: American Psychological Association.

Kostić, J. S., Nešić, M., Stanković, M., Žikić, O., & Marković, J. (2016). Evaluating empathy in adolescents with conduct disorders. *Vojnosanitetski Pregled, 73*, 429–434.

Kotler, M., Cohen, H., Segman, R., Gritsenko, I., Nemanov, L., Lerer, B., . . . Ebstein, R. P. (1997). Excess dopamine D4 receptor (D4DR) exon III seven repeat allele in opioid-dependent subjects. *Molecular Psychiatry, 2*, 251–254.

Kraepelin, E. (1909–1913). *Psychiatrie* (8th ed.). Leipzig: Barth.

Kranzler, H. R. (2006). Evidence-based treatments for alcohol dependence: New results and new questions. *JAMA: Journal of the American Medical Association, 295*, 2075–2076.

Kring, A. M., Kerr, S. L., Smith, D. A., & Neale, J. M. (1993). Flat affect in schizophrenia does not reflect diminished subjective experience of emotion. *Journal of Abnormal Psychology, 102*, 507–517.

Kring, A. M., & Neale, J. M. (1996). Do schizophrenic patients show a disjunctive relationship among expressive, experiential, and psychophysiological components of emotion? *Journal of Abnormal Psychology, 105*, 249–257.

Krueger, R. F., & Markon, K. E. (2006). Reinterpreting comorbidity: A model-based approach to understanding and classifying psychopathology. *Annual Review of Clinical Psychology, 2*, 111–133.

Kruesi, M. J., Fine, S., Valladares, L., Phillips, R. A., Jr., & Rapoport, J. L. (1992). Paraphilias: A double-blind cross-over comparison of clomipramine versus desipramine. *Archives of Sexual Behavior, 21*, 587–593.

Krug, I., Penelo, E., Fernandez-Aranda, F., Anderluh, M., Belodi, L., Cellini, E., . . . Treasure, J. (2013). Low social interaction in eating disorder patients in childhood and adulthood: A multi-centre European case control study. *Journal of Health Psychology, 18*, 26–37.

Kryger, M. H. (2001). Waking up to the consequences of sleep disorders. Winnipeg: St. Boniface Hospital Research Centre. Retrieved from http://www.sbrc.umanitoba.ca/framekryger.htm

Kuehn, B. M. (2007). Opiod prescriptions soar. *JAMA: Journal of the American Medical Association, 297*, 249–251.

Kuo, J. R., Khoury, J. E., Metcalfe, R., Fitzpatrick, S., & Goodwill, A. (2015). An examination of the relationship between childhood emotional abuse and borderline personality disorder features: The role of difficulties with emotion regulation. *Child Abuse & Neglect, 39*, 147–155.

Kurlansik, S. L., & Ibay, A. M. D. (2012). Seasonal affective disorder. *American Family Physician, 86*(11), 1037–1041.

Kurlansik, S. L., & Maffei, M. S. (2016). Somatic symptom disorder. *American Family Physician, 93*, 49–54.

Kurtz, J. E., & Blais, M. A. (2007). Introduction to the special issue on the Personality Assessment Inventory. *Journal of Personality Assessment, 88*(1), 1–4.

Kymalainen, J. A., & Weisman, A. G. (2008). Expressed emotion, communication deviance, and culture in families of patients with schizophrenia: A review of the literature. *Cultural Diversity and Ethnic Minority Psychology, 14*, 85–91.

Kymalainen, J. A., Weisman, A. G., Resales, G. A., & Armesto, J. C. (2006). Ethnicity, expressed emotion, and communication deviance in family members of patients with schizophrenia. *Journal of Nervous and Mental Disease, 194*, 391–396.

L

Labonté, B., Suderman, M., Maussion, G., Navaro, L., Yerko, V., Mahar, I., . . . Turecki, G. (2012). Genome-wide epigenetic regulation by early-life trauma. *Archives of General Psychiatry, 69*, 722–731.

Lacourse, E. (2012). Late childhood risk factors associated with conduct disorder subtypes in early adolescence: A latent class analysis of a Canadian sample. Research Report: 2012-2. Ottawa: National Crime Prevention Centre, Public Safety Canada.

Lacourse, E., Baillargeon, R., Dupéré, V., Vitaro, F., Romano, E., & Tremblay, R. (2010). Two-year predictive validity of conduct disorder subtypes in early adolescence: A latent class analysis of a Canadian longitudinal sample. *Journal of Child Psychology and Psychiatry, 51*(12), 1386–1394.

Ladouceur, R. (2002). *Understanding and treating the pathological gambler.* New York: Wiley.

LaGrange, B., Cole, D. A., Jacquez, F., Ciesla, J., Dallaire, D., Pineda, A., . . . Felton, J. (2011). Disentangling the prospective relations between maladaptive cognitions and depressive symptoms. *Journal of Abnormal Psychology, 120*, 521–527.

Lahey, B. B., Loeber, R., Hart, E. L., Frick, P. J., Applegate, B., Zhang, Q., . . . Russo, M. F. (1995). Four-year longitudinal study of conduct disorder in boys: Patterns and predictors of persistence. *Journal of Abnormal Psychology, 104*, 83–93.

Laishes, J. (2002). The 2002 mental health strategy for women offenders. Ottawa: Correctional Services Canada. Retrieved from http://www.csc-scc.gc.ca/text/prgrm/fsw/mhealth/toc-eng.shtml

Lakhan, R. (2013). The coexistence of psychiatric disorders and intellectual disability in children aged 3–18 years in the Barwani District, India. *ISRN Psychiatry, 875873.*

Lakhan, S. E., & Callaway, H. (2010). Deep brain stimulation for obsessive-compulsive disorder and treatment-resistant depression: Systematic review. *BMC Research Notes, 3*(1), 60.

Lalonde, J. K., Hudson, J. I., Gigante, R. A., & Pope, H. G., Jr. (2001). Canadian and American psychiatrists' attitudes toward dissociative disorders diagnoses. *Canadian Journal of Psychiatry, 46*, 407–412.

Lam, R. W., Levitt, A. J., Levitan, R. D., Enns, M. W., Morehouse, R., Michalak, E. E., & Tam, E. M. (2006). The CAN-SAD study: Randomized controlled trial of the effectiveness of light therapy and fluoxetine in patients with winter seasonal affective disorder. *American Journal of Psychiatry, 163*, 805–812.

Lamberg, L. (2003). Advances in eating disorders offer food for thought. *JAMA: Journal of the American Medical Association, 290*, 1437–1442.

Landau, S. M., Harvey, D., Madison, C. M., Reiman, E. M., Foster, N. L., Aisen, P. S., . . . Jagust, W. J. (2010). Comparing predictors of conversion and decline in mild cognitive impairment. *Neurology, 75*, 230–238.

Landy, S., & Tam, K. K. (1998). *Understanding the contribution of multiple risk factors on child development at various ages* (Catalogue No. MP32-28/98-22E). Ottawa: Human Resources Development Canada. Retrieved from http://publications.gc.ca/pub?id=81774&sl=0

Lane-Donovan, C., & Herz, J. (2017). ApoE, apoE receptors, and the synapse in Alzheimer's disease. *Trends in Endocrinology & Metabolism, 28*, 273–284.

Laney, C., & Loftus, E. F. (2013). Recent advances in false memory research. *South African Journal of Psychology, 43*, 137–146.

Lang, P. J., & Lazovik, A. D. (1963). Experimental desensitization of phobia. *Journal of Abnormal and Social Psychology, 66*(6), 519.

Laporte, L., Paris, J., Guttman, H., Russell, J., & Correa, J. A. (2012). Using a sibling design to compare childhood adversities in female patients with BPD and their sisters. *Child Maltreatment, 17*, 318–329.

Larøi, F. (2006). The phenomenological diversity of hallucinations: Some theoretical and clinical implications. *Psychologica Belgica, 46*, 163–183.

Laumann, E. O., Gagnon, J. H., Michael, R. T., & Michaels, S. (1994). *The social organization of sexuality: Sexual practices in the United States.* Chicago: University of Chicago Press.

Lavallée, C., & Bourgault, C. (2000). The health of Cree, Inuit and southern Quebec women: Similarities and differences. *Canadian Journal of Public Health, 91*, 212–216.

Lavender, J. M., Mason, T. B., Utzinger, L. M., Wonderlich, S. A., Crosby, R. D., Engel, S. G., . . . Peterson, C. B. (2016). Examining affect and perfectionism in relation to eating disorder symptoms among women with anorexia nervosa. *Psychiatric Research, 241*, 267–272.

Learning Disabilities Association of Canada. (2003a). Advocating for your child with learning disabilities: IV. Programming plans, placement options. Retrieved from http://www.ldac-taac.ca/english/indepth/advocacy/yorchild/6.htm

Learning Disabilities Association of Canada. (2003b). Fact sheet: Assistive technology and learning disabilities. Retrieved from http://www.ldac-taac.ca/english/indepth/assistiv/ATandLD.pdf

Learning Disabilities Association of Canada. (2015). Official definition of learning disabilities. Retrieved from http://www.ldac-acta.ca/learn-more/ld-defined/officialdefinition-of-learning-disabilities

LeBlanc, H. (2014). *Eating disorders among girls and women in Canada.* Report of the Standing Committee on the Status of Women. Ottawa: House of Commons.

Lee, H.-J., Woo, H. G., Greenwood, T. A., Kripke, D. F., & Kelsoe, J. R. (2013). A genome-wide association study of seasonal pattern mania identifies NF1A as a possible susceptibility gene for bipolar disorder. *Journal of Affective Disorders, 145*, 200–207.

Lee, J. K. P., Jackson, H. J., Pattison, P., & Ward, T. (2002). Developmental risk factors for sexual offending. *Child Abuse & Neglect, 26*, 73–92.

Lee, J. Y., Brook, J. S., Finch, S. J., & Brook, D. W. (2016). An adverse family environment during adolescence predicts marijuana use and antisocial personality disorder in adulthood. *Journal of Child and Family studies, 25*, 661–668.

Lee, S. (2001). From diversity to unity: The classification of mental disorders in 21st-century China. *Psychiatric Clinics of North America, 24*, 421–431.

Leger Marketing. (2002). Canadians and sleep: Report. Retrieved from http://www.legermarketing.com/documents/spclm/020121eng.pdf

Lehmann, H. E., & Hanrahan, G. E. (1954). Chlorpromazine: New inhibiting agent for psychomotor excitement and manic states. *Archives of Neurology and Psychiatry, 71*, 227–237.

Leiblum, S. R. (2006). *Principles and practice of sex therapy* (4th ed.). New York: Guilford.

Leichsenring, F., & Leibing, E. (2003). The effectiveness of psychodynamic therapy and cognitive behavior therapy in the treatment of personality disorders: A meta-analysis. *American Journal of Psychiatry, 160*, 1223–1232.

Leichsenring, F., & Rabung, S. (2008). Effectiveness of long-term psychodynamic psychotherapy: A meta-analysis. *JAMA: Journal of the American Medical Association, 300*, 1551–1565.

Leit, R. A., Gray, J. J., & Pope, H. G., Jr. (2002). The media's representation of the ideal male body: A cause for muscle dysmorphia? *International Journal of Eating Disorders, 31*, 334–338.

Lentillon-Kaestner, V., Berchtold, A., Rousseau, A., & Ferrand, C. (2014). Validity and reliability of the French versions of the Body Shape Questionnaire. *Journal of Personality Assessment, 96*, 471–477.

Leonardo, E. D., & Hen, R. (2006). Genetics of affective and anxiety disorders. *Annual Review of Psychology, 57*, 117–137.

Leszcz, M., MacKenzie, R., el-Guebaly, N., Atkinson, M. J., & Wiesenthal, S. (2002). Part V: Canadian psychiatrists' use of psychotherapy. *Canadian Psychiatric Association: The Bulletin, 34*(5), 28–31.

Letendre, A. D. (2002). Aboriginal traditional medicine: Where does it fit? *Crossing Boundaries—An Interdisciplinary Journal, 1*(2), 78–87.

Leue, A., Borchard, B., & Hoyer, J. (2004). Mental disorders in a forensic sample of sexual offenders. *European Psychiatry, 19*, 123–130.

LeVine, E. S. (2012). Facilitating recovery for people with serious mental illness employing a psychobiosocial model of care. *Professional Psychology: Research and Practice, 43*, 58–64.

Levinger, D. M. (2011) Neurobiological basis of drug reward and reinforcement. In B. A. Johnson (Ed.), *Addiction medicine: Science and practice* (pp. 255–281). New York: Springer.

Levitan, R. D., Kaplan, A. S., Joffe, R. T., Levitt, A. J., & Brown, G. M. (1997). Hormonal and subjective responses to intravenous metachlorophenylpiperazine in bulimia nervosa. *Archives of General Psychiatry, 54*, 521–527.

Levitt, A. J., Boyle, M. H., Joffe, R. T., & Baumal, Z. (2000). Estimated prevalence of the seasonal subtype of major depression in a Canadian community sample. *Canadian Journal of Psychiatry, 45*, 650–654.

Lewinsohn, P. M., Antonuccio, D. O., Steinmetz Breckenridge, J., & Teri, L. (1984). *The Coping with Depression course: A psychoeducational intervention for unipolar depression*. Eugene, OR: Castalia.

Lewinsohn, P. M., Sullivan, J. M., & Grosscup, S. J. (1980). Changing reinforcing events: An approach to the treatment of depression. *Psychotherapy: Theory, Research, & Practice, 17*, 322–334.

Lewis, R. W., Fugl-Meyer, K. S., Corona, G., Hayes, R. D., Laumann, E. O., Moreira, E. D., . . . Segraves, T. (2010). Definitions/epidemiology/risk factors for sexual dysfunction. *Journal of Sexual Medicine, 7*, 1598–1607.

Leyton, M., & Stewart, S. (Eds.). (2014). *Substance abuse in Canada: Childhood and adolescent pathways to substance use disorders*. Ottawa: Canadian Centre on Substance Abuse.

Lezak, M. D., Howieson, D. B., & Loring, D. W. (2004). *Neuropsychological assessment* (4th ed.). New York: Oxford University Press.

Liebowitz, M. R., Asnis, G., Mangano, R., & Tzanis, E. (2009). A double-blind, placebo-controlled, parallel-group, flexible-dose study of venlafaxine extended release capsules in adult outpatients with panic disorder. *Journal of Clinical Psychiatry, 70*, 550–561.

Lilienfeld, S. O., & Lynn, S. J. (2003). Dissociative identity disorder: Multiple personalities, multiple controversies. In S. O. Lilienfeld, S. J. Lynn, & J. M. Lohr (Eds.), *Science and pseudoscience in clinical psychology* (pp. 109–142). New York: Guilford.

Lim, A., Hoek, H. W., Deen, M. L., Blom, J. D., Bruggeman, R., Cahn, W., . . . Wiersma, D. (2016). Prevalence and classification of hallucinations in multiple sensory modalities in schizophrenia spectrum disorders. *Schizophrenia Research, 176*, 493–499.

Lim, J., & Dinges, D. F. (2010). A meta-analysis of the impact of short-term sleep deprivation on cognitive variables. *Psychological Bulletin, 136*, 375–389.

Lindahl, V., Pearson, J. L., & Colpe, L. (2005). Prevalence of suicidality during pregnancy and the postpartum. *Archives of Women's Mental Health, 8*, 77–87.

Linde, K., Berner, M., Egger, M., & Mulrow, C. (2005). St John's wort for depression: Meta-analysis of randomised controlled trials. *British Journal of Psychiatry, 186*, 99–107.

Linehan, M. M. (1993). *Cognitive-behavioral treatment of borderline personality disorder*. New York: Guilford.

Linehan, M. M., Camper, P., Chiles, J. A., Strosahl, K., & Shearin, E. (1987). Interpersonal problem solving and parasuicide. *Cognitive Therapy and Research, 11*, 1–12.

Ling, W., Casadonte, P., Bigelow, G., Kampman, K. M., Patkar, A., Bailey, G. L., . . . Beebe, K. L. (2011). Buprenorphine implants for treatment of opioid dependence: A randomized controlled trial. *JAMA: Journal of the American Medical Association, 304*, 1576–1583.

Links, P. S., Heslegrave, R., & Van Reekum, R. (1998). Prospective follow-up study of borderline personality disorder: Prognosis, prediction of outcome, and Axis II comorbidity. *Canadian Journal of Psychiatry, 43*, 265–270.

Lipps, G., & Frank, J. (1997). The National Longitudinal Survey of Children and Youth, 1994–1995: Initial results from the school component (Catalogue no. 81-003-XPB) *Education Quarterly Review, Statistics Canada, 4*(2), 43–57.

Litman, L. C. (2003). Sexual sadism with lust-murder proclivities in a female? *Canadian Journal of Psychiatry, 48*, 127.

Liu, H., Liao, J., Jiang, W., & Wang, W. (2014). Changes in low-frequency fluctuations in patients with antisocial personality disorder revealed by resting-state functional MRI. *PLoS ONE, 9*, e89790. doi:10.1371/journal.pone.0089790

Livesley, W. J. (2001). Conceptual and taxonomic issues. In W. J. Livesley (Ed.), *Handbook of personality disorders: Theory, research, and treatment* (pp. 3–38). New York: Guilford.

Livesley, W. J. (2005). Principles and strategies for treating personality disorder. *Canadian Journal of Psychiatry, 50*, 442–450.

Livesley, W. J., Jang, K. L., Jackson, D. N., & Vernon, P. A. (1993). Genetic and environmental contributions to dimensions of personality disorder. *American Journal of Psychiatry, 150*, 1826–1831.

Livingston, J. D., Wilson, D., Tien, G., & Bond, L. (2003). A follow-up study of persons found not criminally responsible on account of mental disorder in British Columbia. *Canadian Journal of Psychiatry, 48*, 408–415.

Livingstone, M. S., Rosen, G. D., Drislane, F. W., & Galaburda, A. M. (1991). Physiological and anatomical evidence for a magnocellular defect in developmental dyslexia. *Proceedings of the National Academy of Sciences, 88*, 7943–7947.

Lo, H. T., & Fung, K. P. (2003). Culturally competent psychotherapy. *Canadian Journal of Psychiatry, 48*, 161–170.

Lobbestael, J., Leurgans, M., & Arntz, A. (2011). Inter-rater reliability of the Structured Clinical Interview for DSM-IV axis I disorders (SCID I) and axis II disorders

(SCID II). *Clinical Psychology and Psychotherapy, 18,* 75–79.

Lochman, J. E., & Dodge, K. A. (1994). Social-cognitive processes of severely violent, moderately aggressive, and nonaggressive boys. *Journal of Consulting and Clinical Psychology, 62,* 366–374.

Lochman, J. E., & Lenhart, L. A. (1993). Anger coping intervention for aggressive children: Conceptual models and outcome effects. *Clinical Psychology Review, 13,* 785–805.

Loftus, E. F. (1996). The myth of repressed memory and the realities of science. *Clinical Psychology: Science and Practice, 3,* 356–365.

Loftus, E. F., & Davis, D. (2006). Recovered memories. *Annual Review of Clinical Psychology, 2,* 469–498.

López, S. R., Nelson Hipke, N., Polo, A. J., Jenkins, J. H., Karno, M., Vaughn, C., & Snyder, K. S. (2004). Ethnicity, expressed emotion, attributions, and course of schizophrenia: Family warmth matters. *Journal of Abnormal Psychology, 113,* 428–439.

LoPiccolo, J., & Stock, W. E. (1986). Treatment of sexual dysfunction. *Journal of Consulting and Clinical Psychology, 54,* 158–167.

Loranger, A. W., Sartorius, N., Andreoli, A., Berger, P., Buchheim, P., Channabasavanna, S. M., . . . Regier, D. A. (1994). The International Personalty Disorder Examination: The World Health Organization/Alcohol, Drug, Abuse and Mental Health Administration International Pilot Study of Personality Disorders. *Archives of General Psychiatry, 51,* 215–224.

Løvaas, O. I. (1987). Behavioral treatment and normal educational and intellectual functioning in young autistic children. *Journal of Consulting and Clinical Psychology, 55,* 3–9.

Løvaas, O. I., Koegel, R. L., & Schreibman, L. (1979). Stimulus overselectivity in autism: A review of the research. *Psychological Bulletin, 86,* 1236–1254.

Lowe, M. R., Thomas, J. G., Safer, D. L., & Butryn, M. L. (2007). The relationship of weight suppression and dietary restraint to binge eating in bulimia nervosa. *International Journal of Eating Disorders, 40,* 640–644.

Lowe, M. R., Witt, A. A., & Grossman, S. (2013). Dieting in bulimia nervosa is associated with increased food restriction and psychopathology but decreased binge eating. *Eating Behaviors, 14,* 342–347.

Lukassen, J., & Beaudet, M. P. (2005). Alcohol dependence and depression among heavy drinkers in Canada. *Social Science & Medicine, 61,* 1658–1667.

Luntz, B. K., & Widom, C. S. (1994). Antisocial personality disorder in abused and neglected children grown up. *American Journal of Psychiatry, 151,* 670–674.

Lydiard, R. B. (2003). The role of GABA in anxiety disorders. *Journal of Clinical Psychiatry, 64*(Suppl. 3), 21–27.

Lyons, M. J., Goldberg, J., Eisen, S. A., True, W., Tsuang, M. T., Meyer, J. M., & Henderson, W. G. (1993). Do genes influence exposure to trauma? A twin study of combat. *American Journal of Medical Genetics, 48,* 22–27.

M

MacDonald, C. (2002). Treatment resistance in anorexia nervosa and the pervasiveness of ethics in clinical decision making. *Canadian Journal of Psychiatry, 47,* 267–270.

Macgowan, M. J., & Engle, B. (2010). Evidence for optimism: Behavior therapies and motivational interviewing in adolescent substance abuse treatment. *Child and Adolescent Psychiatric Clinics of North America, 19,* 527–545.

MacLatchy-Gaudet, H. A., & Stewart, S. H. (2001). The context-specific positive alcohol outcome expectancies of university women. *Addictive Behaviors, 26,* 31–49.

Macnaughton, E. (2000). Cultural competence and "the knowledge resource base." *Visions: BC's Mental Health Journal, 9*(Winter), 14–15.

Maggi, M. (2012). *Hormonal therapy for male sexual dysfunction.* Hoboken, NJ: Wiley.

Magnusson, A., & Partonen, T. (2005). The diagnosis, symptomatology, and epidemiology of seasonal affective disorder. *CNS Spectrums, 10,* 625–634.

Maher, W. B., & Maher, B. A. (1985). Psychopathology: I. From ancient times to the eighteenth century. In G. A. Kimble & K. Schlesinger (Eds.), *Topics in the history of psychology: Vol. 2.* Hillsdale, NJ: Erlbaum.

Mahler, M., & Kaplan, L. (1977). Developmental aspects in the assessment of narcissistic and so-called borderline personalities. In P. Hartocollis (Ed.), *Borderline personality disorders: The concept, the syndrome, the patient* (pp. 71–85). New York: International Universities Press.

Maier, S. F., & Seligman, M. E. P. (1976). Learned helplessness: Theory and evidence. *Journal of Experimental Psychology (General), 105,* 3–46.

Maletzky, B. M. (1991). *Treating the sexual offender.* Newbury Park, CA: Sage.

Maletzky, B. M. (1998). The paraphilias: Research and treatment. In P. E. Nathan & J. M. Gorman (Eds.), *A guide to treatments that work* (pp. 472–500). New York: Oxford University Press.

Maletzky, B. M., & Steinhauser, C. (2002). A 25-year follow-up of cognitive/behavioral therapy with 7,275 sexual offenders. *Behavior Modification, 26,* 123–147.

Malla, A. K., Norman, R. M. G., & Joober, R. (2005). First-episode psychosis, early intervention, and outcome: What have we learned? *Canadian Journal of Psychiatry, 50,* 881–891.

Mann, J. J., Underwood, M. D., & Arango, V. (1996). Postmortem studies of suicide victims. In S. J. Watson (Ed.), *Biology of schizophrenia and affective disease* (pp. 179–221). Washington, DC: American Psychiatric Press.

Marcantonio, E. R. (2012). Postoperative delirium: A 76-year-old woman with delirium following surgery. *JAMA: Journal of the American Medical Association, 308,* 73–81.

Marco, J. H., Pérez, S., & Garcia-Alandete, J. (2016). Meaning in life buffers the association between risk factors for suicide and hopelessness in participants with mental disorders. *Journal of Clinical Psychology, 72,* 689–700.

Marcus, D. K., Gurley, J. R., Marchi, M. M., & Bauer, C. (2007). Cognitive and perceptual variables in hypochondriasis and health anxiety: A systematic review. *Clinical Psychology Review, 27,* 127–139.

Marengo, J. T., & Harrow, M. (1997). Longitudinal courses of thought disorder in schizophrenia and schizoaffective disorder. *Schizophrenia Bulletin, 23,* 273–285.

Marin, A. (2001). Report to the Minister of National Defence: Systematic treatment of CF members with PTSD. Ottawa: Department of National Defence.

Marin, J. M., Agusti, A., Villar, I., Forner, M., Nieto, D., Carrizo, S. J., . . . Jelic, S. (2012). Association between treated and untreated obstructive sleep apnea and risk of hypertension. *JAMA: Journal of the American Medical Association, 307,* 2169–2176.

Markkula, N., Suvisaari, J., Saarni, S. I., Pirkola, S., Peña, S., Saarni, S., . . . Härkänen, T. (2015). Prevalence and correlates of major depressive disorder and dysthymia in an eleven-year follow-up—Results from the Finnish Health 2011 Survey. *Journal of Affective Disorders, 173,* 73–80.

Markowitz, J. C. (2006a). Adaptations of interpersonal psychotherapy. *Psychiatric Annals, 36,* 559–563.

Markowitz, J. C. (2006b). Interpersonal psychotherapy for depression and dysthymic disorder. In D. J. Stein, D. J. Kupfer, & A. F. Schatzberg (Eds.), *American Psychiatric Publishing textbook of mood disorders* (pp. 373–388). Washington, DC: American Psychiatric Publishing.

Marlatt, G. A. (1978). Craving for alcohol, loss of control, and relapse: A cognitive-behavioral analysis. In P. E. Nathan, G. A. Marlatt, & T. Løberg (Eds.), *Alcoholism: New directions in behavioral research and treatment* (pp. 271–314). New York: Plenum.

Marlatt, G. A., Demming, B., & Reid, J. B. (1973). Loss of control drinking in alcoholics: An experimental analogue. *Journal of Abnormal Psychology, 81,* 233–241.

Marlatt, G. A., Larimer, M. E., Baer, J. S., & Quigley, L. A. (1993). Harm reduction for alcohol problems: Moving beyond the controlled drinking controversy. *Behavior Therapy, 24,* 461–504.

Marsh, R., Steinglass, J. E., Gerber, A. J., O'Leary, K. G., Wang, Z., Murphy, D., . . . Peterson, B. S. (2009). Deficient activity in the neural systems that mediate self-regulatory control in bulimia nervosa. *Archives of General Psychiatry, 66,* 51–63.

Marshall, D. (1971). Sexual behavior on Mangaia. In D. S. Marshall & R. C. Suggs (Eds.), *Human sexual behavior: Variations in the ethnographic spectrum*. Englewood Cliffs, NJ: Prentice Hall.

Marshall, W. L. (2001). Attachment problems in the etiology and treatment of sexual offenders. In W. Everaerd, E. Laan, & S. Both (Eds.), *Sexual appetite, desire and motivation: Energetics of the sexual system* (pp. 135–143). Amsterdam: Royal Netherlands Academy of the Arts and Sciences.

Marshall, W. L., & Eccles, A. (1993). Pavlovian conditioning processes in adolescent sex offenders. In H. E. Barbaree, W. L. Marshall, & S. M. Hudson (Eds.), *The juvenile sex offender* (pp. 118–142). New York: Guilford.

Marshall, W. L., & Marshall, L. E. (2015). Psychological treatment of the paraphilias: A review and an appraisal of effectiveness. *Current Psychiatric Reports, 17*, 47.

Marshall, W. L., Marshall, L. E., Serran, G. A., & O'Brien, M. D. (2008). Sexual offender treatment: A positive approach. *Psychiatric Clinics of North America, 31*, 681–696.

Marshall, W. L., & Moulden, H. (2001). Hostility toward women and victim empathy of rapists. *Sexual Abuse: A Journal of Research and Treatment, 13*, 249–255.

Marshall, W. L., Serran, G. A., & Cortoni, F. A. (2000). Childhood attachments, sexual abuse, and their relationship to adult coping in child molesters. *Sexual Abuse: Journal of Research and Treatment, 12*, 17–26.

Martinez, D., Greene, K., Broft, A., Kumar, D., Liu, F., Narendran, R., . . . Kleber, H. D. (2009). Lower level of endogenous dopamine in patients with cocaine dependence: Findings from PET imaging of D2/D3 receptors following acute dopamine depletion export. *American Journal of Psychiatry, 166*, 1170–1177.

Martinez-Garcia, M., Campos-Rodriguez, F., Almendros, I., & Farré, R. (2015). Relationship between sleep apnea and cancer. *Archivos de Bronconeumologia, 51*, 456–461.

Martinsen, E. W. (2005). Exercise and depression. *International Journal of Sport and Exercise Psychology, 3*, 469–483.

Mason, B. J., Crean, R., Goodell, V., Light, J. M., Quello, S., Shadan, F., . . . Rao, S. (2012). A proof-of-concept randomized controlled study of gabapentin: Effects on cannabis use, withdrawal and executive function deficits in cannabis-dependent adults. *Neuropsychopharmacology, 37*, 1689–1698.

Mason, T. B., & Heron, K. E. (2016). Do depressive symptoms explain associations between binge eating symptoms and later psychosocial adjustment in young adulthood? *Eating Behaviors, 23*, 126–130.

Masters, W. H., & Johnson, V. E. (1970). *Human sexual inadequacy*. Boston: Little, Brown.

Mata, J., Thompson, R. J., Jaeggi, S. M., Buschkuehl, M., Jonides, J., & Gotlib, I. H. (2012). Walk on the bright side: Physical activity and affect in major depressive disorder. *Journal of Abnormal Psychology, 121*, 297–308.

Matheson, K., & Anisman, H. (2003). Systems of coping associated with dysphoria, anxiety and depressive illness: A multivariate profile perspective. *Stress: The International Journal on the Biology of Stress, 6*, 223–234.

Mathews, A., & MacLeod, C. (2005). Cognitive vulnerability to emotional disorders. *Annual Review of Clinical Psychology, 1*, 167–195.

Maughan, B., Collishaw, S., & Stringaris, A. (2013). Depression in childhood and adolescence. *Journal of the Canadian Academy of Child and Adolescent Psychiatry, 22*, 35–40.

Maxwell, J. C. (2005). Emerging research on methamphetamine. *Current Opinion in Psychiatry, 18*, 235–242.

Mayo-Smith, M. F. (1997). Pharmacological management of alcohol withdrawal: A meta-analysis and evidence-based practice guideline. American Society of Addiction Medicine Working Group on Pharmacological Management of Alcohol Withdrawal. *JAMA: Journal of the American Medical Association, 278*, 144–151.

Mazurek, M. O., Kanne, S. M., & Miles, J. H. (2012). Predicting improvement in social-communication symptoms of autism spectrum disorders using retrospective treatment data. *Research in Autism Spectrum Disorders, 6*, 535–545.

McCarthy, B. W., & Bodnar, L. E. (2005). Couple sex therapy: Assessment, treatment, and relapse prevention. In J. L. Lebow (Ed.), *Handbook of clinical family therapy* (pp. 464–493). New York: Wiley.

McCaul, M. E., & Furst, J. (1994). Alcoholism treatment in the United States. *Alcohol Health & Research World, 18*, 253–260.

McCord, W., & McCord, J. (1964). *The psychopath: An essay on the criminal mind*. New York: Van Nostrand.

McCormick, R. M. (2000). Aboriginal traditions in the treatment of substance abuse. *Canadian Journal of Counselling, 34*(1), 25–32.

McCracken, J. T., McGough, J., Shah, B., Cronin, P., Hong, D., Aman, M. G., . . . McMahon, D. (2002). Risperidone in children with autism and serious behavioral problems. *New England Journal of Medicine, 347*, 314–321.

McDonald, K., Bulloch, A. G. M., Duffy, A., Bresee, L., Williams, J. V. A., Lavorato, D. H., & Patten, S. B. (2015). Prevalence of bipolar I and II disorder in Canada. *Canadian Journal of Psychiatry, 60*(3), 151–156.

McDonough, M. (2015). Update on medicines for smoking cessation. *Australian Prescriber, 38*, 106–111.

McEachin, J. J., Smith, T., & Løvaas, O. I. (1993). Long-term outcome for children with autism who received early intensive behavioral treatment. *American Journal on Mental Retardation, 97*, 359–372.

McGillivray, J. A., & Kershaw, M. M. (2013). The impact of staff initiated referral and intervention protocols on symptoms of depression in people with mild intellectual disability. *Research in Developmental Disabilities, 34*, 730–738.

McGuire, P. K., Shah, G. M. S., & Murray, R. M. (1993). Increased blood flow in Broca's area during auditory hallucinations in schizophrenia. *Lancet, 342*, 703–706.

McKellar, J., Stewart, E., & Humphreys, K. (2003). Alcoholics Anonymous involvement and positive alcohol-related outcomes: Cause, consequence, or just a correlate? A prospective 2-year study of 2,319 alcohol dependent men. *Journal of Consulting and Clinical Psychology, 71*, 302–308.

McLawsen, J. E., Scalora, M. J., & Darrow, C. (2012). Civilly committed sex offenders: A description and interstate comparison of populations. *Psychology, Public Policy, and Law, 18*, 453–476.

McLellan, A. T., Alterman, A. I., Metzger, D. S., Grissom, G. R., Woody, G. E., Luborsky, L., & O'Brien, C. P. (1994). Similarity of outcome predictors across opiate, cocaine, and alcohol treatments: Role of treatment services. *Journal of Consulting and Clinical Psychology, 62*, 1141–1158.

McMain, S. F., Links, P. S., Gnam, W. H., Guimond, T., Cardish, R. J., Korman, L., & Streiner, D. L. (2009). A randomized trial of dialectical behavior therapy versus general psychiatric management for borderline personality disorder. *American Journal of Psychiatry, 166*, 1365–1374.

McMurran, M. (2006). Controlled drinking goals for offenders. *Addiction Research & Theory, 14*, 59–65.

Mead, M. (1935). *Sex and temperament in three primitive societies*. New York: Morrow.

Meador-Woodruff, J. H., Haroutunian, V., Powchik, P., Davidson, M., Davis, K. L., & Watson, S. J. (1997). Dopamine receptor transcript expression in striatum and prefrontal and occipital cortex: Focal abnormalities in orbitofrontal cortex in schizophrenia. *Archives of General Psychiatry, 54*, 1089–1095.

Meany, R., Hasking, P., & Reupert, A. (2016). Prevalence of borderline personality disorder in university samples: Systematic review, meta-analysis and meta-regression. *PLoS ONE, 11*(5), e0155439. doi:10.1371/journal.pone.0155439

Medalia, A., Aluma, M., Tryon, W., & Merriam, A. E. (1998). Effectiveness of attention training in schizophrenia. *Schizophrenia Bulletin, 24*, 147–152.

Mednick, S. A. (1970). Breakdown in individuals at high risk for schizophrenia: Possible predispositional perinatal factors. *Mental Hygiene, 54*, 50–63.

Mednick, S. A., Parnas, J., & Schulsinger, F. (1987). The Copenhagen High-Risk Project, 1962–86. *Schizophrenia Bulletin, 13*, 485–495.

Mednick, S. A., & Schulsinger, F. (1968). Some pre-morbid characteristics related to breakdown in children with schizophrenia mothers. In D. Rosenthal & S. S. Kety (Eds.), *The transmission of schizophrenia: Proceedings of the second research conference of the Foundations' Fund for Research in Psychiatry, Dorado, Puerto Rico, 26 June to 1 July 1967* (pp. 267–291). New York: Pergamon.

Meehl, P. E. (1962). Schizotaxia, schizotypy, schizophrenia. *American Psychologist, 17,* 827–838.

Meehl, P. E. (1972). A critical afterword. In I. I. Gottesman & J. Shields (Eds.), *Schizophrenia and genetics: A twin study vantage point* (pp. 367–415). New York: Academic.

Meichenbaum, D. (1976). Toward a cognitive theory of self-control. In G. Schwartz & D. Shapiro (Eds.), *Consciousness and self-regulation: Advances in research: Vol 1.* New York: Plenum.

Meichenbaum, D. (1977). *Cognitive-behavior modification: An integrative approach.* New York: Plenum.

Meichenbaum, D. (1993). Changing conceptions of cognitive behavior modification: Retrospect and prospect. *Journal of Consulting and Clinical Psychology, 61,* 202–204.

Meichenbaum, D. (2005). 35 years of working with suicidal patients: Lessons learned. *Canadian Psychology, 46,* 64–72.

Meier, M. H., Slutske, W. S., Heath, A. C., & Martin, N. G. (2011). Sex differences in the genetic and environmental influences on childhood conduct disorder and adult antisocial behavior. *Journal of Abnormal Psychology, 120,* 377–388.

Mellings, T. M. B., & Alden, L. E. (2000). Cognitive processes in social anxiety: The effects of self-focus, rumination and anticipatory processing. *Behaviour Research and Therapy, 38,* 243–257.

Mellor, C. S. (1970). First rank symptoms of schizophrenia. *British Journal of Psychiatry, 177,* 15–23.

Melrose, S. (2015). Seasonal affective disorder: An overview of assessment and treatment approaches. *Depression Research and Treatment, 2015,* Article ID 178564.

Menary, K. R., Corbin, W. R., Leeman, R. F., Fucito, L. M., Toll, B. A., DeMartini, K., & O'Malley, S. S. (2015). Interactive and indirect effects of anxiety and negative urgency on alcohol-related problems. *Alcoholism Clinical & Experimental Research, 39,* 1267–1274.

Meng, X., & D'Arcy, C. (2015). Comorbidity between lifetime eating problems and mood and anxiety disorders: Results from the Canadian Community Health Survey of Mental Health and Well-Being. *European Eating Disorders Review, 23,* 156–162.

Mental Health Commission of Canada. (2009). *Toward recovery & well-being: A framework for a mental health strategy for Canada.* Calgary, AB: Author.

Mental Health Commission of Canada. (2012). *Changing directions, changing lives: The mental health strategy for Canada.* Calgary, AB: Author.

Mental Health Commission of Canada. (2015). Informing the future: Mental health indicators for Canada. Retrieved from https://www.mentalhealthcommission.ca/English/document/68796/informing-future-mental-health-indicators-canada

Mental Health Commission of Canada. (2016). Advancing the Mental Health Strategy for Canada: A Framework for Action (2017–2022). https://www.mentalhealthcommission.ca/English/media/3746

Menzies, P. (2014). Intergenerational trauma. In V. Harper, P. Menzies, & L. Lavallée (Eds.), *Journey to healing: Aboriginal people with addiction and mental health issues: What health, social service and justice workers need to know* (pp. 61–72). Toronto: Centre for Addiction & Mental Health.

Messenger, J. (1971). Sex and repression in an Irish folk community. In D. S. Marshall & R. C. Suggs (Eds.), *Human sexual behavior: Variations in the ethnographic spectrum.* Englewood Cliffs, NJ: Prentice Hall.

Meston, C. M., & Bradford, A. (2006). Sexual dysfunctions in women. *Annual Review of Clinical Psychology, 3,* 81–104.

Metsänen, M., Wahlberg, K.-E., Saarento, O., Tarvainen, T., Miettunen, J., Koistinen, P., . . . Tienari, P. (2004). Early presence of thought disorder as a prospective sign of mental disorder. *Psychiatry Research, 125,* 193–203.

Meyer, G. J., Mihura, J. L., & Smith, B. L. (2005). The interclinician reliability of Rorschach interpretation in four datat sets. *Journal of Personality Assessment, 84,* 296–314.

Meyer, G. J., Viglione, D. J., Mihura, J. L., Erard, R. E., & Erdberg, P. (2011). *Rorschach Performance Assessment System: Administration, coding, interpretation, and technical manual.* Toledo, OH: Rorschach Performance Assessment System.

Meyers, B. S. (2006). Psychotic depression. *Psychiatric Annals, 36,* 7–9.

Mianji, F., & Semnani, Y. (2015). *Zār* spirit possession in Iran and African countries: Group distress, culture-bound syndrome or cultural concept of distress? *Iranian Journal of Psychiatry, 10,* 225–232.

Michalek, J. E., Kepa, A., Vincent, J., Frissa, S., Goodwin, L., Hotopf, M., . . . Powell, T. R. (2017). Genetic predisposition to advanced biological ageing increases risk for childhood-onset recurrent major depressive disorder in a large UK sample. *Journal of Affective Disorders, 213,* 207-213.

Michaud, J.-P., Hallé, M., Lampron, A., Thériault, P., Préfontaine, P., Filali, M., . . . Rivest, S. (2013). Toll-like receptor 4 stimulation with the detoxified ligand monophosphoryl lipid A improves Alzheimer's disease-related pathology. *PNAS, 110,* 1941–1946.

Micco, J. A., Hirshfeld-Becker, D. R., Henin, A., & Ehrenreich-May, J. (2013). Content specificity of threat interpretation in anxious and non-clinical children. *Cognitive Therapy and Research, 37,* 78–88.

Miklowitz, D. J. (2004). The role of family systems in severe and recurrent psychiatric disorders: A developmental psychopathology view. *Development and Psychopathology, 16,* 667–688.

Miklowitz, D. J., & Johnson, S. L. (2006). The psychopathology and treatment of bipolar disorder. *Annual Review of Clinical Psychology, 2,* 199–235.

Miller, E. (1987). Hysteria: Its nature and explanation. *British Journal of Clinical Psychology, 26,* 163–173.

Miller, J. D., Morse, J. Q., Nolf, K., Stepp, S. D., & Pilkonis, P. A. (2012). Can DSM-IV borderline personality disorder be diagnosed via dimensional personality traits? Implications for the DSM-5 personality disorder proposal. *Journal of Abnormal Psychology, 121,* 944–950.

Miller, W. R., & Hester, R. K. (1986). Inpatient alcoholism treatment: Who benefits? *American Psychologist, 41,* 794–805.

Miller, W. R., Leckman, A. L., Delaney, H. D., & Tinkcom, M. (1993). Long-term follow-up of behavioral self-control training. *Journal of Studies on Alcohol, 53,* 249–261.

Miller, W. R., & Muñoz, R. F. (1983). *How to control your drinking* (2nd ed.). Albuquerque: University of New Mexico Press.

Miller, W. R., & Rollnick, S. (2013). *Motivational interviewing: Helping people change* (3rd ed.). New York: Guilford Press.

Millon, T. (1981). *Disorders of personality: DSM-III, Axis II.* New York: Wiley.

Mills, P. D., Watts, B. V., Huh, T. J. W., Boar, S., & Kemp, J. (2013). Helping elderly patients to avoid suicide: A review of case reports from a national veterans affairs database. *Journal of Nervous & Mental Disease, 201,* 12–16.

Milner, P. (2006). Trains of neural thought. *Canadian Psychology, 47*(1), 36–43.

Mineka, S., & Zinbarg, R. (2006). A contemporary learning theory perspective on the etiology of anxiety disorders. *American Psychologist, 61,* 10–26.

Minuchin, S. (1974). *Families & family therapy.* Cambridge, MA: Harvard University Press.

Miron, J. (2006). "Open to the public": Touring Ontario asylums in the nineteenth century. In D. Wright and J. E. Moran (Eds.), *Mental health and Canadian society: Historical perspectives.* Montreal: McGill-Queen's University Press.

Mischel, W. (1979). On the interface of cognition and personality: Beyond the person-situation debate. *American Psychologist, 34,* 740–754.

Mitchell, P. B., & Loo, C. K. (2006). Transcranial magnetic stimulation for depression. *Australian and New Zealand Journal of Psychiatry, 40,* 406–413.

Mitte, K. (2005). Meta-analysis of cognitive-behavioral treatments for generalized anxiety disorder: A comparison with pharmacotherapy. *Psychological Bulletin, 131,* 785–795.

Mockus, D. S., Macera, C. A., Wingard, D. L., Peddecord, M., Thomas, R. G., & Wifley, D. E. (2011). Dietary self-monitoring and its impact on weight loss in overweight children. *International Journal of Pediatric Obesity, 6,* 197–205.

Moffitt, T. E., Caspi, A., & Rutter, M. (2006). Measured gene-environment interactions in psychopathology: Concepts, research strategies, and implications for research, intervention, and public understanding of genetics. *Perspectives on Psychological Science, 1,* 5–27.

Mohee, A., & Eardley, I. (2011). Medical therapy for premature ejaculation. *Therapeutic Advances in Urology, 3,* 211–222.

Monahan, J. (1981). *A clinical prediction of violent behavior.* (DHHS Publication No. ADM. 81-921). Rockville, MD: National Institute of Mental Health.

Money, J., & Lamacz, M. (1990). *Vandalized lovemaps: Paraphilic outcome of seven cases in pediatric sexology.* Buffalo, NY: Prometheus.

Monroe, S. M., & Harkness, K. L. (2011). Recurrence in major depression: A conceptual analysis. *Psychological Review, 118*(4), 655–674.

Montgomery, S. (2006). Serotonin noradrenaline reuptake inhibitors: Logical evolution of antidepressant development. *International Journal of Psychiatry in Clinical Practice, 10*(Suppl. 2), 5–11.

Monti, P. M., Rohsenow, D. J., Rubenois, A. V., Niaura, R. S., Sirota, A. D., Colby, S. M., . . . Abrams, D. B. (1994). Cue exposure with coping skills treatment for male alcoholics: A preliminary investigation. *Journal of Consulting and Clinical Psychology, 61,* 1011–1019.

Montorsi, F., Adaikan, G., Becher, E., Giuliano, F., Khoury, S., Lue, T. F., . . . Wasserman, M. (2010). Summary of the recommendations on sexual dysfunctions in men. *Journal of Sexual Medicine, 7,* 3572–3588.

Moos, R. H., & Moos, B. S. (2004). Long-term influence of duration and frequency of participation in Alcoholics Anonymous on individuals with alcohol use disorders. *Journal of Consulting and Clinical Psychology, 72,* 81–90.

Moore, B. A., Fazzino, T., Garnet, B., Cutter, C. J., & Barry, D. T. (2011). Computer-based treatments for drug abuse and dependence: A systematic review. *Journal of Substance Abuse Treatment, 40,* 215–223.

Mor, N. & Winquist, J. (2002). Self-focused attention and negative affect: A meta-analysis. *Psychological Bulletin, 128*(4), 638–662.

Moretti, M. M., Emmrys, C., Grizenko, N., Holland, R., Moore, K., Shamsie, J., & Hamilton, H. (1997). The treatment of conduct disorder: Perspectives from across Canada. *Canadian Journal of Psychiatry, 42,* 637–648.

Moretz, M. W., & McKay, D. (2009). The role of perfectionism in obsessive-compulsive symptoms: "Not just right" experiences and checking compulsions. *Journal of Anxiety Disorders, 23,* 640–644.

Morey, L. C., Skodol, A. E., & Oldham, J. M. (2014). Clinician judgments of clinical utility: A comparison of DSM-IV-TR personality disorders and the alternative model for DSM-5 personality disorders. *Journal of Abnormal Psychology, 123,* 398–405.

Morin, C. M., LeBlanc, M., Bélanger, L., Ivers, H., Mérette, C., & Savard, J. (2011). Prevalence of insomnia and its treatment in Canada. *Canadian Journal of Psychiatry, 56,* 540–548.

Morin, C. M., LeBlanc, M., Daley, M., Gregoire, J. P., & Mérette, C. (2006). Epidemiology of insomnia: Prevalence, self-help treatments, consultations, and determinants of help-seeking behaviors. *Sleep Medicine, 7*(2), 123–130.

Morin, C. M., & Wooten, V. (1996). Psychological and pharmacological approaches to treating insomnia: Critical issues in assessing their separate and combined effects. *Clinical Psychology Review, 16,* 521–542.

Morris, J. K., Alberman, E., Scott, C., & Jacobs, P. (2008). Is the prevalence of Klinefelter syndrome increasing? *European Journal of Human Genetics, 16,* 163–170.

Morrison, T., Waller, G., & Lawson, R. A. (2006). Attributional style in the eating disorders. *Journal of Nervous and Mental Disease, 194,* 303–305.

Mottron, L., Bouvet, L., Bonnel, A., Samson, F., Burack, J. A., Dawson, M., & Heaton, P. (2013). Veridical mapping in the development of exceptional autistic abilities. *Neuroscience and Biobehavioral Reviews, 37,* 209–228.

Mowrer, O. H. (1948). Learning theory and the neurotic paradox. *American Journal of Orthopsychiatry, 18,* 571–610.

Muckle, W., & Turnbull, J. (2006). Sheltering the homeless. *Canadian Medical Association Journal, 175,* 1177.

Mueller, B., Ahnert, P., Burkhardt, J., Brauer, J., Czepezauer, I., Quente, E., . . . Kirsten, H. (2014). Genetic risk variants for dyslexia on chromosome 18 in a German cohort. *Genes, Brain, and Behavior, 13*(3), 350–356.

Mueser, K. T., & Liberman, R. P. (1995). Behavior therapy in practice. In B. Bongar & L. E. Beutler (Eds.), *Comprehensive textbook of psychotherapy: Theory and practice* (pp. 84–110). New York: Oxford University Press.

Mukherjee, R. A. S., Hollins, S., & Turk, J. (2006). Psychiatric comorbidity in foetal alcohol syndrome. *Psychiatric Bulletin, 30,* 194–195.

Müller, N. (2004). Immunological and infectious aspects of schizophrenia. *European Archives of Psychiatry and Clinical Neuroscience, 254,* 1–3.

Muran, J. C., Eubanks-Carter, C., & Safran, J. D. (2010). A relational approach the treatment of personality dysfunction. In J. J. Magnavita (Ed.), *Evidence-based treatment of personality dysfunction: Principles, methods, and processes* (pp. 167–192). Washington, DC: American Psychological Association.

Muraven, M. (2005). Self-focused attention and the self-regulation of attention: Implications for personality and pathology. *Journal of Social and Clinical Psychology, 24,* 382–400.

Murphy, M. L. M., Slavich, G. M., Rohleder, N., & Miller, G. E. (2013). Targeted rejection triggers differential pro- and anti-inflammatory gene expression in adolescents as a function of social status. *Clinical Psychological Science, 1,* 30–40.

Murphy, R., Straebler, S., Basden, S., Cooper, Z., & Fairburn, C. G. (2012). Interpersonal psychotherapy for eating disorders. *Clinical Psychology and Psychotherapy, 19,* 150–158.

Murphy, W. D., & Page, I. J. (2012). Exhibitionism: Psychopathology and theory. In I. D. R. Laws & W. T. O'Donohue (Eds.), *Sexual deviance: Theory, assessment, and treatment* (pp. 61–75). New York: Guilford Press.

Murray, H. A. (1943). *Thematic Apperception Test manual.* Cambridge, MA: Harvard University Press.

Murstein, B. I., & Mathes, S. (1996). Projection on projective techniques and pathology: The problem that is not being addressed. *Journal of Personality Assessment, 66,* 337–349.

Mussell, B. (2014). Mental health from an Indigenous perspective. In V. Harper, P. Menzies, & L. Lavallée (Eds.), *Journey to healing: Aboriginal people with addiction and mental health issues: What health, social service and justice workers need to know* (pp. 187–200). Toronto: Centre for Addiction & Mental Health.

Mustafa, N., Zaidi, A., & Weaver, R. R. (2017). Conspiracy of silence: Cultural conflict as a risk factor for the development of eating disorders among second-generation Canadian South Asian women. *South Asian Diaspora, 9,* 33–49.

Myers, N. L. (2011). Update: Schizophrenia across cultures. *Current Psychiatry Reports, 13,* 305–311.

Myrick, H., Anton, R. F., Li, X., Henderson, S., Randall, P. K., & Voronin, K. (2008). Effect of naltrexone and ondansetron on alcohol cue–induced activation of the ventral striatum in alcohol-dependent people. *Archives of General Psychiatry, 65,* 466–475.

N

Naj, A. C., Jun, G., Beecham, G. W., Wang, L. S., Vardarajan, B. N., Buros, J., . . . Schellenberg, G. D. (2011). Common variants at MS4A4/MS4A6E, CD2AP, CD33 and EPHA1 are associated with late-onset Alzheimer's disease. *Nature Genetics, 43,* 436–441.

Najavits, L. M. (2002). *Seeking safety: A treatment manual for PTSD and substance abuse.* New York: Guilford.

Nasser, E. H., & Overholser, J. C. (2005). Recovery from major depression: The role of support from family, friends, and spiritual beliefs. *Acta Psychiatrica Scandinavica, 111,* 125–132.

National Council on Ethics in Human Research. (2002). Who we are. Retrieved from http://ncehr-cnerh.org/english/mstr_frm.html

National Institute for Clinical Excellence. (2005). *Post-traumatic stress disorder (PTSD): The management of PTSD in adults and children in primary and secondary care.* London: Royal College of Psychiatrists and British Psychological Society.

National Institute of Nutrition. (2001). Giving adolescents a fighting chance against eating disorders. Retrieved from http://www.nin.ca/public_html/Publications

Nauert, R. (2011, June 11). Numerous genetic factors tied to autism. *PsychCentral.* Retrieved from http://psychcentral.com/news/2011/06/09/numerous-genetic-factors-tied-to-autism/26801.html

Naumann, E., Tuschen-Caffier, B., Voderholzer, U., Schäfer, J., & Svaldi, J. (2016). Effects of emotional acceptance and rumination on media-induced body dissatisfaction in anorexia and bulimia nervosa. *Journal of Psychiatric Research, 82,* 119–125.

Navaneelan, T. (2012). Suicide rates: An overview. *Health at a Glance.* Statistics Canada, Catalogue No. 82-624-X. Retrieved from http://www.statcan.gc.ca/pub/82-624-x/2012001/article/11696-eng.pdf

Needles, D. J., & Abramson, L. Y. (1990). Positive life events, attributional style, and hopefulness: Testing a model of recovery from depression. *Journal of Abnormal Psychology, 99,* 156–165.

Neill, J. (1990). Whatever became of the schizophrenogenic mother? *American Journal of Psychotherapy, 44,* 499–505.

Nelson, N. W., Sweet, J. J., & Heilbronner, R. L. (2007). Examination of the new MMPI-2 response bias scale (Gervais): Relationship with MMPI-2 validity scales. *Journal of Clinical and Experimental Neuropsychology, 29*(1), 67–72.

Nemiah, J. C. (1978). Psychoneurotic disorders. In A. M. Nicholi, Jr. (Ed.), *Harvard guide to modern psychiatry.* Cambridge: Belknap Press.

Nes, R. B., Czajkowski, N. O., Røysamb, E., Ørstavik, R. E., Tambs, K., & Reichborn-Kjennerud, T. (2013). Major depression and life satisfaction: A population-based twin study. *Journal of Affective Disorders, 144*(1–2), 51–58.

Neufeld, R. W. J., Vollick, D., Carter, J. R., Boksman, K., & Jetté, J. (2002). Application of stochastic modeling to the assessment of group and individual differences in cognitive functioning. *Psychological Assessment, 14,* 279–298.

Neugebauer, R. (1979). Medieval and early modern theories of mental illness. *Archives of General Psychiatry, 36,* 477–483.

Neurological basis of depression following sports concussion found. (2008, January 21). *ScienceDaily.* Retrieved from http://www.sciencedaily.com/releases/2008/01/080118115428.htm

Nevid, J. S., Fichner-Rathus, L., & Rathus, S. A. (1995). *Human sexuality in a world of diversity* (2nd ed.). Boston: Allyn & Bacon.

Newman, S. C., Bland, R. C., & Thompson, A. H. (2012). Long-term course and outcome in schizophrenia: A 34-year follow-up study in Alberta, Canada. *Psychological Medicine, 42,* 2137–2143.

New marker for Alzheimer's discovered. (2009, September 14). *ScienceDaily.* Retrieved from http://www.sciencedaily.com/releases/2009/09/090914131906.htm

New research tool can detect autism at 9 months of age. (2008, May 20). *ScienceDaily.* Retrieved from http://www.sciencedaily.com/releases/2008/05/080520112133.htm

Newton-Howes, G., Levack, W. M. M., McBride, S., Gilmor, M., & Tester, R. (2016). Non-physiological mechanisms influencing disulfiram treatment of alcohol use disorder: A grounded theory study. *Drug and Alcohol Dependence, 165,* 126–131.

Nezu, A. M. (1994). Introduction to special section: Mental retardation and mental illness. *Journal of Consulting and Clinical Psychology, 62,* 4–5.

Nezu, A. M., Wilkins, V. M., & Nezu, C. M. (2004). Social problem solving, stress, and negative affect. In E. C. Chang, T. J. D'Zurilla, & L. J. Sanna (Eds.), *Social problem solving: Theory, research, and training* (pp. 49–65). Washington, DC: American Psychological Association.

Nicolosi, A., Laumann, E. O., Glasser, D. B., Brock, G., King, R., & Gingell, C. (2006). Sexual activity, sexual disorders and associated help-seeking behavior among mature adults in five Anglophone countries from the Global Survey of Sexual Attitudes and Behaviors (GSSAB). *Journal of Sex & Marital Therapy, 32,* 331–342.

Nicolson, R. I., & Fawcett, A. J. (2008). *Dyslexia, learning, and the brain.* Cambridge, MA: MIT Press.

Nicolson, R. I., & Fawcett, A. J. (2011). Dyslexia, dysgraphia, procedural learning and the cerebellum. *Cortex, 47*(1), 117–127.

Nicolson, R., & Szatmari, P. (2003). Genetic and neurodevelopmental influences in autistic disorder. *Canadian Journal of Psychiatry, 48,* 526–537.

Nides, M. A., Rakos, R. F., Gonzales, D., Murray, R. P., Tashkin, D. P., Bjornson-Benson, W. M., . . . Connett, J. E. (1995). Predictors of initial smoking cessation and relapse through the first 2 years of the Lung Health Study. *Journal of Consulting and Clinical Psychology, 63,* 60–69.

Niemz, K., Griffiths, M., & Banyard, P. (2005). Prevalence of pathological Internet use among university students and correlations with self-esteem, the General Health Questionnaire (GHQ), and disinhibition. *CyberPsychology & Behavior, 8,* 562–570.

Nierenberg, A. A., Friedman, E. S., Bowden, C. L., Sylvia, L. G., Thase, M. E., Ketter, T., . . . Calabrese, J. R. (2013). Lithium Treatment Moderate-Dose Use Study (LiTMUS) for bipolar disorder: A randomized comparative effectiveness trial of optimized personalized treatment with and without lithium. *American Journal of Psychiatry, 170,* 102–110.

Nigg, J. T., Lohr, N. E., Western, D., Gold, L. J., & Silk, K. R. (1992). Malevolent object representations in borderline personality disorder and major depression. *Journal of Abnormal Psychology, 101,* 61–67.

Nolen-Hoeksema, S., & Corte, C. (2004). Gender and self-regulation. In R. F. Baumeister & K. D. Vohs (Eds.), *Handbook of self-regulation: Research, theory, and applications* (pp. 411–421). New York: Guilford.

Norcross, J. C., & Karpiak, C. P. (2012). Clinical psychologists in the 2010s: 50 years of the APA Division of Clinical Psychology. *Clinical Psychology: Science and Practice, 19,* 1–12.

Norman, R. M. G., Manchanda, R., Malla, A. K., Windell, D., Harricharan, R., & Northcott, S. (2011). Symptom and functional outcomes for a 5 year early intervention program for psychoses. *Schizophrenia Research, 129,* 111–115.

Norton, E. (2012). Rewiring the autistic brain. *Science.* Retrieved from http://news.sciencemag.org/sciencenow/2012/09/rewiring-the-autistic-brain.html?ref=hp

Nowell, P. D., Buysse, D. J., Morin, C., Reynolds, C F., III, & Kupfer, D. J. (1998). Effective treatments for selected sleep disorders. In P. E. Nathan & J. M. Gorman (Eds.), *A guide to treatments that work* (pp. 531–543). New York: Oxford University Press.

Nunes, K. L., Hermann, C. A., Malcom, J. R., & Lavoie, K. (2013). Childhood sexual victimization, pedophilic interest, and sexual recidivism. *Child Abuse & Neglect, 37,* 703–711.

Nunes, J., & Simmie, S. (2002). *Beyond crazy: Journeys through mental illness.* Toronto: McClelland & Stewart.

O

O'Brien, C. P. (1996). Recent developments in the pharmacotherapy of substance abuse. *Journal of Consulting and Clinical Psychology, 64,* 677–686.

O'Brien, C. P., & McKay, J. (1998). Psychopharmacological treatments of substance use disorders. In P. E. Nathan & J. M. Gorman (Eds.), *A guide to treatments that work* (pp. 127–155). New York: Oxford University Press.

O'Brien-Teengs, D., & Monette, L, (2014). Beyond LGBT: Two-spirit people. In V. Harper, P. Menzies, & L. Lavallée (Eds.), *Journey to healing: Aboriginal people with addiction and mental health issues: What health, social service and justice workers need to know* (pp. 161–172). Toronto: Centre for Addiction & Mental Health.

Ochs, R. (1998, March 9). Alcohol: Sorting the contradictions. *Newsday.*

O'Connor, B. P., & Dyce, J. A. (2001). Personality disorders. In M. Hersen & V. B. Van Hasselt (Eds.), *Advanced abnormal psychology* (2nd ed., pp. 399–417). New York: Kluwer Academic/Plenum.

O'Farrell, T. J., Choquette, K. A., Cutter, H. S. G., Floyd, F. J., Bayog, R., Brown, E. D., . . . Deneault, P. (1996). Cost-benefit and cost-effectiveness analyses of behavioral marital therapy as an addition to out-patient alcoholism treatment. *Journal of Substance Abuse, 8,* 145–166.

Oldenbeuving, A. W., de Kort, P. L., Jansen, B. P., Algra, A., Kappelle, L. J., & Roks, G. (2011). Delirium in the acute phase after stroke: Incidence, risk factors, and outcome. *Neurology, 76,* 993–999.

Oldham, J. M. (1994). Personality disorders: Current perspectives. *JAMA: Journal of the American Medical Association, 272,* 1770–1776.

Olff, M., Langeland, W., Draijer, N., & Gersons, B. P. (2007). Gender differences in posttraumatic stress disorder. *Psychological Bulletin, 133,* 183–204.

Oliffe, J. L., Ogrodniczuk, J. S., Gordon, S. J., Creighton, G., Kelly, M. T., Black, N., & Mackenzie, C. (2016). Stigma in male depression and suicide: A Canadian sex comparison study. *Community Mental Health Journal, 52,* 302–310.

Olley, M. C., & Ogloff, J. R. P. (1995). Patients' rights advocacy: Implications for program design and implementation. *Journal of Mental Health Administration, 22,* 368–376.

Olson, K. R., Durwood, L., DeMeules, M., & McLaughlin, K. A. (2016). Mental health of transgender children who are supported in their identities. *Pediatrics, 137*(3), e20153223.

Oltmanns, T. F., & Emery, R. E. (2010). *Abnormal psychology* (6th ed.). Upper Saddle River, NJ: Prentice Hall.

O'Neill, P. (2004). The ethics of problem definition. *Canadian Psychology, 46*(1), 13–20.

Orchowski, L. M., Mastroleo, N. R., & Borsari, B. (2012). Correlates of alcohol-related sex among college students. *Psychology of Addictive Behaviors, 26,* 782–790.

Orešič, M., Hyötyläinen, T., Herukka, S.-K., Sysi-Aho, M., Mattila, I., Seppänen-Laakso, T., . . . Soininen, H. (2011). Metabolome in progression to Alzheimer's disease. *Translational Psychiatry, 1,* e57.

Organisation for Economic Co-operation and Development. (2016). CO4.4: Teenage suicide (15–19 years old). *OECD Family Database.* Retrieved from http://www.oecd.org/els/family/database.htm

Osborne, L. (2001, May 6). Regional disturbances. *New York Times Magazine,* 98–102.

Öst, L.-G. (1987). Age of onset in different phobias. *Journal of Abnormal Psychology, 96*(3), 223–229.

Overmier, J. B. L., & Seligman, M. E. (1967). Effect of inescapable shock upon subsequent escape and avoidance learning. *Journal of Comparative and Physiological Psychology, 63,* 28–33.

P

Pagnin, D., de Queiroz, V., Pini, S., & Cassano, G. B. (2004). Efficacy of ECT in depression: A meta-analytic review. *Journal of ECT, 20,* 13–20.

Paris, J. (2008). *Treatment of borderline personality disorder: A guide to evidence-based practice.* New York: Guilford.

Paris, J. (2015). Clinical implications of biological factors in personality disorders. *Canadian Psychology, 56,* 263–266.

Parnas, D. J., Cannon, T. D., Jacobsen, B., Schulsinger, H., Schulsinger, F., & Mednick, S. A. (1993). Lifetime DSM-III-R diagnostic outcomes in the offspring of schizophrenic mothers: Results from the Copenhagen High-Risk Study. *Archives of General Psychiatry, 50,* 707–714.

Patra, A. P., Bharadwaj, B., Shaha, K. K., Das, S., Payamane, A. P., & Tripathi, S. (2013). Impulsive frotteurism: A case report. *Medicine, Science and the Law, 53,* 235–238.

Patten, S. B., Wang, J. L., Williams, J. V. A., Currie, S., Beck, C. A., Maxwell, C. J., & el-Guebaly, N. (2006). Descriptive epidemiology of major depression in Canada. *Canadian Journal of Psychiatry, 51,* 84–90.

Patten, S. B., Williams, J. V., Lavorato, D. H., Fiest, K. M., Bulloch, A. G. M., & Wang, J. (2015). The prevalence of major depression is not changing. *The Canadian Journal of Psychiatry, 60,* 31-34.

Paul, G. L., & Lentz, R. J. (1977). *Psychosocial treatment of chronic mental patients: Milieu versus social-learning programs.* Cambridge, MA: Harvard University Press.

Paulesu, E., Demonet, J. F., Fazio, F., McCrory, E., Chanoine, V., Brunswick, N., . . . Frith, U. (2001). Dyslexia: Cultural diversity and biological unity. *Science, 291,* 2165–2167.

Paulesu, E., Frith, C. D., & Frackowiak, R. S. J. (1993). The neural correlates of the verbal component of working memory. *Nature, 362,* 342–344.

Pearson, C., Janz, T., & Ali, J. (2013). Mental and substance use disorders in Canada. *Health at a glance.* Statistics Canada. Retrieved from http://www.statcan.gc.ca/pub/82-624-x/2013001/article/11855-eng.pdf

Peat, C. M., Von Holle, A., Watson, H., Huang, L., Thornton, L. M., Zhang, B., . . . Bulik, C. M. (2014). The association between Internet and television access and disordered eating in a Chinese sample. *International Journal of Eating Disorders, 48,* 663–669.

Pendery, M. L., Maltzman, I. M., & West, L. J. (1982). Controlled drinking by alcoholics? New findings and a reevaluation of a major affirmative study. *Science, 217,* 169–174.

Penn, D. L., Combs, D., & Mohamed, S. (2001). Social cognition and social functioning in schizophrenia. In P. W. Corrigan & D. L. Penn (Eds.), *Social cognition and schizophrenia* (pp. 97–121). Washington, DC: American Psychological Association.

Perkins, D. O., Gu, H., Boteva, K., & Lieberman, J. A. (2005). Relationship between duration of untreated psychosis and outcome in first-episode schizophrenia: A critical review and meta-analysis. *American Journal of Psychiatry, 162,* 1785–1804.

Perlis, R. (2007). Review: Adding second generation antipsychotics to mood stabilisers reduces acute mania symptoms. *Evidence-Based Mental Health, 10*(4), 111.

Petersen, T. J. (2006). Enhancing the efficacy of antidepressants with psychotherapy. *Journal of Psychopharmacology, 30*(Suppl. 3), 19–28.

Peterson, A. V., Jr., Leroux, B. G., Bricker, J., Kealey, K. A., Marek, P. M., Sarason, I. G., & Andersen, M. R. (2006). Nine-year prediction of adolescent smoking by number of smoking parents. *Addictive Behaviors, 31,* 788–801.

Peto, R., Lopez, A. D., Boreham, J., & Thun, M. (2006). *Mortality from smoking in developed countries 1950–2000* (2nd ed.). Oxford: Oxford University Press. Retrieved from http://www.ctsu.ox.ac.uk/deathsfromsmoking/publications.html

Pettinati, H. M., O'Brien, C. P., & Dundon, W. D. (2013). Current status of co-occurring mood and substance use disorders: A new therapeutic target. *American Journal of Psychiatry, 170,* 23–30.

Petty, S. C., Sachs-Ericsson, N., & Joiner, T. E., Jr. (2004). Interpersonal functioning deficits: Temporary or stable characteristics of depressed individuals? *Journal of Affective Disorders, 81,* 115–122.

Pfaus, J. G., Kippin, T. E., & Centeno, S. (2001). Conditioning and sexual behavior: A review. *Hormones and Behavior, 40,* 291–321.

Pianta, R. C., & Egeland, B. (1994). Relation between depressive symptoms and stressful life events in a sample of disadvantaged mothers. *Journal of Consulting and Clinical Psychology, 62,* 1229–1234.

Pihl, R. O., & Smith, S. (1983). Of affect and alcohol. In L. A. Pohorecky & J. Brick (Eds.), *Stress and alcohol use: Proceedings of the First International Symposium on Stress and Alcohol Use, held June 9–11, 1982, at Rutgers University, New Brunswick, New Jersey, U.S.A.* (pp. 203–228). New York: Elsevier.

Pike, K. M., & Rodin, J. (1991). Mothers, daughters, and disordered eating. *Journal of Abnormal Psychology, 101,* 198–204.

Pinhas, L., Toner, B. B., Ali, A., Garfinkel, P. E., & Stuckless, N. (1999). The effects of the ideal of female beauty on mood and body satisfaction. *International Journal of Eating Disorders, 25*(2), 223–226.

Piper, A., & Merskey, H. (2004). The persistence of folly: A critical examination of dissociative identity disorder. Part I. The excesses of an improbable concept. *Canadian Journal of Psychiatry, 49,* 592–600.

Pistorello, J., Fruzzetti, A. E., MacLane, C., Gallop, R., & Iverson, K. M. (2012). Dialectical behavior therapy (DBT) applied to college students: A randomized clinical trial.

Journal of Consulting and Clinical Psychology, 80, 982–994.

Plomin, R., Owen, M. J., & McGuffin, P. (1994). The genetic basis of complex human behaviors. Science, 264, 1733–1739.

Pogue-Geile, M. F., & Yokley, J. L. (2010). Current research on the genetic contributors to schizophrenia. Current Directions in Psychological Science, 19, 214–219.

Pottier, C., Hannequin, D., Coutant, S., Rovelet-Lecrux, A., Wallon, D., Rousseau, S., . . . Campion, D. (2012). High frequency of potentially pathogenic SORL1 mutations in autosomal dominant early-onset Alzheimer disease. Molecular Psychiatry, 17, 875–879.

Polaschek, D. L. L., Ward, T., & Hudson, S. M. (1997). Rape and rapists: Theory and treatment. Clinical Psychology Review, 17, 117–144.

Polivy, J., & Herman, C. P. (2002). Causes of eating disorders. Annual Review of Psychology, 53, 187–213.

Pompili, M., Serafini, G., Innamorati, M., Biondi, M., Siracusano, A., Di Giannantonio, M., . . . Möller-Leimkühler, A. M. (2012). Substance abuse and suicide risk among adolescents. European Archives of Psychiatry and Clinical Neuroscience, 262, 469–485.

Poole, R., Higgo, R., & Robinson, C. A. (2014). Mental health and poverty. New York: Cambridge University Press.

Poonwassie, A., & Charter, A. (2001). An Aboriginal worldview of helping: Empowering approaches. Canadian Journal of Counselling, 35(1), 63–73.

Pope, H. G., Jr., & Yurgelun-Todd, D. (1996). The residual cognitive effects of heavy marijuana use in college students. JAMA: Journal of the American Medical Association, 275, 521–527.

Porter, M., & Haslam, N. (2001). Forced displacement in Yugoslavia: A meta-analysis of psychological consequences and their moderators. Journal of Traumatic Stress, 14(4), 817–834.

Porter, S., Birt, A. R., Yuille, J. C., & Lehman, D. R. (2000). Negotiating false memories: Interviewer and rememberer characteristics relate to memory distortion. Psychological Science, 11, 507–510.

Porter, S., Yuille, J. C., & Lehman, D. R. (1999). The nature of real, implanted, and fabricated childhood emotional events: Implications for the recovered memory debate. Law and Human Behavior, 23, 517–537.

Postma, R., Bicanic, I., van der Vaart, H., & Laan, E. (2013). Pelvic floor muscles mediate sexual problems in young adult rape victims. Journal of Sexual Medicine, 10, 1978–1987.

Potenza, M. N., Hong, K. A., Lacadie, C. M., Fulbright, R. K., Tuit, K. L., & Sinha, R. (2012). Neural correlates of stress-induced and cue-induced drug craving: Influences of sex and cocaine dependence. American Journal of Psychiatry, 169, 406-414.

Potter, S. M., Zelazo, P. R., Stack, D. M., & Papageorgiou, A. N. (2000). Adverse effects of fetal cocaine exposure on neonatal auditory information processing. Pediatrics, 105, E40.

Poulin, F., Denault, A.-S., & Pedersen, S. (2011). Longitudinal associations between other-sex friendships and substance use in adolescence. Journal of Research on Adolescence, 21, 776–788.

Power, M. (2000). Freud and the unconscious. The Psychologist, 13, 612–614.

Prince, R. H. (2000). Transcultural psychiatry: Personal experiences and Canadian perspectives. Canadian Journal of Psychiatry, 45(2), 195–196.

Psychological Assessment Resources (PAR) Inc. (2001). Mini-mental state examination (2nd ed.). Lutz, FL: Author.

Public Health Agency of Canada. (2009). The health of Canadian children. Retrieved from http://www.phac-aspc.gc.ca/cphor-sphc-respcacsp/2009/fr-rc/cphorsphc-resp-cacsp06-eng.php

Public Health Agency of Canada. (2012). Evaluation of the Aboriginal Head Start in Urban and Northern Communities Program at the Public Health Agency of Canada. Retrieved from http://www.phac-aspc.gc.ca/about_apropos/evaluation/reports-rapports/2011-2012/ahsunc-papacun/index-eng.php

Public Health Agency of Canada. (2016). The chief public health officer's report on the state of public health in Canada 2015: Alcohol consumption in Canada. Retrieved from healthycanadians.gc.ca/publications/department-ministere/state-public-health-alcohol-2015-etat-sante-publique-alcool/index-eng.php

Pull, C. B. (2005). Current status of virtual reality exposure therapy in anxiety disorders. Current Opinion in Psychiatry, 18, 7–14.

Pull, C. B. (2007). Combined pharmacotherapy and cognitive-behavioural therapy for anxiety disorders. Current Opinion in Psychiatry, 20, 30–35.

Purdon, C., & Clark, D. A. (1993). Obsessive intrusive thoughts in nonclinical subjects. Part I. Content and relation with depressive, anxious and obsessional symptoms. Behaviour Research and Therapy, 31(8), 713–720.

Purdon, C., Rowa, K., & Antony, M. M. (2005). Thought suppression and its effects on thought frequency, appraisal and mood state in individuals with obsessive-compulsive disorder. Behaviour Research and Therapy, 43, 93–108.

Pyszczynski, T., & Greenberg, J. (1992). Hanging on and letting go: Understanding the onset, progression, and remission of depression. New York: Springer.

Q

Quinsey, V. L. (2003). The etiology of anomalous sexual preference in men. Annals of the New York Academy of Sciences, 989, 105–117.

R

R. v. François (1994) 2 S.C.R. 827.

R. v. Swain (1991) 63 C.C.C. (3d) 481 (S.C.C.).

Rabheru, K. (2001). The use of electroconvulsive therapy in special patient populations. Canadian Journal of Psychiatry, 46, 710–719.

Radel, M., Vallejo, R. L., Iwata, N., Aragon, R., Long, J. C., Virkkunen, M., & Goldman, D. (2005). Haplotype-based localization of an alcohol dependence gene to the 5q34{gamma}-aminobutyric acid type A gene cluster. Archives of General Psychiatry, 62, 47–55.

Radomsky, A. S., Gilchrist, P. T., & Dussault, D. (2006). Repeated checking really does cause memory distrust. Behaviour Research and Therapy, 44, 305–316.

Rajkumar, R. P. (2016). Distinctive clinical features of Dhat syndrome with comorbid sexual dysfunction. Asian Journal of Psychiatry, 19, 1–2.

Ramachandran, V. S., & Hubbard, E. M. (2001). Synaesthesia—A window into perception, thought and language. Journal of Consciousness Studies, 8(12), 3–34.

Ramakrishnan, K., & Scheid, D. C. (2007). Treatment options for insomnia. American Family Physician, 76, 517–526.

Ramanan, V. K., Kim, S., Holohan, K., Shen, L., Nho, K., Risacher, S. L., . . . Aisen, P. S. (2012). Genome-wide pathway analysis of memory impairment in the Alzheimer's Disease Neuroimaging Initiative (ADNI) cohort implicates gene candidates, canonical pathways, and networks. Brain Imaging and Behavior, 6, 634–648.

Ramnerö, J., Folke, F., & Kanter, J. W. (2016). A learning theory account of depression. Scandinavian Journal of Psychology, 57, 73–82.

Ranjith, G., & Mohan, R. (2006). Dhat syndrome as a functional somatic syndrome: Developing a sociosomatic model. Psychiatry, 69, 142–150.

Rapin, I. (1997). Autism. New England Journal of Medicine, 337, 97–104.

Rapoport, M. J., Mamdani, M., & Herrmann, N. (2006). Electroconvulsive therapy in older adults: 13-year trends. Canadian Journal of Psychiatry, 51, 616–619.

Rastad, C., Ulfberg, J., & Lindberg, P. (2011). Improvement in fatigue, sleepiness, and health-related quality of life with bright light treatment in persons with seasonal affective disorder and subsyndromal SAD. Depression Research and Treatment, 2011, Article ID 543906.

Rathod, S., & Turkington, D. (2005). Cognitive-behaviour therapy for schizophrenia: A review. Current Opinion in Psychiatry, 18, 159–163.

Rathus, S. A. (2011). Psychology: Concepts and connections, Brief Version (10th ed). Florence, KY: Cengage.

Rathus, S. A., & Nevid, J. S. (1977). BT: Behavior therapy: Strategies for solving problems. Garden City, NY: Doubleday.

Rathus, S. A., Nevid, J. S., Fichner-Rathus, L., & Herold, E. S. (2010). *Human sexuality in a world of diversity* (3rd Canadian ed.). Toronto: Pearson Education Canada.

Ratti, L. A., Humphrey, L. L., & Lyons, J. S. (1996). Structural analysis of families with a polydrug-dependent, bulimic, or normal adolescent daughter. *Journal of Consulting & Clinical Psychology, 64*, 1255–1262.

Ray, R. A. (2012). Clinical neuroscience of addiction: Applications to psychological science and practice. *Clinical Psychology: Science and Practice, 19*, 154–166.

Rector, N. A., & Beck, A. T. (2012). Cognitive behavioral therapy for schizophrenia: An empirical review. *Journal of Nervous and Mental Disease, 200*, 832–839.

Regehr, C., LeBlanc, V. R., Barath, I., Balch, J., & Birze, A. (2013). Predictors of physiological stress and psychological distress in police communicators. *Police Practice and Research, 14* (6), 451–463.

Reger, G., & Gahm, G. A. (2008). Virtual reality exposure therapy for active duty soldiers. *Journal of Clinical Psychology, 64*, 940–946.

Reger, G. M., Holloway, K. M., Candy, C., Rothbaum, B. O., Difede, J., Rizzo, A. A., & Gahm, G. A. (2011). Effectiveness of virtual reality exposure therapy for active duty soldiers in a military mental health clinic. *Journal of Traumatic Stress, 24*, 93–96.

Rehm, J., Ballunas, D., Brochu, S., Fischer, B., Gnam, W., Patra, J., . . . Taylor, B. (2006). *The costs of substance abuse in Canada 2002*. Ottawa: Canadian Centre on Substance Abuse.

Reichborn-Kjennerud, T. (2010). The genetic epidemiology of personality disorders. *Dialogues in Clinical Neuroscience, 12*, 104–114.

Reichborn-Kjennerud, T., Ystrom, E., Neale, M. C., Aggen, S. H., Mazzeo, S. E., Knudsen, G. P., . . . Kendler, K. S. (2013). Structure of genetic and environmental risks factors for symptoms of DSM-IV borderline personality disorder. *JAMA Psychiatry, 70*, 1206–1214.

Reisner, A. D. (2003). The electroconvulsive therapy controversy: Evidence and ethics. *Neuropsychology Review, 13*, 199–219.

Reitan, R. M., & Wolfson, D. (2012). Detection of malingering and invalid test results using the Halstead-Reitan Battery. In C. R. Reynolds & A. M. Horton (Eds.), *Detection of malingering during head injury litigation* (pp. 241–272). New York: Springer.

Renaud, J., Chagnon, F., Turecki, G., & Marquette, C. (2005). Completed suicides in a youth centres population. *Canadian Journal of Psychiatry, 50*, 690–694.

Renneberg, B., Goldstein, A. J., Phillips, D., & Chambless, D. J. (1990). Intensive behavioral group treatment of avoidant personality disorder. *Behavior Therapy, 21*, 363–377.

Reuter, M., Stark, R., Hennig, J., Walter, B., Kirsch, P., Schienle, A., & Vaitl, D. (2004). Personality and emotion: Test of Gray's personality theory by means of an fMRI study. *Behavioral Neuroscience, 118*, 462–469.

Rey, J. M. (1993). Oppositional defiant disorder. *American Journal of Psychiatry, 150*, 1769–1778.

Ricciardelli, L. A., & McCabe, M. P. (2004). A biopsychosocial model of disordered eating and the pursuit of muscularity in adolescent boys. *Psychological Bulletin, 130*(2), 179–205.

Ricciardelli, L. A., McCabe, M. P., Williams, R. J., & Thompson, J. K. (2007). The role of ethnicity and culture in body image and disordered eating among males. *Clinical Psychology Review, 27*, 582–606.

Rice, J. L., & Tan, T. X. (2017). Youth psychiatrically hospitalized for suicidality: Changes in familial structure, exposure to familial trauma, family conflict, and parental instability as precipitating factors. *Children and Youth Services Review, 73*, 79–87.

Ridenour, T. A. (2005). Inhalants: Not to be taken lightly anymore. *Current Opinion in Psychiatry, 18*, 243–247.

Rieber, R. W., Takooshian, H., & Iglesias, H. (2002). The case of Sybil in the teaching of psychology. *Journal of Social Distress and the Homeless, 11*, 355–360.

Rief, W., & Barsky, A. J. (2005). Psychobiological perspectives on somatoform disorders. *Psychoneuroendocrinology, 30*, 996–1002.

Rief, W., & Sharpe, M. (2004). Somatoform disorders—New approaches to classification, conceptualization, and treatment. *Journal of Psychosomatic Research, 56*, 387–390.

Rimland, B. (1978). The savant capabilities of autistic children and their cognitive implications. In G. Serban (Ed.), *Cognitive defects in the development of mental illness*. New York: Brunner/Mazel.

Ritterband, L. M., Thorndike, F. P., Gonder-Frederick, L. A., Magee, J. C., Bailey, E. T., Saylor, D. K., & Morin, C. M. (2009). Efficacy of an Internet-based behavioral intervention for adults with insomnia. *Archives of General Psychiatry, 66*, 692–698.

Rivas-Vazquez, R. A., & Blais, M. A. (2002). Pharmacologic treatment of personality disorder. *Professional Psychology: Research and Practice, 33*(1), 104–107.

Robinson, J. A., Sareen, J., Cox, B. J., & Bolton, J. M. (2009). Correlates of self-medication for anxiety disorders: Results from the National Epidemiologic Survey on Alcohol and Related Conditions. *Journal of Nervous and Mental Disease, 297*, 873–878.

Rock, C. L., & Curran-Celentano, J. (1996). Nutritional management of eating disorders. *Psychiatric Clinics of North America, 19*, 701–713.

Rodin, G., Olmsted, M. P., Rydall, A. C., Maharaj, S. I., Colton, P. A., Jones, J. M., . . . Daneman, D. (2002). Eating disorders in young women with type 1 diabetes mellitus. *Journal of Psychosomatic Research, 53*, 943–949.

Roelofs, J., Muris, P., Braet, C., Arntz, A., & Beelen, I. (2015). The Structured Clinical Interview for DSM-IV childhood diagnoses (Kid-SCID): First psychometric evaluation in a Dutch sample of clinically referred youths. *Child Psychiatry and Human Development, 46*, 367–375.

Rogers, C. (1951). *Client-centered therapy: Its current practice, implications and theory*. London: Constable.

Rogers, J. (2009, August 5). Alzheimer disease and inflammation: More epidemiology, more questions. *Journal Watch Neurology*. Retrieved from http://neurology.jwatch.org/cgi/content/full/2009/804/3?q=etoc_jwneuro

Romano, E., Baillargeon, R. H., Fortier, I., Hong-Wu, X., Robaey, P., Zoccolillo, M., & Tremblay, R. E. (2005). Individual change in methylphenidate use in a national sample of children aged 2 to 11 years. *Canadian Journal of Psychiatry, 50*, 144–152.

Romano, E., Baillargeon, R. H., & Tremblay, R. E. (2002). *Prevalence of hyperactivity-impulsivity and inattention among Canadian children: Findings from the first data collection cycle (1994–1995) of the National Longitudinal Survey of Children and Youth* (Catalogue No. RH63-1/561-01-03E). Ottawa: Human Resources Development Canada.

Ronald, J., Delaive, K., Roos, L., Manfreda, J., Bahammam, A., & Kryger, M. H. (1999). Health care utilization in the 10 years prior to diagnosis in obstructive sleep apnea syndrome patients. *Sleep, 22*(2), 225–229.

Rosa, M. A., Gattaz, W. F., Pascual-Leone, A., Fregni, F., Rosa, M. O., Rumi, D. O., . . . Marcolin, M. A. (2006). Comparison of repetitive transcranial magnetic stimulation and electroconvulsive therapy in unipolar non-psychotic refractory depression: A randomized, single-blind study. *International Journal of Neuropsychopharmacology, 9*, 667–676.

Rosenberg, H. (1993). Prediction of controlled drinking by alcoholics and problem drinkers. *Psychological Bulletin, 113*, 129–130.

Rosenfarb, I. S., Bellack, A. S., & Aziz, N. (2006). Family interactions and the course of schizophrenia in African American and White patients. *Journal of Abnormal Psychology, 115*, 112–120.

Rosenthal, D., Wender, P. H., Kety, S. S., Schulsinger, F., Welner, J., & Ostergaard, L. (1968). Schizophrenics' offspring reared in adoptive homes. In D. Rosenthal & S. S. Kety (Eds.), *The transmission of schizophrenia: Proceedings of the second research conference of the Foundations' Fund for Research in Psychiatry, Dorado, Puerto Rico, 26 June to 1 July 1967*. Oxford: Pergamon.

Rosenthal, D., Wender, P. H., Kety, S. S., Schulsinger, F., Welner, J., & Rieder, R. O. (1975). Parent–child relationships and psychopathological disorder in the child. *Archives of General Psychiatry, 32*, 466–476.

Ross, C. A. (2001). *Dissociative identity disorder: Diagnosis, clinical features, and treatment of multiple personality* (2nd ed.). New York: Wiley.

Ross, C. A., & Ness, L. (2010). Symptom patterns in dissociative identity disorder patients and the general population. *Journal of Trauma & Dissociation, 11,* 458–468.

Rotermann, M., & Langlois, K. (2015). Prevalence and correlates of marijuana use in Canada, 2012. *Health Reports, 25,* 10–15. Statistics Canada, catalogue no. 82-003-X.

Rotter, J. B. (1972). Beliefs, social attitudes, and behavior: A social learning analysis. In J. B. Rotter, J. E. Chance, & E. J. Phares (Eds.), *Applications of a social learning theory of personality.* New York: Holt, Rinehart and Winston.

Rowa, K., & Antony, M. M. (2005). Psychological treatments for social phobia. *Canadian Journal of Psychiatry, 50,* 308–316.

Rowland, D., McMahon, C. G., Abdo, C., Chen, J., Jannini, E., Waldinger, M. D., & Ahn, T. Y. (2010). Disorders of orgasm and ejaculation in men. *Journal of Sexual Medicine, 7,* 1668–1686.

Rowland, D. L., Cooper, S. E., & Slob, A. K. (1996). Genital and psychoaffective response to erotic stimulation in sexually functional and dysfunctional men. *Journal of Abnormal Psychology, 105,* 194–203.

Rudnick, A., Montgomery, P., Coatsworth-Puspoky, R., Cohen, B., Forchuk, C., Lahey, P., Perry, S., & Schofield, R. (2014). Perspectives of social justice among people living with mental illness and poverty: A qualitative study. *Journal of Poverty and Social Justice, 22,* 147–157.

Rueger, S. Y., & George, R. (2017). Indirect effects of attributional style for positive events on depressive symptoms through self-esteem during early adolescence. *Journal of Youth and Adolescence, 46,* 701–708.

Russell, J. M., Newman, S. C., & Bland, R. C. (1994). Drug abuse and dependence. *Acta Psychiatrica Scandinavica, 89*(Suppl. 376), 54–62.

Russo, N., Foxe, J. J., Brandwein, A. B., Altschuler, T., Gomes, H., & Molholm, S. (2010). Multisensory processing in children with autism: High-density electrical mapping of auditory-somatosensory integration. *Autism Research, 3,* 253–267.

Rutter, M. (2006). *Genes and behavior: Nature–nurture interplay examined.* Malden, MA: Blackwell.

Ryder, A. G., Yang, J., Zhu, X., Yao, S., Yi, J., Heine, S. J., et al. (2008). The cultural shaping of depression: Somatic symptoms in China, psychological symptoms in North America? *Journal of Abnormal Psychology, 117,* 300–313.

S

Sabri, O., Sabbagh, M. N., Seibyl, J., Barthel, H., Akatsu, H., Ouchi, Y., . . . Florbetaben Phase 3 Study Group. (2015). Florbetaben PET imaging to detect amyloid beta plaques in Alzheimer's disease: Phase 3 study. *Alzheimer's & Dementia, 11,* 964–974.

Saha, S., Welham, J., Chant, D., & McGrath, J. (2006). Incidence of schizophrenia does not vary with economic status of the country. *Social Psychiatry and Psychiatric Epidemiology, 41,* 338–340.

Salovey, P. (2008). Foreword. In R. J. Emmerling, V. K. Shanwal, & M. K. Mandal (Eds.), *Emotional intelligence: Theoretical and cultural perspectives* (pp. vii–viii). New York: Nova Science Publishers.

Samuel, D. B., & Widiger, T. A. (2009). Comparative gender bias in models of personality disorder. *Personality and Mental Health, 3,* 12–25.

Samuels, J. (2011). Personality disorders: Epidemiology and public health issues. *International Journal of Psychiatry, 23,* 223–233.

Sanchez-Craig, M., Annis, H. M., Bornet, A. R., & MacDonald, K. R. (1984). Random assignment to abstinence or controlled drinking: Evaluation of a cognitive-behavioral program for problem drinkers. *Journal of Consulting and Clinical Psychology, 52,* 390–403.

Sanchez-Craig, M., & Wilkinson, D. A. (1986/1987). Treating problem drinkers who are not severely dependent on alcohol. In M. B. Sobell & L. C. Sobell (Eds.), *Moderation as a goal or outcome of treatment for alcohol problems: A dialogue* (pp. 39–67). New York: Haworth.

Sanders, S. J., Ercan-Sencicek, A. G., Hus, V., Luo, R., Murtha, M. T., Moreno-De-Luca, D., . . . State, M. W. (2011). Multiple recurrent de novo CNVs, including duplications of the 7q11.23 Williams syndrome region, are strongly associated with autism. *Neuron, 70,* 863–885.

Santini, E., Huynh, T. N., MacAskill, A. F., Carter, A. G., Pierre, P., Ruggero, D., . . . Klann, E. (2013). Exaggerated translation causes synaptic and behavioural aberrations associated with autism. *Nature, 493,* 411–415.

Sarró, S., Pomarol-Clotet, E., Canales-Rodriguez, E. J., Salvador, R., Gomar, J. J., Ortiz-Gil, J., . . . McKenna, P. J. (2013). Structural brain changes associated with tardive dyskinesia in schizophrenia. *British Journal of Psychiatry, 203,* 51–57.

Sartorius, N., & Schulze, H. (2005). *Reducing the stigma of mental illness: A report from a global programme of the World Psychiatric Association.* New York: Cambridge University Press.

Satir, V. (1967). *Conjoint family therapy: A guide to theory and technique* (rev. ed.). Palo Alt, CA: Science and Behavior Books.

Sawyer, T. M., & Stevenson, J. F. (2008). Perceived parental and peer disapproval toward substances: Influences on adolescent decision-making. *Journal of Primary Prevention, 29,* 465–477.

Scahill, L., McDougle, C. J., Aman, M. G., Johnson, C., Handen, B., Bearss, K., . . . Vitiello, B. (2012). Effects of risperidone and parent training on adaptive functioning in children with pervasive developmental disorders and serious behavioral problems. *Journal of the American Academy of Child & Adolescent Psychiatry, 51,* 136–146.

Schachar, R., Jadad, A. R., Gauld, M., Boyle, M., Booker, L., Snider, A., . . . Cunningham, C. (2002). Attention-deficit hyperactivity disorder: Critical appraisal of extended treatment studies. *Canadian Journal of Psychiatry, 47,* 337–348.

Schachter, H. M., Pham, B., King, J., Langford, S., & Moher, D. (2001). How efficacious and safe is short-acting methylphenidate for the treatment of attention-deficit disorder in children and adolescents? A meta-analysis. *Canadian Medical Association Journal, 165,* 1475–1488.

Schaefer, A., Braver, T. S., Reynolds, J. R., Burgess, G. C., Yarkoni, T., & Gray, J. R. (2006). Individual differences in amygdala activity predict response speed during working memory. *Journal of Neuroscience, 26,* 10120–10128.

Schaffer, A., Cairney, J., Cheung, A., Veldhuizen, S., & Levitt, A. (2006). Community survey of bipolar disorder in Canada: Lifetime prevalence and illness characteristics. *Canadian Journal of Psychiatry, 51,* 9–16.

Scheier, L. M., Botvin, G. J., & Baker, E. (1997). Risk and protective factors as predictors of adolescent alcohol involvement and transitions in alcohol use: A prospective analysis. *Journal of Studies on Alcohol, 58,* 652–667.

Schepis, M. M., Reid, D. H., & Fitzgerald, J. R. (1987). Group instruction with profoundly retarded persons: Acquisition, generalization, and maintenance of a remunerative work skill. *Journal of Applied Behavior Analysis, 20,* 97–105.

Schiff, R., & Joshi, R. M. (2016). *Interventions in learning disabilities: A Handbook on systematic training programs for individuals with learning disabilities.* New York: Springer.

Schliebs, R., & Arendt, T. (2006). The significance of the cholinergic system in the brain during aging and in Alzheimer's disease. *Journal of Neural Transmission, 113,* 1625–1644.

Schmidt, N. B., & Keough, M. E. (2010). Treatment of panic. *Annual Review of Clinical Psychology, 6,* 241–256.

Schmidt, N. B., Zvolensky, M. J., & Maner, J. K. (2006). Anxiety sensitivity: Prospective prediction of panic attacks and Axis I pathology. *Journal of Psychiatric Research, 40,* 691–699.

Schmits, E., Mathys, C., & Quertemont, E. (2016). Is social anxiety associated with cannabis use? The role of cannabis use effect expectancies in middle adolescence. *Journal of Child & Adolescent Substance Abuse, 25*(4), 348–359.

Schneider, K. (1957). Primäre und sekundäre Symptome bei der Schizophrenia. *Fortschritte der Neurologie Psychiatrie, 25,* 487–490.

Schneider, R. D., Glancy, G. D., Bradford, J. M., & Seibenmorgen, E. (2000). Canadian landmark case, *Winko v. British Columbia:* Revisiting the conundrum of the mentally disordered accused. *Journal of the American Academy of Psychiatry and Law, 28,* 206–212.

Schoeneman, T. J. (1984). The mentally ill witch in textbooks of abnormal psychology: Current status and implications of a fallacy. *Professional Psychiatry, 15,* 299–314.

Schreiner-Engel, P., Schiavi, R. C., White, D., & Ghizzani, A. (1989). Low sexual desire in women: The role of reproductive hormones. *Hormones and Behavior, 23,* 221–234.

Schruers, K., Koning, K., Luermans, J., Haack, M. J., & Griez, E. (2005). Obsessive-compulsive disorder: A critical review of therapeutic perspectives. *Acta Psychiatrica Scandinavica, 111,* 261–271.

Schuckit, M. A., Daeppen, J.-B., Danko, G. P., Tripp, M. L., Smith, T. L., Li, T.-K., . . . Bucholz, K. K. (1999). Clinical implications for four drugs of the DSM-IV distinction between substance dependence with and without a physiological component. *American Journal of Psychiatry, 156,* 41–49.

Schuller, R. A., & Ogloff, J. R. P. (2000). *Introduction to psychology and law: Canadian perspectives.* Toronto: University of Toronto Press.

Schulze, B., & Angermeyer, M. C. (2003). Subjective experiences of stigma. A focus group study of schizophrenic patients, their relatives and mental health professionals. *Social Science and Medicine, 56,* 299–312.

Schulze-Rauschenbach, S. C., Harms, U., Schlaepfer, T. E., Maier, W., Falkai, P., & Wagner M. (2005). Distinctive neuro-cognitive effects of repetitive transcranial magnetic stimulation and electroconvulsive therapy in major depression. *British Journal of Psychiatry, 186,* 410–416.

Schumacher, A., & Petronis, A. (2006). Epigenetics of complex diseases: From general theory to laboratory experiments. *Current Topics in Microbiology and Immunology, 310,* 81–115

Schwartz, D. R., & Carney, C. E. (2012). Mediators of cognitive-behavioral therapy for insomnia: A review of randomized controlled trials and secondary analysis studies. *Clinical Psychology Review, 32,* 664–675.

Schwartz-Mette, R. A., & Rose, A. J. (2016). Depressive symptoms and conversational self-focus in adolescents' friendships. *Journal of Abnormal Child Psychology, 44,* 87–100.

Schwitzer, G. (2012, December 3). Critic calls American Psychiatric Association approval of DSM-V "a sad day for psychiatry." *Health News Review.* Retrieved from https://www.healthnewsreview.org/2012/12/critic-calls-american-psychiatric-assoc-approval-of-dsm-v-a-sad-day-for-psychiatry/

Scott, K. (1994). Substance use among indigenous Canadians. In D. McKenzie (Ed.), *Aboriginal substance use: Research issues.* Ottawa: Canadian Centre on Substance Abuse.

Scotto Rosato, N., Correll, C. U., Pappadopulos, E., Chait, A., Crystal, S., & Jensen, P. S. (2012). Treatment of maladaptive aggression in youth: CERT guidelines II. Treatments and ongoing management. *Pediatrics, 129,* e1577–e1586.

Sealy, P., & Whitehead, P. C. (2004). Forty years of deinstitutionalization of psychiatric services in Canada: An empirical assessment. *Canadian Journal of Psychiatry, 49,* 249–257.

Seeman, P., & Kapur, S. (2001). The dopamine receptor basis of psychosis. In A. Breier, P. V. Tran, J. M. Herrea, G. D. Tollefson, & F. P. Bymaster (Eds.), *Current issues in the psychopharmacology of schizophrenia* (pp. 73–84). Philadelphia: Lippincott Williams & Wilkins.

Segal, Z. V., Williams, M. G., & Teasdale, J. D. (2002). *Mindfulness-based cognitive therapy for depression: A new approach to preventing relapse.* New York: Guilford.

Segarra, P., Ross, S. R., Pastor, M. C., Montañés, S., Poy, R., & Moltó, J. (2007). MMPI-2 predictors of Gray's two-factor reinforcement sensitivity theory. *Personality and Individual Differences, 43,* 437–448.

Seidman, L. J., Valera, E. M., & Makris, N. (2005). Structural brain imaging of attention-deficit/hyperactivity disorder. *Biological Psychiatry, 57,* 1263–1272.

Seligman, M. E. P. (1975). *Helplessness: On depression, development, and death.* San Francisco: Freeman.

Seligman, M. E. P. (1991). *Learned optimism.* New York: Knopf.

Selten, J.-P., Cantor-Graae, E., & Kahn, R. S. (2007). Migration and schizophrenia. *Current Opinion in Psychiatry, 20,* 111–115.

Sorene, J. A., Ashtari, M., Szeszko, P. R., & Kumra, S. (2007). Neuroimaging studies of children with serious emotional disturbances: A selective review. *Canadian Journal of Psychiatry, 52,* 135–145.

Serin, R., Forth, A., Brown, A., Nunes, K., Bennell, C., & Pozzulo, J. (2011). *Psychology of criminal behaviour: A Canadian perspective.* Toronto: Pearson Education Canada.

Seroczynski, A. D., Cole, D. A., & Maxwell, S. E. (1997). Cumulative and compensatory effects of competence and incompetence on depressive symptoms in children. *Journal of Abnormal Psychology, 106,* 586–597.

Seto, M. C. (2004). Pedophilia and sexual offenses against children. *Annual Review of Sex Research, 15,* 321–361.

Seto, M. C. (2008). *Pedophilia and sexual offending against children: Theory, assessment, and intervention.* Washington, DC: American Psychological Assocation.

Seto, M. C. (2009). Pedophilia. *Annual Review of Clinical Psychology, 5,* 391–407.

Seto, M. C., Lalumière, M. L., Harris, G. T., & Chivers, M. (2012). The sexual responses of sexual sadists. *Journal of Abnormal Psychology, 121,* 739–753.

Seto, M. C., Maric, A., & Barbaree, H. E. (2001). The role of pornography in the etiology of sexual aggression. *Aggression and Violent Behavior, 6,* 35–53.

Seyffert, M., Lagisetty, P., Landgraf, J., Chopra, V., Pfeiffer, P. N., Conte, M. L., & Rogers, M. A. M. (2016). Internet-delivered cognitive behavioral therapy to treat insomnia: A systematic review and metal-analysis. *PLoS ONE, 11*(2), e0149139.

Shams, G., & Milosevic, I. (2015). A comparative study of obsessive beliefs in obsessive-compulsive disorder, anxiety disorder patients and a normal group. *Acta Medica Iranica, 53*(5), 301–310.

Shapiro, C. M., Trajanovic, N. N., & Fedoroff, J. P. (2003). Sexsomnia—A new parasomnia? *Canadian Journal of Psychiatry, 48*(5), 311–317.

Sharan, P., Kulhara, P., Verma, S. K., & Mohanty, M. (2002). Reliability of the ICD-10 International Personality Disorder Examinataion (IPDE) (Hindi version): A preliminary study. *Indian Journal of Psychiatry, 44,* 362–364.

Shaywitz, S. E. (1998). Dyslexia. *New England Journal of Medicine, 338,* 307–312.

Shean, G. D. (2007). Recent developments in psychosocial treatments for schizophrenic patients. *Expert Review of Neurotherapeutics, 7,* 817–827.

Shedler, J., Beck, A., Fonagy, P., Gabbard, G. O., Gunderson, J. G., Kernberg, O., . . . Westen, D. (2010). Personality disorders in DSM-5. *American Journal of Psychiatry, 167,* 1026–1028.

Sheitman, B. B., Kinon, B. J., Ridgway, B. A., & Lieberman, J. A. (1998). Pharmacological treatments of schizophrenia. In P. E. Nathan & J. M. Gorman (Eds.), *A guide to treatments that work* (pp. 167–189). New York: Oxford University Press.

Sher, K. J., Grekin, E. R., & Williams, N. A. (2005). The development of alcohol use disorders. *Annual Review of Clinical Psychology, 1,* 493–523.

Sher, L., Siever, L. J., Goodman, M., McNamara, M., Hazlett, E. A., Koenigsberg, H. W., & New, A. S. (2015). Gender differences in the clinical characteristics and psychiatric comorbidity in patients with antisocial personality disorder. *Psychiatry Research, 229,* 685–689.

Shields, M. (2004a). Social anxiety disorder—beyond shyness. *Health Reports, 15*(Suppl.), 47–81.

Shields, M. (2004b). Stress, health and the benefit of social support. *Health Reports, 15*(1), 9–38.

Shiffman, S., Hickcox, M., Paty, J. A., Gnys, M., Kasiel, J. D., & Richards, T. J. (1996). Progression from a smoking lapse to relapse: Prediction from abstinence violation effects, nicotine dependence, and lapse characteristics. *Journal of Consulting and Clinical Psychology, 64,* 993–1002.

Shin, D. H., & Spitz, A. (2014). The evaluation and treatment of delayed ejaculation. *Sexual Medicine Review, 2,* 121–133.

Shneidman, E. S. (1994). Clues to suicide, reconsidered. *Suicide and Life-Threatening Behavior, 24,* 395–397.

Shneidman, E. S., Farberow, N. L., & Litman, R. E. (1994). *The psychology of suicide: A clinician's guide to evaluation and treatment.* Northvale, NJ: Aronson.

Shrivastava, A., Johnston, M., Terpstra, K., & Bureau, Y. (2015). Pathways to psychosis in cannabis abuse. *Clinical Schizophrenia & Related Psychosis, 9,* 30–35.

Sidani, J. E., Shensa, A., Hoffman, B., Hanmer, J., & Primack, B. A. (2016). The association between social media use and eating concerns among US young adults. *Journal of the Academy of Nutrition and Dietetics, 116,* 1465–1472.

Siddique, J., Chung, J. Y., Brown, C. H., & Miranda, J. (2012). Comparative effectiveness of medication versus cognitive-behavioral therapy in a randomized controlled trial of low-income young minority women with depression. *Journal of Consulting and Clinical Psychology, 80,* 995–1006.

Siegel, J. M. (2004). Hypocretin (orexin): Role in normal behavior and neuropathology. *Annual Review of Psychology, 55,* 125–148.

Siegel, S. (2005). Drug tolerance, drug addiction, and drug anticipation. *Current Directions in Psychological Science, 14,* 296–300.

Siever, L. J., & Davis, K. L. (2004). The pathophysiology of schizophrenia disorders: Perspectives from the spectrum. *American Journal of Psychiatry, 161,* 398–413.

Simeon, D., & Abugel, J. (2006). *Feeling unreal: Depersonalization disorder and the loss of the self.* New York: Oxford University Press.

Simmie, S. (1998, October 4). I'd sit in the kitchen and just shake. *Toronto Star.*

Simon, G. E. (2006). The antidepressant quandary—considering suicide risk when treating adolescent depression. *New England Journal of Medicine, 355,* 2722–2723.

Simpkins, J. W., & Van Meter, R. (2005). Potential testosterone therapy for hypogonadal sexual dysfunction in women. *Journal of Women's Health, 14,* 449–451.

Simpson, D. D., Joe, G. W., Fletcher, B. W., Hubbard, R. L., & Anglin, M. D. (1999). A national evaluation of treatment outcomes for cocaine dependence. *Archives of General Psychiatry, 57,* 507–514.

Singh, N. N., McKay, J. D., & Singh, A. N. (1998). Culture and mental health: Nonverbal communication. *Journal of Child and Family Studies, 7,* 403–409.

Sinnamon, G. (2017). Psychopathology as a mediator of antisocial and criminal behavior. In W. Petherick & G. Sinnamon (Eds.), *The psychology of criminal and antisocial behavior: Victim and offender perspectives.* London: Academic Press.

Sitharthan, T., Sitharthan, G., Hough, M. J., & Kavanagh, D. J. (1997). Cue exposure in moderation drinking: A comparison with cognitive-behavior therapy. *Journal of Consulting and Clinical Psychology, 65,* 878–882.

Skinner, B. F. (1938). *The behavior of organisms: An experimental analysis.* New York: Appleton-Century.

Skodol, A. E. (2012). Personality disorders in DSM-5. *Annual Review of Clinical Psychology, 8,* 317–344.

Skodol, A. E., Gunderson, J. G., Pfohl, B., Widiger, T. A., Livesley, W. J., & Siever, L. J. (2002). The borderline diagnosis I: Psychopathology, comorbidity, and personality structure. *Biological Psychiatry, 51,* 936–950.

Skodol, A. E., Siever, L. J., Livesley, W. J., Gunderson, J. G., Pfohl, B., & Widiger, T. A. (2002). The borderline diagnosis II: Biology, genetics, and clinical course. *Biological Psychiatry, 51,* 951–963.

Slovenko, R. (2006). Patients who deceive. *International Journal of Offender Therapy and Comparative Criminology, 50,* 241–244.

Smith, D. (1982). Trends in counseling and psychotherapy. *American Psychologist, 37,* 802–809.

Smith, D. B., & Morrissette, P. J. (2001). The experiences of white male counsellors who work with First Nations clients. *Canadian Journal of Counselling, 35*(1), 74–88.

Smith, G. N., Boydell, J., Murray, R. M., Flynn, S., McKay, K., Sherwood, M., & Honer, W. G. (2006). The incidence of schizophrenia in European immigrants to Canada. *Schizophrenia Research, 87,* 205–211.

Smith, G. N., Ehmann, T. S., Flynn, S. W., MacEwan, G. W., Tee, K., Kopala, L. C., . . . Honer, W. G. (2011). The assessment of symptom severity and functional impairment with DSM-IV Axis V. *Psychiatric Services, 62,* 411–417.

Smith, G. N., Flynn, S. W., McCarthy, N., Meistrich, B., Ehmann, T. S., MacEwan, G. W., . . . Honer, W. G. (1999). Low birthweight in schizophrenia: Prematurity or poor fetal growth? *Schizophrenia Research, 47,* 177–184.

Smith, G. T., Goldman, M. S., Greenbaum, P. E., & Christiansen, B. A. (1995). Expectancy for social facilitation from drinking: The divergent paths of high-expectancy and low-expectancy adolescents. *Journal of Abnormal Psychology, 104,* 32–40.

Smith, M. L., & Glass, G. V. (1977). Meta-analysis of psychotherapy outcome studies. *American Psychologist, 32,* 752–760.

Smith, M. L., Glass, G. V., & Miller, T. I. (1980). *The benefits of psychotherapy.* Baltimore, MD: Johns Hopkins University Press.

Smith, M. L., Klim, P., & Hanley, W. B. (2000). Executive function in school-aged children with phenylketonuria. *Journal of Developmental and Physical Disabilities, 12,* 317–332.

Smith, R., Ronald, J., Delaive, K., Walld, R., Manfreda, J., & Kryger, M. H. (2002). What are obstructive sleep apnea patients being treated for prior to this diagnosis? *Chest, 121*(1), 164–172.

Smith, S. B. (1983). *The great mental calculators: The psychology, methods, and lives of calculating prodigies, past and present.* New York: Columbia University Press.

Smith, Y. L. S., Van Goozen, S. H. M., Kuiper, A. J., & Cohen-Kettenis, P. T. (2005). Sex reassignment: Outcomes and predictors of treatment for adolescent and adult transsexuals. *Psychological Medicine, 35,* 89–99.

Smits, D. J. M., & Boeck, P. D. (2006). From BIS/BAS to the Big Five. *European Journal of Personality, 20,* 255–270.

Smoking will be world's biggest killer. (1996, September 17). *Newsday,* p. A21.

Snell, M. E. (1997). Teaching children and young adults with mental retardation in school programs: Current research. *Behaviour Change, 14,* 73–105.

Sobell, L. C., Toneatto, A., & Sobell, M. B. (1990). Behavior therapy. In A. S. Bellack & M. Hersen (Eds.), *Handbook of comparative treatments for adult disorders* (pp. 479–505). New York: Wiley.

Sobell, M. B., & Sobell, L. C. (1973). Alcoholics treated by individualized behavior therapy: One year treatment outcome. *Behaviour Research and Therapy, 11,* 599–618.

Sobell, M. B., & Sobell, L. C. (1976). Second year treatment outcome of alcoholics treated by individualized behavior therapy: Results. *Behaviour Research and Therapy, 14,* 195–215.

Sobell, M. B., & Sobell, L. C. (1984). The aftermath of heresy: A response to Pendery et al.'s critique of "Individualized behavior therapy for alcoholics." *Behaviour Research and Therapy, 22,* 413–440.

Sobell, M. B., & Sobell, L. C. (2011). It is time for low-risk drinking goals to come out of the closet. *Addiction, 106,* 1715–1717.

Söchting, I. (2004). Painful pasts: Post-traumatic stress in women survivors of Canada's Indian residential schools. *Visions: BC's Mental Health and Addictions Journal, 2*(4), 13–14.

Söderpalm Gordh, A. H. V., & Söderpalm, B. (2011). Healthy subjects with a family history of alcoholism show increased stimulative subjective effects of alcohol. *Alcoholism: Clinical and Experimental Research, 35,* 1426–1434.

Sohn, C.-H., & Lam, R. W. (2005). Update on the biology of seasonal affective disorder. *CNS Spectrums, 10,* 635–646.

Somers, J. M., Goldner, E. M., Waraich, P., & Hsu, L. (2006). Prevalence and incidence studies of anxiety disorders: A systematic review of the literature. *Canadian Journal of Psychiatry, 51,* 100–113.

Sotiropoulos, I., Catania, C., Pinto, L. G., Silva, R., Pollerberg, G. E., Takashima, A., . . . Almeida, O. F. X. (2011). Stress acts cumulatively to precipitate Alzheimer's disease-like tau pathology and cognitive deficits. *Journal of Neuroscience, 31,* 7840–7847.

Southwick, S. M., Vythilingam, M., & Charney, D. S. (2005). The psychobiology of depression and resilience to stress: Implications for prevention and treatment. *Annual Review of Clinical Psychology, 1,* 255–291.

Spanos, N. P. (1978). Witchcraft in histories of psychiatry: A critical analysis and an alternative conceptualization. *Psychological Bulletin, 85,* 417–439.

Spanos, N. P. (2001). *Multiple identities and false memories: A sociocognitive perspective.* Washington, DC: American Psychological Association.

Speed, J., & Mooney, G. (1997). Rehabilitation of conversion disorders: An operant approach. *Neurorehabilitation, 8,* 175–181.

Spencer, T., Biederman, J., Wilens, T., Harding, M., O'Donnell, D., & Griffin, S. (1996). Pharmacotherapy of attention-deficit hyperactivity disorder across the life cycle. *Journal of the American Academy of Child and Adolescent Psychiatry, 35,* 409–432.

Spielmans, G. I., & Gerwig, K. (2014). The efficacy of antidressants on overall well-being and self-reported depression symptom severity in youth: A meta-analysis. *Pychotherapy and Psychosomatics, 83,* 158–164.

Spirito, A., & Esposito-Smythers, C. (2006). Attempted and completed suicide in adolescence. *Annual Review of Clinical Psychology, 2,* 237–266.

Spreen, O. (1988). Prognosis of learning disability. *Journal of Consulting and Clinical Psychology, 56,* 836–842.

Stallman, H. M., & Kohler, M. (2016). Prevalence of sleepwalking: A systematic review and meta-analysis. *PLoS ONE, 11,* e0164769.

Stankovska, G., Osmani, F., Pandilovska, S., & Dimitrovski, D. (2015). Association between puberty, bulimia nervosa and depression. *Bangladesh Journal of Medical Science, 14,* 327–330.

Starr, L. S., & Davila, J. (2008). Excessive reassurance seeking, depression, and interpersonal rejection: A meta-analytic review. *Journal of Abnormal Psychology, 117,* 762–775.

Statistics Canada. (2008). Profile of disability for children. Retrieved from http://www.statcan.gc.ca/pub/89-628-x/2007002/4125020-eng.htm#a4

Statistics Canada. (2012a). Canadian Community Health Survey—Mental health (CCHS). Table 105-1101. Retrieved from http://www.statcan.gc.ca/tables-tableaux/sum-som/l01/cst01/hlth66a-eng.htm

Statistics Canada. (2012b). Mental health profile: Canadian Community Health Survey, by age group and sex, Canada and provinces. Table 105-1101. Retrieved from www5.statcan.gc.ca/cansim

Statistics Canada. (2013a). Fact Sheet—2011: National Household Survey Aboriginal demographics, educational attainment and labour market outcomes. Retrieved from https://www.aadnc-aandc.gc.ca/eng/1376329205785/1376329233875

Statistics Canada. (2013b). Mental health profile, Canadian Community Health Survey—Mental health (CCHS), by age group and sex, Canada and provinces. CANSIM Table 105-1101. Retrieved from http://www.statcan.gc.ca/tables-tableaux/sum-som/l01/cst01/hlth66a-eng.htm

Statistics Canada. (2015a). Mental retardation. Retrieved from www.statcan.gc.ca/pub/82-619-m/2012004/sections/sectione-eng.htm

Statistics Canada. (2015b). Suicide and suicide rate, by sex and age group. CANSIM Table 102-0551 (Catalogue No. 84F0209XIE). Retrieved from http://www.statcan.gc.ca/tables-tableaux/sum-som/l01/cst01/hlth66a-eng.htm

Statistics Canada. (2016a). First Nations & Inuit health. Retrieved from www.hc-sc.gc.ca/fniah-spnia/promotion/suicide/index-eng.php

Statistics Canada. (2016b). Immigration and ethnocultural diversity in Canada. Retrieved from https://www12.statcan.gc.ca/nhs-enm/2011/as-sa/99-010-x/99-010-x2011001-eng.cfm

Statistics Canada. (2016c). Population aged 12 and over who reported being a current smoker. CANSIM Table 105-0501 (Catalogue no. 82-221-X). Retrieved from http://www.statcan.gc.ca/tables-tableaux/sum-som/l01/cst01/health73a-eng.htm

Statistics Canada. (2016d). Population aged 12 and over who reported having 5 or more drinks on one occasion, at least once a month in the past 12 months. CANSIM Table 105-0501 (Catalogue no. 82-221-X). Retrieved from www.statcan.gc.ca/tables-tableaux/sum-som/l01/cst01/health79a-eng.htm

Statistics Canada. (2017a). Deaths and mortality rate, by selected grouped causes, age group and sex, Canada, annual. CANSIM Table 102-0551.

Statistics Canada. (2017b). Population size and growth in Canada: Key results from the 2016 census. Retrieved from http://www.statcan.gc.ca/daily-quotidien/170208/dq170208a-eng.htm?HPA=1

Stauffer, V., Case, M., Kollack-Walker, S., Ascher-Svanum, H., Ball, T., Kapur, S., & Kinon, B. J. (2011). Trajectories of response to treatment with atypical antipsychotic medication in patients with schizophrenia pooled from 6 double-blind, randomized clinical trials. *Schizophrenia Research, 130,* 11–19.

Steensma, T., McGuire, J. K., Kreukels, B. P. C., Beekman, A. J., & Cohen-Kettenis, P. T. (2013). Factors associated with desistence and persistence of childhood gender dysphoria: A quantitative follow-up study. *Journal of the American Academy of Child & Adolescent Psychiatry, 52,* 582–590.

Stefanatos, G. A., & Baron, I. S. (2007). Attention-deficit/hyperactivity disorder: A neuropsychological perspective towards DSM-V. *Neuropsychology Review, 17*(1), 5–38.

Stefanovics, E., He, H., Cavalcanti, M., Neto, H., Ofori-Atta, A., Leddy, M., . . . Rosenheck, R. (2016). Witchcraft and biopsychosocial causes of mental illness. *Journal of Nervous and Mental Disease, 204,* 169–174.

Stegemann, K. C. (2016). Learning disabilities in Canada. *Learning Disabilities: A Contemporary Journal, 14,* 53–62.

Steiger, H. (2007). Eating disorder paradigms for the new millennium: Do "attachment" and "culture" appear on brain and genome scans? *Canadian Journal of Psychiatry, 52,* 209–211.

Steiger, H., & Bruce, K. R. (2007). Phenotypes, endophenotypes, and genotypes in bulimia spectrum eating disorders. *Canadian Journal of Psychiatry, 52,* 220–227.

Stein, D. J., Solms, M., & van Honk, J. (2006). The cognitive-affective neuroscience of the unconscious. *CNS Spectrums, 11,* 580–583.

Stein, M. B., Jang, K. L., & Livesley, W. J. (2002). Heritability of social anxiety-related concerns and personality characteristics: A twin study. *Journal of Nervous and Mental Disease, 190,* 219–224.

Stein, M. B., Jang, K. L., Taylor, S., Vernon, P. A., & Livesley, W. J. (2002). Genetic and environmental influences on trauma exposure and posttraumatic stress disorder symptoms: A general population twin study. *American Journal of Psychiatry, 159,* 1675–1681.

Stein, M. B., & Walker, J. R. (2002). *Triumph over shyness: Conquering shyness and social anxiety.* New York: McGraw-Hill.

Stephane, M., Barton, S., & Boutros, N. N. (2001). Auditory verbal hallucinations and dysfunction of neural substrates of speech. *Schizophrenia Research, 50,* 61–78.

Stern, S., Biron, D., & Moses, E. (2016). Transmission of trisomy decreases with maternal age in mouse models of Down syndrome, mirroring a phenomenon in human Down syndrome mothers. *BMC Genetics, 17,* 105.

Stewart, S. E., Manion, I. G., & Davidson, S. (2002). Emergency management of the adolescent suicide attempter: A review of the literature. *Journal of Adolescent Health, 30,* 312–325.

Stewart, S. H. (1996). Alcohol abuse in individuals exposed to trauma: A critical review. *Psychological Bulletin, 120,* 83–112.

Stewart, S. H., Taylor, S., Jang, K. L., Cox, B. J., Watt, M. C., Fedoroff, I. C., & Borger, S. C. (2001). Causal modeling of relations among learning history, anxiety sensitivity, and panic attacks. *Behaviour Research and Therapy, 39,* 443–456.

Stewart, S. M., Kennard, B. D., Lee, P. W. H., Hughes, C. W., Mayes, T. L., Emslie, G. J., & Lewinsohn, P. M. (2004). A cross-cultural investigation of cognitions and depressive symptoms in adolescents. *Journal of Abnormal Psychology, 113,* 248–257.

Stoller, R. J. (1969). Parental influences in male transexualism. In R. Green & J. Money (Eds.), *Transsexualism and sex reassignment.* Baltimore, MD: Johns Hopkins University Press.

Stoltenborgh, M., van Ijzendoorn, M. H., Euser, E. M., & Bakermans-Kranenburg, M. J. (2011). A global perspective on child sexual abuse: Meta-analysis of prevalence around the world. *Child Maltreatment, 16,* 79–101.

Stone, J., Smyth, R., Carson, A., Warlow, C., & Sharpe, M. (2006). *La belle indifférence* in conversion symptoms and hysteria: Systematic review. *British Journal of Psychiatry, 188,* 204–209.

Stone, M. H. (1980). *The borderline syndromes: Constitution, personality, and adaptation.* New York: McGraw-Hill.

Stonnington, C. M., Barry, J. J., & Fisher, R. S. (2006). Conversion disorder. *American Journal of Psychiatry, 163,* 1510–1517.

Storebø, O. J., Ramstad, E., Krogh, H. B., Nilausen, T. D., Skoog, M., Holmskov, M., . . . Gluud, C. (2015). Methylphenidate for children and adolescents with attention deficit hyperactivity disorder (ADHD). *Cochrane Database of Systematic Reviews 2015*(11). doi: 10.1002/14651858.CD009885.pub2

Strasser, A. A., Kaufmann, V., Jepson, C., Perkins, K. A., Pickworth, W. B., & Wileyto, E. P. (2005). Effects of different nicotine replacement therapies on postcessation psychological responses. *Addictive Behaviors, 30,* 9–17.

Strassnig, M., Stowell, K. R., First, M. B., & Pincus, H. A. (2006). General medical and psychiatric perspectives on somatoform disorders: Separated by an uncommon language. *Current Opinion in Psychiatry, 19,* 194–200.

Stricker, G., & Gold, J. R. (1999). The Rorschach: Toward a nomothetically based, idiographically applicable configurational model. *Psychological Assessment, 11,* 240–250.

Strober, M., & Humphrey, L. L. (1987). Familial contributions to the etiology and course of anorexia nervosa and bulimia. *Journal of Consulting and Clinical Psychology, 55,* 654–659.

Stroup, T. S., McEvoy, J. P., Ring, K. D., Hamer, R. H., LaVange, L. M., Swartz, M. S., . . . Schizophrenia Trials Network. (2011). A randomized trial examining the effectiveness of switching from olanzapine, quetiapine, or risperidone to aripiprazole to reduce metabolic risk: Comparison of antipsychotics for metabolic problems (CAMP). *American Journal of Psychiatry, 168*(9), 947–956.

Strupp, H. H. (1992). The future of psychodynamic psychotherapy. *Psychotherapy: Theory, Research, Practice, Training, 29,* 21–27.

Stuart, F. M., Hammond, D. C., & Pett, M. A. (1987). Inhibited sexual desire in women. *Archives of Sexual Behavior, 16,* 91–106.

Stuart, H. L. (2005). Fighting stigma and discrimination is fighting for mental health. *Canadian Public Policy, 31*(Suppl.), 21–28. Retrieved from http://economics.ca/cgi/jab?journal=cpp&view=v31s1/CPPv31s1p021.pdf

Sullivan, H. S. (1962). *Schizophrenia as a human process.* New York: Norton.

Sulloway, F. J. (1983). *Freud: Biologist of the mind: Beyond the psychoanalytic legend.* New York: Basic Books.

Sussman, S. (1998). The first asylums in Canada: A response to neglectful community care and current trends. *Canadian Journal of Psychiatry, 43,* 260–264.

Sussman, S. (1999). *Dr. Ruth Kajander: A pioneer of Canadian psychiatry.* London, ON: Sussco Publishing Company.

Sutandar-Pinnock, K., Woodside, D. B., Carter, J. C., Olmsted, M. P., & Kaplan, A. S. (2003). Perfectionism in anorexia nervosa: A 6–24-month follow-up. *International Journal of Eating Disorders, 33*(2), 225–229.

Suzdak, P. D., Glowa, J. R., Crawley, J. N., Schwartz, R. D., Skolnick, P., & Paul, S. M. (1986). A selective imidazobenzodiazepine antagonist of ethanol in the rat. *Science, 225,* 1243–1247.

Swann, A. C., Lafer, B., Perugi, G., Frye, M. A., Bauer, M., Bahk, W.-M., . . . Suppes, T. (2013). Bipolar mixed states: An international society for bipolar disorders task force report of symptom structure, course of illness, and diagnosis. *American Journal of Psychiatry, 170,* 1–42.

Swinson, R. P. (2005). Social anxiety disorder. *Canadian Journal of Psychiatry, 50,* 305–307.

Szabadi, E. (2014). Selective targets for arousal-modifying drugs: Implications for the treatment of sleep disorders. *Drug Discovery Today, 19,* 701–708.

Szasz, T. S. (1961). *The myth of mental illness: Foundations of a theory of personal conduct.* New York: Hoeber-Harper.

Szatmari, P. (2011). Is autism, at least in part, a disorder of fetal programming? *Archives of General Psychiatry, 68,* 1091–1092.

Szechtman, H., & Woody, E. Z. (2004). Obsessive-compulsive disorder as a disturbance of security motivation: Constraints on comorbidity. *Psychological Review, 111,* 111–127.

Szegedi, A., Kohnen, R., Dienel, A., & Kieser, M. (2005). Acute treatment of moderate to severe depression with hypericum extract WS 5570 (St John's wort): Randomised controlled double blind non-inferiority trial versus paroxetine. *British Medical Journal, 330,* 503–509.

Szyf, M. (2006). Letter from the editor. *Epigenetics, 1*(1), i.

Szymanski, S., Kane, J. M., & Lieberman, J. A. (1991). A selective review of biological markers in schizophrenia. *Schizophrenia Bulletin, 17,* 99–111.

T

Tackett, J. L., Silberschmidt, A. L., Krueger, R. F., Sponheim, S. R. (2008). A dimensional model of personality disorder: Incorporating DSM cluster A characteristics. *Journal of Abnormal Psychology, 117,* 454–459.

Tadić, A., Wagner, S., Hoch, J., Başkaya, Ö., von Cube, R., Skaletz, C., . . . Dahmen, N. (2009). Gender differences in axis I and axis II comorbidity in patients with borderline personality disorder. *Psychopathology, 42,* 257–263.

Talbot, J. D., & McMurray, L. (2004). Combining cognitive-behavioural therapy and pharmacotherapy in the treatment of anxiety disorders. *Canadian Psychiatric Association Bulletin, 36*(1), 20–22.

Tanguay, P. E. (2011). Autism in DSM-5. *American Journal of Psychiatry, 168,* 1142–1144.

Taylor, C. T., & Alden, L. E. (2005). Social interpretation bias and generalized social phobia: The influence of developmental experiences. *Behaviour Research and Therapy, 43,* 759–777.

Taylor, S., (Ed.). (1999). *Anxiety sensitivity: Theory, research, and treatment of the fear of anxiety.* Mahwah, NJ: Erlbaum.

Taylor, S. (2000). *Understanding and treating panic disorder: Cognitive-behavioural approaches.* New York: Wiley.

Taylor, S. (2005). *Clinician's guide to PTSD: A cognitive-behavioral approach.* New York: Guilford.

Taylor, S., Abramowitz, J. S., & McKay, D. (2006). Cognitive-behavioral models of obsessive-compulsive disorder. In M. M. Antony, C. Purdon, & L. Summerfeldt (Eds.), *Psychological treatment of obsessive-compulsive disorder: Fundamentals and beyond* (pp. 9–29). Washington, DC: American Psychological Association.

Taylor, S., & Asmundson, G. J. G. (2004). *Treating health anxiety: A cognitive-behavioral approach.* New York: Guilford.

Taylor, S., Asmundson, G. J. G., & Coons, M. J. (2005). Current directions in the treatment of hypochondriasis. *Journal of Cognitive Psychotherapy, 19,* 285–304.

Taylor, S., & Jang, K. L. (2011). Biopsychosocial etiology of obsessions and compulsions: An integrated behavioral–genetic and cognitive–behavioral analysis. *Journal of Abnormal Psychology, 120,* 174–186.

Taylor, S., McKay, D., & Abramowitz, J. S. (2005). Is obsessive-compulsive disorder a disturbance of security motivation? *Psychological Review, 112,* 650–657.

Taylor, S., & Stein, M. B. (2006). The future of selective serotonin-reuptake inhibitors (SSRIs) in psychiatric treatment. *Medical Hypotheses, 66,* 14–21.

Taylor, S., Thordarson, D. S., Jang, K. L., & Asmundson, G. J. G. (2006). Genetic and environmental origins of health anxiety: A twin study. *World Psychiatry, 5,* 47–50.

Teachman, B. A., Smith-Janik, S. B., & Saporito, J. (2007). Information processing biases and panic disorder: Relationships among cognitive and symptom measures. *Behaviour Research & Therapy, 45*(8), 1791–1811.

Teunisse, R. J., Cruysberg, J. R., Hoefnagels, W. H., Verbeek, A. I., & Zitman, F. G. (1996). Visual hallucinations in psychologically normal people: Charles Bonnet's syndrome. *Lancet, 347,* 794–797.

Thapar, A., Gottesman, I. I., Owen, M. J., O'Donovan, M. C., & McGuffin, P. (1994). The genetics of mental retardation. *British Journal of Psychiatry, 164,* 747–758.

Thibaut, F. (2011). Pharmacological treatment of sex offenders. *Sexologies, 20,* 166–168.

Thibaut, F. (2016). Pharmacological treatment of sex offenders. *European Psychiatry, 33S,* S18-S55.

Thomas, M., & Lovell, A. (2015). Anxiety and compulsion patterns in the maintenance of bingeing/purging behaviours by individuals with bulimia nervosa. *Journal of Psychiatric and Mental Health Nursing, 22,* 20–29.

Thompson, D. F., Ramos, C. L., & Willett, J. K. (2014). Psychopathy: Clinical features, developmental basis and therapeutic challenges. *Journal of Clinical Pharmacy and Therapeutics, 39,* 485–495.

Thompson, P. A., Hulme, C., Nash, H. M., Gooch, D., Hayiou-Thomas, E., & Snowling, M. J. (2015). Developmental dyslexia: Predicting individual risk. *Journal of Child Psychology and Psychiatry, 56,* 976–987.

Thompson, R. G., Alonzo, D., Hu, M., & Hasin, D. S. (2017). Substance use disorders and poverty as prospective preditors of adult first-time suicide ideation or attempt in the United States. *Community Mental Health Journal, 53,* 324–333.

Thorpy, M. (2007). Therapeutic advances in narcolepsy. *Sleep Medicine, 8,* 427–440.

Thylstrup, B., Schrøder, S., & Hesse, M. (2015). Psycho-education for substance use and antisocial personality disorder: A randomized trial. *BMC Psychiatry, 15,* 283.

Tiefer, L. (2001). Arriving at a "new view" of women's sexual problems: Background, theory, and activism. In E. Kachak & L. Tiefer (Eds.), *A new view of women's sexual problems* (pp. 63–98). New York: Haworth.

Tienari, P. (1991). Interaction between genetic vulnerability and family environment: The Finnish adoptive family study of schizophrenia. *Acta Psychiatrica Scandinavica, 84,* 460–465.

Tienari, P. (1992). Implications of adoption studies on schizophrenia. *British Journal of Psychiatry, 161*(Suppl. 18), 52–58.

Tienari, P., Lahti, L., Sorri, A., Naarala, M., Moring, J., Kaleva, M., . . . Wynne, L. C. (1990). Adopted-away offspring of schizophrenics and controls: The Finnish adoptive family study of schizophrenia. In L. N. Robbins & M. Rutter (Eds.), *Straight and devious pathways from childhood to adulthood.* New York: Cambridge University Press.

Tienari, P., Sorri, A., Naarala, M., Wahlberg, K.-E., Moring, J., Pohjola, J., . . . Wynne, L. C. (1987). Genetic and psychosocial factors in schizophrenia: The Finnish Adoptive Family Study. *Schizophrenia Bulletin, 13,* 477–484.

Tienari, P., Wahlberg, K.-E., & Wynne, L. C. (2006). Finnish adoption study of schizophrenia: Implications for family interventions. *Families, Systems, and Health, 24,* 442–451.

Tjepkema, M. (2002). Health of the off-reserve Aboriginal population. *Health Reports, 13*(Suppl.), 73–86.

Tjepkema, M. (2005). Insomnia. *Health Reports, 17*(1), 9–25.

Toichi, M., Kamio, Y., Okada, T., Sakihama, M., Youngstrom, E. A., Findling, R. L., & Yamamoto, K. (2002). A lack of self-consciousness in autism. *American Journal of Psychiatry, 159,* 1422–1424.

Tolin, D. F. (2010). Is cognitive-behavioral therapy more effective than other therapies? A meta-analytic review. *Clinical Psychology Review, 30,* 710–720.

Tolin, D. F., & Foa, E. B. (2006). Sex differences in trauma and posttraumatic stress disorder: A quantitative review of 25 years of research. *Psychological Bulletin, 132,* 959–992.

Tolomiczenko, G. S., & Goering, P. N. (1998). Pathways into homelessness: Broadening the perspective. *Psychiatry Rounds, 2*(8), 1–6.

Tomko, R. L., Trull, T. J., Wood, P. K., & Sher, K. J. (2014). Characteristics of borderline personality disorder in a community sample: Comorbidity, treatment utilization, and general functioning. *Journal of Personality Disorders, 28,* 734–750.

Tough, S. C., Butt, J. C., & Sanders, G. L. (1994). Autoerotic asphyxial deaths: Analysis of nineteen fatalities in Alberta, 1978 to 1989. *Canadian Journal of Psychiatry, 39,* 157–160.

Toward Optimized Practice. (2007). Adult primary insomnia: Assessment to diagnosis. Retrieved from http://www.topalberta doctors.org/download/439/insomnia_management_guideline.pdf

Town, J. M., Diener, M. J., Abbass, A., Leichsenring, F., Driessen, E., & Rabung, S. (2012). A meta-analysis of psychodynamic psychotherapy outcomes: Evaluating the effects of research-specific procedures. *Psychotherapy, 49,* 276–290.

Trask, P. C., & Sigmon, S. T. (1997). Munchausen syndrome: A review and new conceptualization. *Clinical Psychology: Science and Practice, 4,* 346–358.

Treasure, J., & Ward, A. (1997). Cognitive analytical therapy in the treatment of anorexia nervosa. *Clinical Psychology & Psychotherapy, 4*(1), 62–71.

Treffert, D. A. (1988). The idiot savant: A review of the syndrome. *American Journal of Psychiatry, 145,* 563–572.

Triebwasser, J., Chemerinski, E., Roussos, P., & Siever, L. J. (2012). Schizoid personality disorder. *Journal of Personality Disorders, 26,* 919–926.

Trigger, B. G., & Swagerty, W. R. (1996). Entertaining strangers: North America in the sixteenth century. In B. G. Trigger and W. E. Washburn (Eds.), *The Cambridge history of the Native peoples of the Americas: Vol. 1. North America, part 1* (pp. 325–398). New York: Cambridge University Press.

Triggs-Raine, B., Richard, M., Wasel, N., Prence, E. M., & Natowicz, M. R. (1995). Mutational analyses of Tay-Sachs disease: Studies on Tay-Sachs carriers of French Canadian background living in New England. *American Journal of Human Genetics, 56,* 870–879.

True, W. R., Rice, J., Eisen, S. A., Heath, A. C., Goldberg, J., Lyons, M. J., & Nowak, J. (1993). A twin study of genetic and environmental contributions to liability for posttraumatic stress symptoms. *Archives of General Psychiatry, 50,* 257–265.

Trzepacz, P. T., Baker, R. W., Greenhouse, J. (1988). A symptom rating scale for delirium. *Psychiatry Research, 23,* 89–97.

Turkington, D., & Morrison, A. P. (2012). Cognitive therapy for negative symptoms of schizophrenia. *Archives of General Psychiatry, 69,* 119–120.

Turnbridge, E. M., Dunn, G., Murray R. M., Evans, N., Lister, R., Stumpenhorst, K., . . . Freeman, D. (2015). Genetic moderation of the effects of cannabis: Catechol-O-methyltransferase (COMT) affects the impact of Δ9-tetrahydrocannabinol (THC) on working memory performance but not on the occurrence of psychotic experiences. *Journal of Psychopharmacology, 29,* 1146–1151.

Turner, S. M., Beidel, D. C., Dancu, C. V., & Keys, D. J. (1986). Psychopathology of social phobia and comparison to avoidant personality disorder. *Journal of Abnormal Psychology, 95,* 389–394.

Tuvblad, C., Narusyte, J., Grann, M., Sarnecki, J., & Lichtenstein, P. (2011). The genetic and environmental etiology of antisocial behavior from childhood to emerging adulthood. *Behavioral Genetics, 41,* 629–640.

Tyhurst, J. S., Chalke, F. C. R., Lawson, F. S., McNeel, B. H., Roberts, C. A., Taylor, G. C., Griffin, J. D. (1963). *More for the mind: A study of psychiatric services in Canada.* Toronto: Canadian Mental Health Association.

U

Uchida, M., Spencer, T. J., Faraone, S. V., & Biederman, J. (2015). Adult outcome of ADHD: An overview of results from the MGH longitudinal family studies of pediatrically and psychiatrically referred youth with and without ADHD of both sexes. *Journal of Attention Disorders, 2015,* 1–12. doi:10.1177/1087054715604360

US Department of Health and Human Services. (1986). *NIDA Capsules: Designer drugs.* No. 10. U.S. Department of Health and Human Services, Public Health Service, Alcohol, Drug Abuse, and Mental Health Administration, National Institute on Drug Abuse. Rockville, MD: National Institute on Drug Abuse.

US Department of Health and Human Services. (1992). *NIDA Capsules: LSD (Lysergic acid diethylamide)* No. 39. U.S. Department of Health and Human Services, Public Health Service, Alcohol, Drug Abuse, and Mental Health Administration, National Institute on Drug Abuse. Rockville, MD: National Institute on Drug Abuse.

US Department of Health and Human Services. (2001). *Healthy people 2000: National health promotion and disease prevention objectives.* Washington, DC: US Government Printing Office.

Ullman, S. E., (2016). Sexual revictimization, PTSD, and problem drinking in sexual assault survivors. *Addictive Behaviors, 53,* 7–10.

Ullmann, L. P., & Krasner, L. (1975). *A psychological approach to abnormal behavior* (2nd ed.). Englewood Cliffs, NJ: Prentice-Hall.

Urbanoski, K. A., & Kelly, J. F. (2012). Understanding genetic risk for substance use and addiction: A guide for non-geneticists. *Clinical Psychology Review, 32,* 60–70.

V

Van Ameringen, M., Mancini, C., Patterson, B., & Boyle, M. H. (2008). Post-traumatic stress disorder in Canada. *CNS Neuroscience & Therapeutics, 14,* 171–181.

Van Ameringen, M., Mancini, C., Pipe, B., & Boyle, M. (2004, October). Canadian PTSD epidemiology study. Paper presented at the annual convention of the Canadian Psychiatric Association, Montreal.

Van der Oord, S., Prins, P. J. M., Oosterlaan, J., & Emmelkamp, P. M. G. (2008). Efficacy of methylphenidate, psychosocial treatments and their combination in school-aged children with ADHD: A meta-analysis. *Clinical Psychology Review, 28,* 783–800.

Van Lankveld, J. J. D. M., Granot, M., Schultz, W. C. M. W., Binik, Y. M., Wesselmann, U., Pukall, C. F., . . . Achtrari, C. (2010). Women's sexual pain disorders. *Journal of Sexual Medicine, 7,* 615–631.

Van Orden, K. A., & Joiner, T. E. (2006). The inner and outer turmoil of excessive reassurance seeking: From self-doubts to social rejection. In K. D. Vohs & E. J. Finkel (Eds.), *Self and relationships: Connecting intrapersonal and interpersonal processes* (pp. 104–129). New York: Guilford.

Van Os, J., Krabbendam, L., Myin-Germeys, I., & Delespaul, P. (2005). The schizophrenia envirome. *Current Opinion in Psychiatry, 18,* 141–145.

Vazza, G., Bertolin, C., Scudellaro, E., Vettori, A., Boaretto, F., Rampinelli, S., . . . Mostacciuolo, M. L. (2007). Genomewide scan supports the existence of a susceptibility locus for schizophrenia and bipolar disorder on chromosome 15q26. *Molecular Psychiatry, 12,* 87–93.

Veen, V. C., Stevens, G. W. J. M., Andershed, H., Raaijmakers, Q. A. W., Doreleijers, T. A. H., & Vollebergh, W. A. M. (2011). Cross-ethnic generalizability of the three-factor model of psychopathy: The Youth Psychopathic Traits Inventory in an incarcerated sample of native Dutch and Moroccan immigrant boys. *International Journal of Law and Psychiatry, 34,* 127–130.

Veilleux, J. C., Colvin, P. J., Anderson, J., York, C., & Heinz, A. J. (2010). A review of opioid dependence treatment: Pharmacological and psychosocial interventions to treat opioid addiction. *Clinical Psychology Review, 30,* 155–166.

Vellante, M., Larøi, F., Cella, M., Raballo, A., Petretto, D. R., & Preti, A. (2012), Hallucination-like experiences in the nonclinical population. *Journal of Nervous and Mental Disease, 200,* 300–315.

Verkerk, G. J. M., Pop, V. J. M., Van Son, M. J. M., & Van Heck, G. L. (2003). Prediction of depression in the postpartum period: A longitudinal follow-up study in high-risk and low-risk women. *Journal of Affective Disorders, 77,* 159–166.

Vermani, M., Milosevic, I., Smith, F., & Katzman, M. A. (2005). Herbs for mental illness: Effectiveness and interaction with conventional medicines. *Journal of Family Practice, 54,* 789–800.

Vermote, R., Luyten, P., Verhaest, Y., Vandeneede, B., Vertommen, H., & Lowyck, B. (2015). A psychoanalytically informed hospitalization-based treatment of personality disorders. *International Journal of Psychoanalysis, 96,* 817–843.

Vespia, K. M. (2009). Culture and psychotic disorders. In S. Eshun & R. A. R. Gurung (Eds.), *Culture and mental health: Sociocultural influenes, theory, and practice.* Chichester, UK: Blackwell Publishing.

Viens, M., De Koninck, J., Mercier, P., St-Onge, M., & Lorrain, D. (2003). Trait anxiety and sleep-onset insomnia: Evaluation of treatment using anxiety management training. *Journal of Psychosomatic Research, 54*(1), 31–37.

Viguera, A. C., Tondo, L., Koukopoulos, A. E., Reginaldi, D., Lepri, B., & Baldessarini, R. J. (2011). Episodes of mood disorders in 2,252 pregnancies and postpartum periods. *American Journal of Psychiatry, 168,* 1179–1185.

Vincent, N., & Walsh, K. (2013). Hyperarousal, sleep scheduling, and time awake in bed as mediators of outcome in computerized cognitive-behavioral therapy (cCBT) for insomnia. *Behaviour Research and Therapy, 5,* 161–166.

Vine, C., & Challen, P. (2002). *Gardens of shame: The tragedy of Martin Kruze and the sexual abuse at Maple Leaf Gardens.* Vancouver: Greystone.

Vissers, L. E. L. M., de Ligt, J., Gilissen, C., Janssen, I., Steehouwer, M., de Vries, P., . . . Veltman, J. A. (2010). A de novo paradigm for mental retardation. *Nature Genetics, 42,* 1109–1112.

Vocci, F. J., & Elkashef, A. (2005). Pharmacotherapy and other treatments for cocaine abuse and dependence. *Current Opinion in Psychiatry, 18,* 265–270.

Volkow, N. D., Wang, G. J., Fischman, M. W., Foltin, R. W., Fowler, J. S., Abumrad, N. N., . . . Shea, C. E. (1997). Relationship between subjective effects of cocaine and dopamine transporter occupancy. *Nature, 386,* 827–830.

W

Waddell, C., McEwan, K., Shepherd, C. A., Offord, D. R., & Hua, J. M. (2005). A public health strategy to improve the mental health of Canadian children. *Canadian Journal of Psychiatry, 50,* 226–233.

Waddell, C., & Shepherd, C. (2002). *Prevalence of mental disorders in children and youth: A research update prepared for the British Columbia Ministry of Children and Family Development, October 2002.* Vancouver: The University of British Columbia.

Wade, M., Prime, H., & Madigan, S. (2015). Using sibling designs to understand neurodevelopmental disorders: From genes and environments to prevention programming. *BioMed Research International, 2015,* 1–16.

Wadsworth, M. E., & Achenbach, T. M. (2005). Explaining the link between low socioeconomic status and psychopathology: Testing two mechanisms of the social causation hypothesis. *Journal of Consulting and Clinical Psychology, 73,* 1146–1153.

Wald, J., & Taylor, S. (2003). Preliminary research on the efficacy of virtual reality exposure therapy to treat driving phobia. *CyberPsychology and Behavior, 6,* 459–465.

Wald, J., Taylor, S., & Scamvougeras, A. (2004). Cognitive behavioural and neuropsychiatric treatment of posttraumatic conversion disorder: A case study. *Cognitive Behaviour Therapy, 33,* 12–20.

Waldram, J. B. (2001). The problem of "culture" and the counselling of Aboriginal peoples. In L. J. Kirmayer, M. E. MacDonald, & G. M. Brass (Eds.), *The mental health of indigenous peoples: Proceedings of the Advanced Study Institute* (pp. 145–158). Montreal: McGill Summer Program in Social & Cultural Psychiatry.

Waldram, J. B. (2004). *Revenge of the Windigo: The construction of the mind and mental health of North American Aboriginal peoples.* Toronto: University of Toronto Press.

Walker, E., Shapiro, D., Esterberg, M., & Trotman, H. (2010). Neurodevelopment and schizophrenia: Broadening the focus. *Psychological Science, 19,* 204–208.

Walsh, B. T., Fairburn, C. G., Mickley, D., Sysko, R., & Parides, M. K. (2004). Treatment of bulimia nervosa in a primary care setting. *American Journal of Psychiatry, 161,* 556–561.

Walsh, B. T., Kaplan, A. S., Attia, E., Olmsted, M., Parides, M., Carter, J. C., . . . Rockert, W. (2006). Fluoxetine after weight restoration in anorexia nervosa: A randomized controlled trial. *JAMA: Journal of the American Medical Association, 295,* 2605–2612.

Wampold, B. E. (2001). *The great psychotherapy debate: Models, methods, and findings.* Mahwah: Erlbaum.

Wampold, B. E., Budge, S. L., Laska, K. M., Del Re, A. C., Baardseth, T. P., Flückiger, C., . . . Gunn, W. (2011). Evidence-based treatments for depression and anxiety versus treatment-as-usual: A meta-analysis of direct comparisons. *Clinical Psychology Review, 31,* 1304–1312.

Wampold, B. E., Mondin, G. W., Moody, M., Stick, F., Benson, K., & Ahn, H. (1997). A meta-analysis of outcome studies comparing bona fide psychotherapies: Empirically, "All must have prizes." *Psychological Bulletin, 122,* 203–215.

Wang, Q., Chan, R., Sun, J., Yao, J., Deng, W., Sun, X., . . . Li, T. (2007). Reaction time of the continuous performance test is an endophenotypic marker for schizophrenia: A study of first-episode neuroleptic-naive schizophrenia, their non-psychotic first-degree relatives and healthy population controls. *Schizophrenia Research, 89,* 293–298.

Warme, G. (2006). *Daggers of the mind: Psychiatry and the myth of mental disease.* Toronto: House of Anansi Press.

Wasylenki, D. (2001). The paradigm shift from institution to community. In Q. Rae-Grant (Ed.), *Psychiatry in Canada: 50 years* (pp. 95–110). Ottawa: Canadian Psychiatric Association.

Watkins, K. E., Hunter, S. B., Hepner, K. A., Paddock, S. M., de la Cruz, E., Zhou, A. J., & Gilmore, J. (2011). An effectiveness trial of group cognitive behavioral therapy for patients with persistent depressive symptoms in substance abuse treatment. *American Journal of Psychiatry, 68,* 577–584.

Watson, J. B., & Rayner, R. (1920). Conditioned emotional reactions. *Journal of Experimental Psychology, 3*(1), 1–14.

Webber, C., Hehir-Kwa, J. Y., Nguyen, D.-Q., de Vries, B. B. A., Veltman, J. A., & Ponting, C. P. (2009). Forging links between human mental retardation–associated CNVs and mouse gene knockout models. *PLoS Genetics, 5*(6), e10000531. Retrieved from http://www.plosgenetics.org/article/info:doi/10.1371/journal.pgen 1000531

Webster-Stratton, C., & Hammond, M. (1997). Treating children with early-onset conduct problems: A comparison of child and parent training interventions. *Journal of Consulting and Clinical Psychology, 65,* 93–109.

Wechsler, D. (1975). Intelligence defined and undefined: A relativistic appraisal. *American Psychologist, 30,* 135–139.

Weinberger, D. R. (1997). On localizing schizophrenic neuropathology. *Schizophrenia Bulletin, 23,* 537–540.

Weinhold, B. (2006). Epigenetics: The science of change. *Environmental Health Perspectives, 114*(3), A160–A167.

Weir, K. (2012, June). The roots of mental illness. *Monitor on Psychology, 43,* 30–33.

Weisman, A. G., Nuechterlein, K. H., Goldstein, M. J., & Snyder, K. S. (1998). Expressed emotion, attributions, and schizophrenia symptom dimensions. *Journal of Abnormal Psychology, 107,* 355–359.

Weiss, R. D., Mirin, S. M., & Bartel, R. L. (1994). *Cocaine* (2nd ed.). Washington, DC: American Psychiatric Press.

Weissman, M. M. (2011). Can epidemiology translate into understanding major depression with borderline personality disorder? *American Journal of Psychiatry, 168,* 231–233.

Weissman, M. M., Bland, R. C., Canino, G. J., Greenwald, S., Hwu, H.-G., Joyce, P. R., . . . Yeh, E.-K. (1999). Prevalence of suicide ideation and suicide attempts in nine countries. *Psychological Medicine, 29,* 9–17.

Weissman, M. M., Markowitz, J. C., & Klerman, G. L. (2000). *Comprehensive guide to interpersonal psychotherapy.* New York: Basic Books.

Weisz, J. R., McCarty, C. A., & Valeri, S. M. (2006). Effects of psychotherapy for depression in children and adolescents: A meta-analysis. *Psychological Bulletin, 132,* 132–149.

Welch, E., Lagerström, M., & Ghaderi, A. (2012). Body Shape Questionnaire: Psychometric properties of the short version (BSQ-8C) and norms from the general Swedish population. *Body Image, 9,* 547–550.

Welch, M. R., & Kartub, P. (1978). Sociocultural correlates of incidence of impotence: A cross-cultural study. *Journal of Sex Research, 14,* 218–230.

Weltzin, T. E., Cameron, J., Berga, S., & Kaye, W. H. (1994). Prediction of reproductive status in women with bulimia nervosa by past high weight. *American Journal of Psychiatry, 151,* 136–138.

Wender, P. H., Rosenthal, D., Kety, S. S., Schulsinger, F., & Welner, J. (1974). Cross-fostering: A research strategy for clarifying the role of genetic and experiential factors in the etiology of schizophrenia. *Archives of General Psychiatry, 30,* 121–128.

Wente, M. (2006, July 6). Post-traumatic stress is felling more troops than the enemy. *Globe and Mail,* p. A15.

Werner, K. B., Few, L. R., & Bucholz, K. K. (2015). Epidemiology, comorbidity, and behavioral genetics of antisocial personality disorder and psychopathy. *Psychiatric Annals, 45,* 195–199.

Westen, D., & Shedler, J. (1999). Revising and assessing Axis II, Part I: Developing a clinically and empirically valid assessment method. *American Journal of Psychiatry, 156,* 258–272.

Westmoreland, P., Krantz, M. J., & Mehler, P. S. (2016). Medical complications of anorexia nervosa and bulimia. *The American Journal of Medicine, 129,* 30–37.

Whaley, A. L., & Hall, B. N. (2009). Effects of cultural themes in psychotic symptoms on the diagnosis of schizophrenia in African Americans. *Mental Health, Religion & Culture, 12,* 457–471.

White, J. (2005). A summary of suicide risk and protective factors (youth and young adults). *Visions: B.C.'s Mental Health and Addictions Journal, 2*(7), 8.

Whittington, C. J., Kendall, T., & Pilling, S. (2005). Are the SSRIs and atypical antidepressants safe and effective with children and adolescents? *Current Opinion in Psychiatry, 18,* 21–25.

Wicks, S., Hjern, A., & Dalman, C. (2010). Social risk or genetic liability for psychosis? A study of children born in Sweden and reared by adoptive parents. *American Journal of Psychiatry, 167,* 1240–1246.

Widaman, K. F. (2009). Phenylketonuria in children and mothers: Genes, environments, behavior. *Current Directions in Psychological Science, 18,* 48–52.

Widiger, T. A., & Costa, P. T. (2012). Integrating normal and abnormal personality structure: The five-factor model. *Journal of Personality, 80,* 1472–1506.

Widiger, T. A., Livesley, W. J., & Clark, L. A. (2009). An integrative dimensional classification of personality disorders. *Psychological Assessment, 21,* 243–255.

Widiger, T. A., & Lowe, J. R. (2008). A dimensional model of personality disorder: Proposal for DSM-V. *Psychiatric Clinics of North America, 31,* 363–378.

Widiger, T. A., & Mullins-Sweatt, S. (2005). Categorical and dimensional models of personality disorder. In J. Oldham, A. Skodol, & D. Bender (Eds.), *The APA textbook of personality disorders* (pp. 35–53). Washington, DC: American Psychiatric Press.

Widiger, T. A., & Simonsen, E. (2005). Alternative dimensional models of personality disorder: finding a common ground. *Journal of Personality Disorders, 19,* 110–130.

Wieman, C. (2001). An overview of Six Nations mental health services. In L. J. Kirmayer, M. E. MacDonald, & G. M. Brass (Eds.), *The mental health of Indigenous peoples: Proceedings of the Advanced Study Institute* (pp. 177–185). Montreal: McGill Summer Program in Social & Cultural Psychiatry.

Wiersma, D., Jenner, J. A., van de Willige, G., Spakman, M., & Nienhuis, F. J. (2001). Cognitive behaviour therapy with coping training for persistent auditory hallucinations in schizophrenia: A naturalistic follow-up study of the durability of effects. *Acta Psychiatrica Scandinavica, 103,* 393–399.

Wilfley, D. E., Crow, S. J., Hudson, J. I., Mitchell, J. E., Berkowitz, R. I., Blakesley, V., & Walsh, B. T. (2008). Efficacy of sibutramine for the treatment of binge-eating disorder: A randomized multicenter placebo-controlled double-blind study. *American Journal of Psychiatry, 165,* 51–58.

Williams, P., Narciso, L., Browne, G., Roberts, J., Weir, R., & Gafni, A. (2005). The prevalence, correlates, and costs of depression in people living with HIV/AIDS in Ontario: Implications for service directions. *AIDS Education and Prevention, 17,* 119–130.

Wilson, G. T., & Fairburn, C. G. (1998). Treatments for eating disorders. In P. E. Nathan & J. M. Gorman (Eds.), *A guide to treatments that work* (pp. 501–530). New York: Oxford University Press.

Wilson, P. (2000, May 16). Keeping pain at a distance. *The Hamilton Spectator.*

Winblad, B., Andreasen, N., Minthon, L., Floesser, A., Imbert, G., Dumortier, T., . . . Graf, A. (2012). Safety, tolerability, and antibody response of active Aß immuno-therapy with CAD106 in patients with Alzheimer's disease: Randomised, double-blind, placebo-controlled, first-in-human study. *The Lancet Neurology, 11,* 597–604.

Winnicott, D. W. (1953). Übergangsobjekte und Übergangsphänomene: Eine Studie über den ersten, nicht zum Selbst gehörenden Besitz. (First presented 1951). *Psyche, 23,* 1969.

Witkiewitz, K., Bowen, S., Douglas, H., & Hsu, S. H. (2013). Mindfulness-based relapse prevention for substance craving. *Addictive Behaviors, 38,* 1563–1571.

Witkiewicz, K., & Marlatt, G. A. (2004). Relapse prevention for alcohol and drug problems: That was Zen, this is Tao. *American Psychologist, 59,* 224–235.

Witkiewitz, K., Warner, K., Sully, B., Barricks, A., Stauffer, C., Thompson, B. L., & Luoma, J. B. (2014). Randomized trial comparing mindfulness-based relapse prevention with relapse prevention for women offenders at a residential addiction treatment center. *Substance Use & Misuse, 49,* 536–546.

Wolf, N. J., & Hopko, D. R. (2008). Psychosocial and pharmacological interventions for depressed adults in primary care: A critical review. *Clinical Psychology Review, 28,* 131–136.

Wolfe, K. L., Foxwell, A., & Kennard, B. (2014). Identifying and treating risk factors for suicidal behaviors in youth. *International Journal of Behavioral Consultation and Therapy, 9,* 11–14.

Wolff, J. J., Gu, H., Gerig, G., Elison, J. T., Styner, M., Gouttard, S., . . . IBIS. (2012). Network differences in white matter fiber tract development present from 6 to 24 months in infants with autism. *American Journal of Psychiatry, 169,* 589–600.

Wolpe, J. (1958). *Psychotherapy by reciprocal inhibition.* Stanford, CA: Stanford University Press.

Wong, C. L., Holroyd-Leduc, J., Simel, D. L., & Straus, S. E. (2010). Does this patient have delirium? Value of bedside instruments. *JAMA: Journal of the American Medical Association, 304,* 779–786.

Wong, S. L., Gilmour, H., & Ramage-Morin, P. L. (2016). Alzheimer's disease and other dementias in Canada. *Health Reports.* Statistics Canada, catalogue no. 82-003-X.

Wong, T. P. T. (2002). INPM: Who we are and what we do. International Network on Personal Meaning. Retrieved from http://www.meaning.ca/about_us/june02_letter.htm

Wood, J. M., Bootzin, R. R., Rosenham, D., Nolen-Hoeksma, S., & Jourden, F. (1992). Effects of the 1989 San Francisco earthquake on frequency and content of nightmares. *Journal of Abnormal Psychology, 101,* 219–234.

Wood, J. M., Lilienfeld, S. O., Nezworski, M. T., Garb, H. N., Allen, K. H., & Wildermuth, J. L. (2010). Validity of Rorschach inkblot scores for discriminating psychopaths from non-psychopaths in forensic populations: A meta-analysis. *Psychological Assessment, 22,* 336–349.

Woods, B., Spector, A. E., Prendergast, L., & Orrell, M. (2012). Cognitive stimulation to improve cognitive functioning in people with dementia. *The Cochrane Review,* published online. doi: 10.1002/14651858.CD005562

Woodside, D. B., Bulik, C. M., Halmi, K. A., Fichter, M. M., Kaplan, A. S., Berrettini, W. H., . . . Kaye, W. H. (2002). Personality, perfectionism, and attitudes toward eating in parents of individuals with eating disorders. *International Journal of Eating Disorders, 31,* 290–299.

Working Group for the Canadian Psychiatric Association and Canadian Alliance for Research on Schizophrenia. (1998). Canadian clinical practice guidelines for the treatment of schizophrenia. *Canadian Journal of Psychiatry, 43*(Suppl. 2), 25S–39S.

World Health Organization. (n.d.). WHO definition of health. Retrieved from http://www.who.int/about/definition/en

World Health Organization. (2001, June 25). ICD-10 Description. Geneva, Switzerland: Author. Retrieved from https://apps.who.int/whosis/icd10/descript.htm

World Health Organization. (2016). WHO guidelines on the management of health complications from female genital mutilation. Retrieved from https://www.who.int/entity/reproductivehealth/topics/fgm/management-health-complications-fgm/en/

Wright, J. H., Wright, A. S., Albano, A. M., Basco, M. R., Goldsmith, L. L., Raffield, T., & Otto, M. W. (2005). Computer-assisted cognitive therapy for depression: Maintaining efficacy while reducing therapist time. *American Journal of Psychiatry, 162,* 1158–1162.

Y

Yang, L. H., Phillips, M. R., Licht, D. M., & Hooley, J. M. (2004). Causal attributions about schizophrenia in families in China: Expressed emotion and patient relapse. *Journal of Abnormal Psychology, 113,* 592–602.

Yang, M., Wong, S. C., & Coid, J. (2010). The efficacy of violence prediction: A meta-analytic comparison of nine risk assessment tools. *Psychological Bulletin, 136,* 740–746.

Yang, Y., & Raine, A. (2009). Prefrontal structural and functional brain imaging findings in antisocial, violent, and psychopathic individuals: A meta-analysis. *Psychiatry Research: Neuroimaging, 174,* 81–88.

Yatham, L. N., Kennedy, S. H., O'Donovan, C., Parikh, S. V., MacQueen, G., McIntyre, R. S., . . . Gorman, C. P. (2006). Canadian Network for Mood and Anxiety Treatments (CANMAT) guidelines for the management of patients with bipolar disorder: Update 2007. *Bipolar Disorders, 8,* 721–739.

Yirmiya, N., & Sigman, M. (1991). High functioning individuals with autism: Diagnosis, empirical findings, and theoretical issues. *Clinical Psychology Review, 11,* 669–683.

Z

Zadra, A., Desautels, A., Petit, D., & Montplaisir, J. (2013). Somnambulism: Clinical aspects and pathophysiological hypotheses. *The Lancet Neurology, 12,* 285–294.

Zakzanis, K. K., & Heinrichs, R. W. (1999). Schizophrenia and the frontal brain: A quantitative review. *Journal of the International Neuropsychological Society, 5,* 556–566.

Zakzanis, K. K., Poulin, P., Hansen, K. T., & Jolic, D. (2000). Searching the schizophrenic brain for temporal lobe deficits: A systematic review and meta-analysis. *Psychological Medicine, 30,* 491–504.

Zanardi, R., Franchini, L., Gasperini, M., Perez, J., & Smeraldi, E. (1996). Double-blind controlled trial of sertraline versus paroxetine in the treatment of delusional depression. *American Journal of Psychiatry, 153,* 1631–1633.

Zanarini, M. C., Skodol, A. E., Bender, D., Dolan, R., Sanislow, C., Schaefer, E., . . . Gunderson, J. G. (2000). The Collaborative Longitudinal Personality Disorders Study: Reliability of axis I and II diagnoses. *Journal of Personality Disorders, 14,* 291–299.

Zhong, C.-B., & Liljenquist, K. (2006). Washing away your sins: Threatened morality and physical cleansing. *Science, 313,* 1451–1452.

Zhou, X., Dere, J., Zhu, X., Yao, S., Chentsova-Dutton, Y. E., & Ryder, A. J. (2011). Anxiety symptom presentations in Han Chinese and Euro-Canadian outpatients: Is distress always somatized in China? *Journal of Affective Disorders, 135,* 111–114.

Zhu, A. J., & Walsh, B. T. (2002). Pharmacologic treatment of eating disorders. *Canadian Journal of Psychiatry, 47,* 227–234.

Ziegler, J. C., Pech-Georgel, C., Dufau, S., & Grainger, J. (2010). Rapid processing of letters, digits and symbols: What purely visual-attentional deficit in developmental dyslexia? *Developmental Science, 13,* F8–F14.

Zilberman, M., Tavares, H., & el-Guebaly, N. (2003). Gender similarities and differences: The prevalence and course of alcohol- and other substance-related disorders. *Journal of Addictive Diseases, 22,* 61–74.

Zimmerman, B. J., & Schunk, D. H. (2002). Albert Bandura: The man and his contributions to educational psychology. In B. J. Zimmerman & H. Schunk (Eds.), *Educational psychology: A century of contributions* (pp. 431–459). Mahwah, NJ: Erlbaum.

Zimmerman, M., Martinez, J., Young, D., Chelminski, I., Morgan, T. A., & Dalrymple, K. (2014). Comorbid bipolar disorder and borderline personality disorder and history of suicide attempts. *Journal of Personality Disorders, 28,* 358–364.

Zimmerman, M., Rees, C., Posick, C., & Zimmerman, L. A. (2016). The power of (mis)perception: Rethinking suicide contagion in youth friendship networks. *Social Science & Medicine, 157,* 31–38.

Zimmerman, M., Rothschild, L., & Chelminski, I. (2005). The prevalence of DSM-IV personality disorders in psychiatric outpatients. *American Journal of Psychiatry, 162,* 1911–1918.

Zotter, D. L., & Crowther, J. H. (1991). The role of cognitions in bulimia nervosa. *Cognitive Therapy & Research, 15,* 413–426.

Zubin, J., & Spring, B. (1977). Vulnerability—A new view of schizophrenia. *Journal of Abnormal Psychology, 86,* 103–126.

Zucker, K. J. (2005). Gender identity disorder in children and adolescents. *Annual Review of Clinical Psychology, 1,* 467–492.

Zucker, K. J., Lawrence, A. A., & Kreukels, B. P. C. (2016). Gender dysphoria in adults. *Annual Review of Clinical Psychology, 12,* 217–247.

Zuckerman, M. (1980). Sensation seeking. In H. London & J. Exner, Jr. (Eds.), *Dimensions of personality.* New York: Wiley.

Zwan, M. D., Bouwman, F. H., Konijnenberg, E., Van der Flier, W. M., Lammertsma, A. A., Verhey, F. R. J., . . . Schelten, P. (2017). Diagnostic impact of [18F]flutemetamol PET in early-onset dementia. *Alzheimer's Research & Therapy, 9,* 2.

Zweig-Frank, H., & Paris, J. (1991). Parents' emotional neglect and overprotection according to the recollections of patients with borderline personality disorder. *American Journal of Psychiatry, 148,* 648–651.

Burke, A., 179
Burke, J. D., 413
Burke, R. S., 275
Burkhardt, J., 407
Burlina, A., 401
Burns, D. D., 77n, 159
Buros, J., 427
Burt, S. A., 238
Busch, A. M., 168
Buschkuehl, M., 175
Bush, G., 410
Bushnik, T., 294
Butcher, J. N., 47
Butler, M., 419
Butryn, M. L., 300
Butt, J. C., 334
Buysse, D. J., 314
Byrne, S. M., 305

C

Cadrin, C., 401
Caffier, P. P., 311
Cahn, W., 364, 375
Cairney, J., 154
Calabrese, J. R., 173
Calamari, J. E., 123
Calati, R., 237
Calhoun, K. S., 334, 341
Calhoun, P. S., 47
Callaway, H., 69
Callicott, J. H., 368
Callinan, P. A., 19
Camara, W. J., 50
Cameron, J., 299
Campbell, L. A., 61
Camper, P., 179
Campi, S., 177
Campion, D., 427
Campling, S., 329
Campos, J. A., 304
Campos-Rodriguez, F., 311
Canadian Centre for Justice
   Statistics, 90, 328
Canadian Centre on Substance
   Abuse (CCSA), 250, 281
Canadian Collaboration for
   Immigrant and Refugee Health
   (CCIRH), 119
Canadian Institute for Health
   Information (CIHI), 59, 392
Canadian Lung Association, 315
Canadian Mental Health Associa-
   tion (CMHA), 12, 37, 386,
   430, 445
Canadian Press, 118n
Canadian Psychological Associa-
   tion (CPA), 65, 89, 435, 445
Canales-Rodriguez, E. J., 382
Candy, C., 136
Canfield, M. L., 50
Canino, G. J., 175
Canli, T., 238
CANMAT Depression Work
   Group, 67
Cannon, T. D., 364, 378
Cantor-Graae, E., 376
Cantu, R., 178
Cao, L., 302
Caplan, R., 396
Capps, L., 395
Cardeña, E., 117, 198
Cardish, R. J., 242
Carey, G., 238
Carey, M. P., 348

Cargo, M., 177
Carlson, E., 117
Carmichael, K. L. C., 227
Carnes, P. J., 329
Carney, C. E., 169, 316
Carpenter, S., 309
Carr, J. L., 339
Carrasquillo, M., 427
Carrillo, M. C., 425
Carrizo, S. J., 311
Carson, A., 202
Carson, R. C., 161
Carter, A. G., 397
Carter, J. C., 300, 305
Carter, J. R., 375–376
Cartwright, J. L., 270
Casadonte, P., 281
Casañas i Comabella, C., 177
Case, M., 383
Casey, D. E., 382
Casey, K. F., 20
Cashman, L., 329
Caspi, A., 127, 156, 165, 238–239,
   272, 376
Cassano, G. B., 174
Cassem, N. H., 424
Castellanos, F. X., 396, 410
Castellvi, P., 420
Castro-Fornieles, J., 374
Catalan-Serra, P., 311
Catania, C., 427
Cavalcanti, M., 6
Cechnicki, A., 379
Celik, S., 345
Celis, W., 339
Cella, M., 365
Cellini, E., 301
Centeno, S., 335
Centre for Addiction and Mental
   Health, 250
Centre for Addictions Research,
   BC, 256
Cernovsky, Z., 258
Chabernaud, C., 396
Chachamovich, E., 177
Chagnon, F., 177
Chaimowitz, G., 89
Chait, A., 415
Chalke, F. C. R., 12
Challen, P., 334
Chambers, C., 261
Chambers, L. W., 425
Chambless, D. J., 241
Chambless, D. L., 227
Chan, R., 368
Chan, S. M., 419
Chand, P. K., 198
Chandrashekar, C. R., 208
Chang, L., 271
Chang, Z., 410
Channabasavanna, S. M., 239
Chanoine, V., 407
Chant, D., 361
Charney, D. S., 164
Charter, A., 7, 81
Chartier, I. S., 168
Chelminski, I., 221, 222
Chemerinski, E., 216
Chen, J., 62, 351, 353
Chen, L., 272
Chen, Y. Y., 309
Cheng, C., 315
Cheng, S. T., 208
Chentsova-Dutton, Y. E., 6
Cheung, A., 154

Cheung, A. H., 419
Cheung, C., 397
Cheung, F. M., 56
Chilcoat, H. D., 274
Chiles, J. A., 179
Chiu, W. T., 106
Chivers, M., 335
Chodirker, B. N., 401
Choi, S.-H., 423
Chokka, P., 104, 117
Chopra, V., 316
Choquette, K. A., 284
Chorpita, B. F., 419
Chou, C., 254
Chou, P., 217
Chou, S. P., 287
Chow, C. K., 267
Chow, E. W. C., 372
Chowdhury, A. N., 208
Choy, Y., 62
Christ, M. A., 414
Christensen, H., 419
Christiansen, B. A., 275
Chung, J. Y., 170
Chung, S. A., 311
Chung, T.-S., 285, 423
Ciccarelli, S. K., 399t
Ciesla, J., 161
Ciszewski, A., 120
Claes, L., 239
Clark, D. A., 113, 114, 123, 124,
   135, 136, 162
Clark, D. M., 124
Clark, L. A., 229, 231
Clark, W., 283
Clausen, M., 272
Clay, R. A., 59
Cleary, M., 401
Clinton, A. M., 260
Cloos, J.-M., 131
Coan, J. A., 223
Coatsworth-Puspoky, R., 33
Cockerham, W. C., 277
Cohen, B., 33
Cohen, F. L., 310
Cohen, H., 272
Cohen, N. L., 67
Cohen, R., 300
Cohen, S., 309
Cohen-Kettenis, P. T., 325, 327
Coid, J., 88
Coifman, K. G., 222
Colapinto, J., 326
Colby, S. M., 274, 285
Cole, D. A., 161, 418
Cole, T. B., 338
Coleman, E., 327
Collerton, D., 366
Collishaw, S., 418
Colman, I., 155, 156, 175
Colpe, L., 148
Colton, P. A., 304
Coluccia, A., 334
Colvin, P. J., 281
Combs, D., 368
Combs, J. L., 338
Committee on Sexual Offences
   Against Children and Youth,
   338
Compas, B. E., 305
Compton, W. M., 151
Condron, L., 254
Congdon, E., 238
Conner, B. T., 413
Connett, J. E., 287

Connolly Gibbons, M. B., 84
Conron, K., 287
Conte, M. L., 316
Conway, K. P., 151
Coolidge, F. L., 229
Cools, A. R., 368
Cooney, N. L., 285
Coons, M. J., 207
Coons, P. M., 199
Cooper, P. J., 304
Cooper, S. E., 346
Cooper, Z., 294, 304, 305
Copeland, J., 270
Coplan, J. D., 127, 128
Corbett, A., 428
Corbett, J., 272
Corbin, J., 345
Corbin, W. R., 274
Cornblatt, B. A., 368
Corona, G., 342
Corr, P. J., 238, 239
Correa, J. A., 222
Correa, J. B., 275
Correctional Services Canada,
   337n
Correll, C. U., 415
Corsi, D. J., 267
Corsini-Munt, S., 353
Corte, C., 149, 150
Cortese, S., 396
Cortoni, F. A., 333
Coryell, W., 127
Cossette, L., 405
Cossrow, N., 307
Costa, P. T., 231
Costello, E. J., 151, 413, 418
Cotton, A. J., 119
Cottraux, J., 134
Coursey, R. D., 374
Coutant, J., 427
Cox, B. J., 109, 121, 124, 149,
   156, 274
Coyle, J. R., 368
Coyne, J. C., 158
Craig, I. W., 238–239
Craske, M. G., 108
Crawley, J. N., 260
Crean, R., 270
Creighton, C. D., 340
Creighton, G., 177
Crespo-Facorro, B., 382
Crits-Christoph, P., 84
Cronin, P., 398
Crosby, R. D., 300, 302, 307
Cross-National Collaborative
   Group, 151
Crow, S. J., 305, 307
Crowell, S. E., 223
Crowther, J. H., 300
Crowther, R., 315
Crozier, J. C., 414
Crozier, W. R., 110, 112
Cruysberg, J. R., 365
Crystal, S., 415
CTS Sleep Disordered Breathing
   Committee, 310
Cuijpers, P., 6, 84, 170, 175,
   419
Cullumbine, H., 263
Culverhouse, R., 272
Cummings, E. M., 302
Cummings, J. L., 425
Cummings, T. J., 424
Cunningham, C., 412
Cunningham, C. E., 414

Cunningham, J. A., 287
Curran, N., 353
Curran-Celentano, J., 296, 304
Currie, S., 146, 156
Currie, S. R., 146, 260, 279
Cutter, C. J., 81
Cutter, H. S. G., 284
Cuvo, A. J., 404
Czajkowski, N. O., 164
Czepezauer, I., 407

D

Dabholkar, D., 401
Daeppen, J.-B., 254
Dahl, A., 240
Dahl, R. E., 312, 313, 315
Dahmen, N., 221
Daiuto, A. D., 352
Daleiden, E. L., 419
Dalenberg, C. J., 198
Daley, M., 308
Dallaire, D., 161
Dalman, C., 372
Dalrymple, K., 222
D'Amico, E. J., 285
Dancu, C. V., 61
Daneman, D., 304
Danesh, J., 217
Danko, G. P., 254
D'Arcy, C., 301
Dare, C., 304
Daren, A., 379
Darrow, C., 329
Das, S., 332
da Silva, W. R., 304
Daskalakis, Z. J., 69, 174
David, A. S., 199
Davidson, M., 373
Davidson, S., 176
Davies, B. A., 294, 302
Davies, G. A. L., 401
Davies, M., 339
Davies, M. F., 30
Davies, P. T., 302
Davila, J., 158
Davis, D., 199, 200
Davis, D. D., 77, 241
Davis, J. O., 374
Davis, K. L., 217, 373, 411
Davis, M. C., 345, 352, 353
Davis, R., 305
Davis, S. R., 92, 345
Davis, T. L., 305
Dawe, S., 285
Dawson, D. A., 61, 105, 106, 287
Dawson, G., 396
Dawson, M., 403
Day, H. R., 423
Dean, D. D., 400
De Barros, V. V., 287
de Beurs, D. P., 84
de Bruin, N. M., 368
de Castella, A., 69
Decker, S. L., 51
De Clercq, B., 214
Decouflé, P., 402
DeCuypere, G., 327
Deen, M. L., 364
DeFina, L. F., 428
Deforce, D., 131
DeFries, J. C., 406
De Fruyt, F., 214
DeKeseredy, W. S., 338
De Koninck, J., 309

de Kort, P. L., 423
de la Cruz, E., 287
de la Cruz-Moron, I., 311
Delahanty, D. L., 119
Delaive, K., 311
Delaney, H. D., 286
de la Pena, D., 428
Delespaul, P., 374
de Ligt, J., 399
DeLisi, L. E., 370, 374
Dell'Osso, B., 131
Del Re, A. C., 84
De Luca, R. V., 334
DeMartini, K., 274
DeMeules, M., 327
Demmer, D. H., 414
Demming, B., 276, 276f
Demonet, J. F., 407
Denault, A.-S., 277–278
Deneault, P., 284
Deng, W., 368
Dennerstein, L., 342, 343
Denov, M. S., 332
Denys, D., 131
Department of Justice Canada, 93
de Queiroz, V., 174
Dere, J., 6
Déry, M., 413
Desautels, A., 313
Desco, M., 374
De Souza, I. C. W., 287
Desrochier, M., 120
De Strooper, B., 427
De Sutter, P., 343, 346, 348
Deter, H. C., 306
Detera-Wadleigh, S. D., 372
Devanand, D. P., 68, 428
de Vries, B. B. A., 399
de Vries, P., 399
Dewey, R., 10
de Zubicaray, G. I., 427
de Zwaan, M., 300, 301
Diamond, F. R., 395
Diamond, S., 395
Dias, J. C., 304
Dickens, B. M., 286
Dickerson, F. B., 384
Dienel, A., 173
Diener, M. J., 83
Dietz, L. J., 167
Difede, J., 136
Di Giannantonio, M., 421
DiLalla, D. L., 238
DiLalla, L. F., 238
Di Martino, A., 396
Dimidjian, S., 168
Dimitrovski, D., 418
Dimsdale, J. E., 311
Di Nardo, P. A., 61
Dinges, D. F., 309
Dingle, G., 256, 261f
Dinh, K. T., 275
di Padova, C., 257
Dishion, T. J., 277
Distel, M. A., 237
Dix, D. L., 11
Dmochowski, S., 300
Dobbs, D., 362, 373
Dobson, K. S., 76, 168, 169
Dodge, E., 304
Dodge, K. A., 237, 414
Dogan, Z., 425, 427
Dohrenwend, B. P., 118
Dolan, R., 43
Doll, B., 413

Doll, H. A., 294, 302, 305
Dome, P., 177
Donatucci, C., 345
Donker, T., 175
Donnellan, M. B., 238
Donovan, P., 161
Doob, A. N., 286
Dorahy, M. J., 198
Doran, N., 275
Doreleijers, T. A. H., 219
Douglas, H., 287
Downey, G., 222
Doyle, W. J., 309
Dozois, D. J. A., 49n, 76, 169–170
Draijer, N., 117
Drewnowski, A., 300
Drewry, W. F., 10
Drews, C. D., 402
Drexler, K. P. G., 274
Driessen, E., 83
Drislane, F. W., 407
Drummond, D. C., 285
Dryden, J., 13
Dryden, W., 30, 76, 78
Duan, T., 425
Dubovsky, S., 272
Ducci, F., 272
Duclos, E., 405
Duda, S., 421
Dufau, S., 407
Duffy, A., 154
Dugas, M. J., 124
Dulit, R. A., 222
Duman, R. S., 165
Dumortier, T., 428
Dundon, W. D., 287
Dunham, Y., 324
Dunn, G., 270
Dunner, D. L., 170, 171
Dupéré, V., 414
Durbin, A., 404
Durbin, J., 404
Durkheim, E., 178
Durwood, L., 327
Dussault, D., 123
Dutra, L. M., 267
Dvorak, J., 178
Dwork, A. J., 68
Dyce, J. A., 229
Dykens, E. M., 402
Dzokoto, V. A., 62, 208

E

Eardley, I., 345, 353
Earnst, K. S., 373
Easson, A., 421
Eaves, L., 303
Eberhardy, F., 394n
Ebert, D. D., 419
Ebesutani, C., 419
Ebstein, R. H., 239
Ebstein, R. P., 272
Eccles, A., 335
Eck, L. H., 268
Ecker, C., 396
Edenberg, H., 272
Edman, J. L., 6
Edwards, H. P., 65
Edwards, V., 153
Egeland, B., 444
Egger, M., 173
Ehmann, T. S., 61
Ehrenreich-May, J., 418

Ehrlich, S., 296
Ehud, K., 149
Eikeseth, S., 397
Eisen, S. A., 126, 126t
Eisler, I., 304
Ekstrom, R. D., 148
Elbe, D., 419
Elbert, T., 119
el-Guebaly, N., 22, 146, 156, 257, 260, 279
Elison, J. T., 396
Elkashef, A., 399
Elkin, A., 164
Elkin, I., 67
Ellason, J. W., 199
Ellenbroek, B. A., 368
Elliot, R., 75
Ellis, A., 30, 31, 76, 78
El-Meliegy, A., 345
Ely, T. D., 274
Emery, G., 31, 54, 159, 277
Emery, R. E., 426f
Emmelkamp, P. M. G., 411
Emmrys, C., 416
Emsley, R., 365
Emslie, G. J., 419
Emslie, G. L., 419
Engel, S. G., 300
Engelsmann, F. F., 61
Engle, B., 285
Enns, M. W., 148, 149, 156
Erard, R. E., 50
Ercan-Sencicek, A. G., 397
Erdberg, P., 50
Erder, M. H., 307
Erdleyi, M. H., 200
Erkanli, A., 151
Erlenmeyer-Kimling, L., 377, 378
Ernberg, G., 6
Erowid, E., 368
Eshler, B., 310
Esposito-Smythers, C., 176
Esses, J. A., 424
Esterberg, M., 373
Eubanks-Carter, C., 241
Euser, E. M., 333
Evans, N., 270
Everett, B., 41
Ewing, B. A., 285
Exner, J. E., 50
Eysenck, H. J., 238
Eysenck, M. W., 238

F

Faber, B., 372
Fagan, A. M., 428
Fagiolini, A., 334
Fairburn, C. G., 294, 302, 303, 304, 305
Fairchild, A. J., 302
Fairley, C. K., 342, 343
Falato, W. L., 329
Falkai, P., 69, 362
Fallon, B. A., 207
Fallon, W., 119
Fang, M., 385
Faraone, S. V., 410
Farber, B. A., 75
Farberow, N. L., 181
Farley, M., 119
Farmer, A., 164
Farmer, A. E., 371f
Farré, R., 311

Farrell, A. D., 278
Farrell, M., 256
Fathalli, G., 370
Fawcett, A. J., 405, 407
Fazel, S., 217
Fazio, F., 407
Fazzino, T., 81
Fearon, R. P., 195, 196
Fecteau, S., 285
Fedoroff, I. C., 124
Fedoroff, J. P., 313
Feinberg, A. P., 19
Feldman, H. S., 261
Feldman, J., 327
Feldman, M., 414, 415
Feltner, C., 281
Felton, J., 161
Feng, Y., 396
Ferguson, K., 310
Ferguson, M., 337
Fernandez, A., 281
Fernández-Aranda, F., 296, 301, 305
Fernández del Río, E., 228
Ferrand, C., 304
Ferrans, C. E., 310
Ferrarese, L., 272
Ferretti, F., 334
Few, L. R., 237
Fichner-Rathus, L., 338, 344n, 352n
Fichter, M. M., 302
Fiedorowicz, C., 407
Field, A. P., 121
Fiest, K. M., 151
Fiez, J. A., 50
Filali, M., 428
Finch, S. J., 236
Findlay, C., 242
Findlay, L., 416
Findling, R. L., 396
Fine, S., 337
Finke, B., 296
Finke, K., 410
Finkelhor, D., 332, 334
Finney, J. W., 284
Firestone, P., 49n
First, M. B., 203
First Nations Information
    Governance Centre, 258
Fischer, B., 253, 281
Fischman, M. W., 265
Fisher, L., 91
Fisher, M., 383, 411
Fisher, R. S., 206
Fittig, E., 296
Fitzgerald, J. R., 404
Fitzgerald, L. F., 341
Fitzgerald, P. B., 69, 174
Fitzpatrick, M., 310
Fitzpatrick, S., 223
Flament, M. F., 131, 294
Flanagan, E. H., 230
Flaskerud, J. H., 196
Fleetham, J., 310
Fleischhaker, W., 370
Fletcher, B. W., 287
Flett, G. L., 160
Floesser, A., 428
Florbetaben Phase 3
    Study Group, 426
Flores, C., 370
Florian, C., 309
Floyd, F. J., 284
Fluckiger, C., 84

Flynn, S., 376
Flynn, S. W., 61, 374
Foa, E. B., 117, 135, 136
Folke, F., 158
Folstein, M. F., 424
Folstein, S. E., 424
Foltin, R. W., 265
Fombonne, E., 394, 396
Fonagy, P., 62, 231
Fontaine, R. G., 414
Forcano, L., 296
Forchuk, C., 33
Forner, M., 311
Foroud, T., 272
Forsell, Y., 175
Forsman, M., 328
Forste, B. B., 220
Forth, A. E., 339
Fortier, I., 411
Foster, N. L., 426
Foubert, J. D., 340
Fountain, S., 174
Fountoulakis, K. N., 240
Fouquereau, E., 281
Fowler, J. S., 265
Fox, N. C., 428
Foxe, J. J., 396
Foxwell, A., 420
Frackowiak, R. S. J., 366
Frahm, S., 272
Frances, A. J., 62, 63, 222
Franchini, L., 171
Francis, D. J., 414
Frank, G. K. W., 303
Frank, J., 405
Frankenfield, G., 304
Franklin, M. E., 135, 136
Franks, R., 368
Frasquilho, F., 195, 196
Freedman, R., 368
Freeman, A., 77, 241
Freeman, C. P., 300
Freeman, D., 270
Fregni, F., 69
Frei, B., 148
Frenkel, E., 378
Freud, S., 23, 156, 178, 232
Frezza, M., 257
Friborg, O., 227
Fricchione, G. L., 424
Frick, P. J., 413, 414
Friedlander, L., 128
Friedman, E. S., 173
Frigge, M. L., 372
Frissa, S., 419
Frith, C. D., 366
Frith, U., 407
Fritzley, V. H., 399t
Frodl, T., 410
Froehlich, T., 411
Fromm-Reichmann, F., 378
Fruzzetti, A. E., 242, 306
Frye, M. A., 152
Fu, J., 411
Fu, S., 270
Fucito, L. M., 274
Fugl-Meyer, K. S., 342
Fukumoto, H., 426
Fulbright, R. K., 274
Fulero, S. M., 89
Fulkerson, J. A., 418
Fulton, J. J., 207
Fung, K. P., 83
Fursland, A., 305
Furst, J., 282

Furukawa, K., 426
Furukawa, T. A., 62
Furumoto, S., 426
Fydrich, T., 227
Fyer, A., 127
Fyer, M. R., 222

G

Gabbard, G. O., 62, 231
Gabbrielli, M., 334
Gabert-Quillen, C. A., 119
Gafni, A., 155
Gage, F. H., 20
Gagnon, J. H., 322
Gahm, G. A., 136
Galaburda, A. M., 407
Galambos, N. L., 155, 156, 175
Galea, S., 118
Gallagher, S. M., 400
Gallop, R., 84, 242
Gansera, L., 345
Gantchev, K., 296
Gao, A., 428
Garand, I., 249
Garb, H. N., 49, 50, 230
Garbutt, J. C., 281
Garcia-Alandete, J., 181
Gard, M. C., 300
Gardner, D. M., 131, 414, 415
Garfinkel, P. E., 296, 299, 304
Garland, A. J., 172, 413, 419
Garland, O. M., 413
Garner, D. M., 296
Garnet, B., 81
Garson, C., 165
Gasbarrini, G., 272
Gasperini, M., 171
Gattaz, W. F., 69
Gauld, M., 412
Gaupp, L., 285
Gauthier, J. G., 66
Gaviria, A. M., 222
Gawin, F. H., 265
Gaynes, B. N., 148
Gearhardt, A. N., 305
Geist, R., 305
Gelboin-Burkhart, C., 20
Géonet, M., 343, 346, 348
George, C., 310
George, M. S., 174
George, M. W., 302
George, R., 419
George, W. H., 285
Georges, J., 425
Gerber, A. J., 303
Gerhardt, G. A., 368, 410
Gerig, G., 396
Gerwig, K., 419
Gex-Fabry, M., 169
Gfellner, B. M., 258
Ghaderi, A., 304
Ghizzani, A., 345
Ghionoulakis, C., 281
Gibbs, N., 411, 412
Gi?ewska, M., 401
Gigante, R. A., 191
Gilbertson, M. W., 120
Gilchrist, P. T., 123
Gilissen, C., 399
Gilmor, M., 280
Gilmore, J., 287
Gilmour, H., 425
Gilston, J., 339

Ginestet, C., 396
Gingell, C., 342
Giovancarli, C., 285
Giuliano, F., 345, 351
Glancy, G. D., 89, 92
Glantz, S. A., 267
Glaser, P. E., 410
Glaskin, K., 5
Glass, G. V., 82
Glasser, D. B., 342
Glautier, S., 285
Gleaves, D. H., 193, 198
Glowa, J. R., 260
Gluud, C., 411
Gnam, W., 253, 281
Gnam, W. H., 242
Gnys, M., 286
Goate, A., 272, 428
Goering, P., 16
Goering, P. N., 16
Gohm, C. L., 338
Golbasi, Z., 345
Gold, J. M., 118, 375
Gold, J. R., 50
Gold, L. J., 236
Goldapple, K., 165
Goldberg, J., 126, 126t
Goldberg, T. E., 368
Golden, C. J., 51
Golden, R. N., 148
Goldfield, G. S., 294, 300
Goldfried, M. R., 79
Goldman, D., 272
Goldman, M. S., 275
Goldman, R. N., 75
Goldman-Rakic, P. S., 375
Goldner, E. M., 103
Goldsmith, L. L., 81
Goldstein, A. J., 241, 263
Goldstein, M. J., 380
Goldstein, R. B., 61, 105, 106, 217
Goleman, D., 225, 418
Gomar, J. J., 382
Gombart, A. F., 148
Gomes, H., 396
Gomide, H. P., 287
Gonçalves, S., 302
Gonda, X., 177
Gonder-Frederick, L. A., 316
Gonzales, D., 287
Gonzalez-Gadea, M. L., 410
González-Pinto, A., 374
Gooch, D., 407
Goodell, V., 270
Goodman, L. A., 341
Goodman, M., 217
Goodstadt, M., 13
Goodwill, A., 223
Goodwin, L., 419
Gordon, S. J., 177
Gorman, C. P., 172, 173
Gorman, D. A., 414, 415
Gorman, J., 127, 128
Gorwood, P., 237
Gotlib, I. H., 150, 175
Gottesman, I. I., 238, 371f, 377, 399
Gouttard, S., 396
Gower, M. W., 398
Grace, A. A., 373
Graf, A., 428
Graham, C. A., 353
Graham, J. R., 47
Grainger, J., 407

Granero, R., 296, 305
Granic, I., 239
Grann, M., 237
Granot, M., 344
Grant, A., 370
Grant, B. F., 61, 105, 106, 151, 217, 287
Gratz, K. L., 223
Gratzer, T. G., 91
Gray, J. A., 238
Gray, J. E., 90, 92
Gray, J. J., 300
Gray, J. R., 237, 239
Graziottin, A., 353
Green, B. A., 329
Green, P. A., 407
Greenbaum, P. E., 275
Greenberg, J., 157
Greenberg, L. S., 29, 75
Greenberg, R. M., 174
Greenberg, R. P., 228
Greene, K., 272
Greenhouse, J., 424
Green-Paden, L. D., 384
Greenspan, E. L., 92
Greenwald, S., 175
Greenwood, T. A., 164
Greeven, A., 207, 209
Gregg, L., 366
Gregoire, J. P., 308
Grekin, E. R., 237
Gressier, F., 237
Griez, E., 131
Griffin, J. D., 12
Griffin, S., 411
Griffiths, M., 254
Grigsby, J., 400
Grilo, C. M., 223, 230, 307
Grissett, N. I., 301
Grissom, G. R., 279
Gritsenko, I., 272
Grizenko, N., 416
Groleau, D., 83, 164
Grønbæk, M., 260
Gropalis, M., 207
Gross, A. M., 338
Gross, R. E., 274
Gross, S. R., 249
Grosscup, S. J., 157
Grossman, S., 298
Grover, S., 174
Gruber-Baldini, A. L., 423
Grubert, C., 174
Grunberg, N. E., 267
Gu, H., 386, 396
Gualtieri, G., 334
Guerreiro, R., 427
Guertin, T. L., 298
Guimond, T., 242
Gunderson, J. G., 43, 62, 221, 222, 223, 230, 231, 237, 241, 242
Gunewardene, R., 69
Gunn, W., 84
Guo, X., 385
Gupta, N., 174
Gurley, J. R., 205
Gutheil, T. G., 90
Gutiérrez-Zotes, J. A., 222
Guttman, H., 222
Guydish, J., 283
Guzder, J., 83, 119
Guze, S. B., 229
Gvirts, H. Z., 222

H

Haack, M. J., 131
Haaga, D. A., 305
Haas, B. W., 238
Habib, R., 131
Habif, V. L., 334
Haddock, G., 365
Hadley, D., 174
Hadrysiewicz, B., 174
Haggarty, J., 258
Haggarty, J. M., 177
Hahn, B., 375
Haider, I. I., 240
Halassa, M. M., 309
Halbreich, U., 148
Haley, J., 378, 379n
Hall, B. N., 363
Hall, G. C., 339, 340
Hall, T. M., 62
Hallé, M., 428
Halleguen, O., 337
Hallgren, M., 175
Halmi, K. A., 302
Hamer, R. H., 382
Hamer, R. M., 148
Hamid, F., 240
Hamid, S., 83
Hamilton, H. A., 144, 267, 392, 416
Hamilton, J., 84
Hamish, J. D., 414
Hammeke, T. A., 51
Hammen, C., 149, 155, 156, 444
Hammond, D. C., 345
Hammond, M., 415
Han, J., 425
Hancock, L., 412
Handen, B., 398
Haning, W., 271
Hanley, W. B., 401
Hanmer, J., 300
Hannequin, D., 427
Hanrahan, G. E., 382
Hansen, K. T., 374
Hansen, T. E., 382
Hanson, K., 414
Hansson, O., 428
Hanuszkiewicz, I., 379
Harada, R., 426
Harari, H., 222
Harding, M., 411
Hare, R. D., 220
Hariri, A. R., 127, 368
Härkänen, T., 151
Harkins, L., 337
Harkness, K. L., 147, 156
Harms, U., 69
Haro, J. M., 383
Haroutunian, V., 373
Harrell, P. T., 275
Harricharan, R., 386, 387
Harrigan, T. R., 399t
Harrington, H., 238–239
Harris, A. D., 423
Harris, G. T., 335
Harris, M. G., 146
Harris, S., 30
Harrow, M., 364
Hart, E. L., 413
Hart, M. A., 82
Hartikainen, A.-L., 272, 378
Hartz, S. M., 272
Harvey, A. G., 116
Harvey, D., 426
Hasin, D. S., 61, 105, 106, 421

Haskell, W. L., 428
Hasking, P., 220, 222
Haslam, N., 119
Hatzenbuehler, M. L., 61
Hatzimouratidis, K., 345
Haugen, E. C., 302
Haugh, J. A., 156
Haughton, E., 370
Havercamp, S. M., 404
Haw, C., 177
Hawke, J. L., 406
Hawkrigg, J. J., 104n
Hawton, K., 177
Hayden, J. A., 270
Haydon, P. G., 309
Hayes, R. D., 342, 343
Hayiou-Thomas, E., 407
Haynos, A. F., 306
Hayward, C., 300, 301
Hazlett, E. A., 217
He, H., 6
Health Canada, 7, 13, 150, 151, 172, 249, 250, 250t, 256, 258, 259, 260, 265, 267, 281, 314, 361, 362, 402, 412, 445
Healy, A., 401
Healy, D., 280
Heath, A. C., 126t, 237, 303
Heather, N., 285, 286
Heaton, P., 403
Hebb, D. O., 30
Heffelfinger, S. K., 123
Hehir-Kwa, J. Y., 399
Heidkamp, D., 373, 374
Heilbronner, R. L., 47
Heilbronner, U., 362
Heiman, J. R., 352
Heine, S. J., 6
Heinmaa, M., 305
Heinrichs, R. W., 372, 374
Heinz, A. J., 281
Hellstrom, W. J. G., 344
Hempel, S., 173
Hen, R., 126, 127
Hendershot, C. S., 285
Henderson, J., 392
Henderson, K., 294
Henderson, S., 281
Henderson, W. G., 126, 126t
Henein, M., 92
Henin, A., 418
Hennig, J., 237, 239
Hennig-Fast, K., 410
Henningsen, K. H., 84
Henriksen, T. B., 296
Hepner, K. A., 287
Herman, B. K., 307
Herman, C. P., 299
Herman, L. I., 327
Hermann, C. A., 333
Hernandez, A., 222
Hernandez, E., 193
Herold, E. S., 338, 344n, 352n
Heron, K. E., 307
Herpertz, S. C., 237
Herrmann, N., 68
Herrup, K., 427
Hersen, M., 443, 443f
Herukka, S.-K., 427
Herz, J., 427
Herzog, W., 306
Heslegrave, R., 221
Hesse, M., 218
Hester, R. K., 283
Hewitt, P. L., 160

Hickcox, M., 286
Hickey, A., 149
Hidaka, B. H., 151
Hidaka, H., 426
Higgo, R., 33
Hilker, I., 305
Hiller, W., 207
Himelhoch, S. S., 423
Hinshaw, S. P., 411
Hinton, D. E., 6, 62
Hiripi, E., 294
Hirshfeld-Becker, D. R., 418
Hjern, A., 372
Ho, M.-H. R., 124
Hoch, J., 221
Hodapp, R. M., 402
Hodgins, D., 286
Hoefnagels, W. H., 365
Hoek, H. W., 306, 364
Hoffman, B., 300
Hoffman, W. F., 382
Hofmann, S. G., 6, 62, 123
Hogan, M. E., 161, 164
Hogarty, G. E., 383
Holbrook, A. M., 315
Holland, A. J., 303
Holland, R., 416
Hollander, E., 131
Hollingworth, A., 375
Hollins, S., 261
Hollon, S. D., 54, 161, 162, 168, 169, 170, 175
Holloway, K. M., 136
Holmes, E. A., 195, 196
Holmskov, M., 411
Holohan, K., 427
Holroyd-Leduc, J., 423
Holz, B., 236
Holze, S., 345
Hölzl, M., 311
Hone-Blanchet, A., 285
Honer, W. G., 61, 376
Hong, D., 398
Hong, K. A., 274
Hongpaisan, J., 427
Hong-Wu, X., 411
Hooker, C. I., 383
Hooley, J. M., 361, 362, 379, 380, 384
Hooley, M., 414
Hopkins, I. M., 398
Hopkins, T. A., 329
Hopko, D. R., 158, 171
Hops, H., 168
Hopwood, C. J., 238
Hoste, R. R., 473
Hotaling, G., 332, 334
Hotopf, M., 419
Hottenga, J.-J., 237
Hough, M. J., 287
Houston, D. A., 332, 333
Howard, C. E., 307
Howard, R., 428
Howard, S., 13
Howes, O. D., 373
Howes, S., 256
Howieson, D. B., 194
Hoyer, J., 331
Hsu, L., 103
Hsu, S. H., 287
Hu, M., 421
Hua, J. M., 392
Hua, X., 396
Huang, B., 61, 105, 106
Huang, L., 299

Huang, W., 404
Hubbard, E. M., 330
Hubbard, R. L., 287
Huber, K. M., 400
Hucker, S. J., 334
Hudac, C. M., 397
Hudon, T., 416, 419
Hudson, C. G., 33
Hudson, J. I., 191, 294, 307
Hudson, S. M., 338, 339
Hudziak, J. J., 229
Huffman, J. C., 209
Hughes, A. E., 223
Hughes, C. W., 419
Huh, T. J. W., 176
Huibers, M. J. H., 84
Hulme, C., 407
Hulshoff Pol, H., 375
Hultquist, C. M., 268
Humphrey, L. L., 302
Humphreys, K., 282
Hundelby, J. D., 258
Hunter, E. C. M., 195, 196, 199
Hunter, S. B., 285, 287
Huntsman, S., 69
Hur, Y.-M., 312
Hurd, H. M., 10
Hurlemann, R., 174
Hus, V., 397
Hussain, M. R., 311
Hutchinson, E. R., 68
Huynh, T. N., 397
Hwu, H.-G., 175
Hyötyläinen, T., 427

I

Iacono, W. G., 238
Iacovides, A., 240
Ibanez, A., 410
Ibañez-Tallon, I., 272
Ibay, A. M. D., 148
IBIS, 396
Iglesias, H., 191
Ilgen, M. A., 282
Iliadou, A., 222
Imbert, G., 428
Imel, Z. E., 171
Infurna, M. R., 236
Ingraham, L. J., 372, 378
Innamorati, M., 421
Inouye, S. K., 423
Ioannidou, C., 240
Irfan, M., 240
Isaac, M., 198
IsHak, W. W., 345, 352, 353
Ishigami, N., 426
Ishiki, A., 426
Isohanni, M., 272, 378
Israël, M., 20
Ivers, H., 309
Iverson, K. M., 242
Iwata, N., 272

J

Jabeen, Q., 280
Jablensky, A., 6, 376
Jackson, D. N., 237
Jackson, H. J., 329
Jackson, J., 334
Jacobi, C., 300, 301
Jacobs, P., 400
Jacobsen, B., 372, 378
Jacobsen, F. M., 148

Jacobson, N. S., 168
Jacquez, F., 161
Jadad, A. R., 412
Jaeggi, S. M., 175
Jagiellowicz, J., 413
Jagust, W. J., 426
Jahanshad, N., 427
Jahr, E., 397
Jairam, S., 311
Jakob, A., 311
Janca, A., 207
Janeck, A. S., 123
Jang, K. L., 123, 124, 126, 164,
    205, 237, 238, 272
Janicki-Deverts, D., 309
Jannini, E., 351, 353
Jansen, B. P., 423
Janssen, I., 399
Jansson, L., 372
Januszkowski, T., 83
Japuntich, S. J., 280
Jardri, R., 237
Järvelin, M.-R., 272
Jarvis, E., 83
Jarvis, G. E., 83
Javelot, H., 337
Jeffery, R. W., 73
Jeffrey, J. K., 345, 352, 353
Jelic, S., 311
Jellinek, E. M., 259
Jenkins, J. H., 380
Jenkins, P. E., 473
Jenkins, R., 256
Jenner, J. A., 385
Jensen, P. S., 415
Jeppesen, P., 386
Jepson, C., 280
Jermann, F., 169
Jetté, J., 375–376
Jiang, W., 220
Jiang, X. L., 309
Jilek, W. G., 294
Jiménez-Murcia, S., 296, 305
Jin, R., 106
Joe, G. W., 287
Joffe, R. T., 47, 131, 303
Johansson, A., 328
Johns, L. C., 366
Johnson, A. K., 239
Johnson, B. R., 13
Johnson, C., 398
Johnson, P. A., 6, 13, 13f
Johnson, R. C., 6
Johnson, S. L., 153, 154, 156,
    165, 173, 177
Johnson, V. E., 349
Johnson, W. G., 304
Johnston, K., 178
Johnston, M., 270
Johnston, P., 396
Joiner, T. E., Jr., 158, 177, 179,
    181
Jolic, D., 374
Jonas, D. E., 281
Jones, A. C., 340
Jones, E., 15
Jones, H. E., 261
Jones, J. M., 294, 300, 304
Jones, K. L., 261
Jones, P. B., 378
Jones, R., 305
Jonides, J., 175
Jonsdottir, I., 427
Jonsson, P. V., 427
Jonsson, T., 427

Joober, R., 20, 336, 370
Joormann, J., 150
Jordan, C. E., 338
Jorm, A. F., 146
Joshi, R. M., 407
Jou, J., 20
Jourden, F., 312
Jouriles, E. N., 414
Joyce, P. R., 175
Jun, G., 427
Jun, H. L., 124
Jung, J., 217
Jung, Y. C., 423

K

Kaakinen, M., 272
Kaback, M., 401
Kaess, M., 236
Kahan, B., 13
Kahn, R. S., 375, 376, 411
Kahn, S., 258
Kaiser, M. D., 397
Kaiser, S. T., 227, 375
Kaldo, V., 175
Kaleva, M., 377
Kambeitz, J., 373
Kamio, Y., 396
Kampman, K. M., 281
Kandel, D. B., 270
Kandil, S., 416, 418, 419
Kane, J. M., 373, 377, 382
Kanne, S. M., 397
Kanner, L., 394
Kanter, J. W., 158, 168
Kao, K., 261
Kaplan, A. S., 300, 302, 303,
    304, 305
Kaplan, B., 407
Kaplan, L., 233
Kaplan, S. J., 415n
Kappelle, L. J., 423
Kaprinis, G., 240
Kaprio, J., 306
Kapur, S., 373, 383
Karakula, H., 364
Karamanolaki, H., 222
Karkun, S., 148
Karlsson, P., 397
Karno, M., 380
Karpiak, C. P., 79
Karran, E., 427
Kartub, P., 348
Karyotaki, E., 84
Kasai, K., 120
Kasai, T., 426
Kasari, C., 395
Kasiel, J. D., 286
Katon, W. J., 137
Katzman, D. K., 305
Katzman, M. A., 104, 117, 173
Kaufmann, V., 280
Kavanagh, D. J., 287
Kaye, W. H., 299, 302
Kayser, S., 174
Kazdin, A. E., 52, 235, 237, 415,
    419, 443
Kealey, K. A., 275
Kealy, D., 223
Keane, T. M., 117
Kearins, J. M., 45
Keefe, F. J., 305
Keel, P. K., 305
Keilp, J. G., 368
Keita, G. P., 341

Keith, S. J., 362
Kelleci, M., 345
Kellner, C. H., 174
Kelly, A. M., 280
Kelly, C. M., 146, 396
Kelly, J. F., 272
Kelly, M. T., 177
Kelsoe, J. R., 164
Kemp, J., 176
Kempton, M. J., 374
Kendall, P. C., 54
Kendall, T., 172
Kendler, K. S., 126, 127,
    155, 157, 164, 237, 272,
    273, 303, 371, 372, 377,
    414, 440
Kennard, B. D., 419, 420
Kennedy, S. H., 67, 165, 172,
    173, 175
Kent, A., 302
Kent, J. M., 127, 128
Keo-Meier, C. L., 327
Keon, W. J., 12, 13, 16, 41
Keough, M. E., 137
Kepa, A., 419
Kermeen, P., 258
Kernberg, O., 62, 231
Kernberg, O. F., 233
Kerr, D. C. R., 148
Kerr, S. L., 367
Kershaw, M. M., 404
Kershner, R., 340
Keshavan, M. S., 374
Keski-Rahkonen, A., 306
Kesner, P., 425
Kessler, R. C., 106, 294, 303
Ketelaars, C., 397
Ketter, T., 173
Kety, S. S., 372
Keyes, K., 61
Keys, D. J., 61
Keysers, C., 397
Khan. S. A., 410
Khatami, R., 310
Khatri, N., 169
Khoury, J. E., 223
Khoury, S., 345, 351
Kiehl, K. A., 220
Kielland, N., 7
Kieser, M., 173
Kihlstrom, J. K., 191, 193, 194,
    197, 198, 199
Killackey, E., 386, 387
Kilpatrick, D., 118
Kilts, C. D., 274
Kim, E., 373
Kim, J.-J., 423
Kim, S. I., 423, 427
Kimerling, R., 341
King, D., 315
King, J., 411
King, R., 342
King, S., 373, 374
Kingston, D. A., 339
Kinney, D. K., 372
Kinon, B. J., 382, 383
Kinoshita, Y., 62
Kippin, T. E., 335
Kirby, M. J. L., 12, 13, 16, 41
Kirisci, L., 275
Kirmayer, L. J., 61, 82, 83,
    119, 150, 164, 177, 203,
    204, 205
Kirsch, P., 237, 239
Kirsten, H., 407

SUBJECT INDEX

cognitive-behaviour treatments, 76
for antisocial and aggressive behaviours, 415
for attention-deficit/hyperactivity disorder (ADHD), 413
for binge-eating disorder (BED), 307
cognitive-behavioural therapy (CBT), 78–79
cognitive therapy, 77–78
for dissociative disorders, 198
for generalized anxiety disorder (GAD), 137
panic disorders and, 128
problem-solving therapy, 237
rational-emotive behaviour therapy (REBT), 76, 78
cognitive-behavioural modification (CBM), 32
cognitive-behavioural perspectives, 30–32
ABC approach, 30
applicability of, 33
on autism spectrum disorder (ASD), 396
core irrational beliefs, 30
evaluation of, 32–33
on personality disorders, 236
cognitive-behavioural therapy (CBT), 31, 32, 78–79
for bulimia nervosa, 305
for children and adolescents with depression, 419
coping-skills model of, 419
for dissociative disorders, 198–199
for insomnia, 316
for panic disorder, 137, 137t
with social skills training (SST) for schizophrenia, 384–385
for somatic symptom and related disorders, 208
cognitive distortions, 32–33, 159, 161
all-or-nothing thinking, 159–160
alternative responses to, 169, 170t
disqualifying the positive, 160
emotional reasoning, 160
jumping to conclusions, 160
labelling and mislabelling, 160–161
magnification (catastrophizing), 160
mental filter, 160, 161
minimization, 160
overgeneralization, 160
personalization, 161
should statements, 160
cognitive errors, 31, 31t
cognitive impairment, 426
cognitive psychology, 25
cognitive restructuring, 134
cognitive schemas, 159
cognitive therapy, 77, 134
for major depressive disorder (major depression), 169
for mood disorders, 169
for persistent depressive disorder (dysthymia), 170
cognitive triad of depression, 159, 159t, 161
Columbia University, 303

Columbine High School massacre (1999), 118
communication deviance, 379
expressed emotion (EE) and, 379–381, 380f
high-EE families and, 381, 380f
low-EE families and, 381, 380f
communication disorders, 393
competency to stand trial, 93
criteria for, 93
compulsion, 113–114
learning theories on, 122
computer technology,
computer-assisted therapy, 81
interactive program for autism spectrum disorder (ASD), 397
online information, 445
computer-assisted therapy, 81, 136
cognitive-behavioural for insomnia, 316
computerized tomography (CT scan), 50, 57t, 373
concordance (rates of), 440
Concordia University, Montreal, 123, 124, 137
shootings (1992), 118
Concordia University College of Alberta, 229
conditioned response (CR), 26, 27f
phobias and, 121
conditioned stimulus (CS), 26, 27f
conditioning model of cravings, 274–275
conduct disorder (CD), 393t, 412–413
aggressive parenting factor in, 414
causal factors in, 414
compared to attention-deficit/hyperactivity disorder (ADHD), 412–413
compared to oppositional defiant disorder (ODD), 413
family and parenting factors in, 414
genetic factors in, 414
prevalence in childhood and adolescence, 392
prevalence of, 412–413
treatments for, 414–416
confidentiality, 435, 436
conscious, 23
control subjects, 438
controlled social drinking, 286
conversion disorder (functional neurological symptom disorder), 15, 187, 201–202, 205, 206, 207
diagnostic criteria for, 201–202, 201t
histrionic personality disorder and, 223
learning theories of, 206
psychodynamic theories of, 206
Coons, P. M., 199
Coping with Depression (CWD) Course, 168
coprophilia, 335
correlation, 436
correlational research, 436–437
longitudinal study type of, 437
prediction objective of, 436

Corte, C., 149, 150
countertransference, 71
crack cocaine, 264–265
craving-for-stimulus model, 219–220
criminality, 218
antisocial personality disorder (APD) and, 218–219
psychopathy and, 218–219
critical thinking, 443–445
about abnormal psychology, 444–445
assumptions weighing feature of, 444
correlation not causation feature of, 444
evidence consideration feature of, 444
features of, 444
no overgeneralization feature of, 445
no oversimplification feature of, 445
online information and, 445
skeptical attitude feature of, 444
skills, 444
term definitions feature of, 444
cross-fostering study (of schizophrenia), 372
Cruise, Tom, 403, 405
cue-exposure training, 285
Cullen, William, 103
cultural consultation services (CCS) model, 83
cultural differences, 6
mental health care and, 83
specific phobias and, 110
cultural-familial intellectual disorder, 402
culture-bound disorders, 62
Dhat syndrome, 208
DSM system and, 64
Koro syndrome, 208
cyclic vomiting syndrome (abdominal migraine), 306
cyclothymic disorder, 143, 141t, 154
hypomanic episodes, 154
cytomegalovirus, 401

D

d'Aiguillon, Duchesse, 10
Daily Record of Dysfunctional Thoughts, 54
Dalhousie University, 304
Dallaire, André, 91
Dallaire, Roméo, 118
da Vinci, Leonardo, 441
Dawson College, Montreal, shootings (2006), 118
de Sade, Marquis, 334
debriefed, 436
deep brain stimulation (DBS), 69, 174
defence mechanisms, 24–25, 24t, 25
denial, 24t
displacement, 24t
projection, 24t
rationalization, 24t
reaction formation, 24t
regression, 24t, 25

repression, 24, 24t
sublimation, 24t
deinstitutionalization, 12
results of, 11–12
DeKeseredy, W. S., 338
delayed ejaculation, 343
delirium, 251, 392, 422–424. *See also* schizophrenia
dementia disorder, 392
diagnostic criteria for, 423t
diagnostic tools for, 423–424
features of, 424t
neuroleptics (antipsychosis drugs) for, 424
outcomes, 424
treatments for, 424
Delirium Rating Scale (DRS), 424
delirium tremens ("the DTs"), 251
delta-9-tetrahydrocannabinol, 269
delusions, 4, 113, 362, 363
dementia praecox, 14
dementia, 424, 425–428
acetycholine (Ach) neurotransmitter and, 425
Alzheimer's disease as cause of, 426
amyloid plaques in, 425
brain abnormalities characteristic of, 425
brain inflammation in, 425
causes of, 425–426
diagnosis of, 425–426
features of, 424t
memory loss with, 425
neurofibrillary tangles in, 425
neuropathy, 425
progressive symptoms of, 425
screening tools for, 426
spinal fluid cause of, 426
Demming, B., 276
demonological model (of abnormal behaviour), 8, 9, 14, 15
dendrites, 20, 21f
denial (defence mechanism), 24t
deoxyribonucleic acid (DNA), 18
analysis for gene mutations, 401
sequence, 20
dependent personality disorder, 227–228
characteristics of, 227
gender and, 227–228
linkage to other disorders, 227
dependent variable, 437, 437t
depersonalization, 194–196
depersonalization/derealization disorder, 195
diagnostic criteria for, 196t
depressants (drugs), 256–264
barbiturates, 262–263
depression, 3, 4, 22
in adolescence, 416
adolescent girls and, 419
antidepressants for, 67–68
biochemical factors in, 164–165
brain abnormalities in, 164–165
in childhood, 416
common features of, 144, 144t
deep brain stimulation (DBS) for, 174–175

major depressive disorder
(*Continued*)
   prevalence of, 146
   risk factors for, 149–151
   seasonal affective disorder
    (SAD), 147
   with seasonal pattern, 147–148
   stress and, 155–156
major depressive episode (MDE),
   145*t*
male erectile disorder (erectile
   dysfunction), 349
   biological perspectives on, 345
   testosterone and, 345
Maletzky, B. M., 336
malingering, 194, 204
Malleus Maleficarum ("The
   Witches' Hammer"), 9
Mangaia peoples,
   sexual behaviour of, 322
manic, 144
manic-depressive psychosis, 14
manic episodes, 152–153
   characteristics of, 153
   diagnostic criteria for, 152*t*
   self-esteem in, 153
marijuana (cannabis), 249, 268,
   269–270
   dependence, 269
   schizophrenia and, 376
   withdrawal, 270
marital therapy, 79–80
Marlatt, G. A., 276
Marsh, Rachel, 303
Marshall, William L., 338
Masters, William, 349, 350, 351
McCord, J., 236
McCord, W., 236
McGill University, 12, 30, 61, 83,
   177, 178, 223, 249, 303, 382
McMain, Shelley, 242
McMaster University, 111, 314,
   412, 414
Mead, Margaret, 4
medical model perspective, 2,
   14–15
   classification system for diag-
    nosis, 14–15
Mednick, Sarnoff, 377
Meehl, Paul, 375
Meichenbaum, Donald, 32, 76,
   79, 175
melancholia, 9
Mellor, C. S., 363
memory loss, 425
menarche, 295
mental age (MA), 44
mental disorders. *See* psychological (mental) disorders
mental health care
   community system of, 12, 16
   cultural diversity and, 83
   deinstitutionalization and, 12
   epigenetics and, 19–20
   two-tier system of, 12
Mental Health Commission of
   Canada (MHCC), 37
mental health professionals, 65
   cultural diversity and, 83
   duty to warn, 89
mental health promotion, 13
mental status examination, 43
Merskey, Harold, 191
mescaline, 268
Messenger, John Cowan, 322*n*

meta-analysis, 81
methadone treatments, 280–281
methylenedioxymethamphetamine
   (MDMA), 249
Métis peoples, 258. *See also*
   Aboriginal peoples
mild cognitive impairment (MCI),
   426
Miller, T. I., 82
Millon, Theodore, 234
mindfulness-based cognitive
   therapy (MBCT), 169
Mini-Mental State Examination
   (MMSE), 423–424, 424*t*
Minnesota Multiphasic Personality Inventory (MMPI), 46, 47,
   51, 52
   clinical scales of, 47*t*
   form, 48*f*
modelling, 72–73, 121, 443
   schizophrenia and, 370
   suicide and, 179
Mohan, R., 208
Moldofsky, H., 296
Money, John, 327, 336
monoamine oxidase (MAO)
   inhibitors, 67, 171
monogyzotic (MZ) twins, 440
Monroe, Marilyn, 263
Montreal Neurological Institute,
   McGill University, 178
mood disorders
   biological perspectives on,
    164–165
   borderline personality disorder
    (BPD) and, 221
   cognitive theories of, 159–164
   depressive types of, 143–151
   genetic factors in, 164
   learned helplessness (attribu-
    tional) theory of, 162–164
   learning perspectives of, 158–
    159
   mood swing types of, 143,
    152–154
   psychodynamic perspectives
    on, 156–157
   psychodynamic treatments for,
    167–168
   stress and, 155–156
moods, 143
moral principle, 24, 25
moral therapy, 11
*More for the Mind: A Study
   of Psychiatric Services in
   Canada,* 12
motivational enhancement
   therapy (MET), 285
motor disorders, 393
mourning (normal bereavement),
   156
Mowrer, O. Hobart, 121
Mozart, Wolfgang Amadeus, 188
multiple (split) personality, 190,
   192
   compared to schizophrenia,
    193
multiple-baseline design, 443
   feedback from, 443
   modelling in, 443
   rehearsal in, 443
Münchausen by proxy syndrome
   (MBPS), 204
Mundugumor people, 4
Murray, Henry, 50

muscle dysmorphia (bigorexia or
   reverse anorexia nervosa), 306

N

naloxone, 281
naltrexone, 281
narcissistic personality disorder,
   224–226
   borderline personality disorder
    (BPD) and, 224–225
   characteristics of, 224–225
   healthy *versus* destructive, 225*t*
   prevalence of, 225
   relationships of, 225
   self psychology and, 233
narcolepsy, 309–310
   diagnosis of, 309
   as neurological disorder, 315
   prevalence of, 310
Narcotics Anonymous, 281
narcotics, 263
Narkissos, 224
National Sex Offender Program,
   Correctional Services Canada,
   337
natural sciences, 14
naturalistic-observation method,
   436
   unobtrusive observations in,
    436
necrophilia, 335
negative correlation, 436
negative dimension (of schizophrenia), 368
negative reinforcers, 27
negative symptoms (of schizophrenia), 366–367
neo-Freudians, 25
neo-humanistic perspective, 29–30
neologisms, 364
Neufeld, Richard W. J., 375
neurocognitive disorders, 422–428
   delirium, 422–424, 423*t*, 424*t*
   dementia, 424*t*, 425–428
neurodevelopmental disorder,
   393–398
   attention-deficit/hyperactivity
    disorder (ADHD), 392, 393,
    408–410
   autism spectrum disorder
    (ASD), 393–398
   communication disorders, 393
   intellectual disability (intellec-
    tual developmental disorder),
    393, 398–405
   motor disorders, 393
   specific learning disorder, 393
neurofibrillary tangles, 425
neuroleptics (antipsychosis drugs),
   67, 373, 382
neurons, 20
neuropeptide, 310
neuropsychological assessment,
   50–51
neuroscience theory of fetishistic
   disorder, 330
neuroscience theory of personality, 238–239
   behavioural approach system
    (BAS), 238–239
   behavioural inhibition system
    (BIS), 238–239
   fight-flight-freeze system
    (FFFS), 238–239

neuroses, 103, 187
neurosurgery, 131
neuroticism, 127
neurotransmitters, 20, 171, 265,
   268, 271–272, 280, 302, 303,
   365, 373
   anxiety disorders and, 127
New View classification system,
   344
Nicolson, R. I., 397
nicotine, 265–268
   dependence, 267
   as form of self-medication for
    depression, 274
   tobacco products and, 267
nicotine replacement therapy, 280
night-eating syndrome, 306
nightmare disorder, 312–313
   during rapid eye movement
    (REM) sleep, 313
   prevalence of, 312
nocturnal sleep-related eating
   disorder, 306
Nolen-Hoeksema, S., 149
nonspecific treatment factors, 84
norepinephrine, 22, 272
not criminally responsible on
   account of a mental disorder
   (NCRMD), 91, 93
not guilty by reason of insanity
   (NGRI), 91, 92

O

objective tests, 46
observational learning, 275
obsession, 113, 121
   normal, 123
obsessive-compulsive and related
   disorders, 113–115
   obsessive-compulsive disorder
    (OCD), 108, 113–115
obsessive-compulsive disorder
   (OCD), 108, 113–115
   antidepressant drugs for, 131
   behavioural treatment for,
    135–136
   biological aspects of, 128
   checking and cleaning rituals
    in, 113, 114
   compulsive behaviour patterns,
    114*t*
   irrational beliefs and, 122–123
   obsession–delusion line, 113
   obsessive thought patterns,
    114*t*
   prevalence of, 113
   self-defeating thoughts and,
    122–123
obsessive-compulsive personality
   disorder (OCPD), 228
   characteristics of, 228
   normal *versus* abnormal
    perfectionism, 229
O'Connor, Brian, 229
Oedipus complex, 121, 232, 335
Offord, D. R., 218*f*
Olff, M., 117
*One Flew Over the Cuckoo's
   Nest,* 90
O'Neill, Patrick, 33
Ontario,
   asylums in, 10
operant conditioning, 27–28, 121
   behaviour therapy and, 73

psychic, 23
psychoactive substances, 249,
    251. *See also* individual drugs
    operant conditioning and, 273
    prevalence of, 249
psychoanalysis, 69–70
    for anxiety disorders, 130
    countertransference, 71
    displacement, 70
    for dissociative disorders,
        198–199
    free association, 70
    for paraphilic disorders, 335
    for somatic symptom and
        related disorders, 207, 209
    transference relationship, 70
psychoanalytic theory, 22–23
psychodynamic model, 15, 103
    of alcoholism, 277
    of anxiety disorders,
        120–121
    of cigarette smoking, 277
    of conversion disorder
        (functional neurological
        symptom disorder), 206
    of dissociative disorders, 196
    evaluation of, 25
    of gender dysphoria (gender
        identity disorder), 325
    neo-Freudian, 25
    newer approaches, 71–72
    of paraphilic disorders,
        335–336
    of personality disorders,
        232–234
    personality structure, 23–24
    projective personality tests and,
        49
    of schizophrenia, 369
    of somatic symptom and
        related disorders, 205–206
    structure of mind, 23
    substance abuse treatments,
        283
    of suicide, 177
psychodynamic theory of
    depression, 156–157
psychodynamic therapies, 69–70
    modern approaches, 71–72
    for personality disorders, 241
psychological assessment, 41
psychological dependence, 254
psychological (mental) disorders, 2
    in adolescence, 392
    in childhood, 392
    prevalence among aging people
        of, 392
    stigmatization of, 15
    as a term, 2
psychological model perspective,
    14, 15, 22–24
    on sexual dysfunction, 346
psychology, 2
psychometric approach, 51
psychopathology, 258
psychopathy, 218. *See also* anti-
    social personality disorder
    (APD)
    behavioural factor in,
        218–219
    craving-for-stimulus model of,
        219–220
    criminality and, 218–219
    lack of emotional responsive-
        ness in, 219

lack of restraint on impulsivity,
    220
limbic abnormalities, 220
personality profile, 218
psychopharmacology, 66–67
    anti-anxiety drugs (anxiolytics),
        66–67
    antidepressants, 67–68
    antipsychotic drugs
        (neuroleptics), 67
    anxiety disorders and, 131
    drug addiction, 66
    drug tolerance, 66
    lithium, 68
    problems, 131
    rebound anxiety, 67
psychosis, 25
    early-intervention programs
        for, 386–387
    early psychosis intervention
        programs, 385–386
psychosocial rehabilitation, 385
psychosocial stress, 33
psychotherapy, 65
    for anorexia nervosa, 304
    effectiveness of, 81
    multicultural issues in, 83
    placebo-control groups in
        research, 438
Ptito, Dr. Alain, 178
Public Health Agency of Canada,
    256, 392
pulse generator, 69
punishments, 28, 235
Purdon, Christine, 123
Pussin, Jean-Baptiste, 10, 11

Q

Quebec, asylums in, 10
Queen's University, 73, 155,
    338

R

R. v. François (1994), 199
R. v. Swain (1991), 92
Radomsky, Sean, 123
Rain Man, 403
Ramachandran, V. S., 330
random sampling, 439
Ranjith, G., 208
rapid eye movement (REM) sleep,
    310
    nightmares during, 312
rapid flight of ideas, 153
Raspe, Rudolf Erich, 205
Rational Recovery, 282
rational-emotive behaviour ther-
    apy (REBT), 30, 31, 76, 78
rationalization (defence
    mechanism), 24t
Rayner, Rosalie, 27
reaction formation (defence
    mechanism), 24t
reality principle, 23, 24
rebound anxiety, 67
receptor site, 22
reciprocal determinism, 32
recovered memories, 199, 444
reformulated helplessness theory,
    162, 163
regression (defence mechanism),
    24t, 25
    schizophrenia and, 369

rehearsal (in behaviour therapy),
    443
Reid, J. B., 276
reinforcement, 27, 235
    depression and, 157–158
    dissociative identity (multiple
        personality) disorder and, 192
reinforcement sensitivity theory
    (RST), 238
relapse, 285
relapse-prevention training,
    285–287
reliable, 61
Renaissance, 9, 10
repetitive transcranial magnetic
    stimulation (rTMS), 68,
    174–175
*Report on Mental Illness in
    Canada*, 2
repression (defence mechanism),
    24, 24t
research ethics boards (REBs),
    435
research methods, 433–445
    case-study method, 441–443
    correlation of variables in,
        436–437
    epidemiological method, 439
    ethical principles in, 435–436
    experimental, 437–439
    feedback in, 443
    kinship studies, 440–441
    longitudinal study, 437
    naturalistic observation, 436
    scientific, 434–435
    survey method, 439
residual phase (of schizophrenia),
    362
reversal designs, 441, 442f, 442
    baseline phase in, 441, 442f
    illustration of, 442, 442f
    second baseline phase in, 441,
        442f
    second treatment phase in,
        441, 442f
    treatment phase in, 441, 442f
Reynolds, J. R., 303
Ritterband, L. M., 316
Rogers, Carl, 74, 75
role-playing model,
    dissociative identity (multiple
        personality) disorder, 192
Roman Catholic Church, 9
Rorschach, Hermann, 49
Rorschach inkblot test, 49, 50,
    51, 52
    scoring approach for, 50
    validity of, 49
Royal Canadian Mounted Police
    (RCMP), 91, 363
rubella (German measles), 373,
    401
rumination disorder, 306
Rutherford, Mel, 397
Ryerson University, 110
Rypien, Rick, 178

S

Sacks, Oliver, 403
sadistic rapists, 335
sadomasochism, 335
Salk Institute for Biological
    Studies, California, 20
sample, 439

San Francisco earthquake (1989),
    312
sanguine, 9
Satir, Virginia, 80
savant syndrome, 403
    hereditary factors in, 403
    males and, 403
    prevalence of, 403
    theories for, 403
schizoid personality disorder,
    215–216
    characteristics of, 215–216
schizophrenia, 6, 14, 103. *See
    also* delusions; hallucinations
    adoption studies of, 372
    antipsychotic drugs for, 11–12
    atypical antipsychotic drugs
        for, 382
    biochemical factors in, 373
    biological perspectives on,
        370–375
    biological treatments for,
        382–383
    blockage of goal-directed activ-
        ities in, 368
    brain abnormalities and,
        373–375
    brain circuitry defects and, 375
    brain-imaging techniques for,
        373–375
    characteristics of, 359
    in childhood, 393
    chronic pattern of, 362
    clinical criteria for, 360–362,
        361t
    clinical guidelines for treatment
        of, 383
    communication deviance as
        stress factor in, 379
    compared to multiple (split)
        personality, 192
    cross-fostering study of, 372
    diathesis-stress model of, 375–
        378, 375f
    disconnected speech, 363–364
    disturbance in thought form,
        363–364
    dopamine and, 22
    dopamine theory of, 373
    double-bind communications
        and, 378
    dynamic vulnerability model
        of, 375
    early-intervention programs
        for, 386–387
    early treatment outcomes for,
        386
    environmental factors in, 376
    environmental stressors and,
        375–376
    epigenetics and, 20
    expressed emotion (EE) in fam-
        ily communication and, 379,
        380f
    familial studies of, 371, 371f
    family factors in, 381
    family-intervention programs
        for, 385–386
    family stress as factor in, 379
    family theories of,
        378–381
    first-rank symptom of, 360
    flat affect in, 367
    four A's (primary features of),
        359–360, 363

sociocultural model perspective, 14, 15–17, 33–34
  on alcohol and drug consumption, 277–278
  downward drift hypothesis and, 33
  drug abuse from, 33
  evaluation of, 33–34
  of feeding and eating disorders, 299–300
  of personality disorders, 239–240
  of sexual assault, 340
  on sexual dysfunction, 348–349
  of suicide, 177
  stress and, 165–166
socioeconomic status (SES), 219
  alcohol abuse and, 258
  antisocial personality disorder (APD) and, 239–240
  risk factors, 239
sociopathy, 218
soma, 20
somatic symptom and related disorders, 187, 201–209
  behavioural treatments for, 207
  biological theories of 19th century of, 205–206
  conversion disorder (functional neurological symptom disorder), 201–202
  environmental factors in, 205
  genetic factors in, 205
  hypochondriacal features of, 205
  illness anxiety disorder, 202–203, 203t
  pain disorder, 203
  psychoanalysis treatments for, 207
  psychodynamic model of, 206
  psychological theories of 19th century of, 205–206
  somatic symptom disorder, 203–204
somatic symptom disorder, 201, 203–204
  essential feature of, 204
  prevalence of, 204
somatoform disorders, 103
"soul loss," 6
Spanos, Nicholas, 191, 192, 197
specific attribution, 162, 163
specific learning disorder, 405–408
specific phobias, 110–112
  acrophobia, 110
  claustrophobia, 110
  cultural factors in, 110
  diagnostic criteria for, 111t
  prevalence of, 110
  subtypes of, 110
speech impairment, 405
splitting, 223, 233, 236
Spring, B., 375
stable attribution, 162
Stanford University, 44
Stanford-Binet Intelligence Scale (SBIS), 43–44
St. Boniface General Hospital Research Centre, Winnipeg, 311
Steiger, Howard, 303

stem cells, 20
  intervention, 66
St. John's wort (Hypericum perforatum), 173
stimulants (drugs), 255, 264–268
  amphetamines, 264
  cocaine, 264–265, 266t
  nicotine, 265–268
stimulus generalization, 122
stressors, 155–156
structural hypothesis, 23
Structured Clinical Interview for the DSM (SCID), 43
structured (standardized) interviews, 43
stupor, 366
subject expectancies (in treatments), 438–439
sublimation (defence mechanism), 24t
substance use disorder, 254–255
  addiction or dependence stage, 255
  biological treatments for, 279
  experimentation stage, 255
  problems with treatments for, 285
  routine use stage, 255
substance-induced disorders, classification of, 251–252
  psychodynamic treatments for, 283
  self-efficacy expectations, 275–276
substance-related disorders, 251
  cognitive perspectives on, 275–277
  consequences of, 252
  learning perspectives on, 273–275
  negative reinforcement and withdrawal, 274
  recurrent use pattern, 252
  substance-induced disorder category, 251–252
  substance-use disorder category, 251, 252–253
substance use disorders, 16, 22
  classification of, 252–253
  residential approaches, 282–283
  self-control strategies for, 283, 284t
  support groups for, 281–282
sudden infant death syndrome (SIDS), 261
suicide
  adolescent, 176
  age factor in adolescent, 420
  age factor in childhood, 420
  alcohol abuse and, 256
  biological factors in, 179
  bipolar disorder and, 177
  classic psychodynamic model of, 177–178
  depression and hopelessness factors in adolescent, 420
  depression and hopelessness factors in childhood, 420
  depression and, 177
  electroconvulsive therapy (ECT) and, 69
  ethnicity factor in adolescent, 420
  ethnicity factor in childhood, 420

family problems factor in adolescent, 420
  family problems factor in childhood, 420
  gender differences and, 176–177
  gender factor in adolescent, 420
  gender factor in childhood, 420
  genetic factors in, 179
  learning theory of, 179
  older adults, 176
  postpartum depression (PPD) and, 148
  prevention, 181
  previous suicidal behaviour factor in adolescence, 420
  previous suicidal behaviour factor in childhood, 420
  rates of Aboriginal youth and, 420
  rates of, 175–176, 176f
  reasons for, 177
  risk factors for, 180–181, 180t
  social contagion factor in adolescence, 421
  social contagion factor in childhood, 421
  social-cognitive theory of, 179
  sociocultural theory of, 178–179
  stress and, 177
  stressful life events factor in adolescence, 421
  stressful life events factor in childhood, 421
  substance abuse factor in adolescence, 421
  substance abuse factor in childhood, 421
  teen, 179
Sullivan, Harry Stack, 25, 167, 369, 383
superego, 23–24, 232
Supreme Court of Canada, 199
survey method, 439
  incidence in, 439
  populations in, 439
  prevalence in, 439
  random assignment in, 439
  random sampling in, 439
  samples in, 439
Swain, Owen, 92
Swinson, Richard, 111
Sybil, 191, 192
symbiotic, 233
synapse, 21, 21f
  antidepressants and, 171f
syphilis, 401
systematic desensitization, 72, 132
systems perspective, 302
Szasz, Thomas, 15, 17
Szatmari, P., 397

T

tachycardia, 251
taijin-kyofu-sho (TKS), 62
Tarasoff, Tatiana, 89
Tarasoff v. the Regents of the University of California, 89
tardive dyskinesia (TD), 67, 382
Tay-Sachs disease, 401
  prevalence of, 401

telephone scatologia, 335
tension-reduction theory, 273–274
Terman, Louis, 44
terminals, 20
testosterone, 345
Thematic Apperception Test (TAT), 49, 50, 50f, 51, 52
  criticism of, 50
theories of behaviour, 434
  as explanations and predictions, 434
theory of mind, 396
Thonga peoples, sexual behaviour of, 323
thought disorder (looseness of associations), 360, 363–364
thought records, 54
Three Faces of Eve, The, 191, 192
Tiefer, Leonore, 344
time out, 415
Tjepkema, M., 258
tobacco, 249, 250t, 265–268
  decline in usage of, 250
token economies, 73
token economy systems, 384
tolerance, 66
Toronto Western Hospital, 311
Tourette syndrome, 69
trait theory, 234
tranquillizers, 66, 249
transcranial magnetic stimulation (TMS), 66
transference neurosis, 71
transference relationship, 71
transgender identity, 323
transvestic disorder, 330–331
  diagnosis of, 330
  psychodynamic theory for, 335
trauma- and stressor-related disorders, 115–120
  acute stress disorder (ACD), 116–120
  adjustment disorders, 115–116
  posttraumatic stress disorder (PTSD), 116–120
  prevalence of trauma exposure, 117, 117t
treatment, 2
  behaviour-based approaches to anxiety disorders, 131–138
  biological approaches to anxiety disorders, 131
  deinstitutionalization, 11–12
  exorcism as, 9
  humanistic approaches to anxiety disorders, 130
  modern era of, 10–11
  moral therapy, 11
  psychodynamic approaches to anxiety disorders, 130
  psychotic drugs, 11
treatment methods, 64–65
  for anxiety disorders, 130–138
  behaviour therapy, 72–73, 168
  biological approaches for mood disorders, 170–175
  biological approaches for schizophrenia, 382–383
  for childhood and adolescent depression, 418–419
  cognitive therapy for mood disorders, 168–170